Eighth Edition

Essentials of Entrepreneurship and Small Business Management

Norman M. Scarborough

Presbyterian College

Jeffrey R. Cornwall

Belmont University

Boston Columbus Indianapolis New York San Francisco
Amsterdam Cape Town Dubai London Madrid Milan Munich Paris Montréal Toronto
Delhi Mexico City São Paulo Sydney Hong Kong Seoul Singapore Taipei Tokyo

Vice President, Business Publishing: Donna Battista
Editor-in-Chief: Stephanie Wall
Acquisitions Editor: Dan Tylman
Program Manager Team Lead: Ashley Santora
Program Manager: Claudia Fernandes
Editorial Supervisor: Linda Albelli
Vice President, Product Marketing: Maggie Moylan
Director of Marketing, Digital Services and Products: Jeanette Koskinas
Executive Product Marketing Manager: Anne Fahlgren
Field Marketing Manager: Lenny Ann Raper
Senior Strategic Marketing Manager: Erin Gardner
Project Manager Team Lead: Judy Leale
Project Manager: Kelly Warsak
Operations Specialist: Diane Peirano
Creative Director: Blair Brown
Senior Art Director: Janet Slowik

Text Designer: S4Carlisle Publishing Services
Cover Designer: S4Carlisle Publishing Services
Cover Art: alphaspirit/Fotolia
VP, Director of Digital Strategy & Assessment: Paul Gentile
Manager of Learning Applications: Paul Deluca
Digital Editor: Brian Surette
Digital Studio Manager: Diane Lombardo
Digital Studio Project Manager: Robin Lazrus
Digital Studio Project Manager: Alana Coles
Digital Studio Project Manager: Monique Lawrence
Digital Studio Project Manager: Regina DaSilva
Full-Service Project Management and Composition: Lori Bradshaw, S4Carlisle Publishing Services
Printer/Binder: LSC Communications
Cover Printer: LSC Communications
Text Font: 8/10 Times LT Std

Library of Congress Cataloging-in-Publication Data
Scarborough, Norman M.
    Essentials of entrepreneurship and small business management / Norman M. Scarborough, Jeffrey R. Cornwall.—Eighth Edition.
      pages cm
    Includes index.
    ISBN 978-0-13-384962-2—ISBN 0-13-384962-7
    1. Small business—Management. 2. New business enterprises—Management. 3. Entrepreneurship. I. Cornwall, Jeffrey R.
II. Zimmerer, Thomas. Essentials of entrepreneurship and small business management. III. Title.
    HD62.7.S273 2014
    658.02'2—dc23
                                                                                            2014021098

6

PEARSON

ISBN 10:   0-13-384962-7
ISBN 13: 978-0-13-384962-2

To Cindy, whose patience is always tested during a writing project
of this magnitude. Your love, support, and understanding
are a vital part of every book.
You are the love of my life.

—NMS

To Ann, for her wisdom and love. Your encouragement
and support is the foundation for each new entrepreneurial
adventure we take.

—JRC

"May your own dreams be your only boundaries."

—The Reverend Purlie Victorious Judson,
in "Purlie," Broadway Theater, 1970

Brief Contents

Contents

Preface

Entrepreneurship is a fast-growing and ever-changing discipline. People of all ages, backgrounds, and nationalities are launching businesses of their own and, in the process, are reshaping the world's economy. The purpose of this book is to open your mind to the possibilities, the challenges, and the rewards of owning your own business and to provide the tools you will need to be successful if you choose the path of the entrepreneur. It is not an easy road to follow, but the rewards—both tangible and intangible—are well worth the risks. Not only may you be rewarded financially for your business ideas, but like entrepreneurs the world over, you will be able to work at something you love!

Now in its eighth edition, *Essentials of Entrepreneurship and Small Business Management* has stood the test of time by bringing you the material you need to launch and manage a small business successfully in a hotly competitive environment. In writing this edition, we have worked hard to provide plenty of practical, "hands-on" tools and techniques to make new business ventures successful. Many people launch businesses every year; only some of them succeed. This book provides the tools to help teach students the *right* way to launch and manage a small business with the staying power to succeed and grow.

What's New to This Edition?

This edition includes many new features that reflect this dynamic and exciting field of study.

- One of the first changes you will notice is the addition of Jeff Cornwall as coauthor. Jeff, who holds the Jack C. Massey Chair of Entrepreneurship and is Professor of Entrepreneurship at Belmont University, is an experienced and successful entrepreneur, a dedicated teacher, a respected author, and an acknowledged expert in the field of entrepreneurship. The United States Association for Small Business and Entrepreneurship has honored Jeff on numerous occasions, naming him a Longenecker/USASBE Fellow in 2006 and presenting the center that he headed at Belmont University the USASBE National Model Undergraduate Program of the Year Award in 2008. USASBE also recognized Jeff in 2013 with the prestigious Outstanding Educator of the Year award. He also served as USASBE's president in 2010. Jeff's blog, the Entrepreneurial Mind, is one of the most popular small business blogs on the Internet, named by *Forbes* as a "best of the Web" selection.

- Almost all of the real-world examples in this edition are new and are easy to spot because they are accompanied by an icon. These examples allow you to see how entrepreneurs are putting into practice the concepts you are learning about in the book and in class. These examples are designed to help you to remember the key concepts in the course. The business founders in these examples also reflect the diversity that makes entrepreneurship a vital part of the global economy.

- We have added a new chapter on "Ethics and Entrepreneurship: Doing the Right Thing" that provides you with a framework for making ethical decisions in business and with the opportunity to wrestle with some of the ethical dilemmas entrepreneurs face in business, including the controversial issues surrounding employers' responses to employees' postings on social media sites. Encouraging you to think about and discuss these issues now prepares you for making the right business decisions later.

- This edition provides expanded and updated coverage of important topics such as using the business model canvas to refine a business idea; using social media, including Facebook, Twitter, and YouTube, as bootstrap marketing tools; attracting capital using crowd funding; using "pop-up" stores to test potential permanent locations; and identifying the factors that drive employee engagement.

- To emphasize the practical nature of this book, we have updated the content of the very popular "Hands On: How To . . ." feature, which selects a concept from each chapter and explains how you can put it to practice in your own company. These features include topics such as how to "Be a Successful Innovator," "Use a Mobile-First, Responsive Web Design to Increase Online Sales," "Manage Cash Flow in a Highly Seasonal Business," and "Make Your Small Business a Great Place to Work."

- Another feature that is popular with both students and professors is "You Be the Consultant." Every chapter contains at least one of these inserts, which describe a decision an entrepreneur faces and asks you to play the role of consultant and advise the entrepreneur on the best course of action. This feature includes the fascinating stories of how entrepreneurs came up with their business ideas (including one on decoding the DNA of the entrepreneur that introduces beekeepers Tim Dover and Susan Gardner, who turned their hobby into a successful bee supply business), setting the right price for a company's custom-made shirts in a highly competitive market (direct sales company J. Hilburn, founded by Hil Davis), helping entrepreneurs revamp their Web site (New Columbia Distillers, the first new distillery to open in Washington, D.C., since Congress passed the Eighteenth Amendment to the U.S. Constitution), and advising companies on their strategies for becoming micro-multinational businesses (Zee Wines USA and Somnio, which makes unique running shoes that accommodate runners' foot shapes and running styles). Each one poses a problem or an opportunity and includes questions that focus your attention on key issues and help you to hone your analytical and critical thinking skills.

- This edition includes ten brief cases, eight of them new to this edition, covering a variety of topics (see the Case Matrix that appears on the inside cover). All of the cases are about small companies, and most are companies you can research online. These cases challenge you to think critically about a variety of topics that are covered in the text—from developing a business strategy and building a brand to protecting intellectual property and financing a business.

- The content of every chapter reflects the most recent statistics, studies, surveys, and research about entrepreneurship and small business management. You will learn how to launch and manage a business the *right* way by studying the most current concepts in entrepreneurship and small business management.

Entrepreneurship has become a major force in the global economy. Policymakers across the world are discovering that economic growth and prosperity lie in the hands of entrepreneurs—those dynamic, driven men and women who are committed to achieving success by creating and marketing innovative, customer-focused new products and services. Not only are these entrepreneurs creating economic prosperity, but as social entrepreneurs, many of them are also striving to make the world a better place in which to live. Those who possess this spirit of entrepreneurial leadership continue to lead the economic revolution that has proved time and again its ability to raise the standard of living for people everywhere. We hope that by using this book in your small business management or entrepreneurship class, you will join this economic revolution to bring about lasting, positive changes in your community and around the world. If you are interested in launching a business of your own, *Essentials of Entrepreneurship and Small Business Management* is the ideal book for you!

This eighth edition of *Essentials of Entrepreneurship and Small Business Management* introduces you to the process of creating a new venture and provides you with the knowledge you need to launch a business that has the greatest chance for success. One of the hallmarks of every edition of this book has been a very practical, "hands-on" approach to entrepreneurship. We strive to equip you with the tools you will need for entrepreneurial success. By combining this textbook with your professor's expertise, you will be equipped to follow your dream of becoming a successful entrepreneur.

Other Text Features

- This edition once again emphasizes the importance of conducting a feasibility analysis and creating a business plan for a successful new venture. Chapter 4 offers comprehensive coverage of how to conduct a feasibility study for a business idea and then how to create a sound business model for the ideas that pass the feasibility test.

- This edition features an updated, attractive, full-color design and a user-friendly layout that includes an in-margin glossary and learning objectives. Each chapter begins with learning objectives, which are repeated as in-margin markers within the chapter to guide you as you study.

- Chapter 3, "Inside the Entrepreneurial Mind: From Ideas to Reality," explains the creative process entrepreneurs use to generate business ideas and to recognize entrepreneurial opportunities. This chapter helps you learn to think like an entrepreneur.

- Chapter 9, "E-Commerce and the Entrepreneur," serves as a practical guide to using the Internet as a marketing and business tool and offers helpful advice for engaging successfully in mobile commerce.

- Chapter 13, "Sources of Financing: Equity and Debt," gives you a useful overview of the various financing sources that are available to entrepreneurs with plenty of practical advice for landing the financing you need to start or grow your business. Given the changes that have resulted from recent turmoil in the financial industry, this is a particularly important chapter.

- Through a partnership with Palo Alto Software, we're able to provide 6-month access to LivePlan at a reduced rate with the purchase of a new textbook. LivePlan simplifies business planning, budgeting, forecasting, and performance tracking for small businesses and startups. Set business goals, compare performance to industry benchmarks, and see all your key numbers in an easy-to-use dashboard so you know exactly what's going on in your business. To order LivePlan with the textbook, use package ISBN 0134113756.

Instructor Resources

At the Instructor Resource Center, www.pearsonhighered.com/irc, instructors can easily register to gain access to a variety of instructor resources available with this text in downloadable format. If assistance is needed, our dedicated technical support team is ready to help with the media supplements that accompany this text. Visit http://247.pearsoned.com for answers to frequently asked questions and toll-free user support phone numbers.

The following supplements are available with this text:

- **Instructor's Resource Manual**
- **Test Bank**
- **TestGen® Computerized Test Bank**
- **PowerPoint Presentations**

Essentials of Entrepreneurship and Small Business Management contains a multitude of both student- and instructor-friendly features. We trust that this edition will help you, the next generation of entrepreneurs, to reach your full potential and achieve your dreams of success as independent business owners. It is your dedication, perseverance, and creativity that keep the world's economy moving forward.

Acknowledgments

Supporting every author is a staff of professionals who work extremely hard to bring a book to life. They handle the thousands of details involved in transforming a rough manuscript into the finished product you see before you. Their contributions are immeasurable, and we appreciate all they do to make this book successful. We have been blessed to work with the following outstanding publishing professionals:

- Dan Tylman, acquisitions editor, who has assisted us in many ways as we developed a revision plan for this edition. His input and vision proved to be a valuable resource.

- Claudia Fernandes, our exceptionally capable program manager, who was always just an e-mail away when we needed her help with a seemingly endless number of details. She did a masterful job of coordinating the many aspects of this project. Her ability to juggle many aspects of multiple projects at once is amazing!

- Kelly Warsak, project manager, who skillfully guided the book through the long and sometimes difficult production process with a smile and a "can-do" attitude. She is always a pleasure to work with and a good friend.

- Nancy Moudry, photo researcher, who took our ideas for photos and transformed them into the meaningful images you see on these pages. Her job demands many hours of research and hard work, which she did with aplomb.

- Lenny Ann Rapper, marketing manager, whose input helped focus this edition in an evolving market.

We also extend a big "Thank You" to the corps of Pearson sales representatives, who work so hard to get our books into customers' hands and who represent the front line in our effort to serve our customers' needs. They are the unsung heroes of the publishing industry.

Special thanks to the following academic reviewers, whose ideas, suggestions, and thought-provoking input have helped to shape this and previous editions of our two books, *Essentials of Entrepreneurship and Small Business Management* and *Entrepreneurship and Effective Small Business Management*. We always welcome feedback from customers!

Lon Addams, *Weber State University*
Sol Ahiarah, *Buffalo State College*
Professor M. Ala, *California State University–Los Angeles*
Annamary Allen, *Broome Community College*
Tammy Yates Arthur, *Mississippi College*
Jay Azriel, *York College of Pennsylvania*
Bruce Bachenheimer, *Pace University*
Kevin Banning, *University of Florida*
Jeffrey Bell, *Dominican University*
Tom Bergman, *Northeastern State University*
Nancy Bowman, *Baylor University*
Jeff Brice, *Texas Southern University*
Michael S. Broida, *Miami University*
James Browne, *University of Southern Colorado*
Rochelle Brunson, *Alvin Community College*
John E. Butler, *University of Washington*
R. D. Butler, *Trenton State College*
Pamela Clark, *Angelo State University*
Richard Cuba, *University of Baltimore*
Kathy J. Daruty, *Los Angeles Pierce College*
Gita DeSouza, *Pennsylvania State University*
Stuart Devlin, *New Mexico State University*
John deYoung, *Cumberland Community College*
Michael Dickson, *Columbus State Community College*
Judy Dietert, *Southwest Texas State University*

Robert M. Donnelly, *St. Peter's College*
Steve Dunphy, *Indiana University Northwest*
Art Elkins, *University of Massachusetts*
W. Bruce Erickson, *University of Minnesota*
Frances Fabian, *University of Memphis*
Jan Feldbauer, *Austin Community College*
George J. Foegen, *Metropolitan State College of Denver*
Caroline E. W. Glackin, *Delaware State University*
Stephen O. Handley, *University of Washington–Bothell*
Charles Hubbard, *University of Arkansas*
Fred Hughes, *Faulkner University*
Samira B. Hussein, *Johnson County Community College*
Ralph Jagodka, *Mt. San Antonio College*
Theresa Janeczek, *Manchester Community College*
Robert Keimer, *Florida Institute of Technology*
E. L. (Betty) Kinarski, *Seattle University*
Kyoung-Nan Kwon, *Michigan State University*
Dick LaBarre, *Ferris State University*
Paul Lamberson, *Riverton, Wyoming*
Mary Lou Lockerby, *College of DuPage*
Martin K. Marsh, *California State University–Bakersfield*

Charles H. Matthews, *University of Cincinnati*

John McMahon, *Mississippi County Community College*

Michael L. Menefee, *Purdue University*

Julie Messing, *Kent State University*

William Meyer, *TRICOMP*

Milton Miller, *Carteret Community College*

John Moonen, *Daytona Beach Community College*

Linda Newell, *Saddleback College*

Marcella Norwood, *University of Houston*

David O'Dell, *McPherson State College*

John Phillips, *University of San Francisco*

Louis D. Ponthieu, *University of North Texas*

Ben Powell, *University of Alabama*

Frank Real, *St. Joseph's University*

William J. Riffe, *Kettering University*

Matthew W. Rutherford, *Virginia Commonwealth University*

Joseph Salamone, *State University of New York at Buffalo*

Manhula Salinath, *University of North Texas*

Nick Sarantakes, *Austin Community College*

Khaled Sartawi, *Fort Valley State University*

Terry J. Schindler, *University of Indianapolis*

Thomas Schramko, *University of Toledo*

Peter Mark Shaw, *Tidewater Community College*

Jack Sheeks, *Broward Community College*

Lakshmy Sivaratnam, *Johnson Community College*

Bill Snider, *Cuesta College*

Deborah Streeter, *Cornell University*

Ethné Swartz, *Fairleigh Dickinson University*

Yvette Swint-Blakely, *Lancing Community College*

John Todd, *University of Arkansas*

Charles Toftoy, *George Washington University*

Barry L. Van Hook, *Arizona State University*

Ina Kay Van Loo, *West Virginia University Institute of Technology*

William Vincent, *Mercer University*

Jim Walker, *Moorhead State University*

Bernard W. Weinrich, *St. Louis Community College*

Donald Wilkinson, *East Tennessee State University*

Gregory Worosz, *Schoolcraft College*

Bernard Zannini, *Northern Essex Community College*

We also are grateful to our colleagues who support us in the often grueling process of writing a book: Foard Tarbert, Sam Howell, Jerry Slice, Suzanne Smith, Jody Lipford, Tobin Turner, Cindy Lucking, and Uma Sridharan of Presbyterian College and Mark Schenkel, Mark Phillips, Matthew Wilson, and Jose Gonzalez of Belmont University.

Finally, we thank Cindy Scarborough and Ann Cornwall for their love, support, and understanding while we worked many long hours to complete this book. For them, this project represents a labor of love.

Special Note to Students

We trust that this edition of *Essentials of Entrepreneurship and Small Business Management* will encourage and challenge you to fulfill your aspirations as an entrepreneur and to make the most of your talents, experience, and abilities. We hope that you find this book to be of such value that it becomes a permanent addition to your personal library. We look forward to the day when we can write about your entrepreneurial success story on these pages.

Norman M. Scarborough
William Henry Scott III Associate Professor of Entrepreneurship
Presbyterian College
Clinton, South Carolina
nmscarb@presby.edu

Jeffrey R. Cornwall
Jack C. Massey Chair and Professor of Entrepreneurship
Belmont University
Nashville, Tennessee
Jeff.cornwall@belmont.edu

1

The Foundations of Entrepreneurship

Hero Images / Getty Images, Inc.

Learning Objectives

On completion of this chapter, you will be able to:

1. Define the role of the entrepreneur in business in the United States and around the world.

2. Describe the entrepreneurial profile.

3A. Describe the benefits of entrepreneurship.

3B. Describe the drawbacks of entrepreneurship.

4. Explain the forces that are driving the growth of entrepreneurship.

5. Explain the cultural diversity of entrepreneurship.

6. Describe the important role that small businesses play in our nation's economy.

7. Put failure into the proper perspective.

8. Explain how an entrepreneur can avoid becoming another failure statistic.

LO1
_____

Define the role of the
entrepreneur in business
in the United States and
around the world.

The World of the Entrepreneur

Welcome to the world of the entrepreneur! Around the world, growing numbers of people are realizing their dreams of owning and operating their own businesses. Entrepreneurship continues to thrive in nearly every corner of the world. Globally, one in eight adults is actively engaged in launching a business.[1] Research by the Kauffman Foundation shows that in the United States alone, entrepreneurs launch 476,000 businesses each month.[2] This entrepreneurial spirit is the most significant economic development in recent business history. In the United States and around the globe, these heroes of the new economy are reshaping the business environment and creating a world in which their companies play an important role in the vitality of the global economy. With amazing vigor, their businesses have introduced innovative products and services, pushed back technological frontiers, created new jobs, opened foreign markets, and, in the process, provided their founders with the opportunity to do what they enjoy most. "Small businesses have been at the core of our economy's growth over the last few years," says Winslow Sargeant, chief counsel of the U.S. Small Business Administration's Office of Advocacy.[3]

Entrepreneurial activity is essential to a strong global economy. Many of the world's largest companies continue to engage in massive downsizing campaigns, dramatically cutting the number of employees on their payrolls. This flurry of "pink slips" has spawned a new population of entrepreneurs: "castoffs" from large corporations (in which many of these individuals thought they would be lifetime ladder climbers) with solid management experience and many productive years left before retirement. According to the Small Business Administration, during a recent one-year period, the largest companies in the United States (those with 500 or more employees) _shed_ 1.7 million net jobs; during the same period, small businesses with fewer than 20 employees _created_ 287,000 net jobs![4]

One casualty of this downsizing has been the long-standing notion of job security in large corporations. As a result, many people no longer see launching a business as a risky career path. Having been victims of downsizing or having witnessed large companies execute layoffs with detached precision, these people see entrepreneurship as the ideal way to create their own job security and success. Rather than pursue corporate careers after graduation, many college students are choosing to launch companies of their own. They prefer to control their own destinies by building their own businesses.

ENTREPRENEURIAL PROFILE: Christopher Kelley: Badd Newz BBQ For years, Christopher Kelley had dreamed of becoming a mobile restaurateur by launching a food truck that specialized in barbecue but was hesitant to give up the security of his job at the company where he had worked in maintenance for 14 years. Like many entrepreneurs, Kelley refused to give up on his dream, bought a food truck, outfitted it, and started Bad Newz BBQ as a part-time business, catering local school events, church gatherings, and fundraisers in Huntsville, Alabama. Two months later, Kelley's employer announced a massive layoff, and Kelley's job was eliminated. The layoff prompted Kelley to transform Bad Newz BBQ into a full-time business, and he began marketing his food truck via social and traditional media, even landing a regular spot at a nearby army post. Kelly, who is 43 years old and has lost three jobs over the last 20 years to layoffs, decided it was time to take control of his own destiny by starting a business. He advises other entrepreneurs to believe in their abilities even when others do not and to devote all of their energy into building a successful business.[5] ∎

The downsizing trend among large companies has created a more significant philosophical change. It has ushered in an age in which "small is beautiful." Twenty-five years ago, competitive conditions favored large companies with their hierarchies and layers of management; today, with the pace of change constantly accelerating, fleet-footed, agile, small companies have the competitive advantage. These nimble competitors can dart into and out of niche markets as they emerge and recede, they can move faster to exploit market opportunities, and they can use modern technology to create, within a matter of weeks or months, products and services that once took years and all the resources a giant corporation could muster. The balance has tipped in favor of small, entrepreneurial companies. Howard Stevenson, Harvard's chaired professor of entrepreneurship, says, "Why is it so easy [for small companies] to compete against giant corporations? Because while they [the giants] are studying the consequences, [entrepreneurs] are changing the world."[6]

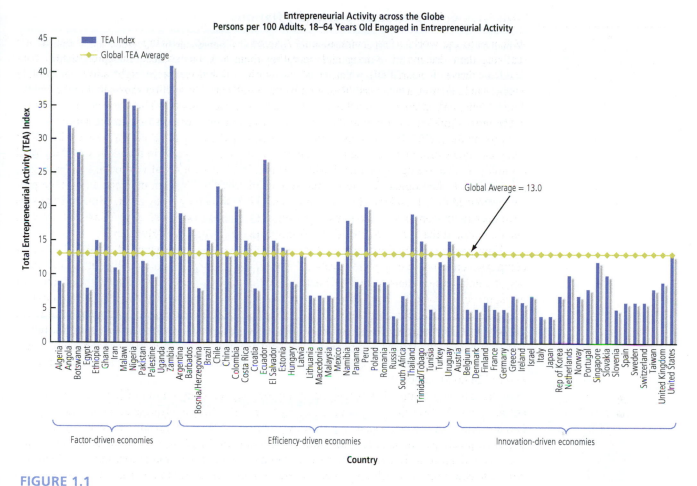

FIGURE 1.1

Entrepreneurial Activity Across the Globe

Source: Based on data from José Ernesto and Neils Bosma, *Global Entrepreneurship Monitor 2013 Global Report*, Babson College, Universidad del Desarrollo, Universiti Tun Abdul Razak, and London Business School, 2014, pp. 30–31.

One of the most comprehensive studies of global entrepreneurship conducted by the Global Entrepreneurship Monitor (GEM) shows significant variation in the rate of new business formation among the nations of the world when measured by total entrepreneurial activity or TEA (see Figure 1.1). The most recent edition of the study reports that 12.7 percent of the adult population in the United States—one in eight people—is working to start a business. The GEM study also reports that globally men are nearly twice as likely to start a business as women; that entrepreneurs are most likely to launch their companies between the ages of 35 and 44; and that the majority of people in the world see entrepreneurship as a good career choice.[7] The health of the global economy and the level of entrepreneurial activity are intertwined. "The world economy needs entrepreneurs," says GEM researcher Kent Jones, "and increasingly, entrepreneurs depend on an open and expanding world economy for new opportunities and growth—through trade, foreign investment, and finance."[8]

The United States and many other nations are benefiting from this surge in global entrepreneurial activity. Eastern European countries, China, Vietnam, and many other nations whose economies were state controlled and centrally planned are now fertile ground for growing small businesses. Table 1.1 shows some of the results from a recent study that ranks 118 nations according to the quality of the entrepreneurial environment they exhibit. Although troubled by corruption, a poor "ease of doing business" ranking, and a low quality entrepreneurial environment, Kenya is home to entrepreneurs of all ages who are hard at work solving problems that range from healthcare and electricity shortages to providing clean water and fashionable clothing to the nation's 41 million residents.

TABLE 1.1 Entrepreneurship-Friendly Nations

Which nations provide the best environment for cultivating entrepreneurship? A recent study ranked 121 countries on the quality of the entrepreneurial environment using the Global Entrepreneurship and Development Index (GEDI), which includes a variety of factors that range from the availability of capital and workforce quality to attitudes toward entrepreneurs and technology available. The maximum GEDI score is 100.

GEDI Score, Top Ten Countries	GEDI Score, Bottom Ten Countries
1. United States 82.5	109. Madagascar 19.6
2. Canada 81.7	110. Ivory Coast 19.4
3. Australia 77.9	111. Uganda 19.3
4. Sweden 73.7	112. Mali 18.8
5. Denmark 72.5	113. Pakistan 18.7
6. Switzerland 70.9	114. Mauritania 18.5
7. Taiwan 69.5	115. Sierra Leone 17.6
8. Finland 69.3	116. Burundi 15.5
9. Netherlands 69.0	117. Chad 15.0
10. United Kingdom 68.6	118. Bangladesh 13.8

Source: "GEDIndex 2014," The Global Entrepreneurship and Development Institute, 2013, http://www.thegedi.org/.

Courtesy of Stawi Foods and Fruits

ENTREPRENEURIAL PROFILE: Eric Muthomi: Stawi Foods and Fruits Eric Muthomi grew up in Meru, Kenya, and studied law at the Catholic University of East Africa. While Muthomi was earning his law degree, his goal was to start his own business. After graduating in 2010, Muthomi, just 26 years old, launched Stawi Foods and Fruits, a company that makes a unique banana flour that is used for baking, making baby food, and preparing ugali, a staple dish in Kenya. Muthomi, who also studied entrepreneurship and banana processing, says that coming up with his business idea was simple because his hometown of Meru is a center for banana growers and processors. Stawi Foods and Fruits benefited from the publicity and recognition that came after Muthomi won Jitihada, Kenya's national business plan competition, beating out 3,439 other business ideas. Getting into business in Kenya was not easy, however; Muthomi says getting necessary permits and licenses for a food business from various government entities is time-consuming and "tiresome." Despite facing challenges, Stawi Foods and Fruits, which employs five people, reached its breakeven point in less than one year, and Muthomi is reinvesting profits into the company to fuel its growth. The determined entrepreneur already has his sights set on exporting his company's banana flour to other African nations and eventually other continents. When asked what advice he could offer to other aspiring entrepreneurs, Muthomi recommends that they should not wait for conditions to be perfect before they launch their businesses; instead, they should start with whatever resources they have and grow from there.[9] ■

Wherever they may choose to launch their companies, these business builders continue to embark on one of the most exhilarating—and frightening—adventures ever known: launching a business. It's never easy, but it can be incredibly rewarding, both financially and emotionally. It can be both thrilling and dangerous, like living life without a safety net. Still, true entrepreneurs see owning a business as the real measure of success. Indeed, entrepreneurship often provides the only avenue for success to those who otherwise might have been denied the opportunity.

Who are these entrepreneurs, and what drives them to work so hard with no guarantee of success? What forces lead them to risk so much and to make so many sacrifices in an attempt to achieve an ideal? Why are they willing to give up the security of a steady paycheck working for someone else to become the last person to be paid in their own companies? This chapter will examine the entrepreneur, the driving force behind the U.S. economy.

What Is an Entrepreneur?

An **entrepreneur** is one who creates a new business in the face of risk and uncertainty for the purpose of achieving profit and growth by identifying significant opportunities and assembling the necessary resources to capitalize on them. Although many people come up with great business ideas, most never act on their ideas. Entrepreneurs do. In his 1911 book *The Theory of Economic Development*, economist Joseph Schumpeter wrote that entrepreneurs are more than just business creators; they are change agents in society. The process of creative destruction, in which entrepreneurs create new ideas and new businesses that make existing ones obsolete, is a sign of a vibrant economy. Although this constant churn of businesses—some rising, others sinking, new ones succeeding, and many failing—concerns some people, in reality it is an indication of a healthy, growing economic system that is creating new and better ways of serving people's needs and improving their quality of life and standard of living. Schumpeter compared the list of leading entrepreneurs to a popular hotel's guest list: always filled with people but rarely the same ones.[10]

High levels of entrepreneurial activity translate into high levels of business formation and destruction and make an economy more flexible and capable of adapting to structural changes in the competitive landscape. One reason the U.S. economy has been so successful over time is the constant churn that results from the rapid pace at which entrepreneurs create new businesses, destroy old ones, and upend entire industries with their creativity and ingenuity. Entrepreneurs are important change agents in the global economy, uprooting staid industries with fresh new business models that spot market opportunities and deliver the products and services customers want.

ENTREPRENEURIAL PROFILE: Jennifer Hyman and Jenny Fleiss: Rent the Runway
While in college, Jenn Hyman came up with the idea for a designer clothing rental business, Rent the Runway, that would disrupt the fashion industry after she witnessed one of her sister's "closet full of clothes, but nothing to wear" moments during Thanksgiving break. When she returned to school, she shared her idea with a suitemate, Jenny Fleiss, and the two collegiate entrepreneurs launched the company that rents high-end, designer clothing, accessories, and jewelry to customers at a fraction of the regular retail price. To test their business model (think "Netflix meets high fashion"), they used their savings to purchase 100 dresses and set up a pop-up shop on campus that proved to be a hit. The shop's success convinced the entrepreneurial pair that their business idea was valid and led them to conduct focus groups with more than 1,000 women, which gave them valuable insight into refining their business model and pricing strategy. Since starting Rent the Runway in 2009, Hyman and Fleiss have raised nearly $55 million in four rounds of financing from a "who's who" list of venture capital firms and assembled an inventory of tens of thousands of dresses from more than 170 designers, such as Nicole Miller, Vera Wang, Versace, and Dolce and Gabbana. Customers go online, select the dress they want, enter their size (a backup size comes free), and specify the rental date; returns are as easy as dropping the dress into a prepaid return envelope. "We deliver Cinderella moments," says Hyman. Rent the Runway, which became cash-flow positive in less than one year, now has more than 3 million members, and financial experts estimate its value at $240 million.[11] ■

LO2

Describe the entrepreneurial profile.

entrepreneur
one who creates a new business in the face of risk and uncertainty for the purpose of achieving profit and growth by identifying significant opportunities and assembling the necessary resources to capitalize on them.

Steven Kelly and Jeff Parker, Dustin, King Features Syndicate

FIGURE 1.2

Percentage of Start-Up Companies in the United States

Source: Business Dynamics Statistics Data Tables: Firm Characteristics, U.S. Department of Commerce, U.S. Census Bureau, 2013, http://www.census.gov/ces/dataproducts/bds/data_firm.html.

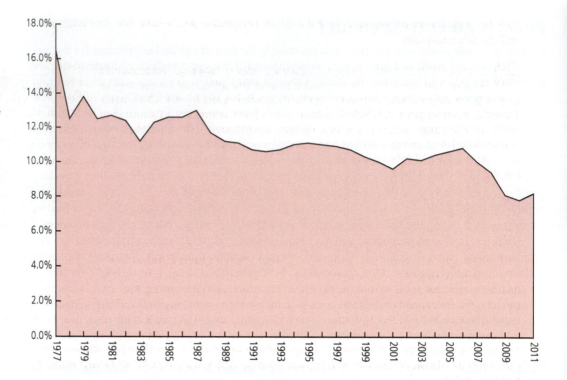

Unfortunately, in the United States, the percentage of private companies that are start-up businesses (those companies that are less than one year old), the primary source of the economy's healthy churn, has been declining since the late 1970s (see Figure 1.2). Although many entrepreneurs fail, some more than once, those who succeed earn the satisfaction of creating value for their customers and wealth for themselves—all while working at something they love to do. Some of them create companies that change the world.

Researchers have invested a great deal of time and effort over the last few decades trying to paint a clear picture of "the entrepreneurial personality." Although these studies have identified several characteristics entrepreneurs tend to exhibit, none of them has isolated a set of traits required for success. We now turn to a brief summary of the entrepreneurial profile.[12]

1. *Desire for responsibility.* Entrepreneurs feel a deep sense of personal responsibility for the outcome of ventures they start. They prefer to be in control of their resources, and they use those resources to achieve self-determined goals. Deborah Sullivan, a lifelong serial entrepreneur realized at the age of 16 that she did not want to spend her life working for others. "You're stuck by all of these different rules [when you work for someone else]," she says. "I wanted to create something for myself." Sullivan has been an entrepreneur since she was 22 years old, when she launched a hair salon and spa in Atlanta, Georgia. In 2012, at the age of 60, Sullivan started Consign Werks, a consignment shop in Greenville, South Carolina, which she says has been the most gratifying of her entrepreneurial ventures perhaps because she knew almost nothing about the business until she spent months researching and learning everything she could about consignment shops.[13]

2. *Preference for moderate risk.* Entrepreneurs are not wild risk takers but are instead calculated risk takers. Lee Lin, who left his job at a large investment bank to start RentHop, an online service that helps renters find the ideal apartment in New York City, says that entrepreneurs who risk everything typically do not stay in business very long. Lin says that to minimize risk, he manages his company's finances carefully and focuses on profitable growth opportunities.[14] A study of the founders of the businesses listed as *Inc.* magazine's fastest-growing companies found no correlation between risk tolerance and entrepreneurship. The common belief that entrepreneurs prefer taking big risks is a myth. Unlike "high-rolling, riverboat gamblers," entrepreneurs rarely gamble. Their goals may appear to be high—even impossible—in others' eyes,

but entrepreneurs see the situation from a different perspective and believe that their goals are realistic and attainable.

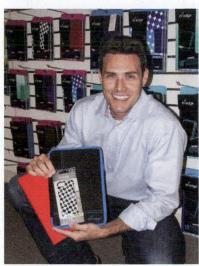

ENTREPRENEURIAL PROFILE: Patrick Mish: M-Edge Accessories Patrick Mish took his father's advice to take the safe route by earning an engineering degree and getting a stable job. After earning a PhD in aero-acoustics from Virginia Polytechnic Institute and State University, Mish went to work for Northrop Grumman, where he was a member of the team that was responsible for creating the next generation of super-stealthy destroyers, but he wasn't happy. Mish spent his days in a cubicle dealing with corporate bureaucracy but dreamed of owning a business of his own. He and his wife, Devon, had purchased one of the first e-readers on the market and discovered that there were very few accessories to enhance its use. That's when the idea to start a business that sells e-reader accessories came to him. Mish began contacting manufacturers with his designs and found one that could produce quality products and was willing to make them in the small quantities Mish ordered at first. Although he was not yet ready to take the plunge into full-time entrepreneurship, Mish began selling a small selection of accessories online after work. Realizing that he needed sales experience, Mish left his engineering job and became a sales representative for a small information technology firm before leaving to operate M-Edge full time. Mish says that by then, starting a business was not a huge risk because he had taken the necessary steps to prepare himself to be a successful entrepreneur. Today, M-Edge generates more than $37 million in annual sales of e-book accessories and has appeared on *Inc.* magazine's list of fastest-growing companies.[15] ■

Courtesy of M-Edge Accessories

Like Patrick Mish, entrepreneurs usually spot opportunities in areas that reflect their passions, knowledge, backgrounds, or experiences, which increases their probability of success. Successful entrepreneurs are not as much risk *takers* as they are risk *eliminators*, systematically removing as many obstacles to the successful launch of their ventures as possible. One of the most successful ways of eliminating risks is to build a viable business plan for a venture.

3. *Self-reliance.* Entrepreneurs must fill multiple roles to make their companies successful, especially in the early days of a start-up. Because their resources usually are limited, they end up performing many jobs themselves, even those they know little about. Yet, entrepreneurs demonstrate a high level of self-reliance and do not shy away from the responsibility for making their businesses succeed. Perhaps that is why many entrepreneurs persist in building businesses even when others ridicule their ideas as follies.

4. *Confidence in their ability to succeed.* Entrepreneurs typically have an abundance of confidence in their ability to succeed and are confident that they chose the correct career path. Entrepreneurs' high levels of optimism may explain why some of the most successful entrepreneurs have failed in business—often more than once—before finally succeeding.

ENTREPRENEURIAL PROFILE: David Steinberg: XL Marketing In 2004, David Steinberg's company, InPhonic, a business that sold mobile phones and services, made it to the top of *Inc.* magazine's list of the fastest-growing small companies in the United States. By 2007, however, the company's fast growth outstripped its cash flow, and InPhonic filed for Chapter 11 bankruptcy before Steinberg sold it to an investment firm. While he was closing the InPhonic chapter of his entrepreneurial experience, Steinberg was launching another company, XL Marketing, which provides lead-generation and customer-acquisition services for other businesses. With his second venture, Steinberg learned from the mistakes he made with InPhonic, securing adequate financing, managing carefully XL Marketing's financial resources, and controlling the company's growth rate. Like Steinberg, smart entrepreneurs recognize that their failures can be the source of some of the lessons that lead them to their greatest successes.[16] ■

5. *Determination.* Some people call this characteristic "grit," the ability to focus intently on achieving a singular, long-term goal. Studies show that grit is a reliable predictor of achievement and success, whether the goal involves launching a successful business,

winning the Scripps National Spelling Bee, or excelling in professional sports.[17] (One recent study concludes that top performance in the National Football League's Combine, in which players who are entering the league's draft perform short physical and mental tasks, has no consistent statistical relationship to subsequent performance in the league.) Successful entrepreneurs demonstrate high levels of determination, especially in the face of challenging circumstances. "Failure was not an option for me," says Alexander Gomez, founder of New Wave Surgical, a highly successful company that designs, patents, and markets laparoendoscopic medical devices used in surgery. "I had everything on the line. It was all or nothing for me."[18] Research by Robert Fairlie of the University of California, Santa Cruz, shows that the Great Recession, which began in late 2007, spawned a surge in entrepreneurship in the same types of businesses typically launched in prosperous times.[19] Perhaps that explains why 57 percent of the *Fortune* 500 companies were launched in either a recession, a "bear" market, or both.[20]

ENTREPRENEURIAL PROFILE: Romesh Wadhwani: Aspect Development Five years after starting a canteen with several other students on the campus of Mumbai's Indian Institute of Technology in 1964 with an investment of 100 rupees (about $10), Romesh Wadhwani arrived in the United States with just $3.48 in his pocket. He earned a master's degree and a PhD in bioengineering from Carnegie Mellon University in Pittsburgh, Pennsylvania, and renewed his passion for entrepreneurship by launching a company that provided computer-based security and energy management services during the short recession of 1991. Wadhwani convinced an angel investor to invest $30,000 and pitched his idea to 125 venture capital firms before he found one that was willing to finance a business started by an entrepreneur with no experience. Just nine years later, Wadhwani sold Aspect Development to i2 technologies for $9.3 billion. Wadhwani says it never occurred to him to give up, and ultimately his tenacity paid off.[21] ∎

6. *Desire for immediate feedback.* Entrepreneurs enjoy the challenge of running a business, and they like to know how they are doing and are constantly looking for feedback. The feedback they receive from their businesses drives them to set higher standards of performance for their companies and themselves.[22]

7. *High level of energy.* Entrepreneurs are more energetic than the average person. That energy may be a critical factor given the incredible effort required to launch a start-up company. Long hours and hard work are the rule rather than the exception, and the pace can be grueling. According to a recent survey by Bank of America, 72 percent of small business owners work more than 40 hours per week.[23] Another recent survey by Sage Software reports that 37 percent of business owners work more hours per week than they did just five years ago.[24] Will Schroter, an entrepreneur who has launched numerous companies, including Go Big Network, an online community for entrepreneurs, says that he works at 1:30 in the morning because he is the founder of a start-up and start-up founders often don't have time to sleep because their work is never-ending. He laughs, adding that he can catchup on his sleep in several years when his company has grown and matured and has levels of managers to handle the immense workload that he currently manages himself.[25]

8. *Future orientation.* Entrepreneurs have a well-defined sense of searching for opportunities. They look ahead and are less concerned with what they did yesterday than with what they might do tomorrow. Not satisfied to sit back and revel in their success, real entrepreneurs stay focused on the future. A year after William Roetzheim's software company, Marotz, landed on *Inc.* magazine's list of the 500 fastest-growing companies in the United States, he sold it and launched another company, Cost Xpert Group, which sells a cost-estimating tool he had developed at Marotz. When Cost Xpert Group reached about $5 million in annual sales, he sold it. "I always plan to sell when I get to $5 million," says Roetzheim. "I like starting companies. I don't want to run something big." Roetzheim recently started another company, Level 4 Ventures, which provides project management software. His plan for the future? Expand Level 4 Ventures to $5 million in sales, sell it, and start another company.[26]

Entrepreneurs see potential where most people see only problems or nothing at all, a characteristic that often makes them the objects of ridicule (at least until their ideas become huge successes). Whereas traditional managers are concerned with managing available *resources*, entrepreneurs are more interested in spotting and capitalizing on *opportunities*. In the United States, 59 percent of those engaged in entrepreneurial activity are **opportunity entrepreneurs**, people who start businesses because they spot an opportunity in the marketplace, compared to **necessity entrepreneurs**, those who start businesses because they cannot find work any other way.[27]

ENTREPRENEURIAL PROFILE: AJ Forsythe and Anthony Martin: iCracked After California Polytechnic State University student AJ Forsythe cracked the screen on his iPhone for the sixth time in just 18 months, the long-time tinkerer decided to fix his phone himself using parts he purchased on eBay. A few hours later, with his phone as good as new, Forsythe realized he had discovered a significant business opportunity and decided to launch iCracked, an iPhone, iPad, and iPod repair service, from his dorm room to serve other Cal Poly students. The business grew quickly, and Forsythe teamed up with fellow students Leslee Lambert and Anthony Martin to turn iCracked into a full-time business. The entrepreneurs reworked their business model, choosing to train self-employed technicians, who would buy parts from iCracked to repair their customers' devices. The young entrepreneurs took a chance and used credit cards to finance iCracked, often rolling up credit card balances of $30,000 to $40,000 per month. Today, iCracked generates $1.4 million in annual sales and has thousands of satisfied customers and nearly 350 technicians across the United States and in 11 other countries. To give back to the community, the entrepreneurs recently opened a retail store in a renovated hotel in Long Beach, California, that employs adult foster youth and provides them with a safe place to live. Forsythe says he and his cofounders have had so much fun launching iCracked that they cannot wait to see what their business brings next.[28] ∎

Serial entrepreneurs, those who repeatedly start businesses and grow them to a sustainable size before striking out again, push this characteristic to the maximum. The majority of serial entrepreneurs are *leapfroggers*, people who start a company, manage its growth until they get bored, and then sell it to start another. A few are *jugglers* (or *parallel entrepreneurs*), people who start and manage several companies at once. Serial entrepreneurs instinctively know that the process of creating a company takes time and choose to pursue several ideas at the same time.[29] *The Entrepreneur State of Mind* study reports that 54 percent of business owners are serial entrepreneurs.[30] "The personality of the serial entrepreneur is almost like a curse," admits one entrepreneurial addict. "You see opportunities every day."[31] At age 81, serial entrepreneur David Gilmour says he has been trying to retire for four decades, but opportunities just kept coming his way. "None of my start-ups were based on searching for something to do," claims Gilmour, who has founded 11 companies (some of which failed) that range from a stereo maker and a luxury resort to bottled water and a gold mine. "I get the vision and the passion for the next project," he says. "It must see the light of day."[32]

It's almost as if serial entrepreneurs are addicted to launching businesses. "Starting a company is a very imaginative, innovative, energy-driven, fun process," says Dick Kouri, who has started 12 companies in his career and now teaches entrepreneurship at the University of North Carolina. "Serial entrepreneurs can't wait to do it again."[33]

9. *Skill at organizing.* Building a company "from scratch" is much like piecing together a giant jigsaw puzzle. Entrepreneurs know how to put the right people together to accomplish a task. Effectively combining people and jobs enables entrepreneurs to transform their visions into reality. "Great entrepreneurship is in the execution," says Eric Paley, an entrepreneur-turned-venture-capitalist.[34]

10. *Value of achievement over money.* One of the most common misconceptions about entrepreneurs is that they are driven wholly by the desire to make money. To the contrary, *achievement* seems to be entrepreneurs' primary motivating force; money is simply a way of "keeping score" of accomplishments—a symbol of achievement. What drives

opportunity entrepreneurs entrepreneurs who start businesses because they spot an opportunity in the marketplace.

necessity entrepreneurs entrepreneurs who start businesses because they cannot find work any other way.

serial entrepreneurs entrepreneurs who repeatedly start businesses and grow them to a sustainable size before striking out again.

entrepreneurs goes much deeper than just the desire for wealth. Economist Joseph Schumpeter claimed that entrepreneurs have "the will to conquer, the impulse to fight, to prove oneself superior to others, to succeed for the sake, not of the fruits of success, but of success itself." Entrepreneurs experience "the joy of creating, of getting things done, or simply of exercising one's energy and ingenuity."[35]

Other characteristics that entrepreneurs tend to exhibit include the following:

High degree of commitment. Entrepreneurship is hard work, and launching a company successfully requires total commitment from an entrepreneur. Business founders often immerse themselves completely in their companies. Most entrepreneurs must overcome seemingly insurmountable barriers to launch a company and keep it growing. That requires commitment and fortitude. Oleg Firer, who at age 12 emigrated to the United States from Russia with his family, cofounded Unified Payments when he was 29. The debit and credit card processing company handles $10 billion in transactions for more than 100,000 merchants annually. Many people dream of launching their own companies; entrepreneurs such as Firer muster the commitment to actually do it. Firer says that the primary reasons for his success are his refusal to accept "no" as an answer and his "all-in" attitude toward his business.[36]

Tolerance for ambiguity. Entrepreneurs tend to have a high tolerance for ambiguous, ever-changing situations, the environment in which they most often operate. This ability to handle uncertainty is critical because these business builders constantly make decisions using new, sometimes conflicting information gleaned from a variety of unfamiliar sources. Based on his research, entrepreneurial expert Amar Bhidé says that entrepreneurs exhibit a willingness to jump into ventures even when they cannot visualize what the ultimate outcome may be.[37]

Creativity. One of the hallmarks of entrepreneurs is creativity. They constantly come up with new product or service ideas, unique ways to market their businesses, and innovative business models. Their minds are constantly at work developing unique business models, services, and products. Davide Vigano, Mario Esposito, and Maurizio Macagno, founders of Heapsylon, focused their creativity on developing practical wearable technology designed to improve people's lives. One of the products their company has created is Sensoria fitness socks, which are made from a proprietary fabric equipped with sensors and include an electronic anklet that reads signals from the sensors. The anklet transmits information to the runner's smart phone via an app that shows his or her speed, number of steps, distance traveled, and calories burned. The sophisticated device also tracks the runner's cadence, foot-landing technique, and weight distribution on the foot. If Sensoria detects a problem, such as heel striking or overpronating, it offers the runner real-time verbal coaching cues to remedy it, allowing the runner to avoid injuries.[38] You will learn more about the creative process and how to stimulate entrepreneurial creativity in Chapter 2.

Flexibility. One hallmark of true entrepreneurs is their ability to adapt to the changing needs and preferences of their customers and the changing demands of the business environment. In this rapidly changing global economy, rigidity often leads to failure. Successful entrepreneurs learn to be masters of improvisation, reshaping and transforming their businesses as conditions demand. Research by Saras Sarasvathy, a professor at the University of Virginia's Darden School of Business, shows that entrepreneurs excel at effectual reasoning, which "does not begin with a specific goal." Instead, says Sarasvathy, "it begins with a given set of means and allows goals to emerge contingently over time from the varied imagination and diverse aspirations of the founders and the people they interact with. Effectual thinkers are like explorers setting out on voyages into uncharted waters." Entrepreneurs set goals, but their goals are flexible. Sarasvathy compares entrepreneurs to "iron chefs," who prepare sumptuous meals when handed a hodgepodge of ingredients and given the task of using their creativity to come up with an appetizing menu. Corporate CEOs, on the other hand, develop a plan to prepare a specific dish and then create a process for making that dish in the most efficient, expeditious fashion.[39]

Resourceful. Entrepreneurs excel at getting the most out of the resources that are available, however limited they may be. They are skilled at **bootstrapping**, a strategy that involves conserving money and cutting costs during start-up so that entrepreneurs can pour every available dollar into their businesses.

ENTREPRENEURIAL PROFILE: Ryan Barr: WhippingPost.com After holding a series of uninspiring jobs, Ryan Barr, a musician, started an online company, WhippingPost.com, that markets high-quality leather products, such as guitar cases, guitar straps, tote bags, and "picker's wallets." Like many cash-starved entrepreneurs, Barr used bootstrapping to launch and grow his company. He would save enough money, buy some leather, and make a prototype. Once he had saved enough money, Barr visited a leather manufacturer in Leon, Mexico, to whom he outsourced production of the company's products. Priced at $825, Barr's initial product, guitar cases, appealed to a limited audience, so he came up with the idea of a picker's wallet, one that has a slot designed specifically to hold a guitar pick so that guitar players no longer have to resort to their standard practice of storing picks between their credit cards. Barr sent press releases about his picker's wallet to numerous fashion, design, and music blogs, which generated several posts and good publicity. Priced between $31 and $37, the picker's wallet is now the company's best-selling item and has helped WhippingPost.com surpass $200,000 in annual sales.[40] ∎

Willingness to work hard. Entrepreneurs work hard to build their companies, and there are no shortcuts around the workload. In his book *Outliers: The Story of Success*, Malcolm Gladwell observes that the secret to success in business (or sports, music, art, or any other field) is to invest at least 10,000 hours practicing and honing one's skills. "What's really interesting about this 10,000-hour rule is that it applies virtually everywhere," says Gladwell. For instance, Mark Cuban, billionaire owner of the Dallas Mavericks of the National Basketball Association and founder of Broadcast.com, the leading provider of multimedia and streaming on the Internet (which he sold to Yahoo! for $5.7 billion), says he worked for seven years without taking a day off to launch his first business, MicroSolutions, a computer systems integrator. Cuban spent his days making sales calls, and at night and on weekends he studied and practiced to learn everything he could about computers.[41] Entrepreneurs often capitalize on opportunities through sheer amounts of hard work through which they test, invalidate, test again, and finally validate their ideas. A great idea may come to an entrepreneur in a single moment, but building a successful business from that idea takes time and lots of hard work.[42]

Tenacity. Obstacles, obstructions, and defeat typically do not dissuade entrepreneurs from doggedly pursuing their visions. They simply keep trying. Hurricane Sandy nearly wiped out Jackie Summers's company, Jack from Brooklyn, which produces a unique artisanal alcoholic beverage called sorel in an old warehouse in Brooklyn's historic Red Hook district. Despite the loss of product, equipment, and sales, Summers persevered and rebuilt his business. Summers's spirit of tenacity, willingness to concentrate on a single unsurmountable task each day, and accomplishment of each task enabled him to recover from the devastating loss.[43] Noting the obstacles that entrepreneurs must overcome, economist Joseph Schumpeter argued that success is "a feat not of intellect but of will." Rick Smolan quit his job as a magazine photojournalist to launch A Day in the Life Inc., a company that publishes eye-popping coffee table books that feature photographs by professional photographers who swarm a particular country and capture its essence in 24-hour marathon photo sessions. "I met with 35 publishers," says Smolan. "Every single one of them told me what an incredibly stupid idea A Day in the Life was." Smolan persisted, and his company went on to produce 11 books that sold more than 5 million copies before he sold it to start another business.[44]

What conclusion can we draw from the volumes of research conducted on the entrepreneurial personality? Entrepreneurs are not of one mold; no one set of characteristics can predict who will become entrepreneurs and whether they will succeed. Indeed, *diversity* seems to be a central characteristic of entrepreneurs. One astute observer of the entrepreneurial personality explains, "Business owners are a culture unto themselves—strong, individualistic people who

bootstrapping
a strategy that involves conserving money and cutting costs during start-up so that entrepreneurs can pour every available dollar into their businesses.

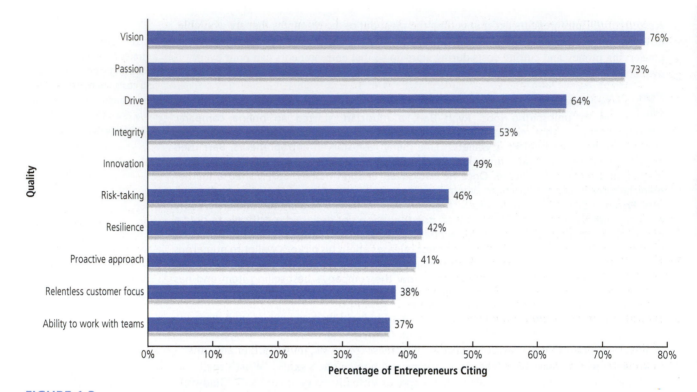

FIGURE 1.3

Most Important Qualities of an Entrepreneur

Source: Nature or Nurture: Decoding the DNA of the Entrepreneur, Ernst & Young, 2011, p. 17, http://www.ey.com/GL/en/Services/ Strategic-Growth-Markets/Nature-or-nurture--Decoding-the-DNA-of-the-entrepreneur---Entrepreneurs-share-core-traits.

scorn convention—and nowadays, they're driving the global economy."[45] Indeed, entrepreneurs tend to be nonconformists, a characteristic that seems to be central to their views of the world and to their success.

As you can see from the examples in this chapter, *anyone*, regardless of age, race, gender, color, national origin, or any other characteristic, can become an entrepreneur (although not everyone should). There are no limitations on this form of economic expression. Entrepreneurship is not a mystery; it is a practical discipline. Entrepreneurship is not a genetic trait; it is a skill that most people can learn. It has become a very common vocation. The editors of *Inc.* magazine claim, "Entrepreneurship is more mundane than it's sometimes portrayed. . . . You don't need to be a person of mythical proportions to be very, very successful in building a company."[46] Figure 1.3 summarizes the qualities that company founders say are most important to entrepreneurs.

LO3A

Describe the benefits of entrepreneurship.

The Benefits of Entrepreneurship

Surveys show that owners of small businesses believe they work harder, earn more money, and are more satisfied than if they worked for someone else. Before launching any business venture, every potential entrepreneur should consider the benefits of small business ownership.

Opportunity to Create Your Own Destiny

Owning a business provides entrepreneurs the independence and the opportunity to achieve what is important to them. Entrepreneurs want to "call the shots" in their lives, and they use their businesses to make that desire a reality. "Owning your own business means you have some say in deciding what your destiny is going to be," says Kathy Mills, founder of Strategic Communications, a highly successful information technology company in Louisville, Kentucky.[47]

For many entrepreneurs, living where and how they choose is one of the principal benefits of controlling their destinies through business ownership.

ENTREPRENEURIAL PROFILE: Alan Blado: Liquid Descent Alan Blado had a successful career as a stockbroker in Colorado Springs, Colorado, but found his work unsatisfying. Nor did he enjoy wearing a suit to work every day. Blado had worked as a whitewater rafting guide in college and loved the thrill and beauty of being on the river. Several prime rivers, including the Colorado River and the Eagle River, were nearby, and Blado decided to open his own whitewater rafting business. Blado bootstrapped his business, keeping his job and living with his parents for a few years so that he could save enough money to get into business. With the money he saved, Blado purchased a failed rafting business, renamed it Liquid Descent, and began marketing rafting trips with an emphasis on safety and customer satisfaction. Now with two Colorado locations in Idaho Springs and Kremmling, Blado works seven days a week during the busy summer season. Blado does not consider his calling to be work because he spends most of his days on the water in beautiful places with his clients doing what he loves.[48] ∎

Courtesy of Liquid Descent

Like Alan Blado, entrepreneurs reap the intrinsic rewards of knowing that they are the driving forces behind their businesses.

Opportunity to Make a Difference

Increasingly, entrepreneurs are starting businesses because they see an opportunity to make a difference in a cause that is important to them. Known as **social entrepreneurs**, these business builders seek innovative solutions to some of society's most vexing problems. They use their skills not only to create profitable business ventures but also to achieve social and environmental goals for society as a whole. Their businesses often have a triple bottom line that encompasses economic, social, and environmental objectives. These entrepreneurs see their businesses as mechanisms for achieving social goals that are important to them as individuals. Whether it is providing low-cost, sturdy housing for families in developing countries or establishing a recycling program to preserve Earth's limited resources, these entrepreneurs are finding ways to combine their concerns for social issues and their desire to earn a good living.

social entrepreneurs
entrepreneurs who use their skills not only to create profitable businesses but also to achieve economic, social, and environmental goals for the common good.

ENTREPRENEURIAL PROFILE: Jessica Matthews and Julia Silverman: Uncharted Play Jessica Matthews and Julia Silverman drew the inspiration for their business, Uncharted Play, from their travels abroad during college. Everywhere they went, even in the most poverty-stricken areas, they saw children playing soccer, an observation that led them to create the Soccket ball, an energy-harnessing soccer ball, as part of an engineering class for non-engineers. Their goal was to create a for-profit company whose goal is to improve the lives of the 1.4 billion people around the world who have no access to electricity. The Soccket ball is a regulation-size soccer ball that contains a motion-activated chargeable battery pack surrounded by a foam core and acts as a portable generator, capturing and storing energy during play that people can use later to operate lights, cell phones, mini-refrigerators, and other devices. The Soccket ball has a small flip cap that covers an electric socket into which users can plug various devices. For every 15 minutes of play, the Soccket ball can power an LED lamp for three hours. "We're also thinking of how everything from basketballs to volleyballs can be useful," Matthews says. "Making a difference doesn't have to be serious and boring. It can be as simple and fun as playing soccer."[49] ∎

Evan Agostini/AP Photo

Matthews and Silverman are just two of millions of social entrepreneurs who have started for-profit businesses with a broader goal of making the world a better place to live.

You Be the Consultant

Decoding the DNA of the Entrepreneur

Management consulting firm Ernst & Young has developed the following model of an entrepreneur:

Nucleus. At the center of the model lie the entrepreneur's complementary characteristics of an opportunistic mindset and an attitude of tolerance of risk and failure.

Opportunistic mindset. One of the hallmarks of entrepreneurs is their ability to spot opportunities where others do not. They know that although disruptions create problems, they also create opportunities for those who are prepared to capitalize on them. Avid beekeepers Tim Dover and Susan Gardner turned their hobby into a bee supply business that they operated out of their homes and then into a retail store in tiny Traveler's Rest, South Carolina, when a new state law required beekeepers who produce more than 400 gallons of honey per year for resale to process their honey in a Department of Agriculture-approved honey house. "That's when we decided to turn our little home-based hobby business into a store," says Gardner. The entrepreneurs launched Carolina Honey Bee Company, purchased a building in the town's revitalized business district, and converted it into a state-approved honey house that includes retail space for beekeeping supplies and local honey for nearby residents and area tourists. Although Gardner and Dover are not yet drawing salaries, Carolina Honey Bee Company is generating positive cash

flow. "We started this business on a shoestring budget," says Dover, "and we're at a point that it's funding its own growth." Surging interest in both beekeeping and in local food products are fueling their company's growth. The entrepreneurs' goal is to have multiple stores in several states within five years. "We want it to be a brand," says Dover.

Tolerance of risk and failure. Most people are risk averse. Most entrepreneurs don't take extraordinary risks, but they accept risk as a natural part of achieving big goals. Lyn Strong studied graphic design and painting at Western Carolina University in Cullowhee, North Carolina, where she took a class on jewelry making on a whim. She was captivated by the medium and, after graduation, purchased jewelry-making equipment to set up a studio in her small apartment. To learn the industry, she also took a job at a local jewelry store and worked her way into the store's workshop. As her skills improved, Strong decided to go out on her own, selling her hand-crafted jewelry at arts and crafts shows and eventually opening a retail store in Greenville, South Carolina. Customers appreciate her highly detailed pieces, which feature precious gemstones, silver, platinum, and gold, because of their "everyday wearability," she says. Recently, Strong made significant investments in technology and equipment so that she can produce pieces faster and expand her customer base nationally

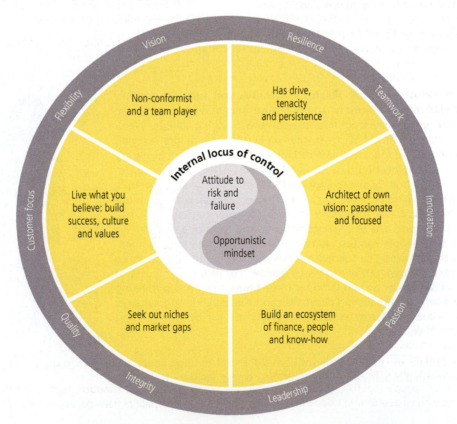

You Be the Consultant (continued)

and internationally. "I've stood out on a limb most of my life," says the successful entrepreneur. "You have to take risks to be successful, and I don't think you always are."

Inner Ring. The inner ring of the model shows six characteristics that are integral parts of the entrepreneurial personality:

Drive, tenacity, and persistence. To bring their business ideas to life, entrepreneurs must demonstrate drive, tenacity, and persistence. Entrepreneurs must overcome countless obstacles on their way to building successful businesses.

Architect of own vision; passionate and focused. As teens, copreneurs Larkin and Mark Hammond worked at fast-food restaurants before going to college and taking corporate jobs in California. For years, the Hammonds dreamed of owning a restaurant. Finally, they decided to leave their corporate jobs behind, sell everything they owned, and move to the East Coast, where they purchased a small lakeside restaurant in Lake Lure, North Carolina. Risky? "That's where Larkin comes in," laughs Mark. "She has a lot of confidence." The Hammonds quizzed all of their customers about their favorite dishes, items they would like to see on the menu, and décor ideas and integrated everything they learned into revamping the restaurant. Within three years, Larkins on the Lake was earning a profit and providing the couple with salaries that exceeded their former corporate paychecks. Fourteen years after they started, the entrepreneurial couple owns six restaurants and a catering business, but both of them agree that success is doing something that they love *together*.

Build an ecosystem of finance, people, and know-how. Smart entrepreneurs know that they cannot do everything themselves and build a team of professionals to nurture and protect the business. While attending the University of South Carolina, Allen Stephenson dreamed of starting a business. Having operated a successful lawn care business in high school, Stephenson had a head start on the road to entrepreneurship. His inspiration came one day as a result of a semester he spent abroad in Italy, where he saw firsthand fine clothing made with attention to detail; he took a pair of scissors to his collection of polo shirts, cut away what he considered to be the best features of each one, and stitched them back together into a model "Frankenstein" shirt. He spent the next year working with several textile industry veterans, perfecting his design for the perfect polo shirt and having samples made by 11 factories in four countries. Stephenson launched Southern Tide, ordered 5,500 shirts, and began calling on independent men's shops to sell them. Most shop owners declined, which prompted him to start giving the owners a few shirts to wear or to give to their best customers. "I started getting phone calls saying, 'We need more. We need more,'" he recalls. Sales accelerated quickly, and Stephenson made an important and selfless decision to bring in an experienced CEO, Jim Twining. "I was sure [the business] was going to work if I just kept working at it and getting the right people together," he says. "I knew it wouldn't work with what and who I alone knew at the

time." Twining led Southern Tide in a $1.8 million round of equity financing and developed a strategic plan to guide its growth. Today, Southern Tide's product line has grown well beyond the perfect polo shirt to include pants, T-shirts, hats, belts, shoes, swimwear, and more and is sold in nearly 600 stores in 43 states and on its Web site. Many publications, including *Inc.* and *Forbes*, have recognized Stephenson's Southern Tide as one of the fastest-growing small companies in the United States.

Seek out market niches and gaps. Entrepreneurs are adept at finding lucrative niches and gaps in the market that large businesses often overlook. After graduating from Clemson University, Craig Pavlish, a fan of craft beers, worked with his partners, who were experienced brew masters, to open Growler Station (a growler is a special amber-colored container used to carry fresh craft beer home from a brewery), a craft brewery in Greenville, South Carolina. With a vibrant downtown district filled with restaurants, performance venues, and shops; a growing population of upscale, educated young people; and a large international community, Greenville proved to be the ideal location for a niche business such as a craft brewery. "The trail has been blazed here in Greenville," says Pavlish. Growler Station's unique process and technology allows the small brewery to bottle beer in growlers so that customers can take it home, unlike typical growlers, which must be consumed immediately.

Live what you believe; build success, culture, and values. As you have seen, entrepreneurs create company cultures that reflect their values and belief systems. Entrepreneurs often build businesses that seek to achieve financial, social, and environmental goals that make their communities—and the world—better places to live.

Be a nonconformist and a team player. Entrepreneurs tend to be nonconformists, choosing to do things their own way. Just as many traditional managers would find the life of an entrepreneur unsettling, so too would entrepreneurs find the boundaries, rules, and traditions of corporate life stifling and boring. Yet successful entrepreneurs recognize the importance of being team players. They understand that accomplishing big goals requires a broad set of skills that no one person has. Sisters Sophie LaMontagne and Kallinis Berman were close growing up but went their separate ways after college. LaMontagne became a biotech expert, and Berman worked in the fashion industry. In 2007, the sisters reunited to realize a dream they had had since childhood: owning a bakery together. "We quit our jobs, borrowed our grandmother's cake recipes, and took a leap of faith," says LaMontagne. Today, the sisters are at the helm of Georgetown Cupcake, a bakery that has grown from a two-person shop outside of Washington, DC, to a 350-person operation with stores in New York City, Boston, Atlanta, and Los Angeles. "Having your sister as your business partner gives you a huge head start," says La Montagne. "I'm not saying it's easy, but if anything goes wrong, you know you've got your sister behind you."

Outer Ring. The model's outer ring includes many of the entrepreneurial traits discussed in this chapter, including

(continued)

You Be the Consultant (continued)

resilience, teamwork, innovation, passion, leadership, integrity, quality, customer focus, flexibility, and vision.

1. How do the characteristics at the model's nucleus, opportunistic mindset and tolerance of risk and failure, fit together in the entrepreneur's mind?

2. Work with a team of your classmates to interview at least one entrepreneur. Does he or she fit the model

described here? Explain, giving specific examples from your interview.

Sources: Based on "Nature or Nurture? Decoding the DNA of the Entrepreneur," Ernst & Young, 2011, pp. 14–21; Amy Clarke Burns, "The Buzz About Honey," *Greenville News*, January 20, 2013, pp. 1E–2E; Lillia Callum-Penso, "An Original by Design," *Greenville News*, October 14, 2012, pp. 1E–2E; Lillia Callum-Penso, "Feeding a Passion," *Greenville News*, November 11, 2012, pp. 1E–2E; Julia Savacool, "The Sweet Success of Sisters," *USA Weekend*, August 3–5, 2012, pp. 6–7; Amy Clarke Burns, "Riding the Tide," *Greenville News*, August 5, 2012, pp. 1E–2E; Lillia Callum-Penso, "Crafting a Culture," *Greenville News*, July 29, 2012, pp. 1E–2E.

Opportunity to Reach Your Full Potential

Too many people find their work boring, unchallenging, and unexciting. But not entrepreneurs! To them, there is little difference between work and play; the two are synonymous. Entrepreneurs' businesses become their instruments for self-expression and self-actualization. They know that the only boundaries on their success are those imposed by their own creativity, enthusiasm, and vision. Owning a business gives them a sense of empowerment. While Elizabeth Elting was in college, she worked in the translation industry, where she saw plenty of room for improvement. After she met Phil Shawe at New York University's Stern School of Business, the pair decided to start TransPerfect Translations to provide timely, accurate translation services to companies across the globe. Launched from a dorm room, TransPerfect Translations now employs more than 2,000 people in 80 offices on six continents and generates annual sales of more than $350 million. Elting and Shawe have financed the companies' growth without any external financing. Elting says she and Shawe enjoy having the freedom to make their own business decisions and not having to explain them to investors or anyone else. The duo also agree there is nothing they would rather be doing than running their own business.[50]

Opportunity to Reap Impressive Profits

Although money is not the primary force driving most entrepreneurs, the profits their businesses can earn are an important motivating factor in their decisions to launch companies. A recent survey by Wells Fargo reports that 72 percent of small business owners believe they are in a better financial position running their own businesses than working for a company in the same field.[51] Several studies, including one by the Institute for the Study of Labor, confirm this belief; the median salary for entrepreneurs is 18 percent higher than that for employed workers.[52] What explains the earning differential? "While employees suffer from the 'guard rails' and 'iron cages' of corporate America, entrepreneurs are able to create environments over time that maximize the value of their education and skills," notes one writer.[53] Entrepreneurs are not constrained by the boundaries that corporate hierarchies impose on their employees; they are free to create value by making the best use of their experience, skills, abilities, and ideas and, as a result, reap the financial benefits of their creative efforts. Most entrepreneurs never become superrich, but many of them do become quite wealthy. In fact, more than two-thirds of the billionaires on the *Forbes* list of the 400 richest Americans are first-generation entrepreneurs![54] People who own their own businesses are more likely to be millionaires than those who are employed by others. According to Russ Alan Prince and Lewis Schiff, authors of *The Middle Class Millionaire*, more than 80 percent of middle-class millionaires, those people with a net worth between $1 million and $10 million, own their own businesses or are part of professional partnerships. (They also work an average of 70 hours a week.)[55] Indeed, the typical millionaire's business is not a glamorous, high-tech enterprise; more often, it is something much less glamorous—scrap metal, welding, auctioneering, garbage collection, and the like.

ENTREPRENEURIAL PROFILE: Madison Robinson: Fish Flops When Madison Robinson was just eight years old, she was living at the beach in Galveston Island, Texas, and came up with the idea of flip flops for children adorned with sea creature motifs and LED lights. Five years later, her father, Dan, a former banker, helped her turn her sketches into an actual product, Fish Flops, and get some samples made so that she could display them at a trade show, which resulted in more than 30 boutique stores placing orders. Using family and friend financing, Madison also launched a Web site and wrote to buyers at upscale department stores Nordstrom and Macy's, which not only agreed to sell Fish Flops but also asked Madison to design a line of Fish Flops for women. Madison used social media marketing to catch the attention of reporters, television show hosts (including *Entertainment Tonight's* Nancy O'Dell), and HSN's Tony Little. Her company also received publicity after Madison convinced celebrities to sign 300 pairs of Fish Flops that she donated to patients at a children's hospital. As she enters the tenth grade, Madison already has sold more than 60,000 pairs of Fish Flops, generating more than $1.2 million in sales. In business just two years, Madison's company has diversified into apparel and children's books and is already profitable, earning more than enough to cover her tuition for college, where she plans to study business.[56] ■

Opportunity to Contribute to Society and Be Recognized for Your Efforts

Playing a vital role in their local business systems and knowing that their work has a significant impact on the nation's economy is yet another reward for small business managers. Often, small business owners are among the most respected and most trusted members of their communities. Business deals based on trust and mutual respect are the hallmark of many established small companies. These owners enjoy the trust and recognition they receive from the customers and the communities they have served faithfully over the years. A recent Public Affairs Council survey reports that 87 percent of adults have a favorable view of small businesses, compared to just 41 percent who view the federal government favorably.[57] An earlier version of the same survey reports that 68 percent of adults say they prefer doing business with a small local company that charges somewhat higher prices than a large national company that offers lower prices.[58]

Opportunity to Do What You Enjoy and Have Fun at It

A common sentiment among small business owners is that their work really isn't work. Most successful entrepreneurs choose to enter their particular business fields because they have an interest in them and enjoy those lines of work. They have made their avocations (hobbies) their vocations (work) and are glad they did! In a recent Gallup poll, 51 percent of entrepreneurs said that if money were no object, they would continue to work either full- or part-time in their businesses, and 18 percent said they would start another business.[59] These entrepreneurs are living Harvey McKay's advice: "Find something you love to do, and you'll never have to work a day in your life." The journey rather than the destination is the entrepreneur's greatest reward. "Rather than have money be your primary motivator," says Tony Hsieh, CEO of online shoe retailer Zappos, a company that Hsieh sold to Amazon for $1.2 billion, "think about what you would be so passionate about doing that you'd be happy doing it for 10 years, even if you never made any money from it. *That's* what you should be doing. Your passion is what's going to get you through the hard times. Your passion is going to be contagious and rub off onto employees and have a ripple effect on customers and business partners as well."[60]

ENTREPRENEURIAL PROFILE: Ian McMenamin: Anything Coral When Ian McMenamin was in high school, he worked in a pet store and spent a lot of time near the saltwater aquariums because he was fascinated by the beautifully colored coral in them. McMenamin learned that the more colorful the coral, the higher its selling price and that it is possible to grow coral. He took some of the money he had saved from his part-time job and invested in the equipment he needed to grow coral. His early efforts failed, but over time, McMenamin engaged in extensive research and conducted his own experiments to learn which diets produced the best results for his coral and was able to produce enough to sell to customers he found through Craigslist. As his knowledge base grew, McMenamin began growing rare varieties of coral, which attracted more customers, many of whom were willing and able to pay premium prices for rare specimens of coral. While he was a sophomore at the University of Oregon, McMenamin invested $12,000 in more sophisticated equipment and officially launched his company, Anything Coral. His customer base grew, and today, McMenamin, who recently graduated from the University of Oregon with a degree in business and entrepreneurship, rents a 1,500-square-foot room in the basement of his apartment building in Eugene, Oregon, where he grows more than 400 varieties of coral using environmentally sustainable methods. Anything Coral sells to more than 300 retail and 30 wholesale customers around the world, including some of the world's wealthiest coral collectors, and has become one of the most successful coral distributors on the West Coast.[61] ■

Not only has McMenamin found a way to earn a living, but, more important, he is doing something he loves!

LO3B

Describe the drawbacks of entrepreneurship.

The Potential Drawbacks of Entrepreneurship

Owning a business has many benefits and provides many opportunities; however, anyone planning to enter the world of entrepreneurship should be aware of its potential drawbacks. Although operating a successful business has never been easy, 59 percent of small business owners say running their companies is harder now than it was five years ago. In addition to a soft economy, entrepreneurs cited difficulty keeping pace with technology and more competition from direct rivals and large companies as the primary reasons that business is more difficult today.[62] Entrepreneurship is not a suitable career path for the timid. Individuals who prefer the security of a steady paycheck, a comprehensive benefits package, a two-week paid vacation, and the support of a corporate staff probably should not go into business for themselves. Some of the disadvantages of entrepreneurship include the following.

Uncertainty of Income

Opening and running a business provides no guarantee that an entrepreneur will earn enough money to survive. Although the mean and median incomes for entrepreneurs are higher than those for employees, so is the *variability* of entrepreneurs' incomes. In other words, some entrepreneurs earn far more through their companies than they could working for someone else, but other entrepreneurs' businesses barely earn enough to provide them with an adequate income. In the early days of a start-up, a business often cannot provide an attractive salary for its owner and meet all its financial obligations, meaning that the entrepreneur may have to live on savings or a spouse's income. The steady income that comes with working for someone else is absent because the owner is always the last one to be paid.

ENTREPRENEURIAL PROFILE: Gary Whitehill: Entrepreneur Week Gary Whitehill, a former investment banker on Wall Street, decided to forego his six-figure salary and invest his life savings into a start-up venture, Entrepreneur Week. Whitehill and his cofounders estimate that they saved $350,000 in the first year by bootstrapping their start-up, which sponsors events around the world that are designed to provide other entrepreneurs with the skills and inspiration they need to launch their companies. The cofounders agreed that they would not draw salaries for at least one year, used their network of contacts to secure publicity and in-kind start-up services, and worked from their homes to avoid the cost of renting office space. Whitehill had interns sleeping on his couches and managers staying in spare bedrooms and held weekly strategy sessions on his patio.[63] ■

Risk of Losing Your Entire Investment

Business failure can lead to financial ruin for an entrepreneur, and the small business failure rate is relatively high. According to research by the Bureau of Labor Statistics, 34 percent of new businesses fail within two years, and 51 percent shut down within five years. Within 10 years, 66 percent of new businesses will have folded.[64] Business failure can mean financial ruin for an entrepreneur. Before "reaching for the golden ring," entrepreneurs should ask themselves if they can cope psychologically with the consequences of failure:

- What is the worst that could happen if I open my business and it fails?

- How likely is the worst to happen? (Am I truly prepared to launch my business?)

- What can I do to lower the risk of my business failing?

- If my business were to fail, what is my contingency plan for coping?

Long Hours and Hard Work

Business start-ups usually demand long hours and hard work from their owners. The average small business owner works 51 hours a week, compared to the 40.2 hours per week the typical U.S. production employee works.[65] Adam Warren, founder of Syinc.tv and Sportyourself, companies that allows users to incorporate links to retailers' Web sites for the products that appear in their online photographs and receive payment when someone purchases a tagged item, says that his business is nothing like a 9-to-5 job. Warren's workday typically starts at 6:30 A.M. and does not end until 10 p.m. or later, but Warren does not view it as work. Operating his own business is a passion that he sees as a calling.[66] In many start-ups, six- or seven-day work-weeks with no paid vacations are the *norm*. A recent survey by American Express OPEN reports that only 49 percent of small business owners were planning to take a summer vacation of at least one week. The primary reason entrepreneurs don't take vacations? "Too busy."[67] The demands of owning a business make achieving a balance between work and life difficult for entrepreneurs. Many entrepreneurs find that they must work 60 to 80 hours a week as they build their businesses and must push their personal lives aside until their companies are established.[68]

Lower Quality of Life Until the Business Gets Established

The long hours and hard work needed to launch a company can take their toll on the other aspects of an entrepreneur's life. Business owners often find that their roles as husbands or wives and fathers or mothers take a backseat to their roles as company founders. In fact, according to a survey by American Express, 67 percent of entrepreneurs say that owning a business requires them to make sacrifices, most often in the areas of family relationships and friendships.[69] Meg Hirshberg, whose husband Gary founded Stonyfield Farm, a maker of organic yogurt, says that an entrepreneur's family members actually are his or her most important investors because no one will sacrifice more or be affected more by the outcome of the business venture. Because launching a business consumes so much of an entrepreneur's time, energy, and focus, his or her family members often wonder whether the business takes priority over family.[70] Part of the problem is that more than three-fourths of all entrepreneurs launch their businesses between the ages of 20 and 44, just when they marry and start their families.[71] As a result, marriages, families, and friendships are too often casualties of small business ownership.

ENTREPRENEURIAL PROFILE: Frances and Michael Weldon: Cattail Ridge Family Market   Four years after launching Cattail Ridge Family Market in Sackville, New Brunswick, Frances Weldon was exhausted from the constant challenges of starting and running a business and felt isolated because the business consumed almost all of her time and energy. To regain balance in her life, she asked her husband Michael to join the company. Frances now manages the sales floor because customer service is her strength, and Michael handles the company's operations, which is his strength. The change saved the company. The Weldons spend more time with their friends and family and will soon take their first vacation since starting the business.[72] ■

High Levels of Stress

Starting and managing a business can be an incredibly rewarding experience, but it also can be a highly stressful one (see Figure 1.4). Entrepreneurs often have made significant investments in their companies, have left behind the safety and security of a steady paycheck and benefits, and have mortgaged everything they own to get into business. Failure may mean total financial ruin, and that creates intense levels of stress and anxiety! Sometimes entrepreneurs unnecessarily bear the burden of managing alone because they cannot bring themselves to delegate authority and responsibility to others in the company, even though their employees are capable.

Complete Responsibility

It's great to be the boss, but many entrepreneurs find that they must make decisions on issues about which they are not really knowledgeable. Many business owners have difficulty finding advisers. When there is no one to ask, the pressure can build quickly. The realization that the decisions they make are the cause of their company's success or failure has a devastating effect on some people.

Discouragement

Launching a business is a substantial undertaking that requires a great deal of dedication, discipline, and tenacity. Along the way to building a successful business, entrepreneurs will run headlong into many different obstacles, some of which appear to be insurmountable. In the face of such difficulties, discouragement and disillusionment are common emotions. Successful entrepreneurs know that every business encounters rough spots along the way, and they wade through difficult times with lots of hard work and an abundant reserve of optimism.

Despite the challenges that starting and running a business pose, entrepreneurs are very satisfied with their career choices. A Wells Fargo/Gallup Small Business Index survey reports that 83 percent of small business owners say that if they were choosing a career again, they would still

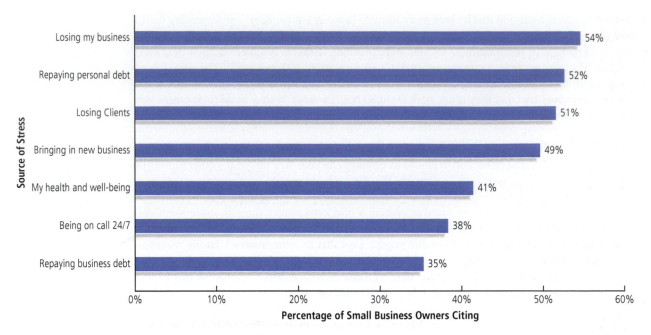

FIGURE 1.4

Sources of Stress for Small Business Owners

Source: Based on *Q1 U.S. Small Business Survey: Health and Well-Being*, Hiscox, April 2012, p. 12.

become small business owners.[73] "I absolutely love what I'm doing," says Scott Badger, founder of KPI Direct, a consulting company that helps businesses create direct marketing programs. "I have no regrets."[74] Many entrepreneurs are so happy with their work that they want to continue it indefinitely. In fact, 63 percent of entrepreneurs polled in a recent survey say they never intend to fully retire, choosing instead to work either full- or part-time, and 4 percent say they intend to start a new business.[75]

LO4

Explain the forces that are driving the growth of entrepreneurship.

Behind the Boom: What's Feeding the Entrepreneurial Fire

What forces are driving this entrepreneurial trend in our economy? Which factors have led to this age of entrepreneurship? Some of the most significant ones include the following:

Entrepreneurs as heroes. An intangible but compelling factor is the attitude that Americans have toward entrepreneurs. As a nation, we have raised them to hero status and have held out their accomplishments as models to follow. Business founders such as Bill Gates (Microsoft Corporation), Kevin Plank (Under Armour), Oprah Winfrey (Harpo Productions and OWN [the Oprah Winfrey Network]), Jeff Bezos (Amazon), Robert Johnson (Black Entertainment Television), Steve Jobs (Apple), and Mark Zuckerberg (Facebook) are to entrepreneurship what LeBron James, Michael Phelps, and Tom Brady are to sports.

Entrepreneurial education. Colleges and universities have discovered that entrepreneurship is an extremely popular course of study. Disillusioned with corporate America's downsized job offerings and less promising career paths, a rapidly growing number of students sees owning a business as their best career option. Increasingly, students enroll in college knowing that they want to start their own companies rather than considering entrepreneurship as a possibility later in life; indeed, many are starting companies while they are in college. Today, more than two-thirds of the colleges and universities in the United States (more than 2,300) offer more than 5,000 courses in entrepreneurship or small business, up from just 16 in 1970. More than 400,000 students are enrolled in entrepreneurship courses taught by nearly 9,000 faculty members, and many colleges and universities have difficulty meeting the demand for courses in entrepreneurship and small business.[76]

ENTREPRENEURIAL PROFILE: Jeremy Young: HillFresh Laundry When Jeremy Young enrolled at Hamilton College in Clinton, New York, he declared a major in art history, but joining the entrepreneurship club on campus in his sophomore year changed his future. During one of the club's meetings, Young pitched the idea of a prepaid laundry service aimed at busy students and soon had partnered with four other students to research the market and prepare a business plan. Rather than raise capital to start a laundry business, Hill and his partners decided to become laundry brokers. Impressed with the young entrepreneurs' business plan and professionalism, college administrators approved their request to launch their company, Hillfresh Laundry, on campus. The entrepreneurs mailed materials promoting their laundry service and within 18 months had recouped their initial investments and were earning a profit. Young immediately began preparing a succession plan to ensure that HillFresh Laundry continues to operate after he graduates. The founders donate a portion of the company's sales to the entrepreneurship club that helped them get started.[77] ∎

Demographic and economic factors. More than 75 percent of entrepreneurs start their businesses between the ages of 20 and 44, and the number of Americans in that age range currently is nearly 103 million! In addition, the economic growth that spanned most of the last 25 years created a significant amount of wealth among people of this age group and many business opportunities on which they can capitalize.

ENTREPRENEURIAL PROFILE: Michelle Lam and Aarthi Ramamurthy: True & Co. After Michelle Lam, 33, a former research associate with several large multinational consulting firms, spent two hours in a fruitless search for a new bra at a San Francisco department store, she decided that there had to be a better way and decided to improve the customer buying experience that has remained the same since the modern bra was invented in the mid-1930s. Lam worked with Aarthi Ramamurthy, a former program manager for Microsoft, to develop an online quiz using guidelines that experts use to fit customers without using a tape measure. After testing the quiz, which is based on a computer algorithm that accounts for more than 2,000 body variations, with the help of a professional fitter at bra-fitting parties they hosted, Lam and Ramamurthy raised $2 million from angels and venture capital firms and launched True & Co., their bra-fitting business and online retail store. After a shopper completes the fitting quiz, the algorithm identifies her "best fits," and after receiving a $45 fully-refundable deposit, True & Co. ships her up to five bras. Customers pay only for those they keep; shipping and returns are free. Sales are growing rapidly, and Lam and Ramamurthy have expanded their product line to include other lingerie and are planning to introduce their own private label line of bras. One investor says True & Co. has identified a customer pain point in the $12 billion intimate apparel industry and is offering a valuable solution to it.[78] ∎

Shift to a service economy. The service sector accounts for 82.5 percent of the jobs and 79.7 percent of the private sector gross domestic product (GDP) in the United States, both of which represent a sharp rise from just a decade ago.[79] Because of their relatively low start-up costs, service businesses have become very popular among entrepreneurs. The booming service sector continues to provide many business opportunities, from educational services and computer maintenance to pet waste removal and iPod repair.

Technology advancements. With the help of modern business machines such as personal computers, laptop computers, smart phones, fax machines, copiers, color printers, answering machines, and voice mail, even one person working at home can look like a big business. At one time, the high cost of such technological wizardry made it impossible for small businesses to compete with larger companies that could afford the hardware. Today, however, powerful computers, smart phones, and communication equipment are priced within the budgets of even the smallest businesses and have drastically reduced the cost of launching a business. Noting how technology has made testing an idea and starting a business much easier, David Kappos, head of the U.S. Patent and Trademark Office, says, "The distance between an idea and the marketplace has decreased dramatically."[80] Although entrepreneurs may not be able to manufacture heavy equipment in their spare bedrooms, they can run a service- or information-based company from their homes—or almost anywhere—very effectively and look like any *Fortune* 500 company to customers and clients. Jimbo Wales, founder of Wikipedia, says, "Wherever my laptop is, that's my office."[81]

Independent lifestyle. Entrepreneurship fits the way Americans want to live—independent and self-sustaining. People want the freedom to choose where they live, what hours they work, and what they do. Although financial security remains an important goal for most entrepreneurs, many place top priority on lifestyle issues, such as more time with family and friends, more leisure time, and more control over work-related stress.

The Internet, cloud computing, and mobile marketing. The proliferation of the Internet, the vast network that links computers around the globe and opens up oceans of information to its users, has spawned thousands of entrepreneurial ventures since its beginning in 1993. **Cloud computing**, Internet-based subscription or pay-per-use software services that allow business owners to use a variety of business applications, from database management and inventory control to customer relationship management and accounting, has reduced business start-up and operating costs. Fast-growing small companies can substitute cloud computing applications for networks of computers and large office spaces, which allows entrepreneurs to build their companies without incurring high overhead costs.

Online retail sales, which currently account for 10 percent of total retail sales, are forecasted to continue to grow rapidly (see Figure 1.5), creating many opportunities for Web-savvy entrepreneurs. Computer software and hardware, books, music, consumer electronics, office supplies, and apparel are among the best-selling items on the Internet, but entrepreneurs are learning that they can use this powerful tool to sell just about anything! In fact, entrepreneurs are using the Internet to sell services such as tours to the sites of their favorite television shows and movies (including *Sex and the City* and *The Sopranos*), pajama parties for women, products such as crocheted cotton thong underwear, and recordings by musicians who perform for tips in the New York City subway.[82] Sami Bay launched the Something Store, an online store where customers pay $10 (shipping is free) and receive "something," a random item that the company guarantees sells for at least $10. Tens of thousands of customers have ordered something from the store and have received surprises that range from coffee mugs and USB hubs to cool toys and iPods.[83]

Currently, about 60 percent of small businesses have Web sites, double the number that had Web sites in 1997, and 67 percent of business owners say they use their Web sites to

cloud computing
internet-based subscription or pay-per-use software services that allow business owners to use a variety of business applications, from database management and inventory control to customer relationship management and accounting.

FIGURE 1.5

U.S. Online Retail Sales

Source: Forrester Research, 2013.

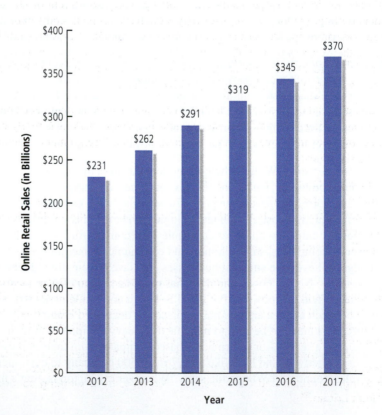

market to their customers, second only to word-of-mouth as a marketing tool.[84] Business owners are discovering the importance of connecting with online customers through their mobile devices. In fact, 37 percent of the time users spend on the Internet is on a mobile device, but only 26 percent of small companies have mobile-friendly Web sites.[85] Small companies that make their Web sites mobile friendly typically reap benefits quickly, however, in the form of new customers and increased sales. According to one study, 84 percent of small businesses report an increase in new business as a result of their mobile marketing efforts.[86]

ENTREPRENEURIAL PROFILE: Andy Kurtzig: Pearl.com When Andy Kurtzig's wife was pregnant with their first child, she called her doctor so often with questions that the physician finally asked her to call less often. The situation gave Kurtzig the idea to create a Web site, Pearl.com, that connects people who have questions to experts in hundreds of fields, ranging from medicine to home repairs. "I thought, 'Why not program a Web site so she could talk to a doctor anytime she wanted?'" he says. Pearl.com screens its experts with background checks and an eight-step vetting process. Fees range from $10 to $90 with an average of $30, and the average response time to a customer's question is 7.5 minutes. Pearl.com, now with 140 full-time employees, has a stable of 10,000 experts and operates in 196 countries. Kurtzig used bootstrapping to launch his company and get it to 10 million unique monthly users before he raised $51.3 million in two rounds of venture capital financing to fuel its growth and to develop mobile versions of the Web site.[87] ■

International opportunities. No longer are small businesses limited to pursuing customers within their own borders. The shift to a global economy has opened the door to tremendous business opportunities for entrepreneurs willing to reach across the globe. Although the United States is an attractive market for entrepreneurs, approximately 95 percent of the world's population and 80 percent of its purchasing power lie outside U.S. borders.[88] The emergence of potential markets across the globe and crumbling barriers to international business because of trade agreements have opened the world to entrepreneurs who are looking for new customers. Whereas companies once had to grow into global markets, today small businesses can have a global scope from their inception. Called **micromultinationals**, these small companies focus more on serving customers' needs than on the countries in which their customers live. More than 305,000 small businesses export goods and services. In fact, small businesses make up nearly 98 percent of all businesses engaged in exporting, yet they account for only 33 percent of the nation's export sales.[89] Many small companies that could export do not take advantage of export opportunities, often because their owners don't know how or where to start an export initiative. Although regional unrest and recessions remain challenges to international trade, global opportunities for small businesses have a long-term positive outlook.

micromultinationals
small companies that operate globally from their inception.

Although going global can be fraught with dangers and problems, many entrepreneurs are discovering that selling their products and services in foreign markets is really not so difficult. Small companies that have expanded successfully into foreign markets tend to rely on the following strategies:

- Researching foreign markets thoroughly
- Focusing on a single country initially
- Utilizing government resources designed to help small companies establish an international presence
- Forging alliances with local partners

ENTREPRENEURIAL PROFILE: Lawrence Sheer: Magnificent Baby Lawrence Sheer's business, Magnificent Baby, has been a global company since he started it in 2010. Sheer's company, which is based in New York City, manufactures its baby products, which use magnetic fasteners rather than snaps or buttons, in China and distributes them in 20 countries around the world. Sheer entered international markets only when enough customers in a particular country demonstrated interest in the company's products. Magnificent Baby generates nearly 10 percent of its sales from exports, and Sheer recently signed agreements with foreign distributors in Canada, Hong Kong, Australia, and New Zealand. Currently, he is working to find a foreign distributor in Great Britain.[90] ■

You Be the Consultant

College: The Ideal Place to Launch a Business

For growing numbers of students, college is not just a time of learning, partying, and growing into young adulthood; it is fast becoming a place for building a business. More than 2,300 colleges and universities offer courses in entrepreneurship and small business management (an increase from just 200 schools in the 1970s) to more than 400,000 students, and many of them have trouble keeping up with demand for these classes. "Students used to come to college and assume that five to ten years down the road, they'd start a business," says Gerry Hills, cofounder of the Collegiate Entrepreneurs Organization. "[Today], they come in preparing to get ideas and launch."

Many collegiate entrepreneurs realize that if they are going to have a job when they graduate, it is likely to be one they have created for themselves. According to a recent survey by Accenture, only 16 percent of college graduates who applied for a job had one waiting for them after graduation. For a growing number of college students, landing a job in corporate America, starting on the bottom rung of an uncertain career ladder, has lost much of its allure. While studying at Harvard (where she majored in the history of science), Windsor Hanger worked in internships at *OK! Magazine* and at Bloomingdale's, which offered her a marketing position when she graduated. Hanger turned down the job offer, choosing instead to focus on the business, *HerCampus*, an online magazine aimed at college women, that she had started with classmates Stephanie Kaplan and Annie Wang. "It's not a pure dichotomy anymore that entrepreneurship is risky and other jobs are safe, so why not do what I love?" she says. For their work at *HerCampus*, which is now profitable, Hanger, Kaplan, and Wang recently were named to *Inc.* magazine's "30 Under 30 Coolest Young Entrepreneurs" list.

Perhaps because of their stage in life, college entrepreneurs are particularly keen at spotting business opportunities. When Derek Pacqué was a senior at Indiana University, he was at a nightclub one cold evening and tucked his coat away in a corner for safekeeping. When he went to get his coat later, however, it was gone. Pacqué never found his coat, but he did find the inspiration for a business when he realized that none of the bars in town had a coat check. Pacqué approached several bar owners around town to see whether they were interested in a coat check service. Many were, and Pacqué launched Hoosier Coat Check, investing $500 to build portable coat racks and hiring several college students to staff them. Hoosier Coat Check collected between 10 percent and 30 percent of the $2 to $3 check fee the bars charged and in just six months generated $50,000 in revenue. The business was more profitable than Pacqué had expected, but numerous unanticipated problems cropped up as well, including lost tickets and matching customers with the wrong coats.

After graduating, Pacqué worked with a former professor to reformulate his business model to eliminate paper tickets and incorporate digital technology. Now, an app uses photographs and QR codes to check customers' coats, increasing both the speed and the reliability of the service. He also changed the name of the company to CoatChex and began to focus on events at large venues rather than local bars. He landed contracts to provide coat check services for the ESPN and Maxim Super Bowl parties

in Indianapolis, and the company grew from there. Pacqué also discovered an unexpected angle on his company's digital coat check service. His customers wanted access to the information that CoatChex collected on its customers through its app so that they could connect with customers through social media such as Facebook, Twitter, and Instagram.

Pacqué is searching for $1 million from private investors to fuel CoatChex's growth so that the company can live up to its potential. He appeared on television's Shark Tank, offering 10 percent of the company in exchange for a $200,000 investment. Indiana University alumnus Mark Cuban offered Pacqué $200,000 for one-third of CoatChex, but Pacqué refused, not wanting to give up that much equity so early in the life of his business. Although Pacqué did not get the investment deal he had hoped for from *Shark Tank*, the brand exposure that CoatChex received from appearing on the show has proved to be as valuable as an infomercial that would cost $500,000.

While working on a master's degree in computer science and electrical engineering, Limor Fried enjoyed applying the skills she was learning in the classroom, building MP3 players and laser toys from custom-ordered parts. Fried posted the instructions on her Web site and soon was flooded with requests from people asking for pre-assembled kits so that they could build their own devices. "At first, I was like, 'I'm really busy. Leave me alone,'" she recalls. Then she realized the entrepreneurial potential that selling kits had and convinced her parents to allow her to use $10,000 of the money they had set aside for tuition to purchase parts in bulk, assemble the kits, and sell them. As word spread, the number of orders grew, and Fried began hiring some of her friends to help fill them. Soon, she was designing a new project every week for her customers, who ranged from elementary school kids and tech geeks to hobbyists and retirees.

Today, Fried owns Adafruit Industries, a New York City-based company that generates more than $10 million in annual sales by selling pre-assembled kits of parts for building cool objects such as MintyBoost, a portable USB mobile device charger made from an Altoids tin and various electronic components (50,000 kits sold so far). Other popular kits include the iNecklace, which allows customers to build a pendant shaped like the "on" button on Apple gadgets (complete with pulsating light), and the MaKey MaKey, a device that uses circuitry and alligators clips to turn anything that conducts electricity (bananas, plants, your dog . . .) into a keyboard or touchpad. AdaFruit Industries' 50 employees are constantly developing new kits and shipping them worldwide.

Budding entrepreneurs at a growing number of colleges can take advantage of a special programs designed to create a culture for entrepreneurship. A growing number of schools provide on-campus business accelerators that offer promising student entrepreneurs amenities such as low-cost (sometimes free) office space, start-up funding, professionally appointed conference rooms, wireless Internet access, smartboards, ample computer facilities, videoconferencing equipment, copiers, and others. Presentations from entrepreneurs, venture capitalists, bankers, attorneys, and others help students define their business ideas and develop their

You Be the Consultant (continued)

business plans. "It's often over those late-night pizzas where the best ideas are born," says one official. One student entrepreneur in the program agrees: "A lot of it is the community. Being around people in the [entrepreneurship] program inspires one to think about other opportunities out there. What I've learned here is how to plan, how to make a business actually work."

1. In addition to the normal obstacles of starting a business, what other barriers do collegiate entrepreneurs face?

2. What advantages do collegiate entrepreneurs have when launching a business?

3. What advice would you offer a fellow college student about how to start a business?

4. Work with a team of your classmates to develop ideas about what your college or university could do to create a culture of entrepreneurship on your campus or in your community.

Sources: Based on Jodi Helmer, "May I Take Your Coat?" *Entrepreneur*, May 2013, p. 80; Carol Tice, "Why One Young Entrepreneur Turned Down Mark Cuban on Shark Tank," *Entrepreneur*, October 19, 2012, http://www.entrepreneur.com/blog/224699; *Accenture 2013 College Graduate Employment Survey*, Accenture, 2013, p. 4; Jennifer Wang, "Entrepreneur of 2012: Limor Fried, Adafruit," *Entrepreneur*, January 2013, pp. 46–48; David Whitford, "Can You Learn to Be an Entrepreneur?," *Fortune*, March 22, 2010, pp. 63–66; Glenn Rifkin, "A Classroom Path to Entrepreneurship," *New York Times*, May 1, 2008, http://www.nytimes.com/2008/05/01/business/smallbusiness/01sbiz.html?_r=1&pagewanted=print&oref=slogin; Joel Holland, "Putting Your School to Work," *Entrepreneur*, December 2009, p. 78; Ellen McCarthy, "Dorm Incubates Captains of Industry." *Chicago Tribune*, December 1, 2002, http://articles.chicagotribune.com/2002-12-01/features/0212010363_1_dorm-joint-venture-college-park/2; Max Raskin and Sommer Saadi, "Startup Fever: College Students Have It Bad," *Bloomberg Business Week*, October 19, 2010; and Jason Daley, "From the Blackboard to the Boardroom," *Entrepreneur*, April 2010, p. 58. Nichole L. Torres, "Big Biz on Campus." *Entrepreneur*, November 30, 2004, http://www.entrepreneur.com/article/73758; Hannah Seligson, "No Jobs? Young Graduates Make Their Own," *The New York Times*, December 11, 2010, http://www.nytimes.com/2010/12/12/business/12yec.html?pagewanted=all&_r=0; Based on Jodi Helmer, "May I Take Your Coat?" *Entrepreneur*, May 2013, p. 8; Jodi Helmer, *Inside a College Entrepreneur's Unique Coat Check Business Entrepreneur*, June 1, 2013 www.entrepreneur.com/article/226384.

The Cultural Diversity of Entrepreneurship

LO5

Explain the cultural diversity of entrepreneurship.

As we have seen, virtually anyone has the potential to become an entrepreneur. Indeed, diversity is a hallmark of entrepreneurship. We now explore the diverse mix of people who make up the rich fabric of entrepreneurship.

Young Entrepreneurs

Young people are embracing entrepreneurship enthusiastically as a career choice. A recent survey by the Kauffman Foundation reports that 40 percent of young people between the ages of 8 and 24 have already started a business or would like to do so in the future. The top five reasons these young people want to start their own businesses include the opportunity to use their skills and abilities, build something for their future, be their own bosses, earn lots of money, and see their ideas realized. Although entrepreneurial activity tends to increase with age, many members of the Millennial generation (or Generation Y, those people born between 1982 and 2000) show high levels of interest in entrepreneurship. Disenchanted with their prospects in corporate America and willing to take a chance at controlling their own destinies, scores of young people are choosing entrepreneurship as their initial career path. People between the ages of 15 and 29, nearly 64 million strong, are deciding that owning their own companies is the best way to create job security and to achieve the balance between work and life that they seek. "People are realizing they don't have to go to work in suits and ties and don't have to talk about budgets every day," says Ben Kaufman, founder of Mophie, a company (named after his golden retrievers, Molly and Sophie) that he started at age 18 while still in high school that makes iPod accessories such as cases, armbands, and belt clips. "They can have a job they like. They can create a job for themselves."[91] Because of young people such as Kaufman, the future of entrepreneurship looks very bright.

Women Entrepreneurs

Despite years of legislative effort, women still face discrimination in the workforce. However, small business has been a leader in offering women opportunities for economic expression through entrepreneurship. Increasing numbers of women are discovering that the best way to break the "glass ceiling" that prevents them from rising to the top of many organizations is to start their own companies. Women entrepreneurs have even broken through the comic strip barrier. Blondie Bumstead, long a typical suburban housewife married to Dagwood, now owns her own catering business with her best friend and neighbor Tootsie Woodly!

The number of women-owned businesses is growing 1.5 times faster than the national average.[92] Women now own 30.4 percent of all privately held businesses in the United States, but their companies generate just 11 percent of business sales.[93] Although women-owned businesses are smaller

FIGURE 1.6

Characteristics of Women-Owned Businesses

Source: Based on data from *The 2013 State of Women-Owned Businesses Report*, American Express OPEN, 2013, p. 7.

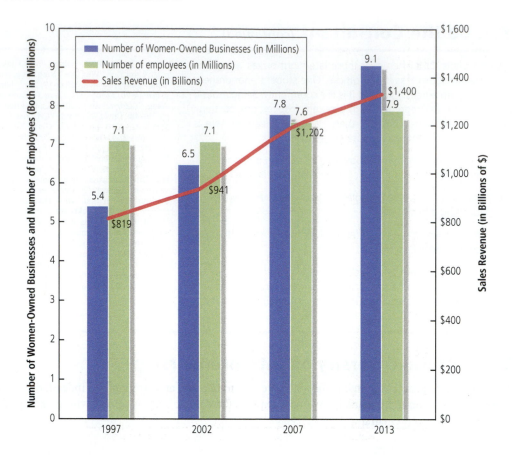

and far less likely to attract equity capital investments than those that men start, their impact is significant.[94] The more than 9.1 million women-owned companies in the United States employ nearly 7.9 million workers and generate sales of more than $1.4 trillion a year (see Figure 1.6)![95] A study by Guardian Life Small Business Research Institute projects that women-owned companies will generate between 5 million and 5.5 million jobs in the United States by 2018, which represents more than half the total jobs small companies will generate in that period.[96]

Neil Rasmus/BFAnyc/Sipa USA/Newscom

ENTREPRENEURIAL PROFILE: Sophia Amoruso: Nasty Gal In 2006, Sophia Amoruso, just 21 years old, started a business in her garage selling vintage clothing on eBay. Today, Amoruso is CEO of Nasty Gal (named after a 1975 song by Betty Davis), an online clothing store that has a "crazy, freakishly loyal" customer base of young women who clamor to purchase the company's vintage-inspired clothing, much of which she purchases from up-and-coming designers. Just four years after launch, Nasty Gal's annual sales hit $128 million, a dramatic increase from its first-year sales of $223,000. Nasty Gal now has 300 employees, a 10,000-square-foot headquarters in downtown Los Angeles, and a 50,000-square-foot warehouse in Louisville, Kentucky. Amoruso recently launched a mobile Web site, a *Super Nasty* magazine, and an in-house brand that includes collections of dresses, tops, jeans, swimwear, and more. Amoruso's goal is to transform Nasty Gal from a mere retailer to a full-fledged brand. She revels in meeting the challenges that a fast-growing business present, saying that the business changes so quickly, it is almost like working for a new business each month.[97] ■

Minority Enterprises

Another rapidly growing segment of the small business population is minority-owned businesses. Hispanics, African Americans, and Asians are the minority groups that are most likely to be entrepreneurs. Hispanics, who now make up the largest minority population in the United States, own 8.5 percent of all businesses. African Americans, who make

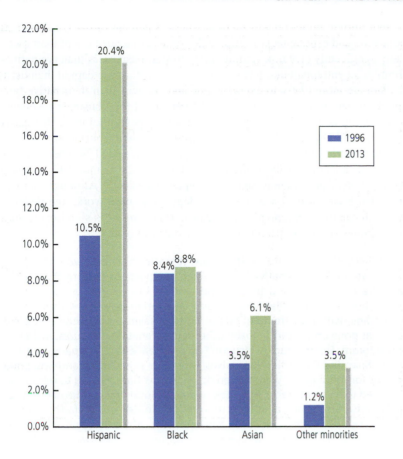

FIGURE 1.7

Percentage of New Entrepreneurs by Minority Group, 1996 vs. 2013

Source: Based on Robert W. Fairlie, *Kauffman Index of Entrepreneurial Activity, 1996–2013*, Kauffman Foundation, April 2014, p. 10.

up about 13 percent of the U.S. population, own 7 percent of all businesses, and Asians own 5.9 percent of all businesses.[98] Minority-owned businesses have come a long way in the last two decades (see Figure 1.7), however, and their success rate is climbing.

ENTREPRENEURIAL PROFILE: Britta Aragon: Cinco Vidas SkinLabs Inspired by her father's battle with cancer, Britta Aragon, a cancer survivor herself, worked with a team of leading dermatologists, toxicologists, and holistic skin-care chemists to develop a line of nontoxic skin care products that soothe, repair, and hydrate skin that has been damaged by the devastating effects of cancer treatments, skin sensitivity, or skin disorders such as eczema. To sell her innovative products, the former skin care therapist and makeup artist launched Cinco Vidas ("Five Lives" in Spanish) SkinLabs in New York City in 2008. "After I went through cancer and later lost my father to the disease, I knew that my purpose was to make a difference for other people going through similar challenges—whether from cancer or from battling a variety of skin conditions," says Aragon. "Sometimes in tragedy, we find our life's purpose."[99] ■

Minority entrepreneurs own 22.5 percent of all businesses, and their economic impact is significant. Minority-owned businesses generate $871 billion in annual revenues and employ more than 5.9 million workers.[100] The future is promising for this new generation of minority entrepreneurs, who are better educated, have more business experience, and are better prepared for business ownership than their predecessors.

Immigrant Entrepreneurs

The United States, which has long been a melting pot of diverse cultures, is the leading destination in the world for immigrants drawn to this nation by its promise of economic freedom and prosperity. The immigrant population in the United States is more diverse than in the past, with people coming from a larger number of countries. In 1960, 75 percent of the foreign-born population came from Europe; today, most immigrants come from Mexico, and just 12 percent of the immigrant population emigrates from Europe.[101] Unlike the unskilled "huddled masses" of the past, today's 40.4 million immigrants, which make up 13 percent of the U.S. population, arrive with more education and experience and often a desire to start a business of their own.[102] In fact, immigrants are significantly (1.9 times) more likely to start businesses than are native-born U.S. citizens.[103] Immigrant entrepreneurs start their businesses with more capital than do native-born entrepreneurs and are more likely to export goods and services than their native-born counterparts. Immigrant-owned businesses account for 12 percent of total business revenues; however, the annual sales immigrants' businesses generate are just 71 percent of those that native-born entrepreneurs generate ($434,000 vs. $609,000).[104] Immigrant-owned businesses play an important role in many key industries. In fact, immigrant entrepreneurs founded 24.3 percent of all the high technology companies started in the United States between 2006 and 2012. These companies employ 560,000 workers and generate $63 billion in annual sales.[105] Although many immigrants come to the United States with few assets, their dedication, hard work, and desire to succeed enable them to achieve their entrepreneurial dreams. Their impact is significant; immigrants or children of immigrants started 41 percent of *Fortune* 500 companies.[106]

ENTREPRENEURIAL PROFILE: Ruben and Rosalinda Montalvo. After emigrating to the United States from his native Mexico as an engineer for Gillette, Ruben Montalvo decided to leave the corporate world behind and embark on a career as an entrepreneur. He launched his first business, Cantinflas Mexican and Vegetarian Gourmet Cuisine, a restaurant in Greer, South Carolina, with his wife Rosalinda using their savings and credit cards in 1994. Since then, Montalvo has gone on to start a dozen other entrepreneurial ventures, including a healthy quick service restaurant, Senor Wraps, a bistro in France, a real estate company, and an investment company. Before financing Cantinflas themselves, Montalvo says that he and Rosalinda turned to family and friends for funding but were turned down. At the time, having to rely on only on their own capital seemed to be an obstacle, but, looking back, Motalvo says it turned out to be a blessing. Montalvo admits that starting a business requires one to step out on faith, but he knows that it was the right decision for him. Like most entrepreneurs, Montalvo sees needs—and business opportunities—everywhere that serve as open doors for new business ventures.[107] ■

Part-Time Entrepreneurs

Starting a part-time business is a popular gateway to entrepreneurship. Part-time entrepreneurs have the best of both worlds: They can ease into business for themselves without sacrificing the security of a steady paycheck and benefits. The Internet (and particularly eBay) and mobile communication devices make establishing and running a part-time business very easy; many part-time entrepreneurs run online businesses from a spare bedroom in their homes or from wherever they are.

ENTREPRENEURIAL PROFILE: Anthony Lau: Cyclehoop When Anthony Lau was a student at London's University College, a thief stole his bicycle even though he had chained it to a signpost on one of the city's busy streets. A short time later, the architectural student noticed a design competition for a secure bicycle parking solution and began researching the problem. He came up with a simple yet effective design involving two simple hoops that proved to be easy to use and hard for thieves to defeat. He entered his design in the competition and won. After winning the competition, Lau launched a part-time business, Cyclehoop, which he financed with his own money, from his bedroom to market his invention. He landed contracts for the Cyclehoop from two London boroughs, Islington and Southwark, and went on to win several business plan competitions. Lau learns something from each business plan competition he enters and uses the feedback he gets to refine his ideas and business model. Today, Cyclehoop generates annual sales of £1.7 million and boasts an international presence, exporting its products to markets all over the world, including the United States, Canada, Australia, New Zealand, Denmark, Sweden, and many others. Lau also worked with a partner, Jessica Lee, to win a competition to design an indoor bicycle shed for Google's New York City office that he also plans to bring to market. Lau and Lee came up with a system for storing bicycles vertically, stacking them on two levels and suspending them from the ceiling, which conserves space.[108] ■

A major advantage of going into business part-time is the lower risk in case the venture flops. Many part-timers are "testing the entrepreneurial waters" to see whether their business ideas will work, whether there is sufficient demand for their products and services, and whether they enjoy being self-employed. As they grow, many successful part-time enterprises absorb more of entrepreneurs' time until they become full-time businesses. Starting part-time businesses on a small scale means that entrepreneurs can finance their companies themselves, allowing them to retain complete ownership.

Home-Based Businesses

Home-based businesses are booming! An entrepreneur starts a home-based business on average every 12 seconds.[109] Fifty-two percent of all small businesses are home based, and half of these have at least one employee, which means that home-based companies employ 13.2 million workers (including the owner).[110] Home-based businesses are an important economic force; they generate $427 billion a year in sales.[111] Several factors make the home the first choice location for many entrepreneurs:

- Operating a business from home keeps start-up and operating costs to a minimum. In fact, 44 percent of home-based entrepreneurs start their businesses for less than $5,000.[112]

- Home-based companies allow owners to maintain flexible life and work styles. Many home-based entrepreneurs relish being part of the "open-collar workforce."

- Technology, which is transforming many ordinary homes into "electronic cottages," allows entrepreneurs to run a wide variety of businesses from their homes.

- Many entrepreneurs use the Internet to operate e-commerce businesses from their homes that literally span the globe. They also rely heavily on social media to promote their home-based businesses.

In the past, home-based businesses tended to be rather mundane cottage industries, such as making crafts or sewing. Today's home-based businesses are more diverse; modern "homepreneurs" are more likely to be running high-tech or service companies with annual sales of hundreds of thousands of dollars. Twenty percent of home-based businesses generate between $100,000 and $500,000 in annual revenue.[113]

Family Businesses

A **family-owned business** is one that includes two or more members of a family with financial control of the company. Family businesses are an integral part of our economy. Of the nearly 28 million businesses in the United States, 90 percent are family owned and managed. These companies account for 62 percent of total employment in the United States and 78 percent of all new jobs, pay 65 percent of all wages, and generate 64 percent of the nation's GDP. Not all of them are small; 33 percent of the *Fortune* 500 companies are family businesses.[114]

family-owned business
one that includes two or more members of a family with financial control of the company.

"When it works right," says one writer, "nothing succeeds like a family firm. The roots run deep, embedded in family values. The flash of the fast buck is replaced with long-term plans. Tradition counts."[115] Indeed, the lifespan of the typical family business is 24 years.[116] Despite their magnitude, family businesses face a major threat, a threat from within: management succession. In a recent survey by PriceWaterhouseCoopers, one-third of family business owners expressed apprehension about transferring the business to the next generation, and 9 percent of owners saw the potential for family conflict as a result of the transition.[117] Only 30 percent of family businesses survive to the second generation, just 12 percent make it to the third generation, and only 3 percent survive into the fourth generation and beyond. Business periodicals are full of stories describing bitter feuds among family members that have crippled or destroyed once thriving businesses. The co-owner of one family business explains the challenges of operating a family business this way: "The best part is working with family. The worst part is working with family."[118] To avoid the senseless destruction of thriving family businesses, owners should do the following:

- Work to build positive relationships among family members both at and away from work

- Demonstrate respect for other family members' abilities and talents

- Separate responsibilities in the company based on each person's interests, abilities, and talents

- Develop plans for minimizing the potentially devastating effects of estate taxes

- Develop plans for management succession long before retirement looms before them

ENTREPRENEURIAL PROFILE: Antonio, Mario, and Robert Pasin: Radio Flyer Since 1917, millions of children have played with red Radio Flyer wagons. At age 16, Antonio Pasin, the son of an immigrant cabinet maker, started a business, The Liberty Coaster Company, making wooden wagons in a Chicago workshop. Several years later, Pasin opened his own factory and began making his wagons from metal and called them Radio Flyers. "They were simply the buzzwords of the day," explains Robert Pasin, Antonio's grandson, who now runs the company. Antonio retired from the family business when he was in his 70s, turning the company over to his son, Mario, who expanded the product line and renamed the business Radio Flyer. In 1997, Mario turned over the reins of the family business to his son, Robert, who also introduced new products, including tricycles, scooters, training bikes, and a line of wagons made from plastic that customers can trick out with a plethora of nifty options. The third-generation family business is still going strong with 70 employees and more than $100 million in annual sales.[119] ■

Copreneurs

copreneurs
entrepreneurial couples who work together as co-owners of their businesses.

Copreneurs are entrepreneurial couples who work together as co-owners of their businesses. Nearly 4 million couples operate businesses together in the United States, but unlike the traditional "Mom and Pop" (Pop as "boss" and Mom as "subordinate"), copreneurs "create a division of labor that is based on expertise as opposed to gender," says one expert.[120] Managing a small business with a spouse may appear to be a recipe for divorce, but most copreneurs say not. Caterina Fake, who with her husband Sewart Butterfield launched Flickr, a photo-sharing Web site, says that sharing with someone you love the intensity of launching a business, with its long hours, terrifying moments of despair, crushing defeats, joyous victories, and raging uncertainty, brings a couple closer together.[121] Successful copreneurs learn to build the foundation for a successful working relationship before they ever launch their companies. Some of the characteristics they rely on include the following:

- An assessment of whether their personalities will mesh—or conflict—in a business setting

- Mutual respect for each other and one another's talents

- Compatible business and life goals—a common vision

- Similar work ethic

- A view that they are full and equal partners, not a superior and a subordinate

- Complementary business skills that each acknowledges and appreciates and that lead to a unique business identity for each spouse

- The ability to keep lines of communication open, talking and listening to each other about personal as well as business issues

- A clear division of roles and authority, ideally based on each partner's skills and abilities, to minimize conflict and power struggles

- The ability to encourage each other and to lift up a disillusioned partner

- Separate work spaces that allow them to escape when the need arises

- Boundaries between their business life and their personal life so that one doesn't consume the other

- A sense of humor

- The realization that not every couple can work together

Although copreneuring isn't for everyone, it works extremely well for many couples and often leads to successful businesses. Both spouses work for a common purpose and bring their unique talents to the business. Combining their skills with their dedication to the company produces a synergistic effect, in which one plus one equals more than two.[122]

ENTREPRENEURIAL PROFILE: David Horvath and Sun-Min Kim After graduation in 2001, David Horvath sent a letter to his college sweetheart, Sun-Min Kim, who had returned to Korea because her student visa had expired, and signed it with a silly drawing of a wide-eyed monster with long arms, fangs, stubby legs, and a large head. As a surprise, Kim took the drawing and made it into a plush, hand-sewn doll. Horvath happened to show the funny creature to a friend who owned a toy store in Los Angeles, who was intrigued and ordered 20 dolls, which sold quickly. When Horvath's friend called to order more dolls, the couple, who were married in 2005, began designing a collection of brightly colored dolls based on an "Ugly-verse" of 60 characters they created. Orders trickled—and then poured—in, and the copreneurs started Pretty Ugly LLC to market their line of dolls. Today, Pretty Ugly, which is based in Green Brook, New Jersey, employs a dozen workers and sells a complete line of Uglydolls, books, games, apparel, accessories, and other items in more than 10,000 retail stores worldwide. The company Horvath and Kim started together has generated sales of more than $100 million and sells more than 2 million Uglydolls-branded items each year.[123] ∎

Corporate Castoffs

Concentrating on shedding the excess bulk that took away their flexibility and speed, many large American corporations have been downsizing in an attempt to regain their competitive edge. For decades, one major corporation after another has announced layoffs—and not just among blue-collar workers. According to placement firm Challenger, Gray, and Christmas, from 2002 to 2012, corporations laid off an average of 80,200 employees per month.[124] Executives and line workers alike have experienced job cuts, and these corporate castoffs have become an important source of entrepreneurial activity. Some 20 percent of discharged corporate managers have become entrepreneurs, and many of those left behind in corporate America would like to join them. "There is really no safe job anymore," says Marty Bauer, who left the banking industry to launch a start-up business after he witnessed one of his mentors being laid off just three years before he was to retire. Bauer and three friends started RidePost, a Web site that allows travelers to meet and find safe rides from one destination to another.[125]

Many corporate castoffs are deciding that the best defense against future job insecurity is an entrepreneurial offense. Accustomed to the support of the corporations they left, many corporate castoffs decide to purchase franchises, where there is a built-in management system already in place. *Entrepreneur* magazine surveyed the companies on its Franchise 500 list recently and discovered that 77 percent of franchisors report that "second-career executives" (i.e., corporate castoffs) are among the primary purchasers of their franchises.[126]

Corporate Dropouts

The dramatic downsizing of corporate America has created another effect among the employees left after restructuring: a trust gap. The result of this trust gap is a growing number of dropouts from the corporate structure who then become entrepreneurs. Although their workdays may grow longer and their incomes may shrink, those who strike out on their own often find their work more rewarding and more satisfying because they are doing what they enjoy. Other entrepreneurs are inspired to launch their companies after being treated unfairly by large, impersonal corporate entities.

ENTREPRENEURIAL PROFILE: Olivia DeCastro: A Public Affair PR and Diana Classic Children After graduating from college, Olivia DeCastro embarked on a career in corporate America, first with an advertising agency and then as public relations director for a large hospital system. However, DeCastro became disenchanted with the limitations that corporate hierarchies imposed and wanted to control her own destiny. In 2010, the 25-year-old set aside a promising corporate career to launch her own public relations firm, A Public Affair PR, and an upscale children's clothing boutique, Diana Classic Children, in Palm Beach Gardens, Florida. "I didn't feel like I had freedom in the corporate world," says DeCastro. Within two years, A Public Affair PR had a staff of six and offices in Miami, Florida, and Greenville, South Carolina.[127] ∎

Because they have college degrees, a working knowledge of business, and years of management experience, both corporate dropouts and castoffs may ultimately increase the small business survival rate. A recent survey by Manta, an online small business community, reports that 69 percent of small business owners have college degrees, and 61 percent say a college degree was important to their business success.[128] Better-trained, more experienced entrepreneurs are more likely to succeed.

Retiring Baby Boomers

Because people are living longer and are remaining active as they grow older, the ranks of older entrepreneurs are growing. In fact, according to studies by the Kauffman Foundation, the level of entrepreneurial activity among people ages 55 to 64 actually exceeds that of people ages 20 to 34 (see Figure 1.8). The average age of the first-time entrepreneurs in the United States is nearly 44.[129] One advantage that older entrepreneurs have is wisdom that has been forged by experience.

ENTREPRENEURIAL PROFILE: Don Shula: Shula's Steak Houses, LLC At age 64, Don Shula, retired National Football League coach and Pro Football Hall of Fame member, and several members of his family, including his son Dave who was also an NFL coach, started a restaurant company, Shula's Steak Houses, LLC. The coaching legend, who racked up 347 career wins and is the only coach to complete a perfect season in the NFL, applies the same work ethic to the restaurant business and now has more than 30 restaurants across the United States. In addition to 14 Shula's Steak Houses, the Shulas also own four Shula's Bar and Grills, one Shula's On the Beach, two Shula's 2 Steak and Sports, and eight Shula's 347 Grills. The family's most recent start-up is Shula Burger, an upscale burger eatery that features patties made from a combination of fresh steak and ground beef, veggie burgers, turkey burgers, a large menu of side items, and an impressive wine list. The décor is all sports, with sports events playing on large-screen televisions, football memorabilia, and massive paintings of favorite plays from Shula's playing and coaching days. "I'm just a guy who rolls up his sleeves and goes to work," says Shula, now 83. "The bottom line in coaching is winning. The bottom line in the restaurant business is winning. You want to win every meal."[130] ■

FIGURE 1.8

Entrepreneurial Activity by Age Group

Source: Based on Robert W. Fairlie, *Kauffman Index of Entrepreneurial Activity, 1996–2013*, Kauffman Foundation, April 2014, p. 13.

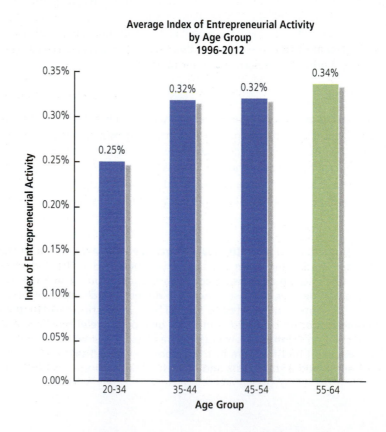

Average Index of Entrepreneurial Activity by Age Group 1996-2012

Hands On . . . How To

Launch a Successful Business While You Are Still in College

Collegiate entrepreneurs are becoming increasingly common as colleges and universities offer more courses and a greater variety of courses in the areas of entrepreneurship and small business management. Launching a business while in college offers many advantages, including access to research and valuable advice, but starting an entrepreneurial career also poses challenges, including a lack of financial resources, business experience, and time. What are some of the most common myths that prevent young people (not just college students) from launching businesses?

- **I don't have enough money to launch a business.** One of the greatest benefits of the shift in the United States to a service economy is that service businesses usually are inexpensive to start. One young entrepreneur worked with a friend to launch a Web development company while in high school, and their total start-up cost was just $80.

- **I don't have enough time.** Many companies that have grown into successful, mature businesses were started by entrepreneurs in their spare time. Everyone has the same 24 hours in a day. What matters is what you do with those hours.

- **I'm not smart enough to start a company.** SAT scores and grades have little correlation to one's ability to launch a successful business. Quite a few successful entrepreneurs, including Michael Dell (Dell Inc.), Richard Branson (Virgin), Walt Disney (Disney), Mark Zuckerberg (Facebook), and Debbi Fields (Mrs. Fields Cookies), dropped out of college to start their businesses.

- **I'm not majoring in business.** Success in entrepreneurship is not limited to students who earn business degrees. *Anyone* has the potential to be a successful entrepreneur. At the University of Miami, only 20 percent of the students who have participated in The Launch Pad, the school's start-up accelerator, have been business majors.

- **I'm not creative enough to come up with a good idea for a business.** As you will learn in Chapter 3, *everyone* has the potential to be creative. Some of the most successful businesses are the result of an entrepreneur who recognized a simple need that people had and created a business to meet that need.

- **I don't have any experience.** Neither did Bill Gates (Microsoft) and Michael Dell (Dell Inc.) when they launched their companies, and things worked out pretty well for both of them. Business experience can be an important factor in a company's success, but every entrepreneur has to start somewhere to gain that experience.

- **I might fail.** Failure *is* a possibility. In fact, the survival rate of new companies after five years is 51 percent. Ask yourself this: What is the worst that can happen if I launch a business and it fails? Entrepreneurs do not allow the fear of failure to stop them from trying to realize their dreams.

If you want to become a successful collegiate entrepreneur, what can you do to increase the chances of your success? The following tips will help.

Recognize That Starting a Business at an Early Age May Be to Your Advantage

Young people tend to be highly creative, and that can provide your company with a competitive advantage. In addition, young people often accomplish things simply because they don't know that they are not supposed to be able to do them!

Build a Business Plan

One of the best ways to lower the probability that your business will fail is to create a business plan. Doing so forces you to ask and then answer some tough questions about your idea and your proposed venture. "It's all about 'derisking' your idea," says Gregg Fairbrothers, who teaches entrepreneurship at Dartmouth's Tuck School of Business. "Identifying, unblinkingly, what could go wrong and taking whatever steps necessary to slash the odds that it will."

Use All of the Resources Available to You

Many colleges and universities now offer courses in entrepreneurship and small business management and have faculty members who are experts in the field. In many cases, the people who are teaching these classes are veteran entrepreneurs themselves with tremendous reservoirs of knowledge and experience. Some colleges provide special dorms for budding entrepreneurs that serve as business incubators. Smart collegiate entrepreneurs tap into the pool of resources that their campuses offer.

Don't Go It Alone

Research from MIT's Sloan School of Business suggests that starting a business with cofounders increases the company's probability of success. Each additional founder up to four increases the likelihood that a start-up will succeed. "Two or three cofounders seems to be the sweet spot," says one expert. Another study reports that solo entrepreneurs take 3.6 times as long to launch than teams of two or more cofounders. Cofounders bring complementary skill sets to the venture, share the burden of the huge volume of work required to launch, and provide an important support system when things get tough. Four students at MIT who met at the school's entrepreneurship center launched Ministry of Supply (MoS), a company whose goal is to revolutionize men's business clothing by adding "tech under the hood." Aman Advani, Kit Hickey, Kevin Rustagi, and Gihan Amarasiriwardena pooled their individual talents to create garments that incorporate high-tech fabrics that regulate the wearer's body heat, wick moisture, and neutralize bacteria that cause body odor. MoS, whose products are based on technology used to keep astronauts comfortable in space, began by selling men's shirts but has added a line of high-tech T-shirts and pants.

(continued)

Hands On . . . How To (continued)

Find a Mentor

Most young entrepreneurs have not had the opportunity to gain a wealth of business experience, but they do have access to mentors who do. Mike Brown, who recently won the top prize at the annual Global Student Entrepreneur Awards for his company ModBargains.com, a business that sells aftermarket products for modifying cars and trucks, says his first boss, who owns several businesses, served as his mentor. ModBargains.com, which Brown started with fellow car enthusiast Ron Hay, now has more than 4,000 products available and has surpassed annual sales of $1 million.

Learn to Be a "Bootstrapper"

Learning to start and manage a company with few resources is good training for any entrepreneur. In the early days of their start-ups, many successful entrepreneurs find creative ways to finance their businesses and to keep their operating expenses as low as possible. Because they lack the deep pockets of their larger rivals, entrepreneurs must use their creativity, ingenuity, and street smarts to market their companies effectively.

Manage Your Time Wisely

Taking college classes and running a business place a large workload on any collegiate entrepreneur, one that demands good time management skills. The most successful entrepreneurs recognize the importance of controlling their schedules (as much as possible) and working as efficiently as they can.

Remember to Have Fun

College is supposed to be one of the best times of your life! Starting and running a business also can be one of the most rewarding experiences of your life. Doing both can double the fun, but it also can create a great deal of stress. Balance is the key.

Sources: Based on Colleen Taylor, "For Start-Ups Pitching VCs, Three Is the Magic Number," Gigaom, May 13, 2011, http://gigaom.com/2011/05/13/multiple-founder-startups/; "No Entrepreneur Is an Island: Cofounders Help Start-Ups Succeed," Nevada Institute for Renewable Energy and Commercialization, January 21, 2013, http://nirec.org/no-entrepreneur-is-an-island-co-founders-help-startups-succeed/; Michael Hughes, "Top 10 Articles to Help Entrepreneurs Find a Cofounder," CoFounders Lab, May 31, 2012, http://blog.cofounderslab.com/founders/how-to-find-a-co-founder; Millie Kerr, "Fashion's Final Frontier," *Entrepreneur*, May 2013, p. 78; Claire Martin, "Rolling Up Their Sleeves, as a Team," *New York Times*, May 18, 2013, http://www.nytimes.com/2013/05/19/business/at-ministry-of-supply-team-work-in-making-high-tech-apparel.html?pagewanted=all&_r=0; Adam Bluestein and Amy Barrett, "Revitalize the American Dream: Bring on the Entrepreneurs!," *Inc.*, July/August 2010, pp. 76–88; David Whitford, "Can You Learn to Be an Entrepreneur?," *Fortune*, March 22, 2010, p. 66; Robert Sherman, "Student Entrepreneur Shares Hard-Won Lessons at YoungMoney.com," *Orange Entrepreneur*, Syracuse University, Fall 2007, p. 5; Daniel Jimenez, "The Best College Entrepreneurs of 2006," *Young Money*, July 2007, http://www.youngmoney.com/entrepreneur/student_entrepreneurs/070126; Michael Simmons, "Why Starting a Business Now May Be the Best Way to Achieve Your Dreams," *Young Money*, July 2003, http://www.youngmoney.com/entrepreneur/student_entrepreneurs/031010_01; and Scott Reeves, "How to Swing with Guerrilla Marketing," *Forbes*, June 8, 2006, http://www.forbes.com/2006/06/08/entrepreneurs-marketing-harley-davidson cx_sr_0608askanexpert.html.

LO6

Describe the important role that small businesses play in our nation's economy.

small business
one that employs fewer than 100 people.

The Power of "Small" Business

Of the 27.9 million businesses in the United States, approximately 27.8 million, or 99.7 percent, are considered small. Although there is no universal definition of a small business (the U.S. Small Business Administration has more than 800 definitions of a small business based on industry categories), a common delineation of a **small business** is one that employs fewer than 100 people. They thrive in virtually every industry, although the majority of small companies are concentrated in the service, construction, and retail industries (see Figure 1.9). Although they

FIGURE 1.9

Small Businesses by Industry

Source: Statistics of U.S. Businesses: U.S. All Industries by Sector, U.S. Census Bureau, http://www.census. gov/epcd/susb/2008/us/US--.HTM.

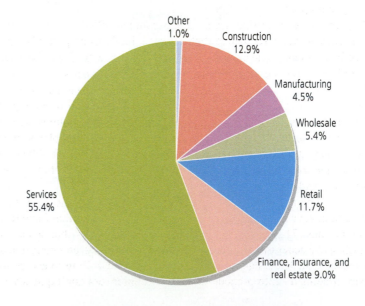

- Other 1.0%
- Construction 12.9%
- Manufacturing 4.5%
- Wholesale 5.4%
- Retail 11.7%
- Finance, insurance, and real estate 9.0%
- Services 55.4%

may be small businesses, their contributions to the economy are anything but small. For example, small companies employ 49.2 percent of the nation's private sector workforce, even though they possess less than one-fourth of total business assets. Almost 90 percent of businesses with paid employees are small, employing fewer than 20 workers, but small companies account for 43 percent of total private payroll in the United States. Because they are primarily labor intensive, small businesses actually create more jobs than do big businesses. In fact, between 1993 and 2013, small companies created 63 percent of the net new jobs in the U.S. economy.[131]

The ability to create jobs is not distributed evenly across the small business sector, however. Research shows that the top-performing 5 percent of small companies create 67 percent of the net new jobs in the economy, and they do so across all industry sectors, not just in "hot" industries, such as high-tech. These young, job-creating small companies are known as **gazelles**, businesses that grow at 20 percent or more per year for four years with at least $100,000 in annual sales. Nearly 85 percent of these high-impact companies are located in urban areas. Not surprisingly, cities with high levels of entrepreneurial activity boast higher levels of job creation than those that are home to heavier concentrations of existing businesses.[132] "Mice" are small companies that never grow much and don't create many jobs. The majority of small companies are mice.[133] In fact, 75 percent of small business owners say they are not seeking rapid growth for their businesses and want to keep them small.[134] The country's largest businesses, "elephants," have continued to shed jobs for several years.[135]

gazelles
small companies that are growing at 20 percent or more per year with at least $100,000 in annual sales; they create 70 percent of net new jobs in the economy.

Small businesses also produce 46 percent of the country's private GDP and account for 47 percent of business sales.[136] In fact, the U.S. small business sector is the world's third-largest "economy," trailing only the entire U.S. economy and China! One business writer describes the United States as "an entrepreneurial economy, a system built on nimble, low-overhead small companies with fluid workforces, rather than the massive conglomerates that upheld the economy for decades."[137]

Small companies also are incubators of new ideas, products, and services. Small firms create 16 times more patents per employee than large companies.[138] Traditionally, small businesses have played a vital role in innovation, and they continue to do so today. Many important inventions trace their roots to an entrepreneur, including the zipper, laser, brassiere, escalator, light bulb, personal computer, automatic transmission, air conditioning, and FM radio.

Putting Failure into Perspective

LO7

Put failure into the proper perspective.

Because of their limited resources, inexperienced management, and lack of financial stability, small businesses suffer relatively high mortality rates. As you learned earlier in this chapter, two years after start-up, 34 percent of small companies have failed, and after five years, 51 percent have failed.[139] Figure 1.10 shows the failure rate for small businesses over time, clear evidence of the constant "churn" that exists as entrepreneurs create new businesses and others close. New companies that replace old ones with better ideas, market approaches, and products actually are a sign of a healthy, entrepreneurial economy.

Because they are building businesses in an environment filled with uncertainty and shaped by rapid change, entrepreneurs recognize that failure is likely to be part of their lives, but they are not paralyzed by that fear. "The excitement of building a new business from scratch is greater than the fear of failure," says one entrepreneur who failed in business several times before finally succeeding.[140] Entrepreneurs use their failures as a rallying point and as a means of refocusing their business ventures for success. They see failure for what it really is: an opportunity to learn what does not work! Successful entrepreneurs have the attitude that failures are simply stepping-stones along the path to success. Basketball legend Michael Jordan displayed the same attitude. "I've missed more than 9,000 shots in my career," he says. "I lost almost 300 games. Twenty-six times, I've been trusted to take the game-winning shot and *missed*. I've failed over and over and over again in my life. And that is why I succeed."[141]

Failure is a natural part of the creative process. The only people who never fail are those who never do anything or never attempt anything new. Baseball fans know that Babe Ruth held the record for career home runs (714) for many years, but how many know that he also held the record for strikeouts (1,330)? Successful entrepreneurs know that hitting an entrepreneurial home run requires a few business strikeouts along the way, and they are willing to accept them. Failure is an inevitable part of being an entrepreneur, and true entrepreneurs don't quit when they fail. One

FIGURE 1.10

Small Business Failure Rate

Source: Based on data from "Business Employment Dynamics: Establishment Survival," Bureau of Labor Statistics, 2013, http://www .bls.gov/bdm/us_age_naics_ 00_table7.txt.

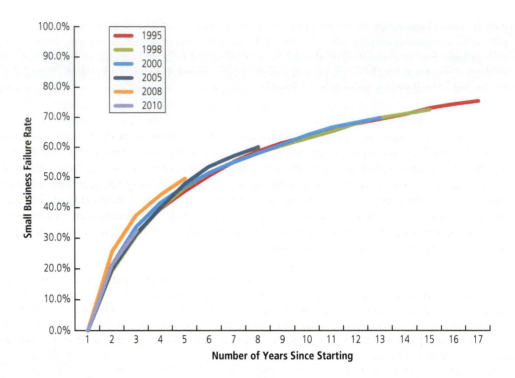

entrepreneur whose business burned through $800 million of investors' money before folding says, "If you're an entrepreneur, you don't give up when times get tough."[142]

One hallmark of successful entrepreneurs is the ability to fail *intelligently*, learning why they failed so that they can avoid making the same mistake again. James Dyson, whose company makes one of the best-selling vacuum cleaners in the world, made 5,127 prototypes of his bagless vacuum cleaner before he hit on one that worked. Dyson points out that he failed 5,126 times but that he learned from each failure. Each failure brought him closer to a successful solution, so, to him, failure is nothing to fear; it is part of the creative process.[143] Like Dyson, entrepreneurs know that business success depends on their ability not to avoid making mistakes but rather to be open to the lessons that each mistake teaches. They learn from their failures and use them as fuel to push themselves closer to their ultimate target. "Failure can teach not only what one is doing wrong but also how to do it right the next time," says one business writer. "It can be a useful, even transformational, force for better business practices. It is best not to shove it under the rug because it is, at some point, inevitable."[144] Entrepreneurs are less worried about what they might lose if they try something and fail than about what they might lose if they fail to try.

Entrepreneurial success requires both persistence and resilience, the ability to bounce back from failure. Thomas Edison, who earned 1,093 patents (a record that still stands), discovered about 1,800 ways not to build a light bulb before hitting on a design that worked. "Results!" Edison once exclaimed. "I have gotten a lot of results. I know several thousand things that won't work."[145] Walt Disney was fired from a newspaper job because, according to his boss, he "lacked imagination and had no good ideas." Disney also went bankrupt several times before he created Disneyland. R. H. Macy failed in business seven times before his retail store in New York City became a success. In the spirit of true entrepreneurship, these visionary business leaders refused to give up in the face of failure; they simply kept trying until they achieved success. When it comes to failure, entrepreneurs' motto seems to be, Failure is temporary; quitting is permanent.

ENTREPRENEURIAL PROFILE: Ziver Birg: Zivelo When Ziver Birg was an 18-year-old student at Arizona State University, he started Afforablekiosks.com, an online business that sold kiosks to other companies. His business grew, and Birg raised $3 million in equity capital to build his own manufacturing operation. The financing was supposed to last his company three years, but Birg burned through it in just nine months and ended up closing the business. Undaunted, Birg was back in business 18 months later with his second kiosk company, Zivelo. Today, Zivelo has 20 employees, generates annual revenue of $4 million, and is about to build a 100,000-square-foot manufacturing facility.[146] ∎

How to Avoid the Pitfalls

LO8

Explain how an entrepreneur can avoid becoming another failure statistic.

Although failure can be a valuable part of the entrepreneurial process, no one sets out to fail in business. Now we must examine the ways to avoid becoming another failure statistic and gain insight into what makes a successful business.

Know Your Business in Depth

We have already emphasized the need for the right type of experience in the business you plan to start. Get the best education in your business area you possibly can *before* you set out on your own. Become a serious student of your industry. Read everything you can—trade journals, business periodicals, books, and research reports—relating to your industry and learn what it takes to succeed in it. Personal contact with suppliers, customers, trade associations, and others in the same industry is another excellent way to get that knowledge. Smart entrepreneurs join industry trade associations and attend trade shows to pick up valuable information and to make key contacts before they open their doors for business.

ENTREPRENEURIAL PROFILE: Steve Ells: Chipotle Mexican Grill Steve Ells has had a passion for food his entire life. As a child, while his friends watched cartoons, he watched cooking shows starring famous chefs Julia Child and Graham Kerr, the Galloping Gourmet. "In grammar school, I learned how to make hollandaise from my Mom, and in high school, I started throwing dinner parties and collecting cookbooks," he recalls. After graduating from the University of Colorado in Boulder, he enrolled in the Culinary Institute of America to refine his cooking skills. From there, he moved to San Francisco, where he worked at Stars, a restaurant that launched the careers of many renowned chefs, and learned the details of operating a restaurant. One day, while dining in a small taqueria in the Mission district of San Francisco, Ells noted the volume of customers the restaurant handled and the system it used to serve them extremely efficiently. Inspired by the experience, Ells decided to return to Denver, Colorado, where he launched the first Chipotle Mexican Grill in 1993 with the help of an $85,000 loan from his father. "My friends and family thought I was crazy," recalls Ells, "but I had a very clear vision of the way Chipotle was going to look and taste and feel. It was going to incorporate all of the things I had learned while at the Culinary Institute and at Stars." Ells's knowledge and experience in the restaurant industry has paid off. Today, Chipotle, a publicly held company, has nearly 1,600 restaurants and generates more than $3.2 billion in annual sales![147] ■

Build a Viable Business Model—and Test It

Before launching a business, an entrepreneur should define the business model on which he or she plans to build a company and test it, preferably with actual customers or potential customers, to verify that it can be successful. Grand assumptions about capturing market share and "hockey stick" revenue growth that never materialize have been the downfall of many start-up businesses. Creating a successful business model requires entrepreneurs to identify all of the model's vital components, including the resources, the partners, the activities they must assemble, the customer segments they are targeting, the channels they will use to reach them, the value proposition they offer customers, and the sources of revenue and accompanying costs they will incur.

ENTREPRENEURIAL PROFILE: Justin Mares: RoommateFit After encountering the "classic horrible roommate" experience when he enrolled at the University of Pittsburgh, Justin Mares thought he could come up with a better way to match roommates with the technology used by online dating sites than the scant questionnaires most colleges use. To test the feasibility of his idea, Mares researched and developed a basic screening model and pitched his idea to 100 college administrators, who expressed a great deal of interest in the service. "Schools are concerned about retention, and this is one tool that can increase student satisfaction,"[148] he says. Using a prize he won from the Collegiate Entrepreneurs' Organization, Mares worked with a psychologist to hone his software, which he named RoommateFit and which measures a variety of personality traits. To test his business model, Mares convinced officials at Ohio University to participate in a pilot study, and the results not only were impressive but also gave him the hard data he needed to demonstrate RoommateFit's effectiveness. Out of the 1,000 freshmen who used RoommateFit, 40 percent planned to stay with their roommates the following year. Mares then applied for a slot in a Pittsburgh business accelerator, AlphaLab. AlphaLab accepted the start-up and provided Mares with $30,000 in start-up funds, office space, and access to office equipment. Within six months, Mares had signed three more universities, which license RoommateFit's proprietary software for a fee of $2 to $3 per student. In addition to marketing RoommateFit to other colleges and universities, the young entrepreneur also is planning to launch a consumer version for roommate-seekers in New York City and San Francisco.[149] ■

We will discuss the process of building and testing a business model in Chapter 4.

Develop a Solid Business Plan

If an entrepreneur's business model passes the feasibility test, the next step is to prepare a business plan. For any entrepreneur, a well-written business plan is a crucial ingredient in preparing for business success. Without a sound business plan, a company merely drifts along without any real direction. Yet entrepreneurs, who tend to be people of action, too often jump right into a business venture without taking time to prepare a written plan outlining the essence of the business. Not only does a plan provide a pathway to success, but it also creates a benchmark against which an entrepreneur can measure actual company performance. Building a successful business begins with implementing a sound business plan with laser-like focus.

A business plan allows entrepreneurs to replace sometimes-faulty assumptions with facts before making the decision to go into business. The planning process forces entrepreneurs to ask and then answer some difficult, challenging, and crucial questions about target customers, market potential, competition, costs of doing business, pricing, realistic revenue forecasts, and other matters.

ENTREPRENEURIAL PROFILE: Frank Mobley: Immedion At 43, Frank Mobley bowed to his independent streak, left a well-paying steady job with a successful data solutions business, and started his own data support and security company, Immedion. Building on his experience in the telecommunications and data solutions industries, Mobley saw a growing need among mid-size companies for reliable servers that could store data securely and keep companies' Web sites up and running under any circumstances. He spent two months writing a business plan, which was all he had to convince investors to put up the $2.5 million he needed to launch Immedion. Mobley was able to use the business plan to sell his idea to investors, including friends, family members, and even his former employers. When Mobley started his company in Greenville, South Carolina, he had one data center and no clients. Today, Immedion has four data centers, 300 clients, and is growing rapidly. Mobley considers his business to be successful because his customers are satisfied, his investors are happy, and his employees enjoy their work.[150] ■

We will discuss the process of developing a business plan in Chapter 5.

Understand Financial Statements

Every business owner must depend on records and financial statements to know the condition of his or her business. All too often, entrepreneurs use these only for tax purposes and not as vital management control devices. To truly understand what is going on in the business, an owner must have at least a basic understanding of accounting and finance.

When analyzed and interpreted properly, these financial statements are reliable indicators of a small firm's health. They can be quite helpful in signaling potential problems. For example, declining sales, slipping profits, rising debt, and deteriorating working capital are all symptoms of potentially lethal problems that require immediate attention. We will discuss financial statement analysis in Chapter 11.

Manage Financial Resources

The best defense against financial problems is to develop a practical information system and then use this information to make business decisions. No entrepreneur can maintain control over a business unless he or she is able to judge its financial health.

The first step in managing financial resources effectively is to have adequate start-up capital. Too many entrepreneurs start their businesses undercapitalized. One experienced business owner advises, "Estimate how much capital you need to get the business going and then double that figure." His point is well taken; it almost always costs more (and takes longer) to launch a business than any entrepreneur expects. Jake Burton, founder of Burton Snowboards, a company that dominates the snowboard industry with 58 percent market share, made that mistake when he started his now successful company in 1977 straight out of college. Looking back, Burton acknowledges that he underestimated both the cost and the time that it would take to start the business, mistakes that almost cost him the business.[151]

The most valuable financial resource to any small business is *cash*. Although earning a profit is essential to its long-term survival, a business must have an adequate supply of cash to pay its bills. Some entrepreneurs count on growing sales to supply their company's cash needs, but this almost never happens. Growing companies usually consume more cash than they generate, and the faster they grow, the more cash they gobble up! Business history is littered with failed companies whose founders had no idea how much cash their businesses were generating and were spending cash as if they were certain there was "plenty more where that came from." Four years after former professional baseball player Curt Schilling launched 38 Studios, a company he started to produce massive multiplayer online games, the company ran short of cash and defaulted on a $1.1 million interest payment that was part of a $75 million guaranteed loan. The company soon folded, 400 people lost their jobs, lenders lost $110 million, and Schilling himself lost $50 million.[152]

We will discuss cash management techniques in Chapter 12.

Learn to Manage People Effectively

No matter what kind of business you launch, you must learn to manage people. Every business depends on a foundation of well-trained, motivated employees. No business owner can do everything alone. The people an entrepreneur hires ultimately determine the heights to which the company can climb—or the depths to which it can plunge. Attracting and retaining a corps of quality employees is no easy task, however. It remains a challenge for every small business owner. "In the end, your most dominant sustainable resource is the quality of the people you have," says one small business expert.[153] At Chipotle Mexican Grill, Steve Ells is quick to point to the company's dedicated 45,000 employees as one key to success. "We develop our people and promote from within," says Ells, noting that 85 percent of Chipotle's salaried managers and 96 percent of its hourly managers are promoted from within the company, and many of them started as burrito rollers in a restaurant.[154] We will discuss the techniques of managing and motivating people effectively in Chapter 16.

Set Your Business Apart from the Competition

The formula for almost certain business failure involves becoming a "me-too business"—merely copying whatever the competition is doing. Most successful entrepreneurs find a way to convince their customers that their companies are superior to their competitors even if they sell similar products or services. It is especially important for small companies going up against larger, more powerful rivals with greater financial resources. Ideally, the basis for differentiating a company from its competitors is founded in what it does best. For small companies, that basis often is customer service, convenience, speed, quality, or whatever else is important to attracting and keeping satisfied customers. We will discuss the strategies for creating a unique footprint in the marketplace in Chapters 5 and 8.

Maintain a Positive Attitude

Achieving business success requires an entrepreneur to maintain a positive mental attitude toward business and the discipline to stick with it. Successful entrepreneurs recognize that their most valuable resource is their time, and they learn to manage it effectively to make themselves and their companies more productive. None of this, of course, is possible without passion—passion for their businesses, their products or services, their customers, and their communities. Passion is what enables a failed business owner to get back up, try again, and make it to the top! One business writer says growing a successful business requires entrepreneurs to have great faith in themselves and their ideas, great doubt concerning the challenges and inevitable obstacles they will face as they build their businesses, and great effort—lots of hard work—to make their dreams become reality.[155]

Conclusion

As you can see, entrepreneurship lies at the heart of this nation's free enterprise system: Small companies truly are the backbone of our economy. Their contributions are as many and as diverse as the businesses themselves. Indeed, diversity is one of the strengths of the U.S. small business sector. Although there are no secrets to becoming a successful entrepreneur, entrepreneurs can take steps to enhance the probability of their success. The remainder of this book will explore those steps and how to apply them to the process of launching a successful business with an emphasis on building a sound business plan.

- Chapter 2, "Ethics and Social Responsibility," describes a framework for making ethical decisions and ensuring that a business lives up to its social responsibility. Chapter 3, "Inside the Entrepreneurial Mind: From Ideas to Reality," explores the creative process that lies at the heart of entrepreneurship and offers practical tips on how you can stimulate your own creativity and that of your employees.

- Section 2, "The Entrepreneurial Journey Begins" (Chapters 4 to 7), discusses the classic start-up questions every entrepreneur faces, particularly conducting a feasibility analysis, creating a business model, developing a strategy, building a business plan, choosing a form of ownership, and alternative methods for becoming a business owner (franchising and buying an existing business).

- Section 3, "Launching a Business" (Chapters 8 to 13), focuses first on creating an effective bootstrap marketing plan for a small company. These chapters address creating an effective e-commerce strategy and establishing pricing and credit strategies. This section also explains how to develop the financial component of a business plan, including creating projected financial statements and forecasting cash flow. These chapters offer existing business owners practical financial management tools and explain how to find the sources of funding, both debt and equity, necessary to launch a business.

- Section 4, "Growing the Business" (Chapters 14 to 16), explains how to find the ideal location for a business and plan for an efficient layout and how to penetrate global markets successfully. This section also provides useful techniques for assembling a strong new venture team and leading its members to success and discusses the importance of creating a management succession plan to ensure that a company successfully makes the transition to the next generation of owners.

As you can see, the journey down the road of entrepreneurship will be fascinating and exciting. Let's get started!

Chapter Summary by Learning Objective

1. Define the role of the entrepreneur in business in the United States and around the world.

Entrepreneurship is thriving in the United States, but the current wave of entrepreneurship is not limited to the United States; many nations across the globe are seeing similar growth in their small business sectors. A variety of competitive, economic, and demographic shifts have created a world in which "small is beautiful."

Capitalist societies depend on entrepreneurs to provide the drive and risk taking necessary for the system to supply people with the goods and services they need.

2. Describe the entrepreneurial profile.

Entrepreneurs have some common characteristics, including a desire for responsibility, a preference for moderate risk, confidence in their ability to succeed, desire for immediate feedback, a high energy level, a future orientation, skill at organizing, and a value of achievement over money. In a phrase, they are tenacious high achievers.

3A. Describe the benefits of entrepreneurship.

Driven by these personal characteristics, entrepreneurs establish and manage small businesses to gain control over their lives, make a difference in the world, become self-fulfilled, reap unlimited profits, contribute to society, and do what they enjoy doing.

3B. Describe the drawbacks of entrepreneurship.

Entrepreneurs also face certain disadvantages, including uncertainty of income, the risk of losing their investments (and more), long hours and hard work, a lower quality of life until the business gets established, high stress levels, and complete decision-making responsibility.

4. Explain the forces that are driving the growth of entrepreneurship.

Several factors are driving the boom in entrepreneurship, including the portrayal of entrepreneurs as heroes, better entrepreneurial education, economic and demographic factors, a shift to a service economy, technological advances, more independent lifestyles, and increased international opportunities.

5. Explain the cultural diversity of entrepreneurship.

Several groups are leading the nation's drive toward entrepreneurship: young people, women, minorities, immigrants, part-timers, home-based business owners, family business owners, copreneurs, corporate cast-offs, corporate dropouts, social entrepreneurs, and retired baby boomers.

6. Describe the important role that small businesses play in our nation's economy.

The small business sector's contributions are many. They make up 99.7 percent of all businesses, employ 49.2 percent of the private sector workforce, have created nearly two-thirds of the net new jobs in the economy, produce 46 percent of the country's private GDP, and account for 47 percent of all business sales.

7. Put failure into the proper perspective.

Entrepreneurs recognize that failure is a natural part of the creative process. Successful entrepreneurs have the attitude that failures are simply stepping-stones along the path to success, and they refuse to be paralyzed by a fear of failure.

8. Explain how an entrepreneur can avoid becoming another failure statistic.

Entrepreneurs can employ several general tactics to avoid these pitfalls. They should know their businesses in depth, prepare a solid business plan, manage financial resources effectively, understand financial statements, learn to manage people, set their businesses apart from the competition, and maintain a positive attitude.

Discussion Questions

1-1. What forces have led to the boom in entrepreneurship in the United States and across the globe?

1-2. What is an entrepreneur? Give a brief description of the entrepreneurial profile.

1-3. *Inc.* magazine claims, "Entrepreneurship is more mundane than it's sometimes portrayed . . . you don't need to be a person of mythical proportions to be very, very successful in building a company." Do you agree? Explain.

1-4. What are the major benefits of business ownership?

1-5. Which of the potential drawbacks to business ownership are most critical?

1-6. Briefly describe the role of the following groups in entrepreneurship: young people, women, minorities, immigrants, part-timers, home-based business owners, family business owners, copreneurs, corporate castoffs, corporate dropouts, social entrepreneurs, and retired baby boomers.

1-7. What contributions do small businesses make to our economy?

1-8. Describe the small business failure rate.

1-9. Outline the causes of business failure. Which problems cause most business failures?

1-10. How does the typical entrepreneur view the possibility of business failure?

1-11. How can the small business owner avoid the common pitfalls that often lead to business failures?

1-12. Why is it important to study the small business failure rate and to understand the causes of business failures?

1-13. Explain the typical entrepreneur's attitude toward risk.

1-14. Are you interested in some day launching a small business?

1-15. If you are interested in launching a business, when do you intend to start it?

1-16. If you intend to start a business, what steps can you take to increase the likelihood that it will succeed?

Beyond the Classroom . . .

1-17. Choose an entrepreneur in your community and interview him or her. What's the "story" behind the business?

1-18. How well does the entrepreneur fit the entrepreneurial profile described in this chapter?

1-19. What advantages and disadvantages does the entrepreneur see in owning a business?

1-20. What advice would he or she offer to someone considering launching a business?

1-21. Select one of the categories under the section "The Cultural Diversity of Entrepreneurship" in this chapter and research it in more detail. Find examples of business owners in that category and prepare a brief report for your class.

1-22. Search through recent business publications (especially those focusing on small companies) and find an example of an entrepreneur, past or present, who exhibits the entrepreneurial spirit of striving for success in the face of failure. Prepare a brief report for your class.

Endnotes

Scan for Endnotes or go to www.pearsonhighered.com/scarborough

Ethics and Social Responsibility: Doing the Right Thing

KidStock/Blend Images/Corbis

Learning Objectives

On completion of this chapter, you will be able to:

1. Define business ethics and describe the three levels of ethical standards.

2. Determine who is responsible for ethical behavior and why ethical lapses occur.

3. Explain how to establish and maintain high ethical standards.

4. Explain the difference between social entrepreneurs and traditional entrepreneurs.

5. Define social responsibility.

6. Understand the nature of business's responsibility to the environment.

7. Describe business's responsibility to employees.

8. Explain business's responsibility to customers.

9. Discuss business's responsibility to investors.

10. Describe business's responsibility to the community.

Business ethics involves the moral values and behavioral standards that businesspeople draw on as they make decisions and solve problems. It originates in a commitment to do what is right. Ethical behavior—doing what is "right" as opposed to what is "wrong"—starts with the entrepreneur. The entrepreneur's personal values begin to shape the business from day one. Entrepreneurs' personal values and beliefs influence the way they lead their companies and are apparent in every decision they make, every policy they write, and every action they take. Additionally, the entrepreneurs' values set the tone for the culture that will guide the ethical actions of every employee they bring into their business. Entrepreneurs who succeed in the long term have a solid base of personal values and beliefs that they articulate to their employees, put into practice in ways that others can observe, and are demonstrated throughout the culture of the organization. Values-based leaders do more than merely follow rules and regulations; their consciences dictate that they do what is right.

For many entrepreneurs, the ability to determine the values and ethics that will shape how business will be conducted is a major motivation to launching a venture. For example, Blake Jones spent several years working as an engineer in Nepal and Egypt. Jones found the caste system in Nepal and the rigid social structure of Egypt appalling. When he returned to the United States, Jones joined with two partners to form a company, Namasté Solar, built on their shared value of the importance of full participation of all employees in the governance of the business. To bring these values to life, Jones and his partners structured Namasté Solar as an employee owned cooperative. The company Web site describes its business model as follows: "We choose co-ownership over hierarchy, democratic decision-making over centralized leadership, sustainable growth over aggressive expansion, and collaboration over competition."[1] Namasté Solar designs and installs residential and commercial solar electric systems in Colorado. Seventy percent of the employees are owners of the company, with each owning one share valued at $5,000. All employee owners have an equal vote in important issues facing the company. "A 22-year-old recent college grad who is an apprentice installing solar panels on rooftops has the same vote as I have," says Jones. "I regularly don't get my way."[2]

The values and morals that entrepreneurs draw on to guide their ethical behaviors come from a variety of sources, including their family upbringing, their faith traditions, mentors who have shaped their lives, and the communities they grew up in. Bringing their personal values into their decision making and actions in their businesses helps ensure that entrepreneurs will act with integrity. Acting with integrity means that entrepreneurs do what is right no matter what the circumstances.

In some cases, ethical dilemmas are apparent. Entrepreneurs must be keenly aware of the ethical entrapments awaiting them and know that society will hold them accountable for their actions. More often, however, ethical issues are less obvious, cloaked in the garb of mundane decisions and everyday routine. Because they can easily catch entrepreneurs off guard and unprepared, these ethical "sleepers" are most likely to ensnare business owners, soiling their reputations and those of their companies. Repeated enough times, these unethical acts can become habits that shape the moral character of the entrepreneur. To make proper ethical choices, entrepreneurs must first be aware that a situation with ethical implications exists.

Complicating the issue even more is that, in some ethical dilemmas, no clear-cut right or wrong answers exist. There is no direct conflict between good and evil, right and wrong, or truth and falsehood. Instead, there is only the issue of conflicting interests among a company's **stakeholders**, the various groups and individuals who affect and are affected by a business. These conflicts force entrepreneurs to identify their stakeholders and to consider the ways in which entrepreneurs will deal with them (see Figure 2.1). For instance, when the founders of a local coffee shop make business decisions, they must consider the impact of those decisions on many stakeholders, including the team of employees who work there, the farmers and companies that supply the business with raw materials, the union that represents employees in collective bargaining, the government agencies that regulate a multitude of activities, the banks that provide the business with financing, the founding partners and other external investors who helped fund the start-up, the general public the business serves, the community in which the company operates, the customers who buy the company's products, and their families. When making decisions,

stakeholders
the various groups and individuals who affect and are affected by a business.

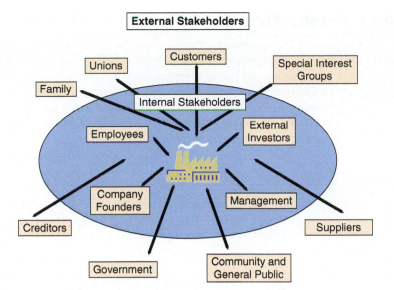

FIGURE 2.1

Key Stakeholders

entrepreneurs often must balance the needs and demands of a company's stakeholders, knowing that whatever the final decision is, not all groups will be satisfied.

Ethical leaders approach their organizational responsibilities with added dimensions of thought and action. They link ethical behaviors to organizational outcomes and incorporate social responsibility into daily decisions. They establish ethical behavior and concern for the environment as an integral part of organizational training and eventually as part of company culture. How does a commitment to "doing the right thing" apply to employees, customers, and other stakeholders, and how does it affect an entrepreneur's daily decision making? Large technology companies such as Apple, Google, Yahoo, Facebook, Microsoft, and Verizon have been facing an ethical dilemma as they attempt to comply with the National Security Administration's request for information. The NSA operates a program known as Prism, which gathers telephone and Internet data to capture information about foreign nationals living in America. The NSA gets this information from technology companies that provide Internet and telephone services to consumers and businesses. Technology companies gain significant revenue from the data they gather from their users. For example, although Google offers many of its products such as Gmail and the Google search engine free to most users, these products generate significant revenue from the information Google amasses from its users' Internet searches and emails. Google sells the data to advertisers, which then use it to target ads to specific consumers. Although their customers generally are aware that data mining is commonly a part of having access to technologies at no cost, there is an implied understanding that this data will be protected beyond Google's internal use. However, Google and other large technology companies have a duty to comply with the federal government's request for information tied to national security concerns and have turned over large amounts of customer data to the NSA.[3] As evidenced by this example, balancing the demands of various stakeholders to make ethical decisions is no easy task.

Business operates as an institution in our often complex and ever-evolving society. As such, every entrepreneur is expected to behave in ways that are compatible with the value system of society. It is society that imposes the rules of conduct for all business owners in the form of ethical standards of behavior and responsibilities to act in ways that benefit the long-term interest of all. Society expects business owners to strive to earn a profit on their investment. Ethics and social responsibility simply set behavioral boundaries for decision makers. **Ethics** is a branch of philosophy that studies and creates theories about the basic nature of right and wrong, duty, obligation, and virtue. **Social responsibility** involves how an organization responds to the needs of the many elements in society, including shareholders, lenders, employees, consumers, governmental agencies, and the environment. Because business is allowed to operate in society, it has an obligation to behave in ways that benefit all of society.

ethics
a branch of philosophy that studies and creates theories about the basic nature of right and wrong, duty, obligation, and virtue.

social responsibility
how an organization responds to the needs of the many elements in society.

An Ethical Perspective

Business ethics consists of the fundamental moral values and behavioral standards that form the foundation for the people of an organization as they make decisions and interact with stakeholders. Business ethics is a sensitive and highly complex issue, but it is not a new one. In 560 BC, the Greek philosopher Chilon claimed that a merchant does better to take a loss than to make a dishonest profit.[4] Maintaining an ethical perspective is essential to creating and protecting a company's reputation, but it is no easy task. Ethical dilemmas lurk in the decisions—even the most mundane ones—that entrepreneurs make every day. Succumbing to unethical temptations ultimately can destroy a company's reputation, one of the most precious and most fragile possessions of any business.

Building a reputation for ethical behavior typically takes a long time; unfortunately, destroying that reputation requires practically no time at all, and the effects linger for some time. One top manager compares a bad reputation to a hangover: "It takes a while to get rid of, and it makes everything else hurt."[5] Many businesses flounder or even fail after their owners or managers are caught acting unethically.

ENTREPRENEURIAL PROFILE: Brian Whitfield, Edwin Todd, and Marsha Whitfield: Sommet Group Brian Whitfield and his father-in-law Edwin Todd founded Sommet Group to provide business services, including payroll, human resources, employee benefits, and staffing, to small- and medium-sized companies. Outsourcing these functions allowed their clients to focus on growing their business. Marsha Whitfield, Brian's wife and Edwin Todd's daughter, served as Vice President of Payroll for the company. To help build brand awareness, the Sommet Group entered into a multi-year naming rights agreement in 2007 with the Nashville Predators of the National Hockey League. The company was seeking to become a nationally known provider of outsourced business services. The home arena for the Predators became known as the Sommet Center. However, soon the empire being built by the family-owned business began to unravel. In 2009, just two years after signing the agreement, the Nashville Predators sued the Sommet Group to revoke the naming rights, alleging nonpayment of the agreed-upon naming rights fees. In July 2010 the FBI raided Sommet Group's headquarters, looking for evidence of fraud. In 2011 federal agents also raided the home of Brian and Marsha Whitfield seeking additional evidence. That same year Marsha filed for divorce. On March 1, 2012, the Whitfields and Todd were indicted in federal court on 15 criminal counts, including wire fraud, conspiracy, theft from an ERISA plan, and money laundering charges. The Whitfields allegedly stole more than $650,000 from an employee pension plan to help pay for the arena naming rights obligations, to buy a houseboat, and to build a pool at their home. The indictment also alleged that the Whitfields failed to report almost $80 million of gross wages paid on behalf of Sommet clients, leading to an underpayment of more than $20 million in income taxes. In July 2013, two former executives of Sommet reached a plea deal with federal prosecutors. Edwin Todd agreed to plead guilty to one count of conspiracy. Marsha Whitfield agreed to testify against her former husband Brian Whitfield and pleaded guilty to one count of conspiracy and one count of wire fraud.[6] ■

Three Levels of Ethical Standards

As displayed in Figure 2.2, there are three levels of ethical standards:

1. *The law*, which defines for society as a whole those actions that are permissible and those that are not. The law is the narrowest level of ethical standards. The law merely establishes the minimum standard of behavior. Actions that are legal, however, may not be ethical. Simply obeying the law is insufficient as a guide for ethical behavior; ethical behavior requires more. Few ethical issues are so simple and one dimensional that the law can serve as the acid test for making a decision.

2. *Organizational policies and procedures*, which serve as specific guidelines for people as they make daily decisions. Policies and procedures include a broader definition of ethical standards that go beyond what is defined by the law. Many colleges and universities have created honor codes, and companies rely on policies covering everything from sexual harassment and gift giving to hiring and whistle blowing.

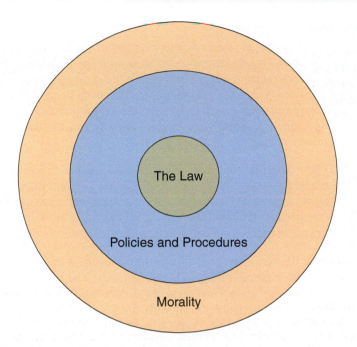

FIGURE 2.2

**Three Levels of
Ethical Standards**

3. The *moral stance* that employees take when they encounter a situation that is not governed by levels 1 and 2. It is the broadest and most fundamental definition of ethical standards. The values people learn early in life at home, from their religious upbringing, in the communities they were raised in, in school, and at work are key ingredients at this level. Morality is what shapes a person's character. A strong determinant of moral behavior is *training*. As Aristotle said thousands of years ago, you get a good adult by teaching a child to do the right thing. A company's culture can serve either to support or undermine its employees' concepts of what constitutes ethical behavior.

Ethics is something that every businessperson faces daily; most decisions involve some degree of ethical judgment. Over the course of a career, entrepreneurs can be confident that they will face some tough ethical choices. However, that is not necessarily bad! Situations such as these give entrepreneurs the opportunity to flex their ethical muscles and do what is right. Entrepreneurs set the ethical tone for their companies. The ethical stance employees take when faced with difficult decisions often reflects the values that entrepreneurs have used to intentionally shape the culture within their businesses.

ENTREPRENEURIAL PROFILE: Joey Prusak, Dairy Queen manager Joey Prusak was working at the Dairy Queen franchise where he had been employed for the previous five years. A blind man, who was a regular customer, was standing at the counter paying his bill. While the customer was getting money out of his wallet, he unknowingly dropped a twenty-dollar bill. A woman standing behind him in line quickly picked up the twenty-dollar bill and put it in her purse. When the woman stepped up to the counter to be served, Prusak asked her to return the money to the man who had dropped it. She refused, claiming it was her money that she had dropped. Prusak refused to serve her, saying that he would not serve her if she was going to be so "disrespectful" to another customer. The woman became belligerent and stormed out of the store. Prusak served the remaining customers in line, apologizing to each one for the incident. Prusak then went over to the blind man, pulled out a twenty-dollar bill, and handed him the money, telling him that he had dropped it on the floor when he was paying for his food. A customer who witnessed the entire incident wrote a comment card describing what had happened. The owner of the franchise put the comment card on a bulletin board for all of the employees to see. One of the employees took a picture of the card and posted it on Facebook. The story then went viral. Billionaire Warren Buffet, whose company Berkshire Hathaway owns American Dairy Queen Corporation, heard the story and invited Prusak to be his special guest at the annual shareholder meeting of Berkshire Hathaway.[7] ∎

Moral Management

Although companies may set ethical standards and offer guidelines for employees, the ultimate decision on whether to abide by ethical principles rests with the *individual*. In other words, companies really are not ethical or unethical; individuals are. Managers, however, can greatly influence individual behavior within the company. That influence must start at the *top* of the organization. The entrepreneur who practices ethical behavior establishes the moral tone for the entire organization. Table 2.1 summarizes the characteristics of the three ethical styles of management: immoral, amoral, and moral management.

IMMORAL MANAGEMENT Immoral managers are motivated by selfish reasons such as their own gains or those of the company. The driving force behind immoral management is *greed*: achieving personal or organizational success at any cost. Immoral management is the polar opposite of ethical management; immoral managers do what they can to circumvent laws and moral standards and are not concerned about the impact their actions have on others.

AMORAL MANAGEMENT The principal goal of amoral managers is to earn a profit, but their actions differ from those of immoral managers in one key way: They do not purposely violate laws or ethical standards. Instead, amoral managers neglect to consider the impact their decisions have on others; they use free-rein decision making without reference to ethical standards. Amoral management is not an option for socially responsible businesses.

MORAL MANAGEMENT Moral managers also strive for success but only within the boundaries of legal and ethical standards. Moral managers are not willing to sacrifice their values and violate

TABLE 2.1 Approaches to Business Ethics

Organizational Characteristics	Immoral Management	Amoral Management	Moral Management
Ethical norms	Management decisions, actions, and behavior imply a positive and active opposition to what is moral (ethical). Decisions are discordant with accepted ethical principles. An active negation of what is moral is implicit.	Management is neither moral nor immoral; decisions are not based on moral judgments. Management activity is not related to any moral code. A lack of ethical perception and moral awareness may be implicit.	Management activity conforms to a standard of ethical, or right, behavior. Management activity conforms to accepted professional standards of conduct. Ethical leadership is commonplace.
Motives	Selfish. Management cares only about its or its company's gains.	Well-intentioned but selfish in the sense that impact on others is not considered.	Good. Management wants to succeed but only within the confines of sound ethical precepts such as fairness, justice, and due process.
Goals	Profitability and organizational success at any price.	Profitability. Other goals are not considered.	Profitability within the confines of legal obedience and ethical standards.
Orientation toward law	Legal standards are barriers that management must overcome to accomplish what it wants.	Law is the ethical guide, preferably the letter of the law. The central question is, what we can do legally?	Obedience toward letter and spirit of the law. Law is a minimal ethical behavior. Prefer to operate well above what law mandates.
Strategy	Exploit opportunities for corporate gain. Cut corners when it appears useful.	Give managers free rein. Personal ethics may apply but only if managers choose. Respond to legal mandates if caught and required to do so.	Live by sound ethical standards. Assume leadership position when ethical dilemmas arise. Enlightened self-interest.

Source: Archie B. Carroll, "In Search of the Moral Manager," reprinted from *Business Horizons*, March/April, Copyright 1987 by the Foundation for the School of Business at Indiana University. Used with permission.

ethical standards just to make a profit. Managers who operate with this philosophy see the law as a minimum standard for ethical behavior.

The Benefits of Moral Management

One of the most common misconceptions about business is that there is a contradiction between earning a profit and maintaining high ethical standards. In reality, companies have learned that these two goals are consistent with one another. Elizabeth Riley, program manager of Impact Engine, a Chicago-based business accelerator that supports for-profit start-ups with strong social missions, says, "Much too often, business leaders are faced with an unnecessary choice between profits and making the world a better place. This is a false construct that has been perpetuated for far too long—profit and purpose should not be mutually exclusive."[8] Many entrepreneurs launch businesses with the idea of making a difference in society. They quickly learn that to "do good," their companies must first "do well." Bridget Hilton, founder of Jack's Soap, a for-profit company that addresses the problem of child mortality due to hygiene by donating one bar of soap to a child in need for every bar of soap sold, says, "Cynics believe there's no way to do good while reaping financial rewards. We beg to differ."[9]

According to a survey by the public relations firm Edelman, 83 percent of U.S. consumers say transparent and honest practices and operating as a business that one can trust are the most important factors in a company's reputation.[10] The Edelman survey also reports that people in the United States (and globally) trust small businesses more than big businesses.[11]

ENTREPRENEURIAL PROFILE: Patrick Woodyard and Nick Meyer: Nisolo Patrick Woodyard began developing the for-profit social venture he cofounded in 2011, called Nisolo, when he was working in a microfinance project in Peru. Woodyard observed talented craftsmen and artisans who were struggling to find a market for their products. Woodyard launched Nisolo to help Peruvian shoemakers expand the market for their handmade shoes. Nisolo sells high quality, fashionable men's and women's shoes handmade by artisans in Peru through e-commerce and out of its showroom in Nashville, Tennessee. Nisolo sells shoes that are both fashionable and help support the shoemakers living in impoverished regions. With each purchase, customers receive a business card from the shoemaker who makes their shoes. Nisolo's goal is to help Peruvian shoemakers receive a fair price and have steady sales for their shoes. The shoes are high quality and retail for an average price of $120 per pair. Nisolo pays the shoemakers an average of $30 per pair, which is enough to pull them out of poverty and provide a sustainable living for their families. "It's about giving them jobs and empowering them," says cofounder Nick Meyer. Nisolo seeks to earn a profit while at the same time helping to provide economic empowerment for the artisans who supply its handmade shoes by offering them a fair price for their products.[12] ∎

Patrick Woodyard, CEO

Although behaving ethically has value in itself, there are many other benefits to companies that adhere to high ethical standards. First, companies avoid the damaging fallout from unethical behavior on their reputations. Unethical businesses usually gain only short-term advantages; over the long run, unethical decisions don't pay. It's simply not good business.

Second, a solid ethical framework guides managers as they cope with an increasingly complex network of influence from external stakeholders. Dealing with stakeholders is much easier if a company has a solid ethical foundation on which to build.

Third, businesses with solid reputations as ethical companies find it easier to attract and retain quality workers. Max Lubarsky gets paid to volunteer for a variety of projects in Washington, D.C., including cleaning up the bird exhibit at the National Zoo, participating in Habitat for Humanity building projects, and helping to beautify the grounds around various national monuments. Lubarsky works for the Carlyle Group, which offers employees two paid days off a year to perform volunteer work around the community. "It's been a great opportunity to give

TABLE 2.2 Reasons to Run a Business Ethically and the Factors That Drive Business Ethics

Top Five Reasons to Run a Business Ethically

1. Protect brand and company reputation
2. It is the right thing to do
3. Maintain customers' trust and loyalty
4. Maintain investors' confidence
5. Earn public acceptance and recognition

Top Five Factors That Drive Business Ethics

1. Corporate scandals
2. Marketplace competition
3. Demands by investors
4. Pressure from customers
5. Globalization

Source: *The Ethical Enterprise: A Global Study of Business Ethics 2005–2015* (American Management Association/Human Resource Institute, 2006), p. 2.

back to the community," says Lubarsky. Lubarsky has a strong loyalty to Carlyle Group, as he wants to work for a company where he can make a difference within both his profession and his community.[13]

Fourth, ethical behavior has a positive impact on a company's bottom line. Research on the relationship between corporate ethics and financial performance suggests that companies that outperform their competitors ethically also outperform them financially due to the strong employee commitment that an ethical culture creates.[14] However, financial rewards should never become the motivating force behind acting ethically. Entrepreneurs must strive to do the right thing simply because it is the right thing to do!

Finally, a company's ethical philosophy has an impact on its ability to provide value for its customers. The "ethics factor" is difficult to quantify, yet it is something that customers consider when deciding where to shop and which company's products to buy. "Do I want people buying Timberland boots as a result of the firm's volunteer efforts?" asks CEO Jeffrey Swartz. "You bet."[15] Timberland's commitment to "doing good" in addition to "doing well" is expressed in its slogan, "Boots, Brand, Belief." Like other social entrepreneurs, Swartz's goal is to manage the company successfully so that he can use its resources to combat social problems.

Entrepreneurs must recognize that ethical behavior is an investment in the company's future rather than merely a cost of doing business. Table 2.2 shows the results of a comprehensive study that was conducted by the American Management Association of global human resources directors who were asked about the reasons for their companies' engaging in ethical behavior and the factors that drive business ethics today.

Establishing an Ethical Framework

To cope successfully with the many ethical decisions they face, entrepreneurs must develop a workable ethical framework to guide themselves and the organization. Although many frameworks exist, the following five-step process works quite well:

Step 1. *Identify the personal moral and ethical principles that shape all business decisions.* Entrepreneurs build the foundation for making ethical decisions by understanding how their personal values come to life in business situations. This starts with an inventory of the important principles that define one's personal values. The entrepreneur then determines how each of these principles affects each of the major stakeholders of the business. Many entrepreneurs integrate this proactive approach to ethical decision making into their business plans to ensure the integrity of their business actions as they launch and grow their business ventures.

Bradford Veley/www.CartoonStock.com

Step 2. ***Recognize the ethical dimensions involved in the dilemma or decision.*** Before entrepreneurs can make informed ethical decisions, they must recognize that an ethical situation exists. Only then is it possible to define the specific ethical issues involved. Too often, business owners fail to take into account the ethical impact of a particular course of action until it is too late. To avoid ethical quagmires, entrepreneurs must consider the ethical forces at work in a situation—honesty, fairness, respect for the community, concern for the environment, trust, and others—to have a complete view of the decision.

Step 3. ***Identify the key stakeholders involved and determine how the decision will affect them.*** Every business influences and is influenced by a multitude of stakeholders. Frequently, the demands of these stakeholders conflict with one another, putting a business in the position of having to choose which groups to satisfy and which to alienate. Before making a decision, managers must sort out the conflicting interests of the various stakeholders by determining which ones have important stakes in the situation. Although this analysis may not resolve the conflict, it will prevent the company from inadvertently causing harm to people it may have failed to consider. More companies are measuring their performance using a **triple bottom line (3BL)** that, in addition to the traditional measure of profitability, includes the commitment to ethics and social responsibility and the impact on the environment ("profit, people, and planet").

triple bottom line (3BL)

measuring business performance using profitability, its commitment to ethics and social responsibility, and its impact on the environment ("profit, people, and planet").

Jason Adkins, Owner

ENTREPRENEURIAL PROFILE: Jason Adkins: BrightHouse Luxury Green Home Cleaning BrightHouse Luxury Green Home Cleaning is a healthy, eco-friendly green home cleaning service, operating out of offices in Jacksonville, Florida, and Nashville, Tennessee. BrightHouse uses all natural and allergy-reducing products, HEPA filtrations, microfiber, and recyclable packaging. BrightHouse is affiliated with Cleaning for a Reason Foundation, which provides free home cleaning services for women undergoing treatment for cancer. Cleaning for a Reason partners with local cleaning companies such as BrightHouse throughout the United States and Canada. Adkins says that all of BrightHouse's employees can attest to the fact that home cleaning is strenuous work. Providing cleaning for cancer patients enables them to save their strength to tolerate treatment and get well. BrightHouse's non-toxic cleaning solution do not cause problems for cancer patients whose immune systems are compromised by chemotherapy. Adkins hopes that a clean home can comfort patients during their treatment and recovery.[16] ■

Step 4. *Generate alternative choices and distinguish between ethical and unethical responses.* When entrepreneurs are generating alternative courses of action and evaluating the consequences of each one, they can use the questions in Table 2.3 to guide them. Asking and answering questions such as these ensure that everyone involved is aware of the ethical dimensions of the issue.

TABLE 2.3 Questions to Help Identify the Ethical Dimension of a Situation

Principles and Codes of Conduct

- Does this decision or action meet my standards for how people should interact?
- Does this decision or action agree with my religious teachings or beliefs (or with my personal principles and sense of responsibility)?
- How will I feel about myself if I do this?
- Do we (or I) have a rule or policy for cases like this?
- Would I want everyone to make the same decision and take the same action if faced with these circumstances?
- What are my true motives for considering this action?

Moral Rights

- Would this action allow others freedom of choice in this matter?
- Would this action involve deceiving others in any way?

Justice

- Would I feel this action was just (right) if I were on the other side of the decision?
- How would I feel if this action were done to me or someone close to me?
- Would this action or decision distribute benefits justly?
- Would it distribute hardships or burdens justly?

Consequences and Outcomes

- What will be the short- and long-term consequences of this action?
- Who will benefit from this course of action?
- Who will be hurt?
- How will this action create good and prevent harm?

Public Justification

- How would I feel (or how will I feel) if (or when) this action becomes public knowledge?
- Will I be able to explain adequately to others why I have taken the action?
- Would others feel that my action or decision is ethical or moral?

Intuition and Insight

- Have I searched for all alternatives? Are there other ways I could look at this situation? Have I considered all points of view?
- Even if there is sound rationality for this decision or action, and even if I could defend it publicly, does my inner sense tell me it is right?
- What does my intuition tell me is the ethical thing to do in this situation? Have I listened to my inner voice?

Source: Sherry Baker, "Ethical Judgment," *Executive Excellence*, March 1992, pp. 7–8.

Step 5. *Choose the "best" ethical response and implement it.* At this point, there likely will be several ethical choices from which managers can pick. Comparing these choices to the "ideal" ethical outcome may help managers make the final decision. The final choice must be consistent with the company's goals, culture, and value system as well as those of the individual decision makers.

Why Ethical Lapses Occur

LO2

Determine who is responsible for ethical behavior and why ethical lapses occur.

Although most small business owners run their companies ethically, business scandals involving Enron, WorldCom, Tyco, and other high-profile companies have sullied the reputations of businesses of all sizes. The best way for business owners to combat these negative public perceptions is to run their business ethically. When faced with an ethical dilemma, however, not every entrepreneur or employee will make the right decision. According to KPMG's Integrity Survey, 73 percent of workers say they have observed ethical lapses in their companies within the last year, and 56 percent say the misconduct they observed would cause "a significant loss of public trust if discovered."[17] Normally decent people who believe in moral values commit many unethical acts. Figure 2.3 shows the results of the KPMG Integrity Survey that identifies the primary causes of misconduct in businesses. Let's explore some of the causes if ethical lapses in more detail.

An Unethical Employee

Ethical decisions are individual decisions, and some people are corrupt. Try as they might to avoid them, small businesses occasionally find that they have hired a "bad apple." Eliminating unethical behavior requires eliminating these bad apples.

An Unethical Organizational Culture

In some cases, a company's culture has been poisoned with an unethical overtone; in other words, the problem is not the "bad apple" but the "bad barrel." Pressure to prosper produces an environment that creates conditions that reward unethical behavior, and employees act accordingly. Studies show that companies with strong ethical cultures experience fewer ethical violations than those with weak ethical cultures.[18] In fact, an ethical culture positively influences the behaviors of employees *independently* of the degree to which there is a match between employee and organizational values.[19]

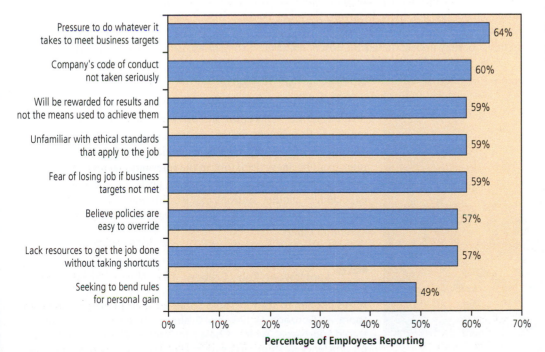

Causes of Ethical Lapses

Cause	Percentage
Pressure to do whatever it takes to meet business targets	64%
Company's code of conduct not taken seriously	60%
Will be rewarded for results and not the means used to achieve them	59%
Unfamiliar with ethical standards that apply to the job	59%
Fear of losing job if business targets not met	59%
Believe policies are easy to override	57%
Lack resources to get the job done without taking shortcuts	57%
Seeking to bend rules for personal gain	49%

Percentage of Employees Reporting

FIGURE 2.3

Causes of Ethical Lapses

Source: KPMG Integrity Survey 2013, p. 12.

Moral Blindness

Sometimes, fundamentally ethical people commit unethical blunders because they are blind to the implications of their conduct. Moral blindness may be the result of failing to realize that an ethical dilemma exists, or it may arise from a variety of mental defense mechanisms. One of the most common mechanisms is rationalization:

"Everybody does it."

"If they were in my place, they'd do it too."

"Being ethical is a luxury I cannot afford right now."

"The impact of my decision/action on (whomever or whatever) is not my concern."

"I don't get paid to be ethical; I get paid to produce results."

Conducting ethics training and creating a culture that encourages employees to consider the ethical impact of their decisions reduces the likelihood of moral blindness. Instilling a sense of individual responsibility and encouraging people at all levels of an organization to speak up when they see questionable actions create a company-wide ethical conscience. However, employees are not the only ones who need guidance when facing ethical decisions. Entrepreneurs themselves should also seek out advice and counsel when it comes to ethics. One reason entrepreneurs should establish advisory boards is to serve as a sounding board to help ensure that they understand the moral and ethical dimensions of major decisions.

Competitive Pressures

If competition is so intense that a company's survival is threatened, managers may begin to view what were once unacceptable options as acceptable. Managers and employees are under such pressure to produce that they may sacrifice their ethical standards to reduce the fear of failure or the fear of losing their jobs. Without a positive organizational culture that stresses ethical behavior regardless of the consequences, employees respond to feelings of pressure and compromise their personal ethical standards to ensure that the job gets done.

Opportunity Pressures

When the opportunity to "get ahead" by taking some unethical action presents itself, some people cannot resist the temptation. The greater the reward or the smaller the penalty for unethical acts, the greater is the probability that such behavior will occur. If managers, for example, condone or even encourage unethical behavior, they can be sure it will occur. Those who succumb to opportunity pressures often make one of two mistakes: They overestimate the cost of doing the right thing, or they underestimate the cost of doing the wrong thing. Either error can lead to disaster.

Robert Grabow, President, Intrepid Sportswear

Globalization of Business

The globalization of business has intertwined what once were distinct cultures. This cultural cross-pollination has brought about many positive aspects, but it has created problems as well. Companies have discovered no single standard of ethical behavior applies to all business decisions in the international arena. Practices that are illegal in one country may be perfectly acceptable, even expected, in another. Actions that would send a businessperson to jail in Western nations are common ways of working around the system in others.

ENTREPRENEURIAL PROFILE: Rob Grabow: Intrepid Sportswear Rob Grabow has always loved playing basketball. His experience wearing poor quality, over-priced uniforms led him to start Intrepid Sportswear from his college dorm room at Gonzaga University. Grabow's business model for Intrepid Sportswear, which is based in Seattle, Washington, focuses on efficiency by shipping product directly from the manufacturer

TABLE 2.4 **Ethics Research Reveals Features of Ethical Cultures**

1. Leaders support and model ethical behavior.
2. Consistent communications come from all company leaders.
3. Ethics is integrated into the organization's goals, business processes, and strategies.
4. Ethics is part of the performance management system.
5. Ethics is part of the company's selection criteria and selection process.
6. The needs of the various stakeholder are balanced when making decisions.
7. A strong set of core values supports the vision and mission of the company.
8. The company maintains a long-term perspective on all decisions.

Source: Based on *The Ethical Enterprise: A Global Study of Business Ethics 2005–2015* (American Management Association/Human Resource Institute, 2006), pp. 5, 6, 10; Alexandre Ardichvili, James A. Mitchell and Douglas Jondle, "Characteristics of Ethical Business Cultures," *Journal of Business Ethics*, 2009 (85:4), pp. 445–451.

to the customer. The savings from eliminating buyers in international markets, wholesalers, and U.S.-based sales representatives is passed along to their customers. Intrepid customers save as much as 50 percent on uniforms compared to other suppliers. In addition to paying overseas workers above-market wages, Intrepid also gives 5 to 10 percent of its net profits back to these workers. Grabow says he gives back to his employees because it is ethical to share success with those who helped create it. However, the practice also creates positive outcomes for his business. Grabow finds that Intrepid Sportswear's profit sharing has improved employee retention and loyalty. His team is more willing to go above and beyond for the company. Grabow believes doing the right thing and sound business practices are not mutually exclusive. Intrepid sells to teams in all 50 states and to teams in eight countries in Europe. More than 6,400 teams have bought uniforms from Intrepid since Grabow started the business in his dorm room in 2002.[20] ∎

Table 2.4 provides a summary of important ethics research concerning the characteristics that are most important to establishing an ethical culture.

Establishing and Maintaining Ethical Standards

LO3

Explain how to establish and maintain high ethical standards.

Establishing Ethical Standards

A study by the Southern Institute for Business and Professional Ethics found that small companies are less likely than large ones to have ethics programs.[21] Although they may not have formal ethics programs, entrepreneurs can encourage employees to become familiar with the following ethical tests for judging behavior:

- *The utilitarian principle.* Choose the option that offers the greatest good for the greatest number of people.

- *Kant's categorical imperative.* Act in such a way that the action taken under the circumstances could be a universal law or rule of behavior.

- *The professional ethic.* Take only those actions that a disinterested panel of professional colleagues would view as proper.

- *The Golden Rule.* Treat other people the way you would like them to treat you.

- *The television test.* Would you and your colleagues feel comfortable explaining your actions to a national television audience?

- *The family test.* Would you be comfortable explaining to your children, your spouse, and your parents why you took this action?[22]

Although these tests do not offer universal solutions to ethical dilemmas, they do help employees identify the moral implications of the decisions they face. People must be able to understand the ethical impact of their actions before they can make responsible decisions. Table 2.5 describes ten ethical principles that differentiate between right and wrong, thereby offering a guideline for ethical behavior.

TABLE 2.5 Ten Ethical Principles to Guide Behavior

The study of history, philosophy, and religion reveals a strong consensus about certain universal and timeless values that are central to leading an ethical life.

1. *Honesty.* Be truthful, sincere, forthright, straightforward, frank, and candid; do not cheat, lie, steal, deceive, or act deviously.

2. *Integrity.* Be principled, honorable, upright, and courageous and act on convictions; do not be two-faced or unscrupulous or adopt an ends-justifies-the-means philosophy that ignores principle.

3. *Promise-keeping.* Be worthy of trust, keep promises, fulfill commitments, and abide by the spirit as well as the letter of an agreement; do not interpret agreements in a technical or legalistic manner to rationalize noncompliance or to create excuses for breaking commitments.

4. *Fidelity.* Be faithful and loyal to family, friends, employers, and country; do not use or disclose information earned in confidence; in a professional context, safeguard the ability to make independent professional judgments by scrupulously avoiding undue influences and conflicts of interest.

5. *Fairness.* Be fair and open-minded, be willing to admit error and, when appropriate, change positions and beliefs; demonstrate a commitment to justice, the equal treatment of individuals, and tolerance for diversity; do not overreach or take undue advantage of another's mistakes or adversities.

6. *Caring for others.* Be caring, kind, and compassionate; share, be giving, and serve others; help those in need and avoid harming others.

7. *Respect for others.* Demonstrate respect for human dignity, privacy, and the right to self-determination for all people; be courteous, prompt, and decent; provide others with the information they need to make informed decisions about their own lives; do not patronize, embarrass, or demean.

8. *Responsible citizenship.* Obey just laws [if a law is unjust, openly protest it]; exercise all democratic rights and privileges responsibly by participation [voting and expressing informed views], social consciousness, and public service; when in a position of leadership or authority, openly respect and honor democratic processes of decision making, avoid secrecy or concealment of information, and ensure others have the information needed to make intelligent choices and exercise their rights.

9. *Pursuit of excellence.* Pursue excellence in all matters; in meeting personal and professional responsibilities, be diligent, reliable, industrious, and committed; perform all tasks to the best of your ability, develop and maintain a high degree of competence, and be well informed and well prepared; do not be content with mediocrity, but do not seek to win "at any cost."

10. *Accountability.* Be accountable; accept responsibility for decisions, for the foreseeable consequences of actions and inactions, and for setting an example for others. Parents, teachers, employers, many professionals, and public officials have a special obligation to lead by example and to safeguard and advance the integrity and reputation of their families, companies, professions, and the government; avoid even the appearance of impropriety and take whatever actions are necessary to correct or prevent inappropriate conduct by others.

Source: Michael Josephson, "Teaching Ethical Decision Making and Principled Reasoning," *Ethics: Easier Said Than Done*, Winter 1988, pp. 28–29, www.JosephsonInstitute.org.

Christopher Redhage,
Co-founder, ProviderTrust Inc.

ENTREPRENEURIAL PROFILE: Christopher Redhage and Michael Rosen, ProviderTrust Christopher Redhage and Michael Rosen launched ProviderTrust to help healthcare providers ensure that their staff and vendors are all fully licensed under Medicare and Medicaid regulations. The 2010 Affordable Care Act (also known as ObamaCare) expanded the reach of these regulations and increased the penalties for noncompliance. The company has experienced high growth from its launch. The founders are committed to building a company that is based on a clear set of core values. Every morning the ProviderTrust employees meet for ten to fifteen minutes. There are two items on the agenda for these daily meetings. The first item on the agenda is to review one of their core values or key business practices, which Redhage thinks it is important because it helps keep employees' values aligned with the company's core values and keeps everyone focused on a healthy, ethical culture. The second item on the daily meeting allows each member of the team to talk about the one thing he or she will to accomplish that day, which is always shared within the context of the core value or key business practice. ∎

Maintaining Ethical Standards

Establishing ethical standards is only the first step in an ethics-enhancing program; implementing and maintaining those standards is the real challenge facing management. What can entrepreneurs do to integrate ethical principles into their companies? To create an environment that encourages ethical behavior, entrepreneurs must make building an intentional culture that is based on a strong ethical foundation a core responsibility as leaders of their businesses.

SET THE TONE "The character of the leader casts a long shadow over the organization and can determine the character of the organization itself," says one business executive.[23] Entrepreneurs must set an impeccable ethical example at all times. Remember that ethics starts at the top. If entrepreneurs and their managers talk about the importance of ethics and then act in an unethical manner, they send mixed signals to employees. Workers believe the *actions* of those in charge more than their words. What you do, how you do it, and what you say set the tone for your employees. The values you profess must be aligned with the behaviors you demonstrate.

CREATE A COMPANY CREDO A **company credo** defines the values underlying the entire company and its ethical responsibilities to its stakeholders. It offers general guidance in ethical issues. The most effective credos capture the elusive essence of a company—what it stands for and why it's important—and they can be a key ingredient in a company's competitive edge. A company credo is especially important for a small company, where the entrepreneur's values become the values driving the business. A credo is an excellent way to transform those values into guidelines for employees' ethical behavior. For example, Trustworth, a residential provider of elderly care operating in England, developed the following credo: "Our residents are a mirror of ourselves should we reach old age. They have been entrusted to our care and we have accepted that trust. We resolve to give them the patience, loving care and understanding we would like to receive for ourselves."[24]

> **company credo**
> a statement that defines the values underlying the entire company and its ethical responsibilities to its stakeholders.

ESTABLISH HIGH STANDARDS OF BEHAVIOR It is essential to emphasize to *everyone* in the organization the importance of ethics. All employees must understand that ethics is *not* negotiable. The role that an entrepreneur plays in establishing high ethical standards is critical; no one has more influence over the ethical character of a company than its founder. One experienced entrepreneur offers this advice to business owners: "Stick to your principles. Hire people who want to live by them, teach them thoroughly, and insist on total commitment."[25]

INVOLVE EMPLOYEES IN ESTABLISHING ETHICAL STANDARDS Encourage employees to offer feedback on how to establish standards. Involving employees improves the quality of a company's ethical standards and increases the likelihood of employee compliance.

CREATE A CULTURE THAT EMPHASIZES TWO-WAY COMMUNICATION A thriving ethical environment requires two-way communication. Employees must have the opportunity to report any ethical violations they observe. A reliable, confidential reporting system is essential to a whistle-blowing program, in which employees anonymously report breaches of ethical behavior through proper channels.

ELIMINATE "UNDISCUSSABLES." One of the most important things entrepreneurs can do to promote ethical behavior is to instill the belief that it is acceptable for employees to question what happens above them. Doing away with undiscussables makes issues transparent and promotes trust both inside and outside the company.[26]

DEVELOP A CODE OF ETHICS A **code of ethics** is a written statement of the standards of behavior and ethical principles a company expects from its employees. A code of ethics spells out what kind of behavior is expected (and what kind will not be tolerated) and offers everyone in the company concrete guidelines for dealing with ethics every day on the job. Although creating a code of ethics does not guarantee 100 percent compliance with ethical standards, it does tend to foster an ethical atmosphere in a company. Workers who will be directly affected by the code should have a hand in developing it.

> **code of ethics**
> a written statement of the standards of behavior and ethical principles a company expects from its employees.

ENFORCE THE CODE OF ETHICS THROUGH POLICIES Set appropriate policies for your organization. Communicate them on a regular basis and adhere to them yourself so that others can see. Show zero tolerance for ethical violations and realize that the adage "Don't do as I do; do as I say" does *not* work. Without a demonstration of real consequences and personal accountability from the CEO, organizational policies are meaningless. Managers must take action whenever they discover ethical violations. If employees learn that ethical breaches go unpunished, the code of ethics becomes meaningless. Enforcement of the code of ethics demonstrates to everyone that you believe ethical behavior is mandatory.

RECRUIT AND PROMOTE ETHICAL EMPLOYEES Ultimately, the decision in any ethical situation belongs to the individual. Hiring people with strong moral principles and values is the best insurance against ethical violations. To make ethical decisions, people must have (1) *ethical commitment*—the personal resolve to act ethically and do the right thing; (2) *ethical consciousness*—the ability to perceive the ethical implications of a situation; and (3) *ethical competency*—the ability to engage in sound moral reasoning and develop practical problem-solving strategies.[27] Find colleges and universities that incorporate business ethics into courses and make them prime recruiting sources. Tina Byles Williams, owner of FIS Group, an investment advising and management firm, understands how important it is to hire honest employees with a strong sense of ethics. Although Williams knows that there is no foolproof hiring method, she has redesigned her company's selection process with an emphasis on screening for integrity.[28]

CONDUCT ETHICS TRAINING Instilling ethics in an organization's culture requires more than creating a code of ethics and enforcing it. Managers must show employees that the organization truly is committed to practicing ethical behavior. One of the most effective ways to display that commitment is through ethical training designed to raise employees' consciousness of potential ethical dilemmas. Ethics training programs not only raise employees' awareness of ethical issues but also communicate to employees the core of the company's value system. Rob Kaplan, professor of management practice at Harvard University, recommends that employees be trained to follow a simple yet powerful three-step process when facing an ethical situation:

1. Slow down.

2. Seek advice and elevate the issue.

3. Don't get bullied into making a quick decision you might later regret.[29]

REWARD ETHICAL CONDUCT The reward system is a large window into the values of an organization. If you reward a behavior, people have a tendency to repeat the behavior.

SEPARATE RELATED JOB DUTIES This is a basic organizational concept. Not allowing the employee who writes checks to reconcile the company bank statement is one example.

PERFORM PERIODIC ETHICAL AUDITS One of the best ways to evaluate the effectiveness of an ethics system is to perform periodic audits. These reviews send a signal to employees that ethics is not just a passing fad.

LO4

Explain the difference between social entrepreneurs and traditional entrepreneurs.

Social Entrepreneurship

Whereas traditional entrepreneurs seek opportunities to create market value, there is a growing trend to use entrepreneurship to pursue opportunities to create social value. These social entrepreneurs, people who start businesses so that they can create innovative solutions to society's most vexing problems, see themselves as change agents for society. Social entrepreneurs are finding the resources to tackle challenging problems confronting the global economy, including pollution, habitat destruction, human rights, AIDS, hunger, poverty, and others. Social entrepreneurship can be characterized by the following:

1. Social entrepreneurs seek solutions for social problems that are met by neither the market nor government.

2. Creating social benefit rather than commercial success motivates social entrepreneurs.

3. Social entrepreneurs tackle social problems by taking full advantage of natural market forces.[30]

You Be the Consultant

Funding Social Ventures Through Franchise Businesses

Nonprofits are facing severe funding challenges. Although the number of social ventures is increasing, funding from grants and donations has declined. A recent survey found that 54 percent of nonprofits were not able to generate enough funding to meet demand for their services. As a result, 39 percent of nonprofits surveyed plan to change the main way they raise funding. To meet this challenge, several nonprofits have turned to a creative way to fund their missions. Rather than rely on grants and donations, a growing number are using franchise businesses to generate new revenue streams to fund their causes.

Sandwich Shop Helps Build Housing

Affordable Homes of South Texas develops affordable housing for low-income families. In the past, the agency relied on federal grants as its main source of funding. However, this source of funding has declined steadily over the past several years due to government budget cuts while demand for its services had continued to climb. Bobby Calvillo, the executive director of Affordable Homes of South Texas, had an inspiration when he noticed lines of people waiting for service in a sandwich shop nearby. Calvillo wondered if Affordable Homes could open its own sandwich shop to help provide badly needed funding for its clients. After getting approval from his board, Calvillo began the process of buying a Blimpie's sandwich franchise. Affordable Homes could not directly own a franchise business because nonprofits are not allowed to own such investments. Affordable Homes set up an investment corporation as a parent entity and, under it, formed a limited liability company that would own the franchise business. Calvillo projects that the franchise will be able to fund the construction of several homes once it is fully operational.

Clients of Training Center Bake Pizzas to Generate Revenue

Dale Rogers Training Center trains and employs more than 1,100 people with disabilities in Oklahoma City each year. Due to declining private funding, the nonprofit partnered with Papa Murphy's Pizza to open a franchise operation to provide additional funding and offer a place for at least 15 of its clients to work. Dale Rogers Training Center is not new to using social enterprises to support its operating budget. The nonprofit generates 83 percent of its revenue from several social enterprises, including janitorial, cleaning, and delivery services. Dale Rogers Training Center receives 100 percent of the profits from the pizza shop and is able to fill 75 percent of the store's jobs with its clients. Even though this Papa Murphy's restaurant hires people with disabilities, it has the same standards for its employees as every other Papa Murphy's store.

Ice Cream Sales Help Several Nonprofits

Ben and Jerry's is a leader in providing franchises to support nonprofits, partnering with a variety of social ventures for more than 20 years. One of the first is a franchise owned by Common Ground, a New York nonprofit working to end homelessness. The partnership with Common Ground operates three Ben and Jerry's stores, which hire 15 clients served by the nonprofit. The stores each took two to three years to break even. Ben and Jerry's partners with several programs providing employment and life skills training for disadvantaged youth. It has five locations owned by Juma Ventures, which supports disadvantaged youth by offering them employment in its social enterprises with the goal of getting them ready to attend and complete college. Latin American Youth Center in Washington, D.C., Metro Community Investment in Minneapolis, Minnesota, and Youth Job Center of Evanston, Illinois, all operate Ben and Jerry's to provide employment and life training for their clients. Ben and Jerry's operates franchises through the Postgraduate Center for Mental Health in New York City and Second Chance in San Diego, California, to provide revenue for these nonprofits and job training for their clients. Finally, youth participating in the Chicago Children's Choir raise money for the choir by singing as they serve customers in a franchise operated in Chicago's theater district.

1. What challenges does owning and operating a franchise business create for these nonprofits? Explain.

2. What advantages do franchise businesses offer nonprofits that seek side businesses to generate revenues to support their causes?

3. Select a local nonprofit and work with a team of your classmates to brainstorm ideas for a franchise business that could help create a sustainable cash flow to support the mission of the social venture. What advice can you offer social entrepreneurs on how to develop alternative revenues to replace declining grants and donations?

Sources: "Nonprofit Finance Fund Survey of 5900+ Nonprofits: Organizations Innovating and Adapting to New Reality," Nonprofit Finance Fund, March 25, 2013, http://nonprofitfinancefund.org/announcements/2013/state-of-the-nonprofit-sector-survey; Elizabeth Findell, "Nonprofit starts sandwich shop to gather revenue to build housing," *The Monitor,* May 24, 2013, www.themonitor.com/news/local/article_032f8f20-c367-11e2-b381-001a4bcf6878.html; Hillary McLain, "Oklahoma City pizza restaurant to provide opportunities for employees with disabilities," *The Oklahoman,* July 11, 2013, http://newsok.com/oklahoma-city-pizza-restaurant-to-provide-opportunities-for-employees-with-disabilities/article/3861000; "Nonprofit-Owned Franchises: A Strategic Business Approach," Community Wealth Ventures, Inc. & IFA Educational Foundation, March 2004, www.franchise.org/uploadedfiles/files/nonprofit_owned.pdf.

Social entrepreneurs use their creativity to develop solutions to social problems that range from cleaning up the environment to improving working conditions for workers around the world; their goal is to use their businesses to make money *and* to make the world a better place to live.

Social entrepreneurship is the fastest growing type of entrepreneurship in most parts of the world. The Global Entrepreneurship Monitor survey of entrepreneurial activity reports that one-third of entrepreneurs in the United States pursue a purely social entrepreneurial venture.[31] Bill Drayton, founder of Ashoka, an organization that promotes social entrepreneurship, says, "Social entrepreneurs are not content just to give a fish or teach [someone] how to fish. They will not rest until they have revolutionized the fishing industry."[32]

ENTREPRENEURIAL PROFILE: Jamie Yang, EGG-energy Jamie Yang wanted to address an important issue facing much of Tanzania: Only 14 percent of its population has access to electricity. Without reliable electricity, residents must rely on unsafe kerosene and disposable batteries. These alternative power sources increase pollution and are expensive. EGG-energy seeks to provide developing countries with affordable electrical service. EGG-energy sends electricians to customers' homes or businesses to install a full electrical system, including high-efficiency LED light bulbs, wiring, and switches for a small one-time fee. These systems are then powered by safe and efficient rechargeable batteries that last about five evenings for a typical household. EGG-energy charges customers a small subscription fee to swap a depleted battery with a fully charged one. The EGG-energy system costs customers less than half of what they spent on kerosene and disposable batteries. As the electrical grid expands in Tanzania, customers can be connected using the wiring already installed by EGG-energy. "We want to concentrate enough demand in an area, such that it makes sense to come in and provide electrical services," says Yang. As a social enterprise, EGG-energy seeks to make a profit while providing low-cost, safe energy to families who have not had this service.[33] ■

LO5

Define social responsibility.

Social Responsibility

The concept of social responsibility has evolved from that of a nebulous "do-gooder" to one of "social steward" with the expectation that businesses will produce benefits not only for themselves but also for society as a whole. Society is constantly redefining its expectations of business and now holds companies of all sizes to high standards of ethics and social responsibility. Companies must go beyond "doing well"—simply earning a profit—to "doing good"—living up to their social responsibility. They also must recognize the interdependence of business and society. Each influences the other, and both must remain healthy to sustain each other over time. A growing recognition of social responsibility is true not only for large public corporations but also for small businesses. Two surveys by SurePayroll shed light on the scope of small business owners' engagement in social responsibility. One survey reports that 55 percent of small businesses' mission statements include a reference to achieving some type of social goal, and a second report finds that 90 percent of small business owners give to charity and 70 percent donate both money and time to local causes.[34]

Companies that are most successful in meeting their social responsibility select causes that are consistent with their core values and their employees' interests and skill sets. In fact, some entrepreneurs allow employees to provide input into the decision concerning which causes to support. A common strategy is to allow employees to provide pro bono work for the charitable organizations they support.

ENTREPRENEURIAL PROFILE: Doral Financial Corporation Doral Financial is a bank holding company that operates Doral Bank in Puerto Rico. The Puerto Rican economy has continued to languish since the Great Recession began in 2008. Doral Bank executives made the decision to create growth for their financial institution by supporting women entrepreneurs. To help differentiate its brand, the bank moved from spending money on traditional advertising to supporting philanthropic causes. In addition to its long-term support for breast cancer research, the bank began to offer free mammograms because breast cancer is a leading cause of death among Puerto Rican women. The bank also donates funding to a nonprofit that provides micro financing to help women start businesses. More than 25 women have received $50,000 loans through this initiative. Doral Bank also hosts several free seminars that target women entrepreneurs.

"It makes all the sense in the world. Rather than spending tons in advertising, our real investment is spending time assisting the community," says Jesus Mendez, executive vice president of Puerto Rico operations at Doral Bank.[35] ■

In a free enterprise system, companies that fail to respond to their customers' needs and demands soon go out of business. Today, customers are increasingly demanding the companies they buy goods and services from to be socially responsible. When customers shop for "value," they no longer consider only the price–performance relationship of the product or service; they also consider the company's stance on social responsibility. Whether a company supports a social or an environmental cause has a significant effect on shoppers' behavior. A study by Penn Schoen Berland, in conjunction with Burson-Marsteller and Landor, reports that more than 75 percent of consumers say social responsibility is important in their purchasing decisions. The survey finds that 55 percent of consumers are more likely to choose a product that supports a certain cause when choosing between otherwise similar products and that 38 percent are willing to pay more for products with added social benefits.[36] Other studies conclude that when price, service, and quality are equal among competitors, customers buy from the company that has the best reputation for social responsibility.

Other studies show a connection between social responsibility and profitability. One team of researchers evaluated 52 studies on corporate social responsibility that were conducted over 30 years and concluded that a positive correlation existed between a company's profitability and its reputation for ethical, socially responsible behavior. The relationship also was self-reinforcing. "It's a virtuous cycle," says Sara Rynes, one of the researchers. "As a company becomes more socially responsible, its reputation and financial performance go up, which causes them to become even more socially responsible."[37] The message is clear: Companies that incorporate social responsibility into their competitive strategies outperform those that fail to do so. Today's socially wired, transparent economy makes ethical and socially responsible behavior highly visible and, conversely, improper behavior more difficult to hide.

One problem businesses face is defining just what socially responsible behavior is. Is it manufacturing environmentally friendly products? Is it donating a portion of profits to charitable organizations? Is it creating jobs in inner cities plagued by high unemployment levels? The nature of a company's social responsibility efforts depends on how its owners, employees, and other stakeholders define what it means to be socially responsible. Typically, businesses have responsibilities to several key stakeholders, including the environment, employees, customers, investors, and the community. Table 2.6 lists simple ways that small businesses can practice social responsibility.

TABLE 2.6 Simple Ways for a Small Business to Be Socially Responsible

1. *Encourage recycling.* Place recycling bins throughout the workplace. If the business sells retail products, encourage customers to bring reusable shopping bags. Use recycled products whenever possible.
2. *Support local fundraisers.* Provide local fundraising events with donated products or services. Encourage employees to participate in fundraising events as a team representing the company.
3. *Join in community service.* Allow employees to participate in community volunteer projects on company time. Designate a day a year for all employees to help with a local charity, such as planting trees on Arbor Day, cleaning up a section of a local highway, helping with a Habitat for Humanity building project, or volunteering at an inner city school.
4. *Reduce energy usage.* Encourage employees to help find ways to reduce energy consumption in your business. Provide recognition to employees whose ideas help reduce energy usage.
5. *Create a grant program.* Set up a fund that local nonprofits can apply to for small grants. Create a matching program to encourage employee giving to the fund by committing to company matching donations for their gifts.
6. *Support local causes.* Work with employees to identify local causes that the business can support by offering publicity for that cause. Promotion can include flyers in the window, promotion on the company website, employee T-shirts supporting the cause, and social media campaigns.
7. *Partner with local schools.* Partner with local schools by providing supplies and encouraging employees to serve as volunteers. Mentor young people through a job shadowing program.

Source: Based on Lisa Mooney, "Ways for a Small Business to Show Social Responsibility," *AzCentral.com*, n.d., http://yourbusiness.azcentral.com/ways-small-business-show-social-responsibility-2392.html; Lalia Helmer, "7 Ways Small Business Can Embrace Social Responsibility," *Business That Cares,* September 21, 2010, http://businessthatcares.blogspot.com/2010/09/7-ways-small-business-can-embrace.html.

LO6

Understand the nature of business's responsibility to the environment.

Business's Responsibility to the Environment

Due to a strong personal belief in environmental protection, many entrepreneurs seek to start ventures that have a positive impact on the environment or take steps to operate their businesses in ways that help protect the environment. Also driven by their customers' interest in protecting the environment, small businesses have become more sensitive to the impact their products, processes, and packaging have on the planet. Environmentalism has become—and will continue to be—one of the dominant issues for companies worldwide because consumers have added another item to their list of buying criteria: environmental friendliness and safety. Companies have discovered that sound environmental practices make for good business. In addition to lowering their operating costs, environmentally safe products attract environmentally conscious customers and can give a company a competitive edge in the marketplace. Socially responsible business owners focus on the three Rs: reduce, reuse, and recycle:

- *Reduce* the amount of energy and materials used in your company, from the factory floor to the copier room.

- *Reuse* whatever you can.

- *Recycle* the materials that you must dispose of.

ENTREPRENEURIAL PROFILE: Scott Kelly and Jenn Rezeli, Re:Vision Architecture Scott Kelly and Jenn Rezeli practice their commitment to the environment in every aspect of their business. Re:Vision Architecture, based in Philadelphia, Pennsylvania, specializes in sustainable architecture consulting and offers targeted consulting services to developers, building owners, government agencies, manufacturers, schools, and design professionals. The company offers a full-service staff of architects and planners who can design a sustainable building to conserve natural resources, lower operating costs, and enrich designs. Beyond its design practices, Re:Vision Architecture's business practices reflect its commitment to the environment. More than 75 percent of office supplies come from recycled materials. The company also rewards employees for using public transportation and car-pooling.[38] ■

Many progressive small companies are taking their environmental policies a step further, creating redesigned, "clean" manufacturing systems that focus on *avoiding* waste and pollution and using resources efficiently. That requires a different manufacturing philosophy. These companies design their products, packaging, and processes from the start with the environment in mind, working to eliminate hazardous materials and by-products and looking for ways to turn what had been scrap into salable products. This approach requires an ecological evaluation of every part of the process, from the raw materials that go into a product to the disposal or reuse of the packaging that contains it.

ENTREPRENEURIAL PROFILE: Alan Machin, a student at the University of Nottingham, looked at the collection of old paint cans in his garage and came up with the idea for a better paint container. His design, which incorporates a tube with a one-way valve that keeps air out so the paint does not dry up, won an award in the prestigious RSA Design competition. A special coating protects the paint in the tube from extreme temperatures, and the hexagonally-shaped outer package is more efficient to ship and store. Both the tube and the outer package are recyclable. Machin's design is far superior to the traditional aluminum paint can, which has not been updated since its invention in 1868. His clever paint package has the potential to reduce the 60 to 70 million gallons of paint that people in the United States discard each year, which creates a serious environmental hazard. Several paint manufacturers have expressed interest in Machin's earth-friendly packaging.[39] ■

LO7

Describe business's responsibility to employees.

Business's Responsibility to Employees

Few other stakeholders are as important to a business as its employees. It is common for managers to *say* that their employees are their most valuable resource, but the truly excellent ones actually *treat* them that way. Employees are at the heart of increases in productivity, and they add the personal touch that puts passion in customer service. In short, employees produce the winning competitive advantage for an entrepreneur. Entrepreneurs who understand the value of their employees follow a few simple procedures by doing the following:

- Listening to employees and respecting their opinions

- Asking for their input and involving them in the decision-making process

- Providing regular feedback—positive and negative—to employees

- Telling them the truth—always

- Letting them know exactly what's expected of them

- Rewarding employees for performing their jobs well

- Trusting them; creating an environment of respect and teamwork

ENTREPRENEURIAL PROFILE: Delight, Co. Delight Co. is a Korean company that makes and distributes affordable hearing aid devices to the elderly population. To keep its products affordable, Delight manufactures standardized devices and distributes them through company-owned stores located throughout the country. Through its efficient operations, Delight sells its product for $299, which is equivalent to the government subsidy for hearing impaired people in Korea. Delight employs senior citizens to deliver the products from the headquarters to the branch stores and other hearing-impaired people to work in its manufacturing plant. Delight offers its employees a wide array of benefits, including subsidized meals, transportation, and housing. Also, Delight employees are eligible for company sponsored training and tuition reimbursement.[40] ∎

Several important issues face entrepreneurs who are trying to meet their social responsibility to employees, including cultural diversity, drug testing, sexual harassment and privacy.

Cultural Diversity in the Workplace

The United States has always been a nation of astonishing cultural diversity (see Figure 2.4), a trait that has imbued it with an incredible richness of ideas and creativity. Indeed, this diversity is one of the driving forces behind the greatest entrepreneurial effort in the world, and it continues to grow. The United States, in short, is moving toward a "minority majority," and significant demographic shifts will affect virtually every aspect of business. Nowhere will this be more visible than in the makeup of the nation's workforce (see Figure 2.5). In 2020, members of five

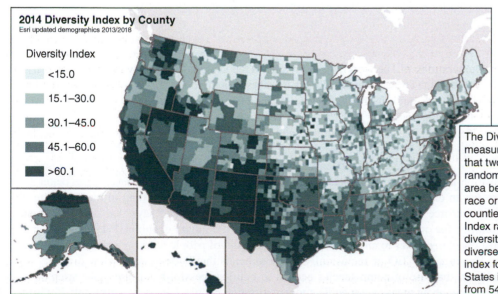

2014 Diversity Index by County
Esri updated demographics 2013/2018

Diversity Index

- <15.0
- 15.1–30.0
- 30.1–45.0
- 45.1–60.0
- >60.1

FIGURE 2.4

Diversity Index by County

Source: Kyle Reese-Cassal, *2014/2019 Diversity Index 2014/2019*, Ersi, September 2014, p. 4.

The Diversity Index measures the probability that two people chosen at random from the same area belong to different race or ethnic groups. For counties, the Diversity Index ranges from 0 (little diversity) to 100 (highly diverse). The diversity index for the entire United States is 62.6, an increase from 54 in 2000.

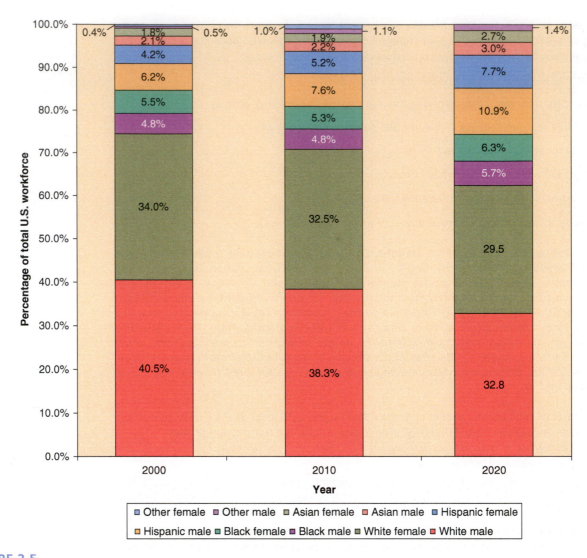

FIGURE 2.5

Projected Composition of the U.S. Workforce in 2020

Source: Mitra Toossi, "Labor Force Projections to 2020: A More Slowly Growing Workforce," *Monthly Labor Review*, January 2012, pp. 43–64.

different generations will be working side by side in the United States.[41] By 2039, the *majority* of the workforce in the United States will be a member of a minority.[42] The Hispanic population is the fastest-growing sector in the United States, and Hispanics now make up the largest minority population in the nation.

This rich mix of generations, cultures, and backgrounds within the workforce presents both opportunities and challenges to employers. One of the chief benefits of a diverse workforce is the rich blend of perspectives, skills, talents, and ideas employees have to offer. Also, the changing composition of the nation's population will change business's customer base. What better way is there for an entrepreneur to deal with culturally diverse customers than to have a culturally diverse workforce? George Chavel, president and CEO of Sodexo says that diversity creates opportunities for organizations to be more effective in the global economy.[43] Diversity is more than just checking boxes to ensure that a broad spectrum of people work in a business, however. Shirley Engelmeier, CEO of InclusionINC, recommends that entrepreneurs view diversity as a way to build the base of competencies needed to build successful businesses. She stresses that diversity is not about meeting a specific quota of different people. Diversity works only if it is tied to improving the profitability of the business.[44]

Managing a culturally diverse workforce presents a real challenge for employers, however. Molding workers with highly varied beliefs, backgrounds, and biases into a unified team takes time and commitment. Stereotypes, biases, and prejudices present barriers workers and managers must constantly overcome. Communication may require more effort because of language differences. In many cases, dealing with diversity causes a degree of discomfort for entrepreneurs because of the natural tendency to associate with people who are similar to us. These reasons and others cause some entrepreneurs to resist the move to a more diverse workforce, a move that threatens their ability to create a competitive edge.

How can entrepreneurs achieve unity through diversity? The only way is by *managing* diversity in the workforce. In its *Best Practices of Private Sector Employers*, an Equal Employment Opportunity Commission task force suggests following a "SPLENDID" approach to diversity:

- *Study.* Business owners cannot solve problems they don't know exist. Entrepreneurs must familiarize themselves with issues related to diversity, including relevant laws.

- *Plan.* Recognizing the makeup of the local population, entrepreneurs must set targets for diversity hiring and develop a plan for achieving them.

- *Lead.* A diversity effort starts at the top of the organization with managers communicating their vision and goals to everyone in the company.

- *Encourage.* Company leaders must encourage employees at all levels of an organization to embrace the diversity plan.

- *Notice.* Entrepreneurs must monitor their companies' progress toward achieving diversity goals.

- *Discussion.* Managers must keep diversity on the company's radar screen by communicating the message that diversity is vital to business success.

- *Inclusion.* Involving employees in the push to achieve diversity helps break down barriers that arise.

- *Dedication.* Achieving diversity in a business does not happen overnight, but entrepreneurs must be persistent in implementing their plans.[45]

The goal of diversity efforts is to create an environment in which all types of workers—men, women, Hispanic, African American, white, disabled, homosexual, elderly, and others—can flourish and can give top performances to their companies. In fact, researchers at Harvard University report that companies that embrace diversity are more productive than those that shun diversity. A distinguishing factor the companies supporting diversity share is the willingness of people to learn from their coworkers' different backgrounds and life experiences.[46]

Managing a culturally diverse workforce requires a different way of thinking, and that requires training. In essence, diversity training will help make everyone aware of the dangers of bias, prejudice, and discrimination, however subtle or unintentional they may be. Managing a culturally diverse workforce successfully requires a business owner to do the following:

Assess your company's diversity needs. The starting point for an effective diversity management program is assessing a company's needs. Surveys, interviews, and informal conversations with employees can be valuable tools. Several organizations offer more formal assessment tools—cultural audits, questionnaires, and diagnostic forms—that also are useful.

Learn to recognize and correct your own biases and stereotypes. One of the best ways to identify your own cultural biases is to get exposure to people who are not like you. By spending time with those who are different from you, you will learn quickly that stereotypes simply don't hold up. Giving employees the opportunity to spend time with one another is an excellent way to eliminate stereotypes. The owner of one small company with a culturally diverse staff provides lunch for his workers every month with a seating arrangement that encourages employees to mix with one another.

Avoid making invalid assumptions. Decisions that are based on faulty assumptions are bound to be flawed. False assumptions built on inaccurate perceptions or personal bias have kept many qualified minority workers from getting jobs and promotions. Make sure that it does not happen in your company.

Push for diversity in your management team. To get maximum benefit from a culturally diverse workforce, a company must promote nontraditional workers into top management. A culturally diverse top management team that can serve as mentors and role models provides visible evidence that nontraditional workers can succeed.

Concentrate on communication. Any organization, especially a culturally diverse one, will stumble if lines of communication break down. Frequent training sessions and regular opportunities for employees to talk with one another in a nonthreatening environment can be extremely helpful.

Make diversity a core value in the organization. For a cultural diversity program to work, top managers must "champion" the program and take active steps to integrate diversity throughout the entire organization.

Continue to adjust your company to your workers. Rather than pressure workers to conform to the company, entrepreneurs with the most successful cultural diversity programs are constantly looking for ways to adjust their businesses to their workers. Flexibility is the key.

As business leaders look to the future, an increasingly diverse workforce stares back. People with varying cultural, racial, gender and lifestyle perspectives seek opportunity and acceptance from coworkers, managers, and business owners. Currently, women make up 46 percent of the U.S. workforce, and minority workers make up more than 33 percent of the labor force.[47] Businesses that value the diversity of their workers and the perspectives they bring to work enjoy the benefits of higher employee satisfaction, commitment, retention, creativity, and productivity more than those companies that ignore the cultural diversity of their workers. In addition, they deepen the loyalty of their existing customers and expand their market share by attracting new customers. In short, diversity is a winning proposition from every angle!

Drug Testing

One of the realities of our society is substance abuse. The second reality, which entrepreneurs now must face head on, is that substance abuse has infiltrated the workplace. In addition to the lives it ruins, substance abuse takes a heavy toll on business and society. Drug and alcohol abuse by employees results in reduced productivity (an estimated $262.8 billion per year), increased medical costs, higher accident rates, and higher levels of absenteeism. Alarmingly, 66 percent of all drug abusers and 77 percent of alcohol abusers are employed.[48] Small companies bear a disproportionate share of the burden because they are less likely to have drug-testing programs than large companies and are more likely to hire people with substance abuse problems. Abusers who know that they cannot pass a drug test simply apply for work at companies that do not use drug tests. In addition, because the practice of drug testing remains a controversial issue, its random use can lead to a variety of legal woes for employers, including invasion of privacy, discrimination, slander, or defamation of character.

An effective, proactive drug program should include the following five elements:

1. *A written substance abuse policy.* The first step is to create a written policy that spells out the company's position on drugs. The policy should state its purpose, prohibit the use of drugs on the job (or off the job if it affects job performance), specify the consequences of violating the policy, explain the drug-testing procedures the company will use, and describe the resources available to help troubled employees.

2. *Training for supervisors to detect substance-abusing workers.* Supervisors are in the best position to identify employees with alcohol or drug problems and to encourage them to get help. The supervisor's job, however, is not to play "cop" or "therapist." The supervisor should identify problem employees early and encourage them to seek help. The focal point of the supervisor's role is to track employees' performances against their objectives to identify the employees with performance problems. Vigilant managers look for the following signs:

   - Frequent tardiness or absences accompanied by questionable excuses
   - Long lunch, coffee, or bathroom breaks

- Frequently missed deadlines
- Withdrawal from or frequent arguments with fellow employees
- Excessive sensitivity to criticism
- Declining or inconsistent productivity
- Inability to concentrate on work
- Disregard for personal safety or the safety of others
- Deterioration of personal appearance

3. *An employee education program.* Business owners should take time to explain the company's substance abuse policy, the reasons behind it, and the help that is available to employees who have substance abuse problems. Every employee should participate in training sessions, and managers should remind employees periodically of the policy, the magnitude of the problem, and the help that is available. Some companies have used inserts in pay envelopes, home mailings, lunch speakers, and short seminars as part of their ongoing educational efforts.

4. *A drug-testing program, when necessary.* Experts recommend that business owners seek the advice of an experienced attorney before establishing a drug-testing program. Preemployment testing of job applicants generally is a safe strategy to follow as long as it is followed consistently, however in many cases you can only test someone if they already have a conditional offer for employment from your company. Testing current employees is a more complex issue, but, again, consistency is the key. If you test one employee, you should test them all.

5. *An employee assistance program.* No drug-battling program is complete without a way to help addicted employees. An **employee assistance program** (EAP) is a company-provided benefit designed to help reduce workplace problems such as alcoholism, drug addiction, a gambling habit, and others and to deal with them when they arise. Although some troubled employees may balk at enrolling in an EAP, the company controls the most powerful weapon in motivating them to seek and accept help: *their jobs.* The greatest fear that substance-abusing employees have is losing their jobs, and the company can use that fear to help workers recover. EAPs, which cost between $18 and $30 per employee each year to operate, are an effective weapon in the battle against workplace substance abuse. Research shows that EAPs can pay for themselves quickly by reducing absenteeism and tardiness by 25 percent and increasing productivity by 25 percent.[49] Unfortunately, only 21 percent of small companies (compared to 76 percent of large companies) offer EAPs.[50]

employee assistance program (EAP)

a company-provided benefit designed to help reduce workplace problems such as alcoholism, drug addiction, a gambling habit, and other conflicts and to deal with them when they arise.

ENTREPRENEURIAL PROFILE: Eastern Industries Eastern Industries, a Pennsylvania-based company that produces building supplies, concrete, asphalt, and stone, operates in an industry that traditionally has been plagued by substance abuse problems. A recent study shows that 15.1 percent of workers in the construction industry had substance abuse problems, second only to the food service industry. Initially, Eastern's substance abuse policy was simple: We test for drugs, and if you fail the test, you are fired. The all-or-nothing policy affected the company's ability to keep and retain skilled workers, so managers decided to adopt a new policy that includes prevention, testing, and rehabilitation. Eastern includes educational sessions on substance abuse in its employee orientation program and ongoing programs for all workers. If an employee fails a drug test, he or she can enroll in an employee assistance program including rehabilitation that, once successfully completed, allows the worker to return to his or her job. Managers at Eastern say the program has been a tremendous success, allowing them to keep good workers they would have lost under the old policy and giving employees the opportunity to correct bad decisions and keep their jobs.[51] ■

Sexual Harassment

Sexual harassment is a problem in the workplace. Thousands of workers file sexual harassment charges with the Equal Employment Opportunity Commission (EEOC) against their employers every year. Since awareness of sexual harassment has increased, there has been a steady decline in charges filed over the past decade. Sexual harassment is a violation of Title VII of the Civil Rights Act of 1964 and is considered to be a form of sex discrimination. Studies show that sexual harassment occurs in businesses of all sizes, but small businesses are especially vulnerable because they typically lack the policies, procedures, and training to prevent it.

sexual harassment
any unwelcome sexual advance, request for sexual favors, and other verbal or physical sexual conduct made explicitly or implicitly as a condition of employment.

Sexual harassment is any unwelcome sexual advance, request for sexual favors, and other verbal or physical sexual conduct made explicitly or implicitly as a condition of employment. Women bring about 82 percent of all sexual harassment charges.[52] Jury verdicts reaching into the millions of dollars are not uncommon. In 2013, there were 7,256 sexual harassment claims filed with the EEOC that yielded a total of $44.6 million in settlements to the victims.[53] Retaliation, such as demotions and assignments to less attractive work against employees who file complaints of sexual harassment, occurs too often, but the most common form of employer retaliation is termination. Types of behavior that may result in sexual harassment charges include the following.

QUID PRO QUO HARASSMENT The most blatant and most potentially damaging form of sexual harassment is quid pro quo ("this for that"), in which a superior conditions the granting of a benefit such as a promotion or raise on the receipt of sexual favors from a subordinate. Only managers and supervisors, not coworkers, can engage in quid pro quo harassment.

HOSTILE ENVIRONMENT Behavior that creates an abusive, intimidating, offensive, or hostile work environment also constitutes sexual harassment. A hostile environment usually requires a *pattern* of offensive sexual behavior rather than a single, isolated remark or display. When judging whether a hostile environment exists, courts base their decisions on how a "reasonable woman" would perceive the situation. (The previous standard was that of a "reasonable person.") Examples of what creates a hostile work environment might include the following:

- Displaying sexually suggestive pictures or posters
- Engaging in sexually related humor within hearing of someone who takes offense
- Talking about sexual matters where others can hear (as in colorfully relating one's "conquests")
- Making sexual comments to other employees
- Dispensing assignments based on sexual orientation
- Repeatedly asking a coworker for a date after having been refused multiple times[54]

Although not easily defined, a hostile work environment is one in which continuing unwelcome sexual conduct in the workplace interferes with an employee's work performance. Sexual harassment is sexually related behavior that is unwelcome, unwanted, and repeated. Most sexual harassment charges arise from claims of a hostile environment.

HARASSMENT BY NONEMPLOYEES An employer can be held liable for third parties (customers, sales representatives, and others) who engage in sexual harassment if the employer has the ability to stop the improper behavior. For example, one company required a female employee to wear an extremely skimpy, revealing uniform. She complained to her boss that the uniform encouraged members of the public to direct offensive comments and physical contact toward her. The manager ignored her complaints, and later she refused to wear the uniform, which resulted in her dismissal. When she filed a sexual harassment claim, the court held the company accountable for the employee's sexual harassment by nonemployees because it required her to wear the uniform after she complained of harassment.[55]

No business wants to incur the cost of defending itself against charges of sexual harassment, but those costs can be devastating for a small business. Multi-million-dollar jury awards in harassment cases are becoming increasingly common because the Civil Rights Act of 1991 allows victims to collect punitive damages and emotional distress awards. A jury awarded eight former employees of Four Amigos Travel, Inc. and Top Dog Travel, Inc. $20,251,963 after they won a lawsuit claiming daily sexual harassment of women employees in the workplace. The complaint was filed against travel agency owner Ronald Schlom and male managers by employees describing unwanted sexual advances, physical touching, and repeated propositions for sex. The suit described a work environment that was filled with sexual banter, abuse of power, and outright disrespect for women. The company fired the manager who brought forward the victims' complaints. The jury returned a unanimous verdict awarding $3.75 million in compensatory damages, $16 million in punitive damages, and $501,963 in back pay to the former employees. "This was a long journey for these women who were forced to work under unspeakable conditions at this workplace," said Gregory Lee McClinton, the EEOC's lead attorney in the case. "Their testimony about how the sexual harassment occurred and how it affected their lives was very powerful."[56]

The U.S. Supreme Court has expanded the nature of an employer's liability for sexual harassment, rejecting the previous standard that the employer had to be negligent to be liable for a supervisor's improper behavior toward employees. In *Burlington Industries v. Ellerth*, the court ruled that an employer can be held liable *automatically* if a supervisor takes a "tangible employment action," such as failing to promote or firing an employee whom he has been sexually harassing. The employer is liable even if he or she was not aware of the supervisor's conduct. If a supervisor takes no tangible employment action against an employee but engages in sexually harassing behavior, such as offensive remarks, inappropriate touching, or sexual advances, the employer is not *automatically* liable for the supervisor's conduct. However, an employer would be liable for such conduct if, for example, he or she knew (or should have known) about the supervisor's behavior and failed to stop it.[57]

A company's best weapons against sexual harassment are education, policy, and procedures.

EDUCATION Preventing sexual harassment is the best solution, and the key to prevention is educating employees about what constitutes sexual harassment. Training programs are designed to raise employees' awareness of what might be offensive to other workers and how to avoid sexual harassment altogether.

POLICY Another essential ingredient is a meaningful policy against sexual harassment that management can enforce. The policy should do the following:

- Clearly define what behaviors constitute sexual harassment
- State in clear language that harassment will not be tolerated in the workplace
- Identify the responsibilities of supervisors and employees in preventing harassment
- Define the sanctions and penalties for engaging in harassment
- Spell out the steps to take in reporting an incident of sexual harassment

In another case, the Supreme Court ruled that an employer was liable for a supervisor's sexually harassing behavior even though the employee never reported it. The company's liability stemmed from its failure to communicate its sexual harassment policy throughout the organization. This ruling makes employers' policies and procedures on sexual harassment the focal point of their defense.

PROCEDURE Socially responsible companies provide a channel for all employees to express their complaints. Choosing a person inside the company (perhaps someone in the human resources area) and one outside the company (a close adviser or attorney) is a good strategy because it gives employees a choice about how to file a complaint. At least one of these people should be a woman. When a complaint arises, managers should do the following:

- Listen to the complaint carefully without judging. Taking notes is a good idea. Tell the complainant what the process involves. Never treat the complaint as a joke.
- Investigate the complaint *promptly*, preferably within 24 hours. Failure to act quickly is irresponsible and illegal. Table 2.7 offers suggestions for conducting a sexual harassment investigation.
- Interview the accused party and any witnesses who may be aware of a pattern of harassing behavior *privately* and separately.
- Keep findings confidential.
- Decide what action to take, relying on company policy as a guideline.

TABLE 2.7 What to Do When an Employee Files a Sexual Harassment Complaint

When an employee files a sexual harassment complaint, the Equal Employment Opportunity Commission (EEOC) recommends that employers (1) gather detailed information about the complaint from both of the parties involved and (2) seek out other evidence that helps explain what happened. The following checklist helps to ensure that EEOC recommendations are adhered to:

- Careful assess the victim's statements to ensure that it is consistent throughout and credible.
- Do not weight the accused party's statement of denial too heavily.
- Seek evidence that supports both party's stories, not just evidence that supports or refutes the accusations through careful interviews of other employees close to the situation and by talking to those who the victim confided in about the events that they claim occurred, such as coworkers or professionals.
- Ask other employees about any changes in how the two parties interact in the workplace both before and after the alleged incident.
- Examine the background of the victim and the accused for other similar incidences looking for patterns, making sure to follow up with other employees who may have claimed similar harassment.

To make a just decision on a sexual harassment complaint, gather as much information as possible, not only about the events in question but also about general information about both parties. Ask probing questions of the victim, the accuser and of all witnesses to the alleged incident.

Source: "Questions for Investigations," Women's Studies Database at the University of Maryland, www.mith2.umd.edu/WomensStudies/GenderIssues/SexualHarassment/questions-for-investigations.

- Inform both the complaining person and the alleged harasser of the action taken.
- Document the entire investigation.[58]

The accompanying "Hands On . . . How To" feature includes a quiz on sexual harassment for both employees and managers.

 **Hands On . . . How To**

How to Avoid Sexual Harassment Charges

The Equal Employment Opportunity Commission handles about 7,500 charges of sexual harassment each year from both women and men. Not surprisingly, women file 82 percent of the charges. Experts say many other employees are sexually harassed but never file charges because of the stigma associated with doing so. What can you do to ensure you provide your employees a safe work environment that is free of sexual harassment? Consider the following case and then take the accompanying quizzes on sexual harassment.

Theresa Waldo was the only woman working in the Transmission Lines Department, a traditionally male-dominated job in which workers maintain and repair high-voltage power lines, sometimes at heights up to 250 feet, for Consumers Energy (CE). Her supervisor told her the company did not "have women in this department" and had never had them there and that "they are not strong enough" to do the job. Despite resistance from her supervisor and coworkers, Waldo, who started her career with CE as a meter reader, was participating in a four-year Line Apprentice Training Program that would entitle her to a higher-paying job.

On several occasions, Waldo's supervisor told her that he would "wash her out" of the apprenticeship program.

During her time in the apprenticeship program, Waldo alleges that she faced an "abusive and dysfunctional environment" in which she was constantly "bombarded with sexually abusive and derogatory language and conduct." Male coworkers subjected her to magazines, calendars, playing cards, and other items that contained photographs of nude women. They also referred to Waldo using derogatory, sexually offensive names and on one 90-degree day intentionally locked her in a port-a-potty for 20 minutes. On another occasion, her supervisor ordered her to clean up the tobacco spit of the male workers; when she refused, her coworkers locked her in a trailer. Waldo complained to the company's management about the sexual harassment on several occasions, but managers failed to take any meaningful action to stop the behavior.

After Waldo had successfully completed three years of the apprenticeship program, CE removed her from it and transferred her to the Sub Metro Department, where her pay was $4 less per hour. She filed a sexual harassment charge, alleging that the company had created a hostile work environment, committed sexual harassment, and engaged in gender discrimination and retaliation.

1. Does Waldo have a legitimate sexual harassment complaint? Explain.

One of the primary causes of sexual harassment in the workplace is the lack of education concerning what constitutes harassment. The following quizzes ask you to assume the roles of an employee and of a manager when answering the questions. Learning from these quizzes can help your company avoid problems with sexual harassment.

[1. Yes. Although the jury in the trial ruled in favor of the employer on all claims, the judge granted Waldo's motion for a new trial, acknowledging that the jury's verdict on the hostile work environment and sexual harassment should be set aside because of the "clear evidence presented" in the case. The court ruled that the evidence "demonstrated egregious actions and sexually offensive and demeaning language" directed at Waldo. The court concluded that the harassment created "an intimidating, hostile, and offensive work environment" and that CE "knew of the harassment and failed to implement proper and appropriate corrective action." At the second trial, a jury ruled in Waldo's favor and granted her $400,000 in compensatory damages and $7.5 million in punitive damages.]

A Test for Employees

Answer the following true/false questions:

1. If I just ignore unwanted sexual attention, it will usually stop.

2. If I don't mean to sexually harass another employee, he or she cannot perceive my behavior as sexually harassing.

3. Some employees don't complain about unwanted sexual attention from another worker because they don't want to get that person in trouble.

4. If I make sexual comments to someone and that person doesn't ask me to stop, I can assume that my behavior is welcome.

5. To avoid sexually harassing a woman who comes to work in a traditionally male workplace, men simply should not haze her.

6. A sexual harasser may be told by a court to pay part of a judgment to the employee he or she harassed.

7. A sexually harassed man does not have the same legal rights as a woman who is sexually harassed.

8. About 84 percent of all sexual harassment in today's workplace is male to female harassment.

9. Sexually suggestive pictures or objects in a workplace don't create a liability unless someone complains.

10. Displaying nude pictures can constitute a hostile work environment even though most employees in the workplace think they are harmless.

11. Telling someone to stop his or her unwanted sexual behavior usually doesn't do any good.

Answers (1) False, (2) False, (3) True, (4) False, (5) False, (6) True, (7) False, (8) True, (9) False, (10) True, (11) False.

A Test for Managers

Answer the following true/false questions:

1. Men in male-dominated workplaces usually have to change their behavior when a woman begins working there.

2. Employers are not liable for the sexual harassment of one of their employees unless that employee loses specific job benefits or is fired.

3. Supervisors can be liable for sexual harassment committed by one of their employees against another.

4. Employers can be liable for the sexually harassing behavior of management personnel even if they are unaware of that behavior and have a policy forbidding it.

5. It is appropriate for a supervisor, when initially receiving a sexual harassment complaint, to determine if the alleged recipient overreacted or misunderstood the alleged harasser.

6. When a supervisor is to tell an employee that an allegation of sexual harassment has been made against him or her by another employee, it is best for the supervisor to ease into the allegation instead of being direct.

7. Sexually suggestive visuals or objects in a workplace don't create a liability unless an employee complains about them and management allows them to remain.

8. The lack of sexual harassment complaints is a good indication that sexual harassment is not occurring.

9. It is appropriate for supervisors to tell an employee to handle unwelcome sexual behavior if they think the employee is misunderstanding the behavior.

10. The *intent* behind employee A's sexual behavior is more important than the *impact* of that behavior on employee B when determining if sexual harassment has occurred.

11. If a sexual harassment problem is common knowledge in a workplace, courts assume that the employer has knowledge of it.

Answers: (1) False, (2) False, (3) True, (4) True, (5) False, (6) False, (7) False, (8) False, (9) False, (10) False, (11) True.

Sources: Reprinted with permission from *Industry Week*, November 18, 1991, p. 40. Copyright Penton Publishing, Cleveland, Ohio; *Sexual Harassment Manual for Managers and Supervisors* (Chicago: Commerce Clearing House), 1992, p. 22; Andrea P. Brandon and David R. Eyler, *Working Together* (New York: McGraw-Hill), 1994; *Theresa Waldo v. Consumers Energy Company*, 2010 U.S. District Lexus 55068; 109 Fair Employment Practices Case (BNA) 11348, June 4, 2010; John Agar, "Consumers Energy Ordered to Pay $8 Million in Sexual Harassment Lawsuit Verdict," *Mlive*, October 8, 2010, www.mlive.com/news/grand-rapids/index.ssf/2010/10/consumers_energy_ordered_to_pa.html.

Privacy

Modern technology has given business owners the ability to monitor workers' performance as they never could before, but where is the line between monitoring productivity and invasion of privacy? With a few mouse clicks, it is possible for managers to view e-mail messages employees send to one another, listen to voice-mail or telephone conversations, and actually see what is on their monitors while they are sitting at their computer terminals. Some employers have begun to demand Facebook usernames and passwords from job applicants although this is a violation of the Facebook terms of use, has been made illegal in several states, and is considered by many experts to be a violation of employee privacy. Employers have established policies that prohibit employees from stating negative information—or in some cases *any* information—about the company in any social media (including Facebook, Twitter, blogs, and so forth). Employers can monitor all activities, including Web usage and text messages that employees send on their employer-issued smart phones. Managers use electronic monitoring to track customer service representatives, word-processing clerks, data entry technicians, and other workers for speed, accuracy, and productivity. Even truck drivers, the "lone rangers of the road," are not immune to electronic tracking. Most trucking companies outfit their trucks with GPS devices they use to monitor drivers' exact locations at all times, regulate their speed, make sure they stop only at approved fueling points, and ensure that they take the legally required hours of rest. Although many drivers support the use of these devices, others worry about their tendency to create George Orwell's "Big Brother" syndrome.

E-mail also poses an ethical problem for employers. Internet users have more than 4.1 billion e-mail accounts worldwide (974 million of which are business e-mail accounts), and people send more than 108 billion business e-mails per day.[59] Most workers do not realize that, in most states, employers legally can monitor their e-mail and voice-mail messages without notification. However, this is limited to company e-mail accounts; employers cannot monitor personal e-mail accounts. Only two states (Connecticut and Delaware) require companies to notify employees that they are monitoring e-mail.

To avoid ethical and legal problems, business owners should follow these guidelines:

- *Establish a clear policy for monitoring employees' communications.* Employees should know that the company is monitoring their e-mails and other forms of communication, and the best way to make sure they do is to create an unambiguous policy. Once you create a policy, be sure to follow it. Some managers ask employees to sign a consent form acknowledging that they have read and understand the company's monitoring policy.

- *Create guidelines for the proper use of the company's communication technology and communicate them to everyone.* A company's policies and guidelines should be reasonable and should reflect employees' reasonable expectations of privacy.

- *Monitor in moderation.* Employees resent monitoring that is unnecessarily invasive. In addition, excessively draconian monitoring may land a company in a legal battle.

LO8

Explain business's responsibility to customers.

Business's Responsibility to Customers

One of the most important group of stakeholders that a business must satisfy is its *customers.* Building and maintaining a base of loyal customers is no easy task because it requires more than just selling a product or a service. The key is to build long-term relationships with customers. Socially responsible companies recognize their duty to abide by the Consumer Bill of Rights, first put forth by President John Kennedy. This document gives consumers the following rights.

Right to Safety

The right to safety is the most basic consumer right. Companies have the responsibility to provide their customers with safe, quality products and services. The greatest breach of trust occurs when businesses produce products that, when properly used, injure customers.

You Be the Consultant

Think before You Tweet

There has been increasing attention given to employee posts on social media sites such as Facebook and Twitter. The National Labor Relations Board (NLRB) and several judges have begun to define what is protected, private speech when it is posted on a personal Facebook or Twitter account. Several cases have helped bring this issue into focus.

Employee Rants about Tip

The owner of a New York City food truck called the Milk Truck fired an employee, Brendan O'Connor, when he tweeted from his personal Twitter account about not receiving a tip. Glass, Lewis & Co. employees ordered $170 worth of grilled cheese sandwiches and milkshakes. After not receiving any tip, O'Conner tweeted, "Shout out to the good people of Glass, Lewis & Co. for placing a $170 order and not leaving a tip. @glasslewis." After Glass, Lewis & Co. employees found the tweets, the company expressed its displeasure to the owner of Milk Truck. O'Connor was promptly fired by the owner, who said O'Conner had embarrassed the company. The owner of Milk Truck apologized to Glass, Lewis & Co., via Twitter. The apology was accepted. However, O'Connor has more than 300 followers on his Twitter account. Most of the discussion on Twitter about O'Connor's firing blasted both Milk Truck and Glass, Lewis & Co.

Tweets about Illegal Activity

Sunith Baheerathan, an employee of Mr. Lube in Toronto, Ontario, used Twitter to try to find dealers to buy marijuana. In his tweets, he suggested that dealers could bring the drugs to Mr. Lube, where he was working. The tweet went viral and soon came to the attention of the police, who joined in the Twitter conversation. "Awesome! Can we come too?" read a tweet sent by the York Regional Police's official Twitter feed. Baheerathan's next tweet read "Just got the call of termination." Another of his tweets said, "Gotta watch what you tweet nowadays, even the freedom of speech & the right to an entitled opinion isn't safe."

New Hire Loses Offer

Connor Riley had just gotten a job offer from CISCO Systems, which is based in San Jose, California. Riley was pursuing a master's degree in information systems and management at the University of California, Berkeley. After receiving her offer, Riley tweeted, "Cisco just offered me a job! Now I have to weigh the utility of a fatty paycheck against the daily commute to San Jose and hating the work." It was not too long before Riley received a

reply tweet from someone who claimed to be a Cisco employee. It read, "Who is the hiring manager? I'm sure they would love to know that you will hate the work. We here at Cisco are versed in the Web." Riley is not working at Cisco, after all.

Although the National Labor Relations Board (NLRB) protects the use of Facebook and Twitter as equivalent to the modern-day water cooler, there are limits on what speech is protected in social media. Employees can use social media to communicate with each other about work conditions, for example. However, there are clear limits on social media posts that are abusive, target individuals, give away company secrets and so forth. The boundaries between protected speech and posts that might leave employees subject to disciplinary action remain a gray area of employment law. Employees should be careful when they tweet, and employers should have clear policies that fall within the emerging guidelines established by the courts and the NLRB.

1. If you were the judge reviewing the O'Connor case, how would you rule? Explain your reasoning.

2. If you were the judge in the Riley case, how would you rule? Explain your reasoning.

3. What policies would you put in place as a business owner about employee comments on social media sites like Facebook and Twitter? Explain your policies based on the cases discussed here.

Sources: Based on Hillary Dixer, "Food Truck Employee Fired for Tip-Shaming on Twitter," *Eater,* July 30, 2013, http://eater.com/archives/2013/07/30/food-truck-employee-fired-for-tipshaming-on-twitter.php; Rachel Tepper, "Brendan O'Connor, Former Milk Truck Employee, Fired for Tip-Shaming Customers on Twitter," *Huffington Post,* July 31, 2013; Rachel Quigley, "Food truck employee fired after he calls company out on Twitter for not leaving a tip on a $170 order - prompting an angry online backlash," *Daily Mail,* July 31, 2013, http://www.dailymail.co.uk/news/article-2381982/Milk-Truck-employee-Brendan-OConnor-fired-calls-company-Twitter-leaving-tip.html; "Guy gets pink slip after apparently requesting pot delivery on Twitter," *MSN Now,* August 15, 2013, http://now.msn.com/sunith-baheerathan-reportedly-asked-for-marijuana-on-twitter-fired-from-job; Michelle McQuigge, "Sunith Baheerathan Loses Job After Tweet Looking for Marijuana," *Huffington Post,* August 14, 2013, http://www.huffingtonpost.ca/2013/08/14/sunith-baheerathan-marijuana-twitter_n_3756992.html; "York Region police ask to tag along after man tweets 'need a spliff'," *The Star,* August 14, 2013, www.thestar.com/news/crime/2013/08/14/man_tweets_need_a_spliff_york_regional_police_asks_to_tag_along.html; "Mr. Lube employee fired after asking for pot via Twitter," *The Province,* August 15, 2013, www.theprovince.com/business/Tweet+seeking+greases+skids+under+Lube+employee+Toronto+suburb/8788823/story.html; Helen A.S. Popkin, "Twitter Gets You Fired in 140 Characters or Less," *NBC News,* March 23, 2009, www.nbcnews.com/id/29796962/ns/technology_and_science-tech_and_gadgets/#.UkSIEBb3B-V; Helen A.S. Popkin, "Getting the Skinny on Twitter's 'Cisco Fatty,'" *NBC News,* March 29, 2013, www.nbcnews.com/id/29901380/ns/technology_and_science-tech_and_gadgets/t/getting-skinny-twitters-cisco-fatty/#.UkSZDRb3B-U; Catharine Smith and Bianca Bosker, "Fired Over Twitter: 13 Tweets That Got People CANNED," *Huffington Post,* July 14, 2010, http://www.huffingtonpost.com/2010/07/15/fired-over-twitter-tweets_n_645884.html#s112801title=Cisco_Fatty_Loses.

Product liability cases can be controversial, such as the McDonald's coffee lawsuit, in which a jury found that the fast-food giant's coffee was too hot when served and caused a serious injury when a customer at a drive-through window spilled coffee in her lap. In other situations, the evidence is clear that a product suffers from fundamental flaws in either design or construction and caused an injury to its user when used properly.

Many companies have responded by placing detailed warning labels on their products that sometimes insult customers' intelligence. Consider the following actual examples from product warning labels:

- "Does not supply oxygen" on a dust mask

- "Caution: Do not swallow" on a clothes hanger

- "Wash hands after using" on a common extension cord

- "Not for human consumption," a warning on a package of plastic fishing worms

- "Combustion of this manufactured product results in the emissions of carbon monoxide, soot and other combustion by-products which are known by the State of California to cause cancer, birth defects, or reproductive harm" on a box of matches

- "Do not use while sleeping," a product warning for a Vidal Sassoon hair dryer

- "This product is not intended for use as a dental drill" on a Dremel rotary power tool[60]

Right to Know

Consumers have the right to honest communication about the products and services they buy and the companies that sell them. In a free market economy, information is one of the most valuable commodities available. Customers often depend on companies for the information they need to make decisions about price, quality, features, and other factors. As a result, companies have a responsibility to customers to be truthful in their advertising.

Unfortunately, not every business recognizes its social responsibility to be truthful in advertising. The Federal Trade Commission reached a settlement requiring Reebok to refund $25 million to customers because its advertising promised, without any evidence, that the company's EasyTone shoes could firm users' butts and legs with every step.[61] Businesses that rely on unscrupulous tactics may profit in the short term, but they will not last in the long run.

Right to Be Heard

The right to be heard suggests that the channels of communication between companies and their customers run in both directions. Socially responsible businesses provide customers with a mechanism for resolving complaints about products and services. Some companies have established a consumer ombudsman to address customer questions and complaints. Others have created customer hot lines, toll-free numbers designed to serve customers more effectively. Today, many businesses actively monitor social media, watching for customer complaints or negative comments that customers make about the company or its products and services and then addressing them promptly.

Another effective technique for encouraging two-way communication between customers and companies is the customer report card. The Granite Rock Company, a business that supplies a variety of building materials to construction companies, relies on an annual report card from its customers to learn how to serve them better. Although the knowledge an entrepreneur gets from customer feedback is immeasurable for making improvements, only 1 in 12 small companies regularly schedules customer satisfaction surveys such as Granite Rock's. This tool can boost a company's profitability significantly.

Right to Education

Socially responsible companies give customers access to educational material about their products and services and how to use them properly. The goal is to give customers enough information to make informed purchase decisions. A product that is the wrong solution to the customer's needs results in a disappointed customer who is likely to blame the manufacturer or retailer for the

You Be the Consultant

But Is It Safe?

Kali Hardig, a 12-year-old from Arkansas, spent a day swimming and enjoying the attractions at Willow Springs Water Park. Willow Springs was a popular local attraction that offered a lake for swimming, a water slide, water trampolines, concessions, and a picnic area. A day after her visit to Willow Springs, Kali's mother rushed her to the hospital. She had a high fever, was vomiting, and had an excruciating headache. Centers for Disease Control and Prevention and the Arkansas Department of Public Health determined that Kali had contracted parasitic meningitis caused by a brain-eating amoeba.

The amoeba, called Naegleria fowleri, enters through the noses of people who come into contact with contaminated water or soil. Most cases occur in the summer because the amoeba is most often found in water that is 115 degrees Fahrenheit. The amoeba can enter a human victim only through the nose. Drinking contaminated water cannot lead to infection. The amoeba moves from the nose into the brain, causing the brain to swell (meningitis), and in 99 percent of cases leads to the death of the infected person. Naegleria is very rare, with only 128 cases ever reported in the United States. However, only two people have survived this infection. Doctors put Kali into a drug-induced coma to help her fight the infection.

This was the second case of Naegleria linked to Willow Springs. Authorities believe that another person was infected at the water park in 2010. However, the owners of the park said they had not been informed about the first infection until Kali's case was diagnosed. Authorities admit that the exact source of the strain is not traceable to a specific location, but were convinced that the chronology of events and other evidence strongly linked both cases to the lake at Willow Springs. The Arkansas Department of Public Health asked the owners of the water park to voluntarily close the park to protect public health. David and Lou Ann Ratliff, owners of Willow Springs Water Park, said in a statement:

"We, David and Lou Ann Ratliff, as general management of Willow Springs Water Park, have received new information regarding Naegleria fowleri, and have elected to close the park as of July 25 at the request of the Arkansas Department of Health. Though the odds of contracting Naegleria are extremely low, they are just not good enough to allow our friends or family to swim. For the thousands of people who love Willow Springs, we will be taking this time to determine the feasibility of installing a solid bottom to the lake. We will not ever reopen as a sand bottom lake. We covet your prayers and our Willow Springs family will continue to be in our thoughts and prayers."

The owners of Willow Springs are not sure about the future of their business or what else they might do with the property. Willow Springs first opened as a water park in 1928. David Ratliff was exploring the possibility of building a hard surface for the lake bottom. However, given the high cost of this alternative, he said he doubts they will be able reopen as a water park. They are exploring alternative businesses that will attract local residents as customers.

By August, Kali was showing signs of recovery. She woke up and spoke briefly to her mother. By early September Kali was able to leave the hospital for short trips with her mother to go to the movies and eat at local restaurants. On September 11, 2013, against all odds, Kali was released to go home from the hospital. She had become only the third person to recover from the Naegleria infection.

1. How could the owners of Willow Springs have ensured the safety of their customers and prevented the infections from occurring? Explain.

2. Would it have been ethical for Willow Springs to remain open after Kali's case came to light even though there could never be definitive evidence linking the infection to their lake? Explain.

3. What do you think the owners of Willow Springs should do with their property? Should they reopen the water park if they can ensure that the water is safe to swim in? Explain.

4. Create a detailed diagram of all of the stakeholders of Willow Springs. How is each of the stakeholders affected by the water park's actions? What conclusions can you draw from this analysis? Explain.

Sources: Based on "Girl Contracts Brain Eating Amoeba after Swimming at Arkansas Water Park," *Fox News,* July 29, 2013, www.foxnews.com/health/2013/07/29/girl-contracts-brain-eating-amoeba-after-swimming-at-arkansas-water-park/; "Naegleria fowleri - Primary Amebic Meningoencephalitis (PAM)," Centers for Disease Control and Prevention, August 23, 2013, www.cdc.gov/parasites/naegleria/treatment.html; "ADH Confirms Case of Parasitic Meningitis," Arkansas Department of Health, July 26, 2013, www.arkansas.gov/health/newsroom/index.php?do:newsDetail=1&news_id=921; Mark Johanson, "Willow Springs Water Park In Little Rock Closed After Second Child Contracts Rare Brain-Eating Amoeba," *International Business Times,* July 29, 2013, www.ibtimes.com/willow-springs-water-park-little-rock-closed-after-second-child-contracts-rare-brain-eating-amoeba; Katie Moisse, "Brain-Eating Amoeba Victim Shows Signs of Recovery," *ABC News,* August 21, 2013; http://abcnews.go.com/blogs/health/2013/08/21/brain-eating-amoeba-victim-shows-signs-of-recovery/; David Harten, "Willow Springs Shuts for Season after Parasite Discovered," *Arkansas Online,* July 26, 2013, www.arkansasonline.com/news/2013/jul/26/willow-springs-shuts-down-season-after-parasite-di/;"Prayers for Kali Le Ann," *Facebook,* n.d., https://www.facebook.com/pages/Prayers-For-Kali-Le-Ann/279567398852251.

---

mistake. Consumer education is an inexpensive investment in customer satisfaction (especially when done online) and the increased probability that a satisfied customer will be a repeat buyer.

Right to Choice

Inherent in the free enterprise system is the consumer's right to choose among competing products and services. Socially responsible companies do not restrict competition, and they abide by

U.S. antitrust policy, which promotes free trade and competition in the market. The foundation of this policy is the Sherman Antitrust Act of 1890, which forbids agreements among sellers that restrain trade or commerce and outlaws any attempts to monopolize markets.

LO9

Discuss business's responsibility to investors.

Business's Responsibility to Investors

Companies have the responsibility to provide investors with an attractive return on their investments. Although earning a profit may be a company's *first* responsibility, it is not its *only* responsibility; meeting its ethical and social responsibility goals is also a key to success. Investors today want to know that entrepreneurs are making ethical decisions and acting in a socially responsible manner. Those who invest in entrepreneurial ventures are a small community (see Chapter 13). Reputation can mean everything for an entrepreneur because most investors invest more on the basis of the entrepreneur's track record than on the entrepreneur's idea. Maintaining high standards of ethics and social responsibility translates into a business culture that sets the stage for future equity investments and in more profitable business operations.

Companies also have the responsibility to report their financial performance in an accurate and timely fashion to their investors. Businesses that misrepresent or falsify their financial and operating records are guilty of violating the fiduciary relationship with their investors.

ENTREPRENEURIAL PROFILE: Russell Daniel, Daniel Enterprises, Inc. Russell Daniel, of Louisville, Kentucky, offered investors a healthy return on their investments in his firm, Daniel Enterprises. Daniel promised his investors returns on their investments of 10 to 15 percent. He said their investments would be used to purchase and rehabilitate houses, which in return would be sold for a profit. Daniel used the money received from investors to pay out returns promised to previous investors and for unrelated personal investments. Daniel provided investors with false and fictitious mortgages totaling more than $530,000, which contained a forged signature of a notary public. Many of the properties that he claimed were located in Kentucky did not exist or were actually located in other states, and Daniel did not have any authority to issue mortgages on those properties. However, Daniel could not maintain his fraud and was eventually caught and prosecuted in federal court. Daniel pleaded guilty to devising a scheme to defraud investors and to obtain money and property from investors by means of false and fraudulent pretenses, representations, and promises. He was sentenced to 37 months in federal prison and was ordered to pay $2,797,000 in restitution for his real estate schemes that resulted in the loss of more than $1 million for investors.[62] ■

LO10

Discuss business's responsibility to the community.

Business's Responsibility to the Community

As corporate citizens, businesses have a responsibility to the communities in which they operate. In addition to providing jobs and creating wealth, companies contribute to the local community in many different ways. Socially responsible businesses are aware of their duty to put back into the community some of what they take out as they generate profits; their goal is to become a neighbor of choice.

Experts estimate that 80 percent of companies worldwide engage in some type of socially responsible activity.[63] The following are just a few examples of ways small businesses have found to give back to their communities:

- Act as volunteers for community groups such as the American Red Cross, United Way, literacy programs, and community food banks.
- Participate in projects that aid the elderly or economically disadvantaged.
- Adopt a highway near the business to promote a clean community.
- Volunteer in school programs, such as Junior Achievement.

In a recent survey, 92 percent of consumers say that given the opportunity, they would buy products with a social and/or environmental benefit.[64] Even small companies that may be short on funding can support causes by choosing them strategically and discovering creative ways to help them. The key to choosing the "right" cause is finding one that makes an impact and whose purpose resonates with customers, employees, and owners. Small companies can commit their employees' talent and know-how, not just dollars, to carefully chosen social causes and then tell the world about their cause and their dedication to serving it. By forging meaningful partnerships, both the businesses and the causes benefit in unique ways. Over the years, companies have helped social causes enjoy financial rewards and unprecedented support. In addition to doing good, companies have been able to enhance their reputations, deepen employee loyalty, strengthen ties with business partners, and sell more products or services.

ENTREPRENEURIAL PROFILE: Melissa Rich: Inter-Schola Melissa Rich started her social enterprise, Inter-Schola, based on a conversation she had about what schools do with old equipment and other materials. After doing some research, she discovered that there was an opportunity to help schools transform unwanted assets and other materials into cash by selling them on eBay. She keeps about 35 percent of the sales' proceeds, and the school gets the rest. For example, InterSchola recently sold five pianos, a vending machine, and a 35–year-old school bus for the Lemon Grove School District in California. The school received $2,400 in cash and helped clean out some badly needed storage space. "We've tried to do our own auctions in-house, but it was pretty rinky dink," said Bret Felix, projects and facilities supervisor for the school district. "InterSchola has been at it long enough they know how to do it with eBay and get the word out to so many more potential buyers." Since the launch of the business in 2004, InterSchola has sold more than $15 million in materials, providing schools with approximately $10 million in badly needed cash.[65] ■

Melissa Rich, founder of InterSchola

Entrepreneurs such as InterSchola who demonstrate their sense of social responsibility not only make their communities better places to live and work but also stand out from their competitors. Their efforts to operate ethical, socially responsible businesses create a strong sense of loyalty among their customers and their employees.

Conclusion

Businesses must do more than merely earn profits; they must act ethically and in a socially responsible manner. Establishing and maintaining high ethical and socially responsible standards must be a top concern of every business owner. Managing in an ethical and socially responsible manner presents a tremendous challenge, however. There is no universal definition of ethical behavior, and what is considered ethical may change over time and may be different in other cultures.

Finally, business owners and managers must recognize the key role they play in influencing their employees' ethical and socially responsible behavior. What owners and managers *say* is important, but what they *do* is even more important! Employees in a small company look to the owner and managers as models; therefore, owners and managers must commit themselves to following the highest ethical standards if they expect their employees to do so.

Chapter Summary by Learning Objective

1. Define business ethics and describe the three levels of ethical standards.

- Business ethics involves the fundamental moral values and behavioral standards that form the foundation for the people of an organization as they make decisions and interact with organizational stakeholders. Small business managers must consider the ethical and social as well as the economic implications of their decisions.

- The three levels of ethical standards are (1) the law, (2) the policies and procedures of the company, and (3) the moral stance of the individual.

2. Determine who is responsible for ethical behavior and why ethical lapses occur.

- Managers set the moral tone of the organization. There are three ethical styles of management: immoral, amoral, and moral. Although moral management has value in itself, companies that operate with this philosophy discover other benefits, including a positive reputation among customers and employees.

- Ethical lapses occur for a variety of reasons:

  Some people are corrupt ("the bad apple").

  The company culture has been poisoned ("the bad barrel").

  Competitive pressures push managers to compromise.

  Managers are tempted by an opportunity to "get ahead."

  Managers in different cultures have different views of what is ethical.

3. Explain how to establish and maintain high ethical standards.

- Philosophers throughout history have developed various tests of ethical behavior: the utilitarian principle, Kant's categorical imperative, the professional ethic, the Golden Rule, the television test, and the family test.

- A small business manager can maintain high ethical standards in the following ways:

  Create a company credo.

  Develop a code of ethics.

  Enforce the code fairly and consistently.

  Hire the right people.

  Conduct ethical training.

  Perform periodic ethical audits.

  Establish high standards of behavior, not just rules.

  Set an impeccable ethical example at all times.

  Create a culture emphasizing two-way communication.

  Involve employees in establishing ethical standards.

4. Explain the difference between social entrepreneurs and traditional entrepreneurs.

- Traditional entrepreneurs seek opportunities to create market value and profit.

- Social entrepreneurs use entrepreneurship to pursue opportunities to create social value by creating innovative solutions to society's most vexing problems.

5. Define social responsibility.

- Social responsibility is the awareness of a company's managers of the social, environmental, political, human, and financial consequences of their actions.

6. Understand the nature of business's responsibility to the environment.

- Environmentally responsible business owners focus on the three Rs: *reduce* the amount of materials used in the company from the factory floor to the copier room, *reuse* whatever you can, and *recycle* the materials you must dispose of.

7. Describe business's responsibility to employees.

- Companies have a duty to act responsibly toward one of their most important stakeholders: their employees. Businesses must recognize and manage the cultural diversity that exists in the workplace, establish a responsible strategy for combating substance abuse in the workplace (including drug testing), prevent sexual harassment, and respect employees' right to privacy.

8. Explain business's responsibility to customers.

- Every company's customers have a right to safe products and services; to honest, accurate information; to be heard; to education about products and services; and to choices in the marketplace.

9. Discuss business's responsibility to investors.

- Companies have the responsibility to provide investors with an attractive return on their investments and to report their financial performances in an accurate and timely fashion to their investors.

10. Describe business's responsibility to the community.

- Increasingly, companies are seeing a need to go beyond "doing well" to "doing good"—being socially responsible community citizens. In addition to providing jobs and creating wealth, companies contribute to the local community in many different ways.

Discussion Questions

2-1. What is ethics?

2-2. Discuss the three levels of ethical standards.

2-3. List the core personal values you intend to bring to your business (e.g., treating people fairly, giving something back to the community, and so on).

2-4. Where does each of your core values come from (e.g., religious faith, family, personal philosophy)?

2-5. Why is each of your core values important to you?

2-6. In any organization, who determines ethical behavior?

2-7. Briefly describe the three ethical styles of management.

2-8. What are the benefits of moral management?

2-9. Why do ethical lapses occur in businesses?

2-10. Describe the various methods for establishing ethical standards.

2-11. Which is most meaningful to you?

2-12. Why is it most meaningful to you?

2-13. What can business owners do to maintain high ethical standards in their companies?

2-14. What is a social entrepreneur?

2-15. How do social entrepreneurs differ from traditional entrepreneurs?

2-16. What are some social problems you think could be tackled by social entrepreneurs?

2-17. What is social responsibility?

2-18. Describe business's social responsibility to the environment.

2-19. Describe business's social responsibility to its employees.

2-20. Describe business's social responsibility to its customers.

2-21. Describe business's social responsibility to its investors.

2-22. Describe business's social responsibility to the community.

2-23. What can businesses do to improve the quality of our environment?

2-24. Explain your stance on whether companies should be allowed to test employees for drugs?

2-25. How should a socially responsible drug-testing program operate?

2-26. Many owners of trucking companies use electronic communications equipment to monitor their drivers on the road. They say the devices allow them to remain competitive and to serve their customers better by delivering shipments of vital materials exactly when their customers need them. They also point out that the equipment can improve road safety by ensuring that drivers get the hours of rest the law requires. Opponents argue that the surveillance devices work against safety. "The drivers know they're being watched," says one trucker. "There's an obvious temptation to push." What do you think about this practice?

2-27. What ethical issues do trucking companies create when they use electronic communications equipment to monitor their drivers on the road?

2-28. How should a small trucking company considering the use of electronic communications equipment to monitor their drivers handle the ethical issues created by this practice?

2-29. What rights do customers have under the Consumer Bill of Rights?

2-30. How can businesses ensure consumers' rights?

Beyond the Classroom . . .

2-31. Interview a social entrepreneur in your community to determine the social need addressed by the entrepreneur and the solution applied to that social need.

2-32. Was the social venture established as a nonprofit or a for-profit social enterprise?

2-33. If the firm is a nonprofit, what are its primary sources of funding?

2-34. If the firm is a for-profit social enterprise, what is the primary source of revenues and how are the profits used to address the social need the company has as its primary focus?

2-35. A key concern with any social enterprise is sustainability of funding. What recommendations can you make to the social entrepreneur to ensure the sustainability of the venture over the long term?

2-36. Work with a team of your classmates to identify an unmet social need in your community. Identify alternative approaches you can develop to address this social need. Describe the social venture you would establish to meet the social need.

2-37. What are the various ways you could generate the funding you would need to operate your social venture?

Endnotes

Scan for Endnotes or go to www.pearsonhighered.com/scarborough

3

Inside the Entrepreneurial Mind: From Ideas to Reality

Andrew Rich/Getty Images, Inc.

Learning Objectives

On completion of this chapter, you will be able to:

1. Explain the differences among creativity, innovation, and entrepreneurship.

2. Describe why creativity and innovation are such an integral part of entrepreneurship.

3. Understand how the two hemispheres of the human brain function and what role they play in creativity.

4. Explain the 10 "mental locks" that limit individual creativity.

5. Understand how entrepreneurs can enhance the creativity of their employees as well as their own creativity.

6. Describe the steps in the creative process.

7. Discuss techniques for improving the creative process.

8. Describe the protection of intellectual property through patents, trademarks, and copyrights.

One of the tenets of entrepreneurship is the ability to create new and useful ideas that solve the problems and challenges people face every day. Entrepreneurs achieve success by creating value in the marketplace when they combine resources in new and different ways to gain a competitive edge over rivals. From Alexander Fleming's pioneering work that resulted in a cure for infections (penicillin) and the founders of the Rocket Chemical Company's fortieth try to create an industrial lubricant (WD-40) to Jeff Bezos's innovative use of the Internet in retailing (Amazon.com) and Ted Turner's around-the-clock approach to the availability of television news (CNN), entrepreneurs' ideas have transformed the world.

As you learned in Chapter 1, entrepreneurs can create value in a number of ways—inventing new products and services, developing new technology, discovering new knowledge, improving existing products or services, finding different ways of providing more goods and services with fewer resources, and many others. Indeed, finding new ways of satisfying customers' needs, inventing new products and services, putting together existing ideas in new and different ways, and creating new twists on existing products and services are hallmarks of the entrepreneur!

Since Earl Dickson invented the Band-aid in 1920 for his wife, who experienced frequent cuts while preparing food, entrepreneurs have been working to improve the simple but effective invention. Tsai Cheng-Yu and Hsu Hao-Ming, two students at Shih Chien University in Taiwan, created the AmoeBAND, a Band-aid with cut-away sections that allow it to be adjusted to fit the location of the wound so that it stays on and a sensor that alerts the wearer if the wound becomes infected. Inventors at the European Center of Innovative Textiles in Lille, France, have developed a new fabric for use in dressing wounds that incorporates antiviral, antibacterial, and other medicines into the fibers. They also are experimenting with nonwoven textiles that serve as seeds for rebuilding human tissue. Jeff Skiba, a former medical consultant and founder of Vomaris Innovations, won approval from the Food and Drug Administration (FDA) for an adhesive bandage called Procellera that is equipped with microscopic batteries that pass a small amount of electrical current (just 1.2 volts) over the injured area to accelerate the healing process.[1] Like many innovators, these entrepreneurs have achieved success by taking a common item, bandages, that had existed for many years and looking at it in a different way.

Creativity, Innovation, and Entrepreneurship

According to the Battelle *R&D Magazine*, U.S. companies, government agencies, and universities invest more than $465 billion annually in research and development (R&D).[2] Small companies are an important part of the total R&D picture. One study by the Small Business Administration reports that small companies produce 16 times more patents per employee than their larger rivals. What is the entrepreneurial "secret" for creating value in the marketplace? In reality, the "secret" is no secret at all: It is applying creativity and innovation to solve problems and to exploit opportunities that people face every day. **Creativity** is the ability to develop new ideas and to discover new ways of looking at problems and opportunities. **Innovation** is the ability to *apply* creative solutions to those problems and opportunities to enhance or enrich people's lives. Harvard's Ted Levitt says creativity is *thinking* new things and innovation is *doing* new things. In short, entrepreneurs succeed by *thinking and doing* new things or old things in new ways. Simply having a great new idea is not enough; transforming the idea into a tangible product, service, or business venture is the essential next step. "Big ideas are just that—ideas—until you execute," says Krisztina Holly, an entrepreneur who serves on the National Advisory Council for Innovation and Entrepreneurship.[3]

Successful entrepreneurs develop new ideas, products, and services that solve a problem or fill a need and, in doing so, create value for their customers and wealth for themselves. As management legend Peter Drucker said, "Innovation is the specific instrument of entrepreneurs, the act that endows resources with a new capacity to create wealth."[4] In a world that is changing faster than most of us ever could have imagined, creativity and innovation are vital to a company's success—and ultimate survival. That's true for businesses in every industry—from automakers to tea growers—and for companies of all sizes. A recent survey by Adobe of people in the world's five largest economies reports that 80 percent of people believe unlocking creative potential is the key to economic and societal growth, yet only one in four people say they are living up to their creative potential. In addition, the survey reveals a creativity gap, in which 75 percent of

LO1

Explain the differences among creativity, innovation, and entrepreneurship.

creativity
the ability to develop new ideas and to discover new ways of looking at problems and opportunities.

innovation
the ability to apply creative solutions to problems and opportunities to enhance or to enrich people's lives.

respondents say they are under increasing pressure to be productive rather than creative; yet just 25 percent of their work time is devoted to creativity. The primary barrier to creativity on the job? Lack of time. In addition, 59 percent of the survey's respondents say their educational systems stifle individual creativity.[5]

Although big businesses develop many new ideas, creativity and innovation are the signatures of small, entrepreneurial businesses. Creative thinking has become a core business skill, and entrepreneurs lead the way in developing and applying that skill. In fact, creativity and innovation often lie at the heart of small companies' ability to compete successfully with their larger rivals. Even though they cannot outspend their larger rivals, small companies can create powerful, effective competitive advantages over big companies by "out-creating" and "out-innovating" them! If they fail to do so, entrepreneurs don't stay in business very long. Leadership expert Warren Bennis says, "Today's successful companies live and die according to the quality of their ideas."[6]

Some small businesses create innovations *reactively* in response to customer feedback or changing market conditions, and others create innovations *proactively*, spotting opportunities on which to capitalize. Sometimes innovation is *revolutionary*, creating market-changing, disruptive breakthroughs that are the result of generating something from nothing. More often, innovation is *evolutionary*, developing market-sustaining ideas that elaborate on existing products, processes, and services that result from putting old things together in new ways or from taking something away to create something simpler or better. Apple did not invent the digital music player, but Steve Jobs's company created a player that was easier to use and offered a "cool" factor that existing MP3 players did not have. One experimenter's research to improve the adhesive on tape resulted in a glue that hardly stuck at all. Although most researchers might have considered the experiment a total failure and scrapped it, this researcher asked a simple, creative question: What can you do with a glue when you take away most of its stickiness? The answer led to the invention of one of the most popular office products of all time: the Post-It note, a product that now includes more than 4,000 variations.

Entrepreneurial innovation encompasses not only new products and services but also new business models. As graduate students, Larry Page and Sergey Brin, cofounders of Google, realized that the Internet's ocean of information had outpaced people's ability to locate the information they wanted with existing search engines. Convinced that Internet users would value more relevant search results, the entrepreneurs developed a new service, Google's PageRank system, an algorithm that screens Internet searches and organizes them to produce the most relevant results. As traffic on their search engine grew, the young entrepreneurs created a new business model that involved selling advertising space (paid listings) by auctioning to businesses key words that visitors used in their searches. Today, their innovative business model accounts for 91 percent of Google's revenue (nearly $51 billion annually), and Google dominates the search engine market with 68 percent of all searches conducted.[7]

Some entrepreneurs stumble onto their ideas by accident but are clever enough to spot the business opportunities they offer.

ENTREPRENEURIAL PROFILE: Brian Levin: Perky Jerky Serial entrepreneur Brian Levin, who created the first text-message voting system (the one used on *American Idol*), and a friend were on a chairlift on the snowy slopes in Snowbird, Utah, one morning when Levin reached into his backpack for a package of beef jerky. Unfortunately, an energy drink had spilled onto the package, soaking the jerky, but Levin and his friend were hungry and ate it anyway. As they skied down the mountain, the duo experienced an energy boost. The jerky, now quite tender because of its soaking, had taken on the characteristics of the energy drink but had retained its peppery flavor. Inspired, Levin spent the next two years working with a food laboratory to refine a process for making an energy-boosting jerky around which he built a company to market the new product, which he named Perky Jerky. The company now generates annual sales of $10 million.[8] ■

More often, creative ideas arise when entrepreneurs look at something old and think something new or different. Legendary Notre Dame football coach Knute Rockne, whose teams dominated college football in the 1920s, got the idea for his constantly shifting backfields while watching a burlesque chorus routine! Rockne's innovations in the backfield (which included the legendary "Four Horsemen") and his emphasis on the forward pass (a legal but largely unused tactic in this era) so befuddled opposing defenses that his teams compiled an impressive 105-12-5 record.[9]

© Bettman/CORBIS

ENTREPRENEURIAL PROFILE: Brian Spaly: Trunk Club Brian Spaly, who cofounded pants retailer Bonobos while in college, recently became CEO of Trunk Club, a Chicago-based company that has taken the concept of a personal shopper that many upscale department stores provide for their best clients and moved it online. Fashion-challenged men around the world who need to dress well but do not enjoy shopping can go to the Trunk Club Web site and join for free. After answering some basic questions about their sizes and fashion preferences, they gain access to a personal shopper, who handles all of their clothing purchases and ships various items in a trunk at the customer's request. The typical trunk includes 6 to 10 items from companies such as Gant, Ben Sherman, Jack Spade, Barbour, Bonobos, and others that include items ranging from outerwear and shoes to suits and jeans, all based on the customer's individual preferences and style. The average price is $150 per item, and customers need only to text or e-mail their personal shoppers with a "send trunk" message to receive a trunk. Trunk Club pays all shipping costs (both ways), and customers pay only for the items they keep. The typical Trunk Club member, a professional man between the ages of 25 and 50 with an annual income that exceeds $100,000, keeps one-third of the items his personal shopper ships. "The apparel business is an area where there's a lot of room for innovation," says Spaly. Trunk Club recently landed an $11 million Round A investment led by venture capital firm U.S. Venture Partners and is on track to generate annual sales of $45 million.[10] ■

Entrepreneurship is the result of a disciplined, systematic process of applying creativity and innovation to needs and opportunities in the marketplace. It involves applying focused strategies to new ideas and new insights to create a product or a service that satisfies customers' needs or solves their problems. It is much more than random, disjointed tinkering with a new gadget. Millions of people come up with creative ideas for new or different products and services; most of them, however, never do anything with them. Entrepreneurs are people who connect their creative ideas with the purposeful action and structure of a business. Thus, successful entrepreneurship is a constant process that relies on creativity, innovation, and application in the marketplace.

Innovation must be a constant process because most ideas don't work and most innovations fail. One writer explains, "Trial—and lots of error—is embedded in entrepreneurship."[11] For every 5,000 to 10,000 new drug discoveries, only about 250 get to preclinical trials, and only 5 of those make it to clinical trials. Just one or two drugs emerge from clinical trials for review by the U.S. Food and Drug Administration, and only one typically gets to the market in a process that typically takes 10 to 15 years.[12] New products are crucial to companies' success, however. According to Robert Cooper, a researcher who has analyzed thousands of new product launches, new products (those launched within the previous three years) account for an impressive 38 percent of sales at top-performing companies.[13] Still, successful entrepreneurs recognize that many failures will accompany innovations, and they are willing to accept their share of failures because they know that failure is merely part of the creative process. Rather than quit when they fail, entrepreneurs simply keep trying. While working as a textbook editor, James Michener had an idea for a book based on his experiences in the Solomon Islands during World War II. He sent the manuscript to a publisher and received the following note: "You are a good editor. Don't throw it all away trying to be a writer. I read your book. Frankly, it's not really that good." Michener persisted and went on to publish *South Pacific*, for which he won a Pulitzer Prize and which became the basis for one of Broadway's most successful musicals of all time.[14]

Entrepreneurship requires business owners to be bold enough to try their new ideas, flexible enough to throw aside those that do not work, and wise enough to learn about what will work based on their observations of what did not. We now turn our attention to creativity, the creative process, and methods of enhancing creativity.

LO2

Describe why creativity
and innovation are
such an integral part of
entrepreneurship.

Creativity—Essential to Survival

In this fiercely competitive, fast-faced, global economy, creativity is not only an important source for building a competitive advantage but also a necessity for survival. When developing creative solutions to modern problems, entrepreneurs must go beyond merely relying on what has worked in the past. "The alternatives are to 'make change' or 'be changed,'" says Langdon Morris, cofounder of InnovationLabs and an expert on innovation. "Making change brings considerable advantages, but being changed carries a huge load of negative consequences. The choice isn't really a choice at all. You've got to pursue innovation, and you've got to do it to obtain long lasting benefits."[15] Companies that fail to become engines of innovation are more likely to lose ground to their more creative competitors and ultimately become irrelevant and close their doors. Transforming their organizations into engines of innovation requires entrepreneurs to cast off the limiting assumptions, beliefs, and behaviors and to develop new insights into the relationship among resources, needs, and value. In other words, they must change their perspectives, looking at the world in new and different ways.

Entrepreneurs must always be on guard against traditional assumptions and perspectives about how things ought to be because they are certain killers of creativity. Such self-imposed mental constraints that people tend to build over time push creativity right out the door. These ideas become so deeply rooted in our minds that they become immovable blocks to creative thinking—even though they may be outdated, obsolete, and no longer relevant. In short, they act as logjams to creativity. That's why children are so creative and curious about new possibilities; society has not yet brainwashed them into an attitude of conformity, nor have they learned to accept *traditional* solutions as the *only* solutions. By retaining their creative "inner child," entrepreneurs are able to throw off the shackles on creativity and see opportunities for creating viable businesses where most people see what they've always seen (or, worse yet, see nothing). Creative exercises, such as the one in Figure 3.1, can help adults reconnect with the creativity they exhibited so readily as children.

FIGURE 3.1

How Creative Are You? Can You Recognize the Well-Known Phrases These Symbols Represent?

Sources: Terry Stickels, "Frame Games," *USA Weekend*, June 28–30, 2013, p. 14; February 24–26, 2012, p. 15; August 30–September 1, 2013, p. 11; August 23–25, 2013, p. 14; July 5–7, 2013, p. 14; July 12–14, 2013, p. 14; July 26–28, 2013, p. 14; August 16–18, 2013, p. 14; August 9–11, 2013, p. 14; June 21–23, 2013, p. 14; August 2–4, 2013, p. 14; February 3–5, 2012, p. 14; March 22–24, 2013, p. 14; July 29–31, 2011, p. 14; March 2–4, 2012, p. 14; September 9–11, 2011, p. 18; May 24–26, 2013, p. 14.

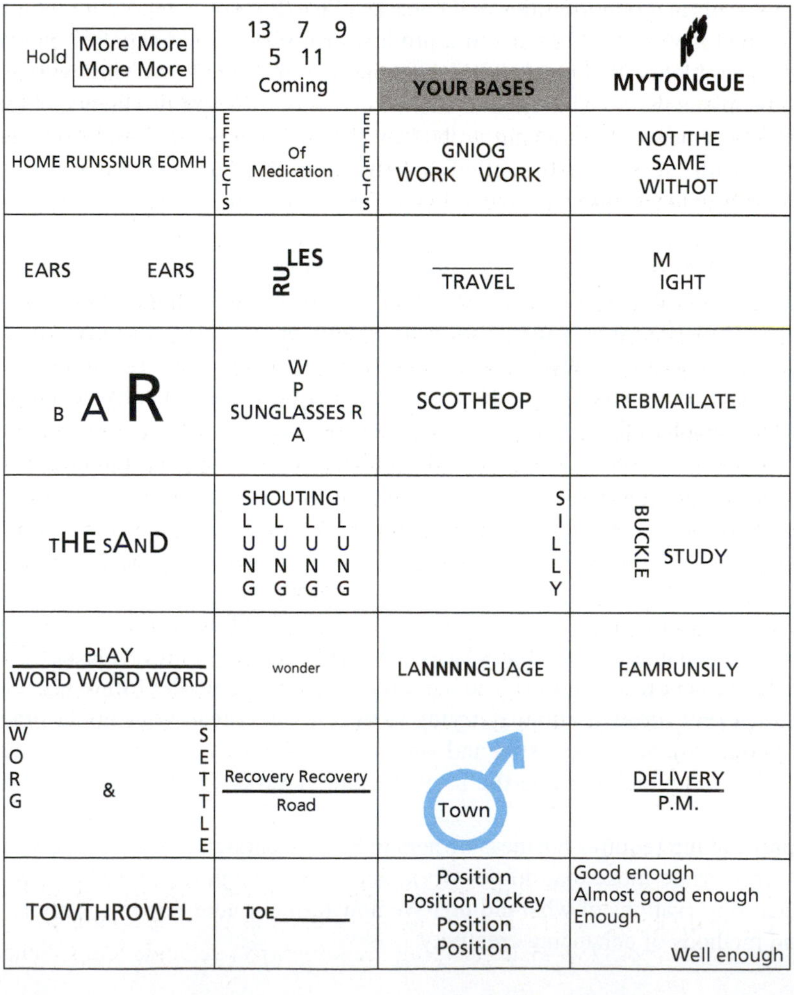

Many years ago, during an international chess competition, Frank Marshall made what has become known as one of the most beautiful—and one of the most creative—moves ever made on a chess board. In a crucial game in which he was evenly matched with a Russian master player, Marshall found his queen under serious attack. Marshall had several avenues of escape for his queen available. Knowing that the queen is one of the most important offensive players on the chessboard, spectators assumed that Marshall would make a conventional move and push his queen to safety.

Using all the time available to him to consider his options, Marshall picked up his queen—and paused—and put it down on the most *illogical* square of all—a square from which the queen could easily be captured by any one of three hostile pieces. Marshall had done the unthinkable! He had sacrificed his queen, a move typically made only under the most desperate of circumstances. All the spectators—even Marshall's opponent—groaned in dismay. Then the Russian (and finally the crowd) realized that Marshall's move was, in reality, a brilliant one. No matter how the Russian opponent took the queen, he would eventually be in a losing position. Seeing the inevitable outcome, the Russian conceded the game. Marshall had won the match in a rare and daring fashion: he had won by sacrificing his queen![16]

What lesson does this story hold for entrepreneurs? By suspending conventional thinking long enough to even consider the possibility of such a move, Marshall was able to throw off the usual assumptions constraining most chess players. He had looked beyond the traditional and orthodox strategies of the game and was willing to take the risk of trying an unusual tactic to win. The result: He won. Although not every creative business opportunity entrepreneurs take will be successful, many who, like Frank Marshall, are willing to go beyond conventional wisdom will be rewarded for their efforts. Successful entrepreneurs, those who are constantly pushing technological and economic boundaries forward, constantly ask, "Is it time to sacrifice the queen?"

Merely generating one successful creative solution to address a problem or a need usually is not good enough to keep an entrepreneurial enterprise successful in the long run, however. Success—even survival—in the modern world of business requires entrepreneurs to tap their creativity (and that of their employees) constantly. Entrepreneurs can be sure that if they have developed a unique, creative solution to solve a problem or to fill a need, a competitor (perhaps one six times zones away) is hard at work developing an even more creative solution to render theirs obsolete. This extremely rapid and accelerating rate of change has created an environment in which staying in a leadership position requires constant creativity, innovation, and entrepreneurship. A company that has achieved a leadership position in an industry but then stands still creatively is soon toppled from its number one perch.

Can Creativity Be Taught?

For many years, conventional wisdom held that a person was either creative—imaginative, free-spirited, entrepreneurial—or not—logical, narrow-minded, rigid. Today, we know better. Research shows that *anyone* can learn to be creative. "Every person can be taught techniques and behaviors that help them generate more ideas," says Joyce Wycoff, author of several books on creativity.[17] The problem is that in most organizations, employees have never been expected to be creative. In addition, many businesses fail to foster an environment that encourages creativity among employees. Restricted by their traditional thinking patterns, most people never tap into their pools of innate creativity, and the company becomes stagnant. Innovation produces a distinct competitive advantage for a company, empowers employees, and leads to higher levels of job satisfaction.

Not only can entrepreneurs and the people who work for them learn to think creatively, but they must for their companies' sake! "Innovation and creativity are not just for artists," says Wycoff. "These are skills with a direct, bottom-line payoff."[18] Before entrepreneurs can draw on their own creative capacity or stimulate creativity in their own organizations, they must understand creative thinking.

Creative Thinking

Research into the operation of the human brain shows that each hemisphere of the brain processes information differently and that one side of the brain tends to be dominant over the other. The human brain develops asymmetrically, and each hemisphere tends to specialize in certain

LO3

Understand how the two hemispheres of the human brain function and what role they play in creativity.

functions. The left brain is guided by linear, vertical thinking (from one logical conclusion to the next), whereas the right brain relies on kaleidoscopic, lateral thinking (considering a problem from all sides and jumping into it at different points). The left brain handles language, logic, and symbols; the right brain takes care of the body's emotional, intuitive, and spatial functions. The left brain processes information in a step-by-step fashion, but the right brain processes it intuitively—all at once, relying heavily on images.

Left-brain vertical thinking is narrowly focused and systematic, proceeding in a highly logical fashion from one point to the next. Right-brain lateral thinking, on the other hand, is somewhat unconventional, unsystematic, and unstructured, much like the image of a kaleidoscope, whirling around to form one pattern after another. It is this right brain–driven, lateral thinking that lies at the heart of the creative process. Those who have learned to develop their right-brain thinking skills tend to do the following:

- Always ask the question, "Is there a better way?"

- Challenge custom, routine, and tradition.

- Be reflective, often staring out windows, deep in thought. (How many traditional managers would stifle creativity by snapping these people out of their "daydreams," chastise them for "loafing," and admonish them to "get back to work"?)

- Be prolific thinkers. They know that generating lots of ideas increases the likelihood of coming up with a few highly creative ideas.

- Play mental games, trying to see an issue from different perspectives.

- Realize that there may be more than one "right answer."

Hövding/Splash News/Newscom

ENTREPRENEURIAL PROFILE: Anna Haupt and Terese Alstin: Hövding Anna Haupt and Terese Alstin, both students at Sweden's Lund University, recognized that many people incurred serious head injuries from bicycle accidents that they could have avoided if they had been wearing bicycle helmets. Their research showed that many people do not like to wear helmets because they are uncomfortable and don't look cool. The entrepreneurs believed that there was more than one solution to the bicycle helmet problem and created the Hövding Invisible Bike Helmet, which really is not a helmet at all but a collar that contains an airbag shaped like a hood. The invisible helmet uses rechargeable battery-powered accelerometers and gyroscopes that detect the motions involved in a bike crash and trigger a tiny gas inflator that fills a nylon airbag with helium in 0.1 seconds, protecting the cyclist's head from impact. Their company, Hövding, already has raised $13 million in venture capital and has 16 employees.[19] ■

- See mistakes as mere "pit stops" on the way to success.

- See problems as springboards for new ideas.

ENTREPRENEURIAL PROFILE: David Williams: Comfe Designs David Williams's idea came to him while he was reading a book that rested uncomfortably in his hands. He realized that tablet users faced the same problem and developed Comfe Hands, two soft PVC corners that fit on the corners of a tablet, giving it a shape that fits the human hand more naturally. Williams designed his first prototype that weekend, creating it out of a piece of scrap cardboard. After testing his prototypes on actual tablet users and receiving positive feedback, Williams launched Comfe Designs as a part-time business. When his job was eliminated, which he says is the best thing that ever happened to him, Williams made Comfe Designs a full-time business. Williams's company is working on designs to improve the performance of other devices, including smartphones, sound systems, and television monitors. The company's strategy is to identify problems with existing products and to create a solution that improves customers' interaction with that product.[20] ∎

- Understand that failure is a natural part of the creative process. James Dyson spent 15 years and nearly his entire savings before he succeeded in developing the bagless vacuum cleaner that made him rich and famous. To discover something truly new, Dyson says, one must make mistakes because success teaches very few lessons.

- Have "helicopter skills," the ability to rise above the daily routine to see an issue from a broader perspective and then swoop back down to focus on an area in need of change.

- Relate seemingly unrelated ideas to a problem to generate innovative solutions.

ENTREPRENEURIAL PROFILE: Charles Kaman: Kaman Aircraft Company and Ovation Instruments After graduating from college, Charles Kaman worked in the helicopter division of United Aircraft Corporation, where he helped to design helicopters for the military. Using a homemade calculator he called the Aeronalyzer, Kaman developed several innovations in rotor and wing designs, in none of which his employer showed any interest. In 1945, with $2,000 and his idea for a new dual rotor system that made helicopters more stable and safer to fly, 26-year-old Kaman, also an accomplished guitarist, turned down an offer to join Tommy Dorsey's famous swing band and decided to pursue his innovative designs for helicopters. He started the Kaman Aircraft Company in his mother's garage. Over the next 50 years, Kaman built his company into a billion-dollar aviation business, creating many important innovations along the way, including turbine engines, blades made of lightweight, sturdy composite materials, and remote-controlled helicopters. Kaman also maintained an avid interest in guitars and in 1964 began working with a small team of aerospace engineers to build a better acoustic guitar. Drawing on their experience of removing vibrations from helicopters, the team reverse-engineered a guitar with a bowl-shaped body made of composite materials that incorporated more vibration into the instrument, giving it a bolder, richer sound. "In helicopters, engineers spend all of their time trying to figure out how to remove vibration," Kaman said. "To build a guitar, you spend your time trying to figure out how to put vibration in." Kaman founded Ovation Instruments in 1966 and began selling the Balladeer, an acoustical guitar that immediately attracted attention for its superior tone and volume among musicians, including famous artists such as John Lennon, Glen Campbell, Bob Marley, Carly Simon, Jimmy Page, and Melissa Etheridge.[21] ∎

Although each hemisphere of the brain tends to dominate in its particular functions, the two halves normally cooperate, with each part contributing its special abilities to accomplish those tasks best suited to its mode of information processing. Sometimes, however, the two hemispheres may even compete with each other, or one half may choose not to participate. Some researchers have suggested that each half of the brain has the capacity to keep information from the other! The result, literally, is that "the left hand doesn't know what the right hand is doing." Perhaps the most important characteristic of this split-brain phenomenon is that an individual can learn to control which side of the brain is dominant in a given situation. In other words, a person can learn to "turn down" the dominant left hemisphere (focusing on logic and linear thinking) and "turn up" the right hemisphere (focusing on intuition and unstructured thinking) when a situation requiring creativity arises.[22] To get a little practice at this "shift," try the visual exercises presented in Figure 3.2. When viewed from one perspective, the picture B on the right portrays an attractive young lady with a feather in her hair and a boa around her shoulders. Once you shift your perspective, however, you will see an old woman with a large nose wearing a scarf on her head! This change in the image seen is the result of a shift from one hemisphere in the viewer's brain to the other. With practice, a person can learn to control this mental shift, tapping the pool of creativity that lies hidden within the right side of the brain. This ability has tremendous power to unleash the creative capacity of entrepreneurs. The need to develop this creative ability means that exploring inner space (the space within our brains)—not outer space—becomes the challenge of the century.

FIGURE 3.2

What Do You See?

In panel A, do you see the vase or the twins?
In panel B, do you see the old woman with a scarf on her head or the young woman looking away?
In panel C, do you see the face of Jesus?

Sources: Thomas W. Zimmerer and Norman M. Scarborough, *Entrepreneurship and New Venture Formation.* © 1995. Reprinted by permission of Prentice Hall, Inc., Upper Saddle River, NJ.

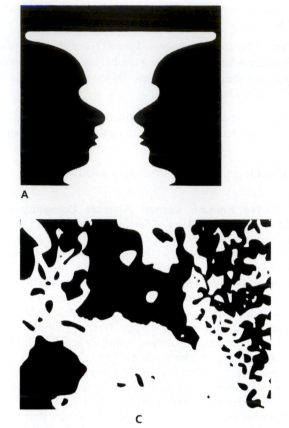

Successful entrepreneurship requires both left- and right-brain thinking. Right-brain thinking draws on the power of divergent reasoning, which is the ability to create a multitude of original, diverse ideas. Left-brain thinking counts on convergent reasoning, the ability to evaluate multiple ideas and choose the best solution to a given problem. Entrepreneurs need to rely on right-brain thinking to generate innovative product, service, or business ideas. Then they must use left-brain thinking to judge the market potential of the ideas they generate. Successful entrepreneurs have learned to coordinate the complementary functions of each hemisphere of the brain, using their brains' full creative power to produce pragmatic innovation. Otherwise, entrepreneurs, who rarely can be accused of being "halfhearted" about their business ideas, run the risk of becoming "halfheaded."

How can entrepreneurs learn to tap their innate creativity more readily? The first step is to break down the barriers to creativity that most of us have erected over the years. We now turn our attention to these barriers and some suggested techniques for tearing them down.

LO4

Explain the 10 "mental locks" that limit individual creativity.

Barriers to Creativity

The number of potential barriers to creativity is virtually limitless—time pressures, unsupportive management, pessimistic coworkers, overly rigid company policies, and countless others. Perhaps the most difficult hurdles to overcome, however, are those that individuals impose on themselves. In his book *A Whack on the Side of the Head*, Roger von Oech identifies 10 "mental locks" that limit individual creativity:[23]

1. *Searching for the one "right" answer.* Recent research by Kyung Hee Kim, a professor at the College of William & Mary, shows that creativity (as measured by the Torrance Test of Creative Thinking) among both children and adults in the United States has declined markedly since 1990. The decline, which Kim says is "very significant," is particularly acute among the youngest segment of the population, children from kindergarten to

You Be the Consultant

10 Keys to Business Innovation

Creativity expert Teresa Amabile identifies three components of creativity: (1) **Expertise**. One must have the technical, procedural, and conceptual knowledge to generate potential solutions to a problem. (2) **Creative thinking skills.** A person must possess the willingness to take risks and to see problems or situations from different perspectives, using many of the techniques described in this chapter. (3) **Motivation**. One must have the internal desire to develop creative solutions. This motivation often comes from the challenge that the work itself presents.

Entrepreneurs and their employees can transform their companies into engines of innovation by combining these three components of creativity with what management consultant The Doblin Group calls the 10 types of innovation.

1. **Business model.** How does your company make money? These are innovations in the value proposition that a company provides its target customers and in the way it delivers value to its customers.

2. **Networks and alliances.** Can you join forces with another company or entity for mutual benefit? A company may forge a synergistic relationship with another organization in which each company's strengths complement the other.

3. **Organizational structure.** How do you support and encourage your employees' creative efforts? The most effective organizations use an appropriate structure and culture to align their talent to spark innovation.

4. **Core process.** How does your company create and add value for customers? These innovations in a company's internal processes result in superior business systems and work methods that result in benefits for customers.

5. **Product or service performance.** What are the most important features and functions of your company's products or services? Innovations in functions and features can give a company's product or service a significant edge over those of competitors.

6. **Product system.** Can you link multiple products into a system or a platform? Bundling products can add value for customers.

7. **Service.** How do you provide value-added service beyond your company's products for customers? Some of the most successful businesses set themselves apart from their competition by providing unparalleled customer service.

8. **Channel.** How do you get your products or services into customers' hands? Some companies provide extra value to their customers by making their products and services available in many venues.

9. **Brand.** What is your company's "identity" in the marketplace? Successful companies use creative advertising, promotion, and marketing techniques to build a desirable brand identity with customers.

10. **Customer experience.** Does your company engage customers and give them reasons to come back to make future purchases? Innovative companies find ways to connect with their customers, creating a loyal base of "fansumers," customers who not only purchase but act like fans who promote the company to their friends and family members.

Boatbound

Serial entrepreneur Aaron Hall took note of the "sharing economy" that emerged during the last recession and launched Boatbound, a peer-to-peer boat rental company that brings together boat owners who are willing to rent their boats when they are not in use and people who want a fun boating experience without the cost of owning a boat. Hall realized that 12.2 million boats are registered in the United States, yet the average owner uses his or her boat just 26 days per year. Boatbound screens all potential renters, verifies the condition and the safety of each boat, carries ample insurance on each boat, and covers general liability. Boat owners select their renters from Boatbound's pool of applicants and set daily rental fees, and Boatbound collects 35 percent of the fee. Boatbound has rented every kind of boat, from kayaks to yachts with captains. Fees range from $200 to $8,500 per day. "As a boat owner and someone in the marine industry, I've been waiting for something like this my whole life," says Aabad Melwani, owner of a marina. "I just didn't know it."

Henrybuilt

Scott Hudson, CEO of Henrybuilt, had created a profitable niche designing and building upscale kitchens that ranged from $30,000 to $100,000. In 2006, Hudson opened a New York City showroom, which doubled in size in just 18 months. By 2008, the company had more than 200 jobs in the United States, Mexico, and Canada. When the recession hit, however, new projects came to a standstill, and customers began cancelling orders. In response, Hudson launched a subsidiary, Viola Park Corporation, that provides customers lower-cost remodeling options that use its software rather than an architect to create "custom" variations on Henrybuilt designs. The result is a process that produces a kitchen much faster and at half the cost of a Henrybuilt kitchen. Henrybuilt sales have recovered, but Viola Park accounts for 20 percent of sales and is growing twice as fast as Henrybuilt.

Unequal Technologies

Robert Vito started Unequal Technologies in 2008 to supply protective clothing and gear, including bullet-proof vests, to military contractors. The protective gear is made from a lightweight yet strong composite material that he developed and patented. Two years later, the equipment manager of the Philadelphia Eagles called to ask whether Unequal Technologies could create a special garment for one of its star players who had suffered a sternum injury. Vito modified the bullet-proof vest for the player and soon had other players in the National Football League asking for protective gear. Unequal technologies went on to develop Concussion Reduction Technology (CRT), peel-and-stick pads for football helmets that are made from

(continued)

You Be the Consultant (continued)

the composite and that absorb and disperse the force of an impact before it reaches the skull. Independent tests show that CRT reduces the risk of head injuries from impact by 53 percent. The company now supplies equipment to 27 of the NFL's 32 teams and has its sights set on an even larger market: amateur sports. Vito says Unequal's technology gives the company a competitive edge that has allowed it to increase sales from $1 million to $20 million in just one year.

1. Select one of these businesses and explain which of the 10 types of innovation the company used to bolster its success.

2. Explain how the company you selected in question 1 could use at least one of the remaining types of innovation to increase its sales and profitability.

Sources: Based on Teresa M. Amabile, "Componential Theory of Creativity," Harvard Business School, Working Paper 12-096, April 26, 2012, pp. 2–3; Robert F. Brands, "Stay Inspired This Holiday Season: The 12 Days of Innovation," *Huffington Post*, December 20, 2012, http://www.huffingtonpost.com/robert-f-brands/stay-inspired-holiday-season_b_2334305.html; Paul Davis, "Innovation White Paper," Scanlon Leadership Network, January 2008, p. 3; Nancy Dahlberg, "Making Waves in 'the Sharing Economy': Peer-to-Peer Rental Companies Arrive in South Florida," *Miami Herald*, September 15, 2013, http://www.miamiherald.com/2013/09/15/3626239/making-waves.html; Sarah E. Needleman, Vanessa O'Connell, Emily Maltby, and Angus Loten, "And the Most Innovative Entrepreneur Is . . ." *Wall Street Journal*, November 14, 2011, pp. R1, R4; April Joyner, "Unequal Technologies," *Inc.*, February 2013, p. 26; Suzanne Barlyn, "New and Improved," *Wall Street Journal*, April 23, 2009, http://online.wsj.com/article/SB124025160159735869.html; Kelly Spors, "Tough Times Call for New Ideas," *Wall Street Journal*, February 15, 2009, http://online.wsj.com/article/SB123466563957289181.html; and Gene Marks, "Why Most Small Businesses Will Beat the Recession," *Bloomberg Business Week*, January 8, 2009, http://www.businessweek.com/smallbiz/content/jan2009/sb2009015_212410.htm.

sixth grade.[24] Part of the problem is that deeply ingrained in most educational systems is the assumption that there is one "right" answer to a problem. In reality, however, most problems are ambiguous. The average student who has completed four years of college has taken more than 2,600 tests; therefore, it is not unusual for this one-correct-answer syndrome to become an inherent part of our thinking. Although everyone has the capacity to be creative, not everyone develops that capacity. Most education systems do not do much to encourage creativity among students; instead, they promote uniformity and standardization. People who go through many years of schooling often come out on the other side drained of their creative potential and focused on conformity rather than on creativity.

Depending on the questions one asks, there may be (and usually are) several "right" answers.

Sam Gangwer/SUMAPRESS/Newscom

ENTREPRENEURIAL PROFILE: Jason Lucash and Mike Szymczak: OrigAudio Jason Lucash and Mike Szymczak grew tired of hauling bulky audio players as part of their jobs with JanSport, a maker of sports, travel, business, and tote bags, and began experimenting with designs for pop-up speakers. (Their early experiments involved putting speakers into Chinese food takeout boxes.) With $10,000 in seed money from Lucash's mother, the entrepreneurs launched OrigAudio (a mash-up of "origami" and "audio") and introduced their first product: speakers made from recycled material that come flat and fold together. "The Chinese takeout box concept inspired us," says Lucash, "but origami is what empowered us." Sales took off quickly, and Lucash and Szymczak left their jobs to manage OrigAudio full time. OrigAudio now has 14 employees and generates $4 million in annual sales from nine products, including the Rock-It, a small, simple device that turns almost anything—a cooler, a cup, a bowl, a box, a painting, a lampshade—into a speaker.[25] ∎

2. *Focusing on "being logical."* Logic is a valuable part of the creative process, especially when evaluating ideas and implementing them. However, in the early imaginative phases of the process, logical thinking can restrict creativity. Focusing too much effort on being logical also discourages the use of one of the mind's most powerful creations: intuition. Von Oech advises us to "think something different" and to use nonlogical thinking freely, especially in the imaginative phase of the creative process. Intuition, which is based on the accumulated knowledge and experiences a person encounters over the course of a lifetime and which resides in the subconscious, can be unlocked. It is a crucial part of the

creative process because using it often requires one to tear down long-standing assumptions that limit creativity and innovation.

ENTREPRENEURIAL PROFILE: Chuck Swoboda: Cree, Inc. Chuck Swoboda, CEO of Cree, Inc., a lighting manufacturer based in Durham, North Carolina, realized that the design of the light bulb had remained virtually unchanged in the 130 years since Thomas Edison invented it. Cree, founded in 1987, produced highly efficient, long-lasting LED lights, but LEDs suffer from one problem: They emit light in only one direction, which makes them poor substitutes for traditional incandescent and fluorescent bulbs, which produce omnidirectional light for broad coverage. Designers at the innovative company redesigned the traditional filament towers (the heart of a bulb) to include up to 20 small LED bulbs of different colors aligned at different (and overlapping) angles that create an omnidirectional glow that mimics the light from an incandescent bulb. When Cree made an initial public offering in 1993, the company had just 30 employees; today, its workforce exceeds 6,000.[26] ■

3. *Blindly following the rules.* We learn at a very early age not to "color outside the lines," and we spend the rest of our lives blindly obeying such rules. Sometimes, creativity depends on our ability to break the existing rules so that we can see new ways of doing things. "Most people's minds are not wired to go against what everybody else is doing," observes neuroscientist Gregory Berns. "When you look at problems, you tend to perceive them in well-worn paths in ways that you've perceived them before. That's the first roadblock in innovating: overcoming your perceptual biases."[27]

ENTREPRENEURIAL PROFILE: King Gillette: Gillette Safety Razor Company In 1895, King Gillette, a traveling salesman who aspired to be an entrepreneur, was shaving with a straight razor, the standard technology of the day, when a creative idea struck him: a "safety razor" that consisted of a small, thin square of sheet steel held in place by a holder equipped with a handle. When a blade became dull, the user would simply replace it. "I saw it all in a moment," Gillette said. "The way the blade would be held in a holder. Then came the idea of sharpening the two opposite edges of a thin piece of steel, and then came the clamping plates for the blades, with a handle centered between the edges. I stood there in a trance of joy." Gillette visited metallurgists at the nearby Massachusetts Institute of Technology, who assured him that it would be *impossible* to produce steel that was thin enough, sharp enough, and inexpensive enough to produce blades for his safety razor. After six years of work, however, two business associates introduced the determined Gillette to William Nickerson, an MIT graduate who produced the blade that Gillette had designed. Gillette received patent number 775,134 for his safety razor from the U.S. Patent and Trademark Office in 1904. The American Safety Razor Company, which later became Gillette Safety Razor Company, began producing blades in Boston in 1903, and the world of shaving was transformed forever because Gillette was willing to question the established "rules" of shaving. Procter and Gamble purchased Gillette in 2005 for $57 billion.[28] ■

4. *Constantly being practical.* Imagining impractical answers to "what-if" questions can be powerful stepping stones to creative ideas. Suspending practicality for a while frees the mind to consider creative solutions that otherwise might never arise. Whenever Thomas Edison hired an assistant to work in his creative laboratory, he would tell the new employee to walk through town and list 20 things that interest him. When the worker returned, Edison would ask him to split the list into two columns. Then he would tell the employee to randomly combine objects from the two columns to come up with as many inventions as he could. Edison's methods for stimulating creativity in his lab proved to be successful; he holds the distinction of being the only person to have earned a patent every year for 65 consecutive years![29]

Periodically setting aside practicality allows entrepreneurs to consider taking a product or a concept from one area and placing it in a totally different application.

ENTREPRENEURIAL PROFILE: GEWOS Chair Researchers at Germany's Fraunhofer Institute for Integrated Circuits threw out practical assumptions when they created an armchair that converts into a rowing machine. Their goal was to develop a device that allows the elderly or the disabled to get fit without having to leave the comfort of their living rooms. The GEWOS (the acronym for the German phrase that translates "Healthy Living with Style") chair, which took three-and-a-half years to develop, features armrests that raise to reveal rowing handles and built-in sensors that monitor the seated person's heart rate, blood pressure, and oxygen saturation levels. Sensors also indicate whether the user is sitting in the proper posture to avoid back injuries. An accompanying tablet includes a virtual fitness assistant that analyzes a user's data over time and recommends customized exercise plans. When not in use as a rowing machine, the chair looks like any other comfortable armchair. Early tests with senior citizens indicate that the GEWOS chair is a big hit.[30] ■

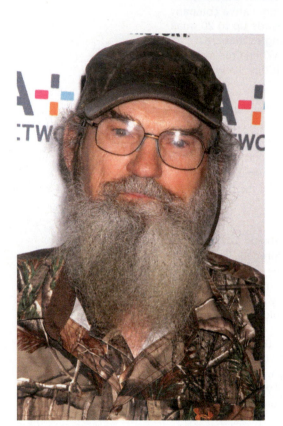

Splash News/Newscom

5. *Viewing play as frivolous.* A playful attitude is fundamental to creative thinking. There is a close relationship between the "haha" of humor and the "aha" of discovery. Play gives us the opportunity to reinvent reality and to reformulate established ways of doing things. Children learn when they play, and so can entrepreneurs. Watch children playing, and you will see them invent new games, create new ways of looking at old things, and learn what works (and what doesn't) in their games.

Entrepreneurs can benefit from playing in the same way that children do. They, too, can learn to try new approaches and discover what works and what doesn't. Creativity results when entrepreneurs take what they have learned at play, evaluate it, corroborate it with other knowledge, and put it into practice. Zappos, the online shoe retailer that makes regular appearances on *Fortune's* Best Places to Work list, includes "create fun and a little weirdness" as one of its core values. "Our company culture is what makes us successful," says CEO Tony Hsieh. "We want to be able to laugh at ourselves. We look for both fun and humor in our daily work."[31] Encouraging employees to have fun when solving problems means that they are more likely to push the boundaries and come up with genuinely creative solutions. What kind of invention would Wile E. Coyote, who seems to have an inexhaustible supply of ideas for catching the Roadrunner in those cartoons, create in this situation? How might the Three Stooges approach this problem? What would Kramer of *Seinfeld* suggest? What solution would Si from *Duck Dynasty* offer? What would a six-year-old do? The idea is to look at a problem or situation from different perspectives.

ENTREPRENEURIAL PROFILE: Stu Snyder: Cartoon Network PlayWorks, an organization dedicated to promoting the creative power of play, recently named Stu Snyder, CEO of the Cartoon Network, as the Most Playful CEO in the country. Employees are likely to see Stu riding his oversized tricycle around company headquarters or hear him ring a gong to celebrate a worker's or team's accomplishment, which is followed by cheers and hoots of laughter from employees. "I'm a believer of leading by play," says Snyder. "We're all teammates. Playing, having fun, and laughing together help us enjoy our jobs and improve our work ethic." Snyder also recognizes the power of play to unleash people's creative spirit. "Stu's playful leadership allows employees to be more creative and to take the risk to go full force with their creative ideas," says one employee.[32] ■

myopic thinking
a type of thinking that destroys creativity because it is narrowly focused and limited by the status quo.

6. *Becoming overly specialized.* A common killer of creativity is **myopic thinking**, which is narrowly focused and limited by the status quo. Because experts are so immersed in what they know, they often are victims of myopic thinking. That's why creative companies include *non-experts* in creative problem solving or idea generation sessions; they are free to ask questions and offer ideas that challenge the status quo and traditional solutions that experts "know" cannot work but often do. Creative thinkers tend to be "explorers," searching for ideas outside their areas of specialty. The idea for the roll-on deodorant stick came from the ballpoint pen. The famous Mr. Potato Head toy was invented by a father sitting with his family at the dinner table who noted how much fun his children had playing with

their food. Velcro (a combination of "velvet" and "crochet") was invented by Swiss engineer Georges de Mestral, who, while hiking one day in 1941 to take a break from work, had to stop to peel sticky cockleburs from his clothing. As he picked them off, he noticed how their hooked spines caught on and held tightly to the cloth. When he resumed his hike, he began to think about the possibilities of using a similar design to fasten objects together. After eight years of research and work, Mestral perfected his design for Velcro, which he patented in 1955.[33]

ENTREPRENEURIAL PROFILE: Lynn Perkins, Daisy Downs, Andrea Barrett, and Hadar Wissotzky: UrbanSitter Late in 2010, Lynn Perkins, a mother of twin boys and founder of on-line clothing company Xuny, was having trouble finding a babysitter, a problem that she and many of her friends encountered often. She wondered why she could book an online restaurant reservation so easily, yet had to spend hours sometimes making phone calls and sending e-mails to find a babysitter. Perkins knew that there had to be a better way and, drawing inspiration from the online restaurant booking service OpenTable, convinced three friends, Daisy Downs, Andrea Barrett, and Hadar Wissotzky, to launch UrbanSitter, a San Francisco-based company that uses Facebook to connect parents and babysitters. Tapping (with permission) into Facebook contacts, groups, and likes, UrbanSitter's software identifies potential babysitters and generates a list that enables parents to review rates, conduct background checks, schedule interviews, and book sitters online. The service also allows parents to see which babysitters their friends have used and reviewed, which, Perkins points out, puts parents' minds at ease when bringing in someone for the first time to care for their

Courtesy of UrbanSitter

children. Just six months after launching UrbanSitter, Perkins and her cofounders expanded the service to New York City, Chicago, Denver, Seattle, St, Louis, and Lake Tahoe/Reno, Nevada.[34] ∎

7. *Avoiding ambiguity.* Ambiguity can be a powerful creative stimulus; it encourages us to "think something different." Being excessively detailed in an imaginative situation tends to stifle creativity. Ambiguity, however, requires us to consider at least two different, often contradictory notions at the same time, which is a direct channel to creativity. Ambiguous situations force us to stretch our minds beyond their normal boundaries and to consider creative options we might otherwise ignore. Although ambiguity is not a desired element when entrepreneurs are evaluating and implementing ideas, it is a valuable tool when they are searching for creative ideas and solutions. Entrepreneurs are famous for asking a question and then going beyond the first answer to explore other possible answers. The result is that they often find business opportunities by creating ambiguous situations.

8. *Fearing looking foolish.* Creative thinking is no place for conformity! New ideas rarely are born in a conforming environment. People tend toward conformity because they don't want to look foolish. The fool's job is to whack at the habits and rules that keep us thinking in the same old ways. In that sense, entrepreneurs are top-notch "fools." They are constantly questioning and challenging accepted ways of doing things and the assumptions that go with them. The noted entrepreneurship theorist Joseph Schumpeter wrote that entrepreneurs perform a vital function—"creative destruction"—in which they rethink conventional assumptions and discard those that are no longer useful. According to Schumpeter, "The function of entrepreneurs is to reform or revolutionize the pattern of production by exploiting an invention or, more generally, an untried technological possibility for producing a new commodity or producing an old one in a new way, by opening up a new source of supply of materials or a new outlet for products, by reorganizing an industry or so on."[35] In short, entrepreneurs look at old ways of doing things and ask, "Is there a better way?" By destroying the old, they create the new.

ENTREPRENEURIAL PROFILE: Neurowear: Mico Headphones Neurowear, a company based in Tokyo, Japan, has developed technology that makes creating a playlists on your smartphone or MP3 player unnecessary. The company's Mico headphones include sensors that monitor the user's brain activity (different patterns in the prefrontal cortex indicate different moods) to select the appropriate type of music. Neurowear says that Mico headphones provide "music inspiration from your subconscious." Tense? Mico will select a soothing ballad or a piece of classical music from your player to relax you. Drowsy? The headphones will select an upbeat, energetic tune to get you moving.[36] ■

9. *Fearing mistakes and failure.* Creative people realize that trying something new often leads to failure; however, they do not see failure as an end. It represents a learning experience on the way to success. As you learned in Chapter 1, failure is an important part of the creative process; it signals entrepreneurs when to change their course of action. Entrepreneurship is all about the opportunity to fail! Many entrepreneurs failed numerous times before finally succeeding. Despite their initial setbacks, they were able to set aside the fear of failure and keep trying.

ENTREPRENEURIAL PROFILE: Arianna Huffington: Huffington Post Arianna Huffington, author of a dozen books and founder of the news and blog Web site Huffington Post, says, "I love talking about my failures more than my successes. Think of failure as a stepping-stone to success. I was rejected by 35 publishers before getting to yes." The highly successful Huffington Post, which Huffington launched in 2005, attracts more than 50 million unique visitors per month, more than the Web sites of any major newspaper in the United States.[37] ■

The key is to see failure for what it really is: a chance to learn how to succeed. Entrepreneurs who willingly risk failure and learn from it when it occurs have the best chance of succeeding at whatever they try. Charles F. Kettering, a famous inventor (he invented the lighting and ignition systems in automobiles, among other things), explains, "You fail because your ideas aren't right, but you should learn to fail intelligently. When you fail, find out *why* you failed and each time it will bring you nearer to the goal."[38] Successful entrepreneurs equate failure with innovation rather than with defeat.

Thanks to technology, the cost of failed attempts at innovation has never been lower. Entrepreneurs and companies can test new ideas at speeds and costs that were unimaginable only a few years ago. Building prototypes, getting them into potential customers' hands, and getting useful feedback on them has never been easier and less expensive. Entrepreneurs use the Internet and social media to test their business models and determine whether customers are interested in purchasing their product and service innovations.

10. *Believing that "I'm not creative."* Some people limit themselves because they believe that creativity belongs only to the Einsteins, Beethovens, and da Vincis of the world. Unfortunately, this belief often becomes a self-fulfilling prophecy. A person who believes that he or she is not creative will, in all likelihood, behave that way and will make that belief come true. Some people who are considered geniuses, visionaries, and inventors actually are no smarter and have no more innate creative ability than the average person; however, they have learned how to think creatively and are persistent enough to keep trying until they succeed.

Successful entrepreneurs recognize that "I'm not creative" is merely an excuse for inaction. *Everyone* has within him or her the potential to be creative; not everyone will tap that potential, however. Successful entrepreneurs find a way to unleash their creative powers on problems and opportunities.

By avoiding these 10 mental locks, entrepreneurs can unleash their own creativity and the creativity of those around them as well. Successful entrepreneurs are willing to take some risks, explore new ideas, play a little, ask "What if?" and learn to appreciate ambiguity. By doing so,

TABLE 3.1 Questions to Spur the Imagination

We learn at an early age to pursue answers to questions. Creative people, however, understand that *good questions* are extremely valuable in the quest for creativity. Some of the greatest breakthroughs in history came as a result of creative people asking thought-provoking questions. Bill Bowerman, contemplating a design for the soles of running shoes over a breakfast of waffles, asked, "What would happen if I poured rubber into my waffle iron?" He did, and that's how Nike shoes came to be. (Bowerman's rubber-coated waffle iron is on display in the Nike Town superstore and museum in Chicago.) Albert Einstein, creator of the theory of relativity, asked, "What would a light wave look like to someone keeping pace with it?"

To jump-start creativity, Steve Gillman suggests writing a short list of adjectives, such as *light, cheap, fast, big, short, small,* and *fun,* and using them to ask what-if questions. What if this product could be lighter? What if this process could be faster? What if this service could be cheaper?

The following questions can help spur your imagination:

1. Is there a new way to do it?
2. Can you borrow or adapt it?
3. Can you give it a new twist?
4. Do you merely need more of the same?
5. Less of the same?
6. Is there a substitute?
7. Can you rearrange the parts?
8. What if you do just the opposite?
9. Can you combine ideas?
10. Are customers using your product or service in ways you never expected or intended? (other markets)
11. Which customers are you not serving? What changes to your product or service are necessary to reach them?
12. Can you put it to other uses?
13. What else could we make from this?
14. Are there other markets for it?
15. Can you reverse it?
16. Can you rearrange it?
17. Can you put it to another use?
18. What idea seems impossible but, if executed, would revolutionize your business?

Bob Purcell, CEO of Protean Electric, based in Auburn Hills, Michigan, asked a simple but profound question: "What if we could convert *any* vehicle into a hybrid?" That question led the employees at the company to develop the Protean Drive Motor, a 68-pound motor that installs directly onto an existing vehicle's wheels and converts them to direct-drive, which eliminates the need for a transmission. Because the Protean Drive Motor contains a power inverter, electronics, and software to drive the system and costs between $1,500 and $1,800, it can be easily integrated into most existing vehicles, converting them to hybrid electric or pure electric vehicles without adding significant weight or cost. A lithium-ion battery pack installed beneath the car's trunk and the car's engine power the drive motors. The sophisticated system also funnels to the drive motors up to 85 percent of the kinetic energy it captures when the car brakes. Studies show that equipping a car with two drive motors adds 220 horsepower and improves its fuel efficiency by 30 percent. Protean Electric recently landed $84 million in venture capital to finance the construction of a factory in Liyang, China, and is working with several automakers around the world to implement its fuel-saving technology. Protean has received 27 patents for its technology and designs.

Sources: Based on Chuck Frey, "How to Develop a Powerful Arsenal of Creative Questions," *Innovation Tools*, March 1, 2011, http://www .innovationtools.com/weblog/innovationblog-detail.asp?ArticleID=1570; David Lidsky, "Brain Calisthenics," *Fast Company*, December 2004, p. 95; Thea Singer, Christopher Caggiano, Ilan Mochari, and Tahl Raz, "If You Come, They Will Build It," *Inc.*, August 2002, p. 70; Creativity Web, "Question Summary," http://www.ozemail.com.au/~caveman/Creative/Techniques/osb_quest.html; *Bits & Pieces*, February 1990, p. 20; *Bits & Pieces*, April 29, 1993; "Creativity Quiz," *In Business*, November/December 1991, p. 18; Doug Hall, *Jump Start Your Brain* (New York: Warner Books, 1995), pp. 86–87; Christine Canabou, "Imagine That," *Fast Company*, January 2001, p. 56; Steve Gillman, "Step Out of Business Mode to Solve Problems," *Regan's Manager's eBulletin*, May 22, 2008, p. 1; Nicole Dyer, "Innovation," *Inc.*, October 12, 2012, pp. 38–39; Angus MacKenzie, "Smack Torque: Protean Electric Launches New In-Wheel Drive System," *GizMag*, April 17, 2013, http://www.gizmag.com/protean-electric-unveils-in-wheel-electric-drive-system-for-hybrids-and-evs/27110/.

they develop the skills, attitudes, and motivation that make them much more creative—one of the keys to entrepreneurial success. Table 3.1 lists some questions designed to spur imagination.

How to Enhance Creativity

Enhancing Organizational Creativity

Creativity doesn't just happen in organizations; entrepreneurs must establish an environment in which creativity can flourish—for themselves and for their workers. "Everyone has a creative spark, but many factors can inhibit its ignition," says one writer. "Part of an [entrepreneur's] role is to see

LO5

Understand how entrepreneurs can enhance the creativity of their employees as well as their own creativity.

the spark in his or her people, encourage its ignition, and champion its success."[39] New ideas are fragile creations, but the right company culture can encourage people to develop and cultivate them. Ensuring that workers have the freedom and the incentive to be creative is one of the best ways to achieve innovation. Entrepreneurs can stimulate their own creativity and encourage it among workers by following these suggestions, which are designed to create a culture of innovation.

INCLUDE CREATIVITY AS A CORE COMPANY VALUE AND MAKE IT AN INTEGRAL PART OF THE COMPANY'S CULTURE Innovative companies do not take a passive approach to creativity; they are proactive in their search for new ideas. One of the best ways to set a creative tone throughout an organization begins with the company's mission statement. Entrepreneurs should incorporate creativity and innovation into their companies' mission statements and affirm their commitment to them in internal communications. Bell Labs, a predecessor to the high-tech companies of Silicon Valley, was the birthplace of some of the world's greatest inventions, including the semiconductor chip, optical fiber, communication satellites, C programming language, and many others, from the 1920s to the 1960s. For most of those years, Mervin Kelly, a former researcher, led the company with his vision of establishing an "institute of creative technology" that fostered "a busy exchange of ideas." Employees at Bell Labs understood that their mission was to transform new knowledge into transformational products that the company could commercialize.[40] As Bell Labs proved, innovation allows a company to shape, transform, and create its future, and the starting point for defining that future is in the mission statement. If creativity and innovation are vital to a company's success (and they usually are!), they also should be a natural part of the performance appraisal process.

Innovation can be a particularly powerful competitive weapon in industries that are resistant to change and are populated by companies that cling to the same old ways of doing business. Even small companies that are willing to innovate can have a significant impact on entire industries by shaking up the status quo with their creative approaches. The result often is growing market share and impressive profits for the innovator.

ENTREPRENEURIAL PROFILE: T. J. Scimone: Slice T. J. Scimone, founder of Slice, a product design firm in Campbell, California, originally intended to improve the design of kitchen and houseware products when he launched his company in 2008. However, after Scimone came up with a better idea for a safer, more effective ceramic blade for opening shrink-wrapped packages that became his company's best-selling item, he decided to focus his efforts on redesigning common tools such as box cutters and scissors. Scimone noted that box cutters were unsafe, antiquated tools and set out to make them safer, more functional, and more aesthetically pleasing. His company's Slice box cutter features a nonslip handle with a wrap-around protective housing that serves as a natural shield for the user's hand and that exposes only half of the double-sided ceramic blade, which lasts up to 10 times longer than steel blades. The slim, comfortable design gives users so much control that they can carve out intricate shapes with surgical accuracy. The keys to the success of Slice's box cutter, which has won numerous design awards, and its other products are simplicity and functionality. "We look for simple, incremental twists to existing products," says Scott Herbst, the company's director of industrial design.[41] ■

HIRE FOR CREATIVITY Research published in the *Sloan Management Review* concludes that the most effective way for companies to achieve continuous innovation over the long term is by hiring and cultivating talented people.[42] Figure 3.3 shows the results of a survey of the CEOs of *Inc.*'s 500 fastest growing companies about the factors that are most important to their companies' ability to innovate. Often the most creative people also tend to be somewhat different, even eccentric. Two researchers call these employees "the odd clever people every organization needs" because they use their creativity to create disproportionate amounts of value for their companies.[43] Hiring creative people was one of the keys to Bell Labs' impressive record of innovation. The company hired the smartest people it could find from a variety of disciplines, backgrounds, and philosophies; encouraged them to interact with and support one another; and gave them the freedom to dream up creative ideas, many of which failed. The ones that succeeded, however, changed the world.[44]

ESTABLISH AN ORGANIZATIONAL STRUCTURE THAT NOURISHES CREATIVITY John Kao, an economist whose nickname is "Mr. Creativity," says innovative companies are structured like spaghetti rather than a traditional pyramid. In a spaghetti-style organization, employees are

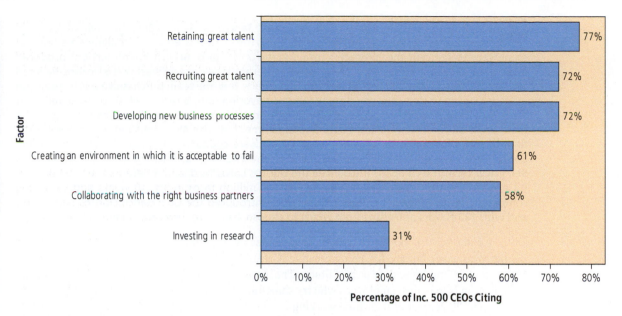

FIGURE 3.3

Factors That Contribute to Companies' Ability to Innovate

Source: Based on "Idea Factories," *Inc.*, September 2013, pp. 104–105.

encouraged to mix and mingle constantly so that creative ideas flow freely throughout the company.[45] At innovative companies, managers create organizational structures and cultures that emphasize the importance of creativity. At FremantleMedia Ltd., the London-based television production company behind hit shows such as *Idols* and *X Factor*, managers have established a structure that encourages and rewards creativity. Every year, the company sponsors Fremantle Market, an event at which executives from production companies around the world pitch their ideas for new television shows to each other, often by showing a trial episode. Show creators explain the premise behind their shows and answer questions from their colleagues about target audiences, production costs, and the potential for links to other media, especially the Internet. Because of FremantleMedia's internal licensing system, executives have the autonomy to decide whether to purchase a show for distribution in their own countries. Shows that attract the most interest receive funding and go on the air.[46]

EMBRACE DIVERSITY One of the best ways to cultivate a culture of creativity is to hire a diverse workforce. When people solve problems or come up with ideas, they do so within the framework of their own experience. Hiring people from different backgrounds, cultural experiences, hobbies, and interests provides a company with crucial raw materials needed for creativity. Smart entrepreneurs enhance organizational creativity by hiring beyond their own comfort zones.

Focusing the talent and creativity of a diverse group of employees on a problem or challenge is one of the best ways to generate creative solutions. Research by Harvard Business School professor Karim Lakhani concludes that the experiences, viewpoints, and thought processes of diverse groups of people are powerful tools for solving problems creatively. "It's very counterintuitive," says Lakhani, "but not only did the odds of a [problem] solver's success actually increase in fields outside his expertise, but also the further a challenge was from his specialty, the greater was the likelihood of success."[47] The lesson for entrepreneurs: to increase the odds of a successful creative solution to a problem, involve in the process people whose background and experience lies *outside* the particular problem area. One manager says, "They create a little grit to stimulate the oyster to produce a pearl."[48]

EXPECT CREATIVITY Employees tend to rise—or fall—to the level of expectations that entrepreneurs have of them. One of the best ways to communicate the expectation of creativity is to encourage them to be creative.

ENTREPRENEURIAL PROFILE: Greg Creed: Taco Bell As Taco Bell, the chain of fast-food Mexican restaurants, approached its 50th birthday, CEO Greg Creed challenged a team of employees to reinvent the company's traditional crunchy taco. Brainstorming sessions produced more than 30 potential ideas, but the one that generated the most interest was a Doritos-flavored taco shell packed with Taco Bell ingredients. In an early test, the team purchased a paint-spray gun at Home Depot so that they could spray Doritos flavoring onto a taco shell. Once Taco Bell's test kitchen developed a prototype, taste tests began, and the product was a flop with customers. The team went back to the drawing board and experimented with 45 recipes before narrowing the field to three for market testing. The tests, which were conducted in a handful of cities around the country, resulted in a clear winner, and soon the Internet was buzzing with hype about Taco Bell's new taco. The company introduced the Doritos Locos Taco, and it became the most successful product launch in Taco Bell history, selling 100 million tacos in just 10 weeks and increasing company sales by 13 percent. Taco Bell has since introduced the Cool Ranch Doritos Locos Taco, and with 123 flavors of Doritos from which to choose, has more new tacos planned.[49] ■

EXPECT FAILURE AND LEARN FROM IT Creative ideas will produce failures as well as successes. People who never fail are not being creative. Creativity requires taking chances, and managers must remove employees' fear of failure. The surest way to quash creativity throughout an organization is to punish employees who try something new and fail. Google allows employees to spend up to 20 percent of their time working on "pet projects" that they find exciting and believe have potential. In addition, Google provides seed capital for its employees' most promising ideas. The company credits its policy with creating some of its most successful product innovations, including Gmail, its Web-based e-mail service.[50]

ENTREPRENEURIAL PROFILE: Jason Seiken: PBS Digital When Jason Seiken became head of PBS's then-struggling digital division, he went beyond expecting failure and announced to employees that failure was required. "If you don't fail enough times during the coming year, you'll be downgraded because if you're not failing enough, you're playing it safe," he says. "The idea was to deliver a clear message: Move fast. Iterate fast. Be entrepreneurial. Don't be afraid that if you stretch and sprint you might break things. Executive leadership has your back." The change among employees was immediate, profound, and exactly what Seiken was trying to achieve. Employees began trying innovative ideas for the PBS Web site, many of which failed and some of which became huge successes. Had Seiken not shaken up the existing culture with the "failure requirement," many of those ideas would never have come to light. One idea, Garden of Your Mind, was a remix of old Mr. Rogers clips in which the genteel host bursts into song; within 48 hours of posting, the video topped the most viewed and most shared video on YouTube. Seiken's attitude toward failure spread across the organization as employees adopted the mantra, "Reinvent PBS."[51] ■

INCORPORATE FUN INTO THE WORK ENVIRONMENT Smart entrepreneurs know work should be fun, and although they expect employees to work hard, they create a company culture that allows employees to have fun. "If you want creative workers, give them enough time to play," says actor John Cleese. At Radio Flyer, the Chicago-based company that makes the classic little red wagon for children, employees routinely participate in fun activities at work that include karaoke, tricycle races, pumpkin-carving contests, a Hollywood Squares game, and others. CEO Robert Pasin intentionally has made fun events a part of the company's culture. "There's method to the madness," says the company's "chief wagon officer," pointing out that the company's success depends on creative employees who are motivated and engaged in their work.[52]

ENCOURAGE CURIOSITY Curiosity is an important ingredient in creativity. Children are innately curious, which is one reason they are so creative. Creativity expert Hal Gregersen says innovators constantly question the world around them and involve others in helping them in answering the questions they pose. Entrepreneurs and their employees constantly should ask "what-if" questions and take a "maybe-we-could" attitude. Challenging standing assumptions about how something should be done ("We've always done it that way.") is an excellent springboard for creativity. Doing so allows people to break out of assumptions that limit creativity. Supporting employees' extracurricular activities also can spur creativity on the job. For instance, M. P. Muller, founder of Door Number 3, a branding agency, paid for a comedy improvisation class for the company's art director, believing that it would enhance the director's creative talents.[53]

DILBERT   *BY SCOTT ADAMS*

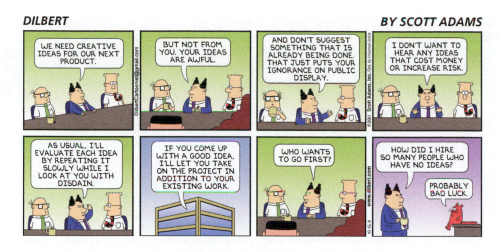

Encouraging employees to "think big" also helps. Creativity expert John Kao points out that, although incremental innovation can be useful, it is not likely to make a company a winner. Instead, the real opportunity for creating a significant competitive edge lies in creating innovations that disrupt and revolutionize an entire industry.

DESIGN A WORK SPACE THAT ENCOURAGES CREATIVITY The physical environment in which people work has an impact on their level of creativity. The cubicles made so famous in the Dilbert cartoon strip can suck creativity right out of a work space. Transforming a typical office space— even one with cubicles—into a haven of creativity does not have to be difficult or expensive. Covering bland walls with funny posters, photographs, murals, or other artwork; adding splashes of color; and incorporating live plants enliven a work space and enhance creativity. Designs that foster employee interaction, especially informal interaction, enhance an organization's creative power.

Because creativity is at the heart of their jobs, employees at Davison Design and Development, a product design company, work in a setting that more closely resembles an amusement park than an office complex. CEO George Davison designed the office, known as Inventionland™, to get employees out of their offices, to interact with one another, and to be inspired by a fun, whimsical environment. The 60,000-square-foot space resembles an amusement park and includes a pirate ship where employees design toys and games for clients and a Thinktank Treehouse for hardware designers. Davison calls Inventionland™ "the world's most innovative workplace" and says the unusual design has helped fuel the company's growth.[54] Even though creating their own version of Inventionland™ may not be practical for most businesses, entrepreneurs can stimulate creativity by starting meetings with some type of short, fun exercise designed to encourage participants to think creatively.

VIEW PROBLEMS AS OPPORTUNITIES Every problem offers the opportunity for innovation. One of the best ways to channel a company's innovative energy productively is to address questions that focus employees' attention on customers' problems and how to solve them.

ENTREPRENEURIAL PROFILE: Roni and Ken Di Lullo: Doggles On a trip to the dog park with their border collie, Midknight, Roni and Ken Di Lullo noticed that Midknight kept missing the Frisbee during their game of fetch. They soon discovered that he was sensitive to sunlight, which led Roni to retrofit a pair of sports goggles for Midknight. People who saw Midknight were so amused that Roni created a Web site with photos of their beloved dog wearing his sports goggles. Before long, dog owners began contacting Roni, asking to purchase a pair of goggles for their pets. To fill each order, Roni purchased a

Rick Roach/ASSOCIATED PRESS

pair of sports goggles and modified them to fit each customer's dog. As sales grew, Roni realized that she had inadvertently launched a unique business, something she never intended to do because she had a full-time job as a software developer. She named the product Doggles and found an eyewear manufacturer in Taiwan who created goggles with a broader nose bridge and deeper lens cup that would fit a wide range of dogs, from Chihuahuas to Great Danes. Every pair of Doggles features shatterproof, anti-fog lenses that block 100 percent of UV rays and adjustable head and chin straps. Doggles also offers goggles with prescription lenses for dogs that have undergone cataract surgery. Doggles sell for $16 to $20 per pair at more than 3,500 pet boutiques and at stores such as Target, Amazon, and Petco. Today, Doggles generates more than $3 million in annual sales.[55] ■

PROVIDE CREATIVITY TRAINING Almost everyone has the capacity to be creative, but developing that capacity requires training. Training accomplished through books, seminars, workshops, and professional meetings can help everyone learn to tap their creative capacity.

ELIMINATE BUREAUCRATIC OBSTACLES AND PROVIDE THE SUPPORT NECESSARY FOR INNO-VATION Just as a good carpenter needs certain tools to do his or her job, employees need certain resources and support to be creative, including freedom from bureaucracy to pursue their ideas. Do innovators need hardware, software, time to collaborate, or other resources? Entrepreneurs also must remember that creativity often requires nonwork phases, and giving employees time to "daydream" is an important part of the creative process. The creativity that employees display when they know managers value innovation can be amazing—and profitable. These **intrapreneurs**, entrepreneurs who operate within the framework of an existing business, sometimes can transform a company's future or advance its competitive edge. To encourage intrapreneurial innovation, Microsoft renovated one of its older buildings, transforming it into the Garage, an incubator equipped with all of the latest technology for employees to explore and develop ideas they have for new products and services. Garage director Quinn Hawkins says the inspiration for the incubator (and its name) came from all of the great companies, such as Apple, Hewlett-Packard, and Amazon, that started in garages. After receiving four e-mails in one week with missing attachments, software engineer Bhavesh Chauhan used the Garage's resources to develop a program that automatically scans e-mails for words that indicate that the user intends to send an attachment. If the e-mail contains no attachment, a notice pops up to alert the user. Chauhan's forgotten attachment detector appeared in Microsoft's Office 2013 software.[56]

DEVELOP A PROCEDURE FOR CAPTURING IDEAS Small companies that are outstanding innovators do not earn that mantle by accident; they have a process in place to solicit and then collect new ideas. When workers come up with creative ideas, however, not every organization is prepared to capture them. The unfortunate result is that ideas that might have vaulted a company ahead of its competition or made people's lives better simply evaporate. Without a structured approach for collecting employees' creative concepts, a business leaves its future to chance. Clever entrepreneurs establish processes within their companies that are designed to harvest the results of employees' creativity. Sadler's Wells, a dance group that operates three theaters in London and whose mission is to be the center of innovation in dance, has fashioned a procedure for capturing and developing creative ideas. Representatives scout a variety of promising dancers and invite them to its studios, where they work together in small teams to develop new dance performances. The dance teams present their creations to Sadler's Wells' producers, theater managers, and dancers. Sadler's Wells invests in the creations that offer the greatest potential, often testing them in its smaller theaters before taking them to its main stage.[57]

TALK WITH CUSTOMERS—OR, BETTER YET, INTERACT WITH THEM Innovative companies take the time to get feedback about how customers use the companies' products or services, listening for new ideas. The voice of the customer can be an important source of creative ideas, and the Internet allows entrepreneurs to hear their customers' voices quickly and inexpensively. Some companies observe their customers actually using their products or services to glean ideas that may lead to improvements and new features. Other companies go further, forging alliances with customers to come up with creative ideas and develop new products based on them. A recent survey of the CEOs of *Inc.*'s 500 fastest growing companies, reports that although customers are

---

intrapreneurs
entrepreneurs who operate within the framework of an existing business.

the most common source of ideas for new products and services, only 37 percent of companies have a formal process for collecting customers' ideas.[58]

MONITOR EMERGING TRENDS AND IDENTIFY WAYS YOUR COMPANY CAN CAPITALIZE ON THEM
Tracking trends is an excellent way to generate ideas for new products, services, or business models. Taco Bell, the quick-service chain of Mexican restaurants, invests resources in monitoring demographic and social trends that influence customers' dining habits. One trend the company recently identified is the demand for healthier menus. To capitalize on this trend, Taco Bell worked with celebrity chef Lorena Garcia to introduce a fresher, lighter, and healthier Cantina Bell product line. Market tests show that the Cantina Bell line is popular among women and older customers and has enhanced customers' perceptions of Taco Bell's quality image. Just one year after its launch, Cantina Bell products accounted for 5 percent of the company's sales. Taco Bell normally creates about 200 new product ideas each year before winnowing them down to about 20 products to introduce into test markets. Those that succeed in the test markets are rolled out nationwide. "Fail to innovate at your own risk," says Taco Bell's chief marketing officer.[59]

LOOK FOR USES FOR YOUR COMPANY'S PRODUCTS OR SERVICES IN OTHER MARKETS Focusing on the "traditional" uses of a product or service limits creativity—and a company's sales. Entrepreneurs can boost sales by finding new applications, often in unexpected places, for their products and services.

ENTREPRENEURIAL PROFILE: Neil Wadhawan and Raj Raheja: Heartwood Studios
In 2002, Neil Wadhawan and Raj Raheja launched Heartwood Studios, a company that produced three-dimensional renderings and animations of buildings and products for architects and designers. Their business was successful, but a brainstorming session helped the entrepreneurs to realize that their company's three-dimensional renderings had applications in other industries as well. Today Heartwood Studios has clients in the defense and aerospace industries as well as in the fields of entertainment and sports. In fact, the company creates animations for use on the giant screens in sports arenas for several professional sports teams.[60] ■

REWARD CREATIVITY Entrepreneurs can encourage creativity by rewarding it when it occurs. Financial rewards can be effective motivators of creative behavior, but nonmonetary rewards, such as praise, recognition, and celebration, usually offer more powerful incentives for creativity.

MODEL CREATIVE BEHAVIOR Creativity is "caught" as much as it is "taught." Companies that excel at innovation find that the passion for creativity starts at the top. Entrepreneurs who set examples of creative behavior, taking chances, and challenging the status quo soon find their employees doing the same.

ENTREPRENEURIAL PROFILE: Jason Fried: 37signals Jason Fried, cofounder of 37signals, a Chicago-based software company, compares his company's product line to the apple trees on his farm. Fried routinely prunes his apple trees, noting that pruning gives them a stronger foundation for the future. Fried applies that same logic to his company, regularly pruning the company's software products. Observers were stunned when Fried sold to another business a service that generated $17,000 per month in profit for 37signals. A few months later, however, at a company meeting, the staff came up with ideas for two new products, one a variation of an existing product, and the other a totally new product. Fried says that the ideas for new products would never have emerged unless 37signals took the bold step of cutting some of its old products. Growing strong new limbs in a business requires the entrepreneur to prune away the old ones.[61] ■

DON'T FORGET ABOUT BUSINESS MODEL INNOVATION As Jason Fried's experience suggests, creating new products and services is the lifeblood of a company's long-term success; however, business model innovations can produce significant impact on a business as well. A study by the consulting firm Doblin Group reveals that although companies focus most of their creative resources on developing new products and product extensions, those investments are least likely to produce a positive return. In fact, the success rate for new products and product extensions is just 4.5 percent. Innovations in a company's business model, customer service process, distribution system, customer value stream, and internal processes produce higher rates of return.[62]

Apple's iTunes store has proved to be a valuable business model innovation, providing a system for billions of people to download music, apps, ebooks, and movies conveniently and easily. Since its launch in 2001, iTune's 500 million-plus active users have downloaded more than 50 billion apps and 25 billion songs (from its library of 35 million songs). Apple's business model innovation now generates $16 billion in annual revenue for the company.[63]

Enhancing Individual Creativity

Just as entrepreneurs can cultivate an environment of creativity in their organizations by using the techniques described previously, they can enhance their own creativity by using the following techniques.

ALLOW YOURSELF TO BE CREATIVE As we have seen, one of the biggest obstacles to creativity occurs when a person believes he or she is not creative. A recent study by Adobe shows that just 52 percent of people in the United States (and only 39 percent of people globally) believe they are creative.[64] Giving yourself the permission to be creative is the first step toward establishing a pattern of creative thinking. Refuse to give in to the temptation to ignore ideas simply because you fear that someone else may consider them "stupid." When it comes to creativity, there are no stupid ideas!

ENTREPRENEURIAL PROFILE: Robert Bigelow: Bigelow Aerospace As a child living in Las Vegas, Robert Bigelow witnessed the mushroom clouds from the first tests of atomic bombs in the Nevada desert. Fascinated by science, Bigelow soon was captivated by stories of space travel. Bigelow went on to build a highly successful hotel chain, Budget Suites America, that made him a billionaire. In 1998, the hotelier launched Bigelow Aerospace, a company that recently signed a contract with NASA to provide a new type of inflatable space pod called the Bigelow Expandable Activity Module (BEAM) to be attached to the International Space Station (ISS). The module, which resembles a large balloon made of kevlar and other high-tech materials, provides many advantages, including low cost and light weight, and is 50 percent cheaper to launch than traditional rigid modules. Once in space, astronauts simply attach the BEAM to the ISS and inflate it to its full 560-cubic-foot volume. Bigelow's long-term goal is to use BEAM technology to create inexpensive commercial space stations to lease to businesses, governments, and wealthy individuals who want to spend time in space.[65] ■

FORGET THE "RULES" Creative individuals take a cue from Captain Jack Sparrow in the Pirates of the Caribbean series of movies. When faced with a difficult (sometimes impossible) situation, Sparrow (played by Johnny Depp) usually operates outside the rules and, as a result, comes up with innovative solutions. Sparrow's unwillingness to be encumbered by rules frees him to develop innovative, often unusual solutions to the problems he encounters.

GIVE YOUR MIND FRESH INPUT EVERY DAY To be creative, your mind needs stimulation. Do something different each day—listen to a new radio station, take a walk through a park or a shopping center, or pick up a magazine you never read.

ENTREPRENEURIAL PROFILE: Doris Raymond: The Way We Wore The Way We Wore, a huge vintage clothing store in Los Angeles started by Doris Raymond in 2004 that stocks garments from the Victorian era to the 1980s, has become a destination for designers from many fashion houses and retailers, ranging from Marc Jacobs to Forever 21, who are looking for inspiration for their clothing collections. Recognizing that meeting customers' demand for fresh designs gives their clothing lines a competitive advantage, many designers are looking to the past for creative ideas, taking note not only of fabrics and patterns but also of the smallest details, such as buttons and the type of stitching used on pockets. These fashion experts have discovered that exposing their minds to "new" designs is a great way to stimulate their own creativity.[66] ■

TAKE UP A HOBBY Hobbies provide not only an avenue to escape your regular routine, but they also give your mind fresh input that can be a source of creative ideas. Izhar Gafni, a bicycling enthusiast, was in a bicycle shop talking about his hobby ("Bicycling is in my soul," he says) when the conversation turned to a man who had invented a cardboard canoe. The concept fascinated him. "Why not make a bicycle out of cardboard?" he wondered. Gafni went to work and invented a low-cost, eco-friendly bicycle made entirely out of recycled cardboard and car tires.

Tight folding gives the cardboard frame strength, and a special coating makes the cardboard waterproof and fireproof. Although the bike weighs just 27 pounds, it is strong enough to support a 275-pound passenger. Gafni, who started Cardboard Technologies to market his invention, says each bike costs between $9 and $12 to build, and he plans to sell them for $20 each.[67]

TRAVEL—AND OBSERVE Visiting other countries (even other states) is a creativity stimulant. Travelers see new concepts and engage in new experiences that can spark creative ideas. While on vacation, Tom Adeyoola watched his girlfriend revel in the inexpensive custom-made clothing available in Vietnam because she was frustrated by the poor fit of most off-the-rack products available in online shops in their native United Kingdom. Adeyoola began to ponder ways of improving the traditional online buying experience and came up with the idea of a tool that allows online shoppers to try on clothing virtually. A Cambridge professor connected him with a former student, and the two young men started Metail, a London-based technology company that allows shoppers to upload basic body measurements and photos of themselves that Metail transforms into a three-dimensional avatar that is 94 to 96 percent accurate. Customers who shop at companies that subscribe to Metail can use their avatars to try on virtual garments to test their fit. With Metail, customers find clothes that fit them better, and retailers experience lower costs due to returns from poor-fitting items.[68]

OBSERVE THE PRODUCTS AND SERVICES OF OTHER COMPANIES, ESPECIALLY THOSE IN COMPLETELY DIFFERENT MARKETS Creative entrepreneurs often borrow ideas from companies that are in businesses totally unrelated to their own. The founders of Project Frog, a San Francisco-based builder, noted the popularity of eco-friendly modular residential homes and applied the concept to building prefabricated schools and government buildings faster and cheaper than traditional "stick-built" structures. CEO Ann Hand soon extended the company's reach into retail and healthcare. "We design a common chassis for different types of buildings that people can reprogram according to their needs," she says. Project Frog uses sophisticated software to create a three-dimensional model of a structure before it actually manufactures all of the individual components for on-site assembly. Its buildings include energy-saving features, optimize the use of natural light, and result in cost savings of up to 30 percent. Project Frog, which has attracted $30 million in venture capital, generates more than $25 million in annual sales.[69]

RECOGNIZE THE CREATIVE POWER OF MISTAKES AND ACCIDENTS Innovations sometimes are the result of serendipity, finding something while looking for something else, and sometimes they arise as a result of mistakes or accidents. Creative people recognize that even their errors may lead to new ideas, products, and services. Louis Daguerre, a scene painter for the Paris Opera, was fascinated with lighting and in 1822 began conducting experiments with the effect of light on translucent screens. In 1829, Daguerre formed a partnership with Joseph Niecpe, who had invented a primitive version of photography called the heliograph in 1829. (The exposure time for Niecpe's first photograph was a mere eight hours!) The two men worked for years trying to capture photographic images on metal plates treated with silver iodide, but they made little progress before Niecpe died in 1833. One evening in 1835, Daguerre placed one of his treated plates in his chemical cupboard, intending to recoat it for other experiments. When he removed it later, he was surprised to see a photographic image with brilliant highlights. Excited but puzzled by the outcome, Daguerre finally discovered that mercury vapors from a broken thermometer in the cupboard had caused the photographic image to appear on the treated metal plate. Daguerre refined the process, naming it Daguerreotype after himself. The world of modern photography was born—and an accident played a significant role.[70]

NOTICE WHAT IS MISSING Sometimes entrepreneurs spot viable business opportunities by noticing something, often very practical and simple, that is *missing*. The first step is to determine whether a market for the missing product or service actually exists (perhaps the reason it does not exist is that there is not market potential), which is one of the objectives of building a business plan.

ENTREPRENEURIAL PROFILE: Mark Bowles and EcoATM Fewer than 20 percent of the discarded electronic devices in the United States are recycled; most are burned or dumped in landfills, where they leak dangerous chemicals into the environment. After spending 25 years in the wireless and technology industries, serial entrepreneur Mark Bowles noticed that no one was doing anything about the problem and decided it was time to take action. Inspired by Coinstar change-counting machines that he saw in many locations, Bowles spent three years developing the ecoATM, an ATM-like machine that uses an artificial intelligence-based vision system to recognize 4,000 types of phones, MP3 players, and tablets and identify any damage. The ecoATM taps into a real-time global auction system to offer customers competitive prices for their old electronic devices. The machine even has thumbprint scanning technology designed to thwart thieves who might try to use the ecoATM as a fence for stolen e-devices. EcoATM resells 75 percent of the devices it collects to refurbishers with the remainder of them going to authorized e-waste recyclers. With 500 kiosks already in place across the United States, Bowles is making plans to expand ecoATM internationally. ■

LOOK FOR WAYS TO TURN TRASH INTO TREASURE Some entrepreneurs achieve success by finding creative ways to turn trash into treasure. Before coffee growers can ship coffee beans to coffee makers, they must strip away the skin of the fruit that surrounds the bean. In Hawaii alone, coffee growers throw away 40 million pounds of coffee fruit skins each year. Serial entrepreneur Shaun Roberts took note and developed a way to transform coffee fruit skin, which also contains caffeine and is packed with antioxidants, into a line of energy drinks called KonaRed. His 15-person company, based in Kalaheo, Hawaii, purchases coffee fruit skins from growers, dries them, and processes them into a thick, molasses-like concentrate that it mixes with various fruit juices to create a line of healthful beverages. In addition to selling KonaRed through retail outlets in Hawaii and on the mainland, Roberts's company offers monthly subscriptions through its Web site.[71]

KEEP A JOURNAL HANDY TO RECORD YOUR THOUGHTS AND IDEAS Creative ideas are too valuable to waste, so always keep a journal nearby to record them as soon as you get them. Leonardo da Vinci was famous for writing down ideas as they struck him. Patrick McNaughton invented the neon blackboards that restaurants use to advertise their specials. In addition to the neon blackboard, McNaughton has invented more than 30 new products, many of which are sold through the company he and his sister, Jamie, own. McNaughton credits much of his creative success to the fact that he writes down every idea he gets and keeps it in a special folder. "There's no such thing as a crazy idea," he insists.[72]

LISTEN TO OTHER PEOPLE No rule of creativity says an idea has to be your own! Sometimes the best business ideas come from someone else, but entrepreneurs are the ones to act on them.

ENTREPRENEURIAL PROFILE: Cameron Roelofson: Splash Mobile Car Wash Cameron Roelofson, owner of Splash Mobile Car Wash in Concord, Ontario, washes 2,500 tractor-trailer trucks per week during warm months, but sales in his highly seasonal business fall to nothing during the frigid winters. On one cold winter day, Roelofson was talking with an acquaintance who asked if he would use his mobile truck-washing equipment to put water into an outdoor skating rink. He agreed and quickly realized the potential for a business that would offset seasonality in sales in his truck-washing business. Roelofson began advertising, and sales took off. For $1,000 to $2,000, Splash builds a frame with a reusable liner and then fills it with water. Three days later, frozen solid in Ontario's winter weather, the rink is ready for skating or hockey. In the spring, Splash returns to disassemble the rink and store it until the next winter.[73] ■

LISTEN TO CUSTOMERS Some of the best ideas for new products and services or new applications of an existing product or service come from a company's customers. Entrepreneurs who take the time to listen to their customers often receive ideas that they may never have come up with on their own. "You must talk to and deeply understand your customers to build products, services, and experiences that work in today's consumer-driven market," says Eric Holtzclaw, founder and CEO of Laddering Works, a marketing and product strategy firm. Middleby Marshall, a foodservice equipment maker founded in 1888, relies on feedback from customers to guide its new product development efforts. The company recently introduced its CTX oven, which combines a griddle, a fryer, and a charbroiler into a single unit that cooks food fasters, uses less energy, and improves the efficiency of commercial kitchens. "Our business is built on a high degree of customer interaction," says president Mark Sieron. "We listen to our customers, and that's what drives our innovation."[74]

GET ADEQUATE SLEEP Sleep restores both our bodies and our brains. A study by the Mental Health Foundation shows a correlation between sound sleep and a person's ability to produce creative ideas and new insights.[75]

WATCH A MOVIE Great business ideas come from the strangest places, even the movies. As a child, Stanley Yang was fascinated by sci-fi movies such as *Star Wars*. That fascination led him to become an engineer so that he could transform his ideas into reality. Yang's company, NeuroSky, has developed headsets that allow people to control video games with their minds using biosensor technology, a concept used by an advanced alien race in the movie *Battle Los Angeles*. "Movies may spark an idea," says Yang, who still dreams of building a functional light saber.

TALK TO A CHILD As we grow older, we learn to conform to society's expectations about many things, including creative solutions to problems. Children place very few limitations on their thinking; as a result, their creativity is practically boundless. (Remember all the games you and your friends invented when you were young?)

DO SOMETHING ORDINARY IN AN UNUSUAL WAY Experts say that simply doing something out of the ordinary can stimulate creativity. To stimulate his own creativity, Scott Jones, an entrepreneur who is known as "the guy who invented voice mail" (and many other items as well), often engages in what other people might consider bizarre behavior—eating without utensils, watching television sitting one foot away from the screen, or taking a shower with his eyes closed. "Anything I normally do, I'll do differently just to see what happens," says Jones.[76]

KEEP A TOY BOX IN YOUR OFFICE Your box might include silly objects, such as wax lips, a yo-yo, a Slinky, fortune cookie sayings, feathers, a top, a compass, or a host of other items. When you are stumped, pick an item at random from the toy box and think about how it relates to your problem.

TAKE NOTE OF YOUR "PAIN POINTS" Do other people experience them as well? Entrepreneurs often create innovations to solve problems they themselves face. Observing "pain points" that result from missing products or services or flaws in existing products or services can be an excellent source of business ideas.

ENTREPRENEURIAL PROFILE: Donna Browning: Sweaty Bands Fitness instructor Donna Browning was tired of elastic headbands that kept slipping out of place during her exercise classes and decided to make one that would stay put. She borrowed a sewing machine and made several prototypes to test. She discovered that velvet–lined ribbon with elastic worked best. Browning made a batch of headbands, gave a few as gifts, and sold the rest out of her gym bag. The positive feedback from her early customers encouraged Browning to start Sweaty Bands with her husband, and the copreneurs soon were selling headbands online at $15 to $18 each. Aggressive marketing and public relations sparked sales, and Sweaty Bands now sells 250,000 headbands per year and employs 100 people. The Brownings recently signed a deal to make sorority-themed Sweaty Bands and are exploring potential relationships with college and professional sports teams. Sales recently hit $12 million and continue to grow rapidly.[77] ∎

DO NOT THROW AWAY SEEMINGLY "BAD" IDEAS Some creative ideas prove to be impractical, too costly, or too silly to work. Creative entrepreneurs, however, do not discard these seemingly bad ideas. Instead, they ask, "What part of this idea can I build on?" and "What could I change about this idea to make it work?" They realize that seemingly bad ideas can be the nucleus of a really good idea. West Paw Design, a company based in Bozeman, Montana, that produces eco-friendly pet toys, sponsors a creativity contest in which its 36 employees, from president to seamstresses, form small teams to develop prototypes of new product ideas. The winning team receives the coveted Golden Hairball Award, a statue reminiscent of the Oscar but with one of the company's cat toys perched atop its head. President Spencer Williams says many of the great ideas for new products come from ideas that don't win the contest. The company's R&D team meets after each contest to review *all* of the ideas employees submit. "We look for one piece of a new idea," he says.[78]

COLLABORATE WITH OTHERS Working with other people to solve a problem or to generate ideas brings a fresh perspective to the situation. Two or more people usually are more creative than one person working alone. GE, a company that owns thousands of patents, recently partnered with

Quirky, a crowdsourcing site that allows an online community of more than 500,000 inventors to collaborate on generating ideas and solving problems, to get new ideas on ways to use its patents. Inventors on Quirky are busy finding new ways to apply technology from GE such as coatings that protect electronics from moisture and a device that cools jet engines. Inventors whose ideas prove commercially viable share in the profits they generate. Ben Kaufman, cofounder of Quirky, says his goal is to create an invention machine.[79]

READ BOOKS ON STIMULATING CREATIVITY OR TAKE A CLASS ON CREATIVITY Creative thinking is a technique anyone can learn. Understanding and applying the principles of creativity can improve dramatically the ability to develop new and innovative ideas.

DOODLE Research shows that engaging in artistic activities, even as simple as doodling, stimulates creativity.[80] Doodling keeps a person's brain engaged even when he or she not focused on a particular task.

TAKE SOME TIME OFF Relaxation is vital to the creative process. Getting away from a problem gives the mind time to reflect on it. It is often during this time, while the subconscious works on a problem, that the mind generates many creative solutions. One study reports that 35 percent of entrepreneurs say they come up with their best ideas during downtime, when they are away from work.[81] One creativity expert claims that fishing is the ideal activity for stimulating creativity. "Your brain is on high alert in case a fish is around," he says, "but your brain is completely relaxed. This combination is the time when you have the 'Aha!' moment."[82]

BE PERSISTENT Entrepreneurs know that one secret to success is persistence and a "don't-quit" attitude. Twelve publishers rejected J. K. Rowling's manuscript about the adventures of a boy wizard and his friends, which she started writing at age 25 when she was a single mother trying to raise her children on welfare. Finally, Bloomsbury, a small London publishing house, agreed to publish 1,000 copies of *Harry Potter and the Philosopher's Stone*. Rowling's seven-part Harry Potter book series went on to sell more than 450 million copies worldwide, making Rowling the first billionaire author.[83]

Hands On . . . How To

Be a Successful Innovator

Creativity and innovation traditionally have played an important part in entrepreneurial success. Today, their role has become an even more vital component as businesses face increasing pressure to produce innovations to remain competitive. One writer notes that until recently people achieved success by copying other people, taking what they know and applying it. Today, however, because unique challenges are a regular part of life, success goes to those brave enough to cross boldly into the unknown.

Entrepreneurs are among the brave souls who challenge existing ideas, norms, values, and business practices and often produce valuable breakthrough products that make them and their companies terrific success stories. What lessons can we learn from successful entrepreneurs about innovation?

Embrace Fear

Creative entrepreneurs face their fears. Ask yourself, "What frightens me about my business?" Are you fearful that a competitor will introduce a new product or service that will make yours obsolete? Are you concerned that customers may find your product or service less appealing? Are trade shows still the best way to reach your customers? Once you have identified the fears that most concern you, address them. Explore them. If you were introducing your company's product or service today, what would it look like? What features would it offer?

Recognize That "Innovation" Is Not Necessarily Synonymous with "Invention"

Some of the most successful entrepreneurs in history actually did not invent the products that made them famous. Henry Ford, founder of Ford Motor Company, said, "I invented nothing new. I simply assembled into a car the discoveries of other men behind whom were centuries of work." Of course, Ford did make innovations in the auto assembly process, creating in 1913 the first mass-assembly process that made cars affordable for the average person. Similarly, Keyvan Mohajer, founder of San Jose, California-based SoundHound, took technology that has been around for years, music recognition, and created an app that made it easier for people to use. His company's Sound2Sound technology recognizes and identifies any song (even those that a person simply hums) and provides the user with instant access to information

Hands On . . . How To (continued)

pertaining to the song, such as biographical sketches of the artist, lyrics, videos, concert dates, upcoming tours, and more. In just two years, the company's customer base has grown from 10 million to more than 100 million. Like Mohajer, successful entrepreneurs often find new ways to connect existing technologies to create value.

Find the Intersection of "Problem" and "Solution"

Some entrepreneurs launch businesses with a focus on marketing their products or services to a particular audience but fail to ask whether their products and services actually solve a real problem customers face. "If you're not solving a problem, the world won't care," explains Ben Kaufman, founder of Quirky, a social product development company that serves aspiring inventors. Successful innovators often spot a "pain point" in their own lives and realize that other people face the same problem as well. As a New York City native, Internet entrepreneur Jay Bregman was very familiar with the inefficiencies in the taxi cab industry. At any given moment, thousands of cabs in major cities are looking for fares, while thousands of people are trying to hail cabs. In fact, Bregman's research shows that taxis in New York City spend 40 percent of their time cruising for fares, while potential passengers have difficulty finding cabs. Bregman, two other Internet entrepreneurs, and three New York City cab drivers found the intersection of "problem" and "solution" when they created Hailo, a company that markets an app that connects cab drivers with passengers for a small fee. Hailo allows passengers to locate a cab within two minutes with just two taps on their smart phones and has become the world's most popular taxi app. Bregman and his cofounders now are turning their attention to developing apps for other markets that suffer from similar inefficiencies.

Entrepreneurs often spot "pain points" by noting the following:

- Complaints they hear from other people
- The inconvenience of buying a product or service
- A fundamental flaw in an existing product or service
- A product or service that can make life easier
- A product or service that can add to one's well-being
- A simpler way to access a product or service

Realize That Innovation Typically Is the Result of an Iterative Feedback Cycle

Innovations often come about when entrepreneurs come up with an idea, test it, discover what works (and what doesn't work), and then modify their idea based on this feedback. This cycle of developing ideas, testing them, and refining them is an essential part of the creative process. Thomas Edison, recipient of a record 1,093 patents, including the patents for the phonograph and the light bulb, once said the real measure of success is the number of experiments that one can squeeze into 24 hours.

Beware of Faulty Assumptions

One of the most dangerous assumptions that innovative entrepreneurs can make is that customers are as excited about their innovations as they themselves are. Like Edison, successful innovators see the pathway to entrepreneurship as a series of experiments. One of the most valuable experiments an entrepreneur can undertake is to get feedback from potential customers. Confirmation of an idea tells an entrepreneur that he or she is on the right track; conversely, lukewarm or negative customer feedback suggests that he or she drop the idea and move to another, more promising one. Andrew Hargadon, director of the Center for Entrepreneurship at the University of California, Davis, recalls a student entrepreneur who had developed a novel pathology device. Part of her feedback cycle included talking with surgeons, whose response was overwhelmingly positive and gave her the confidence to pursue commercializing the device. Her conversations with the surgeons also produced several suggestions for improvement that she had not thought of.

Innovators, says one writer, are "figure-outers." When faced with problems and opportunities, they figure out how to deal with them successfully and in the process create innovations.

Sources: Based on Gwen Moran, "4 Ways to Find Your Next Revolutionary Business Idea," *Entrepreneur*, July 4, 2012, http://www.entrepreneur.com/blog/223893; Kara Ohngren, "Voice of a Generation," *Entrepreneur*, June 2012, p. 68; Katherine Duncan, "A Mobile App That Makes Hailing a Cab Easier and More Efficient," *Entrepreneur*, May 21, 2013, http://www.entrepreneur.com/article/226684; Katherine Duncan, "Brilliant 100: Where To?" *Entrepreneur*, June 2013, p. 54; Andrew B. Hargadon, "7 Ways to Make Students More Entrepreneurial," *Chronicle of Higher Education*, March 28, 2010, http://chronicle.com/article/Teaching-Matters-7-Ways-to/64841; Jeff Cornwall, "The Entrepreneurship Educator," May 2010, p. 1; Donna Fenn, "Will Your New Product Be a Hit or a Flop? Answer These 5 Questions to Find Out," *BNET*, January 20, 2011, http://www.bnet.com/blog/entrepreneurs/will-your-new-product-be-a-hit-or-a-flop-answer-these-5-questions-to-find-out/1571; Dennis Stauffer, "The Best Figure-Outers Win," *Insight Fusion*, June 13, 2011, http://www.insightfusion.com/blog/index.php/.../the-best-figure-outers-win. William S. Pretzer, editor, *Working at Inventing: Thomas A. Edison and the Menlo Park Experience*, (Deerborn: Henry Ford Museum & Greenfield Village, 1989).

The Creative Process

LO6
Describe the steps in the creative process.

Although creative ideas may appear to strike as suddenly as a bolt of lightning, they are actually the result of the creative process, which involves seven steps:

1. Preparation
2. Investigation
3. Transformation
4. Incubation
5. Illumination

6. Verification

7. Implementation

Step 1. Preparation

This step involves getting the mind ready for creative thinking. Preparation might include a formal education, on-the-job training, work experience, and other learning opportunities. This training provides a foundation on which to build creativity and innovation. As one writer explains, "Creativity favors the prepared mind."[84] For example, Dr. Hamel Navia, a scientist at tiny Vertex Pharmaceuticals, was working on a promising new drug to fight the AIDS virus. His preparation included earning an advanced degree in the field of medicine and learning to use computers to create three-dimensional images of the protein molecules he was studying.[85] How can you prepare your mind for creative thinking?

- Adopt the attitude of a lifelong student. Realize that educating yourself is a never-ending process. Look at every situation you encounter as an opportunity to learn.

  ENTREPRENEURIAL PROFILE: Tony Brennan: Sharklet Technologies Tony Brennan, a materials science and engineering professor, was searching for a way to keep barnacles from clinging to ships' hulls. He began studying sharkskin, which is known for its ability to resist microbes, and discovered the key at a microscopic level: the diamond-shaped pattern of tiny tooth-like outcroppings that prevent microbes from sticking. Brennan's research led him to start Sharklet Technologies, a company in Aurora, Colorado, that makes a sharkskin-inspired, micropatterned fabric called SafeTouch that resists the growth of bacteria, including staph, e. coli, and MRSA. It can be applied to almost any high-touch surface. Sharklet is selling SafeTouch to hospitals, labs, research centers, and owners of public spaces that are prone to high concentrations of bacteria. The company recently landed a $2 million investment from Altria Ventures, a venture capital firm.[86] ■

- Read—a lot—and not just in your field of expertise. Many innovations come from blending ideas and concepts from different fields in science, engineering, business, and the arts. Reading books, magazines, and papers covering a variety of subject matter is a great way to stimulate your creativity.

- Clip interesting articles and create a file for them. Over time, you will build a customized encyclopedia of information from which to draw ideas and inspiration.

- Take time to discuss your ideas with other people, including those who know little about it as well as experts in the field. Sometimes, the apparently simple questions that an "unknowledgeable" person asks lead to new discoveries and to new approaches to an old problem. Don Medoff breathed creativity into his Tucson, Arizona–based supplier of windows and doors by bringing in as consultants college students from the nearby University of Arizona. Medoff and his managers briefed teams of students on several of the company's stickiest problems and asked them for ideas on how to solve them. The student teams created new packaging ideas for several products, developed new television commercials, and made suggestions for updating the company's Web site. Medoff, who implemented most of the students' ideas, says that their input has been "invaluable." He is working with the university on other projects for students to tackle.[87]

- Join professional or trade associations and attend their meetings. There you have the chance to interact with others who have similar interests. Learning how other people have solved a particular problem may give you fresh insight into solving it.

- Develop listening skills. It's amazing what you can learn if you take the time to listen to other people—especially those who are older and have more experience. Try to learn something from everyone you meet.

- Eliminate creative distractions. Interruptions from telephone calls, e-mails, and visitors can crush creativity. Allowing employees to escape to a quiet, interruption-free environment enhances their ability to be creative.

Step 2. Investigation

This step requires one to develop a solid understanding of the problem, situation, or decision at hand. To create new ideas and concepts in a particular field, an individual first must study the problem and understand its basic components. Creative thinking comes about when people make careful observations of the world around them and then investigate the way things work (or fail to work). For example, Dr. Navia and another scientist at Vertex had spent several years conducting research on viruses and on a protein that blocks a virus enzyme called protease. His exploration of the various ways to block this enzyme paved the way for his discovery.

ENTREPRENEURIAL PROFILE: Christopher Leamon and Endocyte After earning his PhD in chemistry, Christopher Leamon began researching targeted anticancer therapy using molecules that tumors absorb as "Trojan horses" to deliver drugs that are lethal to them. Initially, Leamon had focused on the vitamin biotin, but after nine months of research and hard work, his experiment was a failure. One morning while sitting at the breakfast table with his wife, Leamon, a longtime cereal lover, was reading the ingredients on the nutrition panel of his box of Kellogg's Frosted Flakes. One of the items, folic acid, caught his attention. Leamon dashed off to the library and found a research paper on how folic acid enters a human cell and realized that this was the breakthrough that he had been seeking. Before long, Leamon had developed a technique for attaching cancer drugs to folic acid so that they would be absorbed and enable cells to fight the disease in much the same way they battle infections. Leamon has licensed the promising therapy to a company called Endocyte, which plans to have drugs on the market within a few years. Leamon says that although he has experienced "Eureka" moments in the lab, none was as significant as his folic acid breakthrough. His encounter with a simple cereal box at breakfast redefined his career and his life.[88] ■

Step 3. Transformation

Transformation involves viewing the similarities and the differences among the information collected. This phase requires two types of thinking: convergent and divergent. **Convergent thinking** is the ability to see the *similarities* and the connections among various and often diverse data and events. "So much of innovation comes from connecting things where other people don't make connections," says Mark Rice, professor of technology entrepreneurship at Olin College.[89]

convergent thinking
the ability to see similarities and the connections among various data and events.

ENTREPRENEURIAL PROFILE: Dominique Ansel: Dominique Ansel Bakery Dominique Ansel, owner of the bakery in New York City's SoHo district that created the wildly popular Cronut, says he and his employees devote time every week to brainstorming new product and menu ideas. "Finding a new idea is a lifestyle, not a moment," he says. Ansel and his team identified the best features of two popular bakery products, the croissant, with its layers of light crust, and the doughnut, which may include lush fillings or decadent toppings, or both, and combined them to create the Cronut. Making Cronuts is a labor-intensive process that can take up to three days. Because lines often form outside the bakery two-and-a-half hours before it opens, Ansel has had to impose a two-Cronut-per-person limit on in-store purchases and a six-Cronut limit on advance orders. Although Ansel has kept the price of the Cronut at $5, some customers resell their Cronuts at markups of up to 950 percent.[90] ■

Emmanuel Dunand/AFP/Getty Images/Newscom

Divergent thinking is the ability to see the *differences* among various data and events. While developing his AIDS-fighting drug, Dr. Navia studied the work of other scientists whose attempts at developing an enzyme-blocking drug had failed. He was able to see the similarities and the differences in his research and theirs and to build on their successes while avoiding their failures.

divergent thinking
the ability to see among various data and events.

How can you increase your ability to transform the information collected into a purposeful idea?

- Evaluate the parts of the situation several times, trying to grasp the "big picture." Getting bogged down in the details of a situation too early in the creative process can diminish creativity. Look for patterns that emerge.

- Rearrange the elements of the situation. By looking at the components of an issue in a different order or from a different perspective, you may be able to see the similarities and the differences among them more readily. Rearranging them also may help uncover a familiar pattern that had been masked by an unfamiliar structure. After graduating with a degree in physics from Bowling Green University, Jerry Barber spent most of his career designing rides for amusement parks and eventually started his own company, Venture Ride Manufacturing, which he operated for 18 years before selling it. The holder of 51 patents, Barber's most famous amusement park invention is the "free fall" ride, such as Disney's Tower of Terror. One day, after visiting with a friend who was delivering an enormous gearbox for a wind turbine, Barber began to think about creating a more efficient wind turbine. Drawing on his knowledge of a Ferris wheel's design, Barber eliminated the need for a complex gearbox and rearranged other turbine components to create the innovative WindWheel. A unique structural ring supports the five-blade turbine that turns with a slower, more efficient rotation, which dramatically reduces the level of noise pollution and makes the turbine more cost effective to operate. Barber's design also includes blades that come in sections, allowing for much easier highway transport.[91]

- Try using synectics (a term derived from the Greek words for "to bring together" and "diversity"), taking two seemingly nonsensical ideas and combining them. For instance, why not launch a bookstore with no physical storefront and no books—an accurate description of what Jeff Bezos did when he came up with the idea for Amazon.com.[92]

- Before locking into one particular approach to a situation, remember that several approaches might be successful. If one approach produces a dead end, don't hesitate to jump quickly to another. Considering several approaches to a problem or opportunity simultaneously would be like rolling a bowling ball down each of several lanes in quick succession. The more balls you roll down the lanes, the greater is the probability of hitting at least one strike. Resist the temptation to make snap judgments on how to tackle a problem or opportunity. The first approach may not be the best one.

Step 4. Incubation

The subconscious needs time to reflect on the information collected. To an observer, this phase of the creative process would be quite boring; it looks as though nothing is happening! In fact, during this phase, it may appear that the creative person is *loafing*. Incubation occurs while the individual is away from the problem, often engaging in some totally unrelated activity. Dr. Navia's creative powers were working at a subconscious level even when he was away from his work, not even thinking about his research on AIDS-fighting drugs.

How can you enhance the incubation phase of the creative process, letting ideas marinate in your mind?

- Walk away from the situation. Time away from a problem is vital to enhancing creativity. A study by Wilson Brill, an expert on creativity, of how 350 great ideas became successful products shows that two-thirds of the ideas came to people while they were *away* from work—in the shower, in their cars, in bed, on a walk, and in other nonwork situations.[93] Doing something totally unrelated to the problem gives your subconscious mind the chance to work on the problem or opportunity. Greg and Meredith Tally own the Best Western Southwest, a hotel in Denver located near Dinosaur Ridge, a famous site where paleontologists found the first fossils of several species of dinosaurs, including the stegosaurus, the allosaurus, and other large sauropods. The copreneurs were about to embark on a major renovation of their 112-room hotel. While on a fossil hunting expedition, Dave, a science and fossil enthusiast, had an idea: Rather than do a generic remodel, why not turn their hotel into an extension of the nearby Morrison Museum of Natural History?

In addition to a heated indoor pool (decorated with a mosaic of the creatures in a Cretaceous Period sea by famous dinosaur artist Larry Felder), the Tallys' renovation includes fossil displays from Dinosaur Ridge and the Morrison Museum ("They have way more stuff than they could ever show," Greg says), museum-like exhibits, and life-size models of dinosaurs. "I could not think of a more unique differentiator than the history of Dinosaur Ridge," Greg says.[94]

- Take the time to daydream. Although it may *look* as if you're doing nothing, daydreaming is an important part of the creative process. That's when your mind is most free from self-imposed restrictions on creativity. Research shows a connection between daydreaming and creativity; people who daydream are better at generating new ideas.[95] Feel free to let your mind wander, and it may just stumble onto a creative solution. Recent research shows that daydreaming is one sign of a well-equipped and active brain. Although daydreaming appears to be a passive activity, it actually keeps the brain in a highly engaged state in which it can make insightful connections and discover brilliant insights.[96]

- Relax—and play—regularly. Perhaps the worst thing you can do for creativity is to work on a problem or opportunity constantly. Soon enough, fatigue walks in, and creativity walks out! Great ideas often are incubated on the golf course, on the basketball court, on a hiking trail, in the hammock, or in a bar.

> **ENTREPRENEURIAL PROFILE: Kazuhide Sekiyama: Spiber Inc.** During an all-night drinking session that included an in-depth conversation about "bug technology," Kazuhide Sekiyama began working to develop a man-made thread that mimics spider web—soft and flexible, yet amazingly strong given its small diameter. In fact, real spider thread is one of nature's miracles; it can stretch 40 percent beyond its original length without breaking and is so strong that a spider web made of strands as thick as a pencil could stop a jumbo jet in flight. Using biomimicry, Sekiyama eventually created an artificial spider thread called Qmonos ("spider web" in Japanese) that he claims is equal to steel in tensile strength with the flexibility of rubber. He created a company, Spiber Inc., to produce and market Spiber Web, which could make lighter, stronger products in many fields, including auto parts, surgical materials, and bulletproof vests.[97] ∎

- Dream about the problem or opportunity. "Dreams have been responsible for two Nobel prizes, the invention of a couple of major drugs, other scientific discoveries, several important political events, and innumerable novels, films, and works of visual art," says Harvard Medical School psychologist Deirdre Barrett.[98] Although you may not be able to dream on command, thinking about an issue just before you drift off to sleep can be an effective way to encourage your mind to work on it while you sleep, a process called *lucid dreaming*. Barrett's research suggests that about 50 percent of people can focus their dreams by contemplating a particular problem before they go to sleep, in essence "seeding" the subconscious to influence their dreams.[99] The idea for Chris and Kella McPhee's business, Suburban Camping, came to Chris after he dreamed that he had created elaborate and unique backyard campouts for birthday parties and summer activities. The McPhees, both of whom are camping enthusiasts, used $15,000 of their savings to start their business. They have invested in a line of customized tents and now offer camping events with a variety of themes, including a Harry Potter campout, a girls night out package, a romantic evening, a movie night, and others. Prices range from $80 to $500, and the McPhees already are planning to expand beyond their New Jersey base and into beach camping.[100]

- Work on the problem or opportunity in a different environment—somewhere other than the office. Take your work outside on a beautiful fall day or sit on a bench in a mall. The change of scenery will likely stimulate your creativity.

Step 5. Illumination

This phase of the creative process occurs at some point during the incubation stage when a spontaneous breakthrough causes "the light bulb to go on." It may take place after five minutes—or five years. "An insight is an unexpected shift in the way we understand things," says Gary Klein, a clinical psychologist and author. "It comes without warning. It's not something that we think is going to happen. It feels like a gift, and, in fact, it is."[101] In the illumination stage, all the previous stages come together to produce the "Eureka factor"—the creation of the innovative idea. In one study of 200 scientists, 80 percent said at least once a solution to a problem had "just popped into their heads"—usually when they were away from the problem.[102] For Dr. Navia, the illumination stage occurred one day while he was reading a scientific journal. As he read, Dr. Navia says he was struck with a "hallucination" of a novel way to block protease.

Although the creative process itself may last for months or even years, the suddenness with which the illumination step occurs can be deceiving, making the process appear to occur much faster than it actually does. One night, Kent Murphy, an electrical engineer, began dreaming about what it would be like to be a photon of light. "I was riding a ray of light moving through the fiber," he recalls about his dream. Murphy, who holds 30 patents, used the insight from his dream to invent a fiber-optic gauge that monitors on a real-time basis the structural wear in airplanes.[103]

Step 6. Verification

For entrepreneurs, validating an idea as realistic and useful may include conducting experiments, running simulations, test-marketing a product or service, establishing small-scale pilot programs, building prototypes, and many other activities designed to verify that the new idea will work and is practical to implement. The goal is to subject the innovative idea to the test of cold, hard reality. At this phase, appropriate questions to ask include the following:

- Is it *really* a better solution to a particular problem or opportunity? Sometimes an idea that appears to have a bright future in the lab or on paper dims considerably when put to the test of reality.

- Will it work?

- Is there a need for it?

- If so, what is the best application of this idea in the marketplace?

- Does this product or service idea fit into our core competencies?

- How much will it cost to produce or to provide?

- Can we sell it at a reasonable price that will produce adequate sales, profit, and return on investment for our business?

- Will people buy it? Tom Ellingson and Dean Curtis, cofounders of Fandeavor, a business that helps sports fans' dreams come true (e.g., locker room and sideline access at a professional football game, tickets for pit row and meet-and-greet drivers at a NASCAR race, and others), kept their jobs at Zappos while they tested their business on a small scale. Fans responded enthusiastically to their business model and less than a year after starting Fandeavor, Ellingson and Curtis left Zappos and made their company (in which Zappos CEO Tony Hsieh invested $525,000) their full-time career.[104]

To test the value of his new drug formulation, Dr. Navia used powerful computers at Vertex Pharmaceuticals to build three-dimensional Tinkertoy-like models of the HIV virus and then simulated his new drug's ability to block the protease enzyme. Subsequent testing of the drug verified its safety. Dr. Navia was convinced he had an insight into solving the AIDS puzzle that no one else had discovered.

Step 7. Implementation

The focus of this step is to transform the idea into reality. Plenty of people come up with creative ideas for promising new products or services, but most never take them beyond the idea stage. What sets entrepreneurs apart is that they *act* on their ideas. An entrepreneur's philosophy is "Ready, aim, fire," not "Ready, aim, aim, aim, aim." Innowattech, a company based in Ra'anana, Israel, has developed a variety of piezoelectric (PE) crystals that possess the ability to transform vibrations, motion, and temperature changes into clean energy. Like miniature generators, the pressure-sensitive ceramic crystals give off small electrical charges when "squeezed, squashed, bent, or slapped," says Markys Cain, a materials scientist. In a recent test, Innowattech placed

PE generators two inches beneath a small section of Israel's busy Highway 4, where passing cars compressed the road, activated the tiny generators, and produced energy. The company estimates that placing the PE crystals under a one-half-mile stretch of highway would generate enough energy to supply 250 homes. Innowattech also has developed crystals for collecting clean energy from railways, airport runways, and pedestrian walkways. Pavegen Systems, a London-based company, has developed a similar technology for pedestrian walkways that captures the kinetic energy from passersby. Installed on a busy thoroughfare, the company's energy-absorbing pads (which are made from recycled material) can generate enough energy to power the area's lighting and signs.[105] The key to both companies' success is their ability to take a creative idea for a useful new product and turn it into a reality. As one creativity expert explains, "Becoming more creative is really just a matter of paying attention to that endless flow of ideas you generate, and learning to capture and act upon the new that's within you."[106]

For Dr. Navia and Vertex Pharmaceuticals, the implementation phase required testing the drug's ability to fight the deadly virus in humans. If it proved to be effective, Vertex would complete the process by bringing the drug to market. In this final phase of testing, Navia was so certain he was on the verge of a major breakthrough in fighting AIDS that he couldn't sleep at night. Unfortunately, the final critical series of tests proved that Dr. Navia's flash of creativity proved to be incorrect. Although his intuition proved to be wrong this time, Dr. Navia's research into fighting AIDS continues. Much of the current work at Vertex is based on Dr. Navia's original idea. Although it proved to be incorrect, his idea has served a valuable purpose: generating new ideas for HIV research.[107]

Techniques for Improving the Creative Process

LO7

Discuss techniques for improving the creative process.

Teams of people working together usually can generate more and more creative ideas. Five techniques that are especially useful for improving the quality of creative ideas from teams are brainstorming, mind mapping, force-field analysis, TRIZ, and rapid prototyping.

Brainstorming

Brainstorming is a process in which a small group of people interact with very little structure with the goal of producing a large *quantity* of novel and imaginative ideas. The goal is to create an open, uninhibited atmosphere that allows members of the group to "freewheel" ideas. Participants should suggest any ideas that come to mind *without evaluating or criticizing them*. As group members interact, each idea sparks the thinking of others, and the spawning of ideas becomes contagious. The free-flowing energy generated by the team becomes the genesis of a multitude of ideas, some of which may be impractical; however, those impractical ideas may lead to one idea that results in a breakthrough product or service for a company. For a brainstorming session to be successful, entrepreneurs should follow these guidelines:

brainstorming
a process in which a small group of people interact with very little structure with the goal of producing a large quantity of novel and imaginative ideas.

- Keep the group small—just five to eight members. Amazon founder Jeff Bezos uses the "two-pizza rule"—if a brainstorming group can eat two pizzas, it's too big.[108]

- Make the group as diverse as possible. Include people with different backgrounds, disciplines, and perspectives. At Joe Design Inc., every employee in the small firm takes part in brainstorming sessions. "We bring in everybody from the bookkeeper to the office manager because they see things completely differently than we do," says cofounder Joe Raia.[109]

- Encourage participants to engage in some type of aerobic exercise before the session. One study found that people who exercise—walking, bicycling, swimming, or running—before brainstorming sessions were more creative than those who did not exercise.[110]

- Ignore company rank and department affiliation. Every member of the brainstorming team is on equal ground.

- Give the group a well-defined problem. Stating the problem in the form of a "why," "how," or "what" question often helps.

- Rather than waste precious group meeting time getting participants up to speed, provide everyone involved in the session with relevant background material about the problem to be solved beforehand. Invite participants to submit at least three ideas by e-mail before the brainstorming session takes place. This gets people's minds focused on the issue.

- Limit the session to 40 to 60 minutes. Beyond that, participants grow weary, and creativity flags because brainstorming is an intense activity.

- Take a field trip. Visit the scene of the problem, if possible. Research shows that brainstorming teams that go "on site" actually come up with more and better ideas.[111]

- Appoint someone (preferably not a brainstorming participant) the job of recorder. The recorder should write every idea on a flip chart or board so that everyone can see it.

- Use a seating pattern that encourages communication and interaction (e.g., circular or U-shaped arrangements).

- Throw logic out the window. The best brainstorming sessions are playful and anything but logical.

- Encourage *all* ideas from the team, even wild and extreme ones. Discourage participants from editing their ideas. Not only can ideas that initially seem crazy get the group's creative juices flowing, but they also can spread creativity like wildfire. In addition, the group often can polish some of these wild ideas into practical, creative solutions.

- Establish a goal of *quantity* of ideas over *quality* of ideas. There will be plenty of time later to evaluate the ideas generated. At Ideo Inc., a Silicon Valley design firm, brainstorming teams shoot for at least 150 ideas in a 30- to 45-minute session.[112] When chemist Linus Pauling received his second Nobel Prize, someone asked him how he came up with so many great ideas. Pauling replied simply, "I come up with lots of ideas."[113]

- *Forbid* evaluation or criticism of any idea during the brainstorming session. No idea is a bad idea. Criticism slams the brakes on the creative process instantly!

- Encourage participants to use "idea hitchhiking," building new ideas on those already suggested. Often, some of the best solutions are those that are piggybacked on others.

- Dare to imagine the unreasonable. Creative ideas often arise when people suspend conventional thinking to consider far-fetched solutions.

ENTREPRENEURIAL PROFILE: John Nottingham: Nottingham Spirk At Nottingham Spirk, an industrial design firm whose success depends on the creativity of its people, employees routinely use brainstorming to come up with new product ideas and designs. The focus of these sessions is to generate a large quantity of ideas, "from mild to wild," says cofounder John Nottingham, rather than to emphasize the quality of the ideas. By the end of the session, the walls are covered with pieces of paper containing scribbles, sketches, and notes, representing 100 or more ideas. Only after the brainstorming session do employees begin to focus on the quality of the ideas generated. In these meetings, employees judge each idea using a simple scale. Each person can display one of three cards: "Who Cares?" "Nice," and "Wow!" (All participants display their cards simultaneously.) A consensus of "Who Cares?" cards means that the group discards the idea, but a strong showing of "Wow!" cards means that the idea moves forward for refinement. A vote of "Nice" usually means that the idea goes back for more brainstorming, hopefully transforming it into a "Wow!" idea. An idea for a Christmas tree stand that uses a swivel joint and a locking pedal initially received a "Nice" rating from the group. The idea's champion kept tinkering with it, ultimately adding a self-regulating automatic watering device and other features before returning to the group. In its second pass, the idea went from "Nice" to "Wow!" Since 2002, the SwivelStraight tree stand has sold 1 million units.[114] ■

Mind Mapping

Another useful tool for jump-starting creativity is **mind mapping**, an extension of brainstorming. One strength of mind mapping is that it reflects the way the brain actually works. Rather than throwing out ideas in a linear fashion, the brain jumps from one idea to another. In many creative sessions, ideas are rushing out so fast that many are lost if a person attempts to shove them into a

mind mapping
a graphical technique that encourages thinking on both sides of the brain, visually displays the various relationships among ideas, and improves the ability to view a problem from many sides.

linear outline. Creativity suffers. Mind mapping is a graphical technique that encourages thinking on both sides of the brain, visually displays the various relationships among ideas, and improves the ability to view a problem from many sides.

The mind-mapping process works this way:

- Start by writing down or sketching a picture symbolizing the problem or area of focus in the center of a large blank page. Tony Buzan, originator of the mind-mapping technique, suggests using ledger paper or covering an entire wall with butcher paper to establish a wide-open attitude toward creativity.

- Write down *every* idea that comes into your mind, connecting each idea to the central picture or words with a line. Use key words and symbols to record ideas in shorthand. Work as quickly as possible for no more than 20 minutes, doing your best to capture the tide of ideas that flows from your brain. Just as in brainstorming, do not judge the quality of your ideas; just get them onto the paper. Build new ideas on the backs of existing ones. If you see a connection between a new idea and one already on the paper, connect them with a line. If not, simply connect the idea to the center symbol. You will organize your ideas later in the process.

- When the flow of ideas slows to a trickle, stop! Don't try to force creativity.

- Allow your mind to rest for a few minutes and then begin to integrate the ideas on the page into a mind map. Use colored pens and markers to connect ideas with similar themes or to group ideas into related clusters. As you organize your thoughts, look for new connections among your ideas. Sometimes the brain needs time to process the ideas in a mind map. (Recall the incubation stage of the creative process.) Walking away from the mind map and the problem for a few minutes or a few hours may lead to several new ideas or to new relationships among ideas. One entrepreneur created the format for his company's business plan with a mind map rather than with a traditional linear outline. When he finished, he not only knew what he should include in his plan but also had a clear picture of the order in which to sequence the elements.

Force-Field Analysis

Force-field analysis is a useful technique for evaluating the forces that support and oppose a proposed change. It allows entrepreneurs to weigh both the advantages and the disadvantages of a particular decision and work to maximize the variables that support it and minimize those that work against it. The process, which, like brainstorming, works well with a group, begins by making three columns and listing the problem to be addressed in the center column. In the column on the left, the group should list driving forces, those that support the issue and move it forward. In the column on the right, the group should list the restraining forces, those that hold back the company from implementing the idea. The specific forces that the group may come up with are almost limitless, but some of the factors the team should consider include people, values, costs, trends, traditions, politics, costs, revenues, environmental impact, regulations, and attitudes.

Once the group has identified a reasonable number of driving and restraining forces (4 to 10 is typical), the next task is to assign a numerical value that reflects the strength of that particular force. For the driving forces column, scores range from 1 (weak) to 4 (strong), and in the restraining forces column, scores range from -1 (weak) to -4 (strong). Adding the scores for the driving forces column and the restraining forces column shows which set of forces dominates the issue. The higher the total score, the more feasible is the idea. If the decision is a "go," the group can focus on ideas to create new driving forces, strengthen existing driving forces, and minimize the impact of restraining forces.

Force-field analysis produces many benefits, particularly when it is combined with other creativity enhancing techniques. It helps entrepreneurs judge the practicality of a new idea, identify resources the company can use to bring the idea to market, recognize obstacles the company must overcome to implement the idea, and suggest ways to conquer those obstacles.

Figure 3.4 shows a sample force-field analysis for a small liberal arts college that is considering an entrepreneurial venture, launching a pharmacy school.

FIGURE 3.4

Sample Force-Field Analysis

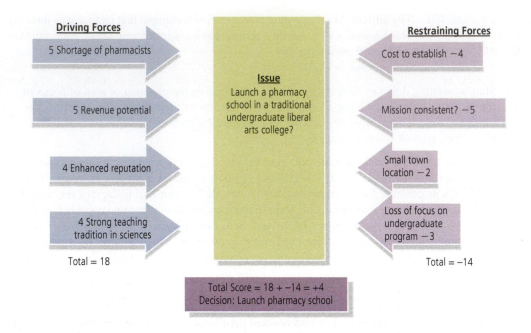

TRIZ

Developed in 1946 by Genrich Altshuller, a 22-year-old naval officer in the former Soviet Union, TRIZ (pronounced "trees") is a systematic approach designed to help solve any technical problem, whatever its source. The name is derived from the acronym for the Russian phrase that translates as "theory of inventive problem solving." Unlike brainstorming and mind mapping, which are right-brain activities, TRIZ is a left-brain, scientific, step-by-step process that is based on the study of hundreds of the most innovative patents across the globe. Altshuller claimed that these innovations followed a particular set of patterns. Unlocking the principles behind those patterns allows one not only to solve seemingly insurmountable problems but also to predict where the next challenges would arise.

Altshuller and his colleagues developed 40 principles underlying these innovative patents and then developed the "TRIZ contradiction matrix," a tool that combines these principles to solve a problem. They recognized that innovations come about when someone is able to overcome the inherent contradictions in a process. For instance, in the packaging industry, a contradiction exists between the effectiveness of childproof safety caps for medicine containers and making those containers easy for authorized users to open. Manufacturers of mattresses face the contradiction of making mattresses that are both hard and soft. Too often, companies rely on a very unimaginative solution to contradictions such as these; they compromise. Rather than settle for a mediocre compromise, the TRIZ contradiction matrix is designed to *resolve* these conflicts using the 40 principles that Altshuller developed. One axis of the matrix displays the characteristic of the process to be improved, and the other axis displays the conflicting characteristic that is becoming worse.

For example, suppose that a candy maker wants to make syrup-filled, bottle-shaped chocolates by molding the chocolate bottles and then pouring syrup into the mold. To speed production of the finished product to meet demand, the business owner tries heating the syrup to allow for faster pouring, but the heated syrup melts the molded chocolate bottles and distorts their shape (the contradiction; see Figure 3.5). Using the TRIZ contradiction matrix, the candy maker recognizes the problem as a conflict between speed and shape. Speed is the characteristic to be improved, and shape is the characteristic that is getting worse. The principles that the matrix suggests for solving this problem include (1) changing the dynamics of the object or the environment (e.g., making a rigid part flexible), (2) discarding or recovering parts of an object (e.g., dissolving a protective case when it is no longer needed), (3) causing an object to vibrate or oscillate (e.g., transforming a standard knife into an electric knife by introducing oscillating blades), and (4) changing the properties of the object (e.g., freezing the chocolate syrup and then molding the bottles around the syrup).

Characteristic to be improved	Characteristic that is getting worse					
	Volume of stationary object	Speed	Force	Stress or pressure	Shape	Stability of the object
Volume of stationary object	—	*	Taking out Mechanical vibration Thermal expansion	Intermediary Parameter changes	Nested doll Taking out Parameter changes	Discarding and recovering Mechanics substitution Parameter changes Composite materials
Speed	*	—	The other way around Mechanics substitution Dynamics Periodic action	Universality Mechanical vibration Strong oxidants Composite materials	Dynamics Discarding and recovering Mechanical vibration Parameter changes	Mechanics substitution Homogeneity Segmentation Mechanical vibration
Force	Taking out Phase transitions Mechanical vibration Thermal expansion	The other way round Mechanics substitution Dynamics Equipotentiality	—	Mechanical vibration Skipping Beforehand cushioning	Preliminary action Parameter changes Composite materials Discarding and recovering	Parameter changes Preliminary action Skipping
Stress or pressure	Parameter changes Intermediary	Universality Parameter changes Phase transitions	Phase transitions Parameter changes Skipping	—	Parameter changes Asymmetry Dynamics Preliminary action	Parameter changes Homogeneity Taking out Composite materials
Shape	Nested doll Taking out Parameter changes	Parameter changes Discarding and recovering Mechanical vibration	Parameter changes Preliminary action Thermal expansion Composite materials	Discarding and recovering Dynamics Preliminary action Spheroidality and curvature	—	Homogeneity Segmentation Mechanical vibration Asymmetry

FIGURE 3.5

TRIZ Contradiction Matrix

Source: Based on, G. Altshuller, TRIZ 40, http://www.triz40.com/aff_Matrix.htm.

Choosing principle 4, the candy maker decides to change the properties of the chocolate syrup by adding a compound that causes it to solidify when exposed to air, making it easier and faster to coat with chocolate. Once enclosed inside the chocolate, the syrup once again becomes a liquid. Problem solved![115]

Rapid Prototyping

Generating creative ideas is a critical step in the process of taking an idea for a product or a service successfully to market. However, recall that many (perhaps most) ideas that entrepreneurs come up with fail. Inventor and serial entrepreneur Scott Jones says his kids still enjoy teasing him about one of his offbeat ideas that flopped: a pair of microturbines embedded in the soles of shoes that would propel the wearer forward. (Jones abandoned the idea after seeing a similar concept fail flamboyantly in the movie *Jackass*.)[116] Rapid prototyping plays an important part in the creative process because it serves as a way to screen ideas that are not practical or just won't work so that entrepreneurs can focus their creative energy on other ideas. The premise behind **rapid prototyping** is that transforming an idea into an actual model points out flaws in the original idea and leads to improvements in its design. "If a picture is worth a thousand words, a prototype is worth ten thousand," says Steve Vassallo of Ideo Inc.[117]

rapid prototyping
the process of creating a model of an idea, enabling an entrepreneur to discover flaws in the idea and to make improvements in the design.

The three principles of rapid prototyping are the three Rs: rough, rapid, and right. Models do not have to be perfect; in fact, in the early phases of developing an idea, perfecting a model usually is a waste of time. The key is to make the model good enough to determine what works and what does not. Doing so allows an entrepreneur to develop prototypes rapidly, moving closer to a successful design with each iteration. The final R, right, means building lots of small models that focus on solving particular problems with an idea. "You're not trying to build a complete model," says Vassallo. "You're just focusing on a small section of it."[118]

LO8

Describe the protection of intellectual property through patents, trademarks, and copyrights.

Intellectual Property: Protecting Your Ideas

Once entrepreneurs come up with innovative ideas for a product or service that has market potential, their immediate concern should be to protect them from unauthorized use. Counterfeit goods pose a real threat to businesses that have created intellectual property and their customers who use the products based on that intellectual property. The World Trade Organization estimates that between 5 and 7 percent of all goods traded globally are counterfeit.[119] Research by the International Chamber of Commerce concludes that the value of counterfeit goods sold globally exceeds $1.7 trillion.[120] Table 3.2 lists the top 10 counterfeit goods seized by U.S. Customs agents. China is the origin of 68 percent of the counterfeit goods seized in the United States.[121]

For many businesses, the value of their intellectual property exceeds the value of their tangible assets. Entrepreneurs must understand how to protect their intellectual property using three common tools—patents, trademarks, and copyrights.

Patents

patent

a grant from the federal government's Patent and Trademark Office to the inventor of a product, giving the exclusive right to make, use, or sell the invention in this country for 20 years from the date of filing the patent application.

A **patent** is a grant from the U.S. Patent and Trademark Office (PTO) to the inventor of a product, giving the exclusive right to make, use, or sell the invention (and to prevent others from making, using or selling it) in this country for 20 years from the date of filing the patent application. The purpose of giving an inventor a 20-year monopoly over a product is to stimulate creativity and innovation. After 20 years, the patent expires and cannot be renewed, and the invention becomes part of the public domain. The popular Keurig single-cup coffee machine is protected by 37 patents, but two of its most crucial patents expired in 2012, opening the door for competitors to introduce their own versions of the device.[122]

Most patents are granted for new product inventions (called *utility patents*), but *design patents*, extending for 14 years beyond the date the patent is issued, are given to inventors who make new, original, and ornamental changes in the design of existing products that enhance their sales.

TABLE 3.2 Top 10 Counterfeit Products Seized by U.S. Customs Agents

In a typical year, U.S. customs agents make about 23,000 seizures of counterfeit goods coming into the United States. These seizures represent only a portion of the total traffic in pirated goods. Which items are most often pirated?

Rank	Product	Percentage of Counterfeit Goods Seized
1	Wearing apparel and accessories	35%
2	Consumer electronics	20%
3	Handbags and wallets	8%
4	Pharmaceuticals and personal care items	8%
5	Watches and jewelry	6%
6	Footwear	6%
7	Optical media	5%
8	Computers and accessories	4%
9	Labels and tags	3%
10	Sporting goods	1%

Source: Intellectual Property Rights: Fiscal Year 2013 Seizure Statistics, U.S. Customs and Border Protection, Office of International Trade, 2014, p. 8.

Inventors who develop a new plant can obtain a *plant patent*, provided that they can reproduce the plant asexually (e.g., by grafting or crossbreeding rather than planting seeds). To be patented, a device must be new (but not necessarily better!), not obvious to a person of ordinary skill or knowledge in the related field, and useful. A device *cannot* be patented if it has been publicized in print anywhere in the world or if it has been used or offered for sale in this country prior to the date of the patent application. A U.S. patent is granted only to the true inventor, not a person who discovers another's invention, and is effective *only* in the United States and its territories. (In 2011, Congress passed the America Invents Act that changed the "first to invent" rule formerly in place to "first to file," which means that a patent goes to the first person to *file* a patent application.) Inventors who want to sell their inventions abroad must file for patents in each country in which they plan to do business. Once a product is patented, no one can copy or sell it without getting a license from its creator. A patent does not give one the right to make, use, or sell an invention but rather the right to exclude others from making, using, or selling it.

Although inventors are never assured of getting a patent, they can enhance their chances by following the basic steps suggested by the PTO. Before beginning the often lengthy and involved procedure, inventors should obtain professional assistance from a patent practitioner—a patent attorney or a patent agent—who is registered with the PTO. Only those attorneys and agents who are officially registered may represent an inventor seeking a patent. A list of registered attorneys and agents is available at the PTO's Web site. Approximately 98 percent of all inventors rely on these patent experts to steer them through the convoluted process. Legal fees for filing a patent application range from $4,000 to $25,000, depending on the complexity of the product.

THE PATENT PROCESS Since George Washington signed the first patent law in 1790, the PTO (www.uspto.gov) has issued patents on everything imaginable (and some unimaginable items, too), including mouse traps (of course!), Robert Fulton's steamboat, animals (genetically engineered mice), Thomas Edison's light bulb, golf tees (764 different patents), games, and various fishing devices. The J. M. Smucker Company even holds a patent issued in 1999 on a "sealed, crustless sandwich," a peanut butter and jelly sandwich it markets very successfully under the name "Uncrustables."[123] The PTO also has issued patents on business processes—methods of doing business—including Amazon.com's controversial patent on its "1-Click" technology, which allows users to store their customer information in a file and then recall it with one mouse click at checkout. Google recently received a patent for a system of "advertising based on environmental conditions." The patent gives Google the exclusive right to use the technology to send targeted ads to users depending on the temperature, for example (e.g., ads for winter coats when the temperature dips into the 30s or rain gear when it rains).[124] To date, the PTO has issued nearly 9 million patents, and it receives more than 575,000 new applications and grants nearly 250,000 patents each year (see Figure 3.6)![125] To receive a patent, an inventor must follow these steps:

Establish the invention's novelty. An invention is not patentable if it is known or has been used in the United States or has been described in a printed publication in this or a foreign country.

Document the device. To protect their patent claims, inventors should be able to verify the date on which they first conceived the idea for their inventions. Inventors should document a device by keeping dated records (including drawings) of their progress on the invention and by having knowledgeable friends witness these records.

Search existing patents. To verify that the invention truly is new, not obvious, and useful, an inventor must conduct a search of existing patents on similar products. The purpose of the search is to determine whether the inventor has a chance of getting a patent. Most inventors hire professionals trained in conducting patent searches to perform the research. Inventors themselves can conduct an online search of all patents granted by the PTO since 1976 from the office's Web site. An online search of these patents does not include sketches; however, subscribers to Delphion's Research Intellectual Property Network can access patents, including sketches, as far back as 1971. Search engine Google also enables entrepreneurs to search patents at its "patents" site.

Study search results. Once the patent search is finished, inventors must study the results to determine their chances of getting a patent. To be patentable, a device must be sufficiently

FIGURE 3.6

Patent Applications and Patents Issued

Source: U.S. Patent and Trademark Office, 2014.

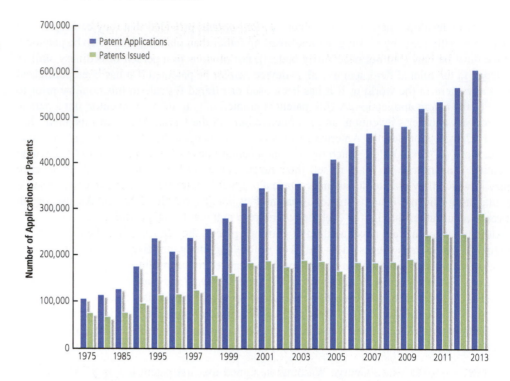

different from what has been used or described before and must not be obvious to a person having ordinary skill in the area of technology related to the invention.

Complete a patent application. If an inventor decides to seek a patent, he or she must file an application describing the invention with the PTO. The patent application must include specific *claims*, which describe the invention—what it does and how it works—and any drawings that are necessary to support the claims. The typical patent application runs 20 to 40 pages although some, especially those for biotech or high-tech products, are tens of thousands of pages long. The longest patent application to date is one for a gene patent that was 6 million pages long![126] Most inventors hire patent attorneys or agents to help them complete their patent applications. Figure 3.7 shows a portion of the application for a rather unusual patent. Inventors also can file a provisional application for a patent for a small fee. Filing for a provisional patent does not require the inventor to file any claims but does give him or her the right to use the phrase "patent pending" on the device. After filing for a provisional patent, an inventor has one year to file a standard patent application.

File the patent application. Before the PTO will issue a patent, one of its examiners studies the application to determine whether the invention warrants a patent. Approval of a patent takes on average 27.5 months from the date of filing.[127] If the PTO rejects the application, the inventor can amend his or her application and resubmit it to the PTO.

Defending a patent against "copycat producers" can be expensive and time consuming but often is necessary to protect an entrepreneur's interest. The number of patent infringement lawsuits has increased sharply. In 2009, patent holders filed 2,800 infringement suits; today, courts see nearly 5,200 patent suits per year. The median time for a patent infringement case to get to trial is 2.3 years. The median cost of a patent infringement lawsuit when the amount in dispute is between $1 million and $25 million is about $2.65 million if the case goes to trial (about 95 percent of patent infringement lawsuits are settled out of court), but the odds of winning are in the patent holder's favor. About two-thirds of patent holders win their infringement suits; since 2007, the median award is $4.95 million, which is most often based on the royalties lost to the infringer.[128] Canada Goose is a company started in 1957 in Toronto, Ontario, that manufactures high-quality, down-insulated vests and coats designed to protect people who wear the company's products from the mind-numbing cold of Antarctica or the gale-force winds on the North Sea. Recently, Canada Goose managers discovered knockoffs of its products that look like the real items but contain no down insulation at all. Instead, the counterfeit garments, many of which are

FIGURE 3.7

A Sample (and Unusual) Patent for Pet Display Clothing

Source: The United States Patent and Trademark Office, an Agency of the Department of Commerce, United States Government, Washington, DC.

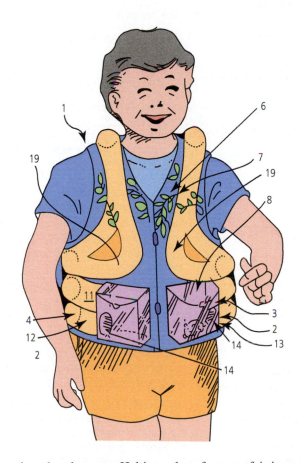

offer no protection against the elements. Halting sales of counterfeit items can be difficult, but CEO Dani Reiss, whose grandfather founded the company, says Canada Goose "employs legal teams all over the world to intercept [counterfeit] shipments." Recently, Canada Goose was successful in shutting down a business that was importing counterfeit jackets bearing its labels and selling them to unsuspecting customers in Sweden. To verify the authenticity of its products, the company recently began adding a hologram to every jacket.[129] With its global reach and speedy convenience, the Internet compounds the problem of counterfeit sales, especially among brand-name products such as shoes, consumer electronics, handbags, apparel, watches, computers, and others. Ninety-three percent of counterfeit goods originate in China and Hong Kong.[130]

Trademarks

A **trademark** is any distinctive word, phrase, symbol, design, name, logo, slogan, or trade dress that a company uses to identify the origin of a product or to distinguish it from other goods

trademark

any distinctive word, phrase, symbol, design, name, logo, slogan, or trade dress that a company uses to identify the origin of a product or to distinguish it from other goods on the market.

You Be the Consultant

How Would You Rule in These Intellectual Property Cases?

Companies in the fashion industry typically defend their trademarks aggressively but traditionally have not relied on patents to protect their intellectual property because few legal protections for clothing designs exist. Fashion designers constantly come up with new designs for garments but find that protecting, say, the shape of a lapel or the cut of a cuff, is difficult because clothing is functional and not "novel, useful, and not obvious" in light of current technology, which receiving a patent requires. Fashion companies usually look to trademarks to protect their brands.

Christian Louboutin SA v. Yves Saint Laurent SA. French luxury shoemaker Christian Louboutin (CL) recently filed a trademark infringement lawsuit against Yves Saint Laurent (YSL), claiming that CL had the right to trademark protection for the "China red" soles the company uses on all of its high heel shoes and that YSL had violated its trademark by introducing a line of "monochrome" high heel shoes in which the red shoes had red soles. CL's attorney argued that Louboutin's use of the red soles had transformed an everyday item, the sole of a shoe, into a work of art and created a well-recognized trademark. "The red sole has become synonymous with Christian Louboutin and high fashion," the company pointed out in its complaint. "Louboutin turned a pedestrian item into a thing of beauty." Celebrities such as Scarlett Johansson, Oprah Winfrey, Gwyneth Paltrow, Halle Berry, Beyoncé, Christina Aguilera, and many others, often sport "Loubs." CL also pointed out that other companies have trademark protection for certain colors, such as Tiffany and Company's robin-egg blue boxes, United Parcel Service's brown trucks and uniforms, and Owens-Corning's pink insulation.

Winning a trademark for color has proven to be more difficult in the fashion industry, where color is a fundamental part of almost any design. That principle became the foundation of YSL's argument. YSL's attorney countered by citing a judge's ruling in a similar case that said, "Granting a producer the exclusive use of a basic element of design (shape, material, color, and so forth) impoverishes other designers' palettes." YSL went on to argue that "allowing Louboutin to claim a monopoly on the use of red on a part of the shoe would have an unprecedented, anti-competitive effect in limiting the design options available to all other designers."

After hearing the parties' arguments, Judge Victor Marrero, a district court judge in New York, ruled in favor of Yves Saint Laurent. "Louboutin's claim would cast a red cloud over the whole industry, cramping what other designers could do while allowing Louboutin to paint with a full palette," he wrote. "Color constitutes a critical attribute of the goods." His ruling meant that Christian Louboutin could not claim trademark protection for its red-soled shoes. Attorneys for Christian Louboutin filed an appeal with the Second Circuit U.S. Court of Appeals with the intent of having the appeals court reverse the trial court's decision.

Lulumon Athletica Inc. v. Calvin Klein Inc. Lulumon, a maker of yoga apparel based in Vancouver, British Columbia,

filed a complaint in a district court in Delaware, claiming that Calvin Klein Inc. (CKI) was selling yoga pants that infringed on three of the company's design patents, including one that included a distinctive waistband made of three overlapping panels of fabric that the company received in 2011. Unlike a utility patent, a design patent protects an item's nonfunctional, ornamental features. To receive a design patent, a product must include the following five elements:

1. The item must be an "article of manufacture."

2. The design must be original.

3. The design must be novel.

4. The design must be non-obvious.

5. The design must be ornamental.

With its three overlapping pieces of Lulumon's trademarked Luon compression fabric, the waistband on the company's Astro yoga pants, which retail for $98, is designed to make the waist look slimmer and, because they can be rolled down to sit lower on the waist, enhance the wearer's athletic performance. Lulumon claimed that the waistband on CKI's yoga pants, which sell for as little as $20, is substantially similar to the waistband on its Astro yoga pants. According to a decision in 2008 by the U.S. Court of Appeals for the Federal Circuit, owners of design patents must prove that to the average observer the alleged infringer's design appears to be substantially the same as its own design (known as the "ordinary observer test").

1. What does a trademark protect? What does a patent protect? What is a design patent?

2. Assume the role of a judge in these two cases. How would you rule? Explain your reasoning. (In the Lulumon Athletica v. Calvin Klein case, you may want to search online for images of the two companies' yoga pants and apply the ordinary observer test before making your decision.)

3. Use a search engine to research the outcomes of these two cases. How were the cases resolved? If a judge rendered a decision, summarize his or her reasoning. Do you agree with the judge's decision?

Sources: Based on Tim Sablik, "Can Creativity and Copying Coexist?" *Region Focus,* Fourth Quarter, 2011, p. 24; Ashby Jones, "The Red Sole Case," *Wall Street Journal,* January 25, 2012, pp. B1–B2; Ray A. Smith and Ashby Jones, "Color Wars: Luxury Makers Battle Over Red-Soled Shoes," *Wall Street Journal,* August 11, 2011, pp. B1, B8; Chad Bray, "Red-Soled Shoes Win Appeal," *Wall Street Journal,* September 6, 2012, p. B10; Ashby Jones, "Downward Docket: The Yoga Pants War," *Wall Street Journal,* September 12, 2012, pp. B1, B5; "Lulumon Settles Yoga Pants Lawsuit with Calvin Klein," *CBC News,* November 21, 2012, http://www.cbc.ca/news/business/lululemon-settles-yoga-pants-patent-lawsuit-with-calvin-klein-1.1183253; Cory Howard, "Lulumon's Yoga-Pant Waistband Stretches the Limits of Design Patent Protection," *Jurist,* October 25, 2012, http://www.cbc.ca/news/business/lululemon-settles-yoga-pants-patent-lawsuit-with-calvin-klein-1.1183253; "Lulumon Settles Patent Dispute with Calvin Klein," *Jurist,* November 22, 2012, http://jurist.org/paperchase/2012/11/lululemon-settles-patent-dispute-with-calvin-klein.php.; Complaint at page 9, Christian Louboutin v Yves Saint Laurent, No. 11-cv-2381, United States District Court, Southern District Court of New York, April 7, 2011; Complaint at page 2, Defendants/Counterclaim Plaintiffs' Memorandum of Law in Opposition to Motion for Preliminary Injunction, No. 11-cv-2381, United States District Court of New York, July 12, 2011.

*"Yeah, Org invented the wheel, but
I invented the patent."*

Larry Lambert/www.CartoonStock.com

goods on the market. (A **service mark** is the same as a trademark except that it identifies and distinguishes the source of a service rather than a product.) A trademark serves as a company's "signature" in the marketplace. A trademark can be more than just a company's logo, slogan, or brand name; it can also include symbols, shapes, colors, smells, or sounds. For instance, Coca-Cola holds a trademark on the shape of its bottle, and Owens-Corning has trademarked the unique pink color of its insulation. NBC owns a "sound mark," the auditory equivalent of a trademark, on its three-toned chime, and MGM has similar protection on the roar of the lion (whose name is Leo) that appears at the beginning of its movies.[131] *Trademark infringement* involves using another company's trademark without permission or using a mark that is so similar to another's trademark that it is likely to create confusion about the origin of the goods. Trademark owners file about 3,600 infringement lawsuits per year.[132]

ENTREPRENEURIAL PROFILE: Heath Scurfield and Calli Baker's Firehouse Bar & Grill Firehouse Subs, a chain of fast-food submarine sandwich shops with more than 450 locations across the United States, filed a trademark infringement suit against Heath Scurfield, a retired firefighter who owns Calli Baker's Firehouse Bar & Grill, claiming that his use of the word "firehouse" in his company's name was likely to confuse customers into believing that his restaurant was affiliated with the national chain. Scurfield argued that the only similarity between his independent, full-service restaurant, which features lunch and dinner entrees, a bar, and a catering service, and the Firehouse Subs chain is the inclusion of the word "firehouse" in their names and the firehouse decor. After three years of legal wrangling, a jury ruled in Scurfield's favor and invalidated Firehouse Subs' trademark because it filed a fraudulent trademark application in 2003, claiming that at the time no other restaurants were using the word "firehouse" in their names when, in reality, the company knew that many restaurants included "firehouse" in their names. Firehouse Subs appealed the ruling, and the parties ultimately entered into a court-approved settlement under which Scurfield would continue to use his company's name and Firehouse Subs would not renew its trademark and would pay all of Scurfield's legal fees, which amounted to hundreds of thousands of dollars.[133] ■

Components of a product's identity are part of its **trade dress**, the unique combination of elements that a company uses to create a product's image and to promote it. For instance, a Mexican restaurant chain's particular decor, color schemes, design, and overall "look and feel" constitute

service mark
offers the same protection as a trademark but identifies and distinguishes the source of a service rather than a product.

trade dress
the unique combination of elements that a company uses to create a product's image and to promote it.

its trade dress. To be eligible for trademark protection, trade dress must be inherently unique and distinctive to a company, and another company's use of that trade dress must be likely to confuse customers.

There are 1.88 million trademarks registered and in active use in the United States (see Figure 3.8).[134] Federal law permits a company to register a trademark, which prevents other companies from employing a similar mark to identify their goods. Before 1989, a business could not reserve a trademark in advance of use. Today, the first party who either uses a trademark in commerce or files an application with the PTO has the ultimate right to register that trademark. Before attempting to register a trademark, an entrepreneur must conduct a search to verify that it is not already in use or is too similar to an existing mark. BizFilings' Trademark Explorer is a handy, low-cost tool for conducting trademark searches. Registering a trademark takes an average of 10.3 months from the time an entrepreneur submits the application.[135] Unlike patents and copyrights, which are issued for limited amounts of time, trademarks last indefinitely as long as the holder continues to use it. However, between 5 and 6 years after a trademark's registration date (and again between 9 and 10 years after the registration date and every 10 years after that), an entrepreneur must file an affidavit of use with the PTO. A trademark cannot keep competitors from producing the same product or selling it under a different name; it merely prevents others from using the same or confusingly similar trademark for the same or similar products.

Many business owners are confused by the use of the symbols ™ and ®. Anyone who claims the right to a particular trademark (or service mark) or has filed a trademark application can use the ™ (or ᔆᴹ) symbol. The claim to that trademark or service mark may or may not be valid, however. Only those businesses that have *registered* their marks with the PTO can use the ® symbol. Entrepreneurs do not have to register trademarks or service marks to establish their rights to those marks; however, registering a mark with the PTO does give entrepreneurs greater power to protect their marks. Filing an application to register a trademark or service mark costs from $275 to $375 and is relatively easy, but it does require a search of existing names.

An entrepreneur may lose the exclusive right to a trademark if it loses its unique character and becomes a generic name. Aspirin, escalator, thermos, brassiere, super glue, corn flakes, yo-yo, and cellophane all were once enforceable trademarks that have become common words in the English language. These generic terms can no longer be licensed as trademarks.

FIGURE 3.8

Trademark Applications and Trademarks and Renewals Issued

Source: US Patent and Trademark Office, 2014.

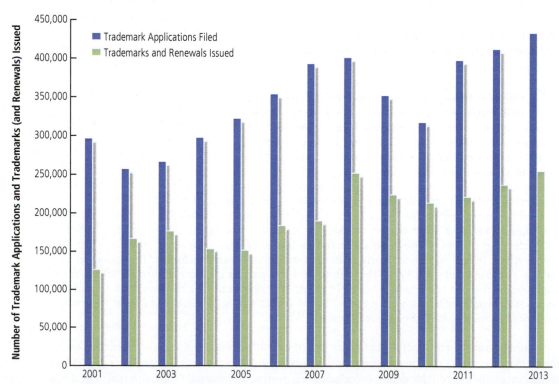

Hands On . . . How To

Protect Your Company's Intellectual Property— Both at Home and Abroad

In 2004, Thomas Dempsey started a company, SylvanSport, in Brevard, North Carolina, to sell a unique recreational camper trailer he invented and patented. SylvanSport marketed the trailer as "more versatile than a Swiss army knife" because it folds into a trailer that can carry boats, bikes, and other gear and, once onsite, convert in minutes into a camper with a self-inflating mattress and tent. By 2011, the company's annual sales had reached $3 million, 15 percent of which came from outside the United States, particularly South Korea, Japan, and Australia. With international sales growth outpacing domestic sales growth, Dempsey saw a bright future for his company.

Then he received an e-mail from a customer that included a link to the Web site of a Chinese company, Wuyi Tiandi Motion Apparatus, that was selling a camper trailer almost identical to the one he had designed. "We were shocked," says Dempsey. "We thought at first that what we saw was our product, but we realized that [their product] was created from scratch."

Since then, several of Dempsey's international distributors in Asia have dropped SylvanSport's camper and are selling the Chinese company's product. A Japanese distributor mistakenly purchased the Chinese company's camper, thinking it was buying one of SylvanSport's products. Thomas Tang, sales manager for Wuyi Tiandi, admits that SylvanSport was the first company "to make this type of trailer, and we followed them to make a similar product." Although Wuyi Tiandi cannot sell its camper in the United States because of SylvanSport's patent, "we can still sell our trailer everywhere else [in the world]," says Tang. Dempsey is concerned about the sales his company has lost to its Chinese competitor. "There's a very real chance that the Chinese company could be the survivor here and we could go out of business," he says matter-of-factly.

Thomas Dempsey took the proper steps to protect his intellectual property by securing a utility patent for his unique camper trailer in the United States. Like many entrepreneurs in today's global economy, Dempsey is conducting business internationally, where his U.S. patent offers no protection. What lessons can entrepreneurs learn from Dempsey's experience about protecting their intellectual property?

1. *Recognize that intellectual property, the rights that result when a person uses his or her knowledge and creativity to produce something of value, can be a business's most valuable asset, even for small companies.* Often intellectual property is the source of a company's competitive advantage. Experts estimate that in the United States alone, 30 to 40 percent of all gains in productivity over the course of the twentieth century originated with intellectual property. The World Intellectual Property Organization estimates that the value of the intellectual property of companies in the United States is $5.8 trillion.

2. *Use the appropriate tool to file for protection of your intellectual property and do so promptly.* The processes of filing for a patent, a trademark, and a copyright are different; make sure you know what each tool protects, which one is right for you, and how to get maximum protection from it for your intellectual property. You may be able to apply for more than one type of protection. For instance, an entrepreneur may be able to trademark a company logo and, if it is a form of artistic expression, copyright it as well.

3. *Use qualified, experienced intellectual property attorneys to gain the proper protection.* The time to involve attorneys in protecting the product of your knowledge and creativity is *before* you have to bring them in to take action against someone who has stolen your intellectual property. Filing for patents, trademarks, and copyrights can be intimidating if you have never done it before, and doing it incorrectly may mean that you have no protection at all. Attorneys, consultants, examiners, and other professionals specialize in the various types of intellectual property protection. Use their expertise! They can refer you to patent draftspeople (who create the sketches required for a patent application), design engineers, manufacturers, and others.

4. *If you do business globally, register your company's patents, trademarks, and copyrights in the countries in which you do business or that are a strategic part of your business.* Once an entrepreneur has made the proper filings to protect his or her intellectual property in the United States, the next step is to file for protection in the countries in which the company does business and in countries that are strategically important to the business. Only 15 percent of companies that do business internationally realize that U.S. patents and trademarks do *not* protect their intellectual property outside the borders of the United States. Although enforcing intellectual property laws in some countries can be difficult, the chances that you will be successful rise significantly if you have registered your IP with the proper offices in those nations. Most nations grant patents and trademarks to the first person or business to file. Inventors file more than 2 million patent applications globally each year, and 2011 marked the first time that businesses and entrepreneurs filed more patents in China than in any other country in the world. Businesses also file more than 4 million applications for trademarks globally each year.

Filing to protect intellectual property rights in many individual countries can be expensive and time-consuming. Fortunately, when applying for trademarks, entrepreneurs benefit from important shortcuts: international registration

(continued)

Hands On . . . How To (continued)

and a community trademark. Entrepreneurs can file an international registration in all 86 nations that participate in the Madrid Protocol with an application in their home nations that they extend to the other 85 nations (although they must pay a registration fee in each country). Entrepreneurs who register a community trademark file a single application and pay a single fee that grants trademark protection in all 28 countries that belong to the European Union. In 2007, the patent offices in the United States, the European Union, and Japan created a common patent application that allows entrepreneurs to streamline the patent process by filing a single application for each country's patent office.

5. **Select your company's business affiliates, especially suppliers, carefully.** Companies in some countries have little concern for others' intellectual property. Some suppliers in foreign countries see no problem manufacturing goods for a business and then running an extra shift to produce the same goods that they themselves sell. In China, which is famous for its copycat culture, the term *shanzai* describes companies' tendency to copy the successful products of other businesses. Entrepreneurs should take extra precautions to ensure that they secure proper protection for

their intellectual property before forging relationships with foreign manufacturers, especially those in Asia.

6. **Protect your rights vigorously.** If you discover that someone is using your intellectual property without permission, pursue your rights vigorously. Recognize that the costs of taking legal action, especially in foreign lands, may outweigh the benefits, at least in the short run. Entrepreneurs must decide whether pursuing costly legal action to protect their intellectual property rights will yield long-term benefits. A "head-in-the-sand" approach never works. After registering their trademarks and filing for patents in foreign countries, entrepreneurs must monitor them carefully and avidly prosecute violators of their intellectual property rights.

Sources: Based on *World Intellectual Property Indicators*, World Intellectual Property Organization, 2012, p. 3; Kathy Chu, "Chinese Copycats Challenge U.S. Small Businesses," *USA Today*, March 18, 2012, http://usatoday30.usatoday.com/money/smallbusiness/story/2012-03-15/china-copycats-patents/53614902/1; Carolyn Surh, "Staying Ahead of Copy Cats," *QSR*, March 2012, http://www.qsrmagazine.com/reports/staying-ahead-copy-cats; "How to Protect Your Trademark Internationally," *Business News Daily*, July 13, 2012, http://www.businessnewsdaily.com/2838-how-to-protect-your-trademark-internationally.html; David Hirschmann, "Intellectual Property Theft: Big Problem, Real Solutions, *The ChamberPost*, March 2008, http://www.chamberpost.com/2008/03/intellectual-pr.html; Merrill Matthews Jr. and Tom Giovanetti, "Why Intellectual Property Is Important," *Ideas*, Institute for Policy Innovation, July 8, 2002, p. 1; and Nichole L. Torres, "Getting Intellectual," *Entrepreneur*, December 2007, p. 110.

Copyrights

copyright
an exclusive right that protects the creators of original works of authorship, such as literary, dramatic, musical, and artistic works.

A **copyright** is an exclusive right that protects the creators of original works of authorship, such as literary, dramatic, musical, and artistic works (e.g., art, sculptures, literature, software, music, videos, video games, choreography, motion pictures, recordings, and others). The internationally recognized symbol © denotes a copyrighted work. A copyright protects only the form in which an idea is expressed, not the idea itself. A copyright on a creative work comes into existence the moment its creator puts that work into a tangible form. Just as with a trademark, obtaining basic copyright protection does *not* require registering the creative work with the U.S. Copyright Office (www.copyright.gov).

Registering a copyright does give creators greater protection over their work, however. Entrepreneurs must file copyright applications with the Copyright Office in the Library of Congress for a fee of $35 to $65 per application (plus recording fees). The mean processing time for a copyright application is 94 days.[136] A valid copyright on a work lasts for the life of the creator plus 70 years after his or her death. When a copyright expires, the work becomes public property and can be used by anyone free of charge.

Because they are so easy to duplicate, computer software programs, CDs, and DVDs are among the most often pirated items by copyright infringers. The Business Software Alliance estimates that the global software piracy rate is 42 percent and that the software industry loses $63.4 billion each year to pirates who illegally copy programs.[137] The motion picture industry loses billions of dollars annually to those who forge counterfeit movies and sell them. Immigration and Customs Enforcement officials recently disabled nine Web sites that were selling downloads of pirated movies, in some cases just hours after the films premiered in theaters.[138]

Table 3.3 provides a summary of the characteristics of patents, trademarks, and copyrights.

Protecting Intellectual Property

Acquiring the protection of patents, trademarks, and copyrights is useless unless an entrepreneur takes action to protect those rights in the marketplace. Unfortunately, not every businessperson respects others' rights of ownership to products, processes, names, and works, and some infringe on those rights with impunity. In other cases, the infringing behavior simply is the result of a

TABLE 3.3 Characteristics of Patents, Trademarks, and Copyrights

Protection	What It Protects	Who Is Eligible	Length of Protection	Approximate Cost
Utility Patent	Exclusive right to make, use, and sell an invention	First person to file for a patent	20 years	$4,000 to $25,000, depending on complexity
Design Patent	New, original changes in the design of existing products that enhance their sales	First person to file for a patent	14 years	$4,000 to $25,000, depending on complexity
Trademark	Any distinctive word, phrase, symbol, design, name, logo, slogan, or trade dress that a company uses to identify the origin of a product or to distinguish it from other goods on the market	Entity currently using the mark in commerce or one who intends to use it within six months	Renewable between 5th and 6th years and 9th and 10th years and every 10 years afterward	$1,000 to $2,500
Service mark	Same protection as a trademark except that it identifies and distinguishes the source of a service rather than a product	Entity currently using the mark in commerce or one who intends to use it within six months	Renewable between 5th and 6th years and 9th and 10th years and every 10 years afterward	$1,000 to $2,500
Copyright	Original works of authorship, such as literary, dramatic, musical, and artistic works	Author or creator	Life of the author or creator plus 70 years	$140 to $200

Source: Based on "Idea Factories," *Inc.*, September 2013, pp. 104–105.

lack of knowledge about others' rights of ownership. After acquiring the proper legal protection through patents, copyrights, or trademarks, entrepreneurs must monitor the market (and the Internet in particular) for unauthorized copycat users. If an entrepreneur has a valid patent, trademark, or copyright, stopping an infringer usually requires nothing more than a stern "cease-and-desist" letter from an attorney. Often, offenders don't want to get into expensive legal battles and agree to stop their illegal behavior. If that tactic fails, the entrepreneur may have no choice but to bring an infringement lawsuit, most of which end up being settled out of court.

The primary weapon an entrepreneur has to protect patents, trademarks, and copyrights is the legal system. The major problem with relying on the legal system to enforce ownership rights, however, is the cost and time of infringement lawsuits, which can quickly exceed the budget of most small businesses and occupy huge blocks of managers' time. Lawsuits always involve costs. Before pursuing what could become an expensive and drawn-out legal battle, an entrepreneur must consider the following issues:

- Can the opponent afford to pay if you win?

- Do you expect to get enough from the suit to cover the costs of hiring an attorney and preparing a case?

- Can you afford the loss of time, money, and privacy from the ensuing lawsuit?

Chapter Summary by Learning Objective

1. Explain the differences among creativity, innovation, and entrepreneurship.

- The entrepreneur's "secret" for creating value in the marketplace is applying creativity and innovation to solve problems and to exploit opportunities people face every day. Creativity is the ability to develop new ideas and to discover new ways of looking at problems and opportunities. Innovation is the ability to apply creative solutions to those problems and opportunities to enhance or to enrich people's lives. Entrepreneurship is the result of a disciplined, systematic process of applying creativity and innovation to needs and opportunities in the marketplace.

2. Describe why creativity and innovation are such an integral part of entrepreneurship.

- Entrepreneurs must always be on guard against paradigms—preconceived ideas of what the world is, what it should be like, and how it should operate—because they are logjams to creativity. Successful entrepreneurs often go beyond conventional wisdom as they ask, "Why not?"

- Success—even survival—in this fiercely competitive, global environment requires entrepreneurs to tap their creativity (and that of their employees) constantly.

3. Understand how the two hemispheres of the human brain function and what role they play in creativity.

- For years, people assumed that creativity was an inherent trait. Today, however, we know better. Research shows that almost anyone can learn to be creative. The left hemisphere of the brain controls language, logic, and symbols, processing information in a step-by-step fashion. The right hemisphere handles emotional, intuitive, and spatial functions, processing information intuitively. The right side of the brain is the source of creativity and innovation. People can learn to control which side of the brain is dominant in a given situation.

4. Explain the 10 "mental locks" that limit individual creativity.

The number of potential barriers to creativity is limitless, but entrepreneurs commonly face 10 "mental locks" on creativity: Searching for the one "right" answer, focusing on "being logical," blindly following the rules, constantly being practical, viewing play as frivolous, becoming overly specialized, avoiding ambiguity, fearing looking foolish, fearing mistakes and failure, and believing that "I'm not creative."

5. Understand how entrepreneurs can enhance the creativity of their employees as well as their own creativity.

- Entrepreneurs can stimulate creativity in their companies by expecting creativity, expecting and tolerating failure, encouraging curiosity, viewing problems as challenges, providing creativity training, providing support, rewarding creativity, and modeling creativity.

- Entrepreneurs can enhance their own creativity by using the following techniques: allowing themselves to be creative, giving their minds fresh input every day, keeping a journal handy to record their thoughts and ideas, reading books on stimulating creativity or taking a class on creativity, and taking some time off to relax.

6. Describe the steps in the creative process.

- The creative process consists of seven steps: Step 1, preparation, involves getting the mind ready for creative thinking; step 2, investigation, requires the individual to develop a solid understanding of the problem or decision; step 3, transformation, involves viewing the similarities and the differences among the information collected; step 4, incubation, allows the subconscious mind to reflect on the information collected; step 5, illumination, occurs at some point during the incubation stage when a spontaneous breakthrough causes "the light bulb to go on"; step 6, verification, involves validating the idea as accurate and useful; and step 7, implementation, involves transforming the idea into a business reality.

7. Discuss techniques for improving the creative process.

- Five techniques are especially useful for improving the creative process:

  - Brainstorming is a process in which a small group of people interact with very little structure with the goal of producing a large *quantity* of novel and imaginative ideas.

  - Mind mapping is a graphical technique that encourages thinking on both sides of the brain, visually displays the various relationships among ideas, and improves the ability to view a problem from many sides.

  - Force-field analysis allows entrepreneurs to weigh both the advantages and the disadvantages of a particular decision and work to maximize the variables that support it and minimize those that work against it.

  - TRIZ is a systematic approach designed to help solve any technical problem, whatever its source. Unlike brainstorming and mind mapping, which are right-brain activities, TRIZ is a left-brain, scientific, step-by-step process that is based on the study of hundreds of the most innovative patents across the globe.

  - Rapid prototyping is based on the premise that transforming an idea into an actual model will point out flaws in the original idea and will lead to improvements in its design.

8. Describe the protection of intellectual property through patents, trademarks, and copyrights.

- A patent is a grant from the federal government that gives an inventor exclusive rights to an invention for 20 years.

- A trademark is any distinctive word, symbol, or trade dress that a company uses to identify its product and to distinguish it from other goods. It serves as a company's "signature" in the marketplace.

- A copyright protects original works of authorship. It covers only the form in which an idea is expressed and not the idea itself and lasts for 70 years beyond the creator's death.

Discussion Questions

3-1. Explain the differences among creativity, innovation, and entrepreneurship.

3-2. How are creativity, innovation, and entrepreneurship related?

3-3. Why are creativity and innovation so important to the survival and success of a business?

3-4. One entrepreneur claims, "Creativity unrelated to a business plan has no value." What does he mean? Do you agree?

3-5. Can creativity be taught or is it an inherent trait? Explain.

3-6. How does the human brain function?

3-7. What operations does each hemisphere of the brain specialize in?

3-8. Which hemisphere is the "seat" of creativity?

3-9. Briefly outline the 10 "mental locks" that can limit individual creativity. Give an example of a situation in which you subjected yourself to one of these mental locks.

3-10. What can entrepreneurs do to stimulate their own creativity and to encourage it among workers?

3-11. Explain the steps of the creative process.

3-12. Use the creative processes in this chapter to come up with as many uses as you can for unmanned aerial vehicles ("drones") other than those employed by the military.

3-13. What can an entrepreneur do to enhance each step of the creative process?

3-14. Explain the differences among a patent, a trademark, and a copyright.

3-15. What form of intellectual property do patents, trademarks, and copyrights protect?

Beyond the Classroom . . .

3-16. Your dinner guests are to arrive in five minutes, and you've just discovered that you forgot to chill the wine!! Wanting to maintain your reputation as the perfect host/hostess, you must tackle this problem with maximum creativity. What could you do? Generate as many solutions as you can in five minutes working alone and then work with two or three students in a small group to brainstorm the problem.

3-17. Work with a group of your classmates to think of as many alternative uses for the commercial lubricant WD-40 as you can. Remember to think *fluidly* (generating a quantity of ideas) and *flexibly* (generating unconventional ideas).

3-18. A Facebook group of more than 25,000 people is trying to convince Cadbury, the venerable British confectioner (now owned by Kraft Foods), to produce a giant chocolate Cadbury Crème Egg that contains a filling made from fondant that resembles the yolk and white of a real egg. (Currently, giant Cadbury chocolate eggs, which are about the size of an ostrich egg, are hollow, a great disappointment to fans of the company's smaller chocolate eggs that are filled with creamy white and yolk-colored fondant.) A Cadbury spokesman says that "creating a [chocolate] shell that is strong enough to contain the sheer weight of the fondant is technically challenging." Use the creativity-enhancing techniques described in this chapter to develop potential solutions that would allow Cadbury to manufacture a giant Crème Egg.

3-19. A major maker of breakfast cereals was about to introduce a new multigrain cereal. Its principal selling point is that it features "three great tastes" in every bowl: corn, rice, and wheat. Because a cereal's name is an integral part of its marketing campaign, the company hired a costly consulting firm to come up with the right name for the new product. The consulting firm tackled the job using "a combination of structural linguistics and personal creativity." One year and many dollars later, the consulting firm gave its recommendation. Take 20 minutes to list names that you think would be appropriate for this cereal. Make brief notes about why you think each name is appropriate. Your professor may choose to prepare a list of names from all the members of your class and may take a vote to determine the "winner."

3-20. Every quarter, Inventables, a creative design company in Chicago, sends its clients a package called a DesignAid that contains 20 items, each with "unexpected properties," as a way to stimulate innovation and ideas for new products or services. One Inventables' recent DesignAid package included the following items:

- Translucent concrete—concrete that contains thin layers of fiber optics, which create semitransparent stripes in the concrete.

- Sound-recording paper—A piece of cardboard-like paper that records and plays sounds with the help of ultrathin electronics embedded in the page.

- Impact-absorbing silicon—Silicon that, despite being only one inch thick, absorbs impact, including microvibrations. If you drop an egg on it, the egg won't break.

- Wireless battery-free speakers—Solar-powered speakers receive sound via infrared waves rather than radio frequencies and are capable of producing directional sound. In other words, only the person at whom the speakers are aimed can hear the sound coming from them.

Select one of these items and work with a small group of your classmates to brainstorm as many alternative uses for the item as you can in 15 minutes. Remember to abide by the rules of brainstorming!

3-21. Each hemisphere of the brain processes information differently, and one hemisphere tends to dominate the other. Consider the following lists of words and decide which one best describes the way you make decisions and solve problems:

Metaphor	Logic
Dream	Reason
Humor	Precision
Ambiguity	Consistency
Play	Work
Approximate	Exact
Fantasy	Reality
Paradox	Direct
Diffused	Focused
Hunch	Analysis
General	Specific
Child	Adult

If you chose the list on the left, you tend to engage in "soft" thinking, which suggests a right-brain orientation. If you chose the list on the right, you tend to engage in "hard" thinking, which suggests a left-brain orientation. Creativity relies on both soft and hard thinking. Each plays an important role in the creative process but at different phases. Identify which type of thinking—soft or hard—would be most useful in each of the seven stages of the creative process.

3-22. List five things you can do to develop your thinking skills in the area (soft or hard) that least describes your decision-making style.

3-23. Interview at least two entrepreneurs about their experiences as business owners. Where did their business ideas originate?

3-24. How important are creativity and innovation to these entrepreneurs' success?

3-25. How do these entrepreneurs encourage an environment of creativity in their businesses?

Endnotes

Scan for Endnotes or go to www.pearsonhighered.com/scarborough

4

Conducting a Feasibility Analysis and Designing a Business Model

Tuomas Kujansuu/Getty Images, Inc.

Learning Objectives

On completion of this chapter, you will be able to:

1. Describe the process of conducting an idea assessment.

2. Explain the elements of a feasibility analysis.

3. Describe the six forces in the macro environment of an industry.

4. Understand how Porter's Five Forces Model assesses the competitive environment.

5. Describe the various methods of conducting primary and secondary market research.

6. Understand the four major elements of a financial feasibility analysis.

7. Describe the process of assessing entrepreneur feasibility.

8. Describe the nine elements of a business model.

For many entrepreneurs, the easiest part of launching a business is coming up with an idea for a new business concept or approach. Business success, however, requires much more than just a great new idea. In addition to coming up with a business idea and launching a business, five critical steps guide the process of going from idea generation to growing a successful business. Together these steps make up the new business planning process. Following these steps increases the entrepreneur's chances for launching a successful and sustainable business.

Once entrepreneurs develop ideas for new businesses, the next step is to assess these ideas. An **idea assessment** is the process of examining a need in the market, developing a solution for that need, and determining the entrepreneur's ability to successfully turn the idea into a business. The best business ideas start with a group of customers with a common problem or need. Successful entrepreneurs learn to apply the creative processes discussed in Chapter 3 to find solutions for these customers. Entrepreneurs often identify multiple possible business ideas for any given market need. The idea assessment process helps an entrepreneur more efficiently and effectively examine multiple ideas to identify the solution with the most potential. Examining multiple business ideas ensures that the entrepreneur does not lock in on a single idea and overlook others that have an even greater chance for success.

After identifying the most promising idea using the idea assessment process, the entrepreneur subjects it to a feasibility analysis to determine whether they can transform the idea into a viable business. A *feasibility analysis* is the process of determining whether an entrepreneur's idea is a viable foundation for creating a successful business. Its purpose is to determine whether a business idea is worth pursuing. A feasibility study answers the question, "Should we proceed with this business idea?" Its role is to serve as a filter, screening out ideas that lack the potential for building a successful business, before an entrepreneur commits the necessary resources to develop and test a business model or to build a business plan. A feasibility study primarily is an investigative tool. It is designed to give an entrepreneur a picture of the market and the sales and profit potential of a particular business idea. Will a ski resort located here attract enough customers to be successful? Will customers in this community support a sandwich shop with a retro rock-n-roll theme? Can we build the product at a reasonable cost and sell it at a price customers are willing and able to pay? Does this entrepreneurial team have the ability to implement the idea successfully?

If the idea passes the feasibility analysis, the entrepreneur moves on to the next steps of the new business planning process. If the idea fails to pass muster, the entrepreneur drops it and moves on to the next idea. He or she has not wasted valuable time, money, energy, and other resources building a plan for launching a business that is destined to fail because it is based on a flawed concept. Although it is impossible for a feasibility study to guarantee an idea's success, conducting a study reduces the likelihood that entrepreneurs will waste their time pursuing fruitless business ventures.

The business model answers the question, "How would we proceed with this business idea?" Developing a business model, which is the third step in planning a new business, helps the entrepreneur to fully understand all that will be required to launch and build the business. Business modeling is another step that determines the potential for success for the new venture. It is a visual process that examines how all the moving parts of the business must work together to build a successful venture. It is the step in the planning process in which the entrepreneur tests the concept and uses what it learned from real customers to refine the business model before the entrepreneur commits the resources to grow the business to its full potential.

The idea assessment, feasibility study, business model, business plan, and strategic plan all play important but separate roles in the start-up and growth of an entrepreneurial venture (see Figure 4.1). This chapter describes the idea assessment, feasibility study, and business model development. Chapter 5 examines how to craft a business plan to guide the start-up of a new business, as well as the strategic planning process that helps navigate the growth of the business.

idea assessment
the process of examining a need in the market, developing a solution for that need, and determining the entrepreneur's ability to successfully turn the idea into a business.

LO1
Describe the process of conducting an idea assessment.

Idea Assessment

Successful entrepreneurs understand that the process of going from ideas to the launch of a new business venture is like a funnel. When the entrepreneur observes a need in the market, using the creative process generates many business ideas that might address this need. Each step in the new

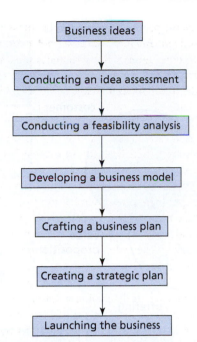

FIGURE 4.1

**New Business
Planning Process**

business planning process narrows down the number of ideas until the entrepreneur is ready to launch a business that he or she has carefully researched and tested. An idea assessment helps the entrepreneur efficiently evaluate the numerous ideas that come out of the creative process before committing the time and effort to craft a business plan, design a business model, or even conduct a feasibility analysis. One effective tool used to help assess ideas is the idea sketch pad.[1]

Entrepreneurs too often jump ahead and begin modeling or planning their business ideas. They get excited about the potential they imagine if they launched a business based on the idea. However, most ideas do not become successful businesses. Alex Bruton, developer of the idea sketch pad, says it is human nature to misjudge how unlikely it is for a new business idea to actually become a successful business.[2] Rather than act on a hunch, successful entrepreneurs are disciplined in evaluating each new idea. Because it takes so many ideas to come up with a viable business concept, entrepreneurs must become adept at quickly sorting through all of them.

The idea sketch pad helps an entrepreneur assess ideas in a relatively short period of time. When using the sketch pad, the entrepreneur asks a series of key questions addressing five key parameters (see Figure 4.2).

1. *Customers.* Start with a group of customers who have a clear need that is not being addressed. This may be a need that no business is currently addressing, or it may be a need that no business is fully or adequately meeting for these customers. The entrepreneur assesses the customers by answering basic questions about the potential users of the product or service and the potential buyers if they are different than the users. For instance, for sugary cereals, children are the users and their parents are the buyers. Specifically who would be the users of the offering? How would they use the offering? How many potential customers are there?

2. *Offering.* Describe your idea for a product or service to offer the customers. Are you offering a product, a service, an experience, or a combination of one or more of these? What are its key features? Describe it in detail and sketch out an image of it if you can.

3. *Value proposition.* Explain why your product or service will be important to the customers. Why would your offering be valuable to the user and/or buyer? How does it address the need these customers currently have that is not being met?

4. *Core competencies.* Does your offering include any technologies or unique features that will help differentiate it from competitors? Is it based on intellectual property that you can protect?

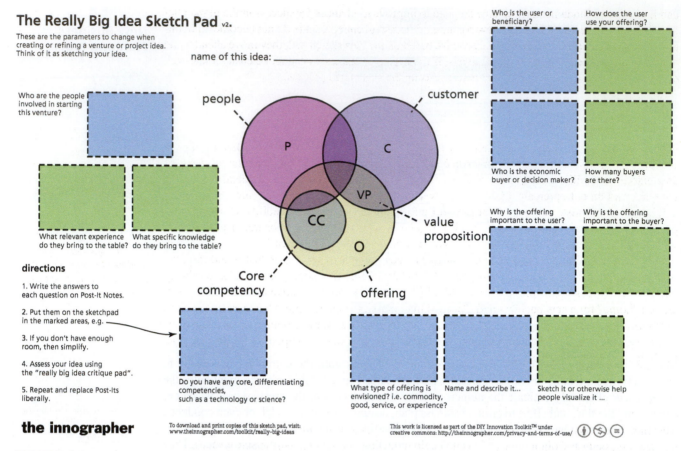

The Really Big Idea Sketch Pad v2.

These are the parameters to change when creating or refining a venture or project idea. Think of it as sketching your idea.

name of this idea: _____

Who are the people involved in starting this venture?

people

customer

P

C

VP

CC

O

value proposition

Core competency

offering

Who is the user or beneficiary?

How does the user use your offering?

Who is the economic buyer or decision maker?

How many buyers are there?

Why is the offering important to the user?

Why is the offering important to the buyer?

What relevant experience do they bring to the table?

What specific knowledge do they bring to the table?

directions

1. Write the answers to each question on Post-It Notes.

2. Put them on the sketchpad in the marked areas, e.g.

3. If you don't have enough room, then simplify.

4. Assess your idea using the "really big idea critique pad".

5. Repeat and replace Post-Its liberally.

Do you have any core, differentiating competencies, such as a technology or science?

What type of offering is envisioned? i.e. commodity, good, service, or experience?

Name and describe it...

Sketch it or otherwise help people visualize it ...

the innographer

To download and print copies of this sketch pad, visit: www.theinnographer.com/toolkit/really-big-ideas

FIGURE 4.2

Idea Sketch Pad

Source: Dr. Alex Bruton, The Innographer, Ltd., theinnographer.com/toolkit/ idea-modeling.

5. *People.* Identify the key people on the team who will launch this business. Who are the founding entrepreneurs of this venture? Do they have the skills and knowledge needed to successfully turn the idea into a start-up venture? Can they attract key team members who will fill in any gaps in knowledge, skills, and experience?

By placing the answers to these questions on the sketch pad, entrepreneurs can clearly visualize gaps or weaknesses in their idea. Rather than use the tool to make minor changes in an idea, they

"MAYBE WE SHOULD HAVE HAD A FEASIBILITY STUDY" FOR UNDERGROUND PARKING BY THE PIER

Joseph Rank, www.cartoonstock.com

can find ways to fundamentally change the idea to improve its chances for success in the market before they move ahead and launch a new business.[3] Successful entrepreneurs do not become emotionally attached to ideas. If the idea shows promise based on the idea sketch pad, they move ahead to the next step of conducting a feasibility analysis. If the gaps or weaknesses cannot be easily addressed, entrepreneurs turn to the next idea and assess it using the sketch pad process.

Feasibility Analysis

After conducting the idea assessment, an entrepreneur scrutinizes the idea further through a **feasibility analysis**. A feasibility analysis consists of four interrelated components: an industry and market feasibility analysis, a product or service feasibility analysis, a financial feasibility analysis, and an entrepreneur feasibility analysis (see Figure 4.3). Rhonda Abrams, nationally-syndicated columnist, author, and successful entrepreneur, says that feasibility analysis is an opportunity to take a hard look at your idea to see whether it needs minor or major pivots, or if warranted, to be completely abandoned so you can move on to another idea.[4]

When evaluating the feasibility of a business idea, an analysis of the industry and targeted market segments serves as the starting point for the remaining three components of a feasibility analysis. The focus in this phase is two-fold: (1) To determine how attractive an industry is overall as a "home" for a new business and (2) to evaluate possible niches a small business can occupy profitably. When examining an industry, an entrepreneur should examine both the macro environment that can have an impact across many industries and the specific competitive environment of the industry of interest (see Figure 4.4).

LO2

Explain the elements of a feasibility analysis.

feasibility analysis
an analysis of the viability of a business idea that includes four interrelated components: an industry and market analysis, the product or service analysis, a financial analysis, and an entrepreneur analysis.

Industry and Market Feasibility

The first step in assessing industry attractiveness is to paint a picture of the industry in broad strokes, assessing it from a "macro" level. Most opportunities for new businesses within an industry are due to changes taking place in that industry. Foundational macro forces shape industries and the markets they serve. Changes in any of these macro forces can dramatically change the competitive nature of an industry and fundamentally change the needs and wants in its target market. Entrepreneurs must be vigilant when monitoring macro forces. Changes in macro forces may have created the initial opportunity the entrepreneur pursued when launching the business, and change will likely continue. If the entrepreneur does not adapt the business to meet the changes these macro forces create in the industry and market, even the most innovative new business may become outdated and left behind in the competitive landscape.

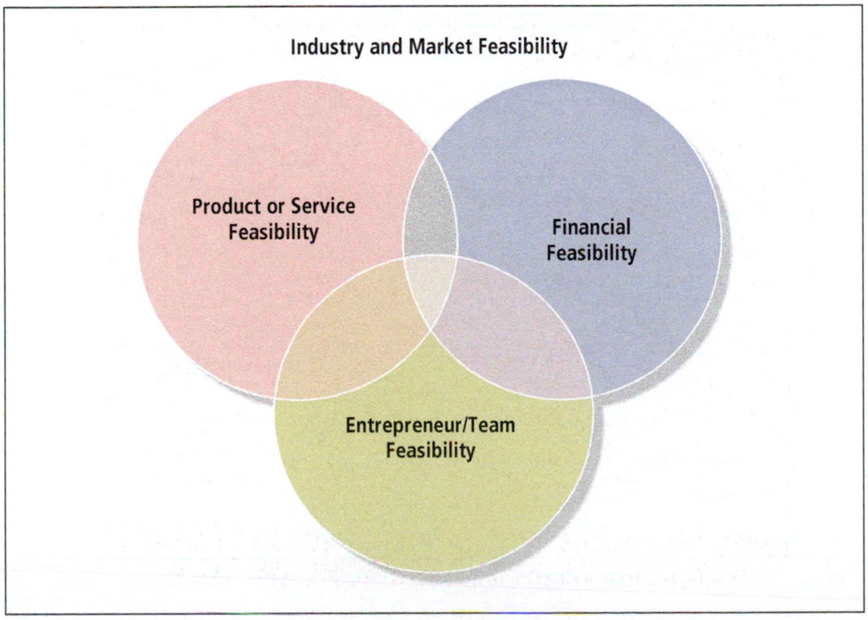

LO3

Describe the six forces in the macro environment of an industry.

FIGURE 4.3

Elements of a Feasibility Analysis

Industry and Market Feasibility

Product or Service Feasibility

Financial Feasibility

Entrepreneur/Team Feasibility

FIGURE 4.4

Environmental Forces and New Ventures

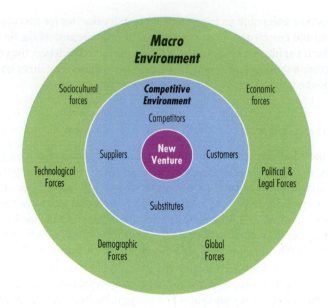

Six foundational macro forces create change in industries and the markets they serve:

1. *Sociocultural.* Social and cultural change can lead to dramatic changes that can create whole new industries and fundamentally transform existing industries. For example, in the 1970s and 1980s women began entering the workforce at much higher rates than had been the case previously. This change was a result of the women's movement of the 1960s. Figure 4.5 displays the dramatic increase in the size of the American workforce that resulted from this cultural change. Not only did more women enter the workforce, but they also had career aspirations to compete for jobs that previously had been dominated by male workers. This cultural change led to the birth of the daycare industry. It also resulted in a new segment within the women's fashion industry for women's business attire. It led to rapid growth in the restaurant industry as families began eating in restaurants much more frequently than previous generations and to a growth period for the auto industry as the percentage of families with two cars doubled from 1960 to 2011.[5]

Technological. Technological breakthroughs lead to the development of new products and entirely new industries. For example, the Internet is a technology that has had a profound impact on many industries. Before the Internet age, a few large companies dominated the music industry. The Internet led to the creation of many new businesses within the music industry, including Pandora, Spotify, and Apple's iTunes, which changed

FIGURE 4.5

American Labor Force Participation Rate

Source: Labor Force Statistics from the Current Population Survey, U.S. Department of Labor, November 14, 2013, http://data.bls.gov/timeseries/LNS11300000

how customers buy and listen to music. The Internet also changed how people consume information. As the news became available online, there was a dramatic decrease in the number of people reading print newspapers. As result, advertising revenues have plummeted for print newspapers, while online newspapers have experienced steady growth in advertising.

ENTREPRENEURIAL PROFILE: Hill Kemp and Suns River The world's limited water supply is a growing concern. Hill Kemp, founder and CEO of Suns River, is using solar technology to help turn poor quality water into safe, distilled water. The device is a solar still that purifies even the saltiest water into safe, clean water. Although technology is not new, Kemp's process is much more efficient. Using Suns River technology, a family can convert 80 percent of brackish water into distilled water. What is left is a block of salt. Each Suns River unit can supply a family of four with all the clean water they need. Kemp is targeting his product for coastal desert areas that would benefit from an affordable means to generate clean water. Suns River systems sell for $3,000 to $5,000. Kemp plans to expand the Suns River product line to include solar stills that can produce enough water to use for agricultural greenhouses.[6] ∎

2. *Demographic.* Changing demographics create opportunities for entrepreneurs. For example, as Generation Y (those born during the 1980s to early 1990s) reaches adulthood, businesses will begin to pay attention to the next generation, Generation Z. Although Generation Y is optimistic and idealistic, those who are part of Generation Z (those born between the mid-1990s to about 2013) are much more realistic. School violence and the Great Recession (which began in 2008) have shaped their lives. Generation Z is more realistic in how they view the world. Because they have watched their parents' generation struggle with prolonged unemployment and economic uncertainty, they intend to be careful with their money. Those in Generation Z will seek products and services that offer value. In a survey of members of Generation Z conducted by the Intelligence Group, 57 percent said they would rather save money than spend it![7]

ENTREPRENEURIAL PROFILE: Jason Greenspan and Silver Stars Fitness Jason Greenspan targets a different market than most fitness clubs. Rather than cater to young working professionals, Greenspan's Silver Stars Fitness located in New York City is specifically designed for the fitness needs of baby boomers. Silver Stars Fitness offers classes such as Mature Boot Camp for basic strength and cardiovascular workouts, Burn Baby Burn that targets fat loss, Balance and Fall Prevention, Zumba Silver, Central Park Walking, Arthritis Soothing, and Osteoporosis Bone Blast. Silver Stars offers smaller classes that are all held during the middle of the day to make them most convenient for retired baby boomers. Greenspan plans to expand to more locations to keep up with the growing population of retired baby boomers.[8] ∎

Silver Star Fitness

3. *Economic.* Although many companies struggle during economic downturns, some businesses are able to grow. For example, businesses in the e-learning industry thrived during the Great Recession. Web-based learning provides customers with opportunities to improve their education and skills at an affordable price. Given the highly competitive job market during a recession, additional knowledge and skills offer job seekers a competitive advantage when applying for a new position. However, those who were unemployed or afraid of becoming unemployed were unwilling to pay the growing cost of tuition for traditional educational programs. Companies that provide high quality Web-based e-learning at a fraction of the cost of traditional university-based education filled this gap in the market.

4. *Political and legal.* The enactment of new legislation creates opportunities for entrepreneurs. For example, when the Affordable Health Care Act (also known as ObamaCare)

was passed in 2010, entrepreneurs recognized that the legislation created a complex array of new requirements for healthcare companies. Because of this legislation, payment for healthcare is shifting from fee-for-service (healthcare providers are paid a set amount for each procedure or service they provide) to a system based on pay-for-performance. In a pay-for-performance system, insurance companies reward healthcare providers and hospitals for initiatives that improve the quality, efficiency, and overall value of health care. Because pay-for-performance is new to healthcare, savvy entrepreneurs are creating new companies that help healthcare providers and hospitals to track and report performance-related metrics based on the value of the healthcare they provide, measure and improve quality of healthcare outcomes, and enhance efficiency in their healthcare delivery systems.

5. *Global.* Global trends create opportunities for even the smallest of companies. More open global markets allow businesses to seek customers and suppliers from all corners of the world.

Ethan Siegl, Orb Audio LLC

ENTREPRENEURIAL PROFILE: Ethan Siegel and Orb Audio Orb Audio, headquartered in New York City, manufactures high-end speakers for home theater systems from its factory in Sherman Oaks, California. Rather than sell through traditional retail outlets, Orb Audio sells directly to the customer through its Web site. When the dollar weakened against other currencies in 2008, cofounder Ethan Siegel noticed a sharp increase in orders from international markets. The weak dollar made American-made goods more attractive to international customers whose buying power improved with the declining dollar. Siegel started running Internet advertisements aimed at consumers in the markets where most of the increase in international sales were coming from, including Great Britain, Canada, Finland, and Australia. Global sales for Orb Audio now comprise 35 percent of sales. Finland alone accounts for 10 percent of total sales for Orb Audio. Although domestic sales for Orb Audio have declined since 2008, total revenue continues to grow due to the expansion of international sales for this small manufacturer.[9] ■

While evaluating the six foundational macro trends, entrepreneurs should answer the following questions to help further evaluate the attractiveness of that industry in light of the impact of the macro forces for change:

- How large is the industry?

- How fast is it growing?

- Is the industry as a whole profitable?

- Is the industry characterized by high profit margins or razor-thin margins?

- How essential are its products or services to customers?

- What trends are shaping the industry's future?

- What threats does the industry face?

- What opportunities does the industry face?

- How crowded is the industry?

- How intense is the level of competition in the industry?

- Is the industry young, mature, or somewhere in between?

Addressing these questions helps entrepreneurs determine whether the potential for sufficient demand for their products and services exist.

LO4

Understand how Porter's Five Forces Model assesses the competitive environment.

Porter's Five Forces Model

After evaluating the broader macro environment, the entrepreneur changes focus to the more immediate competitive environment. A useful tool for analyzing a specific industry's attractiveness within the competitive environment is the Five Forces Model developed by Michael Porter

Hands On . . . How To

Forces Shaping Innovation: The Driverless Car

Driverless cars have been the stuff of science fiction for several decades. As a result of several recent technological breakthroughs, a fully functional driverless car may soon become possible. However, all of the macro forces shaping the automobile industry must come into alignment for the driverless car to become a true market opportunity.

Sociocultural environment. For generations, the automobile has been enmeshed within the American culture. While other countries developed advanced mass transit systems, Americans stayed loyal to their cars and the freedom they offered to allow them to drive when, where, and how they wanted to. However, research from KPMG suggests that there may be a change in consumer attitudes. People are growing weary of ever-longer and more congested commutes. The KPMG study finds that Americans would enthusiastically demand driverless cars if they offered the promise of cheaper and quicker commutes *and* if the cars still allowed people to turn off the driverless feature for pleasure driving. A survey conducted by CarInsurance.com found that 20 percent of drivers would "hand over the keys tomorrow" if a safe, driverless car were available for consumers to purchase. Ninety percent of those surveyed would consider a driverless car if it could bring down insurance costs.

Technological environment. Due to advances in sensors, microcontrollers, GPS, radar, lasers, and cameras, the technological feasibility for a driverless car has advanced quickly in recent years. Traditional automobile companies, including Nissan, General Motors, and Lexus, all have driverless car technologies under development. Google is a leader in the development of technology to enable driverless cars. Google has logged hundreds of thousands of miles of testing for its driverless technology with no reported safety issues. In addition, upstart electric car company Tesla is developing an autopilot system it plans to offer with its cars by 2020.

Demographic environment. As baby boomers age, driverless car technologies offer this generation the promise of continued autonomy even after they reach the age that is no longer safe for them to drive.

Economic environment. With continuing concerns about the cost and supply of energy, driverless cars may offer significant fuel savings. Computers in the driverless cars will be able to determine the most direct route with least traffic congestion and will drive at controlled speeds, all of which will improve fuel consumption for every car on the road.

Political/legal environment. Although the other macro forces all seem to favor the emergence of a market for driverless cars, the political and legal environment is not all favorable. Toyota has been fighting multiple lawsuits for several years that are tied to allegations that its cars are prone to unintended acceleration. The complaints allege that the cars would unexpectedly begin to accelerate under various conditions, and that these accelerations led to numerous accidents. A main cause of the problems may be in the software in the computers that control all modern automobiles. In a pivotal case in Oklahoma, Toyota has been put in a position where it must prove that its software *does not* have any bugs that may have caused the unexpected acceleration events. If this case goes against Toyota, auto makers can assume that they must be prepared to demonstrate that any critical software system that controls the operation of a car must be free of any bugs under any and all possible circumstances. Some legal experts believe this seemingly impossible standard leaves auto companies no choice but shelve any products with software that directs the operation of the vehicle.

1. What changes in the macro environmental forces are shaping the feasibility of the driverless car?

2. If you were an executive at an automobile company, would you pursue your own model of a driverless car? Why or why not?

3. What other opportunities for new businesses can you envision that may result from the introduction of the driverless car into the market?

Based on: "Self-driving Cars: Are We Ready?," KPMG, 2013, www.kpmg.com/ US/en/IssuesAndInsights/ArticlesPublications/Documents/self-driving-cars-are-we-ready.pdf; Mark Vallet, "Survey: Drivers ready to trust robot cars?," *CarInsurance .com*, November 1, 2013, www.carinsurance.com/Articles/autonomous-cars-ready .aspx; Christina DesMarais, "Driverless cars: Tesla, Google, Nissan and Others Shift Gears," *GreenBiz.com*, November 19, 2013, www.greenbiz.com/blog/2013/11/19/ driverless-cars-tesla-google-nissan-shift-gear?mkt_tok=3RkMMJWWfF9wsRolu K7NZKXonjHpfsX56u4rUa63lMI%2F0ER3fOvrPUfGjI4CTMtqI%2BSLDwEYGJ lv6SgFSLHEMa5qw7gMXRQ%3D; Holman W. Jenkins, Jr., "Will Tort Law Kill Driverless Cars?," *Wall Street Journal*, December 17, 2013, http://online.wsj.com/ news/articles/SB10001424052702304403804579264261779925166.

of the Harvard Business School (see Figure 4.6). Five forces interact with one another to determine the setting in which companies compete and hence the attractiveness of the industry: (1) the rivalry among competing firms, (2) the bargaining power of suppliers, (3) the bargaining power of buyers, (4) the threat of new entrants, and (5) the threat of substitute products or services.

Rivalry among companies competing in the industry. The strongest of the five forces in most industries is the rivalry that exists among the businesses competing in a particular

FIGURE 4.6

Five Forces Model of Competition

Source: Adapted from Michael E. Porter, "How Competitive Forces Shape Strategy," *Harvard Business Review* 57, no. 2 (March-April 1979): 137–145.

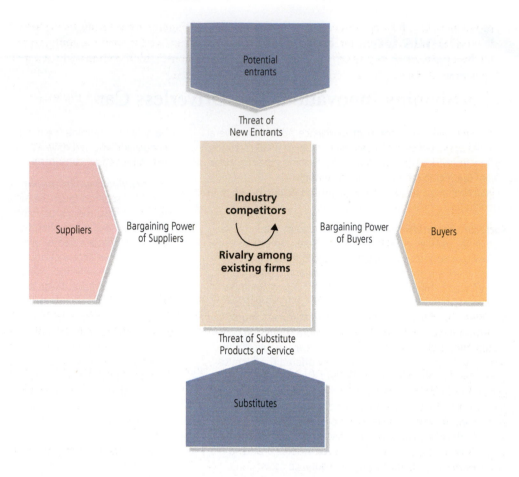

market. Much like the horses running in the Kentucky Derby, businesses in a market are jockeying for position in an attempt to gain a competitive advantage. When a company creates an innovation or develops a unique strategy that transforms the market, competing companies must adapt or run the risk of being forced out of business. This force makes markets a dynamic and highly competitive place. Generally, an industry is more attractive when:

- The number of competitors is large or, at the other extreme, quite small (fewer than five).
- Competitors are not similar in size or capability.
- The industry is growing at a fast pace.
- The opportunity to sell a differentiated product or service is present.

Bargaining power of suppliers to the industry. The greater the leverage suppliers of key raw materials or components have, the less attractive is the industry. For instance, Under Armour, which is in the athletic footwear and apparel industry, has agreements with 27 manufacturers in 14 countries. Its top 10 suppliers manufacture less than half of its products. Because of its diversity in suppliers, Under Armour has a favorable bargaining position with them. It is not dependent on any one or even a small group of its suppliers.[10] Generally, an industry is more attractive when:

- Many suppliers sell a commodity product to the companies in it.
- Substitute products are available for the items suppliers provide.
- Companies in the industry find it easy to switch from one supplier to another or to substitute products (i.e., "switching costs" are low).
- The items suppliers provide the industry account for a relatively small portion of the cost of the industry's finished products.

Bargaining power of buyers. Just as suppliers to an industry can be a source of pressure, buyers also have the potential to exert significant power over businesses, making it less attractive. When the number of customers is small and the cost of switching to competitors' products is low, buyers' influence on companies is high. Famous for offering its customers low prices, Wal-Mart, the largest retailer in the world, is also well known for applying relentless pressure to its 21,000 suppliers for price concessions, which it almost always manages to get.[11] Generally, an industry is more attractive when:

- Industry customers' "switching costs" to competitors' products or to substitutes are relatively high.
- The number of buyers in the industry is large.
- Customers demand products that are differentiated rather than purchase commodity products they can obtain from any supplier (and subsequently can pit one company against another to drive down price).
- Customers find it difficult to gather information on suppliers' costs, prices, and product features—something that is becoming much easier for customers in many industries to do by using the Internet.
- The items companies sell to the industry account for a relatively small portion of the cost of their customers' finished products.

Threat of new entrants to the industry. The larger the pool of potential new entrants to an industry, the greater is the threat to existing companies in it. This is particularly true in industries where the barriers to entry, such as capital requirements, specialized knowledge, access to distribution channels, and others are low. Generally, an industry is more attractive to new entrants when:

- The advantages of economies of scale are absent. Economies of scale exist when companies in an industry achieve low average costs by producing huge volumes of items (e.g., computer chips).
- Capital requirements to enter the industry are low.
- Cost advantages are not related to company size.
- Buyers are not extremely brand-loyal, making it easier for new entrants to the industry to draw customers away from existing businesses.
- Governments, through their regulatory and international trade policies, do not restrict new companies from entering the industry.

ENTREPRENEURIAL PROFILE: Jesse Parker and John Montague and Aspire Beverages The market for sports drinks has been dominated by two major brands, Gatorade and PowerAde. However, new competitors are entering the market due to growing concern that the major brands contain high-fructose corn syrup, artificial coloring, and other unhealthy ingredients. Jesse Parker and John Montague, two self-described hockey dads, launched Aspire Beverages to compete in this well-established market with a healthier alternative. As parents, they were concerned about the unhealthy ingredients their children were consuming with the sports drinks they drank. The Minneapolis-based company promotes its drinks as having no artificial sugars, artificial colors, or artificial flavors. Distribution of Aspire is through traditional retail outlets such as grocery stores, so it is competing for shelf space with the major national brands.[12] ■

Threat of substitute products or services. Substitute products or services can turn an entire industry on its head. For instance, many makers of glass bottles have closed their doors in recent years as their customers—from soft drink bottlers to ketchup makers—have switched to plastic containers, which are lighter, less expensive to ship, and less subject to breakage. Printed newspapers have seen their readership rates decline as new generations of potential readers turn to their iPads and smart phones for sources of news that are constantly updated. Generally, an industry is more attractive when:

- Quality substitute products are not readily available.
- The prices of substitute products are not significantly lower than those of the industry's products.
- Buyers' cost of switching to substitute products is high.

After surveying the power these five forces exert on an industry, entrepreneurs can evaluate the potential for their companies to generate reasonable sales and profits in a

TABLE 4.1 Five Forces Matrix

Assign a value to rate the importance of each of the five forces to the industry on a 1 (not important) to 5 (very important) scale. Then assign a value to reflect the threat that each force poses to the industry.

Multiply the importance rating in column 2 by the threat rating in column 3 to produce a weighted score.

Add the weighted scores in column 3 to get a total weighted score. This score measures the industry's attractiveness. The matrix is a useful tool for comparing the attractiveness of different industries.

Minimum Score = 5 (Very attractive)
Maximum Score = 125 (Very unattractive)

Force	Importance (1 to 5) (1 = Not Important, 5 = Very Important)	Threat to Industry (1 to 5) (1 = Low 3 = Medium 5 = High)	Weighted Score Col 2 × Col 3
Rivalry among companies competing in the industry	5	2	10
Bargaining power of suppliers in the industry	2	2	4
Bargaining power of buyers	2	4	8
Threat of new entrants to the industry	3	4	12
Threat of substitute products or services	4	1	4
		Total	38

particular industry. In other words, they can answer the question, "Is this industry a good home for my business?" Table 4.1 provides a matrix that allows entrepreneurs to assign quantitative scores to the five forces influencing industry attractiveness. Note that the lower the score for an industry, the more attractive it is.

Market niches. The next step in assessing an industry is to identify potentially attractive niches that exist in the industry. Many small businesses prosper by sticking to niches in markets that are too small to attract the attention of large competitors; occupying an industry niche enables these businesses to shield themselves to some extent from the power of the five forces. The key question entrepreneurs address about a possible niche market is "Can we identify a niche that is large enough to produce a profit, or can we position our company uniquely in the market to differentiate it from the competition in a meaningful way?" Entrepreneurs who have designed successful focus or differentiation strategies for their companies can exploit these niches to their advantage. Questions entrepreneurs should address in this portion of the feasibility analysis include:

- Which niche in the market will we occupy?
- How large is this market segment, and how fast is it growing?
- What is the basis for differentiating our product or service from competitors?
- Do we have a superior business model that will be difficult for competitors to reproduce?

Companies can shield themselves from some of the negative impact of these five forces by finding a niche and occupying it. For example, Taylor Morrison found a niche market in residential real estate that addresses the needs of immigrant families seeking housing: Allow multiple generations of the same family to live together. He is building townhouses in Arizona that allow children, parents, and grandparents to live together comfortably in a single townhouse unit. Each townhouse has a bedroom and a bathroom on the ground floor for the grandparents. The second level has the kitchen, living room, and dining room. The third floor has three bedrooms and two bathrooms for the parents and their children.[13]

Generally, a niche strategy is a good way for a new business to enter the market. It usually takes fewer resources for the start-up due to lower marketing costs and the ability to start on a smaller scale. Success rates tend to be higher for niche businesses because they have less direct competition. Without much competition, niche businesses can charge higher prices, which allows for quicker positive cash flow during start-up and better margins once profitable.

However, entrepreneurs should be aware of some cautions with a niche strategy:

- *Entering a niche requires adaptability in your initial plan.* While developing their business models, entrepreneurs can misjudge what customers actually need within a niche market. Unless they are willing and able to adjust their business models to react to the realities of the market niche, the business will fail if it does not offer the customers what they really want.
- *Niches change.* Even if an entrepreneur evaluates the market correctly in the beginning, niche markets (like any market) change over time. Success in a niche requires that entrepreneurs adapt as the market changes. Too many entrepreneurs get stuck doing the same thing or offering the same product while their customers' needs and wants evolve. Even though it is a niche, the market is not isolated and is subject to the same forces and trends that can impact any market.
- *Niches can go away.* Although many niches can last for years, no market is forever. Niches can dry up—sometimes quite suddenly. Again, adaptation can offer some hope, but if the decline is too rapid, niche businesses can fail.
- *Niches can grow.* Although significant growth in a market may not sound bad, it can attract more competitors. If a niche market grows large enough, it can attract some very large competitors. At some point the entrepreneur's cozy market niche can become quite crowded. Eventually, it may no longer be a true market niche, which requires that the entrepreneur adapt his or her business strategies to meet this more competitive market. Prices will be forced downward, while at the same time the costs of business may go up due to increased marketing costs, greater expectations from customers, and higher labor costs due to more competition for qualified employees.

Although finding a market niche is the most common and a relatively safe entry strategy for new entrepreneurial businesses, it still requires continued attention to competitive forces in the market.

ENTREPRENEURIAL PROFILE: Kurt Nelson, Tyler Seymour, and Drew Burchfield and Aloompa Kurt Nelson, Tyler Seymour, and Drew Burchfield launched their business, Aloompa, to develop a variety of mobile apps for the music industry. During the early stages of the business, they realized that their most promising avenue for scaling their business was to focus on one specific niche within the music industry—live music festivals. Aloompa's mobile app for the Bonnaroo Music Festival, a popular four-day rock music festival in Manchester, Tennessee, attracted the attention of several other music festival organizers. Kurt Nelson, president of Aloompa, says focusing on that single niche allowed the company to develop a core framework that could be adapted to any music festival and to many other similar events. Aloompa has become known as a market leader in music festival apps. Although Aloompa operates in a niche market, it is a large and growing market that has allowed the company to expand to music festivals throughout Europe and in other countries around the world.[14] ■

Product or Service Feasibility Analysis: Is There a Market?

LO5

Describe the various methods of conducting primary and secondary market research.

Once entrepreneurs discover that sufficient market potential for their product or service idea actually exists, they sometimes rush in with their exuberant enthusiasm ready to launch a business without actually considering whether they can actually produce the product or provide the service at a reasonable cost. A product or service feasibility analysis determines the degree to which a product or service idea appeals to potential customers and identifies the resources necessary to

primary research
the process of collecting data firsthand and analyzing it.

secondary research
the process of gathering data that has already been compiled and is available, often at a reasonable cost or sometimes even free.

produce the product or provide the service. This portion of the feasibility analysis addresses the question, "Are customers willing to purchase our goods and services?" Entrepreneurs need feedback from potential customers to successfully answer this question. Conducting **primary research** involves collecting data firsthand and analyzing it; **secondary research** involves gathering data that has already been compiled and is available, often at a reasonable cost or sometimes even free. In both types of research, gathering both quantitative and qualitative information is important to drawing accurate conclusions about a product's or service's market potential. Primary research tools include customer surveys, focus groups, construction of prototypes, in-home trials, and "windshield" research (driving around and observing the competition). The goal of primary and secondary research should not only be to find support to validate the business concept. An overly optimistic entrepreneur may overlook important information about the true feasibility of the business if he or she only searches for information that affirms starting the business. It also is important to search for information that does not support the concept. Depending on the nature and severity of any negative evidence, the entrepreneur can either adapt the concept if it is possible to do so or, if necessary, abandon the idea entirely.

CUSTOMER SURVEYS AND QUESTIONNAIRES Keep them short. Word your questions carefully so that you do not bias the results, and use a simple ranking system (e.g., a 1-to-5 scale, with 1 representing "definitely would not buy" and 5 representing "definitely would buy"). Test your survey for problems on a small number of people before putting it to use. Web surveys are inexpensive, easy to conduct, and provide feedback fast. Do not only survey people you know or those who are convenient to reach. Survey people who represent the target market of the business.

FOCUS GROUPS A focus group involves enlisting a small number of potential customers (usually 8 to 12) to give you feedback on specific issues about your product or service (or the business idea itself). Listen carefully for what focus group members like and don't like about your product or service as they tell you what is on their minds. The founders of one small snack food company that produced apple chips conducted several focus groups to gauge customers' acceptance of the product and to guide many key business decisions, ranging from the product's name to its packaging. Once again, consider creating virtual focus groups on the Web. One small bicycle retailer conducts 10 online focus groups each year at virtually no cost and gains valuable marketing information from them. Feedback from online customers is fast, convenient, and real-time.

PROTOTYPES An effective way to gauge the viability of a product is to build a prototype of it. A prototype is an original, functional model of a new product that entrepreneurs can put into the hands of potential customers so that they can see it, test it, and use it. Prototypes usually point out potential problems in a product's design, giving inventors the opportunity to fix them even before they put the prototype into customers' hands. The feedback customers give entrepreneurs based on prototypes often leads to design improvements and new features, some of which the entrepreneurs might never have discovered on their own. Makers of computer software frequently put prototypes of new products into customers' hands as they develop new products or improve existing ones. Known as beta tests, these trials result in an iterative design process in which software designers collect feedback from users and then incorporate their ideas into the product for the next round of tests. Three-dimensional printing creates a less expensive way for entrepreneurs to develop a basic prototype of a product based on drawings. Although the output of a three-dimensional printer is not a fully functional product, it does provide a method of creating a model to test and to use to source manufacturing of component parts.

in-home trial
a market research technique that involves sending researchers into customers' homes to observe them as they use a company's product or service.

IN-HOME TRIALS One technique that reveals some of the most insightful information into how customers actually use a product or service is also the most challenging to coordinate: in-home trials. An **in-home trial** involves sending researchers into customers' homes to observe them as they use the company's product or service. However, in-home trials can be expensive to conduct and therefore may not be affordable for the budgets of most entrepreneurs.

"WINDSHIELD" RESEARCH A good source of information is to observe customers interacting with existing businesses within an industry. Windshield research involves driving around and observing customers interacting with similar kinds of businesses and learning what customers like and don't like about those businesses. For example, before one potential investor was willing to commit funding for a new coffee shop, he required that the entrepreneur get traffic counts at local competitors' outlets. He observed heavy demand and often long lines, which helped provide support for the need for a new coffee shop.

Secondary research should be used to support, not replace, primary research. Secondary research, which is usually less expensive to collect than primary data, includes the following sources:

TRADE ASSOCIATIONS AND BUSINESS DIRECTORIES To locate a trade association, use *Business Information Sources* (University of California Press) or the *Encyclopedia of Associations* (Gale Research). To find suppliers, use *The Thomas Register of American Manufacturers* (Thomas Publishing Company) or *Standard and Poor's Register of Corporations, Executives, and Industries* (Standard and Poor Corporation). *The American Wholesalers and Distributors Directory* includes details on more than 18,000 wholesalers and distributors.

INDUSTRY DATABASES Several online business databases are available through university libraries, such as BizMiner, *Encyclopedia of American Industries, Encyclopedia of Emerging Industries, Encyclopedia of Global Industries, Encyclopedia of Products & Industries—Manufacturing, IBISWorld, Manufacturing & Distribution USA: Industry Analyses, Statistics and Leading Companies*, and *Market Share Reporter*. These databases offer a rich variety of information on specific industries, including statistical analyses, geographic reports, trend analyses, and profiles.

DEMOGRAPHIC DATA To learn more about the demographic characteristics of customers in general, use *The State and Metropolitan Data Book* (Government Printing Office) and *The Sourcebook of Zip Code Demographics* (CACI, Inc.), which provides detailed breakdowns of the population in every zip code in the country. *Sales and Marketing Management's Survey of Buying Power* (Bill Communications) has statistics on consumer, retail, and industrial buying.

CENSUS DATA The Bureau of the Census publishes a wide variety of reports that summarize the wealth of data found in its census database, which is available at most libraries and at the Census Bureau's Web site at www.census.gov.

FORECASTS *The U.S. Industry & Trade Outlook* published by the Department of Commerce, International Trade Administration traces the growth of 200 industries and gives a five-year forecast for each one. Many government agencies, including the U.S. Department of Commerce (www.commerce.gov). offer forecasts on everything from interest rates to the number of housing starts. Again, a government research librarian can help you find what you need.

MARKET RESEARCH Someone may already have compiled the market research you need. The *FINDex Worldwide Directory of Market Research Reports, Studies, and Surveys* (Cambridge Information Group) lists more than 10,600 studies available for purchase. Other directories of business research include *Simmons Study of Media and Markets* (Simmons Market Research Bureau Inc.) and the *A.C. Nielsen Retail Index* (A.C. Nielsen Company).

ARTICLES Magazine and journal articles pertinent to your business are a great source of information. Use the *Reader's Guide to Periodical Literature*, the *Business Periodicals Index* (similar to the Reader's Guide but focusing on business periodicals), and *Ulrich's Guide to International Periodicals* to locate the ones you need.

LOCAL DATA Your state Department of Commerce and your local Chamber of Commerce will very likely have useful data on the local market of interest to you. Call to find out what is available.

THE INTERNET Entrepreneurs can benefit from the vast amount of market research information available on the Internet. This is an efficient resource with up-to-date information, and much of it is free. Entrepreneurs must use caution, however, to ensure the credibility of online sources.

Hands On . . . How To

Do You Want Fries with Those Crickets?

Insects are a common source of food protein for people in many parts of the world. One study suggests that 80 percent of the world population regularly includes insects in their diets. However, in much of the Western world the thought of eating bugs is considered less than appetizing! This soon may be changing. With continued global population growth, concerns about the sustainability of Western agricultural practices, and rising meat and grain prices, Western cultures are beginning to entertain the notion of edible insects as a good source of protein. Entrepreneurs have taken note of these changes in attitudes and are beginning to develop business models that will benefit from the growing acceptance of worms, crickets, and other bugs as a food source.

Insects in Energy Bars

Patrick Crowley introduced his energy bars, called Chapul, as a means to offer an environmentally friendly source of protein to customers. Through his research, Crowley discovered that crickets are 10 times more efficient than cows or pigs at turning vegetable matter into protein. Crowley partnered with a friend who is a chef to develop a recipe for energy bars using cricket flour and had the bars approved by the Food and Drug Administration. Crowley ran a Kickstarter campaign that raised enough money to make 2,000 bars, which sold quickly through online and retail sales. Based on his early success, Crowley contracted with a company to make larger batches of the bars. Chapul cricket bars are sold in 75 stores, and Crowley is negotiating with larger national chains including Whole Foods. Chapul is trending to reach $1 million in annual revenues within its first two years of operations.

Insect Farming Supply

One of the advantages of cultivating insects as a source of protein is that it does not take much space to run an insect farm. In fact, a California company called Tiny Farms sells kits that allow anyone to farm edible insects in their homes or businesses. Andrew Brentano, cofounder of Tiny Farms, notes that there is a shortage of food-grade insects available in the United States due to the increasing acceptance and demand for edible insects. Each

Don Bugito

kit includes a starter package of bugs (locusts, grasshoppers, and worms), insect farming tools and equipment, bug food, and an instruction manual for growing insects for food. Tiny Farms also provides online support, forums, and consulting for aspiring insect farmers. In addition to serving those raising bugs for personal consumption, Tiny Farms intends to become a major supplier for the growing number of commercial bug farmers.

Insect Food Cart

Monica Martinez loved snacking on bugs when she was a young child growing up in Mexico. She decided to find a way to share her taste for insects with residents of her new home, San Francisco, California. Martinez's food cart, Don Bugito, offers menu items such as wax moth larvae tacos, chocolate covered salted crickets, and toffee mealworms over vanilla ice cream. Martinez also offers in-home catering services, featuring a full five-course meal of edible insects, and has begun to sell prepackaged versions of some of her creations.

1. What are the macro trends that support businesses selling edible insects to American consumers?

2. What are the risks that come with being an early entrant into the edible insect market?

3. Do you believe an edible insect business would be successful where you live? Why or why not?

Daniel Imrie-Situnayake, Tiny Farms

Based on: Parija Kavilanz, "This Energy Bar Gets its Kick From . . . Crickets," *CNNMoney*, July 23, 2013, http://money.cnn.com/2013/07/23/smallbusiness/cricket-bar/index.html; Victoria Woollaston, "Forget the Vegetable Patch! This Kit Lets You Grow Your Own Edible INSECTS," *Daily Mail*, November 29, 2013, www.dailymail.co.uk/sciencetech/article-2515043/Forget-vegetable-patch-This-kit-lets-grow-edible-INSECTS-help-cut-meat-eating.html; Kristine A. Wong, "Does Fake Meat Have Legs? The Business Case for Alt-proteins," *Green Biz*, November 27, 2013, www.greenbiz.com/blog/2013/11/27/fake-meat-have-legs-proteins-meatless?mkt_tok=3RkMMJWWfF9wsRoluKXKZKXonjHpfsX56u4rUa631MI%2F0ER3f0vrPUfGjI4CTcRqI%2BSLDwEYGJl v6SgFSLHEMa5qw7gMXRQ%3D; Katharine Schwab, "Don Bugito Introducing Insects to American Diet," *SF Gate*, September 3, 2013, www.sfgate.com/food/article/Don-Bugito-introducing-insects-to-American-diet-4784046.php; Spencer Michels, "Bugs for Dinner?" *PBS News Hour*, May 7, 2012, www.pbs.org/newshour/rundown/2012/05/bugs-for-dinner.html.

Financial Feasibility Analysis: Is There Enough Margin?

LO6

Understand the four major elements of a financial feasibility analysis.

The third component of a feasibility analysis involves assessing the financial feasibility of a proposed business venture. At this stage of the process, a broad financial analysis that examines the basic economic feasibility is sufficient. This component of the feasibility analysis answers the question, "Can this business generate adequate profits?" If the business concept passes the overall feasibility analysis, an entrepreneur should conduct a more thorough financial analysis when developing the business model and creating a full-blown business plan. The four major elements to be included in a financial feasibility analysis include the initial capital requirement, estimated earnings, time out of cash, and resulting return on investment.

CAPITAL REQUIREMENTS Just as a boy scout needs fuel to start a fire, an entrepreneur needs capital to start a business. Some businesses require large amounts of capital, but others do not. Typically, service businesses require less capital to launch than do manufacturing or retail businesses. Start-up companies often need capital to purchase equipment, buildings, technology, and other tangible assets as well as to hire and train employees, promote their products and services, and establish a presence in the market. A good feasibility analysis provides an estimate of the amount of start-up capital an entrepreneur will need to get the business up and running.

When preparing to launch his microbrewery, Cigar City Brewing, Joey Redner needed $585,000 to purchase the brewing system, other equipment, and inventory and to cover initial operating expenses. Redner was able to secure a bank loan after his father agreed to pledge business property as collateral. To help bootstrap his operations, Redner was able to get a large contingent of volunteers to help staff the business, who all agreed to work for free beer. He also set up distribution agreements with two beer distributors before he began brewing his craft beers.[15]

It is important to keep in mind that the typical start-up in the United States can successfully launch with an average of only $10,000,[16] and one in five start-ups get launched with no funding at all.[17] How do entrepreneurs get started with so little funding? Most entrepreneurs employ a variety of techniques called *bootstrapping*. Bootstrapping is the process of finding creative ways to exploit opportunities to launch and grow businesses with the limited resources available for most start-up ventures. It includes a variety of strategies and techniques that cover all of the functions of running a business: marketing, staffing, inventory and production management, cash flow management, and administrative processes needed to keep a business operating.[18]

You will learn more about bootstrapping in Chapter 8 and more about finding sources of business funding, both debt and equity, in Chapter 14.

ESTIMATED EARNINGS In addition to producing an estimate of the start-up company's capital requirements, an entrepreneur also should forecast the earning potential of the proposed business. Industry trade associations and publications such as the *RMA Annual Statement Studies* offer guidelines on preparing sales and earnings estimates for specific types of businesses. From these, entrepreneurs can estimate the financial results they and their investors can expect to see from the business venture if the start-up is executed according to plan.

TIME OUT OF CASH A common cause of business failure is running out of cash before the business breaks even and can support itself through the cash flow from operations. According to a study by U.S. Bank, four out of five small business failures can be attributed to "starting out with too little money."[19] During the planning stage, the entrepreneur should estimate the total cash it will take to sustain the business until the business achieves break-even cash flow. This estimate should be based on a less-than-optimistic scenario because there are almost always unexpected costs and delays in the start-up and growth of a new business. For an operating business, to calculate the number of months until the business runs out of cash, simply divide the amount of available cash remaining in the business by the negative cash flowing from the business each month. The result is the number of months the business can survive at its current rate of negative cash flow. Ideally, the business will be able to grow quickly enough to avoid reaching the point of no more cash.

RETURN ON INVESTMENT The final aspect of the financial feasibility analysis combines the estimated earnings and the capital requirements to determine the rate of return the venture is expected to produce. One simple measure is the rate of return on the capital invested, which is calculated by dividing the estimated earnings the business yields by the amount of capital invested in the business. This aspect of financial feasibility is generally of most concern to investors. Although financial estimates at the feasibility analysis stage typically are rough, they are an important part of the entrepreneur's ultimate "go" or "no go" decision about the business ventures. A venture must produce an attractive rate of return relative to the level of risk it requires. This risk–return trade-off means that the higher the level of risk a prospective business involves, the higher the rate of return it must provide to the entrepreneur and investors. Why should an entrepreneur take on all of the risks of starting and running a business that produces a mere 3 or 4 percent rate of return when he or she could earn that much in a risk-free investment at a bank or other financial institution? Although entrepreneurs should pay more attention to this calculation, many do not because they tend to get wrapped up in the emotion and excitement of their business ideas. You will learn more about developing detailed financial forecasts for a business start-up in Chapter 11.

Wise entrepreneurs take the time to subject their ideas to a feasibility analysis like the one described here, whatever outcome it produces. If the analysis suggests that transforming the idea into a viable business is not feasible, the entrepreneur can move on to the next idea, confident that he or she has not wasted valuable resources launching a business destined to fail.

If the analysis so far finds that there is a market for the idea and that it has real potential as a profitable business, the entrepreneur can move to the final component of the feasibility analysis.

LO7

Describe the process of assessing entrepreneur feasibility.

Entrepreneur Feasibility: Is This Idea Right for Me?

Suppose that the feasibility analysis thus far has established that the industry and market are favorable, there is strong evidence of demand for the product or service in the market, and the concept appears financially feasible. There is one last component of feasibility to examine—the readiness of the entrepreneur (and, if applicable, the entrepreneur's team) to launch the venture successfully. Many new businesses require that an entrepreneur have a certain set of knowledge, experiences, and skills to have any chance of being successful. This is called *entrepreneurial readiness*. Some of these can be simple skills. For example, starting a landscaping business requires knowing how to operate a lawnmower and other equipment. Being successful in a landscaping business also depends on some level of knowledge about plants and grasses. Other new businesses may require a higher level of knowledge and skills. For example, starting an accounting firm requires a high level of knowledge and experience in the laws and practice of accounting. Entrepreneurs can gain the knowledge and skills they need from previous jobs, from their formal education, or from their interests or hobbies. They can also acquire knowledge as part of what they work on during the planning process. Entrepreneurial readiness also involves issues such as temperament, work ethic, and so forth. Performing an entrepreneurial self-assessment can help evaluate entrepreneurial readiness (see Figure 4.7).

Another way to ensure the necessary knowledge and skills are in place is through building a team. For example, an aspiring entrepreneur may have an idea for a new app for smart phones but may not have any programming or design skills. He or she would be best served by exploring the possibility of adding people to the team with that skill set. If there is more than one entrepreneur starting the business, all of them should complete an assessment and use this as a launching point to examine their collective entrepreneurial feasibility.

Beyond the entrepreneur's readiness to start a business, the second aspect of entrepreneur feasibility is to assess whether the business can meet the financial and nonfinancial needs of the entrepreneur and the team. Will the business be able to generate enough profit to support everyone's income needs? If it is successful, will it also meet the wealth goals of the founding team? Just because a business is profitable does not mean that it is profitable enough to support the entrepreneur and his or her team. This can vary from entrepreneur to entrepreneur. A 22-year-old single entrepreneur fresh out of college has very different financial needs than a 42-year-old married entrepreneur who has a mortgage, car payments, and tuition for private schools for his or her children! But making money is not the only thing that matters for most people. Does business fit with goals and aspirations the entrepreneur has outside of work? A business that demands

Personal Aspirations and Priorities
- What gets you excited, gives you energy, and motivates you to excel?
- What do you like to do with your time?
- What drains energy from you?
   In the work you do:
   In personal relationships:
- How do you measure success in your personal life?
   Family:
   Friends and relationships:
   Personal interests and hobbies:
   Contributions to community and society:
- What do you consider success in your business and career?
   Short-term:
   Long-term:
- What are your specific goals for your personal life?
   Family:
   Friends and relationships:
   Personal interests and hobbies:
   Contributions to community and society:
- What are your goals for your business and career?
   Income and lifestyle:
   Wealth:
   Free time:
   Recognition and fame:
   Impact on community:
   Other:
- What do you want to be doing:
   In one year:
   In five years:
   In ten years:
   At retirement:

Core Values
- List the core personal values that you intend to bring to your business (e.g., treating people fairly, giving something back to the community).
- Where does each of these core values come from (religious faith, family, etc.)?
- Why is each of them important to you?

Personal Entrepreneurial Readiness
- What are the major reasons you want to start a business?
- How many hours are you willing and able to put into your new venture?
- How would you describe your tolerance for uncertainty and risk?
- Do you easily trust other people working with you on a common activity? Why or why not?
- How much financial risk are you willing to take with your new venture (personal assets, personal debt, etc.)?
- Assume you decide not to start your business. A short time later, you see that someone has started the same business and is doing well. How would you feel? Why?
- What are the nonfinancial risks for you in starting a new business?
- How do you react to failure? Give examples.
- How do you react in times of personal stress? How do you deal with stress in your life?
- How much income do you need to support your current lifestyle?
- How long could you survive without a paycheck?
- How much money do you have available to start your business?
- Which of your personal assets would you be willing to borrow against, or sell, to start your business?
- Whose support (nonfinancial) is important for you to have before starting your business (family, spouse, etc.)?

FIGURE 4.7

Entrepreneurial Self-Assessment

Source: This self-assessment is adapted from J. Cornwall and N. Carter, *University of St. Thomas Entrepreneurial Self-Assessment: Start-Up*, monograph published by the John M. Morrison Center for Entrepreneurship, University of St. Thomas, St. Paul, Minnesota, 1999. Used with permission.

extensive travel may not fit with an entrepreneur who has a goal of being highly involved with his or her family. A restaurant, which often demands that the entrepreneur be involved 6 or 7 days a week, 52 weeks a year, may not be a good business model for an entrepreneur who wants to travel and take extended vacations.

Once an entrepreneur tests his or her business idea using the four components of a feasibility assessment, the next stage of the new business planning process is to develop a business model.

LO8

Describe the nine elements of a business model.

Developing and Testing a Business Model

In their groundbreaking study of how successful entrepreneurs develop business models, Osterwalder and Pigneur identified the common elements that successful entrepreneurs and investors use when developing and evaluating a business model. They found that most entrepreneurs use a visual process, such as diagraming their business on a whiteboard, when developing their business ideas.[20] They don't just start writing the text of a business plan. Rather, they map out the key components required to make their businesses successful. A business model adds more detail to the evaluation of a new business begun during the feasibility analysis by graphically depicting the "moving parts" of the business and ensuring that they are all working together.

When building a business model, the entrepreneur addresses a series of key questions that will explain how a business will become successful. What value does the business offer customers? Who is my target market? What do they expect of me as my customers? How do I get information to them, and how do they want to get the product? What are the key activities to make this all come together, and what will they cost? What resources do I need to make this happen, including money? Who are key partners I will need to attract to be successful?

In their study, Osterwalder and Pigneur found a pattern of how entrepreneurs use a visual representation of their business model to answer these questions. They used these findings to develop a Business Model Canvas that provides entrepreneurs with a dynamic framework to guide them through the process of developing, testing, and refining their business models (see Figure 4.8). The canvas is comprised of nine elements:

1. *Customer segments.* A good business model always starts with the customer. The entrepreneur's first step is to identify a segment of customers who have a clearly defined need. In the previous steps outlined in this chapter, the entrepreneur begins to define the market for the new business. For most entrepreneurs, the initial market is defined much too broadly. The entrepreneur uses demographic, geographic, socioeconomic, and other characteristics that add specificity to defining the target market. Narrowing the target market enables a small company to focus its limited resources on serving the needs of a specific

FIGURE 4.8

The Business Model Canvas

Source: Osterwalder, Alexander and Pigneur, Yves, "Business Model Generation" © Alexander Osterwalder and Yves Pigneur 2010 (Hoboken: John Wiley and Sons Publisher).

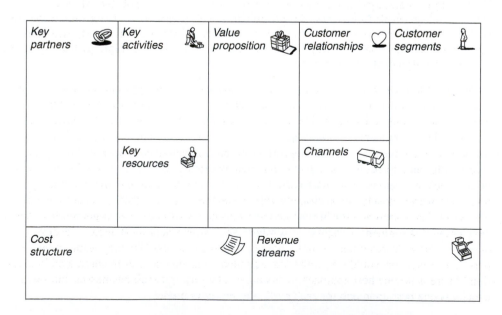

group of customers rather than attempting to satisfy the desires of the mass market. Creating a successful business depends on an entrepreneur's ability to attract real customers who are willing and able to spend real money to buy its products or services. Perhaps the worst marketing error an entrepreneur can commit is failing to define a target market and trying to make the business "everything to everybody." Small companies usually are much more successful focusing on a specific market niche or niches where they can excel at meeting customers' special needs or wants. Who is it, specifically, that has the needs the new business will be addressing with its products and/or services? It may be a market niche. It may be a mass market. Or it may be a segmented market based on age, gender, geography, or socioeconomic grouping.

2. *Value proposition.* A compelling value proposition is at the heart of every successful business. The value proposition is the collection of products and/or services the business will offer to meet the needs of the customers. It is all the things that will set the business apart from its competitors, such as pricing, quality, features, product availability, and other features. Most value propositions for new businesses come from fundamental macro trends within the economy, demographics, technology, or society and culture discussed earlier in the chapter. Trends lead to changes within industries. These trends are first uncovered in the industry and market feasibility analysis. A fundamental role of being an entrepreneur is to find solutions for the problems and needs customers have that result from the change that follows disruptive trends such as these. It could be something about the product itself, such as its price and value, features, performance, durability, or design, or it might be something emanating from the personnel of the company, including their expertise, responsiveness, or reliability.

   It is best to identify and focus on one or two benefits that will make the new business stand out to customers and motivate them to purchase from the new business. The best way to develop the key benefits that are at the heart of a strong value proposition is to listen to customers. Although entrepreneurs may think they know what their customers want, most of the time they will not have it quite right. The entrepreneur will probably have to adjust the product or service to fit it with what the customer actually wants or needs.

   ENTREPRENEURIAL PROFILE: George Bukhov and Burger & Lobster Less than two years after opening his first location, George Bukhov expanded his Burger & Lobster restaurants to four locations across London, England. Burger & Lobster's business model offers a meal that feels like an indulgence at a price point that most people can afford. It is not unusual for a Burger & Lobster restaurant to serve 1,000 customers per day on weekends. Even on weeknights the wait to get into a Burger & Lobster can reach two hours. To keep customers engaged while waiting for their tables, Burger & Lobster offers a large bar area that plays classic Motown music in a fun and lively atmosphere. Once seated, patrons choose from a limited menu of burgers or lobster, which helps control quality and costs. By finding a winning value proposition, Bukhov created a business with high quality, high sales volume, and high profit margins.[21] ■

3. *Customer relationships.* Not every business provides the same type and same level of customer service. This is what defines the customer relationship in the business model. For example, several effective business models provide meals to consumers. Customers may choose to buy food from a vending machine, a fast-food restaurant, a fast casual sit-down restaurant, or an exclusive fine dining establishment. Each of these business models has a very different approach to define the relationship with customers. The vending business offers quick, convenient, and impersonal service. At the other extreme, the fine dining restaurant works closely and personally with customers to ensure they get exactly what they want. Each approach is effective and appropriate for its particular target market. When developing this segment of the business model, the entrepreneur must answer several questions. How do customers want to interact with the business? Do they want intensive personal service, or would they rather have limited engagement or even automated interaction? There is no one best approach to customer relationship for all businesses, but there usually is one best approach for each particular business model.

4. *Channels.* In the business model canvas, channels refer to both communication channels (promotion) and distribution channels (product placement). Communication channels define how the customers seek out information about this type of product. Where do potential customers go to when they want to get information about products and services? It could be Web sites, social networks, blogs, advertisements, experts, and so forth. Again, there is no one best way to communicate for all businesses, but there will be one or more that is most effective with the specific target market for a given business model. The distribution channel defines the most effective way to get products to the customers for this type of business. For some business models it may be best to use in-home sales through Web sites such as Amazon because the target market may prefer to order online from the comfort of their living rooms. For other business models, the customer may want to see the merchandise, touch it, and interact with it in an exciting new retail location. The entrepreneur must determine where the customer wants to make the purchase and then determine the most effective way to get it to the customer at that location.

5. *Key activities.* What important things must the entrepreneur do to ensure a successful launch and to sustain the growth of the business? In the business model, the goal is to build a basic checklist of what needs to be done to open the business and what activities are necessary to ensure its long-term success. The development of the business plan will then take this list and expand on it in much greater detail. We will explore creating a business plan in detail in Chapter 5.

6. *Key resources.* What are the human, capital, and intellectual resources needed for the business to be successful? Again, this will serve as an initial checklist to ensure that the entrepreneur has identified all key resources necessary to support a successful launch and to sustain the business as it grows. The business plan provides the opportunity to explain these in much greater detail and develop all necessary cost estimates for the financial forecasts.

7. *Key partners.* This segment of the business model includes key suppliers, key outsourcing partners, investors, industry partners, advisers, and all other external businesses or entities that are critical to make the business model work. Entrepreneurs cannot expect to become successful all by themselves. They must build a network of relationships when launching and growing their businesses.

8. *Revenue streams.* How will the value proposition generate revenue? Will it be a one-time sale, ongoing fees, advertising, or some other sources of cash into the business? The entrepreneur should answer these questions using the information discovered in the value proposition, customer segments, customer relationship, and channel components of the business model (the right side of the business model canvas). The revenue streams information serves as the framework for the more detailed revenue forecasts developed for the business plan.

9. *Cost structure.* What are the fixed and variable costs that are necessary to make the business model work? The key activities, key resources, and key partners components of the plan (the left side of the business model canvas) identify the basic types of costs and give some estimate of their scope. Just like the revenue streams, the cost structure of the business model becomes the framework for developing more detailed costs that the entrepreneur will incorporate into the financial forecasts of the business plan. Chapter 11 examines the financial plan in more detail.

Developing a business model is a four-phase process[22] (see Figure 4.9). The first phase is to create an initial business model canvas, as outlined previously. It is best to do this on a white board, on the wall using Post-it Notes, or using free business model software such as Business Model Fiddle (www.bmfiddle.com). As the entrepreneur goes through the next three phases, the business model will change. At this point in the process, much of the information in the business model is only a series of hypotheses to be tested. The entrepreneur will update the business model

FIGURE 4.9

**The Business
Modeling Process**

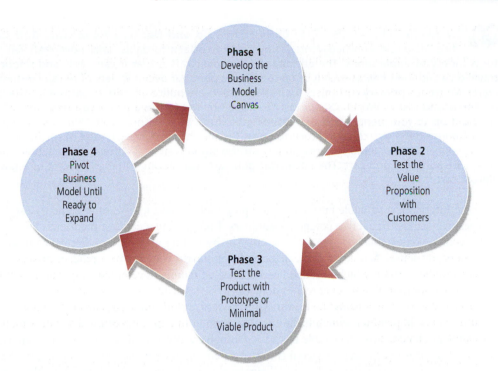

as he or she learns more about the customers and the resources it will take to launch and grow the business. The business model canvas allows all of the team members involved in the start-up to work from a common framework. The team documents all of the hypotheses about the business model that require further investigation and keeps track of changes in the model that result from testing the hypotheses. The entrepreneurial team also estimates the total market size and the size of the specific target market that would be feasible to attract to the new business when it launches.

The second phase in designing the business model is to test the problem that the team thinks the business solves through its core value proposition. This is best done with primary research data. That means the entrepreneurial team must "get out of the office" and test the model with real customers. By engaging potential customers early in the development of a new business and listening to what they have to say, the team has a much better chance of developing a business model that will attract customers. By engaging with real customers, the entrepreneurial team asks the following questions:[23]

- Do we really understand the customer problem the business model is trying to address?

- Do these customers care enough about this problem to spend their hard-earned money on our product?

- Do these customers care enough about our product to help us by telling others through word-of-mouth?

By answering these questions the entrepreneur assesses the actual need for the product and the intensity of that need.

The third phase is to test the solution to the problem in the market. One technique to test the solution offered by the business model involves **business prototyping**, in which entrepreneurs test their business models on a small scale before committing significant resources to launch a business that might not work. Business prototyping recognizes that every business idea is a hypothesis that must be tested before an entrepreneur takes it to full scale. If the test supports the hypothesis and its accompanying assumptions, the entrepreneur takes the next step of building a business plan. If the prototype flops, the entrepreneur scraps the business idea with only minimal losses and turns to the next idea.

business prototyping
the process by which entrepreneurs test their business models on a small scale before committing significant resources to launch a business that might not work.

ENTREPRENEURIAL PROFILE: Chris Fitzgerald and Neoteric Hovercraft Golf Cart
Chris Fitzgerald launched Neoteric Hovercraft to offer affordable, small hovercraft vehicles for a variety of applications. The advantage of a hovercraft is that it can easily and smoothly travel on a cushion of air at speeds of up to 50 miles per hour over a variety of terrain, including water. Neoteric's primary customers for its hovercrafts are police and fire departments, the U.S. Air Force, and Disney World. One model developed by Neoteric is a hovercraft golf cart, which can hold up to four people and two sets of golf clubs. Windy Knoll Golf Club in Springfield, Ohio, bought two hovercraft golf carts to assess the feasibility of everyday use of the devices on a golf course and customer interest in paying the significant cost difference of a hovercraft versus a traditional golf cart. The hovercraft golf cart costs about 10 times the cost of a gas or electric cart.[24] ■

The Internet is a valuable business prototyping tool because it gives entrepreneurs easy and inexpensive access to real live potential customers. Entrepreneurs can test their ideas by selling their products on established sites such as eBay or by setting up their own Web sites to gauge customers' response. A process that can guide testing early versions of a product or service is known as *lean start-up*, which is defined as a process of rapidly developing simple prototypes to test key assumptions by engaging real customers.[25]

To launch a business using the lean start-up process, entrepreneurs begin with what is called a **minimal viable product**, which is the simplest version of a product or service with which an entrepreneur can create a sustainable business. Dropbox was founded in 2007 by Drew Houston and Arash Ferdowsi as a free service that lets users easily share photos, documents, and videos among any devices using their software. When developing the idea for their business, they knew that it would take years to create the software to power it and that developing a simple working prototype was not possible. To test their idea, they created a three-minute video that demonstrated how their new product would work once it was fully developed. The video drove hundreds of thousands of viewers to their Web site and created a long waiting list of people willing to use the product in its beta version. The high level of interest convinced the founders and the investment community that Dropbox was a product for which there was strong demand. Dropbox now has more than 50 million users around the globe and has raised $257 million in funding.[26]

ENTREPRENEURIAL PROFILE: Aayush Phumbhra and Chegg The original business model of Chegg was to establish a site like Craigslist that specialized in connecting college students with each other to offer things they wanted to buy and sell. Company cofounder Aayush Phumbhra noticed that most of the traffic at the site was buying and selling textbooks. Phumbhra wondered whether students would just rather rent their books and avoid the hassle of buying and selling their textbooks every semester. To test the hypothesis, Chegg purchased 2,000 used textbooks online and sent out e-mails to customers about the new service. Within a short time, Chegg's customers clearly demonstrated their preference for renting over buying and selling. Based on the success of the market experiment, Phumbhra pivoted the business model to one that focuses on renting textbooks to college students. Chegg now rents more than a million textbooks each year and employees 150 people.[27] ■

The fourth phase of designing a business model is to make changes and adjustments in the business, called **pivots**, based on what the entrepreneur learns from engaging the market about the problem and the solution that the new business intends to pursue. Some pivots may be subtle adjustments to the business model, while others may be fundamental changes to key parts of the model, including in the value proposition, markets served, or ideal revenue streams. There are three major types of pivots:

- *Product pivot.* The features that make up a product may not match what the customer really wants or needs. Sometimes the entrepreneur adds features that are not really important to the customer. Although customers may be willing to accept these features as part of the product, they are not willing to pay extra for them. This creates a product that is not clearly focused on the market need: It costs more than it should due to the extra features. For example, when Paul Orfalea founded his first Kinko's store (now FedEx Office), he sold a variety of school and office supplies to his fellow University of Southern California students. He also had a copy machine in the back of the store. Students did not buy many

---

minimal viable product
the simplest version of a product or service with which an entrepreneur can create a sustainable business.

pivots
the process of making changes and adjustments to a business model on the basis of the feedback a company receives from customers.

RendezWoof: Creating a Minimal Viable Product for a Mobile App

Entrepreneurs create minimal viable products to allow them to test their product with real customers as quickly as possible. Testing the product this way helps to determine whether consumers really want the product, provides feedback from these customers to help improve the product, and gathers hard data that demonstrates the proof of concept many investors want before they fund an emerging business.

Judson Aikens wanted to start a business but had a good paying job and was concerned about taking on too much risk. While brainstorming about possible businesses he could launch, Aikens came up for an idea for a new dating app. He had observed that it is easy to meet new people at places like dog parks.

Aikens's idea was to develop an app called RendezWoof that created a virtual dog park. "The app would not only connect dog owners with each other, it would connect them with dog-friendly resources around them," says Aikens. "Using GPS, the app's map would populate restaurants with patios and parks convenient to users interested in meeting up to grab a beer or throw a Frisbee."

Aikens reached out to an entrepreneur, Ben Dolgoff, who had spoken to one of the entrepreneurship classes he had taken in graduate school. Ben was an experienced app developer who had developed and launched several successful apps. After asking Ben to sign a nondisclosure agreement, Aikens shared his idea. Ben said he thought the app had promise as a commercially viable product. He suggested that Aikens develop some designs for his idea and then get back with him. If the idea had promise, Ben said he might be willing to develop the app in exchange for some equity in the new business.

Aikens shared his app idea with a friend who was a graphic designer. She was eager to help him with the designs and was willing to provide ongoing graphic design services in exchange for equity.

The next step was for Aikens to work with the graphic designer to develop a wireframe of the app. A wireframe is a drawing of the various screens that make up an app; it includes the kinds of information displayed, the functions of the app, and the basic flow from screen to screen.

Aikens took the wireframe designs to Ben, who was eager to move forward. Ben's company would develop the app in exchange for equity.

"This arrangement was very acceptable to me," says Aikens. "It simultaneously removed the financial burden of development and provided an experienced go-to consultant I could work with through the life of the app."

Aikens formed an LLC and secured the RendezWoof name on all social platforms and for the Web domain. He opened an Apple developer account and applied for copyrights and trademarks.

Judson Aikens, RendezWoof, LLC

Because he is still working his day job, Aikens spends many late nights working with the developers to improve the app's user interface and user experience.

Because the goal of the initial version of the app is to gain users and prove the concept, RendezWoof initially offered the app for free through the Apple Store. Future versions of the app will have more features, which will allow the company to charge a small fee for the app.

1. Why would you recommend that an entrepreneur develop a minimal viable product or a prototype?

2. Can you think of additional market research that Aikens could have done before developing his product?

3. What are the advantages and disadvantages of offering equity in exchange for work done on a new product?

Source: Judson Aikens, personal communication, December 17, 2013.

supplies, but they were constantly using the copy machine. He narrowed his offering to become primarily a copy shop and grew the business to a multinational company with more than 1,200 locations. On the other hand, sometimes the entrepreneur does not offer enough features to fully address the customers' problem. In this situation, the entrepreneur must add the additional features the customer expects.

- *Customer pivot.* Although a product might solve a real market problem or need, sometimes the initial business model targets the wrong customer segment or even the wrong market. For example, PayPal targeted the handheld device market that included the Palm Pilot for its electronic payment system. However, the founders of PayPal soon realized by listening to customer feedback that there was a much larger market for its product. Businesses were beginning to engage in commerce on their Web sites. PayPal pivoted its business model and as a result rapidly grew to become a $1.6 billion company facilitating Internet commerce.

- *Revenue model pivot.* There are many ways in which the revenue model may pivot. One of the most basic revenue decisions is whether to use a high margin/low volume model or low margin/high volume model. For example, Best Buy began as a single location stereo equipment store called the Sound of Music back in the 1960s. Like all of its competitors, the revenue model was high margin/low volume. The owners would mark up inventory two to three times what the product cost them to purchase. As a result, the store would turn its inventory over about once a year. After a tornado destroyed the building but left the inventory undamaged, the Sound of Music owners rented a large tent and ran a drastic sale. The demand was so overwhelming that when they reopened, they changed their revenue model to low margin/high volume and within a short time renamed the business Best Buy. The low prices created so much demand that the stores would sell their entire inventory about once a month, rather than once a year. Other revenue model pivots change the type of payment received. The model may change from a single payment to recurring revenue, or it may shift from hourly billing to charging a fixed price per service. Social entrepreneurs can pivot from a revenue model based on a nonprofit that raises money through grants and donations to a social enterprise that generates revenues from a product or service.

Several minor pivots may also be necessary for a business model around operational aspects of the business, including promotion, distribution, staffing, or outsourcing.

If pivots to the existing business model are not enough, occasionally a company may completely change its business model. For example, when IBM was facing possible failure in the 1990s, the company drastically shifted its business model from a company that manufactured and sold computer and other office hardware to focus primarily on software and information technology consulting. It is now one of the largest and most profitable information technology companies in the world.

Conclusion

Entrepreneurs can follow five steps to guide the process of turning a great new idea into a successful business. This chapter examines the first three steps in this process.

The best business ideas start with a group of customers with a common problem or need. Once entrepreneurs develop ideas for new businesses, the first step is to assess these ideas by examining a need in the market, developing a solution for that need, and determining the entrepreneur's ability to successfully turn the idea into a business. The idea assessment process helps an entrepreneur more efficiently and effectively examine multiple ideas to identify the solution with the most potential.

The second step is to conduct a feasibility analysis to determine whether the entrepreneur can transform the idea into a viable business. The role of a feasibility analysis is to serve as a filter, screening out ideas that lack the potential for building a successful business, before an entrepreneur commits the necessary resources to develop and test a business model or to build a business plan.

You Be the Consultant

When to Call It Quits on a New Business

Jake Jorgovan had become a successful entrepreneur while he was in college. Jorgovan and a classmate started a video production company. They began by making videos of senior recitals for music students at their school. By the time they had graduated, their company had hired several employees and was booked up with a combination of music industry work and shoots for corporate clients needing videos. Jorgovan won several local and national business plan competitions based on the plans he developed for the company. Shortly after graduation, Jorgovan was recognized as the Youth Entrepreneur of the Year in Nashville, Tennessee, where the business was headquartered.

Not long after that, Jorgovan made the decision to move away from the video industry and start a new business. After extensive research, Jorgovan identified an opportunity within the healthcare industry. Telemedicine was a growth sector within the industry. Jorgovan started his new company, Telehealth PT, to develop a telemedicine application for physical therapists. Telehealth's business model was to provide a framework that would allow physical therapists to provide care through live video conferencing sessions on patients' mobile devices or computers.

Jorgovan began developing the basic technology he could use to demonstrate that his concept could work. His goal was to offer a simple version of the product and test it with a few physical therapy clinics. However, not long after beginning work on the basic product, Jorgovan began to have doubts about his ability to get the business launched. He persevered, trying to overcome the many technical hurdles and personal challenges the new business kept throwing in front of his path.

Even though it soon became clear that his new business was not going to work, Jorgovan had a hard time accepting this failure, mainly because he had known so much success with his previous business. He continued to try to uncover ways to salvage the venture, but eventually he had to admit he had failed.

One of the possible outcomes of conducting feasibility analyses and developing business models is that, like Jake Jorgovan, the entrepreneur discovers the business just won't work. Entrepreneurs should consider this a positive outcome because they are able to discover fatal flaws in a business concept early, saving time and money. The reality is that it can be hard for entrepreneurs to

admit failure and walk away from an idea even when it becomes clear it is doomed to fail. Why? What clouds their judgment?

- **Pride and ego.** It is easy for entrepreneurs to let their egos get too wrapped up in their businesses, even very early in the life of their new ventures. They receive affirmation and encouragement from family and friends for taking the risk to start a business. Soon, their pride in being an entrepreneur can get in the way of making a sound business decision and closing a failing venture.

- **Their "baby."** Many long and lonely hours go into getting a business started. Entrepreneurs can quickly become emotionally attached to the new venture. They can reach a point where they could not even imagine thinking about giving up on it.

- **Getting stuck on sunk costs.** It can be difficult for entrepreneurs to look at the time, money, and reputation they have put into a failing concept as a *sunk cost*. That is, entrepreneurs can never recover the resources they have already committed to a venture.

The purpose of feasibility analysis is to ask the question: Can this business work? Sometimes the answer will be "no." The entrepreneur must be ready to accept this answer and move on to the next opportunity.

1. Why was it hard for Jake to admit his newest venture was not going to work?

2. What would you recommend that entrepreneurs do to ensure they don't hang on too long to a failed business concept?

3. A failed business concept does not mean the entrepreneur has failed. How would you explain this to an entrepreneur facing a failed business concept?

Based on: Jeff Cornwall, "Why Entrepreneurs Never Say Die, But Maybe Should," *Inc.*, December 18, 2013, www.inc.com/jeff-cornwall/why-entrepreneurs-never-say-die-but-maybe-should.html; Jake Jorgovan, personal communication, December 6, 2013; Jake Jorgovan, "Accepting Failure," *jake-jorgovan.com*, December 2, 2013, http://jake-jorgovan.com/blog/2013/12/1/accepting-failure.

The third step in the process of evaluating ideas is to develop and test the business model. Developing a business model helps the entrepreneur better understand all that will be required to launch and build the business. In this step in the planning process, the entrepreneur tests the concept and uses what he or she learned from real customers to refine the business model before committing the resources to grow the business to its full potential.

Once the entrepreneur completes the idea assessment, feasibility study, and business model steps, he or she is ready to develop a business plan. As the business becomes more successful, the strategic plan becomes an essential management tool. The business plan and strategic plan are covered in Chapter 5.

Chapter Summary by Learning Objective

1. Describe the process of conducting an idea assessment.

- An idea sketch pad is a tool that helps entrepreneurs assess ideas. The idea sketch pad has five parameters:

  Customers. Start with a group of customers who have a clear need that is not being addressed.

  Offering. Describe your idea for a product or service to offer the customers.

  Value proposition. Explain why your product or service will be important to customers.

  Core competencies. Determine if your offering has any technologies or unique features that will help differentiate it from competitors?

  People. Identify the key people on the team who will launch this business.

2. Explain the elements of a feasibility analysis.

- Determine how attractive an industry is overall as a "home" for a new business.

- Evaluate possible niches a small business can occupy profitably.

3. Describe the six forces in the macro environment of an industry.

- Sociocultural trends can lead to dramatic changes, creating whole new industries and fundamentally transforming existing industries.

- Technological breakthroughs lead to the development of new products and entirely new industries.

- Changing demographics create opportunities for entrepreneurs.

- Economic trends, both positive and negative, create opportunities.

- Political and legal change, such as new laws and regulations, create opportunities for entrepreneurs.

- Global trends that open global markets allow businesses to seek customers and suppliers from all corners of the world and can help in even the smallest business.

4. Understand how Porter's Five Forces Model assesses the competitive environment.

- Entrepreneurs should assess five forces that shape the competitive environment for every business:

  The rivalry among competing firms

  The bargaining power of suppliers

  The bargaining power of buyers

  The threat of new entrants

  The threat of substitute products or services

5. Describe the various methods of conducting primary and secondary market research.

- Primary research tools include customer surveys, focus groups, building prototypes, conducting in-home trials, and "windshield" research (driving around and observing the competition).

- Secondary research gathers existing data from trade associations and business directories, industry databases, demographic data, census data, forecasts compiled by government agencies, market research reports, articles in magazines and journals, local data, and the Internet.

6. Understand the four major elements of a financial feasibility analysis.

- *Capital requirements.* Start-up companies often need capital to purchase equipment, buildings, technology, and other tangible assets and to hire and train employees, promote their products and services, and establish a presence in the market.

- *Estimated earnings.* In addition to producing an estimate of the start-up company's capital requirements, an entrepreneur should forecast the earning potential of the proposed business.

- *Time out of cash.* To estimate time out of cash, take the negative cash flow from the business each month and divide by how much available cash is left in the business. This gives the number of months the business can survive at its current rate of negative cash flow.

- *Return on investment.* A venture must produce an attractive rate of return relative to the level of risk it requires. This risk–return tradeoff means that the higher the level of risk a prospective business involves, the higher the rate of return it must provide to the entrepreneur and investors.

7. Describe the process of assessing entrepreneur feasibility.

- Many new businesses require that an entrepreneur possess a certain set of knowledge, experiences, and skills to have a chance of being successful.

- Entrepreneurial readiness also involves issues such as temperament and work ethic.

8. Describe the nine elements of a business model.

- *Customer segments.* A good business model always starts with the customer. The entrepreneur's first step is to identify a segment of customers who have a clearly defined need.

- *Value proposition.* The value proposition is the collection of products and/or services the business will offer to meet customers' needs.

- *Customer relationships.* Not every business provides the same type and same level of customer service.

- *Channels.* Channels refer to both communication channels (promotion) and distribution channels (product placement). Communication channels define how the customers seek out information about this type of product. The distribution channel defines the most effective way to get products to the customers for this type of business.

- *Key activities.* The goal is to build a basic checklist of what needs to be done to open the business and what activities are necessary to ensure its long-term success.

- *Key resources.* This will serve as an initial checklist to ensure that all key resources have been identified that will support a successful launch and sustain the business as it grows.

- *Key partners.* This segment of the business model includes important suppliers, outsourcing partners, investors, industry partners, advisers, and all other external businesses or entities that are critical to make the business model work.

- *Revenue streams.* How will the value proposition generate revenue?

- *Cost structure.* The key activities, key resources, and key partners components of the plan help identify the basic types of costs and give some estimate of their scope.

Discussion Questions

4-1. Describe the new business planning process.

4-2. Explain the parameters of the idea sketch pad.

4-3. What are the risks for an entrepreneur who becomes emotionally attached to an idea for a new business?

4-4. Describe the four components of a feasibility analysis.

4-5. Why is it important for an entrepreneur to be aware of the macro forces that shape a new business venture?

4-6. List and describe the six foundational forces that shape the macro environment of a business venture.

4-7. Describe in detail Porter's Five Forces Model.

4-8. What is a market niche?

4-9. Explain the advantages an entrepreneur gains by pursuing a niche market.

4-10. List and describe the various tools for conducting primary market research.

4-11. What are the four elements of a financial feasibility analysis?

4-12. Even a business that passes a market and a financial feasibility analysis may not be a good business for an entrepreneur to launch. Explain.

4-13. Why is it essential to develop a sound business model before writing a business plan?

4-14. List and describe the nine elements of the business model canvas.

4-15. Describe the four phases that go into developing a business model.

4-16. A sound business model should always begin with a market need. Explain this statement.

4-17. What is a pivot in a business model?

4-18. Explain the various types of pivots an entrepreneur may need to consider for a business model.

Beyond the Classroom . . .

4-19. Identify an idea for a new business for an industry you would like to work within.

4-20. Evaluate the idea using the idea sketch pad.

4-21. Assess how the six macro forces are creating change within this industry.

4-22. Examine the idea using Porter's Five Forces Model.

4-23. Develop a plan to conduct market research on your idea using both primary and secondary methods of research.

4-24. Complete an entrepreneurial self-assessment.

4-25. What do you take away from this self-assessment about your entrepreneurial readiness?

4-26. Discuss your findings with someone who knows you well.

4-27. Did they offer any insights about your entrepreneurial readiness that you may have overlooked?

Endnotes

Scan for Endnotes or go to www.pearsonhighered.com/scarborough

5 Crafting a Business Plan and Building a Solid Strategic Plan

Xavier Arnau/Getty Images

Learning Objectives

On completion of this chapter, you will be able to:

1. Explain the benefits of an effective business plan.

2. Describe the elements of a solid business plan.

3. Explain the "five Cs of credit" and why they are important to potential lenders and investors reviewing business plans.

4. Understand the keys to making an effective business plan presentation.

5. Understand the importance of strategic management to a small business.

6. Explain why and how a small business must create a competitive advantage in the market.

7. Develop a strategic plan for a business using the nine steps in the strategic management process.

A business plan is a planning tool that builds on the foundation of the idea assessment, feasibility analysis, and business model discussed in Chapter 4. A business plan provides a more comprehensive and detailed analysis than the first three steps in the new business planning process. Together with a well-developed business model, it functions primarily as a planning tool describing in greater detail how to turn the model into a successful business. The primary goals of the business plan are to guide entrepreneurs as they launch their businesses and to help them acquire the necessary financing to launch. Research suggests that, whatever their size, companies that engage in business planning outperform those that do not. A business plan offers:

- a systematic, realistic evaluation of a venture's chances for success in the market.

- a way to determine the principal risks facing the venture.

- a "game plan" for managing the business successfully during its start-up.

- a tool for comparing actual results against targeted performance.

- an important tool for attracting capital in the challenging hunt for money.

Few activities in the life of a business are as vital—or as overlooked—as that of developing a strategy for success that guides a business beyond the start-up detailed in the business plan. Companies without clear strategies may achieve some success in the short run, but as soon as competitive conditions stiffen or an unanticipated threat arises, they usually "hit the wall" and fold. Without a basis for differentiating itself from a pack of similar competitors, the best a company can hope for is mediocrity in the marketplace.

In today's global competitive environment, any business, large or small, that is not thinking and acting strategically is extremely vulnerable. Every business is exposed to the forces of a rapidly changing competitive environment, and in the future small business executives can expect even greater change and uncertainty. From sweeping political changes around the planet and rapid technology advances to more intense competition and newly emerging global markets, the business environment has become more turbulent and challenging to business owners. Although this market turbulence creates many challenges for small businesses, it also creates opportunities for those companies that have in place strategies to capitalize on them. Entrepreneurs' willingness to adapt, to create change, to experiment with new business models, and to break traditional rules has become more important than ever. "It's not the strongest or the most intelligent [companies that] survive," says American Express CEO Ken Chenault, "but those most adaptive to change."[1]

LO1

Explain the benefits of an effective business plan.

The Benefits of Creating a Business Plan

When based on the foundation of a fully developed and tested business model, a well-conceived and factually based business plan increases the likelihood of success of a new business. For decades, research has proved that companies that engage in business planning outperform those that do not. One study by the Small Business Administration reports that entrepreneurs who write business plans early on are two-and-a-half times more likely to actually start their businesses than those who do not.[2] Unfortunately, many entrepreneurs never take the time to engage in the new business planning process, of which the business plan is an important element. The implications of the lack of planning are all too evident in the high failure rates that small companies experience.

A **business plan** is a written summary of an entrepreneur's proposed business venture, its operational and financial details, its marketing opportunities and strategy, and its managers' skills and abilities. There is no substitute for a well-prepared business plan, and there are no shortcuts to creating one. The plan serves as an entrepreneur's road map on the journey toward building a successful business. A business plan describes which direction the company is taking, what its goals are, where it wants to be, and how it intends to get there. The plan is written proof that an entrepreneur has performed the necessary research, has studied the business opportunity adequately, and is prepared to capitalize on it with a sound business model. Crafting a business plan is an entrepreneur's last insurance against launching a business destined to fail or mismanaging a potentially successful company.

business plan

a written summary of an entrepreneur's proposed business venture, its operational and financial details, its marketing opportunities and strategy, and its managers' skills and abilities.

A business plan serves two essential functions. First, it provides a battery of tools—a mission statement, goals, objectives, budgets, financial forecasts, target markets, and entry strategies—to help entrepreneurs subject their ideas to one last test of reality before launching the business. The business plan also helps the entrepreneur to lead the company successfully through its launch and early start-up phases.

The second function of the business plan is to attract lenders and investors. A business plan must prove to potential lenders and investors that a venture will be able to repay loans and produce an attractive rate of return. They want proof that an entrepreneur has evaluated the risk involved in the new venture realistically and has a strategy for addressing it. Unfortunately, many small business owners approach potential lenders and investors without having prepared to sell their business concepts. Given the increased challenges in funding small businesses since the beginning of the recession in 2008, being prepared for *any* funding meeting has become even more important. Tim Williamson, cofounder of The Idea Village, an incubator for entrepreneurs, says that of the thousands of entrepreneurs seeking funding, only about 1 percent are ready to get the money.[3] A collection of figures scribbled on a note pad to support a loan application or investment request is not enough. Applying for loans or attempting to attract investors without a solid business plan rarely lands needed capital. The best way to secure the necessary capital is to prepare a sound business plan. The quality of an entrepreneur's business plan weighs heavily in the final decision to lend or invest funds. It is also potential lenders' and investors' first impression of the company and its managers. Therefore, the finished product should be highly polished and professional in both form and content.

Preparing a sound business plan requires time and effort, but the benefits greatly exceed the costs. Building a plan forces a potential entrepreneur to look at his or her business idea in the harsh light of reality by putting the concepts developed in the business model into specific detail. To get external financing, an entrepreneur's plan must pass three tests with potential lenders and investors: (1) the reality test, (2) the competitive test, and (3) the value test. The first two tests have both an external and internal component:

REALITY TEST The external component of the reality test involves proving that a market for the product or service really does exist. It focuses on industry attractiveness, market niches, potential customers, market size, degree of competition, and similar factors. Entrepreneurs who pass this part of the reality test prove in the marketing portion of their business plans that there is strong demand for their business idea. Evidence that is gathered during the testing of the business model should be an integral part of the marketing plan to bolster the proof for the idea using real customers.

The internal component of the reality test focuses on the product or service itself. Can the company really build it for the cost estimates in the business plan? Is it truly different from what competitors are already selling? Does it offer customers something of value?

COMPETITIVE TEST The external part of the competitive test evaluates the company's relative position to its key competitors. How do the company's strengths and weaknesses match up with those of the competition? Do these reactions threaten the new company's success and survival? Recall from Chapter 4 that a compelling value proposition must clearly define the problem the target market is facing. Are current choices to address the problem for target market unworkable? Is some sort of solution for the problem facing the target market inevitable? Is the problem urgent, critical, and clear for the target market? Is the target market underserved? Successful entrepreneurs carefully and honestly evaluate the strength of their product ideas. Do we offer a solution that looks at the problem differently than competitors? Can we protect our intellectual property (if applicable) and/or create a protectable niche? Do we disrupt the market but not so much that the "cost" of changing to us is too high? A value proposition that is properly constructed answers the following questions:[4]

- Who is our target market?

- What current options exist for this target market?

- What do/will we offer the target market?

- What is the key problem it solves?

- Why is it better than other options the target market has to choose from?

A strong and compelling value proposition guides everything entrepreneurs and their employees do while starting and growing their businesses.[5]

The internal competitive test focuses on management's ability to create a company that will gain an edge over existing rivals. To pass this part of the competitive test, a plan must prove the quality, skill, and experience of the venture's management team. What other resources does the company have that can give it a competitive edge in the market?

VALUE TEST To convince lenders and investors to put their money into the venture, a business plan must prove to them that it offers a high probability of repayment or an attractive rate of return. Entrepreneurs usually see their businesses as good investments because they consider the intangibles of owning a business, such as gaining control over their own destinies and freedom to do what they enjoy. Lenders and investors, however, look at a venture in colder terms: dollar-for-dollar returns. A plan must convince lenders they will be repaid the money they lend to the business, and it must convince investors they will earn an attractive return on their money.

Even after completing a feasibility analysis and building a business model, entrepreneurs sometimes do not come to the realization that "this business just won't work" until they build a business plan. Have they wasted valuable time? Not at all! The time to find out that a business idea will not succeed is in the planning stages before committing significant money, time, and effort to the venture. It is much less expensive to make mistakes on paper than in reality. In other cases, a business plan reveals important problems to overcome before launching a company. Exposing these flaws and then addressing them enhances the chances of a venture's success. Business plans also help nascent entrepreneurs nail down important aspects of their concept and sometimes prevent costly mistakes.

The real value in preparing a plan is not as much in the plan itself as it is in the process the entrepreneur goes through to create the plan—from the idea assessment, to the feasibility analysis, through the development and testing of the business model, and finally with the crafting of the written business plan. Although the finished product is extremely useful, the process of building the plan requires entrepreneurs to explore all areas of the business and subject their ideas to an objective, critical evaluation from many different angles. What entrepreneurs learn about their industry, target customers, financial requirements, competition, and other factors is essential to making their ventures successful. Building a business plan is one controllable factor that can reduce the risk and uncertainty of launching a company.

The Elements of a Business Plan

LO2

Describe the elements of a solid business plan.

Wise entrepreneurs recognize that every business plan is unique and must be tailor-made. They avoid the off-the-shelf, "cookie-cutter" approach that produces a look-alike business plan. The elements of a business plan may be standard, but the way entrepreneurs tell their stories should be unique and reflect the specific strengths of their business model, the experience of their team, their personality and how it will shape the culture of the business, and their enthusiasm for the new venture. In fact, the best business plans usually are those that tell a compelling story in addition to the facts. For those making a first attempt at writing a business plan, seeking the advice of individuals with experience in this process often proves helpful. Accountants, business professors, attorneys, advisers working with local chapters of the Service Corps of Retired Executives (SCORE), and consultants with Small Business Development Centers (SBDCs) are excellent sources of guidance when creating and refining a plan. (For a list of SBDCs, go to the Small Business Administration Web site and see its SBDC Web page; for a list of SCORE chapters, go to the SCORE Web site). Remember, however, you should be the one to author your business plan, not someone else. A sample outline of a business plan is displayed at the end of this chapter.

Initially, the prospect of writing a business plan may appear to be overwhelming. Many entrepreneurs would rather launch their companies and "see what happens" than invest the necessary time and energy defining and researching their target markets, defining their strategies, and mapping out their finances. After all, building a plan is hard work—it requires time, effort, and thought. However, in reality the entrepreneur should do both. By getting started and seeing what happens, the entrepreneur can test and improve the basic business model. The plan is essential as the entrepreneur gets ready to build the business and scale its growth. The business plan pays many dividends, but not all of them are immediately apparent. Entrepreneurs who invest their time and energy building plans are better prepared to face the hostile environment in which their companies will compete than those who do not.

Entrepreneurs can use business planning software available from several companies to create their plans. Some of the most popular programs include Business Plan Pro (Palo Alto Software), PlanMaker (Power Solutions for Business), and Plan Write (Business Resources Software). These packages help entrepreneurs organize the material they have researched and gathered, and they provide helpful tips on plan writing with templates for creating financial statements. Business planning software may help to produce professional-looking business plans with a potential drawback: The plans they produce look as if they came from the same mold. That can be a turn-off for professional investors who review hundreds of business plans each year. Entrepreneurs benefit by making the content and appearance of their plan look professional and unique.

In the past, conventional wisdom was that business plans should be 20 to 40 pages in length, depending on the complexity of the business. More recently experts have begun to recommend that plans should be shorter, typically suggesting that they be limited to 10 to 20 pages. There is mixed opinion on how complex the financial forecasts should be. If the forecasts are based on evidence that is substantiated by testing the business model, more detail will strengthen your case. If the numbers appear to be unsubstantiated or even fabricated, more detail can actually hurt the presentation. In many ways, having to write shorter business plans can make writing them even more of a challenge. A shorter business plan does not mean that any of the elements of the plan be omitted. Instead the entrepreneur must work hard to communicate all of the key aspects of the plan as succinctly as possible. Although entrepreneurs find it difficult to communicate all the important elements of their story within the shorter page length recommendations, they run the risk of never getting used or read if their plans get too long.

This section explains the most common elements of a business plan. However, entrepreneurs must recognize that, like every business venture, every business plan is unique. An entrepreneur should use the following elements as the starting point for building a plan and should modify them as needed to better tell the story of his or her new venture.

TITLE PAGE AND TABLE OF CONTENTS A business plan should contain a title page with the company's name, logo, and address as well as the names and contact information of the company founders. Many entrepreneurs also include the copy number of the plan and the date on which it was issued on the title page. Business plan readers appreciate a table of contents that includes page numbers so that they can locate the particular sections of the plan in which they are most interested.

THE EXECUTIVE SUMMARY To summarize the presentation to each potential financial institution or investors, the entrepreneur should write an executive summary. It should be concise—a maximum of one page—and should summarize all of the relevant points of the proposed deal. After reading the executive summary, anyone should be able to understand the entire business concept, the attributes that differentiate the company from the competition, and the financing that is being requested. The executive summary is a synopsis of the entire plan, capturing its essence in a capsulized form. It should explain the basic business model and the problem the business will solve for customers, briefly describing the owners and key employees, target market(s), financial highlights (e.g., sales and earnings projections, the loan or investment requested, plans for using the funds, and projections for repaying any loans or cashing out investments), and the company's competitive advantage. The executive summary is a written version of what is known as "the elevator pitch." Imagine yourself on an elevator with a potential lender or investor. Only the two of you are on the elevator, and you have that person's undivided attention for the duration of the ride, but the building is not very tall! To convince the investor that your business idea is a great investment, you must condense your message down to its essential elements—key points that you can communicate in a matter of no more than two minutes. In the Pitch George Elevator Competition at George Washington University, students actually make their pitch to judges in an elevator, where they have the opportunity to make their elevator pitches in just three minutes. Winners receive a small cash prize and earn the opportunity to present at the GW Business Plan Competition where they compete to earn prizes totaling $101,000.

The following five-part framework helps entrepreneurs develop a meaningful elevator pitch:

1. *Context.* What does your company do in easy-to-understand words?

2. *Benefit.* What benefit or advantage does your company offer customers?

3. *Target customers.* For whom does your company provide the benefit?

4. *Point of differentiation.* How is your company different from other companies that provide similar products, services, or solutions?

5. *Clincher.* Can you leave the listener or reader with a memorable, bottom-line sound bite about your company.[6]

Like a good movie trailer, an executive summary is designed to capture readers' attention and draw them into the plan. If it misses, the chances of the remainder of the plan being read are minimal. What is different between an executive summary and a movie trailer is that the executive summary needs to give away the ending! If it does not, potential funders will never read the full plan. A coherent, well-developed summary of the full plan establishes a favorable first impression of the business and the entrepreneur behind it and can go a long way toward obtaining financing. A good executive summary should allow the reader to understand the business concept and how it will make money, and it should answer the ultimate question from investors or lenders: "What's in it for me?" Although the executive summary is the first part of the business plan, it should be the last section written to ensure that it truly captures all of the important points as they appear in the full plan.

MISSION AND VISION STATEMENT   A mission statement expresses an entrepreneur's vision for what his or her company is and what it is to become. It is the broadest expression of a company's purpose and defines the direction in which it will move. It anchors a company in reality and serves as the thesis statement for the entire business plan by answering the question, "What business are we in?" Every good plan captures an entrepreneur's passion and vision for the business, and the mission statement is the ideal place to express them. Avoid the use of too much business jargon and business clichés. It should clearly state the product or service the business sells, its target market, and the basic nature of the business (e.g., manufacturing, consulting, service, outsourcing). Mission statements should be limited to no more than 25 words.

DESCRIPTION OF FIRM'S PRODUCT OR SERVICE   An entrepreneur should describe the company's overall product line, giving an overview of how customers will use its goods or services. Drawings, diagrams, and illustrations may be required if the product is highly technical. It is best to write product and service descriptions so that laypeople can understand them. A statement of a product's position in the product life cycle might also be helpful. An entrepreneur should include a summary of any patents, trademarks, or copyrights that protect the product or service from infringement by competitors.

One danger entrepreneurs must avoid in this part of the plan is the tendency to dwell on the features of their products or services. This problem is the result of the "fall-in-love-with-your-product" syndrome, which often afflicts inventors. Customers, lenders, and investors care less about how much work, genius, and creativity went into a product or service than about what it will do for them. This part of the plan builds off the value proposition developed in the business model. The emphasis of this section should be on defining the benefits customers get by purchasing the company's products or services, rather than on just a "nuts and bolts" description of the features of those products or services. A **feature** is a descriptive fact about a product or service (e.g., "an ergonomically designed, more comfortable handle"). A **benefit** is what the customer gains from the product or service feature (e.g., "fewer problems with carpal tunnel syndrome and increased productivity"). Benefits are at the core of the value proposition of the business model. This part of the plan must describe how a business will transform tangible product or service features into important but often intangible customer benefits—for example, lower energy bills, faster access to the Internet, less time writing checks to pay monthly bills, greater flexibility in building floating structures, shorter time required to learn a foreign language, or others. Remember: Customers buy benefits, not product or service features.

feature
a descriptive fact about a product or service.

benefit
what a customer gains from the product or service.

   ENTREPRENEURIAL PROFILE: Ami Kassar and Multifunding   Ami Kassar came up with the idea for his Philadelphia-based business, Multifunding, from his experience in the small business credit industry. He had seen the difficulty small businesses had when trying to find financing, and yet he knew that there was financing available for many these businesses if they could just get connected to the right sources. Although the value of the service was apparent from the beginning, it took Kassar several pivots of his business model to finally offer small business customers what they wanted, in the way they wanted it. "There is a fundamental difference between a vision and a business model," said Kassar. "While the core model of how we make our money has not changed from day one, we are constantly testing it, and looking for ways to improve it, evolve it, and grow it. Every few months an entrepreneur should take a cold shower, and take the time to look in the rear view mirror, and come up with some new things to try and test." After getting a profile of a small business client and an assessment of its financing needs, Multifunding puts together a report that gives the small business owner various financing options. Multifunding gets paid only when the financing is completed, taking a small percentage of the approved amount of financing. Multifunding funded 7 small businesses in its first year and 48 in its second. As part of the process of testing and refining its business model, the company began looking into new sources of revenue streams during its third year.[7] ■

Ami Kassar, Founder and CEO of Kassar

BUSINESS AND INDUSTRY PROFILE If one goal of creating a plan to raise funding, the entrepreneur should include a section that acquaints lenders and investors with the industry in which a company competes. This section should provide readers with an overview of the industry or market segment in which the new venture will operate. Industry data such as key trends or emerging developments within the industry, market size and its growth or decline, and the relative economic and competitive strength of the major firms in the industry set the stage for a better understanding of the viability of a new business. Strategic issues such as ease of market entry and exit, the ability to achieve economies of scale or scope, and the existence of cyclical or seasonal economic trends further help readers to evaluate the new venture. This part of the plan also should describe significant industry trends and key success factors as well as an overall outlook for its future. Information about the evolution of the industry helps the reader comprehend its competitive dynamics. *The U.S. Industrial Outlook Handbook* is an excellent reference that profiles a variety of industries and offers projections for future trends. Another useful resource of industry and economic information is the *Summary of Commentary on Current Economic Conditions*, more commonly known as the *Beige Book.* Published eight times a year by the Federal Reserve, the *Beige Book* provides detailed statistics and trends in key business sectors and in the overall economy. It offers valuable information on topics ranging from tourism and housing starts to consumer spending and wage rates. Entrepreneurs can find this wealth of information at their fingertips on the Web site of the Minneapolis Federal Reserve. This section should cover all of the relevant information the entrepreneur uncovered during the market and industry feasibility analysis.

COMPETITOR ANALYSIS An entrepreneur should describe the new venture's competition and the ways in which the chosen business strategy will position it effectively against key competitors. Failing to assess competitors realistically makes entrepreneurs appear to be poorly prepared, naive, or dishonest, especially to potential lenders and investors. The plan should include an analysis of each significant competitor and how well the competing business is meeting the important criteria that target customers are currently using to make their purchase decisions among the various companies. Entrepreneurs who believe they have no competitors are only fooling themselves and are raising a huge red flag to potential lenders and investors. Gathering information on competitors' market shares, products, and strategies is usually not difficult. Trade associations, customers, industry journals, marketing representatives, and sales literature are valuable sources of data. This section of the plan should focus on demonstrating that the entrepreneur's company has an advantage over its competitors and address these questions:

- Who are the company's key competitors?
- What are their strengths and weaknesses?

- What are their strategies?
- What images do they have in the marketplace?
- How successful are they?
- What distinguishes the entrepreneur's product or service from others already on the market, and how will these differences produce a competitive edge?

Firsthand competitor research is particularly valuable.

MARKET ENTRY STRATEGY This section addresses the question of how to attract customers. By laying out a market entry strategy, an entrepreneur explains how he or she plans to enter the market and gain a competitive edge and how his or her value proposition sets the business apart from the competition. A key component of this section is defining what makes the company unique in the eyes of its customers. One of the quickest routes to business failure is trying to sell "me-too" products or services that offer customers nothing newer, better, bigger, faster, or different.

MARKETING STRATEGY One of the most important tasks a business plan must fulfill is proving that a viable market exists for a company's goods or services. The business modeling process helped to identify and describe a company's target customers and their characteristics and habits. Defining the target audience and its potential is one of the most important—and most challenging—parts of the business planning process.

Proving that a profitable market exists involves two steps: showing customer interest and documenting market claims. Both of these steps should have been part of the business modeling process and should be part of the business plan.

Showing Customer Interest An important element of any business plan is showing how a company's product or service provides a customer benefit or solves a customer problem. Entrepreneurs must be able to prove that their target customers actually need or want their goods or services and are willing to pay for them. This is why using customers to validate the business model is so important. Validation from real customers provides the proof of concept that investors look for in a business plan.

Proving that a viable market exists for a product or service is relatively straightforward for a company already in business but can be quite difficult for an entrepreneur with only an idea. In this case, the key is to find a way to get primary customer data. The feasibility analyses and the process of validating the value proposition during the development of the business model provide this type of real data from real customers. During the development of the business model, an entrepreneur might build a prototype and offer it to several potential customers to get written testimonials and evaluations to show to investors. The entrepreneur also could sell the product to several customers, perhaps at a discount on the condition that they provide evaluations. Doing so proves that there are potential customers for the product and allows customers to experience the product in operation. Getting a product into customers' hands is also an excellent way to get valuable feedback that can lead to significant design improvements and increased sales down the road. Integrating this type of primary data into the actual business plan demonstrates that the plan has a stronger chance of success.

ENTREPRENEURIAL PROFILE: Matt Cooper and Canoe and Kayak Rental Matt Cooper quit his job as an investment banker in New York to start Soggy Bottom Canoe and Kayak Rental in the backwoods of Mississippi. Cooper was tired of the corporate grind and was ready for a change of pace. When Cooper arrived in Mississippi, he went full steam ahead buying the land, building the facilities, and buying canoes, kayaks, trailers, and vans. He did no market research such as talking to any prospective customers before investing in the business. In the seven years the business operated, it never reached even half of the revenues it needed to be successful. As a result, Cooper used up all of his savings and much of his parents' savings trying to keep the business afloat. In the end, Cooper closed the business and moved to California to take a job in Silicon Valley. Cooper attributes his business failure to spending his money on buildings and equipment rather than basic market research and marketing.[8] ■

Documenting Market Claims Too many business plans rely on vague generalizations such as, "This market is so huge that if we get just 1 percent of it, we will break even in eight months." Statements such as these usually reflect nothing more than an entrepreneur's unbridled optimism; in most cases, they are quite unrealistic. In *The Art of the Start*, entrepreneur and venture capitalist Guy Kawasaki calls this the Chinese Soda Lie: "If just 1 percent of the people in China drink our soda, we will be more successful than any company in the history of mankind."[9] The problems with this reasoning are (1) few markets, especially the niche markets that small businesses often pursue, are as large as that, and (2) capturing 1 percent of a big market is extremely difficult to do, especially for a small company. Capturing a large share of a small, well-defined niche market is much more realistic for a small company than is winning a small share of a huge market.

Entrepreneurs must support claims of market size and growth rates with facts, and that requires market research. Results of market surveys, customer questionnaires, and demographic studies developed in the feasibility analyses and business modeling steps in the business planning process lend credibility to an entrepreneur's frequently optimistic sales projections contained within the formal business plan. (Refer to the market research techniques and resources in Chapter 8.) Quantitative market data are important because they form the basis for all of the company's financial projections in the business plan. Fortunately, entrepreneurs who follow the business planning process will already have this type of data from their feasibility analyses and from building and testing their business models.

As you learned in Chapter 4 on conducting a feasibility analysis and business models, one effective documentation technique involves business prototyping, in which entrepreneurs test their business models on a small scale before committing serious resources to a business that might not work. Business prototyping recognizes that every business idea is a hypothesis that should be tested before an entrepreneur takes it to full scale. If the test supports the hypothesis and its accompanying assumptions, it is time to launch a company. If the prototype flops, the entrepreneur scraps the business idea with only minimal losses and turns to the next idea.

One of the main purposes of the marketing section of the plan is to lay the foundation for financial forecasts that follow. Sales, profit, and cash forecasts must be founded on more than wishful thinking. An effective market analysis should address the following items in detail based on the framework developed in the business model:

Target Market Who are the company's target customers? How many of them are in the company's trading area? What are their characteristics (e.g., age, gender, educational level, income)? What do they buy? Why do they buy? When do they buy? What expectations do they have about the product or service? Will the business focus on a niche? How does the company seek to position itself in the market(s) it will pursue? Knowing my customers' needs, wants, and habits, what should be the basis for differentiating my business in their minds?

Advertising and Promotion Only after entrepreneurs understand their companies' target markets can they design a promotion and advertising campaign to reach those customers most effectively and efficiently. When developing an advertising and promotion strategy, an entrepreneur should keep in mind what he or she learned when defining the communication channel in the business modeling process. Which media are most effective in reaching the target market? How will they be used? How much will the promotional campaign cost? How will the promotional campaign position the company's products or services? How can the company benefit from publicity? How large is the company's promotional budget?

Market Size and Trends Assessing the size of the market is a critical step. How large is the potential market? Is it growing or shrinking? Why? Are customers' needs changing? Are sales seasonal? Is demand tied to another product or service?

 ENTREPRENEURIAL PROFILE: James Park and Eric Friedman and Fitbit James Park and Eric Friedman cofounded Fitbit as a solution for a problem that Park, like many of the

146 million working adults in the United States, was facing after several years of focusing on his work and not himself. Fitbit is a wireless, wearable fitness device that tracks the number of steps taken, distance traveled, stairs climbed, and calories burned. Fitbit's customers lose an average of 13 pounds as a result of becoming 43 percent more active than when they start using the device. Fitbit sends the data to a dashboard customers access through either the Web or with a mobile app. The software provides customers with graphs that show their progress. Fitbit also allows customers to connect with each other through social media, where they can compete with each other on their progress. By targeting the 25 percent of Americans who are trying to lose weight, Fitbit has grown rapidly and now has more than 75 employees.[10] ■

Location For many businesses, choosing the right location is a key success factor. For retailers, wholesalers, and service companies, the best location usually is one that is most convenient to their target customers. Using census data and other market research, entrepreneurs can determine the sites with the greatest concentrations of their customers and locate there. Which sites put the company in the path of its target customers? Maps that show customer concentrations (available from census maps and other sources), traffic counts, the number of customers using a particular train station and when, and other similar types of information provide evidence that a solid and sizable customer base exists. Do zoning regulations restrict the use of a site? For manufacturers, the location issue often centers on finding a site near their key raw materials or near their primary customers. Using demographic reports and market research to screen potential sites takes the guesswork out of choosing the "right" location for a business.

Pricing What does the product or service cost to produce or deliver? Before opening a restaurant, for example, an entrepreneur should know exactly what it will cost to produce each item on the menu. Failing to know the total cost (including the cost of the food as well as labor, rent, advertising, and other indirect costs) of putting a plate in front of a customer is a recipe for failure. As we will discover in Chapter 10, "Pricing and Credit Strategies," cost is just one part of the pricing equation. Another significant factor to consider is the image a company is trying to create in the market. Pricing helps communicate and reinforce key elements of the value proposition, such as quality and value.

Other pricing issues that a plan should address include: What is the company's overall pricing strategy? Will the planned price support the company's strategy and desired image? Given the company's cost structure, will the price produce a profit? How does the planned price compare to those of similar products or services? Are customers willing to pay it? What price tiers exist in the market? How sensitive are customers to price changes? Will the business sell to customers on credit? Will it accept credit cards? Will the company offer discounts? All of these questions help develop the revenue forecasts in the business plan. Remember, revenues are calculated with a simple formula: Price × Quantity. Therefore, understanding the proper pricing strategy is half the battle of developing accurate revenue forecasts.

Distribution Developed from the distribution channel component of the business model, this portion of the plan should describe the specific channels of distribution the business will use (e.g., the Internet, direct mail, in-house sales force, sales agents, retailers) to distribute its products and services. Will distribution be extensive, selective, or exclusive? What is the average sale? How large will the sales staff be? How will the company compensate its sales force? What are the incentives for salespeople? How many sales calls does it take to close a sale? What can the company do to make it as easy as possible for customers to buy?

ENTREPRENEURS' AND MANAGERS' RÉSUMÉS The most important factor in the success of a business venture is its management, and financial officers and investors weight heavily the ability and experience of a company's managers in financing decisions. Investors will never invest in just a good idea: There must be a strong team in place to ensure the idea will be implemented successfully. A plan should include the résumés of business officers, key directors, and any person with at least 20 percent ownership in the company. This is the section of the plan in which entrepreneurs have the chance to sell the qualifications and the experience of their management team. Remember: Lenders and investors prefer experienced managers. Ideally, they look for managers with at least two years of operating experience in the industry they are targeting.

In a technology business, investors are looking for partners that have both management and technology expertise.

A résumé should summarize each individual's education, work history (emphasizing managerial responsibilities and duties), and relevant business experience. Lenders and investors look for the experience, talent, and integrity of the people who will breathe life into the plan. This portion of the plan should show that the company has the right people organized in the right fashion for success. An entrepreneur can enhance the strength of the management team with a capable, qualified board of advisers. A board of directors or advisers consisting of industry experts lends credibility and can complement the skills of the management team.

PLAN OF OPERATION To complete the description of the business, an entrepreneur should construct an organization chart identifying the business's key positions and the people who occupy them. Assembling a management team with the right stuff is difficult, but keeping it together until the company is established can be even harder. Most small companies cannot match the salaries that employees can earn at larger competitors, but offering stock options, profit-sharing, shares of ownership, and other perks helps retain and motivate key employees. A plan of operation should also describe how the business operates, including space requirements, inventory management if applicable, staffing plans, and accounting processes and policies.

Finally, a description of the form of ownership (e.g., sole proprietorship, partnership, joint venture, C corporation, S corporation, LLC) and of any leases, contracts, and other relevant agreements pertaining to the operation is helpful.

PRO FORMA (PROJECTED) FINANCIAL STATEMENTS One of the most important sections of the business plan is an outline of the proposed company's financial statements—the "dollars and cents" of the proposed venture. An entrepreneur should carefully prepare projected (pro forma) financial statements for the operation for the next year using past operating data (if available), published statistics, and research to derive forecasts of the income statement, balance sheet, cash forecast (always!), and a schedule of planned capital expenditures. (You will learn more about creating projected financial statements in Chapter 11 and cash flow forecasts in Chapter 12.) Although including only most likely forecasts in the business plan is acceptable, entrepreneurs also should develop forecasts for pessimistic and optimistic conditions that reflect the uncertainty of the future in case potential lenders and investors ask for them.

It is essential that financial forecasts be realistic. Entrepreneurs must avoid the tendency to "fudge the numbers" just to make their businesses look good. Experienced lenders and investors can detect unrealistic forecasts easily. In fact, some venture capitalists automatically discount an entrepreneur's financial projections by as much as 50 percent. One experienced angel investor says that when looking at the financial forecasts compiled by an entrepreneur, he always doubles the start-up costs and triples the time it will take to launch.

After completing these forecasts, an entrepreneur should perform a break-even analysis for the business. The break-even point is critical for an entrepreneurial venture as it signals the point where the business is able to sustain itself through cash generated by operations and should not need any additional start-up capital. It also is the point when the entrepreneur is able to get paid by the business!

It is important to include a statement of the assumptions on which these financial projections are based. Potential lenders and investors want to know how an entrepreneur derived forecasts for sales, cost of goods sold, operating expenses, accounts receivable, collections, accounts payable, inventory, taxes, and other items. Spelling out realistic assumptions gives a plan more credibility and reduces the tendency to include overly optimistic estimates of sales growth and profit margins. Greg Martin, a partner in the venture capital company Redpoint Ventures, says, "I have problems with start-ups making unrealistic assumptions—how much money they need or how quickly they can ramp up revenue. Those can really kill a deal for me."[11]

In addition to providing valuable information to potential lenders and investors, projected financial statements help entrepreneurs run their businesses more effectively and more efficiently after start-up. They establish important targets for financial performance and make it easier for an entrepreneur to maintain control over routine expenses and capital expenditures. An entrepreneur also should construct a financial dashboard that he or she can use to track the progress of the business and assess how well the actual outcomes match the key assumptions made in the business plan.

THE LOAN OR INVESTMENT PROPOSAL The loan or investment proposal section of the business plan should state the purpose of the financing, the amount requested, and the plans for repayment or, in the case of investors, an attractive exit strategy. When describing the purpose of the loan or investment, an entrepreneur must specify the planned use of the funds. Entrepreneurs should state the precise amount requested and include relevant backup data, such as vendor estimates of costs or past production levels. The proposal should include all sources of funding for the business from all intended sources including money the entrepreneur is investing into the business. Most bankers and investors will want to see evidence that the entrepreneur is willing to "put skin in the game" and put some of his or her own money at risk in the venture.

Another important element of the loan or investment proposal is the repayment schedule or exit strategy. A lender's main consideration when granting a loan is the reassurance that the applicant will repay, whereas an investor's major concern is earning a satisfactory rate of return. Financial projections must reflect a company's ability to repay loans and produce adequate returns. Without this proof, a request for funding stands little chance of being approved. It is necessary for the entrepreneur to produce tangible evidence that shows the ability to repay loans or to generate attractive returns. Developing an exit strategy, such as the option to cash out through an acquisition or a public offering, is important. Include specific examples of other firms in the same industry that have already exited to increase the confidence that there is a viable path for the investors to exit the business and realize a return on their investments.

Finally, an entrepreneur should include a realistic timetable for implementing the proposed plan. This should include a schedule showing the estimated start-up date for the project and noting all significant milestones along the way.

A business plan must present an honest assessment of the risks facing the new venture. Evaluating risk in a business plan requires an entrepreneur to walk a fine line, however. Dwelling too much on everything that can go wrong discourages potential lenders and investors from financing the venture. Ignoring the project's risks makes those who evaluate the plan see the entrepreneur as naïve, dishonest, or unprepared. The best strategy is to identify the most significant risks the venture faces and then to describe the plans the entrepreneur has developed to avoid them altogether or to overcome the negative outcome if the event does occur. Figure 5.1 explains how two simple diagrams communicate effectively to investors both the risks and the rewards of a business venture.

There is a difference between a working business plan (the one the entrepreneur is using to guide the business) and the presentation business plan (the one he or she is using to attract capital). Although coffee rings and penciled-in changes in a working plan don't matter (in fact, they're a good sign that the entrepreneur is actually using the plan), they have no place on a plan going to someone outside the company. A plan is usually the tool an entrepreneur uses to make

FIGURE 5.1

Visualizing a Venture's Risks and Rewards

Source: Based on William A. Sahlman, "How to Write a Great Business Plan," *Harvard Business Review*, July/August 1997, pp. 98–108.

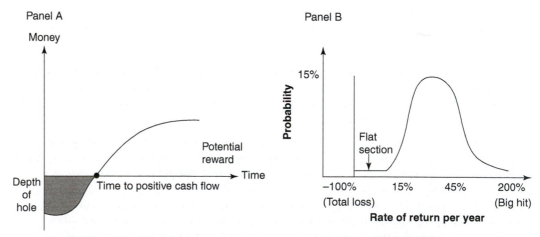

In panel A, the depth of the hole shows lenders and investors how much money it will take to start the business. The length of the chasm shows how long it will take to reach positive cash flow.

Panel B shows investors the range of possible returns and the probability of achieving them. In this example, investors see that there is a 15 percent chance of a total loss and an equal chance that they will earn between 15 and 45 percent on their investment. There is also a small chance that their initial investment will yield a 200 percent return.

a first impression on potential lenders and investors. To make sure that impression is a favorable one, an entrepreneur should follow these tips:

- Realize that first impressions are crucial. Make sure the plan has an attractive (but not an expensive) cover.

- Make sure the plan is free of spelling and grammatical errors and typos. It is a professional document and should look like one.

- Make it visually appealing. Use color charts, figures, and diagrams to illustrate key points. Don't get carried away, however, and end up with a "comic book" plan.

- Include a table of contents with page numbers to allow readers to navigate the plan easily. Reviewers should be able to look through a plan and quickly locate the sections they want to see.

- Make it interesting. Boring plans seldom get read; a good plan tells an interesting story.

- Make the case that the business will make money. Start-ups do not necessarily have to be profitable immediately, but sooner or later (preferably sooner), they must make money.

- Use computer spreadsheets to generate a set of realistic financial forecasts. They allow entrepreneurs to perform valuable "what if" (sensitivity) analysis in just seconds.

- Always include cash flow projections. Entrepreneurs sometimes focus excessively on their proposed venture's profit forecasts and ignore cash flow projections. Although profitability is important, lenders and investors are much more interested in cash flow because they know that's where the money to pay them back or to cash them out comes from.

- Keep the plan "crisp," long enough to say what it should but not so long that it is a chore to read.

- Tell the truth. Absolute honesty is always critical when preparing a business plan.

Business plans are forecasts about the future that an entrepreneur plans to create, something that one expert compares to "taking a picture of the unknown," which is a challenging feat! As uncertain and difficult to predict as the future may be, an entrepreneur who launches a business without a plan, arguing that "trying to forecasting the future is pointless," is misguided. In the *Harvard Business Review*, William Sahlman says, "the best business plans . . . are like movies of the future. They show the people, the opportunity, and the context from multiple angles. They offer a plausible, coherent story of what lies ahead. They unfold the possibilities of action and reaction."[12] That's the kind of "movie" an entrepreneur should strive to create in a plan.

What Lenders and Investors Look for in a Business Plan

LO3

Explain the "five Cs of credit" and why they are important to potential lenders and investors receiving business plans.

To increase their chances of success when using their business plans to attract capital, entrepreneurs must be aware of the criteria lenders and investors use to evaluate the creditworthiness of businesses seeking financing. Lenders and investors refer to these criteria as the *five Cs of credit*: capital, capacity, collateral, character, and conditions.

CAPITAL A small business must have a stable capital base before any lender will grant a loan. Otherwise the lender would be making, in effect, a capital investment in the business. Most lenders refuse to make loans that are capital investments because the potential for return on the investment is limited strictly to the interest on the loan, and the potential loss would probably exceed the reward. In fact, the most common reasons banks give for rejecting small business loan applications are undercapitalization or too much debt. Investors also want to make sure entrepreneurs have invested enough of their own money into the business to survive the tenuous start-up period.

CAPACITY A synonym for capacity is cash flow. Lenders and investors must be convinced of a company's ability to meet its regular financial obligations and to repay the bank loan, and that takes cash. In Chapter 12, "Managing Cash Flow," you will see that more small businesses fail from lack of cash than from lack of profit. It is possible for a company to be earning a profit and still run out of cash. Lenders expect a business to pass the test of liquidity; they study closely a small company's cash flow position to decide whether it has the capacity required to succeed. Most lenders have become extremely cautious when evaluating cash flow since the financial crisis of 2008.

COLLATERAL Collateral includes any assets an entrepreneur pledges to a lender as security for repayment of the loan. If an entrepreneur defaults on the loan, the bank has the right to sell the collateral and use the proceeds to satisfy the loan. Typically, lenders make very few unsecured loans (those not backed by collateral) to business start-ups. Bankers view an entrepreneur's willingness to pledge collateral (personal or business assets) as an indication of dedication to making the venture a success. Bankers always look first at the personal assets of the entrepreneur because they represent the easiest way for them to get repaid on a loan if the business fails. Entrepreneurs must be ready to sign personal guarantees for all business loans, which state that they are personally liable for all bank loans to the business should the business fail. Business assets are lenders' last resort because, selling inventory, equipment, and buildings owned by the business to repay loans is not an easy or effective means of repayment for the bank.

CHARACTER Before putting money into a small business, lenders and investors must be satisfied with the owner's character. An evaluation of character frequently is based on intangible factors such as honesty, competence, polish, determination, knowledge, experience, and ability. Although the qualities judged are abstract, this evaluation plays a critical role in a lender's or investor's decision. Banks have also begun to use what potential clients post on social networking sites such as Facebook, LinkedIn, and Twitter to assess character. If the entrepreneur is closely tied to successful business people, this can help bolster the bank's assessment of character. On the other hand, posts and links that are unprofessional damage the lender's impression of the entrepreneur's character.

Lenders and investors know that most small businesses fail because of poor management, and they try to avoid extending loans to high-risk entrepreneurs. Preparing a solid business plan and a polished presentation can go far in convincing potential lenders and investors of an entrepreneur's ability to manage a company successfully.

CONDITIONS The conditions surrounding a loan request also affect the owner's chance of receiving funds. Banks consider factors relating to the business operation such as potential growth in the market, competition, location, form of ownership, and loan purpose. Again, the owner should provide this relevant information in an organized format in the business plan. Another important condition influencing the banker's decision is the shape of the overall economy, including interest rate levels, the inflation rate, and demand for money. Although these factors are beyond an entrepreneur's control, they still are an important component in a lender's decision. Conditions have not been as favorable for bank loans since the financial crisis in 2008, which has made getting business loans more difficult for all small businesses.

The higher a small business scores on these five Cs, the greater its chance will be of receiving a loan or an investment. Wise entrepreneurs keep this in mind when preparing their business plans and presentations.

LO4

Understand the keys to making an effective business plan presentation.

The Pitch: Making the Business Plan Presentation

Entrepreneurs who are informed and prepared when requesting a loan or investment impress lenders and investors. When entrepreneurs try to secure funding from lenders or investors, the written business plan most often precedes the opportunity to meet face-to-face. In recent years, some investors have moved away from requiring the submission of a formal business plan and instead based their interest on the entrepreneur's presentation of the business model. The written plan must first pass muster before an entrepreneur gets the opportunity to present the plan in person. Usually, the time for presenting a business opportunity is short, often no more than just a few minutes. (When presenting a plan to a venture capital forum, the allotted time is usually less than 20 minutes and rarely more than 30.) When the opportunity arises, an entrepreneur must be well prepared. It is important to rehearse, rehearse, and then rehearse some more. It is a mistake to begin by leading the audience into a long-winded explanation about the technology on which the product or service is based. Within minutes most of the audience will be lost, and so is any chance the entrepreneur has of obtaining the necessary financing for the new venture. A business plan presentation should cover five basic areas:

- Your company and its products and services. The presentation should answer in simple terms the first question that every potential lender and investor has: What does your company do?

- The problem to be solved, preferably told in a personal way through a compelling story. Is it eliminating the time, expense, and anxiety of waiting for the results of medical tests with a device that instantly reads blood samples? Or making hearing aids more effective at filtering out background noise while enhancing the dominant sound for the user?

- A description (again in simple terms) of your company's solution to the problem. Ideally, the solution your company has developed is unique and serves as the foundation of your company's competitive edge in the marketplace.

- Your company's business model. This part of the presentation explains how your company makes money and includes figures such as revenue per sale, expected gross profit and net profit margins, and other relevant statistics. This is your opportunity to show lenders and investors how your company will produce an attractive payback or payoff.

- Your company's competitive edge. Your presentation should identify clearly the factors that set your company apart from the competition.

No matter how good a written business plan is, entrepreneurs who stumble through the presentation will lose the deal. Entrepreneurs who are successful raising the capital their companies need to grow have solid business plans and make convincing presentations of them. Some helpful tips for making a business plan presentation to potential lenders and investors include:

- Prepare. Good presenters invest in preparing their presentations and knowing the points they want to get across to their audiences.

- Practice your delivery and then practice some more.

- Demonstrate enthusiasm about the business but don't be overemotional. Be genuine and be yourself.

- Focus on communicating the dynamic opportunity your idea offers and how you plan to capitalize on it. Fight the temptation to launch immediately into a lengthy discourse about the details of your product or service or how much work it took to develop it. Otherwise, you'll never have the chance to describe the details to lenders and investors.

- Hook investors quickly with an up-front explanation of the new venture, its opportunities, and the anticipated benefits to them. For some businesses a story of its impact can be a good hook to start a presentation.

- Use visual aids. They make it easier for people to follow your presentation. Don't make the mistake of making the visuals the "star" of the presentation, however. Visual aids should punctuate your spoken message and focus the audience's attention on the key points.

- Follow Guy Kawasaki's 10/20/30 rule for PowerPoint presentations. Use 10 slides that you can cover in 20 minutes. Use 30-point font to ensure you do not try to put too many words on each slide.[13]

- Explain how your company's products or services solve some problem and emphasize the factors that make your company unique.

- Offer proof. Integrate relevant facts into your presentation to prove your plan's claims, customers' satisfaction with your company's products or services, and its profit potential.

- Hit the highlights. Specific questions will bring out the details later. Don't get caught up in too much detail in early meetings with lenders and investors.

- Keep the presentation "crisp," just like your business plan. Otherwise, says one experienced investor, "Information that might have caused an investor to bite gets lost in the endless drone."[14]

- Avoid the use of technical terms that will likely be above most of the audience. Do at least one rehearsal before someone who has no special technical training. Tell him or her to stop you anytime he or she does not understand what you are talking about. When this occurs (and it likely will), rewrite that portion of your presentation.

- Remember that every potential lender and investor you talk to is thinking "What's in it for me?" Be sure to answer that question in your presentation.

- Close by reinforcing the potential of the opportunity. Be sure you have sold the benefits the investors will realize when the business succeeds.

- Be prepared for questions. In many cases, there is seldom time for a long "Q&A" session, but interested investors may want to get you aside to discuss the details of the plan.

- Anticipate the questions the audience is most likely to ask and prepare for them in advance.

- Be sensitive to the issues that are most important to lenders and investors by reading the pattern of their questions. Focus your answers accordingly. For instance, some investors may be interested in the quality of the management team whereas others are more interested in marketing strategies. Be prepared to offer details on either.

- Follow up with every investor to whom you make a presentation. Don't sit back and wait; be proactive. They have what you need—investment capital. Demonstrate that you have confidence in your plan and have the initiative necessary to run a business successfully.

You Be the Consultant

The Battle of the Plans

The Richards Barrentine Values and Ventures® Business Plan Competition, run by the Neeley Entrepreneurship Center at Texas Christian University, focuses on for-profit enterprises owned by current undergraduate students that specifically impact society in meaningful ways. Plans must demonstrate a societal or environmental need to be filled, such as contributions to sustainability, innovations in the health and life sciences, innovations in energy, or opportunities for underrepresented groups in business. Business plans submitted for the Values and Ventures competition must be for-profit values-centered enterprises. The competition defines a values-centered enterprise as one that assures sustainable prosperity while also supporting the needs of company owners and shareholders, employees and their families, suppliers, customers, communities, and the environment. This is not a competition for nonprofit social enterprises.

Values and Ventures is a two-day event. During the first day, teams present in concurrent sessions. The teams are grouped into flights. The first place team in each flight automatically advances to the finals. The second place teams in each flight compete in a "lightning round." The top two teams from the lightening round also make the finals. In the second day of competition, each

Mathew Wallis

finalist presents again to the judges. Each team gets 12 minutes to present and 10 minutes to respond to questions from the judges.

You Be the Consultant *(continued)*

Teams that do not make the finals compete in an elevator pitch competition. One member from each non-finalist team is invited to participate in a 90-second elevator pitch on the second day of the competition.

One recent competition fielded teams from 28 universities. The third place team, winner of $5,000, was Sneeze4 from Texas Christian University. The venture sells tissues that support issues directed by the consumer. The second place team, winner of $10,000, was SoundSense from Christopher Newport University. SoundSense offers a home communication system for the hearing impaired. The first place team, winner of $15,000, was Crowdvance from George Washington University, founded by Dylan Fox, a self-taught Web site designer. Fox came up with the idea for Crowdvance while working on his design software and was able to attract a couple of fraternity brothers to help him launch the company.

Crowdvance supports small community groups, such as a Little League team struggling to pay for its uniforms or a high school debate team that needs money to enter a national competition. Donors to Crowdvance get a menu of exclusive deals, such as discounts on tickets or various products from national companies such as Hulu and Fathead. Crowdvance gets its revenues from its donors buying products through its Web site. Crowdvance charges no fee against the actual donation, which differentiates the company from its competitors, which charge a 3 to 10 percent fee. The small community groups get 100 percent of the donated funds.

After graduation, Fox began working full-time on Crowdvance. The company raised a seed round of financing.

Crowdvance reports that it increases the percentage of first-time donors for the charities it serves by 78 percent and has a 92 percent approval rating from its donors.

1. What benefits do entrepreneurs who compete in business plan competitions such as the one at Texas Christian University gain?

2. Work with a team of your classmates to brainstorm ideas for establishing a business plan competition on your campus. How would you locate judges? What criteria would you use to judge the plans? What prizes would you offer the winners, and how would you raise the money to give those prizes? Who would you allow to compete in your competition?

3. Using the ideas you generated in question 2, create a two-page proposal for establishing a business plan competition at your school.

Sources: "Neeley Entrepreneurship Center, Values and Ventures® Business Plan Competition," Neeley School of Business, Texas Christian University, n.d., www.neeley .tcu.edu/vandv/; "Case Studies," Crowdvance, n.d., www.crowdvance.com/case-studies/; Vanessa Small, "GWU students help small groups raise money," *Washington Post,* May 5, 2013, www.washingtonpost.com/business/capitalbusiness/gwu-students-help-small-groups-raise-money/2013/05/05/fffbc452-b422-11e2-9a98-4be1688d7d84_story.html; Annabelle Massey Malloy, "Profit and Virtue," *Fort Worth Weekly,* June 5, 2013, www.fwweekly.com/2013/06/05/profit-and-virtue/; "Crowdvance .com Now the Only Fundraising Platform on the Planet to not Charge a Service Fee and to Reward Donors," *Boston Globe,* June 18, 2013, http://finance.boston.com/boston/news/read/24447209/Crowdvance.com_Now_the_Only_Fundraising_Platform_on_the_Planet_to_not_Charge_a_Service_Fee_and_to_Reward_Donors.

Building a Strategic Plan

LO5

Understand the importance of strategic management to a small business.

The rules of the competitive game are constantly changing. To be successful, entrepreneurs must adapt to changes in the marketplace. Fortunately, entrepreneurs have at their disposal a powerful weapon to cope with an often hostile, ever-changing environment: the process of strategic planning. Strategic planning involves developing a game plan to guide a company as it strives to accomplish its vision, mission, goals, and objectives and to keep it from straying off course.

A solid strategic plan provides managers and employees a sense of direction when everyone is involved in creating and updating it. As more team members become committed to making the plan work, it takes on special meaning. It gives everyone targets to shoot for, and it provides a yardstick for measuring actual performance against those targets, especially in the crucial and chaotic start-up phase of the business.

Clate Mask, cofounder and CEO of Infusionsoft, credits strategic planning for the successful growth of his company from a small start-up to a 450-employee company funded with venture capital. Infusionsoft's strategic planning is built from a bold three- to five-year vision of what the business can become and what it can achieve. From there, the company develops three to five annual priorities that ensure progress toward the vision. Finally, managers develop the quarterly priorities and operational tactics necessary to reach their annual goals. "Strategic planning isn't a one-time event," says Mask. "Once you've laid out your strategy, it's crucial to stay focused over the long-term. I've found that it's vital to schedule a steady rhythm of productive meetings—annually, quarterly, monthly, weekly, and daily."[15]

ENTREPRENEURIAL PROFILE: Abt Electronics Abt Electronics is a family-owned business founded by David and Jewel Abt in Chicago, Illinois, in 1936. To compete with large national chains, such as Best Buy, Abt pursues several successful strategies. Abt installed several activity and play stations throughout its 350,000-square-foot store, including a flight simulator, a giant granite ball that floats on water, and aquariums teaming with sharks and other fish. Abt employees treat their customers well, offering them coffee and fresh-baked cookies. Abt offers extensive training for its employees and empowers them to offer customers discounts without the need for a supervisor's approval. Abt ties part of employee bonuses to customer service, rather than only to sales targets. Abt offers more than just electronics. Customers can buy watches, gourmet food, exercise equipment, furniture, and many other specialty products. Abt was an early entrant into online retailing, beginning Internet sales in 1998. Jon Abt, co-president of the company, says Best Buy's advertising helps build awareness of the products Abt sells in its store. Abt offers more than just its products—it offers an enjoyable experience for the entire family.[16] ■

Perhaps the biggest change that entrepreneurs face is unfolding now: the shift in the world's economy from a base of *financial to intellectual* capital. "Knowledge is no longer just a factor of production," says futurist Alvin Toffler. "It is the *critical* factor of production."[17] Today, a company's intellectual capital is likely to be the source of its competitive advantage in the marketplace. **Intellectual capital** is comprised of three components:[18]

intellectual capital
one source of a company's competitive advantage that consists of human, structural, or customer capital.

1. *Human capital* consists of the talents, creativity, skills, and abilities of a company's workforce and shows up in the innovative strategies, plans, and processes the people in an organization develop and then passionately pursue.

2. *Structural capital* is the accumulated knowledge and experience that a company possesses. It can take many forms, including processes, software, patents, copyrights, and, perhaps most important, the knowledge and experience of the people in a company.

3. *Customer capital* is the established customer base, positive reputation, ongoing relationships, and goodwill that a company builds up over time with its customers.

Increasingly, entrepreneurs are recognizing that the capital stored in these three areas forms the foundation of their ability to compete effectively and that they must manage this intangible capital base carefully. Every business uses all three components in its strategy, but the emphasis on each one varies from company to company.

ENTREPRENEURIAL PROFILE: Gabe Newell and Mike Harrington and Valve Corporation Valve Corporation, based in Bellevue, Washington, is a video game development and digital distribution company. Gabe Newell and Mike Harrington founded Valve in 1996, after leaving their positions at Microsoft. Valve's first video game success was Half-Life, which it released in 1998. Valve's 300 employees work in an organization that has no bosses and no formal managers. Any employee has the power to approve a new project and hire new employees. All desks are on wheels, allowing employees to move around freely and join any project that interests them. Valve CEO Gabe Newell, to whom nobody in the company officially reports, says the structure makes sense for what they produce. He says managers are good at creating procedures and processes. Because Valve must continuously create new games that have never existed, Newell believes managers would get in the way of employees' creativity.[19] ■

This knowledge shift is creating as much change in the world's business systems as the Industrial Revolution did in the agriculture-based economies of the 1800s. The Knowledge Revolution threatens the existence of those companies that are not prepared for it, but it is spawning tremendous opportunities for those entrepreneurs who are equipped with the strategies to exploit these opportunities. Management legend Jack Welch, who masterfully guided General Electric for many years, says, "Intellectual capital is what it's all about. Releasing the ideas of people is what we've got to do if we are going to win."[20] However, in practice, releasing people's ideas is much more difficult than it appears. The key is to encourage employees to generate a large volume of ideas, recognizing that only a few (the best) will survive. According to Gary Hamel, author of *Inside the Revolution*, "If you want to find a few ideas with the power to enthrall customers, foil competitors, and thrill investors, you must first generate hundreds and potentially thousands of unconventional strategic ideas. Put simply, you have to crush a lot of rock to find a diamond."[21] In other words, small companies must use the creativity-stimulating techniques discussed in Chapter 3 as one source of competitive advantage over their rivals.

Building a Competitive Advantage

The goal of developing a strategic plan is to create for the small company a **competitive advantage**—the value proposition that sets a small business apart from its competitors and gives it a unique position in the market that is superior to its rivals. It is the differentiating factor that makes customers want to buy from your business rather than from your competitors. From a strategic perspective, the key to business success is to develop a sustainable competitive advantage, one that is durable, creates value for customers, and is difficult for competitors to duplicate. For example, Whole Foods competes successfully with giant chains such as Wal-Mart and Kroger not on price but by emphasizing superior customer service, higher-quality products, a more extensive inventory of local and organic products, and a commitment to fair-trade suppliers. Its stores are well organized, attractive, and entertaining. Asked to describe his recently opened Whole Foods store, team leader Matthew Mell says, "It's a Disney World for foodies."[22] Companies that fail to define their competitive advantage fall into "me-too" strategies that never set them apart from their competitors and do not allow them to become market leaders or to achieve above-average profits.

Entrepreneurs should examine five aspects of their businesses to define their companies' competitive advantages:

LO6

Explain why and how a small business must create a competitive advantage in the market.

competitive advantage
the value proposition that sets a small business apart from its competitors and gives it a unique position in the market that is superior to its competition.

1. *Products they sell.* What is unique about the products the company sells? Do they save customers time or money? Are they more reliable and more dependable than those that competitors sell? Do they save energy, protect the environment, or provide more convenience for customers? By identifying the unique customer benefits of their companies' products, entrepreneurs can differentiate their businesses. Jason Lucash and Mike Szymczak developed their first audio speakers to solve their own problem. They wanted to develop speakers that would be easy to take along on trips. Their solution was speakers made of recycled cardboard that come flat and open up like an origami paper model. OrigAudio cardboard speakers caught on quickly with customers looking for inexpensive speakers with an edgy design. OrigAudio added eight more products to its line of audio speakers, including custom printed headphones that let customers choose their own unique designs. OrigAudio headphones sell for one-fifth the price of most major brands. "It's hard to be in a huge sector," says Lucash. "But if we stick to what we are good at, we will be successful."[23]

2. *Service they provide.* Many entrepreneurs find that the service they provide their customers is an excellent way to differentiate their companies. Because they are small, friendly, and close to their customers, small businesses can provide customer service that is superior to that which their larger competitors can provide. What services does the company provide (or which ones can it provide) to deliver added value and a superior shopping experience for customers?

3. *Pricing they offer.* As we will see later in this chapter, some small businesses differentiate themselves using price. Price can be a powerful point of differentiation; offering the lowest price gives some customers a great incentive to buy. However, offering the lowest price is not always the best way to create a unique image. Small companies that do not offer the lowest prices must emphasize the value their products offer.

4. *Way they sell.* Customers today expect to be able to conduct business when they want to, meaning that companies that offer extended hours—even 24-hour service seven days a week (perhaps via the Internet)—have the basis for an important competitive advantage. Zoots, a small chain of dry-cleaning stores in the Northeast, offers customers extended hours seven days a week and allows a secure 24-hour pickup and drop-off service. The company also offers a home pickup and delivery service that customers can book online and an environmentally friendly cleaning process, all of which maximize customers' convenience and set the company apart from its competition.[24]

5. *Values to which they are committed.* The most successful companies exist for reasons that involve far more than merely making money. The entrepreneurs behind these companies understand that one way to connect with customers and establish a competitive

edge is to manage their companies from a values-based perspective and operate them in an ethical and socially responsible fashion. In other words, they recognize that there is no inherent conflict between earning a profit and creating good for society and the environment.

Building a competitive advantage alone is not enough; the key to success over time is building a *sustainable* competitive advantage. In the long run, a company gains a sustainable competitive advantage through its ability to develop a set of core competencies that enable it to serve its selected target customers better than its rivals. **Core competencies** are a unique set of capabilities that a company develops in key areas, such as superior quality, customer service, innovation, team building, flexibility, and responsiveness, that allow it to vault past competitors. As the phrase suggests, they are central to a company's ability to compete successfully and are usually the result of important skills and lessons that a business has learned over time.

core competencies
a unique set of capabilities that a company develops in key areas that allow it to vault past competitors.

Typically, a company develops core competencies in no more than five or six (often fewer) areas. These core competencies become the nucleus of a company's competitive advantage and are usually quite enduring over time. Markets, customers, and competitors may change, but a company's core competencies are more durable, forming the building blocks for everything a company does. To be effective strategically, these competencies should be difficult for competitors to duplicate, and they must provide customers with an important perceived benefit. Small companies' core competencies often have to do with the advantages of their size, such as agility, speed, closeness to their customers, superior service, or the ability to innovate. Smart entrepreneurs use their companies' size to their advantage, recognizing that it allows them to do things that their larger rivals cannot. The key to success is building the company's strategy on its core competencies and concentrating them on providing value for target customers (see Figure 5.2).

Successful small companies are able to build strategies that exploit all the competitive advantages that their size gives them by doing the following:

- Responding quickly to customers' needs

- Providing the precise desired level of customer service

- Remaining flexible and willing to change

- Constantly searching for new, emerging market segments

- Building and defending small market niches

- Erecting "switching costs," the costs a customer incurs by switching to a competitor's product or service, through personal service and loyalty

- Remaining entrepreneurial and willing to take risks and act with lightning speed

- Constantly innovating

ENTREPRENEURIAL PROFILE: Kevin Reddy and Noodles & Company Noodles & Company is a restaurant chain that has grown to more than 350 U.S. locations since it opened

FIGURE 5.2

Building a Sustainable Competitive Advantage

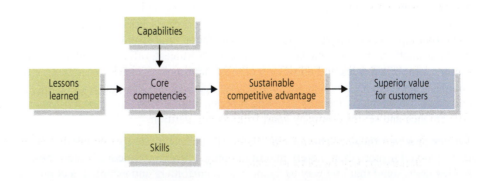

its first store in 1996. The company has achieved this growth even after moving away from a franchising model, which is the most common strategic approach for growing restaurant chains. Kevin Reddy, Chairman and CEO of Noodles & Company, says the company may start selling franchises again at some point in the future, but its strategy is to build a solid base by staying close to customers and offering a simple menu built on noodles and pasta. Although the company has faced some pressure to grow more quickly since its IPO in 2013, managers are holding firm to their long-term strategic focus. The company continues to use feedback from its customers to adapt its business model and strategies. The company views its core competency as operational excellence used to build a strong brand. By owning most of the stores, Reddy says, the company focuses on growing its customers rather than adding a certain number of franchises. He says it also offers more opportunity for employees to grow and develop within the company, which creates a stronger team.[25] ∎

No business can (or should) be everything to everyone. In fact, one of the biggest pitfalls many entrepreneurs stumble into is failing to differentiate their companies from the crowd of competitors. Entrepreneurs often face the challenge of setting their companies apart from their larger, more powerful competitors (who can easily outspend them) by using their creativity and the special abilities their businesses offer customers. Developing core competencies does *not* necessarily require a company to spend a great deal of money. It does, however, require an entrepreneur to use creativity, imagination, and vision to identify those things that it does best and that are most important to its target customers. Businesses have an infinite number of ways to create a competitive edge, but building a strategy around a company's core competencies allows it to gain a sustainable competitive advantage based on what it does best.

Strategic management enhances a small company's effectiveness, but entrepreneurs first must have a process designed to meet their needs and their business's special characteristics. It is a mistake to attempt to apply a big business's strategic development techniques to a small business because a small business is not merely "a little big business." Because of their size and their particular characteristics—small resource base, flexible managerial style, informal organizational structure, and adaptability to change—small businesses need a different approach to the strategic management process. The strategic management procedure for a small business should include the following features:

- Use a relatively short planning horizon—two years or less for most small companies.

- Be informal and not overly structured; a shirtsleeve approach is ideal.

- Encourage the participation of employees and outside parties to improve the reliability and creativity of the resulting plan.

- Do not begin with setting objectives because extensive objective setting early on may interfere with the creative process of strategic management.

- Maintain flexibility; competitive conditions change too rapidly for any plan to be considered permanent.

- Focus on strategic *thinking*, not just planning, by linking long-range goals to day-to-day operations.

- Be an ongoing process because businesses and the competitive environment in which they operate constantly change.

The Strategic Management Process

LO7

Develop a strategic plan for a business using the nine steps in the strategic management process.

Strategic management is a continuous process that consists of nine steps:

Step 1. Develop a clear vision and translate it into a meaningful mission statement.

Step 2. Assess the company's strengths and weaknesses.

Step 3. Scan the environment for significant opportunities and threats facing the business.

Step 4. Identify the key factors for success in the business.

Step 5. Analyze the competition.

Step 6. Create company goals and objectives.

Step 7. Formulate strategic options and select the appropriate strategies.

Step 8. Translate strategic plans into action plans.

Step 9. Establish accurate controls.

Step 1. Develop a Clear Vision and Translate It into a Meaningful Mission Statement

VISION Throughout history, the greatest political and business leaders have been visionaries. Whether the vision is as grand as Martin Luther King Jr.'s "I have a dream" speech or as simple as Ray Kroc's devotion to quality, service, cleanliness, and value at McDonald's, the purpose is the same: to focus everyone's attention on the same target and to inspire them to reach it. The vision is future oriented and touches everyone associated with the company—its employees, investors, lenders, customers, and the community. It is an expression of what an entrepreneur stands for and believes in. Highly successful entrepreneurs communicate their vision and their enthusiasm about that vision to those around them.

A vision is the result of an entrepreneur's dream of something successful that does not exist yet and the ability to paint a compelling picture of that dream for everyone to see. It answers the question, "Where are we going?" Former NFL player Nick Buoniconti started the Miami Project to Cure Paralysis with a vision to "cure spinal cord injury" after his son, Mark, was paralyzed by a football injury. This was considered an audacious goal at that time because spinal cord injuries were considered permanent and incurable. Buoniconti created a bold vision to help bring together supporters and researchers to move toward real progress in spinal cord treatment. Since its founding, the Miami Project has raised hundreds of millions of dollars for research that has led to critical breakthroughs in treating spinal cord injuries.[26] A strong vision helps a company in four ways:

1. *Vision provides direction.* Entrepreneurs who spell out the vision for their company focus everyone's attention on the future and determine the path the business will take to get there.

2. *Vision determines decisions.* The vision influences the decisions, no matter how big or how small, that owners, managers, and employees make every day in a business. This influence can be positive or negative, depending on how well defined the vision is.

3. *Vision inspires people.* A clear vision excites and ignites people to action. People want to work for a company that sets its sights high.

4. *Vision allows for perseverance in the face of adversity.* Young companies, their founders, and their employees often face many hardships from a multitude of sources. Having a vision that serves as a company's "guiding star" enables people to overcome imposing obstacles.

Vision is based on an entrepreneur's values. Explaining how an entrepreneur's values are the nucleus around which a company grows, author and consultant Ken Blanchard says, "Winning companies first emphasize values—the beliefs that you, as the business owner, have about your employees, customers, quality, ethics, integrity, social responsibility, growth, stability, innovation, and flexibility. Managing by values—not by profits—is a powerful process."[27] Successful entrepreneurs build their businesses around a set of three to seven core values that might range from respect for the individual and innovation to creating satisfied customers and making the world a better place. Indeed, truly visionary entrepreneurs see their companies' primary purpose as more than just "making money."

Business writer Thomas Stewart explains that works in small businesses don't just fill out forms and do menial work; they are also making important decisions. The entrepreneur must ensure that the workers' decisions are aligned with the company's strategic compass. The extent of that alignment depends on the entrepreneur's values and how well he or she transmits them throughout the company.* Table 5.1 offers useful tips for creating a vision for your company.

The best way to put values into action is to create a written mission statement that communicates those values to everyone the company touches.

MISSION The **mission statement** addresses another basic question of any business venture: "What business are we in?" Establishing the purpose of the business in writing must come first in order to give the company a sense of direction. "As an entrepreneur, your company's mission statement should be concise and specific so your customers understand your purpose and how you provide value to them," says serial entrepreneur Patrick Hull.[28] As an enduring declaration of a company's purpose, a mission statement is the mechanism for making it clear to everyone the company touches "why we are here" and "where we are going."

mission statement
an enduring declaration of a company's purpose that addresses the first question of any business venture: What business are we in?

TABLE 5.1 Creating a Vision for Your Company

Ari Wienzweig, founder of Zingerman's Community of Businesses, emphasizes the importance of creating a vision to achieve entrepreneurial success. A vision is a picture of what success will look like in a business at a particular time in the future. "The power that comes out of visioning is huge," he says. "Effective visioning allows us to move toward the future we want, not just react to a present-day reality we don't like."

How does an entrepreneur start the visioning process? First, select the time frame, ideally 3 to 10 years out. The next step is to write the first draft of your vision, remembering to shoot for something *great*, even those things that other people have told you repeatedly were unachievable. As you proceed, write as if your vision already has happened. The following questions will help you get started:

1. How big is your business?
2. What has your business achieved that you are most proud of?
    a. Relative rank in your industry
    b. Financial success
    c. Product or service quality
    d. Contribution to the community
    e. Awards and recognitions
3. What are your most important product lines or services?
4. What products or services do you refuse to offer?
5. What is a customer's shopping experience like at your business? What makes that experience different from your competition?
6. Who are your customers? How did you find them?
7. If you asked your customers to list the three most noteworthy characteristics of your business, what would they be?
8. How do you describe your management style?
9. What kind of people do you hire as employees and managers?
10. What kind of relationship do you have with your employees? What do they say about their jobs?
11. What do you do every day when you go to work? How many hours a week do you work?
12. How does the community view your business?
13. What do suppliers say about your business?
14. What do industry experts say about your business?

You will probably write several drafts of your vision before sharing it with others, especially with the people who will be involved in making it a reality. Ask for their feedback and input, but remember: It's *your* vision. When people ask (and they inevitably will) "How will we achieve that?" remember that vision is about the "*what*"; strategy—the "*how*"—comes later.

Source: Based on Ari Weinzweig, "Creating a Company Vision," *Inc.*, February 1, 2011, www.inc.com/magazine/20110201/creating-a-company-vision.html/2.

Source: Thomas A. Stewart, "Why Values Statements Don't Work," *Fortune*, June 10, 1996, p. 137.

Without a concise, meaningful mission statement, a small business risks wandering aimlessly in the marketplace, with no idea of where to go or how to get there. A great mission statement sets the tone for the entire company and focuses its attention in the right direction.

Elements of a Mission Statement   A sound mission statement need not be lengthy to be effective. In fact, shorter usually is better. The four key questions entrepreneurs and their employees should address as they develop a mission statement for their businesses are the following:

- What are we in business to accomplish?

- Who are we in business to serve?

- How are we going to accomplish that purpose?

- What principles and beliefs form the foundation of the way we do business?

A company's mission statement may be the most essential and basic communication that it puts forward. It should inspire and motivate employees by communicating the company's overarching values. If the people on the plant, shop, retail, or warehouse floor don't know what a company's mission is, then, for all practical purposes, it does not have one! The mission statement expresses a company's character, identity, and scope of operations, but writing it is only half the battle, at best. The most difficult and important part is *living* that mission every day. *That's* how employees decide what really matters. To be effective, a mission statement must become a natural part of the organization, embodied in the minds, habits, attitudes, and decisions of everyone in the company every day. In other words, a good mission statement is translated into positive performance within an organization. Five years after founding Field Trip Factory Inc., a business that organizes life skill educational field trips for students, Susan Singer saw the need to update the company's mission statement. At a company retreat, she and her employees decided that their existing mission statement no longer reflected what the company actually stood for and did. A brainstorming session yielded a new mission statement that Singer says is helping her company improve its bottom line. "It became so clear what we do vs. what we want to be," she says.[29]

A well-used mission statement serves as a strategic compass for a small company, guiding both managers and employees as they make decisions in the face of uncertainty. Some companies use short, one- or two-sentence mission statements that are easy to remember and understand, and others create longer mission statements with multiple components. Consider the following examples:

- Bongo World is the parent company of five coffee shops in Nashville, Tennessee all committed to serving organic, fair-trade coffee. Bongo World's mission: "Bongo World supports communities by expanding the definition of quality to include how stuff is produced, purchased and served."[30]

- Badger Mining Corporation, Berlin, Wisconsin: "We will be the leader in the industrial sand industry with a team of associates committed to excellence and a passion for satisfying our stakeholders."[31]

- Putney, Inc., located in Portland, Maine, manufactures generic prescription drugs for pets. Its mission is to "partner with veterinary practices to provide high-quality medicines that meet pet medical needs and offer cost-effective medicines for pet owners."[32]

- Nisolo Shoes is a social enterprise that supports artisans in developing countries by creating distribution and branding for their products. Co-founder Patrick Woodyard says its mission is as follows: "Nisolo is a socially conscious brand dedicated to offering a unique product that fuses quality and fashion with a vision to spur sustainable development throughout impoverished regions of the world."[33]

- The Clymb is a retailer of outdoor gear and apparel located in Portland, Oregon. "Our mission is to increase the well-being of the planet and its inhabitants by inspiring human-powered adventure."[34]

A company may have a powerful competitive advantage, but it is wasted unless (1) the owner has communicated that advantage to workers, who, in turn, work hard to communicate it to customers and potential customers and (2) customers recommend the company to their friends because they understand the benefits they are getting from it that they cannot get elsewhere. *That's* the real power of a mission statement. Table 5.2 offers some useful tips on writing a mission statement.

TABLE 5.2 Tips for Writing a Powerful Mission Statement

A mission statement is a useful tool for getting everyone fired up and heading in the same direction, but writing one is not as easy as it may first appear. Here are some tips for writing a powerful mission statement:

- *Keep it short.* The best mission statements are just a few sentences long. If they are short, people tend to remember them better.

- *Keep it simple.* Avoid using fancy jargon just to impress outsiders such as customers or suppliers. The first and most important use of a mission statement is inside a company.

- *Know what makes your company different.* Your competitors are trying to reach the same customers that you are. A mission statement should address what is unique about your company and what sets it apart from the competition.

- *Take a broad view, but not too broad.* If it is too specific, a mission statement can limit a company's potential. Similarly, a mission statement is too broad if it applies to any company in the industry. When asked what business his company was in, Rob Carter, a top manager at FedEx, did not mention shipping packages quickly; instead, his response was, "We're in the business of engineering time."

- *Get everyone involved.* If the boss writes the company mission statement, who is going to criticize it? Although the entrepreneur has to be the driving force behind the mission statement, everyone in the company needs the opportunity to have a voice in creating it. Expect to write several drafts before you arrive at a finished product.

- *Keep it current.* Mission statements can get stale over time. As business and competitive conditions change, so should your mission statement. Make a habit of evaluating your mission periodically so that it stays fresh.

- *Make sure your mission statement reflects the values and beliefs you hold dear.* They are the foundation on which your company is built.

- *Make sure your mission includes values that are worthy of your employees' best efforts.* One entrepreneur says a mission statement should "send a message to employees, suppliers, and customers as to what the purpose of the company is aside from just making profits."

- *Make sure your statement reflects a concern for the future.* Business owners can get so focused on the present that they forget about the future. A mission statement should be the first link to the company's future.

- *Keep the tone of the statement positive and upbeat.* No one wants to work for a business with a pessimistic outlook of the world.

- *Use your mission statement to lay an ethical foundation for your company.* This is the ideal time to let employees know what your company stands for—and what it won't stand for.

- *Look at other companies' mission statements to generate ideas for your own.* Two books, *Say It and Live It: The 50 Corporate Mission Statements That Hit the Mark* (Currency/Doubleday) and *Mission Statements: A Guide to the Corporate and Nonprofit Sectors* (Garland Publishing), are useful resources. Internet searches also produce useful examples of mission statements.

- *Make sure your mission statement is appropriate for your company's culture.* Although you should look at other companies' missions, do not make the mistake of trying to copy them. Your company's mission is unique to you and your company.

- *Revise it when necessary.* No business is static, which means that your company's mission statement should change as your company changes. Work with a team of employees on a regular basis to review and revise your company's mission statement.

- *Use it.* Don't go to all of the trouble of writing a mission statement just to let it collect dust. Post it on bulletin boards, print it on buttons and business cards, stuff it into employees' pay envelopes. Talk about your mission often, and use it to develop your company's strategic plan. That's what it's for!

Source: Based on "Ten Tips for Writing a Mission Statement," AllBusiness, http://www.allbusiness.com/marketing/advertising-copywriting/12185-1.html; Ken Blanchard, "The New Bottom Line," *Entrepreneur*, February 1998, pp. 127–131; Alan Farnham, "Brushing Up Your Vision Thing," *Fortune*, May 1, 1995, p. 129; Sharon Nelton, "Put Your Purpose in Writing," *Nation's Business*, February 1994, pp. 61–64; Jacquelyn Lynn, "Single-Minded," *Entrepreneur*, January 1996, p. 97.

Step 2. Assess the Company's Strengths and Weaknesses

strengths

positive internal factors that a company can use to accomplish its mission, goals, and objectives.

Having defined the vision they have for their company and translated that vision into a meaningful mission statement, entrepreneurs can turn their attention to assessing company strengths and weaknesses. Building a successful competitive strategy requires a business to magnify its strengths and overcome or compensate for its weaknesses. **Strengths** are positive internal factors that a company can draw on to accomplish its mission, goals, and objectives. They might include special skills or knowledge, a superior proprietary product or process, a positive public image, an experienced sales force, an established base of loyal customers, and many other factors. For instance, 1366 Technologies, a company in Lexington, Massachusetts, has developed a revolutionary process called the Direct Wafer method for producing the silicon wafers inside most solar panels. The process represents a major strength for the small company because it reduces wafer manufacturing costs 60 percent and reduces the time required to make a wafer from more than two days to just seconds.[35] **Weaknesses** are negative internal factors that inhibit a company's ability to accomplish its mission, goals, and objectives. Lack of capital, a shortage of skilled workers, the inability to master technology, and an inferior location are examples of weaknesses.

weaknesses

negative internal factors that inhibit the accomplishment of a company's mission, goals, and objectives.

Identifying strengths and weaknesses helps owners understand their businesses as they exist (or that, for start-ups, will exist). An organization's strengths should originate in the core competencies that are essential to gaining an edge in each of the market segments in which the firm competes. The key to building a successful strategy is using the company's underlying strengths as its foundation and matching those strengths against competitors' weaknesses.

One technique for taking this strategic inventory is to prepare a "balance sheet" of the company's strengths and weaknesses (see Table 5.3). The left side should reflect important skills, knowledge, or resources that contribute to the firm's success. The right side should record honestly any limitations that detract from the company's ability to compete. This balance sheet should analyze all key performance areas of the business—human resources, finance, production, marketing, product development, organization, and others. This analysis should give owners a realistic perspective of their businesses, pointing out foundations on which they can build future strengths and obstacles that they must remove for the business to progress. This exercise can help entrepreneurs determine the best way to move from their current position to a desired one.

Step 3. Scan the Environment for Significant Opportunities and Threats Facing the Business

opportunities

positive external options that a company can exploit to accomplish is mission, goals, and objectives.

OPPORTUNITIES Once entrepreneurs have taken an internal inventory of company strengths and weaknesses, they must turn to the external environment to identify any opportunities and threats that might have a significant impact on the business. **Opportunities** are positive external options that a firm can exploit to accomplish its mission, goals, and objectives. The number of potential opportunities is limitless; therefore, entrepreneurs should analyze only those that are most significant to the business (probably two or three at most). The key is to focus on the most promising opportunities that fit most closely with the company's strengths and core competencies. That requires entrepreneurs to say "no" to opportunities, even promising ones, that do not fit their companies' strategic vision.

TABLE 5.3 Identifying Company Strengths and Weaknesses

Strengths (Positive Internal Factors)	Weaknesses (Negative Internal Factors)

When identifying opportunities, an entrepreneur must pay close attention to new potential markets and product offerings. Are competitors overlooking a niche in the market we could easily exploit? Is there a better way to reach our customers, such as a greater focus on online sales? Are there new markets we can expand into with our existing business? Can we develop new products that offer customers better value? What opportunities are trends in the industry creating?

ENTREPRENEURIAL PROFILE: World Wrestling Entertainment The rapid growth in online streaming of video content led World Wrestling Entertainment (WWE) to shift away from relying on cable television distribution of its shows to launching its own 24/7 online streaming network. WWE Network airs all of the WWE live pay-per-view events, original programming, reality shows, documentaries, classic matches from its archives, and more than 1,500 hours of video on demand. Customers pay a flat monthly subscription fee to gain access to all WWE network content through its Web site and through apps that are compatible with most tablets and smart phones. Viewership of pay-per-view over cable and satellite television has been declining, while online streaming has continued to grow as a new medium for video content. WWE believes that the new business model provides an opportunity to generate more predictable and growing revenues.[36] ■

As WWE Network's experience illustrates, opportunities arise as a result of factors that are beyond entrepreneurs' control. Constantly scanning for those opportunities that best match their companies' strengths and core competences and pouncing on them ahead of competitors is the key to success.

Threats are negative external forces that inhibit a company's ability to achieve its mission, goals, and objectives. Threats to the business can take a variety of forms, such as new competitors entering the local market, a government mandate regulating a business activity, an economic recession, rising interest rates, mounting energy prices, or technology advances making a company's product obsolete. For instance, the growing reach of cellular phone networks and advances in smart phone technology pose a threat to companies that provide traditional landline

threats
negative external forces that inhibit a company's ability to achieve its mission, goals, and objectives.

Hands On . . . How To

Beat the Big Guys

It's the news that sends shivers down the spines of small business owners everywhere: Wal-Mart (or any other "big-box" retailer) is coming to town. "How can my small business compete against the largest retailer in the world?" they wonder. "Can my business survive?"

Although no business owner welcomes a threat of this magnitude from a giant competitor with greater buying power, more name recognition, and a reputation for driving small companies out of business, it is no reason to fold up the tent and go home. Smart entrepreneurs know that, by formulating and executing the proper strategy, they can not only survive in the face of larger competitors but also *thrive* in their presence.

Rule 1. Don't Play Their Game

A fundamental concept in strategy is to avoid matching your company's weaknesses against a competitor's strengths. For instance, because Wal-Mart buys in such huge volume from its suppliers, it can extract the lowest prices from them. Small companies purchasing from those same suppliers cannot; therefore, it makes little sense for small companies to try to compete with Wal-Mart and other giant retailers on price. Unless your small company has another more significant cost advantage, competing on the basis of price is a recipe for disaster. Entrepreneurs who compete successfully emphasize features that giant discounters cannot provide—extensive product

knowledge, better selection, superior customer service, a hassle-free buying experience, higher quality, and others. "Not everyone wants the lowest quality at the lowest price," says one expert.

Rule 2. Emphasize the Unique Aspects of Your Company and How They Benefit Your Customers

Joe Runyan, founder of Hangers Cleaners of Kansas City, Missouri, was faced with the challenge of competing with Proctor & Gamble's entry into the dry cleaning market with its national rollout of Tide Dry Cleaners. Hangers Cleaners had been able to differentiate its service by offering an environmentally safe dry cleaning process. Hangers Cleaners uses liquid carbon dioxide instead of the harsh chemicals traditionally used by dry cleaners. However, Tide Dry Cleaning also offered eco-friendly dry cleaning services. To compete with a large national brand, Runyan pursued several strategies. Hangers focused on its offbeat image. The company sent out entertaining promotional e-mails, gave away T-shirts bearing the invitation to "Sniff Me," put funny messages on its hangers, and held a St. Patrick's Day tailgate party in the parking lot. The company also pays close attention to customer service. Hangers has several programs to help with fundraising for local nonprofits and schools. The company offers van service for pick-up and delivery to affluent neighborhoods willing to pay a premium

(continued)

Hands On . . . How To *(continued)*

for the extra service. Although many of the other local dry cleaners suffered after the entry of Tide Dry Cleaners, Runyan's business has continued to experience growth in revenues and profits.

Rule 3. Hit 'em Where They Ain't

Big companies usually aim at big markets and often ignore small but profitable niche markets, which are ideal targets for small companies. Ashley Rosebrook and Stefan Peters entered a crowded personalized photo printing industry with their Web site Pinhole Press. When researching the industry, they found that most of the competition offered too many choices for the most common customer—new grandparents and parents. By creating a simple site that is easy to use, Pinhole found a niche in the market. The founders recently sold Pinhole for $33 million to a large software company.

Rule 4. Hire the Best—and Train Them

Small companies usually cannot afford to pay the highest wages in an area; however, because their companies are small, entrepreneurs have the opportunity to create a work environment in which employees can thrive. For instance, one small company attracts and retains quality workers by allowing them to use flexible work schedules that make it easier for them to manage their busy lives. The owner also invests heavily in training workers so that they can move up the organization—and the pay scale—faster. The training pays off, however, in the form of greater productivity, lower turnover, increased customer satisfaction, and higher sales per employee. Paying attention to seemingly small details, such as more communication, frequent recognition for jobs well done, less bureaucracy, and flexible benefits, enables small companies to build a loyal, motivated workforce that can outperform those at larger companies.

Rule 5. Bring Back What the Big Boys Have Eliminated

Ron Samuels founded Avenue Bank in Nashville, Tennessee, in 2007, not long before the financial crisis rocked the banking industry. However, Avenue Bank not only survived one of the most difficult times in banking since the Great Depression, but the company's old-fashioned approach to banking also resulted in strong and steady growth. Avenue focuses on highly personalized service, which is no longer available in many national bank chains. Avenue Bank offers the same personalized service to small businesses and entrepreneurs. The bank works with start-ups by offering concierge services, working to meet their unique needs from start-up through growth.

Rule 6. Use the Cost Advantages of the Internet to Gain an Edge

Ernesto Perez-Carrillo Jr. and his family launched EPC Cigar as a premium cigar company. The promotional channels for cigars include taxi-top advertising in large cities, commercials on cable channels, radio ads in large markets, and print ads in national business magazines and specialty publications that cater to the wealthy. This type of advertising is quite costly and not always highly effective. One ad might cost up to half EPC Cigar's total marketing budget. Because the company could not afford a traditional advertising campaign, the company put its marketing budget into the Internet, social media initiatives, trade shows, and

special events. EPC Cigar's sales grew to more than $1.5 million in revenue within the first year.

Rule 7. Be *Great* at Something Customers Value, Such as Service and Personal Attention

Do not make the mistake of choosing a "middle-of-the-road" strategy where, one writer says, there "are yellow lines, dead armadillos, and once-great companies that are slowly going out of business." Successful small companies differentiate themselves from their larger, more powerful rivals by emphasizing superior, friendly, personal service, something their size makes them uniquely capable of doing. Successful small companies also treat their customers like VIPs. Many small business owners know their customers by name, something that large companies cannot achieve. One of the best ways to determine exactly how to provide superior service and personal attention is to identify your top five customers and periodically ask them, "How can we serve you better?"

Rule 8. Get Involved in the Community

Entrepreneurs can make their small companies stand out from the crowd by supporting events in their local communities. A big budget is not a prerequisite. For instance, Pizza Ranch franchises host "community impact" nights. Family members and friends of employees bus tables to help fundraising for local causes. Pizza Ranch donates all of the evening's tips plus a matching share of the profits. The events generally draw additional donations from the community. The events help the franchises build relationships in the community and make genuine and enduring relationships with customers.

1. Why do many small businesses fail when a big discount retailer such as Wal-Mart enters their market?

2. Work with a team of your classmates to identify a local small business that competes with a bigger competitor. Which of these strategies has the small company employed to become a stronger competitor? What other strategies would you recommend to the owner of this business?

3. Based on your work in question 2, develop a one-page report summarizing your strategic suggestions.

Sources: Based on Chad Brooks, "10 Ways You Can Beat Wal-Mart," Business News Daily, April 20, 2011, http://www.businessnewsdaily.com/walmart-small-stores-1201; Norm Brodsky, "How Independents Can Hold Their Ground," *Inc.*, August 2007, pp. 65–66; Thomas M. Box, Kent Byus, Chris Fogliasso, and Warren D. Miller, "Hardball and OODA Loops: Strategy for Small Firms," *Proceedings of the Academy of Strategic Management* 6, no. 1 (2007): 5–10; Matthew Maier, "How to Beat Wal-Mart," *Business 2.0*, May 2005, pp. 108–114; Rhonda Abrams, "Small Businesses Can Compete with the Big Guys," *Business*, September 26, 2004, p. 8; Barry Cotton and Jean-Charles Cachon, "Resisting the Giants: Small Retail Entrepreneurs against Mega-Retailers—An Empirical Study," paper presented at the International Council for Small Business 2005 World Conference, June 2005; Amy Merrick, Gary McWilliams, Ellen Byron, and Kortney Stringer, "Targeting Wal-Mart," *Wall Street Journal*, December 1, 2004, pp. B1, B2; William C. Taylor, "The Fallacy of the 'Middle of the Road' Strategy," *BNET*, February 23, 2011, http://www.bnet.com/blog/innovator/the-fallacy-of-the-8220middle-of-the-road-8221-strategy/195; Jessica Shambora, "David vs. Goliath," *Fortune*, November 15, 2010, p. 55; Pamela Ryckman, "A Local Dry Cleaner Tries to Compete Against P.&G.," *New York Times*, April 14, 2010, www.nytimes.com/2010/04/15/business/smallbusiness/15sbiz.html?_r=1&; Judith Ohikuare, "How Pinhole Press Cut the Complexity and Got Noticed," *Inc.*, April 11, 2013, www.inc.com/best-industries-2013/judith-ohikuare/pinhole-press-cuts-the-complexity.html; "Avenue Bank Adds Four to the Team," *Nashville.com*, September 3, 2013, www.nashville.com/news/nashville-business-news/avenue-bank-adds-four-to-the-team; Jane Levere, "Choosing a Marketing Plan: Traditional or Social Media," *New York Times*, February 24, 2010, www.nytimes.com/2010/02/25/business/smallbusiness/25sbiz.html?ref=casestudies.

phone service and equipment. Landline phones reached their peak in 2001 when there were 57 fixed landlines (business and residential) for every 100 people. Just a decade later, more than half of all American households did not have or use a landline phone. A survey of Chief Information Officers found that 65 percent believed landline phones will likely disappear from everyday use by 2017. AT&T plans to end all landline service by the year 2020. Businesses that based their business models on the traditional landline phone system, such as companies manufacturing copper wire and telephone switching systems, face the ultimate threat to their future survival.[37]

Many small businesses face a threat from larger rivals who offer lower prices because of their high-volume purchasing power, huge advertising budgets, and megastores that attract customers for miles around. However, small businesses with the proper strategies in place do *not* have to fold in the face of intense competition. The accompanying "Hands On . . . How To" feature explains that, with the proper strategy, small companies cannot only survive but also thrive in the shadow of larger, more powerful rivals.

Opportunities and threats are products of the interactions of forces, trends, and events outside the direct control of the business. These external forces have direct impact on the behavior of the markets in which the business operates, the behavior of competitors, and the behavior of customers. The number of potential threats facing a business is huge, but entrepreneurs should focus on the three or four most significant threats confronting their companies. Table 5.4 provides a simple analytical tool to help entrepreneurs identify the threats that pose the greatest danger to their companies.

The interactions of strengths, weaknesses, opportunities, and threats can be the most revealing aspects of using a SWOT analysis as part of a strategic plan. This analysis also requires entrepreneurs to take an objective look at their businesses and the environment in which they operate, as they address many issues fundamental to their companies' success in the future.

TABLE 5.4 Identifying and Managing Threats

Every business faces threats, but entrepreneurs cannot afford to be paranoid or paralyzed by fear when it comes to dealing with them. At the same time, they cannot afford to ignore threats that have the potential to destroy their businesses. The most productive approach to dealing with threats is to identify those that would have the most severe impact on a small company and those that have the highest probability of occurrence.

Research by Greg Hackett, president of management think tank MergerShop, has identified 12 major sources of risk that can wreak havoc on a company's future. The following table helps entrepreneurs to determine the threats on which they should focus their attention.

Source	Specific Threat	Severity (1 = Low, 10 = High)	Probability of Occurrence (0 to 1)	Threat Rating (Severity × Probability, Max = 10)
1. Channels of distribution				
2. Competition				
3. Demographic changes				
4. Globalization				
5. Innovation				
6. Waning customer or supplier loyalty				
7. Offshoring or outsourcing				
8. Stage in product life cycle				
9. Government regulation				
10. Influence of special interest groups				
11. Influence of stakeholders				
12. Changes in technology				

Once entrepreneurs have identified specific threats facing their companies in the 12 areas (not necessarily all 12), they rate the severity of the impact of each one on their company on a 1 to 10 scale. Then they assign probabilities (between 0 and 1) to each threat. To calculate the Threat Score, entrepreneurs simply multiply the severity of each threat by its probability. (Maximum Threat Score is 10.) The higher a threat's score, the more attention it demands. Typically, one or two threats stand out above all of the others, and entrepreneurs should focus on those.

Source: Based on Edward Teach, "Apocalypse Soon," *CFO*, September 2005, pp. 31–32.

Step 4. Identify the Key Factors for Success in the Business

KEY SUCCESS FACTORS Every business is characterized by controllable variables that determine the relative success of market participants. By focusing efforts to maximize their companies' performance on these key success factors, entrepreneurs can achieve dramatic market advantages over their competitors. Companies that understand these key success factors tend to be leaders of the pack, whereas those that fail to recognize them become also-rans.

key success factors
the factors that determine a company's ability to compete successfully in an industry.

Key success factors (KSFs, also called key performance indicators) come in a variety of patterns, depending on the industry. Simply stated, these factors determine a company's ability to compete successfully in an industry. Every company in an industry must understand the KSFs that drive the industry; otherwise, they are likely to become industry also-rans like the horses trailing the pack in the Kentucky Derby. Many of these sources of competitive advantages are based on cost factors, such as manufacturing cost per unit, distribution cost per unit, or development cost per unit. Some are less tangible and less obvious but are just as important, such as superior product quality, solid relationships with dependable suppliers, superior customer service, a highly trained and knowledgeable sales force, prime store locations, readily available customer credit, and many others. For example, one restaurant owner identified the following KSFs:

- Experience in the industry
- Sufficient start-up capital
- Tight cost control (labor costs, 15 to 18 percent of sales, and food costs, 35 to 40 percent of sales)
- Accurate sales forecasting, which minimizes wasted food
- Proper inventory control
- Meticulous cash management
- Choosing locations that maximize customer convenience
- Cleanliness
- High food quality
- Friendly and attentive service from a well-trained wait staff
- Consistency in quality and service over time
- Speed, particularly at lunch, when the restaurant attracts businesspeople who must dine quickly and get back to work
- A clear definition of the restaurant's distinctive concept—its food, decor, service, and ambiance

These controllable variables determine the ability of any restaurant in this market segment to compete. Restaurants lacking these KSFs are not likely to survive, but those that build their strategies with these factors in mind will prosper. However, before entrepreneurs can build a strategy around the industry's KSFs, they must identify them. Table 5.5 presents a form to help owners identify the most important success factors in the industry and their implications for their companies.

Identifying the KSFs in an industry allows entrepreneurs to determine where they should focus their companies' resources strategically. It is unlikely that a company, even a large one, can excel on every KSF it identifies. Therefore, as they begin to develop their strategies, successful entrepreneurs focus on surpassing their rivals on one or two KSFs to build a sustainable competitive edge. As a result, KSFs become the cornerstones of a company's strategy. The last recession took a heavy toll on the casual dining sector of the restaurant industry, forcing many restaurants to refocus their attention on the KSFs in their respective market segments. At Chili's and Cracker Barrel, managers targeted lunch customers by making changes designed to reduce food preparation and service times. Recognizing that shaving even a few minutes from a lunch visit makes a huge difference for the lunch crowd, managers simplified lunch menus, streamlined their service procedures, retrained wait staff, and redesigned their kitchen layouts for maximum efficiency.[38]

TABLE 5.5 Identifying Key Success Factors

List the specific skills, characteristics, and core competences your business must possess if it is to be successful in its market segment.

Key Success Factor	How Your Company Rates . . .
1	Low 1 2 3 4 5 6 7 8 9 10 High
2	Low 1 2 3 4 5 6 7 8 9 10 High
3	Low 1 2 3 4 5 6 7 8 9 10 High
4	Low 1 2 3 4 5 6 7 8 9 10 High
5	Low 1 2 3 4 5 6 7 8 9 10 High

Conclusions:

In the hotly competitive gourmet burger segment of the industry, entrepreneurs behind chains such as Five Guys Burgers and Fries, Blazing Onion Burger Company, and In-N-Out are emphasizing KSFs to fuel their growth: high-quality burgers made from fresh ingredients, clean restaurants, superior service, and prices that offer good value. Because customers wait 10 minutes and pay anywhere from $5 to more than $10 for a burger at fast-growing chains such as these, managers make sure that customers understand that "this is not a typical fast-food burger joint." At Five Guys, which was founded in 1986 by CEO Jerry Murrell, his wife, and three sons, customers enjoy French fries that are hand cut daily and burgers made from fresh beef. Five Guys, now with more than 1,000 locations, is the fastest-growing restaurant chain in the United States. The Blazing Onion Burger Company, a small chain based in Mill Creek, Washington, offers customers 25 gourmet burgers made from fresh beef as well as a turkey burger, a veggie burger, a meatloaf burger, and an assortment of homemade desserts. Service at Blazing Onion, founded by David Jones in 2007, is paramount. Each table has a "Service Alert" card that resembles a stop sign; when customers post it, "we'll be there in 30 seconds," says Jones, who plans to open a new location every 10 months and recently began franchising.[39]

Step 5. Analyze the Competition

Ask most small business owners to identify the greatest challenge their companies face, and the most common response is *competition*. The Internet and e-commerce have increased the ferocity and the scope of the competition entrepreneurs face and have forced many business owners to change completely the ways in which they do business.

ENTREPRENEURIAL PROFILE: PJ's Coffee PJ's Coffee of New Orleans was founded seven years after Starbucks. While Starbucks grew to become the dominant global brand, PJ's Coffee has focused on establishing a strong local brand in New Orleans and growing locations in the Gulf Coast region. PJ's Coffee's strong regional brand has made it difficult for Starbucks to penetrate this region. PJ's Coffee follows a strategy that has been successful for many other regional brands competing against strong national brands. PJ's measures its success based on quality rather than quantity. Although Starbucks measures its success by the growth in number of retail outlets and market share, PJ's developed strong relationships with its farmers and local roasters. PJ's knows its customers and has developed niche products in response. Its growth strategy is based on organic growth and expanding distribution into regional grocery outlets.[40] ∎

Keeping tabs on rivals' movements through competitive intelligence programs is a vital strategic activity. "Business is like any battlefield. If you want to win the war, you have to know who you're up against," says one small business consultant.[41] Unfortunately, most businesses are not very good at competitive intelligence: 97 percent of U.S. businesses do not systematically track the progress of their key competitors.[42] A study of business executives around the world by McKinsey and Company reports that just 23 percent of companies discovered a major competitive innovation by a competitor in time to be able to plan a response before the innovation hit the market.[43] The primary goals of a competitive intelligence program include the following:

- Conducting continuous rather than periodic analysis of competition
- Avoiding surprises from existing competitors' new strategies and tactics
- Identifying potential new competitors
- Improving reaction time to competitors' actions
- Anticipating rivals' next strategic moves

COMPETITOR ANALYSIS Sizing up the competition gives a business owner a realistic view of the market and his or her company's position in it. Yet not every competitor warrants the same level of attention in the strategic plan. *Direct competitors* offer the same products and services,

 ## You Be the Consultant

Digital Franchise Seeks to Expand Nationwide

When Chris Jeffery was in college at Penn State in 2003, he noticed that very few restaurants had their menus posted on a Web site. Those that did have an Internet presence did not have online ordering for delivery or takeout. Jeffery started OrderUp to help restaurants and customers connect through its online platform.

After college, Jeffery proved the concept by licensing it to a small number of people. Once he had proof of concept, Jeffery was ready to scale and expand into other markets. He looked into raising venture capital but came away convinced that he would rather find a way to grow the business in a way that he could maintain control of the company.

After operating as LionsMenu while Jeffery was in college and LocalUp when he was first testing the concept, he eventually chose the name OrderUp for his venture. Jeffery was able to raise seed money from an angel investor but relied mostly on bootstrapping to establish a franchising model to grow the concept. However, Jeffery faced the challenge that no one had ever franchised an online business before.

OrderUp offers its franchises for an up-front cost of $42,000, which covers the software system, training, and territorial rights to a specific area defined by phone number area codes. OrderUp handles all of the order processing and customer support via online chat or telephone. OrderUp pays the restaurant for each order, after keeping 5 percent for the company and 5 to 9 percent for its franchisee. Customers have the convenience of viewing a wide variety of menu items from several restaurants on one online location.

The franchisees are responsible for selling the service to local restaurants and for connecting OrderUp with the local community. Social media also is an important tool for expanding the sales for each territory. Quick service restaurants are the most receptive to the OrderUp model. In many markets, franchisees are forging partnerships with restaurants to create special promotions, featured menu items, and even new products. Franchisees who are able to meet sales targets can earn more than $100,000 a year.

Bill Proferes, a veteran restaurateur, is an example of a successful OrderUp franchisee. After one year as owner of the Norfolk, Virginia, franchise, Proferes bought additional franchise rights in Norfolk. Proferes has signed up dozens of local restaurants to be partners with his OrderUp franchise.

By its 10th year in business, OrderUp had grown to 32 markets in 18 states, had more than 1,000 restaurants signed up to participate in its program, and had more than 400,000 registered users.

The company plans to continue this growth into mid-sized markets across the country, but faces competition from other companies developing online restaurant ordering Web sites and mobile applications.

1. Visit OrderUp Web site at https://orderup.com to learn more about the company. Work with a team of your classmates to identify the company's strengths and weaknesses.

2. What opportunities and threats does OrderUp face?

3. Identify OrderUp's major competitors. What are their strengths and weaknesses?

4. Write a short memo (two pages maximum) to Chris Jeffery and his management team describing your strategic recommendations for helping OrderUp gain and maintain a competitive advantage in their industry and realize their goals grow the company to become a national industry leader.

Sources: "OrderUp Celebrates One Year of Success Servicing the Norfolk Area," *Franchising.com,* October 30, 2013, www.franchising.com/news/20131030_orderup_celebrates_one_year_of_success_servicing_t.html; Minda Zetlin, "Digital Franchises: New Spin on an Old Business Model," *Inc.,* March 7, 2013, www.inc.com/minda-zetlin/orderup-founder-tells-vcs-to-get-lost-and-creates-first-digital-franchise-instea .html; "Online Ordering Platform Keeps It All in the Community," *QRS,* May 31, 2013, www.qsrmagazine.com/news/online-ordering-platform-keeps-it-all-community; Andrew Zaleski, "OrderUp: Canton Startup Invests in 'Digital Franchising' to Bring Online Food-ordering Nationwide," *Technically Baltimore,* January 28, 2013, http://technical .ly/baltimore/2013/01/28/orderup-localup-digital-franchise/; "We're in 32 Markets across the Country and Growing," OrderUp.com, n.d., https://orderup.com.

and customers often compare prices, features, and deals from these competitors as they shop. *Significant competitors* offer some of the same products and services. Although their product or service lines may be somewhat different, there is competition with them in several key areas. *Indirect competitors* offer the same or similar products or services only in a small number of areas, and their target customers seldom overlap yours. Entrepreneurs should monitor closely the actions of their direct competitors, maintain a solid grasp of where their significant competitors are heading, and spend only minimal resources tracking their indirect competitors.

Collecting competitive intelligence enables entrepreneurs to update their knowledge of top competitors by answering the following questions:

- What are the primary criteria customers used to choose among competitive businesses in your industry?

- Who are your primary competitors? Where are they located?

- What distinctive competencies have they developed?

- How do their cost structures compare to yours? Their financial resources?

- How do they promote their products and services?

- What do customers say about them? How do customers describe their products or services, their way of doing business, and the additional services they might supply?

- What are their key strategies?

- What are their strengths? How can your company counteract them?

- What are their major weaknesses? How can your company capitalize on them?

- Are new competitors entering the business?

According to the Society of Competitive Intelligence, 95 percent of the competitive intelligence information is available from public sources that anyone can access—if they know how.[44] Gathering competitive intelligence does not require entrepreneurs to engage in activities that are unethical, illegal, or unsavory (such as dumpster diving). One expert says competitive intelligence involves "taking information from the public domain, adding it to what you know about your company and your industry, and looking for patterns."[45] By collecting many nuggets of information about their competitors, entrepreneurs can assemble the pieces to make reliable inferences about their rivals' overall strategies. Entrepreneurs can use the following low-cost competitive intelligence methods to collect information about their rivals:

- Read industry trade publications for announcements and news stories about competitors.

- Ask questions of customers and suppliers about what they hear competitors may be doing. In many cases, this information is easy to gather because some people love to gossip.

- Regularly debrief employees, especially sales representatives and purchasing agents. Experts estimate that 70 to 90 percent of the competitive information a company needs already resides with employees who collect it in their routine dealings with suppliers, customers, and other industry contacts.[46]

- Attend industry "meet-ups" in your local community.

- Attend trade shows and collect competitors' sales literature.

- Monitor social media for insights into your direct competitors.

- Watch for employment ads and job postings from competitors; knowing what types of workers they are hiring can tell you a great deal about their future plans.

- Conduct patent searches for patents competitors have filed. This gives important clues about new products they are developing.

- Learn about the kinds and amounts of equipment and raw materials that competitors are importing by studying the *Journal of Commerce Port Import Export Reporting Service (PIERS)* database. These clues can alert an entrepreneur to new products that a competitor is about to launch.

- If appropriate, buy competitors' products and assess their quality and features. Benchmark their products against yours.

- Obtain credit reports on each of your major competitors to evaluate their financial condition. For less than $200, Dun & Bradstreet and other research firms provide detailed credit reports of competitors that can be helpful in a strategic analysis.

- Publicly held companies must file periodic reports with the Securities and Exchange Commission, including quarterly 10-Q and annual 10-K reports. Information on publicly held companies is available at the Securities and Exchange Commission Web site.

- Investigate Uniform Commercial Code reports. Banks file these with the state whenever they make loans to businesses. These reports often include the amount of the loan and what it is for.

- Check out the resources of your local library, including articles, computerized databases, and online searches. Press releases, which often announce important company news, can be an important source of competitive intelligence. Many companies supply press releases through the PR Newswire. For local competitors, review back issues of the area newspaper for articles on and advertisements by competitors.

- Visit competitors' Web sites periodically to see what news is contained there. The Web enables small companies to uncover valuable competitive information at little or no cost.

- Sign up for competitors' social media feeds for current news about their businesses.

- Visit competing businesses periodically to observe their operations. Tom Stemberg, CEO of Staples, a chain of office supply superstores, says, "I've never visited a store where I didn't learn something."[47]

- Don't resort to unethical or illegal practices.

competitive profile matrix
a tool that allows business owners to evaluate their companies against major competitors using the key success factors for that market segment.

Entrepreneurs can use the results of their competitive intelligence efforts to construct a competitive profile matrix for its most important competitors. A **competitive profile matrix** allows owners to evaluate their firms against the major competitor using the KSFs for that market segment. The first step is to list the KSFs identified in step 4 of the strategic planning process (refer to Table 5.5) and to attach weights to them reflecting their relative importance. (For simplicity, the weights in this matrix sum add up to 1.00.) In this example, notice that product quality is weighted twice as heavily (twice as important) as price competitiveness.

The next step is to identify the company's major competitors and to rate each one (and your company) on each of the KSFs:

If Factor Is a . . .	Rating Is . . .
Major weakness	1
Minor weakness	2
Minor strength	3
Major strength	4

Once the rating is completed, the owner simply multiplies the weight by the rating for each factor to get a weighted score and then adds up each competitor's weighted scores to get a total weighted score. Table 5.6 shows a sample competitive profile matrix for a small company. The results show which company is strongest, which is weakest, and which of the KSFs each one is best and worst at meeting. By carefully studying and interpreting the results, an entrepreneur can begin to envision the ideal strategy for building a competitive edge in his or her corner of the market. Notice that the small company profiled in Table 5.6 should emphasize the competitive advantages it holds over its rivals in quality and perception of value in its business strategy.

TABLE 5.6 Sample Competitive Profile Matrix

Key Success Factors (from Step 4)	Weight	Your Business		Competitor 1		Competitor 2	
		Rating	Weighted Score	Rating	Weighted Score	Rating	Weighted Score
Quality	0.25	4	1.00	2	0.50	2	0.50
Customer retention	0.20	3	0.60	3	0.60	3	0.60
Location	0.15	4	0.60	3	0.45	4	0.60
Perception of value	0.20	4	0.80	2	0.40	3	0.60
Cost control	0.20	3	0.60	1	0.20	4	0.80
Total	1.00		**3.60**		**2.15**		**3.10**

 ## You Be the Consultant

Finding a Niche with a Subscription Business Model

In his book *Break from the Pack*, Oren Harari explains how business owners can escape the problems of the "Copycat Economy, where everyone has access to the same resources and talent, where the Web is the great equalizer, and where the market's twin foundations are imitation and commoditization." He argues that too many businesses are stuck in the pack with "me-too" products and services that customers see as commodities. The danger of being stuck in the pack (or relying on a "middle-of-the-road strategy") is becoming what entrepreneur Terry Brock calls "disgustingly generic." What can small companies, which often lack the resources that large companies have, do to break from the pack strategically? Consider the lessons we can learn from the following small businesses that all rely on subscription services.

Dollar Shave Club

Michael Dubin, CEO of Dollar Shave Club, effectively uses social media to successfully compete with well-established national brands Schick and Gillette. Dollar Shave Club sends out razors to its subscribers that cost $1, $3, or $9 per month. The products are simple in design but are made of high quality materials. Dollar Shave Club partners with an overseas manufacturer. The 38 employees who work for Dollar Shave Club focus on marketing, order fulfillment, and product development. The company's YouTube video features Dubin, who uses humor and passion to try to convince people to buy shaving goods by mail rather than from the grocery store. The YouTube Dollar Shave Club commercial was viewed more than 13 million times in just two years and attracted hundreds of thousands of subscribers.

Citrus Lane

Mauria Finley used her own experience as a new mother to develop the business model for her company, Citrus Lane. Like many first-time mothers planning for the arrival of their first babies, Finley spent months planning her business model. She sent out e-mails to all her friends who already had babies, seeking advice on their favorite products and brands. Her e-mail in box was soon full of recommendations for a wide variety of products for her new baby. She realized other new mothers could benefit from the same wisdom from experienced mothers that she had received. Citrus Lane is a subscription service that sends new parents "care packages" of products recommended by a panel of advisers and by Citrus Lane customers. Subscribers pay $25 per month to get a package with age-appropriate products for their children. Venture capital firms have endorsed the Citrus Lane concept with two rounds of financing of more than $6 million.

For the Makers

For the Makers is a subscription business built on the popularity of at-home craft projects. For the Makers sends its subscribers a monthly box that contains instructions and materials for four to six small craft projects. Most of the projects are jewelry or similar trinkets and take less than an hour to complete. Cofounders Janet Crowther and Katie Covington, who have past experience designing for national fashion brands, dream up the projects and develop the detailed instructions on how to make each project. The company also provides online tutorials for all of the projects it sells. For the Makers charges subscribers $29 per month for the materials and online support.

1. Which of the strategies discussed in this chapter are these companies using? Explain.

2. What competitive advantages does the successful execution of their subscription-based strategies produce for these businesses?

3. What are the risks associated with these companies' strategies?

Sources: Erica Swallow, "Ten Internet Startups That Thrive by Mail," *Forbes,* April 26, 2012, www.forbes.com/sites/ericaswallow/2012/04/26/internet-startups-by-mail/; Kathleen Davis, "Moss of the Month Club? 15 Unique Subscription Services," *Entrepreneur,* November 15, 2013, www.entrepreneur.com/slideshow/229916#0; Daniel Gross, "After 100 Years, the Shaving Industry Is Finally Being Disrupted," *Daily Beast,* January 24, 2014, www.thedailybeast.com/articles/2014/01/24/after-100-years-the-shaving-industry-is-finally-being-disrupted.html; Jennifer Van Grove, "Oh baby, Citrus Lane bags $5.1M to send care packages to new moms," *Venture Beat,* April 24, 2012, http://venturebeat.com/2012/04/24/citrus-lane-funding/; "Our Story," Citrus Lane, n.d., www.citruslane.com/about-us/; Fiorella Valdesolo, "What Do You Subscribe To?," *New York,* May 13, 2012, http://nymag.com/shopping/features/subscriptions-2012-5/; Ryan Kim, "For the Makers creates monthly boxes for DIY crafters," *Gigaom,* December 18, 2012; http://gigaom.com/2012/12/18/for-the-makers-creates-monthly-boxes-for-diy-crafters/.

Step 6. Create Company Goals and Objectives

Before entrepreneurs can build a comprehensive set of strategies, they must first establish business goals and objectives, which give them targets to aim for and provide a basis for evaluating their companies' performance. Without them, it is impossible to know where a business is going or how well it is performing. The following conversation between Alice and the Cheshire Cat, taken from Lewis Carroll's *Alice in Wonderland*, illustrates the importance of creating meaningful goals and objectives as part of the strategic management process:[48]

"Would you tell me please, which way I ought to go from here?" asked Alice.

"That depends a good deal on where you want to get to," said the Cat.

"I don't much care where . . .," said Alice.

"Then it doesn't matter which way you go," said the Cat.

A small business that "doesn't much care where" it wants to go (i.e., one that has no goals and objectives) will find that "it really doesn't matter which way" it chooses to go (i.e., its strategy is irrelevant).

goals
broad, long-range attributes that a business seeks to accomplish; they tend to be general and sometimes abstract.

GOALS   The broad, long-range attributes that a business seeks to accomplish are its **goals**; they tend to be general and sometimes even abstract. Goals are not intended to be specific enough for a manager to act on but simply state the general level of accomplishment sought. Do you want to boost your market share? Does your cash balance need strengthening? Would you like to enter a new market or increase sales in a current one? Do you want to develop new products or services? Researchers Jim Collins and Jerry Porras studied a large group of businesses for their book *Good to Great* and determined that one of the factors that set apart successful companies from unsuccessful ones was the formulation of ambitious, clear, and inspiring long-term goals. Collins and Porras called them BHAGs ("Big Hairy Audacious Goals," pronounced "bee-hags") and suggest that their main benefit is to inspire and focus a company on important actions that are consistent with its overall mission.[49] Figure 5.3 shows that effective BHAGs originate at the intersection of a company's mission, vision, and values; its distinctive competencies; and its KSFs. Addressing these broad issues will help entrepreneurs focus on the next phase—developing specific, realistic objectives.

objectives
more specific targets of performance, commonly addressing areas such as profitability, productivity, growth, and other key aspects of a business.

OBJECTIVES   **Objectives** are more specific targets of performance. Common objectives concern profitability, productivity, growth, efficiency, sales, financial resources, physical facilities, organizational structure, employee welfare, and social responsibility. Because some of these objectives might conflict with one another, it is important to establish priorities. Which objectives are most important? Which are least important? Arranging objectives in a hierarchy according to their priority can help an entrepreneur resolve conflicts when they arise. Well-written objectives have the following characteristics:

They are specific. Objectives should be quantifiable and precise. For example, "to achieve a healthy growth in sales" is not a meaningful objective; however, "to increase retail sales

FIGURE 5.3

What Makes an Effective BHAG?

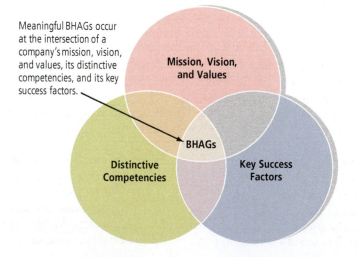

Meaningful BHAGs occur at the intersection of a company's mission, vision, and values, its distinctive competencies, and its key success factors.

Mission, Vision, and Values

Distinctive Competencies

Key Success Factors

BHAGs

by 12 percent and wholesale by 10 percent in the next fiscal year" is precise and spells out exactly what management wants to accomplish.

They are measurable. Managers should be able to plot the organization's progress toward its objectives; this requires a well-defined reference point from which to start and a scale for measuring progress.

They are action commitments. Objectives are linked to specific actions. Ideally, managers and employees should be able to see how their jobs lead to the company achieving its objectives. ProviderTrust is a healthcare software company that is backed by venture capital, which means that the management team has specific revenue growth objectives investors expect the company to reach. The company holds 10- to 15-minute meetings with all 11 employees at the start of every day during which team members can talk about what they are working on to help the company achieve its revenue objectives.[50]

They are assignable. Unless an entrepreneur assigns responsibility for an objective to an individual, it is unlikely that the company will ever achieve it. Creating objectives without giving someone responsibility for accomplishing them is futile. Accountability is the key.

They are realistic yet challenging. Objectives must be within the reach of the organization, or motivation will disappear. In any case, managerial expectations must remain high. In other words, the more challenging an objective is (within realistic limits), the higher the performance will be. Set objectives that will challenge your business and its employees.

They are timely. Objectives must specify not only what is to be accomplished but also when it is to be accomplished. A time frame for achievement is important.

They are written down. Setting objectives does not have to be complex; in fact, an entrepreneur should keep the number of objectives relatively small (from 5 to 10). Writing down objectives makes them more concrete and makes it easy to communicate them to everyone in the company.

The strategic planning process works best when managers and employees work together to set goals and objectives. Developing a plan is top management's responsibility, but executing it falls to managers and employees; therefore, encouraging them to participate broadens the plan's perspective and increases the motivation to make the plan work. Unfortunately, although 65 percent of companies have a clear strategy, only 14 percent of employees understand their role in implementing the company's strategies.[51] A recent study by SuccessFactors reports that companies that set goals, align them with their companies' overall strategy, and measure employees' performance against those goals using multiple benchmarks financially outperform companies that do not. SuccessFactors cites three primary benefits of an effective goal-setting process: (1) increased profitability, (2) faster execution of company strategy, and (3) reduced employee turnover.[52]

Step 7. Formulate Strategic Options and Select the Appropriate Strategies

By this point in the strategic management process, entrepreneurs should have a clear picture of what their businesses do best and what their competitive advantages are. They also should understand their firms' weaknesses and limitations as well as those of their competitors. The next step is to evaluate strategic options and then prepare a game plan designed to achieve the stated mission, goals, and objectives.

STRATEGY A **strategy** is a road map of the actions an entrepreneur draws up to accomplish a company's mission, goals, and objectives. In other words, the mission, goals, and objectives spell out the ends, and the strategy defines the means for reaching them. A strategy is the master plan that covers all the major parts of the organization and ties them together into a unified whole. The plan must be action oriented; it should breathe life into the entire planning process. An entrepreneur must build a sound strategy based on the preceding steps that uses the

strategy
a road map of the actions an entrepreneur draws up to fulfill the company's mission, goals, and objectives.

"Stay with me now, people, because in Step C, things get a bit delicate."

Bradford Veley, www.cartoonstock.com

company's core competencies and strengths as the springboard to success. Joseph Picken and Gregory Dess, authors of *Mission Critical: The 7 Strategic Traps That Derail Even the Smartest Companies*, write, "A flawed strategy—no matter how brilliant the leadership, no matter how effective the implementation—is doomed to fail. A sound strategy, implemented without error, wins every time."[53]

ENTREPRENEURIAL PROFILE: Zina and Jason Santos and August Kitchen August Kitchen offers a meal starter for hamburgers, called J-BURGER, which was born in the kitchen of Zina and Jason Santos. Their friends kept wanting to take home some of the meal starter the couple used to zest up their burgers. In 2009, they invested about $100,000 of their own funds to try commercializing their product. Their first product was J-BURGER (the "J" is for Jason). To ensure that its product is fresh, which is a big selling point, August Kitchen partnered with a packager that could produce small batches tied to grocery store orders. Getting shelf space and building consumer awareness of J-BURGER has been a challenge. The Santoses spent many hours cooking mini-burgers to entice shoppers to take J-BURGER home with them. By working with stores that support local products and by listening to what consumers want, the company is gaining market acceptance. More than 60 retailers in 11 states now carry August Kitchen products. August Kitchen has added J-CHILI and J-MEATLOAF meal starters to its product line.[54] ∎

A successful strategy is comprehensive and well integrated, focusing on establishing the KSFs that the entrepreneur identified in step 4. For instance, if maximum shelf space is a KSF for a small manufacturer's product, the strategy must identify techniques for gaining more in-store shelf space (e.g., offering higher margins to distributors and brokers than competitors do, assisting retailers with in-store displays, or redesigning a wider, more attractive package).

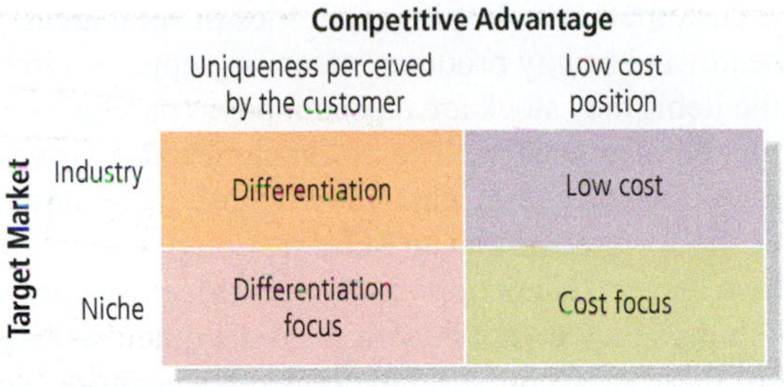

FIGURE 5.4

Three Strategic Options

Source: Michael E. Porter, *Competitive Strategy* (New York: Free Press, 1980), chap. 2.

THREE STRATEGIC OPTIONS Obviously, the number of strategies from which the small business owner can choose is infinite. When all the glitter is stripped away, however, three basic strategies remain. In his classic book *Competitive Strategy*, Michael Porter defines these strategies: (1) cost leadership, (2) differentiation, and (3) focus (see Figure 5.4).[55]

COST LEADERSHIP A company pursuing a **cost leadership strategy** strives to be the lowest-cost producer relative to its competitors in the industry. Many companies attempt to compete by offering low prices, but low costs are a prerequisite for success. Low-cost leaders have a competitive advantage in reaching buyers whose primary purchase criterion is price, and they have the power to set the industry's price floor. This strategy works well when buyers are sensitive to price changes, when competing firms sell the same commodity products and compete on the basis of price, and when companies can benefit from economies of scale. Not only is a low-cost leader in the best position to defend itself in a price war, but it also can use its power to attack competitors with the lowest price in the industry.

cost leadership strategy
a strategy in which a company strives to be the low-cost producer relative to its competitors in the industry.

There are many ways to build a low-cost strategy, but the most successful cost leaders know where they have cost advantages over their competitors, and they use these as the foundation for their strategies. Successful cost leaders often find low-cost suppliers (or use a vertical integration strategy to produce their own products), eliminate the inefficiencies in their channels of distribution, use the Internet to cut costs, and operate more efficiently than their competitors. They are committed to squeezing every unnecessary cost out of their operations.

ENTREPRENEURIAL PROFILE: Eric Casaburi and Retro Fitness Eric Casaburi, founder and CEO of Retro Fitness, pursues a low-cost strategy in a highly competitive industry. Retro Fitness offers gym memberships at a rock bottom price of $19.99 per month in its more than 100 fitness centers in 13 states. Featuring a 1980s theme, Retro Fitness offers quality equipment and service with no additional frills. Casaburi keeps costs down by negotiating deals with suppliers and by carefully selecting low-cost sites. Instead of building 30,000-square-foot gyms, Retro Fitness is able to fit everything its customers need within a space one-third that size, which saves a significant amount of rent expense each month. Retro Fitness also offers additional products its customers want, such as smoothies, training sessions, and clothing, which adds to the monthly revenue per customer. The company offers an app as part of membership that allows customers to track their workouts, measure progress toward goals, make an appointment with a trainer, and order a smoothie from the smoothie bar. Casaburi plans to have 300 locations by 2018.[56] ■

Of course, there are dangers in following a cost leadership strategy. Sometimes a company focuses exclusively on lower manufacturing costs, without considering the impact of purchasing, distribution, or overhead costs. Another danger is incorrectly identifying the company's true cost drivers. Although their approach to managing is characterized by frugality, companies that understand cost leadership are willing to invest in those activities that drive costs out of doing business, whether it is technology, preventive maintenance, or some other factor. In addition, over time, competitors may erode a company's cost advantage by finding ways to lower their own costs. Finally, a firm may pursue a low-cost leadership strategy so zealously that, in its drive to push costs downward, it eliminates product or service features that customers consider to be essential.

Under the right conditions, a cost leadership strategy executed properly can be an incredibly powerful strategic weapon. Small discount retailers that live in the shadows of Wal-Mart and thrive even when the economy slows succeed by relentlessly pursuing low-cost strategies. Small chains, such as Fred's, Dollar General, Family Dollar, 99 Cents Only, and Dollar Tree, cater to low- and middle-income customers who live in inner cities or rural areas. They offer inexpensive products such as food, health and beauty products, cleaning supplies, clothing, and seasonal merchandise, and many of the items they stock are closeout buys (purchases made as low as 10 cents on the dollar) on brand-name merchandise. These companies also strive to keep their overhead costs as low as possible. For instance, 99 Cents Only, whose name describes its merchandising strategy, is housed in a no-frills warehouse in an older section of City of Commerce, California.[57] By keeping their costs low, these retailers offer customers prices that are within 1 to 2 percent of those at Wal-Mart, even though they do not benefit from the quantity discounts that the low-cost giant does. The success of these stores proves that companies pursuing a cost leadership strategy must emphasize cost containment in *every* decision, from where to locate the company headquarters to which items to stock.

differentiation strategy
a strategy in which a company seeks to build customer loyalty by positioning its goods or services in a unique or different fashion.

DIFFERENTIATION A company following a **differentiation strategy** seeks to build customer loyalty by selling goods or services that provide unique attributes and that customers perceive to be superior to competing products. That, in turn, enables the business to command higher prices for its products or services than competitors. There are many ways to create a differentiation strategy, but the key is to be unique at something that is important to the customer. In other words, a business strives to be better than its competitors at something customers value.

Phillip Tompkins, Tompkins Venture LLC, DBA Rent the Chicken

ENTREPRENEURIAL PROFILE: Jenn and Phillip Tompkins and RentTheChicken.com Jenn and Phillip Tompkins started RentTheChicken.com in Freeport, Pennsylvania, to take advantage of the growing interest in backyard, suburban farms. RentTheChicken.com takes the risk out of backyard farming for the first-time urban farmers. Every spring, the company brings two egg-laying chickens and all of the necessary supplies to its customers who are all located within about an hour of the company's headquarters. The Tompkins offer lessons to clients to help ensure their success at raising chickens. The chicken rental and supplies costs $350 a season. Then in the fall, RentTheChicken.com picks up the chickens to keep them safe and warm over the winter. If predators eat any of the rented chickens, the chickens are replaced at no cost. However, if a chicken dies from neglect, RentTheChicken.com picks up the equipment and charges the customer a fee. Environmentalists praise the business model because it reduces the number of chickens that end up in animal shelters after would-be urban farmers find raising chickens to be more work than they had assumed.[58] ∎

If a small company can improve a product's (or service's) performance, reduce the customer's cost and risk of purchasing it, or provide intangible benefits that customers value (such as status, prestige, exclusivity, or a sense of safety), it has the potential to be a successful differentiator. Companies that execute a differentiation strategy successfully can charge premium prices for their products and services, increase their market share, and reap the benefits of customer loyalty and retention. To be successful, a business must make its product or service truly different, at least in the eyes of its customers.

Although few businesses are innately as unique as RentTheChicken.com, the goal for a company pursuing a differentiation strategy is to create that kind of uniqueness in the minds of its customers. The key to a successful differentiation strategy is to build it on a core competency something a small company is uniquely good at doing in comparison to its competitors. Common bases for differentiation include superior customer service, special product features, complete product lines, instantaneous parts availability, absolute product reliability, supreme product quality, and extensive product knowledge. To be successful, a differentiation strategy must create the perception of value in the customer's eyes. No customer purchases a good or service that fails to produce its perceived value, no matter how real that value may be. One business consultant advises, "Make sure you tell your customers and prospects what it is about your business that makes you different. Make sure that difference is on the form of a true benefit to the customer."[59]

Small companies encounter risks when pursuing a differentiation strategy. One danger is trying to differentiate a product or service on the basis of something that does not boost its performance or lower its cost to customers. Another pitfall is trying to differentiate on the basis of something customers do not see as important. Business owners also must consider how long they can sustain a product's or service's differentiation; changing customer tastes may make the basis for differentiation temporary. Imitations and "knockoffs" from competitors also pose a threat to a successful differentiation strategy. For instance, designers of high-priced original clothing see much cheaper knockoff products on the market shortly after their designs hit the market. Another pitfall is over-differentiating and charging so much that the company prices its products out of the market. The final risk is focusing only on the physical characteristics of a product or service and ignoring important psychological factors, such as status, prestige, and image, which can be powerful sources of differentiation.

FOCUS A **focus strategy** recognizes that not all markets are homogeneous. In fact, in any given market, there are many different customer segments, each having different needs, wants, and characteristics. Businesses with a focus strategy sell to these specific segments rather than try to sell to the mass market. Chris Anderson, editor-in-chief of *Wired Magazine,* in his book *The Long Tail*, explains that the digital age has opened up smaller niche market segments to smaller businesses, creating a long tail of niche markets (see Figure 5.5). Three drivers create the long tail of the market:[60]

1. *The tools of production are more affordable.* Software and hardware are now much cheaper to buy and easier to use. For instance, in the past, musical artists recorded their work in a studio at a cost of thousands of dollars per song. Today, musicians no longer have to rely on large record companies to produce their music. With affordable software such as Pro Tools, artists can record and edit music with a personal computer or laptop anywhere. The quality of these recordings is so high that it is almost impossible to tell the difference between a recording made in a professional recording studio and one made in an artist's living room.

2. *The Internet has created better access to niche markets.* Internet aggregators can pull together all of the products consumers may possibly want. Amazon, iTunes, eBay, and many other Internet retailers have opened up distribution to many small businesses that would never have been able to achieve such broad market exposure. In addition, the company Web site is now a tool to reach consumers directly through digital advertising and social media.

3. *Search tools make it easier to reach specific consumers.* Search engines and recommendations available through Web sites and social media drive consumers to specific products and services on the Internet that meet their particular needs. For example, a consumer who traveled to the Czech Republic and wanted to buy some Czech crystal after getting home can easily search for Czech crystal manufacturers that ship abroad.

focus strategy
a strategy in which a company selects one or more market segments; identifies customers' special needs, wants, and interests; and approaches them with a good or service designed to excel in meeting those needs, wants, and interests.

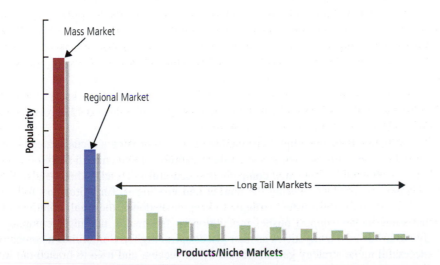

FIGURE 5.5

Long Tail Markets

Source: Anderson, Chris. *The long tail: Why the future of business is selling less of more.* (New York: Hyperion Books, 2008).

The principal idea of a focus strategy is to select one (or more) segment(s); identify customers' special needs, wants, and interests; and provide them with goods or services designed to excel in meeting these needs, wants, and interests. By focusing on small market niches, focus strategies build on *differences* among market segments. Because they are small, flexible, and attentive to their customers' particular needs, small companies can be successful in niches that are too narrow for their larger competitors to enter profitably. These companies focus on a narrow segment of the overall market and set themselves apart either by becoming cost leaders in the segment or by differentiating themselves from competitors.

Focus strategies will become more prevalent among small businesses in the future as industries increasingly become dumbbell shaped, with a few large companies dominating one end, a relatively small number of mid-sized businesses in the middle, and a large number of small businesses operating at the other end. A study by Intuit and the Institute for the Future on the small business environment in 2018, *The Intuit Future of Small Business Report*, cites increasingly fragmented markets, customers who demand products and services that are tailored to their specific needs, and advancements that give small companies affordable access to increasingly sophisticated technology as key factors that will make narrow markets increasingly suitable for small businesses to thrive. The report concludes that "there will be increasing opportunities for small businesses to flourish in niches left untouched by global giants."[61]

In fact, serving specific target segments or niches rather than the attempting to reach the total market is the essence of a focus strategy, making it ideally suited to small businesses, which often lack the resources to reach the overall market. Their goal is to serve their narrow target markets more effectively and efficiently than competitors that pound away at the broad market. Common bases for building a focus strategy include zeroing in on a small geographic area, targeting a group of customers with similar needs or interests (e.g., left-handed people), specializing in a specific product or service (e.g., Batteries Plus Bulbs, a store that sells and services every kind of battery and bulb imaginable), or selling specialized knowledge (e.g., restoring valuable and priceless works of art).

Because of their size and agility, small companies are particularly well suited for serving niche markets that are part of the long tail. The most successful focusers build a competitive edge by concentrating on specific market niches and serving them better than competitors—even powerful giants—can. Norm Brodsky, a highly successful serial entrepreneur, says that small companies can develop close relationships with their customers. He stresses that they can be much more nimble and react more quickly than their larger competitors, which often take a cookie-cutter approach to running their portfolio of stores.[62]

A focus strategy depends on creating value for customers either by being the lowest-cost producer or by differentiating the product or service in a unique fashion but doing it in a narrow target segment. To be worth targeting, a niche must be large enough to be profitable, reachable with marketing media, and capable of sustaining a business over time (i.e., not a passing fad). Many small companies operate quite successfully in small, yet profitable, niches.

Market niches do not have to be glamorous to be profitable. Joshua Opperman lost a fiancée, but discovered a market need and a simple business model to exploit it. When his fiancée called off their marriage, he tried to sell the engagement ring he had purchased back to the jeweler. When the store only offered him just $3,500 for a ring he paid $10,000 for just a few months earlier, he started his company, I Do, Now I Don't, to help people to sell engagement rings and other jewelry with a system that works like Craigslist. The company facilitates more than 150 transactions a month, taking a 15 percent commission on all successful sales through its Web site.[63]

Although it can be a highly profitable strategy, pursuing a focus strategy is not without risks. Companies sometimes struggle to capture a large enough share of a small market to be profitable. If a small company is successful in a niche, there is also the danger of larger competitors entering the market and eroding it. Entrepreneurs following this strategy often face a constant struggle to keep costs down; the small volume of business that some niches support pushes production costs upward, making a company vulnerable to lower-cost competitors as their prices spiral higher. Sometimes a company with a successful niche strategy gets distracted by its success and tries to branch out into other

Joshua Opperman, Founder and CEO of I Do Now I Don't

areas. As it drifts farther away from its core strategy, it loses its competitive edge and runs the risk of confusing or alienating its customers. Muddying its image with customers puts a company in danger of losing its identity.

Step 8. Translate Strategic Plans into Action Plans

No strategic plan is complete until it is put into action; planning a company's strategy and implementing it go hand in hand. Entrepreneurs must convert strategic plans into operating plans that guide their companies on a daily basis and become a visible, active part of the business. No small business can benefit from a strategic plan sitting on a shelf collecting dust. Unfortunately, failure to implement a strategy effectively is a common problem. The lesson is that even sound strategies, unless properly implemented, will fail.

EXECUTING THE STRATEGY Research by Mark Huselid, Brian Becker, and Richard Beatty shows that proper execution of a company's strategy accounts for 85 percent of a company's financial performance.[64] Implementing a strategy successfully requires both a process that fits a company's culture and the right people committed to making that process work. Getting the right people in place starts with the selection process but includes every other aspect of the human resources function—from job design and training to motivational methods and compensation. To make their strategic plans workable, entrepreneurs should divide them into projects, carefully defining each one by the following:

Purpose. What is the project designed to accomplish?

Scope. Which areas of the company will be involved in the project?

Contribution. How does the project relate to other projects and to the overall strategic plan?

Resource requirements. What human and financial resources are needed to complete the project successfully?

Timing. Which schedules and deadlines will ensure project completion?

Once entrepreneurs assign priorities to projects, they can begin to implement the strategic plan. Involving employees and delegating adequate authority to them is essential because these projects affect them most directly. If an organization's people have been involved in the strategic management process to this point, they will have a better grasp of the steps they must take to achieve the organization's goals as well as their own professional goals. Early involvement of the workforce in the strategic management process is a luxury that larger businesses cannot achieve. Commitment to reaching the company's objectives is a powerful force, but involvement is a prerequisite for achieving total employee commitment. The greater the level of involvement of those who will implement a company's strategy (often those at the lower levels of an organization) in the process of creating the strategy (often the realm of those at the top of an organization), the more likely the strategy is to be successful. Without a team of committed, dedicated employees, a company's strategy, no matter how precisely planned, usually fails.

Step 9. Establish Accurate Controls

So far, the planning process has created company objectives and has developed a strategy for reaching them, but rarely, if ever, will the company's actual performance match stated objectives. Entrepreneurs quickly realize the need to control actual results that deviate from plans.

CONTROLLING THE STRATEGY Planning without control has little operational value; therefore, a sound planning program requires a practical control process. The plans and objectives created in the strategic planning process become the standards against which actual performance is measured. It is important for everyone in the organization to understand—and to be involved in— the planning and controlling process. Unless entrepreneurs measure progress against the goals and objectives established in step 6, their companies make little progress toward accomplishing them.

Controlling plans and projects and keeping them on schedule means that an entrepreneur must identify and track key performance indicators. The source of these indicators is the operating data from the company's normal business activity; they are the guideposts for detecting deviations from established standards. Financial, production, sales, inventory, quality, customer service and satisfaction, and other operating records are primary sources of data managers can use to control activities. For example, on a customer service project, performance indicators might include the number of customer complaints, the number of orders returned, the percentage of on-time shipments, and a measure of order accuracy.

The most commonly used indicators of a company's performance are financial measures; however, judging a company's performance solely on the basis of financial measures can lead to strategic myopia. To judge the effectiveness of their strategies, many companies are developing **balanced scorecards**, a set of multidimensional measurements that are unique to a company and that incorporate both financial and operational measures to give managers a quick yet comprehensive picture of the company's overall performance. As one writer explains, a balanced scorecard

> is a sophisticated business model that helps a company understand what's really driving its success. It acts a bit like the control panel on a spaceship—the business equivalent of a flight speedometer, odometer, and temperature gauge all rolled into one. It keeps track of many things, including financial progress and softer measurements—everything from customer satisfaction to return on investment—that need to be managed to reach the final destination: profitable growth.[65]

Rather than sticking solely to the traditional financial measures of a company's performance, the balanced scorecard gives managers a comprehensive view from *both* a financial and an operational perspective. The premise behind such a scorecard is that relying on any single measure of company performance is dangerous. Just as a pilot in command of a jet cannot fly safely by focusing on a single instrument, an entrepreneur cannot manage a company by concentrating on a single measurement. The complexity of managing a business demands that an entrepreneur be able to see performance measures in several areas simultaneously. "Knowing whether an enterprise is viable or not doesn't mean looking at just the bottom line," says one manager.[66] Scoreboards that combine relevant results from all aspects of the operation allow everyone in the organization to see how their job performance connects to a company's mission, goals, and objectives.

When creating balanced scorecards for their companies, entrepreneurs should create meaningful measures for each mission-related objective they established in step 6. If used properly, a balanced scorecard serves as a call to action. When a key indicator is out of control, everyone in the company knows it and can work together to do something about it quickly. The keys to using scorecards successfully are making sure that the measures included are important to the company's success and that each one tells a different story.

ENTREPRENEURIAL PROFILE: Alex Phinn: Griff Paper and Film Alex Phinn, president of Griff Paper and Film, a maker of protective films, silicone-coated liners, and specialty labeling materials, looks over his company's balanced scorecard with his morning cup of coffee. Rather than use one of the many balanced scorecard software packages available, Phinn designed his own scorecard. His one-page report includes operating data such as new orders received, the number of quotations submitted to potential customers (both measures of future sales), the number of customer complaints, employee absentee rates (both quality indicators), and financial data, such as daily accounts receivables, accounts payables, and cash balances. Phinn's easy-to-use scorecard gives him and his employees the ability to spot problem areas and positive trends in the company quickly.[67] ■

Ideally, a balanced scorecard looks at a business from five important perspectives (see Figure 5.6).[68]

CUSTOMER PERSPECTIVE How do customers see us? Customers judge companies by at least four standards: time (how long it takes the company to deliver a good or service), quality (how well a company's product or service performs in terms of reliability, durability, and accuracy), performance (the extent to which a good or service performs as expected), and service (how well a company meets or exceeds customers' expectations of value). Because customer-related goals

---

balanced scorecards
a set of multidimensional measurements that are unique to a company and that incorporate both financial and operational measures to give managers a quick but comprehensive picture of a company's performance.

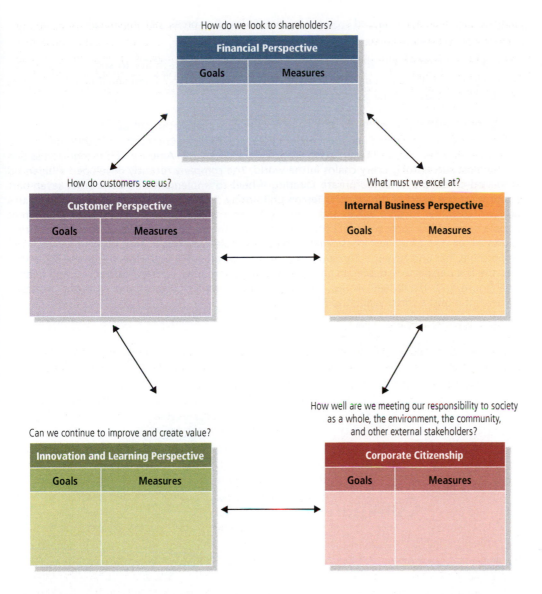

FIGURE 5.6

The Balanced Scorecard Links Performance Measures

Source: Robert S. Kaplan and David P. Norton, "The Balanced Scorecard—Measures That Drive Performance," *Harvard Business Review*, January–February 1992, pp. 71–79.

are external, managers must translate them into measures of what the company must do to meet customers' expectations.

INTERNAL BUSINESS PERSPECTIVE At what must we excel? The internal factors on which managers should focus are those that have the greatest impact on customer satisfaction and retention and on company effectiveness and efficiency. Developing goals and measures for factors such as quality, cycle time, productivity, cost control, and others that employees directly influence is essential.

INNOVATION AND LEARNING PERSPECTIVE Can we continue to improve and create value? This view of a company recognizes that the targets required for success are never static; they are constantly changing. If a company wants to continue its pattern of success, it cannot stand still; it must continuously innovate and improve. Employee training and development are essential ingredients of this component. A company's ability to innovate, learn, and improve determines its future. These goals and measures emphasize the importance of continuous improvement in customer satisfaction and internal business operations.

FINANCIAL PERSPECTIVE How do we look to shareholders? The most traditional performance measures, financial standards, tell how much the company's overall strategy and its execution are contributing to its bottom line. These measures focus on such factors as profitability, growth, and shareholder value. On balanced scorecards, companies often break their financial goals into three categories: survival, success, and growth.

CORPORATE CITIZENSHIP How well are we meeting our responsibility to society as a whole, the environment, the community, and other external stakeholders? Even small companies must recognize that they must be good business citizens.

ENTREPRENEURIAL PROFILE: Tesco's Corporate Steering Wheel Tesco is a chain of nearly 5,400 food and general merchandise stores based in Cheshunt, Hertfordshire, United Kingdom, that operates in 14 markets in Europe, Asia, and North America. It is recognized as one of the most successful grocery chains in the world. The company recently developed a balanced scorecard called the Tesco Corporate Steering Wheel to implement and control its seven-part strategy. At the heart of the wheel is Tesco's philosophy, "Every little bit helps." Surrounding this are two customer-focused values statements ("No one tries harder for customers" and "Treat people how we like to be treated") that drive the way the company does business. The next ring shows 20 areas in which Tesco has developed specific objectives (e.g., "earn lifetime loyalty," "be responsible, fair and honest," "grow sales," "an interesting job," and others) that are separated into the five perspectives described earlier: customer, community, operations, people, and finance (see Figure 5.7). The Wheel works; Tesco's sales increased 31 percent, and its profit increased 36 percent in just a three-year period.[69] ■

FIGURE 5.7

Corporate Steering Wheel, an Application of the Balanced Scorecard

Source: Based on *Delivering Success: How Tesco Is Managing, Measuring, and Maximizing Its Performance,* Advanced Performance Institute, June 23, 2009, p. 4.

Although the balanced scorecard is a vital tool that helps managers keep their companies on track, it is also an important tool for changing behavior in an organization and for keeping everyone focused on what really matters. Used properly, balanced scorecards allow managers to see how actions in each of the five dimensions of performance influence actions in the others. As competitive conditions and results change, managers can use the balanced scorecard to make corrections in plans, policies, strategies, and objectives to get performance back on track. A practical control system is also economical to operate. Most small businesses have no need for a sophisticated, expensive control system. The system should be so practical that it becomes a natural part of the management process.

Conclusion

A solid business plan is essential to raising the capital needed to start a business; lenders and investors demand it. "There may be no easier way for an entrepreneur to sabotage his or her request for capital than by failing to produce a comprehensive, well-researched, and, above all, credible business plan," says one small business expert.[70] Creating a successful business requires entrepreneurs to put the plan into action and then manage the company's growth with a sound strategic plan.

The strategic planning process does *not* end with the nine steps outlined here; it is an ongoing procedure entrepreneurs must repeat. With each round, managers and employees gain experience, and the steps become easier. The planning process described here is designed to be simple. No small business should be burdened with an elaborate, detailed formal planning process it cannot easily use. Some planning processes require excessive amounts of time to operate and generate a sea of paperwork. Entrepreneurs need neither.

What does this strategic planning process lead to? It teaches business owners a degree of discipline that is important to business survival. It helps them learn about their businesses, their core competencies, their competitors, and, most important, their customers. Although strategic planning cannot guarantee success, it does dramatically increase a small company's chances of survival in a hostile business environment.

Sample Business Plan Outline

Although every company's business plan will be unique, reflecting its individual circumstances, certain elements are universal. The following outline summarizes these components.

I. Executive Summary (not to exceed one page)
   A. Company name, address, and phone number
   B. Name(s), addresses, and phone number(s) of all key people
   C. Brief description of the business, its products and services, the customer problems they solve, and the company's competitive advantage
   D. Brief overview of the market for your products and services
   E. Brief overview of the strategies that will make your company successful
   F. Brief description of the managerial and technical experience of key people
   G. Brief statement of the financial request and how the money will be used
   H. Charts or tables showing highlights of financial forecasts

II. Vision and Mission Statement
   A. Entrepreneur's vision for the company
   B. "What business are we in?"
   C. Values and principles on which the business stands
   D. What makes the business unique? What is the source of its competitive advantage?

III. Company History (for existing businesses only)
   A. Company founding
   B. Financial and operational highlights
   C. Significant achievements

IV. Company Products and Services
    A. Description
        1. Product or service features
        2. Customer benefits
        3. Warranties and guarantees
        4. Unique Selling Proposition (USP)
    B. Patent or trademark protection
    C. Description of production process (if applicable)
        1. Raw materials
        2. Costs
        3. Key suppliers
        4. Lead times
    D. Future product or service offerings

V. Industry Profile and Overview
    A. Industry analysis
        1. Industry background and overview
        2. Significant trends
        3. Growth rate
        4. Barriers to entry and exit
        5. Key success factors in the industry
    B. Outlook for the future
    C. Stage of growth (start-up, growth, maturity)

VI. Competitor Analysis
    A. Existing competitors
        1. Who are they? Create a competitive profile matrix.
        2. Strengths
        3. Weaknesses
    B. Potential competitors: Companies that might enter the market
        1. Who are they?
        2. Impact on your business if they enter

VII. Business Strategy
    A. Desired image and position in market
    B. Company goals and objectives
        1. Operational
        2. Financial
        3. Other
    C. SWOT analysis
        1. Strengths
        2. Weaknesses
        3. Opportunities
        4. Threats
    D. Competitive strategy
        1. Cost leadership
        2. Differentiation
        3. Focus

VIII. Marketing Strategy
    A. Target market
        1. Problem to be solved or benefit to be offered
        2. Demographic profile
        3. Other significant customer characteristics
    B. Customers' motivation to buy
    C. Market size and trends
        1. How large is the market?
        2. Is it growing or shrinking? How fast?

    D. Personal selling efforts
       1. Sales force size, recruitment, and training
       2. Sales force compensation
       3. Number of calls per sale
       4. Amount of average sale
    E. Advertising and promotion
       1. Media used (reader, viewer, listener profiles)
       2. Media costs
       3. Frequency of usage
       4. Plans for generating publicity
    F. Pricing
       1. Cost structure
         a. Fixed
         b. Variable
       2. Desired image in market
       3. Comparison against competitors' prices
       4. Discounts
       5. Gross profit margin
    G. Distribution strategy (if applicable)
       1. Channels of distribution used
       2. Sales techniques and incentives for intermediaries
    H. Test market results
       1. Surveys
       2. Customer feedback on prototypes
       3. Focus groups

IX. Location and Layout
    A. Location
       1. Demographic analysis of location vs. target customer profile
       2. Traffic count
       3. Lease/rental rates
       4. Labor needs and supply
       5. Wage rates
    B. Layout
       1. Size requirements
       2. Americans with Disabilities Act compliance
       3. Ergonomic issues
       4. Layout plan (suitable for an appendix)

X. Description of management team
    A. Key managers and employees
       1. Their backgrounds
       2. Experience, skills, and know-how they bring to the company
    B. Résumés of key managers and employees (suitable for an appendix)
    C. Future additions to management team
    D. Board of directors or advisers

XI. Plan of Operation
    A. Form of ownership chosen and reasoning
    B. Company structure (organization chart)
    C. Decision-making authority
    D. Compensation and benefits packages
    E. Staffing plans

XII. Financial Forecasts (suitable for an appendix)
    A. Key assumptions
    B. Financial statements (year 1 by month, years 2 and 3 by quarter)

           1. Income statement
           2. Balance sheet
           3. Cash flow statement
       C. Break-even analysis
       D. Ratio analysis with comparison to industry standards (most applicable to existing businesses)

    XIII. Loan or Investment Proposal
       A. Amount requested
       B. Purpose and uses of funds
       C. Repayment or "cash out" schedule (exit strategy)
       D. Timetable for implementing plan and launching the business

    XIV. Appendices (Supporting documentation, including market research, financial statements, organization charts, résumés, and other items)

Chapter Summary by Learning Objective

1. Explain the benefits of an effective business plan.

- A business plan, which builds off of information from the feasibility analysis and business model, serves two essential functions. First and more important, it guides the company's operations by charting its future course and devising a strategy for following it. The second function of the business plan is to attract lenders and investors. Applying for loans or attempting to attract investors without a solid business plan rarely attracts needed capital. Rather, the best way to secure the necessary capital is to prepare a sound business plan.

- An effective business plan should pass these three tests:

  - Reality test. The external component of the reality test revolves around proving that a market for the product or service really does exist. The internal component of the reality test focuses on the product or service itself.

  - Competitive test. The external part of the competitive test evaluates the company's relative position to its key competitors. The internal competitive test focuses on the management team's ability to create a company that will gain an edge over existing rivals.

  - Value test. To convince lenders and investors to put their money into the venture, a business plan must prove to them that it offers a high probability of repayment or an attractive rate of return.

2. Describe the elements of a solid business plan.

- Although a business plan should be unique and tailor-made to suit the particular needs of a small company, it should cover these basic elements: executive summary, mission statement, company history, business and industry profile, description of the company's business strategy, profile of its products or services, statement explaining its marketing strategy, competitor analysis, owners' and officers' résumés, plan of operation, financial data, and loan or investment proposal.

3. Explain the "five Cs of credit" and why they are important to potential lenders and investors reviewing business plans.

- Small business owners need to be aware of the criteria bankers use in evaluating the creditworthiness of loan applicants, known as the *five Cs of credit*: capital, capacity, collateral, character, and conditions.

- Capital—Lenders expect small businesses to have an equity base of investment by the owner(s) that will help support the venture during times of financial strain.

- Capacity—A synonym for capacity is cash flow. The bank must be convinced of the firm's ability to meet its regular financial obligations and to repay the bank loan, and that takes cash.

- Collateral—Collateral includes any assets the owner pledges to the bank as security for repayment of the loan.

- Character—Before approving a loan to a small business, the banker must be satisfied with the owner's character.

- Conditions—The conditions–interest rates, the health of the nation's economy, industry growth rates, etc.—surrounding a loan request also affect the owner's chance of receiving funds.

4. Understand the keys to making an effective business plan presentation.

- Entrepreneurs who are informed and prepared when requesting a loan or investment favorably impress lenders and investors.

- Tips include: Demonstrate enthusiasm about the venture, but don't be overemotional; "hook" investors quickly with an up-front explanation of the new venture, its opportunities, and the anticipated benefits to them; use visual aids; hit the highlights of your venture; don't get caught up in too much detail in early meetings with lenders and investors; avoid the use of technological terms that will likely be above most of the audience; rehearse your presentation before giving it; close by reinforcing the nature of the opportunity; and be prepared for questions.

5. Understand the importance of strategic management to a small business.

- Companies without clear strategies may achieve some success in the short run, but as soon as a competitive threat arises, they often fail.

6. Explain why and how a small business must create a competitive advantage in the market.

- The goal of developing a strategic plan is to create for the small company a competitive advantage—the combination of factors that sets the small business apart from its competitors and gives it a unique position in the market.

- Every small firm must establish a plan for creating a unique image in the minds of its potential customers.

- A company builds a competitive edge on its core competencies, which are a unique set of capabilities that a company develops in key operational areas, such as quality, service, innovation, team building, flexibility, responsiveness, and others, that allow it to vault past competitors. They are what the company does best and are the focal point of the strategy. This step must identify target market segments and determine how to position the firm in those markets.

- Entrepreneurs must identify some way to differentiate their companies from competitors.

7. Develop a strategic plan for a business using the nine steps in the strategic management process.

- Small businesses need a strategic planning process designed to suit their particular needs. It should be relatively short, be informal and not structured, encourage the participation of employees, and not begin with extensive objective setting.

- Linking the purposeful action of strategic planning to an entrepreneur's little ideas can produce results that shape the future.

- **Step 1.** Develop a clear vision and translate it into a meaningful mission statement. Highly successful entrepreneurs communicate their vision to those around them. The firm's mission statement answers the first question of any venture: What business am I in? The mission statement sets the tone for the entire company.

- **Step 2.** Assess the company's strengths and weaknesses. Strengths are positive internal factors; weaknesses are negative internal factors.

- **Step 3.** Scan the environment for significant opportunities and threats facing the business. Opportunities are positive external options; threats are negative external forces.

- **Step 4.** Identify the key factors for success in the business. In every business, key factors determine the success of the firms in it, so they must be an integral part of a company's strategy. KSFs are relationships between a controllable variable and a critical factor influencing the firm's ability to compete in the market.

- **Step 5.** Analyze the competition. Business owners should know their competitors almost as well as they know their own. A competitive profile matrix is a helpful tool for analyzing competitors' strengths and weaknesses.

- **Step 6.** Create company goals and objectives. Goals are the broad, long-range attributes that the firm seeks to accomplish. Objectives are quantifiable and more precise; they should be specific, measurable, assignable, realistic, timely, and written down. The process works best when managers and employees are actively involved.

- **Step 7.** Formulate strategic options and select the appropriate strategies. A strategy is the game plan the firm plans to use to achieve its objectives and mission. It must center on establishing for the firm the KSFs identified earlier.

- **Step 8.** Translate strategic plans into action plans. No strategic plan is complete until the owner puts it into action.

- **Step 9.** Establish accurate controls. Actual performance rarely, if ever, matches plans exactly. Operating data from the business assembled into a comprehensive scorecard serves as an important guidepost for determining how effective a company's strategy is. This information is especially helpful when plotting future strategies.

- The strategic planning process does not end with these nine steps; rather, it is an ongoing process that an entrepreneur will repeat.

- The three basic strategies a business can pursue are low cost, differentiation, and focus.
- Controls are essential for the effective implementation of a strategic plan. A balanced scorecard is a set of measurements unique to a company that includes both financial and operational measures and gives managers a quick yet comprehensive picture of the company's total performance.

Discussion Questions

5-1. Why should an entrepreneur develop a business plan?

5-2. Why do entrepreneurs who are not seeking external financing need to prepare business plans?

5-3. Describe the major components of a business plan.

5-4. How can an entrepreneur seeking funds to launch a business convince potential lenders and investors that a market for the product or service really does exist?

5-5. What are the 5 Cs of credit?

5-6. How do lenders and investors use the 5 Cs of credit when evaluating a request for financing?

5-7. How would you prepare to make a formal presentation of your business plan to a venture capital forum?

5-8. Why is strategic planning important to a small company?

5-9. What is a competitive advantage?

5-10. Why is a competitive advantage important for a small business to establish one?

5-11. What are the steps in the strategic management process?

5-12. A common criticism of mission statements is that entrepreneurs spend too much time crafting them and not enough time implementing them in the business. What is meant by this criticism?

5-13. Discuss the importance of what you do with a mission statement.

5-14. What are strengths, weaknesses, opportunities, and threats?

5-15. Give an example of strengths, weaknesses, opportunities, and threats.

5-16. Explain the characteristics of effective objectives.

5-17. Why is setting objectives important?

5-18. What are business strategies?

5-19. Describe the three basic strategies available to small companies.

5-20. Under what conditions is each of the three basic strategies most successful?

5-21. Explain how a company can gain a competitive advantage using each of the three strategies described in this chapter: cost leadership, differentiation, and focus.

5-22. Give an example of a company that is using each of the three strategies.

5-23. How is the controlling process related to the planning process?

5-24. What is a balanced scorecard?

5-25. What value does a balanced scorecard offer entrepreneurs who are evaluating the success of their current strategies?

Beyond the Classroom . . .

5-26. Contact the owner of a small business that competes directly with an industry giant, such as Home Depot, Wal-Mart, or Barnes & Noble.

5-27. What does the owner see as his or her competitive advantage?

5-28. How does the business communicate this competitive advantage to its customers?

5-29. What competitive strategy is the owner using?

5-30. How successful is the competitive strategy?

5-31. What changes would you suggest the owner make?

5-32. In his book *The HP Way*, Dave Packard, cofounder of Hewlett-Packard, describes the seven commitments of the HP Way:

- Profit—the ultimate source of corporate strength.
- Customers—constant improvement in the value of the products and services the company offers them.
- Field of interest—seeking new opportunities but limiting them to complementary products and services based on company core competencies.
- Growth—a measure of strength and a requirement for survival.
- Employees—provide opportunities for advancement, share in their success, and offer job security based on performance.
- Organization—foster individual motivation, initiative, and creativity by giving employees the

freedom to work toward established goals and objectives.

- Citizenship—contribute in a positive way toward the community and society at large.

In what ways do these values help HP define its vision?

5-33. In what way do these values help HP define its competitive edge?

5-34. How important is it for entrepreneurs to define a system of values to guide their companies?

5-35. Contact a local entrepreneur and help him or her devise a balanced scorecard for his or her company.

5-36. What goals did you and the owner establish in each of the four perspectives?

5-37. What measures did you use to judge progress of the owner toward those goals?

5-38. Use the strategic tools provided in this chapter to help a local small business owner discover his or her firm's strengths, weaknesses, opportunities, and threats.

5-39. Use the strategic tools provided in this chapter to help identify the relevant KSFs.

5-40. Use the strategic tools provided in this chapter to help analyze its competitors.

5-41. Help the owner devise a strategy for success for his or her business.

5-42. Choose an entrepreneur in your community and interview him or her.

5-43. Does the company have a strategic plan?

5-44. Does the company have a mission statement?

5-45. Explain why the company does or does not have a mission statement.

5-46. What does the owner consider the company's strengths and weaknesses to be?

5-47. What opportunities and threats does the owner perceive?

5-48. What image is the owner trying to create for the business?

5-49. Has the effort been successful?

5-50. Do you agree with the owner's assessment of its effectiveness?

5-51. Which of the generic competitive strategies is the company following?

5-52. Who are the company's primary competitors?

5-53. How does the owner rate his or her chances for success in the future using a low [1] to high [10] scale?

5-54. Compare your evaluation with other classmates.

5-55. What, if any, generalizations can you draw from the interview?

Endnotes

Scan for Endnotes or go to www.pearsonhighered.com/scarborough

6 Forms of Business Ownership and Buying an Existing Business

MachineHeadz/Getty Images, Inc.

Learning Objectives

On completion of this chapter, you will be able to:

1. Explain the advantages and disadvantages of a sole proprietorship and a partnership.

2. Describe the similarities and differences of the C corporation and the S corporation.

3. Understand the characteristics of the limited liability company.

4. Explain the process of creating a legal entity for a business.

5. Understand the advantages and disadvantages of buying an existing business.

6. Define the steps involved in the *right* way to buy a business.

7. Understand how the negotiation process works and identify the factors that affect it.

Once an entrepreneur makes the decision to launch a business, one of the first issues he or she faces is choosing a form of ownership. Too often, entrepreneurs invest insufficient time and effort evaluating the impact that the various forms of ownership will have on them and on their businesses. They simply select a form of ownership by default or choose the form that appears to be most popular at the time. Choosing a form of ownership is a decision that has far-reaching effects for both the entrepreneur and the business. Although the decision is not irreversible, changing from one ownership form to another can be difficult, time consuming, complicated, and expensive. In many instances, switching an existing business from one form of ownership to another can trigger onerous tax consequences for the owners. Therefore, it is important for entrepreneurs to get it right the first time.

There is no one "best" form of ownership. The form of ownership that is best for one entrepreneur may not be suitable for another. Choosing the "right" form of ownership means that entrepreneurs must understand the characteristics of each form and how well those characteristics match their business and personal circumstances. Only then can they make an informed decision about a form of ownership. One attorney advises that entrepreneurs should choose a structure that offers them protection, while being only as complex as their business will really need.[1] The following are some of the most important issues entrepreneurs should consider when they are evaluating the various forms of ownership:

Tax considerations. The amount of net income an entrepreneur expects the business to generate and the tax bill the owner must pay are important factors when choosing a form of ownership. The graduated tax rates that apply to each form of ownership, the government's constant tinkering with the tax code, and the year-to-year fluctuations in a company's income make some forms of ownership more attractive than others.

Liability exposure. Certain forms of ownership offer business owners greater protection from personal liability that might result from financial problems, faulty products, lawsuits, and a host of other difficulties. Entrepreneurs must decide the extent to which they are willing to assume personal responsibility for their companies' financial obligations. Two entrepreneurs who started a company with a portable climbing wall formed a limited liability company to limit their personal liability exposure because of the high-risk nature of their business.

Start-up and future capital requirements. Forms of ownership differ in their ability to raise start-up capital. Depending on how much capital an entrepreneur needs and where he or she plans to get it, some forms are superior to others. In addition, as a business grows, so does its appetite for capital, and some forms of ownership make it easier to attract external growth capital than others.

Control. By choosing certain forms of ownership, an entrepreneur automatically gives up some control over the company. Entrepreneurs must decide early on how much control they are willing to sacrifice in exchange for help from other people to build a successful business.

Managerial ability. Entrepreneurs must assess their skills and abilities to manage a business effectively. If they lack ability or experience in key areas, they may need to choose a form of ownership that allows them to bring in other owners who can provide the necessary skills for the company to succeed.

Business goals. How big and how profitable an entrepreneur plans for the business to become influences the form of ownership chosen. Businesses often switch forms of ownership as they grow, but moving from some formats to others can be extremely complex and expensive.

Management succession plans. When choosing a form of ownership, business owners must look ahead to the day when they will pass their companies on to the next generation or to a buyer. Some forms of ownership make this transition much easier than others.

Cost of formation. Some forms of ownership are much more costly and involved to create. Entrepreneurs must weigh carefully the benefits and the costs of the particular form they choose.

When it comes to organizing their businesses, entrepreneurs have a wide choice of forms of ownership, including a sole proprietorship, a general partnership, a limited partnership, a corporation, an S corporation, and a limited liability company. Figure 6.1 provides a breakdown of

FIGURE 6.1

**Forms of Business
Ownership.
(A) Percentage
of Businesses;
(B) Percentage
of Sales;
(C) Percentage
of Net Income**

Source: Based on data from
Sources of Income, Internal
Revenue Service.

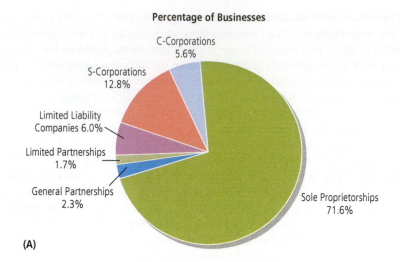

Percentage of Businesses

C-Corporations
5.6%

S-Corporations
12.8%

Limited Liability
Companies 6.0%

Limited Partnerships
1.7%

General Partnerships
2.3%

Sole Proprietorships
71.6%

(A)

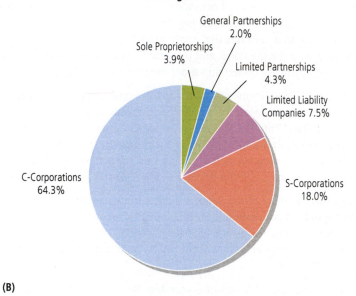

Percentage of Sales

General Partnerships
2.0%

Sole Proprietorships
3.9%

Limited Partnerships
4.3%

Limited Liability
Companies 7.5%

C-Corporations
64.3%

S-Corporations
18.0%

(B)

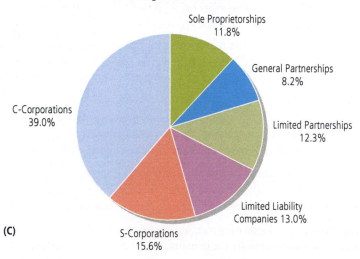

Percentage of Net Income

Sole Proprietorships
11.8%

General Partnerships
8.2%

Limited Partnerships
12.3%

C-Corporations
39.0%

Limited Liability
Companies 13.0%

S-Corporations
15.6%

(C)

these forms of ownership. Notice that sole proprietorships account for the greatest percentage of businesses, but corporations generate the largest portion of business sales. This chapter discusses the key features of these various forms of ownership, beginning with the three most basic forms (from simplest to most complex): the sole proprietorship, the partnership, and the corporation.

Hands On . . . How To

Come Up with the Perfect Moniker for Your Business

Dan Loh/Associated Press

Eminem, known for being hard-core and controversial, is a top rap artist. However, even with this persona, would he still sell out concerts if he performed under the name Marshall Bruce Mathers, III, his real name? Perhaps. However, Eminem's stage name is an important part of his brand and his marketing success. Similarly, choosing the right name for a company can enhance its success by creating the proper image and telling customers what it does. A good business name should do the following:

- Reinforce the company's brand positioning. A good name communicates to potential customers something about the brand's personality. For example, Twitter conjures up images of a flock of birds twittering in a tree or excitement over some event ("all atwitter"), both of which reinforce the company's purpose: allowing users to share short bursts of information about their lives.

- Resonate with the company's target audience. PayPal puts a warm and friendly image on a product that simply aids financial transactions on the web. This image helps to build trust and confidence among the businesses and customers who make payments over the Internet.

- Suggest to customers what your company does. The name Under Armour suggests that its sportswear products protect the person wearing them and conveys an image of being strong, which is very appealing to its target market of people who are active and physically fit.

- Be clever and differentiate your company from its competitors. For example, Tequila Mockingbird (Mexican restaurant), Sherlock Homes (locksmith), Planet of the Grapes (wine store), Florist Gump (flower shop), Curl Up & Dye (hair salon), Character Eyes (optometrist) and Pita Pan (sandwich shop) are all examples of small business names that are clever and memorable!

- Be short, fun, attention getting, and memorable. Not only is Google fun to say, but it is also quite memorable. Naming experts say a great name has "emotional hang time," a football metaphor to describe a name that stays in your mind.

- Be easy to spell and pronounce. This is especially important for companies that operate solely online because their names often serve as the URLs for their Web sites. "Wikipedia" works, but "Eefoof," a failed video-sharing site, did not.

- Grow with your business. When choosing a name, it is a good idea to keep an eye on the future. Many entrepreneurs select names for their businesses that can be limiting as their companies grow beyond their existing product lines, geographic areas, and target markets. Apple Computer moved beyond computers as its only product line with the introduction of its iPhone. With the announcement of the first iPhone, Steve Jobs also announced that Apple Computer was changing its name to Apple. Revenues of iPhones and iPads both outpace revenues from Apple's computers.

Choosing a memorable name can be one of the most fun—and most challenging—aspects of starting a business. It also is an extremely important task because it has long-term implications, is the single most visible attribute of a company, and has the capacity to either engage or repel customers. The business name is the first connection that many customers will have with a company, and it should create an appropriate image in their minds. The president of one small design firm specializing in branding says a company name is the cornerstone for branding. If done properly, a company's name portrays the business's personality, stands out in a crowd, and sticks in the minds of consumers. Large companies may spend hundreds of thousands of dollars in their search for just the right name. Although entrepreneurs don't have the resources to enable them to spend that kind of money finding the ideal name, they can use the following process to come up with the perfect name for their businesses:

1. Decide on the image you want your company to project to customers, suppliers, bankers, the press, the community,

(continued)

Hands On . . . How To (continued)

and others. Do you want to create an air of sophistication, the suggestion of a bargain, a sense of adventure, the implication of trustworthiness and dependability, or a spirit of fun and whimsy? The right name can go a long way toward communicating the right image for a company.

2. Make a list of your competitors' business names. The idea is *not* to borrow from their ideas but to try to come up with a name that is unique. Do you notice any trends among competitors' names? What are the similarities? What are the differences?

3. Work with a group of the most creative people you know to brainstorm potential names for your business. One entrepreneur called on 10 customers and 10 vendors to help him come up with a business name. Don't worry about quality at this point; the goal is to generate a large quantity of names—at least 100 potential names, if possible. Having a dictionary, a thesaurus, a rhyming dictionary, and samples (or graphics) of your company's products and services help to stimulate creativity. Consider names from unrelated sources that might be meaningful.

4. After allowing them to percolate for a few days, evaluate the names generated in the brainstorming session. Narrow the list of choices to 10 or so names with the greatest potential. Print each name in a large font on a single page and look at them. Which ones are visually appealing? Which ones lend themselves to being paired with a clever logo?

5. Reassemble your creative group, present each name you have printed, and discuss its merits and challenges. Having a designated person to record the group's comments helps. The group may come to a consensus on a preferred name; if not, you can use a round-by-round voting process to move the group toward a consensus.

6. Conduct a search at the U.S. Patent and Trademark Office Web site (www.uspto.gov) to see whether the leading names on your list are already registered trademarks for existing businesses. Remember, however, that the same name can be registered as a trademark as long as the product, service, or company's business does not overlap.

7. Conduct searches with domain name companies, such as GoDaddy.com, to see whether other businesses are using your desired business name as a domain name. When the founders of Emma, an e-mail marketing firm, searched for the availability of emma.com, they found that the name was already taken. They chose, instead, the domain myemma.com, but kept the name Emma for the business. Several years later. this resulted in a legal dispute with the company that owned the emma.com domain name.

8. Conduct a Google or Safari search to see whether other businesses conducting business within your intended market have the same or very similar names.

9. Make your choice. Including input from others is useful when selecting a business name, but the final choice is yours.

10. Register your company name with the U.S. Patent and Trademark Office. Doing so gives you maximum protection from others using the name you worked so hard to create. Diane Dassow thought she had the ideal name for her personal history and memoir service business in Lombard, Illinois: Bridging Generations. However, Dassow soon discovered a funeral home in Pennsylvania that was using that name. She checked with the U.S. Patent and Trademark Office and learned that the funeral home had already registered "Bridging Generations." She changed the name of her company to Binding Legacies and registered it as a trademark to protect her business.

Other helpful tips for creating the ideal business name include the following:

• Look at your name from your potential customer's perspective. Do customers need reassurance (Gentle Dentistry), or do they prefer a bit of humor (Barking Lot Dog Grooming)? Other options include using a name that conveys an image to your customers that expresses your business strategy, such as Tires Now, Quality Muffler, or Pay-Less Auto Detailing.

• Decide the most appropriate quality of your business that you want to convey and incorporate it into your business name. Avoid sending a mixed or inappropriate message. Avoid business names that might leave potential customers confused about what your business does. Remember that the company name will be displayed on all of your advertising, packaging, and printed materials.

There are millions of names in the marketplace. Coming up with the one that is just right for your business can help greatly in creating a brand image for your business. Choosing a name that is distinctive, memorable, and positive can go a long way toward helping you achieve success in your business venture. Naming experts at Landor, an international branding firm, say a name "acts as the primary handle for a brand; it's a recall and recognition device, it communicates desired attributes or specific benefits, and, through time and consistent use, it becomes a valuable asset and intellectual property." What's in a name? Everything!

Sources: Based on Denise Lee Yohn, "How to Name Your Concept (and Do It Right)," *QSR,* March 10, 2011, http://www.qsrmagazine.com/denise-lee-yohn/how-name-your-concept-and-do-it-right; Emily Maltby, "And Now, the Tricky Part: Naming Your Business," *Wall Street Journal,* http://online.wsj.com/article/SB100014240527 48704103904575336942902327092.html; Laurel Sutton, "10 Best and Worst Internet Company Names of the Decade," *Marketing Profs,* December 29, 2009, http://www.marketingprofs.com/articles/2009/3278/10-best-and-worst-internet-company-names-of-the-decade; Scott Trimble, "18 Strategies and Tools for Naming Your Business or Product," *Marketing Profs,* January 24, 2008, https://www.marketingprofs.com/login/join.asp?adref=rdblk&source=%2F8%2Fhow%2Dto%2Dname%2D products%2Dcompanies%2Dtrimble%2Easp; Alex Frankel, "The New Science of Naming," *Business 2.0,* December 2004, pp. 53–55; Jeff Wuorio, "'Oedipus Wrecks' and Other Business Names to Avoid," *bCentral,* www.bCentral.com/articles/wuorio/153.asp; and Suzanne Barlyn, "Name That Firm," *Wall Street Journal,* March 17, 2008, p. R7; "14 Clever Business Names You Just Want to Take Your Money," WildAmmo, October 12, 2013, http://wildammo.com/2013/10/12/14-clever-business-names-you-just-want-to-take-your-money/; "The Worst (and Best) Company Name Changes," *CNNMoney,* December 6, 2013, http://money.cnn.com/gallery/leadership/2013/12/06/worst-best-corporate-name-changes.fortune/2.html; Darren Dahl, "The Best (and Worst) Business Names," *AOL Small Business,* May 5, 2010, http://smallbusiness.aol.com/2010/05/10/the-best-and-worst-business-names/.

Sole Proprietorships and Partnerships

The Sole Proprietorship

The simplest and most popular form of ownership remains the **sole proprietorship**. The sole proprietorship, as its name implies, is a business owned and managed by one individual. Sole proprietorships make up about 72 percent of all businesses in the United States.

LO1

Explain the advantages and disadvantages of a sole proprietorship and a partnership.

sole proprietorship
a business owned and managed by one individual.

The Advantages of a Proprietorship

SIMPLE TO CREATE One of the most attractive features of a proprietorship is how fast and simple it is to begin. If an entrepreneur wants to operate a business under his or her own name (e.g., Strossner's Bakery), he or she simply obtains the necessary licenses from state, county, and/or local governments and begins operation. Entrepreneurs who operate a business under a trade name usually must file a certificate of trade name (or fictitious business name statement) with the secretary of state. Filing this statement notifies the public of the identity of the person behind the business. For most entrepreneurs, it is possible to start a proprietorship in a single day.

LEAST COSTLY FORM OF OWNERSHIP TO BEGIN In addition to being easy to begin, the proprietorship is generally the least expensive form of ownership to establish. There is no need to create and file legal documents that are recommended for partnerships and required for corporations. An entrepreneur simply goes to the city or county government, states the nature of the business he or she will start, and purchases the necessary business licenses. Businesses with employees (including sole proprietorships) must obtain from the Internal Revenue Service (IRS) (at no charge) an employer identification number, a nine-digit number that serves as the equivalent of a business Social Security number. In addition, companies that have employees may be required to register with the state labor department that administers the unemployment insurance and the workers' compensation programs. Businesses that sell goods or services must obtain a state sales tax license from the state tax office that allows them to collect sales tax from their customers and pass it on to the state department of revenue.

PROFIT INCENTIVE One major advantage of proprietorships is that once owners pay all of their companies' expenses, they can keep the remaining profits (less taxes, of course). The profit incentive is a powerful one, and profits represent an excellent way of "keeping score" in the game of the business. Sole proprietors report the net income of their businesses on Schedule C of IRS Form 1040, and the amount is taxed at the entrepreneur's personal tax rate. Because they are self-employed, sole proprietors' income from their business activities also is subject to the self-employment tax, which currently stands at 15.3 percent (12.4% for Social Security and 2.9% for Medicare program) of the proprietor's income. A ceiling on the Social Security portion of the self-employment tax does apply.

TOTAL DECISION-MAKING AUTHORITY Because the sole proprietor is in total control of operations, he or she can respond quickly to changes, which is an asset in a rapidly shifting market. The freedom to set the company's course of action is a major motivational force. For those who thrive on the challenge of seeking new opportunities in business, the freedom of fast, flexible decision making is vital. Many sole proprietors relish the feeling of control they have over their personal financial futures and the recognition they earn as the owners of their businesses.

NO SPECIAL LEGAL RESTRICTIONS The proprietorship is the least-regulated form of business ownership. In a time when government regulation seems never ending, this feature has much merit.

EASY TO DISCONTINUE If an entrepreneur decides to discontinue operations, he or she can terminate the business quickly even though he or she will still be personally liable for any outstanding debts and obligations the business cannot pay.

The Disadvantages of a Proprietorship

Entrepreneurs considering the sole proprietorship as a form of ownership also must be aware of its disadvantages.

unlimited personal liability
a situation in which the owner of a business is personally liable for all of the business's debts.

UNLIMITED PERSONAL LIABILITY Probably the greatest disadvantage of a sole proprietorship is the **unlimited personal liability** of the owner, meaning that the sole proprietor is personally liable for all of the business's debts. In a proprietorship, the owner *is* the business. He or she owns all of the business's assets, and if the business fails, creditors can force the sale of these assets to cover its debts. If unpaid business debts remain, creditors can also force the sale of the proprietor's *personal* assets to recover payment. In short, the *company's* debts are the *owner's* debts. Laws vary from one state to another, but most states require creditors to leave the failed business owner a minimum amount of equity in a home, a car, and some personal items. The reality is that failure of a business can ruin a sole proprietor financially.

Larry Kim, WordStream, Inc.

ENTREPRENEURIAL PROFILE: Larry Kim: WordStream Larry Kim launched WordStream in 2007 as a sole proprietorship. WordStream began as a keyword software tool developer for Web-based marketing. Kim said that early on he treated the business as if it were his own personal bank account. After paying for business expenses, Kim kept the rest of the money he made for his own personal expenses. He eventually realized that to grow his business, he needed to leave some funds in the business and pay himself a lower salary. The investment back into the business began to pay off in growth. He was able to add a partner and then begin to hire employees to take on the growing number of customers. WordStream has evolved from a sole proprietorship into a full-service paid search marketing company with more than 80 employees.[2] ∎

LIMITED SKILLS AND CAPABILITIES A sole proprietor has total decision-making authority, but that does not mean that he or she has the range of skills that running a successful business requires. Each of us has areas in which our education, training, and work experiences have taught us a great deal, yet there are other areas in which our decision-making ability is weak. Many business failures occur because owners lack the skills, knowledge, and experience in areas that are vital to business success. Owners tend to push aside problems they don't understand or don't feel comfortable with in favor of those they can solve more easily. Unfortunately, the problems they set aside seldom solve themselves. By the time an owner decides to ask for help in addressing these problems, it may be too late to save the company.

FEELINGS OF ISOLATION Running a business alone allows an entrepreneur maximum flexibility, but it also creates feelings of isolation; there is no one else to turn to for help when solving problems or getting feedback on a new idea. Most sole proprietors admit that there are times when they feel the pressure of being alone and completely responsible for every major business decision.

LIMITED ACCESS TO CAPITAL If a business is to grow and expand, a sole proprietor often needs additional financial resources. However, many proprietors have already put all of the resources they have into their businesses and have used their personal assets as collateral to acquire loans, making it difficult to borrow additional funds. A sole proprietorship is limited to whatever capital the owner can contribute and whatever money he or she can borrow. In short, proprietors find it difficult to raise additional money and maintain sole ownership. Most banks and other lending institutions have well-defined formulas for determining borrowers' eligibility. Unfortunately, many sole proprietors cannot meet those borrowing requirements, especially in the early days of business.

LACK OF CONTINUITY OF THE BUSINESS Lack of continuity is inherent in a sole proprietorship. If the proprietor dies, retires, or becomes incapacitated, the business automatically terminates. Unless a family member or employee can take over (which means that person is now a sole proprietor), the business will disappear. Because people look for secure employment and an opportunity for advancement, proprietorships often have trouble recruiting and retaining good employees. If no one is willing to step in to run the business in the founder's absence, creditors can petition the courts to liquidate the assets of the dissolved business to pay outstanding debts.

Some entrepreneurs find that forming partnerships is one way to overcome the disadvantages of the sole proprietorship. For instance, when one person lacks specific managerial skills or has insufficient access to needed capital, he or she can compensate for these weaknesses by forming a partnership with someone with complementary management skills or money to invest. In fact, businesses that have multiple owners (not necessarily partners) are more likely to be larger and to survive longer than sole proprietorships.[3]

The Partnership

A **partnership** is an association of two or more people who co-own a business for the purpose of making a profit. In a partnership, the co-owners (partners) share the business's assets, liabilities, and profits according to the terms of a previously established partnership agreement (if one exists).

partnership
an association of two or more people who co-own a business for the purpose of making a profit.

ENTREPRENEURIAL PROFILE: Tom Colicchio, Jeffrey Zurofsky, and Sisha Ortuzar: 'wichcraft Tom Colicchio, Jeffrey Zurofsky, and Sisha Ortuzar co-founded the first 'wichcraft sandwich shop in New York City in 2003. Colicchio, chef/owner of craft restaurant, celebrity chef, documentary producer, and former chef/partner of Gramercy Tavern in New York, has also been head judge on the reality television show "Top Chef." Before going into business together to launch 'wichcraft, the three partners had worked together in several fine dining restaurants, which formed the basis for 'wichcraft's culinary roots in sourcing, production, and service. 'wichcraft sources seasonal ingredients from local farms and was an early practitioner of the farm-to-table movement. The company works with local nonprofit organizations to employ inner-city kids as part of its commitment to the community. 'wichcraft has 15 locations in New York as well as locations in San Francisco and Las Vegas.[4] ■

'wichcraft

The law does not require a partnership agreement (also known as the articles of partnership), but it is wise to work with an attorney to develop one that spells out the exact status and responsibility of each partner. All too often, the parties think they know what they are agreeing to only to find later that no real meeting of the minds took place. A **partnership agreement** is a document that states in writing the terms under which the partners agree to operate the partnership and that protects each partner's interest in the business. Every partnership should be based on a written agreement. A partnership agreement helps focus the entrepreneurial energy of business partners in a common direction. A sound written agreement helps guide the partners through inevitable bumps in the road that every business partnership experiences from time to time.[5]

ENTREPRENEURIAL PROFILE: Ted Weitzel and Matthew Greer: Sawyer's Walk/Crosswinds Ted Weitzel, president of Indian River Investments of Miami, Inc., entered into a partnership agreement with Matthew Greer, CEO of affordable housing developer Carlisle Development Group, to develop new residential project in Miami's blighted Overtown neighborhood. Weitzel and Greer formed the partnership to develop Sawyer's Walk/Crosswinds in Overtown to help spur new development in an area that had become a virtual ghost town.[6] ■

partnership agreement
a document that states in writing the terms under which the partners agree to operate the partnership and that protects each partner's interest in the business.

The Revised Uniform Partnership Act

The Revised Uniform Partnership Act (RUPA) codifies the body of law dealing with partnerships in the United States. Under the RUPA, the three key elements of any partnership are common ownership interest in a business, agreement on how the business's profits and losses will be shared, and the right to participate in managing the operation of the partnership. Under the act, each partner has the *right* to do the following:

- Participate in the management and operations of the business
- Share in any profits the business might earn from operations
- Receive interest on loans made to the business
- Be compensated for expenses incurred in the name of the partnership

- Receive his or her original capital contributions if the partnership terminates
- Have access to the business's books and records
- Receive a formal accounting of the partnership's business affairs

The RUPA also sets forth the partners' general obligations. Each partner is *obligated* to do the following:

- Share in any losses sustained by the business
- Work for the partnership without salary
- Submit differences that may arise in the conduct of the business to majority vote or arbitration
- Give the other partners complete information about all business affairs
- Give a formal accounting of the partnership's business affairs
- Live up to a fiduciary responsibility of the partnership and place the interest of the partnership above his or her personal interests

Partnership Agreement

When no partnership agreement exists, the Revised Uniform Partnership Act governs a partnership. If a partnership agreement contains gaps in its coverage, the act will fill them. However, its provisions may not be as favorable as a specific agreement hammered out among the partners. Creating a partnership agreement is not necessarily costly. In most cases, the partners can discuss their preferences for each of the provisions in advance. Once they have reached an agreement, an attorney can draft the formal document. Bankers often want to see a copy of a partnership agreement before lending money to a partnership. Perhaps the most important feature of the partnership agreement is that it resolves potential sources of conflict that, if not addressed in advance, could later result in partnership battles and the dissolution of an otherwise successful business. Spelling out details—especially sticky ones such as profit splits, contributions, workloads, decision-making authority, dispute resolution, dissolution, and others—in a written agreement at outset helps to avoid damaging tension in a partnership that could lead to a business "divorce." Business divorces, like marital ones, are almost always costly and unpleasant for everyone involved.

David Gage, a partnership mediator, suggests that partners also create a "partnership charter," a document that serves as a guide for running the partnership and dealing with each other as business partners. Whereas a partnership agreement addresses the legal and business issues of running a business, a partnership charter covers the interpersonal aspects of the partners' relationships and serves as a helpful tool for managing the complexity of partnership relations.[7] Even with a partnership charter and a partnership agreement, a partnership must have two more essential elements above all others: mutual trust and respect. Any partnership missing these elements is destined to fail.

The Advantages of the Partnership

EASY TO ESTABLISH Like the proprietorship, the partnership is easy and inexpensive to establish. The owner must obtain the necessary business licenses and submit a minimal number of forms. In most states, partners must file a Certificate for Conducting Business as Partners if the business is run under a trade name.

COMPLEMENTARY SKILLS In a sole proprietorship, the owner must wear lots of different hats, and not all of them will fit well. In successful partnerships, the parties' skills and abilities usually complement one another, strengthening the company's managerial foundation. A common need for many entrepreneurs today is the need for partners with technical skills. Many new businesses have strong Web-based components or are app-based business models. If an entrepreneur lacks the requisite technical skills, bringing in a "tech partner" who can handle the technical elements of the business may be necessary.

DIVISION OF PROFITS There are no restrictions on how partners distribute the company's profits as long as they are consistent with the partnership agreement and do not violate the rights of any partner. The partnership agreement should articulate each partner's contribution to the business and his or her share of the profits. If the partners fail to create an agreement, the RUPA says the partners share equally in the partnership's profits, even if their original capital contributions were unequal.

LARGER POOL OF CAPITAL The partnership form of ownership can significantly broaden the pool of capital available to a business. Each partner's asset base enhances the business's pool of capital and improves its ability to borrow needed funds; together, partners' personal assets provide a larger capital base and support greater borrowing capacity.

ABILITY TO ATTRACT LIMITED PARTNERS When partners share in owning, operating, and managing a business, they are **general partners**. General partners have unlimited liability for the partnership's debts and usually take an active role in managing the business. Every partnership must have at least one general partner, although there is no limit on the number of general partners a business can have.

Limited partners are financial investors in a partnership, cannot participate in the day-to-day management of a company, and have limited liability for the partnership's debts. If the business fails, they lose only what they have invested in it and no more. A limited partnership can attract investors by offering them limited liability and the potential to realize a substantial return on their investments if the business is successful. Many individuals find it very profitable to invest in high-potential small businesses but only if they avoid the disadvantages of unlimited liability while doing so. If limited partners are "materially and actively" engaged in a business (defined as spending more than 500 hours per year in the company) or if they hold themselves out as general partners, they will be treated as general partners and will lose their limited liability protection. Two types of limited partners are silent partners and dormant partners. **Silent partners** are not active in a business but generally are known to be members of the partnership. **Dormant partners** are neither active nor generally known to be associated with the business.

A **limited partnership** is composed of at least one general partner and at least one limited partner. There is no limit on the total number of limited partners. In a limited partnership, the general partner is treated, under the law, the same as in a general partnership. Limited partners are treated as investors in the business venture, and they have limited liability for the partnership's debts. They can lose only the amount they have invested in the business. Because of this advantage, limited partnerships own many professional sports teams, including the Miami Heat, Chicago Bulls, and Minnesota Timberwolves of the National Basketball Association (NBA).

Forming a limited partnership requires its founders to file a Certificate of Limited Partnership with the secretary of state's office. A limited partnership must include "limited partnership," "L.P.," or "LP" in its business name.

The limited partner does not have the right to engage actively in managing the business. In fact, limited partners who take an active part in managing the business (more than 500 hours per year) forfeit their limited liability status and are treated just like general partners. Limited partners can, however, make management suggestions to the general partners, inspect the business, and make copies of business records. A limited partner is, of course, entitled to a share of the business's profits as specified in the Certificate of Limited Partnership. The primary disadvantage of limited partnerships is the complexity and cost of establishing and maintaining them.

ENTREPRENEURIAL PROFILE: Casey Carter, Taylor Hunt, and James Dean: CryptPro Casey Carter, an Internet programmer, wanted to share some code with Taylor Hunt, with whom he was collaborating on a project. However, Carter wanted to ensure that nobody except Hunt would see the code. The experience led Carter, Hunt, and James Dean, an art director at a logo

general partners
partners who have unlimited liability for the partnership's debts and usually take an active role in managing the business.

limited partners
partners who are financial investors in a partnership, cannot participate in the day-to-day management of a company, and have limited liability for the partnership's debts.

silent partners
partners who are not active in a business but generally are known to be members of the partnership.

dormant partners
partners who are neither active nor generally known to be members of the partnership.

limited partnership
a partnership composed of at least one general partner and at least one limited partner.

US Logo, Inc. and CryptPro, LLC

development company, to form a limited partnership called CryptPro. The partners, who are working on the project outside of their full-time jobs, are developing a secure messaging system that allows two parties to exchange messages over a secure network. Users can send a small number of secure messages for free, and heavier users will pay a monthly subscription fee.[8] ∎

MINIMAL GOVERNMENT REGULATION Like the sole proprietorship, partnerships are not burdened with excessive red tape.

FLEXIBILITY Although not as flexible as a sole proprietorship, a partnership can generally react quickly to changing market conditions because the partners can respond quickly and creatively to new opportunities. In large partnerships, however, getting partners' approval can slow a company's strategic actions. Unless the partnership agreement states otherwise, each partner has a single vote in the management of the company no matter how large his or her contribution to the partnership is.

TAXATION A partnership itself is not subject to federal taxation. It serves as a conduit for the profit or losses it earns or incurs; its net income or loss is passed through to the partners as personal income, and the partners pay income tax on their distributive shares at their individual tax rates. The partnership files an informational return, Form 1065, with the IRS that reports its net income for the tax year and the percentages of the business that each partner owns. The partnership provides each partner with a Schedule K-1 that shows his or her share of partnership's net income (or loss). Partners must pay taxes on their respective shares of the partnership's net income, even if none of that income actually is distributed to them. A partnership, like a sole proprietorship, avoids the "double-taxation" disadvantage associated with the corporate form of ownership.

The Disadvantages of the Partnership

Before entering into a partnership, every entrepreneur should double-check the decision to be sure that the prospective business partner will add value to the business. A partnership is like a business marriage, and before entering into one, an entrepreneur should be aware of the disadvantages.

UNLIMITED LIABILITY OF AT LEAST ONE PARTNER At least one member of every partnership must be a general partner. The general partner has unlimited personal liability for any debts that remain after the partnerships assets are exhausted. In addition, general partners' liability is *joint and several*, which means that creditors can hold all general partners equally responsible for the partnership's debts or can collect the entire debt from just one partner.

ENTREPRENEURIAL PROFILE: AmyLynn Keimach and Kenneth Tran: Border7 Studios AmyLynn Keimach and Kenneth Tran operate their Web-services firm, Border7 Studios, based in Simi Valley, California, as a general partnership. Even though they recognize the liability risks in choosing to operate as a partnership, Keimach and Tran, who started the company after they were laid off from their jobs without severance pay, say they cannot yet afford to form an S corporation, their desired form of ownership. Keimach says if one of Border7's clients sues the company, a resulting judgment could conceivably take everything the two partners own.[9] ∎

CAPITAL ACCUMULATION Although the partnership form of ownership is superior to the proprietorship in its ability to attract capital, it is generally not as effective as the corporate form of ownership, which can raise capital by selling shares of ownership to outside investors.

DIFFICULTY IN DISPOSING OF PARTNERSHIP INTEREST Most partnership agreements restrict how partners can dispose of their shares of the business. Usually, an agreement requires a partner to sell his or her interest to the remaining partner(s). Even if the original agreement contains such a requirement and clearly delineates how the value of each partner's ownership will be determined, there is no guarantee that the other partner(s) will have the financial resources to buy the seller's interest. When the money is not available to purchase a partner's interest, the other partner(s) may be forced to accept a new partner or dissolve the partnership, distribute the remaining assets, or begin again. Under prior versions of the RUPA, when a partner withdrew from a partnership (an act called disassociation), the partnership automatically dissolved, requiring the remaining partners to form a new partnership. Current provisions of the RUPA, however, do not require dissolution and allow the remaining partners to continue to operate the business without the disassociated partner through a continuation agreement. The disassociated partner no longer has the authority to represent the business or to take part in managing it.

A similar problem arises when a partner dies. The deceased partner's interest in the partnership passes to his or her heirs, in which case the partnership is dissolved and the heirs receive the value of the deceased partner's share of the business. However, the partnership agreement may provide for the partnership to continue to operate with the remaining partner(s) purchasing the deceased partner's share of the business from his or her estate. To ensure that sufficient funds are available to purchase a deceased partner's interest in the business, the partnership should purchase life insurance policies on all partners and use the proceeds to purchase the deceased partner's share of the business for the surviving partner(s).

POTENTIAL FOR PERSONALITY AND AUTHORITY CONFLICTS Being in a partnership is much like being in a marriage. Making sure that partners' work habits, goals, ethics, and general business philosophy are compatible is an important step in avoiding a nasty business divorce. Engaging in serious discussions with potential partners before launching a business together is a valuable and revealing exercise. A better way to "test-drive" a potential partnership is to work with a prospective partner on a joint project to get a sense of how compatible your work styles, business philosophies, and personalities really are. That project might be a small business venture or working together to create a business plan for the proposed partnership. The idea is to work together before committing to a partnership to determine how compatible the potential partners' values, goals, personalities, views, and ethics are.

ENTREPRENEURIAL PROFILE: René Siegel and High Tech Connect René Siegel and her partner launched their business, High Tech Connect, based on a need they discovered among their colleagues in Silicon Valley. Companies required the skills of specialized marketing consultants to work on specific projects, some of which might last for years. High Tech Connect built a strong network of highly skilled, experienced freelancers to provide those marketing services. However, after a few years in business, the partnership became quite contentious. The partners had established High Tech Connect as a 50/50 partnership with no exit clause in their agreement. The dissolution of the partnership included many accounting and legal disputes, which led to litigation. Siegel eventually took full ownership of the business. She credits finding the right attorney, keeping employees focused on moving the business ahead, being able to rely on strong support from her family, and building a strong advisory team with getting through the transition to sole ownership. High Tech Connect now manages a network of more than 2,000 consultants who assist clients with content development, editing, communications, speechwriting, public relations, and marketing through social media. Its consultants serve more than 500 clients, including companies such as IBM, Cisco Systems, Intuit, and McAfee.[10] ■

High Tech Connect, LLC

No matter how compatible partners are, friction among them is inevitable. The key is to have a mechanism such as a partnership agreement and open lines of communication for managing conflict. The demise of many partnerships can be traced to interpersonal conflicts and the lack of a process to resolve those conflicts.

PARTNERS ARE BOUND BY THE LAW OF AGENCY Each partner is an agent for the business and can legally bind the partnership and, hence, the other partners, to contracts—even without the remaining partners' knowledge or consent. Because of this agency power, all partners must exercise good faith and reasonable care when performing their responsibilities. For example, if a partner signs a three-year lease for a business jet, a move that only worsens the small company's cash flow struggles, the partnership is legally bound by the agreement even though the remaining partners may not be in favor of the decision.

Some partnerships survive a lifetime, but others struggle because they suffer from many of the problems described here. Conflicts between or among partners can force an otherwise thriving business to close. Too many partners never put into place a mutually agreed-on method of conflict resolution such as a partnership agreement. Without such a mechanism, disagreements can escalate to the point where the partnership dissolves and the business ceases to operate.

 **You Be the Consultant**

Making a Partnership Work

Structured properly, a partnership can be very successful and quite rewarding for its founders. Nick Friedman and Omar Soliman met in the tenth grade and became best friends. In his senior year at the University of Miami in Coral Gables, Florida, Soliman enrolled in an entrepreneurship class where he created a business plan for College Hunks Hauling Junk, the moving and junk-hauling company that he and Friedman operated during their summer breaks from college. He submitted his plan to the Leigh Rothschild Entrepreneurship Competition, where it won first prize and $10,000. After graduating from Pomona College, Friedman accepted a job at a Washington, D.C., consulting firm but quickly became disenchanted with his corporate career. At age 22, he and Soliman decided to launch College Hunks Hauling Junk and became the youngest franchisors in the United States.

Today their company, which recycles 50 percent of the material they process, has grown into a $3.5 million junk removal business with 35 franchisees and has been featured in the *Inc.* 500 list of fastest-growing small companies and on *Shark Tank*. Friedman and Soliman are best friends, something that has strengthened their business partnership and made their company a success. However, that is not always the outcome when best friends go into business together. Friedman and Soliman offer the following lessons for making a business partnership work:

- **Make certain that you have a common vision before you start.** Friedman says the key to their successful partnership is that they share a common vision and common values. Before they officially launched College Hunks Hauling Junk, each of them wrote separately about where they expected their business to be in five years. They were amazed at how strong their visions for the company matched with each other. While they have day-to-day disagreements, like any partnership, the two partners never disagree on the direction of the business nor the values that underpin how they conduct their business.

- **The ideal partner is one whose skills, experience, talents, and abilities complement yours rather than mirror them.** While their company has grown, Friedman

and Soliman have developed distinctive roles that support one another. Soliman is more of the strategic thinker, while Friedman is stronger with business operations and implementation of strategy.

- **Create a partnership agreement—always.** No matter how strong a friendship is, partners should create a partnership agreement. Discussing and then putting in writing how partners will handle sensitive issues, such as financing, daily decision making, deadlocks in decisions, compensation, and withdrawal from the partnership, not only helps resolve disputes down the road but also allows the partners to avoid disputes.

- **Create an advisory board.** Friedman and Soliman are equal owners of College Hunks Hauling Junk. What happens when they disagree on an important decision? In the early stages of the business, they simply "duked it out." (Friedman laughingly concedes that actual punches have been involved on occasion.) Today, the business partners consult with the advisory board they created that includes professors, executives from large companies, and other entrepreneurs who can offer valuable insight.

In other cases, forming a partnership can be the beginning of an extended nightmare. Three entrepreneurs formed a partnership to sell male enhancement products but never created a partnership agreement. The partner who controlled the company's finances and operations distributed more than $11 million to himself from the partnership but less than $1 million to his partners. The two partners became suspicious and demanded a full accounting of the partnership's records. The managing partner refused, prompting the two partners to file an arbitration claim against him. During the arbitration hearing, the managing partner claimed that because there was no partnership agreement, no partnership existed. The two partners argued that the parties' original intent was to create a partnership and that they should receive equal shares of the partnership's profits. A panel of arbitrators agreed with the two partners and ordered the managing partner to pay them $4.5 million. Of course, the business did not survive the dispute.

You Be the Consultant (continued)

Avoiding ugly and costly business divorces that too often bring an end to businesses requires an ongoing and active effort. Experts suggest that partners follow these guidelines to keep their partnerships going strong:

- Ask yourself, "Do I really need a partner?" You should take on a partner only if doing so is essential to your company's success. A potential partner should bring to the business skills, contacts, financing, knowledge, or something else you don't have.

- Take a close look at what you're getting. How well do you really know your potential partner? One of the best ways to test your compatibility is to work on small projects together before you decide to go into business with one another. Doing so allows you to judge how compatible your management styles, business philosophies, and values are.

- Invest in the relationship, not just the deal making. Partners must constantly work to strengthen their relationships. You cannot delegate or ignore this role; otherwise, the partnership is destined to fail.

- Respect your differences but expect to work out conflicts. When potential sources of conflict exist, address them immediately. Festering wounds seldom heal themselves.

- Divide business responsibilities and duties according to each partner's skills, interests, and abilities.

- Be prepared to change. Be open to new opportunities and share with your partners what you see. Partnerships must evolve to survive.

- Help your partners to succeed. Work hard to see that every partner plays a role in the business that affords him or her the opportunity to be successful.

- Make sure your partners are people you admire, respect, and enjoy being around.

David and Jason Benham, who are identical twins, share interests in athletics, family, and business. After attempting short careers in professional baseball, the brothers found themselves doing odd jobs to get by. However, David and Jason had bigger dreams. They wanted to get into real estate and build a company that could support their families and their commitment to various religious charities. In 2003 they recognized a niche in foreclosed properties and launched Beanham Companies. When the mortgage meltdown occurred in 2008, Benham Companies was positioned to succeed in an otherwise dismal real estate market. Their business now provides tax planning, business consulting, and real estate services, operating out of more than 100 offices in 35 states.

1. Research relationships between partners and add at least three guidelines to those listed here.

2. Develop a list of the behaviors that are almost certain to destroy a partnership.

3. Suppose that two of your friends are about to launch a business together with nothing but a handshake. "We've been best friends since grammar school," they say. What advice would you give them?

Sources: Based on Donna Fenn, "Advice from College Hunks: How to Start a Company with Your Best Friend," *BNET*, September 7, 2010, http://www.bnet.com/blog/entrepreneurs/advice-from-college-hunks-how-to-start-a-company-with-your-best-friend/1213; Laura Petrecca, "A Partner Can Give Your Business Shelter or a Storm," *USA Today*, October 9, 2009, http://www.usatoday.com/money/smallbusiness/startup/week4-partnerships.htm; Patricia Laya, "This Guy Quit His Consulting Job to Haul People's Junk, and Is Making Millions," *Business Insider*, August 8, 2011, http://www.businessinsider.com/business-tips-nick-friedman-college-hunks-hauling-junk-08-2011?op=1; "$4.5 Million Judgment for Aiken Schenk Clients in Partnership Dispute," Aiken Schenk, 2011, http://www.ashrlaw.com/news/oral-partnership.htm; John Jessup, "Twin Brothers Boost Business Through 'Missioneering,'" *CBN News*, September 23, 2012, www.cbn.com/cbnnews/us/2012/September/Twin-Brothers-Boost-Business-through-Missioneering/.

Limited Liability Partnerships

Many states now recognize **limited liability partnerships (LLPs)**, in which *all* partners in a business are limited partners, giving them the advantage of limited liability for all of the partnership's debts. Most states restrict LLPs to certain types of professionals, such as attorneys, physicians, dentists, and accountants. However, many states restrict the limited liability advantage of LLPs to the results of actions taken by other partners. For instance, if an LLP sells a defective product that injures a customer, the injured customer could sue the business *and* the partners as individuals. The partners' unlimited personal liability exposure means that their personal assets would be at risk.

Just as with any limited partnership, the partners must file a Certificate of Limited Partnership in the state in which the partnership will conduct business, and the partnership must identify itself as an LLP to those with whom it does business. In addition, like every partnership, an LLP does not pay taxes; its income is passed through to the limited partners, who pay taxes on their shares of the company's income.

Corporations

The corporation is the most complex of the three major forms of business ownership. It is a separate entity apart from its owners and may engage in business, make contracts, sue and be sued, own property, and pay taxes. The Supreme Court has defined the **corporation** as "an artificial

limited liability partnerships (LLPs)
partnerships in which all partners in the business are limited partners, giving them the advantage of limited liability for the partnership's debts.

LO2
Describe the similarities and differences of the C corporation and the S corporation.

corporation
a separate legal entity apart from its owners that receives the right to exist from the state in which it is incorporated.

being, invisible, intangible, and existing only in contemplation of the law."[11] Because the life of the corporation is independent of its owners, the shareholders can sell their interests in the business without affecting its continuation. Corporations are creations of the states. When a corporation is founded, it accepts the regulations and restrictions of the state in which it is incorporated and any other state in which it chooses to do business.

Because it is a separate legal entity, a corporation allows investors to limit their liability to the total amount of their investment in the business. In other words, creditors of the corporation cannot lay claim to shareholders' personal assets to satisfy the company's unpaid debts. The legal protection of personal assets from business creditors is of critical concern to many potential investors. John Gazzola, founder of Toyopolis, a company that sells toys, games, and collectibles online, chose the corporate form of ownership because of his desire to limit his personal liability and for "peace of mind."[12]

This shield of limited liability may not be impenetrable, however. Because start-up companies are so risky, lenders and other creditors often require the founders of corporations to personally guarantee loans made to the business. Experts estimate that 95 percent of small business owners have to sign personal guarantees to get the debt financing they need. Banks, landlords, and vendors may all required personal guarantees from small business owners. By making these guarantees, owners are putting their personal assets at risk (just as in a proprietorship) despite choosing the corporate form of ownership.

The corporate form of ownership also does not protect its owners from being held personally liable for fraudulent or illegal acts. Court decisions have extended the personal liability of the owners of small corporations beyond the financial guarantees that banks and other lenders require, "piercing the corporate veil" much more than ever before. Courts increasingly are holding entrepreneurs *personally* liable for environmental, pension, and legal claims against their corporations. Courts will pierce the corporate veil and hold entrepreneurs liable for the company's debts and obligations if the owners deliberately commit criminal or negligent acts when handling corporate business. Courts ignore the limited liability shield the corporate form of ownership provides when an entrepreneur:

- Uses corporate assets for personal reasons or commingles them with his or her personal assets

- Fails to act in a responsible manner and creates an unwarranted level of financial risk for the stockholders

- Makes financial misrepresentations, such as operating with more than one set of books

- Takes actions in the name of the corporation that were not authorized by the board of directors

closely held corporation
a corporation whose shares are controlled by a relatively small number of people, often family members, friends, or employees.

publicly held corporation
a corporation that has a large number of shareholders and whose stock usually is traded on one of the large stock exchanges.

Corporations have the power to raise large amounts of capital by selling shares of ownership to outside investors, but many corporations have only a handful of shareholders. A **closely held corporation** has shares that are controlled by a relatively small number of people, often family members, friends, or employees. Its stock is not traded on any stock exchange but instead is passed from one generation to the next. Most small corporations are closely held. A **publicly held corporation** has a large number of shareholders, and its stock usually is traded on one of the large stock exchanges.

In general, a corporation must report annually its financial operations to its home state's secretary of state. These financial reports become public record. If a corporation's stock is sold in more than one state, the corporation must comply with federal regulations governing the sale of corporate securities. There are substantially more reporting requirements for a corporation than for the other forms of ownership.

Liability problems associated with piercing the corporate veil almost always originate from actions and decisions that fail to maintain the integrity of a corporation. The most common cause of these problems, especially in closely held corporations, is corporate owners and officers failing to keep their personal funds and assets separate from those of the corporation. Table 6.1 offers some useful suggestions for avoiding legal tangles in a corporation.

Unless a corporation fails to pay its taxes or is limited to a specific length of life by its charter, it can continue indefinitely. The corporation's existence does not depend on the fate of any

TABLE 6.1 Avoiding Legal Tangles in a Corporation

Entrepreneurs should take these steps to avoid legal problems if they own a corporation:

- *Identify the company as a corporation by using "Inc." or "Corporation" in the business name.* This alerts all who do business with a company that it is a corporation.

- *File all reports and pay all necessary fees required by the state in a timely manner.* Most states require corporations to file reports with the secretary of state on an annual basis. Failing to do so will jeopardize the validity of your corporation and will open the door for personal liability problems for its shareholders.

- *Hold annual meetings to elect officers and directors.* In a closely held corporation, the officers elected may *be* the shareholders, but that does not matter. Corporations formed by an individual are not required to hold meetings, but the sole shareholder must file a written consent form.

- *Keep minutes of every meeting of the officers and directors, even if it takes place in the living room of the founders.* It is a good idea to elect a secretary who is responsible for recording the minutes.

- *Make sure that the corporation's board of directors makes all major decisions.* Problems arise in closely held corporations when one owner makes key decisions alone without consulting the elected board.

- *Make it clear that the business is a corporation by having all officers sign contracts, loan agreements, purchase orders, and other legal documents in the corporation's name rather than their own names.* Failing to designate their status as agents of the corporation can result in the officers being held personally liable for agreements they think they are signing on the corporation's behalf.

- *Keep corporate assets and the personal assets of the owners separate.* Few things make courts more willing to hold shareholders personally liable for a corporation's debts than commingling corporate and personal assets. In some closely held corporations, owners have been known to use corporate assets to pay their personal expenses (or vice versa) or to mix their personal funds with corporate funds into a single bank account. Protect the corporation's identity by keeping it completely separate from the owner's personal identities.

Source: U.S. Small Business Administration, 2010.

single individual. Unlike a proprietorship or partnership in which the death of a founder ends the business, a corporation lives beyond the lives of those who gave it life. This perpetual life gives rise to another major advantage—transferable ownership. However, with most small businesses the ability of any individual shareholder to sell shares is limited and must follow the processes agreed on by the company founders when they incorporated.

The C Corporation

C corporations are the traditional form of incorporation. All large publically traded companies and some small businesses are C corporations. C corporations are separate legal entities and therefore must pay taxes on their net income at the federal level, in most states, and to some local governments as well. Before stockholders receive a penny of its net income as dividends, a C corporation must pay taxes at the *corporate* tax rate, a graduated tax on corporate profits. Then, stockholders must pay taxes on the dividends they receive from these same profits at their *individual* tax rates. Thus, a corporation's profits are taxed twice. This **double taxation** is a distinct disadvantage of the C corporation form of ownership. If a company plans to seek investment from venture capital or other forms of private equity (sources of financing will be discussed in Chapter 13), it should be established as a C corporation. A C corporation provides the appropriate structure for investments by corporations, an eventual acquisition, and a future public stock offering.

double taxation
a disadvantage of the corporate form of ownership in which the corporation's profits are taxed twice, once at the corporate rate and again at the individual rate on the portion of profits distributed to shareholders as dividends.

The S Corporation

In 1954, the IRS Code created the Subchapter S corporation, more commonly known as *S corporation* or *S Corp.* Unlike a C corporation, S corporations do not pay taxes on corporate income. Income earned by S corporations is passed through to the owners, just as it is in a sole proprietorship and a partnership. The **S corporation** was established specifically for small, closely held businesses to alleviate the owners from the double taxation that occurs with a C corporation. Table 6.2 shows a comparison of the tax bill for a small company organized as a C corporation and the tax liability of the same company organized as an S corporation (or a limited liability company, which shares the same tax treatment as an S corporation). An S corporation is a distinction that is made only for federal income tax purposes and is, in terms of all other legal characteristics, no different from any other corporation.

S corporation
a corporation that retains the legal characteristics of a regular C corporation but has the advantage of being taxed as a partnership if it meets certain criteria.

TABLE 6.2 Tax Rate Comparison: C Corporation and S Corporation or Limited Liability Company

Entrepreneurs must consider the tax bills that their companies incur under the various forms of ownership. For example, S corporations do not pay taxes on their net income. Instead, that income passes through to the owners, who pay taxes on it at their individual tax rates. C corporations, on the other hand, pay a corporate tax on their net income. If the C corporation pays out some or all of its net income as dividends to shareholders, the dividends are taxed a second time at the shareholders' individual tax rates. Therefore, the tax obligations for an owner of an S corporation may be considerably lower than that of a C corporation.

The following example illustrates the effect of these tax rate differentials. This somewhat simplified example assumes that a small company generates a net income of $500,000 and that all after-tax income is distributed to the owner.

	C Corporation	S Corporation or LLC
Corporate or limited liability company net income	$500,000	$500,000
Maximum corporate tax	35%	0%
Corporate tax	**$175,000**	**0**
After-tax income	$325,000	$500,000
Maximum shareholder tax rate	39.6%	39.6%
Shareholder tax	**$65,000***	**$198,000****
Total tax paid	**$240,000**	**$198,000**

(Corporate tax plus shareholder tax)

Total tax savings by choosing an S corporation or limited liability company = $42,000

*Using the marginal 20% tax rate on dividends: $325,000 × 20% = $65,000.

**Using the marginal 39.6% tax rate on ordinary income: $500,000 × 39.6% = $198,000.

Source: U.S. Small Business Administration, 2010.

A corporation seeking S status must meet the following criteria:

- It must be a domestic corporation.

- It can only have only allowable shareholders, including individuals, certain trusts, and estates.

- It cannot include partnerships, corporations, or nonresident aliens as shareholders.

- It cannot have more than 100 shareholders.

- It can only issue one class of stock. However, S corporations can issue shares of stock with different voting rights.

- It cannot be an ineligible corporation, such as certain financial institutions, insurance companies, and domestic international sales corporations.

If a corporation meets the criteria of an S corporation, its shareholders must elect to be treated as one. Shareholders may file for S corporation status at any time during the 12 months that precede the taxable year for which the election is to be effective. (The corporation must have been eligible for S status for the entire year.) To make the election of S status effective for the current tax year, entrepreneurs must file Form 2553 with the IRS within the first 75 days of the corporation's fiscal year. *All* shareholders must consent to have the corporation treated as an S corporation. Jennifer Chu launched Chu Shu, a company that makes odor-absorbing liners for women's shoes, after she was laid off from her investment banking job. Chu incorporated her business and intended to transform it into an S corporation but missed the filing deadline the first year, causing her to forgo several thousands of dollars in tax savings.[13]

An S corporation files an informational return (1120-S) with the IRS and provides its shareholders with Schedule K-1, which reports their proportionate shares of the company's profits. The shareholders report their portions of the S corporation's earnings on their individual income tax returns (Form 1040) and pay taxes on those profits at the individual tax rates (even if they never take the money out of the business). This tax treatment can cause problems for individual shareholders, however. If an S corporation earns a profit but managers choose to plow that income back into the business in the form of retained earnings to fuel its growth and expansion, shareholders still must pay taxes on their share of the company's net income. In that case, shareholders will end up paying taxes on "phantom income" they never actually received. S corporations should always distribute enough cash to ensure that shareholders have the funds they need to pay taxes on the income that is passed through from the corporation. S corporations (and other pass through entities, such as partnerships) should follow the **1/3, 1/3, 1/3 rule of thumb**: distribute one-third of earnings to the shareholders to cover the taxes they will owe, retain one-third of earnings to fund its growth, and earmark the final one-third to pay down debt, add to funding for its growth, or distribute to the owners as a return on their investment.

S corporations' earnings are not subject to the self-employment tax that sole proprietors and general partners must pay; however, they are responsible for payroll taxes (for Social Security and Medicare) on the wages and salaries the S corporation pays its employees. Therefore, owners of S corporations must be sure that the salaries they draw are reasonable; salaries that are too low or too high draw scrutiny from the IRS.

Before 1998, if an entrepreneur owned separate but affiliated companies, he or she had to maintain each one as a distinct S corporation with its own accounting records and tax return. Under current law, business owners can set up all of these affiliated companies as qualified S corporation subsidiaries ("Q subs") under the umbrella of a single company, each with its own separate legal identity, and still file a single tax return for the parent company. For entrepreneurs with several lines of businesses, this change means greatly simplified tax filing. Owners also can use losses from one subsidiary company to offset profits from another to minimize their tax bills.

ENTREPRENEURIAL PROFILE: Joseph Rotella: Spencer Organ Company Joseph Rotella is the owner of Spencer Organ Company, an organ maintenance and restoration business based in Waltham, Massachusetts. Spencer Organ Company is an S Corporation, and Rotella is the only shareholder. Therefore, all of the company's profits flow through to Rotella as personal income. In a typical year, Spencer Organ Company's profits are about $250,000. Rotella only draws a salary of about one half of that amount. Therefore, he not only owes income taxes on his salary, but also on the profits earned by his company.[14] ∎

The Limited Liability Company

The **limited liability company (LLC)**, like an S corporation, offers its owners limited personal liability for the debts of the business, providing a significant advantage over sole proprietorships and partnerships. LLCs, however, are not subject to many of the restrictions currently imposed on S corporations and offer more flexibility than S corporations. For example, S corporations cannot have more than 100 shareholders, and none of them can be foreigners or corporations. S corporations are also limited to only one class of stock. LLCs eliminate those restrictions. Although an LLC can have just one owner, most have multiple owners (called "members"). LLCs offer their owners limited liability without imposing any requirements on their characteristics or any ceiling on their numbers. LLC members can include non-U.S. citizens, partnerships, and corporations. Unlike a limited partnership, which prohibits limited partners from participating in the day-to-day management of the business, an LLC does not restrict its members' ability to become involved in managing the company. Today most entrepreneurs form LLCs for their new businesses.

In addition to offering its members the advantage of limited liability, LLCs also avoid the double taxation imposed on C corporations. Like an S corporation, an LLC does not pay income taxes; its income passes through to the members, who are responsible for paying income taxes on their shares of the LLC's net income. Because they are not subject to the many restrictions imposed on other forms of ownership, LLCs offer entrepreneurs another significant advantage: flexibility. An LLC permits its members to divide income (and thus tax liability) as they see fit, including allocations that differ from their percentages of ownership. Like an S corporation, the members' shares of an LLC's earnings are not subject to the self-employment tax. However, the managing member's share of the LLC's earnings is subject to the self-employment tax (15.3 percent) just as a sole proprietor's or a general partner's earned income is.

These advantages make the LLC an ideal form of ownership for many small companies across many industries—retail, wholesale, manufacturing, real estate, or service. Because it offers the tax advantage of a partnership, the legal protection of a corporation, and maximum operating flexibility, the LLC is the fastest-growing form of business ownership. Mark Cuban, billionaire

1/3, 1/3, 1/3 rule of thumb
a guideline that calls for an S corporation (and other pass-through entities) to distribute one-third of its earnings to shareholders to cover the taxes they will owe, retain one-third to to fund its growth, and earmark one-third to pay down debt, add to funding for growth, or distribute to shareholders as a return on their investment.

LO3
Understand the characteristics of the limited liability company.

limited liability company (LLC)
a form of ownership that, like an S corporation, is a cross between a partnership and a corporation; it is not subject to the restrictions imposed on S corporations.

owner of the NBA's Dallas Mavericks, recently created an LLC, Radical Football LLC, a company whose mission is to fund the creation of a playoff system that will crown a real champion in major college football. The current collegiate football postseason consists of 35 bowl games in which many of the teams that compete are determined by computerized formulas. Cuban says he started the LLC so that the best teams will be the ones playing for the national championship.[15]

Creating an LLC is much like creating a corporation. Forming an LLC requires an entrepreneur to create two documents: the articles of organization (which must be filed with the secretary of state) and the operating agreement. The LLC's **articles of organization**, similar to the corporation's articles of incorporation, actually create the LLC by establishing its name and address, its method of management (board managed or member managed), its duration, and the names and addresses of each organizer. In most states, the company's name must contain the words "limited liability company," "limited company," or the letters "L.L.C." or "L.C."

Once the members form an LLC, they must adopt an operating agreement. The **operating agreement**, similar to a corporation's bylaws, outlines the provisions that govern the way the LLC will conduct business, such as members' capital contributions to the LLC; members' rights, roles, and responsibilities; the admission or withdrawal of members; distributions from the business; and the way the LLC will be managed. To ensure that their LLCs are classified as a partnership for tax purposes, entrepreneurs must draft the operating agreement carefully. The operating agreement must create an LLC that has more characteristics of a partnership than of a corporation to maintain this favorable tax treatment.

Despite their universal appeal to entrepreneurs, LLCs suffer some disadvantages. They can be expensive to create, often costing between $1,500 and $5,000. Some states also impose annual fees on LLCs. Unlike corporations, which can operate "for perpetuity," LLCs have limited life spans. Entrepreneurs who want to provide attractive benefits to themselves and their employees will not find this form of ownership appealing because the cost of those benefits is not tax deductible in an LLC. Because there is no stock involved, this form of ownership also is not suitable for companies whose owners plan to raise money through an IPO or who want to use stock options or an ESOP as incentives for employees.

ENTREPRENEURIAL PROFILE: Anya Sapozhnikova: Lady Circus Anya Sapozhnikova is a partner in a business that is based on risk taking. Sapozhnikova is both a partner and a performer in Lady Circus of Brooklyn, New York, a circus that elevates traditional circus acts to new heights. Sapozhnikova says that because society expects more extreme experiences, a circus also must offer more extreme shows for its audiences. Circuses limit their business risk by requiring performers to sign waivers of liability and to carry performers insurance. To limit her personal liability, Sapozhnikova and her partners organized Lady Circus as an LLC. To further protect from liability, she has her venue, the Sky Box, and her costuming and prop-making studio organized under a separate corporation. ■

Although an LLC may be ideally suited for an entrepreneur launching a new company, it may pose problems for business owners considering converting an existing business to an LLC. Switching to an LLC from a general partnership, a limited partnership, or a sole proprietorship to bring in new owners is usually not a problem. However, owners of corporations and S corporations could incur large tax obligations if they convert their companies to LLCs.

How to Create a Legal Business Entity

C corporations, S corporations, and LLCs can be costly and time consuming to establish and to maintain. The owners are giving birth to an artificial legal entity, and the gestation period can be prolonged, especially for a novice. Many entrepreneurs hire attorneys to handle the process, but in most states entrepreneurs can complete all of the required forms, most of which are online, themselves. However, entrepreneurs must exercise great caution when proceeding without the help of an attorney. Incorporating a business requires a variety of fees that are not applicable to proprietorships or partnerships. The average cost to create a legal business entity is around $1,000, but, depending on the complexity of the organization and the type of entity the entrepreneur chooses for the business, fees can range from $500 to $5,000.

articles of organization
the document that creates an LLC by establishing its name and address, method of management, its duration, and other details.

operating agreement
the document that establishes for an LLC the provisions governing the way it will conduct business.

LO4
Explain the process of creating a legal entity for a business.

Most states allow entrepreneurs to establish a legal business entity without the assistance of an attorney. Some states even provide kits to help in the process. Many entrepreneurs use Web sites such as MyCorporation, BizFilings, and LegalZoom to create legal business entities because they can incorporate for as little as $100.

ENTREPRENEURIAL PROFILE: James O'Leary and Ansar Khan: Refulgent Software
James O'Leary and Ansar Khan are cofounders of Refulgent Software, located in Amherst, New York. The company develops point-of-sale software, called Ambur, for restaurants. The partners relied on family support and bootstrapping to launch their new business. To keep their start-up costs down, O'Leary and Khan ran their business out of their apartment and set up their company using LegalZoom. "I would advise folks using services like LegalZoom to do some additional research to make sure they are meeting all the requirements," suggests Khan. "We incorporated in August of 2010 and started selling our product in April of 2011. We had a few hundred dollars in expenses in 2010 and no revenue. We did not realize that we still had to file a tax return for the company for 2010. We did not end up doing that until late 2011 shortly after receiving a letter from the IRS stating that we owed them about $10,000 in fines for not filing a return in 2010. Luckily, we were able to talk to them and the fine was waived. Surprisingly, we figured out pretty much everything else on our own and avoided any other major mistakes!" Refulgent Software grew quickly. Within the first year, it grew to 400 customers and earned six-figure revenues.[16] ∎

Although it is cheaper for entrepreneurs to complete the process of creating a legal business entity themselves, it is not always the best idea. In some states, the application process is complex, and the required forms are confusing. The price for filing incorrectly can be high. If an entrepreneur completes the process of forming a legal business entity improperly, it is generally invalid. In addition, if there are multiple founders, it is important to get assistance from an attorney to develop shareholder or member agreements. These agreements set the ground rules and expectations for shareholders or members, guide the process for major decisions, and mitigate any possible future shareholder or member disputes.

Once entrepreneurs decide to form a legal business entity, they must choose a state in which to establish the entity. If the business will operate within a single state, it is most logical to form the business entity in that state. States differ—sometimes dramatically—in the requirements they place on the legal business entities they charter and how they treat the entities created within their borders. Some states, like Delaware, Vermont, and Nevada, offer low business formation fees, favorable laws concerning the sale of securities, low taxes, and minimal legal requirements; many *Fortune* 500 corporations are chartered in these states. However, for most entrepreneurs, creating the legal business entity in the state from which they intend to operate the business usually is best because they are not likely to reap any significant benefits by forming the business out of state.

Table 6.3 provides a summary of the key features of the major forms of ownership discussed in this chapter.

Buying an Existing Business

LO5
Understand the advantages and disadvantages of buying an existing business.

Rather than launch their own businesses, some entrepreneurs opt for a more direct route to business ownership: They buy an existing business. Each circumstance of buying an existing business is unique, but the process of evaluating a potential business acquisition is not. The due diligence process that involves analyzing and evaluating an existing business for possible purchase is no less time consuming than developing a comprehensive business plan for a start-up. Done correctly, this due diligence process reveals both the negative and the positive aspects of an existing business. Glossing over or skipping altogether the due diligence process is a mistake because a business that looks good on the surface may have serious flaws hidden at its core. Investigating a business to discover its real condition and value requires time, dedication, and, as the name implies, diligence, but the process is worthwhile because it can prevent an entrepreneur from purchasing a business destined for failure.

When considering purchasing a business, the first rule is, "Do not rush into a deal." Taking shortcuts when investigating a potential business acquisition almost always leads to nasty—and

TABLE 6.3 Characteristics of the Major Forms of Ownership

Characteristic	Sole Proprietorship	General Partnership	Limited Partnership	C Corporation	S Corporation	LLC
Definition	A for-profit business owned and operated by one person	A for-profit business jointly owned and operated by two or more people	One general partner and one or more partners with limited liability and no rights of management	An artificial legal entity separate from its owners and formed under state and federal laws	An artificial legal entity that is structured like a C corporation but taxed by the federal government like a partnership	A business entity that provides limited liability like a corporation but is taxed like a partnership; owners are referred to as *members*
Ease of formation	Easiest form of business to set up; if necessary, acquire licenses and permits, register fictitious name, and obtain taxpayer identification	Easy to set up and operate; a written partnership agreement is highly recommended; must acquire an employer ID number; if necessary, register fictitious name	File a Certificate of Limited Partnership with the secretary of state; name must show that business is a limited partnership; must have written agreement and must keep certain records	File articles of incorporation and other required reports with the secretary of state; prepare bylaws and follow corporate formalities	Must meet all criteria to file as an S corporation; must file timely election with the IRS (within two and a half months of first taxable year	File articles of organization with the secretary of state; adopt operating agreement and file necessary reports with secretary of state; the name must show that it is an LLC
Owner's personal liability	Unlimited	Unlimited for general partners; limited for limited partners	Limited	Limited	Limited	Limited
Number of owners	One	Two or more	At least one general partner and any number of limited partners	Any number	Maximum of 100 with restrictions as to who they are	One (a few states require two or more)
Tax liability	Single tax: personal tax rate	Single tax: partners pay on their proportional shares at their individual rate	Same as general partnership	Double tax: corporation pays tax, and shareholders pay tax on dividends distributed	Single tax: owners pay on their proportional shares at individual rate	Single tax: members pay on their proportional shares at individual rate
Current maximum tax rate	39.6%	39.6%	39.6%	35% corporate plus 39.6% individual	39.6%	39.6%
Transferability of ownership	Fully transferable through sale or transfer of company assets	May require consent of all partners	Same as general partnership	Fully transferable	Transferable (but transfer may affect S status)	Usually requires consent of all members
Continuity of the business	Ends on death or insanity of proprietor or on termination by proprietor	Dissolves on death, insanity, or retirement of a general partner (business may continue)	Same as general partnership	Perpetual life	Perpetual life	Perpetual life
Cost of formation	Low	Moderate	Moderate	High	High	High
Liquidity of the owner's investment in the business	Poor to average	Poor to average	Poor to average	High	High	High
Ability to raise capital	Low	Moderate	Moderate to high	Very high	High	High
Formation procedure	No special steps required other than buying necessary licenses	No written partnership agreement required (but highly advisable)	Must comply with state laws regarding limited partnership	Must meet formal requirements specified by state law	Must follow same procedures as C corporation, then elect S status with IRS	Must meet formal requirements specified by state law

expensive—surprises. Prospective buyers must be sure they discover the answers to the following fundamental questions:

- Is the right type of business for sale in a market in which you want to operate?

- What experience do you have in this particular business and the industry in which it operates? How critical to your ultimate success is experience in the business?

- What is the company's potential for success?

- What changes will you have to make—and how extensive will they be—to realize the business's full potential?

- What price and payment method are reasonable for you and acceptable to the seller?

- Is the seller willing to finance part of the purchase price?

- Will the company generate sufficient cash to pay for itself and leave you with a suitable rate of return on your investment?

- Should you be starting a business and building it from the ground up rather than buying an existing one?

Figure 6.2 shows a profile of the four major categories of buyers and their characteristics that business brokers have identified.

The Advantages of Buying an Existing Business

A recent survey by Securian Financial Group shows that 60 percent of business owners intend to leave their companies within the next decade and that their most likely exit strategy is selling the business to someone.[17] Over the next decade, as these small business owners decide to retire and sell, entrepreneurs looking to buy existing businesses will have ample opportunities to consider. Those who purchase an existing business may reap the benefits discussed in the following sections.

SUCCESSFUL EXISTING BUSINESSES OFTEN CONTINUE TO BE SUCCESSFUL Purchasing a thriving business at a reasonable price increases the likelihood of success. Although buying an existing business brings with it certain risks, it tends to be less risky than starting a company from scratch. The previous management team already has established a customer base, built supplier relationships, and set up a business system. The customer base inherited in a business purchase

FIGURE 6.2

Types of Business Buyers

Source: "Meet the Buyers," by Darren Dahl, *Inc.*, April 1, 2008, pp. 98–99. © 2008 by Inc. Magazine. Reprinted with permission.

Main Street Buyers

Want: A business that is manageable and easy to run alone or with a small group of employees.

Revenue Range: Up to $1 million.

Risk Tolerance: Low

Focus: Current and past earnings; often want seller to stay on to assist with transition.

Examples: Car wash, dry cleaners, cafés.

Corporate Refugees

Want: Service businesses with commercial clients and existing contract revenue.

Revenue Range: Less than $5 million.

Risk Tolerance: Low to medium

Focus: Ability to build on his or her corporate experience.

Examples: consulting firms, landscaping, advertising, manufacturing.

Serial Entrepreneurs

Want: Profitable companies with sound management in place.

Revenue Range: Less than $10 million.

Risk Tolerance: Medium to high.

Focus: Building a portfolio of companies in different industries, sectors, or markets; want businesses they can run themselves.

Examples: computer services, rental properties.

Financial Buyers

Want: Profitable companies that offer "hot" products or services and are ready to grow rapidly.

Revenue Range: $10 million to $100 million (or more).

Risk Tolerance: Medium to high (often are VCs or angels).

Focus: Highly profitable exit within five to seven years. Goal is to add capital to the company to turbocharge its growth.

Examples: health care, communications, energy.

can carry an entrepreneur while he or she learns how to build on the company's success. The new owner's objective is to make modifications that attract new customers without alienating the company's existing customers.

SUPERIOR LOCATION When the location of the business is critical to its success (as is often the case in retailing), purchasing a business that is already in the right place may be the best choice. Opening in a second-choice location and hoping to draw customers usually proves fruitless.

EMPLOYEES AND SUPPLIERS ARE IN PLACE An existing business already has experienced employees who can help the new owner through the transition phase. Experienced employees enable a company to continue to earn money while a new owner learns the business. Many new owners find soliciting ideas from employees about methods for increasing sales or reducing costs to be valuable. In many cases, the previous owner may not have involved employees in this fashion and never gained the advantages found in their wisdom and experience. Few people know a job better than the people who perform it every day.

In addition, an existing business has an established set of suppliers with a history of business dealings. Those vendors can continue to supply the business while the new owner investigates the products and services of other suppliers.

INSTALLED EQUIPMENT WITH KNOWN PRODUCTION CAPACITY Acquiring and installing new equipment exerts a tremendous strain on a fledgling company's financial resources. A buyer of an existing business can determine the condition of the plant and equipment and its capacity before making the purchase. In many cases, entrepreneurs can purchase physical facilities and equipment at prices significantly below their replacement costs.

INVENTORY IN PLACE The proper amount of inventory is essential to both controlling costs and generating adequate sales volume. Carrying too little inventory means that a business will not have the quantity and variety of products to satisfy customer demand, and holding too much inventory ties up excessive capital unnecessarily, thereby increasing costs, reducing profitability, and putting a strain on cash flow. Owners of successful established businesses have learned the proper balance between these extremes.

TRADE CREDIT IS ESTABLISHED Previous owners have established trade credit relationships with vendors that can benefit the new owner. The business's proven track record gives the new owner leverage in negotiating favorable trade credit terms.

THE TURNKEY BUSINESS Starting a company can be a daunting, time-consuming task, and buying an existing business is one of the fastest pathways to entrepreneurship. When things go well, purchasing an existing business saves the time and energy required to plan and launch a new business. The buyer gets a business that is already generating cash and perhaps profits as well. The day the entrepreneur takes over the ongoing business is the day revenues begin.

THE NEW OWNER CAN USE THE EXPERIENCE OF THE PREVIOUS OWNER In many business sales, the agreement calls for the seller to spend time with a new owner during the transition period, giving the new manager the time to become acclimated to the business and to learn about the keys to success. Previous owners also can be extremely helpful in unmasking the unwritten rules of business in the area, critically important intangibles such as how to keep customers happy and whom one can trust. Hiring the previous owner as a consultant for at least several months can be a valuable investment and increase the probability that the business will continue to be successful.

EASIER ACCESS TO FINANCING Attracting financing to purchase an existing business often is easier than finding the money to launch a company from scratch. Many existing businesses already have established relationships with lenders, which may open the door to financing through traditional sources such as banks.

HIGH VALUE Some existing businesses are real bargains. If the current owner must sell quickly, he or she may have set a bargain price for the company that is below its actual worth. Special skills or training that are required to operate the business limits the number of potential buyers; therefore, the more specialized the business is, the greater the likelihood is that a buyer will find a bargain. If the owner wants a substantial down payment or the entire selling price in cash, there may be few qualified buyers, but those who do qualify may be able to negotiate a good deal.

Disadvantages of Buying an Existing Business

CASH REQUIREMENTS One of the most significant challenges to buying a business is acquiring the necessary funds for the initial purchase price. The Small Business Administration advises that because the buyer of a company is purchasing the business concept, existing customers, the company's brands, and other existing elements of the business, the costs of acquiring an existing business are usually greater then starting one from scratch.[18]

THE BUSINESS IS LOSING MONEY A business may be for sale because it is struggling and the owner wants out. In these situations, a prospective buyer must be wary. Business owners sometimes attempt to disguise the facts and employ creative accounting techniques to make the company's financial picture appear much brighter than it really is. Few business sellers honestly state "It's losing money" as the reason for putting their companies up for sale. If there is one area of business where the maxim "let the buyer beware" still prevails, it is in the purchase of an existing business. Any buyer unprepared to do a thorough analysis of a business may be stuck with a real money loser. One expert cautions that entrepreneurs who purchase troubled companies in hopes of turning them around face an 85 percent failure rate.[19]

Although buying a money-losing business is risky, it is not necessarily taboo. If a company is poorly managed or suffering from neglect, a new owner may be able to turn it around. However, a prospective buyer who does not have well-defined plan for improving a struggling business should *not* consider buying it!

ENTREPRENEURIAL PROFILE: Chuck and Alan Bush: Fuzzy's Taco Shop Former restaurateur Chuck Bush was enjoying a meal at Fuzzy's Taco Shop in Fort Worth, Texas, and observing the restaurant's operating system in action. He saw the potential of the restaurant but realized that it suffered from a sloppy operating system. There were no control systems in the business. When Bush asked how many shrimp would be served on a particular dish, each employee gave a different answer. Chuck Bush and his father, Alan, an accountant, put together a group of investors to buy the money-losing restaurant for $80,000. They also assumed $10,000 in liabilities and invested another $15,000 for working capital. Chuck became the on-site manager, and his first step was to close the restaurant for four days, power wash every surface, repaint and redecorate the interior, and retrain the staff. He transcribed all of the recipes, which existed only in one cook's head, and assembled them into a notebook to ensure consistency and cost control. Chuck Bush noted that the food at Fuzzy's was good, which is what made him interested in buying the business. The business needed tightening of systems and better operation. The changes the Bushes made were successful, and the business became profitable the first year they owned it. They soon opened a second location in Fort Worth and began fielding inquiries about franchises. Today, 78 Fuzzy's operate across Texas and in 10 other states.[20] ■

Like Fuzzy's, unprofitable businesses often result from at least one of the following problems:

- High inventory levels
- Excessively high wage and salary expenses due to excess pay or inefficient use of personnel
- Excessively high compensation for the owner
- Inadequate accounts-receivable collection efforts
- Excessively high rental or lease rates
- High-priced maintenance costs or service contracts
- Poor location or too many locations for the business to support
- Inefficient equipment
- Intense competition from rivals
- Prices that are too low
- Low profit margins
- Losses due to employee theft, shoplifting, and fraud

Like Chuck Bush, a potential buyer usually can trace the causes of a company's lack of profitability by analyzing a company and its financial statements. The question is, Can the new owner take steps to resolve the problems and return the company to profitability?

PAYING FOR ILL WILL Just as sound business dealings can create goodwill, improper business behavior or unethical practices can create ill will. A business may look great on the surface, but customers, suppliers, creditors, or employees may have negative feelings about their dealings with it. Too many business buyers discover—after the sale—that they have inherited undisclosed credit problems, poor supplier relationships, soon-to-expire leases, lawsuits, mismanaged customer relationships, building code violations, and other problems created by the previous owner. Vital business relationships may have begun to deteriorate, but their long-term effects may not yet be reflected in the company's financial statements. Ill will can permeate a business for years. The only way to avoid these problems is to investigate a prospective purchase target thoroughly *before* moving forward in the negotiation process.

EMPLOYEES INHERITED WITH THE BUSINESS MAY NOT BE SUITABLE Previous managers may have kept marginal employees because they were close friends or because they started with the company. A new owner, therefore, may have to make some very unpopular termination decisions. For this reason, employees often do not welcome a new owner because they feel threatened by change. Some employees may not be able to adapt to the new owner's management style, and a culture clash may result. If the due diligence efforts reveal that existing employees are a significant cause of the problems a business faces, the new owner will have no choice but to terminate them and hire new ones.

UNSATISFACTORY LOCATION What was once an ideal location may have become obsolete as market and demographic trends change. Large shopping malls, new competitors, or highway reroutings can spell disaster for small retail shops. Prospective buyers should always evaluate the existing market in the area surrounding an existing business as well as its potential for expansion. Buyers must remember that they are buying the future of a business, not its past. If business success is closely linked to a good location, acquiring a business in a declining area or where demographic trends are moving downward is not a good idea. The value of the business can erode faster than the neighborhood surrounding it.

OBSOLETE OR INEFFICIENT EQUIPMENT AND FACILITIES Potential buyers sometimes neglect to have an expert evaluate a company's facilities and equipment before they purchase it. Only later do they discover that the equipment is obsolete and inefficient and that the business is suffering losses from excessively high operating costs. Modernizing equipment and facilities is seldom inexpensive.

THE CHALLENGE OF IMPLEMENTING CHANGE It is easier to plan for change than it is to implement it. Methods, policies, and procedures the previous owner used in a business may have established precedents that a new owner finds difficult to modify. Employees and customers may resist changes to established procedures.

OBSOLETE INVENTORY Inventory is valuable only if it is salable. Smart buyers know better than to trust the inventory valuation on a firm's balance sheet. Some of it may actually appreciate in value in periods of rapid inflation, but inventory is more likely to depreciate. A prospective buyer must judge inventory by its market value, *not* by its book value.

WORTHLESS ACCOUNTS RECEIVABLE MAY BE WORTH LESS THAN FACE VALUE Like inventory, accounts receivable rarely are worth their face value. Prospective buyers should age a company's accounts receivable (a breakdown of accounts 30, 60, 90, and 120 days old and beyond) to determine their collectability. The older the receivables are, the less likely they are to be collected, and, consequently, the lower their value. Generally, receivables that are more than 90 days old are difficult, if not impossible, to collect.

THE BUSINESS MAY BE OVERPRICED At BizBuySell, an online marketplace for small companies that are for sale, the median asking price is $200,000, and the median actual sale price is $189,000.[21] Unfortunately, many people purchase businesses at prices far in excess of their value, which can impair the companies' ability to earn a profit and generate a positive cash flow. Some sellers attach an emotionally driven value on their businesses. Others set the value based on what they need to fund their retirement. If a buyer accurately values a business's accounts receivable, inventories, and other assets, he or she will be in a better position to negotiate a price that will allow the business to be profitable. Making payments on a business that is overpriced is a millstone around the new owner's neck, making it difficult to keep the business afloat.

Although most buyers do not realize it, the price they pay for a company typically is not as crucial to its continued success as the terms on which they make the purchase. Of course, wise business buyers will try to negotiate a fair and reasonable price, but they are often equally interested in the more specific terms of the deal. For instance, how much cash they must pay out and when, how much of the price the seller is willing to finance and for how long, at what interest rate the deal is financed, and other such terms can make or break a deal. A buyer's primary concern is making sure that the terms of the deal do not endanger the company's future financial health and that they preserve the company's cash flow.

The Steps in Acquiring a Business

LO6

Define the steps involved in the *right* way to buy a business.

Buying an existing business can be risky if approached haphazardly. Kevin Mulvaney, a senior lecturer of entrepreneurship at Babson College and CEO of a mergers and acquisitions consulting firm, says 50 to 75 percent of all business sales that are initiated fall through.[22] Figure 6.3 summarizes the acquisition process. To avoid blowing a deal or making costly mistakes, an entrepreneur-to-be should follow these seven steps:

1. Conduct a self-inventory, objectively analyzing skills, abilities, and personal interests to determine the type(s) of business that offer the best fit.

2. Develop a list of the criteria that define the "ideal business" for you.

3. Prepare a list of potential candidates that meet your criteria.

4. Thoroughly investigate the potential acquisition targets that meet your criteria. This *due diligence process* involves practical steps, such as analyzing financial statements and making certain that the facilities are structurally sound. The goal is to minimize the pitfalls and problems that arise when buying any business.

5. Explore various financing options for buying the business.

6. Negotiate a reasonable deal with the existing owner.

7. Ensure a smooth transition of ownership.

Mike Mosedale, www.cartoonstock.com

| 1. Identify and approach candidate | 2. Sign nondisclosure statement | 3. Sign letter of intent | 4. Buyer's due diligence investigation | 5. Draft the purchase agreement | 6. Close the final deal | 7. Begin the transition |

Negotiations

1. Approach the candidate. If a business is advertised for sale, the proper approach is through the channel defined in the ad. Sometimes buyers will contact business brokers to help them locate potential target companies. If you have targeted a company in the "hidden market," an introduction from a banker, accountant, or lawyer often is the best approach. During this phase, the seller checks out the buyer's qualifications, and the buyer begins to judge the quality of the company.

2. Sign a nondisclosure document. If the buyer and the seller are satisfied with the results of their preliminary research, they are ready to begin serious negotiations. Throughout the negotiation process, the seller expects the buyer to maintain strict confidentiality of all of the records, documents, and information he or she receives during the investigation and negotiation process. The nondisclosure document is a legally binding contract that ensures the secrecy of the parties' negotiations.

3. Sign a letter of intent. Before a buyer makes a legal offer to buy the company, he or she typically will ask the seller to sign a letter of intent. The letter of intent is a nonbinding document that says that the buyer and the seller have reached a sufficient "meeting of the minds" to justify the time and expense of negotiating a final agreement. The letter should state clearly that it is nonbinding, giving either party the right to walk away from the deal. It should also contain a clause calling for "good faith negotiations" between the parties. A typical letter of intent addresses terms such as price, payment terms, categories of assets to be sold, and a deadline for closing the final deal.

4. Buyer's due diligence. While negotiations are continuing, the buyer is busy studying the business and evaluating its strengths and weaknesses. In short, the buyer must "do his or her homework" to make sure that the business is a good value.

5. Draft the purchase agreement. The purchase agreement spells out the parties' final deal. It sets forth all of the details of the agreement and is the final product of the negotiation process.

6. Close the final deal. Once the parties have drafted the purchase agreement, all that remains to making the deal "official" is the closing. Both buyer and seller sign the necessary documents to make the sale final. The buyer delivers the required money, and the seller turns the company over to the buyer.

7. Begin the transition. For the buyer, the *real* challenge now begins: making the transition to a successful business owner!

FIGURE 6.3

The Acquisition Process

Sources: Based on *Buying and Selling: A Company Handbook* (New York: Price Waterhouse, 1993), pp. 38–42; Charles F. Claeys, "The Intent to Buy," *Small Business Reports,* May 1994, pp. 44–47.

Analyze Your Skills, Abilities, and Interests

The first step in buying a business is *not* searching out potential acquisition candidates. Every entrepreneur who is considering buying a business should begin by conducting a self-audit to determine the ideal business for him or her. The primary focus is to identify the type of business that *you* will be happiest and most successful owning. Consider, for example, the following questions:

- What business activities do you enjoy most? Least? Why?

- Which industries or markets offer the greatest potential for growth?

- Which industries interest you most? Least? Why?

- What kind of business would you enjoy running?

- What kinds of businesses do you want to *avoid*?

- What do you expect to get out of the business?

- How much time, energy, and money can you put into the business?

- What business skills and experience do you have? Which ones do you lack?

- How easily can you transfer your skills and experience to other types of businesses? In what kinds of businesses would that transfer be easiest?

- How much risk are you willing to take?

- Are you willing and able to turn around a struggling business?

- What size company do you want to buy?

- Is there a particular geographic location you desire?

Answering these and other questions beforehand allows you to develop a list of criteria a company must meet to become a purchase candidate. Addressing these issues early in the process will also save a great deal of time, trouble, and confusion as you wade through a multitude of business opportunities. The better you know yourself and your skills, competencies, and interests, the more likely you will be to find and manage a successful business.

Develop a List of Criteria

Based on the answers to the self-inventory questions, the next step is to develop a list of criteria that a potential business acquisition must meet. Investigating every business that you find for sale is a waste of time. The goal is to identify the characteristics of the "ideal business" for you so that you can focus on the most viable candidates as you wade through a multitude of business opportunities. These criteria will provide specific parameters against which you can evaluate potential acquisition candidates.

Prepare a List of Potential Candidates

Once you know what your goals are for acquiring a business, you can begin your search. Do *not* limit yourself to only those businesses that are advertised as being "for sale." In fact, the **hidden market** of companies that might be for sale but are not advertised as such is one of the richest sources of top-quality businesses. Many businesses that can be purchased are not publicly advertised but are available either through the owners themselves or through business brokers and other professionals. Although they maintain a low profile, these hidden businesses represent some of the most attractive purchase targets a prospective buyer may find.

hidden market
low-profile companies that might be for sale but are not advertised as such.

ENTREPRENEURIAL PROFILE: Art and Alan McCraw: B. W. Burdette and Sons When brothers Art and Alan McCraw, two enterprising college graduates, returned to their hometown, they approached the owners of B. W. Burdette and Sons, a local hardware store that had been founded by the current owners' father 80 years earlier about buying the business. The company was not listed for sale, but because the McCraws were familiar with the business, they knew that the current owners might be interested in selling. After several months of due diligence and negotiations, the young entrepreneurs closed the deal. They have since expanded the business to include two more locations, expanded its market reach, and increased its profitability many times over. ■

How can you tap into this hidden market of potential acquisitions? Typical sources include the following:

- The Internet, where several sites such as Bizbuysell.com and Bizquest, include listings of business brokers and companies for sale

- Business brokers—to locate a broker near you, visit the Web site for the International Business Brokers Association at www.ibba.org

- Professionals who provide business services, such as bankers, accountants, attorneys, investment bankers, and others

- Industry contacts—suppliers, distributors, customers, insurance brokers, and others

- Networking—social and business contact with friends and relatives

- Knocking on the doors of businesses you would like to buy (even if they're not advertised as being "for sale")

- Trade associations

- Newspapers and trade journals listing businesses for sale

The more opportunities an entrepreneur has to find and evaluate potential acquisitions, the greater the likelihood of finding a match that meets his or her criteria.

Investigate and Evaluate Potential Companies: The Due Diligence Process

Finding the right company requires patience. Although some buyers find a company after only a few months of looking, the typical search takes much longer, sometimes as much as two or three years. Once you have a list of prospective candidates, it is time to do your homework. The next step is to investigate the candidates in more detail:

- What are the company's strengths? Weaknesses?

- Is the company profitable? What is its overall financial condition?

- What is its cash flow cycle? How much cash will the company generate?

- Who are its major competitors?

- How large is the customer base? Is it growing or shrinking?

- Are the current employees suitable? Will they stay?

- What is the physical condition of the business, its equipment, and its inventory?

- What new skills must you learn to be able to manage this business successfully?

Determining the answers to these and other questions addressed in this chapter allow a prospective buyer to develop a list of the most attractive prospects and to prioritize them in descending order of attractiveness. This process also makes the task of valuing the business much easier. The next section of this chapter explains the due diligence process in more detail.

Explore Financing Options

According to a recent survey of business brokers by BizBuySell, an online marketplace for businesses that are for sale, the principal cause of business sales failing to close is lack of available financing.[23] Although financing the purchase of an existing business usually is easier than financing a new one, some traditional lenders shy away from deals involving the purchase of an existing business, especially in the wake of the financial crisis. Those that are willing to finance business purchases normally lend only a portion of the value of the assets, and buyers often find themselves searching for alternative sources of funds. Fortunately, most business buyers have access to a ready source of financing: the seller. Seller financing often is more flexible, faster, and easier to obtain than loans from traditional lenders; in fact, it is currently an essential part of most deals. BizBuySell estimates that in 90 percent of business sales, at least some portion of the financing is provided by the seller. Once a seller finds a suitable buyer, he or she typically will agree to finance anywhere from 25 to 80 percent of the purchase price.

Usually, a deal is structured so that the buyer makes a sizable down payment to the seller, who then finances a note for the balance. The buyer makes regular principal and interest payments over 5 to 10 years—perhaps with a larger balloon payment at the end—until the note is paid off. The terms and conditions of the loan are a vital concern to both buyer and seller. They cannot be so burdensome that they threaten the company's continued existence; that is, the buyer must be able to make the payments to the seller out of the company's cash flow. At the same time, the deal must give the seller the financial security he or she is seeking from the sale. Defining reasonable terms is the result of the negotiation process between the buyer and the seller.

ENTREPRENEURIAL PROFILE: Jamey Hamm: Roots Café Jamey Hamm purchased Roots Café in Brooklyn, New York, from its previous owner. Hamm was eating a meal at Roots Café and mentioned to the owner that he would like to own a business of his own some day. The owner also had purchased the restaurant but was never able to make it a profitable business. The owner offered to sell Hamm Roots Café. Intrigued, Hamm studied the business, liked what he saw, and was able to secure a loan from a family member. Because the owner was eager to sell Roots Café, Hamm was able to purchase the company's assets for $8,000 less than the seller's asking price.[24] ■

Negotiate a Reasonable Deal with the Owner

The buyer must sit down with the seller to negotiate the actual selling price for the business and, more important, the terms of the deal. The final deal the buyer strikes depends, in large part, on his or her negotiating skills. The first "rule" of negotiating a deal is to avoid confusing price with value. *Value* is what the business is actually worth; *price* is what the buyer agrees to pay. In a business sale, the party who is the better negotiator usually comes out on top. Buyers seek to do the following:

- Get the business at the lowest possible price.

- Negotiate favorable payment terms, preferably over time.

- Get assurances that they are buying the business they think they are getting.

- Avoid putting the seller in a position to open a competing business.

- Minimize the amount of cash paid up front.

Sellers are looking to do the following:

- Get the highest price possible for the business.

- Sever all responsibility for the company's liabilities.

- Avoid unreasonable contract terms that might limit his or her future opportunities.

- Maximize the cash they get from the deal.

- Minimize the tax burden from the sale.

- Make sure the buyer will be able to make all future payments.

One factor that makes the process of negotiating the purchase of a business challenging is that many business founders overestimate the value of their companies because of all of the "sweat equity" they have poured into their businesses over the years. Indeed, the second most common reason that business brokers say keeps business purchases from closing is the seller's unwillingness to lower the asking price.[25] One entrepreneur recalls a negotiation that he was involved in for the potential purchase of a rival's business. The company had $4 million in sales but had incurred losses of more than $1 million in the previous two years, owed more than $2.5 million in unpaid bills, and had no machinery that was less than 30 years old. Much to the prospective buyer's amazement, the owner was asking $4 million for the business![26]

Ensure a Smooth Transition

Once the parties strike a deal, the challenge of making a smooth transition immediately arises. No matter how well planned the sale is, there are *always* surprises. For instance, the new owner may have ideas for changing the business—sometimes radically—that cause a great deal of stress and anxiety among employees and the previous owner. Charged with such emotion and uncertainty, the transition phase is always difficult and frustrating—and sometimes painful. To avoid a bumpy transition, a business buyer should do the following:

- Concentrate on communicating with employees. Business sales are fraught with uncertainty and anxiety, and employees need reassurance.

- Be honest with employees. Avoid telling them only what they want to hear. Share with the employees your vision for the business in the hope of generating a heightened level of motivation and support.

- Listen to employees. They have firsthand knowledge of the business and its strengths and weaknesses and usually can offer valuable suggestions for improving it.

- Consider asking the seller to serve as a consultant until the transition is complete. The previous owner can be a valuable resource, especially to an inexperienced buyer.

- Be ready to act if it becomes clear that there are problem employees. Most small business owners wait too long to terminate employees who are not working out. The previous owner may have avoided addressing these issues prior to selling the business.

LO7

Understand how the negotiation process works and identify the factors that affect it.

Negotiating the Deal

On the surface, the negotiation process appears to be strictly adversarial. Although each party may be trying to accomplish objectives that are at odds with those of the opposing party, the negotiation process does not have to turn into a nasty battle of wits with overtones of "If you win, then I lose." The negotiation process will go much more smoothly and much faster if both parties work to establish a cooperative relationship based on honesty and trust from the outset. A successful deal requires both parties to examine and articulate their respective positions while trying to understand the other party's. Recognizing that neither of them will benefit without a deal, both parties must work to achieve their objectives while making certain concessions to keep the negotiations alive.

To avoid a stalled deal, a buyer should go into the negotiation with a list of objectives ranked in order of priority. Once he or she has developed a list of priorities, it is useful to develop what he or she perceives to be the seller's list of priorities. That requires learning as much as possible about the seller. Knowing which terms are most important (and which are least important) to him or her and to the seller enables a buyer to make concessions without "giving away the farm" and without getting bogged down in "nitpicking," which often leads to a stalemate. If, for instance, the seller insists on a term the buyer cannot agree to, he or she can explain why and then offer to give up something in exchange. The buyer also should identify the one concrete objective that sits at the top of that list, the one thing he or she absolutely must come away from the negotiations with. The final stage of preparing for the actual negotiation is to study his or her list and the one that he or she has developed based on his or her perceptions of the seller to determine where the two mesh and where they conflict. The key to a successful negotiation is to use this analysis to look for areas of mutual benefit and to use them as the foundation for the negotiation. The accompanying "Hands On: How To . . ." feature offers tips to help entrepreneurs become more effective negotiators.

Hands On . . . How To

Become a Successful Negotiator

Buying or selling a business always involves a negotiation, and so do many other business activities, whether an entrepreneur is dealing with a bank, a customer, or a vendor. Roger Fisher and William Ury, authors of *Getting to Yes,* say everyone negotiates several times every day. That's why negotiating skills are among the most important skills that entrepreneurs can learn. How can you become a more successful negotiator? The following advice will help.

1. **Prepare.** Good negotiators know that the formula for a successful negotiation is 90 percent preparation and 10 percent bargaining. What you do—or don't do—*before* the actual negotiation ever begins is a primary determinant of how successful your negotiation will be. The key is to learn as much as possible about the party with whom you will be negotiating, the issues that are most important to him or her, and his or her likely positions on those issues. Leo Riley, president of his own training and consulting firm, says remembering people's hobbies, families, interests, religious affiliations, and so forth serves as ice breakers and helps to avoid awkward mistakes.

    Your preparation for a negotiation also should include a statement of the outcome you desire from the negotiation. John Patrick Nolan, a negotiation specialist,

recommends that you develop a clear and precise set of goals when going into any negotiation. You also should write down what you think your *counterpart's* goals from the negotiation are. This encourages you to look at the negotiation from a different perspective and can be a valuable and revealing exercise.

2. **Remember the difference between a "position" and an "interest."** The outcome a person wants from a negotiation is his or her position. What is much more important, however, is his or her interest, the reason behind the position he or she hopes to achieve. Focusing strictly on their positions usually leads two parties into a win–lose mentality in a negotiation in which they try to pound one another into submission. When the parties involved in a negotiation focus on their *interests* rather than on their *positions*, however, they usually discover that there are several different solutions that both will consider acceptable and reasonable.

    The parable of the orange provides an excellent lesson on the difference between the two. Two parties each want an orange, but there is only one orange. After much intense negotiating, the two agree to cut the orange in half. As it turns out, however, one party wanted only the rind of the orange to make cookies, and the other party wanted

Hands On . . . How To *(continued)*

the orange to make orange juice. If the parties involved in the negotiation had focused on their interests and taken a problem-solving approach, both could have gotten exactly what they wanted from the negotiation!

3. ***Develop the right mindset.*** Inexperienced negotiators see a negotiation as a zero-sum, win–lose game. "If you win, then I lose." Entrepreneurs who want or need to maintain ongoing relationships with the other party (e.g., buying a business from the company founder, whom you want to convince to stay on through a transition period to help you learn the business) must see negotiations in a different light. Their goal is to work toward a mutually beneficial agreement that both parties consider to be fair and reasonable.

   Successful negotiations almost always involve compromise on both sides, meaning that *neither* party gets *everything* he or she wanted. Mike Staver, a negotiation consultant, says many times you may not be completely satisfied with the results of a negotiation. In other words, successful negotiators see a negotiation not just as deal making but also as problem solving.

4. ***Always leave yourself an escape hatch.*** In any negotiation, you should be prepared to walk away without making a deal. Doing so, however, requires you to define what negotiation experts call a best alternative to a negotiated agreement (BATNA), which is the next best alternative to a negotiated outcome. You cannot determine whether a negotiated agreement is suitable unless you know what your alternatives are, and one alternative (although not always the best one) is to walk away from the negotiation without an agreement—your BATNA. Although you may never need to use your BATNA, it is good to know you have it in your "back pocket" to give you confidence and help you remain calm throughout the negotiating process.

   Having a BATNA increases your power in a negotiation, but you should use that power judiciously. Do not use your BATNA as a threat to coerce an agreement. In addition,

don't kill the deal just because you can. Instead, use your BATNA as the baseline against which you measure your negotiated alternatives.

5. ***Keep your emotions in check.*** Negotiations can become emotionally charged, especially if those involved allow their egos to enter into the process. It is always best to abide by the golden rule of negotiating: treat others the way you want to be treated in the negotiation. Be fair but firm. If the other party forgets the golden rule of negotiating, remember that you can always walk away from the negotiation and fall back on your BATNA.

6. ***Don't fall into the "rules" trap.*** Successful negotiations involve give-and-take by both parties. There are no hard and fast rules that prohibit either party from making changes in contracts or agreements throughout the negotiating process. Nothing is settled until both parties sign the final documents. Until then, the parties can change anything. The goal is not to win specific points in the negotiating process; the goal is to reach an agreement viewed as fair and reasonable to both sides of the negotiation.

7. ***Sometimes it's best to remain silent.*** A common mistake many people make in the negotiation process is talking too much. Not only does remaining silent allow you to listen to the other party, but it also encourages the other party to make the first offer. Some people are disconcerted by prolonged periods of silence and begin talking, only to erode the strength of their negotiation base.

Source: Based on "How to Negotiate Effectively," *Inc. Guidebook*, vol. 2, no. 7, pp. 1–4; "My Best Negotiation Tips," *Paul's Tips*, June 11, 2006, http://www .paulstips.com/brainbox/pt/home.nsf/link/10062006-My-eight-best-negotiation-tips; Rhonda Abrams, "Know What You Need Before Starting to Negotiate Deal," *Greenville News Business*, May 29, 2005, p. 8; "Negotiating to Resolve Conflict," Fed Ex Small Business Center, January 22, 2003, http://www.mysmallbizcenter.com/rawdoc .asp?docID=7169&temp=6378; Scott Smith, "Negotiate from Strength," *Success*, July/August 2000, pp. 74–75; Susan St. John, "Five Steps to Better Negotiating," *E-Merging Business*, Fall–Winter 2000, pp. 212–214; and Rob Walker, "Take It or Leave It: The *Only* Guide to Negotiating You Will *Ever* Need, *Inc.*, August 2003, pp. 75–82; Susan St. John, "Five Steps to Better Negotiating," *E-Merging Business*, Fall–Winter 2000, pp. 212–214.

Chapter Summary by Learning Objective

1. **Explain the advantages and disadvantages of a sole proprietorship and a partnership.**

   - A sole proprietorship is a business owned and managed by one individual and is the most popular form of ownership.

   - Sole proprietorships offer these *advantages*: They are simple to create, they are the least costly form to begin, the owner has total decision-making authority, there are no special legal restrictions, and they are easy to discontinue.

   - Sole proprietorships also suffer from these *disadvantages*: unlimited personal liability of the owner,

   limited managerial skills and capabilities, limited access to capital, and lack of continuity.

   - A partnership is an association of two or more people who co-own a business for the purpose of making a profit. Partnerships offer these *advantages*: ease of establishing, complementary skills of partners, division of profits, larger pool of capital available, ability to attract limited partners, little government regulation, flexibility, and tax advantages.

   - Partnerships suffer from these *disadvantages*: unlimited liability of at least one partner, difficulty in disposing of partnership, lack of continuity, potential for personality and authority conflicts, and partners bound by the law of agency.

2. Describe the similarities and differences of the C corporation and the S corporation.

- Both C corporations and S corporations are separate legal entities. To form a corporation, an entrepreneur must file the articles of incorporation with the state in which the company will incorporate.

- Both types of corporations offer these *advantages*: limited liability of stockholders, ability to attract capital, ability to continue indefinitely, and transferable ownership.

- C corporations suffer from these *disadvantages*: double taxation, potential for diminished managerial incentives, legal requirements and regulatory red tape, and potential loss of control by the founder(s).

- S corporations are pass-through entities and do not have taxation of profits at the corporate level.

3. Understand the characteristics of the limited liability company.

- An LLC is not a corporation but offers the advantage of limited liability to its owners.

- An LLC is a cross between a partnership and a corporation yet operates without the restrictions imposed on an S corporation. To create an LLC, an entrepreneur must file the articles of organization with the secretary of state and create an operating agreement.

4. Explain the process of creating a legal entity for a business.

- C corporations, S corporations, and LLCs can be costly and time consuming to establish and to maintain.

- Many entrepreneurs hire attorneys to handle the process, but in most states entrepreneurs can complete all of the required forms, most of which are online, themselves.

5. Understand the advantages and disadvantages of buying an existing business.

- The *advantages* of buying an existing business include the following: a successful business may continue to be successful, the business may already have the best location, employees and suppliers are already established, equipment is installed and its productive capacity known, inventory is in place and trade credit established, the owner hits the ground running, the buyer can use the expertise of the previous owner, and the business may be a bargain.

- The disadvantages of buying an existing business include the following: an existing business may be for sale because it is deteriorating, the previous owner may have created ill will, employees inherited with the business may not be suitable, its location may have become unsuitable, equipment and facilities may be obsolete, change and innovation are hard to implement, inventory may be outdated, accounts receivable may be worth less than face value, and the business may be overpriced.

6. Define the steps involved in the *right* way to buy a business.

- Buying a business can be a treacherous experience unless the buyer is well prepared.

- The right way to buy a business is to analyze your skills, abilities, and interests to determine the ideal business for you; prepare a list of potential candidates, including those that might be in the "hidden market"; investigate and rank candidate businesses and evaluate the best one; explore financing options before you actually need the money; and ensure a smooth transition.

7. Understand how the negotiation process works and identify the factors that affect it.

- The first rule of negotiating is to never confuse price with value.

- In a business sale, the party who is the better negotiator usually comes out on top. Before beginning negotiations, a buyer should identify the factors that are affecting the negotiations and then develop a negotiating strategy.

- The best deals are the result of a cooperative relationship between the parties based on trust.

Discussion Questions

6-1. What factors should an entrepreneur consider before choosing a form of ownership?

6-2. Why are sole proprietorships so popular as a form of ownership?

6-3. How does personal conflict affect partnerships?

6-4. What issues should the articles of partnership address?

6-5. Why are the articles important to a successful partnership?

6-6. Explain why one partner cannot commit another to a business deal without the other's consent.

6-7. What issues should the Certificate of Incorporation cover?

6-8. How does an S corporation differ from a regular corporation?

6-9. What role do limited partners play in a partnership?

6-10. What happens if a limited partner takes an active role in managing the business?

6-11. What advantages does an LLC offer over an S corporation?

6-12. What advantages does an LLC offer over a partnership?

6-13. How is an LLC created?

6-14. What criteria must an LLC meet to avoid double taxation?

6-15. What advantages can an entrepreneur who buys a business gain over one who starts a business "from scratch"?

6-16. How would you go about determining the value of the assets of a business if you were unfamiliar with them?

6-17. Why do so many entrepreneurs run into trouble when they buy an existing business?

6-18. Outline the steps involved in the *right* way to buy a business.

6-19. What tips would you offer someone about to enter into negotiations to buy a business?

6-20. One entrepreneur who recently purchased a business advises buyers to expect some surprises in the deal no matter how well prepared they may be. He says potential buyers must build some "wiggle room" into their plans to buy a company. What steps can a buyer take to ensure that he or she has sufficient wiggle room?

Beyond the Classroom . . .

6-21. Interview four local small business owners.

6-22. What form of ownership did each of the business owners choose?

6-23. Why did the business owners you interviewed choose the form of ownership they did?

6-24. Prepare a brief report summarizing your findings and explain the advantages and disadvantages those owners face because of their choices.

6-25. Explain why you think these business owners have or have not chosen the form of ownership that is best for their particular situations.

6-26. Invite entrepreneurs who operate as partners to your classroom.

6-27. Do they have a written partnership agreement?

6-28. Are their skills complementary?

6-29. How do they divide responsibility for running their company?

6-30. How do they handle decision making?

6-31. What do they do when disputes and disagreements arise?

6-32. Interview several new owners who purchased existing businesses.

6-33. How did they determine the value of the business?

6-34. Visit a business broker and ask him or her how he or she brings a buyer and seller together.

6-35. What does the broker do to facilitate the sale?

6-36. What methods does the broker use to determine the value of a business?

6-37. Invite an attorney to speak to your class about the legal aspects of buying a business.

6-38. How does he or she recommend that a business buyer protect himself or herself legally in a business purchase?

Endnotes

Scan for Endnotes or go to www.pearsonhighered.com/scarborough

7

Franchising and the Entrepreneur

Steve Hix, Getty Images, Inc.

Learning Objectives

On completion of this chapter, you will be able to:

1. Describe the three types of franchising: trade name, product distribution, and pure.

2A. Explain the benefits of buying a franchise.

2B. Explain the drawbacks of buying a franchise.

3. Understand the laws covering franchise purchases.

4. Discuss the *right* way to buy a franchise.

5. Outline the major trends shaping franchising.

Samantha Goldsmith learned about business from her father, Harvey, who owned a company that rented equipment for businesses to use when taking inventory. "I've wanted to be like my Dad since I was five years old," she says. Goldsmith began working part-time at a Bed Bath and Beyond store on her native Long Island, New York, when she was 16 years old and was promoted twice in less than two years. When she was just 21 years old, Goldsmith attended a franchise expo with her father and was intrigued by the "delicious and healthy" product line of the Red Mango all-natural yogurt and smoothie franchise. She applied for a franchise and, with her father's help, became the youngest franchisee in the Red Mango chain. Now only 25, Goldsmith owns 10 Red Mango franchises, which makes her the largest multi-unit operator in the system. "I want my stores to be as profitable as they can be, and I want people to see how clean and well-run the stores are," she says. Goldsmith works closely with her husband, Tim Gatto, who serves as Goldsmith Companies' chief operations officer, but her father remains her greatest fan. "He tells me how proud he is all the time," she says. *Multi-Unit Franchisee* magazine recently honored Goldsmith by naming her the winner of one of its prestigious MVP Awards.[1]

Samantha Goldsmith

Like Goldsmith's business, most franchised outlets are small, but as a whole, they have a significant impact on the U.S. economy. In the United States alone, about 3,000 franchisors operate more than 770,000 franchise outlets (see Figure 7.1), and more are opening constantly both in the United States and around the world. Franchises generate more than $800 billion in annual sales, account for 4.1 percent of the U.S. GDP, and employ nearly 8.1 million workers in the United States in more than 300 industries.[2] Much of the popularity of franchising stems from its ability to offer those who lack business experience the chance to own and operate a business with a high probability of success. This booming industry has moved far beyond the traditional boundaries of fast food and hotels into fields as diverse as mosquito spraying, used clothing, mold detection, and pet resorts. In 2008, Daniel Rella, Chris Couri, and Tom Darrow launched a part-time parking lot striping business, We Do Lines, in Richfield, Connecticut, that quickly became a full-time business. They soon discovered that the parking lot striping business was a $1 billion a year industry with no national players and in 2009 began selling franchises. Currently with 10 franchisees, the entrepreneurs have plans to expand to more than 100 franchises within five years. "We'll teach you everything you need to know," says Rella.[3] Figure 7.2 provides a breakdown of the franchise market by industry.

Franchising also has a significant impact on the global economy. U.S. franchisors are expanding globally to reach their growth targets. A survey by the International Franchise Association reports that 61 percent of its members operate in international markets and that 74 percent of international franchisors plan to accelerate the growth of their global franchised units in the near future.[4] Countries that are attracting the greatest attention for international expansion among

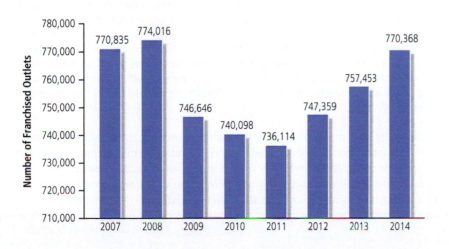

FIGURE 7.1

Number of Franchised Outlets in the United States

Source: "Number of Franchised Outlets in the US" from Franchise Business Economic Outlook for 2013, International Franchise Association Educational Foundation, IHS Global Insight. Copyright © 2012 IHS Inc. All rights reserved. Permission to use this content granted by IHS Inc. in advance. Further reuse or redistribution is strictly prohibited.

FIGURE 7.2

Franchised Outlets by Industry

Source: Based on *Franchise Business Economic Outlook for 2014*, International Franchise Association Educational Foundation, HIS Global Insight, January 13, 2014, p. 3.

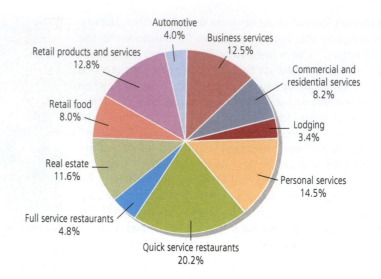

franchising

a system of distribution in which semi-independent business owners (franchisees) pay fees and royalties to a parent company (franchisor) in return for the right to become identified with its trademark, to sell its products or services, and often to use its business format and system.

franchisors include Brazil, India, China, and nations in the Middle East and North Africa region. With their fast-growing populations, rising levels of disposable income, spreading urbanization, and keen interest in American brands, these nations offer prime growth opportunities for U.S. franchisors.

In **franchising**, semi-independent business owners (franchisees) pay fees and royalties to a parent company (franchisor) in return for the right (license) to become identified with its trademark, to sell its products or services, and often to use its business format and system. Franchisees do not establish their own autonomous businesses; instead, they buy a "success package" from the franchisor, who shows them how to use it. Franchisees, unlike independent business owners, don't have the freedom to change the way they run their businesses—for example, shifting advertising strategies or adjusting product lines—but they do have access to a formula for success that the franchisor has worked out. "As a franchisee, your role is to operate," says franchising expert Mark Spriggs. "You have to be willing to follow the rules."[5] Fundamentally, when franchisees buy franchises, they are purchasing a successful business model. The franchisor provides the business model and the expertise to make it work; the franchisee brings the investment, spirit, and drive necessary to implement the model successfully. Many successful franchisors claim that neglecting to follow the formula is one of the chief reasons some franchisees fail. "If you are overly entrepreneurial and you want to invent you own wheel, or if you are not comfortable with following a system, don't go down [the franchise] path," says Don DeBolt, former head of the International Franchise Association.[6]

ENTREPRENEURIAL PROFILE: Schlachter's Maaco Auto Painting and Bodyworks Anita Schlachter, co-owner of a highly successful Maaco (automotive services) franchise with her husband and her son, is convinced that the system the franchisor taught them is the key to their company's progress and growth to date. The Schlachters follow the franchisor's plan, using it as a road map to success. Schlacter says franchisees who listen to their franchisors and follow their policies and procedures are likely to be successful. Entrepreneurs who believe they know more about the business than the franchisor should avoid franchising and launch independent businesses.[7] ■

Franchising is built on an ongoing relationship between a franchisor and a franchisee (see Figure 7.3). The franchisor provides valuable services, such as a proven business system, training and support, name recognition, and many other forms of assistance; in return, the franchisee pays an initial franchise fee as well as an ongoing percentage of his or her outlet's sales to the franchisor as a royalty and agrees to operate the outlet according to the franchisor's terms. Because franchisors develop the business systems that their franchisees use and direct their distribution

FIGURE 7.3
The Franchising Relationship

Source: From *Economic Impact of Franchised Businesses: A Study for the International Franchise Association Educational Foundation,* Copyright 2004 by the International Franchise Association. Reprinted with permission.

Element	The Franchisor	The Franchisee
Site selection	Oversees and approves; may choose site.	Chooses site with franchisor's approval.
Design	Provides prototype design.	Pays for and implements design.
Employees	Makes general recommendations and training suggestions.	Hires, manages, and fires employees.
Products and services	Determines product or service line.	Modifies only with franchisor's approval.
Prices	Can only recommend prices.	Sets final prices.
Purchasing	Establishes quality standards; provides list of approved suppliers; may require franchisees to purchase from the franchisor.	Must meet quality standards; must purchase only from approved suppliers; must purchase from supplier if required.
Advertising	Develops and coordinates national ad campaign; may require minimum level of spending on local advertising.	Pays for national ad campaign; complies with local advertising requirements; gets franchisor approval on local ads.
Quality control	Sets quality standards and enforces them with inspections; trains franchisees.	Maintains quality standards; trains employees to implement quality systems.
Support	Provides support through an established business system.	Operates business on a day-to-day basis with franchiser's support.

methods, they maintain substantial control over their franchisees. Yet this standardization lies at the core of franchising's success as a method of distribution.

Types of Franchising

Many experts trace the roots of modern franchising to the 1850s when Isaac Singer, founder of the Singer Sewing Machine Company, decided to expand his young business by granting licenses to other businesses that would sell his company's sewing machines in specific geographic areas.[8] Three basic types of franchises operate in almost every industry: trade-name franchising, product distribution franchising, and pure franchising. **Trade-name franchising** involves a brand name, such as True Value Hardware or Western Auto. Here, the franchisee purchases the right to use the franchisor's trade name without distributing particular products exclusively under the franchisor's name. **Product distribution franchising** involves a franchisor licensing a franchisee to sell specific products under the franchisor's brand name and trademark through a selective, limited distribution network. This system is commonly used to market automobiles (Chevrolet, Lexus, Ford), gasoline products (ExxonMobil, Sunoco, Texaco), soft drinks (Pepsi Cola, Coca-Cola), appliances, cosmetics, and other products. These two methods of franchising allow franchisees to affiliate with the parent company's identity.

Pure franchising (also called comprehensive or business format franchising) involves providing the franchisee with a complete business format, including a license for a trade name, the products or services to be sold, the store layout, the methods of operation, a marketing plan, a quality control process, a two-way communications system, and the necessary business support services. In short, the franchisee purchases the right to use all of the elements of a fully integrated

trade-name franchising
a system of franchising in which a franchisee purchases the right to use the franchisor's trade name without distributing particular products exclusively under the franchisor's name.

LO1
Describe the three types of franchising: trade name, product distribution, and pure.

product distribution franchising
a system of franchising in which a franchisor licenses a franchisee to sell its products under the franchisor's brand name and trademark through a selective, limited distribution network.

pure franchising
a system of franchising in which a franchisor sells a franchisee a complete business format and system.

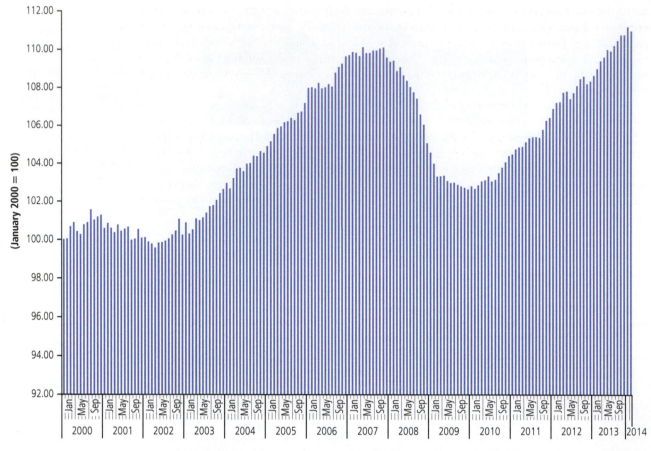

FIGURE 7.4

Franchise Business Index

Source: Based on data from Franchise Business Index, International Franchise Association, 2014, http://franchiseeconomy.com/what-is-the-current-state-of-the-franchise-industry/.

business operation. Business format franchising is the most common and the fastest growing of the three types of franchising and accounts for nearly 95 percent of all franchised outlets.[9] It is common among quick service restaurants, hotels, business service firms, car rental agencies, educational institutions, beauty aid retailers, and many other types of businesses.

The franchise industry is not immune to cyclical swings in the economy. Recessions, high unemployment, declining business and consumer confidence, and tight credit conditions lead to failures of both independent and franchised businesses. Figure 7.4 shows the International Franchise Association's Franchise Business Index, a composite measure of the economic health of the franchise industry that includes six different indicators (January 2000 = 100).

LO2A

Explain the benefits of buying a franchise.

The Benefits of Buying a Franchise

A franchisee gets the opportunity to own a small business relatively quickly and, because of the identification with an established product and brand name, often reaches the break-even point faster than an independent business would. Still, most new franchise outlets don't break even for at least 6 to 18 months.

Franchisees also benefit from the franchisor's business experience. In fact, experience is the essence of what a franchisee is buying from a franchisor. As you learned in Chapter 1, many entrepreneurs go into business by themselves and make costly mistakes. Given the thin margin for error in the typical start-up, a new business owner cannot afford to make many mistakes. In a franchising arrangement, the franchisor already has worked out the kinks in the system by trial and error, and franchisees benefit from that experience. A franchisor has climbed up the learning curve and shares with franchisees the secrets of success it has discovered in the industry. "A great franchisor has developed all of the tools that you need to start a business," says Lori Kiser-Block, president of a franchise consulting firm. "They've developed the marketing system, the training and operation system, the brand, and the marketing tools you need. They've made all of the mistakes for you."[10]

For many first-time entrepreneurs, access to a business model with a proven track record is the safest way to own a business. Still, every potential franchisee must consider one important question: "What can a franchise do for me that I cannot do for myself?" The answer to this question depends on one's particular situation and requires a systematic evaluation of a franchise opportunity. After careful deliberation, one person may conclude that a franchise offers nothing that he or she could not do independently, and another may decide that a franchise is the key to success as a business owner. Franchisees often cite the advantages discussed in the following sections.

A Business System

One of the biggest benefits of buying a franchise is gaining access to a business system that has a proven record of success. In many cases, the business system that a franchisor provides allows franchisees to get their businesses up and running faster than if they had tried to launch them on their own. Fran Lubin, who left the corporate office of Goddard School, an early education franchise, to become a Goddard franchisee, recalls, "I understood that the business was mine to run. Goddard was there to help me and to provide multiple resources and a proven system, but it was up to me to take all of those things and to make my business successful."[11]

Using the franchisor's business system as a guide, franchisees can be successful even though they may have little or no experience in the industry. According to Jerry Perch, director of franchise development for Express Oil Change, the franchisor looks first for candidates who are financially qualified. The company does not require franchisees to have experience as mechanics; instead, the ideal candidate is someone with business skills whom the franchisor can train to operate a million-dollar business successfully.[12]

ENTREPRENEURIAL PROFILE: Spencer Smith: Aaron's and Big O Tires Spencer Smith started "working" in his father's tire store every day after he got out of kindergarten, so it was only natural that, as an adult, he would purchase a Big O Tires franchise. Smith, who now owns two Big O Tire franchises and 39 Aaron's franchises in eight western states that generate $49 million in annual sales, emphasizes the importance of following the franchisor's business system in his operation. "When you buy into a franchise, you're buying into doing business that particular way," says Smith. "If you have to be a maverick and reinvent the wheel all the time, both you and the franchisor will be frustrated. When I look at a potential franchise, I ask myself: 'Am I fully on board with doing business the way they're doing business?' If not, I keep looking."[13] ∎

TUR. Inc. dba: Aaron's

Management Training and Support

Franchisors want to give their franchisees a greater chance for success than independent businesses and offer management training programs to franchisees prior to opening a new outlet. Many franchisors, especially well-established ones, also provide follow-up training and consulting services. This service is vital because most franchisors do not require franchisees to have experience in the industry. These programs teach franchisees the fundamentals they need to know for day-to-day operations as well as the nuances of running their businesses successfully. After John Grassia and David Smith retired as pilots for large airlines, they embarked on their second careers as franchisees when they opened an Express Oil Change near Orlando, Florida. The franchisor's support and training were primary drivers in their decision to go with Express Oil Change. Unlike some franchisors that sell franchises and say, "Good luck" to the buyer, Express Oil wants its franchisees to succeed and offers them the support they need to achieve success. Grassia says that Express Oil is proactive in its support, noting that if franchise officials see a franchise struggling in a particular area, they are quick to offer help to resolve the problem.[14]

Training programs often involve both classroom and on-site instruction to teach franchisees the basic operations of the business. McDonald's is famous for Hamburger University, where franchisees and their employees go to learn the proper systems and procedures for operating a restaurant successfully. Training involves classroom instruction from 19 faculty members from around the world, hands-on activities, simulations of events that franchisees are likely to encounter, and computerized e-learning modules at one of seven Hamburger University centers around the world. More than 275,000 people have graduated from Hamburger University, earning their degrees in Hamburgerology.[15]

To ensure franchisees' continued success, many franchisors supplement their start-up training programs with ongoing instruction and support. For instance, Ben & Jerry's sends regional trainers to new franchisees' locations for additional training before they open their Scoop Shops. Once they are up and running, franchisees also benefit from ongoing training programs from Ben & Jerry's field-based support team.[16] Franchisors offer these training programs because they realize that their ultimate success depends on their franchisee's success.

Brand-Name Appeal

A franchisee purchases the right to use a nationally known and advertised brand name for a product or service. Thus, the franchisee has the advantage of identifying his business with a widely recognized trademark, which provides a great deal of drawing power, particularly for franchisees of established systems. Customers recognize the identifying trademark, the standard symbols, the store design, and the products of an established franchise. Because of the franchise's name recognition, franchisees who have just opened their outlets often discover a ready supply of customers ready to purchase their products or services. Entrepreneurs who launch independent businesses may have to work for years and spend many thousands of dollars in advertising to build a customer base of equivalent size. "One of the reasons I bought an AAMCO [transmission repair] franchise was its name recognition," says Stephen Rogers, who owns a franchise in Lockport, New York.[17]

One of the basic tenets of franchising is cloning the franchisor's success. For example, nearly everyone recognizes the golden arches of McDonald's or the pigtailed little girl on the Wendy's sign (founder Dave Thomas named the company after his daughter) and the standard products and quality offered at each. A customer can be confident that the quality and content of a meal at a Fort Lauderdale McDonald's will be consistent with a meal at a San Francisco McDonald's. However, franchisees must be equally aware that negative actions by the franchisor or other franchisees can undermine the value of the brand name and have a negative impact on other stores in the chain. From franchisees' perspective, one of the most important functions that a franchisor performs is promoting and enhancing the company's brand because a stellar brand perception among customers and potential customers translates directly into sales for franchisees. Guillermo Perales, who owns 398 franchises from seven different companies, ranging from Arby's and Burger King to Del Taco and T-Mobile, is one of the most successful franchisees in the United States and understands the necessity of proper brand management. "It's very important for the franchisor to take care of the brand," he says. "We [franchisees] all have a lot riding on this business. Good management of the brand is essential."[18]

Standardized Quality of Goods and Services

Because a franchisee purchases a license to sell the franchisor's product or service and the privilege of using the associated brand name, the quality of the goods or service sold determines the franchisor's reputation. Building a sound reputation in business can take many years, but destroying a good reputation takes no time at all. If some franchisees are allowed to operate at substandard levels, the image of the entire chain suffers irreparable damage; therefore, franchisors normally demand compliance with uniform standards of quality and service throughout the entire chain. In many cases, the franchisor conducts periodic inspections of local facilities to assist in maintaining acceptable levels of performance.

ENTREPRENEURIAL PROFILE: John Schnatter: Papa John's John Schnatter, founder of Papa John's, a fast-growing pizza franchise with more than 4,400 outlets in every state and 34 global markets, makes personal visits to some of his franchisees' stores four or five times each week to make sure they are performing up to the company's high quality standards. Franchisees say Schnatter, known for his attention to detail, often checks pizzas for air bubbles in the crust or tomato sauce for freshness. "Pizza is Schnatter's life, and he takes it very seriously," says one industry analyst.[19] ■

Maintaining quality is so important that most franchisors retain the right to terminate the franchise contract and to repurchase the outlet if the franchisee fails to comply with established standards.

National Advertising Programs and Marketing Assistance

An effective advertising program is essential to the success of every franchise operation. Marketing a brand-name product or service across a wide geographic area requires a far-reaching advertising campaign. A regional or national advertising program benefits all franchisees, and most franchisors have one. In fact, one study reports that 79 percent of franchisors require franchisees to contribute to a national advertising fund (the average amount is 2 percent of sales).[20] Typically, these advertising campaigns are organized and controlled by the franchisor, but franchisees actually pay for the campaigns. In fact, they are financed by each franchisee's contribution of a percentage of monthly sales, usually 1 to 5 percent, or a flat monthly fee. For example, franchisees at Subway, the sandwich chain with more than 42,000 restaurants in 107 countries, pay 4.5 percent of weekly gross sales to the company's national advertising program. Subway pools these funds and uses them for a cooperative advertising program; doing so has more impact than if franchisees spent the same amount of money separately.

Many franchisors also require franchisees to spend a minimum amount on local advertising. In fact, 41 percent of franchisors require their franchisees to invest in local advertising (once again, the average amount is 2 percent of sales).[21] To supplement their national advertising efforts, both Wendy's and Burger King require franchisees to spend at least 3 percent of gross sales on local advertising. Some franchisors assist franchisees in designing and producing local ads. Many companies also help franchisees create marketing plans and provide professionally designed marketing materials, including outdoor advertisements, newspaper inserts, posters, banners, brochures, direct-mail pieces, and platforms for social media and mobile marketing campaigns. Both Google and Facebook now offer marketing features that enable franchisors and franchisees to collaborate on social media promotions and are designed to increase companies' reach by promoting posts on news feeds for a flat rate. Some franchisors provide a corporate social media presence with links to franchisees' local pages that allow franchisees to add their own content that is relevant to their customers. For example, McDonald's manages a corporate Facebook page where visitors can type in their zip codes to access the pages of their local franchises that feature content customized for them. Other franchises, particularly those whose franchisees' businesses vary depending on their location, allow their franchisees to control their own social media presence. Buffalo Wild Wings follows this approach, and its franchisees use their own social media pages to promote local events, festivals, games featuring local teams, and specials.[22]

Nearly 27 percent of e-commerce Web traffic now originates from mobile devices such as smart phones and tablets.[23] As mobile marketing becomes more prevalent, franchisors are developing mobile apps that make it easy for customers to purchase from their franchisees. LaVida Massage, a chain with more than 50 franchises in the United States and Canada, recently unveiled a mobile app that allows clients to schedule massages at its franchised locations, view their operating hours, and read about message therapists' qualifications and specialties.[24] Domino's Pizza, a pizza franchise with nearly 11,000 outlets in

Domino's Pizza LLC

more than 70 countries, is the leader in mobile marketing in the pizza industry, with 35 percent of its online sales originating from mobile devices. Domino's mobile app, which has been downloaded by more than 10 million customers, allows customers to place their orders in just seconds and includes a "Pizza Tracker," that permits customers to monitor their pizzas' progress ("Our expert pizza maker, Antonio, put your pizza in the oven at 7:08 P.M.") and know when it will arrive. The latest version includes a Siri-like virtual assistant named Dom that enables customers to speak their orders (I'd like a large pepperoni pizza with extra cheese") without having to type them in.[25]

Financial Assistance

Purchasing a franchise can be just as expensive (if not more so) than launching an independent business, and the recent upheaval in the financial markets has made many lenders hesitant to fund business start-ups, including franchises. A study by FRANdata shows that the funding gap between the capital that franchises need to grow and the capital that lenders actually provide has averaged nearly 9 percent per year for the last several years (see Figure 7.5). In one year alone, that lack of funding translated into the "loss" of 2,200 outlets that franchisees could not open and would have added $6.1 billion to U.S. GDP.[26]

ENTREPRENEURIAL PROFILE: Guillermo Perales: Sun Holdings LLC After graduating from college in Mexico and working for a large Mexican company, Guillermo Perales moved to Dallas, Texas, where he spotted many business opportunities. In 1997, Perales opened his first Golden Corral restaurant with the help of a $100,000 loan supported by an SBA guarantee. Today, Perales's company, Sun Holdings LLC, owns 398 franchises from seven different companies and generates annual sales of $400 million. "It's better to be a part of a bigger [franchise] system," says Perales. "It takes away some of the risk when you have a recognizable name, and it makes financing easier to get."[27] ■

Although franchisees typically invest a significant amount of their own money in their businesses, most need additional financing. In some cases, the franchisor will provide at least

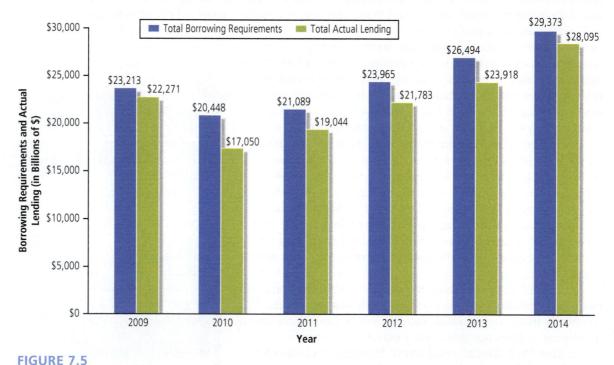

FIGURE 7.5

The Franchise Lending Gap

Source: Based on Data from *Small Business Lending Matrix and Analysis: The Impact of the Credit Crisis on the Franchise Sector,* The International Franchise Association and FRANdata, Volume VI, March 2014, p. 16.

some of that additional financing. A basic principle of franchising is to use franchisees' money to grow their businesses, but some franchisors realize that because start-up costs have reached breathtakingly high levels, they must provide financial help for franchisees. In fact, a study by FRANdata, a franchising research company, reports that 20 percent of franchisors offer direct financing to their franchisees.[28] However, the credit crunch has caused a growing number of franchisors to provide financial assistance to franchisees. "Helping franchisees access financing wasn't a franchisor function a couple of years ago," says Shelly Sun, founder and CEO of Bright-Star Franchising LLC, which provides in-home care service for senior citizens and children. "Now it's job number one."[29]

Small franchise systems are more likely to provide direct financial assistance to franchisees than are larger, more established franchisors. Traditionally, franchisors rarely make loans to enable franchisees to pay the initial franchise fee. However, once a franchisor locates a suitable prospective franchisee, it may offer the qualified candidate direct financial assistance in specific areas, such as purchasing equipment, inventory, or even the franchise fee.

In most instances, financial assistance from franchisors takes a form other than direct loans, leases, or short-term credit. Franchisors usually are willing to help qualified franchisees establish relationships with banks, nonbank lenders, and other sources of financing. The support and connections from the franchisor enhance a franchisee's credit standing because lenders recognize the lower failure rate among established franchises. For instance, Domino's Pizza, the popular pizza franchise, recently forged a relationship with Balboa Capital, a lender that specializes in loans to small and mid-sized companies and franchises, to be the preferred lender for its franchisees. Balboa Capital provides customized financing so that new franchisees can have sufficient working capital and can purchase furniture, fixtures, and equipment and existing franchisees can remodel their stores, make lease-hold improvements, and upgrade to the latest technology. As Domino's Pizza's preferred lender, Balboa Capital offers franchisees a simplified application and approval process with faster processing times.[30]

In an attempt to reignite their chains' growth, some franchisors are reducing fees, cutting royalties, and extending credit to help franchisees open outlets. Papa John's Pizza, the pizza franchise based in Louisville, Kentucky, recently offered an incentive package of discounts on its franchise fee and equipment worth $78,000 and a waiver for 18 months on royalties to new and existing franchisees. Joe Smith, Papa John's global sales and development manager, says that the company wants its franchisees to get off to a good start. By investing less to open their restaurants, they are able to invest more in marketing and attracting large customer bases more quickly. Erik Severinghaus and his business partners have opened seven Papa John's restaurants in Chicago in just three years and are about to open another one. He says that he and his partners would not have opened as many outlets as quickly if it were not for the discounts that Papa John's offered on capital equipment and the reductions in franchise fees and royalties.[31]

The Small Business Administration (SBA) has created a program called the Franchise Registry that is designed to provide financing for franchisees through its loan guarantee programs (more on these in Chapter 13). The Franchise Registry streamlines the loan application process for franchisees who pass the screening tests at franchises that are members of the Registry. Franchisors submit their franchise agreements and other documents to the Registry for preapproval by the SBA, which expedites the loan application process for prospective franchisees. Nearly 1,500 franchises ranging from AAMCO Transmissions (automotive repair) to Zaxby's (fast-food chicken restaurants) participate in the Franchise Registry program. Approximately 9.5 percent of all SBA loan guarantees go to franchisees. SBA-guaranteed loans to franchisees experience an average 6.5 percent charge-off rate (the percentage of the loan amount written off due to nonpayment), which is higher than the overall average charge-off rate of 1.3 percent for all SBA-guaranteed loans.[32] Franchisees who are interested in the Franchise Registry program should visit its Web site at www.franchiseregistry.com.

In January 2011, the International Franchise Association created the VetFran program to help military veterans gain access to franchising opportunities by providing training, financial assistance, and information. More than 580 franchisors participate in the VetFran program, offering financial incentives and mentoring to prospective franchisees. So far, the program has produced nearly 5,200 new franchise owners who are military veterans.[33]

ENTREPRENEURIAL PROFILE: Kevin and Laurel Wilkerson: Boomer Pizza LLC Kevin and Laurel Wilkerson, both of whom served in the Army (Kevin as an Infantry Officer and Laurel as an attorney in the JAG Corps), decided that franchising was a natural fit for a second career. The VetFran program, which gave them a $5,000 discount on their franchise fee, and their combined 44 years of military service have helped them become successful Marco's Pizza franchisees. "What I enjoyed about the Army was the variety of things I did every day," says Kevin. "Franchising tends to be similar to that." Through their company, Boomer Pizza LLC, the Wilkersons own seven Marco's Pizza outlets in Edmond, Oklahoma. The copreneurs' management skills are complementary. "I tend to be more involved in site selection, design, operations, and finance," says Kevin. "[Laurel] handles the HR, client, and government issues. She's also involved with store openings and training."[34] ■

Proven Products, Processes, and Business Formats

As we have seen, franchisees essentially purchase a franchisor's experience in the form of a business system. A franchise owner does not have to build the business from scratch. Instead of being forced to rely solely on personal ability to establish business processes and attract a clientele, a franchisee can depend on the methods and techniques of an established business. At Papa John's, researchers are constantly looking for ways to improve their pizza and their franchisees' operations. Recent improvements include a simple system for making sauce measurements more precise and an oven calibration process to ensure more even heating throughout franchisees' pizza ovens, thereby producing more consistent pizzas.[35] These standardized procedures and operations greatly enhance the franchisee's chances of success and avoid the most inefficient type of learning—trial and error. In addition, franchisees do not have to struggle for recognition in the local marketplace as much as independent owners do.

ENTREPRENEURIAL PROFILE: John Grassia and David Smith: Express Oil Change John Grassia and David Smith, the former airline pilots who became Express Oil Change franchisees when they retired, understand better than most the importance of standard processes. They cite Express Oil Change's standardized processes as one of the factors that drew them to the franchise. As former pilots, the franchisees were accustomed to following standard operating procedures (SOPs) and were impressed by Express Oil's extensive system of SOPS, which they know from experience minimize errors and improve performance.[36] ■

Centralized Buying Power

A significant advantage a franchisee has over an independent small business owner is participation in the franchisor's centralized, volume buying power. If franchisors sell goods and supplies to franchisees (not all do), they may pass on to franchisees cost savings from quantity discounts they earn by buying in volume. Tom Curdes, owner of two Weed Man franchises in Toledo, Ohio, cites the lawn care franchisor's buying power as a major advantage. "The national buying power and the negotiations [with vendors] they do behind the scenes . . . I couldn't do that myself," says Curdes, whose franchises generate $750,000 in sales and employ 25 people.[37]

Site Selection and Territorial Protection

A proper location is critical to the success of any small business, and franchises are no exception. In fact, franchise experts consider the three most important factors in franchising to be *location*, *location*, and *location*. Most franchisors offer franchisees site selection assistance to increase the probability that their outlets will attract sufficient numbers of customers, reach their break-even points quickly, and generate consistent profits. CiCi's Pizza, a family-oriented, buffet-style restaurant chain based in Coppell, Texas, with nearly 500 locations in 34 states, recently entered into a partnership with Newmark Grubb Knight Frank, one of the top real estate advisory firms in the world, to enhance the company's comprehensive site selection software and process. The goal is to find the ideal location for every new restaurant the company opens, including non-traditional locations such as universities, airports, casinos, military bases, and others.[38]

Sometimes, entrepreneurs discover that becoming affiliated with a franchisor is the best way to get into prime locations. Many franchisors conduct an extensive location analysis for each new outlet, including researching traffic patterns, zoning ordinances, accessibility, and population density. McDonald's, for example, is well known for its ability to obtain prime locations in high-traffic areas. Although choosing a location usually is the franchisee's responsibility, some franchisors control the site selection process. Stephen Rogers decided to leave a family business to purchase an AAMCO transmission service franchise and relied on the franchisor to select a location for his service center because of the company's experience in selecting prime locations for their outlets. (AAMCO has been selling franchises since 1963.)[39] Even when the franchisee makes the location decision, the franchisor reserves the right to approve the final site. Choosing a suitable location requires a thorough location analysis, including studies of traffic patterns, zoning ordinances, accessibility, population density, and demographics. You will learn more about the location decision in Chapter 14.

Some franchisors offer franchisees territorial protection, which gives existing franchisees the right to exclusive distribution of brand-name goods or services within a particular geographic area. A clause establishing such a protective zone that bars other outlets from the same franchise from locating there gives franchisees significant protection and security. Even when a franchisor grants territorial protection, the size of a franchisee's territory can vary significantly. The purpose of territorial protection is to prevent an invasion of the existing franchisee's territory and the resulting dilution of sales. One study of successful franchises reports that the failure rate for franchisees is lower in systems that offer exclusive territories than in those that do not.[40]

As existing markets have become increasingly saturated with franchise outlets, the placement of new outlets has become a source of friction between franchisors and franchisees. Existing franchisees complain that franchisors are encroaching on their territories by granting new franchises so close to them that their sales are diluted. Before signing a franchise contract, every prospective franchisee must know exactly the scope of territorial protection, if any, the franchisor guarantees. A fast-growing franchise may be a sign of a healthy business model, but it also may indicate future conflicts between the franchisor and franchisees over encroachment. Why invest years building a successful franchise in a particular location only to have the franchisor allow another franchisee to open nearby, siphoning off sales of the existing outlet?

Greater Chance for Success

Investing in a franchise is not risk free. In a typical year, between 150 and 200 new franchises enter the market each year, but not all of them survive.[41] A study by The Coleman Report provides an indicator of the failure rate of franchises; over a recent 13-year period, an average of 12.5 percent of franchisees who received SBA-guaranteed loans failed to repay them, but the nonpayment rate ranged from 0 to 67 percent, depending on the chain.[42] Despite the fact that franchising offers no guarantees of success, experts contend that franchising is less risky than building a business from the ground up. The tradition of success for franchises is attributed to the broad range of services, assistance, standard procedures, and the comprehensive business system that the franchisor provides. Statistics regarding the success of a given franchise must be interpreted carefully, however. For example, sometimes when a franchise is in danger of failing, the franchisor often repurchases or relocates the outlet and does not report it as a failure.* As a result, some franchisors boast of never experiencing a failure.

A recent study of franchises reports that the success rate of franchisees is higher when a franchise system does the following:

- Requires franchisees to have prior industry experience
- Requires franchisees to actively manage their stores (no "absentee" owners)
- Has built a strong brand name
- Offers training programs designed to improve franchisees' knowledge and skills[43]

The risk involved in purchasing a franchise is two pronged: Success—or failure—depends on the franchisee's managerial skills and motivation and on the franchisor's business experience, system, and support. Many franchisees are convinced that franchising has been the key to their success in business. Their success is proof of the common sentiment that franchising offers the

*As long as an outlet's doors never close, most franchisors do not count it as a failure even if the outlet has struggled for survival and has been through a series of owners who have tried unsuccessfully to turn around its performance.

You Be the Consultant

Would You Buy This Franchise?

Although opening a franchise is not a "sure thing," franchising's immense popularity is due, in part, to the support, experience, and training that franchisors provide their franchisees. Many would-be entrepreneurs believe that franchising reduces their risk of failure and see it as the key to their success. Large, established franchises have systems in place that have been replicated thousands of times and allow franchisees to follow a formula for success that the franchisor has worked out over many years. Many small franchisors don't have the benefit of learning from the mistakes of setting up thousands of outlets to fine-tune their business systems. Some franchisors build their business models on fads that will fade while others tap into meaningful trends. Some of these small franchises have the potential to become tomorrow's franchise giants; others will fall by the wayside.

TITLE Boxing Club

Americans now live longer than ever before, but obesity represents a significant threat to public health. According to the International Health, Racquet, and Sportsclub Association, the number of gym or health club memberships has increased from 41.3 million in 2005 to 50.2 million today, although many clubs, especially those offering a full range of services and the resulting higher fees, struggled during the last recession. Danny Campbell, a retired professional boxer, knew firsthand what a great workout a boxing regime offers (burning up to 1,000 calories in an hour) but realized that most boxing gyms were located in seedy parts of town and were a bit rough around the edges. In 2008, Campbell and Tom Lyons, founder of travel club agency Global Connections, opened a boxing fitness club in Overland Park, Kansas that offered one-hour ("Power Hour") boxing workouts minus the sparring led by experienced trainers aimed at young people who want to stay in shape but who lack the time for lengthy workouts. They soon struck a deal with boxing equipment maker TITLE to use its well-known name and created a retail space in the club to sell gear. TITLE Boxing Club was a hit with customers, and after opening two more clubs, Campbell and Lyons began making plans to sell franchises. They approached John Rotche, who had been a top manager at Domino's Pizza and Krispy Kreme before starting two franchises of his own, Ductz (a duct-cleaning business) and Hoodz (a commercial kitchen hood-cleaning business) for advice. Rotche joined the company full time, and TITLE Boxing Club sold its first franchise in 2010. Rotche expanded the number of franchises from 60 to 500 in just 18 months and generated system-wide sales of $25 million. Sales continue to grow rapidly; the company is on track to double its annual sales to $50 million this year. Rotche says that TITLE's appeal comes from the company's strategy of taking an engaging workout that produces results and typically exists only in the grittiest sections of a town and offering it to customers in a convenient location near traditional retailers such as Target or Starbucks.

Purchasing a TITLE Boxing Club franchise requires an investment of between $187,000 and $364,000, including a $35,000 franchise fee ($29,000 for three or more outlets). Franchisees also pay a royalty of 7 percent of their sales to the franchisor.

Associated Press

"A big part of TITLE's success is a direct result of the short time franchisees take to break even," says Rotche. A club can operate in a relatively small space and requires only about 10 employees. On the revenue side, each club generates sales from both monthly membership fees and its retail store that sells workout gear. Because TITLE is a partner in the business, franchisees can purchase the equipment for their clubs at cost. The franchisor provides franchises with a one-week training program, an annual conference, and daily webinars. Multi-unit ownership is common; the typical TITLE Boxing Club franchisee owns three outlets.

LYFE Kitchen

Only 24 percent of people who eat at restaurants eat a healthy meal, and the founders of LYFE (Love Your Food Everyday) Kitchen want to change that. The fast-casual restaurant offers meals that contain no more than 600 calories and 1,000 milligrams of sodium, including dishes such as sweet corn chowder, fish tacos, roasted salmon, baked sweet potato fries, seasonal flatbread sandwiches, fruit smoothies, and many others. LYFE Kitchen uses whole grains, local fruits and vegetables, responsibly raised meats, and organic ingredients (when possible). The menu also contains vegetarian, vegan, and gluten-free items as well. Typical lunch prices are from $6 to $8, and dinner prices are $14 to $18. The company also markets a line of LYFE Kitchen-branded frozen foods through 2,000 grocery stores nationwide.

In 2010, Stephen Sidwell, a former executive with Gardein, a company that sells a meat substitute, took his idea for a healthy fast-casual restaurant to former McDonald's top executives Mike Roberts and Mike Donahue. The business partners brought two other key players into the business: celebrity chef Art Smith and Tal Ronnen, a famous vegetarian and vegan chef. They opened the first LYFE Kitchen in Palo Alto, California, in 2011. It was so successful that within months they opened a second location in Culver City, California. The founders began developing plans to franchise LYFE Kitchen, and the first franchise opened in Chicago in 2013. The initial investment to open a LYFE Kitchen is $1.5 million, which includes a $35,000 franchise fee and the latest restaurant equipment that is designed to ensure proper and consistent preparation of the restaurant's fresh dishes. Franchisees also pay a 5 percent (of sales) royalty to the franchisor. Currently with three franchised locations, LYFE Kitchen plans to have 250 locations, primarily in urban areas, across the United States within five years. The company seeks as franchisees people who have at least 15 years of business experience (preferably in the hospitality industry), $3 million in net worth, and a desire to open multiple outlets within a defined territory.

1. What are the advantages and the disadvantages of purchasing an outlet from small franchise systems?

2. Suppose that one of your friends is considering purchasing one of the franchises described here and asks your opinion. What advice would you offer him or her?

3. Develop a list of questions that a prospective franchisee should ask the franchisor and existing franchisees before deciding to invest in the franchises described here.

Sources: Based on Maze, Jonathan, In-Depth Franchising: Next Generation Franchises, *Sky Magazine For Delta Airlines*, November 2013, pg. 90. Lawrence Fagan, "Most Current Fitness Industry Statistics," *Gym Insight*, May 20, 2013, http://blog.gyminsight.com/2013/05/most-current-fitness-industry-statistics/; Laurie Kulikowski, "Top 5 Fitness Franchises," *Nuwire Investor*, September 3, 2012, http://www.nuwireinvestor.com/articles/top-5-fitness-franchises-59734.aspx; Neema P. Roshania, "8 Growing Health and Fitness Franchises," *Kiplinger*, June 2012, http://www.kiplinger.com/slideshow/business/T049-S001-8-growing-health-and-fitness-franchises/index.html; William White, "Where LYFE Kitchen Franchises Are Set to Pop Up Across U.S.," *Investor Place*, July 25, 2013, http://investorplace.com/2013/07/where-lyfe-kitchen-franchises-are-set-to-pop-up-across-u-s/#.UrB72id0nkY; Lisa Jennings, "LYFE Kitchen Launches Franchising Program," Nation's Restaurant News, December 6, 2012, http://nrn.com/latest-headlines/lyfe-kitchen-launches-franchising-program; Jody Shee, "5 Brands You Should Know About (But Don't)," *QSR Magazine*, June 2011, http://www.qsrmagazine.com/franchising/5-brands-you-should-know-about-don-t.

opportunity to be in business *for* yourself but not *by* yourself. In a recent survey by Franchise Direct, the main reason (cited by 51 percent of respondents) that prospective franchisees give for considering investing in a franchise is that they want to be their own bosses without having to start completely from "scratch."[44] "[Franchising is] the perfect combination of having an independently owned and operated office, but with support," says Olivier Hecht, who left his corporate job to open a Handyman Matters home repair franchise.[45]

The Drawbacks of Buying a Franchise

LO2B

Explain the drawbacks of buying a franchise.

The benefits of buying a franchise can mean the difference between success and failure for some entrepreneurs. Prospective franchisees must understand the disadvantages of franchising before choosing this method of doing business. Perhaps the biggest drawback of franchising is that a franchisee must sacrifice some freedom to the franchisor. Other disadvantages are discussed in the following sections.

Franchise Fees and Ongoing Royalties

Virtually every franchisor imposes some type of fees and demands a share of franchisees' sales revenue in return for the use of the franchisor's name, products or services, and business system. The fees and the initial capital requirements vary among the different franchisors. The total investment required for a franchise varies from around $3,500 for some home-based service franchises to $20 million or more for hotel and motel franchises. For example, Jazzercise, an aerobics exercise franchise, requires a capital investment that ranges from just $4,300 to $76,500, and Subway, the sandwich and salad chain, estimates that the total cost of opening a franchise ranges from $85,700 for a kiosk location to $262,850 for a traditional restaurant. Culver's, a fast-growing regional chain that sells sandwiches (including the delicious ButterBurger®), salads, dinners, and frozen custard, requires an investment of $1.44 million to $3.08 million, depending on land acquisition and building construction costs. Franchisees use many of the same sources to finance franchises that independent entrepreneurs use to finance their start-up companies (see Figure 7.6).

Start-up costs for franchises often include a variety of fees. Most franchises impose an initial franchise fee for the right to use the company name. The average up-front fee that franchisors charge is $25,147.[46] Subway's franchise fee is $15,000, but Culver's charges a franchise fee of $55,000. Other franchise start-up costs might include fees for location analysis, site purchase and preparation, construction, signs, fixtures, equipment, management assistance, and training. Some franchise fees include these costs, but others do not. Before signing any contract, a prospective franchisee should determine the total cost of a franchise, something that every franchisor is required to disclose in item 7 of its Franchise Disclosure Document (see the section "Franchising and the Law" later in this chapter).

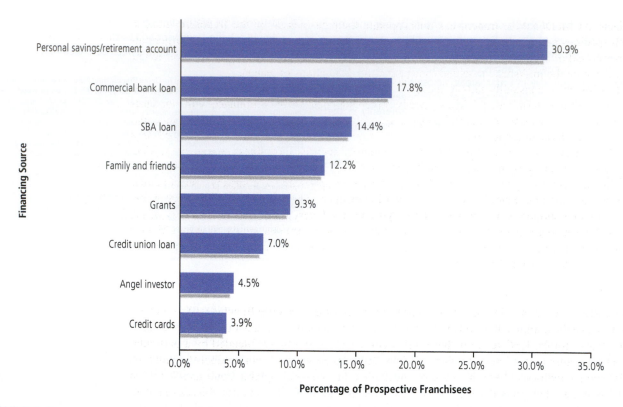

FIGURE 7.6

Planned Sources of Financing for Prospective Franchisees

Source: Prospective Franchisee Survey Results, Franchise Direct, 2013, http://www.franchisedirect.com/information/trendsfacts/
prospectivefranchiseesurveyresults2013franchiseeprofessionalfinancialbackground2/8/2384/.

Franchisors also impose continuing royalty fees as revenue-sharing devices. The royalty usually involves a percentage of gross sales with a required minimum, or a flat fee levied on the franchise. (In fact, 82 percent of franchisors charge a royalty based on a percentage of franchisees' sales.[47]) Royalty fees range from 1 to 11 percent, and the average royalty rate is 6.7 percent.[48] Culver's charges franchisees a royalty of 4 percent of gross sales, which is payable weekly, and Subway charges a royalty of 8 percent of weekly gross sales. These ongoing royalties increase a franchisee's overhead expenses significantly. Because the franchisor's royalties and fees (the total fees the average franchisor collects amount to 8.4 percent of a franchisee's sales) are calculated as a percentage of a franchisee's sales, the franchisor gets paid even if the franchisee fails to earn a profit.[49] Sometimes, unprepared franchisees discover (too late) that a franchisor's royalties and fees are the equivalent of the normal profit margin for a business. To avoid this problem, prospective franchisees should determine exactly how much fees will be and then weigh the benefits of the services and benefits the fees cover. One of the best ways to do this is to itemize what you are getting for your money and then determine whether the cost is worth the benefits provided. Be sure to get the details on all expenses—the amount, the timing of payments, and financing arrangements; find out which items, if any, are included in the initial franchise fee and which ones are "extra."

Strict Adherence to Standardized Operations

Although franchisees own their businesses, they do not have the autonomy that independent owners have. To protect its image, a franchisor requires that franchisees maintain certain operating standards. In fact, conformity is standard operating procedure in franchising. The franchisor controls the layout and the color schemes that its franchisees use in their stores, the products they sell, the personnel and operating policies they use, and many other aspects of running the business. At McDonald's, franchisees must operate their businesses by the franchise manual, which specifies nearly every detail of running a franchise—including how many hamburger patties per pound of beef (10), how long to toast a bun (17 seconds), and how much sanitizer to use when cleaning the milkshake machine (one packet for 2.5 gallons of water).

If a franchise constantly fails to meet the minimum standards established for the business, the franchisor may terminate its license. Many franchisors determine compliance with standards with periodic inspections and secret shoppers. Secret shoppers work for a survey company and, although they look like any other customer, are trained to observe and then later record on a checklist a franchise's performance on key standards, such as cleanliness, speed of service, employees' appearances and attitudes, and others. At Five Guys Burgers and Fries, founder Jerry Murrell uses secret shoppers to ensure that franchisees comply with the company's strict quality and service standards. Five Guys conducts two independent audits of every store every week. One is a secret shopper who poses as a customer and rates everything from the courtesy of the crew and the appearance of the food to the cleanliness of the bathrooms and the time required for service; the other audit focuses on safety.[50] At times, strict adherence to franchise standards may become a burden to some franchisees.

Restrictions on Purchasing and Prices

In the interest of maintaining quality standards, franchisors may require franchisees to purchase products, special equipment, or other items from the franchisor or from a list of "approved" suppliers. For example, KFC requires that franchisees use only seasonings blended by a particular company because a poor image could result from franchisees using inferior products to cut costs. Under some conditions, these purchase arrangements may be challenged in court as a violation of antitrust laws, but generally franchisors have a legal right to ensure that franchisees maintain acceptable quality standards. Franchisees recently filed another round of lawsuits against Quiznos, a chain of sandwich shops, in which they allege that the franchisor, based in Denver, Colorado, engaged in fraud and misdealing by requiring franchisees to purchase food and supplies from the franchisor's supply division. The complaints contend that Quiznos, whose domestic franchisee count has declined by 2,500 since 2006, earned millions in profits using "hidden markups" on items that the contract requires franchisees to purchase from the franchisor, while most franchisees were "losing money or barely breaking even."[51]

For many years, franchisors could legally set the prices they charge for the products they sell to franchisees but could not control the retail prices franchisees charge for products. However, two U.S. Supreme Court decisions (*State Oil Company vs. Khan* in 1997 and *Leegin Creative Leather Products vs. PSKS, Inc.* in 2007) opened the door for franchisors to establish maximum prices that franchisees can charge. Many franchisors do not impose maximum prices, choosing instead to provide franchisees with suggested prices, but some do establish price limits. "Value menus" have become a source of contention for franchisees of many quick-service restaurants because franchisors impose price limits on items that appear on their value menus. Value menus are an important revenue source for franchises, accounting for 13 to 15 percent of sales, but franchisees complain that making a profit on low-priced items is difficult. To address its franchisees' concerns, McDonald's replaced its "Dollar Menu" with the "Dollar Menu and More," which includes 25 items priced between $1 and $2. The new menu gives franchisees more flexibility in pricing and allows them to offset rising commodity and labor costs.[52] Several Steak 'n Shake franchisees have been locked in a legal battle with the franchisor over the franchisor's insistence that all franchisees comply with its "4 Meals for $4" promotion. The franchisees recently won an injunction against Steak 'n Shake, effectively blocking the policy that required franchisees to abide by the prices the franchisor sets for its menu items. Stuller, Inc., the chain's oldest franchisee, argued that the policy would cost its five franchises nearly $700,000 per year.[53]

Limited Product Line

In most cases, the franchise agreement stipulates that the franchisee can sell only those products approved by the franchisor. Unless they are willing to risk the cancellation of their licenses, franchisees must avoid selling any unapproved products through the franchise. A franchise may be required to carry an unpopular product or be prevented from introducing a desirable one by the franchise agreement. A franchisee's freedom to adapt a product line to local market conditions is restricted. However, some franchisors actively solicit innovations and product suggestions from their franchisees. Subway's wildly successful "$5 Footlong" idea did not come from corporate headquarters but originated with Miami franchisee Stuart Frankel.[54] Some of McDonald's most successful products came not from the corporate kitchen but from franchisees such as Jim Delligatti, who invented the legendary Big Mac in 1967. In 1968, McDonald's put the sandwich on franchisees' menus, where its original price was 49 cents. Today, McDonald's sells 560 million Big Macs each year—an average of more than 17 sandwiches per second![55] Some franchisees are concerned that McDonald's has developed no "home run" products for its menu since the successful introduction of McGriddles, a pancake sandwich, in 2003. Many franchisees also complain that they throw away more of the chain's "healthy" menu items, such as salads, which make up only 2 to 3 percent of sales, than they sell.[56]

ENTREPRENEURIAL PROFILE: Diana Tavary: Curves Some franchisees of Curves, a chain of exercise outlets that offer a 30-minute workout aimed at busy women, claim that the company ignored their requests to update its exercise format to help them retain members and attract new ones. Diana Tavary walked away from her Curves franchise after 10 years because the company failed to adapt to new exercise trends. One business broker in the fitness industry, agrees, pointing out that Curves allowed franchisees to offer only the standard 30-minute workout, despite feedback from franchisees indicating that customers wanted other exercise options. Franchisees say they have lost business to rival gyms that allow customers to exercise at any time without supervision because the company does not allow that practice. Curves, which started franchising in 1995, has 4,000 franchised outlets, about half the number it had at its peak in 2005.[57] ∎

Contract Terms and Renewal

Because franchise contracts are written by the franchisor's attorneys, they always are written in favor of the franchisor. Some franchisors are willing to negotiate the terms of their contracts, but many of the well-established franchisors are not because they know they don't have to. The franchise contract is extremely important because it governs the franchisor–franchisee relationship over its life, which may last as long as 20 years. In fact, the average length of a franchise contract is 10.5 years.[58]

Franchisees also should understand the terms and conditions under which they may renew their franchise contracts at the expiration of the original agreement. In most cases, franchisees are required to pay a renewal fee and to repair any deficiencies in their outlets or to modernize and upgrade them. One study by the International Franchise Association and FRANdata reports that the renewal rate of franchise agreements is 94 percent.[59]

Unsatisfactory Training Programs

A major benefit of purchasing a franchise is the training that the franchisor provides franchisees so that they are able to run successful operations. The quality of franchise training programs can vary dramatically, however. "Many franchisees think they will get a lot of training but find out it's a one-week crash course," says Marko Grunhagen, a franchising expert at Southern Illinois University.[60] Before signing on with a franchise, it is wise to find out the details of the training program the franchisor provides to avoid unpleasant surprises.

Market Saturation

Franchisees in fast-growing systems reap the benefits of the franchisor's expanding reach, but they also may encounter the downside of a franchisor's aggressive growth strategy: market saturation. As the owners of many fast-food, sandwich shops, and yogurt and ice cream franchises have discovered, market saturation is a very real danger. One researcher has determined that only one place in the contiguous 48 states, a high plain in northwestern South Dakota, is more than 100 miles from a McDonald's restaurant.[61] Subway, which started franchising in 1974, has grown from just 166 outlets in 1981 to more than 42,000 outlets today![62] Any franchise growing that rapidly runs the risk of having outlets so close together that they cannibalize sales from one another, causing them to struggle to reach their break-even points.

As you learned in the previous section, although some franchisors offer franchisees territorial protection, others do not. Territorial encroachment, competition from within the franchise, has become a hotly contested issue in franchising as growth-seeking franchisors have exhausted most of the prime locations and are now setting up new franchises in close proximity to existing ones. Franchise experts consistently site territorial encroachment as the primary threat to franchisees.

Less Freedom

When franchisees sign a contract, they agree to sell the franchisor's product or service by following its prescribed formula. This feature of franchising is the source of the system's success, but it also gives many franchisees the feeling that they are reporting to a "boss." Franchisors want to ensure franchisees' success, and most monitor their franchisees' performances closely to make sure that franchisees follow the system's specifications. "Everything you do in a franchise will be dictated [by the franchisor] from the moment you turn the key in the door in the morning," warns Eric Karp, a Boston attorney who teaches franchising at Babson College.[63]

Strict uniformity is the rule rather than the exception. For example, a group of franchisees filed a lawsuit against Burger King, claiming that the company had no right to require them to open their stores as early as 6 a.m. and to stay open as late as 2 A.M., but the court dismissed their argument, ruling that the franchise contract, which authorized the extended hours, is unambiguous and enforceable.[64] "There is no independence," says one writer. "Successful franchisees are happy prisoners."[65] As a result, highly independent, "go-my-own-way" entrepreneurs often are frustrated with the basic "go-by-the-rules" philosophy of franchising. Table 7.1 describes 10 myths of franchising.

Franchising and the Law

LO3

Understand the laws covering franchise purchases.

The franchising boom spearheaded by McDonald's and others in the late 1950s brought with it many prime investment opportunities. However, the explosion of legitimate franchises also ushered in with it numerous fly-by-night franchisors who defrauded their franchisees. By the 1970s, franchising was rife with fraudulent practitioners. David Kaufman, a renowned franchise expert with more than 30 years of experience, says, "In the late 1960s and 1970s, the words 'franchise' and 'fraud' had almost become synonymous."[66] Thousands of people lost millions of dollars to criminals and unscrupulous operators who sold flawed business concepts and phantom franchises to unsuspecting investors. In an effort to control the rampant fraud in the industry and the potential for deception inherent in a franchise relationship, California in 1971 enacted the first Franchise Investment Law. The law (and those of 14 other states that passed similar laws) required franchisors to register a Uniform Franchise Offering Circular (UFOC) and deliver a copy to prospective franchisees before any offer or sale of a franchise. In October 1979, the Federal Trade Commission (FTC) adopted similar legislation at the national level that established full disclosure guidelines for any company selling franchises and was designed to give potential franchisees the information they needed to protect themselves from unscrupulous franchisors.

In 2008, the FTC replaced the UFOC with a similar document, the **Franchise Disclosure Document (FDD)**, which requires all franchisors to provide detailed information on their operations at least 14 days before a franchisee signs a contract or pays any money. The FDD applies to all franchisors, even those in the 35 states that lack franchise disclosure laws. The purpose of the regulation is to assist potential franchisees' investigations of a franchise deal and to introduce consistency into the franchisor's disclosure statements. The FTC also established a "plain English" requirement for the FDD that prohibits legal and technical jargon and makes a document easy to read and understand. The FTC's philosophy is not so much to prosecute abusers as to provide information to prospective franchisees and help them to make intelligent decisions. Although the FTC requires each franchisor to provide a potential franchisee with this information, it does not verify its accuracy. Prospective franchisees should use this document only as a starting point for their investigations.

The Trade Regulation Rule requires a franchisor to include 23 major topics in its disclosure statement:

Franchise Disclosure Document (FDD)
a document that every franchisor is required by law to give prospective franchisees before any offer or sale of a franchise; it outlines 23 important pieces of information.

1. Information identifying the franchisor and its affiliates and describing the franchisor's business experience and the franchises being sold.

2. Information identifying and describing the business experience of each of the franchisor's officers, directors, and managers responsible for the franchise program.

TABLE 7.1 10 Myths of Franchising

Myth #1. Franchising is the safest way to go into business because franchises never fail: Although the failure rate for franchises is lower than that of independent businesses, there are no guarantees of success. Franchises can—and do—fail. Potential franchisees must exercise the same degree of caution in judging the risk of a franchise as they would any other business.

Myth #2. I'll be able to open my franchise for less money than the franchisor estimates: Launching a business, including a franchise, normally takes more money and more time than entrepreneurs estimate. Be prepared. One franchisee of a retail computer store advises, "If a franchisor tells you you'll need $100,000 to get started, you better have $150,000."

Myth #3. The bigger the franchise organization, the more successful I'll be: Bigger is not always better in the franchise business. Some of the largest franchise operations are struggling to maintain their growth rates because the best locations are already taken and their markets have become saturated. Market saturation is a significant problem for many large franchises, and smaller franchises are accounting for much of the growth in the industry. Early franchisees in new franchise systems often can negotiate better deals and receive more individual attention from the franchisor than those who purchase units in well-established systems.

Myth #4. I'll use 80 percent of the franchisor's business system, but I'll improve on it by substituting my experience and know-how: When franchisees buy a franchise, they are buying, in essence, the franchisor's experience and knowledge. Why pay all of that money to a franchisor if you aren't willing to use their system? When franchisors screen potential franchisees, they look for people who are willing to fit into their systems rather than fiercely independent entrepreneurs. "[Franchisors] have spent years building the company," says Jeff Elgin, founder of FranChoice, a franchise referral consulting firm. "They don't want someone who will come in and try to innovate because that produces chaos." Ideally, franchisors look for franchisees who exhibit a balance between the freewheeling entrepreneurial spirit and a system-focused approach.

Myth #5. All franchises are basically the same: Each franchise has its own unique personality, requirements, procedures, and culture. Naturally, some will suit you better than others. Avoid the tendency to select the franchise that offers the lowest cost. If the franchise does not fit your needs, it is not a bargain, no matter how inexpensive it is. Ask the franchisor and existing franchisees lots of questions to determine how well you will fit into the system. One of the best ways to get a feel for a franchise's personality is to work in a unit for a time.

Myth #6. I don't have to be a hands-on manager. I can be an absentee owner and still be very successful: Most franchisors shy away from absentee owners, and some simply do not allow them in their systems at all. They know that franchise success requires lots of hands-on attention, and the franchise owner is the best person to provide that.

Myth #7. Anyone can be a satisfied, successful franchise owner: With more than 3,000 franchises available, the odds of finding a franchise that appeals to your tastes are high. However, not everyone is cut out to be a franchisee. "If a person is highly entrepreneurial, he or she should not even consider a franchise investment," says Kevin Murphy, a franchise attorney. Those "free spirits" who insist on doing things their way most likely will be miserable in a franchise.

Myth #8. Franchising is the cheapest way to get into business for yourself: Although bargains do exist in franchising, the price tag for buying into some well-established systems is breathtaking, sometimes running more than $1 million. Franchisors look for candidates who are on solid financial footing.

Myth #9. The franchisor will solve my business problems for me; after all, that's why I pay an ongoing royalty: Although franchisors offer franchisees start-up and ongoing training programs, they will not run their franchisees' businesses for them. As a franchisee, your job is to take the formula that the franchisor has developed and make it work in your location. Expect to solve many of your own problems.

Myth #10. Once I open my franchise, I'll be able to run things the way I want to: Franchisees are not free to run their businesses as they see fit. Every franchisee signs a contract that requires him or her to run the business according to the franchisor's requirements. Franchisees who violate the terms of that agreement run the risk of having their franchise relationship terminated.

Sources: Based on Mark Henricks, "Finding the Perfect Fit: How Franchisers Select Franchisees," Advertising Insert, *Inc.*, February 2011, p. 110; April Y. Pennington, "The Right Stuff," *Entrepreneur B.Y.O.B.*, September 2004, pp. 90–100; Andrew A. Caffey, "There's More to a Franchise Than Meets the Eye," *Entrepreneur*, May 1998, http://www.entrepreneur.com/article/0,4621,228443,00.html; Andrew A. Caffey, "Myth vs. Reality," *Entrepreneur*, October 1998, http://www.entrepreneur.com/mag/article/0,1539,229435,00.html; Chieh Chieng, "Do You Want to Know a Secret?" *Entrepreneur*, January 1999, pp. 174–178; "Ten Most Common Mistakes Made by Franchise Buyers," Franchise Doctor, http://www.franchisedoc.com/mistakes.html; and Devlin Smith, "The Sure Thing," *Entrepreneur B.Y.O.B.*, May 2004, p. 100.

3. A description of the lawsuits in which the franchisor and its officers, directors, and managers have been involved. Although most franchisors will have been involved in some type of litigation, an excessive number of lawsuits, particularly if they relate to the same problem, is alarming. Another red flag is an excessive number of lawsuits brought against the franchisor by franchisees. "The history of the litigation will tell you the future of your relationship [with the franchisor]," says the founder of a maid-service franchise.[67]

4. Information about any bankruptcies in which the franchisor and its officers, directors, and managers have been involved.

5. Information about the initial franchise fee and other payments required to obtain the franchise, the intended use of the fees, and the conditions under which the fees are refundable.

6. A table that describes all of the other fees that franchisees are required to make after start-up, including royalties, service fees, training fees, lease payments, advertising or marketing charges, and others. The table also must include the due dates for the fees.

7. A table that shows the components of a franchisee's total initial investment. The categories included are preopening expenses, the initial franchise fee, training expenses, equipment, opening inventory, initial advertising fee, signs, real estate (purchased or leased), equipment, opening inventory, security deposits, business licenses, initial advertising fees, and other expenses, such as legal and accounting fees. Also included is an estimate of amount of working capital a franchisee should have on hand to sustain the company in its first three months of operation. (Franchisees should be aware that the actual amount of capital required to keep a franchise going until it generates positive cash flow is probably much higher.) These estimates, usually stated as a range, give prospective franchisees an idea of how much their total start-up costs will be. Franchising expert Don Schadle says that for a typical franchisee, the total cost to open a franchise is $150,000; only 5 percent of franchisees invest more than $500,000.[68]

8. Information about quality requirements of goods, services, equipment, supplies, inventory, and other items used in the franchise and where franchisees may purchase them, including required purchases from the franchisor. When interviewing existing franchisees, prospective franchisees should ask whether the prices the franchisees pay for products and services are reasonable.

9. A cross-reference table that shows the location in the FDD and in the franchise contract of the description of the franchisee's obligations under the franchise contract.

10. A description of the financial assistance (if any) available from the franchisor in the purchase of the franchise. Although many franchisors do not offer direct financial assistance to franchisees, they may have special arrangements with lenders who help franchisees find financing.

11. A description of all obligations the franchisor must fulfill to help a franchisee prepare to open and operate a unit, including site selection, advertising, computer systems, pricing, training (a table describing the length and type of training is required), and other forms of assistance provided to franchisees. This usually is the longest section of the FDD.

12. A description of any territorial protection that the franchise receives and a statement as to whether the franchisor may locate a company-owned store or other franchised outlet in that territory. The franchisor must specify whether it offers exclusive or nonexclusive territories. Given the controversy in many franchises over market saturation, franchisees should pay close attention to this section. Prospective franchisees should recognize the risk of investing in a franchise that provides no territorial protection or exclusive territories.

13. All relevant information about the franchisor's trademarks, service marks, trade names, logos, and commercial symbols, including where they are registered. Prospective franchisees should look for a strong trademark or service mark that is registered with the U.S. Patent and Trademark Office.

14. Similar information on any patents, copyrights, and proprietary processes that the franchisor owns and the rights that franchisees have to use them.

15. A description of the extent to which franchisees must participate personally in the operation of the franchise. Many franchisors look for hands-on franchisees and discourage or even prohibit absentee owners.

16. A description of any restrictions on the goods or services that franchises are permitted to sell and with whom franchisees may deal. The agreement usually restricts franchisees to selling only those items the franchisor has approved.

17. A table that describes the conditions under which the franchise may be repurchased or refused renewal by the franchisor, transferred to a third party by the franchisee, and terminated or modified by either party. This section also addresses the methods established for resolving disputes, usually either mediation or arbitration, between franchisees and the franchisor. One recent study reports that 44 percent of franchisors' contracts contain arbitration clauses, which means that if a dispute arises, the parties must submit the dispute to arbitration rather than resolve it in the courts.[69]

18. A description of the involvement of celebrities and public figures in the franchise. Less than 1 percent of franchise systems use public figures as part of their promotional strategies.[70]

19. A complete statement of the basis for any earnings claims made to the franchisee, including the percentage of existing franchises that have actually achieved the results that are claimed. Franchisors that make earnings claims must include them in the FDD, and the claims must "have a reasonable basis" at the time they are made. However, franchisors are *not* required to make any earnings claims at all; in fact, 60 to 70 percent of franchisers do not, primarily because of liability concerns about committing earnings estimates to writing.[71]

20. A table that displays systemwide statistical information about the expansion or the contraction of the franchise over the last three years. This section also includes the current number of franchises, the number of franchises projected for the future and the states in which they are to be sold, the number of franchises terminated, the number of agreements the franchisor has not renewed, the number of franchises that have been sold to new owners, the number of outlets the franchisor has repurchased, and a list of the names and addresses (organized by state) of other franchisees in the system and of those who have left the system within the last year. Contacting some of the franchisees who have left the system can alert would-be franchisees to potential problems with the franchise.

21. The franchisor's audited financial statements.

22. A copy of all franchise and other contracts (leases, purchase agreements, and others) that the franchisee will be required to sign.

23. A standardized, detachable receipt to prove that the prospective franchisee received a copy of the FDD. The FTC now allows franchisors to provide the FDD to prospective franchisees electronically.

The typical FDD is from 100 to 200 pages long, but every potential franchisee should read and understand it. Unfortunately, many do not, often resulting in unpleasant surprises for franchisees. The information contained in the FDD neither fully protects a potential franchise from deception nor guarantees success. The FDD does, however, provide enough information to begin a thorough investigation of the franchisor and the franchise deal, and prospective franchisees should use it to their advantage.

The *Right* Way to Buy a Franchise

LO4

Discuss the *right* way to buy a franchise.

The FDD is a powerful tool designed to help would-be franchisees select the franchise that is right for them and to avoid being duped by dishonest franchisors. The best defenses a prospective entrepreneur has against unscrupulous franchisors are preparation, common sense, and patience. By asking the right questions and resisting the urge to rush into an investment decision, potential franchisees can avoid being taken by unscrupulous operators.

"We would like to visit with you about the possibility of expanding our franchise into new territory."

Dave Carpenter/www.CartoonStock.com

Not every franchise "horror story" is the result of dishonest franchisors. More often than not, the problems that arise in franchising have more to do with franchisees who buy legitimate franchises without proper research and analysis. They end up in businesses that they don't enjoy and that they are not well suited to operate. Fortunately, most franchisees are happy with the franchise decision they made; 72 percent of franchisees say that if given the chance, they would choose the same franchise again.[72] How can you avoid choosing the wrong franchise? The steps discussed in the following sections will help you to make the right choice.

Evaluate Yourself

Before looking at any franchise, entrepreneurs should study their own traits, goals, experience, likes, dislikes, risk orientation, income requirements, time and family commitments, and other characteristics. Knowing how much you can invest in a franchise is important, but it is not the only factor to consider. "You not only have to understand simple things such as what kind of investment you're willing to make, but also what kind of risks you are willing to take, how hard you want to work, how many hours you want to work, and what kind of environment you want to work in," advises Lori Kiser-Block, head of franchise consulting service FranChoice.[73] Will you be comfortable working in a structured environment? In what region of the country or world do you want to live and work? What is your ideal job description? Do you want to sell a product or a service? What hours do you expect to work? Do you want to work with people, or do you prefer to work alone? Knowing what you enjoy doing (and what you *don't* want to do) will help you to narrow your search. Which franchises are a good match for your strengths, weaknesses, interests, and professional experience? The goal is to find the franchise that is right—for *you*!

ENTREPRENEURIAL PROFILE: Todd and Bambi Stringham: Signs by Tomorrow After spending 15 years in the corporate world, Todd and Bambi Stringham grew disillusioned and decided to make a career change. After evaluating their experience, strengths, and finances, they decided to make their dream of owning a business a reality by buying a franchise. The Stringhams spent months reviewing the features of more than 30 franchisors that matched their profile of what they were looking for in a franchise before settling on Signs by Tomorrow, a Maryland-based company with 150 outlets that makes a variety of signs, primarily for businesses. They wanted a franchisor that would support their operation with a solid business system and that would allow them to use their own creativity. "I have always wanted to own my own business," says Todd. "After a lot of research, we found that Signs by Tomorrow had the business model and support system we were looking for."[74] ■

Prospective franchisees also must determine how much they can invest in a franchise. Although the FDD shows prospective franchisees the total investment amount required, including working capital, experts recommend that franchisees have additional cache of capital as a contingency fund to cover the cost of unexpected surprises. Keith Gerson, a top manager for FranConnect, a provider of franchise management software, points out that franchisees start burning through their start-up capital the day they sign their franchise contracts and that the time gap before they begin to generate revenue can be lengthy.[75] Prospective franchisees must realize that despite their best plans, delays in opening a franchise often crop up, pushing back the date when the revenue stream begins. Having a sufficient amount of working capital (experts recommend two to three times the amount the FDD lists) to keep the franchise afloat until it becomes cash flow positive is essential. Gerson notes that insufficient working capital is the number one cause of franchise failure.[76]

Alex Gashkevich decided to leave behind a career in finance on Wall Street for the opportunity to own a franchise. After months of research, he decided to invest in Aaron's, a franchise that sells furniture, electronics, and appliances under lease-to-own contracts. He invested $400,000 of his own money to renovate and build out a location in Rockaway, New Jersey, and to hire employees. Gashkevich says that the renovations took much longer than he had planned, during which time he paid the employees he had already hired. His franchise reached its breakeven point in just 16 months, but Gashkevich has not yet paid himself a salary, choosing instead to use the profits from his first store to open a second one. He also has signed an area development contract with Aaron's under which he agrees to open Aaron's stores in seven territories in the New York area. Gashkevich says that he is having an incredible amount of fun as a franchisee.[77]

Table 7.2 is designed to help prospective franchisees to evaluate their potential as successful franchisees.

Research Your Market

Before shopping for a franchise, research the market in the area you plan to serve. How fast is the overall area growing? In which areas is that growth occurring fastest? How many competitors already operate in the area? How strong is the competition? Investing some time to develop a profile of the customers in your target area is essential; otherwise, you will be flying blind. Who are your potential customers? How many of them are in your proposed trading area? What are their characteristics? What are their income and education levels? What kinds of products and services do they buy? What gaps exist in the market? These gaps represent potential franchise opportunities for you. Market research also should confirm that a franchise is not merely a fad that will quickly fade. Steering clear of fads and into long-term trends is one way to sustain the success of a franchise. Before Papa John's Pizza allows franchisees to open a franchise, the company requires them to spend six months to a year evaluating the market potential of the local area. "We don't just move into an area and open up 200 stores," says one manager. "We do it one store at a time."[78]

Consider Your Franchise Options

Small business magazines (and their Web sites), such as *Entrepreneur* and *Inc.*, devote at least one issue to franchising in which they often list hundreds of franchises. These guides can help you find a suitable franchise within your price range. Another useful resource is *Bond's Franchise Guide* (Source Book Publications), which provides detailed profiles of nearly 900 North American franchisers and lists of franchise attorneys, consultants, and service providers. The Internet is another valuable tool for gathering information on franchises. The Web sites of organizations such as the International Franchise Association, the American Association of Franchisees and Dealers, the Canadian Franchise Association, and others offer valuable resources and advice for prospective franchisees. In addition, many cities host franchise trade shows throughout the year where hundreds of franchisors gather to sell their franchises. Attending one of

TABLE 7.2 Are You Franchisee Material?

Not everyone is cut out to be a franchisee. What characteristics do successful franchise owners have?

- *Commitment.* Like all entrepreneurs, successful franchisees must be committed to making their businesses successful. For franchisees, that means learning how the franchisor's system works and how to apply it in their individual markets.
- *Learning attitude.* Franchisees must exhibit a learning attitude and be willing to learn from the franchisor, other franchisees, and other experts. "Franchisors are not necessarily looking for experts in their industry," says one franchise consultant, "but for individuals with a great work ethic, broad business knowledge, and a willingness to follow a proven system."
- *Willingness to work with others.* Franchising success requires a willingness to work with the franchisor in a close, mutually beneficial relationship.
- *Patience.* Franchisees must understand that franchising is *not* a ticket to overnight success; success often requires years of hard work.
- *Positive attitude.* Franchisors look for franchisees who have a positive outlook and are focused on success.
- *General business skills.* Although franchisors usually do not require franchisees to have years of experience in the particular industry in which they operate, they do look for people who have general business experience. Sound leadership and communication skills are important in every industry.
- *Leadership ability.* Getting a franchise up and running successfully requires every ounce of leadership ability that a franchisee has.
- *Coachability.* In addition to being successful leaders, franchisees also must be good followers. Franchisors say that their most successful franchisees are coachable and are willing to learn from the experience of others. Reaping the advantages of the franchisor's experience is one of the primary benefits of franchising, and franchisees should take advantage of it. "Be prepared to listen to others who have blazed the path for you," says John Hewitt, founder of the Jackson Hewitt Tax Service franchise.
- *Perseverance.* Successful franchisees are dedicated to making their franchises successful and work hard to get the job done.
- *Solid people skills.* Whatever field they enter, successful franchisees require good people skills because they will be managing employees and working with customers.
- *Adequate capital.* Franchisors look for franchisees who have adequate financial resources to launch their businesses and to keep them going until they can generate enough cash flow to support themselves.
- *Compatible values.* Successful franchisees have value systems that are compatible with those of the franchisor.
- *Willingness to follow the system.* Some people enter the world of franchising because they have an entrepreneurial streak, which could be a mistake. Although creativity and a fresh approach are valuable assets in any business, franchising boils down to following the system that the franchisor has established. Why pay a franchisor for the benefit of experience if you are not willing to put that experience to work for yourself?

Sources: Based on Jerry Chautin, "Tips to Help Succeed at Owning a Franchise," *Herald Tribune*, September 27, 2010, http://www.heraldtribune.com/article/20100927/COLUMNIST/9271021; Jeff Elgin, "Are You Franchisee Material?," *Entrepreneur*, April 4, 2005, http://www.entrepreneur.com/franchises/buyingafranchise/franchisecolumnistjeffelgin/article76896.html; Kim Ellis, "Key Characteristics of Successful Franchise Owners," *Bison*, July 1, 2007, http://www.bison.com/articles_investigationellis_07012007; Jennifer Openshaw, "Five Keys to Success as a Franchise Owner," *AOL Small Business*, October 8, 2007, http://smallbusiness.aol.com/article/_a/five-keys-to-success-as-a-franchise/2007101217280999000; and Sara Wilson, "Show Me the Way," *Entrepreneur*, September 2006, p. 120.

these franchise showcases is a convenient, efficient way to collect information about a variety of available opportunities.

Many franchisors offer prospective franchisees visits to corporate headquarters where they have the opportunity to learn more about the franchise, the people who manage it, and its products and services. Known as "Discovery Days," these visits are an excellent way for prospective franchisees to peek behind the curtain of a franchise operation and for franchisors to size up potential franchisees.

ENTREPRENEURIAL PROFILE: Bob and Kathy Summers: Spring-Green Lawn Care
Bob and Kathy Summers traveled nearly 900 miles to the corporate headquarters of Spring-Green Lawn Care, a franchise they were considering purchasing. They met with a top executive who explained the sales that franchisees typically generate in their first year of operation, had lunch with the office staff, and saw firsthand the equipment they would purchase for their business. Their visit convinced them that Spring-Green was the right franchise for them.[79] ■

Some franchisors use technology to allow prospective franchisees to make virtual visits to the company's headquarters, watch online videos, and talk with executives in videoconferences.

Get a Copy of the Franchisor's FDD

Once you narrow your franchise choices, you should contact each franchise (at least two in the industry that you have selected) and get a copy of its FDD. Then read it! This document is an important tool in your search for the right franchise, and you should make the most of it. When Ali Saifi was looking for a franchise, he reviewed disclosure documents from 130 different franchises before selecting Subway. Today, Saifi owns 390 Subway restaurants in South Carolina that employ 4,000 people and generate more than $200 million in annual sales.[80] Figure 7.7 shows the number of franchisors from which prospective franchisees solicit information before selecting a franchise in which to invest.

When evaluating a franchise opportunity, what should a potential franchisee look for? Although there is never a guarantee of success, the following characteristics make a franchise stand out:

- *A unique concept or marketing approach.* "Me-too" franchises are no more successful than me-too independent businesses. Franchisees of Pizza Fusion, a pizza chain with 21 outlets based in Boca Raton, Florida, are drawn not only to the company's vision and values but also to its unique position in the market, which includes a focus on fresh, organic, and natural ingredients and eco-friendly stores and delivery vehicles. Pizza Fusion's slogan is "Saving the earth, one pizza at a time."

- *Profitability.* A franchisor should have a track record of profitability, and so should its franchisees. If a franchisor is not profitable, its franchisees are not likely to be either. Franchisees who follow the business format should expect to earn a reasonable rate of return.

- *A registered trademark.* Name recognition is difficult to achieve without a well-known and protected trademark.

- *A business system that works.* A franchisor should have in place a system that is efficient and is well documented in its manuals and training materials.

- *A solid training program.* One of the most valuable components of a franchise system is the training it offers franchisees. The system should be relatively easy to teach.

FIGURE 7.7

Number of Franchisees from Which Prospective Franchisees Solicit Information Before Selecting a Franchise

Source: Based on data from Prospective Franchisee Survey Results, Franchise Direct, 2013, http://www.franchisedirect .com/information/trendsfacts/ prospectivefranchiseesurvey- results2013franchiseeprofessional- financialbackground2/8/2384/.

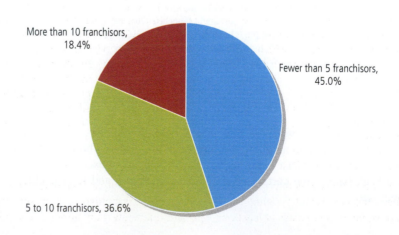

More than 10 franchisors, 18.4%

Fewer than 5 franchisors, 45.0%

5 to 10 franchisors, 36.6%

- *Affordability.* A franchisee should not have to take on an excessive amount of debt to purchase a franchise. Being forced to borrow too much money to open a franchise outlet can doom a business from the outset. Respectable franchisors verify prospective franchisees' financial qualifications as part of the screening process rather than hand out franchises to anyone who has the money to buy one.

- *A positive relationship with franchisees.* The most successful franchises see their franchisees as partners—and treat them accordingly.

The FDD covers the 23 items discussed in the previous section and includes a copy of the company's franchise agreement and any contracts accompanying it. Although the law requires an FDD to be written in plain English rather than "legalese," it is best to have an attorney experienced in franchising review the FDD and discuss its provisions with you. Watch for clauses that give the franchisor absolute control and discretion. The franchise contract summarizes the details that will govern the franchisor–franchisee relationship over its life. It outlines *exactly* the rights and the obligations of each party and sets the guidelines that govern the franchise relationship. Because franchise contracts typically are long term (more than 70 percent run for 10 years or more), it is extremely important for prospective franchisees to understand their terms *before* they sign them.

One of the most revealing items in the FDD is the **franchisee turnover rate**, the rate at which franchisees leave the system. If the turnover rate is less than 5 percent, the franchise is probably sound. However, a double-digit franchise turnover rate is cause for concern, and one approaching 20 percent is a sign of serious underlying problems in a franchise. Satisfied franchisees are not inclined to leave a successful system.

franchisee turnover rate the rate at which franchisees leave a franchise system.

Item 3, the description of the lawsuits in which the franchise has been involved, provides valuable insight into the franchisor–franchisee relationship. Although franchise lawsuits are not uncommon, an unusual number of lawsuits relating to the same issue should alert a potential franchisee to problems. For instance, a judge recently upheld a settlement concerning four class-action lawsuits filed by more than 8,000 current or former franchisees against Quiznos Subs. The lawsuits involved complaints concerning the franchisor's supply chain and food costs, marketing and advertising funds, and fees and royalties on territories that franchisees purchased but in which they never opened restaurants. Although Quiznos paid $206 million to the franchisees, the settlement involved no admission of wrongdoing on the franchisor's part.[81]

Another important aspect of investigating a potential franchise is judging how well you fit into the company culture. Unfortunately, the FDD isn't much help here. The best way to determine this is to actually work for a unit for a time (even if it's without pay). Doing so not only gives prospective franchisees valuable insight into the company culture but also enables them to determine how much they enjoy the daily activities involved in operating the franchise. "Many people don't do enough research, digging into what a company is about, what they believe in, what they're trying to accomplish, and whether they will fit into the culture," says Kevin Hogan, a consultant who works with the Whattaburger franchise.[82]

ENTREPRENEURIAL PROFILE: Reynolds Corea: BrightStar After Reynolds Corea was laid off from his executive position at a large consulting firm, he decided that buying a franchise was the best way to realize his entrepreneurial dreams. He went to work at $10 per hour at a local Chick-Fil-A restaurant, serving chicken sandwiches, mopping floors, and closing the store "to get a better feel for the business." After nine months, Corea decided that owning a restaurant franchise was not for him and worked with a franchise consultant to find a franchise that better suited his interests, goals, and skills. Corea ultimately chose to purchase a franchise from BrightStar, an in-home care service for senior citizens and children. Corea tapped his retirement accounts for the franchise fee and start-up costs, which totaled about $200,000. Corea's franchise is off to a solid start, with two full-time employees and 10 part-time caregivers and plans to hire more.[83] ■

Talk to Existing Franchisees

As valuable as the FDD is, it is only a starting point for researching a franchise opportunity thoroughly. Perhaps the best way to evaluate the reputation of a franchisor is visit several franchise owners who have been in business at least one year and interview them about the positive and the negative features of the agreement and whether the franchisor delivered on its promises. Were their start-up costs consistent with the franchisor's estimates in item 7 of the FDD? Do they get the support the franchisor promised them? Was the training the franchisor provided helpful? How long did it take to reach the break-even point? Have they incurred any unexpected expenses? What risks are involved in purchasing a franchise? Has the franchise met their expectations concerning sales, profitability, and return on investment? What is involved in operating the franchise on a typical day? How many hours do they work in a typical week? What do they like best (and least) about their work? Knowing what they know now, would they buy the franchise again? When you are on site, note the volume of customer traffic and the average transaction size. Are they large enough for an outlet to be profitable? How well managed are the franchises you visit? Michael Whalen, who left a management position with a large office supply chain after 20 years to purchase a Huntington Learning Center franchise, says the most helpful part of his franchise evaluation process "was meeting with current franchise owners."[84] Monitoring franchisees' blogs also enables prospective franchisees to learn the "real story" of running a franchise.

Another revealing exercise is to spend an entire day with at least one (preferably more) franchisee to observe firsthand what it is like to operate a franchise unit. Item 20 of the FDD lists all of a company's current franchisees and former franchisees who have left the system within the last year and their contact information, which makes it easy for potential franchisees to contact them. It is wise to interview former franchisees to get their perspectives on the franchiser-franchisee relationship. Why did they leave the system? If their franchises were unsuccessful, what were the causes?

Table 7.3 offers a list of questions prospective franchisees should ask existing franchisees.

Ask the Franchisor Some Tough Questions

Take the time to ask the franchisor questions about the company and its relationship with its franchisees. As a franchisee, you will be in this relationship a long time, and you need to know

TABLE 7.3 Questions to Ask Existing Franchisees

One of the most revealing exercises for entrepreneurs who are evaluating potential franchises is to visit and interview franchisees who already are operating outlets for a franchise. This is the chance to get the "inside scoop" from people who know best how a particular franchise system works. Following are some questions to ask:

1. Are you happy with your relationship with the franchisor? Explain.
2. How much control does the franchisor exercise over you and the way you run your franchise?
3. What did it actually cost you to get your franchise running? How close was the actual amount to the amount the franchisor told you it would cost?
4. Is your franchise profitable? How long did it take for your franchise to break even? How much does your franchise earn? Are the earnings consistent with your expectations?
5. Did the franchisor estimate accurately the amount of working capital necessary to sustain your business until it began generating positive cash flow?
6. What is the training program like? Were you pleased with the training you received from the franchisor? Did the training prepare you adequately for operating your franchise successfully?
7. Did you encounter any unexpected franchise fees or hidden costs? If so, what were they?
8. Are you pleased with the size of your territory? Is it large enough for you to reach your sales and profitability goals? What kind of territorial protection does the franchisor offer?
9. What restrictions do you face on the products and services that you can sell? Are you required to purchase from approved suppliers? Are their prices reasonable?
10. Does the franchisor advertise as much as it said it would? Is the advertising effective in producing sales?
11. What kind of education and business experience do you have? How important have they been to your success in the franchise?
12. Given what you know now, would you purchase this franchise again?

Sources: Based on Sara Wilson, "Final Answer," *Entrepreneur*, December 2007, pp. 122–126, and "Ten Questions to Ask Other Franchisees in the Franchise Chain," *AllBusiness*, 2006, http://www.allbusiness.com/buying-exiting-businesses/franchising-franchises/2188-1.html.

as much about it as you possibly can beforehand. What is the franchisor's philosophy concerning the relationship? Is there a franchise association made up of franchisees who consult and work with the franchisor's management team? What is the company culture like? How much input do franchisees have into the system? What are the franchise's future expansion plans? How will they affect your franchise? Are you entitled to an exclusive territory? Under what circumstances can either party terminate the franchise agreement? What happens if you decide to sell your franchise in the future? Under what circumstances would you not be entitled to renew the agreement? What kind of earnings can you expect? (If the franchisor made no earnings claims in item 19 of the FDD, why not?) Does the franchisor have a well-formulated strategic plan? How many franchisees own multiple outlets? (A significant percentage of multi-unit franchisees is a good sign that a franchise's brand name and business system are strong.) Has the franchisor terminated any franchisee's contracts? If so, why? How many franchisees have failed? What caused their failure? How are disputes between the franchisor and franchisees settled?

Make Your Choice

The first lesson in franchising is, "Do your homework *before* you get out your checkbook." Robyn Vescovi left behind a 25-year career as an executive in the financial industry to become a Tasti D-Lite franchisee in Boynton Beach, Florida. Before making the career switch, Vescovi spent a year studying her franchise options before making Tasti D-Lite her final choice. "Franchising seemed right for me," she says. "I learned about the board. I knew what the product could do, and I knew who was behind it."[85] Once you have done your research, you can make an informed choice about which franchise is right for you. Then it is time to put together a solid business plan that will serve as your road map to success in the franchise you have selected. The plan is also a valuable tool to use as you arrange the financing for your franchise. Appendix A at the end of this chapter offers a checklist of questions a potential franchisee should ask before entering into any franchise agreement.

Trends Shaping Franchising

LO5

Outline the major trends shaping franchising.

Franchising has experienced three major growth waves since its beginning. The first wave occurred in the early 1970s when fast-food restaurants used the concept to grow rapidly. The fast-food industry was one of the first to discover the power of franchising, but other businesses soon took notice and adapted the franchising concept to their industries. The second wave took place in the mid-1980s as the U.S. economy shifted heavily toward the service sector. Franchises followed suit, springing up in every service business. A third wave began in the early 1990s and continues today. It is characterized by new low-cost franchises that focus on specific market niches. In the wake of major corporate downsizing and the burgeoning costs of traditional franchises, these new franchises allow would-be entrepreneurs to get into proven businesses faster and at reasonable costs. These companies feature start-up costs in the range of about $4,000 to $250,000 and span a variety of industries—from leak detection in homes and auto detailing to day care and tile glazing.

Other significant trends affecting franchising are discussed in the following sections.

Changing Face of Franchisees

Franchisees today are a more diverse group than in the past. A study by the International Franchise Association reports that minorities own 20.5 percent of all franchises compared to 14.2 percent of independent businesses. Although the percentage of women who own franchises has declined to 20.5 percent from 25 percent in 2002, the percentage of franchises jointly owned by women and men increased from 17.1 to 24.4 percent over the same period.[86] Finding the necessary financing to purchase a franchise is one of the biggest obstacles minorities face. To encourage diversity among their franchisees, some franchisors have established programs that offer special discounts and financing opportunities to members of minority groups. Focus Brands, a company that operates several franchises, including Cinnabon, Carvel, Moe's Southwest Grill, and Schlotsky's, has a Growth Through Diversity program that gives minority franchisees discounts on the initial franchise fee and operating fees. Focus Brands is also one of more than 100 franchises that are members of MinorityFran, a program created by the International

Franchise Association in 2006 that has the goal of recruiting minority franchisees.[87] Nearly 60 percent of the largest 500 franchises offer similar discounts and financing opportunities to military veterans who want to become franchisees.[88]

ENTREPRENEURIAL PROFILE: Ronald and Ella Avery-Smothers: Burger King and Denny's Growing up, Ronald Smothers dreamed of owning his own business. After graduating from UCLA and a short stint in the business world, Smothers opened his first franchise, a Burger King outlet in the Crenshaw neighborhood of Los Angeles. Over the next several years, Smothers, an African-American, opened several more Burger King stores before adding a Denny's restaurant to his multi-unit holdings in 2006. Ronald's wife, Ella, also is a successful franchisee, owning nine-and-a-half Burger King franchises. (She brought in a long-time, dedicated employee as co-owner of her eighth restaurant.) Ella says that she originally started working in the business to help her husband but then became interested in the restaurant business, which led her to purchase a franchise of her own . . . and then another . . . and another. . . .[89] ■

Modern franchisees also are better educated, are more sophisticated, have more business acumen, and are more financially secure than those of just 20 years ago. People of all ages and backgrounds are choosing franchising as a way to get into business for themselves. Franchising also is attracting skilled, experienced businesspeople who are opening franchises in their second careers and whose goal is to own multiple outlets that cover entire states or regions. Many of them are former corporate managers—either corporate castoffs or corporate dropouts—looking for a new start on a more meaningful and rewarding career. They have the financial resources, management skills and experience, and motivation to operate their franchises successfully. David Omholt, owner of a franchise brokerage company, says that former executives often make ideal franchisees because they exhibit financial discipline, understand how businesses grow, and are comfortable working with in a business system.[90]

ENTREPRENEURIAL PROFILE: Edith Kelly-Green and Lenny's Sub Shop Edith Kelly-Green had retired from FedEx after 30 years when her college-age daughter, Jayna, suggested that she purchase a franchise of her favorite restaurant, Lenny's Sub Shop, which is headquartered in Memphis, Tennessee. Kelly-Green knew the CEO of the company and called him with the idea that she would become an investor in the business. "He convinced me that I'd be happier as a franchisee," she recalls. Kelly-Green opened her first Lenny's Sub Shop franchise in Oxford, Mississippi, near the University of Mississippi. "After I opened my first unit in Oxford, I decided I didn't want to be a one-location owner," she says. Today, Kelly-Green is the largest multi-unit owner in the chain with 10 stores in Oxford, Mississippi, and Memphis, Tennessee, and her sons, James Kelly and Ryan Green, work with her.[91] ■

International Opportunities

One of the major trends in franchising is the internationalization of American franchise systems. Franchising has become a major export industry for the United States, where franchises are focusing on international markets to boost sales and profits as the domestic market has become saturated. "If you look at long-term growth potential, not to focus significantly on the international opportunity would be a big miss," says Roland Smith, CEO of Wendy's/Arby's.[92] Two-thirds of the members of the International Franchise Association say that international markets will be important to the future success of their franchise operations.[93] Yum! Brands, the parent company of Taco Bell, KFC, and Pizza Hut, earns 75 percent of its revenue from international franchises.[94] McDonald's, which had restaurants in 28 countries in 1980, now operates more than 15,500 outlets in 118 nations outside the United States; international locations account for nearly 70 percent of the company's sales.[95] Only 105 nations in the world, including Bermuda, Cambodia, Montenegro, and North Korea, do not have at least one McDonald's restaurant.[96] International markets are attracting franchisors because they are growing rapidly and offer rising personal incomes, strong demand for consumer goods, growing service economies, and spreading urbanization. Yum! Brands was an early entry into China, opening its first KFC store there in 1987. Today, the company has nearly 4,600 KFC locations in China and opens on average one new store in China every day.[97] The company launched its first Pizza Hut in China in 1990, and the brand, which is regarded by Chinese customers as an upscale, trendy restaurant (often requiring reservations), now holds the top position in the pizza market in China.[98] McDonald's, which opened its first

Rob Culpepper

Hands On . . . How To

Select the Ideal Franchise—*For You*!

When Aaron Miller was a student at the University of Vermont, he wrote a business plan for a sports bar as part of an entrepreneurship class he was taking. More than 15 years later, Miller, a former Olympic and professional ice hockey player, and Martti Matheson, close friends since their college days, transformed that business plan into reality when they opened their first Buffalo Wild Wings Grill and Bar franchise in Burlington, Vermont. What lessons can prospective franchisees learn from Miller and Matheson's experience and that of other franchisees?

Lesson 1. Don't be in a rush; start with a self-evaluation to determine whether franchising is right for you. Finding the right franchise can take months—sometimes years. The first step to finding the right franchise is not screening potential franchises; it is to consider whether franchising is the proper route for you. For would-be entrepreneurs who are independent and have definite ideas about how they want their businesses to operate, franchising is not the path they should follow to get into business. Miller and Matheson considered launching their own independent sports bar but after evaluating their lack of experience in the restaurant business decided to go with a franchise because of the support system it offers on everything from establishing the menu and setting up the kitchen to advertising and choosing a location.

Lesson 2. Make sure that you understand both the advantages and the disadvantages of franchising before making a commitment. The best franchisors offer their franchisees a recipe for success and the support to help them make it work. "You can take your capital and apply it to the franchise and grow quicker than you could on your own," says Gary Robins, owner of 41 Supercuts franchises. However, franchisors require that franchisees pay them for the recipe with up-front fees and ongoing royalties and then stick to the recipe as they operate their businesses. "Someone who really likes their independence and doing things their way will find franchising a very uncomfortable setting," says Francine LaFontaine, a franchising expert. Matheson recognizes that operating a franchise can be frustrating because the contract restricts franchisees' decision making authority on basic business issues. However, pointing out that the benefits that the franchisor provides far outweigh the costs, he says that he does not mind paying the 5 percent (of sales) royalty fee. The average Buffalo Wild Wings Grill and Bar generates $3 million in annual sales, and Matheson knows that getting to that level of sales as an independent restaurateur would take much longer than it would with a franchisor's support.

Lesson 3. Review the FDD with the help of an experienced attorney. The FDD is an extremely valuable resource for anyone who is considering purchasing a franchise. Poring over the document alone can be frustrating, however, because it covers so much. "The typical FDD is enormously complex because it is so multifaceted," says Eric Karp, an attorney who teaches franchising courses at Babson College. Karp says some franchisees are so overwhelmed by the size of the FDD that they make the mistake of not reading it at all.

Lesson 4. Use the FDD to screen potential franchises and don't be shy about asking lots of questions. Rob Parsons worked as the franchise development director for Popeyes Louisiana Kitchen for six years before he decided to switch sides and become one of the company's franchisees. "Something a franchisee said kept ringing in my head," he recalls. "He said, 'You did all the work. Why are you letting me reap all the benefits?'" Parsons, who has experienced the FDD from both the franchisor's and the franchisee's perspective, says that the FDD can be extremely useful to prospective franchisees. "The FDD has a list of all of the franchisees in a system," says Parsons. "That's a huge resource." Use the list to contact current and past franchisees to discover what it's really like to operate an outlet in the franchisor's system. If they were making the decision today, would they still purchase the franchise?

Lesson 5. Make sure that you can afford the franchise without getting in over your head. Some franchises cost millions of dollars; others require only a few thousand dollars. Prospective franchisees should know how much they can afford to spend on a franchise. Changes in financial markets have required franchisors to get more creative when it comes to helping franchisees finance the purchase of their outlets. Marco's Pizza, which operates nearly 250 restaurants, offers qualified franchisees personal guarantee insurance that repays a bank 70 percent of a franchisee's loan in case the franchisee cannot repay the loan. Marco's also has assembled a group of private investors to create a $5 million private equity fund that will invest up to $100,000 in each Marco's restaurant. In addition, Marco's has established a leasing program that finances the $250,000 cost of opening one of its pizza outlets. When Remi Tessler approached a bank for a loan to open a Marco's Pizza franchise in Warner Robbins, Georgia, the bank told him that it could finance only the cost of the equipment for just five years, despite his stellar credit score. "I was shocked," says Tessler, who then turned to his franchisor for financing assistance. Tessler made a down payment of $62,500 and used Marco's leasing program to finance the remaining $187,500, which he will repay over eight years.

Lesson 6. Visit your top franchise candidates. After narrowing the list of potential franchises to your top choices, go visit them. Most franchisors sponsor Discovery Days events in

(continued)

Hands On . . . How To (continued)

which they host potential franchisees at their headquarters. Be observant and, once again, ask lots of questions. Ted Dowell says his visit to the operations center of TSS Photography, a franchise that specializes in taking photographs of sports, school, and special events, convinced him to become a franchisee. Dowell was particularly impressed with the franchise's production system, which is a key component in its franchisees' success. He points out that that getting a behind-the-scenes, firsthand look at the franchise's system won him over as a franchisee. In addition, recognize that franchisors use these on-site visits to evaluate prospective franchisees.

Lesson 7. Realize that no business, not even a franchise, runs itself. Some new franchisees believe that they can be absentee owners because the business system they purchase from the franchisor will allow their franchises to operate by themselves. It's just not true. "Some people think that running a franchise won't be a lot of work," says Matt Haller of the International Franchise Association. "They think that all they have to do is pay the franchise fee and then sit back and watch the money roll in." Although the franchisor provides franchisees with a formula for success, franchisees must implement the formula and make it work. "In franchising, like anything else, hard work pays off," says Haller.

Sources: Based on Uri Berliner, "The Roots of Franchising Took Hold in a Hair Salon," *NPR*, October 17, 2013, http://www.npr.org/2013/10/17/234929759/the-roots-of-franchising-took-hold-in-a-hair-salon-chain; Melissa Pasanen, "Chain Restaurant Model Works for Many Vermont Entrepreneurs," *Burlington Free Press*, June 7, 2010, http://www.burlgingtonfreepress.com/article/20100607/NEWS01; Dianne Molvig, "Buying a Franchise: Potential and Precautions," Educational Employees Credit Union, January 10, 2011, http://hffo.cuna.org/11270/article/3171/html; Anne Fisher, "Risk Reward," *FSB*, December 2005/January 2006, pp. 45–61; Julie Bennett, "The Road to Discovery," *Entrepreneur*, February 2011, pp. 83–87; Kermit Patterson, "Tight Credit Is Turning Franchisors into Lenders," *New York Times*, June 9, 2010, http://www.nytimes.com/2010/06/10/business/smallbusiness/10sbiz.html; Jason Daley, "The Cross Over," *Entrepreneur*, March 2011, pp. 101–105; and Emily Maltby, "Want to Buy a Franchise: The Requirements Went Up," *Wall Street Journal*, November 15, 2010, p. R9.

outlet in China in 1990, also sees the country as a prime growth market and recently built its first Hamburger University training center in Shanghai to support its expansion in China.[99]

As they venture into foreign markets, franchisors have learned that adaptation is one key to success. Although a franchise's overall business format may not change in foreign markets, some of the details of operating its local outlets must. For instance, fast-food chains in other countries often must make adjustments to their menus to please locals' palates. In addition to Original Recipe chicken, KFC restaurants in China also include an extensive menu of beef, seafood, vegetable, and rice dishes (spicy prawn rice and beef rice) as well as soups, breakfast items, and desserts (sugared egg tart) that appeal to Chinese customers' tastes. In Japan, McDonald's (known as "Makudonarudo") outlets sell teriyaki burgers, rice burgers, a bacon potato pie (mashed potatoes and bacon deep fried inside a pastry roll), and katsu burgers (cheese wrapped in a roast pork cutlet topped with katsu sauce and shredded cabbage) in addition to their traditional American fare. In Canada, the McDonald's menu includes poutine, a classic comfort dish that consists of French fries topped with cheese curds and gravy. McDonald's has eliminated beef and pork from its menu and has substituted mutton for beef in its burgers in India, a nation that is predominantly Hindu and Muslim. In India, McDonald's sells the Maharaja Mac (two specially seasoned chicken patties with locally flavored condiments), the McAloo (a patty made from potatoes, peas, and special spices), and the McSpicy Paneer (a spicy cottage cheese patty made from buffalo milk topped with a tandoori sauce).[100] In India, Pizza Hut restaurants offer customers a selection of beer and wine.[101] In China, KFC quickly learned that residents were not interested in coleslaw, so the company dropped the item from its menu and added local delicacies, such as the Dragon Twister (a chicken wrap soaked in a spicy Peking duck sauce), congee (rice porridge), bamboo shoots, and soy milk.[102]

As China's economy continues to grow and its capital markets expand, increasing numbers of franchisors are opening locations there. In China, Subway, known as Sai Bei Wei (which translates as "tastes better than others" in Mandarin), learned the importance of patience in building a franchise presence in challenging international markets. When the company opened its first outlet in China, managers had to print signs explaining how to order a sandwich. Sales of tuna salad were dismal because residents, accustomed to seeing their fish whole, did not believe that the salad was made from fish at all. In addition, because Chinese diners do not like to touch their food, many of them held their sandwiches vertically, peeled the paper wrapper away gradually,

You Be the Consultant

Franchising in Africa: Potential Abounds but So Do Challenges

U.S. franchises are growing faster abroad than they are in the domestic market. As franchisors have found wringing impressive growth rates from a franchise-saturated domestic market increasingly difficult, they have begun to export their franchises to international markets. Even small franchises, those with fewer than 100 locations, are opening outlets in global markets, including those with developing economies. Indeed, franchising is ideally suited for developing economies because it allows people with limited business experience and financial resources to become part of an established business. China and India, with combined populations of 2.4 billion people with rising incomes, are drawing franchisors from across the globe. Despite the challenges it presents, Africa also is becoming the target of many franchisors because of its size, growing middle class, insatiable appetite for American brands, relative scarcity of franchised outlets, and economic growth. In fact, Africa is home to 6 of the 10 fastest growing economies in the world. Economists forecast that the continent's economy will grow by 5 percent per year through 2017. Quick-service restaurant franchises in particular are drawn to Africa because the World Bank estimates that food demand across the continent will double between 2012 and 2020.

Initially, franchisors focused their development efforts on Africa's largest economy, South Africa (where franchising accounts for 12 percent of total GDP), but many are now turning their attention to Nigeria, Ghana, Kenya, Egypt, and Tanzania. "Africa is the last continent," says Jeff Spear, vice-president of development for CKE Restaurants, the parent company of Hardee's and Carl Jr.'s. "If we don't start today, it will never happen." Franchisors are entering African markets cautiously. McDonald's has 177 restaurants in South Africa but has not expanded into other African nations. Yum! Brands, owner of KFC, Long John Silver, and Taco Bell, has about 1,000 KFC franchises in Africa. Domino's Pizza reports that its five outlets in Nigeria are its busiest stores in the entire world by sales volume. The franchisor also has more than two dozen restaurants in Egypt and Morocco and is making plans to enter South Africa and Kenya. Potential franchisees in Africa find that the nation's banks prefer to make loans for franchised outlets because they perceive the risk to be lower.

Franchising in Africa is fraught with challenges, however. "Africa is not for sissies," says Eric Parker, cofounder of Nando's, a South African chicken franchise. "You're going to take some hard knocks." One of the biggest challenges is establishing a reliable, consistent supply chain. To open his first four KFC franchises in Ghana, entrepreneur Ashok Mohinani had to import chicken, which increased his food cost significantly, because local farmers could not produce enough chickens and meet the chain's quality standards. When Gavin Bell, a KFC franchisee in Kenya, opened

his first outlets, the government prohibited chicken imports, so Bell invested $500,000 into a local chicken operation, which took 13 months to get its production up to speed. Nigeria also prohibits poultry imports, so the KFC restaurants there have added fish to their menus because local farmers cannot meet all of the restaurants' demand for chicken. Getting supplies to individual stores can be a challenge because of the distances to refrigerated warehouses and the limited supply of reliable refrigerated trucks required to keep products fresh.

Water shortages can be problematic as well. Eric Andre, a Domino's Pizza franchisee in Nigeria, has had to dig wells and install water treatment plants at a cost of $60,000 each at each one of his five restaurants in Nigeria. Because only two of his employees had ever tasted pizza, Andre sent his managers to the United States to tour pizzerias. "It is important to enter the [African] market with your eyes wide open," says one top government official.

All of these challenges produce a significantly higher cost structure, often two to five times higher than franchisees in other parts of the world experience. For example, in the United States, tomatoes cost $3.45 per kilogram, but in Nigeria, the cost is $10.73 per kilogram. Similar cost comparisons exist for cheddar cheese ($4.12 vs. $13.88 per kilogram), ground beef ($4.17 vs. $7.57 per kilogram), iceberg lettuce ($2.16 vs. $10.09 per kilogram), and other commodities. The result, of course, is higher menu prices. Chris Nahman, who left a law practice in California, to open the first Johnny Rockets hamburger franchise in Nigeria, charges $14 for a Rocket Single, compared to the typical $5.50 price in the United States. Nevertheless, Nahman says that his restaurant serves between 300 and 400 customers a day.

1. What steps should U.S.-based franchisors take when establishing outlets in foreign countries?

2. Describe the opportunities and challenges franchisors face when entering emerging markets such as the nations of Africa.

3. Use the Internet as a resource to develop a list of at least five suggestions that will help new franchisors looking to establish outlets in Africa. Which countries do you recommend they focus on? Explain.

Sources: Tosin Sulaiman, "Franchises Target Africa with Fashion, Food, and Fitness," Reuters, September 7, 2012, http://in.reuters.com/article/2012/09/07/africa-money-idINL6E8K74WM20120907; Nancy Weingartner, "Franchising in Africa with Eyes Wide Open," *Franchise Times*, July 2, 2013, http://www.franchisetimes.com/franchise/July-2013/Franchising-in-Africa-with-eyes-wide-open/; Drew Hinshaw, "KFC Leads Fast-Food Race to Africa," *Wall Street Journal*, February 9–10, 2013, pp. B1–B2; Drew Hinshaw, "Hamburgers Come to Africa," *Wall Street Journal*, December 11, 2013, pp. B1–B2.

and ate the contents as they would eat a banana![103] McDonald's faced similar challenges in India, where customers were puzzled by placing their orders at a counter and had no understanding of the golden arches; the company's signs read "McDonald's Family Restaurant" so that customers would know that it was a restaurant.[104]

Smaller, Nontraditional Locations

intercept marketing
the principle of putting a franchise's products or services directly in the paths of potential customers, wherever they may be.

As the high cost of building full-scale locations continues to climb, more franchisors are searching out nontraditional locations in which to build smaller, less expensive outlets. Based on the principle of **intercept marketing**, the idea is to put a franchise's products or services directly in the paths of potential customers, wherever that may be. Locations within locations have become popular. Franchises are putting scaled-down outlets on college campuses; in high school cafeterias, sports arenas, churches, hospitals, museums, and zoos; and on airline flights. Subway has more than 8,000 franchises in nontraditional locations that range from airports and military bases to college campuses and convenience stores. The company has restaurants located in a Goodwill store in Greenville, South Carolina, and inside the True Bethel Baptist Church in Buffalo, New York. Subway put store number 40,000 inside an AppleGreen gas station in Ipswich, England.[105] Perhaps Subway's most unusual location was a temporary restaurant that served only the construction workers building the skyscraper at 1 World Trade Center in New York City. As work progressed on the 105-story building, a hydraulic lift elevated the restaurant, which was housed inside 36 shipping containers welded together.[106]

Many franchisees have discovered that smaller outlets in nontraditional locations often generate more sales per square foot than full-size outlets and at just a fraction of the cost. Locations that emphasize convenience by being close to their customers will continue be a key to continued franchise growth in the market.

Conversion Franchising

conversion franchising
a franchising trend in which owners of independent businesses become franchisees to gain the advantage of name recognition.

The recent trend toward **conversion franchising**, in which owners of independent businesses become franchisees to gain the advantage of name recognition, will continue. One study reports that 72 percent of franchisors in North America use conversion franchising as a growth strategy.[107] In a franchise conversion, the franchisor gets immediate entry into new markets and experienced operators; franchisees get increased visibility and often a big sales boost. It is not unusual for entrepreneurs who convert their independent stores into franchises to experience an increase of 20 percent or more in sales because of the instant name recognition the franchise offers.

ENTREPRENEURIAL PROFILE: John Andikian: 7-Eleven John Andikian opened a convenience store in Tustin, California, in 2004 and named it Andy's Market in memory of his father. He sold typical convenience store fare, including his own version of the Slurpee, the Andy Freeze. After 18 months in business, Andy's Market still had not reached its break-even point, and Andikian was running out of cash and time. The problem: "Nobody knew what Andy's Market was," he says. To save his business, Andikian decided to convert it into a 7-Eleven franchise, paying a $20,000 franchise fee and $100,000 for inventory and remodeling costs. The transformation required only 48 hours, and Andikian noticed the dramatic difference that adding the franchisor's well-known name made almost immediately. "As soon as they put the 7-Eleven sign outside, my sales doubled," he says. "I was doing about $70,000 a month in sales; now I'm doing about $160,000."[108] ■

Refranchising

refranchising
a technique in which franchisors sell their company-owned outlets to franchisees.

Another trend that has emerged over the last several years is franchises selling their company-owned outlets to franchisees. Known as **refranchising**, the goal is to put outlets into the hands of operators, who tend to run their franchises more efficiently than the franchisor can. Since 2007, McDonald's has reduced the percentage of company-owned stores in the chain from 23 percent to 19 percent. Quick-service restaurant franchise Jack in the Box recently sold 66 of its company-owned outlets in the Southeast and Midwest to franchisees, bringing the percentage of franchisee-owned stores to 79 percent. The company plans to refranchise more restaurants to reach its goal of having 85 percent of its outlets owned by franchisees.[109] Refranchising not only increases franchisors' profitability because it generates more royalty income for franchisors but also provides capital to finance their international expansion.

Multi-Unit Franchising

Twenty-five years ago, the typical franchisee operated a single outlet. The current generation of franchisees, however, strives to operate multiple franchise units. According to the International Franchise Association, 20 percent of franchisees are multiple-unit owners; however, those multi-unit franchisees own 55 percent of all franchise outlets.[110] Although the typical multiple-unit franchise owns five outlets, it is no longer unusual for a single franchisee to own 25, 75, or even 100 units. At Taco Bell, the Mexican fast-food restaurant chain, the typical franchisee owns 20 outlets.[111]

Franchisors are finding that multi-unit franchising is an efficient way to do business. For a franchisor, the time and cost of managing 10 franchisees each owning 10 outlets are much less than managing 100 franchisees each owning one outlet. A multi-unit strategy also accelerates a franchise's growth rate. Not only is multiple-unit franchising an efficient way to expand quickly, but it also is effective for franchisors who are targeting foreign markets, where having a local representative who knows the territory is essential.

The popularity of multi-unit franchising has paralleled the trend toward increasingly experienced, sophisticated franchisees who set high performance goals that a single outlet cannot meet. For franchisees, owning multiple units offers the opportunity for rapid growth without leaving the safety net of the franchise. Multi-unit franchisees also earn more than single-unit franchisees.[112] In addition, franchisees may be able to get fast-growing companies for a bargain when franchisors offer discounts off their standard fees for buyers who purchase multiple units.

Although operating multiple units offers advantages for both franchisors and franchisees, there are dangers. Operating multiple units requires franchisors to focus more carefully on selecting the right franchisees—those who are capable of handling the additional requirements of multiple units. The impact of selecting the wrong franchise owners is magnified when they operate multiple units and can create huge headaches for the entire chain. Franchisees must be aware of the dangers of losing their focus and becoming distracted if they take on too many units. In addition, operating multiple units means more complexity because the number of business problems that franchisees face also is multiplied.

Area Development and Master Franchising

Driving the trend toward multiple-unit franchising are area development and master franchising. Under an **area development** franchise, a franchisee earns the exclusive right to open multiple outlets in a specific area within a specified time. In 1973, Steve Kuhnau opened a health food store in New Orleans through which he sold the nutritional fruit smoothies he had developed as a way to combat his own food allergies. Kuhnau's smoothies became so popular that he changed the company's name to Smoothie King. Kuhnau began franchising in 1988, and today Smoothie King, which he sold to franchisee Wan Kim in 2012, has more than 700 locations around the world. To accelerate the company's growth, Smoothie King recently signed area development agreements with new and existing franchisees in eight markets across the United States, ranging from large cities such as Chicago, Dallas, and Atlanta to small cities such as Jackson, Mississippi; New Haven, Connecticut; and Sarasota, Florida. As part of the area development agreements, these franchisees will open 28 new outlets within the next three years.[113] "Franchisors are realizing the advantages of dealing with area developers," says franchising expert Bret Lowell. "The franchisor doesn't have to deal with six people opening six different units. There are economies of scale and added efficiency with area developers."[114] Some franchisors are no longer willing to sell individual franchises and are selling franchises only under area development deals.

A **master franchise** (or subfranchise) gives a franchisee the right to create a semi-independent organization in a particular territory to recruit, develop, and support other franchisees. A master franchisee buys the right to develop subfranchises within a territory or sometimes an entire country, takes over many of the duties and responsibilities of the franchisor, and typically earns a portion of the franchise fees and royalties from its subfranchises. Many franchisors use master franchising to open outlets in international markets because the master franchisees understand local laws and the nuances of selling in local markets. Cinnabon, a company founded by Rich and Greg Komen in 1985 that sells cinnamon buns and other baked treats, recently signed a master franchise agreement to develop territories in the Republic of Georgia. To introduce its products to Georgia, the company partnered with Sam Samuelyan and Stepan Panosyn, owners of BrandCity

area development
a method of franchising in which a franchisee earns the exclusive right to open multiple units in a specific territory within a specified time.

master franchise
a method of franchising that gives a franchisee the right to create a semi-independent organization in a particular territory to recruit, sell, and support other franchisees.

LLC, to supervise the opening of seven stores within six years. Although Cinnabon has a significant presence in Europe and Asia, including nearby Azerbaijan, Armenia, Turkey, and Russia, these outlets will be the company's first in Georgia. Cinnabon has more than 1,000 locations in 55 countries, including more than 130 in Russia.[115] Both area development and master franchising "turbocharge" a franchisor's growth.

Cobranding

cobranding

a method of franchising in which two or more franchises team up to sell complementary products or services under one roof.

A growing number of companies are using **cobranding (or piggyback or combination) franchising**—combining two or more distinct franchises under one roof. This "buddy-system" approach works best when the two franchise ideas are compatible and appeal to similar customers. Large franchisors have used the strategy for many years, but many small franchisors are banding together to establish cobranded units that together create synergy and generate more sales and profits than individual, self-standing units. In 2011, Nestlé Toll House Café, which sells cookies, baked goods, coffee, and other treats, began creating cobranded franchises with Häagen-Dazs, which sells a full line of ice cream, sorbet, yogurt, and gelato. "We're a complete dessert café," says Dan Ogiba, a top manager at Häagen-Dazs. "We looked at this as an opportunity to grow and for our franchisees to increase their revenues."[116] Howard Taylor opened his first Nestlé Toll House Café in 2007; today he owns five franchises, all of which are cobranded with the Häagen-Dazs brand. "The two brands complement one another, giving our customers more options," he says.[117]

Cobranded outlets also save their owners money because they lower both real estate and operating costs. The same employees sell both brands, reducing labor costs, and the franchisors share advertising, maintenance, and other costs. Focus Brands, which owns Schlotsky's (sub sandwiches), Cinnabon (cinnamon buns and other baked treats), and Carvel Ice Cream brands often pairs two and sometimes all three of its franchises in a single location. Both Schlotzky's and Cinnabon stores bake their products daily, which means that employees of each franchise already have experience with operating ovens, making it easy for them to master baking the other brand's products. The cobranding strategy appears to be working; the owners of more than 200 of Scholtsky's 350 locations have added a Cinnabon franchise to their stores.[118]

Unless the brands are well-suited complements, cobranding can create more headaches than benefits. Unless well planned and managed, cobranding can increase operational complexity and cause product and service quality to decline. To make sure that cobranding works for them, some franchisors, especially small ones, test the concept in a limited number of locations. Philly Pretzel Factory, with more than 100 locations, and Rita's Frozen Ice, a franchise with more than 600 outlets, recently partnered to open their first cobranded franchise in the Montgomery Mall in North Wales, Pennsylvania.[119]

Conclusion

Franchising has proved its viability in the U.S. economy and has become a key part of the small business sector because it offers many would-be entrepreneurs the opportunity to own and operate a business with a greater chance for success. Despite its impressive growth rate to date, the franchising industry still has a great deal of room to grow. "Franchising is really small business at its best," says Don DeBolt, former head of the International Franchise Association.[120]

Chapter Summary by Learning Objective

1. Describe the three types of franchising: trade name, product distribution, and pure.

- Trade-name franchising involves a franchisee purchasing the right to become affiliated with a franchisor's trade name without distributing its products exclusively.

- Product distribution franchising involves licensing a franchisee to sell products or services under the

franchisor's brand name through a selective, limited distribution network.

- Pure franchising involves a selling a franchisee a complete business format.

2A.   Explain the benefits of buying a franchise.

- Franchises offer many benefits: management training and support, brand-name appeal, standardized quality of goods and services, national advertising programs, financial assistance, proven products and business formats, centralized buying power, territorial protection, and a greater chance of success.

2B. Explain the drawbacks of buying a franchise.

- Franchising also suffers from certain drawbacks: franchise fees and profit sharing, strict adherence to standardized operations, restrictions on purchasing, limited product lines, unsatisfactory training programs, market saturation, and less freedom.

3. Explain the laws covering franchise purchases.

The FTC requires all franchisors to disclose detailed information on their operations in a Franchise Disclosure Document at the first personal meeting or at least 14 days before a franchise contract is signed or before any money is paid. The FTC rule covers *all* franchisors. The FDD requires franchisors to provide information on 23 topics in their disclosure statements. The FDD is an extremely helpful tool for prospective franchisees.

4. Discuss the *right* way to buy a franchise.

The following steps will help you make the right franchise choice: evaluate yourself, research your market, consider your franchise options, get a copy of the franchisor's FDD, talk to existing franchisees, ask the franchisor some tough questions, and make your choice.

5. Outline the major trends shaping franchising.

Key trends shaping franchising today include the changing face of franchisees; international franchise opportunities; smaller, nontraditional locations; conversion franchising; multiple-unit franchising; master franchising; and cobranding (or combination franchising).

Discussion Questions

7-1. What is franchising?

7-2. Describe the three types of franchising and give an example of each.

7-3. Discuss the advantages and the disadvantages of franchising for the franchisee.

7-4. Why might an independent entrepreneur be dissatisfied with a franchising arrangement?

7-5. Fran Lubbs, who after a five-year stint left the corporate office of Goddard School, an early education franchise, to become a franchisee, says, "Follow the system. It's one of the reasons you bought the franchise. Don't try to change it, break it, or fix it." Do you agree with her? Explain.

7-6. What steps should a potential franchisee take before investing in a franchise?

7-7. Two franchising experts recently debated the issue of whether new college graduates should consider franchising as a pathway to entrepreneurship. Jeff Elgin said recent college graduates are not ready to be franchise owners. "First, most recent college graduates don't have the financial resources to fund a franchise start-up. Second, many lack the life experience and the motivation to run a business effectively and stick with it when times get tough." Jennifer Kushell said franchising is the perfect career choice for many recent college graduates, for several reasons: (1) the support system that franchising provides is ideal for young entrepreneurs, (2) young people have grown up with franchising and understand it well, (3) many college graduates already have launched businesses of their own, and (4) they think big. Which view do you think is correct? Explain.

7-8. What is the function of the FDD? Outline the protection the FDD gives prospective franchisees.

7-9. Describe the current trends in franchising.

7-10. One franchisee says franchising works because the franchisor gets its franchisees going, nurtures them, and, at times, shoves them. However, the franchisor cannot make its franchisees successful. Success depends on how committed one is to finding the right franchise for himself or herself, on what each franchisee brings to the business, and on how hard he or she is prepared to work. Do you agree? Explain.

7-11. Robyn Vescovi, a former financial executive who recently became a Tasti D-Lite franchisee, offers the following advice to first-time franchisees:

- Do your homework. Research the brand (both the long- and short-term business model)
- Know the team behind this brand and understand their vision for that product/business. Know them as franchise experts and their proven successes.
- Know yourself and your limits. This will help you determine the right business (e.g., new and innovative franchise or well-established franchise).
- Be involved! Don't expect that things "will just happen." You have your own business, but you are part of something bigger, and it is in your best interest to participate in whatever you can in support of that brand/product. Don't be an "absentee franchisee."

Do you agree? Explain. What other advice can you offer first-time franchisees?

Beyond the Classroom . . .

7-12. Visit a local franchise operation. Is it a trade name, product distribution, or pure franchise?

7-13. To what extent did the franchisee investigate before investing?

7-14. What assistance does the franchisor provide the franchisee?

7-15. How does the franchisee feel about the franchise contract he or she signed?

7-16. What would the franchisee do differently now?

7-17. Use the Internet to locate several franchises that interest you. Contact the franchisors and ask for their franchise disclosure documents and write a report comparing their treatment of the 23 topics the documents cover.

7-18. What are the major differences in the terms of each franchise's contract?

7-19. Are some terms more favorable than others?

7-20. If you were about to invest in this franchise, which terms would you want to change?

Endnotes

Scan for Endnotes or go to www.pearsonhighered.com/scarborough

Appendix A. A Franchise Evaluation Checklist

Yourself

1. Are you qualified to operate a franchise successfully? Do you have adequate drive, skills, experience, education, patience, and financial capacity? Are you prepared to work hard?

2. Are you willing to sacrifice some autonomy in operating a business to own a franchise?

3. Can you tolerate the financial risk? Would business failure wipe you out financially?

4. Can you juggle multiple tasks simultaneously and prioritize various projects so that you can accomplish those that are most important?

5. Are you genuinely interested in the product or service you will be selling? Do you enjoy this kind of business? Do you like to sell?

6. Do you enjoy working with and managing people? Are you a "team player"?

7. Will the business generate enough profit to suit you?

8. Has the franchisor investigated your background thoroughly enough to decide whether you are qualified to operate the franchise?

9. What can this franchisor do for you that you cannot do for yourself?

The Franchisor and the Franchise

1. Is the potential market for the product or service adequate to support your franchise? Will the prices you charge be in line with the market?

2. Is the market's population growing, remaining static, or shrinking? Is the demand for your product or service growing, remaining static, or shrinking?

3. Is the product or service safe and reputable?

4. Is the product or service a passing "fad," or is it a durable business idea?

5. What will the competition, direct or indirect, be in your sales territory? Do any other franchisees operate in this general area?

6. Is the franchise international, national, regional, or local in scope? Does it involve full- or part-time involvement?

7. How many years has the franchisor been in operation? Does it have a sound reputation for honest dealings with franchisees?

8. How many franchise outlets now exist? How many will there be a year from now? How many outlets are company owned?

9. How many franchises have failed? Why?

10. How many franchisees have left the system within the past year? What were their reasons for leaving?

11. What service and assistance will the franchisor provide? What kind of training program does the franchisor offer? How long does it last? What topics does it cover? Does the franchisor offer ongoing assistance and training?

12. Will the franchise perform a location analysis to help you find a suitable site? If so, is there an extra charge for doing so?

13. Will the franchisor offer you exclusive distribution rights for the length of the agreement, or may it sell to other franchises in this area?

14. What facilities and equipment are required for the franchise? Who pays for construction? Is there a lease agreement?

15. What is the total cost of the franchise? What are the initial capital requirements? Will the franchisor provide financial assistance? Of what nature? What is the interest rate? Is the franchisor financially sound enough to fulfill all its promises?

16. How much is the franchise fee? Exactly what does it cover? Are there any ongoing royalties? What additional fees are there?

17. Does the franchisor provide an estimate of expenses and income? Are they reasonable for your particular area? Are they sufficiently documented?

18. How risky is the franchise opportunity? Is the return on the investment consistent with the risks?

19. Does the franchisor offer a written contract that covers all the details of the agreement? Have your attorney and your accountant studied its terms and approved it? Do you understand the implications of the contract?

20. What is the length of the franchise agreement? Under what circumstances can it be terminated? If you terminate the contract, what are the costs to you? What are the terms and costs of renewal?

21. Are you allowed to sell your franchise to a third party? Does the franchisor reserve the right to approve the buyer?

22. Is there a national advertising program? How is it financed? What media are used? What help is provided for local advertising?

23. Once you open for business, *exactly* what support will the franchisor offer you?

24. How does the franchise handle complaints from and disputes with franchisees? How well has the system worked?

The Franchisees

1. Are you pleased with your investment in this franchise?

2. Has the franchisor lived up to its promises?

3. What was your greatest disappointment after getting into this business?

4. How effective was the training you received in helping you run the franchise?

5. What are your biggest challenges and problems?

6. What is your franchise's cash flow like?

7. How much money are you making on your investment?

8. What do you like most about being a franchisee? Least?

9. Is there a franchisee advisory council that represents franchisees?

10. Knowing what you know now, would you buy this franchise again?

8

Building a Powerful Bootstrap Marketing Plan

Rawpixel/Shutterstock

Learning Objectives

On completion of this chapter, you will be able to:

1. Describe the principles of building a bootstrap marketing plan, and explain the benefits of preparing one.

2. Explain how small businesses can pinpoint their target markets.

3. Discuss the role of market research in building a bootstrap marketing plan and outline the market research process.

4. Describe how a small business can build a competitive edge in the marketplace using bootstrap marketing strategies.

As you learned in Chapters 4 and 5, creating a solid business model and business plan improves an entrepreneur's odds of building a successful company. The business model and business plan are valuable tools that help define *what* an entrepreneur plans to accomplish in both quantitative and qualitative terms and *how* he or she plans to accomplish it. The plan consolidates many of the topics we have discussed in preceding chapters with those in this section to produce a concise statement of how an entrepreneur plans to achieve success in the marketplace. This section focuses on building two major components of every business plan: the marketing plan and the financial plan.

Too many business plans describe in great detail what entrepreneurs intend to accomplish (e.g., "the financials") and pay little, if any, attention to the strategies to achieve those targets. Too often, entrepreneurs squander enormous effort pulling together capital, people, and other resources to sell their products and services because they fail to determine what it will take to attract and keep a profitable customer base. Sometimes they fail to determine whether a profitable customer base even exists! To be effective, a solid business plan must contain both a financial plan *and* a marketing plan. Like the financial plan, an effective marketing plan projects numbers and analyzes them but from a different perspective. Rather than focus on cash flow, net income, and owner's equity, a marketing plan concentrates on the *customer*.

This chapter is devoted to creating an effective marketing plan, which is a subset of a total business plan. Before producing reams of computer-generated spreadsheets of financial projections, an entrepreneur must determine what to sell, to whom and how, and on what terms and at what price and how to get the product or service to the customer. In short, a marketing plan identifies a company's target customers and describes how that business will attract and keep them. Its primary focus is cultivating and maintaining a competitive edge for a small business. Table 8.1 explains how to build a seven-sentence bootstrap (also sometimes called "guerrilla") marketing strategy.

Building a Bootstrap Marketing Plan

Marketing is the process of creating and delivering desired goods and services to customers and involves all of the activities associated with winning and retaining loyal customers. The "secret" to successful marketing is to understand what your target customers' needs, demands, and wants are before your competitors can; to offer them the products and services that will satisfy those needs, demands, and wants; and to provide customer service, convenience, and value so that they will keep coming back.

The marketing function cuts across the entire company, affecting every aspect of its operation—from finance and production to hiring and purchasing—as well as the company's ultimate success. As competition for customers becomes more intense, entrepreneurs must understand the importance of developing creative marketing strategies. Their success and survival depend on it. Traditional marketing techniques emphasize pushing messages out to potential customers. However, modern technology gives consumers the ability to filter and block many of these messages, limiting the effectiveness of "push" techniques. Successful entrepreneurs recognize that modern marketing strategies also must include techniques such as social media and cause marketing that pull customers into their companies' sphere of influence. The good news is that many of these "pull" strategies are relatively inexpensive and, when infused with a healthy dose of creativity, are extremely effective.

Although they may be small and cannot match their larger rivals' marketing budgets, entrepreneurial companies are not powerless when it comes to developing effective marketing strategies. By using **bootstrap marketing strategies**—unconventional, low-cost, creative techniques—small companies can wring as much or more "bang" from their marketing bucks. For instance, facing the power of discount giants such as Wal-Mart, Target, and "category killer" superstores such as Best Buy and Home Depot that are determined to increase their market shares, small retail shops are turning to bootstrap marketing tactics to attract new customers and to keep existing ones. Jay Conrad Levinson, the late guerrilla and bootstrap marketing guru, said bootstrap marketing is all about maximizing the efficiency of a small company's marketing budget.

An effective bootstrap marketing campaign does *not* require an entrepreneur to spend large amounts of money, but it does demand creativity, ingenuity, and an understanding of customers'

LO1

Describe the principles of building a bootstrap marketing plan, and explain the benefits of preparing one.

marketing
the process of creating and delivering desired goods and services to customers; involves all of the activities associated with winning and retaining loyal customers.

bootstrap marketing strategies
unconventional, low-cost, creative marketing strategies designed to give small companies an edge over their larger, richer, more powerful rivals.

TABLE 8.1 A Seven-Sentence Bootstrap (Guerrilla) Marketing Strategy

Building a successful bootstrap marketing plan does not have to be complex. Bootstrap marketing expert Jay Conrad Levinson advised entrepreneurs to create a bootstrap marketing plan with just seven sentences:

1. *What is the purpose of your marketing?* In other words, what action do you want customers or prospective customers to take as a result of your marketing efforts? Should they visit your store? Go to your company's Web site? Call a toll-free number for more information?

2. *What primary benefit can you offer customers?* What is your company's competitive advantage, and what does it do for customers? Bootstrap marketers express their companies' competitive advantage as a solution to a customer's problem, which is easier to market than just a positive benefit. Successful bootstrap marketing requires an entrepreneur to have a clear understanding of a company's unique selling proposition, a key customer benefit of a product or service that sets it apart from its competition.

3. *Who is your target market?* At whom are you aiming your marketing efforts? Answering this question often requires some basic research about your target customers, their characteristics, their habits, and their preferences. Bootstrap marketers know that broadcasting is old school; they realize that narrowcasting—focusing their marketing efforts on those people who are most interested in and are likely to purchase their goods and services—is much more efficient and effective. Most small companies have more than one target market; be sure to identify all of them.

4. *Which marketing tools will you use to reach your target audience?* This list should include only those tools your company understands, knows how to use effectively, and can afford. The good news is that marketing tools do not have to be costly to be effective. In fact, bootstrap marketers are experts at using low-cost methods to market their companies.

5. *What is your company's niche in the marketplace?* How do you intend to position your company against your competition? Bootstrap marketers understand that their markets are crowded with competitors, some of them much larger with gigantic marketing budgets that dwarf their own, and that finding a profitable niche to occupy can be highly profitable. Recall from Chapter 4 that many successful entrepreneurs position their companies in profitable niches. One insurance agent markets his agency as specializing in serving the needs of small businesses. It'Sugar, a company founded in 2006 by Jeff Rubin, a veteran of the candy industry, sells many types of candy, ranging from Jelly Belly jelly beans to five-pound Hershey chocolate bars through its Web site and its 70 retail stores. Not a typical candy store aimed at children, It'Sugar stores mainly target adults and resemble Victoria's Secret shops, with mannequins dressed in candy, unique displays, and vibrant colors. Like It'Sugar, the key is to carve out a position that allows your company to differentiate itself from all of its competitors.

6. *What is your company's identity in the marketplace?* A company's identity is a reflection of its personality, its DNA. Small companies often have an advantage over large businesses when it comes to communicating their identities because of the interesting, unique stories behind their creation and the enthusiasm and passion of their founders. Customers enjoy doing business with small companies that have a clear, meaningful, and compelling identity in the marketplace. Southwest Airlines built its business by attracting customers who were drawn to its fun-loving, somewhat irreverent culture and its reputation for taking care of its customers.

7. *How much money will you spend on your marketing?* What is your marketing budget? Entrepreneurs should decide how much they intend to invest in their marketing efforts, an amount usually expressed as a percentage of sales. The average company in the United States devotes 4 percent of its sales revenue to marketing. Small companies should allocate a portion of their budget to marketing; after all, it drives sales. The good news is that many of the bootstrap marketing techniques that small companies can use (and that are described in this chapter) are either low cost or no cost. When allocating their budgets, bootstrap marketers recognize the importance of putting their money where they will get the greatest "bang."

Answering these seven questions will give you an outline of your company's marketing plan. *Implementing* a bootstrap marketing plan boils down to two essentials:

1. Having a thorough understanding of your target market, including what customers want and expect from your company and its products and services.

2. Identifying the obstacles that stand in your way of satisfying customers (competitors, barriers to entry, processes, outside influences, budgets, knowledge, and others) and eliminating them.

Sources: Based on Jay Conrad Levinson and Jeannie Levinson, "Here's the Plan," *Entrepreneur*, February 2008, pp. 92–97; and Alan Lautenslager, "Write a Creative Marketing Plan in Seven Sentences," *Entrepreneur*, April 24, 2006, http://www.entrepreneur.com/marketing/marketingideas/guerrillamarketingcolumnistallautenslager/article159486.html.

buying habits. Levinson estimated that bootstrap marketers spend between 4 percent and 8 percent of sales on marketing, but they put their money into clever, creative marketing efforts that reach their target customers and raise the profile of their products, services, and companies.[1]

ENTREPRENEURIAL PROFILE: Kimberly Causey: Home Décor Press After spending ten years working in the wholesale home furnishings industry, Kimberly Causey realized consumers wanted information on home furnishing bargains. She took her knowledge of the industry and set out to self-publish a home furnishings buying guide. Causey could not afford to get her guide professionally printed, so she made her first run of books in her kitchen. She printed the interior pages on her home printer, folded them by hand, and glued them inside professionally printed covers using a glue gun and a butter knife. She promoted the books by driving all over the Southeast to appear on local morning television shows. Causey used the profits from her home-made books to buy a professionally printed run of books and an RV and began promoting her books across the country. She was able to secure a nationwide contract with Barnes & Noble. Her story eventually caught the attention of the *Today* show. Her appearance on that show pushed her book to a top 10 title on Amazon. Causey continues to promote her books through appearances on both local and national media outlets.[2] ■

A sound bootstrap marketing plan reflects a company's understanding of its customers and acknowledges that satisfying them is the foundation of every business. It recognizes that the customer is the central player in the cast of every business venture. According to marketing expert Ted Levitt, the primary purpose of a business is not to earn a profit; instead, it is to identify and attract customers. If an entrepreneur focuses on this purpose and uses good sense to run the business, profits will follow.[3] In other words, profits are the outcome of creating value for your target customers. Every area of the business must practice putting the customer first in planning and actions.

A bootstrap marketing plan should accomplish three objectives:

1. It should pinpoint the specific target markets the small company will serve.

2. It should determine customer needs and wants through market research.

3. It should analyze the firm's competitive advantages and build a bootstrap marketing strategy around them to communicate its value proposition to the target market.

This chapter focuses on these three objectives of the small company's marketing plan.

Pinpointing the Target Market

One of the first steps in building a bootstrap marketing plan is to identify a small company's **target market**—the specific group of customers at whom the company aims its goods or services. The more a business knows about its local markets and its customers and their buying habits and preferences, the more precisely it can focus its marketing efforts on the group(s) of customers who are most likely to buy its products or services. Most marketing experts contend that the greatest marketing mistake small businesses make is failing to define clearly the target markets they serve. These entrepreneurs develop new products that do not sell because they are not targeted at a specific audience's needs. They broadcast ads that attempt to reach everyone and end up reaching no one. They spend precious time and money trying to reach customers who are not the most profitable, and many of the customers they attract leave because they do not know what the company stands for. Why, then, do so many small companies make this mistake? Because it is easy and does not require market research or a marketing plan! Smart entrepreneurs know they do not have the luxury of wasting resources. They must follow a more focused, laserlike approach to marketing. Entrepreneurs must identify a specific market niche that has a specific need or "pain point" and tailor a solution, be it a product or a service, to address this need. As you learned in Chapter 4, an effective value proposition offers a specific solution to a specific market segment. "It is amazing how many people assume they know what customers want without actually asking customers," says Hunter Phillips, CEO, PRSM Healthcare in Nashville, Tennessee. "Present it as if you are trying to solve a problem for them. Remember, this is about their needs rather than your idea."[4]

LO2

Explain how small businesses can pinpoint their target markets.

target market

the specific group of customers at whom a company aims its goods or services.

To be customer driven, an effective marketing strategy must be based on a clear, comprehensive understanding of a company's target customers and their needs. A customer-driven marketing strategy is a powerful weapon for any company that lacks the financial and physical resources of its competitors. Customers respond when companies take the time to learn about their unique needs and offer products and services designed to satisfy them.

ENTREPRENEURIAL PROFILE: Ron Henry: BlackRapid Ron Henry, a professional photographer for more than fifteen years, never was able to find a camera strap that was both comfortable and designed to make quick shots easier. Using parts purchased at a hardware store, Henry constructed a strap that allowed his camera to hang comfortably at his side until he was ready to take a photograph, when it would glide quickly and easily into place. Henry borrowed $5,000 from a friend to launch BlackRapid to produce and sell camera straps based on his new design. At first Henry bought banner ads at wedding Web sites to promote his camera straps. However, that proved to be an expensive strategy that resulted in very few sales. Henry changed his strategy to promoting BlackRapid through photography blogs. He sent each blogger a free strap hoping that they would spread the word about his product. The strategy worked. After only four years in business, BlackRapid's revenues grew to more than $6 million a year.[5] ■

Most successful businesses have well-defined portraits of the customers they are seeking to attract. From market research, they know their customers' income levels, lifestyles, buying patterns, likes and dislikes, and even their psychological profiles—why they buy. These companies offer prices that are appropriate to their target customers' buying power, product lines that appeal to their tastes, and service they expect. The payoff comes in the form of higher sales, profits, and customer loyalty. For entrepreneurs, pinpointing target customers has become more important than ever before as markets in the United States have become increasingly fragmented and diverse. Mass marketing techniques no longer reach customers the way they did 30 years ago because of the splintering of the population and the influence exerted on the nation's purchasing patterns by what were once minority groups such as Hispanic, Asian, and African Americans (see Figure 8.1). Peter Francese, marketing consultant and author of the research report *2010 America*, says "the average American" no longer exists.[6] The United States is a multicultural nation in

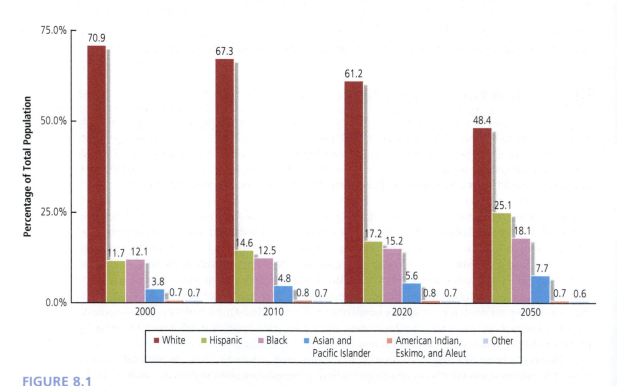

FIGURE 8.1

U.S. Population by Race, 2000, 2010, 20120, and 2050

Source: Based on data from the U.S. Census Bureau.

which no race or ethnicity comprises a majority in its two most populous states, California and Texas. In addition, racial and ethnic minorities accounted for 92 percent of the population growth in the United States between 2000 and 2010.[7] The U.S. Census Bureau predicts that whites will no longer constitute the majority in America by 2043.[8] By 2020, baby boomers' spending will be in decline, the most economically disadvantaged market segments will expand, and household spending will grow at a slow pace, all of which will create a very different world for marketers.[9]

When companies follow a customer-driven marketing strategy, they ensure that their target customers permeate the entire business—from the merchandise sold and the music played on the sound system to the location, layout, and decor of the store. These entrepreneurs have an advantage over their larger rivals because the buying experience they create resonates with their target customers. That's why they prosper.

ENTREPRENEURIAL PROFILE: Orlin Sorensen and Brett Carlile: Woodinville Whiskey Company The Woodinville Whiskey Company, a microdistillery in Woodinville, Washington, founded by Orlin Sorensen and Brett Carlile, builds relationships with its customers by putting them to work. Customers help bottle, label, cork, and case whiskey. During the nightly bottling parties, the company gives 16 customers T-shirts, food, and discounts on any whiskey they buy that evening in return for their efforts. The bottling parties are posted on the company's Facebook page, where the listed parties fill up within a few minutes of posting. Sorenson says the bottling parties build brand awareness and increase customer loyalty. Although it would be less expensive to hire employees to do the bottling, the company has no plans to abandon the parties. The relationship the company has built with its customers far offsets the higher costs associated with the bottling party method of production.[10] ■

Determining Customer Needs and Wants through Market Research

LO3

Discuss the role of market research in building a bootstrap marketing plan and outline the market research process.

demographics
the study of important population characteristics, such as age, income, education, race, and others.

The changing nature of the U.S. population is a potent force altering the landscape of business. Shifting patterns in age, income, education, race, and other population characteristics (which are the subject of **demographics**) have a major impact on new opportunities in the market and on existing small businesses. Entrepreneurs who ignore demographic trends and fail to adjust their strategies accordingly run the risk of becoming competitively obsolete. Entrepreneurs who stay in tune with demographic, social, and economic trends are able to spot growing and emerging market opportunities.

ENTREPRENEURIAL PROFILE: Jennifer Lopez: Viva Móvil Celebrity Jennifer Lopez started the mobile phone reseller, Viva Móvil, to target the growing Latino market. In addition to its online store, Viva Móvil operates brick and mortar locations in New York City, Los Angeles, and Miami. The stores promise a retail experience that caters to the Latino market. Each store has a PlayStation to keep children entertained while their parents shop for new phones and accessories. All employees are bilingual, and the stores offer accessories designed by Lopez to go along with the iPhones and Samsung phones offered through a partnership with Verizon.[11] ■

A demographic trend is like a train: A business owner must find out early on where it's going and decide whether to get on board. Waiting until the train is roaring down the tracks and gaining speed means it's too late to get on board. However, by checking the schedule early and planning ahead, an entrepreneur may find himself or herself at the train's controls wearing the engineer's hat! Similarly, small companies that spot demographic trends early and act on them can gain a distinctive edge in the market. An entrepreneur's goal is to make sure that his or her company's marketing plan is on track with the most significant trends that are shaping the industry. Trend tracking not only keeps a company on the pathway to success but also helps it avoid losing its focus by pursuing opportunities that are out of favor.

Trends are powerful forces and can be an entrepreneur's greatest friend or greatest foe. For entrepreneurs who are observant and position their companies to intercept them, trends can be to their companies what the perfect wave is to a surfer. For entrepreneurs who ignore them or discount their importance, trends can leave their companies stranded like a boat stuck in the mud at low tide.

You Be the Consultant

.CO Internet S.A.S.

Juan Diego Calle was born into an entrepreneurial family in Bogota, Colombia. His parents owned and operated a highly successful wine and beer distribution company. Because of political instability in Colombia, his parents became increasingly worried about the safety of their family. When he was 15 years old, his parents moved Juan and his siblings to Miami. However, his parents chose to stay behind in Colombia to manage the family business.

In 1998 while in college, Calle studied abroad in France. There he became intrigued by the opportunity offered by the Internet. When he returned to Miami, Calle launched an Internet-based business that failed when the Internet bubble burst in 2001. However, Calle continued to pursue Internet-related businesses after the failure of his first endeavor. He had great success with a business that acquired and developed travel domains that matched keywords, such as New York Hotels and London Hotels.

While growing his domain name business, Calle recognized that available domain names ending in .com extensions were becoming scarce. A friend suggested he look into .co extension, which was the domain name designation for his native country of Colombia. After many false starts, Calle was able to convince the government of Colombia to accept his bid to manage the .co extension through his new company called .CO Internet S.A.S.

Calle made the decision to brand the .co extension as a place for start-ups to build their Internet presence. Calle was able to convince trend-setting tech companies to use the .co extension for their Web presence. To achieve his goal, he persuaded executives at Twitter to adopt t.co as its shortened URL address in Colombia. Calle also sold AngelList, the service for connecting entrepreneurs and angel investors, the domain name Angel.co as its Internet address. By associating the .co brand with successful ventures such as these, .CO Internet helped reinforce its branding efforts as the domain of choice for tech start-ups.

The company seeks to position its brand as having more value than just a URL address. .CO Internet offers all businesses that adopt the .co extension "membership," which includes discounts on books and admission to events and forums to connect with other entrepreneurs. To measure the success of its branding efforts, the company conducted a survey after it had been operating for only one year. The results indicated that 80 percent of people thought .co meant "company," while only 3 percent identified it with the country of Colombia

.CO Internet has more than 1.6 million domain names under management in 200 countries, with revenues of more than $21 million. In 2014, Neustar, a publicly-traded company specializing in Internet analytics, agreed to purchase .CO Internet S.A.S. for $109 million.

1. Visit the company's Web site to learn more about the business, the services it offers, and its culture. Work with a team of your classmates to develop a list of bootstrap marketing techniques that the company can use to promote its services and its brand around the globe.

2. What steps can the company take to enhance its brand and build customer recognition of it? Refer to Figure 8.2 on page 303 (the connection between branding and a unique selling proposition) and use the table below to do the following:
   a. List threshold, performance, and excitement attributes for .CO Internet S.A.S.
   b. Identify "proof points" (reasons for customers to believe in the brand) that support each of the attributes you list.
   c. Use the attributes and their proof points to develop a unique selling proposition for .CO Internet.

Threshold Attributes	Performance Attributes	Excitement Attributes
Threshold Proof Points	Performance Proof Points	Excitement Proof Points
Unique selling proposition:		

Sources: Ron Jackson, "The Juan Diego Calle Story: How the .CO CEO Is Turning a Seldom Used ccTLD into a Booming Global Brand," *DN Journal*, December 5, 2010, www.dnjournal.com/cover/2010/november-december.htm; Paul Sloan, ".CO Internet is a Company Cool Enough for Brooklyn Hipsters," *CNET*, March 13, 2012, www.cnet.com/news/co-internet-is-a-company-cool-enough-for-brooklyn-hipsters/; Nancy Dahlberg, "Miami Tech Company .CO Internet to be Acquired for $109 Million," *Miami Herald*, March 22, 2014, www.miamiherald.com/2014/03/21/4009212/miami-tech-company-co-internet.html.

market research
the vehicle for gathering the information that serves as the foundation for the marketing plan; it involves systematically collecting, analyzing, and interpreting data pertaining to a company's market, customers, and competitors.

The Value of Market Research

By performing some basic market research, aspiring entrepreneurs and owners of existing small business can detect key demographic and market trends. Marketing consultants argue that information is just as much a business asset as equipment, machinery, and inventory. **Market research** is the vehicle for gathering the information that serves as the foundation for the marketing plan. It involves systematically collecting, analyzing, and interpreting data pertaining to a company's market, customers, and competitors. The objective of market research is to learn how to improve the level of satisfaction for existing customers and to find ways to attract new customers.

Small companies cannot afford to make marketing mistakes because there is little margin for error when funds are scarce and budgets are tight. Small businesses simply cannot afford to miss their target markets, and market research can help them zero in on the bull's-eye. Market research does *not* have to be time consuming, complex, or expensive to be useful. By applying the same type of creativity to market research that they display when creating their businesses, entrepreneurs can perform effective market research "on the cheap."

ENTREPRENEURIAL PROFILE: John Lusk: Rivet & Sway Before John Lusk launched the designer eyewear company, Rivet & Sway, he and his team spent evenings and weekends conducting market research. They were seeking to identify specific problems that women have when they shop for eyewear. The founding team went through industry reports; interviewed opticians, optometrists, and eyewear boutique owners; conducted surveys of the many people they had all built up in their personal social and professional networks; conducted bootstrap focus groups; and engaged in extensive competitive research. The company's budget for all of the market research was less than $5,000, with most of that being spent on buying a high quality industry report.[12] ∎

Established companies also can conduct market research on the cheap. Ron Shaich, founder of Panera Bread, a chain of bakery cafés with 1,185 locations in 40 states, still visits stores regularly, where he works the cash registers and serves customers so that he can listen to their ideas and concerns.[13] Hands-on market research techniques such as these allow entrepreneurs to get past the barriers that consumers often put up and to uncover their true preferences and hidden thoughts.

Many entrepreneurs are discovering the power, the speed, the convenience, and the low cost of conducting market research over the Internet. Online surveys, customer opinion polls, and other research projects are easy to conduct, cost virtually nothing, and help companies to connect with their customers. With online surveys, businesses can get real-time feedback from customers, often using surveys they have designed themselves. Web sites such as Survey Monkey and Zoomerang allow entrepreneurs to conduct low-cost (sometimes free) online surveys of existing or prospective customers. Many companies are using social media sites such as Facebook and Twitter as market research tools. Entrepreneurs can use surveys and social media to gain insight into the market that used to require hiring a marketing research consultant.

ENTREPRENEURIAL PROFILE: Luca Daniel Lavorato and Mario Christian: Joseph Nogucci Joseph Nogucci, an online jewelry store and manufacturer founded by Luca Daniel Lavorato and Mario Christian, uses Facebook to generate customer reactions to new product offerings. The company gauges customer interest in new designs before it puts them into production. The customer feedback also helps the company determine how much inventory to carry and what demographic to target market with each of its new product offerings. In addition to promoting and managing inventory for new products, the company posts inspirational stories from customers on its Facebook fan page to build customer loyalty. Joseph Nogucci has 75,000 Facebook fans and devotes 80 percent of its marketing budget to Facebook. The company also connects with customers through Twitter, Instagram, and other social media.[14] ∎

Faith Popcorn, a marketing consultant, encourages small business owners to be their own "trend-tracking sleuths." Merely by observing their customers' attitudes and actions, small business owners can shift their product lines and services to meet changing tastes in the market. To spot significant trends, Popcorn suggests the following:[15]

- Read as many current publications as possible, especially ones you normally would not read.

- Watch the top 10 television shows because they are indicators of consumers' attitudes and values and what they're going to be buying.

- See the top 10 movies. They also influence consumer behavior, from language to fashion.

- Talk to at least 150 customers a year. Make a conscious effort to spend time with some of your target customers, preferably in an informal setting, to find out what they are thinking.

Start by asking them two important questions: "Will you buy from us again?" and "Will you recommend us to your friends?"

- Talk with the 10 smartest people you know. They can offer valuable insights and fresh perspectives you may not have considered.

- Listen to your children or younger siblings.

Next, entrepreneurs should make a list of the major trends they spot and should briefly describe how well their products or services match these trends. Companies whose products or services are diverging from major social, demographic, and economic trends rather than converging with them must change their course or run the risk of failing because their markets can evaporate before their eyes. How can entrepreneurs find the right match among trends, their products or services, and the appropriate target markets? Market research!

How to Conduct Market Research

The goal of market research is to reduce the risks associated with making business decisions. For the entrepreneur, there is no bigger decision than the one to start or not start a new business. Market research can replace misinformation and assumptions with facts. Opinion and hearsay are not viable foundations on which to build a solid marketing strategy. Remember, this is a key aspect of developing a sound business model (see Chapter 4). Successful market research consists of four steps: define the problem, collect the data, analyze and interpret the data, and draw conclusions, including how you may need to pivot your business model.

Step 1. *Define the objective.* The first—and most crucial—step in market research is to define the research objective clearly and concisely. For a new business, the objective is to test the assumptions made while developing the business model. For an existing business, the objective is to better understand changes occurring in its business or in its market. A common error at this stage is to confuse a symptom with the true problem. For example, dwindling sales is not a problem; it is a symptom. To get to the heart of the matter, entrepreneurs must list all the possible factors that could have caused it. Do we face new competition? Are our sales representatives impolite or unknowledgeable? Have customer tastes changed? Is our product line too narrow? Do customers have trouble finding what they want? Is our Web site giving customers what they want? Is it easy to navigate?

individualized (one-to-one) marketing
a system based on gathering data on individual customers and developing a marketing program designed to appeal specifically to their needs, tastes, and preferences.

Step 2. *Collect the data.* The marketing approach that dominates today is **individualized (one-to-one) marketing**, which involves gathering data on individual customers and then developing a marketing program designed specifically to appeal to their needs, tastes, and preferences. In a society in which people feel so isolated and interactions are so impersonal, one-to-one marketing gives a business a competitive edge. Companies following this approach know their customers, understand how to give them the value they want, and, perhaps most important, know how to make them feel special and valued. The idea is to treat each customer as an individual, and the goal is to transform a company's best and most profitable customers into loyal, lifetime customers.

Individualized marketing requires business owners to gather and assimilate detailed information about their customers. Fortunately, owners of even the smallest companies now have access to affordable technology that creates and manages computerized databases, allowing them to develop close, one-to-one relationships with their customers. Much like gold nuggets waiting to be discovered, significant amounts of valuable information about customers and their buying habits are hidden *inside* many small businesses, tucked away in computerized databases. For most business owners, collecting useful information about their customers and potential new products and markets is simply a matter of sorting and organizing data that are already floating around somewhere in their companies.

The key is to mine the data that most companies have at their disposal and turn them into useful information that allows the company to "court" its customers with special products, services, ads, and offers that appeal most to them. How can entrepreneurs gather valuable market and customer information? Two basic methods are available: conducting *primary research*, data you collect and analyze yourself, and gathering *secondary research,* data that have already been compiled and that are available, often at a reasonable cost or even free. Primary research techniques include the following:

- *Customer surveys and questionnaires.* Keep them short. Word your questions carefully so that you do not bias the results and use a simple ranking system (e.g., a 1-to-5 scale, with 1 representing "unacceptable" and 5 representing "excellent"). Test your survey for problems on a small number of people before putting it to use. Online surveys are inexpensive, are easy to conduct, and provide feedback fast. VerticalResponse, a self-service marketing firm for small businesses, regularly sends out e-mail surveys to its customers. Because the company relies on word-of-mouth for much of its new business, knowing what its customers like and don't like about how they are doing business and the products it offers is critical to adding new customers.[16]

- *Focus groups.* Enlist a small number of customers to give you feedback on specific issues in your business—quality, convenience, hours of operation, service, and so on. Listen carefully for new marketing opportunities as customers or potential customers tell you what is on their minds. Once again, consider using the Internet; one small bicycle company conducts 10 online focus groups each year at virtually no cost and gains valuable marketing information from them.

- *Social media conversations and monitoring.* With social media, companies have the opportunity to engage in direct conversations with their customers. In addition, monitoring social media for comments about a business and its products or services can provide useful feedback from customers. Many companies use the Google Alerts feature of the leading search engine to track and receive e-mail updates whenever someone writes about their brands online. Most social networking sites, including Facebook and Twitter, offer search features that allow users to track what people are saying about a company and its products or services. Shari's Berries ships more than 5 million gourmet berries every Valentine's Day. When the weather forecast showed that a major snow storm would be sweeping across the country on Valentine's Day, the company proactively e-mailed customers and sent messages on Twitter warning of delivery delays. As the storm hit, the company monitored Facebook and Twitter, responding to every customer who posted comments. Although there was quite a bit of negative chatter in social media about the company when the storm first hit, within four days positive comments significantly outnumbered negative comments throughout social media.[17]

- *Test market.* One of the best ways to gauge customer response to a new product or service is to set up a test market. When Smooth Fitness launched its new unobtrusive, low-cost exercise bicycle designed for aging baby boomers, the company test-marketed the new product on QVC. The company sold 33,000 bikes in one day on QVC, which convinced its managers that the new product would be successful.[18]

- *Daily transactions.* Sift as much data as possible from existing company records and daily transactions—customer warranty cards, personal checks, frequent-buyer clubs, credit applications, and others.

- *Other ideas.* Set up a suggestion system (for customers and employees) and use it. Establish a customer advisory panel to determine how well your company is meeting needs. Talk with suppliers about trends they have spotted in the industry. Contact customers who have not bought anything in a long time and find out why. Contact people who are not customers and find out why. Teach employees to be good listeners and then ask them what they hear.

Secondary research, which is usually less expensive to collect than primary data, includes the following sources:

- *Business directories.* To locate a trade association, use *Business Information Sources* (University of California Press) or the *Encyclopedia of Associations* (Gale Research). To find suppliers, use the *Thomas Register of American Manufacturers* (Thomas Publishing

Company) or *Standard & Poor's Register of Corporations, Executives, and Industries* (Standard & Poor's Corporation). *The American Wholesalers and Distributors Directory* includes details on more than 18,000 wholesalers and distributors.

- *Direct mail lists.* You can buy mailing lists for practically any type of business. The *Standard Rates and Data Service Directory of Mailing Lists* (Standard Rates and Data) is a good place to start looking.

- *Demographic data.* Profiles of more specific regions are available in the *State and Metropolitan Data Book* (Government Printing Office). The *Sourcebook of ZIP Code Demographics* (CACI, Inc.) provides detailed breakdowns of the population in every ZIP code in the country. *Sales and Marketing Management's Survey of Buying Power* (Bill Communications) has statistics on consumer, retail, and industrial buying.

- *Census data.* The Bureau of the Census publishes a wide variety of reports that summarize the wealth of data found in its census database, which is available at most libraries and at the Census Bureau's Web site (www.census.gov).

- *Forecasts.* The *U.S. Global Outlook* tracks the growth of 200 industries and gives a five-year forecast for each one. Many government agencies, including the U.S. Department of Commerce, offer forecasts on everything from interest rates to the number of housing starts. A government librarian can help you find what you need.

- *Market research.* Someone may already have compiled the market research you need. The *FINDex Worldwide Directory of Market Research Reports, Studies, and Surveys* (Cambridge Information Group) lists more than 10,600 studies available for purchase. Other directories of business research include the *Simmons Study of Media and Markets* (Simmons Market Research Bureau Inc.) and the *A. C. Nielsen Retail Index* (A. C. Nielsen Company).

- *Articles.* Magazine and journal articles pertinent to your business are a great source of information. Use the *Reader's Guide to Periodical Literature*, the *Business Periodicals Index* (similar to the *Reader's Guide* but focusing on business periodicals), and *Ulrich's Guide to International Periodicals* to locate the ones you need.

- *Local data.* Your state department of commerce and your local chamber of commerce will very likely have useful data on the local market of interest to you. Call to find out what is available.

- *The Internet.* Most entrepreneurs are astounded at the marketing information that is available on the Internet. Using one of the search engines, you can gain access to a world of information—literally!

Thanks to advances in computer hardware and software, data mining, once available only to large companies with vast computer power and large market research budgets, is now possible for even very small businesses. **Data mining** is a process in which computer software that uses statistical analysis, database technology, and artificial intelligence finds hidden patterns, trends, and connections in data so that business owners can make better marketing decisions and predictions about customers' behavior. By finding relationships among the many components of a data set, identifying clusters of customers with similar buying habits, and predicting customers' buying patterns, data mining gives entrepreneurs incredible marketing power.

data mining
a process in which computer software that uses statistical analysis, database technology, and artificial intelligence finds hidden patterns, trends, and connections in data so that business owners can make better marketing decisions and predictions about customers' behavior.

Step 3. *Analyze and interpret the data.* The results of market research alone do not provide a solution to the problem; business owners must interpret them. What do the data tell you? Is there a common thread running through the responses? Do the results suggest any changes needed in the way the business operates? Can the entrepreneur can take advantage of new opportunities? There are no hard-and-fast rules for interpreting market research results. Entrepreneurs must use judgment and common sense to determine what the results of their research mean.

Step 4. *Draw conclusions and act.* The market research process is not complete until the business owner acts on the information collected. In many cases, the conclusion is obvious once a small business owner interprets the results of the market research. Based on an understanding of what the facts really mean, the owner must then decide how to use the information in the business. For example, the owner of a small ladies' clothing boutique discovered from a survey that her customers preferred evening shopping hours over early morning hours. She made the schedule adjustment, and sales began to climb.

Plotting a Bootstrap Marketing Strategy: How to Build a Competitive Edge

LO4

Describe how a small business can build a competitive edge in the marketplace using bootstrap marketing strategies.

To be successful bootstrap marketers, entrepreneurs must be as innovative in creating their marketing strategies as they are in developing new product and service ideas. Table 8.2 describes several low-cost, creative, and highly effective bootstrap marketing tactics small businesses have used to outperform their larger rivals.

Bootstrap Marketing Principles

The following 14 principles can help business owners create powerful, effective bootstrap marketing strategies.

FIND A NICHE AND FILL IT As you learned in Chapter 4, many successful small companies choose their niches carefully and defend them fiercely rather than compete head-to-head with larger rivals. A focus (niche) strategy allows a small company to maximize the advantages of its size and to compete effectively even in industries dominated by giants by serving its target customers better than its competitors. Focusing on niches that are too small to be attractive to large companies is a common recipe for success among thriving small companies.

ENTREPRENEURIAL PROFILE: Craig Rowe: ClearRisk ClearRisk, founded by Craig Rowe, is a St. Johns, Newfoundland, company that develops risk and claims management apps for government entities and insurance companies around the globe. The company operates in a geographically diverse business-to-business market and relies on social media to reach customers within its narrowly defined niche strategy. The company uses Facebook to connect with its clients and its potential customers and does not use hard sell tactics with social media. Instead, ClearRisk uses Facebook to disseminate valuable information to its niche market. It uses the contacts it generates on Facebook to make calls on potential customers, which is how the company measures its return on its Facebook marketing budget.[19] ∎

USE THE POWER OF PUBLICITY **Publicity** is any commercial news covered by the media that boosts sales but for which a small company does not pay. Publicity has power; because it is from an unbiased source, a news feature about a company or a product that appears in a newspaper or magazine has more impact on people's buying decisions than an advertisement does. Exposure in any medium raises a company's visibility and boosts sales, and, best of all, publicity is free! It does require some creativity and effort, however.

publicity
any commercial news covered by the media that boosts sales but for which a small company does not pay.

The following tactics can help entrepreneurs stimulate publicity for their companies:

Write an article that will interest your customers or potential customers. One marketing and advertising consultant writes a twice-monthly column for the local newspaper on useful topics such as "Unlocking the Mysteries of Big Data," "Advertising Strategies for Small Retailers," and "How CEOs Can Use Social Media." Not only do the articles help build his credibility as an expert, but they also have attracted new customers to his business. Do not focus all your writing on traditional media outlets. Outlets such as blogs provide a wide reach to a very targeted market.

Sponsor an event designed to attract attention. Divurgent Healthcare Advisors, located in Dallas, Texas, sponsors local charitable events for children's healthcare. For example, the company raises $5,000 a year for a children's hospital at an annual trade show and its employees participate in other fundraisers for children's healthcare systems.

TABLE 8.2 Bootstrap Marketing Tactics

- Help organize and sponsor a service- or community-oriented project.
- Sponsor offbeat, memorable events. Build a giant banana split or rent a theater for a morning and invite kids for a free viewing.
- Always be on the lookout for new niches to enter. Try to develop multiple niches.
- Offer to speak about your business, industry, product, or service to local organizations.
- Launch a loyalty program that gives customers a reason to return. Be sure to provide loyalty program members with benefits, such as special offers, discounts, shopping previews, and others.
- Reward existing customers for referring new customers to your company. When customers refer business to Choice Translating, a language translation company in Charlotte, North Carolina, they receive a special gift.
- Sell at every opportunity. One brewery includes a minicatalog advertising T-shirts and mugs in every six-pack it sells. Orders for catalog items are climbing fast.
- Develop a sales "script" that asks customers a series of questions to hone in on what they are looking for and what will lead them to the conclusion that your product or service is *it*!
- Sell gift certificates. They really boost your cash flow.
- Create samples of your product and give them to customers. You'll increase sales later.
- Offer a 100%, money-back, no-hassles guarantee. By removing the customer's risk of buying, you increase your product's attractiveness.
- Create a frequent-buyer program. Remember how valuable existing customers are. Work hard to keep the customers you have! One coffee shop kept its customers coming back with a punch-card promotion that gave a free pound of coffee after a customer purchased nine pounds.
- Clip articles that feature your business and send reprints to customers and potential customers. Keep reminding them of who you are and why you're valuable to them.
- Test how well your ads "pull" with coded coupons that customers bring in. Focus your ad expenditures on those media that produce the best results for you.
- Create "tip sheets" to pass out to customers and potential customers (e.g., landscape tips on lawn maintenance).
- Find ways to make your product or service irresistible to your customers. One furniture company e-mails photos of big-ticket items customers are considering, and sales closing rates have climbed 25 percent.
- Create an award for your community (e.g., a landscape company presented a "best yard" award each season).
- Create a big event of your own: "January is Customer Appreciation Month. Buy one suit and get a second one at 50 percent off."
- Conduct a contest in the community (e.g., a photographer sponsored a juried photo contest for different age groups). One restaurant that targeted the business crowd for lunch encouraged customers to leave their business cards (which gave the restaurateur the ability to e-mail them daily lunch specials) to enter a drawing for a free $50 iTunes gift card.
- Collect testimonials from satisfied customers and use them in ads, brochures, and so on. Testimonials are one of the most effective forms of advertising!
- Purchase customized postage stamps that feature your company's logo (see PhotoStamps at http://photo.stamps.com) and use them on business correspondence.
- Get a former journalist to help you write a story "pitch" for local media.
- Show an interest in your customers' needs. If you spot a seminar that would be of interest to them, tell them! Become a valuable resource for them.
- Find unique ways to thank customers, especially first-time buyers, for their business (e.g., a note, a lunch, a gift basket, and so on).
- Give loyal customers a "freebie" occasionally. You might be surprised at how long they will remember it.
- Create a newsletter that features your customers or clients and their businesses (e.g., a photo of a client using your product in his or her business).
- Cooperate with other businesses selling complementary products and services in marketing efforts and campaigns, a process called fusion marketing. Share mailing lists and advertising time or space or work together on a special promotion.
- Use major competitors' coupons against them. The owner of an independent sandwich shop routinely pulled business from a nearby national chain by advertising that he would accept its coupons.
- Market your company's uniqueness. Many customers enjoy buying from small companies that are different and unique. The owners of the only tea plantation in the United States used that fact to their advantage in establishing a customer base.

Sources: Based on Mickey Meece, "How to Keep Momentum Going for Customers and Employees," *New York Times*, January 3, 2008, http://www .nytimes.com/2008/01/03/business/smallbusiness/03tips.html; Jay Conrad Levinson, "Attention Getters," *Entrepreneur*, March 1998, p. 88; Lynn Beresford, Janean Chun, Cynthia E. Griffin, Heather Page, and Debra Phillips, "Marketing 101," *Entrepreneur*, May 1996, pp. 104–114; Guen Sublette, "Marketing 101," *Entrepreneur*, May 1995, pp. 86–98; Denise Osburn, "Bringing Them Back for More," *Nation's Business*, August 1995, p. 31R; Jay Conrad Levinson, "Survival Tactics," *Entrepreneur*, March 1996, p. 84; Tom Stein, "Outselling the Giants," *Success*, May 1996, pp. 38–41; and Gwen Moran, "Get Noticed," *Entrepreneur*, October 2008, pp. 58–61.

Involve celebrities "on the cheap." Few small businesses can afford to hire celebrities as spokespersons for their companies. Some companies have discovered other ways to get celebrities to promote their products, however. For instance, when the founders of Lookout Mobile Security were launching their company, they went to the Academy Awards and set up hardware to extend their Bluetooth signal to more than a mile. Using this technology, they identified all of the celebrities whose mobile devices were vulnerable to being hacked. The stunt got the new company considerable attention in the media. The company has since grown to more than 20 million customers.[20]

Contact local television and radio stations and offer to be interviewed. Many local news or talk shows are looking for guests to talk about topics of interest to their audiences (especially in January and February). Even local shows can reach new customers.

Publish a newsletter. With a personal computer and desktop publishing software, any entrepreneur can publish a professional-looking newsletter. Freelancers can offer design and editing advice. Use the newsletter to reach present and potential customers, providing them with timely and useful information.

Contact local business and civic organizations and offer to speak to them. A powerful, informative presentation can win new business. (Be sure your public speaking skills are up to par first! If not, consider joining Toastmasters.)

Offer or sponsor a seminar. Teaching people about a subject you know a great deal about builds confidence and goodwill among potential customers. The owner of a landscaping service and nursery offers a short course in landscape architecture and always sees sales climb afterward.

Write news releases and fax or e-mail them to the media. The key to having a news release picked up and printed is finding a unique angle on your business or industry that would interest an editor. Keep it short, simple, and interesting. E-mail press releases should be shorter than printed ones—typically four or five paragraphs rather than one or two pages—and they should include a link to the company's Web site.

Volunteer to serve on community and industry boards and committees. You can make your town a better place to live and work and raise your company's visibility at the same time.

Sponsor a community project or support a nonprofit organization or charity. Not only will you be giving something back to the community, but you will also gain recognition, goodwill, and, perhaps, customers for your business. The key is to partner with charities that match the company's values and mission, whether that involves rescuing homeless pets or providing back-to-school supplies for underprivileged kids. Sweetwater Brewery in Atlanta, Georgia, sponsors an annual bike ride that raises money for Camp Twin Lake, a camp providing life-changing experiences to children facing serious illnesses, disabilities, and other life challenges.[21]

Participants in bike ride for Camp Twin Lake sponsored by Sweetwater Brewing Company.
Courtesy of Sweetwater Brewing Co.

Promote a cause. According to the Cone Communications Social Impact Study, 89 percent of customers (compared to only 66 percent of customers in the study conducted twenty years earlier) say that, other things being equal, they are likely to switch from one brand to another if the other brand is associated with a good cause.[22] By engaging in cause marketing, entrepreneurs can support a worthy cause that is important to them and generate publicity and goodwill for their companies at the same time. The key is choosing a cause that is important to your customers. One marketing expert offers the following formula for selecting the right cause: mission statement + personal passion + customer demographics = ideal cause.[23]

ENTREPRENEURIAL PROFILE: Michael Houlihan and Bonnie Harvey: Barefoot Cellars When Michael Houlihan and Bonnie Harvey first launched their San Francisco, California, winemaking company, Barefoot Cellars, they did not have the minimum of $100,000 to commit to advertising that the bigger retail stores require to stock a new brand. To help gain awareness, Barefoot Cellars began to give away free wine to local nonprofits to support their fundraising events. The strategy worked. People enjoyed the new wine and appreciated the company supporting their favorite causes. As the company grew into new markets, it continued to use the same strategy. As its primary market entry strategy, Barefoot Cellars hired staff to find nonprofits to support in each new market. After becoming a national brand, the founders sold Barefoot Cellars to E&J Gallo.[24] ■

Blendtec

DON'T JUST SELL; ENTERTAIN Today, gaining word-of-mouth support via social media is essential to a company's marketing success. However, accomplishing this requires entrepreneurs to engage and even entertain their customers. Companies spend more than $4 billion each year for online video advertising. A video that stands out, is "liked," and is shared with others must be entertaining. For instance, Tom Dickson, CEO and founder of Blendtec, stars in a series of YouTube videos where he sticks a variety of objects into a Blendtec blender. Dickson has put an iPhone, a glow stick, a crowbar, golf balls, an iPad, Bic lighters, and a can of Spam in a Blendtec Total Blender to answer the question, "Will it blend?" Many of the videos receive millions of views. The ads have helped grow the company from a start-up to an industry leader employing more than 450 people.[25]

STRIVE TO BE UNIQUE One of the most effective bootstrap marketing tactics is to create an image of uniqueness for your business. As you learned in Chapter 5, entrepreneurs can achieve a unique place in the market in a variety of ways, including through the products and services they offer, the marketing and promotional campaigns they use, the store layouts they design, and the business strategies they employ. The goal is to stand out from the crowd. Few things are as uninspiring to customers as a "me-too" business that offers nothing unique. Table 8.3 offers suggestions on ways that a retail store can stand out from the competition.

BUILD A COMMUNITY WITH CUSTOMERS Some of the most successful companies interact with their customers regularly, intentionally, and purposefully to create meaningful, lasting relationships with them. Etsy, an e-commerce Web site that offers handmade or vintage items and art and craft supplies, has fueled growth by connecting its customers into communities referred to as "teams." Etsy has teams that include artists with a common interest (one team of almost 400 is focused on painting miniatures), customers from a common city (the Little Rock, Arkansas, team has more than 400 members), or teams that cross interests and locations (fashion designers in Miami, Florida). The teams help each other promote their goods and expand their offerings sold through the Etsy Web site.[26]

Company Web sites and social media also are important tools for building a community with customers. Brendan's Irish Pub used Facebook to build a list of 3,500 fans before the restaurant opened. Tyler Rex, owner of Brenan's, uses Facebook to generate "buzz" for parties, sell merchandise, and promote various events. Burt's Bees uses Facebook to create new products interactively with its customers. Pacific Bioscience Laboratories, the maker of Clarisonic face brushes, shows customers how to use the product on its Facebook page and conducts a contest to encourage customers to send photos of themselves using a Clarisonic. Pacific Bioscience pledged to donate $1 to charity each new "like" on Facebook, which raised $30,000 to help women with cancer.[27]

CONNECT WITH CUSTOMERS ON AN EMOTIONAL LEVEL Closely linked to building a community with customers is the strategy of creating an emotional attachment with them. Companies that establish a deeper relationship with their customers than one based merely on making a sale have the capacity to be exceptional bootstrap marketers. These businesses win because customers receive an emotional boost every time they buy these companies' products or services. They connect with their customers emotionally by providing captivating products, supporting causes that are important to their customer base, taking exceptional care of their customers, surpassing customers' expectations in quality and service, or making doing business with them a fun and

TABLE 8.3 Seven Principles That Make Your Shop Pop

Pamela Danziger, president of the marketing consulting firm Unity Marketing, offers seven principles that can transform any store into a shop that "pops."

1. *Offer high levels of customer involvement and interaction.* When customers have the opportunity to interact with a product, they spend more time in the store, which increases the probability that they will buy something. That's the guiding principle behind Barnes & Noble's decision to incorporate chairs and couches as well as coffee and snack bars into its bookstores.

2. *Evoke shoppers' curiosity to explore with a unique displays, store layout, and selection of merchandise.* One jewelry store captured the attention of passersby with a window display that featured not only unique pieces of jewelry but also a collection of interesting fossils, crystals, geodes, and unusual rock formations. The display increased the number of walk-in shoppers and sales.

3. *Exude a contagious air of excitement, energy, and "electricity."* Apple Stores generate an astonishing volume of sales per square foot by creating an energized atmosphere. The decor is modern and minimalist so that products stand out. iPads located next to every product on display provide interactive product, service, and support information and allow shoppers to summon a salesperson in a flash. Shoppers who have questions or technical problems can ask a highly trained expert at the Genius Bar. Employees periodically offer free classes on using Apple products.

4. *Create a synergistic convergence of atmosphere, store design, and merchandise that results in a special place for customers.* The goal is to create a "paradox environment," one that offers customers displays and products they expect but also surprises them with something that is unique and unusual, even bizarre. To promote a new loyalty card program called Sprize with the tagline "Turning shopping on its head," a Gap store in London surprised shoppers by displaying 32 mannequins suspended from the ceiling upside down and arranged for three cars and a hot dog stand parked in front of the store to be flipped on their tops.

5. *Provide an authentic values-driven experience.* Godfrey's Welcome to Dogdom, a pet boutique located in Mohnton, Pennsylvania, sees the world from a dog's point of view and stocks a full line of dog-related products, ranging from essentials such as specialty foods, health-related products, and pet care items to luxuries such as hand-cast stone sculptures, cast bronze statues, dog apparel, and healthy fresh-baked dog biscuits in a multitude of flavors. Customers can book their pets for a doggie play group or schedule family time with their pets at one of the store's play parks. Special events such as a Valentine's Day Whine and Dine Brunch, a Pooch Smooch Easter photography session, and a Howl-o-ween Pawrade and Pawty keep customers and their beloved pets coming back to Godfrey's.

6. *Provide a price-value model that customers understand and support.* The Great Recession has made shoppers value conscious, but that does not mean discounting is the best way to attract customers. Businesses that show customers the value their products provide create a good value proposition without having to resort to price cuts. "Our focus is on solutions to our customers' problems and issues with their dogs and is not based on commodity price and product selling," says Barb Emmett of Godfrey's Welcome to Dogdom.

7. *Maintain a friendly, welcoming store that gives customers a reason to return.* In some stores, salespeople act as if they are doing customers a favor by waiting on them. Stores that pop take the opposite approach, welcoming customers and treating them as if they are important (because they are!). At an Arby's franchise in Camp Hill, Pennsylvania, 89-year-old Pearl Weaver greets customers with waving pom-poms, a big smile, and a happy "Welcome to Arby's." The store's manager, Christian Stakes, says not a week goes by without "Miz Pearl," as customers affectionately call her, being mentioned in online and in-store customer satisfaction surveys. "If she's off for a week, people ask about her," he says.

The goal is to create a store with "soul" that engages customers on many different levels; that creates a fun, festive atmosphere; and that has a mission that goes far beyond merely selling products.

Sources: Based on Paula Holewa, "Does Your Shop Pop?," *JCK*, January 13, 2011, http://www.jckonline.com/blogs/retail-details/2011/01/13/does-your-shop-pop; Kerry Bodine, "Apple Store 2.0: Why Customer Experience Leaders Should Care," *Forbes*, May 26, 2011, http://www.forbes.com/sites/forrester/2011/05/26/apple-store-2-0-why-customer-experience-leaders-should-care; Pam Danziger, "A Shop That Pops: How Godfrey's, a Pet Boutique, Creates the Ultimate Customer Experience," Unity Marketing, Shops That Pop, http://www.shopsthatpop.com/cms/Home_Page/White_Papers_Articles.php; Pam Danziger, "Does Your Shop Pop?," Unity Marketing, Shops That Pop, http://www.shopsthatpop.com/cms/Home_Page/White_Papers_Articles.php; Glen Stansberry, "10 Examples of Shockingly-Excellent Customer Service," *American Express OPEN Forum*, May 4, 2010, http://www.openforum.com/idea-hub/topics/managing/article/10-examples-of-shockingly-excellent-customer-service-1; and Lara Brenckle, "Camp Hill Woman, 89, Hands Out Cheers with Sandwiches at Fast-Food Restaurant," *PennLive*, August 10, 2009, http://www.pennlive.com/midstate/index.ssf/2009/08/camp_hill_woman_89_hands_out_c.html.

enjoyable experience. Building and nurturing an ongoing relationship with customers establishes a relationship of trust, a vital component of every marketing effort. The Cone Communications Social Impact Study reports that 82 percent of Americans (84 percent of those in Millennial generation) consider a company's business practices when making purchase decisions.[28]

The goal is not only to create lifelong, loyal customers but also to transform customers into passionate brand advocates, people who promote a company's products or services to friends, family members, and others. Although many companies manufacture tablet PCs, few have achieved the iconic status of Apple's iPad, which allows customers to perform a variety of tasks, ranging from word processing and downloading e-books and music to accessing the Internet and making face-to-face video calls. Its sleek, lightweight, touch-screen design resonates with customers because it reflects the way they want to use a tablet PC and evokes an image of "cool." The result of this emotional connection with customers: sales of 25 million units in a little more than a year and a base of loyal fans who happily promote the company to their friends—at no cost to the company.

One important aspect of connecting with customers is defining the company's **unique selling proposition (USP)**, a key customer benefit of a product or service that sets it apart from its competition. To be effective, a USP must actually *be* unique—something the competition does not (or cannot) provide—as well as compelling enough to encourage customers to buy. Unfortunately, many business owners never define their companies' USP, and the result is an uninspiring me-too message that cries out "buy from us" without offering customers any compelling reason to do so.

A successful USP answers the critical question that every customer asks: "What's in it for me?" A USP should express in no more than 10 words what a business can do for its customers. Can your product or service save your customers time or money, make their lives easier or more convenient, improve their self-esteem, or make them feel better? If so, you have the foundation for building a USP. For instance, Toms donates a pair of shoes to an impoverished child for every pair of shoes it sells. Toms also sells eyewear and donates to a charity that helps restore sight to people in developing countries. Toms has a simple but clear USP: "One for one." Saddleback Leather, a maker of high-end leather bags, has a USP that communicates the quality of its products: "They'll Fight Over It When You're Dead." Naomi Dunford, founder of IttyBiz, a marketing consulting firm that helps small companies with no more than five employees create bootstrap marketing strategies, says her company's USP is "Marketing for businesses without marketing departments."[29]

The best way to identify a meaningful USP that connects a company to its target customers is to describe the primary benefit(s) its product or service offers customers and then to list other, secondary benefits it provides. A business is unlikely to have more than three primary benefits, which should be unique and able to set it apart. When describing the top benefits the company offers its customers, entrepreneurs must look beyond just the physical characteristics of the product or service. Sometimes the most powerful USP emphasizes the *intangible, psychological, and emotional* benefits a product or service offers customers—for example, safety, "coolness," security, acceptance, and status. The goal is to use the USP to enable a company to stand out in customers' minds.

It is also important to develop a brief list of the facts that support your company's USP, such as 24-hour service, a fully trained staff, awards won, and so on. By focusing the message on these top benefits and the facts supporting them, business owners can communicate their USPs to their target audiences in meaningful, attention-getting ways. Building a firm's marketing message around its core USP spells out for customers the specific benefit they get if they buy that product or service and why they should do business with your company rather than with the competition. Finally, once a small company begins communicating its USP to customers, it has to fulfill the promise! Nothing erodes a company's credibility as quickly as promising customers a benefit and then failing to deliver on that promise.

Many small companies are finding common ground with their customers on an issue that is becoming increasingly important to many people: the environment. Small companies selling everything from jeans to toothpicks are emphasizing their "green" products and are making an emotional connection with their customers in the process. Companies must be truthful, however, or their marketing pitches can backfire and damage their reputations. Consumers are becoming more vigilant in their search for companies that are guilty of "greenwashing," touting unsubstantiated or misleading claims about the environmental friendliness of their products. Customers feel good about doing business with companies that manufacture products according to green principles, support environmental causes, donate a portion of their pretax earnings to philanthropic organizations, and operate with a clear sense of fulfilling their social responsibility.

CREATE AN IDENTITY FOR YOUR BUSINESS THROUGH BRANDING One of the most effective ways for entrepreneurs to differentiate their businesses from the competition is to create a unique identity for it through **branding**. Although they may not have the resources to build a brand name as well known as Google (Google's brand is estimated to be worth more than $159 billion), entrepreneurs can be successful in building a brand identity for their companies on a smaller

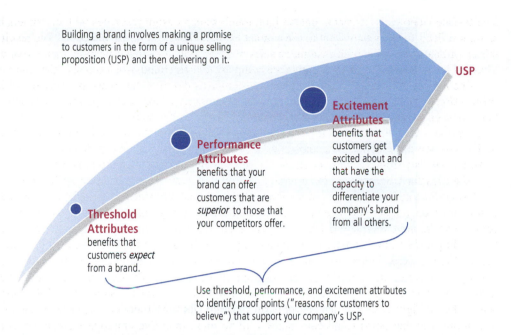

Building a brand involves making a promise to customers in the form of a unique selling proposition (USP) and then delivering on it.

USP

Excitement Attributes
benefits that customers get excited about and that have the capacity to differentiate your company's brand from all others.

Performance Attributes
benefits that your brand can offer customers that are *superior* to those that your competitors offer.

Threshold Attributes
benefits that customers *expect* from a brand.

Use threshold, performance, and excitement attributes to identify proof points ("reasons for customers to believe") that support your company's USP.

FIGURE 8.2

The Connection between Branding and a USP

Source: Based on Brand-Savvy, Highlands Rance, Colorado.

scale in the markets they serve. A large budget is not a prerequisite for building a strong brand, but creating one does take a concerted, well-coordinated effort that connects every touch point a company has with its customers with the company's desired image. A strong brand evokes the company's story in customers' minds.[30]

Branding involves communicating a company's unique selling proposition to its target customers in a consistent and integrated manner. A brand is a company's "face" in the marketplace, and it is built on a company's promise of providing quality goods or services to satisfy multiple customer needs. A brand sends an important message to customers; it signals that the benefits a company offers (which may be intangible) are worth more than those its competitors can offer. Companies that build brands successfully benefit from increased customer loyalty, the ability to command higher prices, greater visibility, and increased name recognition. Small companies that attempt to lure customers with discounts or constant sales often dilute their brands and cheapen them in the customers' eyes. Figure 8.2 shows the connection between a company's brand and its unique selling proposition.

EMBRACE SOCIAL MARKETING   Although social networking sites such as Facebook and Twitter are better known for their personal applications, they also have significant potential as marketing tools. Seventy-three percent of Internet users participate in at least one social networking site, more than double the 34 percent in 2008.[31] Businesses recognize that many of their current and potential customers use social networking sites and are reaching out to them with social marketing efforts. A recent survey of 600 small business owners found that 90 percent of them use social media to connect with existing and potential customers.[32] Figure 8.3 shows the most common social media tools used by small business owners. Most experts suggest that entrepreneurs find the best social media for their particular business instead of trying to use all of them at once. Keep in mind that it may take several months for social media marketing to make an impact on a small business; persistence and consistency are key.

Social networking sites are an ideal type of bootstrap marketing tool because they allow entrepreneurs to market their companies effectively and at little or no cost. One recent survey reports that 89 percent of marketers say their social media marketing efforts have generated greater exposure for their companies and many other benefits (see Figure 8.4).[33] Small companies use a variety of social networking tools to market their companies, but three of the most popular are LinkedIn, Facebook, and Twitter:

LinkedIn. LinkedIn has overtaken Facebook as the most widely used social media site by entrepreneurs. To use LinkedIn as a marketing tool, entrepreneurs should create a personal

FIGURE 8.3

Social Media Entrepreneurs Use as Marketing Tools

Source: "Small Biz Owners Say LinkedIn Offers Them More Potential Than Facebook, Twitter," *Marketing Charts,* February 1, 2013, http://www.marketingcharts.com/wp/online/small-biz-owners-say-linkedin-offers-them-more-potential-than-facebook-twitter-26648/.

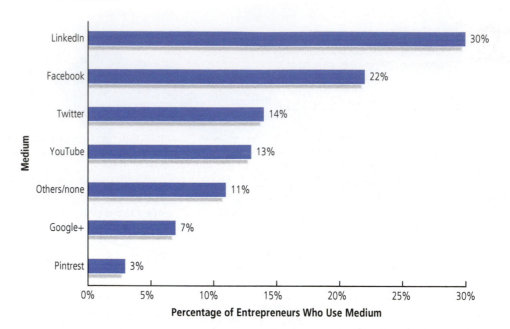

profile that focuses on their role as owner of a business, send invitations to people with whom they have connections, join (or form) groups that are of interest to customers, and use Answers to demonstrate their expertise. LinkedIn is a good forum for generating leads and advice from like-minded business owners. Entrepreneurs also should create a link to their company's Web sites, blog, and Twitter feed. They also can post upcoming events at their businesses and conduct polls among other LinkedIn users. The updates feature allows users to share blog posts, newsletters, and other timely information.

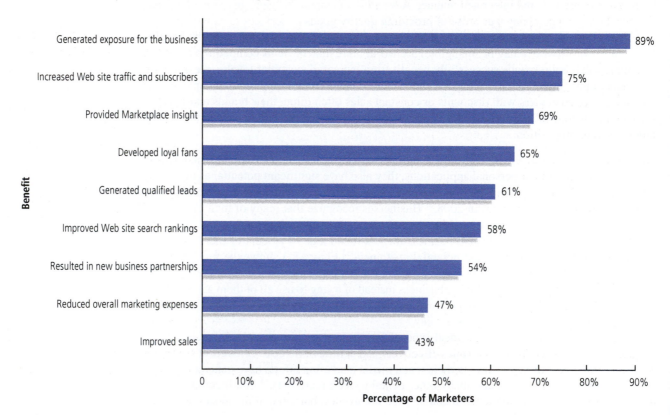

FIGURE 8.4

Benefits of Social Media Marketing

Source: "Want Social to Boost Sales? Be Prepared to Spend the Necessary Time," *Marketing Charts,* May 22, 2013, http://www.marketingcharts.com/wp/online/want-social-to-boost-sales-be-prepared-to-spend-the-necessary-time-29686/.

You Be the Consultant

Auto Repair Goes Social

Victory Auto Service and Glass, founded in 1997 by Jeff Matt, built its base of loyal customers with strong personal relationships. Personal customer service is at the heart of Victory Auto's business model. The company has five locations and a mobile auto glass service in the Minneapolis, Minnesota, metro area.

As the business grew from its first location, Matt found that maintaining the personal relationships with his customers, which was the core of his company's success, became more difficult to maintain. Matt decided to turn to social media to complement face-to-face connections with Victory Auto's customers and sought the help of Stephanie Gutierrez, a communications specialist and loyal customer, to help create a social media strategy for Victory Auto.

Gutierrez experimented with various social media tactics until she found a strategy that supported the personal connection with customers that Matt relied on to build his company. Facebook is the heart of Victory Auto's social media strategy. When Gutierrez developed the company's Facebook page, she took the time to think like the business's average customer: car owners who were not necessarily interested in cars. The typical customer interacts with Victory Auto because they have to, not because they want to. Instead of creating a page with information on cars, she adds posts related to traffic, commuting, and travel that everyone who owns a car would be interested in reading. At first, she posted longer articles with links to articles about cars. However, these posts did not seem to register with the typical customer. Now Gutierrez posts much shorter text entries that are written in a personal style with many photos.

The second major aspect of Victory Auto's social media strategy involves YouTube videos. Gutierrez developed several short videos that are geared toward people who do not know much about cars. The videos on Victory Auto's YouTube channel include short how-to videos and tours of its various store locations around Minneapolis. For example, the most popular video is one that shows how to top off windshield wiper fluid!

Matt believes that success in the auto service business is based on trust, and that trust is built by getting to know the people who work at Victory Auto. Many of the social media posts are about employees of Victory Auto, focusing on their birthdays, other celebrations, and day-to-day casual interactions while at work. About 20 percent of Victory Auto employees are active on Facebook. When they become Facebook and sometimes even personal friends with customers, they are encouraged to share photos on Facebook. These photos can then be tagged to help build more traffic at the Victory Auto Facebook page.

Victory Auto Glass uses social media to promote the various charities, including Mothers Against Drunk Drivers and Toys for Tots. A local charity that Victory Auto is heavily involved with is Free2Be, which provides auto care and donated cars for economically disadvantaged people in Anoka County, Minnesota. Volunteers with Free2Be can use the repair bays at Victory Auto free of charge to repair donated cars. Victory Auto also gives free or discounted car repairs for people helped by the Free2Be program. Gutierrez then posts some of these stories on the company's Facebook page to help promote the charity.

Results

Victory Auto has seen significant returns on its investment in social media:

- The company opened two of its five locations since implementing its social media strategy.

- Most of the customers of the two newest locations heard about Victory Auto from word of mouth or online.

- More than 60% of fans and people "talking about" the company's Facebook page are female.

- Victory Auto became a certified female-friendly auto repair shop with AskPatty, a Web site that provides automotive advice for women.

- The company estimates that 50 to 60 percent of its customers are female, which is far above the industry average.

- Victory Auto has more than 1,200 "likes" on its Facebook page.

- The most popular YouTube video, on how to top off windshield wiper fluid, has more than 6,500 views.

1. Identify at least three lessons that entrepreneurs can learn from the Victory Auto's use of social media.

2. Work with a team of your classmates to select a local business that has no social media presence and develop a plan to boost its visibility, sales, and profits with a social media strategy.

3. Identify at least three additional bootstrap marketing strategies discussed in this chapter that Victory Auto can use to increase its visibility, sales, and profits. Explain how the company should implement each one.

Sources: Based on Louise Julig, "How an Auto Repair Shop Is Winning Female Customers with Social Media," *Social Media Examiner,* September 25, 2013, www .socialmediaexaminer.com/social-media-case-study-victory-auto/; "About Us," Victory Auto Service and Glass, n.d., www.victoryautoservice.com/AboutUs.html; "Victory Auto Service and Glass," Facebook, n.d., www.facebook.com/VictoryAutoService; "Victory Auto Service," YouTube, n.d., www.youtube.com/channel/UCsBv4zmSqaa4CrLXmN0jMTQ.

Facebook. People spend nearly 12 *billion* hours per month on Facebook, the world's largest social network. Creating a Facebook business page is not the same as creating a personal profile page, however. On Facebook, an entrepreneur should create a Welcome page that is designed to create interest in the company's products or services and that encourages visitors to "like" the business. Businesses can generate likes by posting the Facebook URL on in-store signs, business cards, shopping bags, and anything else customers are likely to see. E-mail and "refer-a-friend" campaigns and links to Facebook from a company's Web site and blog also increase the number of likes the company receives. One key to using Facebook successfully as a marketing tool is to keep a company's page fresh, just like the merchandise displays in a physical store. Adding photographs, announcements of upcoming events, polls and surveys, and games and contests or promoting a cause the company supports are excellent ways to create buzz and keep fans coming back. Entrepreneurs must invest time in their social media marketing effort; nearly 58 percent of marketers spend at least six hours a week on social media marketing.[34]

Twitter. Twitter users send more than 1 billion tweets per week, and 42 percent of users look to Twitter for information about the products and services they buy.[35] Twitter, a microblogging (no more than 140 characters) service, is ideal for interacting with customers or potential customers, promoting daily specials and upcoming events, and driving traffic to a company's Web site or blog. Small business expert Steve Strauss recommends Twitter as a good way for entrepreneurs to establish their expertise. Strauss also says that 80 percent of content sent out should be about customers, while only 20 percent should promote the entrepreneur's business.[36] Weetabix, a whole-grain cereal company, used Twitter to promote a new line of On the Go Breakfast Biscuits. The company posted short videos of people going through normal morning routines. Consumers would then decide what happened next in the video by posting hashtags such as #getup, #hitsnooze, #grabbreakfast, and #leavethehouse. The videos reached more than 262,000 people on Twitter, leading to a five-fold growth in the company's followers. As part of its sponsorship of the French Open Tennis Tournament, BNP Paribas Bank offered a social media game that allowed Twitter users to play a game of tennis against Jo-Wilfried Tsonga, a French professional player. Participants dragged-and-dropped a tennis ball on a virtual screen that controlled a robot hitting balls at Tsonga live on a tennis court.[37] Twitter also is a useful tool for monitoring a company's customer service performance, something that companies are discovering is essential to preserving the quality of their brands. A recent poll from RightNow and Harris Interactive reports that 85 percent of customers who posted a negative shopping experience with a company and were subsequently contacted by that company ultimately took an action online that benefited the business (such as changing their negative review to a positive one).[38] The following tips help entrepreneurs use Twitter successfully as a bootstrap marketing tool:

- Connect with others as a person, not as a brand. Twitter users want to talk with people, not companies.
- Engage in conversations. Twitter is a two-way communication tool, not an outlet for sending one-way messages, such as press releases and marketing copy.
- Give people a reason to follow you. Reveal the "inside story" of your company, ask customers for feedback, or offer special deals to followers.
- Link Twitter to your company's Web site. Refer followers to your company's Web site, blog, or a video about your company and its products or services.[39]

ENTREPRENEURIAL PROFILE: Curtis Kimball: The Crème Brûlée Man Curtis Kimball grew his highly successful food cart, The Crème Brûlée Man, with no marketing budget. Kimball uses Twitter to promote his food cart as it travels among various neighborhoods in San Francisco. Kimball has more than 12,000 followers on Twitter, who rely on his posts to let them know where his cart will be and what flavors he is offering each day. He also uses Twitter to get customer feedback on what flavors he should offer and on new locations he should try. To engage his followers, Kimball uses humor in his posts.[40] ■

Hands On . . . How To

Make Social Media Work for Your Business

Social media, such as Facebook, Twitter, LinkedIn, YouTube, and others, can be a vital and productive component of a company's bootstrap marketing strategy. Because the typical customer sees more than 20,000 advertising and sales messages each week, small businesses' marketing efforts, particularly their social media marketing efforts, must be well planned, consistent, and focused. Otherwise, they will become lost in a sea of ads, posts, tweets, and blogs.

The first key to a successful social media marketing strategy is understanding your customers and knowing where they are in the social media universe and what they expect from you. Entrepreneurs can use the following tips and success stories to develop a social media marketing strategy that works for their businesses:

Use social media to level the playing field. One of the greatest advantages of using social media is its low cost, which means that large companies have no more of a marketing advantage than small businesses. "We've never been able to compete with larger casual dining restaurants that own the airwaves," says Jen Gulvik, vice president of marketing for Houlihan's Restaurants, a small restaurant chain based in Leawood, Kansas. "We can't outshout them with our marketing budget, but it's still essentially free to play in social media. We can be in this space and do as well, if not better, than our larger competitors."

Build your brand—and your customer base—with social media. Einstein Bros. Bagels, a bagel, sandwich, and coffee chain with nearly 450 locations across the United States, had amassed 4,700 Facebook fans before launching a social media–based bagel giveaway during the fall. Customers responded and within one week, the number of fans had increased to 300,000. When Einstein Bros. repeated the promotion on Facebook the following spring, its fan base jumped to more than 600,000! "We're not a national advertiser," says James O'Reilly, the company's chief concept officer. "We decided to make social media a pillar of our marketing efforts. It's a whole new channel for businesses to engage their customers in a two-way dialogue." Today, Einstein Bros. boasts nearly 700,000 Facebook fans who ask about new products and upcoming promotions, post photos of themselves (and their pets) enjoying an Einstein Bros. bagel, and respond to questions the company posts on its Wall ("Which bagel and shmear combination do you crave most—sweet or savory?").

Remember that no matter what media you use to promote your business, no one really cares what you do; potential customers care only about what you can do for them. One of the greatest advantages for small businesses that use social media is its ability to naturally showcase their uniqueness, their informal culture, and their staff's passion for what they do. Once prospects understand the value that a company's products or services hold for them, selling to

them becomes much easier. Use social media to showcase the results your company can create for customers.

Be creative in your social media promotions. Using a creative Facebook campaign, California Tortilla, a 26-unit restaurant chain in Rockville, Maryland, increased the number of Facebook fans by 50 percent and generated a 10 percent increase in same-store sales—and spent less than $700. The company offered a free order of chips and queso to its Facebook fans but promised to upgrade the offer to a free taco if its fan base reached 13,000 people. The viral nature of social media took over, and California Tortilla ended up with more than 16,000 likes. "The people who got involved were super-passionate fans," says marketing director Stacey Kane. "Based on customer engagement, it was a win."

Listen before you talk. Success with social media marketing requires a different approach than traditional advertising, which relies primarily on one-way communication, telling your audience about your business and its products and services. Social media marketing requires that businesses *listen* before they engage their audience in a two-way conversation. Mari Luangrath, owner of Foiled Cupcakes, an upscale cupcake bakery in Chicago, has no physical storefront for her business yet manages to sell 1,000 dozen cupcakes each month at an average price of $38 per dozen. Luangrath says she developed 94 percent of her customers using social media marketing tools, especially Twitter. Her strategy is to identify online conversations about food, baking, and cupcakes that she and her employees can join naturally and build trust by providing useful content and comments. "I'm very comfortable with traditional marketing," says Luangrath, "but I don't want to market to everybody. I want to find people who want to hear what I have to say and then, at the end of the engagement, purchase my product." Luangrath also has joined groups of Chicago administrative professionals—the people who plan office parties and events—on LinkedIn and posts useful articles for them. "You want to engage people, get feedback, and start a conversation. Then you can say, 'Why don't we drop some cupcakes by and show you what we can do?'"

Use social media to reward loyal customers, fans, followers, and promoters of your brand. Jordan Zweigoron, founder and "chief psycho" of Psycho Donuts, a doughnut shop in Campbell, California, that sells uniquely flavored doughnuts served by employees wearing nurse uniforms, uses Fanminder, a mobile marketing service that allows businesses to send text messages containing special offers and promotions to customers who opt in. The company also uses Twitter to reward its loyal customers, but Zweigoron says Psycho Donuts's Fanminder offers generate a response that is three to four times greater than its Twitter promotions.

(continued)

Hands On . . . How To *(continued)*

Use online video to show off your products and services. Television advertisers have known for decades that video is the ideal way to show people how a product or service works. Social media sites such as YouTube give even the smallest businesses the opportunity to show their products and services in action at minimal cost. BBQ Guys, a store in Baton Rouge, Louisiana, that sells everything related to barbecuing, began posting videos featuring its grills on YouTube in 2006. The videos were so successful that the company recruited a local chef to host them. BBQ Guys has posted more than 400 videos on YouTube that have more than 1.4 million views. A visitor who watches a video is twice as likely to make a purchase as one who does not. "We see the videos almost like a TV commercial," says Troy Olson, the company's digital advertising manager. "We're planting our brand name."

Give customers a reason to tune in to your business. Create a destination by posting fresh content and promoting upcoming specials, sales, and events. Resist the tendency to let the hectic nature of your schedule drive out the time necessary to make social marketing work for your business. To make social media marketing pay off, entrepreneurs must make social media marketing a regular part of their work schedules.

Use social media to encourage your customers to talk—and then listen. Social media are ideal for engaging customers in two-way conversations. Beachbody, a producer of fitness videos based in Santa Monica, California, realized that many of the online conversations in which its employees participated originated from faith-based sites. It was a market niche that the company had never considered until its employees began listening to potential customers' conversations. The company introduced Body Gospel, a series of workouts set to contemporary Christian music that have been successful.

Use analytics to measure your company's social media results. Entrepreneurs should measure the results of their social media marketing efforts so that they know which ones work best. Social media marketing efforts are always evolving, and entrepreneurs need useful feedback on their results. Many tools are available to measure success, but many of the standards that fit traditional advertising media, such as sales leads, sales, Web site traffic, customer engagement and retention, and profits, apply to social media.

Sources: Based on Heidi Cohen, "How to Jump into the Social Media Pool without Drowning," *SmartBlogs*, May 10, 2011, http://smartblogs.com/socialmedia/2011/05/10/how-to-jump-into-the-social-media-pool-without-drowning; Courtney Jeffries, "How 3 Brands Generate Buzz by Employing Social Technologies," *Social Media Club*, August 24, 2011, http://socialmediaclub.org/blogs/from-the-clubhouse/social-business-snapshot-how-3-brands-generate-buzz-employing-social-techno; Jason Ankeny, "Social Climbers," *Entrepreneur*, January 2011, pp. 116–123; Lisa Nicole Bell, "3 Rules for Selling in the New Economy," *Reuters*, January 10, 2011, http://blogs.reuters.com/small-business/2011/01/10/3-rules-for-selling-in-the-new-economy; Mark Brandau, "California Tortilla: Lessons Learned from Facebook Promo," *Nation's Restaurant News*, March 30, 2011, http://www.nrn.com/article/california-tortilla-lessons-learned-facebook-promo; Brian Quinton, "Baking, Listening, and Selling," *Entrepreneur*, February 2011, pp. 60–61; Jason Ankeny, "Crazy for Mobile Deals," *Entrepreneur*, October 2010, pp. 40–41; Kermit Pattison, "Online Video Offers Low-Cost Marketing for Your Company," *New York Times*, March 16, 2011, http://www.nytimes.com/2011/03/17/business/smallbusiness/17sbiz.html; and April Joyner, "Social Networking: Who's Talking About You?," *Inc.*, September 2010, pp. 63–64.

Start a Blog A Web log ("blog") is a frequently updated online journal that contains a writer's ideas on a multitude of topics and links to related sites. A recent survey by HubSport[41] reports that:

- 62 percent of companies now use blogs as part of their marketing strategies.

- 82 percent of companies that publish blogs on a daily basis say they have acquired a customer through their blogs.

- 57 percent of companies that publish blogs monthly say they have acquired a customer through their blogs.

- 55 percent of marketers spent more time than money on blogging, reinforcing blogs as a strong tool for bootstrap marketing.

Business blogging can be an effective part of a bootstrap marketing strategy, enabling small businesses to communicate with large numbers of potential customers economically.

Blogs that attract the attention of existing and potential customers boost a company's visibility and sales. Companies post their blogs, promote them on their Web sites and in other social media, and then watch as the viral nature of the Internet takes over with visitors posting comments and telling their friends about the blog. Many small companies allow customers to contribute to their blogs, offering the potential for one of the most valuable marketing tools: unsolicited endorsements from satisfied users. Blogging's informal dialogue is an ideal match for small companies whose culture and style also are casual. Linked to a company's other social media marketing efforts (such as Facebook, LinkedIn, and Twitter), a blog can serve as its social media hub. Blogs can keep customers updated on new products, enhance customer service, and promote the company. If monitored regularly, blogs also can give entrepreneurs keen insight into their customers' viewpoints and preferences. Creating a blog is not risk free, however. Companies must be prepared to deal with negative feedback from some visitors. Common platforms for creating blogs include WordPress, Blogger, Tumblr, Weebly, SquareSpace, and TypePad.

The following tips can help entrepreneurs implement a successful blogging strategy:

- *Strive to cultivate the image of an expert or a trusted friend on a topic that is important to your customers.* In his blog, the owner of a company that installs water gardens posts tips for maintaining a healthy water garden and answers questions his readers post.

- *Be patient.* A blog takes months to build up traffic and interest. To be successful, an entrepreneur must be willing to commit to writing regularly for a long time before the blog generates new business.

- *Be honest, balanced, and interesting when writing a blog.* High-pressure sales pitches do not work in the blogging world. Telling an interesting "inside story" about the company, its products or services, or some aspect of the business attracts readers. However, experts recommend the 80–20 rule for posting topics. Keep 80 percent of the posts about more general topics related to your industry or about your customers and only 20 percent of the posts about your company.

- *Post blog entries consistently so that readers have a reason to return.* Entrepreneurs should make blog posts at least once a week. Successful bloggers schedule time each day or several times a week to work on their blog posts.

- *Ask customers for feedback.* Blogs are powerful tools for collecting real-time market research inexpensively. It is easy to insert instant polls that allow readers to offer quick feedback.

- *Use services such as Google Alerts that scan the Web for a company's name and send e-mail alerts when it finds posts about a company.* Entrepreneurs must monitor the online "buzz" about their companies; if they discover negative comments, they can address the issues in their blogs.

- *Be cautious.* If you are blogging to promote your business, be careful what you write about. Avoid making negative comments about competitors, addressing controversial topics, or making unsubstantiated claims.

- *Promote the blog via social media and e-mail.* It is easy to push out blog posts via Twitter, Facebook LinkedIn, and e-mail marketing software. Include a link to your blog in your e-mail signature.[42]

Create Online Videos Video hosting sites such as YouTube give creative entrepreneurs the opportunity to promote their businesses at no cost by creating videos that feature their company's products and services in action. Unlike television ads, uploading a video to YouTube costs nothing, and in some cases, the videos reach millions of potential customers. Watching online videos is pervasive; YouTube reports that visitors view 3 billion videos per day.[43] Of those marketers using social media, 56 percent actively use YouTube to post videos about their company and its products.[44] Successful online video campaigns don't just educate and inform, they also entertain and engage customers. Although YouTube is still the most commonly used platform for videos, Facebook, Twitter, and Instagram offer alternative outlets for video content.

ENTREPRENEURIAL PROFILE: Dr. Irena Vaksman Dr. Irena Vaksman, a San Francisco dentist, uses a variety of social media tools to promote her practice. In addition to Twitter and Facebook, Vaksman has a YouTube channel. On her channel, she shares several educational videos about dental procedures. Vaksman says her efforts have helped her practice stand out in a crowed market.[45] ■

Host a Special Event Another effective bootstrap marketing strategy is to host a special event that reinforces the company's brand in customers' minds. Mashable, an online social-media news site, hosts events to connect with its users. The company sees a benefit in connecting with its users in person, rather than only through its online platform. For instance, Mashable hosted an award show in Las Vegas to celebrate the best of social media. The event, which sold out all its tickets, blended online voting with a live event to feature the awardees. Mashable also hosts live meet-ups across the country to connect with users and to learn what is happening in different communities.[46]

BE DEDICATED TO SERVICE AND CUSTOMER SATISFACTION Many businesses have lost sight of the most important component of every business: the customer. Entrepreneurs must realize that everything in the business—even the business itself—depends on creating a satisfied customer. The rewards for providing excellent customer service are great, and the penalties for failing to do so are severe. Excellent customer service, as you learned in Chapter 4 is an key component of a company's business model, does not look the same for every business. Excellence in customer service means that a company must meet the expectations its business model creates for customers. Excellent customer service may mean quick, efficient service, or it may mean absolute attention to customers' specific wants and needs. A recent survey by Harris Interactive reports that 55 percent of consumers have become customers of a company just because of the company's reputation for providing outstanding customer service. The study also revealed that 85 percent of customers are willing to pay extra (as much as 25 percent more) for products that are accompanied by excellent customer service.[47] Conversely, another Harris Poll reports that 80 percent of customers say they will never return to a business after a negative customer service experience.[48]

Lost sales are only the beginning of a company's woes, however. Unhappy customers are likely to tell their poor service stories to family members and friends. The Harris Interactive survey also shows that 79 percent of customers who have negative customer service experiences tell others about them.[49] This negative word of mouth has a detrimental effect on the offending company. A study by the Jay H. Baker Retailing Initiative at the University of Pennsylvania reports that 48 percent of shoppers say they will not patronize stores where they know that other customers have had bad service experiences.[50] Most of these customers never complain; in fact, for every complaint a company receives, 17 other complaints go unspoken.[51] These disgruntled customers exact revenge over their poor treatment, however. These days, a company that provides poor service may find itself being panned on Yelp, Twitter, Facebook, a YouTube video, a blog, or a Web site. A survey by Social Media Marketing University found that 74 percent of companies receive customer complaints via social media. However, 61 percent take up to a week to respond, and 21 percent of these companies never respond to these complaints. Consumers expect a quick response to their complaints on social media. Companies that do not meet customer expectations for addressing their complaints face the potential of even more negative comments from frustrated customers. The following tips can help you to more effectively address online comments, suggestions, and complaints:[52]

- *Consistently track all social media.* Conduct frequent searches on Twitter, Facebook, Instagram, and on the Web to catch comments in blogs.

- *Respond and take responsibility.* If someone has a bad experience and tells the world through social media, post an apology and promise corrective action. Then send that person a private message to attempt to resolve the issue.

- *The customer is always right.* If there is a problem, fix it and let the person who complained know what you have done. Even if there is nothing to change, offer the customer his or her money back or a discount in the future.

- *Never be defensive.* Think about the situation from the customer's perspective and empathize with his or her frustrations. Don't argue. Let the customer know you feel his or her frustration.

- *Keep a database of all complaints and suggestions.* Rather than read and delete them, keep all complaints and suggestions and organize them into a database, which can help show trends and consistent issues. Organize the database by specific issue addressed in the complaint, date, employee responsible for that part of the business, and other relevant facts.

Smart companies are rediscovering that unexpected, innovative, customized service can be a powerful marketing weapon. Perhaps the most effective marketing tool is a satisfied customer who becomes a passionate brand evangelist for a company. Providing incomparable service—not necessarily low prices—is one of the most effective ways to attract and maintain a growing customer base. Successful businesses recognize that superior customer service is only an intermediate step toward the goal of customer *satisfaction*. The best companies seek to go beyond customer satisfaction, striving for *customer astonishment*! One way to achieve customer astonishment is to "underpromise and overdeliver." Smart entrepreneurs create reasonable expectations among their customers and then exceed them, knowing that those customers will generate positive "buzz" for the companies, which is more valuable and more effective than the most expensive advertising campaign.

Certainly the least expensive—and the most effective—way to achieve customer satisfaction is through friendly, personal service. Numerous surveys of customers in a wide diversity of industries—from manufacturing and services to banking and high tech—conclude that the most important element of service is "the personal touch." Calling customers by name; making attentive, friendly contact; and truly caring about their needs and wants is much more essential than any other factor—even convenience, quality, and speed! In our society, business transactions have become so automated that the typical customer is starved for personal attention. Genuine customer service requires that a business bridge that service gap, treat each customer as an individual, and transform "high-tech" applications into a "high-touch" attitude.

How can a company achieve stellar customer service and satisfaction?

Listen to customers. The best companies constantly listen to their customers and respond to what they hear! This allows them to keep up with customers' changing needs and expectations. The best way to find out what customers really want and value is to ask them. Businesses rely on a number of techniques, including surveys, focus groups, telephone interviews, comment cards, suggestion boxes, toll-free hotlines, and regular one-on-one conversations (perhaps the best technique). The Internet is another useful tool for getting feedback from customers; many companies solicit complaints, suggestions, and ideas through their Web sites.

Keeping customer feedback in its proper perspective is important, however. Although listening to customers produces valuable feedback for business owners in many areas, it is *not* a substitute for an innovative company culture, solid market research, and a well-devised marketing plan. Companies that rely solely on their customers to guide their marketing efforts often find themselves lagging the competition. Customers rarely have the foresight to anticipate market trends and do not always have a clear view of how new products or services could satisfy their needs.

Define superior service. Based on what customers say, managers and employees must decide exactly what "superior service" means in the company. Such a statement should (1) be a strong statement of intent, (2) differentiate the company from others, and (3) have value to customers. This is a critical component of any successful business model. Deluxe Corporation, a printer of personal checks, defines superior service quite simply; the company promises 48 hour turnaround with zero defects.[53]

Set standards and measure performance. To be able to deliver on its promise of superior service, a business must establish specific standards and measure overall performance against them. Satisfied customers should exhibit at least one of three behaviors: loyalty (increased customer retention rate), increased purchases (rising sales and sales per customer), and resistance to rivals' attempts to lure them away with lower prices (market share and price tolerance).[54] Companies must track their performance on these and other service standards and reward employees accordingly.

Examine your company's service cycle. What steps must a customer go through to purchase your product or service? Business owners often are surprised at the complexity that has seeped into their customer service systems as they have evolved over time. One of the most effective techniques is to work with employees to flowchart each component in the company's service cycle, including *everything* a customer has to do to buy your product or service. The goal is to look for steps, policies, and procedures that are unnecessary, redundant, or unreasonable and then to eliminate them.

See customer complaints as a mechanism for improving customer service. Smart entrepreneurs see customer complaints as an important tool for improving their businesses and as a bridge to long-term customer relationships. Ignoring customers leads to disastrous outcomes. Netflix, the movie rental company, made the decision to split its DVD rental business from its online streaming video business. Netflix made this business decision despite negative reactions from customer focus groups. Customers liked the flexibility of being able to get video content from either format. The other negative impact for customers was a 40 percent average increase in monthly cost of using Netflix services. The result was the loss of 800,000 subscribers during the first three months after the split.[55]

When you create a negative customer experience, apologize and fix it—fast. No customer service system is perfect, and companies can recover from creating a negative customer experience. A recent survey shows that 92 percent of customers say they would return to a company after a negative customer experience if the company offered an apology, a discount, or proof that its customer service would be better.[56]

Hire the right employees. A company's customer service process is important, but the key ingredient in the superior service equation is the *people* who make it work. There is no substitute for friendly, courteous sales and service representatives, and hiring them requires a sound selection process. Business owners must always be on the lookout for employees who emanate a customer service attitude and are empathetic, flexible, articulate, creative, and able to think for themselves. Four Seasons Hotels and Resorts, a company with a business model based on customer service, hires people for their attitudes toward other people. The company's philosophy on hiring is that skills and processes can be taught, but attitude is ingrained in people's character.[57]

Train employees to deliver superior service. Successful businesses train *every* employee who deals directly with customers; they don't leave customer service to chance. Superior service companies devote 1 to 5 percent of their employees' work hours to training, concentrating on how to meet, greet, and serve customers. Apple spends as much time training its technicians who work in its retail stores on communication skills as it does on processes and technical knowledge.[58]

Empower employees to offer superior service. One of the most important variables that determines whether employees deliver superior service is the degree to which they perceive they have permission to do so. The goal is to push decision making down the organization to the employees who have contact with customers. This includes giving them the latitude to circumvent "company policy" if it means improving customer satisfaction. If frontline workers don't have the power to solve disgruntled customers' problems, they fear being punished for overstepping their boundaries and become frustrated, and the superior service cycle breaks down. Zytec, a manufacturing company in southern Minnesota, authorizes all employees to spend up to $1,000 without any approval to improve their work processes or satisfy a customer. The CEO of Zytec says employees are prudent with these funds and use

Dilbert cartoon from 3/20/14 used by permission of Universal UClick

them responsibly.[59] To be empowered, employees need knowledge and information, adequate resources, and managerial support.

Treat employees with respect and demonstrate to them how valuable they are. Creating a positive work environment, good work-life balance through policies such as flextime and vacation, and meaningful work leads to satisfied workers. Satisfied employees tend to create satisfied customers. In fact, a recent Gallup survey finds that although work environment is important, creating engaging work is the strongest predictor of satisfaction among employees.[60]

ENTREPRENEURIAL PROFILE: Caitlin McCabe, Real Bullets Branding Caitlin McCabe, founder of Real Bullets Branding, a market research and strategy agency in Boston, asks her employees how they want to be rewarded when they have done exceptional work. She says this is an advantage a small business has over a large corporation that has to follow consistent policies. Her employees have asked for things such as funding to attend a conference, a more flexible schedule, and the latest iPhone. McCage says her employees appreciate their personalized rewards. McCabe's personal approach shows she has taken the time to get to know what each one of them really wants for a job well done.[61] ■

Real Bullets Branding

Use technology to provide improved service. The role of technology is not to create a rigid bureaucracy but to free employees from routine clerical tasks, giving them more time and better tools to serve customers more effectively. Ideally, technology gives workers the information they need to help customers and the time to serve them.

Reward superior service. What gets rewarded gets done. Companies that want employees to provide stellar service must offer rewards for doing so. However, pay is not always the most powerful reward for recognizing employees who provide outstanding service. Zendesk uses weeble wobble toys as a reward for truly outstanding customer service. Although the toys have little monetary value, employees are proud of the recognition they get for being able to display weeble wobbles on their desks because everyone in the company knows what they mean.[62]

Get top managers' support. The drive toward superior customer service will fall far short of its target unless top managers support it fully. Success requires more than just a verbal commitment: It calls for managers' involvement and dedication to making service a core company value. Achieving customer satisfaction must become ingrained in the strategic planning process and work its way into every nook and cranny of the organization. Once it does, employees will be able to provide stellar customer service with or without a checklist of "dos and don'ts."

Give customers an unexpected surprise. In Louisiana, locals call it a lagniappe ("lan-yap"), a small gift that a merchant gives to a customer. The surprise does not have to be expensive to be effective. For instance, when a customer makes a sizable purchase at Wilson Creek Outfitters, a fly-fishing shop in Morganton, North Carolina, the owner includes a dozen flies in the order for free. The cost of the lagniappe is minimal, but the goodwill and loyalty it garners is significant.

View customer service as an investment, not an expense. The companies that lead the way when it comes to retaining their customers view the money they spend on customer service as an investment rather than an expense. One of the most effective ways for entrepreneurs to learn this lesson is to calculate the cost of poor customer service to their companies. Once they calculate it, the cost of lost customers due to poor service is so astonishing to most business owners that they quickly become customer service zealots. For instance, the owner of a small restaurant calculated that if every day he lost to poor service just one customer who spent just $5 per week, his business was losing $94,900 in revenue per year! The restaurateur immediately changed his approach to customer service.

RETAIN EXISTING CUSTOMERS Loyal, long-term customers are the bedrock of every business. High customer retention rates translate into superior financial performance. Earning customers' loyalty requires businesses to take customer focus and service to unprecedented levels, and that means building long-term relationships with customers. Research shows that customers who are satisfied with a company's products and customer service are more likely to be repeat customers and are less sensitive to price increases.[63]

Many studies also show that high levels of customer retention result in above-average profits and superior growth in market share.[64] Powell's Books, a Portland, Oregon, landmark known as the "City of Books" for its 68,000-square-foot store and huge inventory, has built a solid base of loyal customers in its 40-plus-year history, enabling the company to compete successfully against industry giants Amazon and Barnes & Noble. Powell's Books has hosted several weddings for customers who met there, and one customer's ashes are interred (at his request) in one of the columns that is made to look like a stack of books at the northwest entrance to the store. Now *that's* customer loyalty![65]

Because about 20 percent of a typical company's customers account for about 80 percent of its sales, focusing resources on keeping the best (and most profitable) customers is a better investment than chasing "fair-weather" customers who will defect to any better deal that comes along. Suppose a company increases its customer base by 20 percent each year but retains only 85 percent of its existing customers. Its effective growth rate is just 5 percent per year [20% − (100% − 85%) = 5%]. If this same company can raise its customer retention rate to 95 percent, its net growth rate *triples* to 15 percent [20% − (100% − 5%) = 15%].[66]

Although winning new customers keeps a company growing, keeping existing ones is essential to success. Dunnhumby, a global customer loyalty consulting firm, reports that a company must land 12 to 20 new customers to offset the impact of one lost loyal customer.[67] Research shows that repeat customers spend 67 percent more than new customers. In addition, attracting a new customer actually costs the typical business *seven to nine times* as much as keeping an existing one.[68] Therefore, small business owners would be better off asking "How can we improve customer value and service to encourage our existing customers to do more business with us?" than "How can we increase our market share by 10 percent?" One way that companies can entice current customers to keep coming back is with a loyalty program, which many companies' are linking to their social media presence.

Metal Mafia

ENTREPRENEURIAL PROFILE: Vanessa Merit Nornberg and Metal Mafia Metal Mafia, a wholesaler of body and costume jewelry, surprises customers when they call to report a problem with defective or damaged goods. Metal Mafia tells customers to throw away the defective item, rather than waste their valuable time returning it to the company. Vanessa Merit Nornberg, owner of Metal Mafia, says most customers are surprised when they are told to just throw the item away and that the company will replace it. Metal Mafia's customers are happy with the company's customer focus, which turns them into repeat customers and makes them eager to tell others about their shopping experience with the company.[69] ■

The most successful small businesses have developed a customer focus and have instilled a customer satisfaction attitude *throughout* the company. They understand that winning customers for life requires practicing **customer experience management**, systematically creating the optimum experience for their customers every time they interact with the company. Companies with world-class customer experience management attitudes set themselves apart by paying attention to "little things," such as responding to questions or complaints promptly, remembering a customer's unique product or service preferences, or sending a customer a copy of an article of interest to him or her. Small companies cannot always be leaders in creating product or technology innovations. However, because their size allows them to have more personal contact with their customers than large companies, small companies can develop *experience* innovations that keep customers coming back and create a competitive advantage. Taking care of every small interaction a company has with its customers over time adds up to a positive service experience and can create a strong bond with them.

customer experience management
the process of systematically creating the optimum experience for customers every time they interact with the company.

You Be the Consultant

A Company with Soul

In 1974, Bill Crutchfield was living in his mother's house and working as the general manager of a forklift company after an unsuccessful stint in Hollywood, where he tried to sell a screenplay he wrote to a movie studio. He took $1,000 he had saved and started a mail-order car stereo company after trying in vain to find a stereo that he could install himself in an old Porsche he was restoring for resale. Of course, Crutchfield needed far more than $1,000 to start an electronics catalog company and was able to convince a local banker to extend a $25,000 line of credit to the new company, which he named Crutchfield after himself.

Crutchfield kept his job at the forklift company and ran his business as a one-man operation. After working all day, Crutchfield would drive to the post office to pick up orders, drive to his mother's home where he was living, pack up the products with a personal thank-you note to ship to customers, and drive the packages to UPS for shipment. Unfortunately, only seven months into the venture, Crutchfield was incurring a loss and was about to run out of cash. As a last-ditch effort, he sent a one-page questionnaire to everyone who had ordered a catalog, asking customers what the company could do better and noncustomers why they had not placed an order. Crutchfield says the responses he received not only saved his company but still guide its customer service philosophy to this day. The problem was not with the catalog's products, brands, or prices; instead, customers were intimidated at the idea of installing a car stereo on their own.

That feedback inspired Crutchfield to redesign his catalog (after all, it was the 1970s, long before the Internet) into a more polished product that included easy-to-follow articles on car stereo installation techniques, step-by-step photographs, and customer testimonials. The redesigned catalog worked, and sales increased dramatically in just a few months. That simple survey taught Crutchfield the importance of listening and responding to his customers, a lesson that has stuck with him for 40 years. Crutchfield's product line has expanded to include more than 9,500 high-end audiovisual products ranging from flat-screen televisions to cameras and speaker systems. In the company's research department (yes, a retailer that manufactures no products has a research department), employees are busy dissecting the products Crutchfield sells so they can share the details of their features and designs with the members of the sales, call center, and technical support teams. The technical support department routinely takes apart products to ensure they understand exactly how they work.

Digging into the details of every product the company sells is a vital component in the company's customer service equation, but Crutchfield takes a broad view of customer service. Crutchfield does not define customer service as only fixing problems once they occur. The company tries to think like its customers and put in place customer support features to make the customer experience better. Toward that end, Crutchfield has developed detailed car stereo installation guides for more than 16,100 vehicles, many of which contain how-to photos of the technical crew as they remove a factory radio and install one from the Crutchfield catalog. To enhance customers' experience, Crutchfield also makes a significant investment in training its 500 employees. In addition to the extensive training that technical support workers receive, sales advisers spend 13 weeks of classroom and hands-on installation training before they begin fielding customers' calls.

Crutchfield's focus on his customers pays off. The company generates $250 million in annual sales, is debt free, and has never experienced a layoff in its history. It has earned a five-star rating from Yelp and is the only retailer to win BizRate's Circle of Excellence award for 11 consecutive years. In 2007, Bill Crutchfield was inducted into the Consumer Electronics Hall of Fame, where he joined the ranks of notables such as Steve Jobs and Thomas Edison.

Crutchfield's passion for taking care of customers has never subsided even as the company grows. He recently penned a set of core values—including exceeding customers' expectations, passionately pursuing continuous improvement, and treating employees with respect—that he explains to every employee in face-to-face meetings. Those core values are a significant part of the company's hiring process, in which managers look for candidates who demonstrate an attitude of service. Crutchfield believes that although you can train people for technical skills, it is critical for its business model to hire people who truly enjoy helping other people.

Although Internet sales now account for 70 percent of sales, catalogs remain an important part of the business; Crutchfield mails more than 30 million of them each year. The company can never compete on price with Wal-Mart and the myriad of Internet stores. The company competes with its high level of customer service and its attention to its culture, which the Crutchfield refers to as the company's soul.

1. What impact has Crutchfield's strategy of providing superior customer service had on the company's success? In what ways does the company communicate its superior service strategy to customers?

2. Crutchfield makes it clear that his company does not compete with its rivals using low prices. What lessons can other small businesses learn from Crutchfield about the relationship between prices and customer service?

Source: Based on Kasey Wehrum, "Learning, and Relearning, to Listen," *Inc.*, March 2011, pp. 64–68.

Drexel Building Supply

The goal is to create a total customer experience that is so positive that customers keep coming back and tell their friends about it.

How do these companies manage their customer relationships and stay focused so intently on their customers? They constantly ask customers four basic questions and then act on what they hear:

1. What are we doing right?

2. How can we do that even better?

3. What have we done wrong?

4. What can we do in the future?

Table 8.4 offers some basic strategies for developing and retaining loyal customers.

BE DEVOTED TO QUALITY In this intensely competitive global business environment, quality goods and services are a prerequisite for success. According to one marketing axiom, the worst of all marketing catastrophes is to have great advertising and a poor-quality product. Customers have come to expect and demand quality goods and services, and those businesses that provide them consistently have a distinct competitive advantage. Today, quality is more than just a slogan posted on the company bulletin board; world-class companies treat quality as a strategic objective—an integral part of a company's strategy and culture. This philosophy is called **total quality management (TQM)**—quality not just in the product or service itself but also in *every* aspect of the business and its relationship with the customer and *continuous improvement* in the quality delivered to customers.

Companies on the cutting edge of the quality movement are developing new ways to measure quality. Manufacturers were the first to apply TQM techniques, but retail, wholesale, and service organizations have seen the benefits of becoming champions of quality. They are tracking customer complaints, contacting "lost" customers, and finding new ways to track the cost of quality and their return on quality (ROQ). ROQ recognizes that, although any improvement in quality may improve a company's competitive ability, only those improvements that produce a reasonable rate of return are worthwhile. In essence, ROQ requires managers to ensure that the quality improvements they implement will more than pay for themselves.

The key to developing a successful TQM philosophy is seeing the world from the customer's point of view. In other words, quality must reflect the needs and wants of the customer. TQM supports the value proposition of the business model. How do customers define quality? According to one survey, Americans rank the quality of a product in this order: reliability (average time between failures), durability (how long it lasts), ease of use, a known or trusted brand name, and, last, low price.[71] When buying services, customers look for similar characteristics: tangibles (equipment, facilities, and people), reliability (doing what you say you will do), responsiveness (promptness in helping customers and in solving problems), and assurance and empathy (conveying a caring attitude). For example, the owner of a very successful pest control company offers his customers a unique, unconditional guarantee: if the company fails to eliminate all insect and rodent breeding and nesting areas on a client's premises, it will refund the customer's last 12 monthly payments and will pay for one year's service by another exterminator. The company has had to honor its guarantee only once in 17 years.

Companies that excel at providing quality products and services discover tangible benefits in the form of increased sales, more repeat customers, higher customer retention, and lower costs.

total quality management (TQM)

the philosophy of producing a high-quality product or service and achieving quality in every aspect of the business and its relationship with the customer; the focus is on continuous improvement in the quality delivered to customers.

TABLE 8.4 Strategies for Developing and Retaining Loyal Customers

- Identify your best customers and give them incentives to return. Focus resources on the 20 percent of customers who account for 80 percent of sales.

- When you create a dissatisfied customer, fix the problem *fast*. One study found that, given the chance to complain, 95 percent of customers will buy again *if* a business handles their complaints promptly and effectively. The worst way to handle a complaint is to ignore it, to pass it off to a subordinate, or to let a lot of time slip by before dealing with it. Shortly after luxury car maker Lexus introduced the new ES 350 model, managers discovered that about 700 cars had a small transmission problem that was the result of a factory error. Lexus contacted the affected owners and asked them to take their cars to their local dealers, where they received brand new Lexus 350s—no questions asked. Surveys of these customers that were conducted later showed that they were *more* loyal to Lexus than buyers whose cars did not have the problem in the first place.

- Make sure your business system makes it easy for customers to buy from you. Eliminate unnecessary procedures that challenge customers' patience.

- *Encourage* customer complaints. You can't fix something if you don't know it's broken. Find out what solution the customer wants and try to come as close to that as possible. Smart companies learn from customer complaints and use the feedback to make improvements in their products, services, and processes.

- Contact lost customers to find out why they left. You may uncover a problem you never knew existed.

- Ask employees for feedback on improving customer service. A study by Technical Assistance Research Programs, a customer service research firm, found that frontline service workers can predict nearly 90 percent of the cases that produce customer complaints. Emphasize that *everyone* is part of the customer satisfaction team.

- Get total commitment to superior customer service from top managers—and allocate resources appropriately.

- Allow managers to wait on customers occasionally. It's a great dose of reality. Ron Shaich, founder of Panera Bread, a chain of bakery cafés with 1,185 locations in 40 states, still visits stores regularly, working the cash registers and serving customers so that he can listen to their ideas and concerns.

- Carefully select and train *everyone* who will deal with customers. Never let rude employees work with customers.

- Develop a service theme that communicates your attitude toward customers. Customers want to feel they are getting something special.

- Empower employees to do whatever it takes to satisfy customers. At Ritz-Carlton hotels, employees are authorized to spend up to $2,000 to resolve a customer's complaint. At Zappos, the online shoe retailer, members of the Customer Loyalty Team are authorized to spend as much time as necessary on the phone with customers and to assist with anything customers need, even those that are unrelated to Zappos.

- Reward employees "caught" providing exceptional service to customers.

- Get in the habit of calling customers by name. It's one of the most meaningful ways of connecting with your customers.

- *Remember*: Customers pay the bills; without them, you have no business. Special treatment wins customers and keeps them coming back.

Sources: Based on Kasey Wehrum, "How May We Help You?" *Inc.*, March 2011, p. 63; Brandi Stewart, "Able Baker," *FSB*, December 2007/January 2008, pp. 53–58; Jerry Fisher, "The Secret's Out," *Entrepreneur*, May 1998, pp. 1112–1119; Laura M. Litvan, "Increasing Revenue with Repeat Sales," *Nation's Business*, January 1996, pp. 36–37; "Encourage Customers to Complain," *Small Business Reports*, June 1990, p. 7; Dave Zielinski, "Improving Service Doesn't Require a Big Investment," *Small Business Reports*, February 1991, p. 20; John H. Sheridan, "Out of the Isolation Booth," *Industry Week*, June 19, 1989, pp. 18–19; Lin Grensing-Pophal, "At Your Service," *Business Start-Ups*, May 1995, pp. 72–74; and Bill Taylor, "Lessons from Lexus: Why It Pays to Do the Right Thing," Mavericks at Work, December 12, 2007, http://www.maverickssatwork.com/?p=102.

Small businesses that have succeeded in building a reputation for top-quality products and services rely on the following guidelines to "get it right the first time":

- Build quality into the process; don't rely on inspection to obtain quality.

- Foster teamwork and dismantle the barriers that divide disparate departments.

- Establish long-term ties with select suppliers; don't award contracts on low price alone.

- Provide managers and employees the training needed to participate fully in the quality improvement program.

- Empower workers at all levels of the organization; give them authority and responsibility for making decisions that determine quality.

- Get managers' commitment to the quality philosophy. Otherwise, the program is doomed. Employees look to leadership to see if quality is just talked about or actually a part of what the company does.

- Rethink the processes the company uses to get its products or services to its customers.

- Be willing to make changes in processes wherever they may be necessary.

- Reward employees for quality work. Ideally, workers' compensation is linked clearly and directly to key measures of quality and customer satisfaction.

- Develop a company-wide strategy for constant improvement of product and service quality.

- Back up the company's quality pledge with a guarantee. For instance, gSchool, a software programming school in Denver, Colorado, guarantees all students a $60,000 job in Colorado as professional web developers after completing the program. Students who do not land such a job are guaranteed a full refund of their $20,000 tuition![72]

ATTEND TO CONVENIENCE Ask customers what they want from the businesses they deal with, and one of the most common responses is "convenience." In this busy, fast-paced world of dual-career couples and lengthy commutes to and from work, customers increasingly are looking for convenience. Several studies have found that customers rank easy access to goods and services at the top of their purchase criteria. Unfortunately, too few businesses deliver adequate levels of convenience, and they fail to attract and retain customers. One print and framing shop, for instance, alienated many potential customers with its abbreviated business hours—nine to five daily, except for Wednesday afternoons, Saturdays, and Sundays, when the shop was closed! Other companies make it a chore to do business with them. In an effort to defend themselves against unscrupulous customers, these businesses have created elaborate procedures for exchanges, refunds, writing checks, and other basic transactions.

Successful companies go out of their way to make sure that it is easy for customers to do business with them. To provide their customers with a more convenient way to order, some restaurants are replacing printed menus with iPads. Stacked: Food Well Built, a southern California restaurant chain that offers 61 options just for a burger, uses iPads on every table that allow customers to drag and drop ingredients with the touch of a finger to create the perfect burger, pizza, or salad. Customers also pay their bills without having to flag a waiter.[73] At Do, an upscale pizza restaurant in Atlanta, Georgia, that uses a similar concept, customers not only order and pay for their meals using the iPads on their tables but also can control the music they listen to and alert the valet that they are ready for their cars.[74]

Other restaurants are taking their food to customers in food trucks rather than waiting for customers to come to their brick-and-mortar locations. The Milk Truck, which travels to several locations in New York City, specializes in grilled cheese sandwiches and milkshakes. Customers can purchase gourmet grilled cheese sandwiches made from a variety of cheese from Wisconsin and Vermont and add ingredients such as champagne vinegar pickled onions, caramelized Granny Smith apples, whole grain Dijon mustard, fried eggs, and applewood smoked ham. Milkshake flavors include Tahitian & Madagascar vanilla bean, dark chocolate, and crushed malted ball.[75]

Service companies are focusing on convenience as well. In Las Vegas, a couple can pull up into the Tunnel of Vows at the famous Little White Chapel, and an ordained minister at the drive-through window will marry them! Business has been so brisk that the owner of the chapel recently expanded the tunnel to include a ceiling adorned with cherubs and starlights.[76]

How can entrepreneurs boost the convenience level of their businesses? By conducting a "convenience audit" from the customer's point of view to get an idea of its ETDBW ("Easy-to-Do-Business-With") index:

- Is your business located near your customers? Does it provide easy access?

- Are your business hours suitable to your customers? Should you be open evenings and weekends to serve them better?

- Would customers appreciate pickup and delivery service? To enhance customer convenience, nearly 25 percent of takeout restaurants, especially pizza and sandwich shops, give customers the option of ordering online and have discovered that customer satisfaction, order accuracy, and speed increase.[77]

- Are your employees trained to handle business transactions quickly, efficiently, and politely? Waiting while rude, poorly trained employees fumble through routine transactions destroys customer goodwill.

- Do your employees treat customers with courtesy?

- Does your company provide a sufficient number of checkout stations so that shoppers do not have to stand in long lines to pay for their purchases? Does your company make it easy for customers to make purchases with debit or credit cards?

- Are you using technology to enhance customers' shopping experience? At Stop & Shop and Giant supermarkets in the Northeast, customers can pick up a smart phone–like device called Scan It that allows them to scan and bag their own groceries as they roam the stores' aisles. The device shows a running total of their purchases and periodically provides electronic coupons based on customers' purchases. Shoppers are happy because Scan It eliminates long waits at the checkout counter, and the supermarkets are happy because Scan It shoppers spend 10 percent more on average.[78]

- Does your company offer "extras" that make customers' lives easier? With a phone call to Hoyt Hanvey Jewelers, a small gift store in Clinton, South Carolina, customers in need of a special gift simply tell how much they want to spend, and the owner takes care of the rest—selecting the gift, wrapping it, and shipping it. All customers have to do is pay the invoice when it arrives in the mail.

- Can you "bundle" some of your existing products or services to make it easier for customers to use them? Whether it involves gardening tools or a spa treatment, assembling products and services into ready-made, all-in-one kits appeals to busy customers and can boost sales.

- Can you adapt existing products to make them more convenient for customers?

- Does your company handle telephone calls quickly, efficiently, and with a real person? Long waits "on hold," transfers from one office to another, and too many rings before answering signal to customers that they are not important. New services, such as Ruby Receptionists, give businesses the ability to have a real person answer the phone, rather than struggle through the frustration of navigating an automated answering system.

CONCENTRATE ON INNOVATION Innovation is the key to future success. Markets change too quickly and competitors move too fast for a small company to stand still and remain competitive. Because they cannot outspend their larger rivals, small companies often turn to superior innovation as a way to gain a competitive edge. Thanks to their organizational and managerial flexibility, small businesses often can detect and act on new opportunities faster than large companies. Innovation is one of the hallmarks of entrepreneurs, and it shows up in the new products, unique techniques, and unusual marketing approaches they introduce. Despite their limited resources, small businesses frequently are leaders in innovation. There is much more to innovation than spending megadollars on research and development. How do small businesses manage to maintain their leadership role in innovating new products and services? They use their size to their advantage, maintaining their speed and flexibility much like a martial arts expert does against a larger opponent. Their closeness to their customers enables them to read subtle shifts in the market and to anticipate trends as they unfold. Their ability to concentrate their efforts and attention in one area also gives small businesses an edge in innovation. One venture capitalist explains that small businesses can compete by putting all of their efforts into finding new products and markets.[79]

ENTREPRENEURIAL PROFILE: Fair Oaks Farms, LLC Fair Oaks Farms, LLC uses natural gas derived from the manure produced by its 30,000 milk cows to generate electricity to power its 10 barns, cheese factory, gift store, restaurant, and educational center for children. However, electricity generation uses only half of the 5 million pounds of manure generated by the Fair Oak Farms cows each day. Rather than burn off the excess gas, the farm is now using it to fuel its fleet of 42 tractor-trailer trucks. In addition to saving thousands of dollars in fuel costs, the farm also generates additional revenue from two fueling stations that are open to the general public.[80] ■

EMPHASIZE SPEED Technology, particularly the Internet, has changed the pace of business so dramatically that speed has become a major competitive weapon. Today's customers expect businesses to serve them at the speed of light! Providing a quality product at a reasonable price once was sufficient to keep customers happy, but that is not enough for modern customers who can find dozens of comparable products with a just few mouse clicks. Customers become disgruntled when companies fail to show respect for their busy schedules and corresponding lack of time. At world-class companies, speed reigns. They recognize that reducing the time it takes to develop, design, manufacture, and deliver a product reduces costs, increases quality, improves customer satisfaction, and boosts market share.

time compression management (TCM)
a marketing strategy that relies on three principles: (1) speeding products to market, (2) shortening customer response time in manufacturing and delivery, and (3) reducing the administrative time required to fill an order.

This philosophy of speed is based on **time compression management (TCM)**, which involves three principles: (1) speeding new products to market, (2) shortening customer response time in manufacturing and delivery, and (3) reducing the administrative time required to fill an order. Victory in this time-obsessed economy goes to the company that can deliver goods and services the fastest, not necessarily those that are the biggest and most powerful. Businesses that can satisfy their customers' insatiable appetites for speed have a distinct advantage. CarGurus, a popular Web site for researching and purchasing autos, focuses on speed. Rather than ensuring perfection, CarGurus pushes new products out as soon as they satisfy customers' basic requirements and then works on enhancements and changes over time. CEO Langley Steinert believes that, particularly with Web-based businesses, speed is everything. For example, CarGurus recently launched a newsletter, but rather than trying to ensure it included every feature customers might want, the company published it as soon as it had basic functionality and added new features over time based on customer feedback. Steinert is convinced that if businesses wait too long to make innovations and introduce new products, the speed of the Internet allows competitors to pass them by.[81]

Although speeding up the manufacturing process is a common goal, companies using TCM have learned that manufacturing takes only 5 to 10 percent of the total time between an order and getting the product into the customer's hands. The rest is consumed by clerical and administrative tasks. The primary opportunity for TCM to improve speed is in what it can offer to streamline the administrative process. Companies relying on TCM to help them turn speed into a competitive edge should do the following:

- *"Reengineer" the entire process rather than attempt to do the same things in the same way—only faster.* Peter Schultz, founder of Symyx, a small technology company in Santa Clara, California, applied the principles of rapid drug development used in the pharmaceutical industry to the field of materials science and changed the way new chemical compounds are created. Symyx's technology allows its employees to test small amounts of chemicals and metals in parallel—up to 1,000 combinations per day—to create new materials. Processes that not so long ago required two years of intense work now produce marketable results in less time.

- *Create cross-functional teams of workers and give them the power to attack and solve problems.* In world-class companies, product teams include engineers, manufacturing workers, salespeople, quality experts—even customers.

- *Set aggressive goals for time reduction and stick to the schedule.* Some companies using TCM have been able to reduce cycle time from several weeks to just a few hours!

- *Rethink your supply chain.* Can you electronically link with your suppliers or your customers to speed up orders and deliveries?

- *Instill speed in the culture.* At Domino's Pizza, kitchen workers watch videos of the fastest pizza makers in the country.

- *Use technology to find shortcuts wherever possible.* Properly integrated into a company's strategy for speed, technology can restructure a company's operating timetable. Rather than build costly, time-consuming prototypes, many time-sensitive businesses use computer-aided design and computer-assisted manufacturing to speed product design and testing.

- *Put the Internet to work.* Perhaps nothing symbolizes speed better than the Internet, and companies that harness its lightning-fast power can become leaders in TCM.

Conclusion

Small companies lack the marketing budgets of their larger rivals, but that does not condemn them to the world of second-class marketers and its resulting anonymity. By using clever, innovative bootstrap marketing strategies such as the ones described in this chapter, entrepreneurs can put their companies in the spotlight and create a special connection with their customers.

Chapter Summary by Learning Objective

1. Describe the principles of building a bootstrap marketing plan, and explain the benefits of preparing one.

A major part of the entrepreneur's business plan is the marketing plan, which focuses on a company's target customers and how best to satisfy their needs and wants. A solid marketing plan should do the following:

- Determine customer needs and wants through market research.
- Pinpoint the specific target markets the company will serve.
- Analyze the firm's competitive advantages and build a bootstrap marketing strategy around them.

2. Explain how small businesses can pinpoint their target markets.

Sound market research helps the owner pinpoint his or her target market. The most successful businesses have well-defined portraits of the customers they are seeking to attract.

3. Discuss the role of market research in building a bootstrap marketing plan and outline the market research process.

Market research is the vehicle for gathering the information that serves as the foundation of the marketing plan. Good research does *not* have to be complex and expensive to be useful. The steps in conducting market research include the following:

- Defining the objective: "What do you want to know?"

- Collecting the data from either primary or secondary sources.
- Analyzing and interpreting the data.
- Drawing conclusions and acting on them.

4. Describe how a small business can build a competitive edge in the marketplace using bootstrap marketing strategies.

When plotting a marketing strategy, owners must strive to achieve a competitive advantage—some way to make their companies different from and better than the competition. Successful small businesses rely on 14 sources to develop a competitive edge:

- Find a niche and fill it.
- Use the power of publicity.
- Don't just sell—entertain.
- Strive to be unique.
- Build a community with customers.
- Connect with the customer on an emotional level.
- Create an identity for your business through branding.
- Embrace social marketing.
- Be dedicated to service and customer satisfaction.
- Retain existing customers.
- Be devoted to quality.
- Pay attention to convenience.
- Concentrate on innovation.
- Emphasize speed.

Discussion Questions

8-1. Define the marketing plan. What lies at its center?

8-2. What objectives should a marketing plan accomplish?

8-3. How can market research benefit entrepreneurs when starting up?

8-4. How can market research benefit entrepreneurs as their businesses grow?

8-5. List some possible sources of market information for an entrepreneur.

8-6. Explain why market research does not have to be expensive and sophisticated to be valuable?

8-7. Describe several trends that are driving markets today and their impact on small businesses.

8-8. Why is it important for small business owners to define their target markets as part of their marketing strategies?

8-9. What is a competitive advantage?

8-10. Why is it important for a small business owner to create a plan for establishing a competitive advantage?

8-11. Describe how a small business owner could use finding a niche and fill it for a competitive advantage.

8-12. Describe how a small business owner could use the power of publicity for a competitive advantage.

8-13. Describe how a small business owner could use entertaining instead of just selling for a competitive advantage.

8-14. Describe how a small business owner could use striving to be unique for a competitive advantage.

8-15. Describe how a small business owner could use building a community of customers for a competitive advantage.

8-16. Describe how a small business owner could use connecting with customers at an emotional level for a competitive advantage.

8-17. Describe how a small business owner could use creating an identity for the business through branding for a competitive advantage.

8-18. Describe how a small business owner could use social marketing for a competitive advantage.

8-19. Describe how a small business owner could use dedication for service and customer satisfaction for a competitive advantage.

8-20. Describe how a small business owner could use retaining existing customers for a competitive advantage.

8-21. Describe how a small business owner could use devotion to quality for a competitive advantage.

8-22. Describe how a small business owner could use paying attention to convenience for a competitive advantage.

8-23. Describe how a small business owner could use concentrating on innovation for a competitive advantage.

8-24. Describe how a small business owner could use an emphasis on speed for a competitive advantage.

8-25. One experienced entrepreneur says that when a company provides great service, its reputation benefits from a stronger emotional connection with its customers, as well as from increased confidence that it will stand behind its products. Explain why you agree or disagree with this statement.

8-26. Describe a positive service experience you have had with a company and your impressions of that business.

8-27. What are the implications of a company providing poor customer service?

8-28. Describe a negative service experience you have had with a company and your likeliness of doing business with that company again in the future.

8-29. With a 70 percent customer retention rate (average for most U.S. firms, according to the American Management Association), every $1 million of sales will grow to more than $4 million in 10 years. If you retain 80 percent of your customers, the $1 million will grow to a little over $6 million. If you can keep 90 percent of your customers, that $1 million will grow to more than $9.5 million. What can the typical small business do to increase its customer retention rate?

Beyond the Classroom . . .

8-30. Interview the owner of a local restaurant about its marketing strategy.

8-31. From how large a geographic region does the restaurant owned by the person you interviewed draw its clientele?

8-32. What is the target market of the restaurant?

8-33. What is the demographic profile of the restaurant's target customers?

8-34. Does the restaurant have a competitive edge?

8-35. Visit the Web site for the Small Business Administration's (SBA) page on marketing. Interview a local business owner, using the resources at the SBA Web site as a guide.

8-36. Based on your interview, what sources for developing a competitive edge did you find?

8-37. Based on your interview, what weaknesses do you see and how do you recommend overcoming them?

8-38. What recommendations can you make to help the owner make better use of its marketing techniques?

8-39. What bootstrap marketing strategies can you suggest to the owner to enhance current marketing efforts?

8-40. Contact two local small business owners and ask them about their marketing strategies.

8-41. Based on your discussions with the two business owners, what bootstrap marketing strategies do their companies use?

8-42. What are the similarities and differences in how the two business owners have achieved a competitive edge?

8-43. Select three local businesses (one large and two small) and play the role of "mystery shopper."

8-44. Based on your mystery shopper experience, how easy was it to do business with each of the three companies?

8-45. How would you rate their service, quality, and convenience of each of the businesses based on your mystery shopper experience?

8-46. Compare and contrast the staff at the three stores based on how helpful, friendly, professional, and courteous they were to you during your mystery shopper visits?

8-47. How would you describe each company's competitive advantage based on your mystery shopper visits?

8-48. What future do you predict for each company you visited as a mystery shopper?

8-49. Prepare a brief report for your class on your findings and conclusions based on your three mystery shopper visits.

Endnotes

Scan for Endnotes or go to www.pearsonhighered.com/scarborough

9

E-Commerce and the Entrepreneur

Kevin Dodge/Blend Images/Corbis

Learning Objectives

On completion of this chapter, you will be able to:

1. Understand the factors an entrepreneur should consider before launching into e-commerce.

2. Explain the 10 myths of e-commerce and how to avoid falling victim to them.

3. Explain the basic strategies entrepreneurs should follow to achieve success in their e-commerce efforts.

4. Learn the techniques of designing a killer Web site.

5. Explain how companies track the results from their Web sites.

6. Describe how e-businesses ensure the privacy and security of the information they collect and store from the Web.

E-commerce has created a new way of doing business, one that is connecting producers, sellers, and customers via technology in ways that have never been possible before. The result is a new set of companies built on business models that are turning traditional methods of selling on their heads. Companies that ignore the impact of the Internet on their markets and their operations run the risk of becoming as relevant to customers as a rotary-dial telephone. The most successful companies are embracing the Internet not merely as another advertising medium or marketing tool but as a mechanism for transforming their companies and changing *everything* about the way they do business. As these companies discover innovative ways to use the Internet, social media, computers, and mobile devices to serve their customers better and to connect with their suppliers, they are creating a new industrial order. In short, e-commerce has launched a revolution. Just as in previous revolutions in the business world, some old, established players are being ousted, and new leaders are emerging. The winners are discovering new business opportunities, improved ways of designing work, and better ways of organizing and operating their businesses. Yet one lesson that entrepreneurs engaged in e-commerce have learned is that business basics still apply; companies engaged in e-commerce still have to take care of their customers and earn a profit to stay in business. Web-based business success requires entrepreneurs to strike a balance, creating an e-commerce strategy that capitalizes on the strengths of the Internet while meeting customers' expectations of convenience and service.

In the world of e-commerce, new business models recognize the power the Internet gives customers, whether they buy online or offline. In 2017, online sales and Internet activity are projected to account for or influence 60 percent of total retail sales, or more than $2.16 trillion, in the United States.[1] The Internet makes pricing more transparent than ever before: With a few mouse clicks or swipes on a smart phone, customers can compare the prices of the same or similar products and services from companies across the globe. In the connected economy, the balance of power is shifting to customers who comparison-shop, a habit they have retained since the last recession, and new business models must recognize this fact. Whatever products they may sell—from books and smart phones to cars and flowers—retailers are dealing with customers who are more informed and aware of the price and feature comparisons of the items for which they are shopping. A survey by PriceWaterhouseCoopers reports that 83 percent of Americans (and 80 percent of global shoppers) research products such as electronics, books, music, and movies online before buying them. The survey also shows that 73 percent of Americans (and 60 percent of global shoppers) conduct online research on clothing, shoes, toys, and health and beauty products before making purchases.[2] These informed shoppers are taking price out of the buying equation, causing retailers to emphasize other factors, such as customer service, deep product lines, or convenience, to build long-term relationships.

The connection between online and offline business runs both ways. As a result of offline exposure to a company's ads, shoppers are likely to conduct online Web searches of the products and services they see advertised. In addition, customers value other shoppers' opinions about the products they purchase and their shopping experiences with companies. A recent survey of shoppers in North America by BrightLocal, a company that specializes in local search engine optimization strategies, reports that 79 percent of consumers trust online reviews as much as personal recommendations.[3] These trends point to the need for companies to market their products and services by taking a multichannel selling approach that includes the Internet as one option. Modern shoppers expect to be able to purchase the products and services they want across multiple channels, including the Web, mobile devices, social media, television shopping channels, catalogs, and brick-and-mortar stores. The multichannel approach that today's shoppers utilize blurs the boundaries between physical stores and the Internet. A company's e-commerce strategy must recognize that modern consumers are always connected and that a visit to a company's Web site is just one component, albeit an important one, of a customer's experience with a company. "Brands have limitless opportunities to interact with consumers through the entire buying decision process via multiple channels and media, whether it be in-store, online, via mobile, or social media," says Alex Gonzalez, cofounder of Chatalog, an online social shopping tool.[4]

ENTREPRENEURIAL PROFILE: Janet Holian: Gemvara Gemvara, a retailer of customized jewelry that once operated only online, recently opened its first physical retail store on Boston's high-traffic Newbury Street, where shoppers can see and try on the pieces of jewelry that the company makes from 29 gemstones and 9 precious metals. Shoppers also can work with store employees to create their own custom designs just as they can online. "The [in-store] Gemvara experience brings our online custom jewelry experience to life," explains Janet Holian, Gemvara's CEO.[5] ■

In the fast-paced world of e-commerce, size doesn't matter as much as speed and flexibility. One of the Internet's greatest strengths is its interactive, social nature and its ability to provide companies with instantaneous customer feedback, giving them the opportunity to learn and to make necessary adjustments. Businesses, whatever their size, that are willing to experiment with different approaches to reaching customers and are quick to learn and adapt will grow and prosper; those that cannot will fall by the wayside. E-commerce is transforming the way businesses in almost every industry operate, including the retail auto business. "The whole process of buying a car has been flipped from what it used to be," says Alison Spitzer, vice-president of Spitzer Auto Group in Elyria, Ohio. Rather than spend most of their time in dealerships comparing models and prices, customers today walk into a showroom having already researched online the features and reviews of various models and equipped with the car's invoice price, manufacturers' discounts, and competing bids from several dealers. Research by AutoTrader Group shows that car shoppers spend an average of 11 hours conducting research online and just 3.5 hours researching cars offline, including trips to dealerships. "Everything is transparent for the customers," says Tia Morris, a salesperson at Nissan of Manhattan. Morris, whose title is "product specialist," says her job is "helping customers find the right car and make a smart choice."[6]

A Nielsen study of global e-commerce trends reports that 84 percent of the world's online population has used the Internet to make a purchase, up from 40 percent in 2006. The items purchased most often online are apparel, books, computer hardware and software, toys, videogames, and health and beauty products.[7] However, companies can—and do—sell practically anything over the Web, from antiques and groceries to skeletons (animal and human) and Russian military tanks. eMarketer estimates that nearly 9.0 percent of total retail sales in the United States will occur online in 2018, totaling more than $491 billion (see Figure 9.1).[8]

FIGURE 9.1

U.S. E-Commerce Sales

Source: Based on data from eMarketer, April 10, 2014.

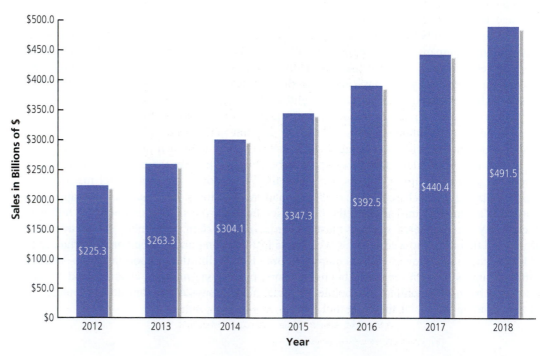

FIGURE 9.2

Internet Penetration Rate by Region

Source: Based on data from "Internet Usage Statistics: The Internet Big Picture," Internet World Stats 2013, www.internetworldstats.com/stats.htm.

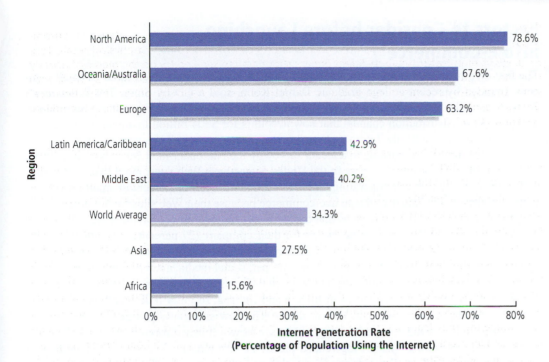

Region

Region	Internet Penetration Rate
North America	78.6%
Oceania/Australia	67.6%
Europe	63.2%
Latin America/Caribbean	42.9%
Middle East	40.2%
World Average	34.3%
Asia	27.5%
Africa	15.6%

Internet Penetration Rate
(Percentage of Population Using the Internet)

Companies of all sizes are busy establishing a presence on the Internet because that's where their customers are. The number of Internet users worldwide now stands at more than 2.4 billion, up from 147 million in 1998 (see Figure 9.2).[9] Consumers have adopted the Internet much more quickly than any other major innovations in the past. It reached 50 percent penetration in the United States in just 7 years, compared to 30 years for the computer, 40 years for electricity, and more than 100 years for steam power.[10]

Starbucks doubles its sales by devising a way to sell coffee over the Internet.

John McPherson, www.cartoonstock.com

LO1

Understand the factors
an entrepreneur should
consider before launching
into e-commerce.

Factors to Consider before Launching into E-Commerce

The first e-commerce transaction took place on August 11, 1994, when NetMarket, a small company founded by recent college graduate Daniel Kohn, sold a CD by Sting, *Ten Summoner's Tales*, to a student at Swarthmore College for $12.48 plus shipping.[11] From these humble beginnings grew a distribution channel that now accounts for $304 billion in annual retail sales.[12] Despite the many benefits the Internet offers, however, not every small business owner is ready to embrace e-commerce. According to a recent survey by the National Small Business Association, 82 percent of small business owners in the United States have Web sites, more than two-and-a-half times as many that were operating online in 1997. However, 28 percent of small businesses with Web sites do not actually engage in e-commerce because their Web sites cannot process customer payments. The primary reasons that business owners give for not having a Web site is that they believe that a Web site is not necessary for their company (27 percent), creating and maintaining a site is too difficult (19 percent), and operating a Web site is too costly (12 percent).[13]

The blurring of the boundaries among the Internet, social media, and brick-and-mortar storefronts has changed the way companies interact with their customers. The RoomPlace, a 100-year-old chain of 21 retail furniture stores in Illinois and Indiana, recently redesigned its entire Web site using feedback from users and Web analytics. The new site shows pictures of entire rooms of furniture sold as bundles so that shoppers can see how a finished room would look. The site emphasizes cross-selling by showing related pieces of furniture and accessories for items that customers view or select. The redesigned site also includes a more visible "add to cart" button that encourages shoppers to buy. The RoomPlace added zoom features that enable shoppers to see product details. Recognizing that many customers want to see, touch, and sit in furniture before making a purchase, The RoomPlace has incorporated multiple purchase options for customers, for example, allowing them to research online and purchase in-store or to research in-store and buy online. Within three months of the site's redesign, the company's sales increased 20 percent, its average order value increased 25 percent, and the site's conversion rate improved by 26 percent.[14]

Like The RoomPlace, small businesses have been allocating more resources to their e-commerce efforts, investing in developing and updating their Web sites, optimizing their sites to achieve top search engine rankings, and encouraging customers to post reviews of their businesses, products, and services. Before launching an e-commerce effort, entrepreneurs should consider the following important strategic issues:

- The way in which a company exploits the Internet's interconnectivity and the opportunities it creates to transform relationships with its suppliers and vendors, its customers, and other external stakeholders are crucial to its success.

- Success requires a company to develop a plan for integrating the Internet into its overall business strategy. The plan should address issues such as Web site design and maintenance, creating and managing a brand name, marketing and promotional strategies, sales, and customer service.

- Developing deep, lasting relationships with customers takes on even greater importance on the Internet. Attracting online customers costs money, and companies must be able to retain their online customers to make their Web sites profitable. That means that online companies must give their customers good reasons to keep coming back.

- Creating a meaningful presence on the Internet requires an ongoing investment of resources—time, money, energy, and talent. Establishing an attractive Web site brimming with catchy photographs and descriptions of products is only the beginning.

- Measuring the success of its Internet-based sales effort is essential if a company is to remain relevant to customers whose tastes, needs, and preferences are always changing. Using Web analytics to continuously improve a Web site is essential.

Doing business on the Internet takes more time and energy than many entrepreneurs expect. The following six factors are essential to achieving e-commerce success:

- *Acquiring customers.* The first e-commerce skill that entrepreneurs must master is acquiring customers, which requires them to drive traffic to their Web sites. Entrepreneurs must develop a strategy for using the many available tools, which range from display ads and Google Adwords to social media and search marketing.

- *Optimizing conversions.* Every online entrepreneur's goal is to convert Web site visitors into paying customers. The efficiency with which an online company achieves this goal plays a significant role in determining its profitability. Unfortunately, more than 97 percent of visitors to the typical retail Web site do not purchase anything.

- *Maximizing Web site performance.* Once shoppers find a company's Web site, they should encounter a site that downloads quickly, is easy to navigate, and contains meaningful content they can find quickly and efficiently. A fast, simple checkout process also is essential. Otherwise, shoppers will abandon the site, never to return.

- *Ensuring a positive user experience.* Achieving customer satisfaction online is just as important as it is offline. Visitors who are satisfied with a site are 71 percent more likely to purchase from the site (and 67 percent more likely to purchase in the future) than visitors who are dissatisfied.[15] An above-average bounce rate (the percentage of single-page visits to a Web site) and shopping cart abandonment rate and a conversion rate that is below average are signs that a company's Web site is not providing a positive customer experience.

- *Retaining customers.* Just as in offline stores, customer retention is essential to the success of online businesses. One study reports that increasing customer retention by 2 percent produces the same financial impact as reducing costs by 10 percent.[16] Entrepreneurs must create an online shopping experience that engages customers, offers them value, and provides them with convenience.

- *Use Web analytics as part of a cycle of continuous improvement.* Entrepreneurs have a multitude of Web analytics tools (many of them free) that they can use to analyze the performance and effectiveness of their Web sites. A Web site is never really "finished"; it is always a work in progress, and analytics tools provide the data for driving continuous improvement. Unfortunately, a survey conducted by The Incyte Group and SiteApps reports that 75 percent of small business owners do not use analytics tools to measure their Web sites' performance. "Small businesses know how important their web presence is for presenting a desirable online identity and attracting new customers, yet don't fully understand how to achieve those goals, implement new technologies, or adapt to new trends as deftly as larger companies," says Phillip Klien, CEO of SiteApps.[17]

We will explain how to achieve these six goals in the "Strategies for E-Success" section of this chapter.

Ten Myths of E-Commerce

LO2

Explain the 10 myths of e-commerce and how to avoid falling victim to them.

Although many entrepreneurs have made their fortunes through e-commerce, setting up shop on the Internet is no guarantee of success. Scores of entrepreneurs have plunged unprepared into the world of e-commerce only to discover that there is more to it than merely setting up a Web site and waiting for orders to start pouring in. Make sure that you do not fall victim to one of the following e-commerce myths.

Myth 1. If I Launch a Site, Customers Will Flock to It

Some entrepreneurs think that once they set up their Web sites, their expenses end there. Not true! Without promotional support, no Web site will draw enough traffic to support a business. With more than 785 million Web sites in existence and 51 million added each year, getting a site noticed in the crowd has become increasingly difficult.[18] Listing a site with popular search engines does not guarantee that online customers will find your company's Web site. Just like traditional retail stores seeking to attract customers, virtual companies have discovered that drawing sufficient traffic to a Web site requires constant promotion—and lots of it! Setting up a Web site and then failing to drive customers to it with adequate promotional support is like setting up a physical store in a back alley: You may be in business, but nobody knows you're there!

Entrepreneurs with both physical and virtual stores must promote their Web sites at every opportunity by printing their Uniform Resource Locators (URLs; a company's address on the Internet) on everything related to their physical stores—on signs, in print and broadcast ads, on shopping bags, on merchandise labels, on employees' uniforms, and anywhere else their customers will see. Quick-response (QR) codes allow smart phone users to go directly to a Web site's relevant page without having to type in a long URL. Entrepreneurs also use social media such as Facebook, Twitter, LinkedIn, Pinterest, YouTube, and others to drive traffic to their Web sites and purchase ads on high-traffic sites such as Google (Google Adsense) and Facebook, both of which allow companies to establish maximum expenditures based on the number of people who click on their ads. Using these tools, companies can aim their ads at specific target customers by location, age, and interests.

State Bicycle - Courtesy of State Bicycle Co.

ENTREPRENEURIAL PROFILE: Mehdi Farsi, Reza Farsi, and Eric Ferguson: State Bicycle Mehdi Farsi, Reza Farsi, and Eric Ferguson, owners of State Bicycle, a manufacturer of quality fixed-gear and single-speed bicycles in Tempe, Arizona, uses Facebook ads to increase its brand recognition, drive new customers to its Web site, and build stronger relationships with existing customers. In addition to adding milestones to the company's Facebook page to promote significant events and accomplishments, the entrepreneurs also ran Facebook ads to people living in cities whose profiles indicated that they were bicyclists or were interested in fixed-gear bicycles (known as "fixies"). They also hosted frequent photo contests on the company Facebook page (e.g., the owner of the "most beaten up bike" won a new State Bicycle bike) and ran "Facebook Friday" specials that included a discount coupon for people who liked the company on Facebook. With only a minimal investment in Facebook ads, the entrepreneurs realized an additional $500,000 in sales in just one year and saw the number of likes increase tenfold in the same time period.[19] ■

Entrepreneurs also should consider buying ads in traditional advertising media as well as using banner ads, banner exchange programs, and cross-marketing arrangements with companies that sell complementary products on their own Web sites. The keys to promoting a Web site are *networking*—building relationships with other companies, customers, trade associations, online directories, and other Web sites that your company's customers visit—and *interacting* with existing and potential customers online through social media outlets.

Myth 2. Online Customers Are Easy to Please

Customers who shop online today tend to be experienced Internet users whose expectations of their online shopping experiences are high and continue to rise. Experienced online shoppers tend to be unforgiving, quickly clicking to another site if their shopping experience is subpar or they cannot find the products and information they want. Because Web shoppers are increasingly more discriminating, companies are finding that they must improve their Web sites constantly to attract and keep their customers.

To be successful online marketers, small companies must create Web sites with the features that appeal to experienced Web shoppers, such as simple navigation; customer reviews; an efficient checkout process; multiple payment options; rock-solid security; quick access to product information, videos, and blogs; and the ability to track their shipments online. In addition, when customers have questions about or experience problems with an online shopping experience, companies that provide easy access to customer assistance and support have the advantage. Giving customers easy access to service representatives through multiple options, such as a toll-free telephone number, live chat, click-to-call, live video chat, and texting (for the growing number of customers who shop from their smart phones and other mobile devices) increases the probability that they will complete their transactions and return to shop again. The payoff for creating a positive online experience for shoppers is significant: Customers are more likely to trust the company, complete their purchases, buy from the company again, recommend the company to someone else, and mention it favorably in social media posts. Conversely, a poor online shopping experience translates into shoppers who abandon their shopping carts, have a negative impression of the company, lose trust in the business, and as a result, purchase from a competing Web site.[20]

ENTREPRENEURIAL PROFILE: David Byun: AccessoryGeeks AccessoryGeeks, an on-line company that sells smart phone, iPod, and iPad accessories, recently redesigned its Web site to make customers' shopping experience easier and better. The company added tabs that allow shoppers to browse its product line by product, manufacturer, or brand and a search tool that enables customers to find a particular accessory even faster. Higher quality photos and more detailed product descriptions are designed to appeal to the company's more discriminating customer base. For customers for whom the FAQ section does not satisfy, AccessoryGeeks employees now respond to customer e-mails around the clock and send text messages to people shopping from mobile devices, which now generate 15 percent of the company's sales. As part of the redesign, the company also added customer reviews and a live chat option. To encourage repeat shopping, the company now awards "Geek Points" for each purchase that shoppers can redeem for discounts, merchandise, and prizes. "Online customers demand more and more as time goes on," says David Byun, AccessoryGeeks' president.[21] ∎

Myth 3. Making Money on the Web Is Easy

Promoters who hawk "get-rich-quick" schemes on the Internet lure many entrepreneurs with the promise that making money online is easy. It isn't. Doing business online can be very profitable, but making money online requires an up-front investment of time, money, and energy. Success online also requires a sound business strategy that is aimed at the appropriate target audience and that an entrepreneur must implement effectively and efficiently—in other words, the same elements that are required for success *offline*. Many entrepreneurs are earning healthy profits from their Web-based businesses, but doing so requires hard work!

As thousands of new sites spring up every day, getting a company's site noticed requires more effort and marketing muscle than ever before. Attracting customers to a Web site is really no different from attracting customers to a brick-and-mortar store; entrepreneurs must define their target customers, devise a marketing plan to reach them, and offer them good value and superior customer service to keep them coming back. Successful e-tailers have discovered that promoting their Web sites via social media and providing comprehensive FAQ (frequently asked questions) pages, e-mail order confirmations and shipment notices, and highly visible telephone and e-mail contact information followed by quick responses enhance their reputations for online customer service.

Myth 4. Privacy Is Not an Important Issue on the Web

The Internet allows companies to gain access to almost unbelievable amounts of information about their customers' online behavior. Tracking tools monitor customers' behavior while they are on a site, giving Internet-based businesses the information they need to make their Web sites more customer friendly. Many sites also offer visitors "freebies" in exchange for information about themselves. Companies then use this information to learn more about their target customers and how to market to them more effectively. Concern over privacy and the proper use of this information has become the topic of debate by many interested parties, including government agencies, consumer watchdog groups, and customers themselves. The TRUSTe Privacy Index reports that 89 percent of adults in the United States worry about their privacy online, and the same percentage of U.S. adults avoid doing business with companies that they believe do not protect their privacy online.[22]

Companies that collect information from their online customers must safeguard their customers' privacy, protect the information they collect from unauthorized use, and use it responsibly. That means that businesses should post a privacy policy on their Web sites, explaining to customers how they intend to use the information they collect. Then they must be sure to follow it! One of the surest ways to alienate online customers is to abuse the information collected from them by selling it to third parties or by spamming customers with unwanted solicitations.

Many customers don't trust Web sites, especially those of companies they don't know. One recent survey reports that 43 percent of U.S. adults do not trust online businesses with their personal information.[23] In addition, 17 percent of online shoppers have abandoned their shopping carts because of security concerns.[24] Therefore, a key component of a successful e-commerce effort, especially for small companies that tend to be less well known, is building trust among customers. Posting security icons from TRUSTe, BBBOnline, McAfee, WhiteHat, Thawte, and other certification services assures customers that a site meets security standards. Another way that businesses can build trust is to create meaningful privacy policies, post them on their Web sites, and then adhere to them. According to John Briggs, director of e-commerce for the Yahoo Network, customers "need to trust the brand they are buying and believe that their online purchases will be safe transactions. They need to feel comfortable that [their] personal data will not be sold and that they won't get spammed by giving their e-mail address. They need to know about shipping costs, product availability, and return policies up front."[25] Privacy *does* matter on the Web, and businesses that respect and protect their customers' privacy win their customers' trust. Trust is the foundation on which the long-term customer relationships that are so crucial to Web success are built.

Myth 5. "Strategy? I Don't Need a Strategy to Sell on the Web! Just Give Me a Web Site, and the Rest Will Take Care of Itself"

Building a successful e-business is no different than building a successful brick-and-mortar business. It requires a well-thought-out strategy. Building a strategy means an entrepreneur must first develop a clear definition of the company's target audience and a thorough understanding of those customers' needs, wants, likes, and dislikes. To be successful, a Web site must be appealing to the customers it seeks to attract just as a traditional store's design and decor must draw foot traffic. If a Web site is to become the foundation for a successful e-business, an entrepreneur must create it with the target audience in mind.

Recall from Chapter 5 that one goal of developing a strategy is to set a business apart from its competition. The same is true for creating a strategy for conducting business online. It is just as important, if not more important, for an online business to differentiate itself from the competition if it is to be successful. Unlike customers in a retail store, who must exert the effort to go to a competitor's store if they cannot find what they want, online customers only have to make a mouse click or two to go to a rival Web site. Competition online is fierce, and to succeed, a company must have a sound strategy.

Courtesy of Adam Fish

ENTREPRENEURIAL PROFILE: Bryan DeLuca, Matt Fry, Tom Browning, Matt McClard, and Kelly Largent: Foot Cardigan Two weeks into a three-month trip to Europe with his wife, Bryan DeLuca ran out of socks. After purchasing "a 10-pack of wacky-designed socks in a retail shop in London," DeLuca says the socks became part of his everyday wardrobe, even after he returned from his trip. The socks generated many comments and questions, inspiring DeLuca to start an online business selling funky socks. He worked with four friends, Matt Fry, Tom Browning, Matt McClard, and Kelly Largent, all of whom are experienced entrepreneurs and brought a unique skill sets to the business, to launch Foot Cardigan, an e-commerce company based in Dallas, Texas. The entrepreneurs decided to base their business model on a subscription service that "delivers one random pair of crazy socks to your mailbox every month." They also kept their day jobs, utilized the lean start-up method, and followed the minimum viable product philosophy. "It's the least amount a business needs to work at the most basic level," explains DeLuca. "Nothing is ever really 'ready' to launch. Just get it out there." The philosophy involves testing almost everything about a business before committing significant resources to it. Foot Cardigan's cofounders tested their subscription business model, their products (all of the company's socks are original designs and are available nowhere else), and the company name to see how customers would respond. "We don't want to put time and money behind something that people really don't want," he says. "If your testing shows that people want it, create it. If it doesn't, don't." Already with more than 2,000 subscribers and growing fast, Foot Cardigan is profitable and has exceeded the young entrepreneurs' expectations. Their next step is to expand into international markets.[26] ∎

Myth 6. The Most Important Part of Any E-Commerce Effort Is Technology

Technology advances have reduced significantly the cost of launching an e-commerce business. Brian Walker, an e-commerce expert at Forrester Research, says that a just decade ago, the cost to launch an online retail business was three to five times higher than it is today. "The technology to run the site, the physical warehouse, site hosting, and staff required a significant investment before the site even went live," says Walker.[27] Modern e-commerce entrepreneurs can build a Web site for next to nothing, outsource the tasks of storing and shipping products, lease space on a server, and rent cloud-computing software to operate their online businesses—all of which lower the cost and the complexity of starting an online company. Julie Wainwright says building the e-commerce company that she helped launch in 1998 cost between $7 million and $10 million (not including the cost of inventory). Wainwright recently launched an online luxury clothing marketplace called TheRealReal at a cost of only $25,000 to $30,000.[28]

As important as having the right technology to support an e-commerce business is, it is *not* the most crucial ingredient in the recipe for success. What matters most is the ability to understand the underlying business and to develop a workable business model that offers customers something of value at a reasonable price and produces a profit for the company. The entrepreneurs who are proving to be most successful in e-commerce are those who know how their industries work inside and out and then build an e-business around that knowledge. They know they can hire Web designers, database experts, and fulfillment companies to handle the technical aspects of their online businesses, but nothing can substitute for a solid understanding of inner workings of their industry, their target market, and the strategy needed to pull the various parts of the business model together. The key is seeing the Web for what it really is: another way to reach and serve customers with an effective business model and to minimize the cost of doing business.

Some entrepreneurs tackle e-commerce by focusing on technology first and then determining how that technology fits their business idea. "If you start with technology, you're likely to going to buy a solution in search of a problem," says Kip Martin, program director of META Group's Electronic Business Strategies. Instead, he suggests, "Start with the business and ask yourself what you want to happen and how you'll measure it. *Then* ask how the technology will help you achieve your goals. Remember: Business first, technology second."[29]

Myth 7. Customer Service Is Not as Important Online as It Is in a Traditional Retail Store

The Internet offers the ultimate in shopping convenience. Numerous studies report that convenience and low prices are the primary drivers of online shopping. In fact, customers say convenience is more important than getting the lowest prices when shopping online.[30] With just a few mouse clicks or taps on the screen of a smart phone or tablet, people can shop for practically anything anywhere in the world and have it delivered to their doorsteps within days. As convenient as online shopping is, customers still expect high levels of service. Unfortunately, some e-commerce companies treat customer service as an afterthought, an attitude that costs businesses in many ways, including lost customers and a diminished public image. The fact is that customer service is just as important (if not more so) on the Web as it is in traditional brick-and-mortar stores.

The average conversion rate for e-commerce sites is just 2.55 percent.[31] In other words, out of 1,000 visitors to the typical company's Web site, only about 26 of them actually make a purchase! Sites that are slow to load and/or difficult to navigate, suffer from complicated checkout systems, or confuse shoppers turn customers away, and many of them never return. Only 28 percent of e-commerce businesses are satisfied with their conversion rates.[32]

ENTREPRENEURIAL PROFILE: Dan Gerler: OnlineShoes.com Dan Gerler, CEO of OnlineShoes.com, a family-owned chain of retail stores based in Seattle, Washington, that became the first online shoe retailer in 1996, was determined to increase the company's conversion rate by making its Web site easier for customers to browse and buy. Web analytics showed

Lynn Stetson, the company's director of e-commerce, marketing, and merchandising, that at checkout, many customers had neglected to select a shoe size, forcing them to backtrack to complete their purchases. Many customers simply abandoned their shopping carts. Stetson added a pop-up reminder that alerted shoppers when they failed to specify a size and included text next to the "add to cart" button that emphasized the company's key selling points: free shipping and exchanges and 365-day-a-year returns. The result was a 20 percent increase in OnlineShoes.com's conversion rate.[33] ■

There is plenty of room for improvement in customer service on the Web. Shoppers' unmet expectations of superior customer service translate into a high shopping cart abandonment rate. Research shows that 67 percent of online shoppers who fill their online shopping carts abandon them without checking out, costing businesses a whopping $1.79 trillion in lost sales. The cart abandonment rate jumps to 97 percent for shoppers who use mobile devices.[34] Figure 9.3 shows the leading causes of shopping cart abandonment. When customers abandon their shopping carts, companies can close a significant percentage of those "lost" sales by sending prompt follow-up "triggered" e-mails designed to convince customers to complete their purchases. On average, 20 percent of shoppers who abandon their carts and receive follow-up ("re-targeted") e-mails from the company (sooner is better) return to complete their purchases, often spending more than shoppers who completed their purchases without abandoning their carts.[35] One recent study concludes that companies that send retargeted e-mails generate an average of $17.90 in revenue per e-mail sent. Including an offer for free shipping to customers who abandon their shopping carts is one of the most effective ways to convince them to complete their purchases.[36]

AP Photo/Al Behrman

ENTREPRENEURIAL PROFILE: Mo and Mark Constantine: Lush Fresh Handmade Cosmetics Mo and Mark Constantine, cofounders of Lush Fresh Handmade Cosmetics, a company based in Poole, Dorset, United Kingdom, sell an extensive line of cosmetics and bath and body products made from natural ingredients (including its popular "bath bombs" and "bubble bars") in 830 retail stores in 51 countries and online. With their company generating annual sales of more than £326 million, the Constantines continue to push for growth, adding new products and expanding sales through the Lush Web site. With the help of Mark Parrott, the company's Internet marketing

FIGURE 9.3

Reasons for Abandoning Online Shopping Carts

Source: Based on data from LivePerson, 2013.

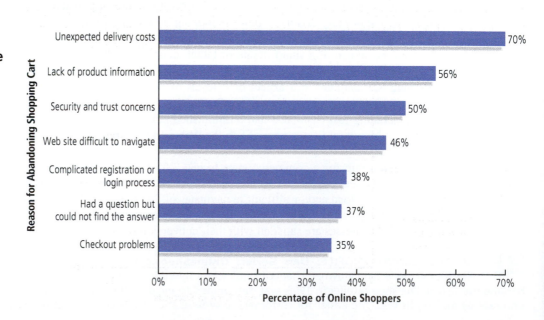

specialist, they recently focused their attention on online customers who had filled shopping carts and then abandoned them. The customers received two retargeted e-mails. The first one, sent just three hours after the abandonment and including the shopper's name and a list of the virtual cart's contents, generated an impressive conversion rate of 36 percent, nearly 11 times the average e-mail conversion rate of 3.34 percent. Shoppers who did not respond to the first e-mail received a second one two days later, which produced a conversion rate of 29 percent. Lush Cosmetics also began another successful e-mail campaign designed to recapture customers who had not made a purchase within the previous six months. This "We miss you!" campaign produced an above-average conversion rate of 10 percent.[37] ■

One tool that increases a company's conversion rate and reduces its cart abandonment rate is live help. In fact, a study by Oracle reports that 57 percent of customers say that live help is one of the most important features a Web site can offer.[38] For reasonable fees, companies can hire virtual assistants, employees who work remotely to answer online shoppers' questions or to offer advice (for example, whether an item's sizes tend to run small) in real time. Even small companies that cannot afford to staff a live chat center can offer customer-responsive chat options on their Web sites by using virtual chat agents. Loaded onto a company's site, these avatar-like creations can step in at the appropriate time to interact with customers, answering their questions or giving them the extra nudge they need, such as an offer of free shipping, to close the deal.

In an attempt to improve the level of service they offer, many sites provide e-mail links to encourage customer interaction. Unfortunately, when responding to e-mail takes a very low priority at some e-businesses, customers take it as a clear sign of poor service. The lesson for e-commerce entrepreneurs is simple: Devote time, energy, and money to developing an effective system for providing superior customer service. Those who do will build a sizable base of loyal customers who will keep coming back.

Myth 8. Flashy Web Sites Are Better Than Simple Ones

Businesses that fall into this trap pour significant amounts of money into designing flashy Web sites with all of the "bells and whistles." The logic is that to stand out online, a site really has to sparkle. That logic leads to a "more-is-better" mentality when designing a site. On the Internet, however, "more" does *not* necessarily equate to "better." A Web site that includes a simple design, easy navigation, clear calls to action on every page, and consistent color schemes show that a company is putting its customers first. A site that performs efficiently and loads quickly is a far better selling tool than one that is filled with "cornea gumbo," slow to download, and confusing to shoppers. "Every millisecond counts," says Arvind Jain, an engineer at Google.[39] Sites that download slowly usually never have the chance to sell because customers click to another site. The time required to download a Web site is one of the most important determinants of its sales effectiveness. Studies show that sites that load slowly have higher bounce rates and lower conversion rates as customers abandon them for faster loading sites (see Figure 9.4).[40] One study reports that a one-second delay in a site's page-load time results in a 7 percent reduction in its conversion rate.[41] In addition, Web sites that load faster earn higher rankings on search engines.[42]

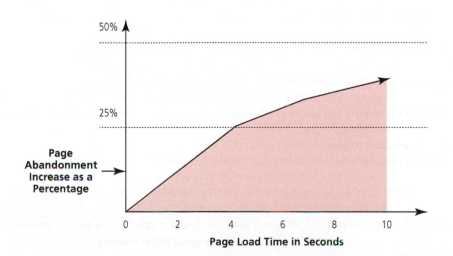

FIGURE 9.4

Page Abandonment Rate vs. Page Load Time

Source: KissMetrics, 2012, http://blog.kissmetrics.com/loading-time/.

To online customers, whose expectations concerning online speed continue to escalate, a good online shopping experience is a fast, uncomplicated one. Successful e-tailers set their sights on meeting the two-second rule: if a Web site does not download within two seconds, users are likely to abandon it. If a Web site takes more than three seconds to load, 40 percent of online shoppers will abandon it.[43] Proper content, formatting, and design are important ingredients in determining a site's performance. Smart e-tailers frequently test their sites on performance, speed, and reliability measures in different browsers using a variety of online tools such as Dotcom-Monitor, WebPageTest, and others. The lesson: Keep the design of your site simple so that pages download in no more than two seconds, and make sure that the site's navigation is easy and intuitive.

ENTREPRENEURIAL PROFILE: Jason Marrone: Jelly Belly Candy Company Jelly Belly Candy Company, a company that sells jelly beans in a multitude of flavors, recently redesigned its Web site to follow a simpler, "minimalistic approach," says e-commerce director Jason Marrone. "We needed less clutter and more focus on the product." The company also upgraded the site's navigation and search capabilities, giving shoppers the ability to search for jelly beans by color, taste, package type, or occasion. Filters for price, color, and container size allow them to narrow their choices further. "People can find what they want more easily now," says Marrone. "It's making a difference." Since the redesign, Jelly Belly's conversion rate has increased 38 percent, and its average order value has gone up by 15 percent.[44] ∎

Myth 9. It's What's Up Front That Counts

Designing an attractive, efficient Web site and driving traffic to it are important to building a successful e-business. However, designing the back office, the systems that take over once customers place their orders on a Web site, is just as important as designing the site itself. If the behind-the-scenes support is not in place or cannot handle the traffic from the Web site, a company's entire e-commerce effort will come crashing down. The potentially large number of orders that a Web site can generate can overwhelm a small company that has failed to establish the infrastructure needed to support the site. Although e-commerce can lower many costs of doing business, it still requires a basic infrastructure in the channel of distribution to process orders, maintain inventory, fill orders, and handle customer service. "The companies with warehouses, supply-chain management, and solid customer service are going to be the ones that survive," says Daryl Plummer, head of the Gartner Group's Internet and new media division.[45]

To customers, a business is only as good as its last order. Web-based entrepreneurs often discover that the greatest challenge their businesses face is not necessarily attracting customers on the Web but creating a viable order fulfillment strategy. Order fulfillment involves everything required to get goods from a warehouse into a customer's hands and includes order processing, warehousing, picking and packing, shipping, and billing.

Some entrepreneurs choose to handle order fulfillment in-house with their own employees, whereas others find it more economical to hire specialized fulfillment houses to handle these functions. **Virtual order fulfillment** (or **drop shipping**) suits many small e-tailers perfectly. When a customer orders a product from its Web site, the company forwards the order to a wholesaler or distributor who then ships the product to the customer with the online merchant's label on it. This strategy allows a small business to avoid the cost and the risk of carrying inventory. Danny Wong and Fan Bi, cofounders of Blank Label, an online retailer of custom-made men's shirts, found a manufacturer in Shanghai, China, that was willing to build shirts to the specifications (fabric, size, collar style, cuff type, button color, and more) that shoppers identify on the Blank Label Web site and drop ship them directly to customers. Their fulfillment strategy minimizes the risk that the entrepreneurs, both in their early twenties, incur and has enabled their company to become one of the fastest-growing online companies in the United States.[46]

Although e-tailers who use virtual order fulfillment avoid the major investments in inventory and the problems associated with managing it, they lose control over delivery times and service quality. In addition, finding a fulfillment house willing to handle a relatively small volume of orders at a reasonable price can be difficult for some small businesses. Major fulfillment providers that focus on small companies include Amazon, Federal Express, UPS, DHL, ShipWire, Webgistix, and WeFullfillIt. Some businesses integrate their brick-and-mortar stores into their online order

virtual order fulfillment (or drop shipping)

a fulfillment strategy in which a company forwards customers' orders to a wholesaler or distributor who then ships the product to the customer with the online merchant's label on it.

fulfillment strategies. They maximize customer convenience by allowing customers to order online and pick up their items (or return them if necessary) to a physical store. Other companies use a ship-from-store fulfillment strategy, in which they fill online orders totally or in part from the inventory in their brick-and-mortar stores. Doing so maximizes the selection of merchandise from which customers can choose but requires the company to manage its inventory carefully to avoid starving its physical stores of goods if online demand surges.

ENTREPRENEURIAL PROFILE: Ned Hamilton: Peter Glenn Ski and Sport Peter Glenn Ski and Sport, a chain of 11 ski and outdoor apparel stores founded in 1958 by Ned Hamilton and headquartered in Fort Lauderdale, Florida, was an early adopter of the ship-from-store strategy. The company typically uses in-store inventory to fill between 10 and 40 percent of its online orders, which maximizes its inventory flexibility and enables it to test new products and brands. Peter Glenn Ski and Sport fills the rest of its orders from its dedicated e-commerce fulfillment center. "Given that ski and snowboard clothing is so fashion driven, we always need to offer the broadest selection possible in our stores and online while at the same time mitigating our inventory risk," says Jason Merrick, the company's e-commerce director. "We can experiment [with new products] with a lot more confidence because we have the extra selling channel on the Web."[47] ∎

Myth 10. My Business Doesn't Need a Web Site

Nearly one in five small businesses does not have a Web site, and many of those that do have sites that lack the ability to make sales online. To online shoppers, especially, these businesses might as well be invisible because doing business online and offline are inextricably connected. Today's shoppers prefer to purchase from companies that offer a multichannel approach, particularly those that offer in-store pick-up for online orders and in-store returns for online purchases.[48] A multichannel approach pays big dividends even for small businesses that consider themselves completely "local." One recent survey reports that 91 percent of shoppers have gone into a store as a result of an online encounter with a business.[49] When looking to purchase products locally, 85 percent shoppers go online to conduct research first, looking for store hours, directions, maps, and special sales.[50] Others prefer the convenience of making online purchases after having a positive encounter with a company's physical location. In addition, customers routinely share their opinions online about products and their shopping experience with companies. These trends point to the need for businesses to use a multichannel approach to selling their products and services that includes the Internet as one option. The key is to meet customers *wherever* they want to do business with a personalized shopping experience like the ones they encounter in the best brick-and-mortar stores. C. Wonder, a retailer of women's clothing and accessories and home décor, is working hard to build brand recognition and loyalty with customers by surprising and delighting its best online customers with special gifts and handwritten thank-you notes in packages. The young company also relies on social media such as Facebook and Twitter to establish connections and to build a sense of community with its customers. For example, if a customer likes a particular purse on Facebook and later logs into the C. Wonder Web site with her Facebook credentials, the site will display that purse on the home page. The company's Web site also can identify individual customers and, based on their past purchase history, customize the landing pages they encounter to suit their tastes and preferences. "Personalized brand experiences for Web sites, apps, and passbook/wallet concepts using location and customer history and preferences wrapped in insight allow your brand to be more relevant and appealing to the customer," says one e-commerce expert. "Those brands that stand out will win the loyalty battle."[51]

Succumbing to this myth often leads entrepreneurs to make a fundamental mistake once they finally decide to go online: They believe they have to have a "perfect" site before they can launch it. Few businesses get their sites "right" the first time. In fact, the most successful e-commerce sites are works in progress; entrepreneurs are constantly changing them, removing what does not work and experimenting with new features to see what does work. Successful Web sites are much like a well-designed flower garden, constantly growing and improving, yet changing to reflect the climate of each season. Their creators worry less about creating the perfect site at the outset than about getting a site online and then using Web analytics to fix it, tweak it, and update it to meet changing customer demands.

LO3

Explain the basic strategies entrepreneurs should follow to achieve success in their e-commerce efforts.

Strategies for E-Success

People now spend more time online than ever before. Today, the average American spends more time with digital media than he or she does watching television.[52] However, converting these digital users into online customers requires a business to do more than merely set up a Web site and wait for the hits to start rolling up. Building sufficient volume for a site takes energy, time, money, creativity, and, perhaps most important, a well-defined strategy.

Although the Web is a unique medium for creating a company, launching an e-business is not much different from launching a traditional offline company. The basic drivers of a successful business are the same on the Internet as on Main Street. To be successful, both offline and online companies require a sound business model and a well-formulated strategy that emphasizes customer service. The goals of e-commerce are no different from traditional offline businesses—to increase sales, improve efficiency, and boost profits by serving customers better. How a company integrates the Internet into its overall business strategy determines how successful it will be. Following are some guidelines for building a successful e-commerce strategy for a small company.

FOCUS ON A NICHE IN THE MARKET Rather than try to compete head-to-head with the dominant players on the Web who have the resources and the brand recognition to squash smaller competitors, many entrepreneurs find success serving market niches. Smaller companies' limited resources usually are better spent focusing on niche markets than trying to be everything to everyone (recall the discussion of the focus strategy in Chapter 5). The idea is to concentrate on serving a small corner of the market that the giants have overlooked. Niches exist in every industry and can be highly profitable given the right strategy for serving them. A niche can be defined in many ways, including by geography, customer profile, product, product usage, and many others.

Because of its pervasive reach and ability to tap large numbers of customers with a common interest, the Web provides an ideal mechanism for implementing a focus strategy.

ENTREPRENEURIAL PROFILE: Paul Geller: Thankster Entrepreneur Paul Geller spotted a niche from the past created by the burgeoning world of electronic communication: handwritten thank-you notes. In 2011, Geller launched Thankster, a Web site that allows users to purchase "handwritten" thank-you notes created with proprietary technology that duplicates customers' actual handwriting and is indistinguishable from the real thing. A customer submits a scanned writing sample, which Thankster turns into a personalized font that the customer uses to "write" thank-you notes that appear to be truly handwritten. Individuals use Thankster to send thank-you notes for weddings, bar/bat mitzvahs, graduations, baby showers, and other special events. Businesses use the service to send notes to valued customers, clients, and employees. "Our digital lifestyles give us an easy way to shoot a quick thank you, but it's one without permanence," says Geller. "Thankster offers people the best way to send a heartfelt, tangible thank you in the easiest, simplest way. You don't even need to worry about buying stamps; we have that covered."[53] ■

DEVELOP A COMMUNITY On the Web, competitors are just a mouse click away. To attract customers and keep them coming back, companies have discovered the need to offer more than just quality products and excellent customer service. Many seek to develop a community of customers with similar interests, the nucleus of which is their Web site. Others include features on their Web sites that allow visitors to share content easily with the people in their social networks. These entrepreneurs intentionally build a social component into their Web sites, with the goal of increasing customers' loyalty by giving them the ability to interact with other like-minded visitors or with experts to discuss and learn more about topics about which they are passionate. A company's social media outlets are natural avenues for small companies to engage their customers because they give visitors the opportunity to have conversations about products, services, and topics that interest them ("What is your favorite sports drink?"). Adding social login options to a Web site allows customers to make purchases from their social media accounts without having to create user profiles. Small businesses that are most successful at building a community enlist their most passionate customers as company evangelists through social media outlets such as Facebook, LinkedIn, Twitter, Pinterest, Instagram, and YouTube. Companies that successfully create a community around their Web sites turn their customers into loyal fans who keep coming back and, better yet, invite others to join them. "Brands build loyalty by developing meaningful and memorable relationships with their customers," says Alex Gonzalez, founder of Chatalog, a social shopping site.[54]

Ideally, a company's Web site provides a mechanism not only for the company to connect with its customers but also for customers to engage one another. The most successful companies are those that seamlessly blend their Web sites with their social media presence and use one to support the other. Engaging customers through social media helps companies build a loyal following of fans who are passionate about its products or services and share news about the company with their friends. A recent survey by Burstmedia reports that 49 percent of active adult social networkers follow at least one brand on social media.[55] Internet users frequent sites of companies that embrace the social aspects of the Internet and give them the opportunity to interact as part of a community with other customers and with company employees.

ENTREPRENEURIAL PROFILE: Tom Amenta and Nick Palmisciano: Ranger Up Military veterans Tom Amenta and Nick Palmisciano founded Ranger Up, an e-commerce company based in Durham, North Carolina, that sells military-themed apparel, signs, and gear. They use social media to engage customers and drive sales. Ranger Up hosts a YouTube channel that features military workout videos and a hit cartoon called "The Damn Few"; the channel has nearly 15,000 subscribers and more than 4 million views. The company's blog, Rhino Den, draws 2.5 million views annually and features a Hero of the Week profile and Warrior Poetry, poems written by soldiers and veterans. Ranger Up also interacts with customers on Facebook, where its fan base is more than 200,000 strong. The company often asks its Facebook fans for input on new T-shirt designs and product ideas. "In 2011, 20 percent of our marketing budget went to social media," says Palmisciano. "In 2014, 90 percent will."[56] ■

Courtesy of Ranger Up

LISTEN TO YOUR CUSTOMERS AND ACT ON WHAT YOU HEAR On social media, customers often talk about the brands they buy and businesses with which they interact. Successful companies make a concerted effort to listen to what their customers are saying about them on social media and respond to the feedback. Because of social media, customer comments, both positive and negative, play a more important role in a company's reputation than ever before. Some negative comments are inevitable, and the worst thing a company can do is ignore them because customers do not. In fact, according to a recent survey by BrightLocal, a search engine optimization company, 85 percent of customers say they read online reviews to determine local businesses' reputations. Smart entrepreneurs take the time to tune in to social media to hear what customers are saying about their businesses so that they can resolve their customers' problems and improve their companies' reputations. Managers at the Land of Nod, an upscale children's furniture store, monitor customer reviews and ratings of its products. Recently, employees analyzed the reviews of a popular activity table that 90 percent of customers said they would recommend to a friend and discovered several negative comments about the table's surface getting scratched easily. Managers worked with the table's manufacturer to redesign the table so that its surface is more durable and then contacted the customers who had reviewed the table and offered them new tables at no cost, transforming those customers into advocates for the Land of Nod brand.[57]

ATTRACT VISITORS BY GIVING AWAY "FREEBIES" One of the most important words on the Internet is "free." Many successful e-merchants have discovered the ability to attract visitors to their sites by giving away something free and then selling them something else. One e-commerce consultant calls this cycle of giving something away and then selling something "the rhythm of the Web."[58] The "freebie" must be something customers value, but it does *not* have to be expensive, nor does it have to be a product. In fact, one of the most common giveaways on the Web is *information*. (After all, that's what most people on the Web are after!) Creating a free online or e-mail newsletter with links to your company's site, of course, and to others of interest is one of the most effective ways of driving potential customers to a site. Meaningful content presented in a clear, professional fashion is a must. Experts advise keeping online newsletters short—no more than about 600 words.

ENTREPRENEURIAL PROFILE: Craig and Tiffany Adamowski: 99 Bottles In 2009, Craig Adamowski, a former delivery driver for a beer and wine distributor, and his wife, Tiffany, opened 99 Bottles, a retail store in Federal Way, Washington, that sells more than 1,200 brands of beer, ranging from local beers and American microbrews to meads (an ancient brew made from honey) and imported brands from 43 countries. "It's important for a small business like ours to use social media to get to know our customers, to share what's new, to educate about beer, and to point them toward shared interests," says Tiffany. "Facebook, Twitter, and our not-so-weekly newsletter, *The Weekly Brews*, are how we do this." Many customers eagerly anticipate the e-mail arrival of *The Weekly Brews*, which is packed with useful and interesting information for beer drinkers, news about upcoming special in-store events, and, of course, promotions about the unique beers 99 Bottle sells. "Many customers treat our newsletter as a shopping list," she explains. "They come in with highlights and notes looking for specific products. A good newsletter promotes your social [media] outlets, links to relevant Web sites, and provides timely information on products and services for your customers." The newsletter, which has an impressive open rate of 30.1 percent, now goes to nearly 3,400 99 Bottles customers.[59] ■

SELL THE "EXPERIENCE" When shoppers enter a retail store, they are courted by an attractive layout, appealing décor, and eye-catching merchandise displays and perhaps are greeted by a salesperson who can offer them information and advice about its products and services. Although e-commerce businesses lack this ability to have face-to-face contact with customers, they can still engender loyalty by creating an engaging and enjoyable online shopping experience. Sites that offer shoppers easy navigation, a simple and fast checkout process, and thorough product descriptions with quality images can provide the same positive shopping experience that the best retail stores do.

MAKE CREATIVE USE OF E-MAIL BUT AVOID BECOMING A "SPAMMER" E-mail is still the backbone of online marketing, especially for small businesses. Numerous studies show that e-mail is the most common marketing tool among small businesses. Used properly and creatively, e-mail can be an effective, low-cost way to build traffic on a Web site. The average **open rate** (the percentage of recipients who open an e-mail) is 26.5 percent, the average **click-through rate** (the percentage of recipients who open an e-mail and click on the link to the company's Web site) for e-mail marketing is 4.6 percent, and the average **conversion rate** (the percentage of recipients who actually make a purchase) for e-mails is 3.34 percent, which is higher than the average conversion rate of 2.55 percent for Web sites as a whole.[60] One recent survey reports that marketers rank e-mail second only to search engine optimization as producing the highest return on investment of their marketing methods, outpacing paid search, social media, affiliate marketing, and mobile marketing.[61]

Just as with newsletters, an e-mail's content should offer something of value to recipients. Customers welcome well-constructed permission e-mail that directs them to a company's site for information or special deals. Unfortunately, spam, those unsolicited and universally despised e-mail messages (which rank below postal "junk mail" and telemarketing calls as the worst form of junk advertising), limits the effectiveness of companies' e-mail legitimate marketing efforts. Spam is a persistent problem for online marketers; Internet security firm Trustwave reports that 75 percent of e-mails sent are spam (and nearly 7 percent of e-mails contain links to malicious Web sites).[62] Companies must comply with the CAN-SPAM Act, a law passed in 2003 that regulates commercial e-mail and sets standards for commercial e-mail messages. (The penalties can be as much as $16,000 per e-mail for companies that violate the law.)

To avoid having their marketing messages become part of that electronic clutter, companies rely on permission e-mails, collecting customers' and visitors' e-mail addresses (and their permission to send them e-mail messages) when they register on a site to receive a freebie. The most successful online retailers post e-mail opt-in messages prominently throughout their Web sites and on their social media pages as well. When customers sign up to receive permission e-mails, a

open rate
the percentage of recipients who open an e-mail.

click-through rate
the percentage of recipients who open an e-mail and click through to the company's Web site.

conversion rate
the percentage of e-mail recipients who actually make a purchase.

company should send them "welcome" e-mails immediately. The most successful marketers give new customers a reason to open welcome e-mails, such as including an offer to "enjoy 10 percent off your first order." To be successful at collecting a sufficient number of e-mail addresses, a company must make clear to customers that they will receive messages that are meaningful to them and that the company will not sell e-mail addresses to others (which should be part of its posted privacy policy). Once a business has a customer's permission to send information in additional e-mail messages, it has a meaningful marketing opportunity to create a long-term customer relationship and to build customer loyalty.

Just as with a newsletter, an e-mail's content should offer something of value to recipients, which means that creating the right subject line is essential to success. A study of the subject lines of more than 2 billion marketing e-mails by Adestra shows that words such as "new," "free delivery," "sale," "video," "alert," "win," and "daily" produce above average open rates. In contrast, words such as "webinar," "register," "report," "offer," "only," "gift," and "save" result in below average open rates.[63] Getting to the point in the subject line also helps; a study by MailChimp shows that subject lines with fewer than 40 characters (28 to 39 characters is the "sweet spot") yield the highest open and click-through rates.[64] Customers welcome well-constructed permission e-mail that directs them to a company's site for information or special deals without resorting to a "hard sell." The experts at MailChimp say, "When it comes to e-mail marketing, the best subject lines *tell* what's inside, and the worst subject lines *sell* what's inside."[65]

MAKE SURE YOUR WEB SITE SAYS "CREDIBILITY" Online shoppers are wary, and with the prevalence of online fraud, they have every right to be. Unless a company can build visitors' trust in its Web site, selling to them is virtually impossible. Visitors begin to evaluate the credibility of a site as soon as they arrive. Studies show that shoppers form an impression of a site's credibility within just 50 milliseconds (about the same amount of time required for a hummingbird to flap its wings five times) of arrival.[66] Although quality content is crucial for converting visitors into paying customers, visitors' initial impressions of a site are almost wholly design related, which means that entrepreneurs must create sites that are simple, consistent, appealing, and easy to navigate. Does the site look professional? Are there misspelled words and typographical errors? If the site provides information, does it note the sources of that information? If so, are those sources legitimate? Are they trustworthy? Is the presentation of the information fair and objective, or is it biased? Are there dead links on the site? Does the company have its privacy and merchandise return policies posted in a prominent place?

One of the simplest ways to establish credibility with customers is to use brand names they know and trust. Whether a company sells nationally recognized brands or its own well-known private brand, using those names on its site creates a sense of legitimacy. People buy brand names they trust, and online companies can use that to their advantage. Businesses selling lesser-known brands should use customer testimonials and endorsements (with their permission, of course) about a product or service.

An effective way to build customer confidence is by joining an online seal program such as McAfee, TrustWave, TRUSTe, Norton, BBBOnline, or others. The online equivalent of the Underwriter Laboratories stamp or the Good Housekeeping Seal of Approval, these seals mean that a company meets certain standards concerning the privacy of customers' information and the resolution of customer complaints. Posting a privacy policy (more on this later in this chapter) is another key ingredient in building trust. Including customer reviews, which Internet users say they believe more than product descriptions from a business, on product Web pages increases customer loyalty and trust in an online business. Testimonials, either in writing or on video, from real customers enhance a company's online credibility, especially among first-time customers. Businesses that are the subject of media coverage should include a "media" or "featured in" page with links to articles or videos about the company so that they can magnify the benefits of publicity. Links to the company's social media accounts using "follow" buttons lend credibility to an online business. Providing a street address, an e-mail address, and a toll-free telephone number also sends a subtle message to shoppers that a legitimate business is behind a Web site.

Another effective technique is to include an "about us" page on the Web site so that customers can read about the company's "story"—its founders, a short summary of how they started the business, the challenges they have overcome, and other details. Customers enjoy supporting small businesses with which they feel a connection, and this is a perfect opportunity for a small company to establish that connection. Many small companies include photographs of their brick-and-mortar stores and of their employees to combat the Web's anonymity and to give shoppers the feeling that they are supporting a friendly small business. One small online retailer includes on his Web site short anecdotes about his dog, Cody, the official company mascot and Cody's "views" on featured products. The response to the technique has been so strong that Cody has become a celebrity among the company's customers and even has her own e-mail account. Table 9.1 offers 12 guidelines for building the credibility of a Web site.

MAKE THE MOST OF THE WEB'S GLOBAL REACH Despite the Web's reputation as an international marketplace, many entrepreneurs fail to utilize fully its global reach. More than 2.4 billion people around the world use the Internet, and nearly 89 percent of them live outside North America.[67] In addition, more than 73 percent of Web users throughout the world speak a language other than English.[68] Limiting a global market to only a small portion of its potential by ignoring foreign customers makes little sense. E-companies wanting to draw significant sales from foreign markets must design their sites with their foreign customers in mind. Global shoppers are much more likely to purchase from sites that are written in their own languages. The most common languages that U.S.-based e-commerce companies translate their content into are French, Spanish, German, Chinese, and Japanese.[69] A common strategy is to include several "language buttons" on the opening page of a site that take customers to pages in the language of their choice. However, experienced e-commerce companies have learned that offering a localized page for every country or region they target pays off in increased sales. Doing so allows entrepreneurs to adapt the terminology they use on their sites and in their search engines to local dialects. For instance, an e-commerce company based in the United States might think it is selling diapers, but its customers in Australia and the United Kingdom are looking for "nappies."

Virtual companies trying to establish a foothold in foreign markets by setting up Web sites dedicated to them run the same risk that actual companies do: offending international visitors by using the business conventions and standards the companies are accustomed to using in the United States. Business practices, even those used online, that are acceptable, even expected, in the United States may be taboo in other countries. Color schemes can be important, too. Selecting the "wrong" colors and symbols on a site targeting people in a particular country can hurt sales and offend visitors. A little research into the subtleties of a target country's culture and business practices can save a great deal of embarrassment and money. Creating secure, simple, and reliable payment methods for foreign customers also will boost sales. International delivery services offer software that small companies can incorporate into their Web sites that calculate the final "landed cost" (including relevant tariffs and duties) of orders and estimate delivery dates.

When translating the content of their Web sites into other languages, entrepreneurs must use extreme caution. This is *not* the time to pull out their notes from an introductory Spanish course and begin their own translations. Hiring professional translation and localization services to convert a company's Web content into other languages minimizes the likelihood of a company unintentionally offending foreign customers.

GO MOBILE The typical online shopper has expanded his or her reach across multiple screens (and screen sizes). Research by Jumptap and comScore shows that 51 percent of the time spent on the Internet is through a mobile device (12 percent on tablets and 39 percent on smart phones).[70] More than 64 percent of mobile phone users own smart phones, and 35 percent of Americans 16 and older own tablets.[71] According to the Pew Internet and American Life Project, 21 percent of mobile phone owners' primary use of their phones is to access the Internet. These mobile users continue to increase the frequency with which they make online purchases from their devices (m-commerce). In fact, the average amount per order for smart phones ($97.82) and tablets ($96.84) is larger than the average amount per order for desktop computers ($91.76). However, conversion rates for mobile devices (1.01 percent for smart phones and 3.12 percent for tablets) are lower than those for desktop computers (3.28 percent).[72] Despite the rapid growth of m-commerce (see Figure 9.5), only 34 percent of small businesses have developed Web sites that are optimized for smart phones.[73] Companies that fail to develop Web sites that display

TABLE 9.1 Twelve Guidelines for Building the Credibility of a Web Site

Guideline	Tips
1. Allow visitors to verify easily the accuracy of the information on your site.	Include references, which you should cite, from credible third parties to support the information you present on your site.
2. Show that there are real people behind your site.	List a physical address for your business and post photographs of your store or office or the people who work there. Photos allow shoppers to put faces with the names of the people with whom they are dealing.
3. Emphasize the skills, experience, and knowledge of the people in your company.	Tell visitors about the experts you have on your team, their credentials, and their accomplishments. Is your company or your employees associated with a well-known, respected national organization? If so, mention it and provide a link to its Web site.
4. Show that honest, trustworthy people stand behind your site.	In addition to posting photographs of the owner and employees, include brief biographical sketches that might include "fun" facts about each person, their hobbies, and links to blogs they create. Erik Leamon, owner of The Ride, a full-service bicycle store in Conway, Arkansas, markets the charm of his business on The Ride's Web site, which profiles the company's five employees, including Pokey, the shop dog, who serves as the shop's unofficial customer service representative.
5. Make it easy for customers to contact you.	One of the simplest ways to enhance your site's credibility is to include contact information in a highly visible location. Be sure to include a physical address, a telephone number, and e-mail addresses. Always respond promptly to customer communications.
6. Make sure your site has a professional look.	Online shoppers evaluate the quality of a Web site by its appearance within the first few seconds of arriving. Pay careful attention to layout, navigation, search tools, images, grammar, spelling, and other seemingly "minor" details because they *do* make a difference. A professional site does not have to look "corporate" to be professional, however. It should reflect your company's unique personality.
7. Make your site easy to use—and useful.	Sites that are easy for customers to use and that are useful to them score high on credibility. Resist the temptation to dazzle visitors with all of the coolest features; instead, focus on keeping your site simple and user friendly. Visitors perceive sites that combine useful information with a purchasing opportunity as more credible than those that merely try to sell them something.
8. Update your site regularly.	Visitors rate sites that show they have been updated or reviewed recently higher than those that contain outdated or obsolete information.
9. Prominently display your company's privacy policy.	Visitors perceive sites that display a meaningful privacy policy—and follow it—as more credible than those that do not.
10. Be vigilant for errors of all types, no matter how insignificant they may seem.	Typographical errors, misspellings, grammatical mistakes, broken links, and other problems cause a site to lose credibility in customers' eyes. Details matter!
11. Post the seals of approval your company has won.	Seals of approval from third parties such as the Better Business Bureau, TRUSTe, WebTrust, and others give shoppers confidence that an online company is reputable and trustworthy.
12. Make sure customers know their online transactions are secure.	To conduct business effectively online, companies must ensure that customers' credit card transactions are secure. Online retailers typically use Secure Sockets Layer technology that is verified as secure by a third party such as VeriSign. Be sure to post the secure seal prominently on your Web site.

Sources: Based on J. Walker, "Instilling Credibility into Your Web Site," GNC Web Creations, 2011, http://www.gnc-web-creations.com/website-credibility.htm; B. J. Fogg, "Stanford Guides for Web Credibility: A Research Summary from the Stanford Persuasive Technology Lab," Stanford University, May 2002, http://www.webcredibility.org/guidelines; and "The Ride: Your Full Service Bicycle Store," http://therideonline.net/index.php?option=com_frontpage&Itemid=1.

effectively on mobile devices suffer from lower search engine results listings and miss out on potential sales. However, the payoff for businesses that cater to mobile shoppers is significant; 84 percent of the companies that have created dedicated mobile Web sites say they have experienced increased sales.[74]

Because mobile devices have smaller screens than desktop PCs, they cannot display traditional Web sites properly. One recent study reports that 93.3 percent of U.S. small business's

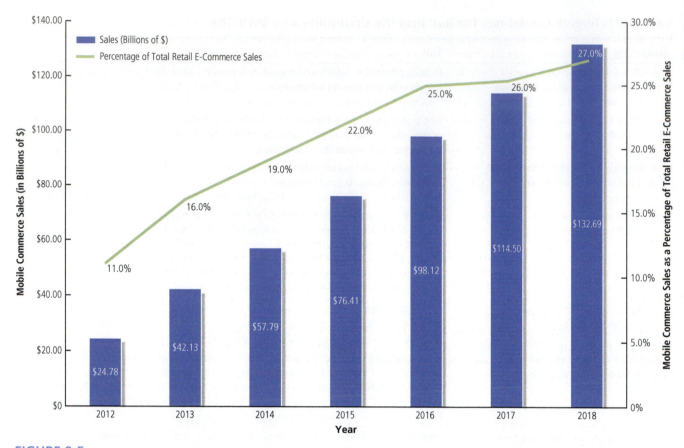

FIGURE 9.5

Mobile Commerce Sales

Source: Based on data from eMarketer, April 10, 2014.

responsive Web sites
Web sites that conform naturally and seamlessly to the size and resolution of the screen on which they are displayed.

Web sites do note render properly on mobile devices.[75] That creates a considerable problem because 61 percent of mobile users say that they quickly move on to other sites when they cannot navigate a site and find the items they want to purchase. Conversely, 67 percent of mobile users say that when they visit a mobile-friendly site, they are *more* likely to make a purchase from the company.[76] By investing a little more time and money to create **responsive Web sites**, those that conform naturally and seamlessly to the size and resolution of the screen on which they are displayed, small companies can accommodate customers on *any* device from which they want to shop. A responsive Web design takes a "one size fits all" approach and eliminates the necessity of creating multiple versions of a Web site for various platforms and moves a company's Web site higher in Google's all-important search engine rankings. Experts say a common mistake many businesses make is assuming that they must present the same Web content on all screens. Smart entrepreneurs design their responsive sites to simplify the content that appears on mobile users' screens and making navigation and "add to cart" buttons easier to see and touch.

social-local-mobile (SoLoMo) strategies
marketing strategies aimed at capitalizing on shoppers' pervasive use of social media, mobile devices, and search engines to find the products and services they want to purchase and the businesses that sell them.

Consumers' pervasive use of mobile devices, social media, and search engines has led businesses to develop integrated **social-local-mobile (SoLoMo) strategies**. Shoppers use these three tools to enhance their shopping experiences, and smart entrepreneurs can use that tendency to their advantage with an appropriate SoLoMo strategy. Eighty percent of smart phone users access social media sites (Facebook, Instagram, and Twitter are most popular) with their devices, and 94 percent use their devices to search for information on local businesses. After searching for a local business, 70 percent of users call the business and 66 percent of them visit the store. Half of all smart phone owners also use their phones to assist them while they are shopping in stores.[77]

What can small companies do to capitalize on the SoLoMo trend? One of the most important steps a company can take is to create a responsive Web site that is optimized for mobile devices. Entrepreneurs also should design their sites for achieve high rankings in local searches. For instance, a jeweler in Birmingham, Alabama, would include location-related terms in the titles, tags, and text of its Web pages and in the key words on which it bids (e.g., Birmingham jewelry, Birmingham diamonds, Birmingham necklaces, and others). Mobile sites also should automatically display the store's address, operating hours, and telephone number (with a click-to-call button) and include a prominent map. Some business owners also offer location-based special offers or discounts to encourage customers to visit the store. Businesses can create listings on Yelp, FourSquare, Google+Local, and other sites to encourage mobile users to locate nearby businesses and "check in" when they arrive. Once inside a store, customers expect free Wi-Fi, which allows local stores to offer apps that allow shoppers to view product features, prices, and customer reviews, all of which can help close a sale. When designing mobile Web sites, companies also must be aware that speed is important (although mobile customers are somewhat more forgiving than those who use desktop PCs). Half of mobile customers say they abandon sites that require more than 10 seconds to load.[78]

ENTREPRENEURIAL PROFILE: Deb Shops Deb Shops, a fashion retailer whose product line is aimed at teenage girls, recently updated the way in which its Web site appears on shoppers' mobile devices, particularly smart phones. The company added a "What's Hot" button to its mobile commerce site that displays all of the apparel that currently is trending on Facebook, Pinterest, and Instagram and allows shoppers to find the latest fashions with one tap. With more than 30,000 products, enabling customers using mobile devices to get to the products they are most interested in is essential. Shoppers who tap the "What's Hot" button are 20 percent more likely to make a purchase and generate 170 percent more revenue than those who do not. In the site update, Deb Shops also added a "More Like This" button that displays for customers other products that are similar to the ones they are viewing. The percentage of traffic that arrives at the company's Web site from smart phones has grown steadily, from 15 percent to more than 50 percent in just two years.[79] ■

PROMOTE YOUR WEB SITE ONLINE AND OFFLINE E-commerce entrepreneurs must use every means available—both online and offline—to promote their Web sites and to drive traffic to them. In addition to using traditional online techniques, such as registering with search engines, using pay-per-click techniques, and creating blogs, Web entrepreneurs must promote their sites offline as well. Ads in other media, such as direct mail or newspapers, that mention a site's URL will bring customers to it. It is also a good idea to put the company's Web address on *everything* a company publishes, from its advertisements and letterhead to shopping bags, business cards, and even employees' uniforms! The techniques for generating publicity for an offline business described in Chapter 8 can be just as effective for online businesses needing to make their domain names better known without breaking their budgets. A passive approach to generating Web site traffic is a recipe for failure; entrepreneurs who are as innovative at promoting their e-businesses as they are at creating them can attract impressive numbers of visitors to their sites.

USE SOCIAL MEDIA TOOLS TO ATTRACT AND RETAIN CUSTOMERS The social aspects of the Internet that are evident in sites such as Facebook, Twitter, LinkedIn, and YouTube have become key components of companies' e-commerce efforts. Social media marketing techniques recognize that shoppers, especially young ones, expect to take a proactive role in their shopping experience by writing (and reading) product reviews, asking questions, reading and writing blogs, watching and creating videos, posting comments, and engaging in other interactive behavior. According to the Pew Internet and American Life Project, 73 percent of online adults participate in social networks, a significant increase from just 8 percent in 2005. The highest level of participation in social media is among adults under 30.[80] In addition, 78 percent of adult Internet users watch online videos (comedy and how-to videos are most popular), 32 percent read blogs, and 32 percent post online reviews of products and services. Shoppers perceive online reviews and blogs as credible, and they influence buying behavior.[81] According to one study, 52 percent of consumers say blogs have influenced their purchasing decisions.[82]

Small businesses are responding to the opportunity to connect with their customers online by adding the following social components to their e-commerce strategies:

- *Mashups.* A **mashup** is a Web site or an application that combines content from multiple sources into a single Web service. For example, Twitzu is a mashup that allows users to manage invitations and responses to events. They invite their Twitter followers to an event—the grand opening of a new location, for example—and then receive responses from guests on Twitter.

mashup
a Web site or an application that combines content from multiple sources.

Use a Mobile-First, Responsive Web Design to Increase Online Sales

Mobile commerce is the hottest trend in e-commerce. Increasingly, shoppers are accessing companies' Web sites from mobile devices such as smart phones and tablets, and entrepreneurs must take this trend into account when designing their companies' Web sites. Shoppers who encounter a Web site designed for a traditional desktop computer on a mobile device will move on to a competitors' site almost immediately rather than attempt to negotiate the garbled mess that appears on their mobile screens. Unfortunately, only 34 percent of small business Web sites are optimized for mobile commerce. Thanks to responsive Web design, the challenge of creating a mobile-friendly Web site is relatively easy to manage. A responsive Web site is one that conforms naturally and seamlessly to the size and resolution of the screen on which it is displayed. In other words, the site's content adapts to fit the screen size and features of the device on which the shopper is using. Skinny Ties, a family-owned business that sells its namesake product online, recently switched from desktop-oriented Web site to a responsive Web site, which required company owners to reconsider the site's content, features, and functions. "It meant throwing out things that weren't really useful," says Brendan Falkowski, the company's e-commerce consultant. Managers used a "mobile-first" philosophy as part of their responsive Web design. "Instead of planning the look of the site on a big screen, where you have a lot of space to move things around, we looked at content on the small screen first, where you don't have that freedom." After Skinny Ties switched to its mobile-first responsive Web design, the company saw sales increase 42.4 percent, its conversion rate increase by 13.6 percent, and its bounce rate decline 23.2 percent. Sales from mobile devices also increased by an impressive 211 percent.

By using the following principles, a small business can create an effective mobile Web site with an above-average conversion rate and a below-average bounce rate.

- *Simplicity reigns.* When designing a responsive Web site, entrepreneurs must remember that mobile shoppers are viewing their companies' sites on the smaller screens of their mobile devices—often just 3 or 4 inches on a smart phone and 10 inches on a tablet. "You've got to rethink your entire page layout for mobile because of the tiny screens," says David Gould, CEO of mShopper, a company that provides mobile commerce platforms. Therefore, simple sites that are well designed and intuitive and allow users to find what they are looking for quickly are most effective. "The context also is a challenge; you're trying to reach a user who is on the go and whose needs are different." Eliminate superfluous content and large graphics, and create tabs users can tap to access more detailed information. Fast download times translate into higher conversion rates, especially on mobile devices.

- *Create a clean layout and easy navigation.* On small screens, every square millimeter is important, and a company's site must make the most of every one. Clean, easy-to-follow layouts and simple navigation are essential for m-commerce success, especially on the home page. Avoid using too many levels of subpages and be sure to give customers an easy way back to the home page from any page in the site. Larger fonts actually work better on small screens. Action buttons (e.g., "Click to add to cart") and links should be large enough for users to tap easily with their fingers.

- *Make sure your company's unique selling proposition (USP) is the focal point of the site.* As you learned in Chapter 8, a company's unique selling proposition explains in just a few words why customers should buy from your business rather than the competition. Toolfetch, an online retailer of tools and construction equipment with an inventory of more than 300,000 products, displays its USP clearly for all shoppers: "Search faster. Done faster." The company also uses a clever tag line its customers can relate to around its search engine box: "Hand me that _____ will ya?"

- *Develop your site's content with your target customer in mind.* As you design your site, think about the needs users are trying to satisfy by visiting it from a mobile device and then focus its content on meeting those needs. Are they trying to find a fast, convenient place to eat lunch, or are they looking for help in selecting the right cordless drill?

- *Include a call to action on every page.* Every page on a company's Web site should include an appropriate call to action. Do you want the customer to register for a newsletter or a Webinar? Download a white paper? Like your company on Facebook? Make a purchase? Making call-to-action buttons so large that they take up the entire width of the screen increases the probability that visitors will take the desired action.

- *Go easy on text and incorporate photographs and videos.* Expecting mobile users to read pages of text on tiny screens is fruitless; instead, rely on videos and photographs to capture their attention. Judicious use of videos also can draw customers into a site.

- *Use tabs, expandable content, and links to avoid scrolling.* Scrolling down a Web site to reach desired content is more difficult for mobile users than for desktop computer users. Therefore, mobile sites should rely on tabs, expandable content, and links to give users access to more detailed information. Outdoor retailer Orvis, for example, uses highly visible tabs shoppers can tap to reach more product details, customer reviews, and size charts for its products.

- *Minimize the number of steps in the checkout process.* Faster, shorter checkout times improve a site's conversion rate. At Toolfetch, 15 percent of Web site traffic comes from smart phones and 20 percent comes from tablets, which led the company to create a one-step checkout process rather than the three to four steps that many companies use on their mobile sites. "We found that a higher percentage of customers would abandon the checkout process with an extra step or two," says Andrew Brown, cofounder and CEO of Toolfetch. "We kept the mobile site very light on its feet."

Sources: Based on Peep Laja, "How Responsive Design Boosts Mobile Conversions," *Conversion XL*, Maarch 22, 2013, http://conversionxl.com/how-responsive-design-boosts-mobile-conversions/#.; Jason Ankeny, "A New Tool to Build a Mobile Storefront," *Entrepreneur*, November 23, 2010, http://www.entrepreneur.com/article/217532; Bill Siwicki, "Skinny Ties Gets a 211% Bump in Mobile Sales with Its Responsive Design Site," *Internet Retailer*, May 2, 2013, http://www.internetretailer.com/2013/05/02/skinny-ties-gets-211-bump-mobile-sales-its-responsive; Bill Siwicki, "Toolfetch.com Retools Its E-commerce and M-commerce Sites," *Internet Retailer*, July 10, 2013, http://www.internetretailer.com/2013/07/10/toolfetchcom-retools-its-e-commerce-and-m-commerce-sites; Hernán Gonzales, "Make It Work," *Website Magazine*, February 2013, p. 38; Ayaz Nanji, "How Small Business Owners Are Using Mobile Technology," *MarketingProfs*, May 17, 2013, http://www.marketingprofs.com/charts/2013/10791/how-small-business-owners-are-using-mobile-technology.

- *Really Simple Syndication.* **Really Simple Syndication (RSS)** is an application that allows subscribers to aggregate content from their favorite Web sites into a single feed that is delivered automatically whenever the content is updated. RSS is ideal for companies whose customers are information junkies. "[RSS] is a must-have for any company Web site or blog because it allows people to track current news via their RSS feeds," says Louis Columbus, an expert on using social media.[83]

- *Social networking.* Many small businesses drive traffic to their Web sites through their Facebook, Pinterest, and Instagram pages; Twitter posts; and LinkedIn accounts. They use their Web sites as a "hub" supported by the "spokes" of social media. Web sites that include a social sign-in feature, which allows social media users to bypass creating accounts and passwords when they log into a company's Web site, create a seamless integration between a company's Web site and social media. Many small businesses have discovered that social media provide an excellent platform for engaging and interacting with their customers and listening to what their customers are saying about their businesses, products, and services. "It is essential that all employees become the eyes and ears of an organization on social media," says entrepreneur Bryan Holmes, founder of HootSuite Media in Vancouver, British Columbia.[84]

ENTREPRENEURIAL PROFILE: Peter and Morton's Steakhouse After a long day of business meetings in Florida, Peter Shankman, CEO of Geek Factory, was about to board a flight back to Newark Airport (EWR) when he jokingly sent a tweet to his favorite restaurant, Morton's Steakhouse, that said "Hey @Mortons – can you meet me at the Newark Airport with a porterhouse when I land in two hours? Thanks." Employees at the Morton's Steakhouse saw the tweet and contacted the manager at the Hackensack, New Jersey, location, which is 23 miles from Newark Airport. When Shankman stepped into the airport terminal, he saw a waiter from Morton's dressed in a tuxedo holding a takeout bag that contained a 24-ounce porterhouse steak, an order of colossal shrimp, a side of potatoes, Morton's signature bread, two napkins, and silverware. "Oh. My. God. I don't believe it. Morton's showed up at EWR WITH A PORTERHOUSE!" read Shankman's next tweet, which went to more than 100,000 followers. He also blogged about the incident, creating even more goodwill for the Morton's Steakhouse chain. Soon, Twitter and other social media were filled with posts from customers around the country saying they had just enjoyed wonderful meals at Morton's.[85] ■

Businesses also have discovered that encouraging customers to post their favorite products to their Facebook pages or sending tweets about them increases sales.

- *Wikis.* A **wiki** is a dynamic collection of Web pages that allows users to add to or edit their content. The most popular wiki is Wikipedia, the user-created online encyclopedia for which users provide the content. Some companies use wikis to encourage customers to participate in the design of their products, a process called *cocreation.*

- *Widgets.* Another tool small companies use to attract attention on the Web is **widgets** (also known as gadgets), low-cost applications that appear like small television screens on Web

Really Simple Syndication (RSS)
an application that allows subscribers to aggregate content from their favorite Web sites into a single feed that is delivered automatically whenever the content is updated.

wiki
a dynamic collection of Web pages that allows users to add to or edit their content.

widget
a low-cost application that appears like a small television screen on a Web site, a blog, or a computer desktop and performs a specific function.

sites, blogs, or computer desktops and perform specific functions. Entrepreneurs can create their own widgets or purchase them from developers and customize them, adding their own names, brands, and logos. Customers and visitors can download the widget to their desktops or, perhaps, post it to their own blogs or social media pages, where other Web users see it and the social nature of the Web exposes the company to thousands of potential customers. A popular widget not only drives customers to a site but also can improve a company's ranking on major search engines.

- *Apps.* Like widgets, apps provide a simple way for businesses to stay in their customers' minds and to generate sales. Sebastian's Café, a five-unit chain of salad and sandwich shops in Boston, uses a loyalty program app that keeps customers engaged. Depending on how much they spend at Sebastian's Café, customers earn points and the opportunity to move their status from "Fresh" to "Fresh-a-licious," earning special deals, discounts, and complimentary meals along the way. The branded app tracks customers' progress and notifies them of menu changes, upcoming events, and specials. Since launching the app, owner Mike Conley says the chain's customer visits have increased 30 percent and total revenue has increased 17 percent.[86]

DEVELOP AN EFFECTIVE SEARCH ENGINE OPTIMIZATION STRATEGY Search engine optimization strategies have become an essential part of online companies' marketing strategies. With nearly 700 million Web sites (and growing) in existence, it is no surprise that online shoppers' first stop usually is a search engine; 89 percent of shoppers rely on search engines to help them find information about business, products, and services before they make purchases.[87] As a result, entrepreneurs are devoting more of their marketing budgets to search engine optimization strategies that are focused on landing their Web sites at or near the top of the most popular search engines. For a company engaged in e-commerce, a well-defined search engine optimization strategy is a vital part of its overall marketing strategy. Search engines drive more traffic to e-commerce sites (33.1 percent) than either e-mail (3.3 percent) or social media (1.46 percent).[88] A recent study by Custora reports that customers who find a company's Web site through a search engine produce a higher lifetime value (54 percent above average) than customers who arrive at a site as a result of e-mail marketing, affiliate ads, banner ads, or social media.[89]

One of the biggest challenges facing e-commerce entrepreneurs is maintaining the effectiveness of their search engine marketing strategies. Because the most popular search engines are constantly updating and refining their algorithms—the secretive formulas and methodology search engines use to find and rank the results of Web searches—entrepreneurs also must evaluate and constantly refine their search strategies. After Google, the leading search engine with 67 percent market share, changed its algorithms recently, many businesses that had ranked highly in searches found that their listings fell sharply down the search engine results page.

natural (organic) listings
search engine listings that are the result of "spiders," powerful programs that crawl around the Web and analyze sites for key words, links, and other data.

search engine optimization (SEO)
the process of managing the content, key words, titles, tags, features, and design of a Web site so that it appears at or near the top of Internet search results.

A company's Web search strategy must incorporate the two basic types of search engine results: natural or organic listings and paid or sponsored listings. Although shoppers more often click on organic listings (60 percent vs. 40 percent for paid listings), paid listings generate higher net revenue per visit than organic listings.[90] **Natural (organic) listings** arise as a result of "spiders," powerful programs that search engines use to crawl around the Web and analyze sites for key words, links, and other data. Based on what they find, spiders use complex algorithms to index Web sites so that a search engine can display a listing of relevant Web sites when a person enters a key word in the engine to start a search. Some search engines use people-powered searches rather than spider-powered ones to assemble their indexes. With natural listings, an entrepreneur's goal is to get his or her Web site displayed at or near the top of the list of search results. **Search engine optimization (SEO)** involves managing the content, key words, titles, tags, features, and design of a Web site so that it appears at or near the top of Internet search results. The reason that SEO is so important is that nearly 92 percent of search engine users click on a link to a site that appears on the first page of the search results (see Figure 9.6).[91] "The difference between being seen on page one and page two of search results can mean thousands, even

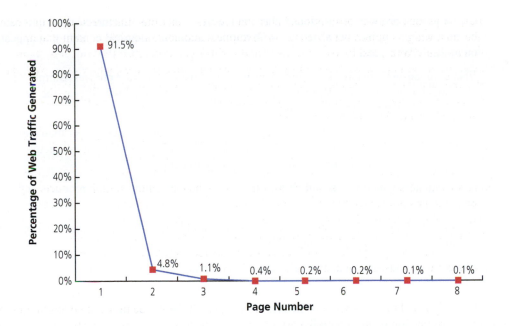

FIGURE 9.6

Percentage of Traffic Generated by Page on Google Search Results

Source: Based on data from Chitika Insights, June 2013.

millions, of dollars for a business in revenue," says Martin Falle, CEO of SEO Research, a search engine marketing company.[92] A useful resource for entrepreneurs is SEO Book, a search engine optimization site (www.seobook.com) that offers both free tools and more than 100 training modules on a variety of SEO topics.

A fierce battle among online competitors rages for landing on the first page of search results. Companies can use the following tips to improve their search placement results:

- Conduct brainstorming sessions to develop a list of key words and phrases that searchers are likely to use when using a search engine to locate a company's products and services and then use those words and phrases on your Web pages. Usually, simple terms are better than industry jargon.

- Use Google's AdWords Keyword Tool or Microsoft Bing Ads to determine how many monthly searches users conduct globally and locally for a key word or phrase. More specific, lower-volume key words and phrases usually produce higher search rankings because they provide potential customers the more focused results they are seeking.

- Use these key words in the title tags (metatags, which are limited to 140 characters) and headlines of your Web pages. Some search engines are geared to pick them up. For best results, you should focus each page of your site on one specific key word or phrase that should appear in the page's title. Placing key words in these critical locations can be tedious, but it produces better search results for the companies that take the time to do it.

- Create meaningful, relevant content for each Web page with your customers and their needs in mind. Each page should contain at least 1,000 to 2,000 words that are relevant to the key word used in the title tag. Entrepreneurs should avoid artificially "stuffing" content (and title tags) with key words because most search engines penalize sites that attempt this maneuver. The average Web page that appears on the first page in Google rankings contains more than 2,000 words.[93] Organize the text into well-structured paragraphs using subheadings and bullets and include photographs and illustrations (that have file names that match the key word of that page) and videos. Content that answers typical questions customers ask increases a site's search ranking.

- Encourage social media shares. The more shares a site's content gets on social media, the more relevant it is to search engines.

- Create unique product descriptions rather than merely copy manufacturers' descriptions because search engines penalize sites with duplicate content, identical content that appears on multiple Web sites.

- Visit competitors' sites for key word ideas but avoid using the exact phrases. Simply right-clicking on a competitor's Web page and choosing "View Source" will display the key words used in the metatags on the site.

- Consider using less obvious key words and brand names. For instance, rather than using simply "bicycles," a small bicycle retailer should consider key words such as "racing bikes" "road racing bike," or "LeMond" to draw customers.

- Ask customers which words and phrases they use when searching for the products and services the company sells.

- Use data analytics tools to find the words and phrases (and the search engines) that brought visitors to the company's Web site.

- Check blogs and bulletin boards related to the company's products and services for potential key terms.

- Don't forget about misspellings; people often misspell the words they type into search engines. Include them in your list.

- Hire services such as Wordtracker that monitor and analyze Web users' search engine tendencies.

- Block irrelevant results with "negative key words," those that are excluded in a search. Twenty percent of small businesses do not use any negative keywords in their Google AdWords accounts.[94]

- Include links to other relevant Web sites and land links to your Web site on high-profile Web sites. Search engines rank sites that have external links to high-volume sites higher than those that do not.

- Start a blog. Well-written blogs not only draw potential customers to your site but also tend to attract links from other Web sites. Blogs also allow entrepreneurs to use key words strategically and frequently, moving their sites up in search result rankings.

- Post videos on your site. In addition to uploading them to video sites such as YouTube, companies can wait for organic listings to appear, or they can submit their videos to search engines for listing. Forrester Research estimates that a properly submitted video is 50 times more likely to achieve a first-page listing on Google than any text-based page.[95]

paid (sponsored) listings

short advertisements with links to the sponsoring company's Web site that appear on the results page of a search engine when the user types in a key word or phrase.

Because organic listings can take months to materialize, many e-commerce companies rely on paid listings, giving them an immediate presence in search engines. **Paid (sponsored) listings** are short text advertisements with links to the sponsoring company's Web site that appear on the results pages of a search engine when a user types in a key word or phrase. Entrepreneurs use paid search listings to accomplish what natural listings cannot. Fortunately, just three search engines—Google, Microsoft Bing, and Yahoo!—account for 96 percent of the searches conducted in the United States.[96] Google, the most popular search engine with 67 percent of all searches, displays paid listings as "sponsored links" at the top and down the side of each results page, and Yahoo! shows "sponsored results" at the top and the bottom of its results pages. Advertisers bid on key words to determine their placement on a search engine's results page. On Google, an ad's placement in search results is a function of the ad's relevance (determined by a quality score of 1 to 10 that Google assigns) and the advertiser's bid on the key word. The average quality score on Google currently is 5.[97] The ad that gets the most prominent placement (at the top) of the search engine's results page when a user types in that key word on the search engine is the one with the highest combination of quality score and bid price. An advertiser pays only when a shopper clicks through to its Web site from the search engine. For this reason, paid listings also are called pay-for-placement, pay-per-click, and pay-for-performance ads. The higher an ad's quality score, the lower is its cost per click. Compared to an ad with an average quality score of 5, an ad with a quality score of just 1 produces a cost-per-click that is 400 percent higher. However, an ad with a perfect quality score of 10 has a cost-per-click that is 50 percent lower than one with an average quality score.[98]

The average cost per click on Google AdWords is 53 cents, up from 38 cents in 2005.[99]* Although paid listings can be expensive, they allow advertisers to evaluate their effectiveness using the statistical reports the search engine generates. Pay-per-click advertisers can control costs by geotargeting their ads, having them appear only in certain areas, and by setting a spending limit per day.

Using generic terms results in large numbers of searches but often produces very small conversion rates and very little in sales; normally, entrepreneurs get better results bidding on more precise, lower-volume ("long-tail") key words. Rather than competing with much larger companies for 5 or 10 common key words, a more effective strategy is to bid on 200 less popular, more specific key words that produce clicks from customers who are more likely to buy. The typical small business spends $1,200 per month on pay-per-click advertising and bids on 212 key words.[100]

ENTREPRENEURIAL PROFILE: Matt Lauzon: Gemvara Jake Sharpless, marketing specialist at online jeweler Gemvara, a company founded by Babson College student Matt Lauzon, has had success focusing on less expensive, specific words and "long-tail" phrases because they are not as popular (or expensive) as more common terms. For instance, rather than bidding on the common term "jewelry," Sharpless bids on specific words such as "necklaces," "ruby necklaces," or "fire opal wedding rings." "By using long-tail terms, you're going to match better with customers and pay less for the terms," he says. Sharpless also bids on common misspellings of key words and blocks irrelevant results with negative key words.[101] ■

Google's **product listing ads (PLAs)** show more information, including product images, prices, business name, and a short promotional message, than do traditional text ads. PLAs appear in their own box separate from plain text ads in Google's search results. Businesses set up PLAs through either their AdWords account or through Google's Merchant Center. One study shows that PLAs offer higher click-through rates (21 percent) and lower cost-per-click (26 percent) than text ads.[102] Online magazine *Search Engine Watch* (http://searchenginewatch.com/) provides many useful resources for entrepreneurs who seek to optimize their search engine strategies.

One problem facing companies that rely on paid listings and display ads to generate Web traffic is **click fraud**, which occurs when a company pays for clicks that are generated by someone with no interest in or intent to purchase a product or service. "Botnets," programs that hijack computers around the world to generate thousands of phony clicks on a Web site, are a common source of click fraud. Botnets also are the source of digital ad fraud, which occurs when they generate phony traffic to Web sites on which businesses then pay for advertising space that no one sees. Although the cost of click fraud is difficult to measure, one security company estimates that botnets drive 29 percent of global display ad traffic and cost companies up to $10 billion annually. A botnet known as ZeroAccess hijacked nearly 2 million computers around the world whose 1.9 billion phony clicks per day cost online companies $90,000 per day before officials could shut it down.[103] Web analytics software can help online merchants detect click fraud. Large numbers of visitors who leave within seconds of arriving at a site, computer IP addresses that appear from all over the world, and pay-per-click costs that rise without any corresponding increase in sales are clues that a company is a victim of click fraud.

Designing a Killer Web Site

Setting up a shop online has never been easier, but creating a Web site that drives sales requires time and commitment. To be successful, entrepreneurs must pay careful attention to the look, feel, efficiency, and navigability of their Web sites and the impression their sites create with shoppers. A site's look and design determine a visitor's first impression of the company. "Your Web site isn't 'about' your company," says one writer. "It's an extension of your company. If it's

product listing ads
paid ads on Google that show more information, including product images, prices, business name, and a short promotional message, than traditional text ads.

click fraud
a situation that occurs when a company pays for clicks that are generated by someone with no interest in or intent to purchase its products or services.

LO4
Learn the techniques of designing a killer Web site.

---

*An online merchant's cost per sale = cost per click ÷ merchant's conversion rate. For example, a merchant with a 1 percent conversion rate who submits a key word bid of 10 cents per click is paying $10 per sale ($0.10 ÷ 0.01 = $10).

You Be the Consultant

A Total Makeover

After Michael Lowe retired from his work as an attorney for Verizon Communications, he was bored and looking for a new challenge in life. His son-in-law, John Uselton, who had experience in the beverage distribution and hospitality industries, approached him with the idea of opening a gin distillery in Washington, DC. Distilling spirits requires a federal permit and is rife with regulations, but the determined entrepreneurs managed to work their way through all of the regulatory requirements and opened New Columbia Distillers, the first distillery in the nation's capital since Congress passed the Eighteenth Amendment to the U.S. Constitution that ushered in Prohibition. To hone their distilling skills, Lowe and Uselton engaged internships at the Dry Fly Distilling School in Spokane, Washington. "We trained to the point where the operators let us make entire product batches," says Uselton.

After returning to Washington, DC, Lowe and Uselton leased an empty warehouse and spent the next year installing all of the infrastructure and equipment their distillery process required. In a clever marketing maneuver, they decided to name their product Green Hat Gin in honor of George Cassiday, who made a successful career providing bootleg liquor to many Congressmen during Prohibition. The dapper Cassiday, who actually set up an office in basement of the House office building and later the Senate office building, was famous for the green fedora he always wore.

Because each batch their company distills produces only about 50 cases of gin, the supply of Green Hat Gin is limited, which heightens the importance of the company's marketing efforts. The entrepreneurial duo and their wives, who also help with the business, knew that their company's Web site would be a significant part of its success and that it had to resonate with their contemporary, tech-savvy target market, yet it also had to reflect the nostalgic feel of the Prohibition era. Lowe and Uselton used a small, local creative firm, Design Army, owned by copreneurs Jake and Pum Lefebure, to design the Green Hat Gin logo and Web site. The distinctive site features the look of a catalog from the 1920s with a distinctive hat motif and includes sections about Prohibition, the company, its namesake, its products, and the distilling process. In addition to its vintage look, it also includes fonts that are reminiscent of newspapers of the era. Visitors also can sign up for e-mail updates about new products, tasting tours, special events, and bottling parties, in which they can show up at the distillery and help bottle the latest batch. The site also includes cocktail recipes that use gin (of course). The design team's goal was to emphasize the unique nature of New Columbia Distillers'

Matt McClain for The Washington Post via Getty Images

Green Hat Gin by creating a Web site that has a look and feel all its own and that is completely different from the Web sites of traditional spirits companies. The design also is consistent with New Columbia Distillers' image, style, and personality. "We didn't want to create just a click, click, click site," says Jake Lefebure. "We wanted something more fluid and smooth, in the same way you would read a newspaper. We also knew a lot of users would be on mobile and tablets, so making it natural to those devices was the way to go." Despite the site's simple navigation and vintage look, its underlying mechanics are very much cutting-edge. The Web site is doing its job. Lowe says many customers who visit the distillery say the company's spectacular Web site convinced them to see it in person. "Good design is no longer just cosmetic or 'making something pretty,'" says Pum Lefebure. "Good designers think strategically."

1. Is creating a Web site that reflects a company's "personality" important? Explain.

2. What benefits does a brick-and-mortar business gain when its Web site becomes an extension of its storefront rather than just another marketing tool?

3. Visit New Columbia Distillery's Web site (www.greenhatgin.com). What suggestions can you offer for improving the site?

Sources: Based on Mike Overturf, "New Columbia Distillers Makes a Home in Ward 5," *Ward 5 Heartbeat,* December 1, 2012, http://www.ward5heartbeat.org/feature/new-columbia-distillers-makes-a-home-in-ward-5/; Stephanie Orma, "A Site That Goes Down Smooth," *Entrepreneur,* September 2013, pp. 32–33.

unprofessional, you're unprofessional. If it's cluttered, you're cluttered. If it's hard to work with, you're hard to work with. By contrast, if it's well put together, smart, and easy to use, so is your company."[104] Unfortunately, according to HubSpot's Marketing Grader, 72 percent of Web sites earn a failing grade. "A Web site is an engine that runs on remarkable content being pumped into it day after day," says one e-commerce expert. "The goal of a Web site is to attract visitors, convert leads, and delight customers. Your business won't see those benefits unless you turn your

Web site into an inbound marketing machine that presents your brand as a thought leader with fresh offers, landing pages, calls-to-action, new media, social conversations, and other content assets. By creating such content, you grow traffic and leads organically without having to rely on paid campaigns."[105]

How can entrepreneurs design Web sites that capture and hold potential customers' attention long enough to make a sale? What can they do to keep customers coming back on a regular basis? There is no surefire formula for providing a best-in-class online shopping experience, but the following suggestions will help:

START WITH YOUR TARGET CUSTOMER Before launching into the design of their Web sites, entrepreneurs must develop a clear picture of their target customers. Only then will they be ready to design a site that appeals to their customers. The goal is create a design in which customers see themselves when they visit. Creating a site with which customers find a comfortable fit requires a careful blend of market research, sales know-how, and aesthetics. The challenge for a business on the Web is to create the same image, style, and ambiance in its online presence as in its offline stores. For example, a Web site that sells discount baby clothing will have an entirely different look and feel than one that sells upscale outdoor gear.

GIVE CUSTOMERS WHAT THEY WANT The main reason people shop online is *convenience*. Online companies that fail to provide a fast, efficient, and flawless shopping experience for their customers will not succeed. A well-designed Web site is intuitive, leading customers to a series of actions that are natural and result in a sale. Sites that provide customers with meaningful content and allow them to find what they are looking for easily and to pay for it conveniently and securely keep customers coming back. High-quality images of products with alternative views that allow customers to zoom in for detail, rotate them 360 degrees, and see color changes showcase a company's products and increase sales. Product descriptions should be simple, detailed, and jargon-free. Videos that show product details or the product in use not only increase customer traffic but also produce higher conversion rates. The goal is to eliminate any element that causes friction—a lengthy registration process, confusing navigation, cluttered pages, and others— in customers' shopping experience. Online customers also expect a personalized shopping experience on a Web site that "remembers" their tastes and preferences and recalls information that maximizes the efficiency of their visit. "By understanding a shopper, a retailer can recommend the right products at the right time," says Rama Ramakrishnan, CEO of CQuotient. "The most effective strategy is to harness big data to find nuanced signals about their tastes, predispositions, and interests and then incorporate that into one-to-one marketing."[106]

SELECT AN INTUITIVE DOMAIN NAME Decide on a domain name that is consistent with the image you want to create for your company and register it. Entrepreneurs should never underestimate the power of the right domain name or URL. It not only tells online shoppers where to find a company but also should suggest something about the company and what it does. Entrepreneurs must recognize that a domain name is part of the brand they are creating and should create the proper image for the company.

The ideal domain name should be as follows:

- *Short.* Short names are easy for people to remember, so the shorter a company's URL is, the more likely it is that potential customers will recall it.

- *Memorable.* Not every short domain name is necessarily memorable. Some business owners use their companies' initials as their domain name (e.g., www.sbfo.com for Stanley Brothers Furniture Outlet). The problem with using initials for a domain name is that customers rarely associate the two, making a company virtually invisible on the Web.

- *Indicative of a company's business or business name.* Perhaps the best domain name for a company is one that customers can guess easily if they know the company's name. For instance, mail order catalog company J.Crew's URL is www.jcrew.com, and New Pig, a maker of absorbent materials for a variety of industrial applications, uses www.newpig .com as its domain name. (The company carries this concept over to its toll-free number, which is 1-800-HOT-HOGS.)

- *Easy to spell.* Even though a company's domain name may be easy to spell, it is usually wise to buy several variations of the correct spelling simply because some customers are not likely to be good spellers!

Just because entrepreneurs come up with the perfect URL for their companies' Web sites does not necessarily mean they can use them. With more than 265 million registered domain names (115 million of which end in ".com"), finding the perfect domain name can be a challenge, but the Internet Corporation for Assigned Names and Numbers, the organization officially in charge of domain names worldwide, recently authorized the use of generic top level domain names (TLDs) such as .app, .dance, .beauty, .pizza, .bike, and others, increasing the number of TLDs from about two dozen to thousands.[107] Domain names are given on a first-come, first-served basis. Before business owners can use a domain name, they must ensure that someone else has not already taken it. The simplest way to do that is to go to a domain name registration service such as Network Solutions' (www.networksolutions.com), Netnames (www.netnames.com), or Go Daddy (www.godaddy.com) to conduct a name search. Once entrepreneurs find an unused name that is suitable, they should register it (plus any variations of it)—and the sooner, the better! Registering is quite easy: simply use one of the registration services cited previously to fill out a form and pay the necessary fees. The next step is to register the domain name with the U.S. Patent and Trademark Office (USPTO) at a cost of $275. The office's Web site (www.uspto.gov) not only allows users to register a trademark online but also offers useful information on trademarks and the protection they offer.

MAKE YOUR WEB SITE EASY TO NAVIGATE Research shows that the primary factor that leads shoppers to choose one Web site over another is ease of navigation and searching.[108] The starting point for evaluating a site's navigability is to conduct a user test. Find several willing shoppers, sit them down in front of a computer, and watch them as they cruise through the company's Web site to make a purchase. It is one of the best ways to get meaningful, immediate feedback on the navigability of a site. Watching these test customers as they navigate the site also is useful. Where do they pause? Do they get lost in the site? Are they confused by the choices the site gives them? Is the checkout process too complex? Are the navigation buttons from one page of the site to another clearly marked, and do they make sense? (One popular Web site critic says sites with vague navigation tools are guilty of "mystery meat navigation.") Web analytics tools (more about these later in this chapter) also offer insight into how long visitors spend on a company's Web site, where they abandon the site, how they arrived, and much other valuable feedback for improving site navigability. The most successful e-commerce companies constantly test various design elements on their sites using "A/B tests" (e.g., sending visitors to two sites, one with less text and more photos) to see which ones produce the highest conversion rates.

landing pages
the pages on which visitors land after they click on a sponsored link in a search engine, e-mail ad, or online ad.

Because many visitors do not start from a Web site's home page, the starting point for easy navigability involves creating the right **landing pages**, the pages on which visitors land after they click on a sponsored link in a search engine, e-mail ad, or online ad. Ideally, each landing page should have the same marketing message as the link that led to it; otherwise, customers are likely to abandon the site immediately (an occurrence that is measured by a site's "bounce rate," the percentage of visits in which customers leave a site from the landing page). In addition to including a clear call to action, a good landing page also allows customers to search or to dig deeper into the company's Web site to the products or services they are seeking. Unfortunately, 20 percent of small businesses send shoppers who click on paid listings to their sites' home page rather than to a customized landing page.[109]

Successful Web sites recognize that shoppers employ different strategies to make a purchase. Some shoppers want to use a search tool, others want to browse through product categories, and still others prefer a company to make product recommendations. Effective sites accommodate all three strategies in their design. Two important Web site design features that online companies often get wrong involve the mechanisms by which customers locate products and then get information about them:

Locating products. Customers won't buy what they cannot find! Products should be easy for customers to find, no matter how many pages a Web site includes. Too often, online companies do a poor job of product categorization, listing their product lines in ways that may make sense to them but that befuddle the typical shopper. User tests can be extremely helpful in revealing product categorization problems. After redesigning its landing pages to include less text, a more visible unique selling proposition above the "fold" (the portion of the screen that does not require a user to scroll down), and a more prominent call to action, Kwik Fit, an insurance company based in the United Kingdom, increased its conversion rate by 78 percent.[110]

In addition to establishing simple product categories that reflect the way customers actually shop (e.g., including categories such as business dress, business casual, sportswear, outerwear, formal wear, shoes, and accessories for a clothing store), another simple solution is to use an internal search tool. An easy-to-use internal search tool can pay for itself many times over in higher conversion rates and increased sales. To make the search feature useful, it should appear in the same place on every page in the site (usually the top right). An internal search tool reveals extremely useful information about which items shoppers are looking for and how they search for them, information that online merchants can use in their key word strategies for paid listings. Rather than building their own internal search engines, many online companies use one of Google's Enterprise Search tools, which can cost as little as $100 a year, to power customer searches on their sites. Managers at Coupon Chief, a directory of online coupons to more than 1,000 e-commerce retailers, replaced the home-grown search function on the company's Web site with a Google search engine and saw the number of successful searches that customers experienced increase by 200 percent.[111]

Getting product information. Once a site is designed to enable shoppers to find products easily, the next task online merchants face is to provide enough product information to convince shoppers to buy. Incomplete product information sends online customers scurrying to competitors' sites. Unlike at brick-and-mortar stores, customers cannot pick up an item, try it on, or engage a salesperson in a face-to-face conversation about its features and merits. Online merchants must walk a fine line because providing too little information may fail to answer the questions customers have, causing them to abandon their shopping carts. On the other hand, providing too much information can overwhelm customers who aren't willing to wade through reams of text just to find the answer to some basic questions. The solution is to provide basic product information in easy-to-understand terms (always including a picture of the item with the option to zoom in on it) and a link to more detailed information (which should be only one click away) that customers can click to if they choose.

OFFER SUGGESTIONS FOR RELATED PRODUCTS Many online merchants increase sales with the help of "searchandising" techniques, which combine internal searches with merchandising techniques that are designed to cross sell. For example, a customer who enters the words "French cuff shirt" into a company's search tool might see a link to the company's selection of cufflinks and ties in addition to all of the French cuff shirts that appear. Amazon.com is famous for the success of its searchandising techniques, including its "customers who bought this item also bought . . . " product suggestions.

ADD WISH LIST CAPABILITY Giving customers the ability to create wish lists of products and services they want and then connecting other people to those lists, often using social media, not only boosts a company's sales but also increases its online visibility.

CREATE A GIFT IDEA CENTER Online retailers have discovered that one of the most successful tools for improving their conversion rates is to offer a gift idea center. A gift idea center is a section of a Web site that includes a variety of gift ideas that shoppers can browse for ideas based on price, gender, or category. Gift centers can provide a huge boost for e-tailers, particularly around holidays, because they offer creative suggestions for shoppers looking for the perfect gift.

PROVIDE CUSTOMER RATINGS AND REVIEWS Customer ratings and reviews are extremely important to online shoppers, second only to the ability to conduct searches as a Web site's most important feature. One recent study reports that 70 percent of shoppers consult reviews or ratings before making a purchase and that 87 percent of shoppers' buying decisions are influenced by positive reviews. In addition, customers who read reviews are 105 percent more likely to make a purchase and spend 11 percent more than those who do not read reviews.[112] Allowing customers to post product reviews and ratings enhances a site's credibility and leads to increased sales. Online companies that include reviews benefit from conversion rates that are 74 percent higher and customer loyalty rates that are 18 percent higher than those of companies that do not offer reviews.[113] Many companies include a review widget that enables customers to post reviews quickly and easily, and some offer incentives for customers to post reviews. Businesses also must monitor their online profiles, being alert to inevitable customer complaints of poor service or product quality problems. Ideally, a company addresses customers' negative reviews and comments quickly with the goal of resolving their problems. The lesson: Companies must focus on earning and maintaining stellar reputations by providing value and excellent shopping experiences for their customers.

USE ONLINE VIDEOS Online shoppers expect to encounter Web sites that feature useful video content. According to a recent study by the e-tailing group Invodo, 35 percent of shoppers watch online videos most or all of the time they encounter them, and 67 percent watch videos at least some of the time. Shoppers who view videos have more confidence in making online purchases and are more likely to make purchases than those who do not. Adding video to a Web site not only increases its customer conversion rate but also increases its average sale and improves its search engine ranking.[114] Smart online entrepreneurs include more than mere product videos on their Web sites, creating instead videos that offer viewers (i.e., potential customers) something of value—a virtual factory tour that shows the company's dedication to quality, customer testimonials about the company's service, or informational videos that teach customers something. Stacks and Stacks, an online retailer founded in 1984 by Mel Ronick with an inventory of more than 40,000 products for organizing and furnishing homes, includes videos on some of its product pages that not only show products in action but also a customer service representative explaining how they work and how to install them. According to the company's analytics, shoppers who view videos are 144 percent more likely to purchase the product than those who do not.[115]

Once companies create video content, they can share it (and encourage others to share it) with potential customers by posting it on social media sites such as YouTube, Vimeo, and Pinterest. A video posted on YouTube, the most popular video Web site, that includes a link to the company's site drives traffic to a company's site. YouTube's Analytics offer business owners analytic tools that give them the ability to determine how effective the videos they post are at reaching potential customers. These tools show entrepreneurs how many times their videos have been viewed over a period of time, how popular their videos are compared to other YouTube videos, how viewers discovered their videos, what the basic demographics of their viewers are, and other useful information.

ESTABLISH THE APPROPRIATE CALL TO ACTION ON EACH PAGE Every page of a Web site should have a purpose, steering customers to take a specific action—place an order, review the company's services, request a consultation, read customer testimonials, and more. Make sure the call to action on every page is highly visible and appropriate. Unfortunately, one recent study reports that 70 percent of small business Web sites had no call to action on their home pages, and 72 percent had no call to action on the internal pages of their sites.[116]

BUILD LOYALTY BY GIVING ONLINE CUSTOMERS A REASON TO RETURN Just as with brick-and-mortar retailers, e-tailers that constantly have to incur the expense of attracting new customers find it difficult to remain profitable because of the extra cost required to acquire customers. One of the most effective ways to encourage customers to return to a site is to establish an incentive program that rewards them for repeat purchases. Frequent-buyer programs that offer discounts or points toward future purchases, giveaways such as T-shirts emblazoned with a company's logo, or special services are common components of incentive programs. Incentive programs that are properly designed with a company's target customer in mind really work.

ESTABLISH HYPERLINKS WITH OTHER BUSINESSES, PREFERABLY THOSE SELLING PRODUCTS OR SERVICES THAT COMPLEMENT YOURS Listing the Web addresses of complementary businesses on a company's site and having them list its address on their sites offer customers more value and can bring traffic to your site that you otherwise would have missed. For instance, the owner of a site selling upscale kitchen gadgets should consider a cross-listing arrangement with sites that feature gourmet recipes, wines, and kitchen appliances.

INCLUDE AN E-MAIL OPTION, A PHYSICAL ADDRESS, AND A TELEPHONE NUMBER Customers appreciate the opportunity to communicate with your company, and your Web site should give them many options for doing so. When you include e-mail access on your site, be sure to respond to it promptly. Nothing alienates customers faster than a company that is slow to respond or that fails to respond to their e-mail messages. Including a physical address (with an interactive map feature) is important because shoppers frequently use their smart phones to locate businesses. Unfortunately, 60 percent of small companies fail to post their business addresses on their Web sites. In addition, businesses should include a toll-free telephone number for customers who prefer to call with their questions. Unfortunately, nearly 50 percent of small companies fail to include their telephone numbers on their sites or bury them so deeply within the site's pages that customers never find them.[117]

GIVE SHOPPERS THE ABILITY TO TRACK THEIR ORDERS ONLINE Many customers who order items online want to track the progress of their orders. One of the most effective ways to keep customers happy is to send an e-mail confirmation that your company received their orders and another e-mail notification when you ship the orders. The shipment notice should include the shipper's tracking number and instructions on how to track the order from the shipper's site. Order and shipping confirmations instill confidence in even the most Web-wary shoppers.

OFFER ONLINE SHOPPERS A SPECIAL ALL THEIR OWN Give online customers a special deal that you don't offer in any other advertising piece. Change your specials often (weekly, if possible) and use clever "teasers" to draw attention to the offer. Regular special offers available only on the Internet give customers an incentive to return to a company's site.

USE THE POWER OF SOCIAL MEDIA Make it easy for customers to connect with your company on social media such as Facebook, Pinterest, Twitter, and others by including social media sharing links and links to your company's social media pages on your Web site.

FOLLOW A SIMPLE DESIGN Catchy graphics and photographs are important to snaring customers, but designers must choose them carefully. Designs that are overly complex take a long time to download, and customers are likely to move on before they appear. Web Site Garage (http://thewebsitegarage.com/), a Web site maintenance company, offers companies a free 21-point inspection of their Web sites and a report that describes problems ranging from slow download speeds to poor search engine rankings and their potential solutions.

Following are some specific design tips:

- Avoid clutter, especially on your site's home page. The best designs are simple and elegant with a balance of both text and graphics. A minimalist approach usually works best.

- Use less text on your site's homepage, landing pages, and initial product or service pages. Although including detailed, text-heavy content deeper in your site is acceptable and even desirable; incorporating too much text early on dissuades customers. Allow customers to drill down to more detailed product and service descriptions.

- Avoid huge graphic headers that must download first, prohibiting customers from seeing anything else on your site as they wait (or, more likely, *don't* wait). Use graphics judiciously so that the site loads quickly. Recall that customers abandon Web sites that load slowly. For impatient online shoppers, faster is better.

- Include a menu bar at the top of the page that makes it easy for customers to find their way around the site.

- Make the site easy to navigate by including navigation buttons at the bottom of pages that enable customers to return to the top of the page or to the menu bar. This avoids what one expert calls the "pogo effect," when visitors bounce from page to page in a Web site looking for what they need. Without navigation buttons or a site map page, a company runs the risk of customers getting lost in its site and leaving. An online merchant never knows which page a customer will land on; therefore, it is important for each page to provide a consistent look, relevant and concise content, and easy navigation.

- Minimize the number of clicks required for a customer to get to any particular page in the site. Long paths increase the likelihood of customers bailing out before they reach their intended destination.

- Incorporate meaningful content in the site that is useful to visitors, well organized, easy to read, and current. The content should be consistent with the message a company sends in the other advertising media it uses. Update the site's content frequently. Although a Web site should be designed to sell, providing useful, current information attracts visitors, keeps them coming back, and establishes a company's reputation as an expert in the field.

- Connect the company's Web site to its social media pages so that posts on social media sites such as Facebook, Twitter, Pinterest, Instagram, and others appear on the company's site.

- Include a "frequently asked questions" (FAQ) section. Adding this section to a page can reduce dramatically the number of telephone calls and e-mails customer service representatives must handle. FAQ sections typically span a wide range of issues—from how to place an order to how to return merchandise—and cover whatever topics customers most often want to know about.

- Be sure to post prominently privacy and return policies as well as product guarantees the company offers.

- If your site is heavy on content, say, 100 or more pages, or has more than 100 products for sale, include a search tool that allows visitors to find the product or information they want. Smaller, simpler sites can get by without a search tool *if* they are organized properly.

- Avoid fancy typefaces and small fonts because they are too hard to read. Limit font and color choices to two or three to avoid a circus look.

- Be vigilant for misspelled words, typographical errors, and formatting mistakes; they destroy a site's credibility.

- Avoid using small fonts on "busy" backgrounds; no one will read them!

- Use contrasting colors of text and graphics. For instance, blue text on a green background is nearly impossible to read.

- Be careful with frames. Using frames that are so thick they crowd out text makes for a poor design.

- Test the site on different Web browsers. A Web site may look exactly the way it was designed to look on one Web browser and be a garbled mess on another.

- Use your Web site to collect information from visitors but don't tie up visitors immediately with a tedious registration process. Most will simply leave the site, never to return. Allow new customers to complete purchases without registering but give them the option of saving their customer information for easy ordering in the future. Be sure to make the registration process short. Offers for a free e-mail newsletter or a contest giveaway can give visitors enough incentive to register with a site.

- Avoid automated music that plays continuously and cannot be cut off.

- Make sure the overall look of the page is appealing. "When a site is poorly designed, lacks information, or cannot support customer needs, that [company's] reputation is seriously jeopardized," says one expert.[118]

- Remember that simpler is almost always better.

CREATE A FAST, SIMPLE CHECKOUT PROCESS One surefire way to destroy an online company's conversion rate is to impose a lengthy, convoluted checkout process that requires customers to wade through pages of forms to fill out just to complete a purchase. When faced with a lengthy checkout process, customers simply abandon a site and make their purchases elsewhere; therefore, businesses should offer a "guest checkout" option but include incentives to encourage shoppers to register. The fewer the steps required for customers to check out, the more successful is a site at generating sales. (A study by *Smashing* magazine reports that the checkout processes of the top 100 grossing Web sites require an average of 5 steps.[119]) A progress indicator that shows customers where they are in the checkout process also can help, and businesses should avoid asking customers to enter the same information more than once.

Entrepreneurs must make sure that their sites' display a prominent "add to cart" button in the same place on every page to ensure that customers can make their purchases easily. Once customers put items into a shopping cart, they should be able to see a complete list and photographs of the products they have selected and should be able to access more information about them with one click. The page also should display security logos to remind shoppers that their online transactions are secure. The cart should display the price of each item in the cart in the shopper's local currency. The cart also should allow customers to change product quantities (and, believe it or not, to remove items from the cart) without having to go back to a product page. Every cart should have a "return to shopping" link in it as well.

PROVIDE CUSTOMERS MULTIPLE PAYMENT OPTIONS Because some customers are skittish about using their credit cards online, online merchants should offer the option to pay by PayPal, Google Checkout, Apple Pay, or other payment services.

ASSURE CUSTOMERS THAT THEIR ONLINE TRANSACTIONS ARE SECURE If you are serious about doing business on the Web, make sure that your site includes the proper security software and encryption devices. The average amount of an online order is $199, and missing a sale because your site lacks proper security makes no sense![120] Web-savvy customers are not willing to divulge their credit card information on sites that are not secure.

ESTABLISH REASONABLE SHIPPING AND HANDLING CHARGES AND POST THEM UP FRONT The number one reason that shoppers do not buy more goods online is high shipping costs. A closely related gripe among online shoppers is that some e-tailers reveal their shipping and handling charges too late in the checkout process. Responsible online merchants keep shipping and handling charges reasonable and display them early on in the buying process to avoid customer "cart shock." Merchants have discovered that free shipping (often with a minimum purchase amount) is a powerful tool for boosting online sales because more shoppers have come to expect it. However, because shipping costs have risen quickly in recent years, online merchants must balance the need to convert browsers into buyers with free or low-cost shipping and keeping costs under control. L. L. Bean, the online and catalog retailer of outdoor clothing and gear, offers free shipping on all orders to its customers, tangible evidence of the company's commitment to superior customer service.

CONFIRM TRANSACTIONS When customers complete their orders, a Web site should display a confirmation page. In addition, order confirmation e-mails, which a company can generate automatically, let customers know that the company received the online order and can be an important first line of defense against online fraud. If a customer claims not to have placed the order, the company can cancel it and report the credit card information as suspicious. Confirmation e-mails can contain ads or coupons for future purchases, but they should be short.

KEEP YOUR SITE UPDATED Customers want to see something new when they visit stores, and they expect the same when they visit virtual stores as well. Entrepreneurs must be diligent about deleting links that have disappeared and keeping the information on their sites current. Yet, making time to update their companies' Web sites often is crowded out by all of the other demands on entrepreneurs' time; 64 percent of small business owners say the greatest challenge they face with their Web sites is finding time to update it.[121] One sure way to run off customers on the Web is to continue to advertise your company's "Christmas Special" in August! Fresh information and new specials keep customers coming back. Smart entrepreneurs are always looking for new ways to engage their customers with interesting, relevant content.

TEST YOUR SITE OFTEN Smart e-commerce entrepreneurs check their sites frequently to make sure they are running smoothly and not causing customers unexpected problems. A good rule of thumb is to check your site at least monthly—or weekly if its content changes frequently.

FIGURE 9.7

The Purchase Funnel and Ways to Improve the Online Shopping Experience

Source: From "Improving the Online Shopping Experience, Part 1: Getting Customers to Your Products," by Lyndon Cerejo, from *Smashing Magazine,* September 15, 2011. Copyright © Smashing Magazine. Reprinted with permission. http://media .smashingmagazine.com/ wp-content/uploads/2011/08/ purchase-funnel-andways-to-improve-online-experience.jpg.

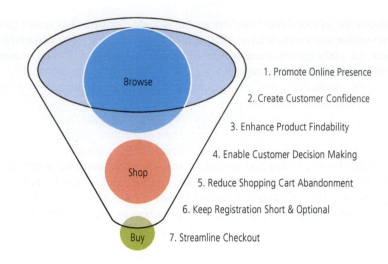

1. Promote Online Presence
2. Create Customer Confidence
3. Enhance Product Findability
4. Enable Customer Decision Making
5. Reduce Shopping Cart Abandonment
6. Keep Registration Short & Optional
7. Streamline Checkout

RELY ON ANALYTICS TO IMPROVE YOUR SITE Web analytics (see the following section) provide a host of useful information, ranging from the key words that shoppers use to find your site and how long they stay on it to the number of visitors and their locations. The best way to increase a site's conversion rate is to use analytics to determine which techniques work best and integrate them throughout the site.

CONSIDER HIRING A PROFESSIONAL TO DESIGN YOUR SITE Pros can do it a lot faster and better than you can. However, don't give designers free rein to do whatever they want to with your site. Make sure it meets your criteria for an effective site that can sell.

Entrepreneurs must remember that on the Internet, every company, no matter how big or small it is, has the same screen size for its site. What matters most is not the size of your company but how you put that screen size to use. Figure 9.7 illustrates the purchase funnel and ways that companies can improve customers' online shopping experience.

LO5

Explain how companies track the results from their Web sites.

Web analytics

tools that measure a Web site's ability to attract customers, generate sales, and keep customers coming back.

Tracking Web Results

Web sites offer entrepreneurs a treasure trove of valuable information about how well their sites are performing—if they take the time to analyze it. **Web analytics,** tools that measure a Web site's ability to attract customers, generate sales, and keep customers coming back, help entrepreneurs to know what works—and what doesn't—on their sites. Online companies that use Web analytics have an advantage over those that do not. Unfortunately, only 25 percent of small businesses use Web analytics to track traffic patterns on their sites and to strategically refashion them to improve their sites' performance.[122] Owners who use analytics review the data collected from their customers' Web site activity, analyze them, make adjustments to their Web sites, and then start the monitoring process over again to see whether the changes improve the site's performance. In other words, Web analytics give entrepreneurs the ability to apply the principles of continuous improvement to their sites. In addition, the changes these e-business owners make are based on facts (the data from the Web analytics) rather than on mere guesses about how customers interact with a site. Google Analytics is the most popular Web analytics system on the market (and is linked to Google's popular AdWords program), but many other companies also offer Web analytics software packages. The most effective ones offer the following types of information, often in real time:

- *Commerce metrics.* These are basic analytics, such as sales revenue generated, number of items sold, and best sellers (and not-so-best sellers).
- *Visitor segmentation measurements.* These measurements provide entrepreneurs with valuable information about online shoppers and customers, including whether they are return or new customers, how they arrived at the site (e.g., via a search engine or a pay-per-click ad), which search terms they used (if they used a search engine), where they are

located, and what type of device they are using. The number of repeat visitors to a site is important because it is an indication of customer loyalty. A high percentage of repeat customers benefits a business because selling to an existing customer is much easier than selling to a first-time customer.

- *Content reports.* This information tells entrepreneurs which products customers are looking for and which pages they view most often (and least often), how they navigate through the site, how long they stay, which pages they are on when they exit, and more. Using this information, an entrepreneur can get an idea of how effective the site's design is.

- *Process measurements.* These metrics help entrepreneurs to understand how their Web sites attract visitors and convert them into customers. Does the checkout process work smoothly? How often do shoppers abandon their carts? At what point in the process do they abandon them? These measures can lead to higher conversion rates for an online business.

Other common measures of Web site performance include the following:

- The **cost per acquisition** is the cost a company incurs to generate each purchase (or customer registration):

    Cost per acquisition = Total cost of acquiring a new customer ÷ Number of new customers

    For example, if a company purchases an advertisement in an e-magazine for $200 and it yields 15 new customers, then the cost of acquisition is $200 ÷ 15 = $13.33.

    cost per acquisition
    measures the cost that a company incurs to generate each purchase (or customer registration).

- The **average number of page views per visit** is a measure of how much time visitors spend on a site (visit duration). Sites that visitors find useful and provide them with meaningful content tend to have longer visit durations that show up as higher numbers of page views per visit.

    average number of page views per visit
    measures how much time visitors spend on a site (visit duration).

- The **bounce rate** is the percentage of visitors to a company's Web site who view a single page and leave without viewing other pages. A high bounce rate indicates that a company's Web site lacks credibility or meaningful content that attracts customers' attention or suffers from some other malady. The bounce rate is calculated as follows:

    Bounce rate = Number of single-page viewers ÷ Total number of visitors

    bounce rate
    measures the percentage of visitors to a company's Web site who view a single page and leave without viewing other pages.

- The **conversion (browse-to-buy) rate** is the proportion of visitors to a site who actually make a purchase. It is one of the most important measures of Web success and is calculated as follows:

    Conversion rate = Number of customers who make a purchase ÷ Number of visitors to the site

    Although conversion rates vary dramatically across industries, the average conversion rate is 2.55 percent.[123] In other words, out of every 1,000 people who visit a typical Web site, about 26 of them actually make a purchase. The longer a site's average visit duration and the lower its bounce rate, the higher its conversion rate. Only 28 percent of companies are satisfied with their conversion rates.[124] The best way for a company to increase its conversion rate is to constantly conduct A/B tests (showing two versions of the same page to visitors) to identify designs, deals, and details that work best.

    conversion (browse-to-buy) rate
    measures the proportion of visitors to a site who actually make a purchase.

- The **cart abandonment rate** is the percentage of shoppers who place at least one item in a shopping cart but never complete the transaction:

    Cart abandonment rate = 1 − (Number of customers who complete a transaction ÷ Number of shoppers who place at least one item in a shopping cart)

    If 500 shoppers place at least one item in a shopping cart but only 175 of them complete their transactions, the company's cart abandonment rate is 1 − (175 ÷ 500) = 65 percent.

    cart abandonment rate
    measures the percentage of shoppers who place at least one item in a shopping cart but never complete the transaction.

- The **search engine ranking** shows where a company's Web site ranks in search engines' results pages. Recall that almost 92 percent of search engine users click on a link to a site that appears on the first page of the search results, which means that unless a company's site shows up on that first page of results, it is almost invisible online.

    search engine ranking
    shows where a company's Web site ranks in search engines' results pages.

LO6

Describe how e-businesses ensure the privacy and security of the information they collect and store from the Web.

Ensuring Web Privacy and Security

Privacy

The Web's ability to track customers' every move naturally raises concerns over the privacy of the information companies collect. Concerns about privacy and security are two of the greatest obstacles to the growth of e-commerce. E-commerce gives businesses access to tremendous volumes of information about their customers, creating a responsibility to protect that information and to use it wisely. To make sure they are using the information they collect from visitors to their Web sites legally and ethically, companies should take the following steps:

Take an inventory of the customer data collected. The first step to ensuring proper data handling is to assess exactly the type of data the company is collecting and storing. How are you collecting them? Why are you collecting them? How are you using them? Do visitors know how you are using the data? Do you need to get their permission to use them in this way? Do you use all of the data you are collecting?

privacy policy

a statement explaining the nature of the information a company collects online, what it does with that information, and what recourse customers have if they believe the company is misusing the information.

Develop a company privacy policy for the information you collect. A **privacy policy** is a statement explaining the nature of the information a company collects online, what it does with that information, and what recourse customers have if they believe the company is misusing the information. Every online company should have a privacy policy, but many do not. Several online privacy firms, such as TRUSTe (www.truste.org), BBBOnline (www.bbbonline.com), and BetterWeb (www.betterweb.com) offer Web "seal programs," the equivalent of the Good Housekeeping seal of privacy approval. To earn a privacy seal of approval, a company must adopt a privacy policy, implement it, and monitor its effectiveness. Many of these privacy sites also provide online policy wizards, which are automated questionnaires that help e-business owners create comprehensive privacy statements.

Post your company's privacy policy prominently on your Web site and follow it. Creating a privacy policy is not sufficient; posting it in a prominent place on the Web site (it should be accessible from *every* page on the Web site) and then abiding by it make a policy meaningful. One of the worst mistakes a company can make is to publish its privacy policy online and then to fail to follow it. Not only is this unethical, but it also can lead to serious damage awards if customers take legal action against the company.

Security

For online merchants, shoppers' concerns over privacy and security translate into lost sales. One recent survey reports that half of online shoppers are concerned about their privacy, security, and safety when they make online purchases.[125] Ninety-eight percent of the data that cybercriminals target involves customer records stolen from companies for the purpose of identity theft, which affects 12.6 million people annually.[126] Every company with a Web site, no matter how small, is a potential target for hackers and other cybercriminals. Cybercrime has become a big business, costing U.S. companies an estimated $100 billion per year.[127] Small companies are not immune to cyberattacks; 44 percent of small business owners say their companies have been victims of a cyber-attack.[128] In fact, security experts have seen a sharp increase in the number of cyberattacks aimed at small companies. The main reason small businesses have become more frequent targets of hackers and criminals is that they typically have in place weaker security measures than large companies. A survey by the National Small Business Association reports that 72 percent of small businesses handle their online security in-house (either the business owner or an employee). Alarmingly, 6 percent of business owners say that *no one* handles their online security.[129] Cyberattacks threaten the very existence of the typical small business; Google usually "blacklists" companies that suffer cyberattacks, which renders them virtual nonentities online. In addition, nearly 60 percent of companies that are victims of cyberattacks close their doors within six months.[130]

Businesses have a number of safeguards available to them, but hackers with enough time, talent, and determination usually can beat even the most sophisticated safety measures. If hackers manage to break into a system, they can do irreparable damage, stealing programs and sensitive customer data, modifying or deleting valuable information, changing the look and content of sites, or crashing sites altogether.

Hands On . . . How To

Build a Web Site That Lands Customers and Creates Conversions

An entrepreneur's quest for the ideal Web site is like legendary King Arthur's knights' search for the Holy Grail: challenging and never-ending. Although creating the "perfect" Web site is an impossible dream, entrepreneurs can build sites that land customers and create conversions by focusing on employing proper design elements and providing relevant content. The following tips and techniques will help:

- **Make sure that your site creates a positive first impression.** Research at several leading universities has revealed that visitors to Web sites make decisions about their appeal and credibility extremely quickly, typically in just 50 to 500 milliseconds. At this point, design rules. A site's content is important, but 94 percent of the typical visitor's first impressions of a Web site are design dependent. Customers who find a Web site visually appealing also perceive it as trustworthy. The following basic design elements are most important:

  - **Color.** Select colors for your site that are consistent with your company's logo and image and that convey its personality. For example, Tiffany and Company, the upscale jeweler, uses its signature Tiffany blue extensively on its Web site.

  - **Fonts.** Fonts must be easy to read.

  - **Photographs.** Whenever possible, use photographs of your company's products and people rather than stock photos. Restaurants, for example, should include photographs of their own dishes.

  - **Consistency.** Avoid using too many colors and too many fonts. Colors, fonts, button styles, and graphics should be consistent throughout the site.

- **Design your site with an understanding of how users interact with it.** Eye-tracking studies show that visitors' eyes follow "F" and "E" patterns, scanning horizontally less often as they move down a page, when viewing Web sites. Therefore, designers should place the most important information in the first two paragraphs of each page so that it appears above the "fold" (the portion of the page visitors see without having to scroll down) because that is where visitors spend 80 percent of their time. The left side of a Web page contains its most valuable real estate because users spend 69 percent of their time looking there. You should put your company logo in the top left corner of each page because visitors remember a logo positioned there 58.4 percent more often than those located in any other area.

- **Simplicity reigns.** Web designers are discovering that the simplest designs usually are most effective, especially given the shift away from desktop computers toward mobile devices. Simple design coupled with intuitive navigation

lead to higher conversion rates. "If you load a page on your desktop and then step back six feet from the monitor, you should still be able to get a general gist of what is going on, what the site does, and how you would start digging in to find something that you came there to shop for," says one expert.

- **Create a site that is mobile friendly.** Transactions conducted from smart phones and tablets account for 21 percent of online sales revenue; therefore, online merchants' sites must be compatible with mobile devices. Mobile users quickly abandon sites that are not. Unfortunately, 93.3 percent of small business Web sites are not mobile compatible and do not render properly on mobile devices.

- **Be social.** Businesses should link their Web sites to their social media accounts, which can be a significant source of traffic to their sites. Unfortunately, 80.5 percent of small business Web sites lack social media widgets. Social media work only when a business has a social media presence and an audience to engage. Every page of a Web site should include appropriate social media widgets with a call to action such as "Like us on Facebook" or "Follow us on Twitter." In addition, a Web site should allow visitors to register or log in via their social media accounts, saving them time. Buttons that allow visitors to share content with others with just one click encourage visitors to become brand ambassadors.

- **Build a call to action into every page.** Every page should drive customers to take a particular action, perhaps registering for a newsletter or blog updates, downloading a free white paper, liking your company on Facebook, or completing a purchase. Remember that if you don't ask customers to take a particular action, they won't. A call to action has four components:

  - **The call.** This is the request to the user to take a particular action.

  - **The action.** This is the specific action you want the user to take.

  - **The outcome.** This is what happens when the user takes the requested action.

  - **The design.** This is how your site visually represents the call to action to the user.

- **Make your contact information easy to find.** Sometimes closing a sale requires answering a customer's question or solving a problem. To make contacting your company easy, a Web site should include an e-mail address and a telephone number. A study by Constant Contact reports that only 6.3 percent of small business Web sites include a contact e-mail address and just over half include a phone number on their home pages.

(continued)

Hands On . . . How To (continued)

- *Use analytics to test and optimize.* The key to building a successful Web site is continuous improvement, which requires entrepreneurs to have access to meaningful information about their sites' performance from analytics and conducting tests to see what works and what doesn't. Analytics give entrepreneurs ideas about how to improve their sites (and conversion rates), and tests confirm or refute those ideas. The simplest tests are A/B tests, which involve driving traffic randomly to two Web sites with only one element that is different (the headline, graphic, call to action, and so on) and monitoring the results to see which one produces a higher conversion rate. Figure out which analytics are most important to your site's success, monitor them, and conduct tests so that you can constantly improve them.

Sources: Based on Allison Howell, "Conversion Via Usability," *Website Magazine*, December 2012, pp. 20–21; Kristin Piombino, "Infographic: Eye Tracking Tops That Will Keep Readers on Your Web Site," *Ragan*, January 14, 2014, http://www.ragan.com/Main/Articles/Infographic_Eye_tracking_tips_that_will_keep_reade_47787.aspx#; "7 Components of Visually Appealing Web Designs and Why It Matters," *Aspire Internet Design*, October 24, 2013, http://aspireid.com/web-design/7-components-of-good-web-design/; Allison Enright, "E-retailers Focus on Mobile and Site Design in 2014," January 29, 2014, *Internet Retailer*, http://www.internetretailer.com/2014/01/29/e-retailers-will-focus-mobile-and-site-design-2014; Jennifer Lonoff Schiff, "6 Ways to Add Social Media to Your Web Design," *CIO*, March 4, 2013, http://www.cio.com/article/729678/6_Ways_to_Add_Social_Media_to_Your_Web_Design; "1 in 4 SMB Web Sites Won't Turn Up in Online Searches," *Marketing Charts*, March 15, 2013, http://www.marketingcharts.com/wp/interactive/1-in-4-smb-web-sites-wont-turn-up-in-online-searches-27767/; Ollie Bigler, "Six Reasons Your Web Site Will Fail," *Marketing Profs*, April 12, 2013, http://www.marketingprofs.com/articles/2013/10531/six-reasons-your-website-will-fail; David Koji, "13 Mistakes You're Making with Your Web Site." *FSR Magazine*, September 2013, http://www.fsrmagazine.com/restaurant-consulting/13-mistakes-youre-making-your-restaurants-website.

Every company, no matter how small, is a potential target. The forensic analysis unit of Verizon Communications reports that 72 percent of the successful cyberattacks they investigate occur in small companies with fewer than 100 employees.[131] Yet a survey by Office Depot Small Business reports that 66 percent of small business owners are confident their data and devices are secure from hackers.[132] The costs associated with a security breach include not only the actual cost of the lost data and the lawsuits that inevitably result from customers but also the long-term impact of the lost trust customers have for a business whose security has been breached.

To minimize the likelihood of invasion by hackers, e-companies rely on several tools, including virus detection software, intrusion detection software, and firewalls. At the most basic level of protection is **virus detection software**, which scans computer drives for viruses and malware, nasty programs written by devious hackers and designed to harm computers and the information they contain. This basic protection is essential; on average, companies come into contact with viruses and malware once every three minutes.[133] The severity of viruses and malware ranges widely, from relatively harmless programs that put humorous messages on a user's screen to those that erase a computer's hard drive or cause the entire system to crash. Because hackers are *always* writing new viruses to attack computer systems, entrepreneurs must keep their virus detection software up to date and must run it often. An attack by one virus can bring a company's entire e-commerce platform to a screeching halt in no time!

Intrusion detection software is essential for any company doing business on the Web. These packages constantly monitor the activity on a company's network server and sound an alert if they detect someone breaking into the company's computer system or if they detect unusual network activity. Intrusion detection software not only can detect attempts by unauthorized users to break into a computer system while they are happening but also can trace the hacker's location. Most packages also have the ability to preserve a record of the attempted break-in that will stand up in court so that companies can take legal action against cyberintruders. Web security companies such as McAfee provide software such as ScanAlert that scans a small business's Web site daily to certify that it is "Hacker Safe." Online companies using the software are able to post a certification mark signifying that their sites are protected from unauthorized access.

A **firewall** is a combination of hardware and software operating between the Internet and a company's computer network that allows employees to have access to the Internet but keeps unauthorized users from entering a company's network and the programs and data it contains. Establishing a firewall is essential to operating a company on the Web, but entrepreneurs must make sure their firewalls are set up properly. Otherwise, they are useless! Even with all of these security measures in place, it is best for a company to run its Web site on a separate server from the network that runs the business. If hackers break into the site, they still do not have access to the company's sensitive data and programs.

virus detection software
programs that scan computer drives for viruses, or nasty programs written by devious hackers and designed to harm computers and the information they contain.

intrusion detection software
programs that constantly monitor the activity on a company's network server and sound an alert if they detect someone breaking into the system or if they detect unusual network activity.

firewall
a combination of hardware and software that allows employees to have access to the Internet but keeps unauthorized users from entering a company's network and the programs and data it contains.

Even though 65 percent of small businesses store customer data on their computer systems, only 44 percent of small companies check their virus detection software and firewalls weekly to ensure that they are up-to-date (and 14 percent *never* check them).[134] The National Cyber Security Alliance (http://staysafeonline.org/) Computer Security Institute (http://www.gocsi.com/) offer articles, information, and seminars to help business owners maintain computer security. *Information Security Magazine* (which can be found at http://searchsecurity.techtarget.com/) also offers helpful advice on maintaining computer security.

In e-commerce, just as in traditional retailing, sales do not matter unless a company gets paid! On the Web, customers demand transactions they can complete with ease and convenience, and the simplest way to allow customers to pay for e-commerce transactions is with credit cards. From a Web customer's perspective, however, one of the most important security issues is the security of his or her credit card information. To ensure the security of their customers' credit card information, online retailers typically use **Secure Sockets Layer (SSL) technology** to encrypt customers' transaction information as it travels across the Internet. By using secure shopping cart features from storefront-building services or Internet service providers, even the smallest e-commerce stores can offer their customers secure online transactions.

Processing credit card transactions requires a company to obtain an Internet merchant account from a bank or financial intermediary. Setup fees for an Internet merchant account typically range from $500 to $1,000, but companies also pay monthly access and statement fees of between $40 and $80 plus a transaction fee of 10 to 60 cents per transaction. Once an online company has a merchant account, it can accept credit cards from online customers.

Online credit card transactions also pose a risk for merchants; online fraud cost companies an estimated $3.5 billion a year, nearly 1 percent of their annual revenues (see Figure 9.8).[135] The most common problem is **charge-backs**, online transactions that customers dispute. Unlike credit card transactions in a retail store, those made online ("card-not-present" transactions) involve no signatures, and Internet merchants incur the loss when a customer disputes an online credit card transaction. One way to prevent fraud is to ask customers for their card verification value (CVV or CVV2), the three-digit number above the signature panel on the back of the credit card, as well as their card number and expiration date. Online merchants also can subscribe to a

Secure Sockets Layer (SSL) technology
an encryption device that secures customers' transaction information as it travels across the Internet.

charge-backs
online transactions that customers dispute.

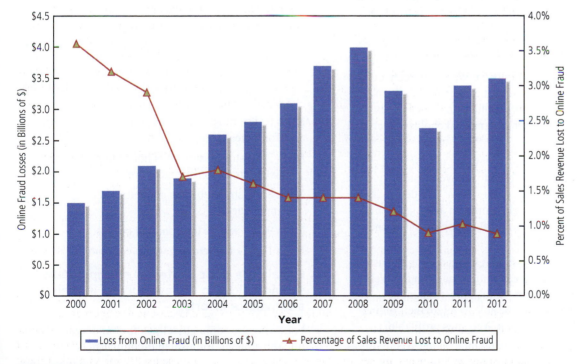

FIGURE 9.8

Losses to Online Fraud

Source: Online Fraud Report: Fourteenth Annual Edition, Cybersource Corporation, Mountain View, California: 2013, p. 1.

real-time credit card processing service that authorizes credit card transactions, but the fees can be high. Sending confirmation e-mails that include the customer's shipping information after receiving an order also reduced the likelihood of a charge-back. In addition, using a shipper that provides the ability to track shipments enables online merchants to prove that the customer actually received the merchandise can help minimize the threat of payment fraud.

Once a company has proper security technology in place, managers must train employees on proper security measures because people often are the weakest link in a company's security chain. Employees must create unique, secure passwords for all accounts and never reveal them to others. Employees must be vigilant for phishing tactics in which scammers pose as legitimate businesses and attempt to extract sensitive information. In addition, employees should never respond to sketchy e-mails (which often are the source of malware, viruses, and attacks) and must exercise extreme caution on social media. As social media have become more prevalent, attackers have shifted their focus away from e-mail attacks to cleverly disguised social media attacks, including fake offerings (inviting users to join a fake group and share sensitive information), "likejacking" (using fake "like" buttons that install viruses and malware on the user's computer), and other malicious techniques.[136]

Chapter Summary by Learning Objective

E-commerce is creating a new economy, one that is connecting producers, sellers, and customers via technology in ways that have never been possible before. In this fast-paced world of e-commerce, size no longer matters as much as speed and flexibility do. The Internet is creating a new industrial order, and companies that fail to adapt to it will soon become extinct.

1. Understand the factors an entrepreneur should consider before launching into e-commerce.

Before launching an e-commerce effort, business owners should consider the following important issues:

- How a company exploits the Web's interconnectivity and the opportunities it creates to transform relationships with its suppliers and vendors, its customers, and other external stakeholders is crucial to its success.

- Web success requires a company to develop a plan for integrating the Web into its overall strategy. The plan should address issues such as site design and maintenance, brand development and management, marketing and promotional strategies, sales, and customer service.

- Developing deep, lasting relationships with customers takes on even greater importance on the Web. Attracting customers on the Web costs money, and companies must be able to retain their online customers to make their Web sites profitable.

- Creating a meaningful presence on the Web requires an ongoing investment of resources—time, money, energy, and talent. Establishing an attractive Web site brimming with catchy photographs of products is only the beginning.

- Measuring the success of its Web-based sales effort is essential to remaining relevant to customers whose tastes, needs, and preferences are always changing.

2. Explain the 10 myths of e-commerce and how to avoid falling victim to them.

Myth 1. If I launch a site, customers will flock to it.

Myth 2. Online customers are easy to please.

Myth 3. Making money on the Web is easy.

Myth 4. Privacy is not an important issue on the Web.

Myth 5. "Strategy? I don't need a strategy to sell on the Web! Just give me a Web site, and the rest will take care of itself."

Myth 6. The most important part of any e-commerce effort is technology.

Myth 7. Customer service is not as important online as it is in a traditional retail store.

Myth 8. Flashy Web sites are better than simple ones.

Myth 9. It's what's up front that counts.

Myth 10. It's too late to get into e-commerce.

3. Explain the basic strategies entrepreneurs should follow to achieve success in their e-commerce efforts.

Following are some guidelines for building a successful Web strategy for a small e-company:

- Focus on a niche in the market.

- Develop a community of online customers.

- Attract visitors by giving away "freebies."

- Make creative use of e-mail but avoid becoming a "spammer."
- Make sure that your Web site says "credibility."
- Make the most of the Web's global reach.
- Promote your Web site online and offline.
- Use social media tools to attract and retain customers.
- Develop an effective search engine optimization strategy.

4. Learn the techniques of designing a killer Web site.

There is no surefire formula for stopping Web shoppers in their tracks, but the following suggestions will help:

- Understand your target customer.
- Give customers want they want.
- Select a domain name that is consistent with the image you want to create for your company and register it.
- Make your Web site easy to navigate.
- Offer suggestions for related products.
- Add wish list capability.
- Create a gift idea center.
- Provide customer ratings and reviews.
- Use online videos.
- Establish the appropriate call to action on each page.
- Build loyalty by giving online customers a reason to return to your Web site.
- Establish hyperlinks with other businesses, preferably those selling products or services that complement yours.
- Include an e-mail option and a telephone number in your site.
- Give shoppers the ability to track their orders online.
- Offer Web shoppers a special all their own.
- Follow a simple design for your Web page.

- Create a fast, simple checkout process.
- Provide customers multiple payment options.
- Assure customers that their online transactions are secure.
- Establish reasonable shipping and handling charges and post them up front.
- Confirm transactions.
- Keep your site updated.
- Test your site often.
- Rely on analytics to improve your site.
- Consider hiring a professional to design your site.

5. Explain how companies track the results from their Web sites.

One option for tracking Web activity is through log-analysis software. Server logs record every page, graphic, audio clip, or photograph that visitors to a site access, and log-analysis software analyzes these logs and generates reports describing how visitors behave when they get to a site. Key metrics for measuring the effectiveness of a site's performance include cost per acquisition, bounce rate, cart abandonment rate, and conversion rate.

6. Describe how e-businesses ensure the privacy and security of the information they collect and store from the Web.

To make sure they are using the information they collect from visitors to their Web sites legally and ethically, companies should take the following steps:

- Take an inventory of the customer data collected.
- Develop a company privacy policy for the information collected.
- Post the company's privacy policy prominently on the Web site and follow it.

To ensure the security of the information they collect and store from Web transactions, companies should rely on virus and intrusion detection software and firewalls to ward off attacks from hackers.

Discussion Questions

9-1. In what ways have the Internet and e-commerce changed how companies do business?

9-2. Discuss the factors entrepreneurs should consider before launching an e-commerce site.

9-3. What are the 10 myths of e-commerce?

9-4. What can an entrepreneur do to avoid falling victim to these 10 myths?

9-5. Most shoppers turn to search engines to find the products and services they want to purchase online.

Very few shoppers look beyond the first page of the search engine results. Suppose that your company, which once ranked on the first results page, has slipped to a spot many pages down and that sales are declining. What steps can you take to remedy this problem?

9-6. What strategic advice would you offer an entrepreneur about to start an e-company?

9-7. What design characteristics make for a successful Web page?

9-8. Explain the characteristics of an ideal domain name.

9-9. Give an example of a company with a good domain name and an example of a company with a poor domain name.

9-10. Describe common metrics that e-companies use to track the effectiveness of their Web sites.

9-11. What advantages does each e-commerce metric offer?

Beyond the Classroom . . .

9-12. Work with a team of your classmates to come up with an Internet business you would be interested in launching. Come up with several suitable domain names for your hypothetical e-company. Once you have chosen a few names, go to a domain name registration service, such as Network Solutions's Internic at www.networksolutions.com or Netnames at www.netnames.com, to conduct a name search.

9-13. How many of the names your team came up with were already registered to someone?

9-14. If an entrepreneur's top choice for a domain name is already registered to someone else, what options does he or she have?

9-15. Select several online companies with which you are familiar and visit their Web sites. What percentage of them have privacy policies posted on their sites?

9-16. How comprehensive are the companies' privacy policies?

9-17. What percentage of the sites you visited belonged to a privacy watchdog agency such as TRUSTe or BBBOnline?

9-18. How important is a posted privacy policy for e-commerce companies? Explain.

9-19. Visit three different e-commerce sites and evaluate them on the basis of the Web site design principles described in this chapter. How well do they measure up?

9-20. What suggestions can you offer for improving the design of each site you selected?

9-21. If you were a customer trying to make a purchase from each site, how would you respond to the design?

Endnotes

Scan for Endnotes or go to www.pearsonhighered.com/scarborough

10

Pricing and Credit Strategies

Tyler Olson/Shutterstock

Learning Objectives

On completion of this chapter, you will be able to:

1. Discuss the relationships among pricing, image, competition, and value.

2. Describe effective pricing techniques for introducing new products or services and for existing ones.

3. Explain the pricing methods and strategies for retailers, manufacturers, and service firms.

4. Describe the impact of credit on pricing.

Setting prices is a business decision governed by both art and science—with a touch of instinct thrown in for good measure. Setting prices for their products and services requires entrepreneurs to balance a multitude of complex forces, many of them working in opposite directions. Entrepreneurs must determine prices for their goods and services that will draw customers and produce a profit. Unfortunately, many small business owners set prices without enough information about their cost of operations and their customers. Price is an important factor in building long-term relationships with customers, and haphazard pricing techniques can confuse and alienate customers and endanger a small company's profitability. Research shows that proper pricing strategies have far greater impact on a company's profits than corresponding increases in unit volume and reductions in fixed or variable costs (see Figure 10.1).[1] For instance, when a company that earns a 10 percent net profit margin raises its prices by just 1 percent, its profits increase by 10 percent (assuming that its unit sales remain the same).

Another complicating factor is a holdover from the Great Recession: Customers have become more price sensitive. As sales slipped during the recession, companies resorted to deals, discounts, and coupons to attract and keep customers. Now those companies are having difficulty weaning customers off of their value-oriented mindset. A recent survey of shoppers' behavior by Parago reports that 75 percent of shoppers say they are more price sensitive than they were just 12 months before. Reflecting this sensitivity, 80 percent of shoppers now look for sales, deals, rebates, or lowest advertised prices at least some of the time before they buy, compared to 69 percent the year before.[2] Modern shoppers use technology such as smart phones and tablet PCs with price comparison apps to shop for the best deals—often right in the middle of a store's aisles, and they expect consistency in prices across all of a company's channels. In a recent survey by SDL, 62 percent of global shoppers say they use their mobile devices to compare product prices, research products, and look for discount coupons or sales.[3] The result is a new age of price transparency entrepreneurs have never before experienced and an environment that makes setting the right prices all the more important—and difficult.

Setting prices is not only one of the toughest decisions small business owners face but also one of the most important. Setting prices too high drives customers away and destroys a company's sales. Establishing prices that are too low, a common tendency among first-time entrepreneurs, robs a business of its ability to generate a profit, creates the impression among customers that the company's products and services are of inferior quality, and threatens its long-term success. Improper pricing has destroyed countless businesses whose owners mistakenly thought that their prices were high enough to generate a profit when, in fact, they were not.

FIGURE 10.1

The Impact of Pricing and Cost Improvements on Profitability

Source: Based on Richard Hayes and Ranjit Singh, "CFO Insights: Pricing for Profitability: What's in Your Pocket?" Deloitte, 2013, http://www.marketingprofs.com/charts/2013/10839/62-of-shoppers-use-mobile-devices-in-stores-to-compare-prices.

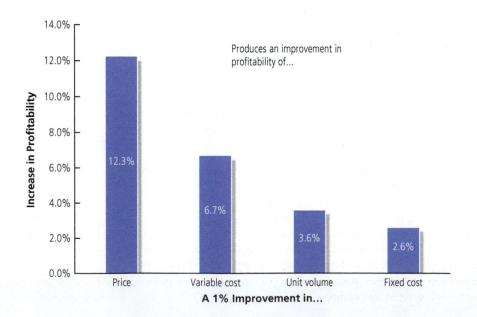

ENTREPRENEURIAL PROFILE: Jeff Trott: Timeless Message After working with a consultant, Jeff Trott, founder of Timeless Message, a company that sells bottles with greeting messages inside them, raised its prices from an average of $30 per bottle to $60 per bottle. The company had underestimated both its costs and the market value of its products. The price increase resulted in a brief sales dip, but, according to Trott, "We started making a profit for the first time in four years. It was like we had been shipping a ten-dollar bill out the door with each order."[4] ∎

Pricing decisions cut across every aspect of a small company, influencing everything from its marketing and sales efforts to its operations and strategy. Price is the monetary value of a product or service in the marketplace; it is a measure of what the customer must give up to obtain various goods and services. Price also is a signal of a product's or service's value to an individual, and different customers assign different values to the same goods and services. From an entrepreneur's viewpoint, price must be compatible with customers' perceptions of value. "Pricing is not just a math problem," says one business writer. "It's a psychology test."[5] The psychology of pricing is an art much more than it is a science. It focuses on creating value in the customer's mind but recognizes that value is what the customer perceives it to be. Customers often look to a product's or service's price for clues about value. Consider the following examples, which illustrate the sometimes puzzling connection between price and perceived value:

- Raymond Cooke started KEF in 1961 in an old Quonset hut located on the former Kent Engineering and Foundry in Kent, England, to manufacture top quality speakers for audio systems. The company, known for its constant innovation in sound technology, recently introduced its Blade speakers, whose unique curved design not only sets them apart visually but also makes them perfect for sound balancing and directing sound across all frequency ranges. Selling for $30,000 a pair, Blade speakers are the ultimate choice for audiophiles. One magazine recently described them as the "Best Money-No-Object Speakers." KEF also made headlines when it sold a limited edition of 100 pairs of Muon speakers, which are six-and-a-half feet tall, at an eye-popping $200,000 per pair.[6]

- An audiophile who buys a set of KEF speakers might also be interested in an MT5 turntable from McIntosh Labs, a company founded by Frank McIntosh in Silver Springs, Maryland, in 1949, that made a name for itself by manufacturing some of the highest quality turntables for vinyl records, which are experiencing a comeback despite their outdated technology. The platter of the MT5 turntable, which retails for $6,500, is magnetically suspended to provide the smoothest track for the tone arm, which is set at the factory to the perfect height so that it produces the highest quality sound. A precision belt-drive motor dampens vibrations so that listeners hear only the sound of the record playing.[7]

- Mike Stewart left his job as chief of police at a large university to open Wildrose Kennels, a kennel near Oxford, Mississippi, that specializes in British Labrador Retrievers trained to be "365 dogs," Stewart's term for a dog that is on its best behavior in the field and at home playing with kids. Seven-week-old puppies from Wildrose Kennels's labs, which come in black, chocolate, yellow, and fox red (a darker shade of yellow), sell for $1,750 to $2,000. An older, "finished" dog that is two to three years old goes for up to $15,000. Despite the lofty prices, Stewart has a one-year waiting list for his labs.[8]

Wildrose Kennels, Inc.

As you can see, setting higher prices sometimes can *increase* the appeal of a product or service ("If you charge more, you must be worth it"). Value for these products is found not solely in their superior technical performance but also in their scarcity and uniqueness and the resulting image they create for the buyer. Although entrepreneurs must recognize the shallow depth of the market for ultraluxury items such as these, the ego-satisfying ownership of limited-edition watches, pens, cars, jewelry, and other items is the psychological force supporting a premium price strategy.

"Great idea, Pete!"

CartoonStock

LO1

Discuss the relationships among pricing, image, competition, and value.

Three Potent Forces: Image, Competition, and Value

Because pricing decisions have such a pervasive influence on all aspects of a small company, one of the most important considerations for entrepreneurs is to take a strategic rather than a piece-meal approach to pricing their companies' products and services. Research by the University of Pennsylvania's Wharton School shows that companies that take a strategic approach to pricing and monitor its results can raise their sales revenue between 1 and 8 percent. After analyzing its existing pricing techniques using price management software, New York City drugstore chain Duane Reade discovered that parents of newborns are less price sensitive than are parents of toddlers. Managers decided to make diaper pricing a function of the child's age, cutting prices to meet those of competitors on toddlers' diapers and raising them on diapers for newborns. A year later, the company's new pricing strategy had produced a 27 percent increase in its baby care revenue.[9]

A company's pricing strategy is a major determinant of its image in the marketplace, is influenced by the pricing strategies of its competitors, and is an important element in the value that customers perceive its products or services provide.

Price Conveys Image

A company's pricing policies communicate important information about its overall image to customers. Pricing sends an important signal to customers about a company, its brand, its position in the market, the quality of its products and services, the image it wants to create, and other important concepts. For example, the prices charged by a posh men's clothing shop reflect a completely different image from those charged by a factory outlet store. Because most people have difficulty judging the quality of many products and services, they typically associate high prices with quality, prestige, and exclusivity. Accordingly, when developing a marketing approach to pricing, entrepreneurs must establish prices that are compatible with what customers expect and are willing to pay. Too often, entrepreneurs *underprice* their goods and services, believing that low prices are the only way they can achieve a competitive advantage.

Carly Otness/BFAnyc/Sipa/Newscom

ENTREPRENEURIAL PROFILE: Neil Blumenthal, David Gilboa, Andrew Hunt, and Jeffrey Raider: Warby Parker While studying at the Wharton School of Business at the University of Pennsylvania, Neil Blumenthal, David Gilboa, Andrew Hunt, and Jeffrey Raider discovered that they all preferred designer eyeglasses but were put off by the $500 prices they paid for them. They began researching the eyeglasses industry and found that it was dominated by a few giant companies and that the typical pair of glasses carried a markup of 20 times its cost. They were amazed because the material used to manufacture eyeglasses (mainly plastic and metal) is inexpensive. They also realized that although eyeglasses were invented several hundred years ago, the industry had experienced very little product innovation and almost none in distribution. The young entrepreneurs decided to change that, pitched in $120,000 of their own money, and launched Warby Parker, an online retailer of vintage-inspired eyeglasses that their original business plan said would design and sell prescription glasses and sunglasses priced at $500 elsewhere for just $45. Their marketing professor told them that their idea would not work, pointing out that their price was less than 10 percent of those of competitors. He explained that such a low price would lead potential customers to assume that Warby Parker's products were of poor quality. Their professor also suggested that the actual cost of producing the glasses would be higher than they had anticipated (he was right; their actual cost of goods sold was almost double what they had projected) and that a low price offered them such a small profit margin that any mistake could cause their business to collapse. Early market research confirmed that customers did not trust prices that are outside the normal range (even on the low side). In the end, the entrepreneurs decided to sell their eyeglasses at $95. Their pricing strategy worked; Warby Parker hit its entire first year sales target just three weeks after it launched. The company has outgrown its office space numerous times and has raised more than $116 million in financing to fuel its continued growth.[10] ∎

Many entrepreneurs make the common pricing mistake of failing to recognize the extra value, convenience, service, and quality they give their customers—all things that many customers are willing to pay for. These companies fall into the trap of trying to compete solely on the basis of price when they lack the sales volume—and, hence, the lower cost structures—of their larger rivals. It is a recipe for failure. "People want quality," says one merchant selling upscale goods at upscale prices. "They want value. But if you lower prices, they think that you are lowering the value and lowering the quality."[11] It is a dangerous cycle that can destroy a business. A study of businesses in multiple industries by Rafi Mohammed, author of *The Art of Pricing*, found that those companies that raised prices by 1 percent saw their profits increase 11 percent. Those that raised their prices by 10 percent realized profit increases of 100 percent![12] The study does not imply that businesses have free rein to raise prices to any level, but it does suggest that many companies can raise their prices enough to improve their financial results significantly as long as they convince customers that their products or services offer superior value. One expert explains the relationship between value and price with the following conceptual equation:

$$(S + P)/D > \$ + E$$

where

S = Company's standards of doing business

P = Product or service quality and performance

D = Doubt in customers' minds that detract from the value of the company's standards and products or services

\$ = Product or service price

E = Customers' expectations of a company and its products and services

According to this equation, the value customers gain from doing business with a company and buying its products or services (after being diminished by doubts they have about the company and its products or services) must exceed the price they pay and the expectations they have about the company and its products or services.[13] When guests visit one of the Walt Disney theme parks, all cast members (Disney-speak for employees) know they must measure up to some of the highest expectations of any business in any industry. (After all, the guests are on vacation, and everything should be perfect.) Ticket prices are not cheap (one-day tickets start at about $100 with discounts for multi-day tickets), but Disney cast members are highly trained in the art of providing stellar customer service and understand the central role that it plays in the company's culture. Cast members also have the freedom to make decisions on the spot to fix any problems that guests may encounter and always strive not only to meet but also to exceed customers' expectations.

A key ingredient to setting prices properly is to understand a company's target market: the customer groups at which the small company is aiming its goods or services. Rather than ask "How much should I charge for my product or service?" entrepreneurs should ask "How much are my target customers willing to pay?" Target market, business image, and pricing strategy are closely related. For example, final prices on T-shirts made in the same factories in Bangladesh for discount retailers and for high-end designer labels often have little connection to their costs but reflect the image the retailer has created for itself. The retail price of a T-shirt made in a Bangladesh factory at Wal-Mart's Asda chain in London is about $6.50. A T-shirt, also made in a Bangladesh factory, from designer brand G-Star Raw sells for $98.50, fifteen times more than the Wal-Mart version. Luxury retailers often choose higher-quality fabrics and include small embellishments such as pockets or contrasting piping on seams that add to their costs, but their final prices are more closely related to reinforcing the brands' image than to recovering costs. The manufacturing cost of a basic T-shirt in Bangladesh is about $1.60 to $2.00; the cost of making a typical designer label T-shirt ranges from $5 to $6. In addition to the additional production costs designer labels incur, their retail prices must cover their higher business costs, such as advertising, rent on boutique shops, and salaries for salespeople.[14] For many of the products upscale brands sell, their final prices are more a reflection of their desired image than the reality of their costs.

Competition and Prices

Competitors' prices can have a dramatic impact on a small company's sales. Today, small companies face competition from local businesses as well as from online businesses that may be many time zones away. Price transparency due to the Internet, the ease of mobile shopping, and customers' persistent post-recession price sensitivity impose constraints on companies' ability to raise prices (see Figure 10.2). About 60 percent of shoppers in North America report using their mobile devices regularly in stores to research prices on items that sell for $100 or more.[15] When setting prices, entrepreneurs must take into account their competitors' prices, but the decision to match or beat them is *not* automatic. A company's pricing policies involve more than covering expenses and generating a profit; they also tell an important story about its position in the marketplace and the extra value it offers customers. However, unless a small company can differentiate itself by creating a distinctive image in customers' minds or by offering superior service, quality, design, convenience, or speed, it must match its competitors' prices or risk losing sales. Before matching any competitor's prices, however, small business owners should consider a rival's motives. A competitor may establish its price structure on the basis of a unique set of criteria and a totally different strategy. Blindly matching competitors' prices can lead a company to financial ruin, and companies that set their prices this way typically do so because they perceive themselves in a position of strategic weakness. Recall from Chapter 5 that companies that execute a successful differentiation strategy can charge prices higher than those of their competitors.

The similarity of competitors' goods and services also influences a company's pricing policies. Entrepreneurs must monitor competitors' prices on products that are identical to or that are close substitutes for those they sell and strive to keep their prices in line with them.

ENTREPRENEURIAL PROFILE: Apple Inc. Apple Inc., long known for its premium pricing strategy, recently introduced a lower priced iPhone, which is the company's leading revenue driver, in an effort to fend off intense competition from low-cost phones from Samsung, HTC, Nokia, LG, and other rivals. Traditionally, phones priced below $300 have generated only 2 percent

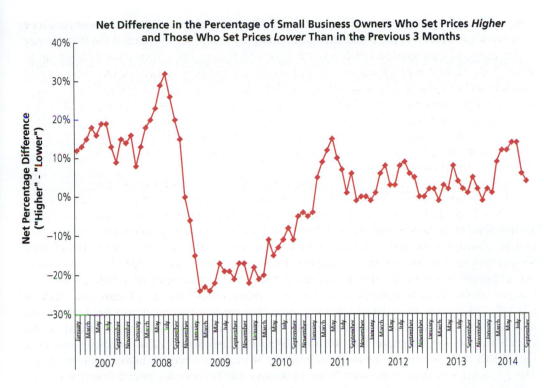

**Net Difference in the Percentage of Small Business Owners Who Set Prices *Higher*
and Those Who Set Prices *Lower* Than in the Previous 3 Months**

FIGURE 10.2

**The Reality of
Setting Prices**

Source: Based on data from
William Dunkelberg and
Holly Wade, "NFIB Small
Business Economic Trends,"
National Federation of
Independent Businesses,
October 2014, p. 8.

of Apple's smart phone sales, compared to an average of 70 percent for its top rivals. The move
was designed to reverse the company's declining market share in the smart phone market and to
introduce new customers, particularly those in foreign markets, to its products. Apple lowered the
cost of the iPhone model by using a plastic case (rather than the aluminum cases on its high-end
phones) and incorporating proven hardware from previous generation phones. Introducing a
lower-priced phone was essential to Apple's global strategy, especially in China, which is its
fastest-growing market and accounts for 15 percent of its sales. Lower-priced phones from
Samsung, Lenovo, Yulong, and Huawei have pushed Apple into fifth place in the Chinese market.
Introducing the lower-priced model enabled Apple to strike a deal with China's largest mobile
carrier with more than 760 million customers, China Mobile, to distribute Apple products.[16] ■

Generally, entrepreneurs should avoid head-to-head price competition with other firms that
can more easily achieve lower prices through lower cost structures. For instance, most locally
owned drugstores cannot compete with the prices of large national drug chains that buy in large
quantities and negotiate significant discounts. However, many local drugstores operate successfully by using nonprice competition; these stores offer more personalized service, free delivery,
credit sales, and other extras that the chains have eliminated. Nonprice competition can be an
effective strategy for a small business in the face of larger, more powerful companies because
experimenting with price changes can be dangerous for small companies. Price changes cause
fluctuations in sales volume that a small company may not be able to tolerate. In addition, frequent price changes may muddle a company's image and damage customer relations.

Recall from Chapter 5 that if a business chooses to offer lower prices than competitors, it
must first create a low cost advantage; otherwise, the strategy is unsustainable. An entrepreneur
can create a low-cost advantage by:

- choosing a low-cost location.

- minimizing operating costs by maximizing efficiency.

- exercising tight control over inventory and restricting product lines to those items that turn
over quickly.

- providing customers with no or limited service (e.g., self-service).

- using low-cost, bootstrap marketing techniques.

- selling basic products but offering customers the option of purchasing additional product or service features that generate higher profit margins.

- achieving high sales volume that allows the business to spread its fixed costs across a large number of units. Stuart Wetanson, fourth generation manager of Dallas BBQ, a chain with 10 locations in New York City that is known for its low-priced, high-quality barbecue, understands that high volume is the key to the company's success, especially given the high costs of its locations. For instance, the company's restaurant in Times Square, which features some of the highest lease rates in the city, can seat 780 people at a time, but on busy nights employees manage to serve 10,000 meals, including catering, takeout, and delivery orders. Dallas BBQ locations are open from 11 A.M. to as late as 1:30 A.M. and offer a simple menu with no desserts, which increases the number of "turns" the restaurants generate each day.[17]

Narrow Street Photography/Alamy

Attempting to undercut competitors' prices is a dangerous strategy, however, and may lead to a price war, one of the deadliest games a small business can play. No business wins a race to the bottom. Price wars can eradicate companies' profit margins and scar an entire industry for years. "Many entrepreneurs cut prices to the point of unprofitability just to compete," says one business writer. "In doing so, they open the door to catastrophe. Less revenue often translates into lower quality, poorer service, sloppier salesmanship, weaker customer loyalty, and financial disaster."[18] Price wars usually begin when one competitor thinks that he or she can achieve higher volume and take market share from rivals instantaneously by lowering prices. Rather than sticking to their strategic guns, competitors believe they must follow suit. Once a highly profitable segment, the market for consumer electronics has become the stage for a price war as retail sales stagnated and frugal customers focused on getting the lowest prices. In attempt to wrest market share from big box competitors Best Buy, Staples, Target, and others, Wal-Mart announced significant price cuts on electronics, including televisions, tablets, videogame consoles, and other devices, heading into the busy holiday season, which for many retailers accounts for as much as 40 percent of their annual sales. The price cuts started a price war that caused the profits of large and small electronics retailers to decline during a critical time of the year as competitors cut prices in an attempt to attract customers and hold on to their market share. One expert likens a price war to competitors holding guns to each other's heads.[19]

Entrepreneurs usually overestimate the power of price cuts. In reality, sales volume rarely increases enough to offset the lower profit margins of a lower price. A business with a 25 percent gross profit margin that cuts its price by 10 percent would have to *triple* its sales volume just to break even.

ENTREPRENEURIAL PROFILE: Steve Richardson: Stave Puzzles When a severe recession caused sales during the crucial holiday season to slow, Steve Richardson, owner of Stave Puzzles, a maker of hand-crafted wooden jigsaw puzzles based in Norwich, Connecticut, resorted to heavy price cuts to stimulate sales. Looking back, Richardson says the 15 percent discount ran contrary to the company's reputation for superior quality and service and was not successful in generating enough traffic to offset the price cuts. Richardson says the stagnant economy frightened him and his management team into cutting prices, but he believes Staves could have earned a profit for the year had he held prices steady or even raised them.[20] ■

As Steve Richardson learned, a company may cut its prices so severely that it is impossible to achieve the volume necessary to offset the lower profit margins. Discounts also threaten to cheapen a company's image for providing quality products and services. Even when price cuts work, their effects often are temporary. Customers lured by the lowest price usually exhibit little loyalty to a business. Rather than join in a price war by cutting prices, entrepreneurs can adjust their product and service offerings to appeal to different market segments: offering lower-priced items that use less expensive materials and offer fewer extras for price-sensitive customers and higher-quality, premium products for those who care less about price and more about quality and service. The lesson: the best way to survive a price war is to stay out of it by differentiating your company, emphasizing the unique features, benefits, and value it offer customers!

Focus on Value

Ultimately, the "right" price for a product or service depends on one factor: the value it provides for a customer. There are two aspects of value, however. Entrepreneurs may recognize the *objective* value of their products and services, which is the price customers would be willing to pay if they understood perfectly the benefits that a product or service delivers for them. Unfortunately, few if any customers can see a product's or a service's true objective value; instead, they see only its *perceived* value, which determines the price they are willing to pay for it. Research into purchasing decisions has revealed a fundamental problem that adds to the complexity of a business owner's pricing decision: People faced with pricing decisions often act irrationally. In one classic study, researchers asked shoppers whether they would travel an additional 20 minutes to save $5 on a calculator that costs $15; most said they would. When asked the same question about a $125 jacket, most of the shoppers said no, even though they would be saving the exact same amount of money![21]

"Value" does not necessarily equate to low price, however. Businesses that underprice their products and services or constantly run special discount price promotions may be short-circuiting the value proposition they are trying to build and communicate to their customers. Norm Brodsky, owner of CitiStorage, a document storage company in New York City, says setting prices too low is more dangerous than setting them too high. The veteran entrepreneur reminds business owners that they can always lower their prices if they initially set them too high. Raising prices that are too low is much more difficult and can create the wrong image for a business.[22]

Customers may respond to price cuts, but companies that rely on them to boost sales risk undermining the perceived value of their products and services. In addition, once customers grow accustomed to buying products and services during special promotions, the habit can be difficult to break. They simply wait for the next sale. The results are extreme swings in sales and diminished value of the brand. In some economic and competitive conditions, however, companies have little choice but to offer lower-priced products. Techniques that companies can use to increase customers' perception of value and, essentially lower their prices with less risk of diminishing their brands, include offering coupons and rebates that are not as closely connected to the product as direct price cuts. Limited-time-only discounts (more on these later in this chapter) used sparingly also increase short-term sales without causing long-term damage to a brand. Another strategy that some companies have used successfully is to launch a "**fighter brand**," a less expensive, no-frills version of a company's flagship product that is designed to confront lower-priced competitors head-on, satisfy the appetites of value-conscious customers, and preserve the image of the company's premium product. Rather than lower the price of its Pentium computer chip, Intel introduced the lower-cost Celeron chip to stave off rival AMD's line of value-priced chips.

One of the most important determinants of customers' response to a price is whether they perceive the price to be a fair exchange for the value they receive from the product or service. The good news is that, through marketing and other efforts, companies can influence customers' perception of value. Because price is one part of a product's or a service's features, it is another way a company can communicate value to its customers. For most shoppers, three reference points define a fair price: the price they have paid for the product or service in the past, the prices competitors charge for the same or similar product or service, and the costs a company incurs to provide the product or service. The price customers have paid in the past for an item serves as a baseline reference point, but people often forget that inflation causes a company's costs to rise from year to year. Therefore, it is important for business owners to remind customers periodically that they must raise prices to offset the increased cost of doing business. Norm Brodsky, owner of the successful document storage company, points out that a business's operating costs go up over time and that customers respond better to small price increases over time rather than big, periodic increases.[23] In addition, customers are less likely to notice small, regular price increases that result from rising costs than a single, steep price increase that could send them running to competitors. In the face of rising food costs and a sluggish economy, McDonald's, the largest restaurant chain in the world, has relied on small, consistent price increases to maintain its profit margins without alienating customers.[24]

fighter brand
a less expensive, no-frills version of a company's flagship product that is designed to confront lower-priced competitors head-on, satisfy the appetites of value-conscious customers, and preserve the image of the company's premium product.

As we have seen already, companies often find it necessary to match competitors' prices on the same or similar items unless they can establish a distinctive image in customers' minds. One of the most successful strategies for companies facing direct competition is to differentiate their products or services by adding value for customers and then charging for it. For instance, a company might offer faster delivery, a longer product warranty, extra service, or something else that adds value to an item for its customers and allows the business to charge a higher price.

Perhaps the least understood of the three reference points is a company's cost structure. Customers often underestimate the costs businesses incur to provide products and services, whether it is a simple cotton T-shirt on a shelf in a beachfront shop or a lifesaving drug that may have cost hundreds of millions of dollars and many years to develop. For instance, in a study on pricing conducted by the University of Pennsylvania's Wharton School, shoppers estimated the average grocery store's net profit margin to be 27 percent when, in reality, it is less than 2 percent.[25] Customers forget that business owners must make or buy the products they sell, market them, pay their employees, and cover a host of other operating expenses, ranging from health care to legal fees. Because customers understand so little about a company's cost of producing a product or providing a service, entrepreneurs should focus on setting prices that communicate value to customers and create the desired image for the company.

One of the biggest mistakes an entrepreneur can make is underestimating the company's actual total cost of a product or service. Calculating the unit cost of a producing a product or providing a service is just the starting point. Entrepreneurs also must calculate the total cost of the product or service, which includes shipping, labor (wages, salaries, and benefits), and overhead costs (marketing, insurance, rent, utilities, and many others). When setting prices, some entrepreneurs think strictly in terms of product or service costs and fail to consider the total cost of providing the product or service. The result is a price that fails to cover the product's or service's total cost and a company that is never able to produce a profit.

ENTREPRENEURIAL PROFILE: Joshua Henderson: Skillet Street Food Joshua Henderson was a pioneer in the gourmet food truck industry when he launched Skillet Street Food in Seattle, Washington, from a converted Airstream trailer. Because there was no model to follow, Henderson says he had to figure out on his own, often using trial and error, how to price his menu offerings. Getting Skillet's prices right took some time, but Henderson eventually found a sweet spot below the prices of brick-and-mortar restaurants but high enough to cover food costs and generate sustainable profit margins. For instance, the original price of Skillet's popular burger and poutine (hand-cut fries covered in cheese and gravy) was $15, but Henderson realized that the company was not making money at that price. Raising the price to $17 produced a profit margin that was in line with the typical restaurant without alienating customers. Skillet Street Food now generates $2 million in annual sales.[26] ■

Entrepreneurs often find themselves squeezed by rising operating and raw material costs but are hesitant to raise prices because they fear losing customers. Businesses facing rapidly rising costs in their businesses should consider the following strategies:

- *Communicate with customers.* Let your customers know why you have to raise prices. Danny O'Neill, owner of The Roasterie, a wholesale coffee business that sells to upscale restaurants, coffeehouses, and supermarkets, operates in a market in which the cost of raw material and supplies can fluctuate wildly because of forces beyond his control. When coffee prices nearly doubled in just three months, O'Neill was able to pass along the rising costs of his company's raw material to customers without losing a single one. He sent his customers a six-page letter and copies of newspaper articles about the increases in coffee prices. The approach gave the Roasterie credibility and helped show customers that the necessary price increases were beyond his control.[27]

- *Rather than raise the price of the good or service, include a surcharge.* Price increases tend to be permanent, but if higher costs are the result of a particular event (e.g., a hurricane that disrupted the nation's ability to process oil and resulted in rapidly rising fuel costs), a company can include a temporary surcharge. If the pressure on its costs subsides, the company can eliminate the surcharge. When fuel prices began climbing rapidly, Mark Bergland, owner of Washington Floral Service, a flower wholesaler in Tacoma, Washington, added to each customer's order a surcharge tied to the average diesel fuel price.[28]

- *Eliminate customer discounts, coupons, and promotions.* Eliminating discounts, coupons, and other freebies is an invisible way of raising prices that can add significantly to a small company's profit margin. Entrepreneurs must exercise care, however, because price-conscious shoppers pay more attention to discounts, coupons, and promotions since the Great Recession. One bookstore chain restructured its generous discount program because it had begun to cut too deeply into the company's profitability. Loyal customers still earn discounts (as do loyal customers at its competitors), but the discounts are smaller and expire faster.[29]

- *Offer products in smaller sizes or quantities.* As food costs have soared, many restaurants have introduced "small plates," reduced-portion items that enabled them to keep their prices in check. In the quick-service sector, slider-style miniburgers billed as "fun food" and offered in bundles have become a popular item on many menus. Buffalo Wild Wings, a chain that specializes in chicken wings, recently saw the cost of wings increase 70 percent in just one year. To cope with the substantial increase in its costs, the company changed the way it sells wings. Buffalo Wild Wings sells wings by portion size—snack, small, medium, and large—rather than by count, giving the company more flexibility over its pricing and greater control over its costs. The chain also began promoting its fresh, never-frozen wings as a premium product. The changes enabled Buffalo Wild Wings to regain control of its cost of goods sold and preserve its profit margins without experiencing a decline in sales.[30]

- *Focus on improving efficiency everywhere in the company.* Although raw materials costs may be beyond a business owner's control, other costs within the company are not. One way to cope with the effects of a rapid increase in costs is to find ways to cut costs and to improve efficiency in other areas. These improvements may not totally offset higher raw materials costs, but they can dampen their impact. Blain Supply, founded in 1955 by brothers Claude and Bert Blain in Janesville, Wisconsin, operates 35 discount stores that sell everything from clothing and kitchen appliances to camping gear and tires in Illinois, Iowa, and Wisconsin. To keep its prices low, Blain Supply, now in its second generation of family ownership (with a third generation in training), participated in Wisconsin's Retail Energy Management Challenge, a program that helps companies manage and reduce their energy consumption. Using energy audits and simple energy conservation measures, the company generated savings of $156,000 in just one year.[31]

- *Emphasize the value your company provides to customers.* Unless a company reminds them, customers can forget the benefits and value its products offer. Entrepreneurs must recognize that providing exceptional value to their customers insulates their businesses from the negative impact of necessary price increases.

- *Raise prices incrementally and consistently rather than rely on large periodic increases.* Companies that do so are less likely to experience resistance due to customers' sticker shock.

- *Shift to less expensive raw materials if possible.* Some small businesses combat rising raw materials cost by adding to their lines new products that cost less. When seafood and beef prices increased, many restaurants revamped their menus to include dishes with less expensive ingredients, such as chicken. After watching beef prices increase significantly, McDonald's added new chicken-based sandwich, wrap, salad, and nugget selections to its menu to control costs and shore up profit margins.[32]

- *Anticipate rising materials costs and try to lock in prices early.* It pays to keep tabs on raw materials prices and be able to predict cycles of inflation. Entrepreneurs who can anticipate rising prices may be able to make purchases early or lock in long-term contracts before prices take off. Starbucks uses this strategy successfully to lock in coffee bean prices with suppliers, thus insulating the company from the risk of price increases that slammed many of its competitors when coffee bean prices hit a 13-year high.[33]

- *Consider absorbing cost increases.* When Norm Brodsky, owner of the document storage company mentioned earlier, saw his competitors add a fuel surcharge to their customers' bills to offset steep increases in gas prices, he decided *not* to add a fuel surcharge. Then he used the pricing decision to attract new accounts, telling them that his company had discovered other ways besides imposing a surcharge to deal with rising costs and assuring them that when the company says its contract price is fixed for a set time, customers can count on it. Brodsky also used the fuel surcharge issue to build loyalty among his existing customers, something he is certain will pay off in the future.[34]

- *Modify the product or service to lower its cost.* Taco Bell introduced the first "value menu" in 1988 with items priced at just 59 cents, and Wendy's, Burger King, McDonald's, and other quick-service restaurants soon followed suit. Price-sensitive customers responded, and value menu items now account for 10 to 15 percent of quick-service restaurants' sales. However, rapidly rising food and energy costs have squeezed or eliminated franchisees' profits on these items, forcing chains to modify the items by eliminating a slice of cheese (which saves six cents) or switching to a sandwich with a single beef patty rather than two to maintain the $1 price.[35] Companies using this strategy must exercise caution, taking care not to reduce the quality of their products and services so much that they damage their reputations. Rather than run that risk, McDonald's introduced its Dollar Menu and More, which includes 15 items priced between $1 and $5, giving the company's franchisees more price flexibility and allowing them to preserve their profit margins. Fast-food competitors, including Burger King and Taco Bell, followed suit, adjusting prices on their value menus.[36]

- *Differentiate your company and its products and services from the competition.* When customers perceive a company's products and services to be superior to those of competitors, they are less sensitive to price increases.

Setting prices with an emphasis on value is more important than trying to choose the ideal price for a product. In fact, for most products, there is an acceptable price range, not a single ideal price. This price range is the area between the price ceiling defined by customers in the market and the price floor established by the company's cost structure. An entrepreneur's goal is to position the company's prices within this acceptable price range. The final price business owners set depends on the desired image they want to create for the business in their customers' minds—discount, middle of the road, or prestige (see Figure 10.3).

FIGURE 10.3

What Determines Price?

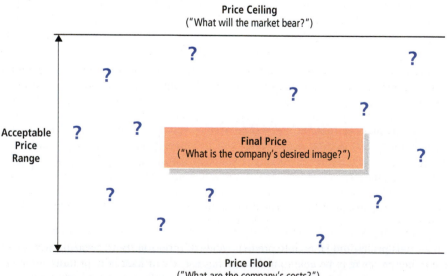

Pricing Strategies and Tactics

There is no limit to the number of variations in pricing strategies and tactics. This wide variety of options is exactly what allows entrepreneurs to be so creative. This section examines some of the more commonly used tactics. Pricing always plays a critical role in a firm's overall strategy; pricing policies must be compatible with a company's total marketing plan and the image it intends to create in the marketplace.

Introducing a New Product

Most entrepreneurs approach setting the price of a new product with a great deal of apprehension because they have no precedent on which to base their decisions. If the new product's price is excessively high, it is in danger of failing because of low sales volume. However, if its price is too low, the product's sales revenue might not cover costs. In addition, the company runs the risk of establishing the product's value at a low level. Management consulting firm McKinsey and Company claims that 80 to 90 percent of the pricing problems on new products are the result of companies setting prices that are too low.[37] When pricing any new product, the owner should try to satisfy three objectives:

1. *Get the product accepted.* No matter how unusual a product is, its price must be acceptable to a company's potential customers. The acceptable price range for a new product depends, in part, on the product's position:

   - **Revolutionary products** are so new and unique that they transform existing markets. The acceptable price range for revolutionary products tends to be rather wide, but the businesses introducing them must be prepared to make an investment in educating customers about them.
   - **Evolutionary products** offer upgrades and enhancements to existing products. The acceptable price range for evolutionary products is not as wide as it is for revolutionary products. Companies that introduce evolutionary products with many new features at prices that are too low may initiate a price war.
   - **Me-too products,** as the name suggests, offer the same basic features as existing products on the market. The acceptable price range for these products is quite narrow, and many companies introducing them find themselves left with me-too pricing strategies that are the same or similar to those of their competitors.

2. *Maintain market share as competition grows.* If a new product is successful, competitors will enter the market, and the small company must work to expand or at least maintain its market share. Continuously reappraising the product's price in conjunction with special advertising and promotion techniques helps to retain market share.

3. *Earn a profit.* A small business must establish a price for a new product that is higher than its total cost. Entrepreneurs should not introduce a new product at a price below cost because it is much easier to lower a price than to increase it once the product is on the market. Pricing their products too low is a common and often fatal mistake for new businesses; entrepreneurs are tempted to underprice their products and services when they enter a new market to ensure their acceptance or to gain market share quickly. Doing so, however, sets customers' value expectations at low levels as well, and that can be a difficult perception to overcome. Steve McKee, president of McKee Wallwork Cleveland Advertising, an advertising agency that targets small companies, says, "It can be odd to feel good about losing customers because of price, but if you're not, you may be backing yourself into a low-margin corner. Don't kid yourself; other than Wal-Mart, very few companies can sustain a low-price position."[38]

Entrepreneurs have three basic strategies to choose from when establishing a new product's price: penetration, skimming, and life cycle pricing.

PENETRATION If a small business introduces a product into a highly competitive market in which a large number of similar products are competing for acceptance, the product must penetrate the market to be successful. To gain quick acceptance and extensive distribution in the mass

LO2

Describe effective pricing techniques for introducing new products or services and for existing ones.

revolutionary products
products that are so new and unique that they transform existing markets.

evolutionary products
products that offer upgrades and enhancements to existing products.

me-too products
products that offer the same basic features as existing products on the market.

You Be the Consultant

What's the Right Price?

To increase sales of a particular product or service, business owners often resort to lowering its price. After all, doing so is consistent with the law of demand, which says that as price decreases, quantity demanded increases. However, there are exceptions to every rule, including the law of demand. A product's or a service's price tag says a great deal about it. Shoppers often have difficulty judging the quality of the goods and services they purchase and look to their prices for clues. Mike Faith, CEO of Headsets.com, an online company that sells a variety of wireless, Bluetooth, and corded headsets, involuntarily conducted an interesting pricing study a few years ago when a computer error caused all of the company's products to be listed at cost rather than their normal retail prices for an entire weekend. Headset sales did not soar despite the price decrease. Faith says that the incident taught him a valuable lesson: The prices his company charges are less important to his target customers than the stellar customer service it offers. Since the incident, Faith has raised prices only once, by 8 percent, and saw the company's sales *increase* by 8 percent.

The prices entrepreneurs set for the products and services they sell are a significant factor in the image they create for their companies in their customers' minds, whether that image is one of a discount store or one of an upscale, exclusive shop. The pricing decisions entrepreneurs make influence the image and ultimately the success of their companies. Hil Davis, cofounder of J. Hilburn, the largest seller of men's custom shirts in the world, uses a direct sales model that involves 2,250 sales representatives. After reading a book by Doris Christopher, the founder of The Pampered Chef, another company that uses a direct sales model, Davis began looking for an industry that he could revolutionize by selling directly to consumers, a business model he believed would enable him to incur lower costs and sell at lower prices. He believed the best opportunities were in luxury products in which customers expected high levels of service. A short time later, Davis's wife, Holly, mentioned that because his favorite shirts were his custom-made shirts, he should buy more of them. Davis declined, pointing out that they cost $250 each—and that's when Davis realized this was the business opportunity he had been seeking. His company would sell custom-shirts directly to upscale customers at prices below those of competing companies.

After much trial-and-error, Davis found mills that could provide high-end fabrics and a factory that could produce quality custom shirts in a timely manner. In fact, the mills that J. Hilburn purchases its fabrics from are the same ones that its competitors, who charge much higher prices, buy from. Because J. Hilburn purchases in smaller quantities and specific sizes that result in more wasted fabric, it pays about 36 percent more per yard of fabric than its larger rivals. J. Hilburn also incurs higher shipping costs because it ships shirts from the factory to customers by air, whereas competing fashion brands ship by sea, which cost less but is much slower. However, by eliminating the markups for wholesalers and retailers, the company can offer top-quality shirts at lower prices. The typical wholesale markup is 2.5 to 3 times the cost of the shirt; the typical retail markup is 2.5 to 3 times the wholesale price. In other words, a shirt that cost $43 to make ends up retailing from $295 to $395.

At J. Hilburn, a similar shirt cost about $60 to manufacture. The sales representative, who takes a customer's measurements and records his preferences for details such as collar style, cuffs, stitching, buttons and others, earns an average commission of about $28. Other sales representatives also earn a share of the sale, which amounts to about $16. A sales incentive program costs the company about $5 per shirt, and the company's profit margin is about $31, making the average final price for a custom-made shirt about $140. Depending on the type of fabric used, J. Hilburn shirts sell at prices that range from $99 to $169. Sales are growing rapidly, and the company has branched out into ties, ready-to-wear casual clothing, accessories, outerwear, and formalwear.

What steps can entrepreneurs take when it comes to setting the right prices? The following tips will help:

- Know the costs, including the direct and the indirect costs, of providing your product or service.

- Don't set your price below your costs. "We lose money on every unit we sell, but we make up for it in volume" is a business philosophy that *never* works.

- Price increases are easier to accomplish when a company faces fewer competitors. The more intense the competition, the more difficult it is to raise prices.

- If you need to raise prices shortly after launching your business, try to soften the blow by bundling products and services to create more value for customers.

- As your costs rise (and they will), adjust your prices in small amounts rather than risk making large, infrequent price increases that may create "sticker shock" among your customers.

- Assign someone in your company to track competitors' prices regularly (at least monthly) and to present the results on a timely basis.

- Do not simply follow your competitors' pricing strategies.

- Base your pricing on the value your product or service offers customers. Remember that sometimes the most valuable components of a product or service are intangible.

- Define the image you want to create for your business and use your pricing strategy to communicate that image to your customers and to position your company in the market. At Five Guys Burgers and Fries, a hamburger, French fries, and a drink cost, on average, $11.76, a good deal higher than the same bundle cost at a typical fast-food restaurant, but customers do not seem to notice. Why? Because Five Guys' value proposition is quality and freshness, not low price.

You Be the Consultant *(continued)*

1. Why do many entrepreneurs underprice their goods and services, especially when they first get into business? Discuss the connection between the prices a company establishes for its goods and services and the image it creates for the company.

2. What advantages does J. Hilburn's pricing strategy create for the company? What risks are associated with the company's low-price strategy?

3. Visit the Web site for J. Hilburn. What advice on pricing can you offer Hil Davis? Work with a group of your classmates to brainstorm various pricing strategies and the impact they might have on the company. How should Davis implement your pricing suggestions?

Sources: Based on Bret Thorn, "Menu Economics: Pricing the Plate," *Nation's Restaurant News*, March 7, 2013, http://nrn.com/purchasing/menu-economics-pricing-plate; Tom Foster, "Made to Measure," *Inc.*, February 2013, pp. 65–70; Eilene Zimmerman, "Real-Life Lessons in the Delicate Art of Setting Prices," *New York Times*, April 20, 2011, http://www.nytimes.com/2011/04/21/business/smallbusiness/21biz.html?_r=1&pagewanted=print; Stephanie Clifford, "How Low Can You Go?," *Inc.*, August 2007, pp. 42–43; and Bridget McCrea, "When Is the Price Right? Effective Pricing Is Crucial to Remain Competitive and Move Product," *Black Enterprise*, July 2004, pp. 78–79.

market, some entrepreneurs introduce the product at a low price. They set the price just above total unit cost to develop a wedge in the market and quickly achieve a high volume of sales. Jeff Bezos, found of Amazon, has used a penetration pricing strategy to introduce each version of the company's Kindle Fire tablet. Bezos says two principles guide Amazon's pricing on its tablets: (1) offer premium products at non-premium prices, and (2) make money when people *use* Amazon devices rather than when they *buy* them. When Amazon introduced its 8.9-inch Kindle Fire HDX tablet, the retailer set the price at $230, but analysts estimate that the tablet actually cost $227 to make ($218 for the components and $9 for a contract manufacturer to assemble them). Amazon priced the Kindle Fire HDX to undercut the iPad Mini, which started at $330, with the goal of generating a profit on the sale of books, apps, and movies for the Fire—and eventually on the tablet itself as the cost of the chips that serve as the device's "brain" declined. Amazon's penetration pricing strategy works; its Kindle Fire tablets are now the second-best selling tablets on the market, although it trails Apple's iPads by a significant amount. In addition, shoppers who own a Kindle tablet spend an average of $1,223 annually on Amazon products compared to an average of $790 annually for shoppers who do not own a Kindle.[39]

A penetration pricing strategy is ideal for introducing relatively low-priced goods into a market where no elite segment and little opportunity for differentiation exists. The introduction is usually accompanied by heavy advertising and promotional techniques, special sales, and discounts. This strategy works best when customers' "switching cost" (the cost of switching to a lower-priced competitor's product) is high (e.g., video game consoles). Entrepreneurs must recognize that penetration pricing is a long-range strategy; until customers accept the product, profits are likely to be small.

A danger of a penetration pricing strategy is that it attracts customers who know no brand loyalty. Companies that garner customers by offering low introductory prices run the risk of losing their customer bases if they raise their prices or a competitor undercuts their prices. If the strategy works and the product achieves mass-market penetration, sales volume increases, and the company earns adequate profits. The objectives of the penetration strategy are to break into the market quickly, generate a high sales volume as soon as possible, and build market share. Many consumer products, such as soap, shampoo, and light bulbs, are introduced with penetration pricing strategies.

ENTREPRENEURIAL PROFILE: Ido Leffler: Yes to Carrots In 2006, Ido Leffler, founder of Yes To Inc., a company that markets a line of skin and hair care products made from carrots, tomatoes, cucumbers, and blueberries introduced the all-natural beauty products at very affordable prices. Leffler says Yes To's pricing is based on offering customers better value than its principal competitors and emphasizes a guilt-free pricing model. Leffler believes customers should not feel guilty buying a moisturizer or shampoo that retails from $9 to $20. Yes to Carrots, which started with 6 products in just 16 stores, now has more than 80 products that are sold in nearly 28,000 stores in 29 countries.[40] ■

SKIMMING A skimming pricing strategy often is used when a company introduces a new product into a market with little or no competition or to establish the company and its products or services as unique and superior to those of its competitors. Sometimes a business employs this tactic when introducing a product into a competitive market that contains an elite group that is able to pay a higher price. Companies that use a skimming strategy often achieve success by emphasizing the intangible benefits of their higher-priced goods and services. For instance, one lawn service that targets busy, upscale professionals commands premium prices by emphasizing the time and trouble doing yard work that they save their clients and the ability to have yards that are the envy of the neighborhood.

Donato Sardella/WireImage/Getty Images

ENTREPRENEURIAL PROFILE: Katrina Markoff: Vosges Haut-Chocolat Vosges Haut-Chocolat, a company started by Katrina Markoff in her Chicago apartment, markets its intriguing chocolate creations with unusual flavor combinations—chocolate bars flavored with bacon, ancho and chipotle chiles and cinnamon, black Hawaiian sea salt and burnt sugar caramel, ginger, wasabi, dark chocolate and black sesame seeds, or blood orange and hibiscus—as an affordable luxury, an inexpensive way for customers to indulge and pamper themselves. Although Vosges Haut-Chocolat's gift boxes range in price from $100 to more than $1,000, customers can purchase 2-ounce bars for prices that range from $4 to $8.50. Markoff, who strives to tell stories about the exotic places she has traveled using chocolate as a medium, says her company sells its unique chocolates through more than 2,000 stores and generates profits in excess of $30 million.[41] ∎

With this strategy, an entrepreneur uses a higher-than-normal price in an effort to quickly recover the initial developmental and promotional costs of the product. The idea is to set a price well above the total unit cost and to promote the product heavily to appeal to the segment of the market that is not sensitive to price. This pricing tactic often reinforces the unique, prestigious image of a business and portrays the product as high quality. Another advantage of this technique is that entrepreneurs can correct pricing mistakes quickly and easily. If a product's price proves to be too low under a penetration strategy, raising the price can be very difficult. If a company using a skimming strategy sets a price too high to generate sufficient sales volume, it can always lower the price. Successful skimming strategies require a company to differentiate its products or services from those of the competition, justifying the above-average price.

LIFE CYCLE PRICING A variation of the skimming price strategy is called life cycle pricing. Using this technique, a small company introduces a product at a high price. Then technological advances enable the firm to lower its costs quickly and to reduce the product's price before its competition can. By beating other businesses in a price decline, the small company discourages competitors and gradually, over time, becomes a high-volume producer. High-definition television sets are a prime example of a product introduced at a high price that quickly cascaded downward as companies forged important technology advances and took advantage of economies of scale. When high-definition televisions were first introduced in 1999, they sold for $19,000; today, they are priced at $300 or less.

Life cycle pricing is a strategy that assumes competition will emerge over time. Even if no competition arises, however, companies almost always lower the product's price to attract a larger segment of the market. Nonetheless, the initial high price contributes to a rapid return of start-up costs and generates a pool of funds to finance expansion and technological advances.

Pricing Established Goods and Services

Each of the following pricing tactics or techniques are part of the toolbox of pricing tactics entrepreneurs can use to set prices of established goods and services.

odd pricing
a pricing technique to set prices that end in odd numbers to create the psychological impression of lower prices.

ODD PRICING Many entrepreneurs use the technique known as **odd pricing** in which they establish prices that end in odd numbers, such as 5, 7, or 9 because they believe that merchandise selling for $12.69 appears to be much cheaper than the item priced at $13.00. Psychological techniques such as odd pricing are designed to appeal to certain customer interests, but research on their effectiveness is mixed. Some studies show no benefits from using odd pricing, but others have concluded that the technique can produce significant increases in sales. Omitting the "$" symbol from prices may help, too. Researchers at Cornell University have discovered that restaurants that list menu prices without the "$" symbol (e.g., "21") achieved $5.55 more in sales on average than those whose menu prices were written in script or included a "$" symbol.[42]

PRICE LINING **Price lining** is a technique that greatly simplifies the pricing decision by pricing different products in a product line at different price points, depending on their quality, features, and cost. Under this system, entrepreneurs sell products in several different price ranges, or price lines. Each category of merchandise contains items that are similar in appearance but that differ in quality, cost, performance, or other features. Many lined products appear in sets of at least three—good (basic), better (upgraded), and best (premium)—at prices designed to satisfy different market segment needs and incomes. Apple uses price lining for its iPad mini with retina display, which is priced at four different points: $399 (16GB), $499 (32 GB), $599 (64 GB), and $699 (128 GB). Price lining can boost a company's sales because it makes goods available to a wide range of shoppers, simplifies the purchase decision for customers, and allows them to choose products with prices that fit within their budgets. Companies that segment their customer bases and use price lines designed to appeal to each segment can improve their profit margins between 1 and 7 percent.[43]

price lining
a technique that greatly simplifies the pricing function by pricing different products in a product line at different price points, depending on their quality, features, and cost.

FREEMIUM PRICING Companies that use **freemium pricing** provide a basic product or service to customers for free but charge a premium for expanded or upgraded versions of the product or service. Products or services that customers must use or experience to appreciate their value, such as software, are ideal candidates for a freemium pricing strategy. The goals of a freemium pricing strategy are to gain rapid and extensive adoption of a product or service and to give potential customers a chance to discover the value it offers, particularly in its upgraded versions. The key to a successful freemium strategy is to expose free users to enough product or service features while reserving the most valuable benefits for customers who are willing to pay for the expanded versions. Typically, only about 2 to 4 percent of customers who use the free version of a product actually purchase its upgraded versions; therefore, for a freemium strategy to be successful, the potential market must be sizable.[44] Suppose, for example, that a company's revenue target is $10 million and its average annual revenue per *paying* customer is $120. The company would need 83,333 paying customers ($10 million ÷ $120 per customer) to reach its target. Assuming a conversion rate of 3 percent, the company would have to attract 2,777,778 free users (83,333 customers ÷ 3 percent) to generate $10 million in annual sales. One of the greatest dangers of a freemium pricing strategy is underestimating the cost of providing service and support for free users.

freemium pricing
a pricing strategy that involves providing a basic product or service to customers for free but charging a premium for expanded or upgraded versions of the product or service.

ENTREPRENEURIAL PROFILE: Eric Wahlforss and Alexander Ljung: SoundCloud While studying at the Royal Institute of Technology in Stockholm, Sweden, Eric Wahlforss, an amateur electronic musician, and Alexander Ljung, a former sound engineer, came up with the idea for a simple sound-sharing tool that allowed them to swap any sound file between their MacBooks. The software worked so well that the entrepreneurs purchased the soundcloud.com domain name and moved to Berlin, Germany, where they tapped into that city's burgeoning electronic music community. Using seed money from private investors and word-of-mouth marketing from about 20,000 users, Wahlforss and Ljung launched SoundCloud with a freemium pricing strategy and watched their user base grow exponentially. Customers, most of whom are musicians, bands, and audio producers or their fans, can register for free and upload a limited amount of music or receive limited access to the site's expansive collection, which they can share with others via social media. Customers who upgrade (about 5 percent do) can pay $4 per month for four hours of sound or $12 per month for unlimited access. So far, the entrepreneurs have raised $123 million in venture capital and have an estimated 55 million users in 200 countries.[45] ■

DYNAMIC PRICING For many businesses, the pricing decision has become more challenging because the Internet gives customers access to real-time pricing information of almost any item ranging from cars to computers. Increasingly, customers are using the Internet to find the lowest prices available. To maintain their profitability, some companies have responded with **dynamic (or customized) pricing**, in which they set different prices for the same products and services for different customers using the information they have collected about their customers. Rather than sell their products at fixed prices, companies using dynamic pricing rely on fluid prices that may change based on supply and demand and on which customer is buying or when a customer makes a purchase. For instance, a first-time customer making a purchase at an online store may pay a higher price for an item than a regular customer who shops there frequently pays for the same item.

dynamic (customized) pricing
a technique in which a company sets different prices for the same products and services for different customers using the information they have collected about their customers.

Dynamic pricing is not a new concept. The standard practice in ancient bazaars involved merchants and customers haggling until they came to a mutually agreeable price, meaning that different customers paid different prices for the same goods. Although the modern version of dynamic pricing often involves sophisticated market research or the Internet, the goal is the same: to charge the right customer the right price at the right time. For example, travelers can use Priceline and similar Web sites to purchase last-minute airline tickets at significant discounts, such as a round-trip ticket from New York to Los Angeles for just $250 rather than for the full-fare price of $750. Travelers benefit from lower prices, and the airlines are able to generate revenue from seats that otherwise would have gone unsold.

Ethics and Entrepreneurship

The Ethics of Dynamic Pricing

In *Casablanca*, the classic romance drama film from 1942, Ilse, the character played by Ingrid Bergman, is looking at a set of lace napkins in a shopping bazaar when she mentions that she is a friend of Rick, the film's lead character played by Humphrey Bogart. The merchant quickly replaces the original 700-franc price tag with one bearing a 100-franc price. "For special friends of Rick's, we have special discounts," he explains to Ilse. The message was clear: Different prices apply to different customers.

Companies now have access to more data on their customers than at any other point in business history, and many of these businesses use that information to serve their customers better, providing them with the goods and services they need just when they need them. One offshoot of this wealth of information is dynamic or customized pricing, a system in which companies charge different prices for the same products and services for different customers using the information they have collected about their customers. The principle is the same as that in *Casablanca*: Different prices apply to different customers. Movie theaters have used a simple version of dynamic pricing for years. Buy a ticket for an afternoon showing, traditionally a slower time for sales of movie tickets, and you get a lower price. Restaurants use the same tactic, offering "early bird" specials at off-peak hours. Airlines have used dynamic pricing for years as well, but their systems are much more complex. (When asked about the pricing strategies of airlines, the CEO of a major airline company said, only half jokingly, "I don't understand airline pricing either!") Business travelers who fly on short notice on weekdays typically pay higher prices than those who book in advance and travel over weekends. Cities such as London, Singapore, San Francisco, and New York use dynamic pricing strategies, charging drivers on toll bridges higher prices at peak commuting times and lower prices during off-peak hours.

Many professional and collegiate sporting events now rely on dynamic pricing, charging higher prices for "high demand" games with arch rivals or stellar matchups between star pitchers and lower prices for games that fans find less appealing or are subject to bad weather. Barry Kahn, CEO of Qcue, a small company that specializes in dynamic pricing for the sports industry, says dynamic pricing has enabled clients to increase their revenue by 30 percent by raising prices for high demand games between 5 and 10 percent and by reducing prices for low demand games.

The practice of dynamic pricing has created controversy, however. Is it ethical for companies to charge different customers different prices for the same goods and services? Many surveys report that customers believe dynamic pricing is *not* an acceptable business practice. However, empirical evidence shows that customized pricing benefits not only the companies using it but also customers, making purchases more affordable for many people. Uber, a company based in Silicon Valley, California, provides an app that allows people in 70 large cities worldwide to use their mobile devices to locate drivers of the company's army of black cars; it uses dynamic pricing, charging higher prices when demand for rides is high and the supply of cars is low, typically on Friday and Saturday evenings, on certain holidays, and during bad weather. Bill Gurley, an investor in Uber, says the company is committed to being a low-price leader in its market niche (the company's basic uberX rate is 40 percent cheaper than the typical taxi) and that its dynamic pricing strategy minimizes customers' wait times and the frequency with which customers experience "no cars available" messages on their phone or tablet screens.

Ragged Mountain, a 49-year-old ski resort in New Hampshire, recently implemented dynamic pricing with the help of Cloud Store, software that gives managers the ability to change prices on lift tickets, equipment rentals, and lessons, depending on weather conditions, holidays, and other factors. A Valentine's Day special, priced at just $14, produced a significant increase in sales of tickets and generated lots of positive buzz for the ski resort. On one occasion, as a big snow storm approached the area, Ragged

Ethics and Entrepreneurship (continued)

Mountain was able to increase its prices gradually each day and still sell out its capacity. Resort managers do not mind reducing prices when demand is low or when conditions are less than ideal because they know that bringing in more customers leads to higher sales of meals, snacks, and beverages.

Dynamic pricing has stood successfully against several legal challenges. Denise Katzman filed a class-action lawsuit against retailer Victoria's Secret when she discovered that a catalog she received listed higher prices than a nearly identical catalog the company sent to a male coworker. She alleged that the company had engaged in illegal price discrimination by charging different prices for identical items to different categories of customers. Because Victoria's Secret had sent the catalogs through the U.S. mail, Katzman claimed that the company's discriminatory pricing structure constituted mail fraud. U.S. District Court Judge Robert W. Sweet upheld the validity of Victoria's Secret's dynamic pricing policies, ruling that "offering different discounts to different catalogue customers does not constitute mail fraud under any reading of the law." On appeal, the U.S. Court of Appeals for the Second Circuit upheld Judge Sweet's decision. This case suggests that businesses can charge different customers different prices as long as the price differences are based on reasonable business practices, such as rewarding loyal customers, and do not discriminate against customers for race, gender, national origin, or some other illegal reason.

Dynamic pricing has emerged as a marketing strategy out of necessity. Entrepreneurs say the Internet has lowered the transaction costs of doing business and moves business along at such a fast pace that the fixed pricing strategies of the past no longer work. To keep up with fluid, fast-changing markets, companies must change their prices quickly. They must be able to adapt the prices they charge their customers on a real-time basis and to charge higher prices to those customers who cost their companies more to serve. Craig Clark, who operates an Amazon storefront that sells more than 2,600 items, recently began using FeedVisor, a service that uses sophisticated algorithms that take into account competitors' prices, sales volume, a company's costs, and other factors to adjust prices. Clark says that after FeedVisor reduced the price on his store's Coobie bras by 10 percent, sales of the bras increased by 25 percent, resulting in higher profits for his company.

1. Work with a team of your classmates to define the ethical issues involved in dynamic pricing.

2. What are the advantages and the disadvantages of dynamic pricing to the companies that use it? To the customers of the companies that use it?

3. According to an old proverb, "The value of a thing is what it will bring." Do you agree? Explain. Should companies be allowed to engage in dynamic pricing?

4. If you owned your own business and had the information required to engage in dynamic pricing, would you do so? Explain.

Sources: Based on Donna Fenn, "Some Businesses Go Creative on Prices, Applying Technology," *New York Times,* January 22, 2014, http://www.nytimes.com/2014/01/23/business/smallbusiness/with-new-thinking-and-technology-some-businesses-get-creative-with-pricing.html?_r=1; Grant Davis, "Snow Job," *Entrepreneur,* January 2014, http://www.entrepreneur.com/article/230219; Bill Gurley, "A Deeper Look at Uber's Dynamic Pricing Model," *Above the Crowd,* March 11, 2014, http://abovethecrowd.com/2014/03/11/a-deeper-look-at-ubers-dynamic-pricing-model/; Patrick Rishe, "Dynamic Pricing: The Future of Ticket Pricing in Sports," *Forbes,* January 6, 2012, http://www.entrepreneur.com/article/230219; Mark Brown, "Indie Royale Bundle Starts a Price War between the Stingy and the Wealthy," *Wired,* October 26, 2011, http://www.wired.co.uk/news/archive/2011-10/26/indie-royale-bundle; Robert M. Weiss and Ajay K. Mehrotra, "Online Dynamic Pricing: Efficiency, Equity, and the Future of E-Commerce," *Virginia Journal of Law and Technology* 6, no. 2 (Summer 2001): 7; Matthew Maier, "Finding Riches in a Mine of Credit Data," *Business 2.0,* October 2005, pp. 72–74; and Peter Coffee, "More 'Dynamic Pricing' Is on the Way," *eWeek,* September 2002, http://www.eweek.com/article2/0,1759,1011178,00.asp.

LEADER PRICING **Leader pricing** is a technique in which a retailer marks down the customary price (i.e., the price consumers are accustomed to paying) of a popular item in an attempt to attract more customers. The company earns a much smaller profit on each unit because the markup is lower, but purchases of other merchandise by customers seeking the leader item often boost sales and profits. In other words, the incidental purchases that consumers make when shopping for the leader item boost sales revenue enough to offset a lower profit margin on the leader. Grocery stores frequently use leader pricing. For instance, during the holiday season, stores often use turkeys as a price leader, knowing that they will earn higher margins on the other items shoppers purchase with their turkeys. Many discount warehouses, such as Sam's Club and Costco, and supermarket chains, such as Albertsons, Kroger, Safeway, and Ingles, sell gasoline as a price leader to encourage customers to make more frequent visits to their retail stores.[46]

leader pricing
a technique that involves marking down the normal price of a popular item in an attempt to attract more customers who make incidental purchases of other items at regular prices.

GEOGRAPHIC PRICING Small businesses whose pricing decisions are greatly affected by the costs of shipping merchandise to customers across a wide range of geographic regions frequently employ one of the geographic pricing techniques. For these companies, freight expenses make up a substantial portion of the cost of doing business and may cut deeply into already narrow profit margins. One type of geographic pricing is **zone pricing**, in which a company sells its merchandise at different prices to customers located in different territories. For example, a manufacturer might sell at one price to customers east of the Mississippi and at another to those west of the Mississippi.

zone pricing
a technique that involves setting different prices for customers located in different territories because of different transportation costs.

delivered pricing
a technique in which a company charges all customers the same price regardless of their locations and different transportation costs.

F.O.B. factory
a pricing method in which a company sells merchandise to customers on the condition that they pay all shipping costs.

discounts (markdowns)
reductions from normal list prices.

A company must be able to show a legitimate basis (e.g., differences in selling or transportation costs) for the price discrimination or risk violating Section 2 of the Clayton Act.

Another variation of geographic pricing is uniform **delivered pricing**, a technique in which a firm charges all of its customers the same price regardless of their location, even though the cost of selling or transporting merchandise varies. A company calculates the proper freight charges for each region and combines them into a uniform fee. The result is that local customers subsidize the company's charges for shipping merchandise to distant customers.

A final variation of geographic pricing is **F.O.B. factory**, in which a small company sells its merchandise to customers on the condition that they pay all shipping costs. In this way, the company can set a uniform price for its product and let each customer cover the freight costs.

DISCOUNTS Many small businesses use **discounts (markdowns)**— reductions from normal list prices—to move stale, outdated, damaged, or slow-moving merchandise or to stimulate sales. A seasonal discount is a price reduction designed to encourage shoppers to purchase merchandise before an upcoming season. For instance, many retail clothiers offer special sales on winter coats in midsummer. Many merchants also offer after-Christmas discounts to make room for their spring merchandise. Some companies grant purchase discounts to special groups of customers, such as senior citizens or college students, to establish a faithful clientele and to generate repeat business.

As tempting as discounts are to businesses when sales are slow, they carry risks. Ideally, discounts win loyal customers who make repeat purchases. Cindy Dickey, owner of a Merle Norman Cosmetics store in Enid, Oklahoma, tied a discount offer to a special promotion that increased her store's sales by requiring customers to return to earn the discount. For a limited time, Dickey allowed customers to select a sealed envelope that contained a gift certificate valued at between $5 and $100 that they could redeem on their next visit.[47] The reality of discounts, however, is that they often attract customers who are merely seeking bargains and who rarely turn into loyal customers. Cacio e Vino, a Sicilian restaurant in New York City's Manhattan borough, offers a limited number of reservations at a 40 percent discount through Groupon Reserve to draw customers on Sundays, Mondays, and Tuesdays, the restaurant's slowest nights. On Wednesdays and Thursdays, Cacio e Vino offers a limited number of diners 30 percent discounts but only between 5 P.M. and 7 P.M. Manager Christine Ehlert says the discounts are a tool to attract new customers to the restaurant during times that it is operating at less than full capacity. Although the discounts have increased sales from an average of $800 to $1,200 to $1,500 on Mondays and Tuesdays, they cut into the restaurant's profit margin, reducing it by 50 percent compared to full-price customers. In addition, fewer than half of Cacio e Vino's discount customers return, and when they do, it almost always is for a discounted meal.[48]

Excessive discounting also diminishes or eradicates altogether a company's profit margin. Perry Schorr, co-owner of Lester's, a 65-year-old retailer that sells clothing for children and teens and targets affluent families, makes limited use of discounts. With four stores in New York, Schorr knows that his customers are more interested in quality products and attentive service than discount prices. During the competitive Black Friday weekend that kicks off the holiday season, which accounts for 15 percent of the company's sales, Lester's offers modest discounts of 20 percent on select items and adds sales staff to ensure that customer service does not suffer. Schorr sees Black Friday as a price-driven event and says small companies such as his cannot build a successful strategy by discounting prices and cheapening their images.[49]

Companies that frequently resort to discounts may ruin their reputation for superior quality and service, thereby diluting the value of their brand and image in the marketplace. Frequent discounting sends customers the message that a company's regular prices are too high and that they should wait for the next sale to make a purchase. As many retailers and restaurants learned from the last recession, weaning customers off of discounts can be difficult; the climb back to "normal" pricing can be long and arduous. One less visible way for companies to offer discounts is to enroll customers in a loyalty program that entitles them to **earned discounts**. Loyalty programs, such as those at supermarkets, pet stores, and bookstores, not only encourage shoppers to return but also provide businesses with meaningful data on customers' buying habits, allowing them to decipher patterns and trends. Belk, a family-owned chain of department stores with more than 300 locations in 16 southern states, offers rewards to customers who make purchases on

earned discounts
discounts customers earn by making repeat purchases at a business.

the store-branded credit card. For every $400 customers spend, they receive $10 in Belk Reward Dollars they can use for future purchases.

Limited time offers (LTOs) are discounts that retailers run for a limited amount of time ("Regular price: $150. Sale price $120 *for three days only.*") with the goal of creating a sense of urgency and excitement among customers. Although LTOs are a common pricing tool for many retailers, quick-service restaurants are perhaps the most frequent users of LTOs. To create a successful LTO, retailers should emphasize the end date of the offer and include a distinct call to action in their advertising, promote the offer on social media as well as in traditional advertising channels, and end the offer on the advertised date. Toppers Pizza, a pizza chain with 41 locations in the Midwest and South, has had great success running periodic, aggressively priced LTOs (such as a one-topping large pizza for just $5) by promoting them among its 50,000 Facebook fans. Scott Iversen, the company's vice-president of marketing, says the number of transactions the company makes during the LTO is twice the number during a normal week and that sales of drinks and side items make up for the lower profit on the LTO.[50]

Recent research suggests that using a **steadily decreasing discount (SDD)**, a limited duration discount that declines over time, is superior to a standard (hi-lo) discount, a common tactic in which a company offers frequent discounts off its standard prices. When one company used a hi-lo discount of 20 percent for three days before returning to the items to full price, sales increased by 75 percent. For the same items, a steadily decreasing discount of 30 percent the first day, 20 percent the second day, and 10 percent the third day (which yielded the same average discount of 20 percent), produced an increase in sales of 200 percent. The researchers conclude that the SDD is more effective because it creates a sense of urgency, especially among wary or indecisive customers.[51] Research also shows that for items other than luxury goods, dollar discounts ("Save $25 now") are more effective at generating sales than percentage discounts ("Save 25% now").[52]

Multiple unit pricing is a promotional technique that offers customers discounts if they purchase in quantity. Many products, especially those with relatively low unit value, are sold using multiple pricing. For example, instead of selling an item for 50 cents, a small company might offer five for $2.

BUNDLING Many small businesses have discovered the marketing benefits of **bundling**, grouping together several products or services or both into a package that offers customers extra value at a special price. Fast-food outlets often bundle items into "meal deals" that customers can purchase at lower prices than if they bought the items separately. Even upscale restaurants use bundled pricing; at New York City's tony Per Se, diners can choose between two nine-course prix fixe chef's tasting menus for $310 per person. Bundling is another way for companies to offer customers discounts without damaging their reputations. Rebecca Kaplan, who operates family-owned Glazer's Camera, in Seattle, Washington, with her brother, Ari Lackman, shuns traditional discounts because the profit margins on the photographic equipment the store sells are too slim to offer price reductions. Instead, Glazer's Camera offers customers limited discounts by bundling cameras with high-end accessories, such as tripods, lenses, and camera bags, at special prices. To differentiate their store from competitors, Kaplan and Lackman invest in training their staff and offer special services, such as in-store photography classes.[53]

OPTIONAL-PRODUCT PRICING **Optional-product pricing** involves selling the base product for one price but selling the options or accessories for it at a much higher markup. Automobiles are often sold at a base price with each option priced separately. In some cases, the car is sold with some of the options "bundled" together, as explained previously.

ENTREPRENEURIAL PROFILE: Amish Backyard Structures Amish Backyard Structures, a small company in tiny Oxford, Pennsylvania, that makes children's playhouses, sheds, barns, gazebos, and lawn furniture, uses an optional-product pricing strategy. The company's playhouses are handcrafted from top-quality materials, range in size from 6 by 8 feet to 10 by 20 feet, and come in designs that resemble Cape Cod cottages and Victorian mansions. Parents can choose to customize their children's playhouses with a variety of options, such as heart-shaped windows, chimneys, porch swings, fully finished interiors, and playhouse furniture, including wooden sink and stove combinations and refrigerators.[54] ∎

---

limited time offers (LTOs)
discounts retailers run for a limited amount of time with the goal of creating a sense of urgency and excitement among customers.

steadily decreasing discount (SDD)
a limited duration discount that declines over time.

multiple unit pricing
a technique offering customers discounts if they purchase in quantity.

bundling
grouping together several products or services or both into a package that offers customers extra value at a special price.

optional-product pricing
a technique that involves selling the base product for one price but selling the options or accessories for it at a much higher markup.

captive-product pricing

a technique that involves selling a product for a low price and charging a higher price for the accessories that accompany it.

by-product pricing

a technique in which a company uses the revenues from the sale of by-products to be more competitive in pricing the main product.

CAPTIVE-PRODUCT PRICING Captive-product pricing is a pricing strategy in which the base product is not functional without the appropriate accessory. King Gillette, the founder of Gillette, taught the business world that the real money is not in selling the razor (the product) but in selling the blades (the accessory)! Manufacturers of electronic games also rely on captive-product pricing, earning lower margins on the game consoles and substantially higher margins on the game cartridges they sell.

BY-PRODUCT PRICING By-product pricing is a technique in which the revenues from the sale of by-products allow a company to be more competitive in its pricing of the main product. For years, sawmills saw the bark from the trees they processed as a nuisance, something they had to discard. Now it is packaged and sold to gardeners who use the bark chips for ground cover. Zoos across the globe offer one of the most creative examples of by-product pricing, packaging once worthless droppings of exotic animals and marketing it as compost under the clever name "Zoo Doo." Zoo Doo is so popular that Seattle Washington's Woodland Park Zoo conducts a lottery to determine which customers can purchase the compost, which is priced at $12.95 for a two-gallon container.[55]

SUGGESTED RETAIL PRICES Many manufacturers print suggested retail prices on their products or include them on invoices or in wholesale catalogs. Small business owners frequently follow these suggested retail prices because doing so eliminates the need to make a pricing decision. Nonetheless, following prices established by a distant manufacturer may create problems for a small company. For example, a men's clothing store may try to create a high-quality, exclusive image through a prestige pricing policy, but manufacturers may suggest prices that are incompatible with the company's image. Another danger of accepting the manufacturer's suggested price is that it does not take into consideration a small company's cost structure or competitive situation. In a U.S. Supreme Court case in 2007, Leegin Creative Products vs. PSKS, Leegin, the maker of Brighton brand belts, refused to sell its products to a small Texas boutique when the retailer discounted its prices on Brighton belts below the minimum prices established in an agreement the parties had signed. The court ruled in favor of Leegin, overturning a nearly 100-year-old ruling and allowing manufacturers to set and enforce minimum prices retailers can charge for the manufacturer's products as long as doing so does not reduce competition. Several states are considering passing new antitrust laws in an attempt to preempt the court's decision.[56]

FOLLOW-THE-LEADER PRICING Some small companies make no effort to be price leaders in their immediate geographic areas and simply follow the prices that their competitors establish. Entrepreneurs should monitor their competitors' pricing policies and individual prices by reviewing their advertisements or by hiring part-time or full-time comparison shoppers. However, some retailers use this information to establish me-too pricing policies, which eradicate any opportunity to create a special price image for their businesses. Although many retailers must match competitors' prices on identical items, maintaining a follow-the-leader pricing policy may not be healthy for a small business because it robs the company of the opportunity to create a distinctive image in its customers' eyes.

The underlying forces that dictate how a business prices its goods or services vary across industries. The next three sections investigate pricing techniques used in retailing, manufacturing, and service businesses.

LO3A

Explain the pricing methods and strategies for retailers.

Pricing Strategies and Methods for Retailers

As customers have become more price conscious, retailers have changed their pricing strategies to emphasize value. This value–price relationship allows for a wide variety of highly creative pricing and marketing practices. As discussed previously, delivering high levels of recognized value in products and services is one key to retail customer loyalty.

markup (markon)

the difference between the cost of a product or service and its selling price.

Markup

The basic premise of a successful business operation is selling a good or service for more than it costs to produce or provide. The difference between the cost of a product or service and its selling price is called **markup (or markon)**. A business's markup must be large enough to produce a reasonable profit. Markup can be expressed in dollars or as a percentage of either cost or selling price:

$$\text{Dollar markup} = \text{Retail price} - \text{Cost of the merchandise}$$

$$\text{Percentage (of retail price) markup} = \frac{\text{Dollar markup}}{\text{Retail price}}$$

$$\text{Percentage (of cost) markup} = \frac{\text{Dollar markup}}{\text{Cost of unit}}$$

For example, if a shirt costs $14, and a retailer plans to sell it for $30, the markup would be as follows:

$$\text{Dollar markup} = \$30 - \$14 = \$16$$

$$\text{Percentage (of retail price) markup} = \frac{\$16}{\$30} = 53.3\%$$

$$\text{Percentage (of cost) markup} = \frac{\$16}{\$14} = 114.3\%$$

The cost of merchandise used in computing markup includes not only the wholesale price of the merchandise but also any other costs (e.g., selling or transportation charges) that the retailer incurs and a profit minus any discounts (quantity, cash) that the wholesaler offers. Markups vary across industries, but in the designer clothing business, markups (of cost) of between 150 and 250 percent are common. However, some brands command much higher markups. For instance, a pair of jeans at Kohl's carries a markup of cost of about 100 percent, but True Religion's Phantom jeans generate an impressive 360 percent markup of cost.[57] The markup on a bottle of wine in a retail shop is 50 percent (of cost), but in New York City's fine dining restaurants, the markup on the same bottles of wine is between 200 and 300 percent.[58] Movie theater popcorn usually carries an even higher markup (of cost) of 1,275 percent.[59] Table 10.1 shows a breakdown of the cost of the components and markup calculations for Apple's third generation iPad and Microsoft's Surface tablets.

Once entrepreneurs create a financial plan, including sales estimates and anticipated expenses, they can compute their companies' initial markup. The initial markup is the *average* markup required on all merchandise to cover the cost of the items, all incidental expenses, and a reasonable profit:

$$\text{Initial dollar markup} = \frac{\text{Operating expenses} + \text{Reductions} + \text{Profit}}{\text{Net sales} + \text{Reductions}}$$

where operating expenses include the cost of doing business, such as rent, utilities, and depreciation, and reductions include employee and customer discounts, markdowns, special sales, and the cost of stock-outs. Entrepreneurs must be aware of the impact that discounts have on their markup percentages. Corey Kaplan, owner of NYC Bagel Deli, a bagel shop with three locations in Chicago, recently sold 10,500 coupons on the discount coupon site Groupon that offered $10 worth of food for just $4, an amount that equals the company's cost of goods sold. The result: a markup of zero percent.[60]

Suppose that a small retailer forecasts sales of $980,000, operating expenses of $544,000, and $24,000 in reductions. If the retailer establishes a target profit of $58,000, the initial markup (of retail price) percentage is calculated as follows:

$$\text{Initial markup percentage} = \frac{544,000 + 24,000 + 58,000}{980,000 + 24,000} = 62\%$$

Any item in the store that carries a markup (of retail price) of at least 62 percent covers costs and meets the owner's profit objective. Any item that has a markup of less than 62 percent reduces the company's net income.

TABLE 10.1 **Costs and Markup Calculations for Apple's iPad and Microsoft's Surface Tablets**

Apple introduced the iPad years before Microsoft launched its Surface tablet and has a commanding 55 percent market share. Although both comparably equipped products sell for $599, Microsoft's Surface has a higher markup. The following table provides a cost breakdown for each device's components and its markup.

Component	Surface	iPad
Memory 32 GB	$34.00	$47.50
Display and touchscreen	$101.00	$127.00
Processors	$21.50	$23.00
Cameras	$5.00	$12.35
User interface and sensors	$20.00	$15.00
Power management device	$8.00	$10.00
Lithium polymer battery	$20.00	$32.00
Mechanical/Electromechanical components	$36.00	$50.50
Box contents	$25.00	$5.50
Assembly cost	$13.00	$10.00
Total Cost	**$283.50**	**$332.85**
Retail Price	$599.00	$599.00
$ Markup = Price − Cost	**$315.50**	**$266.15**
Percentage (of cost) markup =	**111.3%**	**80.0%**

Source: Based on Andrew Rassweiler, "New iPad 32 GB + 4G Carries $364.35 Bill of Materials," *iSuppli*, March 16, 2012, http://www.isuppli.com/Teardowns/News/Pages/New-iPad-32-GB-4G-Carries-364-35-Bill-of-Materials.aspx; Adrian Kingsley-Hughes, "Microsoft's Surface RT 'More Profitable' Than Apple's iPad," *ZDNet*, November 6, 2012, http://www.zdnet.com/microsofts-surface-rt-more-profitable-than-apples-ipad-7000006966/; JP Mangalindan, "Let the Tablet War Begin," *Fortune*, December 24, 2012, p. 34.

Once an entrepreneur determines the initial percentage markup, he or she can compute the appropriate retail price using the following formula:

$$\text{Retail Price} = \frac{\text{Dollar cost}}{(1 - \text{Percentage of retail price markup})}$$

For instance, applying the 62 percent markup to an item that cost the retailer $17.00 gives the following result:

$$\text{Retail price} = \frac{\$17.00}{(1 - .62)} = \$44.74$$

The owner establishes a retail price of $44.74 for this item using a 62 percent (of retail price) markup.

Finally, retailers must verify that the retail price they have calculated is consistent with their companies' image. Will it cover costs and generate the desired profit? Is the final price in line with the company's strategy? Is it within an acceptable price range? How does it compare to the prices charged by competitors? And, perhaps most important, are customers willing and able to pay this price? Figure 10.4 explains the mathematics of markups—and markdowns—at the retail level.

LO3B

Explain the pricing methods and strategies for manufacturers.

Pricing Concepts for Manufacturers

For manufacturers, the pricing decision requires the support of accurate, timely accounting records. The most commonly used pricing technique for manufacturers is **cost-plus pricing**. Using this method, a manufacturer establishes a price that is composed of direct materials, direct

The Sale Rack Shuffle
Have you ever purchased an item of clothing at a significant discount from the sale rack and then wondered if the store actually made any profit on the item? Here is how the markup and mark down process typically works:
1. Clothing company makes dress at a cost of $50.
2. Sells dress to retailer at a wholesale cost of $80.
3. Retailer marks up dress to $200 (60 percent markup (of price).
4. If unsold after eight to twelve weeks, dress is marked down by 25 percent to $150.
5. If dress still does not sell, it is marked down further until it does. Clothing company and retailer negotiate on how to share the cost of the markdown.

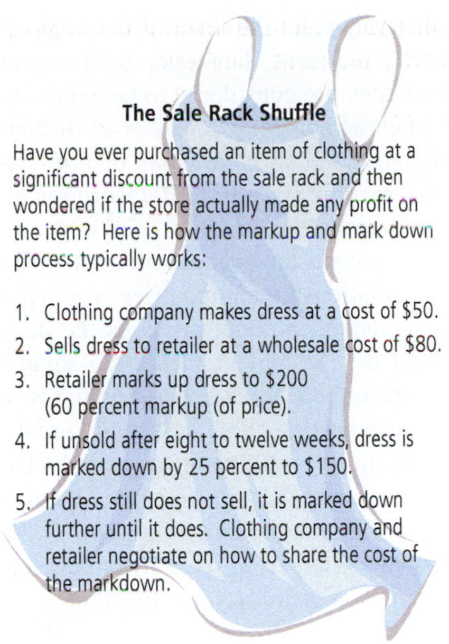

FIGURE 10.4
The Mathematics of Markups and Markdowns

labor, factory overhead, selling and administrative costs, plus a desired profit margin. Figure 10.5 illustrates the cost-plus pricing components.

cost-plus pricing a pricing technique in which a manufacturer establishes a price that covers the cost of direct materials, direct labor, factory overhead, selling and administrative costs, and a desired profit margin.

The main advantage of the cost-plus pricing method is its simplicity. Given the proper cost accounting data, computing a product's final selling price is relatively easy. In addition, because they add a profit onto the top of their companies' costs, manufacturers are likely to achieve their desired profit margins. This process, however, does not encourage the manufacturers to use their resources efficiently. Even if the company fails to employ its resources in the most effective manner, it still earns a profit, and thus there is no motivation to conserve resources in the manufacturing process. Finally, because manufacturers' cost structures vary so greatly, cost-plus pricing fails to consider the competition (and market forces) sufficiently. Despite its drawbacks, the cost-plus method of establishing prices remains popular in industries such as construction and printing.

Direct Costing and Pricing

One requisite for a successful pricing policy in manufacturing is a reliable cost accounting system that can generate timely reports to determine the costs of processing raw materials into finished goods. The traditional method of product costing is called **absorption costing** because all manufacturing and overhead costs are absorbed into a finished product's total cost. Absorption costing includes direct materials, direct labor, plus a portion of fixed and variable factory overhead in each unit manufactured. Full absorption financial statements are used in published annual reports and in tax reports and are very useful in performing financial analysis. However, full absorption statements are of little help to manufacturers when determining prices or the impact of price changes.

absorption costing the traditional method of product costing in which all manufacturing and overhead costs are absorbed into the product's total cost.

A more useful technique for managerial decision making is **variable (direct) costing**, in which the cost of the products manufactured includes only those costs that vary directly with the quantity produced. In other words, variable costing encompasses direct materials, direct labor,

variable (direct) costing a method of product costing that includes in the product's cost only those costs that vary directly with the quantity produced.

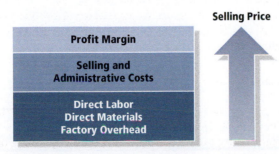

Selling Price
Profit Margin
Selling and Administrative Costs
Direct Labor
Direct Materials
Factory Overhead

FIGURE 10.5
Cost-Plus Pricing Components

and factory overhead costs that vary with the level of the company's output of finished goods. Factory overhead costs that are fixed (rent, depreciation, and insurance) are *not* included in the costs of finished items. Instead, they are considered to be expenses of the period.

A manufacturer's goal when establishing prices is to discover the combination of selling price and sales volume that covers the variable costs of producing a product and contributes toward covering fixed costs and earning a profit. Full-absorption costing clouds the true relationships among price, volume, and costs by including fixed expenses in unit cost. Direct costing, however, yields a constant unit cost for the product no matter what volume of production. The result is a clearer picture of the relationship among price, volume, and costs.

The starting point for establishing product prices is the direct cost income statement. As Table 10.2 indicates, the direct cost statement yields the same net income as does the full-absorption income statement. The only difference between the two statements is the format. The full-absorption statement allocates costs such as advertising, rent, and utilities according to the activity that caused them, but the direct cost income statement separates expenses into their fixed and variable components. Fixed expenses remain constant regardless of the production level, but variable expenses fluctuate according to production volume.

When variable costs are subtracted from total revenues, the result is the manufacturer's **contribution margin**—the amount remaining that contributes to covering fixed expenses and

contribution margin
the amount left over out of a dollar of sales after variable expenses are paid that contributes to covering fixed expenses and earning a profit.

TABLE 10.2 Full-Absorption versus Direct-Cost Income Statement

Full-Absorption Income Statement		
Sales revenue		$790,000
Cost of goods sold		
Materials	250,500	
Direct labor	190,200	
Factory overhead	120,200	560,900
Gross profit		$229,100
Operating expenses		
General and administrative	66,100	
Selling	112,000	
Other	11,000	
Total operating expenses		189,100
Net income (before taxes)		$ 40,000
Direct-Cost Income Statement		
Sales revenue (100%)		$790,000
Variable costs		
Materials	250,500	
Direct labor	190,200	
Variable factory overhead	13,200	
Variable selling expenses	48,100	
Total variable costs (63.5%)		502,000
Contribution margin (36.5%)		288,000
Fixed costs		
Fixed factory overhead	107,000	
Fixed selling expenses	63,900	
General and administrative	66,100	
Other fixed expenses	11,000	
Total fixed expenses (31.4%)		248,000
Net income (before taxes) (5.1%)		$ 40,000

earning a profit. Expressing this contribution margin as a percentage of total revenue yields the company's contribution percentage. Computing the contribution percentage is a critical step in establishing prices through the direct costing method. This manufacturer's contribution margin percentage is 36.5 percent, which is calculated as follows:

$$\text{Contribution percentage} = 1 - \frac{\text{Variable expenses}}{\text{Revenues}}$$

$$= 1 - \frac{\$502,000}{\$790,000} = 36.5\%$$

Computing the Break-Even Selling Price

The manufacturer's contribution percentage tells what portion of total revenues remains after covering variable costs to contribute toward meeting fixed expenses and earning a profit. This manufacturer's contribution percentage is 36.5 percent, which means that variable costs absorb 63.5 percent of total revenue. In other words, variable costs make up 63.5 percent ($1.00 - 0.365 = 0.635$) of the product's selling price. Suppose that this manufacturer's variable costs include the following:

Material	$2.08/unit
Direct labor	$4.12/unit
Variable factory overhead	$0.78/unit
Total variable cost	$6.98/unit

The minimum price at which the manufacturer would sell the item for is $6.98. Any price below this would not cover variable costs. To compute the break-even selling price for this product, we find the selling price using the following equation:

$$\text{Break-even selling price} = \frac{\text{Profit} + (\text{Variable cost per unit} \times \text{Quantity produced}) + \text{Total fixed cost}}{\text{Quantity produced}}$$

To break even, the manufacturer assumes $0 profit. Suppose that plans are to produce 50,000 units of the product and that fixed costs will be $110,000. The break-even selling price is as follows:

$$\text{Break-even selling price} = \frac{\$0 + (\$6.98 \times 50,000 \text{ units}) + \$110,000}{50,000 \text{ units}}$$

$$= \frac{\$459,000}{50,000 \text{ units}}$$

$$= \$9.18/\text{unit}$$

Thus, $2.20 ($9.18/unit − $6.98/unit) of the $9.18 break-even price contributes to meeting fixed production costs. But suppose the manufacturer wants to earn a $50,000 profit. Then the selling price is calculated as follows:

$$\text{Selling price} = \frac{\$50,000 + (\$6.98/\text{unit} \times 50,000 \text{ units}) + \$110,000}{50,000 \text{ units}}$$

$$= \frac{\$509,000}{50,000 \text{ units}}$$

$$= \$10.18/\text{unit}$$

Now the manufacturer must decide whether customers will purchase 50,000 units at $10.18. If not, he or she must decide either to produce a different, more profitable product or to lower the selling price by lowering either its cost or its profit target. Any price above $9.18 will generate some profit although less than that desired. In the short run, the manufacturer could sell the product for less than $9.18 if competitive factors dictate but *not* below $6.98 because a price below $6.98 would not cover the variable cost of production.

pocket price
the price a company receives for a product or service after deducting all discounts and purchase incentives.

Because the manufacturer's capacity in the short run is fixed, pricing decisions should be aimed at employing these resources most efficiently. The fixed costs of operating the plant cannot be avoided, and the variable costs can be eliminated only if the firm ceases offering the product. Therefore, the selling price must be at least equal to the variable costs (per unit) of making the product. Any price above this amount contributes to covering fixed costs and providing a reasonable profit.

Of course, over the long run, a manufacturer cannot sell below total costs and continue to survive. The final selling price must cover total product cost—both fixed and variable—and generate a reasonable profit.

LO3C

Explain the pricing methods and strategies for service firms.

Pricing Strategies and Methods for Service Firms

Service businesses must establish their prices on the basis of the materials used to provide the service, the labor employed, an allowance for overhead, and profit. As in a manufacturing operation, a service business must have a reliable, accurate accounting system to keep a tally of the total costs of providing the service. Most service firms base their prices on an hourly rate, usually the actual number of hours required to perform the service. Some companies, however, base their fees on a standard number of hours, determined by the average number of hours needed to perform the service. For most firms, labor and materials make up the largest portion of the cost

Hands On . . . How To

Calculate Your Company's Pocket Price Band

Pricing decisions have a significant influence on a company's ability to generate a profit. Research by consulting firm Deloitte shows that pricing has four times the impact on profitability as other improvements, such as reducing costs. When entrepreneurs make pricing decisions, they usually look at the retail price or the invoice price they charge. Doing so, however, may be misleading if the company offers significant "off-invoice" discounts, such as cash discounts for paying early, quantity discounts for large purchases, special promotional discounts, and others. These invoice leakages mean that a business is getting less—sometimes far less—than the retail or invoice price listed. In some cases, a company's **pocket price**, the price it receives for a product or a service after deducting all discounts and purchase incentives, is far below the listed retail or invoice price. The impact of these discounts can be significant. Research by the consulting firm McKinsey and Company shows that a decrease of 1 percent in a typical company's average prices will reduce its operating profits by 8 percent if all other factors remain constant.

How are discounts affecting your business? To find out, you must estimate your company's pocket price waterfall and its pocket price band. The pocket price waterfall starts with a company's invoice or retail price on the far left of the diagram and then shows how much every discount or incentive the company offers its customers reduces that price. In the example in Figure 1, this small manufacturer offers a cash discount for early payment that shaves 2.0 percent off of the retail price, a 3.5 percent discount for companies whose purchases exceed a particular volume, a cooperative advertising program (in which it splits the cost of advertising its products with retailers) that amounts to 4.4 percent, and periodic promotional discounts to move products that average 10.8 percent. Other discounts the company offered

customers further reduced its pocket price. In the end, the company's average pocket price is 77.2 percent of the listed invoice price (see Figure 1).

Not every customer qualifies for every discount, however. The type and the amount of the discount vary from one customer to another; the pocket prices they pay can vary a good deal. Therefore, it is important to estimate the width of the company's pocket price band, which shows the percentage of sales that each pocket price (shown as a percentage of the listed invoice or retail price) accounts for (see Figure 2). In this example, pocket prices that are 90 percent or more of the company's invoice price account for just 28.3 percent of its total revenue. Conversely, pocket prices that

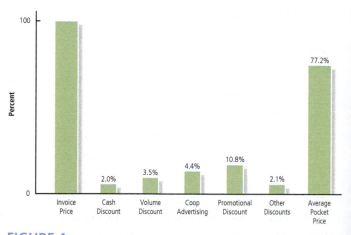

FIGURE 1

Pocket Price Waterfall

Hands On . . . How To (continued)

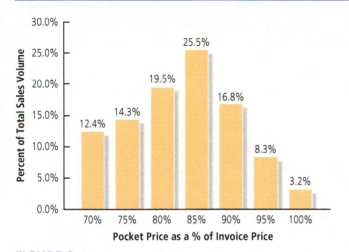

FIGURE 2

Pocket Price Band

are 80 percent or less of its invoice price make up 46.2 percent of its total revenue. The final step in the process is to identify the individual customers that make up each segment of the company's pocket price band. When one manufacturer analyzed its pocket price band, managers discovered that sales to 20 percent of its customers had slipped below its break-even point, causing the company to lose money on sales to those customers. To restore profitability, managers raised prices selectively and lowered their costs by reducing the frequency of deliveries and encouraging customers to place orders online.

A wide pocket price band is not necessarily bad. It simply shows that some customers generate much higher pocket prices than others. When a band is wide, small changes in its shape can produce big results for a company. If an entrepreneur can increase sales at the upper end of the band while reducing or even dropping altogether those at the lower end of the band, the company's revenues and profits will climb. If a company's price band is narrow, an entrepreneur has less room to maneuver prices, changing the shape of the band is more difficult, and any changes the entrepreneur can make tend to have less impact on the company's sales and revenues.

When one lighting company calculated its pocket price band, managers were surprised at its width. Once managers realized how big a dent discounts were putting in its revenues and profits, they worked with the sales force to realign the company's discount structure. Some of the company's smallest accounts had been getting the largest discounts despite their small volume of purchases. Managers also focused on boosting sales to those accounts that were producing the highest pocket prices. These changes resulted in the company's average pocket price rising by 3.8 percent and its profits climbing 51 percent!

Discounts tend to work their way into a company's pricing structure gradually over time, often one transaction at a time, especially if an entrepreneur gives sales representatives latitude to negotiate prices with customers. Few companies make the effort to track these discounts and, as a result, do not realize the impact that discounts have on their profitability. By monitoring their companies' pocket price waterfall and the resulting pocket price band, entrepreneurs can improve significantly the revenue and the profits they generate.

Sources: Adapted from "Pricing for Profitability: What's in Your Pocket," *CFO Insights*, Deloitte, 2013, pp. 1–5; Michael V. Marn, Eric V. Roegner, and Craig C. Zawada, "The Power of Pricing," *McKinsey Quarterly*, no. 1, 2003, http://www.mckinseyquarterly.com; and Cheri N. Eyink, Michael V. Marn, and Stephen C. Moss, "Pricing in an Inflationary Downturn," *McKinsey Quarterly*, September 2008, http://www.mckinseyquarterly.com/Pricing_in_a_downturn_2189.

---

of the service. To establish a reasonable, profitable price for service, small business owners must know the cost of materials, direct labor, and overhead for each unit of service they provide. Using these basic cost data and a desired profit margin, an owner of a small service firm can determine the appropriate price for the service.

Consider a simple example for pricing a common service—computer repair. Ned's Computer Repair Shop uses the direct costing method to prepare an income statement for exercising managerial control (see Table 10.3).

Ned estimates that he and his employees spent about 9,250 hours in the actual production of computer repair service. Therefore, total cost per productive hour for Ned's Computer Repair Shop comes to the following:

$$\frac{\$104,000 + \$68,000}{9,250 \text{ hours}} = \$18.59/\text{hour}$$

Now Ned must add in an amount for his desired profit. He expects a net operating profit of 18 percent on sales. To compute the final price, he uses the following equation:

Price Total cost per hour = productive hour ÷ (1 − net profit target as % of sales)

$$= \$18.59 \div (1 − .18)$$

$$= \$22.68/\text{hour}$$

TABLE 10.3 Direct-Cost Income Statement, Ned's Computer Repair Shop

Sales revenue		$199,000
Variable expenses		
Labor	52,000	
Materials	40,500	
Variable factory overhead	11,500	
Total variable expenses		104,000
Fixed expenses		
Rent	2,500	
Salaries	38,500	
Fixed overhead	27,000	
Total fixed expenses		68,000
Net income		$ 27,000

A price of $22.68 per hour will cover Ned's costs and generate the desired profit. Smart service shop owners compute their cost per production hour at regular intervals throughout the year. Rapidly rising labor costs and material prices dictate that an entrepreneur calculate the company's price per hour even more frequently. As in the case of the retailer and the manufacturer, Ned must evaluate the pricing policies of competitors and decide whether his price is consistent with his company's image.

Of course, the price of $22.68 per hour assumes that each job requires the same amount of materials. If this is not a valid assumption, Ned must recalculate the price per hour *without* including the cost of materials:

$$\text{Cost per productive hour} = \frac{\$172,000 - \$40,500}{9,250 \text{ hours}}$$

$$= \$14.22/\text{hour}$$

Adding in the desired 18 percent net operating profit on sales gives the following:

$$\text{Price per hour} = \$14.22/\text{hour} \div (1.00 - 0.18)$$

$$= \$17.34/\text{hour}$$

Under these conditions, Ned would charge $17.34 per hour plus the actual cost of materials used and any markup on the cost of material. A repair job that takes four hours to complete would have the following price, assuming a 60 percent markup (of cost) on materials.

Cost of service (4 hours × $17.34/hour)	$ 69.36
Cost of materials	$ 41.00
Markup on materials (60%)	$ 24.60
Total price	$134.96

Because services are intangible, their pricing offers more flexibility than do tangible products. One danger that entrepreneurs face is pricing their services too low because prospective customers' perceptions of a service are heavily influenced by its price. In other words, establishing a low price for a service may actually harm a service company's sales. For service companies in particular, the right price reflects both the company's cost of providing the service and the customers' perceived value of the service.

LO4

Describe the impact of credit on pricing.

The Impact of Credit on Pricing

Consumers crave convenience when they shop, and one of the most common conveniences they demand is the ability to purchase goods and services on credit. Small businesses that fail to offer credit to their customers lose sales to competitors who do. One recent study shows that the

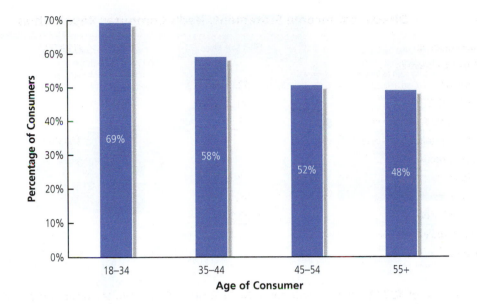

FIGURE 10.6

Percentage of Customers Who Shop Only at Businesses That Accept Multiple Forms of Payment

Source: Based on data from Small Business Payments Survey, WePay, June 23, 2013.

58 percent of small business owners say that their customers expect them to accept credit cards; in addition, the majority of consumers shop only at businesses that accept multiple forms of payment, including credit cards (see Figure 10.6).[61] However, companies that sell on credit incur additional expenses for offering this convenience. Small companies have three options for selling to customers on credit: credit (and debit) cards, installment credit, and trade credit.

Credit Cards

Consumers in the United States hold nearly 1.9 billion credit cards; in fact, the average credit card holder in the United States has 3.75 cards.[62] Shoppers use credit cards to make 26 billion transactions a year that account for more than $2.48 trillion worth of goods and services annually—nearly $78,600 in credit card sales per second.[63] The message is clear: Customers expect to make purchases with credit cards, and small companies that fail to accept credit cards run the risk of losing sales to competitors who do. The average credit card transaction is $94.[64] Research shows that customers who use credit cards make purchases that are 112 percent higher than if they had used cash.[65] In addition, surveys show that customers rate businesses offering credit options higher on key performance measures such as reputation, reliability, and service.[66] In short, accepting credit cards broadens a small company's customer base and closes sales that it would normally lose if customers had to pay in cash.

Companies that accept credit cards incur additional expenses for offering this convenience, however. Businesses must pay to use the system, typically 1 to 6 percent of the total credit card charge, which they must factor into the prices of their products or services. They also pay a transaction fee of 5 to 25 cents per charge. (The average fee is 10 cents per transaction.) Given customer expectations, small businesses cannot afford to drop major cards, even when credit card companies raise the fees merchants must pay. Fees operate on a multistep process (see Figure 10.7). On a typical $100 credit card purchase that a customer makes, the bank that issued the customer's card receives $1.85. This amount includes a 1.75 percent processing fee called the **interchange fee**, the fee that banks collect from retailers whenever customers use a credit or a debit card to pay for a purchase, and a 10-cent flat transaction fee. The credit card company takes 0.13 percent (or 13 cents in this example) of the transaction amount. The retailer's bank, called the processing bank, receives a processing fee of 0.25 percent of the purchase amount plus a 10-cent flat transaction fee (or 35 cents in this example), leaving the retailer with $97.67. Before it can accept credit cards, a business must obtain merchant status from either a bank or an independent sales organization. Square, a company that issues a free credit card reader to merchants that attaches to smart phones and tablets, consolidates all three fees and charges merchants a flat fee of 2.75 percent.

interchange fee
the fee banks collect from retailers whenever customers use a credit or debit card to pay for a purchase.

FIGURE 10.7

How a Typical Credit Card Transaction Works

Source: Based on "Credit Card Processing," Card Fellow, 2013, http://www .cardfellow.com/content/ credit-card-processing-guide .php#MoneyGo; "Credit Cards," United States Government Accounting Office, September 2006, pp. 73–74.

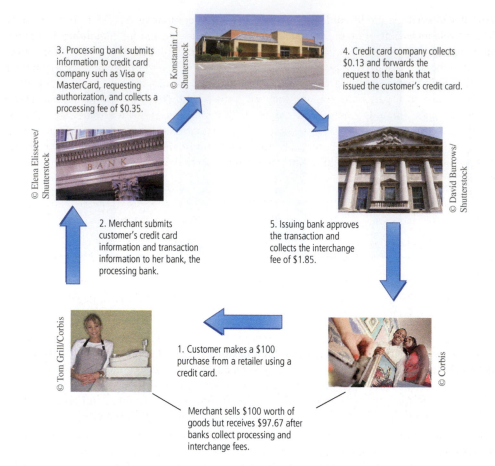

3. Processing bank submits information to credit card company such as Visa or MasterCard, requesting authorization, and collects a processing fee of $0.35.

© Konstantin L./ Shutterstock

4. Credit card company collects $0.13 and forwards the request to the bank that issued the customer's credit card.

© Elena Elisseeva/ Shutterstock

© David Burrows/ Shutterstock

2. Merchant submits customer's credit card information and transaction information to her bank, the processing bank.

5. Issuing bank approves the transaction and collects the interchange fee of $1.85.

© Tom Grill/Corbis

1. Customer makes a $100 purchase from a retailer using a credit card.

© Corbis

Merchant sells $100 worth of goods but receives $97.67 after banks collect processing and interchange fees.

ENTREPRENEURIAL PROFILE: Zack Zilverman and Alex Rein: Kelvin Natural Slush Zack Silverman and Alex Rein, who left their careers as attorneys to start Kelvin Natural Slush, a food truck that navigates the streets of New York City selling all-natural slushies made from real fruit purée, say Square has been an essential part of their mobile business's success. The entrepreneurs say they were considering spending $4,000 on touch-screen computers and software before they learned about Square. Rather than spend $4,000 on hardware and software, Silverman and Rein purchased a $400 iPad, attached Square to it, and process customers' credit cards from wherever they are. Square also gives them the ability to download sales reports at any time.[67] ■

Credit card processing fees, commonly known as "swipe fees," cost merchants $40 billion per year, and small businesses typically pay higher credit card processing fees than their larger counterparts.[68] These fees, especially on small purchases, can wipe out any profit the company might have earned. To minimize the fees associated with credit card transactions, some entrepreneurs offer customers incentives to pay with cash.

ENTREPRENEURIAL PROFILE: Doug Hendrick: Steamer's Café Doug Hendrick, owner of Steamer's Café, a small restaurant in Clinton, South Carolina, conducts a monthly drawing for a $20 gift card for customers who pay with cash rather than with credit cards. Hendrick says that fees absorb 3 percent of every credit card purchase. "Multiply that by thousands of customers and divide it by a thin profit margin, and it's a huge chunk," he says.[69] ■

E-COMMERCE AND CREDIT CARDS When it comes to online business transactions, the most common method of payment is the credit card. Internet merchants are constantly challenged by the need to provide secure methods for safe, secure online transactions. As you learned in Chapter 9, many shoppers are suspicious of online transactions for reasons of security and privacy. Therefore, online merchants must ensure their customers' privacy and the security of their credit card transactions by using encryption software.

Another obstacle is credit card fraud, which cost U.S. companies $11.27 billion annually. Credit card issuers assumed the burden for 63 percent of that loss, and the remaining 37 percent fell on merchants.[70] Because they lack the face-to-face contact with their customers, online merchants face special challenges to avoid credit card fraud. Identity and credit card theft results in customers denying the authenticity of certain purchases and disputing the charges that appear on their bills. Unless merchants are vigilant, they will end up shouldering most of the burden for these charge-backs. About 0.9 percent of online credit card transactions are fraudulent, costing merchants $3.5 billion a year![71] Because small companies are less likely than large businesses to use high-tech online fraud detection tools, they are more likely to be victims of e-commerce fraud. The following steps can help online merchants reduce the probability that they will become victims of credit card fraud:

- Use an address verification system to compare every customer's billing information on the order form with the billing information in the bank or credit card company's records.

- Require customers to provide the CVV2 number from the back of the credit card. Although crooks can get access to this number, it can help screen out some fraudulent orders.

- Check customers' Internet protocol (IP) addresses. If an order contains a billing address in California but the IP address from which the order is placed is in China, chances are that the order is fraudulent.

- Monitor activity on the Web site with the help of a Web analytics software package. There are many packages available, and analyzing log files helps online entrepreneurs pinpoint the sources of fraud.

- Verify large orders. Large orders are a cause for celebration but only if they are legitimate. Check the authenticity of large orders, especially if the order is from a first-time customer.

- Post notices on the Web site that your company uses antifraud technology to screen orders. These notices make legitimate customers feel more confident about placing their orders and crooks trying to commit fraud tentative about running their scams.

- Contact the credit card company or the bank that issued the card. If you suspect that an order may be fraudulent, contact the company *before* processing it. Taking this step could save a company thousands of dollars in losses.[72]

DEBIT CARDS Consumers in the United States carry more than 580 million debit cards that act as electronic checks, automatically deducting the purchase amount immediately from a customer's checking account.[73] Shoppers conduct nearly 53 billion debit card transactions, totaling $2.1 trillion each year. The average debit card transaction is $39.62.[74] In 2003, for the first time in history, shoppers used credit and debit cards more often than cash or checks to make retail purchases.[75] The equipment that allows businesses to accept debit cards is easy to install and to set up, and the cost to the company is negligible. The payoff can be big, however, in the form of increased sales, improved cash flow, and decreased losses from bad checks. In addition, interchange fees on debit cards are lower than those on credit cards. Credit and debit cards account for nearly two-thirds of all consumer and business payments, and that percentage continues to grow.[76] Small businesses that do not accept credit and debit cards operate at a disadvantageous position.

MOBILE WALLETS Modern smart phone technology allows shoppers to carry **mobile wallets** on their smart phones or tablets. Shoppers download software that links their mobile devices to a credit or debit card and then swipe the devices over a near field communication (NFC) or Quick Response (QR) reader to complete a purchase. Today, shoppers make $31 billion in mobile purchases, nearly three times the $11.6 billion in 2012.[77] Google Wallet, the first mobile wallet application, now has competition from other large companies, including AT&T, Verizon Wireless, T-Mobile, and small start-ups such as Square and Dwolla. To accept payments from customers' mobile wallets, some applications require special hardware (which typically cost between $100 and $200), but others use stores' existing checkout equipment that is updated with software business owners usually download for free.[78] The technology not only speeds up the checkout process but also allows merchants to recognize customers when they walk into a store;

mobile wallet
applications that link a smart phone or tablet to a credit or debit card, transforming the device into a digital wallet.

send personalized coupons, incentives, and rewards to them; and generate useful reports, such as how often a shopper buys a particular item or when he or she last shopped. At Marcia and Dean Harris's Itzy Bitzy Ritzy Shop, a store in Norwalk, Connecticut, that sells furniture designed for small spaces, shoppers with mobile devices use Square Wallet to make their furniture purchases quickly and easily, and the money shows up in the store's bank account the next day.[79]

Installment Credit

Small companies that sell big-ticket consumer durables—such as major appliances, cars, and boats—frequently rely on installment credit to support their sales efforts. Because very few customers can purchase such items in a single lump-sum payment, small businesses finance them over an extended time. The time horizon may range from just a few months up to 30 or more years. Most companies require customers to make an initial down payment for the merchandise and then finance the balance for the life of the loan. The customer repays the loan principal plus interest on the loan. One advantage of installment loans for a small business is that the owner retains a security interest as collateral on the loan. If a customer defaults on the loan, the owner still holds the title to the merchandise. Because installment credit absorbs a small company's cash, many rely on financial institutions, such as banks and credit unions, to provide installment credit. When a company has the financial strength to "carry its own paper," the interest income from the installment loan contract often yields more than the initial profit on the sale of the product. For some businesses, such as furniture stores and used car dealerships, this traditionally has been a major source of income.

Trade Credit

Companies that sell small-ticket items frequently offer their customers trade credit—that is, they create customer charge accounts. The typical small business bills its credit customers each month. To speed collections, some offer cash discounts if customers pay their balances early; others impose penalties on late payers. Before deciding to use trade credit as a competitive weapon, business owners must make sure that their companies' cash position is strong enough to support the additional pressure credit sales create.

LAYAWAY Although technically not a form of credit, layaway plans, like trade credit, enable customers to purchase goods over time. In the typical layaway plan, a customer selects an item, pays a deposit on it, and makes regular payments on the item until it is paid in full. Unlike trade credit, the retailer keeps the item until the customer has finished paying. Most stores establish minimum payments and maximum payoff dates, and some charge a service fee. Created during the Great Depression as a way to help shoppers purchase goods, layaway has become popular once again, especially around the holiday season, as stubborn unemployment and slow economic growth have posed challenges for shoppers.

ENTREPRENEURIAL PROFILE: **Marlana Walters: The Everyday Gourmet** Marlana Walters, owner of The Everyday Gourmet, a kitchen and household accessory store with two locations in Mississippi, recently introduced a layaway plan for the holiday season on popular big-ticket items that cost at least $300 after she noted customers' reluctance to purchase her company's higher-priced items. Walters sees layaway as a tool to provide her customers with more time to pay for their purchases. The Everyday Gourmet has a simple layaway plan: Divide the item's price into four equal payments, the last of which must be paid by the week of December 20.[80] ■

Chapter Summary by Learning Objective

1. Discuss the relationships among pricing, image, competition, and value.

- Pricing decisions cut across every aspect of a small company, influencing everything from its marketing and sales efforts to its operations and strategy.

A company's pricing strategy is a major determinant of its image in the marketplace, is influenced by the pricing strategies of its competitors, and is an important element in the value that customers perceive its products or services provide.

- Ultimately, the "right" price for a product or service depends on one factor: the value it provides for a customer. For most shoppers, three reference points define a fair price: the price they have paid for the product or service in the past, the prices competitors charge for the same or similar product or service, and the costs a company incurs to provide the product or service.

2. **Describe effective pricing techniques for introducing new products or services and for existing ones.**

- Pricing a new product is often difficult for business owners, but it should accomplish three objectives: getting the product accepted, maintaining market share as the competition grows, and earning a profit. Generally, three major pricing strategies are used to introduce new products into the market: penetration, skimming, and life cycle.

- Pricing techniques for existing products and services include odd pricing, price lining, dynamic pricing, leader pricing, geographic pricing, discounts, multiple unit pricing, bundling, optional product pricing, captive product pricing, by-product pricing, suggested retail pricing, and follow-the-leader pricing.

3. **Explain the pricing methods and strategies for retailers, manufacturers, and service firms.**

- Pricing for the retailer means pricing to move merchandise. Markup is the difference between the cost of a product or service and its selling price. Most retailers compute their markup as a percentage of retail price.

- A manufacturer's pricing decision depends on the support of accurate cost accounting records. The most common technique is cost-plus pricing, in which the manufacturer charges a price that covers the cost of producing a product plus a reasonable profit. Every manufacturer should calculate a product's break-even price, the price that produces neither a profit nor a loss.

- Service firms often suffer from the effects of vague, unfounded pricing procedures and frequently charge the going rate without any idea of their costs. A service firm must set a price on the basis of the cost of materials used, labor involved, overhead, and a profit. The proper price reflects the total cost of providing a unit of service.

4. **Describe the impact of credit on pricing.**

- Offering consumer credit enhances a small company's reputation and increases the probability, speed, and magnitude of customers' purchases. Small firms offer three types of consumer credit: credit cards, installment credit, and trade credit (charge accounts).

Discussion Questions

10-1. How does pricing affect a small firm's image?
10-2. What competitive factors must the small firm consider when establishing prices?
10-3. Describe the strategies a small business could use in setting the price of a new product.
10-4. What objectives should a company's pricing strategy for a new product seek to achieve?
10-5. Define the following pricing techniques: odd pricing, price lining, leader pricing, geographical pricing, and discounts.
10-6. Why do many small businesses use the manufacturer's suggested retail price?
10-7. What are the disadvantages of using the manufacturer's suggested retail price?
10-8. What is a markup?
10-9. How is the markup for a product calculated?
10-10. What is cost-plus pricing?
10-11. Why do so many manufacturers use cost-plus pricing?
10-12. What are the disadvantages of using cost-plus pricing?
10-13. Explain the difference between full-absorption costing and direct costing.
10-14. How does absorption costing help a manufacturer determine a reasonable price?
10-15. Explain the technique for a small service firm setting an hourly price.
10-16. What benefits does a small business get by offering customers credit?
10-17. What costs does a business incur by selling on credit?

Beyond the Classroom . . .

10-18. Apple Inc. dominates the market for tablets with its line of iPads, which currently includes the classic iPad, the iPad Mini, and the iPad Air. Because the company constantly introduces new models and features, it also adjusts prices on these popular devices. Use the Web to research the history of the iPad and write a brief summary of Apple's pricing strategy on its tablet. Which products compete with the iPad?

10-19. How do the prices of similar models compare to the iPod?

10-20. Is Apple able to command a premium for its brand?

10-21. If so, what factors allow the company to do so?

10-22. Interview a successful small retailer and ask the following questions: Do they seek a specific image through their prices?

10-23. What role do competitors play in the business owner's pricing?

10-24. Does the retailer use specific pricing techniques, such as odd pricing, price lining, leader pricing, and geographic pricing?

10-25. How are discounts calculated?

10-26. What markup percentage does the firm use?

10-27. How are prices derived?

10-28. What are their cost structures?

10-29. Select an industry that has several competing small firms in your area. Contact these firms and compare their approaches to determining prices. Do prices on identical or similar items differ?

10-30. Why are the companies' prices on identical or similar items different?

Endnotes

Scan for Endnotes or go to www.pearsonhighered.com/scarborough

Goodluz/Shutterstock

11 Creating a Successful Financial Plan

Learning Objectives

On completion of this chapter, you will be able to:

1. Describe how to prepare the basic financial statements and use them to manage a small business.

2. Create projected (pro forma) financial statements.

3. Understand the basic financial statements through ratio analysis.

4. Explain how to interpret financial ratios.

5. Conduct a break-even analysis for a small company.

Fashioning a well-designed financial plan as part of a comprehensive business plan is one of the most important steps to launching a new business venture. Entrepreneurs who fail to develop workable strategies for earning a profit from the outset eventually suffer the ultimate business penalty: failure. In addition, potential lenders and investors demand a realistic financial plan before putting their money into a start-up company. More important, a financial plan is a vital tool that helps entrepreneurs to manage their businesses more effectively, steering their way around the pitfalls that cause failures. Proper **financial management** requires putting in place a system that provides entrepreneurs with relevant financial information in an easy-to-read and readily understandable format on a timely basis. It allows entrepreneurs to know not only *how* their businesses are doing financially but also *why* their companies are performing that way. The information in a small company's financial records is one resource to which competitors have no access. Smart entrepreneurs recognize this and put their companies' numbers to work for them so that they can make their businesses more successful. Understanding financial statements and other accounting records can help alert entrepreneurs to emerging problems in their businesses, help them trim costs, and offer clues on how to boost profits.[1]

Unfortunately, failure to collect and analyze basic financial data is a common mistake among entrepreneurs. A recent survey by Sage North America reports that about one in five small business owners lacks sufficient financial literacy to identify the cost that has the greatest impact on a company.[2] A study by the National Federation of Independent Business reports that 79 percent of small business owners have no plans to provide their employees with financial training.[3] Both research and anecdotal evidence suggest that a significant percentage of entrepreneurs run their companies without any kind of financial plan and never analyze their companies' financial statements as part of the decision-making process. Bill Hettinger, business consultant and author of *Finance without Fear*, estimates that 75 percent of business owners do not understand or fail to focus on the financial details of their companies.[4] To reach profit objectives, entrepreneurs must be aware of their companies' overall financial position and the changes in financial status that occur over time. Most accounting experts advise entrepreneurs to use one of the popular computerized small business accounting programs such as QuickBooks, Xero, and others to manage routine record-keeping tasks. More than three-quarters (77 percent) of small business owners use accounting software to help track revenues and expenses.[5] Working with an accountant to set up the system at the outset and then having an employee or a bookkeeping service enter the transactions is most efficient for most businesses. These programs make preparing reports, analyzing a company's financial statements, and summarizing data a snap. Studies show that business owners who use accounting software are more likely to be financially literate than those who do not.[6]

This chapter focuses on some practical tools that help entrepreneurs to develop a workable financial plan, keep them aware of their company's financial performance, and enable them to plan for profit. They can use these tools to help them anticipate changes and plot an appropriate profit strategy to meet these shifts head-on. These profit-planning techniques are not difficult to master, nor are they overly time consuming. We will discuss the techniques involved in preparing projected (pro forma) financial statements, conducting ratio analysis, and performing break-even analysis.

Basic Financial Statements

Before we begin building projected financial statements, it would be helpful to review the basic financial reports that measure a company's financial position: the balance sheet, the income statement, and the statement of cash flows. The level of financial sophistication among small business owners may not be high, but the extent of financial reporting among small businesses is. Most small businesses regularly produce summary financial information, almost all of it in the form of these traditional financial statements.

The Balance Sheet

Like a digital camera, the **balance sheet** takes a "snapshot" of a business's financial position, providing owners with an estimate of its worth on a given date. Its two major sections show the assets the business owns and the claims creditors and owners have against those assets. The balance sheet is usually prepared on the last day of the month. Figure 11.1 shows the balance sheet for Sam's Appliance Shop for the year ended December 31, 2015.

---

financial management

a process that provides entrepreneurs with relevant financial information in an easy-to-read format on a timely basis; it allows entrepreneurs to know not only how their businesses are doing financially but also why they are performing that way.

LO1

Describe how to prepare the basic financial statements and use them to manage a small business.

balance sheet

a financial statement that provides a snapshot of a business's financial position, estimating its worth on a given date; it is built on the fundamental accounting equation: Assets = Liabilities + Owner's equity.

FIGURE 11.1

Sam's Appliance Shop, Balance Sheet

Assets		
Current Assets		
Cash		$49,855
Accounts Receivable	$179,225	
Less Allowance for Doubtful Accounts	$6,000	$173,225
Inventory		$455,455
Prepaid Expenses		$8,450
Total Current Assets		$686,985
Fixed Assets		
Land		$59,150
Buildings	$74,650	
Less Accumulated Depreciation	$7,050	$67,600
Equipment	$22,375	
Less Accumulated Depreciation	$1,250	$21,125
Furniture and Fixtures	$10,295	
Less Accumulated Depreciation	$1,000	$9,295
Total Fixed Assets		$1,57,170
Intangibles (Goodwill)		$3,500
Total Assets		$847,655
Liabilities		
Current Liabilities		
Accounts Payable		$152,580
Notes Payable		$83,920
Accrued Wages/Salaries Payable		$38,150
Accrued Interest Payable		$42,380
Accrued Taxes Payable		$50,820
Total Current Liabilities		$367,850
Long-Term Liabilities		
Mortgage		$127,150
Note Payable		$85,000
Total Long-Term Liabilities		$212,150
Owner's Equity		
Sam Lloyd, Capital		$267,655
Total Liabilities and Owner's Equity		$847,655

The balance sheet is built on the fundamental accounting equation: Assets = Liabilities + Owner's equity. Any increase or decrease on one side of the equation must be offset by an increase or decrease on the other side, hence the name *balance sheet*. It provides a baseline from which to measure future changes in assets, liabilities, and equity. The first section of the balance sheet lists the company's assets (valued at cost, not actual market value) and shows the total value of everything the business owns. **Current assets** consist of cash and items to be converted into cash within one year or within the normal operating cycle of the company, whichever is longer, such as accounts receivable and inventory. **Fixed assets** are those acquired for long-term use in the business. Intangible assets include items such as goodwill, copyrights, and patents that, although valuable, are not tangible.

The second section shows the business's **liabilities**—the creditors' claims against the company's assets. **Current liabilities** are those debts that must be paid within one year or within the normal operating cycle of the company, whichever is longer, and **long-term liabilities** are those

current assets
assets such as cash and other items to be converted into cash within one year or within the company's normal operating cycle.

fixed assets
assets acquired for long-term use in a business.

liabilities
creditors' claims against a company's assets.

current liabilities
those debts that must be paid within one year or within the normal operating cycle of a company.

long-term liabilities
liabilities that come due after one year.

owner's equity
the value of the owner's investment in the business.

that come due after one year. This section of the balance sheet also shows the **owner's equity**, the value of the owner's investment in the business. It is the balancing factor on the balance sheet, representing all of the owner's capital contributions to the business plus all accumulated (or retained) earnings not distributed to the owner(s).

The Income Statement

income statement
a financial statement that represents a moving picture of a business, comparing its expenses against its revenue over a period of time to show its net income (or loss).

The **income statement** (also called the profit-and-loss statement) compares expenses against revenue over a certain period of time to show the firm's net income (or loss). Like a digital video recorder, the income statement is a "moving picture" of a company's profitability over time. The annual income statement reports the bottom line of the business over the fiscal or calendar year. Figure 11.2 shows the income statement for Sam's Appliance Shop for the year ended December 31, 2015.

To calculate net income or loss, an entrepreneur records sales revenues for the year, which includes all income that flows into the business from sales of goods and services. Income from other

FIGURE 11.2
Sam's Appliance Shop, Income Statement

Net Sales Revenue		$1,870,841
Credit Sales	$1,309,589	
Cash Sales	$561,252	
Cost of Goods Sold		
Beginning Inventory, 1/1/xx	$805,745	
+ Purchases	$939,827	
Goods Available for Sale	$1,745,572	
– Ending Inventory, 12/31/xx	$455,455	
Cost of Goods Sold		$1,290,117
Gross Profit		$580,724
Operating Expenses		
Advertising	$139,670	
Insurance	$46,125	
Depreciation		
Building	$18,700	
Equipment	$9,000	
Salaries	$224,500	
Travel	$4,000	
Entertainment	$2,500	
Total Operating Expenses		$444,495
General Expenses		
Utilities	$5,300	
Telephone	$2,500	
Postage	$1,200	
Payroll Taxes	$25,000	
Total General Expenses		$34,000
Other Expenses		
Interest Expense	$39,850	
Bad Check Expense	$1,750	
Total Other Expenses		$41,600
Total Expenses		$520,095
Net Income		$60,629

sources (rent, investments, and interest) also must be included in the revenue section of the income statement. To determine net sales revenue, owners subtract the value of returned items and refunds from gross revenue. **Cost of goods sold** represents the total cost, including shipping, of the merchandise sold during the accounting period. Manufacturers, wholesalers, and retailers calculate cost of goods sold by adding purchases to beginning inventory and subtracting ending inventory. Service-providing companies typically have no cost of goods sold because they do not carry inventory.

Subtracting the cost of goods sold from net sales revenue results in a company's gross profit. Allowing the cost of goods sold to get out of control whittles away a company's gross profit and threatens its ability to generate positive net income because a company must pay all of its operating expenses out of its gross profit. Dividing gross profit by net sales revenue produces the **gross profit margin**, a ratio that every small business owner should watch closely. If a company's gross profit margin slips too low, it is likely that it will operate at a loss (negative net income). A business that operates at a gross profit margin of 50 percent must generate $2 in sales for every $1 of operating expenses just to break even. However, a company with a 10 percent gross profit margin must generate $10 in sales for every $1 of operating expenses to reach its break-even point.

Many business owners whose companies are losing money mistakenly believe that the problem is inadequate sales volume; therefore, they focus on pumping up sales at any cost. In many cases, however, the losses their companies are incurring are the result of an inadequate gross profit margin, and pumping up sales only deepens their losses! Repairing a poor gross profit margin requires a company to raise prices, cut manufacturing or purchasing costs, refuse orders with low profit margins, "fire" unprofitable customers (see Figure 11.3), or add new products with more attractive profit margins. *Increasing sales will not resolve the problem.* Monitoring the gross profit margin over time and comparing it to those of other companies in the same industry are important steps to maintaining a company's long-term profitability.

cost of goods sold
the total cost, including shipping, of the merchandise sold during the accounting period.

gross profit margin
gross profit divided by net sales revenue.

ENTREPRENEURIAL PROFILE: Paul Spiegelman: Stericycle Stericycle, a medical waste company headquartered in Lake Forest, Illinois, is a company that relies on a fundamental set of beliefs to drive how its business operates. The core values that guide Stericycle's culture include accountability to its customers, teamwork in pursuit of a common goal, customers first, continuous improvement, and a strong sense of camaraderie and enjoying work. Paul Spiegelman, Chief Culture Officer of Stericycle, says that if the company's clients don't share these values, the result is a significant negative impact on the company's culture. The founders landed a multi-million-dollar client that shared the values on which they founded the business, but over time the client's priorities shifted from customer service to maximizing its sales. The client began to provide services its customers did not ask for, adding unwanted items to their monthly bills. Despite the negative impact on the company's profits, Stericycle terminated the contract with the client. Employees were pleased to know that Stericycle delivered on its commitment to the customer and sent letters to management thanking them for acting with integrity.[7] ■

Paul Spiegelman, Stericycle

Operating expenses include those costs that contribute directly to the manufacturing and distribution of goods. General expenses are indirect costs incurred in operating the business. "Other expenses" is a catchall category covering all other expenses that don't fit into the other two categories. Subtracting total expenses from total revenue gives the company's net income (or loss) for the accounting period. Reducing expenses increases a company's net income, and even small reductions in expenses can add up to big savings.

ENTREPRENEURIAL PROFILE: Wesley Hutchen: Oak Environmental Wesley Hutchen, owner of Oak Environmental, an environmental remediation rental company based in Calgary, Alberta, switched from tracking its equipment by hand to an automated bar-code system that dramatically increased the accuracy of the company's rental records. Although implementing the new system required three months, error rates fell from 20 percent to less than 2 percent, and employees cut in half the time spent tracking equipment. According to Hutchen, the automated system saves $50,000 a year in costs and allows the company to generate $36,000 more per year in equipment rental revenue.[8] ■

operating expenses
those costs that contribute directly to the manufacture and distribution of goods.

Comparing a company's current income statement to those of prior accounting periods often reveals valuable information about key trends and a company's progress toward its financial

FIGURE 11.3

Customer Profitability Map

Source: Based on Gwen Moran, "Six Weeks to a Better Bottom Line," *Entrepreneur*, January 2010, pp. 47–51; "Retaining and Divesting Customers: An Exploratory Study of Right Customers, 'At Risk' Right Customers, and Wrong Customers," Kashing Woo and Henry K.Y. Fock, *Journal of Services Marketing*, Vol. 18, Issue 2/3, 2004, pp. 187–197.

A classic study reports that 20 percent of the typical company's customers are unprofitable. Many business owners who take the time to analyze their customer bases are surprised to discover that some of the customers they thought were profitable actually are costing their companies money. The solution: Raise prices or fees, or "fire" the unprofitable customers. The following customer profitability map helps entrepreneurs identify which of their customers are best – and worst – for their businesses.

Methodology: Select your biggest customers and assign each one a "resonance score" from 1 (difficult) to 10 (easy) that reflects how easy they are to serve. Then calculate the profit margin (profit as a percentage of sales) your company makes from each customer. Plot each customer's score on the map as a circle. The size of the circle should be proportionate to the percentage of the company's total sales for which the customer accounts. The result is a map that shows how your company's customers fall into each of the 4 quadrants.

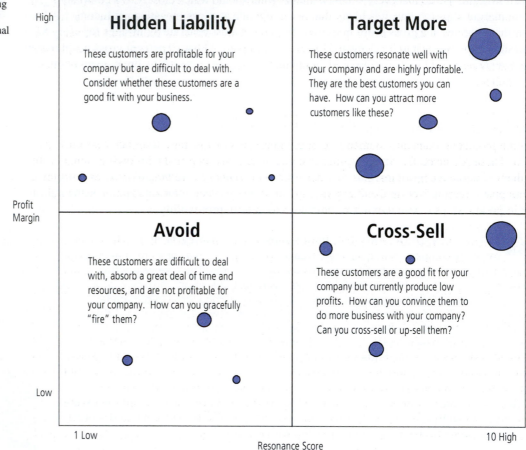

Hidden Liability

These customers are profitable for your company but are difficult to deal with. Consider whether these customers are a good fit with your business.

Target More

These customers resonate well with your company and are highly profitable. They are the best customers you can have. How can you attract more customers like these?

Avoid

These customers are difficult to deal with, absorb a great deal of time and resources, and are not profitable for your company. How can you gracefully "fire" them?

Cross-Sell

These customers are a good fit for your company but currently produce low profits. How can you convince them to do more business with your company? Can you cross-sell or up-sell them?

Profit Margin — High / Low

Resonance Score — 1 Low / 10 High

goals. "Numbers run companies," says Norm Brodsky, serial entrepreneur and owner of Citi-Storage, a successful storage company based in New York City. "It's your responsibility as an owner to know and understand not only the income statement but also the balance sheet of your business. You ignore them at your peril."[9]

The Statement of Cash Flows

statement of cash flows

a financial statement showing the changes in a company's working capital from the beginning of the year by listing both the sources and the uses of those funds.

The **statement of cash flows** show the changes in a company's working capital from the beginning of the accounting period by listing both the sources of funds and the uses of those funds. Many small businesses never need to prepare such a statement; instead, they rely on a cash budget, a less formal managerial tool you will learn about in Chapter 12 that tracks the flow of cash into and out of a company over time. Sometimes, however, creditors, lenders, investors, or business buyers may require this information.

To prepare the statement, owners must assemble the balance sheet and the income statement summarizing the present year's operations. They begin with the company's net income for the period (from the income statement). Then they add the sources of the company's funds: borrowed funds, owner contributions, decreases in accounts receivable, increases in accounts payable, decreases in inventory, depreciation, and any others. Depreciation is listed as a source of funds because it is a noncash expense that has already been deducted as a cost of doing business. Because the owner has already paid for the item being depreciated, however, its depreciation is a source of funds. Next the owner subtracts the uses of these funds: plant and equipment purchases, dividends to owners, repayment of debt, increases in accounts receivable, decreases in accounts payable, increases in inventory, and so on. The difference between the total sources and the total uses is the increase or decrease in working capital. By investigating the changes in their companies' working capital and the reasons for them, owners can create a more practical financial action plan for the future of the enterprise.

These financial statements are more than just complex documents used only by accountants and financial officers. When used in conjunction with the analytical tools described in the following sections, they can help entrepreneurs to map a firm's financial future and actively plan for profit. Mere preparation of these statements is not enough, however; owners and employees must *understand and use* the information contained in them to make the business more effective and efficient.

Creating Projected Financial Statements

LO2

Create projected (pro forma) financial statements.

Creating projected financial statements helps entrepreneurs to transform their business goals into reality. These projected financial statements answer questions such as the following: What profit can the business expect to earn? If the owner's profit objective is x dollars, what sales level must the company achieve? What fixed and variable expenses can the owner expect at that level of sales? The answers to these and other questions are critical in formulating a functional financial plan for the small business.

This section focuses on creating projected income statements and balance sheets for a small start-up. These projected (or pro forma) statements are a crucial component of every business plan because they estimate the profitability and the overall financial condition of a company in the future. They are an integral part of convincing potential lenders and investors to provide the financing needed to get the company off the ground (the topic of Chapter 13). In addition, because these statements project a company's financial position through the end of the forecasted period, they help entrepreneurs to plan the route to improved financial strength and healthy business growth. To be useful, however, these forecasts must be *realistic and well researched*! Entrepreneurs typically find that revenues are the most difficult to forecast. However, even though estimating future revenues is challenging, the accuracy of these forecasts can make or break a business as it grows.

Because an established business has a history of operating data from which to construct projected financial statements, the task is not nearly as difficult as it is for a start-up company. When creating pro forma financial statements for a business start-up, entrepreneurs typically rely on published statistics that summarize the operation of similar-size companies in the same industry. These statistics are available from a number of sources (described later), but this section draws on information found in the *Annual Statement Studies*, a compilation of financial data collected from 250,000 companies across more than 760 industries organized by Standard Industrial Classification (SIC) Code and North American Industry Classification System (NAICS) published by the Risk Management Association (RMA). Because conditions and markets change so rapidly, entrepreneurs developing financial forecasts for start-ups should focus on creating projections for two years into the future. Although these sources offer guidelines to gauge how reasonable a company's projections are, entrepreneurs should use values that apply to their own particular circumstances to derive their forecasts. Remember that any published financial data is based on operating businesses. For a start-up company, the key is accurate forecasts that show how the business will get to these industry standards. Investors want to see that entrepreneurs have developed well-researched, realistic expectations about their companies' income and expenses and when they expect to start earning a profit.

Projected Financial Statements for a Small Business

One of the most important tasks confronting the entrepreneur launching a new enterprise is to determine the amount of funding required to begin operation as well as the amount required to keep the company going until it begins to generate positive cash flow. The amount of money needed to begin a business depends on the type of operation, its location, inventory requirements, sales volume, and many other factors. Every new firm must have enough capital to cover all start-up costs, including funds to rent or buy plant, equipment, and tools, and to pay for advertising, wages, licenses, utilities, and other expenses. In addition, an entrepreneur must maintain a reserve of capital to carry the company until it begins to generate positive cash flow. Too often, entrepreneurs are overly optimistic in their financial plans and fail to recognize that expenses initially exceed income (and cash outflow exceeds cash inflow) for most small firms. This period of net losses (and negative cash flow) is normal and may last from just a few months to several years. During this time, entrepreneurs must be able to pay the company's regular bills, meet payroll, purchase inventory, take advantage of cash discounts, pay the company's regular bills, grant customers credit, and meet their personal financial obligations.

THE PROJECTED INCOME STATEMENT When creating a projected income statement, the first step is to create a sales forecast. An entrepreneur has two options: to develop a sales forecast and work down or to set a profit target and work up. Developing a realistic sales forecast for a business start-up is not always easy, but with creativity and research it is possible. Talking with owners of existing businesses in the industry (outside of the local trading area, of course) can provide meaningful insight into the sales levels a company can expect to generate during its early years. For a reasonable fee, entrepreneurs can access published aggregated financial statistics that industry trade associations collect on the companies in their industries. Other organizations, such as the Risk Management Association and Dun & Bradstreet, publish useful financial information for a wide range of industries. Internet searches and trips to the local library will produce the necessary information. Interviews with potential customers and test-marketing an actual product or service also can reveal the number of customers a company can expect to attract. One method for checking the accuracy of a sales estimate is to calculate the revenue other companies in the same industry generate per employee and compare it to your own projected revenue per employee. A value that is out of line with industry standards is not likely to be realistic. Experienced investors will expect any sales forecasts to be clearly explained by a sound marketing plan.

Many entrepreneurs prefer the second method of creating a projected income statement, targeting a profit figure and then "working up" to determine the sales level they must achieve to reach it. Of course, it is important to compare this sales target against the results of the marketing plan to determine whether it is realistic. Once an entrepreneur determines a reasonable profit target, the next step is to estimate the expenses the business will incur to generate that profit.

The profit a small company produces must be large enough to provide a reasonable return on the time the owners spend operating the business and a return on their investment in the business. Entrepreneurs who earn less in their own businesses than they could earn working for someone else must weigh carefully the advantages and disadvantages of choosing the path of entrepreneurship. Why be exposed to all of the risks, sacrifices, and hard work of beginning and operating a small business if the rewards are less than those of remaining in the secure employment of another? Although there are many nonfinancial benefits of owning a business, the net income a company generates should be at least as much as an entrepreneur could earn by working for someone else.

An adequate profit must also include a reasonable return on the owner's total investment in the business. (The owner's total investment is the amount contributed to the company plus any retained earnings from previous years that were funneled back into the business.) In other words, an entrepreneur's target income is the sum of a reasonable salary for the time spent running the business and a normal return on the amount invested in the company. Determining this amount is the first step in creating the projected income statement.

An entrepreneur then must translate this target profit into a net sales figure for the forecasted period. To calculate net sales from a target profit, the entrepreneur can use published industry statistics. Suppose an entrepreneur wants to launch a small retail comic book store and has determined that his target net income is $30,000. Statistics gathered from BizMiner's *Startup Profit and Loss Profile* show that the typical comic book store's net profit margin (Net profit ÷ Net sales) is 12.7 percent. Using this information, he can compute the sales level required to produce a net profit of $30,000:

$$\text{Net profit margin} = \frac{\text{Net income}}{\text{Sales (annual)}}$$

Solving for net sales produces the following result:

$$\text{Net sales} = \frac{\$30,000}{0.127}$$

$$= \$236,220$$

Now the entrepreneur knows that to make a net profit of $30,000 (before taxes), he or she must achieve annual sales of $236,220. To complete the projected income statement, the owner simply applies the appropriate statistics from the *Startup Profit and Loss Profile* to the annual sales figure. Because the statistics for each income statement item are expressed as percentages of net sales, the entrepreneur merely multiplies the proper percentage by the annual sales figure to obtain the desired value. For example, cost of goods sold usually makes up 60.23 percent of net sales for the typical comic book store; therefore, the owner of this new comic book store expects his cost of goods sold to be the following:

$$\text{Cost of goods sold} = \$236,220 \times 0.6023 = \$142,275$$

The comic book store's complete projected income statement is shown as follows:

Net sales	(100%)	$236,220
−Cost of goods sold	(60.23%)	$142,275
Gross profit margin	(39.77%)	$ 93,945
−Operating expenses	(27.07%)	$ 63,945
Net profit (before taxes)	(12.7%)	$30,000

At this point, the business appears to be a viable venture. However, remember that this income statement represents a sales *goal* the owner may not be able to reach. The next step is to determine whether this required sales volume is reasonable. One useful technique is to break down the required annual sales volume into *daily* sales figures. Assuming that the store will be open six days per week for 52 weeks (312 days), we see that the owner must average $757 per day in sales:

$$\text{Average daily sales} = \frac{\$236,220}{312 \text{ days}} = \$757/\text{day}$$

This calculation gives the owner a better perspective of the sales required to yield an annual profit of $30,000.

To determine whether the profit expected from the business will meet or exceed the target income, the entrepreneur also should use this same process to create income statements that are built on pessimistic, most likely, and optimistic sales estimates. The previous analysis shows an entrepreneur the sales level needed to reach a desired profit. But what happens if sales are lower? Higher? Making these projections requires a reliable sales forecast using the market research techniques described in Chapter 8.

Suppose, for example, that after conducting research on the industry, a marketing survey of local customers, and discussions with owners of comic book stores in other markets, the prospective entrepreneur projects annual sales for the proposed business's first year of operation to be only $210,000. The entrepreneur can take this sales estimate and develop a projected income statement:

Net sales	(100%)	$210,000
−Cost of goods sold	(60.23%)	$126,483
Gross profit margin	(39.77%)	$ 83,517
−Operating expenses	(27.07%)	$ 56,847
Net profit (before taxes)	(12.7%)	$26,670

Based on sales of $210,000, this entrepreneur can expect a net income (before taxes) of $26,670. If this amount is acceptable as a return on the investment of time and money in the business, the entrepreneur should proceed with his or her planning.

At this stage in developing the financial plan, the owner should create a more detailed picture of the venture's expected operating expenses. In addition to gathering information from industry trade associations about typical operating expenses, an entrepreneur can contact potential vendors, suppliers, and providers to get estimates of the expenses he or she can expect to incur in his or her area of operation. One entrepreneur who was preparing a business plan for the launch of an upscale women's clothing store contacted local utility companies, insurance agencies, radio and television stations, newspapers, and other vendors to get estimates of her utility, insurance, advertising, and other expenses.

To ensure that they have not overlooked any business expenses in preparing the business plan, entrepreneurs should list all of the expenses they will incur and have an accountant review the list. Sometimes in their estimates of expenses, entrepreneurs neglect to include salaries for themselves, immediately raising a "red flag" among lenders and investors. Without drawing a salary, how will an entrepreneur pay his or her own bills? At the other extreme, lenders and investors frown on exorbitantly high salaries for owners of business start-ups. Typically, salaries are not the best use of cash in a start-up; one guideline is to draw a salary that is about 25 to 30 percent below the market rate for a similar position (and to make adjustments from there if conditions warrant). In addition, as the company grows, executive salaries should be among the *last* expenses to be increased. Reinvesting the extra money in the company accelerates its growth rate.

THE PROJECTED BALANCE SHEET   In addition to projecting a start-up's net profit or loss, an entrepreneur must develop a pro forma balance sheet outlining the fledgling firm's assets and liabilities. Most entrepreneurs' primary concern is profitability because, on the surface, the importance of a business's assets is less obvious. In many cases, small companies begin their lives on weak financial footing because entrepreneurs fail to determine their firms' total asset requirements. To prevent this major oversight, entrepreneurs should prepare a projected balance sheet listing every asset their businesses will need and all the claims against these assets.

ASSETS   Cash is one of the most useful assets the business owns; it is highly liquid and can quickly be converted into other tangible assets. But how much cash should a small business have at its inception? Obviously, there is no single dollar figure that fits the needs of every small firm. One practical rule of thumb, however, suggests that a company's cash balance should cover its operating expenses (less depreciation, a noncash expense) for at least one inventory turnover period. Using this guideline, we can calculate the cash balance for the small comic book store as follows:

Operating expenses = $56,847 (from projected income statement)

Less depreciation (1.24% of annual sales*) of $2,604 (a noncash expense)

Equals: cash expenses (annual) = $54,243

Annual inventory turnover ratio* = 4.6 times per year

$$\text{Cash requirement} = \frac{\text{Cash expenses}}{\text{Average inventory turnover}}$$

$$= \frac{\$54,243}{4.6}$$

$$= \$11,792$$

*From BizMiner, *Startup Profit and Loss Profile*.

Notice the inverse relationship between the small firm's average turnover ratio and its cash requirement. The higher the number of inventory turns a company generates, the lower its cash requirement. For instance, if this florist could turn its inventory eight times per year, its cash requirement would be $54,243 ÷ 8 = $6,780.

Another decision facing the entrepreneur is how much inventory the business should carry. A rough estimate of the inventory requirement can be calculated from the information found on the projected income statement and from published statistics:

Cost of goods sold = $126,483 (from projected income statement)

$$\text{Average inventory turnover} = \frac{\text{Cost of goods sold}}{\text{Average inventory level}} = 4.6 \text{ times/year}$$

Rearranging the equation to solve for inventory level produces the following:

$$\text{Average inventory level} = \frac{\$126,483}{4.6 \text{ times/year}}$$

$$\text{Average inventory level} = \$27,496$$

The entrepreneur also includes $1,800 in miscellaneous current assets.
The estimate of fixed assets is as follows:

Fixtures	$14,500
Office equipment	5,250
Computers/cash register	5,125
Signs	7,200
Miscellaneous	1,500
Total	$33,575

LIABILITIES To complete the projected balance sheet, the owner must record all of the small firm's liabilities, the claims that creditors have against its assets. The comic book store owner was able to finance 50 percent of the inventory and fixtures ($20,998) through suppliers and has a short-term note payable in the amount of $3,750. The only other major claim against the firm's assets is a note payable to the entrepreneur's father-in-law for $25,000. The difference between the company's assets ($74,592) and its total liabilities ($49,748) represents the owner's investment in the business (owner's equity) of $24,844.

The final step is to compile all of these items into a projected balance sheet, as shown in Figure 11.4.

Ratio Analysis

LO3

Understand the basic financial statements through ratio analysis.

Would you be willing to drive a car on an extended trip without being able to see the dashboard displays showing fuel level, engine temperature, oil pressure, battery status, or the speed at which you were traveling? Not many people would! Yet many small business owners run their companies exactly that way. They never take the time to check the vital signs of their businesses using their "financial dashboards." The result: their companies develop engine trouble, fail, and leave them stranded along the road to successful entrepreneurship. To avoid becoming a failure statistic, entrepreneurs must understand the numbers that drive their businesses. Norm Brodsky, a successful serial entrepreneur, says business owners develop a feel for their financial

FIGURE 11.4

Projected Balance Sheet

Assets		Liabilities	
Current Assets		**Current Liabilities**	
Cash	$11,792	Accounts Payable	$20,998
Inventory	27,496	Note Payable	3,750
Miscellaneous	1,800		
Total Current Assets	$41,088	Total Current Liabilities	$24,748
Fixed Assets		**Long-Term Liabilities**	
Fixtures	$14,500	Note Payable	$25,000
Office Equipment	5,250		
Computer/Cash Register	5,125	Total Liabilities	$49,748
Signs	7,200		
Miscellaneous	1,500		
Total Fixed Assets	$33,575	**Owner's Equity**	$24,915
Total Assets	$74,663	**Total Liabilities and Owner's Equity**	$74,663

statements and the specific numbers that they must watch closely to ensure their companies' success. By watching the numbers over time, successful entrepreneurs learn to identify patterns that can signal problems in their businesses.[10]

Smart entrepreneurs know that once they have their businesses up and running with the help of a solid financial plan, the next step is to keep their companies moving in the right direction with the help of proper financial controls. Establishing these controls—and using them consistently—is one of the keys to keeping a business vibrant and healthy. A sound system of financial controls serves as an early warning device for underlying problems that could destroy a young business. A company's financial accounting and reporting systems help signal entrepreneurs that their businesses are experiencing declining profits, increasing overhead expenses, and growing inventories or accounts receivable. All of these changes have a negative impact on cash flow, the lifeblood of every business. As cash flow suffers, entrepreneurs may struggle to pay vendors, may not be able to order enough raw materials and hire enough workers, and may not be able to maintain equipment properly. To avoid these problems, entrepreneurs must tune into the signals that their businesses send about their performance.

What are these signals, and how does an entrepreneur go about tracking and focusing on these them One extremely helpful tool is ratio analysis. **Ratio analysis**, a method of expressing the relationships between any two elements on financial statements, provides a convenient technique for performing financial analysis. When analyzed properly, ratios serve as barometers of a company's financial health. "You owe it to yourself to understand each ratio and what it means to your business," says one accountant. "Ratios point out potential trouble areas so you can correct them before they multiply."[11] Ratio analysis allows entrepreneurs to determine whether their companies are carrying excessive inventory, experiencing heavy operating expenses, over-extending credit, taking on too much debt, and managing to pay their bills on time and to answer other questions relating to the efficient and effective operation of the overall business. Unfortunately, few business owners actually compute financial ratios and use them to manage their businesses.

Smart business owners use financial ratio analysis to identify problems in their businesses while they are still problems and not business-threatening crises. Tracking these ratios over time permits an owner to spot a variety of red flags that are indications of these problem areas. This is critical to business success because business owners cannot solve problems they do not know exist! Business owners also can use ratio analysis to increase the likelihood of obtaining loans. By analyzing their financial statements with ratios, business owners can anticipate potential problems and identify important strengths in advance. Lenders and investors use ratios to analyze the financial statements of companies looking for financing, comparing them against industry averages and looking for trends over time.

How many ratios should an entrepreneur monitor to maintain adequate financial control over a business? The number of ratios that an owner could calculate is limited only by the number of accounts on a firm's financial statements. However, tracking too many ratios only creates confusion and saps the meaning from an entrepreneur's financial analysis. The secret to successful ratio analysis is *simplicity*, focusing on just enough ratios to provide a clear picture of a company's financial standing.

Twelve Key Ratios

In keeping with the idea of simplicity, we will describe 12 key ratios that enable most business owners to monitor their companies' financial positions without becoming bogged down in financial details. This section presents explanations of these ratios and examples based on the balance sheet and the income statement for Sam's Appliance Shop shown in Figure 11.1 and Figure 11.2. We will group them into four categories: liquidity ratios, leverage ratios, operating ratios, and profitability ratios.

LIQUIDITY RATIOS **Liquidity ratios** tell whether a small business will be able to meet its short-term financial obligations as they come due. These ratios forewarn a business owner of impending cash flow problems. A small company with solid liquidity not only is able to pay its bills on time but also has enough cash to take advantage of attractive business opportunities as they arise. Liquidity ratios measure a company's ability to convert its assets to cash quickly and without a

ratio analysis
a method of expressing the relationship between any two accounting elements that allows business owners to analyze their companies' financial performances.

liquidity ratios
tell whether a small business will be able to meet its short-term financial obligations as they come due.

loss of value to pay its short-term liabilities. The primary measures of liquidity are the current ratio and the quick ratio.

1. Current Ratio. The **current ratio** measures a small firm's solvency by indicating its ability to pay current liabilities (debts) from current assets. It is calculated in the following manner:

$$\text{Current ratio} = \frac{\text{Current assets}}{\text{Current liabilities}}$$

$$= \frac{\$686,985}{\$367,850}$$

$$= 1.87:1$$

Sam's Appliance Shop has $1.87 in current assets for every $1 it has in current liabilities.

Current assets are those that an owner expects to convert into cash in the ordinary business cycle and normally include cash, notes/accounts receivable, inventory, and any other short-term marketable securities. Current liabilities are those short-term obligations that come due within one year and include notes/accounts payable, taxes payable, and accruals.

The current ratio is sometimes called the *working capital ratio* and is the most commonly used measure of short-term solvency. Typically, financial analysts suggest that a small business maintain a current ratio of at least 2:1 (i.e., $2 of current assets for every $1 of current liabilities) to maintain a comfortable cushion of working capital. Generally, the higher a company's current ratio, the stronger its financial position; however, a high current ratio does not guarantee that a company is using its assets in the most profitable manner. For example, a business may have an abundance of accounts receivable (many of which may not even be collectible) or may be over-investing in inventory.

With its current ratio of 1.87, Sam's Appliance Shop could liquidate its current assets at 53.5 percent (1 ÷ 1.87 = 53.5%) of its book value and still manage to pay its current creditors in full.

2. Quick Ratio. The current ratio sometimes can be misleading because it does not reflect the *quality* of a company's current assets. As we have already seen, a company with a large number of past-due receivables and stale inventory could boast an impressive current ratio and still be on the verge of financial collapse. The **quick ratio** (sometimes called the acid test ratio) is a more conservative measure of a company's liquidity because it shows the extent to which its most liquid assets cover its current liabilities. This ratio includes only a company's "quick assets"—those assets that a company can convert into cash immediately if needed—and excludes the most illiquid asset of all, inventory. It is calculated as follows:

$$\text{Quick ratio} = \frac{\text{Quick assets}}{\text{Current liabilities}}$$

$$= \frac{\$686,985 - \$455,455}{\$367,850}$$

$$= 0.63:1$$

Sam's Appliance Shop has 63 cents in quick assets for every $1 of current liabilities.

The quick ratio is a more rigorous test of a company's liquidity. It measures a company's capacity to pay its current debts if all sales income ceased immediately. Generally, a quick ratio of 1:1 is considered satisfactory. A ratio of less than 1:1, as is the case with Sam's Appliance Shop, indicates that the small firm is dependent on inventory and on future sales to satisfy short-term debt. A quick ratio of greater than 1:1 indicates a greater degree of financial security.

ENTREPRENEURIAL PROFILE: Alan Knitowski: Phunware Alan Knitowski, Chairman and CEO of the mobile apps company Phunware, learned about the importance of managing cash flow and liquidity from his two

current ratio
measures a small firm's solvency by indicating its ability to pay current liabilities out of current assets.

quick ratio
a conservative measure of a firm's liquidity, measuring the extent to which its most liquid assets cover its current liabilities.

Alan Knitowski, Phunware

previous start-ups. He underestimated the time and expense required to develop the software products for his first company but was able to raise more funding and eventually sell the company to Cisco Systems. In his second company, in which he was an investor and board member, the outcome was not as happy. Two large customers were unable to pay their bills after they were hit hard by the credit crisis of 2008, which forced Knitowski's company into bankruptcy. In his third start-up, Phunware, Knitowski implemented several practices to ensure effective financial and cash management. Every Friday, Phunware's controller e-mails cash on hand, current accounts payable, and the company's quick ratio to the entire management team, which analyzes the financial data to identify any troublesome trends. If the key financial metrics are trending in the wrong direction, managers identify the reason and take quick corrective actions. The team pays particular attention to accounts receivable to determine whether any customers are paying too slowly and what actions might be necessary as a result of any late payments. Managers monitor cash on hand using a color-coded system. If the company has at least 18 months of cash on hand, managers see a greenbar. If cash on hand would cover 12 to 18 months of expenses, the cash on hand figure is coded yellow, and managers immediately begin to evaluate debt and equity funding sources to improve Phunware's cash position. They do not wait until the company's cash on hand drops too low to act. The company has never dropped below 12 months of cash on hand, which would be coded red.[13] ∎

leverage ratios

measure the financing supplied by a firm's owners against that supplied by its creditors; they are a gauge of the depth of a company's debt.

LEVERAGE RATIOS **Leverage ratios** measure the financing supplied by a firm's owners against that supplied by its creditors; they are a gauge of the depth of a company's debt. These ratios show the extent to which an entrepreneur relies on debt capital (rather than equity capital) to finance the business. They also provide a measure of the degree of financial risk in a company. Generally, small businesses with low leverage ratios are less affected by economic downturns, but the returns for these firms are lower during economic booms. Conversely, small companies with high leverage ratios are more vulnerable to economic slides because their debt loads demolish cash flow; however, they have greater potential for large profits.

Today, 33 percent of small businesses rely on bank loans, a decrease from 50 percent of small companies in 2008. This decline is due to the reduction in available bank credit for small businesses since the financial crisis of 2008. During that same time period, small business owners have looked toward loans from family and friends to meet their borrowing needs. Small business use of private loans from family and friends *increased* from 12 percent to 17 percent over that same time period.[12] Debt is a powerful financial tool, whatever its source, but companies must handle it carefully—just as a demolitionist handles dynamite. Like dynamite, too much debt can be deadly. Unfortunately, some companies push their debt loads beyond the safety barrier and threaten their ability to survive. Heavy debt loads can be deadly, particularly when a company's sales or earnings falter, as often happens during economic downturns.

Managed carefully, however, debt can boost a company's performance and improve its productivity.

debt ratio

measures the percentage of total assets financed by a company's creditors compared to its owners.

3. Debt Ratio. A small company's **debt ratio** measures the percentage of total assets financed by its creditors compared to its owners. The debt ratio is calculated as follows:

$$\text{Debit ratio} = \frac{\text{Total debt (or liabilities)}}{\text{Total assets}}$$

$$= \frac{\$367,850 + \$212,150}{\$847,655}$$

$$= 0.68{:}1$$

Creditors have claims of 68 cents against every $1 of assets that Sam's Appliance Shop owns, meaning that creditors have contributed twice as much to the company's asset base as its owners have.

Total debt includes all current liabilities and any outstanding long-term notes and bonds. Total assets represent the sum of the firm's current assets, fixed assets, and intangible assets. A high debt ratio means that creditors provide a large percentage of a company's total financing and, therefore, bear most of its financial risk. Owners generally prefer higher leverage ratios; otherwise, business funds must come either from the owners' personal assets or from taking on new owners, which means giving up more control over the business. In addition, with a greater portion of a firm's assets financed by creditors, the owner is able to generate profits with a smaller personal investment. Creditors, however, typically prefer moderate debt ratios because a lower debt ratio indicates a smaller chance of creditor losses in case of liquidation. To lenders and creditors, high debt ratios mean a higher risk of default.

ENTREPRENEURIAL PROFILE: Apax Partners and Cengage Learning In 2007 Apax Partners, a private equity firm, purchased Cengage Learning, an education textbook publisher, for $7.75 billion using $5 billion in debt financing. Due to the economic downturn that began in 2008 and to changes in the publishing industry, Cengage experienced a sharp decline in revenue and by 2012, was losing up to $2 billion a year. Cengage tried to renegotiate its debt but was unable to come to terms with its creditors. The company had a debt ratio of 0.96:1, which meant it had $0.96 in debt for every $1 in assets. The company entered into Chapter 11 bankruptcy, which allowed it to continue operations and negotiate while it restructured its financing. After nine months in bankruptcy, the company emerged with a new debt structure. The bankruptcy court gave creditors a majority of equity in the company in exchange for their credit claims against the company. Cengage is pursuing a digital publishing business model, moving away from print publishing, in an attempt to create a sustainable business model.[14] ■

According to a senior analyst at Dun & Bradstreet's Analytical Services, "If managed properly, debt can be beneficial because it's a great way to have money working for you. You're leveraging your assets, so you're making more money than you're paying out in interest." However, excessive debt can be the downfall of a business. "As we pile up debt on our personal credit cards our lifestyles are squeezed," he says. "The same thing happens to a business. Overpowering debt sinks thousands of businesses each year."[15]

4. Debt-to-Net-Worth Ratio. A small company's **debt-to-net-worth (debt-to-equity) ratio** also expresses the relationship between the capital contributions from creditors and those from owners and measures how highly leveraged a company is. This ratio reveals a company's capital structure by comparing what the business "owes" to "what it is worth." It is a measure of a small company's ability to meet both its creditor and owner obligations in case of liquidation. The debt-to-net-worth ratio is calculated as follows:

> **debt-to-net-worth (debt-to-equity) ratio** expresses the relationship between the capital contributions from creditors and those from owners and measures how highly leveraged a company is.

$$\text{Debt-to-net worth ratio} = \frac{\text{Total debt (or liabilities)}}{\text{Tangible net worth}}$$

$$= \frac{\$367,850 + \$212,150}{\$267,655 - \$3,500}$$

$$= 2.20:1$$

Sam's Appliance Shop owes creditors $2.20 for every $1 of equity Sam owns.

Total debt is the sum of current liabilities and long-term liabilities, and tangible net worth represents the owners' investment in the business (capital + capital stock + earned surplus + retained earnings) less any intangible assets (e.g., goodwill) the firm owns.

The higher this ratio, the more leverage a business is using and the lower the degree of protection afforded creditors if the business should fail. A higher debt-to-net-worth ratio also means that the firm has less capacity to borrow; lenders and creditors see the firm as being "borrowed up." Conversely, a low ratio typically is associated with a higher level of financial security, giving the business greater borrowing potential.

ENTREPRENEURIAL PROFILE: The Tribune Company Founded in 1847, the Tribune Company publishes seven newspapers, including the *Los Angeles Times, Chicago Tribune, The Baltimore Sun, Sun Sentinel (South Florida), Orlando Sentinel, Hartford Courant, The Morning Call,* and *Daily Press.* The company also owns 23 television stations, WGN America on national cable, and radio stations including WGN-AM radio in Chicago. In late 2007, real estate entrepreneur Sam Zell purchased the Tribune Company in a leveraged buyout. One year later, following

You Be the Consultant

The Challenges of Debt

Charles Kuhn's business, Kopp's Cycle, is a part of bicycling history. E.C. Kopp founded Kopp's Cycle in Princeton, New Jersey, in 1891. The Kopp family operated the business until the Kuhn family purchased it. Eventually Charles took over the store from his father in the late 1970s. Celebrities from Albert Einstein to Brooke Shields purchased bicycles from Kopp's Cycle. Legendary road racing cyclist Greg LeMond was a customer from the time he was a junior racer.

Kopp's Cycle looks like a typical bike shop. The front of the retail store displays high-end bicycles and accessories. In the back of the store is a repair shop that looks the same as it did when Kuhn's father first purchased the business.

Charles Kuhn purchased the building that houses Kuhn's Cycle in 2004 for about $800,000, which he financed with a $775,000 loan secured by an SBA guarantee. Kuhn was not happy with SBA financing, however, because it came with significant additional paperwork. In addition, the SBA loan had an adjustable rate, which worried him about the actual long-term cost of the loan and the uncertainty about payments as the interest rate changed. As a result, Kuhn refinanced the loan through another bank that offered him a conventional fixed rate loan for $825,000. This new loan was not an SBA guaranteed loan, which pleased Kuhn. At the time of the refinancing, the building was appraised at $1.3 million. Although the loan was amortized over 25 years, it had a balloon payment of $775,000 due in three years. Balloon payments are a common feature of loans to small business owners. At the time of the balloon payment, the borrower must refinance, either with the current lender or with a new lender.

As it did with many small businesses, the economic downturn in 2008 hit Kopp's Cycle hard. In addition, online sales of high-end bicycles were increasing significantly. Online retailers were able to offer prices that a small business like Kopp's Cycle could not compete with due to its lower sales volume and higher overhead. Revenues dropped from $498,000 in 2008 to $393,000 in 2009. Kuhn cut prices in 2010 to compete with online retailers, which did bring his sales levels back up. However, the price cuts resulted in profit margins dropping from 10 to 15 percent down

to 1 percent. To manage cash flow during this time, Kuhn relied on credit cards as a funding source for the business. He amassed credit card debt of more than $100,000.

Kuhn decided to seek new financing for his business. His plan was to borrow $1 million to pay off the $800,000 balance on the building loan, pay off the credit card balances, and provide $100,000 in working capital to help manage cash flow. Kuhn estimated that his building is now worth about $1.5 million, which he believed should be more than enough equity to support the loan.

The first bank Kuhn contacted about a loan declined to make a loan. After reviewing Kopp's Cycle's financial statements, the loan officer said Kopp's Cycle's debt coverage ratio, the ratio of monthly net cash flow divided by debt payments, did not meet the bank's minimum of 1.1 to 1.5. With Kopp's Cycle's declining profit margins, it could not meet the required debt coverage ratio. Bankers want to see a significant cushion in a company's monthly cash flow to ensure that even if the company's financial position declines, it can maintain payments on the loan. The second bank Kuhn approached gave him the same answer. A third banker did not even return Kuhn's phone calls.

Kuhn then turned to a loan broker, who he paid an upfront fee and who would take 10 percent of the loan amount once a loan was closed. However, the bank the loan broker found for Kuhn to talk with also passed on the loan, citing concerns over the true market value of Kuhn's building.

Although Kuhn did not believe that a new loan was essential for the survival of the business, he did hope he could secure new financing to bolster Kopp's Cycle's financial position. In addition, Kiuhn must address the balloon payment that is part of his current building loan sooner or later. There was no guarantee that his current bank would renew this loan, and he had not had much luck finding alternative financing.

1. What are the benefits to entrepreneurs who use debt capital (leverage) to finance their companies' growth?

2. What are the risks associated with debt financing?

3. Why is using ratio analysis to keep track of their companies' financial performance over time so important for entrepreneurs?

4. What lessons concerning the use of debt financing can entrepreneurs learn from Charles Kuhn's experience?

5. Assume the role of a small business banker. Suppose that Kuhn had approached you for a bank loan to refinance his debt. Which financial ratios would you be most interested in? Why? What advice would you offer him?

6. Assume the role of a small business counselor. What advice would you offer him to ensure the long-term survival of Kopp's Cycle?

Blend Images/Moxie Productions/Getty Images

Source: Based on Robb Mandelbaum, "A Bicycle Shop Struggles to Get a Loan," *New York Times*, June 2, 2011, p. B5; "Welcome to Kopp's Cycle," Kopp's Cycle, n.d., http://koppscycle.net/articles/kopps-cycle-history-pg59.htm; Linda Arntzenius, "All in a Day's Work: Charles Kuhn," *Town Topics*, n.d., http://www.towntopics.com/sep1306/other4.html.

the 2008 economic downturn and a prolonged decline in advertising revenues, the Tribune Company filed for protection under Chapter 11 bankruptcy. On December 31, 2012, after four years in bankruptcy, the Tribune Company emerged with its restructured financing in place. Before the restructuring, the company had more than $13 billion in liabilities and a negative equity balance of –$8.27:1 billion, which produced a negative debt to equity ratio. Its debt-to-assets ratio was 2.1:1, which means it owed $2.10 in debt for every $1 in assets! After reorganization, the company had $5.75 billion in liabilities and an equity balance of $4.93 billion, which is a debt-to-equity ratio of 1.16:1. Its debt-to-asset ratio improved to 0.50:1.[16] ■

As a company's debt-to-net-worth ratio approaches 1:1, the creditors' interest in the business approaches that of the owners. If the ratio is greater than 1:1, as is still the case with the Tribune Company after reorganization, creditors' claims exceed those of the owners, and the business may be undercapitalized. In other words, the owner has not supplied an adequate amount of capital, forcing the business to be overextended in terms of debt. Lenders become nervous when a company's debt-to-equity ratio reaches 3:1 or more.

5. **Times-Interest-Earned Ratio.** The **times-interest-earned ratio** is a measure of a small company's ability to make the interest payments on its debt. It tells how many times a company's earnings cover the interest payments on the debt it is carrying. This ratio measures the size of the cushion a company has in covering the interest cost of its debt load. The times-interest-earned ratio is calculated as follows:

times-interest-earned ratio
measures a small firm's ability to make the interest payments on its debt.

$$\text{Times interest earned ratio} = \frac{\text{Earnings before interest and taxes (or EBIT)}}{\text{Total interest expense}}$$

$$= \frac{\$60,629 + \$39,850}{\$39,850}$$

$$= 2.52:1$$

Sam's Appliance Shop's earnings are 2.5 times greater than its interest expense.

EBIT is the firm's profit *before* deducting interest expense and taxes; the denominator measures the amount the business paid in interest over the accounting period. A high ratio suggests that a company has little difficulty meeting the interest payments on its loans; creditors see this as a sign of safety for future loans. Conversely, a low ratio is an indication that the company is overextended in its debts; earnings will not be able to cover its debt service if this ratio is less than one. Many banks look for a times-interest-earned ratio of at least 2:1, but some creditors may want to see 4:1 to 6:1 before pronouncing a small company a good credit risk. Before Vicorp Restaurants Inc., the owner of Village Inn and Bakers Square restaurant chains, filed for bankruptcy, its times-interest-earned ratio had slipped from nearly 3:1 to just 1.85:1.[17] According to a Pepperdine University survey of bankers, the top reason that business loans are denied is inadequate cash flow and profits.[18]

Although low to moderate levels of debt can boost a company's financial performance, trouble looms on the horizon for businesses whose debt loads are so heavy that they must starve critical operations, research and development, customer service, and other vital areas just to pay interest on the debt. Because their interest payments are so large, highly leveraged companies find they are restricted when it comes to spending cash, whether on an acquisition, normal operations, or capital spending. Some entrepreneurs are so averse to debt that they run their companies with little or no borrowing, relying instead on their business's cash flow to finance growth.

ENTREPRENEURIAL PROFILE: Jim Zamichieli: Zamolution When Jim Zamichieli started his digital marketing company, Zamolution, he invested $20,000 in personal savings rather than borrow start-up capital. Zamichieli says he is more careful and thoughtful because it is his money at work in the business. The former corporate executive saw many companies founder when they took on too much debt, something he vows never to do, even though he admits that his company could probably grow more rapidly if he used bank credit.[19] ■

operating ratios

help an entrepreneur evaluate a small company's overall performance and indicate how effectively the business employs its resources.

average-inventory-turnover ratio

measures the number of times its average inventory is sold out, or turned over, during an accounting period.

OPERATING RATIOS Operating ratios help an entrepreneur evaluate a small company's overall performance and indicate how effectively the business employs its resources. The more effectively its resources are used, the less capital a small business will require. These five operating ratios are designed to help an entrepreneur spot those areas he or she must improve if his or her business is to remain competitive.

6. Average-Inventory-Turnover Ratio. A small firm's **average-inventory-turnover ratio** measures the number of times its average inventory is sold out, or turned over, during the accounting period. This ratio tells the owner whether an entrepreneur is managing inventory properly. It indicates whether a business's inventory is understocked, overstocked, or obsolete. The average-inventory-turnover ratio is calculated as follows:

$$\text{Average-inventory-turnover ratio} = \frac{\text{Cost of goods sold}}{\text{Average inventory}}$$

$$= \frac{\$1,290,117}{(\$805,745 + \$455,455) \div 2}$$

$$= 2.05 \text{ times/year}$$

Sam' Appliance Shop turns its inventory about two times a year, or once every 178 days.

Average inventory is the sum of the value of the firm's inventory at the beginning of the accounting period and its value at the end of the accounting period, divided by 2.

This ratio tells an entrepreneur how fast merchandise is moving through the business and helps him or her to balance the company's inventory on the fine line between oversupply and undersupply. To determine the average number of days units remain in inventory, the owner can divide the average-inventory-turnover ratio into the number of days in the accounting period (e.g., 365 days ÷ average-inventory-turnover ratio). The result is called *days' inventory* (or *average age of inventory*).

Auto dealerships often use the average age of inventory as a measure of their performance and consider 50 to 60 days' worth of new cars to be an adequate inventory. Used car dealers' goal is to have 35 to 45 days' worth of used cars in inventory. Slow-turning inventory cannibalizes car dealers' profitability because of the interest and other expenses they incur. Joseph Lescota, a retail automotive expert, says the ability to move inventory drives profits in his industry. At luxury new car dealerships, Lescota says the cost of holding a car in inventory can be as high as $90 per day; at the typical used car dealership, the cost is $21 per day. If a used car dealership sells a car within 20 days, it earns an average gross profit of $2,000. However, if that same car sits on the lot for 80 days before it sells, the average gross profit is just $740 (an occurrence known in the industry as "lot rot.")

ENTREPRENEURIAL PROFILE: Jennifer Cattaui: Babesta Jennifer Cattaui, founder of Babesta in New York City, sells children's clothing and furniture online and through two retail stores. Cattaui uses a financial dashboard that helps the Babesta management team monitor the financial health of the business and make decisions based on financial data. The dashboard gives the team metrics that assess cash balance, cash flow, inventory, and revenue. Babesta uses software that displays key metrics using a gauge. If the gauge is in the red zone, the team digs deeper to find the cause. If it is in the green zone, the team knows that things are going well for that specific financial aspect of the business. For example, when its inventory gauge was in the red, the management team assessed the company's inventory and realized that they had furniture in inventory that was not selling. After cutting back the number of those items in Babesta's inventory, the gauge soon returned to the green zone, telling management that inventory turnover had returned to a satisfactory level.[20] ■

An above-average inventory turnover indicates that the small business has a healthy, salable, and liquid inventory and a supply of quality merchandise that is supported by sound pricing policies. A below-average inventory turnover suggests an illiquid inventory characterized by obsolescence, overstocking, stale merchandise, and poor purchasing procedures. Businesses that turn their inventories more rapidly require a smaller inventory investment to produce a particular sales volume. That means that these companies tie up less cash in inventory that idly sits on shelves. For instance, if Sam's could turn its inventory *four* times each year instead of just *two*, the company would require an average inventory of just $322,529 instead of the current level of $630,600 to generate sales of $1,870,841. Increasing the number of inventory turns would free up more than $308,000 in cash currently tied up in excess inventory! Sam's would benefit from improved cash flow and higher profits.

The inventory turnover ratio can be misleading, however. For example, an excessively high ratio could mean that a company does not have enough inventory on hand and may be losing sales because of stock-outs. Similarly, a low ratio could be the result of planned inventory stockpiling to meet seasonal peak demand. Another problem is that the ratio is based on an inventory balance calculated from two days out of the entire accounting period. Thus, inventory fluctuations due to seasonal demand patterns are ignored, and this may bias the resulting ratio. There is no universal, ideal inventory turnover ratio. Financial analysts suggest that a favorable turnover ratio depends on the type of business, its size, its profitability, its method of inventory valuation, and other relevant factors. The most meaningful benchmark for comparison is other companies of similar size in the same industry. For instance, the typical supermarket turns its inventory on average about 15 times a year, but a jewelry store averages just 1.5 to 2 inventory turns a year.

7. Average-Collection-Period Ratio. A small firm's **average-collection-period ratio** (or days sales outstanding [DSO]) tells the average number of days it takes to collect accounts receivable. To compute the average-collection-period ratio, an entrepreneur must first calculate the company's receivables turnover. Given that Sam's *credit* sales for the year were $1,309,589 (out of the total sales of $1,870,841), the company's receivables turnover ratio is as follows:

average-collection-period ratio
measures the number of days it takes to collect accounts receivable.

$$\text{Receivables turnover ratio} = \frac{\text{Credit sales}}{\text{Accounts receivable}}$$

$$= \frac{\$1,309,589}{\$179,225}$$

$$= 7.31 \text{ times/year}$$

Sam's Appliance Shop turns over its receivables 7.31 times per year. This ratio measures the number of times the firm's accounts receivable turn over during the accounting period. The higher the firm's receivables turnover ratio, the shorter the time lag is between the sale and the cash collection.

Use the following to calculate the firm's average-collection-period ratio:

$$\text{Average-collection-period ratio} = \frac{\text{Days in accounting period}}{\text{Receivables turnover ratio}}$$

$$= \frac{365 \text{ days}}{7.31 \text{ times/year}}$$

$$= 50.0 \text{ days}$$

Sam's Appliance Shop's accounts receivable are outstanding for an average of 50 days. Typically, the higher a firm's average collection period ratio, the greater its chance of incurring bad debt losses. Sales don't count unless a company collects the revenue from them.

One of the most useful applications of the collection period ratio is to compare it to the industry average and to the company's credit terms. This comparison indicates the degree of control a small company exercises over its credit sales and collection techniques. A healthy collection period ratio depends on the industry in which a company operates. For instance, the average collection period for companies that manufacture medical equipment is 56 days; for tire retailers, it is just 16 days.[21] Perhaps the most meaningful analysis is comparing the collection period ratio to a company's credit terms. One rule of thumb suggests that a company's collection period ratio should be no more than one-third greater than its credit terms. For example, if a small company's credit terms are net 30 (payment due within 30 days), its average-collection-period ratio should be no more than 40 days (30 + 30 × 1/3). For this company, a ratio greater than 40 days indicates poor collection procedures.

Slow payers represent a great risk to many small businesses. Many entrepreneurs proudly point to rapidly rising sales only to find that they must borrow money to keep their companies

TABLE 11.1 How Lowering Your Average Collection Period Can Save You Money

Too often, entrepreneurs fail to recognize the importance of collecting their accounts receivable on time. After all, collecting accounts is not as glamorous or as much fun as generating sales. Lowering a company's average collection period ratio, however, *can* produce tangible—and often significant—savings. The following formula shows how to convert an improvement in a company's average collection period ratio into dollar savings:

$$\text{Annual savings} = \frac{(\text{Credit sales} \times \text{Annual interest rate} \times \text{Number of days average collection period is lowered})}{365}$$

where

credit sales = company's annual credit sales in dollars,

annual interest rate = the interest rate at which the company borrows money,

and number of days average collection period is lowered = the difference between the previous year's average collection period ratio and the current one.

Example

Sam's Appliance Shop's average collection period ratio is 50 days. Suppose that the previous year's average-collection-period ratio was 58 days, an eight-day improvement. The company's credit sales for the most recent year were $1,309,589. If Sam borrows money at 8.75%, this six-day improvement has generated savings for Sam's Appliance Shop of

$$\text{Savings} = \frac{\$1,309,589 \times 8.75\% \times 8 \text{ days}}{365 \text{ days}} = \$2,512$$

By collecting his accounts receivable just eight days faster on average, Sam has saved his business more than $2,512! Of course, if a company's average-collection-period ratio rises, the same calculation will tell the owner how much that change costs.

Source: Based on Jill Andresky Fraser, "Days Saved, Thousands Earned," Inc., November, 1995 p. 98.

going because their credit customers are paying their bills in 45, 60, or even 90 days instead of the desired 30. Slow receivables are a real danger because they usually lead to a cash crisis that threatens a company's survival. Table 11.1 shows how to calculate the savings associated with lowering a company's average-collection-period ratio.

8. Average-Payable-Period Ratio. The converse of the average-collection-period ratio, the **average-payable-period ratio** (or days payables outstanding, DPO) tells the average number of days it takes a company to pay its accounts payable. Like the average collection period, it is measured in days. To compute this ratio, an entrepreneur first calculates the payables turnover ratio. Sam's payables turnover ratio is as follows:

average-payable-period ratio

measures the number of days it takes a company to pay its accounts payable.

$$\text{Payables turnover ratio} = \frac{\text{Purchases}}{\text{Accounts payable}}$$

$$= \frac{\$939,827}{\$152,580}$$

$$= 6.16 \text{ times/year}$$

To find the average payable period, use the following computation:

$$\text{Average-payable-period ratio} = \frac{\text{Days in accounting period}}{\text{Payables turnover ratio}}$$

$$= \frac{365 \text{ days}}{6.16 \text{ times per year}}$$

$$= 59.3 \text{ days}$$

Sam's Appliance Shop takes an average of 59 days to pay its accounts with vendors and suppliers.

One of the most meaningful comparisons for this ratio is against the credit terms suppliers offer (or an average of the credit terms offered). If the average payable ratio slips beyond vendors' credit terms, a company probably suffers from a sloppy accounts-payable procedure or from cash shortages, and its credit rating is in danger. An excessively high average-payables-period ratio indicates the presence of a significant amount of past-due accounts payable. Although sound cash management calls for a business owner to keep his or her cash as long as possible, slowing payables too drastically can severely damage the company's credit rating. If this ratio is significantly lower than vendors' credit terms, the company is not using its cash most effectively by paying vendors too quickly.

Comparing a company's average-collection-period ratio (DSO) to its average-payable period ratio (DPO) gives owners meaningful insight into their companies' cash position. Ideally, the average payable period matches (or exceeds) the time it takes to convert inventory into sales and ultimately into cash. In this case, the company's vendors are financing its inventory and its credit sales. Online retailer Amazon benefits from this situation. On average, the company does not pay its vendors until 127 days after it collects payments from its customers.[22] Subtracting DSO from DPO yields a company's **float**, the net number of days of cash that flow into or out of a company. Sam's Appliance Shop's float is

> **float**
> the net number of days of cash flowing into or out of a company; float = days payables outstanding (DPO) – days sales outstanding (DSO).

$$\text{Float} = \text{DPO} - \text{DSO} = 59.3 \text{ days} - 50.0 \text{ days} = 9.3 \text{ days}$$

A positive value for float means that cash will accumulate in a company over time, but a negative number means that the company's cash balance will diminish over time. Multiplying float by the company's average daily sales tells Sam how much the company's cash balance will change over the course of the year as a result of its collection and payable processes:

$$\text{Change in cash position} = \$1,870,841 \div 365 \text{ days} \times 9.3 \text{ days} = \$47,668$$

We will see the impact that these three operating ratios—inventory turnover, accounts receivable, and accounts payable—have on a small company's cash flow in the next chapter.

9. Net-Sales-to-Total-Assets Ratio. A small company's **net-sales-to-total-assets** (also called the **total-asset-turnover) ratio** is a general measure of its ability to generate sales in relation to its assets. It describes how productively the firm employs its assets to produce sales revenue. The total-assets-turnover ratio is calculated as follows:

> **net-sales-to-total-assets (also called the total-asset-turnover) ratio**
> measures a company's ability to generate sales in relation to its asset base.

$$\text{Total-assets-turnover ratio} = \frac{\text{Net sales}}{\text{Net total assets}}$$

$$= \frac{\$1,870,841}{\$847,655}$$

$$= 2.21:1$$

Sam's Appliance Shop is generating $2.21 in sales for every dollar of assets.

The denominator of this ratio, net total assets, is the sum of all of a company's assets (cash, inventory, land, buildings, equipment, tools, and everything it owns) less depreciation. This ratio is meaningful only when compared to that of similar firms in the same industry category. Monitoring it over time is very helpful for maintaining a sufficient asset base as a small business grows. A total-assets-turnover ratio below the industry average indicates that a small company is not generating an adequate sales volume for its asset size.

A recent survey by the National Federation of Independent Business reports "poor sales" as the one of the most commonly cited problems among small businesses, ranking just behind perennial top problems "government regulation" and "taxes."[23] If a company's sales fall below its break-even point, it operates at a loss, which is not sustainable.

PROFITABILITY RATIOS **Profitability ratios** indicate how efficiently a small company is being managed. They provide the owner with information about a company's ability to use its resources to generate a profit, its "bottom line."

> **profitability ratios**
> indicate how efficiently a small company is being managed.

10. Net-Profit-on-Sales Ratio. The **net-profit-on-sales ratio** (also called the profit-margin-on-sales ratio or the net-profit-margin ratio) measures a company's profit per dollar of sales.

> **net-profit-on-sales ratio**
> measures a company's profit per dollar of sales.

This ratio (which is expressed as a percentage) shows the portion of each sales dollar remaining after deducting all expenses. The profit margin on sales is calculated as follows:

$$\text{Net-profit-on-sales ratio} = \frac{\text{Net profit}}{\text{Net sales}}$$

$$= \frac{\$60,629}{\$1,870,841}$$

$$= 3.24\%$$

For every dollar in sales Sam's Appliance Shop generates, Sam keeps 3.24 cents in profit.

A recent study by Sageworks shows that the average net profit margin for privately held companies normally falls between 3 and 7 percent, but this ratio varies from one industry to another. The retail industry typically produces a net-profit-on-sales ratio that falls between 2 and 4 percent, but profit margins in the healthcare field range between 10 and 16 percent.[25] If a company's profit margin on sales is below the industry average, it may be a sign that its prices are too low, that its costs are excessively high, or both.

ENTREPRENEURIAL PROFILE: Villa Enterprises Villa Enterprises operates 360 restaurants, including the Villa Fresh Italian Kitchen chain, Office Beer Bar & Grill restaurants, and several other specialty restaurants serving salads and Asian and Mexican dishes. Andrew Steinberg, senior vice president of business operations, says Villa is able to reduce the impact of increasing food costs by buying in volume. Villa buys food products in half and full truckloads to gain economies of scale. Although it does tie up more cash in inventory, staying ahead of price increases has helped maintain strong profits.[26] ■

A natural reaction to low profitability ratios is to embark on a cost-cutting effort. Although minimizing costs does improve profitability, entrepreneurs must be judicious in their cost cutting, taking a strategic approach rather than imposing across-the-board cuts. The key is to reduce costs without diminishing customer service and damaging employee morale. Cutting costs in areas that are vital to operating success—such as a retail jeweler eliminating its advertising expenditures or a restaurant reducing the quality of its ingredients—usually hurts a company's ability to compete and can lead to failure. For instance, choosing to lay off workers, a common reaction at many companies facing financial challenges, often backfires. Not only does a company risk losing talented workers and the knowledge they have built up over time, but research also shows that repeated rounds of layoffs destroy the morale and productivity of the remaining workers.[27]

If a company's net-profit-on-sales ratio is excessively low, the owner first should check the gross profit margin (net sales minus cost of goods sold expressed as a percentage of net sales). Of course, a reasonable gross profit margin varies from industry to industry. For instance, a service company may have a gross profit margin of 75 percent, while a manufacturer's may be 35 percent. The key is to know what a reasonable gross profit margin is for your particular business. If this margin slips too low, the company's future is in immediate jeopardy. An inadequate gross profit margin cannot cover all of a company's business expenses and still be able to generate a profit.

ENTREPRENEURIAL PROFILE: Chris Siversen: Maritime Parc Maritime Parc restaurant, in Jersey City, New Jersey, is feeling the effects of rising wholesale prices of beef and shrimp. Chris Siversen, chef and co-owner, says that rather than increase prices, his restaurant has been forced to absorb rising food costs. In addition, the continued soft economy does not allow him to increase prices. As a result, profit margins have continued to decline.[24] ■

operating leverage
a situation in which increases in operating efficiency mean that expenses as a percentage of sales revenue flatten or even decline.

Monitoring the net profit margin is especially important for fast-growing companies in which sales are climbing rapidly. Unbridled growth can cause expenses to rise faster than sales, eroding a company's net profit margin. Success can be deceptive: Sales are rising, but profits are shrinking. Ideally, a company reaches a point at which it achieves **operating leverage**, a situation in which increases in operating efficiency mean that expenses as a percentage of sales revenues flatten or even decline. As a result, the company's net profit margin climbs as it grows.

11. Net-Profit-to-Assets Ratio. The **net-profit-to-assets (return-on-assets) ratio** tells how much profit a company generates for each dollar of assets it owns. This ratio describes how efficiently a business is putting to work all of the assets it owns to generate a profit. It tells how much net income an entrepreneur is squeezing from each dollar's worth of the company's assets. It is calculated as follows:

net-profit-to-assets (return-on-assets) ratio
measures how much profit a company generates for each dollar of assets that it owns.

$$\text{Net-profit-to-assets ratio} = \frac{\text{Net profit}}{\text{Total assets}}$$

$$= \frac{\$60,629}{\$847,655}$$

$$= 7.15\%$$

Sam's Appliance shop earns a return of 7.15 percent on its asset base. This ratio provides clues about the asset intensity of an industry. Return-on-assets ratios that are below 5 percent are indicative of asset-intense industries that require heavy investments in assets to stay in business (e.g., manufacturing and railroads). Return-on-assets ratios that exceed 20 percent tend to occur in asset-light industries such as business or personal services—for example, advertising agencies and computer services. A net-profit-to-assets ratio that is below the industry average suggests that a company is not using its assets efficiently to produce a profit. Another common application of this ratio is to compare it to the company's cost of borrowed capital. Ideally, a company's return-on-assets ratio should exceed the cost of borrowing money to purchase those assets. Companies that experience significant swings in the value of their assets over the course of a year often use an average value of the asset base over the accounting period to get a more realistic estimate of this ratio.

12. Net-Profit-to-Equity Ratio. The **net-profit-to-equity ratio** (or return on net worth ratio) measures the owners' rate of return on investment (ROI). Because it reports the percentage of the owners' investment in the business that is being returned through profits annually, it is one of the most important indicators of a firm's profitability or a management's efficiency. The net-profit-to-equity ratio is computed as follows:

net-profit-to-equity ratio
measures the owners' rate of return on investment.

$$\text{Net-profit-to-equity ratio} = \frac{\text{Net profit}}{\text{Owners' equity (or net worth)}}$$

$$= \frac{\$60,629}{\$267,655}$$

$$= 22.65\%$$

Sam is earning 22.65 percent on the money he has invested in this business.

This ratio compares profits earned during the accounting period with the amount the owner has invested in the business at the time. If this interest rate on the owners' investment is excessively low, some of this capital might be better employed elsewhere. A business should produce a rate of return that exceeds its cost of capital.

Interpreting Business Ratios

LO4
Explain how to interpret financial ratios.

Ratios are useful yardsticks when measuring a small firm's performance and can point out potential problems before they develop into serious crises. However, calculating these ratios is not enough to ensure proper financial control. In addition to knowing how to calculate these ratios, entrepreneurs must understand how to interpret them and apply them to managing their businesses more effectively and efficiently. Many entrepreneurs use key financial ratios as a performance dashboard that help them manage by continuously assessing trends in the financial strength of their businesses.

You Be the Consultant

All Is Not Paradise in Eden's Garden: Part 1

Joe and Kaitlin Eden, co-owners of Eden's Garden, a small nursery, lawn, and garden supply business, have just received their

Balance Sheet, Eden's Garden

Assets

Current Assets

Cash		$6,457
Accounts Receivable	$29,152	
Less Allowance for Doubtful Accounts	$3,200	$25,952
Inventory		$88,157
Supplies		$7,514
Prepaid Expenses		$1,856
Total Current Assets		$129,936

Fixed Assets

Land		$59,150
Buildings	$51,027	
Less Accumulated Depreciation	$2,061	$48,966
Autos	$24,671	
Less Accumulated Depreciation	$12,300	$12,371
Equipment	$22,375	
Less Accumulated Depreciation	$1,250	$21,125
Furniture and Fixtures	$10,295	
Less Accumulated Depreciation	$1,000	$9,295
Total Fixed Assets		$150,907
Intangibles (Goodwill)		$0
Total Assets		$280,843

Liabilities

Current Liabilities

Accounts Payable	$54,258
Notes Payable	$20,150
Credit Line Payable	$8,118
Accrued Wages/Salaries Payable	$1,344
Accrued Interest Payable	$1,785
Accrued Taxes Payable	$1,967
Total Current Liabilities	$87,622

Long-Term Liabilities

Mortgage	$72,846
Note Payable	$47,000
Total Long-Term Liabilities	$119,846

Owner's Equity

Sam Lloyd, Capital	$73,375
Total Liabilities and Owner's Equity	$280,843

Income Statement, Eden's Garden

Net Sales Revenue*		**$689,247**

Cost of Goods Sold

Beginning Inventory, 1/1/xx	$78,271	
+ Purchases	$403,569	
Goods available for Sale	$481,840	
− Ending Inventory, 12,31/xx	$86,157	
Cost of Goods Sold		$395,683
Gross Profit		$293,564

Operating Expenses

Advertising	$22,150	
Insurance	$9,187	
Depreciation		
Building	$26,705	
Autos	$7,895	
Equipment	$11,200	
Salaries	$116,541	
Uniforms	$4,018	
Repairs and Maintenance	$9,097	
Travel	$2,658	
Entertainment	$2,798	
Total Operating Expenses		$212,249

General Expenses

Utilities	$7,987	
Telephone	$2,753	
Professional Fees	$3,000	
Postage	$1,892	
Payroll Taxes	$11,589	
Total General Expenses		$27,221

Other Expenses

Interest Expense	$21,978	
Bad check Expense	$679	
Miscellaneous expense	$1,248	
Total Other Expenses		$23,905
Total Expenses		$263,375
Net Income		$30,189

*Credit sales represented $289,484 of this total.

year-end financial statements from their accountant. At their last meeting with their accountant, Shelley Edison, three months ago, the Edens had mentioned that they seemed to be having trouble paying their bills on time. "Some of our suppliers have threatened to put us on 'credit hold,'" said Joe.

You Be the Consultant *(continued)*

"I think you need to sit down with me very soon and let me show you how to analyze your financial statements so you can see what's happening in your business," Edison told them at that meeting. Unfortunately, that was the beginning of Eden's Garden's busy season, and the Edens were so busy running the company that they never got around to setting a time to meet with Shelley.

"Now that business has slowed down a little, perhaps we should call Shelley and see what she can do to help us understand what our financial statements are trying to tell us," said Kaitlin.

"Right. Before it's too late to do anything about it," said Joe, pulling out the financial statements presented here.

1. Assume the role of Shelley Edison. Using the financial statements for Eden's Garden, calculate the 12 ratios covered in this chapter.

2. Do you see any ratios that, on the surface, look suspicious? Explain.

ENTREPRENEURIAL PROFILE: Peter Smith: Golden Spiral Creative
Peter Smith, president and COO of Golden Spiral Creative, a branding and marketing agency based in Nashville, Tennessee, uses a spreadsheet he developed to create a company dashboard. The first key metric is overhead. "This has every employee's salary listed, along with employer taxes (FICA & FUTA), rent, and any other monthly expense," says Smith. "I use this to determine our monthly overhead. It also allows me to quickly project how a new hire or subscription would alter my overhead." Smith also has a section on the same spreadsheet that includes all monthly retainers the company is paying out to its independent contractors. "I also have a section for cost accounting to determine my break-even rate per billable hour," says Smith. "We bill on an hourly basis so this is really helpful." Finally, his dashboard acts as a calculator he can use to help bid on new projects. "I enter the total number of hours that we expect to work and what we are charging for that project," explains Smith. "From there I enter any contractor expenses I will have to pay. The formula takes our break-even per billable hour number and the

Peter Smith Publisher, Inc.

project hours to determine what that project 'costs' us in terms of human capital. All of this together calculates out net income and profit margin on a per project basis. I can toggle the numbers a bit to see how and changes affect our profit margin."[28] ■

Not every business measures its success with the same ratios. In fact, key performance ratios vary dramatically across industries and even within different segments of the same industry. Entrepreneurs must know and understand which ratios are most crucial to their companies' success and focus on monitoring and controlling those indicators. Sometimes business owners develop ratios and measures that are unique to their own operations to help them achieve success. Known as **critical numbers (or key performance indicators, KPIs)**, these indicators measure key financial and operational aspects of a company's performance. When these critical numbers are headed in the right direction, a business is on track to achieve its objectives. Norm Brodsky, owner of a successful document storage and delivery business in New York City, breaks his business into four categories and tracks critical numbers for each one. Every Monday morning, he receives a report comparing the previous week's critical numbers to those of the previous 28 weeks and the same week for the previous three years. With these figures he can quickly assess how the business is performing. If there are problems with any KPI, he can seek out more information to identify any problems or concerns.[29] Examples of critical numbers at other companies include the following:

- A bank's "happy-to-grumpy" ratio, which measures the level of employee satisfaction. Studies show that employees at the bank who score high on this index are more productive and receive higher customer satisfaction ratings.[30]

- Sales per labor hour at a supermarket.

- The number of referrals for a healthcare facility. Managers use this number to predict the number of new patients they can expect and to identify swings in patient revenue. This information helps with staffing decisions and managing cash flow.

- Food costs as a percentage of sales for a restaurant. When rapidly rising flour and cheese prices pushed food costs as a percentage of sales from the normal 34 percent to 40 percent at Mark Parry's pizza restaurant, he was forced to raise prices. Parry knows his restaurant will not make a profit when food costs get above 40 percent.[31] At Dos Caminos, a Mexican restaurant in New York City, chef Ivy Stark's goal is to keep the restaurant's food cost at or below 26 percent of sales. Stark relies on a five-page spreadsheet generated each morning to keep food costs under control.[32]

- The utilization ratio, billable hours as a percentage of total hours worked at an Internet service provider.

- Site traffic and sales dollars per transaction, two critical numbers for an ecommerce business to monitor on a daily basis.

- The load factor, the percentage of seats filled with passengers at an airline.[33]

Critical numbers may be different for two companies that compete in the same industry. The key is identifying *your* company's critical numbers, monitoring them, and then driving them in the right direction. That requires communicating the importance of these critical numbers to employees and giving them feedback on how well the business is achieving them. For instance, one California retail chain established the daily customer count and the average sale per customer as its critical numbers. The company organized a monthly contest with prizes and posted charts tracking each store's performance. Soon, employees were working hard to improve their stores' performances over the previous year and to outdo other stores in the chain. The healthy rivalry among stores boosted the company's performance significantly.[34]

Another valuable way to use ratios is to compare them with those of similar businesses in the same industry. By comparing their companies' financial statistics to industry averages, entrepreneurs are able to locate problem areas and maintain adequate financial controls. Known as **financial benchmarking**, comparing a company's key financial indicators to averages from many firms of similar size in the same industry, can help identify problem areas that the company's own history may not show. Benchmarking also is an effective way to set KPIs to ensure your business is at least doing as well as others in your industry, if not exceeding their performance.

The principle behind calculating these ratios and comparing them to industry norms is the same as that of most medical tests in the healthcare profession. Just as a healthy person's blood pressure and cholesterol levels should fall within a range of normal values, so should a financially healthy company's ratios. A company cannot deviate too far from these normal values and remain successful for long. When deviations from "normal" do occur (and they will), a business owner should focus on determining the cause of the deviations. In some cases, deviations are the result of sound business decisions, such as taking on inventory in preparation for the busy season, investing heavily in new technology, and others. In other instances, however, ratios that are out of the normal range for a particular type of business are indicators of what could become serious problems for a company. When comparing a company's critical numbers to industry standards, entrepreneurs should ask the following questions:

- Is there a significant difference in my company's ratio and the industry average?

- If so, is the difference meaningful?

- Is the difference good or bad?

- What are the possible causes of this difference? What is the most likely cause?

- Does this cause require that I take action?

- If so, what action should I take to correct the problem?

When used properly, critical numbers can help owners to identify potential problem areas in their businesses early on—*before* they become crises that threaten their very survival. Several organizations regularly compile and publish operating statistics, including key ratios, that summarize the financial performance of many businesses across a wide range of industries. The local library should subscribe to most of these publications:

Risk Management Association. Founded in 1914, the RMA publishes its *Annual Statement Studies*, showing ratios and other financial data for more than 760 different

financial benchmarking

a process in which entrepreneurs compare a company's key financial indicators to averages from many companies of similar size in the same industry to identify problem areas that the company's own history may not show.

industrial, wholesale, retail, and service categories that are organized by NAICS and SIC code.

Dun & Bradstreet, Inc. Since 1932, Dun & Bradstreet has published *Industry Norms and Key Business Ratios*, which covers more than 800 business categories. Dun & Bradstreet also publishes Cost of Doing Business, a series of operating ratios compiled from the Statistics of Income reports of the Internal Revenue Service (IRS).

Bizminer. This industry financial data can be segmented by both company size and geographic location.

Almanac of Business and Financial Ratios. Published by CCH, this almanac reports comparative financial data and ratios for nearly 200 industries by company size.

Standard & Poor's Industry Surveys. In addition to providing information on financial ratios and comparative financial analysis, these surveys also contain useful details on industry operations, current industry trends, and key terms in the industry.

Industry Spotlight. Published by Schonfeld & Associates, this publication, which can be customized for any one of 250 industries, contains financial statement data and key ratios gleaned from IRS tax returns. *Industry Spotlight* also provides detailed financial information for both profitable companies and those with losses. Schonfeld & Associates also publishes *IRS Corporate Financial Ratios*, a comprehensive reference book that features 76 financial ratios for more than 250 industries using NAICS codes.

Online resources. Many companies publish comparative financial resources online. Some require subscriptions, but others are free:

- Bizstats publishes common-size financial statements and ratios for 95 business categories for sole proprietorships, S corporations, and corporations.
- Reuters provides an overview of many industries that includes industry trends and news as well as financial ratios.
- A subscription to Lexis/Nexis allows users to view detailed company profiles, including financial reports and analysis, for publicly held companies.

Industry associations. Virtually every type of business is represented by a national trade association that publishes detailed financial data compiled from its membership. For example, owners of small supermarkets could contact the National Association of Retail Grocers or check the *Progressive Grocer*, its trade publication, for financial statistics relevant to their operations.

Government agencies. Several government agencies, including the IRS, the Federal Trade Commission, the Department of Commerce, the Census Bureau, the Department of Agriculture, and the Securities and Exchange Commission, periodically publish reports that provide financial operating data on a variety of industries, although the categories are more general. For instance, the IRS publishes *Statistics of Income*, which includes income statement and balance sheet statistics that are compiled from income tax returns and are arranged by industry, asset size, and annual sales. Every five years (years ending in 2 and 7), the Census Bureau publishes the *Economic Census* (www.census.gov/econ/census), which provides general industry statistics and ratios.

What Do All of These Numbers Mean?

Learning to interpret financial ratios just takes a little practice! This section and Table 11.2 show you how it's done by comparing the ratios from the operating data already computed for Sam's to those taken from the RMA's *Annual Statement Studies.* (The industry median is the ratio falling exactly in the middle when sample elements are arranged in ascending or descending order.) Calculating the variance from the industry median—(company ratio – industry median) ÷ industry median—helps entrepreneurs identify the areas in which the company is out of line with the typical company in the industry.

When comparing ratios for their individual businesses to published statistics, entrepreneurs must remember that the comparison is made against averages. An entrepreneur should strive to achieve ratios that are at least as good as these average figures. The goal should be to manage

TABLE 11.2 Ratio Analysis: Sam's Appliance Shop versus the Industry Median

Sam's Appliance Shop	Industry Median	Variance (%)
Liquidity Ratios—Tell whether a small business will be able to meet its maturing obligations as they come due.		
1. Current Ratio = 1.87:1	1.60:1	16.7%
Sam's Appliance Shop falls short of the rule of thumb of 2:1, but its current ratio is above the industry median by a significant amount. Sam's should have no problem meeting its short-term debts as they come due. By this measure, the company's liquidity is solid.		
2. Quick Ratio = 0.63:1	0.50:1	25.9%
Again, Sam's is below the rule of thumb of 1:1, but the company passes this test of liquidity when measured against industry standards. Sam's relies on selling inventory to satisfy short-term debt (as do most appliance shops). If sales slump, the result could be liquidity problems for Sam's.		
Leverage Ratios—Measure the financing supplied by the company's owners against that supplied by its creditors as a gauge of the depth of a company's debt.		
3. Debt Ratio = 0.68:1	0.62:1	10.4%
Creditors provide 68 percent of Sam's total assets, which is above the industry median of 62 percent. Although Sam's does not appear to be overburdened with debt, the company might have difficulty borrowing additional money, especially from conservative lenders.		
4. Debt-to-Net-Worth Ratio = 2.20:1	2.30:1	−4.5%
Sam's Appliance Shop owes $2.20 to creditors for every $1 the owners have invested in the business (compared to $2.30 in debt to every $1 in equity for the typical business). Although this is not an exorbitant amount of debt by industry standards, many lenders and creditors see Sam's as "borrowed up." Borrowing capacity is somewhat limited because creditors' claims against the business are more than twice those of the owners.		
5. Times-Interest-Earned Ratio = 2.52:1	2.10:1	20.1%
Sam's earnings are high enough to cover the interest payments on its debt by a factor of 2.52, better than the typical firm in the industry, whose earnings cover its interest payments just 2.1 times. Sam's Appliance Shop has a comfortable cushion when meeting its interest payments, although some lenders want to see times-interest-earned ratios of at least 3:1.		
Operating Ratios—Evaluate a company's overall performance and show how effectively it is putting its resources to work.		
6. Average-Inventory-Turnover Ratio = 2.05 times/year	4.4 times/year	−53.5%
Inventory is moving through Sam's at a very slow pace, *half* that of the industry median. The company has a problem with slow-moving items in its inventory and, perhaps, too much inventory. Which items are they, and why are they slow moving? Does Sam need to drop some product lines?		
7. Average-Collection-Period Ratio = 50.0 days	10.5 days	376.3%
Sam's Appliance Shop collects the average accounts receivable after 50 days, compared with the industry median of about 11 days, nearly five times longer. A more meaningful comparison is against Sam's credit terms; if credit terms are net 30 (or anywhere close to that), Sam's has a dangerous collection problem, one that drains cash and profits and demands *immediate* attention!		
8. Average-Payable-Period Ratio = 59.3 days	23.0 days	158.1%
Sam's payables are significantly slower than those of the typical firm in the industry. Stretching payables too far could seriously damage the company's credit rating, causing suppliers to cut off future trade credit. This could be a sign of cash flow problems or a sloppy accounts-payable procedure. This problem, which indicates that the company suffers from cash flow problems, also demands *immediate* attention.		

TABLE 11.2 Ratio Analysis: Sam's Appliance Shop versus the Industry Median (*continued*)

Sam's Appliance Shop	Industry Median	Variance (%)
9. Net-Sales-to-Total-Assets Ratio = 2.21:1	3.4:1	−35.1%
Sam's Appliance Shop is not generating enough sales, given the size of its asset base. This could be the result of a number of factors—improper inventory, inappropriate pricing, poor location, poorly trained sales personnel, and many others. The key is to find the cause—*fast*!		
Profitability Ratios—Measure how efficiently a firm is operating and offer information about its bottom line.		
10. Net-Profit-on-Sales Ratio = 3.24%	4.3%	−24.6%
After deducting all expenses, 3.24 cents of each sales dollar remains as profit for Sam's—nearly 25 percent below the industry median. Sam should review his company's gross profit margin and investigate its operating expenses, checking them against industry standards and looking for those that are out of balance.		
11. Net-Profit-to-Assets Ratio = 7.15%	4.0%	78.8%
Sam's generates a return of 7.15% for every $1 in assets, which is nearly 79 percent *above* the industry median. Given his asset base, Sam is squeezing an above-average return from his company. This could be an indication that Sam's business is highly profitable; however, given the previous ratio, this is unlikely. It is more likely that Sam's asset base is thinner than the industry average.		
12. Net-Profit-to-Equity Ratio = 22.65%	16.0%	41.6%
Sam's Appliance Shop's owners are earning 22.65 percent on the money they have invested in the business. This yield is well above the industry median and, given the previous ratio, is more a result of the owner's relatively low investment in the business than an indication of its superior profitability. Sam is using O.P.M. (other people's money) to generate a profit.		

the business so that its financial performance is above average. As they compare their company's financial performance to those covered in the published statistics, they inevitably will discern differences between them. They should note those items that are substantially out of line from the industry average. However, a ratio that varies from the average does not *necessarily* mean that the small business is in financial jeopardy. Instead of making drastic changes in financial policy, entrepreneurs must explore *why* the figures are out of line.

ENTREPRENEURIAL PROFILE: Greg Smith: Petra Group Greg Smith, CEO of Petra Group, a systems integrator with $1.5 million in annual sales, once gave little thought to comparing his company's financial performance against industry standards. Then Petra Group's sales flattened, and Smith's company faced the prospect of losing money for the first time. Smith worked with an accounting firm, using information from the RMA Annual Statement Studies and a nonprofit organization that provides similar studies, to analyze his company's financial position. Comparing his numbers to industry statistics, Smith quickly saw that payroll expenses for his 15-person company were too high to allow the company to generate a profit. He also discovered that Petra Group's debt ratio was too high. To restore his company's financial strength, Smith reduced his staff by two and began relying more on temporary employees and independent contractors. He realigned Petra Group's financing, reducing the company's line of credit from $100,000 to just $35,000. The analysis also revealed several strengths for the company. For instance, the company's average collection period was 36.5 days compared to an industry average of 73 days! Smith continues to use ratio comparisons to make key decisions for his company, and he credits the initial financial analysis with getting his company back on the track to profitability.[35] ■

In addition to comparing ratios to industry averages, owners should analyze their firms' financial ratios over time. By themselves, these ratios are "snapshots" of a company's financial position at a single instant; however, by examining these trends over time, an entrepreneur can detect gradual shifts that otherwise might go unnoticed until a financial crisis is looming (see Figure 11.5).

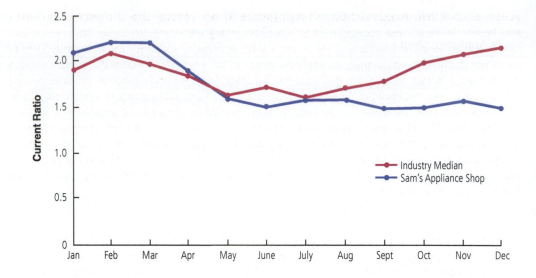

FIGURE 11.5
Trend Analysis of Ratio

break-even point
the level of operation (sales dollars or production quantity) at which a company neither earns a profit nor incurs a loss.

LO5

Conduct a break-even analysis for a small company.

Break-Even Analysis

Another key component of every sound financial plan is a break-even (or cost-volume-profit) analysis. A small company's **break-even point** is the level of operation (typically expressed as sales dollars or production quantity) at which it neither earns a profit nor incurs a loss. At this level of activity, sales revenue equals expenses—that is, the firm "breaks even." A business that

You Be the Consultant

All Is Not Paradise in Eden's Garden: Part 2

Remember Joe and Kaitlin Eden, co-owners of Eden's Garden? Assume the role of Shelley Edison, their accountant. Tomorrow, you have scheduled a meeting with them to review their company's financial statements and to make recommendations about how they can improve their company's financial position. Use the following worksheet to summarize the ratios you calculated earlier in this chapter. Then compare them against the industry averages for businesses of a similar size from the Bizminer's *Industry Financial Report*.

Ratio Comparison

Ratio	Eden's Garden	Nursery, Garden Center, and Farm Supply Stores Industry Median*
Liquidity Ratios		
Current ratio		2.27
Quick ratio		0.84
Leverage Ratios		
Debt ratio		0.57
Debt-to-net-worth ratio		1.34
Times-interest-earned ratio		1.29

Operating Ratios

Average-inventory-turnover ratio	6.74
Average-collection-period ratio	10.79 days
Average-payable-period ratio	37.9 days
Net-sales-to-total-assets ratio	2.95

Profitability Ratios

Net-profit-on-sales ratio	5.51%
Net-profit-to-assets ratio	16.26%
Net-profit-to-equity ratio	38.04%

*Bizminer's *Industry Financial Report*.

1. Analyze the comparisons you have made of Eden's Garden's ratios with those from Bizminer. What red flags do you see?

2. What might be causing the deviations you have observed?

3. What recommendations can you make to the Edens to improve their company's financial performance in the future?

generates sales that are greater than its break-even point will produce a profit, but one that operates below its break-even point will incur a net loss. Many entrepreneurs leave their own salary out of a break-even calculation. This is *not* a wise approach. Although the entrepreneur may forgo paychecks during start-up, the business does not truly break even until the entrepreneur is able to earn a market salary from the business. By analyzing costs and expenses, an entrepreneur can calculate the minimum level of activity required to keep a company in operation. These techniques can then be refined to project the sales needed to generate the desired profit. Most potential lenders and investors expect entrepreneurs to prepare a break-even analysis to assist them in evaluating the earning potential of the new business. In addition to its being a simple, useful screening device for financial institutions, break-even analysis can also serve as a planning device for entrepreneurs. It can show an entrepreneur just how unprofitable a poorly planned business venture is likely to be.

Calculating the Break-Even Point

An entrepreneur can calculate a company's break-even point by using a simple mathematical formula. To begin the analysis, the entrepreneur must determine fixed costs and variable costs. **Fixed expenses** are those that do not vary with changes in the volume of sales or production (e.g., rent, depreciation expense, insurance, lease or loan payments, and others). **Variable expenses**, on the other hand, vary directly with changes in the volume of sales or production (e.g., raw material costs, sales commissions, hourly wages, and others).

Some expenses cannot be neatly categorized as fixed or variable because they contain elements of both. These semivariable expenses change, although not proportionately, with changes in the level of sales or production (electricity is one example). These costs remain constant up to

fixed expenses
expenses that do not vary with changes in the volume of sales or production.

variable expenses
expenses that vary directly with changes in the volume of sales or production.

"CONSIDER YOURSELF LUCKY, EDDIE. 'BREAK-EVEN' IS THE NEW 'WIN-WIN'."

Harley Schwardon/www.CartoonStock.com

a particular production or sales volume and then climb as that volume is exceeded. To calculate the break-even point, an entrepreneur must separate these expenses into their fixed and variable components. A number of techniques are available (which are beyond the scope of this text), but a good cost accounting system can provide the desired results.

Here are the steps an entrepreneur must take to compute the break-even point using an example of a typical small business, the Magic Shop:

Step 1. *Forecast the expenses the business can expect to incur.* With the help of a forecast for a new venture or a budget for an operating small business, an entrepreneur can develop estimates of sales revenue, cost of goods sold, and expenses for the upcoming accounting period. The Magic Shop expects net sales of $950,000 in the upcoming year, with a cost of goods sold of $646,000 and total expenses of $236,500.

Step 2. *Categorize the expenses estimated in step 1 into fixed expenses and variable expenses.* Separate semivariable expenses into their component parts. From the budget, the owner anticipates variable expenses (including the cost of goods sold) of $705,125 and fixed expenses of $177,375.

Step 3. *Calculate the ratio of variable expenses to net sales.* For the Magic Shop, this percentage is $705,125 ÷ $950,000 = 74 percent. The Magic Shop uses 74 cents out of every sales dollar to cover variable expenses, which leaves 26 cents ($1.00 − 0.74) of each sales dollar as a contribution margin to cover fixed costs and make a profit.

Step 4. *Compute the break-even point by inserting this information into the following formula:*

$$\text{Break-even sales (\$)} = \frac{\text{Total fixed cost}}{\text{Contribution margin expressed as a percentage of sales}}$$

For the Magic Shop,

$$\text{Break-even sales} = \frac{\$177,375}{0.26}$$

$$= \$682,212$$

Thus, the Magic Shop will break even with sales of $682,212. At this point, sales revenue generated will just cover total fixed and variable expense. The Magic Shop will earn no profit and will incur no loss. We can verify this with the following calculations:

Sales at break-even point	$ 682,212
−Variable expenses (74% of sales)	−504,837
Contribution margin	177,375
−Fixed expenses	−177,375
Net profit (or net loss)	$ 0

Some entrepreneurs find it more meaningful to break down their companies' annual break-even point into a daily sales figure. If the Magic Shop will be open 312 days per year, the average daily sales it must generate just to break even is $682,212 ÷ 312 days = $2,187 per day.

Adding a Profit

What if the Magic Shop's owner wants to do *better* than just break even? This should be the goal of all entrepreneurs. Just as a track coach tell runners to run through the finish line and football coaches want their players to run over the goal line into the endzone, an entrepreneur should never be satisfied with simply reaching break even. The goal is to move through break-even into profitability. Break-even analysis can be adjusted to consider this goal. Suppose the owner expects a reasonable profit (before taxes) of $80,000. What level of sales must the Magic Shop achieve to generate this? The entrepreneur can calculate this by treating the desired profit as if it were a fixed cost, modifying the break-even formula to include the desired net income:

$$\text{Sales (\$)} = \frac{\text{Total fixed expenses} + \text{Desired net income}}{\text{Contribution margin expressed as a percentage of sales}}$$

$$= \frac{\$177{,}375 + \$80\,000}{0.26}$$

$$= \$989{,}904$$

To achieve a net profit of $80,000 (before taxes), the Magic Shop must generate net sales of $989,904. Once again, if we convert this annual sales volume into a daily sales volume, we get $989,904 ÷ 312 days = $3,173 per day.

Break-Even Point in Units

Some small businesses prefer to express the break-even point in units produced or sold instead of in dollars. Manufacturers often find this approach particularly useful. The following formula computes the break-even point in units:

$$\text{Break-even volume} = \frac{\text{Total fixed costs}}{\text{Sales price per unit} - \text{Variable cost per unit}}$$

For example, suppose that Trilex Manufacturing Company estimates its fixed costs for producing its line of small appliances at $390,000. The variable costs (including materials, direct labor, and factory overhead) amount to $12.10 per unit, and the selling price per unit is $17.50. Trilex computes its contribution margin this way:

$$\text{Contribution margin} = \text{Price per unit} - \text{Variable cost per unit}$$

$$= \$17.50 \text{ per unit} - \$12.10 \text{ per unit}$$

$$= \$5.40 \text{ per unit}$$

So, Trilex's break-even volume is as follows:

$$\text{Break-even volume (units)} = \frac{\text{Total fixed costs}}{\text{Per unit contribution margin}}$$

$$= \frac{\$390{,}000}{\$5.40 \text{ per unit}}$$

$$= 72{,}222 \text{ units}$$

To convert this number of units to break-even sales dollars, Trilex simply multiplies it by the selling price per unit:

$$\text{Break-even sales} = 72{,}222 \text{ units} \times \$17.50 \text{ per unit} = \$1{,}263{,}889$$

Trilex could compute the sales required to produce a desired profit by treating the profit as if it were a fixed cost:

$$\text{Sales (units)} = \frac{\text{Total fixed costs} + \text{Desired net income}}{\text{Per unit contribution margin}}$$

For example, if Trilex wanted to earn a $60,000 profit, its required sales would be

$$\text{Sales (units)} = \frac{390{,}000 + 60{,}000}{5.40} = 83{,}333 \text{ units}$$

which would require 83,333 units × $17.50 per unit = $1,458,328 in sales.

Constructing a Break-Even Chart

The following steps outline the procedure for constructing a graph that visually portrays a company's break-even point (that point where revenues equal expenses):

Step 1. *On the horizontal axis, mark a scale measuring sales volume in dollars (or in units sold or some other measure of volume).* The break-even chart for the Magic Shop shown in Figure 11.6 uses sales volume in dollars because it applies to all types of businesses, departments, and products.

Step 2. *On the vertical axis, mark a scale measuring income and expenses in dollars.*

Step 3. Draw a fixed expense line intersecting the vertical axis at the proper dollar level parallel to the horizontal axis. The area between this line and the horizontal axis represents the company's fixed expenses. On the break-even chart for the Magic Shop shown in Figure 11.6, the fixed expense line is drawn horizontally beginning at $177,375 (point A). Because this line is parallel to the horizontal axis, it indicates that fixed expenses remain constant at all levels of activity.

Step 4. *Draw a total expense line that slopes upward beginning at the point where the fixed cost line intersects the vertical axis.* The precise location of the total expense line is determined by plotting the total cost incurred at a particular sales volume. The total cost for a given sales level is found by using the following formula:

Total expenses = Fixed expenses + Variable expenses expressed as a % of sales × Sales level

Arbitrarily choosing a sales level of $950,000, the Magic Shop's total costs would be as follows:

$$\text{Total expenses} = \$177{,}375 + (0.74 \times \$950{,}000)$$

$$= \$880{,}375$$

Thus, the Magic Shop's total cost is $880,375 at a net sales level of $950,000 (point B). The variable cost line is drawn by connecting points A and B. The area between the total cost line and the horizontal axis measures the total costs the Magic Shop incurs at various levels of sales. For example, if the Magic Shop's sales are $850,000, its total costs will be $806,375.

Step 5. Beginning at the graph's origin, draw a 45-degree revenue line showing where total sales volume equals total income. For the Magic Shop, point C shows that sales = income = $950,000.

FIGURE 11.6

Break-Even Chart for the Magic Shop

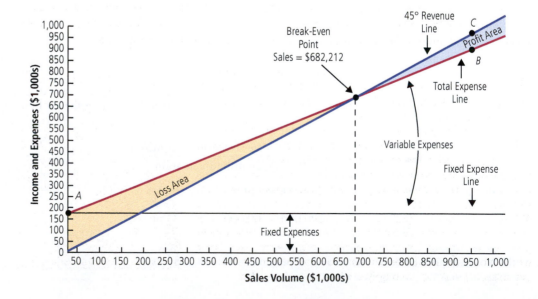

You Be the Consultant

Where Do We Break Even?

Anita Dawson is doing some financial planning for her small gift store. According to her budget for the upcoming year, Anita is expecting sales of $495,000. She estimates the cost of goods sold will be $337,000 and other variable expenses will total $42,750. Using the previous year as a guide, Anita anticipates fixed expenses of $78,100.

Anita recalls a meeting she had recently with her accountant, who mentioned that her store already had passed its break-even point eight and a half months into the year. She was pleased but really didn't know how the accountant had come up with that calculation. Now Anita is considering expanding her store into a vacant building next door to her existing location and taking on three new product lines. The company's cost structure would change, adding another $66,000 to fixed costs and $22,400 to variable expenses. Anita believes the expansion could generate additional sales of $102,000 in the first year.

She wonders what she should do.

1. Calculate Anita's break-even point without the expansion plans. Draw a break-even chart.

2. Compute the break-even point assuming that Anita decides to expand her business.

3. Do you recommend that Anita expand her business? Explain.

Step 6. *Locate the break-even point by finding the intersection of the total expense line and the revenue line.* If the Magic Shop operates at a sales volume to the left of the break-even point, it will incur a loss because the expense line is higher than the revenue line over this range. This is shown by the triangular section labeled "Loss Area." On the other hand, if the firm operates at a sales volume to the right of the break-even point, it will earn a profit because the revenue line lies above the expense line over this range. This is shown by the triangular section labeled "Profit Area."

Using Break-Even Analysis

Break-even analysis is a useful planning tool for the potential small business owner, especially when approaching potential lenders and investors for funds. It provides an opportunity for integrated analysis of sales volume, expenses, income, and other relevant factors. Break-even analysis is a simple, preliminary screening device for an entrepreneur faced with the business start-up decision. It is easy to understand and use. With just a few calculations, an entrepreneur can determine the effects of various financial strategies on the business operation. It is a helpful tool for evaluating the impact of changes in investments and expenditures. Greg Smith, for instance, knows that Petra Group's break-even point is $23,000 per week, and he compares sales to that figure every week.[36]

Calculating the break-even point for a start-up business is important because it tells an entrepreneur the minimum volume of sales required to stay in business in the long run.

ENTREPRENEURIAL PROFILE: Albert Poland: Blue Man
Albert Poland, a Broadway producer and general manager of the Astor Place Theater, an off-Broadway theater in New York City that has been the home of the famous Blue Man Group for many years, knows that the show must generate ticket sales of $40,000 per week to break even. In addition to performers' salaries, the show's costs include weekly rent, a service package fee that covers the salaries of the house and box office staff, and a percentage of the gross weekly box office receipts. The show's break-even point represents sales of about 450 seats per week. The theater's capacity is 300 seats per performance, which means that the show reaches its break-even point by selling out 1.5 of its 9 performances each week. Most of the Blue Man Group performances at the Astor Place Theater are sold out, making it a highly profitable business.[37] ■

© Jeff Moore/ZUMA Press/Alamy

Break-even analysis does have certain limitations. It is too simple to use as a final screening device because it ignores the importance of cash flows. In addition, the accuracy of the analysis depends on the accuracy of the revenue and expense estimates. Finally, the assumptions pertaining to break-even analysis may not be realistic for some businesses. Break-even calculations assume the following: fixed expenses remain constant for all levels of sales volume, variable expenses change in direct proportion to changes in sales volume, and changes in sales volume have no effect on unit sales price. Relaxing these assumptions does not render this tool useless, however. For example, the owner could employ nonlinear break-even analysis to determine a company's break-even point.

Chapter Summary by Learning Objective

1. Describe how to prepare the basic financial statements and use them to manage a small business.

- Entrepreneurs rely on three basic financial statements to understand the financial conditions of their companies:
    1. *The balance sheet*—Built on the accounting equation: Assets = Liabilities = Owner's equity, it provides an estimate of the company's value on a particular date.
    2. *The income statement*—This statement compares the firm's revenues to its expenses to determine its net income (or loss). It provides information about the company's bottom line.
    3. *The statement of cash flows*—This statement shows the change in the company's working capital over the accounting period by listing the sources and the uses of funds.

2. Create projected (pro forma) financial statements.

- Projected financial statements are a basic component of a sound financial plan. They help the manager plot the company's financial future by setting operating objectives and by analyzing the reasons for variations from targeted results. In addition, the small business in search of start-up funds will need these pro forma statements to present to prospective lenders and investors. They also assist in determining the amount of cash, inventory, fixtures, and other assets the business will need to begin operation.

3. Understand the basic financial statements through ratio analysis.

- The 12 key ratios described in this chapter are divided into four major categories: *liquidity ratios*, which show the small firm's ability to meet its current obligations; *leverage ratios*, which tell how much of the company's financing is provided by owners and how much by creditors; *operating ratios*, which show how effectively the firm uses its resources; and *profitability ratios*, which disclose the company's profitability.

- Many agencies and organizations regularly publish such statistics. If there is a discrepancy between the small firm's ratios and those of the typical business, the owner should investigate the reason for the difference. A below-average ratio does not necessarily mean that the business is in trouble.

4. Explain how to interpret financial ratios.

- To benefit from ratio analysis, the small company should compare its ratios to those of other companies in the same line of business and look for trends over time.

- When business owners detect deviations in their companies' ratios from industry standards, they should determine the cause of the deviations. In some cases, such deviations are the result of sound business decisions; in other instances, however, ratios that are out of the normal range for a particular type of business are indicators of what could become serious problems for a company.

5. Conduct a break-even analysis for a small company.

- Business owners should know their firm's break-even point, the level of operations at which total revenues equal total costs; it is the point at which companies neither earn a profit nor incur a loss. Although just a simple screening device, break-even analysis is a useful planning and decision-making tool.

Discussion Questions

11-1. Why is developing a financial plan so important to an entrepreneur about to launch a business?

11-2. How should a small business manager use the 12 ratios discussed in this chapter?

11-3. Outline the key points of the 12 ratios discussed in this chapter.

11-4. What signals does each of the 12 ratios give a business owner?

11-5. Describe the method for building a projected income statement and a projected balance sheet for a beginning business.

11-6. Why are pro forma financial statements important to the financial planning process?

11-7. How can break-even analysis help an entrepreneur planning to launch a business?

Beyond the Classroom . . .

11-8. Ask the owner of a small business to provide your class with copies of his or her company's financial statements (current or past).

11-9. Using these statements, compute the 12 key ratios described in this chapter.

11-10. Compare the company's ratios with those of the typical firm in this line of business.

11-11. Interpret the ratios and make suggestions for operating improvements.

11-12. Prepare a break-even analysis for the owner.

11-13. Find a publicly held company of interest to you that provides its financial statements on the Web. You can conduct a Web search using the company's name, or you can find lists of companies at the Securities and Exchange Commission's EDGAR database or visit AnnualReports.com to download the annual report of a company that interests you.

11-14. Analyze the company's financial statements by calculating the 12 ratios covered in this chapter and compare these ratios to industry averages found in RMA's *Annual Statement Studies, Bizminer,* or one of the other financial analysis resources found in your library.

11-15. Do you spot any problem areas in the company's financials?

11-16. What are the financial strengths of the company?

11-17. What recommendations can you make to improve the company's financial position?

11-18. What do you project the company's future to be?

11-19. Explain why you would or would not recommend investing in the company.

Endnotes

Scan for Endnotes or go to www.pearsonhighered.com/scarborough

12 Managing Cash Flow

Kay/Getty Images

Learning Objectives

On completion of this chapter, you will be able to:

1. Explain the importance of cash management to a small company's success.

2. Differentiate between cash and profits.

3. Understand the five steps in creating a cash budget.

4. Describe fundamental principles involved in managing the "big three" of cash management: accounts receivable, accounts payable, and inventory.

5. Explain the techniques for avoiding a cash crunch in a small company.

Cash—a four-letter word that has become a curse for many small businesses. Lack of this valuable asset has driven countless small companies into bankruptcy. More small businesses fail for a lack of cash than for a lack of profit. Unfortunately, many more firms will become failure statistics because their owners have neglected the principles of cash management that can spell the difference between success and failure. "Everything is about cash," says entrepreneur-turned-venture-capitalist Guy Kawasaki, "raising it, conserving it, collecting it."[1] Indeed, developing a cash forecast is essential for new businesses because start-up companies usually do not generate positive cash flow right away. A common cause of business failures, especially in start-up and fast-growth companies, is overemphasis on increasing sales with little concern for collecting the receivables those sales generate. "Your sales figures may be great, but it's cash flow that determines whether you can keep the doors open," says one business writer.[2] Another problem is that entrepreneurs neglect to forecast how much cash their companies will need to get through the **valley of death**, the time period during which start-up companies experience negative cash flow as they ramp up operations, build their customer bases, and become self-supporting (see Figure 12.1). The result is always the same: a cash crisis.

As you learned in the previous chapter, controlling the financial aspects of a business using the analysis of basic financial statements with ratios is immensely important; however, by themselves, these techniques are insufficient for achieving business success. Entrepreneurs are prone to focus on their companies' income statements—particularly sales and profits. The income statement, of course, shows only part of a company's financial picture. It is entirely possible for a business to earn a profit and still go out of business by *running out of cash*. In other words, managing a company's total financial performance effectively requires an entrepreneur to look beyond the "bottom line" and focus on what it takes to keep a company going—cash. "If a company isn't producing cash from its ongoing business, all the rest is smoke and mirrors," says Michael Connellan, a successful entrepreneur and former investment banker.[3]

valley of death
the time period during which start-up companies experience negative cash flow as they ramp up operations, build their customer bases, and become self-supporting

Cash Management

A survey by American Express OPEN Small Business Monitor reports that 52 percent of small business owners say they experience problems managing cash flow.[4] Managing cash flow is a universal problem for entrepreneurs; a recent survey of Britain's small and medium-sized businesses reports that 46 percent of owners say they had suffered at least one disruption to their companies' cash flow, most often caused by customers paying their bills late or not at all.[5] Although cash flow is a common concern for almost every business owner, the sluggish recovery from the Great Recession has put excess strain on many companies' cash flow. Since 2010, the percentage of small business owners who report that their companies' cash flow is either somewhat or

LO1

Explain the importance of cash management to a small company's success.

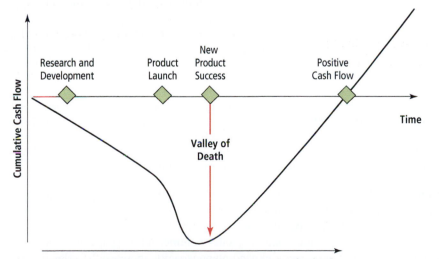

FIGURE 12.1

The Valley of Death

Source: Yoshitaka Osawa and Kumiko Miyazaki, "An Empirical Analysis of the Valley of Death: Large Scale R&D Project Performance in a Japanese Diversified Company," *Asian Journal of Technology Innovation,* vol. 14, no. 2, 2006, pp. 93–116.

A start-up company must have enough cash to survive the depth and the breadth of the valley of death, or it will become another failure statistic.

FIGURE 12.2

Small Business Owners' Ratings of Their Companies' Cash Flow

Source: Based on data from Wells Fargo Small Business Index, 2nd Quarter 2014, p.11.

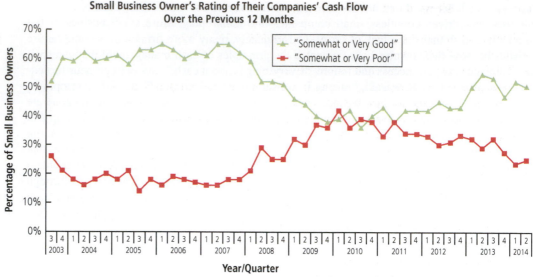

cash management
the process of forecasting, collecting, disbursing, investing, and planning for the cash a company needs to operate smoothly.

very poor has declined, while the percentage of owners who say their companies' cash flow is either somewhat or very good has increased. However, small business's cash positions have not returned to pre-recession levels (see Figure 12.2). The best way to avoid a potentially business-crushing cash crisis is to use the principles of sound cash management. **Cash management** involves forecasting, collecting, disbursing, investing, and planning for the cash a company needs to operate smoothly. Cash management is a vital task because cash is the most important yet least productive asset a small business owns. A business must have enough cash to meet its obligations, or it will be declared bankrupt. Creditors, employees, and lenders expect to be paid on time, and cash is the required medium of exchange. However, some companies retain excessive amounts of cash to meet any unexpected circumstances that might arise. These dormant dollars have an income-earning potential that owners are ignoring; investing this cash, even for a short time, can add to a company's earnings. Proper cash management permits owners to adequately meet the cash demands of their businesses, avoid retaining unnecessarily large cash balances, and stretch the profit-generating power of each dollar their companies own.

Although cash flow difficulties afflict companies of all sizes and ages, young companies, especially, are cash sponges, soaking up every available dollar and always hungry for more. The reason usually is that their cash-generating "engines" are not operating at full speed yet and cannot provide enough power to generate the cash necessary to cover rapidly climbing operating expenses. Entrepreneurs must manage cash flow from the day they launch their businesses.

ENTREPRENEURIAL PROFILE: H.J. Heinz: H.J. Heinz Company Shortly after H.J. Heinz, who started in the food business at age 14 when he began selling horseradish he grew in his garden, and two partners launched their first food business (which sold bottled horseradish) in 1875, their company's rapidly growing sales outstripped their start-up capital, and the company ran out of cash. A local newspaper called the entrepreneurs a "trio in a pickle." After the company failed, Heinz personally was liable for $20,000, a huge sum in that day. Through much determination, he paid off the entire debt. Undaunted, Heinz learned from his mistakes and launched a second food company the very next year. In this venture, he added the product that would eventually make him famous—ketchup—and with the help of careful cash management, the H.J. Heinz Company grew into one of the largest food companies in the world.[6] ∎

Managing cash flow is also an acute problem for rapidly growing businesses. In fact, fast-track companies are most likely to suffer cash shortages. Many successful, growing, and profitable businesses fail because they become insolvent; they do not have adequate cash to meet the needs of a growing business with a booming sales volume. As a company's sales increase, its owner also must hire more employees, expand plant capacity, increase the sales force, build inventory, and incur other drains on the firm's cash supply. During rapid growth, cash collections typically fall behind, compounding the problem. Cash flows out of these high-growth companies

TABLE 12.1 Signs of an Impending Cash Flow Crisis

Following are signs that a company may be on the verge of a cash crisis:

- Excess supplies of inventory
- Large stock of "old" inventory items that never sold
- Significant volume of fixed asset purchases, such as machinery and equipment
- Accounts receivable that are past due
- Failing to take advantage of cash discounts from vendors and suppliers
- Late payments to vendors and suppliers
- Missed quarterly tax payments
- Past due loan payments
- Above average interest expense because of excessive business debt
- Average collection period ratio that is above the industry median
- Missed sales because popular inventory items are out of stock
- Difficulty meeting payroll on time
- Rapid increase in business expenses
- Rapid increase in accounts receivable balance
- Minimal or no financial controls in place to monitor potential theft
- Infrequent preparation and use of financial statements as a managerial tool

Source: Based on Steve LeFever, "Cash Flow Checklist: How Do You Rate?" *Multi-Unit Franchisee*, Issue IV, 2013, p. 76.

much faster than it comes in. The head of the National Federation of Independent Business says many small business owners "wake up one day to find that the price of success is no cash on hand. They don't understand that if they're successful, inventory and receivables will increase faster than profits can fund them."[7] Table 12.1 shows signs that a company is facing an impending cash flow crisis.

ENTREPRENEURIAL PROFILE: Susan Spencer Frustrated by the rigid styles and uncomfortable fit of tennis dresses in the late 1960s, Susan Spencer designed a tennis dress that was more comfortable and flattering to the female figure. When many of her friends asked her to make dresses for them, Spencer, then in her twenties, decided to start a business designing and selling them. She found a clothing manufacturer and took on a partner whose main focus was growing sales as fast as possible. Spencer learned a valuable and costly lesson about fast growth, payment terms, and cash flow; her business failed when it ran out of cash. "One of the most important things is to know the payment terms your customers are setting, what they're going to pay you and when," says Spencer, who went on to become the first female general manager of a National Football League team. "I was in business 4 years, before I figured this out. I didn't know that department stores paid net 90 days, and that sunk me."[8] ∎

Table 12.2 shows how to calculate the additional cash required to support an increase in sales.

The first step in managing cash more effectively is to understand the company's **cash flow cycle**—the time lag between paying suppliers for merchandise or materials and receiving payment from customers after they sell the product or service (see Figure 12.3). The longer this cash flow cycle, the more likely the business owner will encounter a cash crisis. Small companies, especially those that buy from or sell to larger businesses, are finding that their cash flow cycles are growing longer as large companies have stretched their invoice payment times to suppliers and decreased their invoice collection times from customers to improve their cash flow. A recent study by REL Consultancy shows that large companies, those with more than $5 billion in annual sales, have an average days' sales outstanding (DSO) of 41 days but an average days' payable outstanding (DPO) of 55.8 days (a difference of −14.8 days). The numbers for small companies, those with less than $500 million in annual sales, show the "cash squeeze" that large companies are putting them in: Their DSO is 58.9 days, and their DPO is 40.1 days (a difference of 18.8 days).[9]

cash flow cycle
the time lag between paying suppliers for merchandise or materials and receiving payment from customers.

TABLE 12.2 How Much Cash Is Required to Support an Increase in Sales?

Too often, entrepreneurs believe that increasing sales is the ideal solution to a cash crunch, only to discover (often after it is too late) that it takes extra cash to support extra sales. The following worksheet demonstrates how to calculate the amount of additional cash required to support an increase in sales.

To make the calculation, a business owner needs the following information:

- The increase in sales planned ($)
- The time frame for adding new sales (days)
- The company's gross profit margin, gross profit ÷ net sales (%)
- The estimated additional expenses required to generate additional sales ($)
- The company's average collection period (days)

To calculate the amount of additional cash needed, use the following formula:

Extra cash required = [(New sales − Gross profit + Extra overhead) × (Average collection period × 1.20*)] ÷ (Time frame in days for adding new sales)

Consider the following example:

The owner of Ardent Company wants to increase sales by $75,000 over the next year. The company's gross profit margin is 30 percent of sales (so its gross profit on these additional sales would be $75,000 × 30% = $22,500), its average collection period is 47 days, and managers estimate that generating the additional sales will require an increase in expenses of $21,300. To calculate the additional cash that Ardent will need to support this higher level of sales, use the following formula:

Extra cash required = [($75,000 − $22,500 + 21,300) × (47 × 1.2)] ÷ 365 = $11,404

Ardent will need $11,404 in extra cash to support the additional sales of $75,000 it plans to bring in over the next year.

---

*The extra 20 percent is added as a cushion.

Source: Based on Norm Brodsky, "Paying for Growth: How Much Cash You Need to Carry New Sales," Inc. Online Tools & Apps: Worksheet, http://www.inc.com/tools/details/0,6152,CNT61_HOM1_LOC0_NAVhome_TOL11648,00.html.

Once entrepreneurs understand their companies' cash flow cycle, the next step in effective cash management is to analyze it, looking for ways to reduce its length. For the company whose cash flow is illustrated in Figure 12.3, reducing the cycle from 240 days to, say, 150 days would free up incredible amounts of cash that this company could use to finance growth and dramatically reduce its borrowing costs. What steps do you suggest the owner of this business take to reduce its cash flow cycle?

Preparing a cash forecast that recognizes this cycle helps to avoid a cash crisis. Understanding the cash flow patterns of a business over the course of a year is essential to creating a successful cash management strategy. Business owners should calculate their cash flow cycles whenever they prepare their financial statements (or at least quarterly). On a *daily* basis, business

FIGURE 12.3

The Cash Flow Cycle

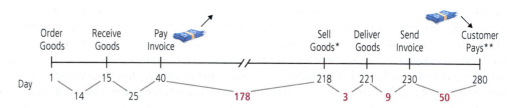

*Based on Average Inventory Turnover:
$$\frac{365 \text{ days}}{2.05 \text{ times/year}} = 178 \text{ days}$$

**Based on Average Collection Period:
$$\frac{365 \text{ days}}{7.31 \text{ times/year}} = 50 \text{ days}$$

Cash Flow Cycle = 240 days

SORRY TO HEAR CASH FLOW IS DOWN

CONGRATULATIONS ON YOUR IMPROVED COMMUNICATION SKILLS

WISHING YOU SUCCESS JUGGLING FAMILY AND WORK

YOU BON

CARDS

Ralph Hughes/Cartoon Stock

owners should generate a report showing the following items: total cash on hand, bank balance, a summary of the day's sales, a summary of the day's cash receipts, a summary of the day's cash disbursements, and a summary of accounts-receivable collections. Compiling these reports into monthly summaries provides the foundation for making reliable cash forecasts and enables entrepreneurs to understand the rhythm of their companies' cash flow.

Cash and Profits Are Not the Same

As important as earning a profit is, a company's survival depends on its ability to generate positive cash flow. Attempting to discern the status of a small company's cash position by analyzing its profitability is futile; profitability is *not* necessarily highly correlated with cash flow. Entrepreneurs often equivocate higher sales with better cash flow, but that is usually not the case. In fact, a company can be growing and earning a profit and still be forced to close its doors because it runs out of cash. For instance, say that a company sells $5,000 of merchandise on credit. The sale shows up as revenue on the income statement, but the company's cash balance does not increase until it actually collects (if it ever collects) the account receivable, which may be months later. An income statement does not tell an entrepreneur anything about the condition of the company's cash flow. "The stumbling block is that a lot of organizations have a hard time getting their arms around cash management and understanding it operationally," says John Cummings, a consultant at KPMG who advises companies on cash management strategies. "They're so used to a profit-and-loss statement world and do not understand the implications of cash flow on operations."[10]

In addition, slow sales also spell problems for a company's cash flow, but in a different way. When sales falter, cash flows in more slowly, which means that the company has less cash to cover its required payments. The result, however, is still the same: a cash crisis. Jay Goltz, owner of five successful art-related and home décor businesses in Chicago, says, "I am dealing with cash flow issues because sales are off, thanks to record snowfall and subzero temperatures, and because we started buying direct from all over the world in bigger quantities—in some cases a

LO2
Differentiate between cash and profits.

year's worth of merchandise. Eventually, this will mean better [profit] margins, a better selection of products, and way more inventory than I had last year at this time, but at the moment, it also means I have way less cash. I am still able to pay the bills, but I have learned that it is always better to have as much cash available as possible."[11]

Profit (or net income) is the difference between a company's total revenue and its total expenses. It measures how efficiently a business is operating. Cash is the money that is free and readily available to use in a business. **Cash flow** is a measure of a company's liquidity and represents the balance of cash payments that flow into and out of a company over a particular period of time. Many small business owners soon discover that profitability does not guarantee liquidity. As important as earning a profit is, no business owner can pay suppliers, creditors, employees, government entities, and lenders in profits; that requires *cash*! Many entrepreneurs focus on their company's earnings because they know that a company must earn a profit to stay in business. However, adequate cash flow also is essential because it represents the money that flows through a business in a continuous cycle without being tied up in any other asset. "Businesses fail not because they are making or losing money," warns one financial expert, "but because they simply run out of cash."[12] A recent survey by Visa Small Business reports that 39 percent of small business owners cite cash flow management as a major or critical concern.[13]

Figure 12.4 shows the flow of cash through a typical small business. Cash flow is the volume of actual cash that comes into and goes out of the business during an accounting period. Decreases in cash occur when the business purchases, on credit or for cash, goods for inventory or materials for use in production. A business sells the resulting inventory either for cash or on credit. When a company takes in cash or collects payments on accounts receivable, its cash balance increases. Notice that purchases for inventory and production *lead* sales; that is, a company typically pays these bills *before* sales are generated. On the other hand, collection of accounts receivable *lags* behind sales; that is, customers who purchase goods on credit do not pay until after the sale, sometimes months later.

cash flow

a method of tracking a company's liquidity and its ability to pay its bills and other financial obligations on time by tracking the flow of cash into and out of the business over a period of time.

The Cash Budget

LO3

Understand the five steps in creating a cash budget.

The need for a cash budget arises because in every business the cash flowing in is rarely "in sync" with the cash flowing out of the business. This uneven flow of cash creates periodic cash surpluses and shortages, making it necessary for entrepreneurs to track the flow of cash through their businesses so that they can project realistically the cash available throughout the year. Many entrepreneurs operate their businesses without knowing the pattern of their cash flows, believing that the process is too complex or time consuming. In reality, entrepreneurs simply cannot afford to disregard the process of cash management. They must ensure that their businesses have on hand an adequate but not excessive supply of cash to meet their operating needs.

FIGURE 12.4

Cash Flow

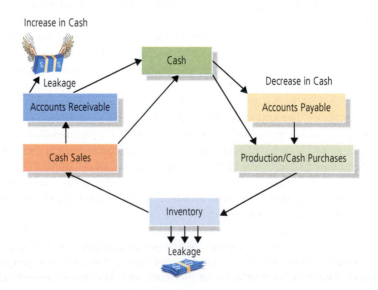

The goal of cash management is to have enough cash available to meet the company's cash needs at a given time.

How much cash is enough? What is suitable for one business may be totally inadequate for another, depending on each firm's size, nature, seasonal pattern of sales, and particular situation. The small business manager should prepare a **cash budget**, which is nothing more than a "cash map" showing the amount and the timing of the cash receipts and the cash disbursements day by day, week by week, or month by month. It is used to predict the amount of cash a company will need to operate smoothly over a specific period of time, and it is a valuable tool in managing a company successfully. A cash budget can illuminate a host of approaching problems, giving entrepreneurs adequate time to handle or, better yet, avoid them. A cash budget reveals important clues about how well a company balances its accounts payable and accounts receivable, controls inventory, finances its growth, and makes use of the cash it has.

Typically, small business owners should prepare a projected monthly cash budget for at least one year into the future and quarterly estimates for another. The forecast must cover all seasonal sales fluctuations. The more variable a firm's sales pattern, the shorter should be its planning horizon. For example, a company whose sales fluctuate widely over a relatively short time frame might require a weekly cash budget. The key is to track cash flow over time. The timing of a company's cash flow is as important as the amounts. "An alert cash flow manager keeps an eye not on cash receipts or on cash demands as average quantities but on cash as a function of the *calendar*," says one business owner.[14]

Creating a written cash plan is not an excessively time-consuming task and can help the owner to avoid unexpected cash shortages, a situation that can cause a business to fail. Someone in the company should have the responsibility of forecasting and tracking the company's cash flow. If the entrepreneur delegates the task to an employee, he or she must be sure that the employee is trained to do the job properly. Joanna Norris, a partner in the Ratio Law Firm in Manchester, England, says that although the firm's cash disbursements tend to be predictable, its cash receipts can be quite variable, which makes daily cash management an essential task. She and her partners have trained their office manager to track the practice's cash flow every day to ensure that the law firm always has sufficient cash on hand.[15] Preparing a cash budget helps business owners avoid nasty cash flow surprises. Most entrepreneurs rely on computer spreadsheets such as Microsoft Excel and others to track their cash flow and to forecast cash receipts and disbursements, but popular small business accounting software includes cash management tools that require very little time and effort and produce reliable results. Many accounting software makers offer cloud-based applications that include cash management modules for less than $20 per month. A recent survey by bill.com, an online bill payment company, reports that 73 percent of small businesses rely on spreadsheets to manage their cash flow and 8.5 percent use an integrated accounting system. Alarmingly, the survey also shows that 8.3 percent track their companies' cash flow "in their heads," and 10.3 percent of business owners do not use any cash management tools at all.[16]

A cash budget is based on the cash method of accounting, meaning that cash receipts and cash disbursements are recorded in the forecast *only when the cash transaction is expected to take place*. For example, credit sales to customers are not reported as cash receipts until the company expects to collect the cash from them. Similarly, purchases made on credit are not recorded until the owner expects to pay them. Because depreciation, bad-debt expense, and other noncash items involve no cash transfers, they are omitted entirely from the cash budget.

A cash budget is nothing more than a forecast of the firm's cash inflows and outflows for a specific time period, and it will never be completely accurate. However, it does give an entrepreneur a clear picture of a company's estimated cash balance for the period, pointing out when it may require external cash infusions or when surplus cash balances are available to invest. In addition, by comparing actual cash flows with projections, an entrepreneur can revise the forecast so that future cash budgets will be more accurate.

ENTREPRENEURIAL PROFILE: Andrew Johnson: Powwownow Andrew Johnson, controller of Powwownow, a small company based in Surrey, England, that provides low-cost, easy-to-use telephone conferencing services, understands how deadly running out of cash can be

cash budget
a "cash map" showing the amount and the timing of cash receipts and cash disbursements on a daily, weekly, or monthly basis.

for a small company and does everything he can to make sure that Powwownow avoids that trap. Johnson uses a spreadsheet he updates weekly to produce accurate forecasts of the company's cash flow for one year into the future.[17] ■

Formats for preparing a cash budget vary depending on the pattern of a company's cash flow. Table 12.3 shows a most likely monthly cash budget for a small department store over a six-month period. (Creating pessimistic and optimistic cash forecasts is a snap once the most likely cash budget is in place.) Each monthly column should be divided into two sections—estimated and actual (not shown)—so that each succeeding cash forecast can be updated to reflect actual cash flows. (The Service Corps of Retired Executives provides a handy set of templates, including one for forecasting cash flow, on its Web site at www.score.org/resources/business-plans-financial-statements-template-gallery.) Comparing forecasted amounts to actual cash flows and learning the causes of any significant discrepancies allows entrepreneurs to improve the accuracy of future cash budgets.

TABLE 12.3 Cash Budget for a Small Department Store

Assumptions:

Cash balance on December 31 is $12,000

Minimum cash balance is $10,000

Sales are 75% credit and 25% cash

Credit sales are collected in the following manner:

* 60% collected in the first month after the sale

* 30% collected in the second month after the sale

* 5% collected in the third month after the sale

* 5% are never collected

Sales forecasts are as follows:	Pessimistic	Most Likely	Optimistic
October (actual)	–	$ 300,000	–
November (actual)	–	350,000	–
December (actual)	–	400,000	–
January	120,000	150,000	175,000
February	160,000	200,000	250,000
March	160,000	200,000	250,000
April	250,000	300,000	340,000
May	260,000	315,000	360,000
June	265,000	320,000	375,000

Rent is $3,000 per month

Interest payments of $664 and $817 are due in April and May, respectively.

A tax prepayment of $18,000 is due in March.

A capital addition payment of $130,000 is due in February.

A bank note payment of $7,500 is due in March.

Insurance premiums are $475 per month.

Other expense estimates include:	Purchases	Wages and Salaries	Utilities	Advertising	Miscellaneous
January	$ 140,000	$ 30,000	$ 1,450	$ 1,600	$ 500
February	140,000	38,000	1,400	1,600	500
March	210,000	40,000	1,250	1,500	500
April	185,000	42,000	1,250	2,000	550
May	190,000	44,000	1,250	2,000	550
June	180,000	44,000	1,400	2,200	550

(continued)

TABLE 12.3 Cash Budget for a Small Department Store (*continued*)

	Oct	Nov	Dec	Jan	Feb	Mar	Apr	May	Jun
Cash Receipts									
Sales	$ 300,000	$ 350,000	$ 400,000	$ 150,000	$ 200,000	$ 200,000	$ 300,000	$ 315,000	$ 320,000
Credit Sales	225,000	262,500	300,000	112,500	150,000	150,000	225,000	236,250	240,000
Collections									
60%—First month after sale				180,000	67,500	90,000	90,000	135,000	141,750
30%—Second month after sale				78,750	90,000	33,750	45,000	45,000	67,500
5%—Third month after sale				11,250	13,125	15,000	5,625	7,500	7,500
Cash Sales				37,500	50,000	50,000	75,000	78,750	80,000
Other cash receipts				25	35	50	60	60	65
Total Cash Receipts				307,525	220,660	188,800	215,685	266,310	296,815
Cash Disbursements									
Purchases				140,000	140,000	210,000	185,000	190,000	180,000
Rent				3,000	3,000	3,000	3,000	3,000	3,000
Utilities				1,450	1,400	1,250	1,250	1,250	1,400
Bank Note				–	–	7,500	–	–	–
Tax Prepayment				–	–	18,000	–	–	–
Capital Additions				–	130,000	–	–	–	–
Wages and Salaries				30,000	38,000	40,000	42,000	44,000	44,000
Insurance				475	475	475	475	475	475
Advertising				1,600	1,600	1,500	2,000	2,000	2,200
Interest				–	–	–	664	817	–
Miscellaneous				500	500	500	550	550	550
Total Cash Disbursements				177,025	314,975	282,225	234,939	242,092	231,625
End-of-Month Balance									
Beginning cash balance				12,000	142,500	48,185	10,000	10,000	14,218
+ Cash receipts				307,525	220,660	188,800	215,685	266,310	296,815
– Cash disbursements				177,025	314,975	282,225	234,939	242,092	231,625
Cash (end-of-month)				142,500	48,185	(45,240)	(9,254)	34,218	79,408
Borrowing				–	–	55,240	19,254	–	–
Repayment				–	–	–	–	20,000	54,944
Final Cash Balance				$ 142,500	$ 48,185	$ 10,000	$ 10,000	$ 14,218	$ 24,464
Monthly Surplus/(Deficit)				130,500	(94,315)	(93,425)	(19,254)	24,218	65,190

Creating a cash budget requires five basic steps:

1. Determining an adequate minimum cash balance

2. Forecasting sales

3. Forecasting cash receipts

4. Forecasting cash disbursements

5. Estimating the end-of-month cash balance

Step 1: Determining an Adequate Minimum Cash Balance

What is considered an excessive cash balance for one small business may be inadequate for another, even though the two companies are in the same industry. Some suggest that a firm's cash balance should equal at least one-fourth of its current liabilities, but this general rule clearly will not work for all small businesses. Many financial experts recommend that businesses build a cash reserve or contingency fund large enough to cover three to six months' of operating expenses. Highly seasonal businesses often require an even larger reserve fund, one large enough to cover its expenses for both its busy and "off" seasons.

The most reliable method of deciding the right minimum cash balance is based on past experience. Past operating records will indicate the cash cushion an entrepreneur needs to cover any unexpected expenses after all normal cash outlays are deducted from the month's cash receipts. For example, past records may indicate that it is desirable to maintain a cash balance equal to five days' sales. Seasonal fluctuations may cause a firm's minimum cash balance to change. For example, the minimum cash balance for a retailer may be greater in June than in December.

Step 2: Forecasting Sales

The heart of the cash budget is the sales forecast. It is the central factor in creating an accurate picture of the firm's cash position because sales ultimately are transformed into cash receipts and cash disbursements. For most businesses, sales constitute the primary source of the cash flowing into the business. Similarly, sales of merchandise require that cash be used to replenish inventory. As a result, the cash budget is only as accurate as the sales forecast from which it is derived.

For an established business, a sales forecast is based on past sales, but owners must be careful not to be excessively optimistic in projecting sales. Economic swings, increased competition, fluctuations in demand, normal seasonal variations, weather, and other factors can drastically affect sales patterns and, therefore, a company's cash flow. Most businesses, from retailers and hotels to accounting firms and builders, have sales patterns that are "lumpy" and not evenly distributed throughout the year.

The Arabian Tent Company

ENTREPRENEURIAL PROFILE: Katherine Hudson: The Arabian Tent Company The Arabian Tent Company, a business that Katherine Hudson, launched in 2004 and operates from her home in East Sussex, England, provides luxurious tents and decorations for outdoor weddings, parties, and festivals. Hudson's business is highly seasonal, with almost all of the company's sales occurring between April and September; sales during the remaining six months of the year are lean. To accommodate the seasonality of her business's cash flow, Hudson requires customers to pay a 25 percent deposit when they book the event and second 25 percent deposit on January 1 of the year of the event. She also has launched a complementary business that provides furniture rental and decorating services for indoor events, particularly during the holiday season. Hudson recently began shipping half of her company's tents to Australia during the winter (which is Australia's summer) to help fill the seasonal gap in her company's cash flow.[18] ■

Many small retailers generate most of their sales and as much as one-third of their profits in the months of November and December. For instance, 40 percent of all toy sales take place in the last six weeks of the year, and companies that make fruitcakes typically generate 50 to 90 percent of their sales during the holiday season.[19] The typical wine and spirits shop makes 15 to 18 percent of its total sales volume for the entire year between December 15 and December 31.[20] Companies that sell television sets and recliners see sales surge in the weeks before the Super Bowl, and Super Bowl Sunday is the busiest day of the year for pizza restaurants, producing revenues that are five times that of a typical Sunday.[21] For fireworks companies, the three weeks before July 4 account for the majority of annual sales with another smaller peak occurring before New Year's Eve.[22] Costume makers generate almost all of their sales before Halloween but must invest in the raw materials and the labor to make the costumes in the spring and summer months, when their cash balances are at their lowest.[23] For companies with highly seasonal sales patterns, proper cash management is an essential activity.

Several quantitative techniques that are beyond the scope of this text (linear regression, multiple regression, time-series analysis, and exponential smoothing) are available to owners of existing businesses with an established sales pattern for forecasting sales. These methods enable the small business owner to extrapolate past and present sales trends to arrive at accurate sales forecasts.

The task of forecasting sales for a start-up is more difficult but not impossible. For example, the entrepreneur might conduct research on similar firms and their sales patterns in the first year of operation to come up with a forecast. The local chamber of commerce and trade associations in various industries also collect such information. Publications such as the *Annual Statement Studies* published by the Risk Management Association (RMA) and BizMiner, which profile financial statements for companies of all sizes in hundreds of industries, are also useful tools. Market research is another source of information that may be used to estimate annual sales for a start-up. Other potential sources that may help to predict sales include census reports, newspapers, radio and television customer profiles, polls and surveys, and local government statistics. Talking with owners of similar businesses (outside the local trading area, of course) can provide entrepreneurs with realistic estimates of start-up sales. Table 12.4 provides an example of how one entrepreneur used such marketing information to derive a sales forecast for his first year of operation.

No matter what techniques entrepreneurs employ, they must recognize that even the best sales estimates will be wrong. Many financial analysts suggest that the owner create *three* estimates—an optimistic, a pessimistic, and a most likely sales estimate—and then make a separate cash budget for each forecast (a very simple task with a spreadsheet). This dynamic forecast enables the owner to determine the range within which his or her sales will likely be as the year progresses.

Step 3: Forecasting Cash Receipts

As you learned earlier, sales constitute the primary source of cash receipts. When a company sells goods and services on credit, the cash budget must account for the delay between the sale and the actual collection of the proceeds. Remember: entrepreneurs cannot spend cash they haven't collected! For instance, an appliance store might not collect the cash from a refrigerator sold in February until April or May, and the cash budget must reflect this delay. To project accurately cash receipts, an entrepreneur must analyze accounts receivable to determine the company's collection pattern. For example, past records may indicate that 20 percent of sales are for cash, 50 percent are paid in the month following the sale, 20 percent are paid two months after the sale, 5 percent are paid after three months, and 5 percent are never collected. In addition to cash and credit sales, a small business may receive cash in a number of forms—interest income, rental income, dividends, and others.

TABLE 12.4 Forecasting Sales for a Business Start-Up

Robert Adler wants to open a repair shop for imported cars. The trade association for automotive garages estimates that the owner of an imported car spends an average of $485 per year on repairs and maintenance. The typical garage attracts its clientele from a trading zone (the area from which a business draws its customers) with a 20-mile radius. Census reports show that the families within a 20-mile radius of Robert's proposed location own 84,000 cars, of which 24 percent are imports. Based on a local consultant's market research, Robert believes he can capture 9.9 percent of the market this year. Robert's estimate of his company's first year's sales are as follows:

Number of cars in trading zone	84,000 autos
× Percent of imports	× 24 %
= Number of imported cars in trading zone	20,160 imports
Number of imports in trading zone	20,160 imports
× Average expenditure on repairs and maintenance	× $485
= Total import repair sales potential	$9,777,600
Total import repair sales potential	$9,777,600
× Estimated share of the market	× 9.9%
= Sales estimate	$967,982

Now Robert Adler can convert this annual sales estimate of $967,982 into monthly sales estimates for use in his company's cash budget.

Hands On . . . How To

Manage Cash Flow in a Highly Seasonal Business

Bruce Schofield and his wife Lucy purchased Good Intents in 2003 from the company founders, who were retiring. With hard work and sound management, the copreneurs have tripled the company's sales since they purchased it. The company, located in Ledbury, Herefordshire, England, provides aluminum-framed marquees and furnishings, which range from tables and chairs to illuminated bars and dance floors, for anniversaries, parties, and corporate, school, and university events. Its primary market, though, is weddings, which means that 75 percent of its sales take place between April and September. Not only does gearing up for the busy wedding season blitz require lots of advance planning, but it also demands some clever cash management techniques, particularly for the slower off-season. Even though sales are concentrated in just a few months of the year, Good Intents's expenses continue year-round. Good Intents's biggest expense is labor. To control labor costs, the Schofields employ a lean staff of four full-time employees, whom they keep busy during the slow winter season cleaning, repairing, and organizing equipment. During the busy season, they hire as many as eight part-time employees to handle the heavy volume of work. The Schofields also market the superior quality of their tents and heaters to their customers for off-season events. In addition, they require clients to pay a 25 percent deposit at booking and collect the balance owed before the event takes place so that they do not have to waste time chasing unpaid invoices. They also offer clients a small discount for early payment.

As the Schofields have learned, seasonal businesses are far more difficult to manage than those that generate sales and cash year-round. How can business owners whose companies face highly seasonal sales patterns manage the uneven cash flow?

- **Be financially disciplined.** Seasonal business owners must establish a realistic budget, stick to it, and avoid the temptation to spend lavishly when cash flow is plentiful. Teevan McManus, owner of the Coronado Surfing Academy in San Diego, failed to heed this advice in his first year of business. "I burned through everything I made in the summer and was living off of my business line of credit before the next season came around," he recalls. "I barely made it to the next June."

- **Manage your time and your employees' time carefully.** During the busy season, employees may be working overtime to serve the rush of customers; during the off-season, a business owner may cut back to 20-hour workweeks or operate with a skeleton crew.

- **Use permanent employees sparingly.** Many owners of seasonal businesses use a small core of permanent employees and then hire part-time workers or student interns during their busy season. Planning for the right number of seasonal employees and recruiting them early ensures that a business will be able to serve its customers properly.

- **Put aside cash in a separate account that you use only for the lean months of your seasonal business.**

- **Maximize your productivity in the off-season.** Use the slow season to conduct market research, perform routine maintenance and repairs, revise your Web site, and stay in touch with customers. Steve Kopelman's company, Haunted House.com, earns all of its $2.6 million in annual revenue in a six-week period leading up to Halloween. Starting in November, Kopelman surveys his customers so that he can refine his marketing efforts for the next season and solicit suggestions for improvement. He visits trade shows to look for the latest technology and gadgets to keep his haunted houses fresh and exciting for his customers. Kopelman also negotiates leases on properties for the next season and studies his competition by visiting every haunted house Web site he can find.

- **Keep inventory at minimal levels during the off-season.** As you will learn in this chapter, holding inventory unnecessarily merely ties up valuable cash uselessly.

- **Negotiate payment terms with vendors that are synchronized with your company's cash flow.** Schedule payments to vendors so that they coincide with your company's cash peaks rather than its cash valleys.

- **Offer off-peak discounts.** Doing so may generate some revenue during slow periods.

- **Consider starting a complementary seasonal business.** The weeks leading up to Halloween are the peak season for Sam Fard, owner of Los Angeles–based Roma Costume, a manufacturer of costumes for women. To reduce the highly seasonal nature of his business, Fard added a line of bikinis and lingerie to his company's product mix.

- **Create a cash flow forecast.** Perhaps one of the most important steps that seasonal business owners can take is to develop a forecast of their companies' cash flow. Doing so allows them to spot patterns and trends and to make plans for covering inevitable cash shortages. Make sure that you include a pessimistic or worst-case scenario in your cash forecast.

- **Establish a bank line of credit.** The line of credit should be large enough to cover at least three months' worth of expenses. Use your cash flow forecast to show the banker how and when your company will be able to repay the loan. A good cash forecast "shows the banker that you know exactly where the peaks and valleys are and what your cash needs are," says one banker.

1. What impact do highly seasonal sales have on a small company's cash flow?

Hands On . . . How To (continued)

2. What other advice can you offer owners of seasonal businesses about coping with the effects of their companies' highly irregular sales patterns? About managing cash flow in general?

Sources: Based on Nick Mead, "Seasonal Businesses: Dealing with Quieter Months Is Critical to Cash Flow," *The Guardian*, January 10, 2014, http://www.theguardian.com/small-business-network/2014/jan/10/seasonal-business-cashflow-income; Rohit Arora, "Winter Brings Seasonal Cash Flow Issues," *Fox Business*, February 5, 2013, http://smallbusiness.foxbusiness.com/marketing-sales/2013/02/05/winter-brings-seasonal-business-cash-flow-issues/; Cindy Vanegas, "Creating a Successful Seasonal Business All Year-Round," *Fox Business*, November 16, 2011, http://smallbusiness.foxbusiness.com/marketing-sales/2011/11/16/creating-successful-seasonal-business-all-year-round; Gwendolyn Bounds, "Preparing for the Big Bang," *Wall Street Journal*, June 29, 2004, pp. B1, B7; Rich Mintzer, "Running a Seasonal Business," *Entrepreneur*, March 16, 2007, http://www.entrepreneur.com/management/operations/article175954.html; Sarah Pierce, "Surviving a Seasonal Business," *Entrepreneur*, July 15, 2008, http://www.entrepreneur.com/startingabusiness/businessideas/article195680.html; Dan Kehrer, "10 Steps to Seasonal Success," *Business.com*, May 2006, http://www.business.com/directory/advice/sales-and-marketing/sales/10-steps-to-seasonal-success; and Amy Barrett, "Basics for Seasonal Business Owners," *BusinessWeek*, April 16, 2008, http://www.businessweek.com/magazine/content/08_64/s0804058908582.htm?chan=smallbiz_smallbiz+index+page_best+of+smallbiz+magazine.

Collecting accounts receivable promptly poses problems for many small companies. Figure 12.5 demonstrates the importance of acting promptly once an account becomes past due. Notice how the probability of collecting an outstanding account diminishes the longer the account is delinquent. Table 12.5 illustrates a concept of which many business owners are not aware: the high cost of failing to collect accounts receivable on time.

ENTREPRENEURIAL PROFILE: Ron Box: Joe Money Machinery Ron Box, chief financial officer of Joe Money Machinery, a family-owned reseller of heavy construction equipment in Birmingham, Alabama, has watched as the company's large customers, mainly construction firms and municipal governments, stretch out payment times on their invoices to 60 or more days, a practice that puts pressure on the small company's cash flow. In an attempt to speed up collections, Box recently began offering customers cash discounts for early payments. About 30 percent of Joe Money Machinery's customers have taken advantage of the discounts, "but they don't always do it," says Box. The company also has encouraged customers to pay with corporate credit cards, but that option has had limited success.[24] ∎

Many banks now offer cash management tools designed to speed up the collection of invoices to small companies that once were reserved only for large businesses. Once set up with a bank, **electronic (Automated Clearing House) collections** automatically deduct invoice amounts from customers' accounts and deposit them into the seller's account within 24 hours. Businesses can use electronic collections for single or periodic transactions, but they are ideal for recurring transactions. **Remote deposit**, which allows businesses to scan customers' checks (still the most widely accepted form of payment among small businesses) and deposit them from anywhere

electronic (Automated Clearing House) collections
a bank service that allows businesses to deduct automatically invoice amounts from customers' accounts and deposit them into the seller's account within 24 hours.

remote deposit
a bank service that allows businesses to scan customers' checks and deposit them from anywhere using a portable scanner, a computer, and an Internet connection.

FIGURE 12.5

Probability of Collecting Accounts Receivable

Source: Based on data from the Commercial Agency Section, Commercial Law League of America, 2011.

TABLE 12.5 The High Cost of Slow Payers

Are your customers who purchase on credit paying late? If so, these outstanding accounts receivable represent a significant leak in your company's cash flow. Slow-paying customers, in effect, are borrowing money from your business interest free. One experienced business owner says, "Whether you realize it or not, you're sort of a banker, and you need to start thinking like one . . . to assess the quality of your [customers' accounts]." Slow-paying customers are using your money without paying you interest while you forgo opportunities to place it in interest-earning investments or pay interest on money that you must borrow to replace the missing funds. Exactly how much is poor credit control costing your company? The answer may surprise you.

The first step is to calculate your company's average collection period ratio (see the section "Operating Ratios" in Chapter 9). The second step is to age your accounts receivable to determine how many accounts are current and how many are overdue. The following example shows how to use these numbers to calculate the cost of past-due accounts for a company whose credit terms are "net 30":

Average collection period	65 days
− Credit terms	−30 days
Excess in accounts receivable	35 days
Average daily sales of $21,500* × 35 days	$752,500
× Normal rate of return	× 8%
Annual cost of excess	$60,200

Slow-paying customers are costing this company more than $60,000 a year! If your business is highly seasonal, quarterly or monthly figures may be more meaningful than annual ones.

*Average daily sales = Annual sales ÷ 365 days = $7,847,500 ÷ 365 = $21,500 per day

Source: Based on Norm Brodsky, "What Are You, a Bank?" *Inc.*, November 2007, pp. 81–82, and "Financial Control," *Inc.* Reprinted with permission of the publisher.

using a check scanner (often provided by the bank at little or no charge), a smart phone, or a tablet, is becoming increasingly popular among small businesses. Scanned checks create an online, digital deposit that eliminates time-consuming runs to the bank and gets customers' payments into the business's account faster. Banks typically charge a monthly fee and a flat amount for each scanned check to provide the remote deposit service. Entrepreneurs should compare the benefits and the costs of these services at various banks, which provide a daily list of transactions to allow entrepreneurs to reconcile payments with their accounts-receivable records. Although only 5 percent of small businesses currently use remote deposit, banks expect that percentage to grow rapidly as business owners become more technologically savvy and more banks offer the service.[25]

Step 4: Forecasting Cash Disbursements

Entrepreneurs must have sufficient cash on hand to pay their bills as they come due (see Figure 12.6). Every entrepreneur should know his or her company's monthly "burn rate," the amount of cash it spends each month. Fortunately, most owners of established businesses can easily develop a clear picture of their companies' pattern of cash disbursements. Many cash payments, such as rent, loan repayments, and interest, are fixed amounts due on specified dates; others, such as purchases of goods and services, vary from one month to another. The key factor when forecasting disbursements for a cash budget is to record them in *the month in which they will be paid, not when the obligation is incurred.* Of course, the number of cash disbursements varies with each particular business, but the following disbursement categories are common: purchase of inventory or raw materials, wages and salaries, rent, utilities, taxes, loan payments, interest, advertising, fixed-asset purchases, and miscellaneous expenses.

When preparing a cash budget, one of the worst mistakes an entrepreneur can make is to underestimate cash disbursements, which can result in a cash crisis. To prevent this, wise entrepreneurs cushion their cash disbursement estimates, assuming they will be higher than expected. This is particularly important for entrepreneurs opening new businesses. In fact, some financial analysts recommend that new owners estimate cash disbursements as best they can and then add another 25 to 50 percent of the total! (Remember Murphy's Law?)

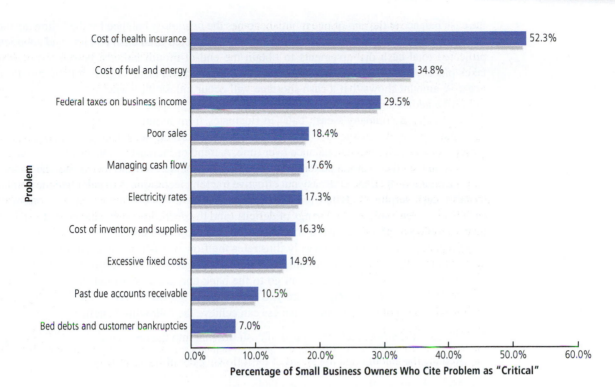

FIGURE 12.6

Cash Flow Concerns among Small Business Owners

Source: Holly Wade, *Small Business Problems and Priorities*, National Federation of Independent Business, August 2012, pp. 13–14.

Sometimes business owners have difficulty developing initial forecasts of cash receipts and cash disbursements. One of the most effective techniques for overcoming the "I don't know where to begin" hurdle is to make a *daily* list of the items that generated cash (receipts) and those that consumed it (disbursements).

ENTREPRENEURIAL PROFILE: Susan Bowen: Champion Awards Susan Bowen, CEO of Champion Awards, a $9 million T-shirt screen printer, monitors cash flow by tracking the cash that flows into and out of her company every day. Focusing on keeping the process simple, Bowen sets aside a few minutes each morning to track updates from the previous day on four key numbers:

Accounts receivable:

1. What did we bill yesterday?
2. How much did we actually collect?

Accounts payable:

1. What invoices did we receive yesterday?
2. How much in total did we pay out?

If Bowen observes the wrong trend—more new bills than new sales or more money going out than coming in—she makes immediate adjustments to protect her cash flow. The benefits produced (not the least of which is the peace of mind in knowing that no cash crisis is looming) more than outweigh the 10 minutes she invests in the process every day. "I've tried to balance my books every single day since I started my company in 1970," says Bowen.[26] ■

Step 5: Estimating the End-of-Month Cash Balance

To estimate a company's cash balance for each month, entrepreneurs first must determine the cash balance at the beginning of each month. The beginning cash balance includes cash on hand as well as cash in checking and savings accounts. As development of the cash budget progresses, the cash balance at the *end* of one month becomes the *beginning* balance for the following month. Next, the owner adds to the beginning balance the projected total cash receipts and subtracts the projected total cash disbursements to obtain the end-of-month balance before any borrowing takes place. A positive amount indicates that the firm has a cash surplus for the month, but a negative amount shows that a cash shortage will occur unless the owner is able to collect, raise, or borrow additional funds.

Normally, a company's cash balance fluctuates from month to month, reflecting seasonal sales patterns in the business. These fluctuations are normal, but business owners must watch closely for *trends* in the cash balance over time. A trend of increases indicates that a company is solvent; on the other hand, a pattern of cash decreases should alert the owner that the business is approaching a cash crisis. One easy but effective tracking technique is to calculate the company's monthly cash surplus or deficit (cash receipts minus cash disbursements) at the bottom of the cash budget (see Table 12.3). Strings of deficits (and the declining cash balance that results from them) should set off alarms that a company is headed for a cash crisis.

Preparing a cash budget not only illustrates the flow of cash into and out of the small business but also allows the owner to *anticipate* cash shortages and cash surpluses. "Then," explains a small business consultant, "you can go to the bank and get a 'seasonal' line of credit for six months instead of twelve. Right there you can cut your borrowing costs in half."[27] By planning cash needs ahead of time, a small business can achieve the following benefits:

- Increase the amount and the speed of cash flowing into the company
- Reduce the amount and the speed of cash flowing out of the company
- Make the most efficient use of available cash
- Take advantage of money-saving opportunities, such as quantity and cash discounts
- Finance seasonal business needs
- Develop a sound borrowing program
- Develop a workable program of debt repayment
- Impress lenders and investors with its ability to plan and repay financing
- Provide funds for expansion
- Plan for investing surplus cash

"Cash flow spells survival for every business," claims one expert. "Manage cash flow effectively, and your business works. If your cash flow is not well managed, then sooner or later your business goes under. It's that simple."[28] Unfortunately, most small business owners forgo these benefits because they fail to track their company's cash flow consistently. Because cash flow problems usually sneak up on a business over time, improper cash management often proves to be a costly—and fatal—mistake. Entrepreneurs cannot track their companies' cash flow "in their heads." There are too many variables involved, including cash sales, credit sales, collections from credit sales, inventory purchases, invoice due dates, seasonal and cyclical fluctuations, and others. Trying to manage a company's cash without a system to record and report receipts and disbursements is like a juggler who can juggle three balls but is overwhelmed as the number of balls increases. One way to avoid this pitfall is to establish a *weekly* report that shows the amount of cash on hand, the cash received, and the cash spent. Some entrepreneurs also monitor the status of the company's accounts receivable and accounts payable balances weekly.

LO4

Describe the fundamental principles involved in managing the "big three" of cash management: accounts receivable, accounts payable, and inventory.

The "Big Three" of Cash Management

It is unrealistic for business owners to expect to trace the flow of every dollar through their businesses. However, by concentrating on the three primary causes of cash flow problems, they can dramatically lower the likelihood of experiencing a devastating cash crisis. The "big three" of cash management are accounts receivable, accounts payable, and inventory. These three variables are leading indicators of a company's cash flow. If a company's accounts receivable balance is

You Be the Consultant

In Search of a Cash Flow Forecast

"I'll never make that mistake again," Douglas Martinez said to himself as he got into his car. Martinez had just left a meeting with his banker, who had not been optimistic about the chances of Martinez's plumbing supply company getting the loan it needed. "I should have been better prepared for the meeting," he muttered, knowing that he could be angry only at himself. "That consultant at the Small Business Development Center [SBDC] was right. Bankers' primary concern when making loans is cash flow."

"At least I salvaged the meeting by telling him I wasn't ready to officially apply for a loan yet," Martinez thought. "But I've got

a lot of work to do. I've got a week to figure out how to put together a cash budget to supplement my loan application. Maybe that consultant can help me."

When he returned to his office, Martinez gathered up the file folders containing all of his fast-growing company's financial reports and printed his projected revenues and expenses using his computer spreadsheet. Then he called the SBDC consultant he had worked with when he was launching his company and explained the situation. When he arrived at the consultant's office that afternoon, they started organizing the information. Here is what they came up with:

Current cash balance	$8,750
Sales pattern	71% on credit and 29% in cash
Collections of credit sales	68% in the same month as the sale
	19% in the first month after the sale
	7% in the second month after the sale
	6% never collected (bad debts)

Sales forecasts:

	Pessimistic	Most Likely	Optimistic
July (actual)	—	$18,750	—
August (actual)	—	$19,200	—
September (actual)	—	$17, 840	—
October	$15,000	$17,500	$19,750
November	$14,000	$16,500	$18,500
December	$11,200	$13,000	$14,000
January	$9,900	$12,500	$14,900
February	$10,500	$13,800	$15,800
March	$13,500	$17,500	$19,900

Utilities expenses	$800 per month
Rent	$1,200 per month
Truck loan	$317 per month

The company's wages and salaries (including payroll taxes) estimates are the following:

October	$2,050
November	$1,825
December	$1,725
January	$1,725
February	$1,950
March	$2,425

(continued)

You Be the Consultant *(continued)*

The company pays 63 percent of the sales price for the inventory it purchases, an amount that it actually pays in the following month. (Martinez has negotiated "net 30" credit terms with his suppliers.)

Other expenses include the following:

Insurance premiums	$1,200, payable in August and February
Office supplies	$95 per month
Maintenance	$75 per month
Computer supplies	$75 per month
Advertising	$550 per month
Legal and accounting fees	$250 per month
Miscellaneous expenses	$60 per month

A tax payment of $1,400 is due in December.

Martinez has established a minimum cash balance of $2,000 and can borrow money at an interest rate of 8.75 percent.

"Well, what do you think?" Douglas asked the consultant.

1. Assume the role of the SBDC consultant and help Douglas put together a cash budget for the six months beginning in October.

2. What conclusions can you draw about Douglas's business from this cash budget?

3. What suggestions can you make to help Douglas improve his company's cash flow?

---

increasing, its cash balance is probably declining. Similarly, accounts payable and inventory balances that are increasing faster than sales are signs of mounting pressure on a company's cash flow. A good cash management "recipe" involves accelerating a company's receivables to collect cash as quickly as possible, paying out cash as slowly as possible (without damaging the company's credit rating), and maintaining an optimal level of inventory. The big three of cash management interact to create a company's **cash conversion cycle**, the length of time required to convert inventory and accounts payable into sales and accounts receivable and finally back into cash. A company's cash conversion cycle equals its days' inventory outstanding + days' sales outstanding − days' payable outstanding. Ideally, a company's cash conversion cycle is negative, meaning that it turns over its inventory quickly and collects payments from its customers before it pays its vendors and suppliers. Amazon Inc. enjoys the benefits of a cash conversion cycle *negative* 14 days (see Figure 12.7).

cash conversion cycle
a measure of the length of time required to convert inventory and accounts payable into sales and accounts receivable and finally back into cash. Equals days' inventory outstanding + days' sales outstanding − days' payable outstanding.

Accounts Receivable

Selling merchandise and services on credit is a necessary evil for most small businesses. Many customers expect to buy on credit, and business owners extend it to avoid losing customers to competitors. However, selling to customers on credit is expensive; it requires more paperwork,

FIGURE 12.7

Amazon's Cash Conversion Cycle

Source: Based on data from "The Cash Conversion Cycle," *Forbes,* March 10, 2012, http://www.forbes.com/sites/ycharts/2012/03/10/the-cash-conversion-cycle/.

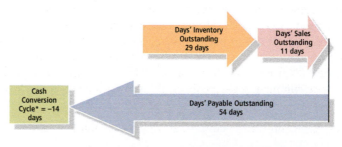

*Cash Conversion Cycle = Days' Inventory + Days' Sales Outstanding − Days' Payable
= 29 + 11 − 54 = −14 days

more staff, and more cash to service accounts receivable. In addition, because extending credit is, in essence, lending money, the risk involved is higher. Every business owner who sells on credit encounters customers who pay late or, worst of all, never pay at all. A recent survey by Visa Small Business reports that the most common cash management challenge for small business owners (36 percent) is collecting accounts receivable. Software publisher Intuit shows that the average small business encounters an average of $5,140 in past-due accounts receivable per month.[29] Caneum, a company based in Newport Beach, California, that provided IT services to businesses and government agencies, experienced a cash crisis when California's legislature failed to pass a budget, which meant that one of the company's major clients, the Los Angeles Unified School District, could not pay the invoice for $660,000 worth of work that Caneum had done. When another client, whom Caneum had billed for $750,000, was late making its payment, Caneum's cash balance could not recover, and the company filed for Chapter 7 bankruptcy (liquidation).[30]

Most small companies operate with very thin cash reserves, and many lack reliable access to credit; therefore, a late payment from a major customer can create a cash crisis. Many business owners speculate that the last recession caused a permanent shift to longer payment terms, especially among large businesses. Before the recession, large companies often paid invoices in 30 to 45 days; now, they routinely take 60 to 100 days to pay them, but small business owners, who lack sufficient bargaining power with large customers, believe they are incapable of doing anything about it. Consumer goods giant Procter and Gamble, which makes $50 billion in purchases annually from 75,000 suppliers, many of them small companies, recently told its vendors that it was extending its payment terms from 45 days to 75 days. Although the move freed up more than $2 billion in cash for P&G, the change has produced a ripple effect on its vendors, creating cash problems for many of them, especially small companies.[31]

A survey by the National Federation of Independent Businesses reports that 74 percent of small companies have accounts receivable outstanding for 60 or more days.[32] Slower payments from customers put more pressure on these small companies' cash flow.

ENTREPRENEURIAL PROFILE: David Schier: Jacobus Energy Jacobus Energy, a petroleum distribution company founded in 1919 in Milwaukee, Wisconsin, faced the problem of slowing receivables. The company had outgrown its manual system for tracking past-due accounts receivable, and nearly 9 percent of its accounts were more than 30 days past due. Credit manager David Schier switched to an online credit-checking and collection system, and the percentage of 30-plus-day past-due accounts declined to just 3.3 percent. In addition, the company's average collection period ratio decreased from 27.3 days to 20.2 days, greatly improving its cash flow.[33] ∎

Selling on credit is a common practice in business. Experts estimate that 90 percent of industrial and wholesale sales are on credit and that 40 percent of retail sales are on account.[34] Because credit sales are so prevalent, an assertive collection program is essential to managing a company's cash flow. A credit policy that is too lenient can destroy a business's cash flow, attracting too many slow-paying or "deadbeat" customers who never pay. On the other hand, a carefully designed policy can be a powerful selling tool, attracting customers and boosting cash flow. Transforming accounts receivable into cash is essential to staying in business; entrepreneurs must remember that a sale does not count until they collect the cash from it! In other words, a business owner cannot use a $10,000 account receivable to meet the company's payroll or pay its bills.

HOW TO ESTABLISH A CREDIT AND COLLECTION POLICY The first step in establishing a workable credit policy is to screen customers carefully *before* granting them credit. Unfortunately, many small businesses neglect to conduct any kind of credit investigation before selling to a new customer. The first line of defense against bad-debt losses is a detailed credit application. Before selling to any customer on credit, a business owner should have the customer fill out a customized application designed to provide the information needed to judge the potential customer's creditworthiness. At a minimum, this credit profile should include the following information about customers:

- Name, address, tax identification number, and telephone number
- Form of ownership (proprietorship, S corporation, LLC, corporation, and so on) and number of years in business

- Credit references (e.g., other suppliers), including contact names, addresses, and telephone numbers

- Bank and credit card references

After collecting this information, a business owner should use it to check the potential customer's credit references! The savings from lower bad-debt expenses can more than offset the cost of using a credit reporting service. Companies such as Dun & Bradstreet (www.dnb.com), Experian (www.experian.com), Equifax (www.equifax.com), TransUnion (www.transunion .com), and KnowX (www.knowx.com) enable entrepreneurs to gather credit information on potential customers. For entrepreneurs who sell to other business, Dun & Bradstreet offers many useful services, including a Small Business Risk New Account Score, a tool for evaluating the credit risk of new businesses. The National Association of Credit Management (www.nacm.org) is another important source of credit information because it collects information on many small businesses that other reporting services ignore. The cost to check a potential customer's credit at reporting services such as these starts at $40, a small price to pay when a small business is considering selling goods or services worth thousands of dollars to a new customer. Unfortunately, few small businesses take the time to conduct a credit check.

ENTREPRENEURIAL PROFILE: Ron Phelps: Boulevard Tire Center Ron Phelps, commercial credit manager at Boulevard Tire Center, a tire retailer with 26 locations in Florida, uses an online business credit reporting service called Cortera Pulse to screen new credit customers and to keep tabs on existing ones. Recently, when Pulse alerted Phelps that the Internal Revenue Service had imposed a large federal tax lien on one of its customers, Phelps immediately cut off the small trucking company's credit, converting it to a "cash only" customer, to avoid the risk of writing off a bad debt.[35] ∎

The next step involves establishing a firm written credit policy and letting every customer know in advance the company's credit terms. The credit agreement must be in writing and should specify a customer's credit limit (which usually varies from one customer to another, depending on their credit ratings), any required deposits (often stated as a percentage of the purchase price), the terms of any discounts (e.g., a 2 percent discount if the invoice is paid within 10 days), and the number of days before payment is due (immediately, 30 days, 60 days, and so on). A credit agreement should state clearly all the terms the business will enforce if the account goes bad, including interest, late charges, attorney's fees, and others. Failure to specify these terms up front in the contract so that the parties have a meeting of the minds means that they *cannot* be added later after problems arise. One entrepreneur compares credit customers to unruly children; unless entrepreneurs set clear boundaries and enforce them, they can expect problems.[36] To maximize a small company's cash flow, its credit policies should be as tight as possible (within federal and state credit laws). Although the goal is to incur no bad debts, achieving that goal is unrealistic. According to the American Collectors Association, if a business is writing off more than 5 percent of sales as bad debts, the owner should tighten its credit and collection policy.[37]

The third step in an effective credit policy is to send invoices promptly because customers rarely pay *before* they receive their bills. Unfortunately, 20 percent of small business owners admit that they forget to send invoices or follow up on past-due invoices.[38] One recent survey of business owners in the United Kingdom estimates that forgotten invoices cost small businesses £3.7 billion per year.[39] Remember: The sooner a company sends invoices, the sooner its customers will pay them.

ENTREPRENEURIAL PROFILE: Sam Goodner: Catapult Systems Sam Goodner, owner of Catapult Systems, an information technology (IT) consulting firm in Austin, Texas, switched from billing his clients every 30 days to every 15 days when he realized the serious cash flow problems that the longer billing cycle created for his company. He continued to extend "net 30" credit terms, and more than 90 percent of the company's clients never complained.[40] ∎

Manufacturers and wholesalers should make sure invoices are en route to customers as soon as the shipments go out the door (if not before). Service companies should keep track of billable hours daily or weekly and bill as often as the contract with the client permits. Online or computerized billing makes managing accounts receivable much easier, is less expensive, and produces faster payments than paper invoices.[41] However, only 34 percent of small businesses use these programs.[42] Some businesses use **cycle billing**, in which a company bills a portion of its credit customers each day or each week of the month, to smooth out uneven cash receipts. Technology, such as cloud computing and smart phone apps, also can speed up a company's collections. Laura Pendlebury, owner of Decorus Academy, a ballet school in Bedfordshire, England, was constantly chasing past due accounts from her students, which put pressure on her small company's cash flow. Pendlebury could not afford to hire a bookkeeper or an administrative assistant to help her, so she turned to a smart phone app called Zapper Scan-to-Pay. Pendlebury simply attaches to each invoice a QR code that contains each customer's payment information. Customers simply scan the code with their phones, confirm the amount, and pay the invoice in just seconds.[43]

cycle billing
a method in which a company bills a portion of its credit customers each day of the month to smooth out uneven cash receipts.

When an account becomes past due, a small business owner must take *immediate* action. The longer an account is past due, the lower is the probability of collecting it. One of the most effective techniques is to have someone in the company who already has a relationship with the customer, perhaps a salesperson or a customer service representative, contact him or her about the past-due account. The best approach is to start with a friendly reminder; getting "tough" too soon can damage the relationship with a good customer. When contacting a delinquent customer, the goal is to get a commitment to pay the full amount of the bill by a specific date (*not* "soon" or "next week"). Following up the personal contact with an e-mail or a letter that summarizes the verbal commitment also helps. If the customer still refuses to pay the bill, collection experts recommend the following:

- Send a letter from the company's attorney.
- Turn the account over to a collection attorney.
- As a last resort, hire a collection agency. The Commercial Law League of America (www.clla.org) can provide a list of reputable agencies.

Decorus Academy image courtesy of Cheeky Chops Photography

Although collection agencies and attorneys typically take 25 to 30 percent of any accounts they collect, they are often worth the price. Companies turn over more than $200 billion annually in past-due debt to collection agencies, which collect about $55 billion for their clients.[44] Seventy percent of the accounts turned over to collection agencies are considered "bad debts," which are 90 days or more past due. According to the American Collectors Association, only 5 percent of accounts more than 90 days delinquent will be paid voluntarily.

Business owners must be sure to abide by the provisions of the federal Fair Debt Collection Practices Act, which prohibits any kind of harassment when collecting debts (e.g., telephoning repeatedly, issuing threats of violence, telling third parties about the debt, or using abusive language). The act also prevents collectors from making false statements and from contacting debtors at inconvenient times (e.g., before 8 A.M. or after 9 P.M.) or places. The primary rule when collecting past-due accounts is "*Never* lose your cool." Establishing a friendly but firm attitude that treats customers with respect is more likely to produce payment than hostile threats. Table 12.6 outlines 10 collection blunders small business owners typically make and how to avoid them.

TECHNIQUES FOR ACCELERATING ACCOUNTS RECEIVABLE Small business owners can rely on a variety of other techniques to speed cash inflow from accounts receivable:

- Speed up orders by having customers e-mail or fax them to you.
- Send invoices when goods are shipped or when the job is completed—not a day or a week later; consider faxing or e-mailing invoices to reduce in-transit time to a minimum. Small business accounting software packages allow users to e-mail the invoices they generate. When Jim Malarney, CEO of Vanguard Services, a company based in Indianapolis, Indiana, that provides contract truck drivers to companies, noticed that the company's collections on its accounts receivable were slowing, he began e-mailing invoices to customers. Malarney also began establishing personal contacts with more people in the companies that Vanguard

TABLE 12.6 Ten Collection Blunders and How to Avoid Them

Business owners often make mistakes when trying to collect the money their customers owe. Checking potential credit customers' credit records and creating a thorough sales contract that spells out exactly what happens if the account becomes past due can help minimize collection problems. Sooner or later, however, even the best system will encounter late payers. What happens then? Business owners should avoid these collection blunders.

Blunder 1: Delaying collection phone calls. Many entrepreneurs waste valuable time and resources sending four or five "past-due" letters to delinquent customers, usually with limited effectiveness.

Instead: Once a bill becomes past due, call the customer within a week to verify that he or she received the bill and that it is accurate. Ask for payment.

Blunder 2: Failing to ask for payment in clear terms. To avoid angering a customer, some entrepreneurs ask meekly, "Do you think you could take care of this bill soon?"

Instead: Firmly but professionally ask for payment (the full amount) by a specific date.

Blunder 3: Sounding desperate. Some entrepreneurs show weakness by saying that they must have payment or they "can't meet payroll" or "can't pay bills." That gives the customer more leverage to negotiate additional discounts or time.

Instead: Ask for payment simply because the invoice is past due—without any other explanation. Don't apologize for your request; it's *your* money.

Blunder 4: Talking tough. Getting nasty with delinquent customers does not make them pay any faster and may be a violation of the Fair Debt Collections Practices Act.

Instead: Remain polite and professional when dealing with past-due customers, even if you think they don't deserve it. *Never* lose your temper. Don't ruin your reputation by being rude.

Blunder 5: Trying to find out the customer's problem. Some entrepreneurs think it is necessary to find out why a delinquent customer has not paid a bill.

Instead: Don't waste time playing private investigator. Focus on the "business at hand," collecting your money.

Blunder 6: Asking customers how much they can pay. When customers claim that they cannot pay the bill in full, inexperienced entrepreneurs ask, "Well, how much can you pay?" They don't realize that they have just turned control of the situation over to the delinquent customer.

Instead: Take charge of negotiations from the outset. Let the customer know that you expect full payment. If you cannot get full payment immediately, suggest a new deadline. Only as a last resort should you offer an extended payment plan.

Blunder 7: Continuing to talk after you get a promise to pay. Some entrepreneurs "blow the deal" by not knowing when to stop talking. They keep interrogating a customer after they have a promise to pay.

Instead: Wrap up the conversation as soon as you have a commitment. Summarize the agreement, thank the customer, and end the conversation on a positive note.

Blunder 8: Calling without being prepared. Some entrepreneurs call customers without knowing exactly which invoices are past due and what amounts are involved. The effort is usually fruitless.

Instead: Have all account details in front of you when you call and be specific in your requests.

Blunder 9: Trusting your memory. Some entrepreneurs think they can remember previous collection calls, conversations, and agreements.

Instead: Keep accurate records of all calls and conversations. Take notes about each customer contact and resulting agreements.

Blunder 10: Letting your computer control your collection efforts. Inexperienced entrepreneurs tend to think that their computers can manage debt collection for them.

Instead: Recognize that a computer is a valuable tool in collecting accounts but that you are in control. "Past-due" notices from a computer may collect some accounts, but your efforts will produce more results. Getting to know the people who handle the invoices at your customers' businesses can be a major advantage when collecting accounts.

Source: Based on "Tips for Collecting Cash," *FSB*, May 2002, p. 72; Janine Latus Musick, "Collecting Payments Due," *Nation's Business*, January 1999, pp. 44–46; Bob Weinstein, "Collect Calls," *Entrepreneur*, August 1995, pp. 66–69; and Elaine Pofeldt, "Collect Calls," *Success*, March 1998, pp. 22–24.

serves. Vanguard's collection strategy has resulted in the percentage of past-due accounts decreasing from 25 percent to just 8 percent.[45]

- Owners of service firms should offer clients retainer packages that provide their clients with a fixed number of hours of work each month that the client pays for in advance. To reduce the variability in her company's cash flow, Yva Yorston, owner of Boost Business Support, a company offering virtual assistance with administration, marketing, and research to small business owners, began offering clients retainer packages. On those accounts, Yorston is paid in advance, and her company's cash flow is much more predictable, giving her peace of mind.[46]

- Ensure that all invoices are clear, accurate, and timely. State clearly a description of the goods or services purchased and an account number and make sure that the prices and the language on invoices agree with the price quotations on purchase orders or contracts.

Newsline Media

- Include a telephone number and a contact person in your organization in case the customer has a question or a dispute.

- Call the customer a week after sending the invoice to make sure it arrived and to ensure that the customer has no problems with the quality of the product or service.

- Highlight the balance due and the terms of sale (e.g., "net 30") on all invoices. A study by Xerox Corporation found that highlighting with color the "balance due" and "due date" sections of invoices increased the speed of collection by 30 percent.[47]

- Allow customers to use multiple payment methods such as checks, credit cards, PayPal, money, orders, and cash.

- Offer incentives to encourage customers to pay invoices early and impose penalties on customers who pay late. Erika Napoletano, owner of RHW Media, a brand strategy firm in Denver, Colorado, recently instituted a payment policy that offers cash discounts to clients who pay early and establishes penalties for those who pay later than the agreed-upon terms. The incentives work; Napoletano says clients now pay early more often than not.[48]

- Restrict a customer's credit until past-due bills are paid. Make sure salespeople know which of their customers are behind in their payments.

- Deposit cash, checks, and credit card receipts *daily*.

- Identify the top 20 percent of your customers (by sales volume), create a separate file system for them, and monitor them closely. Twenty percent of the typical company's customers generate 80 percent of all accounts receivable.

- Ask customers to pay at least a portion of the purchase price up front. To protect her company's cash flow, Erika Napoletano, owner of RHW Media, also requires a deposit of 50 percent (sometimes more) on certain jobs before she starts them. "I'm ready to start for those customers who are ready to pay," she says.[49]

- Watch for signs that a customer may be about to declare bankruptcy. If that happens, creditors typically collect only a small fraction, if any, of the debt owed. If a customer does file for bankruptcy, the bankruptcy court notifies all creditors with a "Notice of Filing" document. If an entrepreneur receives one of these notices, he or she should create a file to track the events surrounding the bankruptcy and take action immediately. To have a valid claim against the debtor's assets, a creditor must file a proof-of-claim form with the bankruptcy court within a specified time, often 90 days. If, after paying the debtor's secured creditors, any assets remain, the court will distribute the proceeds to unsecured creditors who have legitimate proof of claim.

- Use technology to manage cash flow. Cloud-based accounting packages also include modules that allow business owners to monitor their cash flow from anywhere on tablets, smart phones, or laptops.

- Track the results of the company's collection efforts. Managers and key employees should receive a weekly report on the status of the company's outstanding accounts receivable.

Another strategy that small companies, particularly those selling high-priced items, can use to protect the cash they have tied up in receivables is to couple a security agreement with a financing statement. This strategy falls under Article 9 of the Uniform Commercial Code (UCC), which governs a wide variety of business transactions, including the sale of goods and security interests. A **security agreement** is a contract in which a business selling an asset on credit gets a security interest in that asset (the collateral), protecting its legal rights in case the buyer fails to pay. To get the protection it seeks in the security agreement, the seller must file a financing statement called a UCC-1 form with the proper state or county office (a process the UCC calls "perfection"). The UCC-1 form gives notice to other creditors and to the general public that the seller holds a secured interest in the collateral named in the security agreement. The UCC-1 form must include the name, address, and signature of the buyer; a description of the collateral; and the name and address of the seller. If the buyer declares bankruptcy, the small business that sells the asset is not guaranteed payment, but the filing puts its claim to the asset ahead of those of unsecured creditors. A small company's degree of safety on a large credit sale is much higher with a security agreement and a properly filed financing statement than if it did not file the security agreement.

security agreement
a contract in which a business selling an asset on credit gets a security interest in that asset (the collateral), protecting its legal rights in case the buyer fails to pay.

Accounts Payable

The second element of the big three of cash management is accounts payable. The timing of payables is just as crucial to proper cash management as the timing of receivables, but the objective is exactly the opposite. Entrepreneurs should strive to stretch out payables as long as possible *without damaging their companies' credit rating*. Otherwise, suppliers may begin demanding prepayment or cash-on-delivery (C.O.D.) terms, which severely impair a company's cash flow, or they may stop doing business with it altogether. When Borders, once the second-largest bookstore chain in the United States, ran into cash flow problems, the company stopped making payments to book publishers, many of whom halted shipments to the book retailer. In an attempt to survive, Borders downsized to just 400 stores but ultimately succumbed to its cash flow woes, declared bankruptcy, and closed its doors for good.[50] It is perfectly acceptable for small business owners to regulate payments to their companies' advantage. Efficient cash managers set up a payment calendar each month that allows them to pay their bills on time and to take advantage of cash discounts for early payment.

ENTREPRENEURIAL PROFILE: Nancy Dunis: Dunis & Associates Nancy Dunis, CEO of Dunis & Associates, a Portland, Oregon, marketing firm, recognizes the importance of controlling accounts payable. Dunis says that accounts payable are the key to keeping her company's cash flow running smoothly. She has set up a simple five-point accounts-payable system:

1. Set scheduling goals. Dunis strives to pay her company's bills 45 days after receiving them and to collect all her receivables within 30 days. Even though customers do not always pay within 45 days, her goal is to collect her cash as close to 45 days as possible.
2. Keep paperwork organized. Dunis dates every invoice she receives and carefully files it according to her payment plan. The system helps remind her when to write checks to pay her company's invoices, which she attempts to stretch out over a period of days or weeks to avoid having to make large cash disbursements at the same time. Proper scheduling of cash disbursement significantly improves the company's cash flow.
3. Prioritize. Dunis cannot stretch out all of her company's creditors for 45 days; some demand payment sooner. Those suppliers are at the top of the accounts-payable list.
4. Be consistent. Dunis says that companies value customers who pay their bills regularly and consistently. Most companies are willing to extend trade credit for 20 to 30 days as long as they know that the customer will pay the bill in full on time.[51] ■

Other signs that a business is heading for cash flow problems include difficulty making payments on loans and incurring penalties for late payment of routine bills.

Hands On . . . How To

Avoid Losses from Accounts Receivable

Serial entrepreneur Alan Knitowski, founder of Phunware, a mobile apps company that develops and hosts apps for clients such as the National Football League and NASCAR, learned the importance of cash flow when he launched his first company, VoViDa, a communications software provider, in the 1990s. Knitowski cofounded VoViDa with enough cash to fund six months' worth of expenses, but the company began burning cash faster than expected. Fortunately, the cofounders were able to attract equity financing quickly enough to keep the company afloat until Cisco Systems purchased it nearly two years later.

When Knitowski started Phunware, he treated cash as if it were the company's lifeline because his experience taught him that it was. Every Friday afternoon, the Phunware's controller sends a color-coded dashboard that illustrates the company's key financial metrics, including the amount of cash on hand, its current ratio, upcoming receivables, and others. Managers dedicate time regularly to tracking the data, analyzing it, comparing it to past data, and looking for trends. The color-coded dashboard is easy to understand. If Phunware has more than 18 months' worth of cash on hand, the dashboard shows a green light; if its cash balance is between 12 and 18 months' of expenses, the light is yellow; a cash balance less than 12 months of expenses results in a flashing red light. If the red light shows up (so far, it has not), plans call for Phunware to tap its line of credit, an asset-based loan, or some other type of bridge financing.

Phunware has grown to 160 employees and annual sales of $22 million with an average accounts receivable balance of about $5.5 million at any given time. Knitowski and his management team monitor the company's accounts receivable closely, trying to avoid uncollectible accounts. They constantly watch for customers whose accounts have become past-due, taking action to collect them immediately. Although Knitowski admits that his hard-nosed approach to collecting past due accounts has cost Phunware a few customers, he stands by the policy because he understands that the money those customers owe is Phunware's, and it is his job to collect it. The company's accounts receivable policy is firm, insisting on payment within 30 days of delivering an app to a customer. In addition, most clients pay 50 percent of the cost of a job up front when the parties sign the contract. Phunware also has several clients that purchase semi-annual subscriptions, which smoothes out its cash flow and makes it more predictable.

Small businesses report that their customers, particularly large companies, are stretching their accounts payable longer, paying invoices more slowly now than they were just a few years ago. When faced with 30-day credit terms, it is not uncommon for large companies to delay their payments to 45 to 60 days, sometimes longer. The Small Business Network Monitor, a study of small businesses by American Express, confirms the challenge this presents for entrepreneurs. More than half of the small business owners surveyed say their companies experience cash flow problems, and one of their primary concerns is collecting accounts

receivable. The average small business incurs $5,140 in past-due accounts receivables from its customers each month.

"If the money is coming in the front door at 100 miles per hour," explains Brian Hamilton, CEO of Sageworks, a financial consulting firm, "and going out the back door at 110 miles per hour, that's not a good thing. Businesses don't fail because they are unprofitable; they fail because they get crushed on the accounts receivable side." What steps can entrepreneurs take to avoid a cash crisis caused by accounts receivable that turn slowly? The following steps can help:

- **Evaluate your company's collection process.** How many people are involved in generating an invoice? (Fewer is better.) Where do bottlenecks in the billing process occur? (Setting a time limit on processing paperwork helps.) What percentage of your company's invoices are erroneous? (The higher the percentage of errors, the slower the company's collections will be.)

- **Increase your company's cash reserves.** Smart business owners keep at least three months' worth of expenses on hand so that they aren't caught cash short if receivables slow down more than expected or if sales suddenly decline.

- **Boost your company's line of credit.** Business owners can increase their lines of credit with their banks, but the key is to do so *before* you need the money. Be prepared to use your company's financial statements to prove to your banker why you need—and deserve—an increased line of credit.

- **Monitor accounts receivable closely.** Like Knitowski, some entrepreneurs generate weekly (or even daily) summaries of their company's accounts receivable, always on the lookout for disturbing trends. Doing so enables them to spot slow payers who might become nonpayers unless the company takes immediate action.

- **Get to know the people responsible for paying invoices at your biggest customers' or clients' companies.** Collections are easier if you know the right person to call.

- **Take immediate action when an account becomes past due.** Resist the tendency to simply sit back and wait for the customer to pay. If a customer has not paid by the invoice due date, contact him or her immediately and ask for payment.

- **Watch for signs that customers may be about to declare bankruptcy.** When a customer declares bankruptcy, the probability that a company can collect the cash it is owed is miniscule. Terri Oyarzun, founder of Goats R Us, a company that owns a herd of goats that provide fire mitigation services

(continued)

Hands On . . . How To *(continued)*

by eating shrubs and brush that could fuel blazes, realized that when one customer declared bankruptcy, she would never be able to collect the $53,000 the company owed her business. Oyarzun says she had to postpone purchasing a new truck for the farm and hiring new goat herders.

- ***Stick to your credit terms.*** Define the credit terms with every client up front. If clients balk when it comes time for payment, remind them that they have a commitment to live up to the terms of the sales contract.

- ***Raise prices to cover the extra cost of late payments.*** If clients refuse to pay on time, determine how much their slower payments cost your company and raise your rates or your prices enough to cover the cost.

- ***Require customers to pay at least part of total price of a contract up front.*** Because the jobs that one small film production company performs require the owner to incur some rather sizable expenses before they are completed, he

implemented a policy that requires customers to pay one-third of the cost up front, another one-third at mid-project, and the balance on completion.

- ***Offer discounts to encourage early payment.*** Cash discounts (such as "2/10, net 30," which means that you offer the client a 2 percent discount if he or she pays within 10 days; otherwise, the full invoice amount is due in 30 days) can reduce a small company's profit margin, but they also provide an incentive for clients to pay early. Remember: More companies fail for lack of cash than for lack of profit.

Sources: Based on Jill Hamburg-Coplan, "Nice Growth Company You Got There. So How Come You're Running Out of Cash?" *Inc.,* February 2014, pp. 74–78, 106; Christopher Null, "Growth Spurt Secret," May 17, 2012, *Intuit GoPayment Blog,* http://blog.gopayment.com/money-trends/get-growing-small-businesses-miss-an-estimated-100-billion-in-annual-sales-by-denying-credit-cards-infographic/attachment/intuitpayments-getbusinessgrowing-final/; Shivani Vora, "Need Cash? Try Looking Inward," *Inc.,* May 2008, pp. 43–44; Amy Feldman, "The Cash-Flow Crunch," *Inc.,* December 2005, pp. 50–52; and Michael Corkery and Alex Frangos, "Far Away from Wall Street, a Herd Gets Gored," *Wall Street Journal,* January 24–25, 2009, pp. A1, A12.

Business owners should verify all invoices before paying them. Some unscrupulous vendors send out invoices for goods they never shipped or services they never provided, knowing that many business owners will simply pay the bill without checking its authenticity. Two common scams aimed at small business owners involve bogus operators sending invoices for office supplies or ads in nonexistent printed or online "yellow pages" directories. In some cases, the directories actually do exist, but their distribution is so limited that ads in them are useless. To avoid falling victim to such scams, someone in the company—for instance, the accounts-payable clerk—should have the responsibility of verifying *every* invoice received.

A clever cash manager also negotiates the best possible credit terms with his or her suppliers. Almost all vendors grant their customers trade credit, and small business owners should take advantage of it. Favorable credit terms can make a tremendous difference in a company's cash flow. Table 12.7 shows the same most likely cash budget from Table 12.2 with one exception: instead of purchasing on C.O.D. terms as shown in Table 12.2, the owner has negotiated "net 30" payment terms. Notice the drastic improvement in the company's cash flow that results from improved credit terms.

If owners do find themselves financially strapped when payment to a vendor is due, they should avoid making empty promises that "the check is in the mail" or sending unsigned checks. Instead, they should discuss the situation honestly with the vendor. Most vendors will work out payment terms for extended credit. One small business owner who was experiencing a cash crisis claims,

> One day things got so bad I just called up a supplier and said, "I need your stuff, but I'm going through a tough period and simply can't pay you right now." They said they wanted to keep me as a customer, and they asked if it was okay to bill me in three months. I was dumbfounded: *They didn't even charge me interest.*[52]

Entrepreneurs also can improve their firms' cash flow by scheduling controllable cash disbursements so that they do not come due at the same time. For example, paying employees every two weeks (or every month) rather than every week reduces administrative costs and gives the business more time to use its cash. Owners of fledgling businesses may be able to conserve cash by hiring part-time employees or by using freelance workers rather than full-time, permanent workers. Scheduling insurance premiums monthly or quarterly rather than annually also can improve cash flows.

Inventory

Offering customers a wider variety of products is one way a business can outshine its competitors, but product proliferation increases the need for tight inventory control to avoid a cash

TABLE 12.7 Cash Budget—Most Likely Sales Forecast after Negotiating "Net 30" Trade Credit Terms

Cash Receipts	Oct	Nov	Dec	Jan	Feb	Mar	Apr	May	Jun
Sales	$300,000	$350,000	$400,000	$150,000	$200,000	$200,000	$300,000	$315,000	$320,000
Credit sales	225,000	262,500	300,000	112,500	150,000	150,000	225,000	236,250	240,000
Collections	—	—	—	—	—	—	—	—	—
60%—first month after sale				180,000	67,500	90,000	90,000	135,000	141,750
30%—second month after sale				78,750	90,000	33,750	45,000	45,000	67,500
5%—third month after sale				11,250	13,125	15,000	5,625	7,500	7,500
Cash sales				37,500	50,000	50,000	75,000	78,750	80,000
Other cash receipts	—	—	—	25	35	50	60	60	65
Total Cash Receipts				307,525	220,660	188,800	215,685	266,310	296,815
Cash Disbursements									
Purchases*				105,000	140,000	140,000	210,000	185,000	190,000
Rent				3,000	3,000	3,000	3,000	3,000	3,000
Utilities				1,450	1,400	1,250	1,250	1,250	1,400
Banknote				—	—	7,500	—	—	—
Tax prepayment				—	—	18,000	—	—	—
Capital additions				—	130,000	—	—	—	—
Wages and salaries				30,000	38,000	40,000	42,000	44,000	44,000
Insurance				475	475	475	475	475	475
Advertising				1,600	1,600	1,500	2,000	2,000	2,200
Interest				—	—	—	249	—	—
Miscellaneous				500	500	500	550	550	550
Total Cash Disbursements				142,025	314,975	212,225	259,524	236,275	241,625
End-of-Month Balance									
Beginning cash balance				12,000	177,500	83,185	59,760	15,921	45,956
+ Cash receipts				307,525	220,660	188,800	215,685	266,310	296,815
− Cash disbursements	—	—	—	142,025	314,975	212,225	259,524	236,275	241,625
Cash (end of month)				177,500	83,185	59,760	15,921	45,956	101,146
Borrowing				—	—	—	—	—	—
Repayment	—	—	—	—	—	—	—	—	—
Final Cash Balance				$177,500	$83,185	$59,760	$15,921	$45,956	$101,146
Monthly Surplus/(Deficit)				165,500	(94,315)	(23,425)	(43,839)	30,035	55,190

*After negotiating "net 30" trade credit terms.

crisis. The typical grocery store now stocks about 42,700 items, three times as many as it did 20 years ago, and many other types of businesses are following this pattern.[53] Although inventory is the largest investment for many businesses, entrepreneurs often manage it haphazardly, creating a severe strain on their companies' cash flow. As a result, the typical small business has not only too much inventory but also too much of the *wrong* kind of inventory! Because inventory is illiquid, it can quickly siphon off a company's pool of available cash. "Small companies need cash to grow," says one consultant. "They've got to be able to turn [cash] over quickly. That's difficult to do if a lot of money is tied up in excess inventory."[54] After being caught in a cash crisis due to excess inventory early in her entrepreneurial career, Laura Zander, founder of the yarn shop Jimmy Beans Wool, learned from her mistake. Now she ensures that her inventory grows no faster than her business. "We would rather have extra cash than extra inventory," she says.[55]

Courtesy of Jimmy Beans Wool

Surplus inventory yields a zero rate of return and unnecessarily ties up a company's cash. "Carrying inventory is expensive," says one small business consultant. "A typical manufacturing company pays 25 percent to 30 percent of the value of the inventory for the cost of borrowed money, warehouse space, materials handling, staff, lift-truck expenses, and fixed costs. This shocks a lot of people. Once they realize it, they look at inventory differently."[56] Marking down items that don't sell keeps inventory lean and allows it to turn over frequently. Even though volume discounts lower inventory costs, large purchases may tie up the company's valuable cash. Wise business owners avoid overbuying inventory, recognizing that excess inventory ties up valuable cash unproductively. In fact, only 20 percent of a typical business's inventory turns over quickly; therefore, owners must watch constantly for stale items.[57] If a small business must pay its suppliers within 30 days of receiving an inventory shipment and the merchandise sits on the shelf for another 30 to 60 days (or more), the pressure on its cash flow intensifies. Increasing a company's inventory turnover ratio frees surprising amounts of cash. For instance, if a company with $2 million in annual sales that turns its inventory twice each year improves its inventory turnover ratio by just two weeks, it will improve its cash flow by nearly $18,900.

Carrying too little inventory is not the ideal solution to cash flow challenges because companies with excessive "stock-outs" lose sales (and eventually customers if the problem persists). However, carrying too much inventory usually results in slow-moving inventory and a low inventory turnover ratio. Experienced business owners understand the importance of shedding slow-moving inventory during end-of-season sales, even if they must resort to markdowns.

Carrying too much inventory increases the chances that a business will run out of cash. An entrepreneur's goal is to minimize the company's investment in inventory without sacrificing sales, selection, and customer satisfaction. Inventory should grow no faster than a company's sales. "The cash that pays for goods is channeled into inventory," says one business writer, "where its flow is dead-ended until the inventory is sold and the cash is set free again. The cash flow trick is to commit just enough cash to inventory to meet demand."[58] Scheduling inventory deliveries at the latest possible date prevents premature payment of invoices. In addition, given goods of comparable quality and price, an entrepreneur should purchase goods from the fastest supplier to keep inventory levels as low as possible. All of these tactics require entrepreneurs to manage their supply chains carefully and to treat their suppliers as partners in their businesses. Keeping inventory churning rapidly through a small business requires creating a nimble, adaptive supply chain that responds to a company's changing needs.

ENTREPRENEURIAL PROFILE: Zara Zara, a chain of retail stores that sells inexpensive, stylish clothing to young, fashion-conscious people, manages its supply chain so efficiently that its inventory turnover ratio is much higher than the industry average. As a result, the company ties up less cash in inventory than its competition. Zara's fast-fashion approach also keeps customers coming back by keeping stores' inventory fresh, adding new items constantly at a rate that leaves most of its competitors in awe. In fact, Zara can take a garment from design to store shelf in just two to three weeks instead of the five to twelve months that most clothing retailers require. The company tracks the latest fashion trends and manufactures small runs of items, which allows it to avoid being stuck with large quantities of unpopular garments it must mark down. Zara manufactures larger quantities of only those items that sell quickly. The result is that Zara's nearly 1,900 stores, which are located in 86 countries, sell 85 percent of their inventory at full price, compared to the industry average of 60 to 70 percent. Zara has created an irresistible image of scarcity that appeals to its faithful customers who shop at Zara an average of 17 times per year (compared to 4 to 6 times a year for other clothing retailers) and who know that when they find something they like, they had better buy it, or it may be gone—for good. The result is a minimal investment in inventory that ties up little cash but yields above-average sales and profits.[59] ■

Business owners also should take advantage of quantity discounts and cash discounts their suppliers offer. **Quantity discounts** give businesses a price break when they order large quantities of merchandise and supplies and exist in two forms: noncumulative and cumulative. A company earns a noncumulative quantity discount only if it purchases a certain volume of merchandise in a single order. For example, a wholesaler may offer small retailers a 3 percent discount only if they purchase 10 gross of Halloween masks in a single order. Cumulative quantity discounts apply if a company's purchases from a particular vendor exceed a specified quantity or dollar value over a predetermined time period. The time frame varies, but a year is most common. For example, a manufacturer of appliances may offer a small business a 3 percent discount on subsequent orders if its purchases exceed $10,000 per year.

Cash discounts are offered to customers as an incentive to pay for merchandise promptly. Many vendors grant cash discounts to avoid being used as an interest-free bank by customers who purchase merchandise and then fail to pay by the invoice due date. To encourage prompt payment of invoices, many vendors allow customers to deduct a percentage of the purchase amount if they pay within a specified time. Cash discount terms "2/10, net 30" are common in many industries. These terms mean that the total amount of the invoice is due 30 days, but if the bill is paid within 10 days, the buyer may deduct 2 percent from the total. A discount offering "2/10, EOM" (EOM means "end of month") indicates that the buyer may deduct 2 percent if the bill is paid by the tenth of the month after purchase.

In general, it is sound business practice to take advantage of cash discounts because a company incurs an implicit (opportunity) cost by forgoing a cash discount. By failing to take advantage of the cash discount, an entrepreneur is, in effect, paying an annual interest rate to retain the use of the discounted amount for the remainder of the credit period. For example, suppose the Print Shop receives an invoice for $1,000 from a vendor offering a cash discount of 2/10, net 30. Figure 12.8 illustrates this situation and shows how to compute the cost of forgoing the cash discount. Notice that the cost of forgoing this cash discount is 37.25 percent. Table 12.8 summarizes the cost of forgoing cash discounts with different terms.

Monitoring the big three of cash management helps every business owner to avoid a cash crisis while making the best use of available cash. According to one expert, maximizing cash flow involves "getting money from customers sooner; paying bills at the last moment possible; consolidating money in a single bank account; managing accounts payable, accounts receivable, and inventory more effectively; and squeezing every penny out of your daily business."[60]

Avoiding the Cash Crunch

Nearly every small business has the potential to improve its cash position with little or no investment. The key is to make an objective evaluation of the company's financial policies, searching for inefficiency in its cash flow. Young firms cannot afford to waste resources, especially one as

quantity discounts discounts that give businesses a price break when they order large quantities of merchandise and supplies. They exist in two forms: cumulative and noncumulative.

cash discounts discounts offered to customers as an incentive to pay for merchandise promptly.

LO5
Explain the techniques for avoiding a cash crunch in a small company.

FIGURE 12.8
A Cash Discount

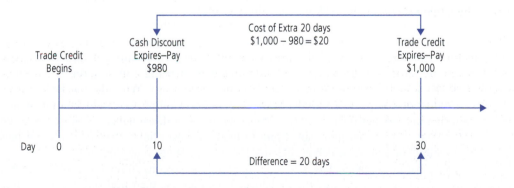

TABLE 12.8 **Cost of Forgoing Cash Discounts**

Cash Discount Terms	Cost of Forgoing the Cash Discount (Annually)
2/10, net 30	37.25%
2/10, net 40	24.83%
3/10, net 30	56.44%
3/10, net 40	37.63%

vital as cash. By using the following techniques, entrepreneurs can get maximum benefit from their companies' pool of available cash.

Barter

bartering
the exchange of goods and services for other goods and services rather than for cash.

Bartering, the exchange of goods and services for other goods and services rather than for cash, is an effective way to conserve cash. An ancient concept, bartering has regained popularity in recent years. Bootstrapping entrepreneurs often use bartering to finance the start-up costs of their businesses, and many exchange equity in their companies for essential services such as legal, accounting, and Web design. To launch BucketFeet, their online retail store selling limited edition sneakers, Raaj Nemani and Aaron Firestein gave up a small percentage of the ownership of their business in exchange for $100,000 worth of high-end Web site design to Dashfire LLC. Nemani points out that by bartering, they were able to conserve precious cash in one of the most critical periods of a company's life.[61] Entrepreneurs also turn to Web sites such as Craigslist to find businesses with which they can barter.

Today, more than 500 barter exchanges operate across the United States (visit the National Association of Trade Exchanges at www.natebarter.com to locate them), and they cater primarily to small- and medium-size businesses looking to conserve cash. Some 400,000 companies—most of them small—engage in more than $12 billion worth of barter each year.[62] Every day, entrepreneurs across the nation use bartering to buy much-needed materials, services, equipment, and supplies—*without* using precious cash.

ENTREPRENEURIAL PROFILE: Judah Schiff: Jmac Supply Jmac Supply, a security equipment supplier founded by Judah Schiff in 2009 in Valley Stream, New York, routinely barters for many professional services, a habit the company developed during the start-up phase. Miki Segal, the company's chief marketing officer, says bartering kept the company alive in its early days. Bartering continues to help the company conserve cash.[63] ∎

In addition to conserving cash, companies that use barter also have the opportunity to transform slow-moving inventory into much-needed products and services. Buying goods and services with barter also offers the benefit of a built-in discount. Although a company gets credit for the retail value of the goods or services it offers, the real cost to the company is less and depends on its gross profit margin. For instance, the owner of an Italian restaurant bartered $1,000 worth of meals for some new furniture, but his actual cost of the meals was only $680, given his gross profit margin of 32 percent. Entrepreneurs who join barter exchanges often find new customers for their products and services, an important benefit for start-ups. When Logan Hale opened his video production company, V3 Media Marketing, in Fort Collins, Colorado, he immediately began bartering his services for legal, accounting, and other professional services—even a gym membership. Hale says bartering enabled him to land business clients that he would not have been able to attract otherwise, which accelerated the growth of his young business.[64]

In a typical barter exchange, businesses accumulate trade credits (think barter dollars) when they offer goods or services through the exchange. Then they use their trade credits to purchase other goods and services from other members of the exchange. The typical exchange charges a $400 to $800 membership fee, a $10 to $15 monthly maintenance fee, and an 8 to 10 percent transaction fee (half from the buyer and half from the seller) on every deal. The exchange acts as a barter "bank," tracking the balance in each member's account and typically sending monthly statements summarizing account activity. Before joining a barter exchange, entrepreneurs should investigate its fee structure, the selection and the prices of its goods and services, and its geographic coverage to make sure the fit is a good one. In addition, barter exchanges report their members' barter transactions because they are subject to taxes.

Trim Overhead Costs

High overhead expenses can strain a small company's cash supply to the breaking point, and simple cost-cutting measures can save big money. Operating a business efficiently improves its cash flow. Larry Parsons, owner of Sackville Cab, a cab company in Sackville, New Brunswick, realized that fuel and maintenance expenses for his fleet of large vehicles were eating into his company's profits. Over time, he replaced his fleet with more fuel-efficient and reliable models that provided room for up to six people and their luggage. Parsons also reduced the number of full-time drivers he employed and replaced them with part-time drivers, which allows him to cover peak demand periods more easily. With the changes, Sackville Cab's costs of operation declined significantly, and the company is thriving once again.[65]

Frugal small business owners can trim their overhead in a number of ways.

ASK FOR DISCOUNTS AND "FREEBIES" Entrepreneurs can conserve cash by negotiating discounts on the purchases they make and using free services whenever possible. For instance, rather than pay a high-priced consultant to assist him with his business plan, one entrepreneur opted instead to use the free services of his local SBDC. The move not only improved the quality of his business plan, enabling him to get the financing he needed to launch his business, but also conserved valuable cash for the start-up.

ENTREPRENEURIAL PROFILE: Sid Jaridly: Original Mr. Cabinet Care Sid Jaridly, CEO of the Original Mr. Cabinet Care, a kitchen remodeling business in Anaheim, California, saw his company's profit margins being squeezed from an industry downturn and approached his top 50 vendors and asked for price reductions of 10 to 15 percent. Nearly 30 of his suppliers agreed to his request for price concessions, a move that saved his company nearly $500,000 in just one year![66] ■

CONDUCT PERIODIC EXPENSE AUDITS Business owners should evaluate their operating costs periodically to make sure they have not gotten out of line. Comparing current expenses with past levels is helpful, and so is comparing a company's expenses against industry standards. Useful resources for determining typical expenses in an industry include the RMA's *Annual Statement Studies*, Dun & Bradstreet's *Industry Norms and Key Business Ratios*, *Bizminer*, and Prentice Hall's *Almanac of Business and Industrial Financial Ratios*.

ENTREPRENEURIAL PROFILE: Sam Goodner: Catapult Systems At least twice a year, Sam Goodner, founder of Catapult Systems, an IT consulting firm in Austin, Texas, reviews every invoice his company pays with a member of his accounting staff, looking for ways to reduce the company's expenses. Recently, Goodner replaced a monthly $600 bottled water service with a water filtration system that cost just $600 annually. He also saved $40,000 a year by switching his public relations firm from a retainer to project-based assignments. "There are tens of thousands of dollars a year I can cut, and the company doesn't feel the difference," says Goodner.[67] ■

WHEN PRACTICAL, LEASE INSTEAD OF BUY Businesses spend about $800 billion on equipment annually, and companies acquire about one-third of that equipment through leases.[68] By leasing automobiles, computers, office equipment, machinery, and many other types of assets rather than buying them, entrepreneurs can conserve valuable cash. The value of these assets is not in *owning* them but in *using* them. Leasing is a popular cash management strategy; about 85 percent of companies lease some or all of their equipment.[69] "These companies are long on ideas, short on capital, and in need of flexibility as they grow and change," says Suzanne Jackson of the Equipment Leasing Association of America. "They lease for efficiency and convenience."[70]

ENTREPRENEURIAL PROFILE: Mark Kolodziej: Hudson Bread In 1994, Mark Kolodziej opened a bakery, Hudson Bread, in New York City and soon was supplying baguettes, focaccias, and other artisanal breads to some of the city's finest restaurants. Hudson Bread grew, and in 2003, Kolodziej opened a 50,000-square-foot baking facility in North Bergen, New Jersey. Bakery equipment is quite expensive, and to conserve capital, Kolodziej decided to lease rather than buy the equipment his company needed. He used the same strategy in 2008 when Hudson Bread turned to GE Capital to lease the $1.5 million equipment to open a second baking facility outside of Philadelphia.[71] ■

Although total lease payments typically are greater than those for a conventional loan, most leases offer 100 percent financing, meaning that the owner avoids the large capital outlays required as down payments on most loans. (Sometimes a lease requires the first and last months' payments to be made up front.) Leasing also protects a business against obsolescence, especially when it comes to equipment such as computer hardware and software, whose technological life is limited to perhaps just two or three years. Furthermore, leasing is an "off-the-balance-sheet" method of financing and requires no collateral. The equipment a company leases does not have to be depreciated because the small business does not actually own it. A lease is considered an operating expense on the income statement, not a liability on the balance sheet. Thus, leasing conserves a company's borrowing capacity. Because lease payments are fixed amounts paid over a particular time period, leasing allows business owners to forecast more accurately their cash flows. Lease agreements also are flexible; entrepreneurs can customize their lease payments to coincide with the seasonal fluctuations in their companies' cash balances. Leasing companies typically allow businesses to stretch payments over a longer time period than do conventional loans.

Entrepreneurs can choose from two basic types of leases: operating leases and capital leases. At the end of an **operating lease**, a business turns the equipment back over to the leasing company with no further obligation. Businesses often lease computer and telecommunications equipment through operating leases because it becomes obsolete so quickly. At the end of a **capital lease**, a business may exercise an option to purchase the equipment, usually for a nominal sum.

operating lease
a lease at the end of which a company turns the equipment back to the leasing company and has no further obligation.

capital lease
a lease at the end of which a company may exercise an option to purchase the equipment, usually for a nominal sum.

AVOID NONESSENTIAL OUTLAYS By forgoing costly ego indulgences like ostentatious office equipment, first-class travel, and flashy company cars, entrepreneurs can make the most efficient use of a company's cash and put their money where it really counts. Before putting scarce cash into an asset, every business owner should put the decision to the acid test: "Will this purchase improve my company's profits and cash flow or enhance its ability to compete?" The secret to successful cost saving is cutting *nonessential* expenditures. Making across-the-board spending cuts to conserve cash is dangerous because the owner runs the risk of cutting expenditures that drive the business. One common mistake during business slowdowns is cutting marketing and advertising expenditures. Economic slowdowns present a prime opportunity for smart business owners to bring increased attention to their products and services and to gain market share if they hold the line on their marketing and advertising budgets as their competitors cut back. "If the lifeblood of your company is marketing, cut it less," advises one advertising executive. "If it is customer service, that is the last thing you want to cut back on. Cut from areas that are not essential to business growth."[72]

BUY USED OR RECONDITIONED EQUIPMENT, ESPECIALLY IF IT IS "BEHIND-THE-SCENES" MACHINERY One restaurateur saved thousands of dollars in the start-up phase of his business by buying used equipment from a restaurant equipment broker.

HIRE PART-TIME EMPLOYEES AND FREELANCE SPECIALISTS WHENEVER POSSIBLE Hiring part-time workers and freelancers rather than full-time employees saves on the cost of salaries, vacations, and benefits.

ENTREPRENEURIAL PROFILE: Gina Kleinworth: HireBetter Gina Kleinworth, CEO of HireBetter, a business based in Austin, Texas, that helps small and midsize companies find the talent they need, relies on an entirely part-time workforce of 35 employees. Kleinworth keeps her company's payroll costs under control, and her workers appreciate the flexibility in their schedules. "Employees have time to get their work done, and go to the gym, take their kids to the park, or volunteer in their communities," she says.[73] ∎

OUTSOURCE One technique that many entrepreneurs use to conserve valuable cash is to outsource certain activities to businesses that specialize in performing them rather than hiring someone to do them in-house (or doing the activities themselves). In addition to saving cash, outsourcing enables entrepreneurs to focus on the most important aspects of running their businesses. "Stick to what you are good at and outsource everything else," advises one entrepreneur.[74] Outsourcing is one principle of building a lean start-up.

USE E-MAIL RATHER THAN MAIL Whenever appropriate, entrepreneurs should use e-mail rather than mail to correspond with customers, suppliers, and others to reduce postage costs.

USE CREDIT CARDS TO MAKE SMALL PURCHASES Using a credit card to make small purchases from vendors who do not offer credit terms allows entrepreneurs to defer payment for up to 30 days. In addition, some credit cards include "cash back" offers that can save entrepreneurs thousands of dollars a year and simplify the accounts payable process by providing a single bill. Entrepreneurs who use this strategy must be disciplined, however, and pay off the entire credit card balance each month. Carrying a credit card balance from month to month exposes an entrepreneur to annual interest rates of 12 to 25 percent—*not* a cash-conserving technique!

NEGOTIATE FIXED LOAN PAYMENTS TO COINCIDE WITH YOUR COMPANY'S CASH FLOW CYCLE Many lenders allow businesses to structure loans so that they can skip specific payments when their cash flow ebbs to its lowest point. Negotiating such terms gives businesses the opportunity to customize their loan repayments to their cash flow cycles.

ESTABLISH AN INTERNAL SECURITY AND CONTROL SYSTEM Too many owners encourage employee theft by failing to establish a system of controls. Reconciling the bank statement monthly and requiring approval for checks over a specific amount—say, $1,000—helps to minimize losses. Separating record-keeping and check-writing responsibilities, rather than assigning them to a single employee, offers additional protection against fraud.

DEVELOP A SYSTEM TO BATTLE CHECK FRAUD Although the use of checks in the United States continues to decline, customers still write more than 18 billion checks per year that total $26 trillion. Unfortunately, about 64 million of those are bad checks that cost businesses nearly $78 billion per year.[75] Bad checks and check fraud can wreak havoc on a small company's cash flow. Simple techniques for minimizing losses from bad checks include requesting proper identification (preferably with a photograph) from customers, recording customers' telephone numbers, and training cashiers to watch for forged or counterfeit checks. Perhaps the most effective way to battle bad and fraudulent checks is to subscribe to an electronic check processing service. The service works at the cash register, and approval takes only seconds. The fee a small business pays to use the service depends on the volume of checks. For most small companies, charges amount to 1 to 2 percent of the cleared checks' value.

CHANGE YOUR SHIPPING TERMS Changing a company's shipping terms from "F.O.B. (free on board) buyer," in which the *seller* pays the cost of freight, to "F.O.B. seller," in which the *buyer* absorbs all shipping costs, improves its cash flow.

START SELLING GIFT CARDS Gift cards are a huge business, generating annual sales of $118 billion, and can provide a real boost to a small company's cash flow.[76] Customers pay for the cards up front, but the typical recipient does not redeem the gift card until later, sometimes much later, giving the company the use of the cash during that time. Selling gift cards also increases a company's revenue because studies show that 60 percent of card recipients spend more than the value of the gift card (and 45 percent of gift card recipients spend at least 60 percent more than the value of the card).[77] Gift cards are an effective way to increase a small company's customer base; 41 percent of customers say they shopped at a business for the first time because they received a gift card for that business, and 72 percent of them returned to that business to make repeat purchases.[78] E-gift cards, digital gift cards that recipients receive via e-mail and can redeem with their smart phones or other mobile devices, represent one of the fastest-growing sectors in the gift card market.

Unfortunately, only 10 percent of small and midsize merchants sell gift cards.[79]

ENTREPRENEURIAL PROFILE: Colleen Stone: Inspa Corporation Colleen Stone, owner of Inspa Corporation, a fast-growing chain of day spas based in Seattle, Washington, uses gift cards to stretch her company's cash flow. Gift cards account for 25 percent of her company's sales, and Stone has discovered that many of the gift cards she sells are not redeemed for a year, giving her a source of interest-free cash in the interim. "We plow all that cash flow right back into opening new stores," says Stone.[80] ∎

SWITCH TO ZERO-BASED BUDGETING Zero-based budgeting (ZBB) primarily is a shift in the philosophy of budgeting. Rather than build the current-year budget on *increases* from the previous year's budget, ZBB starts from a budget of zero and evaluates the necessity of every item. The idea is to start each year's budget with a zero balance and then review each expense category to determine whether it is necessary.

BE ON THE LOOKOUT FOR SHOPLIFTING AND EMPLOYEE THEFT Companies lose an estimated $63 billion each year to shoplifting and employee theft.[81] Although any business can be a victim of shoplifting or employee theft, retailers are particularly vulnerable. Shoplifting is the most common business crime, costing retailers an estimated $13 billion each year. Shoplifting takes an especially heavy toll on small businesses because they usually have the weakest lines of defense against shoplifters. If a shoplifter steals just one item that sells for $100 from a small business with an 8 percent net profit margin, the company must sell an additional $1,250 worth of goods to make up for the loss.

Even though shoplifting is more common than employee theft, businesses lose more money each year to employee theft. Dishonest employees steal 5.5 times more from the businesses for which they work than shoplifters.[82] The Association of Certified Fraud Examiners estimates that companies worldwide lose 5 percent of their annual revenue to fraud by employees.[83] The most common item stolen is, not surprisingly, cash. Because small business owners often rely on informal procedures for managing cash (or have no procedures at all) and often lack proper control procedures, they are most likely to become victims of employee theft, embezzlement, and fraud by their employees. Although 64 percent of small businesses report having experienced employee theft, only 16 percent of business owners reported the theft to police.[84] The median loss suffered by small companies in the United States is a disproportionately large $147,000.[85] The most common methods employees use to steal from small businesses are fraudulent billing schemes, corruption, and check tampering. Alarmingly, the typical fraud goes on for 18 months before the owner discovers it, most often after another employee tips off the owner to the theft.[86] Although establishing a totalitarian police state and trusting no one is not conducive to a positive work environment, putting in place adequate financial control systems is essential. Separating among at least two employees key cash management duties, such as writing checks and handling bank statements and conducting regular financial audits, can be effective deterrents to employee theft.

BUILD A CASH CUSHION Entrepreneurs who have experienced a cash crisis keenly understand the need for every business to build a working capital account as an emergency fund. How much should an entrepreneur put aside? Opinions differ, but most experts say that a small business should put aside enough cash to cover three to six months' worth of expenses—more if conditions warrant.

ENTREPRENEURIAL PROFILE: Carrie Davenport: Century Personnel Carrie Davenport, owner of Century Personnel, a company that specializes in filling jobs in manufacturing, engineering, accounting, and health care, did everything she could to reduce expenses when sales plummeted during a recent recession. She also began putting aside more money into Century Personnel's working capital account, which now has $300,000 more than usual in it in case the economy takes another downturn so that she will have enough cash to keep her business going. Even after reducing her staff from 36 to 14 at the height of the recession, Davenport was concerned that she had only enough cash tucked aside to cover the company's expenses for a couple of months. That prompted her to build a larger cash cushion for her company's protection by adding consistently to Century Personnel's "rainy-day fund."[87] ■

INVEST SURPLUS CASH Because of the uneven flow of receipts and disbursements, a company will often temporarily have more cash than it needs—for a week, month, quarter, or even longer. When this happens, most small business owners simply ignore the surplus because they are not sure how soon they will need it. They believe that relatively small amounts of cash sitting around for just a few days or weeks are not worth investing. However, this is not the case. Small business owners who put surplus cash to work *immediately* rather than allowing it to sit idle soon discover that the yield adds up to a significant amount over time. This money can help ease the daily cash crunch during business troughs. Business owners' goal should be to invest every dollar that they are not using to pay their current bills so that they can improve their cash flow.

You Be the Consultant

Controlling Employee Theft

Looking back, Kelly Morris and her business partner admit they were naïve about employee theft when they opened their first pizza restaurant, believing that if they treated their workers well and paid them fairly, the employees would not steal from them. Experience, however, soon taught them that some people would steal no matter what the young entrepreneurs did. Some employees stole money, some stole inventory and equipment, and others stole food. Initially, Morris and her partner scheduled an employee to go in to set up for the day an hour before anyone else arrived. Unfortunately, that employee, alone in the restaurant, used the opportunity to steal items from the restaurant's inventory. When the entrepreneurs began having a second employee come in to set up, the thefts stopped. Later, an employee alerted Morris and her partner to another theft scheme: an employee was going into the restaurant in the middle of the night, making a few pizzas, and taking them home to eat. They solved that problem by installing an alarm system that required a unique identification code to turn it off. When Morris caught an employee stealing a bottle of soda, she fired him. She admits it was a minor incident, but she recognized the importance of a zero-tolerance policy and the signal it sends to other employees when it comes to stealing. After attending a workshop sponsored by the local police department, Morris and her partner began using clear trash bags to make stealing food items by hiding them in the trash more difficult. Fortunately, Morris and her partner were able to gain control over their employee theft problem before it caused their business to collapse, but some entrepreneurs have to close their businesses because employee theft and fraud destroy their cash flow.

Because small businesses often lack the financial and control procedures that large companies impose, they are disproportionately more likely to be victims of employee theft. Small companies are common targets of employee theft because employees, especially long-term employees, know the weaknesses in the company's systems, procedures, and controls and take advantage when the right opportunity presents itself. Indeed, the longer the tenure of an employee who steals, the greater is the amount stolen. According to a recent study by the Association of Certified Fraud Examiners, the median theft by perpetrators who had been with a company more than 10 years was $229,000; the median theft for those who stolen from a company in their first year of employment was $25,000. One expert cites the following "formula" for employee theft:

Pressure + Rationalization + Opportunity = Employee theft

The only factor in the equation that employers can control is opportunity, which is why entrepreneurs' money is better spent *preventing* employee theft rather than *detecting* it.

Although 64 percent of small businesses report being victims of employee theft, only 16 percent reported the theft to the police. Business owners cite four reasons for failing to report theft by employees: (1) they do not perceive the theft as one warranting

any more attention than firing the employee, (2) their attorneys often advise them that the cost in time and energy to prosecute the thief would likely outweigh any benefits, (3) the decision to prosecute is charged with emotion because the employee has worked alongside the owner for many years or is a family member, and (4) they see the police and criminal justice system as ineffective. The median amount stolen among small companies is $147,000, an amount significant enough to threaten the existence of the businesses themselves. In many cases, the theft leaves the business in a cash bind from which it is unable to recover. In fact, the U.S. Chamber of Commerce estimates that one-third of all small business bankruptcies are the result of employee theft. In small businesses, the typical fraud goes on for 18 months before the owner discovers it. More than 43 percent of the time, an employee tips off the owner to the theft, nearly three times the percentage of thefts that are discovered by management review (14.6 percent). Seven percent of thefts are discovered by accident.

Many entrepreneurs are shocked to discover that the people who are stealing from their businesses are their most trusted, highly valued employees, the *last* people they would suspect. In the United States, employees (43.0 percent) are more likely to steal than are managers (34.3 percent), but thefts by managers cause three times more damage ($182,000) than those by employees ($60,000). Managers' thefts also are more difficult to detect, requiring a median of 24 months to detect, compared to 12 months for those that employees commit. In the United States, 55 percent of the perpetrators are male, 54 percent are between the ages of 31 and 45, and 54 percent have a college or postgraduate degree. The most common "red flags" that lead to detection are employees who are living beyond their means, those who are having financial difficulties, those who are unwilling to share their job duties (for fear of detection), and those who have an unusually close association with a company vendor.

The most effective way to deal with employee theft is to prevent it. Entrepreneurs can take the following steps to reduce the threat of employee theft:

- **Screen potential employees thoroughly.** Statistics show that on average one out of every 40 employees is caught committing employee theft. A business owner's most useful tool against theft is a thorough pre-employment screening process. The best time to weed out prospective criminals is before hiring them.

- **Monitor inventory closely.** Business owners who fail to keep up-to-date, accurate inventory records are inviting employee theft. When the co-owners of two ice cream stores realized that their employees were stealing, they began to take inventory of their stock twice each day. Once employees knew that controls were in place, the thefts stopped, and profits went up.

(continued)

You Be the Consultant (continued)

- **Use technology to discourage theft.** A variety of technology tools help business owners minimize losses to employee theft and fraud at very reasonable prices. Simple video camera systems, such as the ones used on the Food Network's show *Restaurant Stakeout*, are responsible for nabbing many employee thieves, especially cameras that are focused on checkout stations and cash registers.

- **Set up a hotline.** One of the most effective tools for minimizing employee theft is to encourage employees to report suspicious activity and give them a mechanism for reporting. Remember that the most common way that managers detect employee theft is by a tip from another employee.

- **Embrace a zero-tolerance policy.** When business owners catch an employee thief, the best course of action is to fire the perpetrator and to prosecute. Most owners take the attitude: "Resign, return the money, and we'll forget it." Letting thieves off, however, only encourages them to move on to other businesses where they will steal again.

1. Identify the factors that led Kelly Morris and her business partner to become a victim of employee theft and embezzlement. What impact does this crime have on a company's cash flow and survival?

2. Are small businesses more likely to be victims of employee theft? Explain.

3. List at least five additional steps that entrepreneurs should take to prevent their businesses from becoming victims of employee theft and embezzlement.

Sources: Based on Mark Doyle, "25th Annual Retail Theft Survey: Shoplifter and Dishonest Employee Apprehensions and Recovery Dollars," Jack L. Hayes International, June 2013, http://hayesinternational.com/wp-content/uploads/2013/06/SURVEY-2013-25th-Annual-Retail-Theft-Survey-Hayes-International-Thoughts-Behind-Numbers-Final.pdf; Kelly Morris, "Techniques for Preventing or Reducing Employee Theft in Your Restaurant Business," Yahoo! Voices, January 11, 2014, http://voices.yahoo.com/techniques-preventing-reducing-employee-theft-12475702.html?cat=5; Mary-Bridget Reilly, "Surprising Survey: Most Small Businesses Remain Silent Rather Than Report Employee Theft," University of Cincinnati, February 17, 2014, http://www.uc.edu/news/NR.aspx?id=19231; Kent Stolt, "How to Guard Against Theft," Biz Journals, January 24, 2013, http://www.bizjournals.com/bizjournals/how-to/human-resources/2013/04/how-to-guard-against-employee-theft.html?page=all; Neil Williams, "Employee Theft? My Story," Turnkey Parlor, October 25, 2009, http://turnkeyparlor.com/icecreambusinessblog/2009/10/25/employee-theft-my-story/; Kathleen Johnston Jarboe, "Employee Theft at Small Business High and Hard to Detect," *The Daily Record*, October 14, 2005, http://findarticles.com/p/articles/mi_qn4183/is_20051014/ai_n15712876; John Tate, "Little White Thefts," *Small Business Development Center Business Report*, September 5, 2008, p. 2; "Employee Theft Statistics Infographic," *Infographics Showcase*, March 3, 2010, http://www.infographicsshowcase.com/employee-theft-statistics-infographic; and *Report to the Nations on Occupational Fraud and Abuse: 2012 Global Fraud Study*, Association of Certified Fraud Examiners, 2012.

---

money market account
an interest-bearing account that allows depositors to write checks without tying up their money for a specific period of time.

zero-balance account (ZBA)
a checking account that never has any funds in it. A company keeps its money in an interest-bearing master account tied to the ZBA; when a check is drawn on the ZBA, the bank withdraws enough money from the master account to cover it.

sweep account
a checking account that automatically sweeps all funds in a company's checking account above a predetermined minimum into an interest-bearing account.

However, when investing surplus cash, an entrepreneur's primary objective should *not* be to earn the highest yield (which usually carries with it high levels of risk); instead, the focus should be on the safety and the liquidity of the investments. Making high-risk investments with a company's cash cushion makes no sense and could jeopardize its future. The need to minimize risk and to have ready access to the cash restricts an entrepreneur's investment options to just a few such as money market accounts, zero-balance accounts, and sweep accounts. A **money market account** is an interest-bearing account offered by a variety of financial institutions ranging from banks to mutual funds. Money market accounts pay interest while allowing depositors to write checks (most have minimum check amounts) without tying their money up for a specific period of time.

A **zero-balance account (ZBA)** is a checking account that technically never has any funds in it but is tied to a master account. The company keeps its money in the master account, where it earns interest, but it writes checks on the ZBA. At the end of the day, the bank pays all of the checks drawn on the ZBA; then it withdraws enough money from the master account to cover them. ZBAs allow a company to keep more cash working during the float period, the time between a check being issued and its being cashed. A **sweep account** automatically "sweeps" all funds in a company's checking account above a predetermined minimum into an interest-bearing account, enabling it to keep otherwise idle cash invested until it is needed to cover checks.

KEEP YOUR BUSINESS PLAN CURRENT Before approaching any potential lender or investor, a business owner must prepare a solid business plan. Smart owners keep their plans up to date in case an unexpected cash crisis forces them to seek emergency financing. Revising the plan annually also forces the owner to focus on managing the business more effectively.

Conclusion

Successful owners run their businesses "lean and mean." Trimming wasteful expenditures, investing surplus funds, and carefully planning and managing the company's cash flow enable them to compete effectively. The simple but effective techniques covered in this chapter can improve every small company's cash position. One business writer says, "In the day-to-day course of running a company, other people's capital flows past an imaginative CEO as opportunity. By looking forward and keeping an analytical eye on your cash account as events unfold (remembering that if there's no real cash there when you need it, you're history), you can generate leverage as surely as if that capital were yours to keep."[88]

Chapter Summary by Learning Objective

1. Explain the importance of cash management to a small company's success.

- Cash is the most important but least productive asset the small business has. An entrepreneur must maintain enough cash to meet the company's normal requirements (plus a reserve for emergencies) without retaining excessively large, unproductive cash balances.
- Without adequate cash, a small business will fail.

2. Differentiate between cash and profits.

- Cash and profits are *not* the same. More businesses fail for lack of cash than for lack of profits.
- Profits, the difference between total revenue and total expenses, are an accounting concept. Cash flow represents the flow of actual cash (the only thing businesses can use to pay bills) through a business in a continuous cycle. A business can be earning a profit and be forced out of business because it runs out of cash.

3. Understand the five steps in creating a cash budget.

- The cash budgeting procedure outlined in this chapter tracks the flow of cash through the business and enables the owner to project cash surpluses and cash deficits at specific intervals.
- The five steps in creating a cash budget are as follows: determining a minimum cash balance, forecasting sales, forecasting cash receipts, forecasting cash disbursements, and determining the end-of-month cash balance.

4. Describe fundamental principles involved in managing the "big three" of cash management: accounts receivable, accounts payable, and inventory.

- Controlling accounts receivable requires business owners to establish clear, firm credit and collection policies and to screen customers *before* granting them credit. Sending invoices promptly and acting on past-due accounts quickly also improve cash flow. The goal is to collect cash from receivables as quickly as possible.
- When managing accounts payable, a manager's goal is to stretch out payables as long as possible without damaging the company's credit rating. Other techniques include verifying invoices before paying them, taking advantage of cash discounts, and negotiating the best possible credit terms.
- Inventory frequently causes cash headaches for small business managers. Excess inventory earns a zero rate of return and ties up a company's cash unnecessarily. Owners must watch for stale merchandise.

5. Explain the techniques for avoiding a cash crunch in a small company.

- Key strategies include: trimming overhead costs by bartering; leasing assets rather than buying them; avoiding nonessential outlays; buying used equipment; hiring part-time employees; negotiating fixed payments to coincide with a company's cash flow cycle; implementing an internal control system boost a firm's cash flow position; developing a system to battle check fraud; selling gift cards; using zero-based budgeting; being on the lookout for shoplifting and employee theft; building a cash cushion; and keeping the business plan current.
- In addition, investing surplus cash maximizes the firm's earning power. The primary criteria for investing surplus cash are security and liquidity.

Discussion Questions

12-1. Why must entrepreneurs concentrate on effective cash flow management?

12-2. Explain the difference between cash and profit.

12-3. Outline the steps involved in developing a cash budget.

12-4. How can an entrepreneur launching a new business forecast sales?

12-5. What are the big three of cash management?

12-6. What effect do the big three of cash management have on a company's cash flow?

12-7. Outline the basic principles of managing a small firm's receivables, payables, and inventory.

12-8. How can bartering improve a company's cash position?

12-9. What steps can entrepreneurs take to conserve the cash within their companies?

12-10. What should be a small business owner's primary concern when investing surplus cash?

Beyond the Classroom . . .

12-11. Interview several local small business owners about their cash management policies. Do they know how much cash their businesses have during the month? How do they track their cash flows? Do they use some type of cash budget? If not, ask if you can help the owner develop one. Does the owner invest surplus cash? If so, where?

12-12. Volunteer to help a small business owner develop a cash budget for his or her company. What patterns do you detect? What recommendations can you make for improving the company's cash management system?

12-13. Contact the International Reciprocal Trade Association (www.irta.net) and get a list of the barter exchanges in your state. Interview the manager of one of the exchanges and prepare a report on how barter exchanges work and how they benefit small businesses. Ask the manager to refer you to a small business owner who benefits from the barter exchange and interview him or her. How does the owner use the exchange? How much cash has bartering saved? What other benefits has the owner discovered?

12-14. Use the resources of the Internet to research leasing options for small companies. The Equipment Leasing and Financing Association of America (www.elfaonline.org) is a good place to start. What advantages does leasing offer? Disadvantages? Identify and explain the various types of leases.

12-15. Contact a local small business owner who sells on credit. Is collecting accounts receivable on time a problem? What steps does the owner take to manage the company's accounts receivable? Do late payers strain the company's cash flow? How does the owner deal with customers who pay late?

12-16. Conduct an online search for the National Retail Security Survey that the University of Florida Department of Criminology, Law, and Society conducts annually. Summarize the key findings of the survey concerning losses that businesses incur from shoplifting, employee theft, and fraud. What steps can small businesses take to minimize their losses to these problems?

Endnotes

Scan for Endnotes or go to www.pearsonhighered.com/scarborough

13

Sources of Financing:
Equity and Debt

Courtney Keating/Getty Images

Learning Objectives

On completion of this chapter, you will be able to:

1. Describe the differences between equity capital and debt capital.

2. Discuss the various sources of equity capital available to entrepreneurs.

3. Describe the process of "going public."

4. Describe the various sources of debt capital.

5. Describe the various loan programs available from the Small Business Administration.

6. Identify the various federal and state loan programs aimed at small businesses.

7. Explain other methods of financing a business.

Capital is a crucial element in the process of creating new ventures; yet raising the money to launch a new business venture has always been a challenge for entrepreneurs. Capital markets rise and fall with the stock market, overall economic conditions, and investors' fortunes. These swells and troughs in the availability of capital make the search for financing look like a wild roller-coaster ride. Entrepreneurs, especially those in less glamorous industries or those just starting out, face difficulty finding outside sources of financing. Many banks shy away from making loans to start-ups, venture capitalists are looking for ever-larger deals, private investors have grown cautious, and making a public stock offering remains a viable option for only a handful of promising companies with good track records and fast-growth futures. The result has been a credit crunch for entrepreneurs looking for small to moderate amounts of start-up capital. Entrepreneurs and business owners who need between $100,000 and $3 million are especially hard hit because of the vacuum that exists at that level of financing.

In the face of this capital crunch, business's need for capital has never been greater. In a recent survey by the National Federation of Independent Business (NFIB), 41 percent of small business owners say lack of capital is an impediment to the growth of their companies.[1] However, many small business owners have adapted to the new credit conditions. In another survey by the NFIB, 48 percent of small business owners said they did not want to borrow more money.[2] The key is learning to manage capital carefully and knowing the right kind of capital to raise for the right needs in your business. The goal should not be to raise as much capital as you can; you should raise only as much as your business needs.

When searching for the capital to launch their companies, entrepreneurs must remember the following "secrets" to successful financing:

- *Choosing the right sources of capital for a business can be just as important as choosing the right form of ownership or the right location.* It is a decision that will influence a company for a lifetime, and entrepreneurs must weigh their options carefully before committing to a particular funding source. "It is important that companies in need of capital align themselves with sources that best fit their needs," says one financial consultant. "The success of a company often depends on the success of that relationship."[3]

- *The money is out there; the key is knowing where to look.* Entrepreneurs must do their homework *before* they set out to raise money for their ventures. Understanding which sources of funding are best suited for the various stages of a company's growth and then taking the time to learn how those sources work is essential to success.

- *Raising money takes time and effort.* Sometimes entrepreneurs are surprised at the energy and time required to raise the capital needed to feed their cash-hungry, growing businesses. The process usually includes lots of promising leads, most of which turn out to be dead-ends. Meetings with and presentations to lots of potential investors and lenders can crowd out the time needed to manage a growing company. Entrepreneurs also discover that raising capital is an ongoing job. "The fund-raising game is a marathon, not a sprint," says Jerusha Stewart, founder of iSpiritus Soul Spa, a store selling personal growth and well-being products.[4]

- *Creativity counts.* Although some traditional sources of funds now play a lesser role in small business finance than in the past, other sources—from large corporations and customers to international venture capitalists and state or local programs—are taking up the slack. To find the financing their businesses demand, entrepreneurs must use as much creativity in attracting financing as they did in generating the ideas for their products and services. For instance, after striking out with traditional sources of funding, EZConserve, a company that makes software that provides energy management tools for large PC networks, turned to the nonprofit group Northwest Energy Efficiency Alliance and received a sizable grant as well as marketing assistance that fueled its growth.[5]

- *The Internet puts at entrepreneurs' fingertips vast resources of information that can lead to financing. Use it.* The Internet offers entrepreneurs, especially those looking for relatively small amounts of money, the opportunity to discover sources of funds they otherwise might miss. The Internet also provides a low-cost convenient way for entrepreneurs to get their business plans into potential investors' hands anywhere in the world.

- *Put social media to work to locate potential investors.* Social media such as Facebook, Twitter, LinkedIn, and others are useful tools for locating potential investors. For example, LinkedIn has several groups that help investors and entrepreneurs connect with each other, such as *Angel Investors, Impact Investors,* and *Angel Investor Group.*

- *Be thoroughly prepared before approaching potential lenders and investors.* In the hunt for capital, tracking down leads is tough enough; don't blow a potential deal by failing to be ready to present your business idea to potential lenders and investors in a clear, concise, convincing way. That, of course, requires a solid business plan and a well-rehearsed elevator pitch—one or two minutes on the nature of your business and the source of its competitive edge to win over potential investors and lenders. "Entrepreneurs who come across with unsubstantiated market assessments, no competitive analysis, and flimsy marketing and sales plans will be the losers in the race to money," says venture capitalist John May.[6]

- *Entrepreneurs cannot overestimate the importance of making sure that the "chemistry" among themselves, their companies, and their funding sources is a good one.* Too many entrepreneurs get into financial deals because they need the money to keep their businesses growing only to discover that their plans do not match those of their financial partners.

- *Plan an exit strategy.* Although it may seem peculiar for entrepreneurs to plan an exit strategy for investors when they are seeking capital to *start* their businesses, doing so increases their chances of closing a deal. Investors do not put their money into a business with the intent of leaving it there indefinitely. Their goal is to get their money back—along with an attractive return on it. Entrepreneurs who fail to define potential exit strategies for their investors reduce the likelihood of getting the capital their companies need to grow.

- *When capital gets tight, remember to bootstrap.* Because capital is tighter for small businesses, don't forget to use some of the clever ways you employed to get your business going when you had limited funds. Bootstrapping is not just for start-ups!

Rather than rely primarily on a single source of funds as they have in the past, entrepreneurs must piece together capital from multiple sources, a method known as **layered financing**. They have discovered that raising capital successfully requires them to cast a wide net to capture the financing they need to launch their businesses.

layered financing
the technique of raising capital from multiple sources.

ENTREPRENEURIAL PROFILE: John and Patrick Collison: Stripe After launching their first company and selling it in just ten months, brothers John and Patrick Collison launched Stripe, an online payments company, with their own money. While working on several projects, Patrick realized how difficult taking online payments was for merchants and decided that he and his brother could develop a better method. They tested their simple payment solution with online shoppers, made the necessary modifications, and landed a spot (and the seed financing that came with it) in Y Combinator, a prestigious business accelerator in Mountain View, California. Stripe grew quickly, and the Collisons secured investments from several high profile angel investors, including entrepreneurs Elon Musk and Peter Thiel, and eventually venture capital firms. Just four years after start-up, the Collisons had raised more than $120 million in capital, and Stripe was worth an estimated $1.75 billion.[7] ∎

This chapter will guide you through the myriad financing options available to entrepreneurs, focusing on both sources of equity (ownership) and debt (borrowed) financing. Becoming a successful entrepreneur requires one to become a skilled fund-raiser, a job that usually requires more time and energy than most business founders realize. In start-up companies, raising capital can easily consume as much as one-half of the entrepreneur's time and can take many months to complete. In addition, many entrepreneurs find it necessary to raise capital constantly to fuel the hefty capital appetites of their young, fast-growing companies. Although the amount an entrepreneur needs to launch a start-up varies significantly by the type of business being launched, the Global Entrepreneurship Monitor reports that new entrepreneurs need on average about $15,000 to start their businesses and an additional $16,000 in funding after start-up.[8] However, these "small" amounts of capital can be most difficult to secure.

Capital is any form of wealth employed to produce more wealth. It exists in many forms in a typical business, including cash, inventory, plant, and equipment. Entrepreneurs have access to two different types of capital: equity and debt.

capital
any form of wealth employed to produce more wealth.

LO1

Describe the differences between equity capital and debt capital.

equity capital

capital that represents the personal investment of the owner (or owners) of a company; sometimes called risk capital.

Equity Capital versus Debt Capital

Equity capital represents the personal investment of the owner (or owners) in a business and is sometimes called *risk capital* because these investors assume the primary risk of losing their funds if the business fails. If a venture succeeds, however, founders and investors share in the benefits, which can be quite substantial. The founders of and early investors in Yahoo!, Sun Microsystems, Federal Express, Intel, and Microsoft became multimillionaires when the companies went public and their equity investments finally paid off. Michael Moritz, a partner in the venture capital firm Sequoia Capital, recalls a meeting in 1999 that took place around a ping-pong table that doubled as a conference table for Sergey Brin and Larry Page, the founders of a start-up company that had developed a search engine called Google. The young company had just changed its name from Backrub and had only 12 employees when Moritz agreed to invest $25 million in exchange for 16 percent of the company's stock. When Google made an initial public offering five years later, Moritz's original investment was worth $3 billion![9]

To entrepreneurs, the primary advantage of equity capital is that it does not have to be repaid like a loan does. Equity investors are entitled to share in the company's earnings (if there are any) and usually to have a voice in the company's future direction. The primary disadvantage of equity capital is that the entrepreneur must give up some—sometimes even *most*—of the ownership in the business to outsiders. Although 50 percent of something is better than 100 percent of nothing, giving up control of a company can be disconcerting and dangerous. Entrepreneurs are most likely to give up significant amounts of equity in their businesses in the start-up phase than in any other. To avoid having to give up control of their companies early on, entrepreneurs should strive to launch their companies with the least amount of money possible.

debt capital

the financing that an entrepreneur borrows and must repay with interest.

Debt capital is the financing an entrepreneur borrows and must repay with interest. Very few entrepreneurs have adequate personal savings to finance the total start-up costs of a small business; many of them must rely on some form of debt capital to launch their companies. Lenders of capital are more numerous than investors, but small business loans can be just as difficult (if not more difficult) to obtain. Although borrowed capital allows entrepreneurs to maintain complete ownership of their businesses, it must be carried as a liability on the balance sheet, and it must be repaid with interest in the future. In addition, because lenders consider small businesses to be greater risks than bigger corporate customers, they require higher interest rates on loans to small companies because of the risk–return trade-off: The higher the risk, the greater the return demanded. Most small firms pay the prime rate—the interest rate banks charge their most creditworthy customers—*plus* a few percentage points. Still, the cost of debt financing often is lower than that of equity financing. Because of the higher risks associated with providing equity capital to small companies, investors demand greater returns than lenders. In addition, unlike equity financing, debt financing does not require entrepreneurs to dilute their ownership interest in their companies. We now turn our attention to eight common sources of equity capital.

LO2

Discuss the various sources of equity capital available to entrepreneurs.

Sources of Equity Financing

Personal Savings

The *first* place entrepreneurs should look for start-up money is in their own pockets. It's the least expensive source of funds available! A start-up has very little if any financial history, and investors view investments in early-stage companies as high risk. Therefore, the earlier in the life of the company that an entrepreneur must raise capital, the more he or she will likely have to give up in ownership to secure that financing. Entrepreneurs apparently see the benefits of self-sufficiency; tapping their personal savings and using creative, low-cost start-up methods, a technique known as **bootstrapping**, is one of the most common sources of funds used to start a business. According to a survey by the Kauffman Foundation and LegalZoom, more than 86 percent of U.S. entrepreneurs use personal savings and assets as a primary source of financing for their start-ups.[10] However, it is not just small businesses that rely on personal savings. A recent survey of companies in the *Inc.* 500 List of America's Fastest Growing Companies finds that 77 percent of the entrepreneurs who founded these high-growth ventures also relied on personal savings to help fund their businesses.[11] The Global Entrepreneurship Monitor survey reports that entrepreneurs

bootstrapping

a process in which entrepreneurs tap their personal savings and use creative, low-cost start-up methods to launch their businesses.

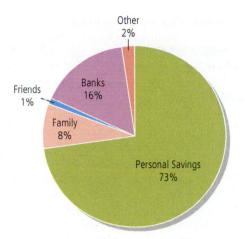

FIGURE 13.1

Sources of Financing for Typical Start-Up Businesses

Source: Donna J. Kelley, Abdul Ali, Candida Brush, Andrew C. Corbett, Mahdi Majbouri, and Edward G. Rogoff, "2012 United States Report," *Global Entrepreneurship Monitor*, p. 23.

in the U.S. rely on personal savings for 73 percent of total funding (see Figure 13.1).[12] Bootstrappers learn quickly to be frugal and stretch the income-generating power of every dollar, especially when most or all of those dollars come from their personal savings.

ENTREPRENEURIAL PROFILE: Sandi Bryant: Americare Pharmacy Sandi Bryant, founder of Americare Pharmacy in Fairview, North Carolina, needed $300,000 to open her long-term care pharmacy business. To fund the business, Bryant used $100,000 from her retirement savings and took out a personal loan using her home as collateral. Although she and her husband were anxious about taking the risk, after analyzing how many prescriptions she would have to fill to break even, they decided that investing their personal savings was worth the risk. Americare Pharmacy broke even after only eight months, and Bryant is now able draw a good salary and put money into her retirement account.[13] ■

Lenders and investors *expect* entrepreneurs to put their own money into a business start-up. If an entrepreneur is not willing to risk his or her own money, potential investors are not likely to risk their money in the business either. Furthermore, failing to put up sufficient capital of their own means that entrepreneurs must either borrow an excessive amount of capital or give up a significant portion of ownership to outsiders to fund the business properly. Excessive borrowing in the early days of a business puts intense pressure on its cash flow, and becoming a minority shareholder may dampen a founder's enthusiasm for making a business successful.

Friends and Family Members

Although most entrepreneurs look to their own bank accounts first to finance a business, few have sufficient resources to launch their businesses alone. After emptying their own pockets, where should entrepreneurs turn for capital? The second place most entrepreneurs look is to friends and family members who might be willing to invest in (or lend to) a business venture. Because of their relationships with the founder, these people are most likely to invest. Often they are more patient than other outside investors and are less meddlesome in a business's affairs (but not always!) than many other types of investors.

ENTREPRENEURIAL PROFILE: Tom Haarlander: ARCiPLEX Tom Haarlander, President of ARCiPLEX, Nashville, Tennessee, has relied on friends and family for most of the funding needs of the company he cofounded. Although Haarlander often has been uncomfortable with the responsibility of using friends' and family members' money, he has had to rely on their support to fund the early growth of his business. In every situation, Haarlander sets up a formal agreement that pays interest every month to those who lend ARCiPLEX money to show his intention to pay them back. Haarlander has always been aggressive in using any excess cash flow to pay back the principal on the loans from friends and family, sometimes to the detriment of the business. By keeping any funding from friends and family structured as a loan, Haarlander says he has been able to keep good relationships with all of those who have helped fund his business.[14] ■

Tom Haarlander, CEO of ARCiPLEX

Investments from family and friends are an important source of capital for entrepreneurs, but the amounts invested typically are small, often no more than just a few thousand dollars. According to the Global Entrepreneurship Monitor, entrepreneurs in the United States receive about 9 percent of total funding from friends and family.[15]

Investments (or loans) from family and friends are an excellent source of seed capital and can get a start-up far enough along to attract money from private investors or venture capital companies. Inherent dangers lurk in family business investments and loans, however. One study reports a default rate of 14 percent on business loans from family and friends, compared to a default rate of 1 percent for bank loans.[16] Unrealistic expectations or misunderstood risks have destroyed many friendships and have ruined many family gatherings. Remember: Thanksgiving comes around every year! To avoid problems, an entrepreneur must honestly present the investment opportunity and the nature of the risks involved to avoid alienating friends and family members if the business fails. Smart entrepreneurs treat family members and friends who invest in their companies in the same way they would treat outside investors. Some investments in start-up companies return more than friends and family members ever could have imagined. In 1995, Mike and Jackie Bezos invested $300,000 in their son Jeff's start-up business, Amazon.com. Today, Mike and Jackie own 6 percent of Amazon.com's stock, and their shares are worth billions of dollars![17] The accompanying "Hands On . . . How To" feature offers suggestions for structuring successful family or friendship financing deals.

Crowd Funding

Historically, securities laws limited who can invest in small businesses. Investing in entrepreneurial businesses has been the realm of those with the knowledge and financial ability to assume the risks that come with such investments. Known as **accredited investors**, these people must have a sustained net worth (excluding their primary residence) of at least $1 million or annual income of at least $200,000. There are between 5 million and 7.2 million accredited investors in the United States; however, only about 756,000 of these accredited investors have made direct investments in entrepreneurial businesses.[18] A few creative entrepreneurs have used a loophole to raise money from investors who do not meet the requirements of accredited investors using a funding technique called **crowdfunding**. Crowdfunding taps the power of the Internet and social networking and allows entrepreneurs to post their elevator pitches and proposed investment terms on specialized Web sites and raise money from ordinary people who invest as little as $100. Crowdfunding primarily has been used to help raise money to support social causes, help fund aspiring artists, or support local small business start-ups. The money received from crowdfunding had to be considered a contribution or a donation, rather than an investment. In most cases, entrepreneurs offer some

accredited investors
investors who have a sustained net worth (excluding their primary residences) of at least $1 million or annual income of at least $200,000.

crowdfunding
a method of raising capital that taps the power of social networking and allows entrepreneurs to post their elevator pitches and proposed investment terms on specialized Web sites and raise money from ordinary people who invest as little as $100.

"It's meat loaf. We didn't make our Kickstarter goal for steak."

Joe Oater/Cartoon Bank

Hands On . . . How To

Structure Family and Friendship Financing Deals

Tapping family members and friends for start-up capital, whether in the form of equity or debt financing, is a popular method of financing business ideas. In a typical year, some 6 million individuals in the United States invest about $100 billion in entrepreneurial ventures. Unfortunately, not all of these deals work to the satisfaction of both parties. The following suggestions can help entrepreneurs avoid needlessly destroying family relationships and friendships:

- ***Family should not be your first financing option.*** Loans and investments from family members should never be considered the easy option for financing a business. Make sure you have done everything you can to bootstrap your business to minimize the cash you actually will need before turning to family for help.

- ***Choose your financier carefully.*** One of the first issues to consider is the impact of the investment on everyone involved. Will it work a hardship on the investor or lender? Is the investor putting up the money because he or she wants to or because he or she feels obligated? Can all parties afford the loan if the business folds? No matter how much capital you may need, accepting more than family members or friends can afford to lose is a recipe for disaster—and perhaps bankruptcy for the investors. Lynn McPhee used $250,000 from family members to launch Xuny, a Web-based clothing store. Her basic rule was that if the investment would cause any financial distress or potential hardship, she would not accept their money. Remember that relationships often suffer if a business fails and friends and family members lose their money.

- ***Keep the arrangement strictly business.*** The parties should treat all loans and investments in a business-like manner, no matter how close the friendship or family relationship, to avoid problems down the line. If the transaction is a loan exceeding $10,000, it must carry a rate of interest at least as high as the IRS minimum rate; otherwise, the Internal Revenue Service may consider the loan a gift and penalize the lender. Treat family investors just like any other early stage investor in the business.

- ***Prepare a business plan.*** Treat friends and family members just as you would angel investors, bankers, venture capitalists, and other professionals by doing your research and preparing a business plan. The most important use of a business plan is to communicate the business model to potential investors, so prepare a thoroughly researched business plan and go over it carefully with any potential family members interested in providing funding for the business. Be honest and be clear about the worst-case scenario in your plan.

- ***Settle the details up front.*** Before any money changes hands, both parties must agree on the details of the deal. How much money is involved? Is it a loan or an investment? How will the investor cash out? How will the loan be paid off? What happens if the business fails?

- ***Create a written contract.*** Don't make the mistake of closing a financial deal with just a handshake. The probability of misunderstandings skyrockets! Putting an agreement in writing demonstrates the parties' commitment to the deal and minimizes the chances of disputes from faulty memories and misunderstandings.

- ***Treat the money as "bridge financing."*** Although family and friends can help you launch your business, it is unlikely that they can provide enough capital to sustain it over the long term. Sooner or later, you will need to establish a relationship with other sources of credit if your company is to survive and thrive. Consider money from family and friends as a bridge to take your company to the next level of financing, as seen in the Entrepreneurial Profile of Tom Haarlander in this chapter.

- ***Develop a payment schedule that suits both the entrepreneur and the lender or investor.*** One of the primary benefits of financing from family members and friends is that the repayment or cash-out schedule usually is flexible. Although lenders and investors may want to get their money back as quickly as possible, a rapid repayment or cash-out schedule can jeopardize a fledgling company's survival. Establish a realistic repayment plan that works for the parties without putting excessive strain on your young company's cash flow. Family members are usually more than willing to be patient funders of your business.

- ***Have an exit plan.*** Every deal should define exactly how investors will "cash out" their investments or loans.

Sources: Based on Luke Landers, "8 Rules for Borrowing Money from Friends and Family," *Consumerism Commentary*, February 26, 2013, www.consumerismcommentary.com/rules-borrowing-money-friends-family/; Caron Beesley, "6 Tips for Borrowing Startup Funds from Friends or Family," *SBA Community*, January 3, 2012, http://community.sba.gov/community/blogs/community-blogs/small-business-cents/6-tips-borrowing-startup-funds-friends-or-family; Rosalind Resnick, "For You, Graduate, Some Start-Up Capital," *Wall Street Journal*, June 7, 2011, http://online.wsj.com/article/SB10001424052702304432304576369842747489336.html; Sarah Dougherty, "'Love Money' Seeds Many Budding Ventures," *Financial Post*, January 30, 2008, http://www.financialpost.com/small-business/business-solutions/story.html?id=269859; Paulette Thomas, "It's All Relative," *Wall Street Journal*, November 29, 2004, pp. RR4, R8; Andrea Coombes, "Retirees as Venture Capitalists," *CBS MarketWatch*, November 2, 2003, http://netscape.marketwatch.com/news/story.asp?dist=feed&siteid=netscape&guid={1E1267CD-32A4-4558-9F7E-40E4B7892D01}; Paul Kvinta, "Frogskins, Shekels, Bucks, Moolah, Cash, Simoleans, Dough, Dinero: Everybody Wants It. Your Business Needs It. Here's How to Get It," *Smart Business*, August 2000, pp. 74–89; Alex Markels, "A Little Help from Their Friends," *Wall Street Journal*, May 22, 1995, p. R10; and Heather Chaplin, "Friends and Family," *Your Company*, September 1999, p. 26.

nominal benefit in return for financial support. For example, a musician might show appreciation to contributors by giving them a free download of a new song. Likewise, an owner of a new restaurant may offer each contributor a special discount. The contributions are motivated by the desire to help out the aspiring musician or restaurateur. The most commonly used websites that promote traditional crowdfunding are Kickstarter, Rock the Post, and IndieGoGo. AngelList is a crowdfunding site for accredited angel investors looking to make small investments. Kiva and Accion are crowd lending sites that link small businesses with people willing to provide micro loans.

ENTREPRENEURIAL PROFILE: Erin Anderson and Dan Ellsworth: Daniel Ellsworth & The Great Lakes Erin Anderson is the manager for an up-and-coming band called Daniel Ellsworth & The Great Lakes. Anderson and Ellsworth set up a crowdfunding campaign for the band's newest release on a crowdfunding site, Pledge Music, which helps them run a pre-order campaign through the band's Web site to raise funding and predict initial demand for new T-shirts, CDs, vinyl albums, and posters. They were able to use the money raised through the Pledge Music campaign to print the T-shirts and posters and produce CDs and albums. The campaign also helped them predict future demand, which helped them order the right amount of inventory.[19] ■

Courtesy of Daniel Ellsworth

The Jumpstart Our Business Startups (JOBS) Act of 2012 significantly expands the use of crowdfunding as a way to raise equity investment for small businesses. Once this law is fully enacted, those who provide funding can now become equity investors with ownership in the business. The JOBS Act opens up funding of start-ups to a much broader group of investors who do not meet the legal criteria to be considered accredited investors. To be eligible for crowdfunding, a business have less than $1 billion in annual revenue. An eligible business can raise up to $1 million from a crowdfunding offering each year. The first phase of the JOBS Act opened up crowdfunding only to accredited investors. Eventually, the JOBS Act will open up equity-based crowdfunding to any investor. When the law is fully enacted, it will establish a ceiling on an individual's crowdfunding investment that is based on his or her income and net worth. The original goal of the JOBS Act was to allow *anyone* to invest some amount in a business start-up. When the law is finally fully implemented, entrepreneurs no longer will be limited to only seeking funding from accredited investors.[20]

Attracting investors through crowdfunding, particularly traditional crowdfunding Web sites, requires a different approach than an entrepreneur uses when pursuing more sophisticated and experienced investors. Unlike experienced investors who invest more in people than in their ideas, crowdfunding investors tend to be attracted to compelling stories and business ideas they can see themselves using. Crowdfunding works through social media, so the entrepreneur's existing network of contacts must be advocates to lend credibility to the business among the broader network.[21] Although the JOBS Act will eventually significantly broaden the pool of people who can invest in small businesses, it also creates new challenges for entrepreneurs who use crowdfunding. Crowdfunding may complicate future fundraising if an entrepreneur uses layered financing, so entrepreneurs should seek advice from financing experts to develop a long-term financing plan. Crowdfunding creates a large number of owners who all have certain expectations and may require attention from the entrepreneur. If adding one additional partner increases the complexity of running a business, imagine what a crowd of partners can do to complicate an entrepreneur's life! The accompanying "Hands On . . . How To" feature offers some additional cautions when using crowdfunding to finance a small business.

Accelerators

accelerator programs
programs, often sponsored by communities and universities, that provide a small amount of seed capital and a wealth of additional support for start-up companies.

Inexperienced entrepreneurs have difficulty finding early stage seed funding. The first-time entrepreneur doesn't have the credibility to attract professional investors and typically doesn't have the personal wealth required to launch a business. To help bridge this gap in funding, many communities and universities have established **accelerator programs** that offer new entrepreneurs a small amount of seed capital and a wealth of additional support. Accelerator programs help move entrepreneurs from the idea stage to a point when the business has a proven story and a strong business model that the founder can pitch for more significant funding. Accelerators offer a structured program that lasts from three months to one year. A select group of entrepreneurs, typically 10 to 20, are invited to participate as a group in an accelerator program. The accelerator provides

Hands On . . . How To

Crowdfunding

Crowdfunding Web sites, such as Kickstarter, are a popular way for small start-ups to get seed funding. There are many success stories of companies that got the start-up capital they needed for a successful launch through a crowdfunding campaign.

Nathan Resnick, founder of Yes Man Watches, had hoped to raise $15,000 using Kickstarter to launch his online retail watch business. Resnick used blogs that write about watches to help build buzz about his new business and its Kickstarter campaign. He asked all of his contacts to post on Twitter and Facebook about Yes Man Watches, sending them pictures of his watches they could include with their posts. When his campaign went live, he had strong support the first day and was able to exceed his goal by raising more than $32,000.

Ilene Ruvinsky, cofounder of a skin care company called Don't Call Me Ma'am, developed a video to support her fundraising campaign on the crowdfunding site Fundable.com. She spent her own money producing the video in hopes that its quality would result in even more funding from her crowdfunding campaign. Ruvinsky met her goal of raising $20,000 through Fundable.com, and the business is moving toward a launch of its product line.

The Dark Side of Crowdfunding

Not every crowdfunding story has a happy ending, however.

Seth Quest launched a Kickstarter campaign to raise $10,000 in seed money to help launch his iPad stand called Hanfree. He put a photo of a prototype on his Kickstarter fundraising page. The description on the Kickstarter page said that for a minimum pledge of $50, backers could preorder a Hanfree, which would be made in San Francisco, California, out of sustainably forested alder wood. He also promised that each one would be hand-numbered and signed by the designer. The campaign was a success, raising more than $35,000 from 440 backers.

However, the excitement over Quest's fundraising success quickly faded. Quest had no business experience and had never manufactured a product before. As a result, he was unable to fill the preorders as promised. Some of the backers became angry, and soon there were hundreds of negative comments on Hanfree's Kickstarter page. Quest realized that he was not going to be able to fill the orders, so he posted a promise that he planned to refund the money given by the backers. However, after several weeks with no refund, some of the backers decided to take action against Quest. One of the backers filed a breach of contract lawsuit against Quest, which eventually forced Quest to file for bankruptcy.

Avoiding a Kickstarter Disaster

Crowdfunding remains a popular tool for entrepreneurs to use to help get hard-to-find seed capital. When approached carefully, crowdfunding can be a highly effective means for raising funding. The following suggestions can help entrepreneurs avoid creating disastrous situations when raising money using crowdfunding:

- ***Start with a business plan.*** Although business plans are not required by crowdfunding Web sites, it is always advisable to develop one as part of your preparation. Remember, one of the most important uses of a business plan is to communicate with investors and bankers. Although Kickstarter backers are not technically investors, developing a plan that spells out what you will do with the money and how you will achieve what you promise benefits both investors and the entrepreneur.

- ***Have contracts in place.*** Because crowdfunding usually involves some sort of a product, make sure you have contacts in place with suppliers or outsource manufacturers to ensure that you can deliver what you promise at the price you have planned for in your projections and budgets.

- ***Be honest about the risks.*** If there are risks and challenges that may prevent you from delivering a product, be open and honest about all of these risks in the information you present at the crowdfunding Web site. Doing so avoids nasty surprises if things do not go as planned.

- ***Remember that backers view themselves as customers, not investors.*** When people provide backing for your project, they are assuming that they have placed a preorder with you that you will fulfill. They do not view themselves as investors who may or may not get any return for the money they give you.

Sources: Based on Karen E. Klein, "How to Get Funded on Kickstarter," *Bloomberg Business Week*, April 18, 2014, www.businessweek.com/articles/2014-04-18/how-to-get-funded-on-kickstarter; Eric Markowitz, "When Kickstarter Investors Want Their Money Back," *Inc.*, January 10, 2013, www.inc.com/eric-markowitz/when-kickstarter-investors-want-their-money-back.html; James Holloway, "Kickstarter Disaster: When Crowdfunding Backfires," *Gizmag*, July 30, 2013, www.gizmag.com/kickstater-disaster/28514/; "Don't Call Me Ma'am," Fundable, n.d., www.fundable.com/dont-call-me-maam; Todd Hixon, "Is Crowdfunding a Boon or a Disaster?" *Forbes*, April 4, 2012, www.forbes.com/sites/toddhixon/2012/04/04/is-crowdfunding-a-boon-or-a-disaster/.

entrepreneurs with about $15,000 to $25,000 in seed capital, gives them temporary space to work on their business and their elevator pitch, and connects them with a team of mentors who each get a small share of equity in the business in return for their guidance. All of this requires the entrepreneur to give up 6 to 10 percent of the ownership in the business. At the end of the program, the accelerator hosts a large pitch event. Local angel investors and venture capitalists are invited to hear all of the pitches of the accelerator participants. Those investors who are interested can join the mentor team as investors in businesses that "graduate" from the accelerator program. Private accelerators are located in most major cities, and a growing number of universities have accelerator programs to assist student and alumni entrepreneurs.

Two of the largest accelerator programs are Y Combinator and TechStars. Although accelerators do provide small investments, the most important contribution they offer is the coaching and mentoring from angel investors and experienced entrepreneurs. Angel investors work alongside the founding entrepreneurs, serving as mentors and advisers. As a result, they help to shape the business model of the companies in which they invest. The Techstars accelerator program reports that 70 percent of its participants receive subsequent funding after going through the program. An amazing 94 percent of businesses launched through the Y Combinator accelerator program receive additional funding.[22]

 ENTREPRENEURIAL PROFILE: Jake Gish: Beyond Right Now Technologies Jake Gish has used two different accelerator programs to help his start-up, Beyond Right Now Technologies. Gish plans to create several products that use the latest technology for resource conservation and management, crop health monitoring, endangered species conservation, land mapping, seed and spore dispersal, and delivery of mitigating solutions. The first accelerator program he participated in was the Next Farm Agriculture Innovation Accelerator based at Northwest Tennessee Entrepreneur Center in Martin, Tennessee, which helped Gish formulate his basic business model. After completing the Next Farm accelerator, he was accepted into the JumpStart Foundry accelerator in Nashville, Tennessee. "Accelerator programs helped me decide exactly which product and customer to focus on," says Gish. "Going into the programs we had enough ideas for over a dozen products for even more customers. Accelerators [also] helped us craft a pitch tailored to communicate clearly to possible investors, strategic partners, and customers."[23] In the JumpStart Foundry accelerator, Gish plans to develop a lead product: Pig Punisher. This product is a drone that helps hunt feral hogs, which are responsible for billions of dollars in crop losses, property damage, and degradation of water quality. A growing concern is that feral hogs carry diseases that infect domestic livestock. The Pig Punisher has an exclusive license for a tool developed at Oak Ridge National Laboratories that helps identify from an aerial drone feral hogs that are infected.[24] ∎

Courtesy of Jake Gish

private investors (angels)

wealthy individuals, often entrepreneurs themselves, who invest in business start-ups in exchange for equity stakes in the companies.

Angels

After dipping into their own pockets and convincing friends and relatives to invest in their business ventures, many entrepreneurs still find themselves short of the seed capital they need. Frequently, the next stop on the road to business financing is private investors. These **private investors (angels)** are wealthy individuals, often entrepreneurs themselves, who are accredited investors and choose to invest their own money in business start-ups in exchange for equity stakes in the companies. Angel investors have provided much-needed capital to entrepreneurs for many years. In 1938, when World War I flying ace Eddie Rickenbacker needed money to launch Eastern Airlines, millionaire Laurance Rockefeller provided it.[25] Alexander Graham Bell, inventor of the telephone, used angel capital to start Bell Telephone in 1877. More recently, companies such as Google, Apple, Starbucks, Kinko's, and the Body Shop relied on angel financing in their early years to finance growth.

In many cases, angels invest in businesses for more than purely economic reasons—for example, because they have a personal interest or experience in a particular industry—and they are willing to put money into companies in the earliest stages, long before venture capital firms and institutional investors jump in. Angel financing, the fastest-growing segment of the small business capital market, is ideal for companies that have outgrown the capacity of investments from friends and family but are still too small to attract the interest of venture capital companies. Angel financing is vital to the nation's small business sector because it fills this capital gap in which small companies need investments ranging from $100,000 or less to perhaps $5 million or more. For instance, after raising the money to launch Amazon.com from family and friends, Jeff Bezos turned to angels for capital because venture capital firms were not interested in investing in a business start-up. Bezos attracted $1.2 million from a dozen angels before landing $8 million from venture capital firms a year later.[26]

Angels are a primary source of start-up capital for companies in the start-up stage through the growth stage, and their role in financing small businesses is significant. Research at the University of New Hampshire shows that nearly 299,000 angels and angel groups invest $24.8 billion a year

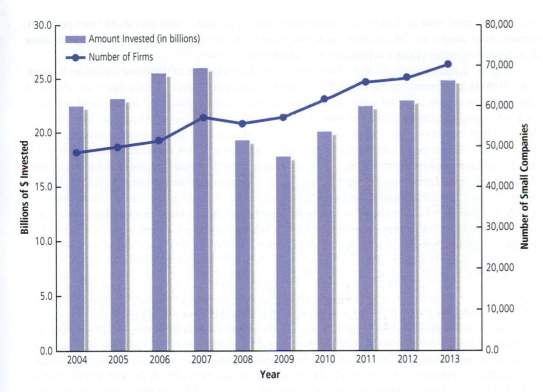

FIGURE 13.2

Angel Financing

Source: Based on data from the Center for Venture Research, Whittemore School of Business, University of New Hampshire, http://paulcollege.unh.edu/center-venture-research.

in more than 70,000 small companies, most of them in the start-up phase.[27] In short, angels are one of the largest and most important sources of external equity capital for small businesses. Their investments in young companies nearly match those of professional venture capitalists, providing vital capital to 18 times as many small companies (see Figure 13.2).

ENTREPRENEURIAL PROFILE: Carter Cleveland: Artsy Artsy, founded by computer scientist Carter Cleveland, seeks to make all of the world's art accessible to anyone with an Internet connection. It is an online platform for discovering, learning about, and collecting art. Artsy provides one of the largest collections of contemporary art available online by partnering with galleries to help broaden their target markets. Artsy's revenues come from the artwork it sells on behalf of its gallery partners. The business model has proved so effective that the company has 1,000 additional galleries on a waiting list to join the Artsy network. Artsy has received investments from more than 20 individual angel investors as well as significant venture capital funding. After raising more than $1.4 million in angel seed investments, Artsy had a successful round of venture capital financing of $6 million. The company is currently raising a new round of up to $18.5 million from venture capital firms.[28] ∎

Angels fill a significant gap in the seed capital market. They are most likely to finance start-ups with capital requirements in the $10,000 to $2 million range, well below the $5 million to $10 million minimum investments most professional venture capitalists prefer. The average angel investment (including angel funds and networks) in a company is $350,000.[29] Because a $1 million deal requires about as much of a venture capitalist's time to research and evaluate as a $20 million deal, venture capitalists tend to focus on big deals where their returns are bigger. Because angels tend to invest in the earliest stages of a business, they incur the highest levels of risk. In fact, 52 percent of angels' investments lose money, returning less than the angels' original investment. The potential for investing in big winners exists as well; 7 percent of angels' investments produce a return of more than 10 times their original investments.[30]

Lewis Gersh, an experienced angel investor, says that out of 10 companies that an angel invests in, 5 will fail, 2 will break even, and 2 will return two to three times the original investment. Just 1 company in 10 will produce a significant return. All of the deals will be high potential, but with high potential comes high risk. Most angels consider a "home-run" investment to be one that results in a return of 10 to 30 times the original investment in five to seven years, somewhat lower than the returns venture capital firms expect.[31] Because of the inherent risks in start-up companies, many venture capitalists have shifted their investment portfolios away from start-ups toward more established businesses. That's why angel financing is so important: Angels often finance deals that no venture capitalist will consider.

Angels accept between 10 and 15 percent of the deals pitched to them and invest an average of $50,000 in a company that is at the seed or start-up growth stages.[32] Most angels are seasoned entrepreneurs themselves; on average, angel investors have founded 2.7 companies and have 14.5 years of entrepreneurial experience. They also are well educated; 99 percent have college degrees. Research also shows that 86 percent of angel investors are men (their average age is 57 years) who have been investing in promising small companies for nine years. The typical angel invests in one company per year.[33] When evaluating a proposal, angels look for a qualified management team (generally not just an individual entrepreneur) and a business with a clearly defined niche, market potential, and competitive advantage. They also want to see market research that proves the existence of a sizable customer base and a viable exit strategy, the avenue by which they get their investments back, ideally with a handsome return. Angels want a path to a clean exit for their investment, rather than a business that might yield dividends over time.

Entrepreneurs in search of capital quickly learn that the real challenge lies in *finding* angels. Most angels have substantial business and financial experience, and many of them are entrepreneurs or former entrepreneurs. Because most angels frown on "cold calls" from entrepreneurs they don't know, locating them boils down to making the right contacts. Networking is the key. Asking friends, attorneys, bankers, stockbrokers, accountants, other business owners, and consultants for suggestions and introductions is a good way to start. Many angel investors use their attorneys and accountants as gatekeepers for potential deals. Angels almost always invest their money locally, so entrepreneurs should look close to home for them—typically within a 50- to 100-mile radius. In fact, 7 out of 10 angels invest in companies that are within 50 miles of their homes or offices.[34] Angels also look for businesses they know something about, and most expect to invest their knowledge, experience, and energy as well as their money in a company. In fact, the advice and the network of contacts that angels bring to a deal can sometimes be as valuable as their money!

Angel investing has become more organized and professional than it was 20 years ago, with investors pooling their resources to form angel networks and angel capital funds, dubbed "super-angels," that operate like miniature versions of professional venture capital firms and draw on investors' skills, experience, and contacts to help the start-ups in which they invest to succeed. Today more than 300 angel capital networks operate in cities of all sizes across the United States (up from just 10 in 1996). Angel networks make the task of locating angels much easier for entrepreneurs in search of capital.

ENTREPRENEURIAL PROFILE: Crista Freeman: Phin & Phebes Ice Cream Crista Freeman, CEO and cofounder of Phin & Phebes Ice Cream, launched her business with the help of an investment by angel investor William Hines, who was part of the company's $150,000 seed funding round. Phin & Phebes Ice Cream is made with no preservatives, conventional stabilizers, or syrups of any kind. It is made with milk, cream, sugar, and egg yolks. Phin & Phebes has expanded into 22 states and more than 260 stores in its first three years in business. Its products are sold in stores such as Whole Foods, Earth Fare, Central Market, Gourmet Garage, Fresh Direct, and Morton Williams. In its second round of funding, Phin & Phebes is raising $5 million in capital to fund its continued growth. The second round of fundraising includes investments by two angel investors, Brad Feld and Joanne Wilson. Feld is part of Foundry Group, which is a venture capital and angel investment group in Boulder, Colorado. Wilson is a businesswoman from New York City who is an active angel investor.[35] ■

The Internet has expanded greatly the ability of entrepreneurs in search of capital and angels in search of businesses to find one another. Dozens of angel networks have set up shop on the Internet many of which are members of the Angel Capital Association. The association reports that its average member group has 42 investors and makes investments in four small companies each year.[36] Entrepreneurs can expand the scope of their hunt for financing by including online angel groups and the Angel Capital Association's membership list in their searches. AngelList is another Web site that connects angel investors with high potential deals.

Angels are an excellent source of "patient money," often willing to wait seven years or longer to cash out their investments. They earn their returns through the increased value of the business, not through dividends and interest. For example, more than 1,000 early investors in Microsoft Inc. are now multimillionaires. Angels' return-on-investment targets tend to be lower than those of professional venture capitalists. Although venture capitalists shoot for 60 to 75 percent returns annually, angel investors usually settle for 20 to 50 percent (depending on the level of risk involved in the venture). A study by the Kauffman Foundation reports that the average return on angels' investments in small companies is 2.6 times the original investment in 3.5 years, which is the equivalent of a 27 percent internal rate of return.[37] Angel investors typically purchase 15 to 30 percent ownership in a small company, leaving the majority ownership to the company founder(s). They look for the same exit strategies that venture capital firms look for: either an initial public offering or a buyout by a larger company. The lesson: If an entrepreneur needs relatively small amounts of money to launch or to grow a company, angels are an excellent source.

Venture Capital Companies

Venture capital companies are private, for-profit organizations that assemble pools of capital and then use them to purchase equity positions in young businesses they believe have high-growth and high-profit potential, producing annual returns of 300 to 500 percent within five to seven years. More than 400 venture capital firms operate across the United States today, investing billions of dollars (see Figure 13.3) in promising small companies in a wide variety of industries. Companies in the high-tech hubs in California's Silicon Valley and Boston's high-tech corridor account for nearly half of all venture capital investments, but "secondary" cities, such as Boulder (Colorado), Salt Lake City (Utah), Ann Arbor (Michigan), Providence (Rhode Island), Norwalk (Connecticut), and Stamford (Connecticut), offer thriving venture capital sectors that invest significant sums of money, especially in local small businesses with high growth potential.[38] Venture capital firms have invested billions of dollars in high-potential small companies over the years, including such notable businesses as Google, Apple, FedEx, Netscape, Home Depot, Microsoft, Intel, Starbucks, Whole Foods Market, and Genentech.[39]

venture capital companies

private, for-profit organizations that purchase equity positions in young businesses that they believe have high-growth and high-profit potential.

ENTREPRENEURIAL PROFILE: Steven DeGennaro, Patrick Parker, and Dirk Gates: Xirrus Xirrus, located in Thousand Oaks, California, develops specialized, Wi-Fi hotspots aimed at high-density and high-performance locations, such as campuses and public areas. Steven DeGennaro, Patrick Parker, and Dirk Gates, all of who remain active in the company, founded

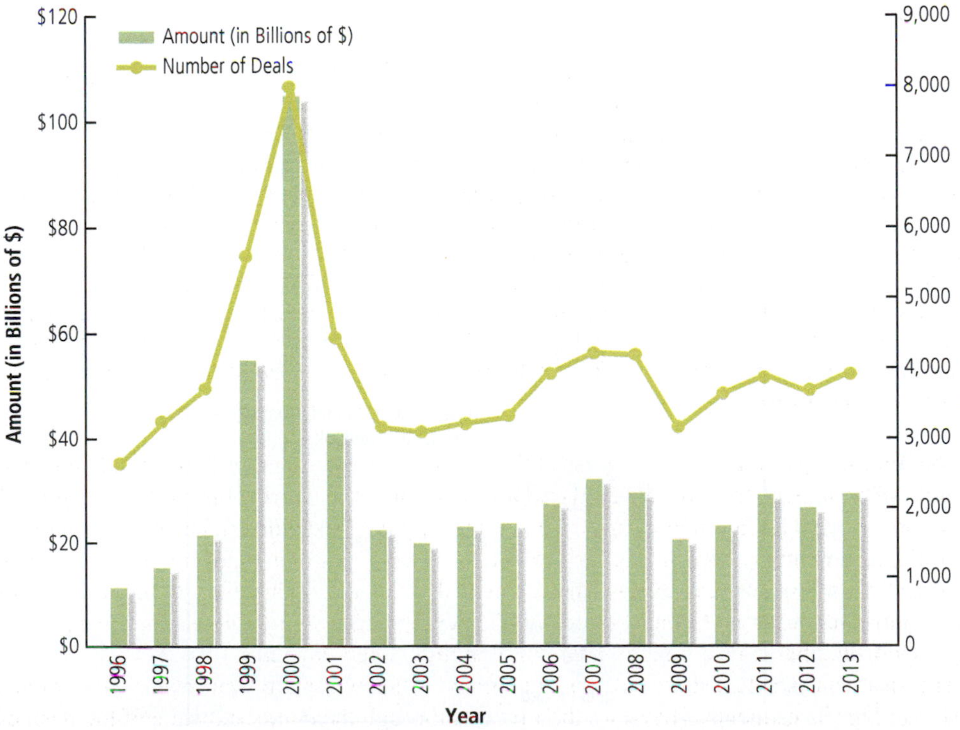

FIGURE 13.3

Venture Capital Funding

Source: Price Waterhouse Coopers, https://www.pwcmoneytree.com/MTPublic/ns/nav.jsp?page=historical.

Xirrus and successfully raised six rounds of venture capital funding totaling $105.9 million. Venture capitalists investing in Xirrus are among the most prominent firms, including August Capital, Canaan Partners, InterWest, QuestMark Partners, and U.S. Venture Partners. These firms participated in more than one of the company's rounds of venture capital funding.[40] ■

POLICIES AND INVESTMENT STRATEGIES Venture capital firms usually establish stringent policies to implement their overall investment strategies.

Investment Size and Screening The average venture capital firm's investment in a small company is $7.4 million.[41] Depending on the size of the venture capital company, minimum investments range from $100,000 to $5 million, but most venture capital firms seek investments in the $5 million to $25 million range to justify the cost of screening the large number of proposals they receive.

In a typical year, venture capital firms invest in about 4,000 of the nearly 28 million small businesses in the United States. The venture capital screening process is *extremely* rigorous. According to the Global Entrepreneurship Monitor, only about 1 in 1,000 businesses in the United States receives venture capital during its existence.[42] The typical venture capital firm receives about 1,200 business plans each year (although some receive many more). For every 100 business plans the average venture capital firm receives, 90 of them are rejected immediately because they do not match the firm's investment criteria or requirements. The firm conducts a thorough due diligence investigation of the remaining 10 companies and typically invests in only 1 of them (see Figure 13.4). The average time required to close a venture capital deal is 60 to 90 days.

Ownership and Control Most venture capitalists prefer to purchase ownership in a small business through common stock or convertible preferred stock. Although many venture capital firms purchase less than 50 percent of a company's stock, others buy a controlling share of a company, leaving its founders with a minority share of ownership. Most venture capitalists prefer to let the founding team of managers employ its skills to operate a business *if* they are capable of managing its growth. However, it is quite common for venture capitalists to join the boards of directors of the companies in which they invest. Sometimes venture investors step in and shake up the management teams in the companies in which they invest. Janet Effland, a partner in the venture capital firm Apax Partners, says her fund changes management in the deals they fund

FIGURE 13.4

The Business Plan Funnel

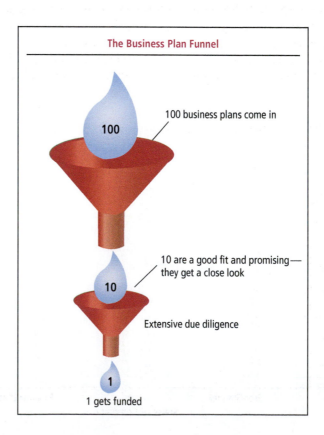

about 40 percent of the time.[43] In other words, entrepreneurs should *not* expect venture capitalists to be passive investors! Some serve only as financial and managerial advisers, but others take an active role managing the company—recruiting employees, providing sales leads, choosing attorneys and advertising agencies, and making daily decisions. The majority of these active venture capitalists say they are forced to step in because the existing management team lacks the talent and experience to achieve growth targets.

Stage of Investment Most venture capital firms invest in companies that are in either the early stages of development (called early-stage investing) or in the rapid-growth phase (called expansion-stage investing). About 96 to 98 percent of all venture capital investments go to businesses in these stages; very few invest in small companies that are in the start-up phase.[44] Most venture capital firms do not make just a single investment in a company. Instead, they invest in a company over time across several stages, where their investments often total $10 million to $15 million or more.

Advice and Contacts In addition to the money they invest, more venture capital companies are providing the small companies in their portfolios with management advice and access to valuable networks of contacts of suppliers, employees, customers, and other sources of capital than they did just a few years ago. One of their goals in doing so is to strengthen the companies in which they have invested, thereby increasing their value.

Investment Preferences Venture capital firms now are larger, more professional, and more specialized than they were 25 years ago. As the industry matures, venture capital funds increasingly are focusing their investments in niches—everything from information technology to biotechnology. Some will invest in almost any industry, but most prefer companies in later stages. Traditionally, fewer companies receiving venture capital financing are in the start-up or seed stage, when entrepreneurs are forming a company or developing a product or service and when angels are most likely to invest (see Figure 13.5). Most of the start-up businesses that attract venture capital are technology companies in "hot" fields such as software, biotechnology, energy, medical devices, and media and entertainment.[45]

WHAT VENTURE CAPITALISTS LOOK FOR Entrepreneurs must realize that it is difficult for any small business, especially fledgling or struggling firms, to pass the intense screening process of a venture capital company and qualify for an investment. A great elevator pitch and a sound business plan are essential to convincing venture capital firms to invest in a company. Geeta Vemuri, a principal in a venture capital firm, says investors want to see proof of concept for deals they consider investing in.[46] Two factors make a deal attractive to venture capitalists: high returns

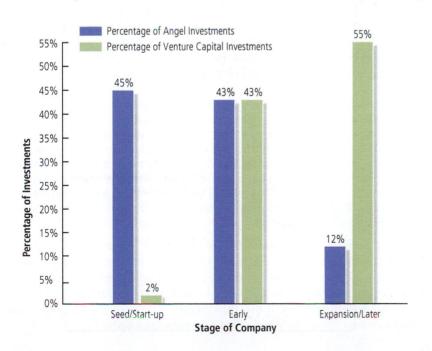

FIGURE 13.5

Angel vs VC Investments

Sources: Based on data from Jeffrey Sohl, "The Angel Investor Market in 2013: A Return to Seed Investing," Center for Venture Research, April 30, 2014,http:// paulcollege.unh.edu/sites/ paulcollege.unh.edu/files/ 2013%20Analysis%20 Report%20FINAL.pdf; https:// www.pwcmoneytree.com/ MTPublic/ns/moneytree/ filesource/displays/notice-D .html "MoneyTree Report," PriceWaterhouseCooper and National Venture Capital Association, April 18, 2014.

and a convenient (and profitable) exit strategy. When evaluating potential investments, venture capitalists look for the following features:

Competent Management The most important ingredient in the success of any business is the ability of the management team, and venture capitalists understand this. To venture capitalists, the ideal management team has experience, managerial skills, commitment, and the ability to expand the team as the business grows.

Competitive Edge Investors are searching for some factor that will enable a small business to set itself apart from its competitors. This distinctive competence may range from an innovative product or service that satisfies unmet customer needs to a unique marketing or research-and-development (R&D) approach. It must be something with the potential to create a sustainable competitive edge, making the company a leader in its industry. Bill Turner, founder of venture capital firm Signature Capital, stresses that he looks for transformational business models, such as his investments in an online music service, a hearing-aid maker, and an HIV-therapy company.[47]

Growth Industry Hot industries attract profits—and venture capital. Most venture capital funds focus their searches for prospects in rapidly growing fields because they believe the profit potential is greater in these areas. Venture capital firms are most interested in young companies that have enough growth potential to become at least $100 million businesses within three to five years. Venture capitalists know that most of the businesses they invest in will flop, so their winners have to be *big* winners.

ENTREPRENEURIAL PROFILE: Chieh Huang: Boxed Chieh Huang, founder and CEO of Boxed, is trying to become a giant killer. Huang founded Boxed with the intent of creating an app to compete with the likes of Amazon, Costco, and Walmart. Boxed is an e-commerce company (like Amazon) offering discounts on large quantities of bulk items (like Costco). Boxed sells its products only through a mobile app and ships to customers anywhere in the United States. Huang raised $6.5 million in an A round of funding that was led by venture capital firms Greycroft Ventures, First Round Capital, and Signia Venture Partners. Three other venture capital firms also participated in the company's first round of funding, which Boxed used to complete the development of the app and launch the company. Boxed plans to attract customers in the Millennial Generation, who typically are not as loyal to companies such as Costco and Sam's Club, preferring to shop online.[48] ∎

Viable Exit Strategy Venture capitalists not only look for promising companies with the ability to dominate a market but also want to see a plan for a feasible exit strategy, typically to be executed within three to five years. Venture capital firms realize the return on their investments when the companies they invest in either make an initial public offering or are acquired by or merged into another business. As the market for initial public offerings has softened, venture capitalists have had to be more patient in their exit strategies. Venture-backed companies that go public now take an average of 5.3 years from the time of their first venture capital investment to their stock offering, up from an average of less than three years in 1998.[49]

ENTREPRENEURIAL PROFILE: Reid Hoffman: LinkedIn The venture capital firms that invested in LinkedIn, the business networking Web site with more than 300 million users in 200 countries, reaped a handsome return on their investments when the company made an initial public offering in 2011. Founder Reid Hoffman guided LinkedIn through five rounds of venture financing from firms including Sequoia Capital, Greylock Partners, Bessemer Venture Partners, and Bain Capital before making an initial public offering. After the initial public offering, the venture capital firms' investments of $103 million, which gave them a 41.4 percent ownership in LinkedIn, were worth $1.76 billion! Hoffman retained 20.1 percent of LinkedIn's stock, worth $853 million at the time of the company's initial public offering.[50] ∎

Intangible Factors Some other important factors considered in the screening process are not easily measured; they are the intuitive, intangible factors that the venture capitalist detects by gut feeling. This feeling might be the result of the small firm's solid sense of direction, its strategic planning process, the chemistry of its management team, or other factors. Venture capital firms want to know that entrepreneurs will use their money wisely—for investments that provide profitable results and not those that merely feed entrepreneurial egos.

ENTREPRENEURIAL PROFILE: Mark Montgomery: FLO {thinkery} and Blue Chair Bay Rum Mark Montgomery, founder of FLO {thinkery}, CEO of Blue Chair Bay Rum, and angel investor, has sat on both sides of the table when it comes to equity investments. Montgomery pays close attention to every detail when assessing an investment in an entrepreneurial venture, particularly early decisions made by the leadership team. "When I go into a startup burning $300,000 a month, and they've got amazing offices with expensive furniture, I immediately think the leadership team's priorities are wrong," says Montgomery, an angel investor from Nashville, Tennessee. "On the other side, I don't think you should have your people sitting on milk crates at a ping pong table. Just be practical."[51] ■

Courtesy of Mark Montgomery

Despite its many benefits, venture capital is not suited for every entrepreneur. Venture capital investments come with many strings attached and can limit entrepreneurs' ability to navigate their companies as they would prefer.

Corporate Venture Capital

Large corporations have gotten into the business of financing small companies and invest in businesses for both strategic and financial reasons. More than 300 large corporations across the globe, including Google, BMW, Comcast, Amazon, Qualcomm, Intel, General Electric, Dow Chemical, Cisco Systems, UPS, Wal-Mart, Unilever, and Johnson & Johnson, invest in small companies, usually companies that are in the later stage of growth and because of their maturity are less risky. Today, more than 17 percent of all venture capital deals involve corporate venture capital. The average investment that large corporations make in small companies is $4.53 million, which represents 10.6 percent of total venture capital investments.[52] Young companies not only get a boost from the capital injections large companies give them but also stand to gain many other benefits from the relationship. The right corporate partner may share technical expertise, distribution channels, and marketing know-how and provide introductions to important customers and suppliers. Another intangible yet highly important advantage an investment from a large corporate partner gives a small company is credibility, often referred to as "market validation." Doors that otherwise would be closed to a small company magically open when the right corporation becomes a strategic partner.

ENTREPRENEURIAL PROFILE: Google Ventures and Shoaib Makani: KeepTruckin In 2009, Google launched Google Ventures, the company's venture capital division, with the goal of investing $200 million a year in small companies with fast-growth potential across all stages of development. Since its inception, Google Ventures has invested amounts ranging from $200,000 to $33 million in promising companies in a variety of industries. Although long-haul trucking is not an industry that sounds like it would attract an investment from Google, KeepTruckin received a seed round of investment of $2.25 million that was led by Google Ventures. Currently, long-haul truckers keep and report the logs that track their mileage and hours using pen, paper, and fax machines. KeepTruckin plans to automate this process using smart phones. According to KeepTruckin cofounder and CEO Shoaib Makani, most of the technological solutions applied to long-haul trucking have focused on solving corporate problems. KeepTruckin, however, is focused on the 3 million truckers in this industry. Its app automatically tracks time and distance driven, generates log files, and automatically sends the files to a dispatcher. The app also alerts drivers when they are over federally mandated driving limits. KeepTruckin plans to move beyond automated drive logs into fleet and truck management.[53] ■

initial public offering (IPO)

a method of raising equity capital in which a company sells shares of its stock to the general public for the first time.

Public Stock Sale ("Going Public")

In some cases, companies can "go public" by selling shares of stock to outside investors. In an **initial public offering (IPO)**, a company raises capital by selling shares of its stock to the general public for the first time. An IPO is an effective method of raising large amounts of capital, but it can be an expensive and time-consuming process filled with regulatory nightmares. Once a company makes an IPO, *nothing* will ever be the same again. Managers must consider the impact of their decisions not only on the company and its employees but also on shareholders and the value of their stock.

LO3

Describe the process of "going public."

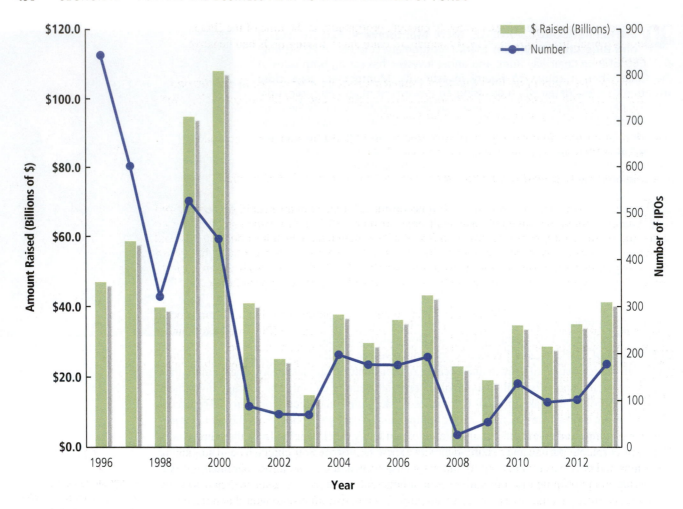

FIGURE 13.6

Initial Public Offerings (IPOs)

Source: Based on data from 2014 IPO Report, WilmerHale, 2014, p. 2.

Going public isn't for every business. In fact, most small companies do not meet the criteria for making a successful public stock offering. Since 2001, the average number of companies that make IPOs each year is 120, and only about 20,000 companies in the United States—less than 1 percent of the total—are publicly held (see Figure 13.6). The dramatic drop in the number of IPOs that occurred in the early part of this century was due in large part to the passage of Sarbanes-Oxley, a law that put significant restrictions and requirements on publicly traded companies. An outcome of this law was to make IPOs unaffordable for smaller companies. Since Sarbanes-Oxley became law, few new companies with less than $25 million in annual sales manage to go public successfully. Since 2001, 68 percent of the companies that have completed IPOs have had annual sales of $50 million or more.[54] For instance, LinkedIn, the professional networking Web site, was generating sales of $243 million at the time of its IPO. When Zygna, the creator of popular Facebook games such as Farmville, Cityville, and Words with Friends, filed for its IPO, the company's sales were $597 million.[55]

It is almost impossible for a start-up company with no track record of success to raise money with an IPO. Instead, the investment bankers who underwrite public stock offerings typically look for established companies with the following characteristics:

- *Consistently high growth rates.* In the three years prior to its IPO, LinkedIn's revenues grew an impressive 212 percent.[56]

- *Scalability.* Underwriters and institutional investors want proof that a company can maintain or improve its efficiency as it experiences the strain that rapid growth imposes.

- *A strong record of earnings.* Strangely enough, profitability at the time of the IPO is not essential; from 2001 to 2013, 49 percent of companies making IPOs had negative earnings.[57]

- *Three to five years of audited financial statements that meet or exceed Securities and Exchange Commission (SEC) standards.* After the Enron and WorldCom scandals, investors are demanding impeccable financial statements.

- *A solid position in a rapidly growing industry.* In 2000, the median age of companies making IPOs was 6 years; today, it is 12 years.[58]

- *A sound management team with experience and a strong board of directors.*

ENTREPRENEURIAL PROFILE: Shayan Zadeh: Zoosk Shayan Zadeh, cofounder and CEO of Zoosk, has taken his business from start-up to IPO in only seven years. During that time, the online dating company has amassed 26 million members, which includes 650,000 paid subscribers, from 80 countries. Although the company has yet to make a profit, it has raised $61.6 million in venture capital and plans to raise another $100 million in its IPO. Merrill Lynch, Pierce, Fenner & Smith, and Citigroup Global Markets provided underwriting for Zoosk's IPO.[59] ■

THE REGISTRATION PROCESS Taking a company public is a complicated, bureaucratic process that usually takes several months to complete. Many experts compare the IPO process to running a corporate marathon, and both the company and its management team must be in shape and up to the grueling task. The typical entrepreneur *cannot* take his or her company public alone. It requires a coordinated effort from a team of professionals, including company executives, an accountant, a securities attorney, a financial printer, and at least one underwriter. The key steps in taking a company public are as follows:

- *Choose the underwriter.* The single most important ingredient in making a successful IPO is selecting a capable **managing underwriter (investment banker)**. The managing underwriter serves two primary roles: helping to prepare the registration statement for the issue and promoting the company's stock to potential investors. The underwriter works with company managers as an adviser to prepare the registration statement that must be filed with the SEC, promotes the issue, prices the stock, and provides aftermarket support. Once the registration statement is finished, the managing underwriter's primary job is selling the company's stock through an underwriting syndicate of other investment bankers it develops.

- *Negotiate a letter of intent.* To begin an offering, the entrepreneur and the underwriter must negotiate a **letter of intent**, which outlines the details of the deal. The letter of intent covers a variety of important issues, including the type of underwriting, its size and price range, the underwriter's commission, and any warrants and options included. It almost always states that the underwriter is not bound to the offering until it is executed—usually the day before or the day of the offering. However, the letter usually creates a binding obligation for the company to pay any direct expenses the underwriter incurs relating to the offer.

- *Prepare the registration statement.* After a company signs the letter of intent, the next task is to prepare the **registration statement** to be filed with the SEC. This document describes both the company and the stock offering and discloses information about the risks of investing. It includes information on the use of the proceeds, the company's history, its financial position, its capital structure, the risks it faces, its managers' experience, and *many* other details. The statement is extremely comprehensive and may take months to develop. To prepare the statement, entrepreneurs must rely on their team of professionals.

- *File with the SEC.* When the statement is finished (with the exception of pricing the shares, proceeds, and commissions, which cannot be determined until just before the issue goes to market), the company officially files the statement with the SEC and awaits the review of the Division of Corporate Finance, a process that takes 30 to 45 days (or more). The division sends notice of any deficiencies in the registration statement to the company's attorney in a comment letter. The company and its team of professionals must cure all of

managing underwriter (investment banker)
a financial company that serves two important roles: helping to prepare the registration statement for an issue and promoting the company's stock to potential investors.

letter of intent
an agreement between the underwriter and the company about to go public that outlines the details of the deal.

registration statement
the document a company must file with the SEC that describes both the company and its stock offering and discloses information about the risk of investing.

the deficiencies in the statement noted in the comment letter. Finally, the company files the revised registration statement along with a pricing amendment (giving the price of the shares, the proceeds, and the commissions).

- *Wait to go effective.* While waiting for the SEC's approval, the managers and the underwriters are busy. The underwriters are building a syndicate of other underwriters who will market the company's stock. (No stock sales can be made prior to the effective date of the offering, however.) The SEC also limits the publicity and information a company may release during this quiet period (which officially starts when the company reaches a preliminary agreement with the managing underwriter and ends 25 days after the effective date).

road show

a gathering of potential syndicate members sponsored by the managing underwriter for the purpose of promoting a company's IPO.

- *Road show.* Securities laws do permit a **road show**, a gathering of potential syndicate members sponsored by the managing underwriter. Its purpose is to promote interest among potential underwriters in the IPO by featuring the company, its management, and the proposed deal. The managing underwriter and key company officials barnstorm major financial centers at a grueling pace.

- *Sign underwriting agreement.* On the last day before the registration statement becomes effective, the company signs the formal underwriting agreement. The final settlement, or closing, takes place a few days after the effective date for the issue. At this meeting the underwriters receive their shares to sell, and the company receives the proceeds of the offering. Typically, the entire process of going public takes from 120 to 180 days, but it can take much longer if the issuing company is not properly prepared for the process.

- *Meet state requirements.* In addition to satisfying the SEC's requirements, a company also must meet the securities laws in all states in which the issue is sold. These state laws (or "blue-sky" laws) vary drastically from one state to another, and the company must comply with them.

NONPUBLIC REGISTRATIONS AND EXEMPTIONS The IPO process just described, called an *S-1 filing,* requires maximum disclosure in the initial filing and discourages most small businesses from using it. Fortunately, the SEC allows several exemptions from this full-disclosure process for small businesses seeking to sell stock through a limited private stock offering. Entrepreneurs can sell stock through a limited private offering to accredited investors, corporations and trusts, and insiders to the business. The SEC has established simplified registration statements and exemptions from the registration process through what is known as Regulation D (Rule 504, 505, and 506).

Regulation D rules minimize the expense and time required to raise equity capital for small businesses by simplifying or eliminating the requirement for registering the offering with the SEC, which often takes months and costs many thousands of dollars. Under Regulation D, the whole process typically costs less than half of what a traditional public offering costs. The SEC's objective in creating Regulation D was to give small companies the access to equity financing that large companies have via the stock market while bypassing many of the costs and filing requirements. A Regulation D offering requires only minimal notification to the SEC.

Rule 504 is the most popular of the Regulation D exemptions because it is the least restrictive. It allows a company to sell shares of its stock to an unlimited number of investors without regard to their experience or level of sophistication. A business also can make multiple offerings under Rule 504 as long as it waits at least six months between them; however, Rule 504 places a cap of $1 million in a 12-month period on the amount of capital a company can raise.

An offering under Rule 505 has a higher capital ceiling ($5 million in a 12-month period) than Rule 504 but imposes more restrictions (no more than 35 nonaccredited investors, no advertising of the offer, and more stringent disclosure requirements).

Rule 506 imposes no ceiling on the amount that can be raised, but most companies that make Rule 506 offerings raise between $1 million and $50 million in capital. Like a Rule 505 offering, it limits the issue to no more than 35 nonaccredited investors and prohibits advertising the offer to the public. There is no limit on the number of accredited investors, however. Rule 506 also requires detailed disclosure of relevant information, but the extent depends on the size of the offering.

Sources of Debt Financing

Debt financing involves the funds that the small business owner borrows and must repay with interest. Debt financing is a popular tool that many entrepreneurs use to acquire capital. In a typical year, small businesses borrow about $1 trillion.[60] Lenders of capital are more numerous than investors, although small business loans can be just as difficult (if not more difficult) to obtain. According to the National Small Business Association, 35 percent of small business owners say they are unable to obtain adequate financing for their companies.[61]

ENTREPRENEURIAL PROFILE: Vicky Vij: Bukhara Grill Vicky Vij, an immigrant from Delhi, India, built a successful restaurant called Bukhara Grill in downtown New York City. The restaurant had sales of more than $2.5 million a year, three straight years of profitability, and excellent credit. However, when Vij decided to buy a catering business to expand the operation, he had no success getting funding from local banks. Vij turned to an online service, Biz2Credit.com, which was able to find a bank in Salt Lake City that was willing to give his business an SBA-guaranteed loan for $3.9 million to purchase a banquet hall and equipment.[62] ■

Although borrowed capital allows entrepreneurs to maintain complete ownership of their businesses, it must be carried as a liability on the balance sheet as well as be repaid with interest at some point in the future. In addition, because small businesses are considered to be greater risks than bigger corporate customers, they must pay higher interest rates because of the risk–return trade-off—the higher the risk, the greater is the return demanded. Most small firms pay well above the **prime rate**, the interest rate that banks charge their most creditworthy customers. A study by David Walker, a professor at Georgetown University, reports that small businesses pay two to three times the prime rate, primarily because they rely heavily on credit cards and other high-cost methods of debt financing.[63] Still, the cost of debt financing often is lower than that of equity financing. Because of the higher risks associated with providing equity capital to small companies, investors demand greater returns than lenders. In addition, unlike equity financing, debt financing does not require an entrepreneur to dilute his or her ownership interest in the company.

Entrepreneurs seeking debt capital are quickly confronted with an astounding range of credit options varying greatly in complexity, availability, and flexibility. Not all of these sources of debt capital are equally favorable, however. By understanding the various sources of debt capital and their characteristics, entrepreneurs can greatly increase the chances of obtaining a loan.

Figure 13.7 shows the financing strategies that existing small businesses use. We now turn to the various sources of debt capital.

LO4

Describe the various sources of debt capital.

prime rate
the interest rate that banks charge their most creditworthy customers.

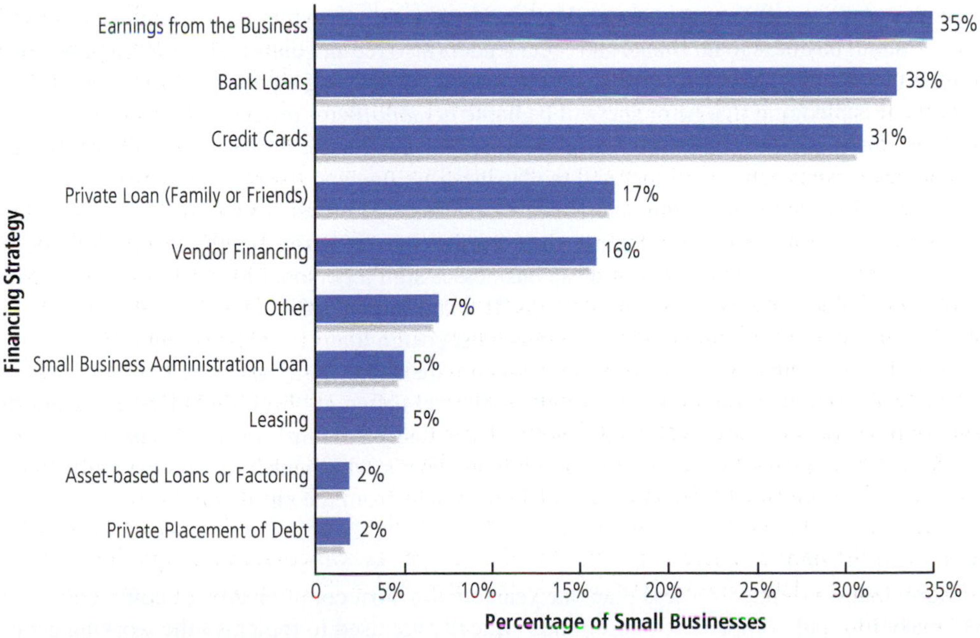

FIGURE 13.7

Small Business Financing Strategies

Source: National Small Business Association, 2013 Mid-Year Report, p.11.

Commercial Banks

Commercial banks are the very heart of the financial market for small businesses, providing the greatest number and variety of loans to small companies. Currently, outstanding small business bank loans total $587.8 billion.[64] For small business owners, banks are lenders of *first* resort. The average microbusiness bank loan (those less than $100,000) is $6,377, and the average small business bank loan (those between $100,000 and $1 million) is $240,428.[65]

Banks tend to be conservative in their lending practices and prefer to make loans to established small businesses rather than to high-risk start-ups. Unfortunately for entrepreneurs, turbulence in the financial markets has caused banks to tighten their lending standards, making it more difficult for small businesses, even established ones, to qualify for loans.

ENTREPRENEURIAL PROFILE: Jeff Goldstein: AcuPOLL Research Even though Jeff Goldstein had a successful track record as a corporate brand manager and consultant, he had a difficult time finding a bank that would lend him the money to buy an existing market research company called AcuPOLL Research. Ten banks turned him down, even though he was seeking a loan with a 75% guarantee from the U.S. Small Business Administration. Eventually, Goldstein was able to find a bank that would fund his purchase of AcuPOLL Research.[66] ■

Because start-up companies are so risky, bankers prefer to make loans to existing businesses with successful track records. They are concerned with a firm's operating past and will scrutinize its financial reports to project its position in the future. They also want proof of the stability of the company's sales and its ability to generate adequate cash flow to repay the loan. If they do make loans to a start-up venture, banks like to see sufficient cash flow to repay the loan, ample collateral to secure it, or an SBA guarantee to insure it. Small banks are more likely than large banks to extend loans to small businesses. Small banks also tend to be "small business friendly" and are more likely than their larger counterparts to customize the terms of their loans to the particular needs of small businesses, offering, for example, flexible payment terms to match the seasonal pattern of a company's cash flow or interest-only payments until a piece of equipment begins generating revenue. Small and midsize banks approve 45 percent of small business loan requests, but large banks approve only 10 percent of loan requests from small companies.[67]

When evaluating a loan application, especially for a business start-up, banks focus on a company's capacity to create positive cash flow because they know that is where the money to repay their loans will come from. The ability of the business to comfortably repay the loan, both interest and principal, is the first source of payment bankers want to see. The first question in most bankers' minds when reviewing an entrepreneur's business plan is, "Can this business generate sufficient cash to repay the loan?"

Bankers look to business owners as the second source of repayment if a company is not able to repay a small business loan. Banks and other lenders also require entrepreneurs to sign personal guarantees for any loan they make to small businesses. By making a personal loan guarantee, an entrepreneur is pledging that he or she will be liable *personally* for repaying the loan in the event that the business itself cannot repay the loan. Recall from Chapter 6 that in the eyes of the law, a sole proprietor or a general partner and the business are one and the same; therefore, for them, personal loan guarantees are redundant. However, because the owners of S corporations, corporations, and LLCs are separate from their businesses, they are not automatically responsible for the company's debts. Once the owners of these businesses sign a personal loan guarantee, however, they become liable for their companies' loans. It is as if these individuals have "cosigned" the loan with the business, not unlike many parents must cosign loans for their young adult children.

Even though bankers rely on collateral to secure their loans, the last thing banks want is for a borrower to default, forcing them to sell the collateral (often at "fire-sale" prices) and use the proceeds to pay off the loan. Therefore, collateral is actually the third source of repayment bankers look to for repayment of a small business loan. That's why bankers stress cash flow when analyzing a loan request and demand personal guarantees from the entrepreneurs.

Short-Term Loans

Short-term loans, extended for less than one year, are the most common type of commercial loan banks make to small companies. These funds typically are used to replenish the working capital account to finance the purchase of inventory, boost output, finance credit sales to customers, or take advantage of cash discounts. As a result, an entrepreneur repays the loan after converting inventory and receivables into cash. There are several types of short-term loans.

HOME EQUITY LOANS Many entrepreneurs use the equity that they have built in their homes to finance their business start-ups. Entrepreneurs borrow from themselves by pledging their homes as collateral for the loans they receive. However, declining real estate values in most parts of the country have reduced or wiped out the equity in many people's homes, making securing home equity loans for their businesses much more difficult. Brother and sister Russell and Julia Lundstrom funded their start-up Simple Smart Science, which produces cognitive and memory nutritional products, with a $125,000 home equity loan from a community bank.[68]

COMMERCIAL LOANS (OR "TRADITIONAL BANK LOANS") A basic short-term loan is the commercial bank's specialty. Business owners typically repay the loan, which often is unsecured because secured loans are much more expensive to administer and maintain, as a lump sum within three to six months. In other words, the bank grants a loan to a business owner without requiring him or her to pledge any specific collateral to support the loan in case of default. The owner repays the total amount of the loan at maturity. Sometimes the interest due on the loan is prepaid—deducted from the total amount borrowed. Until business owners can prove their companies' creditworthiness to the bank's satisfaction, they are not likely to qualify for unsecured commercial loans.

LINES OF CREDIT One of the most common requests entrepreneurs make of banks and commercial finance companies is to establish a commercial **line of credit**, a short-term loan with a preset limit that provides much-needed cash flow for day-to-day operations. A line of credit is ideal for helping business owners smooth out the uneven flow of cash that results from seasonal sales, funding inventory purchases, extending trade credit, and smoothing out fluctuations in a business's working capital. With a commercial line of credit, a business owner can borrow up to the predetermined ceiling at any time during the year by quickly and conveniently drawing down on the line of credit. Bankers often require a company to rest its line of credit during the year, maintaining a zero balance, as proof that the line of credit is not a perpetual crutch. Like commercial loans, lines of credit can be secured or unsecured but normally require a personal guarantee. In a recent NFIB survey, 54 percent of small business owners who applied for a new line of credit received one.[69]

line of credit
a short-term bank loan with a preset limit that provides working capital for day-to-day operations.

ENTREPRENEURIAL PROFILE: Jordan Drake When Jordan Drake was approved to open a State Farm Insurance agency in Hendersonville, Tennessee, he knew that he would need additional financing to supplement the personal savings he was using to start his new business. Drake was able to get a $25,000 line of credit through his local bank by securing the loan with his personal pickup truck. State Farm provided an additional $25,000 unsecured line of credit. Fortunately, through careful negotiation of his lease and prudent cash management, Drake was able to open the business without drawing on either line of credit. However, he says he sleeps easier knowing he has access to additional funding if his start-up hits any bumps in the road.[70] ■

FLOOR PLANNING Floor planning is a form of financing frequently employed by retailers of "big-ticket items" that are easily distinguishable from one another (usually by serial number), such as automobiles, boats, and major appliances. For example, a commercial bank finances Auto City's purchase of its inventory of automobiles and maintains a security interest in each car in the order by holding its title as collateral. Auto City pays interest on the loan monthly and repays the principal as it sells the cars. The longer a floor-planned item sits in inventory, the more it costs the business owner in interest expense. Banks and other floor planners often discourage retailers from using their money without authorization by performing spot checks to verify prompt repayment of the principal as items are sold.

Intermediate- and Long-Term Loans

Banks are primarily lenders of short-term capital to small businesses, although they will make intermediate- and long-term loans. Intermediate- and long-term loans, which are normally secured by collateral, are extended for one year or longer. Commercial banks grant these loans for constructing buildings, purchasing real estate and equipment, expanding a business, and other long-term investments. Matching the amount and the purpose of a loan to the appropriate type and length of loan is important. Loan repayments are normally made monthly or quarterly.

INSTALLMENT LOANS One of the most common types of intermediate-term loans is an installment loan, which banks make to small firms for purchasing equipment, facilities, real estate, and other fixed assets. When financing equipment, a bank usually lends the small business from 60 to 80 percent of the equipment's value in return for a security interest in the equipment. The loan's amortization schedule, which is based on a set number of monthly payments, typically coincides with the length of the equipment's usable life. In financing real estate (commercial mortgages), banks typically lend up to 75 to 80 percent of the property's value and allow a lengthier repayment schedule of 10 to 30 years.

 **Hands On . . . How To**

Get a Bank to Say "Yes" to Your Loan Application

Landing a loan to start or expand a small business is much more difficult today than in the past because of stodgy credit markets and upheaval in the banking and financial industries. Entrepreneurs often complain that bankers don't understand the financial needs they face when starting and operating their businesses. In many instances, however, business owners fail to help themselves when they apply for bank loans. Following are the seven most common reasons bankers reject small business loan applications—and how you can avoid them.

Reason 1. "Our bank doesn't make small business loans."

Cure: Select the right bank. Before applying for a bank loan, research banks to find out which ones actively seek the type of loan you need. Some banks don't make loans of less than $500,000, whereas others focus almost exclusively on small company loans. The SBA's reports *Micro-Business-Friendly Banks in the United States* and *Small Business Lending in the United States* are valuable resources for locating the banks in your area that are most likely to make small business loans. Small, local banks tend to be more receptive to small business loan requests than many large banks, which often rely on formulas and templates to make lending decisions. Other factors that influence the types of loans that banks make include the industry in which the company competes, the company's geographic location, and the length of time it has been in business. Establishing a relationship with a bank before you need a loan also increases the probability that your loan request will be successful. Once you find the right bank for your business, open an account there, seek a small line of credit, and repay it consistently.

Reason 2. "I don't know enough about you or your business."

Cure: Although a business plan that explains what your company does (or will do) is a good first step, develop a personal relationship with the banker so he or she gets to know you better and hears about your business from your perspective. If you already have a physical location for your business, try to get the banker to meet with you there. If not,

try to find a neutral location that gets the banker out of his or her office. Make sure you have your "elevator pitch" honed, as it creates the first impression of you and your business. You should be able to describe your business—what it does, sells, or makes and its competitive edge—in just one or two minutes. Your business plan should address why there is an opportunity in the market, your company's major competition, what it will take to succeed in the market, and how your business will gain a competitive advantage in the market. Keep your plan focused and concise. Do not fill it up with operational details. In addition, be prepared to supply multiple scenarios of your financial projections, business credit references, and a personal credit history.

Reason 3. "You haven't told me why you need the money."

Cure: A solid business plan with clear financial forecasts and budgets will explain how much money you need and how you plan to use it. Make sure your request is specific; avoid requests for loans "for working capital." Don't make the mistake of answering the question "How much money do you need?" with "How much will you lend me?" Also, don't just throw out a rough number without any rationale or justification. If a banker thinks you are just guessing on your financing needs, the conversation will be over immediately. Instead, know how much money you need and be able to explain how the money will benefit your business and get it profitable enough to easily repay the loan. Remember that bankers want to make loans (after all, that's how they generate a profit), but they want to make loans only to those people they believe will repay them. Their primary responsibility is to protect the money that all of us entrust with them in our checking and savings accounts.

Reason 4. "Your numbers don't support your loan request."

Cure: Include a cash flow forecast in your business plan. Bankers analyze a company's balance sheet and income statement to judge the quality of its assets and its profitability, but they lend primarily on the basis of cash flow. "Can you repay the loan

Hands On . . . How To (continued)

balance?" is the question that most concerns bankers, and they know that repaying a loan requires adequate cash flow. Collateral that backs up the loan is their last form of repayment, so do not stress collateral in your presentation—stress cash flow! If your business does not generate adequate cash flow, don't expect to get a loan. Prove to the banker that you understand your company's cash flow and how to manage it properly.

As a measure of a company's ability to repay a loan, bankers calculate the company's *cash coverage ratio*, which is its net income plus its noncash expenses (such as depreciation and amortization) divided by the annual payments on the proposed loan. They want to see a cash coverage ratio of at least 1.5:1 before granting a loan. In other words, to support $100,000 of loan payments, a company should have net cash flow of at least $150,000.

Reason 5. "You don't have enough collateral."

Cure: Be prepared to pledge your company's assets—and your personal assets—as collateral for the loan. If a company's cash flow declines to the point that it cannot make loan payments, banks look for other ways to get their money back. To protect themselves in a worst-case scenario (a business that is unable to repay a loan), bankers want the security of collateral before they make a loan. They will look to your personal assets first through your personal guarantee. They also expect more than $1 in collateral for every $1 of money they lend a business. Banks typically lend 50 to 90 percent of the value of real estate, 50 to 80 percent of the value of accounts receivable, and just 10 to 50 percent of the value of inventory and equipment pledged as collateral.

Reason 6. "Your business does not support the loan on its own."

Cure: Be prepared to provide a personal guarantee on the loan. This is a given for most small business loans until the company has a history of strong financial performance. By giving a personal guarantee, you're telling the banker that if your business cannot repay the loan, you will. Many bankers see their small business clients and their companies as one and the same. Even if you choose a form of ownership that provides you with limited personal liability, bankers will ask you to override

that protection by personally guaranteeing the loan. Another way to lower the risk of a bank extending a loan to a small company is to secure a loan guarantee through one of the SBA's programs.

Reason 7: "You don't have enough 'skin' in the game."

Cure: Increase the amount of money you have invested in the project. A few years ago, entrepreneurs were able to get loans for projects by investing as little as 5 to 10 percent of the total amount. Today, depending on the project, bankers expect entrepreneurs to put up at least 20 to 25 percent of the project's cost—and sometimes much more. Be prepared to use your company's retained earnings to pay for a significant portion of the cost of a project.

David Pitts, owner of Classic Graphics, a printing company in Charlotte, North Carolina, knows firsthand how the small business lending environment has changed. In the company's 30-year history, Pitts has relied on many bank loans to finance the company's growth. Recently, however, securing bank loans has been much more difficult despite Classic Graphics' rapid growth (from $39 million in sales to $50 million in sales in just one year) and strong financial performance. Securing several loans that ranged from $200,000 to more than $1 million became much more difficult than in the past, says Pitts. Although Pitts took realistic financial projections and a strong business plan to banks, several bankers rejected his loan requests for Classic Graphics.

There's no magic to getting a bank to approve your loan request. The secret is proper preparation and building a solid business plan that helps explain your business model and builds your credibility with the banker as a reliable business owner.

Sources: Based on "Five Tips to Increase Your Chances of Getting a Small Business Bank Loan," American Bankers Association, March 25, 2013, www.aba.com/press/pages/032513TipsForSmallBankLoan.aspx; Marla Tabaka, "4 Tips for Getting a Business Loan," *Inc.*, January 21. 2013, www.inc.com/marla-tabaka/4-ways-to-get-a-business-loan.html; Kirsten Valle Pittman, "Small Businesses Ready for Recovery, Lenders Aren't," *MCT/Joplin Globe*, July 18, 2011, http://www.joplinglobe.com/dailybusiness/x357284366/Small businesses-ready-for-recovery-but-their-lenders-aren-t; Emily Maltby, "How to Land a Bank Loan, *CNNMoney*, September 17, 2008, http://money.cnn.com/2008/09/16/smallbusiness/land_a_bank_loan.smb/index.htm; Jim Melloan, "Do Not Say 'I Just Want the Money,'" *Inc.*, July 2005, p. 96; Crystal Detamore-Rodman, "Raising Money: Loan Packaging Help," *Entrepreneur*, October 2008, p. 56; and Kate Lister, "The Numbers That Matter," *Entrepreneur*, November 2010, pp. 98–99.

TERM LOANS Another common type of loan banks make to small businesses is a **term loan.** Typically unsecured, banks grant these loans to businesses whose past operating history suggests a high probability of repayment. Some banks make only secured term loans, however. Term loans impose restrictions (called *covenants*) on the business decisions an entrepreneur makes concerning the company's operations. For instance, a term loan may set limits on owners' salaries, prohibit further borrowing without the bank's approval, or require maintaining certain financial ratios (recall the discussion of ratio analysis in Chapter 11).

The accompanying "Hands On . . . How To" feature describes the seven most common reasons bankers reject small business loan applications and how to avoid them.

term loan
a bank loan that imposes restrictions (covenants) on the business decisions an entrepreneur makes concerning the company's operations.

LO5

Describe the various loan programs available from the Small Business Administration.

The Small Business Administration (SBA) Loan Guarantee Programs

The SBA works with local lenders (both bank and nonbank) to offer many other loan programs that are designed to help entrepreneurs who cannot get capital from traditional sources gain access to the financing they need to launch and grow their businesses. When they were just small companies, Callaway Golf, Outback Steakhouse, and Intel Corporation borrowed through the SBA's loan programs. The SBA has several programs designed to help finance both start-up and existing small companies that cannot qualify for traditional loans because of their thin asset base and their higher risk of failure. The SBA guarantees more than 52,000 small business loans totaling more than $19 billion each year, which enable many entrepreneurs to get the financing they need for start-up or for growth. In the wake of the upheaval in the financial markets, banks have tightened their lending standards, and many small businesses cannot qualify for loans.

SBA loan programs are aimed at entrepreneurs who do not meet lending standards at conventional lending institutions. About 30 percent of SBA-backed loans go to start-up companies.[71] The SBA does *not* actually lend money to entrepreneurs directly; instead, entrepreneurs borrow money from a traditional lender, and the SBA guarantees repayment of a percentage of the loan (at least 50 percent and sometimes as much as 85 percent) in case the borrower defaults. The loan application process can take from three days to several months, depending on how well prepared the entrepreneur is and which bank or lender is involved.

Qualifying for an SBA loan guarantee requires cooperation among the entrepreneur, the participating lender, and the SBA. The participating lender determines the loan's terms and sets the interest rate within SBA limits. Contrary to popular belief, SBA-guaranteed loans do *not* carry special deals on interest rates. The average interest rate on SBA-guaranteed loans is prime-plus-2 percent (compared to prime-plus-1 percent on conventional bank loans).

The average duration of an SBA loan is 12 years—far longer than the average commercial small business loan. In fact, longer loan terms are a distinct advantage of SBA loans. At least half of all bank business loans are for less than one year. By contrast, SBA real estate loans can extend for up to 25 years (compared to just 10 to 15 years for a conventional loan), and working capital loans have maturities of seven years (compared with two to five years at most banks). These longer terms translate into lower loan payments, which are better suited for young, fast-growing, cash-strapped companies.

Because SBA-guaranteed loans are riskier, their default rate is higher than that of standard bank loans. Because the SBA assumes most of the credit risk, lenders are more willing to consider riskier deals that they normally would refuse. With the SBA's guarantee, borrowers also have to come up with less collateral than with a traditional bank loan.

The SBA offers several loan programs, which are summarized in the following sections. Table 13.1 displays a summary of the most popular SBA loan programs.

7(a) loan guaranty program

an SBA program in which loans made by private lenders to small businesses are guaranteed up to a ceiling by the SBA.

7(A) LOAN GUARANTY PROGRAM The **7(a) loan guaranty program** is the SBA's flagship loan program (see Figure 13.8 on page 509). More than 3,500 private lenders in the United States make SBA loans to small businesses, but the SBA guarantees them (85 percent of loans up to $150,000 and 75 percent of loans that range from $150,001 up to the loan cap of $3.75 million for 7(a) loans). The average 7(a) loan is $344,520.[72] A 7(a) loan is a term loan that business owners can use for expansion, renovation, new construction, purchasing land or buildings, purchasing equipment, working capital, a seasonal line of credit, inventory, or starting a business.

ENTREPRENEURIAL PROFILE: Dennis Clem: Clem's Service Station Dennis Clem learned about the business of running a service station from his father, and Clem is teaching his own son what he will need to know to run the family business some day. In 2010, Clem decided he would buy out his siblings who also had inherited a share in the business to allow him to pass the business on to his son when he was ready to retire. All of the siblings agreed because Dennis was the only family member who worked in the service station. The Clem family had never used credit to fund the growth of the business. Each new expansion was funded by the company's retained earnings. However, buying out his siblings would require more cash than the business could generate. Clem was able to secure an SBA guaranteed loan through the 7(a) loan program from his local bank.[73] ■

You Be the Consultant

The Never-Ending Hunt for Financing

The Automobile Film Club of America

Ralph Lucci, owner of The Automobile Film Club of America in Stapleton, New York, operated a true niche market business. Lucci's business rented vintage and specialty cars for use in movies and television shows filmed in the New York City area. The Automobile Film Club of America had been operating since 1993. Although the business suffered in the aftermath of 9/11, it survived that setback, and Lucci was able to rebuild the company as film and television production returned to New York.

At its peak, the business grew to 14 full-time employees who helped support the more than 300 cars the company rented for film and television productions. However, over the next few years the business faced more challenges. The company lost the lease on the lot it used to store the cars, and Lucci could not find a lot large enough to keep his entire inventory, forcing him to sell off many of the cars. Revenues declined, and soon the business could support only him and his wife on the payroll. When hurricane Irene hit in 2011, the company took another financial hit due to damage to its property and lost business.

However, the worst was yet to come.

When hurricane Sandy hit in October 2012, the storm surge flooded his car lot and garage, completely submerging almost all of his cars in salt water. The cars and much of his equipment were a total loss. The building he used for offices and car maintenance also was severely damaged by the flooding. He estimated that the total loss was more than $400,000. The only insurance he carried on the business was for liability, so there was no coverage for his lost property.

Lucci, who is 60 years old, must decide whether he is willing to use his personal assets, including his home, as collateral and attempt to secure a business loan to restart his company.

Eatwhatever

Jacqui Rosshandler, an Australian ex-pat working for an interior design company in New York City, wanted to start a business and leave her corporate career. She had noticed that a popular breath-freshening product sold in Australia was not available in the United States. The product was a gel cap made from meat byproducts, but Rosshandler decided to make her product from organic peppermint oil and parsley seed oil. Much of the source of bad breath is in the stomach, not the mouth, so the gel caps

were very effective. However, she knew that American consumers were used to sucking on breath mints. She decided that she would package the gel cap with a breath mint, so consumers could suck on the mint after swallowing the gel cap. She would market her product as Eatwhatever.

Rosshandler outsourced product formulation and production to a contract manufacturer. She hired a packaging designer to create a package that displayed the product in a clear and attractive way. Eatwhatever is marketed as "2 Steps to Kissable Breath."

Although customers loved her product, she had a difficult time getting contracts with large retailers. She had success selling online and in specialty shops, but it was not enough to fund the growth of the company. Cash was tight. In fact, cash was so tight that she did not have enough to pay for marketing or for a new production run.

Rosshandler met Arthur T. Shorin, an angel investor and former CEO in the candy industry. Shorin liked the product and offered to invest $250,000, connect Rosshandler with people he knew in the industry, and give her a salary on top of the investment in the company. In return, he would take 75 percent ownership in the business. Rosshandler could earn back 15 percent of the company if revenues met certain targets. Although her friends urged her not to accept his terms, she was concerned that her business would not succeed unless it got the cash and connections Shorin offered her.

1. Which of the funding sources described in this chapter do you recommend that Ralph Lucci and Jacqui Rosshandler consider for financing their businesses? Which sources do you recommend they *not* use? Why?

2. What can entrepreneurs do to increase the probability that bankers will approve their loan requests?

3. Work with a team of your classmates to brainstorm ways these entrepreneurs could attract the capital they need for their businesses. What steps do you recommend they take before they approach the potential sources of funding you have identified?

Sources: Based on Suzanne Sataline, "Wiped Out by Sandy, and Owner Sizes Up the Risk in Starting Over," *New York Times*, February 7, 2013, p. B6; "What is Eatwhatever?," Eatwhatever, n.d., www.eatwhatever.com/what/what-is-eatwhatever/; John Grossman, "Help for a Startup, but at a High Price," *New York Times*, January 3, 2103, p. B8.

SECTION 504 CERTIFIED DEVELOPMENT COMPANY PROGRAM The second most popular SBA loan program is the Section 504 program, which is designed to encourage small businesses to purchase fixed assets, expand their facilities, and create jobs. Section 504 loans provide long-term, fixed-asset financing to small companies to purchase land, buildings, or equipment— "brick-and-mortar" loans. Three lenders play a role in every 504 loan: a bank, the SBA, and a

TABLE 13.1 SBA Loan Program Overview

Program	Maximum Loan Amount	Guaranty Percentage	Use of Proceeds	Loan Maturity	Maximum Interest Rates
Standard 7(a)	$5 million	85% on loans up to $150,000; 75 percent on loans greater than $151,000 (up to $3.75 million maximum)	Term Loan. Expansion/renovation; new construction, purchase land or buildings; purchase equipment, fixtures, lease-hold improvements; working capital; refinance debt for compelling reasons; seasonal line of credit, inventory or starting a business	Depends on ability to repay. Generally, working capital, machinery & equipment is 5–10 years; real estate is 25 years.	Loans less than 7 years: $0–$25,000 Prime + 4.25%; $25,001–$50,000 Prime + 3.25%; more than $50,000 Prime + 2.25%. Loans 7 years or longer: 0–$25,000 Prime + 4.75%; $25,001 - $50,000 P + 3.75%; more than $50,000 Prime + 2.75%
SBAExpress	$350,000	50%	Revolving line of credit or term loan [same as 7(a)]	Up to 7 years for revolving line of credit; otherwise, same as 7(a)	Loans of $50,000 or less: prime + 6.5%; Loans of $50,001 to $350,000: prime + 4.5%
Export Express	$500,000	90% on loans of $350,000 or less; 75% on loans greater than $350,000	Same as SBA*Express* plus standby letter of credit	Same as SBA*Express*	Same as SBA*Express*
CAPLines	$5 million	Same as 7(a)	Seasonal and short-term working capital needs including advances for inventory and accounts receivables	Up to 10 years except Builders CAPLine, which is 5 years	Same as 7(a)
International Trade	$5 million	90%	Term loan for working capital, equipment, facilities, land and buildings and debt refinance related to international trade	Up to 25 years	Same as 7(a)
Community Advantage	$250,000	Same as 7(a)	Same as 7(a)	Same as 7(a)	Prime + 6%
Export Working Capital	$5 million	90%	Short-term working capital for exporting	Generally 1 year or less, may go up to 3 years maximum)	No cap
Section 504 through Community Development Corporation (CDC)	$5 to $5.5 million, depending on type of business	CDC: up to 40% Lender: 50% Equity: 10%	Long-term, fixed asset projects such as constructing new buildings, purchasing and renovating existing buildings, and purchasing equipment and machinery	Equipment—up to 10 years; real estate—up to 20 years	Fixed rate depends on when SBA's debenture-backed loan is sold
Microloan	$50,000	N/A	Purchase machinery and equipment, fixtures, leasehold improvements, financing receivables, or working capital. Cannot be used to repay existing debt.	Shortest term possible up to 6 years	7.75 or 8% above intermediary cost of funds

Source: "'Loan Program Quick Reference Guide," U.S. Small Business Administration, Washington, DC, http://www.sba.gov/sites/default/files/files/files/Loan%20Program%20Chart%20March%202014%20Baltimore%20March%202014_20140414.pdf.

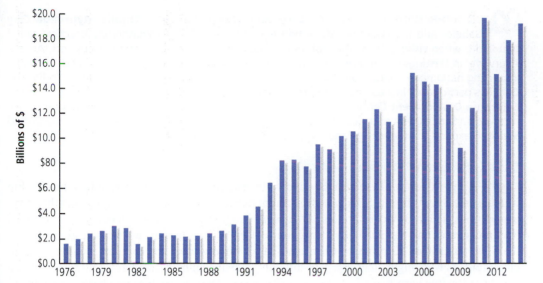

FIGURE 13.8

SBA 7(A) Guaranteed Loans

Source: SBA Guaranteed Loans, U.S. Small Business Administration, http://www .sba.gov/7a-loan-program.

certified development company (CDC), which is a nonprofit organization licensed by the SBA and designed to promote economic growth in local communities. Some 270 CDCs operate across the United States and make about 8,000 loans in a typical year. The entrepreneur is required to make a down payment of just 10 percent of the total project cost rather than the typical 20 to 30 percent traditional bank loans require. The CDC provides 40 percent at a long-term fixed rate, supported by an SBA loan guarantee in case the entrepreneur defaults. The bank provides long-term financing for the remaining 50 percent, also supported by an SBA guarantee. The major advantages of Section 504 loans are their fixed rates and terms, their 10- and 20-year maturities, and the low down payment required. The maximum loan amount that the SBA will guarantee is $5 million, and the average Section 504 loan is $714,000.[74]

certified development company (CDC)
a nonprofit organization licensed by the SBA and designed to promote growth in local communities by working with commercial banks and the SBA to make long-term loans to small businesses.

ENTREPRENEURIAL PROFILE: Joe and Joyce Spatafore: Cubby's Child Care Center
Due to its success in attracting an ever-expanding group of families, Cubby's Child Care Center, located in Bridgeport, West Virginia, needed a larger building. Joe and Joyce Spatafore, Cubby's owners, were able to find a location to construct a new 18,000 square foot building to house their growing business. The Spatafores used the SBA's 504 Certified Development Company loan program to help finance the project through their local bank. The new space allowed Cubby's to double its enrollment from 150 to 300 children. With the added capacity, Cubby's also increased employment by adding 15 new jobs.[75] ■

MICROLOAN PROGRAM About three-fourths of all entrepreneurs need less than $100,000 to launch their businesses. Indeed, most entrepreneurs require less than $50,000 to start their companies. Unfortunately, loans of that amount can be the most difficult to get. Lending these relatively small amounts to entrepreneurs starting businesses is the purpose of the SBA's Microloan Program. Called **microloans** because they range from just $100 to as much as $50,000, these loans have helped thousands of people take their first steps toward entrepreneurship. Banks typically shun loans in such small amounts because they consider them to be risky and unprofitable. In an attempt to fill the void in small loans to start-up companies, the SBA launched the microloan program in 1992, and it has gone on to become the single largest source of funding for microenterprises. Today, nearly 180 authorized lenders make SBA-backed microloans. The average size of a microloan is $13,000, with a maturity of three years (the maximum term is six years) and maximum interest rates that typically are between 8 and 13 percent. Microloans do not carry SBA guarantees, but lenders' standards are less demanding than those on conventional loans. In fact, 37 percent of all microloans go to business start-ups, and more than half of all microloans go to women- and minority-owned businesses.[76] A recent survey found that 54 percent of all start-up microbusiness owners rely on another job as their main source of income.[77] All microloans are made through nonprofit intermediaries that are approved by the SBA. Entrepreneurs can find a listing of microloan intermediaries at the SBA's Web site.

microloans
loans made through an SBA program aimed at entrepreneurs who can borrow amounts of money as small as $100 up to a maximum of $50,000.

ENTREPRENEURIAL PROFILE: Cary and Meryl Gabeler: Anjolie Ayurveda Cary Gabeler and her daughter Meryl had learned the holistic aromatherapy practice, called Ayurvedic, when visiting India. The mother and daughter partners opened their business, Anjolie Ayurveda, in Hastings-On-Hudson, New York, to bring Ayurvedic therapy to the United States by importing handmade skincare products from a women-owned and -operated facility in India. The Gabelers participated in a 60-hour entrepreneurship education program sponsored by the Women's Enterprise Development Center in White Plains, New York. After completing the program, they received an $18,000 SBA microloan to launch a new line of Ayurvedic perfumes made in the United States to expand their inventory and increase their product line.[78] ■

Other SBA Loan Programs

SBA*EXPRESS* PROGRAM To reduce the paperwork requirements and processing time involved in its loans, the SBA offers its SBA*Express* program that gives entrepreneurs responses to their loan applications within 36 hours. In the *SBAExpress* Program, participating lenders use their own loan procedures and applications to make loans of up to $350,000 to small businesses. Because the SBA guarantees 50 percent of the loan, banks often are willing to make smaller loans to entrepreneurs who might otherwise have difficulty meeting lenders' standards. Entrepreneurs can use these flexible term loans for a variety of business purposes, such as purchasing equipment, fixtures, land, or buildings; renovating existing structures or building new ones; buying inventory; and obtaining a seasonal line of credit. Loan maturities on *SBAExpress* loans typically are between 5 and 10 years, but loan maturities for fixed assets can be up to 25 years.

SMALL LOAN ADVANTAGE AND COMMUNITY ADVANTAGE LOAN PROGRAMS In 2011, the SBA introduced two new loan programs, the Small Loan Advantage and the Community Advantage programs. The Small Loan Advantage program is designed to encourage existing, experienced SBA lenders, known as preferred lenders, to make smaller loans, which are most likely to benefit disadvantaged borrowers. The Community Advantage Loan program encourages new lenders that operate in economically challenged communities that have had little or no access to SBA loans to enter the SBA's 7(a) loan program. Both programs include SBA guarantees of 85 percent on loans up to $150,000 and 75 percent on loans between $150,001 and the ceiling of $250,000 and use a streamlined application process.

THE CAPLINE PROGRAM In addition to its basic 7(a) loan guarantee program (through which the SBA makes about 75 percent of its loans), the SBA provides guarantees on small business loans for start-up, real estate, machinery and equipment, fixtures, working capital, exporting, and restructuring debt through several other methods. About two-thirds of all of the SBA's loan guarantees are for machinery and equipment or working capital. The **CAPLine Program** offers short-term capital to growing companies seeking to finance seasonal buildups in inventory or accounts receivable under five separate programs, each with maturities up to five years: seasonal line of credit (provides advances against inventory and accounts receivable to help businesses weather seasonal sales fluctuations), contract line of credit (finances the cost of direct labor and materials costs associated with performing contracts), builder's line of credit (helps small contractors and builders finance labor and materials costs), standard asset-based line of credit (an asset-based revolving line of credit for financing short-term needs), and small asset-based line of credit. CAPLine helps cash-hungry small businesses by giving them a credit line to draw on when they need it. A line of credit is what many small companies need most because they are flexible, efficient, and, unfortunately, quite difficult for small businesses to get from traditional lenders.

LOANS INVOLVING INTERNATIONAL TRADE For small businesses going global, the SBA has the **Export *Express* Program**, which, like its other express programs, offers quick turnaround times on applications for guarantees of 75 to 90 percent on loans up to $500,000 to help small companies develop or expand their export initiatives. Loan maturities range from 5 to 25 years.

The SBA also offers the **Export Working Capital (EWC) Program**, which is designed to provide working capital to small exporters. The SBA works in conjunction with the Export-Import Bank to administer this loan guarantee program. Applicants file a one-page loan application, and the response time normally is 10 days or less. The maximum loan is $5 million with a 90 percent guarantee, and proceeds must be used to finance small business exports.

CAPLine Program
an SBA program that makes short-term capital loans to growing companies seeking to finance seasonal build-ups in inventory or accounts receivable.

Export *Express* Program
an SBA loan program that offers quick turnaround times to small companies that are developing or expanding their export initiatives.

Export Working Capital (EWC) Program
an SBA loan program that is designed to provide working capital to small exporters.

ENTREPRENEURIAL PROFILE: Brenda Marrero Brenda Marrero launched her staffing business after being laid off by a large, multinational corporation. She grew Brenda Marrero & Associates into a leader in its industry. Marrero had started the business in Puerto Rico, but soon saw opportunity to expand the executive staffing business into other markets. The first new markets were the Dominican Republic and Peru. When Marrero wanted to expand into Costa Rica, Panama, Jamaica, Trinidad & Tobago, and Canada, she needed additional financing. Marrero was able to secure an Export Express SBA loan through her local bank in Puerto Rico.[79] ■

The **International Trade Program** is for small businesses that are engaging in international trade or are adversely affected by competition from imports. The SBA allows global entrepreneurs to combine loans from the Export Working Capital Program with those from International Trade Program for up to $5 million with a maximum guarantee of $4.5 million. Loan maturities range from 1 to 25 years.

DISASTER LOANS As their name implies, **disaster loans** are made to small businesses devastated by some kind of financial or physical losses from hurricanes, floods, earthquakes, tornadoes, and other natural disasters. The maximum disaster loan usually is $2 million, but Congress often raises that ceiling when circumstances warrant. Disaster loans carry below-market interest rates as low as 4 percent and terms as long as 30 years. Loans for physical damage above $14,000 require an entrepreneur to pledge some kind of collateral, usually a lien on the business property. In the aftermath of hurricane-force Santa Ana winds in California that damaged or destroyed many small businesses, the SBA approved disaster loans at just 4 percent interest to help entrepreneurs get their companies back up and running.[80]

Nonbank Sources of Debt Capital

Although they usually are the first stop for entrepreneurs in search of debt capital, banks are not the only lending game in town. We now turn our attention to other sources of debt capital that entrepreneurs can tap to feed their cash-hungry companies.

ASSET-BASED LENDERS Across the United States, nearly 3,400 asset-based lenders, which are usually smaller commercial banks, commercial finance companies, specialty lenders, or divisions of bank holding companies that allow small businesses to borrow money by pledging otherwise idle assets, such as accounts receivable, inventory, or purchase orders, as collateral. This method of financing works especially well for manufacturers, wholesalers, distributors, and other companies that have significant stocks of inventory or accounts receivable. Asset-based borrowing is an efficient method of borrowing because business owners borrow only the money they need when they need it. Even unprofitable companies whose financial statements cannot convince loan officers to make traditional loans often can get asset-based loans. These cash-poor but asset-rich companies can use normally unproductive assets—accounts receivable, inventory, and purchase orders—to finance rapid growth and the cash crises that often accompany it.

Like banks, asset-based lenders consider a company's cash flow, but they are more interested in the quality of the assets pledged as collateral. The amount a small business can borrow through asset-based lending depends on the **advance rate**, the percentage of an asset's value that a lender will lend. For example, a company pledging $100,000 of accounts receivable might negotiate a 70 percent advance rate and qualify for a $70,000 asset-based loan. Advance rates can vary dramatically depending on the quality of the assets pledged and the lender. Because inventory is an illiquid asset (i.e., hard to sell), the advance rate on inventory-based loans is quite low, usually 10 to 50 percent. A business pledging high-quality accounts receivable as collateral, however, may be able to negotiate up to an 85 percent advance rate. The most common types of asset-based financing are discounting accounts receivable, inventory financing, and purchase order financing.

Discounting Accounts Receivable The most common form of secured credit is accounts-receivable financing. Under this arrangement, a small business pledges its accounts receivable as collateral; in return, the lender advances a loan against the value of approved accounts receivable. The amount of the loan tendered is not equal to the face value of the accounts receivable, however. Even though the lender screens the firm's accounts and accepts only qualified receivables, it makes an allowance for the risk involved because it will have to write off some of them as uncollectible.

International Trade Program
an SBA loan program for small businesses that are engaging in international trade or are adversely affected by competition from imports.

disaster loans
an SBA loan program that makes loans to small businesses devastated by some kind of financial or physical loss.

advance rate
the percentage of an asset's value that a lender will lend.

A small business usually can borrow an amount equal to 55 to 85 percent of its receivables, depending on their quality. Generally, lenders do not accept receivables that are past due.

Inventory Financing With inventory financing, a small business loan is secured by its inventory of raw materials, work in process, and finished goods. If an owner defaults on the loan, the lender can claim the pledged inventory, sell it, and use the proceeds to satisfy the loan (assuming that the bank's claim is superior to the claims of other creditors). Because inventory usually is not a highly liquid asset and its value can be difficult to determine, lenders are willing to lend only a portion of its worth, usually no more than 50 percent of the inventory's value. Most asset-based lenders avoid inventory-only deals; they prefer to make loans backed by inventory *and* more secure accounts receivable. The key to qualifying for inventory financing is proving that a company has a plan or a process in place to ensure that the inventory securing the loan sells quickly. To ensure the quality of the assets supporting the loans they make, lenders must monitor borrowers' assets, a task that increases the paperwork requirements on these loans.

Purchase Order Financing Small companies that receive orders from large customers can use those purchase orders as collateral for loans. The customer places an order with a small business, which needs financing to fill the order. The small company pledges the future payment from the customer as security for the loan, and the lender verifies the credit rating of the customer (not the small business) before granting the short-term loan, which often carries interest rates of 40 percent or more. Borrowers usually repay the loan within 60 days.

Asset-based loans are more expensive than traditional bank loans because of the cost of originating and maintaining them and the higher risk they involve. Rates usually run from 2 to 7 percent (or more) above the prime rate. Because of this rate differential, small business owners should not use asset-based loans for long-term financing; their goal should be to establish their credit through asset-based financing and then to move up to a line of credit.

VENDOR FINANCING Many small companies borrow money from their vendors and suppliers in the form of trade credit. Because of its ready availability, trade credit is an extremely important source of financing to most entrepreneurs. When banks refuse to lend money to a start-up business because they see it as a high credit risk, an entrepreneur may be able to turn to trade credit for capital. Getting vendors to extend credit in the form of delayed payments (e.g., "net 30" credit terms) usually is much easier for small businesses than obtaining bank financing. Essentially, a company receiving trade credit from a supplier is getting a short-term, interest-free loan for the amount of the goods purchased. Vendors and suppliers often are willing to finance a small business's purchases of goods from 30 to 60 days (sometimes longer), interest free.

EQUIPMENT SUPPLIERS Most equipment vendors encourage business owners to purchase their equipment by offering to finance the purchase. This method of financing is similar to trade credit but with slightly different terms. Equipment vendors offer reasonable credit terms with only a modest down payment, with the balance financed over the life of the equipment (often several years). In some cases, the vendor will repurchase equipment for salvage value at the end of its useful life and offer the business owner another credit agreement on new equipment. Start-up companies often use trade credit from equipment suppliers to purchase equipment and fixtures such as display cases, refrigeration units, and machinery. It pays to scrutinize vendors' credit terms, however, because they may be less attractive than those of other lenders.

COMMERCIAL FINANCE COMPANIES When denied bank loans, small business owners often look to commercial finance companies for the same types of loans. Commercial finance companies are second only to banks in making loans to small businesses, and, unlike their conservative counterparts, they are willing to tolerate more risk in their loan portfolios. Of course, their primary consideration is collecting their loans, but finance companies tend to rely more on obtaining a security interest in some type of collateral, given the higher-risk loans that make up their portfolios. Because commercial finance companies depend on collateral to recover most of their losses, they are able to make loans to small companies with irregular cash flows or to those that are not yet profitable.

Approximately 150 large commercial finance companies, such as AT&T Small Business Lending, GE Capital Small Business Finance, and others, make a variety of loans to small companies, ranging from asset-based loans and business leases to construction and SBA loans. Dubbed "the

Wal-Marts of finance," commercial finance companies usually offer many of the same credit options as commercial banks do. Because their loans are subject to more risks, finance companies charge a higher interest rate than commercial banks. Their most common methods of providing credit to small businesses are asset based—accounts-receivable financing and inventory loans. Rates on these loans vary but can be as high as 15 to 30 percent (including fees), depending on the risk a particular business presents and the quality of the assets involved. Because many of the loans they make are secured by collateral (if not accounts receivable or inventory, then the business equipment, vehicles, real estate, or inventory purchased with the loan), finance companies often impose more onerous reporting requirements, sometimes requiring weekly (or even daily) information on a small company's inventory levels or accounts-receivable balances. However, entrepreneurs who cannot secure financing from traditional lenders because of their short track records, less-than-perfect credit ratings, or fluctuating earnings often find the loans they need at commercial finance companies.

SAVINGS-AND-LOAN ASSOCIATIONS Savings-and-loan associations specialize in loans for real property. In addition to their traditional role of providing mortgages for personal residences, savings-and-loan associations offer financing on commercial and industrial property. In the typical commercial or industrial loan, the savings-and-loan association will lend up to 80 percent of the property's value with a repayment schedule of up to 30 years. Most savings-and-loan associations hesitate to lend money for buildings specially designed for a particular customer's needs. They expect the mortgage to be repaid from the company's future earnings.

STOCKBROKERS Stockbrokers also make loans, and many of the loans they make to their customers carry lower interest rates than those from banks. These **margin loans** carry lower rates because the collateral supporting them—the stocks and bonds in the customer's portfolio—is of high quality and is highly liquid. Moreover, brokerage firms make it easy to borrow. Brokers often set up a line of credit for their customers when they open a brokerage account. To tap that line of credit, the customer simply writes a check or uses a debit card. Typically, there is no fixed repayment schedule for a margin loan; the debt can remain outstanding indefinitely as long as the market value of the borrower's portfolio of collateral meets minimum requirements. Aspiring entrepreneurs can borrow up to 50 percent of the value of their stock portfolios, up to 70 percent of their bond portfolios, and up to 90 percent of the value of their government securities.

There is risk involved in using stocks and bonds as collateral on a loan. Brokers typically require a 30 percent cushion on margin loans. If the value of the borrower's portfolio drops, the broker can make a **margin (maintenance) call**; that is, the broker can call the loan and require the borrower to provide more cash and securities as collateral. Recent swings in the stock market have translated into margin calls for many entrepreneurs, requiring them to repay a significant portion of their loan balances within a matter of days—or hours. If an account lacks adequate collateral, the broker can sell off the customer's portfolio to pay off the loan.

CREDIT UNIONS **Credit unions**, nonprofit financial cooperatives that promote saving and provide loans to their members, are best known for making consumer and car loans. However, many are also willing to lend money to their members to launch and operate businesses. More than 6,500 state-and federally-chartered credit unions with 99 million members operate in the United States, and they make loans to their members totaling more than $684 billion per year.[81] Credit unions make nearly $38 billion in small business loans to their members each year, and at 43.6 percent, the approval rates at credit unions for small business loan requests are higher than those at large banks (18.6 percent) but lower than those at small banks (51.6 percent).[82] Not every credit union makes business loans (about 30 percent of credit unions do), and credit unions don't make loans to just anyone. To qualify for a loan, an entrepreneur must be a member. Lending practices at credit unions are very much like those at banks, but credit unions usually are willing to make smaller loans. Federal law currently limits a credit union's loans to businesses to 12.25 percent of the credit union's assets. The SBA also recently opened its 7(a) loan program to credit unions, providing yet another avenue for entrepreneurs in search of financing. Because banks have tightened their lending requirements, many entrepreneurs are turning to credit unions for start-up and operating business loans.

margin loans
loans from a stockbroker that use the stocks and bonds in the borrower's portfolio as collateral.

margin (maintenance) call
occurs when the value of a borrower's portfolio drops and the broker calls the loan in, requiring the borrower to put up more cash and securities as collateral.

credit unions
a nonprofit financial cooperative that promotes saving and provides loans to its members.

ENTREPRENEURIAL PROFILE: Muhammad Abdullah: Legacy Business Group After his company experienced a sales decline during a recent recession, Muhammad Abdullah, owner of Legacy Business Group, a safety and medical supply company in Des Moines, Iowa, landed several large orders from customers and needed a line of credit to support the company's cash flow while he filled them. After several banks refused his loan requests, Abdullah turned to Veridian Credit Union, which provided Legacy Business Group with a $25,000 line of credit that allows him to take orders that otherwise he would have to refuse.[83] ■

Entrepreneurs in search of a credit union near them can use the online database at the Credit Union National Association's Web site.

PRIVATE PLACEMENTS Private placements are also available for both equity and debt instruments. A private placement involves selling debt to one or a small number of investors, usually insurance companies or pension funds. Private placement debt is a hybrid between a conventional loan and a bond. At its heart, it is a bond, but its terms are tailored to the borrower's individual needs as a loan would be.

In addition to making equity investments in small companies, venture capital firms also provide venture debt financing, often in private placements. Interest rates on venture debt typically vary from prime-plus-1-percent to prime-plus-5-percent, and the loan terms range from 24 to 48 months. Venture debt deals often include warrants, which give the venture capital firm the right to purchase shares of stock in a company at a fixed price. Venture debt financing is a hybrid between a loan and venture capital. Most venture loans also come with covenants, requirements that a company must meet or incur a penalty, such as paying a higher interest rate or giving up more stock.

Small Business Investment Companies (SBICs)

privately owned financial institutions that are licensed by the SBA and use a combination of private capital and federally guaranteed debt to provide long-term venture capital to small businesses.

SMALL BUSINESS INVESTMENT COMPANIES **Small Business Investment Companies (SBICs),** created in 1958 when Congress passed the Small Business Investment Act, are privately owned financial institutions that are licensed and regulated by the SBA. The 292 SBICs operating in the United States use a combination of private capital and federally guaranteed debt to provide growing small businesses with long-term venture capital. Like their venture capital counterparts, most SBICs prefer later-round financing over funding start-ups; about 20 percent of SBIC investments go to start-up businesses.[84] Funding from SBICs helped launch companies such as Costco, Apple, Intel, Gymboree, Cutter and Buck, Build-a-Bear Workshop, Federal Express, Staples, Sun Microsystems, and Callaway Golf.

Since 1958, SBICs have provided more than $60 billion in long-term debt and equity financing to some 107,000 small businesses, adding hundreds of thousands of jobs to the U.S. economy.[85] SBICs must be capitalized privately with a minimum of $5 million, at which point they qualify for up to $3 (but most often $2) in long-term SBA loans for every $1 of private capital invested in small businesses up to a maximum of $150 million. As a general rule, SBICs may provide financial assistance only to small businesses with a net worth of less than $18 million and average after-tax earnings of $6 million during their last two years. However, employment and total annual sales standards vary from industry to industry. SBICs are limited to a maximum investment or loan amount of 20 percent of their private capital to a single client.

SBICs provide both debt and equity financing to small businesses. Most SBIC financing is in the much-needed range of $250,000 to $5 million, and the average investment is $1.55 million, far below the average investment by venture capital firms of $7.4 million.[86] When they make equity investments, SBICs are prohibited from obtaining a controlling interest in the companies in which they invest (no more than 49 percent ownership).

ENTREPRENEURIAL PROFILE: Rand Capital SBIC: Gemcor II, LLC Tom Speller, founder of Gemcor II, LLC, developed the automated riveting machine used worldwide by aircraft manufacturers during World War II. For decades, the company was a major player in the aircraft industry, but when the aircraft manufacturing industry went through a prolonged slump in the early 2000s, Gemcor received an investment from Rand Capital SBIC, Inc., to help reengineer its supply chain and implement a variable cost supply model. After Rand Capital SBIC's investment and the changes it helped fund, Gemcor's revenues grew from $8 million to $19 million seven years later. During that same period, the number of employees at Gemcor for doubled from 31 to 61.[87] ■

LO6
Identify the various federal and state loan programs aimed at small businesses.

Other Federal and State Programs

Federally sponsored lending programs have experienced budget fluctuations over the last several years, but some entrepreneurs have been able to acquire financing from the following programs.

Economic Development Administration

The Economic Development Administration (EDA), a branch of the Commerce Department, offers loan guarantees to create new businesses and to expand existing businesses in areas with below-average incomes and high unemployment rates. Focusing on economically distressed communities, the EDA often works with local governments to finance long-term investment projects needed to stimulate economic growth and to create jobs by making loan guarantees. The EDA guarantees loans up to 80 percent of business loans between $750,000 and $10 million. Entrepreneurs apply for loans through private lenders, for whom an EDA loan guarantee significantly reduces the risk of lending. Start-ups and existing businesses must make equity investments of at least 15 percent of the guaranteed amount. Small businesses can use the loan proceeds in a variety of ways, from supplementing working capital and purchasing equipment to buying land and renovating buildings.

EDA business loans are designed to help revitalize economically distressed areas by creating or expanding small businesses that provide employment opportunities in local communities. To qualify for a loan, a business must be located in a disadvantaged area, and its presence must directly benefit local residents. Some communities experiencing high unemployment or suffering from the effects of devastating natural disasters have received EDA Revolving Loan Fund Grants to create loan pools for local small businesses.

ENTREPRENEURIAL PROFILE: John and Colleen Pfeifer: VoWac Publishing With the help of a revolving credit loan from the EDA-funded Northeast Council of Governments Development Corporation in Aberdeen, South Dakota, John and Colleen Pfeifer purchased VoWac Publishing Company, which publishes phonics and spelling curriculum for public, private, and home schools. VoWac, based in Faulkton, South Dakota, serves more than 2,000 schools in 35 states as well as schools in Asia and Africa. The company has grown enough to employ four full-time employees.[88] ∎

Department of Housing and Urban Development

Although the Department of Housing and Urban Development (HUD) does not extend loans or grants directly to entrepreneurs for launching businesses, it does sponsor several programs that can help qualified entrepreneurs to raise the capital they need. Community Development Block Grants (CDBGs) are extended to cities and counties that, in turn, lend or grant money to entrepreneurs to start or expand small businesses, thereby strengthening the local economy. Grants are aimed at cities and towns that need revitalization and economic stimulation. Some grants are used to construct buildings and factories to be leased to entrepreneurs, sometimes with an option to buy. Others are earmarked for revitalizing a crime-ridden area or making start-up loans to entrepreneurs or expansion loans to existing business owners. No ceilings or geographic limitations are placed on CDBG loans and grants, but projects must benefit low- and moderate-income families.

ENTREPRENEURIAL PROFILE: Cheryl and Stephen Kraus: Upcountry Provisions Bakery & Bistro When Cheryl and Stephen Kraus were renovating a building in downtown Traveler's Rest, South Carolina, to house their retail bakery, the copreneurs received a $5,750 Façade Improvement Grant from a grant funded by HUD's CDBG program. The 1,664-square-foot building on Main Street that serves as the home for the Upcountry Provisions Bakery & Bistro once housed a drugstore but had stood vacant for 20 years. The Kraus's wanted a location with more foot traffic, which this grant allowed them to secure with the Main Street location.[89] ∎

HUD also makes loan guarantees through its Section 108 provision of the CBDG program. These loan guarantees allow a community to transform a portion of CDBG funds into federally guaranteed loans large enough to pursue economic revitalization projects that can lead to the renewal of entire towns.

U.S. Department of Agriculture's Business Programs and Loans

The U.S. Department of Agriculture provides financial assistance to certain small businesses through partnerships with the private sector and the community-based organizations. The various programs fund projects that create or preserve quality jobs and/or promote a clean rural environment in underserved rural communities. For example, through its Business and Industry Guaranteed Loan Program, the Rural Development Rural Business Services (RBS) will guarantee as much as 80 percent of a commercial lender's loan up to $5 million, 70 percent for loans between $5 million and $10 million, and 60 percent for loans in excess of $10 million. Entrepreneurs apply for loans through private lenders, who view applicants with loan guarantees much more favorably than those without guarantees. The guarantee reduces a lender's risk dramatically because the guarantee means that the government agency would pay off the loan balance (up to the ceiling) if the entrepreneur defaults on the loan.

ENTREPRENEURIAL PROFILE: La Rinascente Pasta La Rinascente Pasta, a small maker of pasta, was founded shortly after World War II in the Bronx, New York, but in 2003, a group of investors purchased the company with plans to relocate it to North Dakota. Working with the Hope Development Corporation and the Griggs-Steele Empowerment Zone in Hope, North Dakota, La Rinascente Pasta received a guarantee on a $1.2 million loan from the U.S. Department of Agriculture's Business and Industry Guaranteed Loan Program that allowed the company to purchase the machinery and equipment for its new pasta manufacturing plant.[90] ■

Small Business Innovation Research Program

Started as a pilot program by the National Science Foundation in the 1970s, the Small Business Innovation Research (SBIR) program has expanded to 11 federal agencies, ranging from NASA to the Department of Defense. The total SBIR budget across all 11 agencies is more than $2 billion annually. These agencies award cash grants or long-term contracts to small companies that want to initiate or to expand their R&D efforts. SBIR grants give innovative small companies the opportunity to attract early-stage capital investments *without* having to give up significant equity stakes or taking on burdensome levels of debt.

The SBIR process involves three phases. Phase I ("proof of concept") grants, which determine the feasibility and commercial potential of a technology or product, last for up to six months and have a ceiling of $150,000. Phase II ("prototype development") grants, designed to develop the concept into a specific technology or product, run for up to 24 months and have a ceiling of $1 million. Approximately one-third of all Phase II applicants receive funding. Phase III is the commercialization phase, in which the company pursues commercial applications of the R&D conducted in Phase I and Phase II and must use private or non-SBIR federal funding to bring a product to market.

Competition for SBIR funding is intense; only 17 percent of the small companies that apply for Phase I grants receive funding. So far, more than 135,000 SBIR awards totaling more than $34 billion (72 percent in Phase I and 28 percent in Phase II) have gone to small companies, which traditionally have had difficulty competing with big corporations for federal R&D dollars. The average grant, including Phase I and Phase II, is $342,000.[91] The government's dollars have been well invested. Nearly 45 percent of small businesses receiving Phase II SBIR awards have achieved commercial success with their products.[92]

Small Business Technology Transfer Program

The Small Business Technology Transfer Program (STTR) complements the SBIR program. Whereas the SBIR focuses on commercially promising ideas that originate in small businesses, the STTR helps companies to use the vast reservoir of commercially promising ideas that originate in universities, federally funded R&D centers, and nonprofit research institutions. Researchers at these institutions can join forces with small businesses and can spin off commercially promising ideas while remaining employed at their research institutions. Five federal agencies award grants of up to $750,000 in three phases to these research partnerships.

State and Local Loan Development Programs

Many states have created their own loan and economic development programs to provide funds for business start-ups and expansions. They have decided that their funds are better spent encouraging small business growth rather than "chasing smokestacks"—trying to entice large businesses to locate within their boundaries. These programs come in many forms, but they all tend to focus on developing small businesses that create the greatest number of jobs and economic benefits. Entrepreneurs who apply for state and local funding must have patience and be willing to slog through some paperwork, however.

Although each state's approach to economic development is somewhat special, one common element is some kind of small business financing program: loans, loan guarantees, development grants, venture capital pools, and others. One approach many states have had success with is **Capital Access Programs (CAPs)**. First introduced in Michigan in 1986, many states now offer CAPs that are designed to encourage lending institutions to make loans to businesses that do not qualify for traditional financing because of their higher risk. Under a CAP, a bank and a borrower each pay an upfront fee (a portion of the loan amount) into a loan-loss reserve fund at the participating bank, and the state matches this amount. The reserve fund, which normally ranges from 6 to 14 percent of the loan amount, acts as an insurance policy against the potential loss a bank might experience on a loan and frees the bank to make loans that it otherwise might refuse. One study of CAPs found that 55 percent of the entrepreneurs who received loans under a CAP would not have been granted loans without the backing of the program.[93]

Even cities and small towns have joined in the effort to develop small businesses and help them grow. Many communities across the United States operate **revolving loan funds** that combine private and public funds to make loans to small businesses, often at favorable interest rates, for the purpose of starting or expanding businesses that create jobs and contribute to economic development. As money is repaid into the funds, it is loaned back out to other entrepreneurs.

ENTREPRENEURIAL PROFILE: Oregon Business Development Fund: Krauss Craft, Inc. Krauss Craft, Inc., located in Merlin, Oregon, manufactures commercial playground equipment under the trademark Playcraft Systems and sells its products nationwide to cities, school districts, and park districts. Krauss Craft secured a $500,000 loan through the Oregon Business Development Fund (OBDF) to build a 30 ,000-square-foot building and to purchase two rotational molding machines and related equipment. Krauss Craft added 40 new jobs as a result of the expansion project.[94] ■

In addition to revolving loan funds, nearly 1,000 communities across the United States have created **community development financial institutions (CDFIs)** that designate at least some of their loan portfolios to supporting entrepreneurs and small businesses. CDFIs operate through a variety of institutions, including microenterprise loan funds, community development loan funds, and others to provide capital and credit to otherwise "unbankable" business owners and aspiring entrepreneurs in low-income communities across the United States. Because the loans that they make are higher risk, the interest rates that CDFIs charge are higher than those charged by traditional lenders.

ENTREPRENEURIAL PROFILE: Tina Ferguson-Riffe: Smoke Berkeley Tina Ferguson-Riffe had been unemployed for three years before she started her restaurant, Smoke Berkeley, in Berkeley, California. Ferguson-Riffe needed to buy new equipment to support the growth of her business. Unable to secure a traditional business loan, a program called the Opportunity Fund offered Tina a $20,000 EasyPay loan. Instead of making a fixed monthly payment, Smoke Berkeley repays its loan based on daily credit and debit card sales. Ferguson-Riffe says being able to pay the loan back based on sales helps when seasonal slowdowns occur during the rainy season.[95] ■

Other Methods of Financing

Small business owners do not have to rely solely on financial institutions and government agencies for capital; their businesses have the capacity to generate capital. Other common methods of financing, including factoring, leasing rather than purchasing equipment, and using credit cards, are available to almost every small business.

Factoring Accounts Receivable

Instead of carrying credit sales on its own books (some of which may never be collected), a small business can sell outright its accounts receivable to a factor. A **factor** buys a company's accounts receivable and pays for them in two parts. The first payment, which the factor makes immediately, is for 50 to 80 percent of the accounts' agreed-on (and usually discounted) value. The factor makes the second payment of 15 to 18 percent, which makes up the balance less the factor's service fees, when the original customer pays the invoice. High interest rates (often 36 percent or more) make factoring a more expensive type of financing than loans from either banks or commercial finance companies, but for businesses that cannot qualify for those loans, it may be the only choice. Factoring volume totals more than $101 billion per year.[96]

Capital Access Programs (CAPs)
a state lending program that encourages lending institutions to make loans to businesses that do not qualify for traditional financing because of their higher risk.

revolving loan funds
a program offered by communities that combine private and public funds to make loans to small businesses, often at below-market interest rates.

community development financial institutions (CDFIs)
community-based financial institutions that designate at least a portion of their loan portfolios to otherwise "unbankable" business owners and aspiring entrepreneurs.

LO7
Explain other methods of financing a business.

factor
a financial institution that buys business's accounts receivable at a discount.

Factoring deals are either with recourse or without recourse. Under deals arranged with recourse, a small business owner retains the responsibility for customers who fail to pay their accounts. The business owner must take back these uncollectible invoices. Under deals arranged without recourse, however, the owner is relieved of the responsibility for collecting them. If customers fail to pay their accounts, the factor bears the loss. Nearly 70 percent of factoring deals are without recourse.[97] Because the factor assumes the risk of collecting the accounts, it screens a company's credit customers, accepts those judged to be creditworthy, and advances the small business owner a portion of the value of the accounts receivable. Factors discount anywhere from 2 to 40 percent of the face value of a company's accounts receivable, depending on the following factors related to a small company:

- Customers' financial strength and credit ratings
- The industry and its customers' industries because some industries have a reputation for slow payments
- History and financial strength, especially in deals arranged with recourse
- Credit policies[98]

The discount rate on deals without recourse usually is higher than on those with recourse because of the higher level of risk they carry for the factor.

Although factoring is more expensive than traditional bank loans (a 2 percent discount from the face value of an invoice due in 30 days amounts to an annual interest rate of 24.8 percent), it is a source of quick cash and is ideally suited for fast-growing companies, especially start-ups that cannot qualify for bank loans. Small companies that sell to government agencies and large corporations, both famous for stretching out their payments for 60 to 90 days or more, also find factoring attractive because they collect the money from the sale (less the factor's discount) much faster.

Leasing

Leasing is another common bootstrap financing technique. Today, small businesses can lease virtually any kind of asset, including office space, telephones, computers, and heavy equipment. By leasing expensive assets, the small business owner is able to use them without locking in valuable capital for an extended period of time. In other words, entrepreneurs can reduce the long-term capital requirements of their businesses by leasing equipment and facilities and are not investing their capital in depreciating assets. In addition, because no down payment is required and because the cost of the asset is spread over a longer time (lowering monthly payments), a company's cash flow improves.

ROBS

Rollovers as Business Startups (ROBS)
a method of financing that allows entrepreneurs to use their retirement savings to fund their business start-ups.

Thousands of aspiring entrepreneurs, particularly Baby Boomers, are tapping into their retirement accounts to fund business start-ups or acquisitions of existing small businesses. Many of them are turning to **Rollovers as Business Startups (ROBS)** as a means of using their retirement savings to fund their businesses. By using a 401(k) rollover, entrepreneurs are able to move existing retirement funds into a start-up. The tax laws governing ROBS are complex, and if not set up properly, this form of funding can lead to significant penalties by the IRS. Recent IRS cases show increased scrutiny of these funding plans, so entrepreneurs should exercise extreme care when using a retirement account rollover to fund a business. Once established, ROBS require entrepreneurs to meet certain reporting and fiduciary responsibilities.[99]

Courtesy of Bohnne Jones

ENTREPRENEURIAL PROFILE: Bohnne Jones: Decorating Dens Interiors Bohnne Jones used $260,000 of the $340,000 she had in her retirement savings to purchase a Decorating Den franchise in Nashville, Tennessee. After several lean years caused by the recession, her business is now thriving. Jones says the paperwork to fund her business with a ROBS was quite complicated, and she has to be vigilant with ongoing reporting requirements. She is required to make monthly payments into her 401(k) to repay the loan from her retirement account. If Jones is ever late with a payment, which is due within seven days of each payroll, the IRS imposes a penalty.[100] ∎

Merchant Cash Advance

A **merchant cash advance** is used by small businesses to help finance working capital needs. The provider of the merchant cash advance prepurchases credit and debit card receivables at a discount. Each time a sale is made, a percentage of the card receivable is forwarded to the cash advance provider or purchaser until all of the purchased receivables are paid off. Merchant cash advances are most often used for the purchase of new equipment, purchasing inventory, expansion or remodeling, payoff of debt, and emergency funding. Like factoring accounts receivable, merchant cash advances are an expensive source of funding.

merchant cash advance
a method of financing in which a provider pre-purchases credit and debit card receivables at a discount.

ENTREPRENEURIAL PROFILE: Ivan and Mayra Rincon: Orchid Boutique Ivan and Mayra Rincon, founders of the online swimwear shop Orchid Boutique, needed help funding the highly seasonal nature of their business. Although the business had solid profit margins on its $3 million in annual sales, the Rincons were always scrambling to find cash to fund the next season's inventory purchases. After several banks rejected their loan requests, they were able to secure a merchant cash advance of $200,000. The company had to pay $55,000 for the advance, however, which meant that the Rincons paid 15 percent of sales to the provider until they paid off the $255,000. The funding cost the company an effective annual interest rate of more than 50 percent![101] ∎

Peer-to-peer Lending

New online funding options are emerging to help small businesses with credit. **Peer-to-peer loans** are Web-based vetting platforms, such as Lending Club, Prosper, and Fundation, that create an online community of lenders who provide funding to creditworthy small businesses. Lending Club reports that it is making more than $120 million in loans to small businesses *each month*! Interest rates can range from less than 7 percent to more than 25 percent. Lending Club has a maximum loan limit of $35,000. Lydia Aguinaldo, owner of Pines Home Health Care Services, in Broward County, Florida, secured a $250,000 loan from Fundation at a 19 percent interest rate payable over three years.[102]

peer-to-peer loans
Web-based platforms that create an online community of lenders who provide funding to creditworthy small businesses.

Loan Brokers

Loan brokers specialize in helping small businesses find loans by tapping into a wide network of lenders that include SBA lenders, working capital financing, real estate loans, bridge financing, franchise financing, merchant cash advances, and asset-based lending. Most loan brokers do not charge a fee for the initial evaluation and consulting on financing options for a small business. Loan brokers take a small percentage of the total loan amount, usually 1 to 2.5 percent, once the business is successfully financed. MultiFunding, Biz2Credit, and Loan Finder are a few of the larger companies offering these services to small business clients.

loan brokers
businesses that specialize in helping small companies find loans by tapping into a wide network of lenders.

ENTREPRENEURIAL PROFILE: Patricia and Jim McGrath: Branches Atelier Patricia and Jim McGrath, owners of Branches Atelier, a preschool in Santa Monica, California, wanted to find a larger location to house their growing business. They found a perfect location to buy. The mortgage would cost them no more each month than their current rent, so they were confident that getting a loan would not be difficult. However, when they went to their bank—where they had done business for 20 years—to apply for a loan to buy the building, they were turned down for their loan request. They were shocked because they had enough cash for a down payment and a long waiting list for new students. The McGraths went to a loan brokerage firm, Multifunding, which was able to find a bank willing to give them the loan they needed to buy the building.[103] ∎

Credit Cards

Unable to find financing elsewhere, many entrepreneurs launch their companies using the fastest and most convenient source of debt capital available: credit cards. A study by the Kauffman Foundation reports that 7 percent of the capital for start-up companies comes from credit cards. The study also shows that 58 percent of new businesses rely on credit cards to finance operations in their first year of business.[104] Putting business start-up costs on credit cards charging 20 percent or more in annual interest is expensive, risky, and can lead to severe financial woes. A study by Robert Scott of Monmouth University and the Kauffman Foundation reports that taking on credit card debt *reduces* the likelihood that a start-up company will survive its first three years of operation. Every $1,000 increase in credit card debt results in a 2.2 percent increase in the probability that a company will fail.[105] Putting business start-up costs on credit cards is expensive and risky, especially if sales fail to materialize as quickly as planned, but some entrepreneurs have no other choice. Prudent entrepreneurs rely on credit cards only for making monthly purchases that they are certain can be paid off when the credit card bill comes due.

Chapter Summary by Learning Objective

1. Describe the differences between equity capital and debt capital.

Capital is any form of wealth employed to produce more wealth. Entrepreneurs have access to two different types of capital:

- Equity financing represents the personal investment of the owner (or owners), and it offers the advantage of not having to be repaid with interest.

- Debt capital is the financing a small business owner has borrowed and must repay with interest. It does not require entrepreneurs to give up ownership in their companies.

2. Discuss the various sources of equity capital available to entrepreneurs.

- The most common source of financing a business is the owner's personal savings. After emptying their own pockets, the next place entrepreneurs turn for capital is family members and friends. Crowdfunding taps the power of social networking and allows entrepreneurs to post their elevator pitches and proposed investment terms on crowd-funding Web sites and raise money to fund their ventures from ordinary people who invest as little as $100. Angels are private investors who not only invest their money in small companies but also offer valuable advice and counsel to them. Some business owners have success financing their companies by taking on limited partners as investors or by forming an alliance with a corporation, often a customer or a supplier. Venture capital companies are for-profit, professional investors looking for fast-growing companies in "hot" industries. When screening prospects, venture capital firms look for competent management, a competitive edge, a growth industry, and important intangibles that will make a business successful. Some owners choose to attract capital by taking their companies public, which requires registering the public offering with the SEC.

3. Describe the process of "going public."

- Going public involves (1) choosing the underwriter, (2) negotiating a letter of intent, (3) preparing the registration statement, (4) filing with the SEC, and (5) meeting state requirements.

4. Describe the various sources of debt capital.

- Commercial banks offer the greatest variety of loans, although they are conservative lenders. Typical short-term bank loans include commercial loans, lines of credit, discounting accounts receivable, inventory financing, and floor planning.

- Trade credit is used extensively by small businesses as a source of financing. Vendors and suppliers commonly finance sales to businesses for 30, 60, or even 90 days.

- Equipment suppliers offer small businesses financing similar to trade credit but with slightly different terms.

- Commercial finance companies offer many of the same types of loans that banks do, but they are more risk oriented in their lending practices. They emphasize accounts-receivable financing and inventory loans.

- Savings-and-loan associations specialize in loans to purchase real property—commercial and industrial mortgages—for up to 30 years.

- Stock brokerage houses offer loans to prospective entrepreneurs at lower interest rates than banks because they have high-quality, liquid collateral—stocks and bonds in the borrower's portfolio.

- Small Business Investment Companies are privately owned companies licensed and regulated by the SBA that qualify for SBA loans to be invested in or loaned to small businesses.

- Small Business Lending Companies make only intermediate- and long-term loans that are guaranteed by the SBA.

5. **Describe the various loan programs available from the Small Business Administration.**

- Almost all SBA loan activity is in the form of loan guarantees rather than direct loans. Popular SBA programs include: the SBA *Express* program, the Patriot *Express* program, the 7(a) loan guaranty program, the Section 504 Certified Development Company program, the Microloan program, the CAPLine program, the Export Working Capital program, and the Disaster Loan program.

6. **Identify the various federal and state loan programs aimed at small businesses.**

- The Economic Development Administration, a branch of the Commerce Department, makes loan guarantees to create and expand small businesses in economically depressed areas.
- The Department of Housing and Urban Development extends grants (such as Community Development Block Grants) to cities that, in turn, lend and grant money to small businesses in an attempt to strengthen the local economy.
- The Department of Agriculture's Rural Business Cooperative Service loan program is designed to create nonfarm employment opportunities in rural areas through loans and loan guarantees.
- The Small Business Innovation Research Program involves 11 federal agencies that award cash grants or long-term contracts to small companies wanting to initiate or to expand their R&D efforts.
- The Small Business Technology Transfer Program allows researchers at universities, federally funded R&D centers, and nonprofit research institutions to join forces with small businesses and develop commercially promising ideas.
- Many state and local loan and development programs, such as capital access programs, revolving loan funds, and community development financial institutions, complement those sponsored by federal agencies.

7. **Explain other methods of financing a business.**

- Business owners can get the capital they need by factoring accounts receivable, leasing equipment instead of buying it, borrowing against their retirement accounts, borrowing against future credit card sales, borrowing from peers, using a loan broker, or even using credit cards.

Discussion Questions

13-1. Why is it so difficult for most small business owners to raise the capital needed to start, operate, or expand their ventures?

13-2. What is capital?

13-3. Define equity financing.

13-4. What advantage does equity financing offer over debt financing?

13-5. What is the most common source of equity funds in a typical small business?

13-6. If an owner lacks sufficient equity capital to invest in the firm, what options are available for raising it?

13-7. What guidelines should an entrepreneur follow if friends and relatives choose to invest in her business?

13-8. What is an angel investor?

13-9. Assemble a brief profile of the typical private investor.

13-10. How can entrepreneurs locate potential angels to invest in their businesses?

13-11. What advice would you offer an entrepreneur about to strike a deal with a private investor to avoid problems?

13-12. What types of businesses are most likely to attract venture capital?

13-13. What investment criteria do venture capitalists use when screening potential businesses?

13-14. How do venture capitalist criteria for investing compare to the typical angel's criteria?

13-15. How do venture capital firms operate?

13-16. Describe a venture capitalist procedure for screening investment proposals.

13-17. Summarize the major exemptions and simplified registrations available to small companies wanting to make public offerings of their stock.

13-18. What role do commercial banks play in providing debt financing to small businesses?

13-19. Outline and briefly describe the major types of short-, intermediate-, and long-term loans commercial banks offer.

13-20. What is trade credit?

13-21. How important is trade credit as a source of debt financing to small firms?

13-22. What function do SBICs serve?

13-23. How does an SBIC operate?

13-24. What methods of financing do SBICs rely on most heavily?

13-25. Explain the advantages and disadvantages of using crowdfunding.

13-26. Briefly describe the loan programs offered by the Economic Development Administration.

13-27. Briefly describe the loan programs offered by the Department of Housing and Urban Development.

13-28. Briefly describe the loan programs offered by the Department of Agriculture.

13-29. Explain the purpose and the methods of operation of the Small Business Innovation Research Program and the Small Business Technology Transfer Program.

13-30. What is a factor?

13-31. How does the typical factor operate?

13-32. Explain the advantages and the disadvantages of using factors as a source of funding.

13-33. Explain how an entrepreneur can use retirement funding to start a business using Rollovers as Business Startups (ROBS).

13-34. How do merchant cash advances work as a source of financing a small business?

13-35. What is peer-to-peer lending?

13-36. What is the role and function of loan brokers?

13-37. What role do credit cards play in financing small business?

13-38. Explain the dangers of using credit cards to finance the start-up costs of a small business.

Beyond the Classroom . . .

13-39. Interview several local business owners about how they financed their businesses.

13-40. Where did the initial capital come from for the small business owners you interviewed?

13-41. Ask the small business owners how much money they needed to launch their businesses.

13-42. Ask the small business owners how much of their own money they used to start their businesses.

13-43. Ask the small business owners how they raised the additional capital they needed to start their businesses.

13-44. Ask the small business owners what percentage of the money they raised to start their businesses was debt capital and what percentage was equity capital.

13-45. Ask the small business owners about which of the sources of funds described in this chapter they used.

13-46. Ask the small business owners about any advice they might offer others seeking capital?

13-47. Contact a local private investor and ask him or her to address your class.

13-48. Ask the investor about the kinds of businesses he or she prefers to invest in.

13-49. Ask the investor about the screening criteria he or she uses to select investments.

13-50. Ask the investor about how the deals in which he or she invests are typically structured.

13-51. Contact a local venture capitalist and ask him or her to address your class.

13-52. Ask the venture capitalist about the kinds of businesses his or her company invests in.

13-53. Ask the venture capitalist about the screening criteria used by his or her firm.

13-54. Ask the venture capitalist about how the deals are typically structured when his or her firm invests in an entrepreneurial venture.

13-55. Why are bankers so cautious when making business loans?

13-56. What are the consequences when banks make too many bad business loans?

13-57. How does the cautious attitude of bankers affect entrepreneurs' access to bank financing?

13-58. Contact a local banker who works with small businesses and ask him or her how the small business lending market has changed over the last five years.

13-59. What steps can entrepreneurs take to increase the likelihood that a bank will approve their loan requests?

13-60. Interview the administrator of a financial institution program offering a method of financing with which you are unfamiliar and prepare a short report on its method of operation.

13-61. Contact your state's economic development board and prepare a report on the financial assistance programs it offers small businesses.

13-62. Go to the "IPO Home" section of the Web site for Renaissance Capital, explore the details of a company that is involved in making an initial public offering, and view some of the documents the company has filed with the SEC, especially the IPO filing.

13-63. Prepare a brief report on the company you reviewed at the "IPO Home" section of the Web site for Renaissance Capital, addressing the type of business, its competitors, growth in its industry, risk factors, the money it plans to raise in its IPO, its anticipated stock price, and the number of shares it intends to sell.

13-64. Explain why you would or would not invest in the company you reviewed at the "IPO Home" section of the Web site for Renaissance Capital.

13-65. With a team of classmates, develop a detailed plan for a Kickstarter campaign for a new business that one of the group members is interested in launching.

Endnotes

Scan for Endnotes or go to www.pearsonhighered.com/scarborough

14

Choosing the Right Location and Layout

John Lund/Marc Romanelli/Blend Images/Corbis

Learning Objectives

On completion of this chapter, you will be able to:

1. Explain the stages in the location decision: choosing the region, the state, the city, and the specific site.

2. Describe the location criteria for retail and service businesses.

3. Outline the location options for retail and service businesses: central business districts, neighborhoods, shopping centers and malls, near competitors, shared spaces, inside large retail stores, nontraditional locations, at home, and on the road.

4. Explain the site selection process for manufacturers.

5. Describe the criteria used to analyze the layout and design considerations of a building, including the Americans with Disabilities Act.

6. Explain the principles of effective layouts for retailers, service businesses, and manufacturers.

Location: A Source of Competitive Advantage

LO1

Explain the stages in the location decision: choosing the region, the state, the city, and the specific site.

Much like choosing a form of ownership and selecting particular sources of financing, the location decision has far-reaching and often long-lasting effects on a small company's future. Entrepreneurs who choose their locations wisely—with their customers' preferences and their companies' needs in mind—establish an important competitive advantage over rivals who choose their locations haphazardly. Because the availability of qualified workers, tax rates, quality of infrastructure, traffic patterns, quality of life, and many other factors vary from one site to another, the location decision is an important one that can influence the growth rate and ultimate success of a company. Thanks to widespread digital connectivity, mobile computing, extensive cellular coverage, and affordable air travel, entrepreneurs have more flexibility when choosing a business location than ever before.

Every gardener knows that for a particular plant to thrive and grow, it must be in the right location to suit its needs. Too much shade (or sun), the wrong type of soil, or too much (or too little) water will cause the plants to wither. Similarly, a particular business must have the right location to suit its needs if it is to thrive. Like plants, the conditions that a business requires depend on the type of business involved, but the location decision is important for every business because of its influence on the company's sales. Myriad variables influence an entrepreneur's choice of a location, often making for a difficult decision. However, by conducting research and gathering and analyzing information about potential sites, entrepreneurs can find locations that are ideally suited for their businesses. When screening sites for both Disneyland and Disney World, Walt and Roy Disney hired site selection pioneer Buzz Price to conduct exhaustive studies that included a demographic analysis, population growth projections, future highway construction, accessibility, weather patterns, and other relevant factors. The location analysis successfully pinpointed ideal locations for both Disney theme parks; today the two parks host more than 33 million guests each year. "Buzz nailed both of those locations dead center," says Chip Cleary, head of the International Association of Amusement Parks and Attractions.[1]

The location decision process resembles an inverted pyramid. The first level of the decision is the broadest, requiring an entrepreneur to select a particular region of the country. (We will address locating a business in a foreign country in Chapter 15.) Then an entrepreneur must choose the right state, the right city, and, finally, the right site within the city. The key to selecting the ideal location lies in knowing the factors that are most important to a company's success and then finding a location that satisfies as many of them as possible, particularly those that are most critical. For instance, one of the most important location factors for high-tech companies is the availability of a skilled labor force, and their choice of location reflects this. If physically locating near customers is vital to a company's success, an entrepreneur's goal is to find a site that makes it most convenient for his or her target customers to do business with the company.

ENTREPRENEURIAL PROFILE: Tony and John Calamunci: Johnny's Lunch Tony and John Calamunci sell franchises of the family-owned diner that their grandparents, Johnny and Minnie Colera, started in Brooklyn Square in Jamestown, New York, in 1936 (and that their parents still operate). In launching the franchise operation, they realized that opening outlets in areas in which large concentrations of their target customers lived was essential to their success. They hired an experienced franchise veteran, George Goulson, and worked with Pitney-Bowes Software's MapInfo, using geospatial technology to determine the ideal locations for their restaurants, which sell budget-priced meals such as hot dogs, hamburgers, onion rings, and milkshakes. The Calamuncis started by defining their target customers, which they discovered include people in the lower-middle- to upper-middle-income bracket who fall between the ages of 16 and 24 or over 60. Using the software, they identified 72 types of neighborhoods that best match the demographic and psychographic profile of Johnny's Lunch customers. The next step was to find locations that matched the 72 prototype neighborhoods. Managers identified 4,500 areas across the United States that held large concentrations of potential Johnny's Lunch customers (most of whom lived within one mile of the proposed location) and would be good locations for restaurants. "These models increase our ability to pick 'home-run' locations and avoid the site mistakes that can cripple a budding franchise," says Goulson. Johnny's Lunch is launching its franchising effort in and around Toledo, Ohio, which Goulson says is a microcosm of the United States. "Small restaurant owners like us can use location intelligence to prevent mistakes that could cripple franchising plans from the start. We can't afford not to invest in location intelligence."[2] ∎

"I question your choice of locations."

Frank Cotham/The New Yorker Collection/Conde Nast

The characteristics that make for an ideal location vary dramatically from one company to another because of the nature of their business. In the early twentieth century, companies looked for ready supplies of water, raw materials, or access to railroads; today, they are more likely to look for sites that are close to universities and offer high-speed Internet access and accessible airports. In fact, one study concluded that the factors that make an area most suitable for starting and growing small companies included access to dynamic universities, an ample supply of skilled workers, a nearby airport, a temperate climate, and a high quality of life.[3] The key to finding a suitable location is identifying the characteristics that can give a company a competitive edge and then searching out potential sites that meet those criteria.

Choosing the Region

The first step in selecting the best location is to focus on selecting the right region. This requires entrepreneurs to look at the location decision from the "30,000-foot level," as if he or she were in an airplane looking down. In fact, in the early days of their companies, Sam Walton, founder of retail giant Wal-Mart, and Ray Kroc, who built McDonald's into a fast-food giant, actually used private planes to survey the countryside for prime locations for their stores.

ENTREPRENEURIAL PROFILE: Walt Disney: Disney World In 1963, Walt Disney flew over central Florida in a private plane (which is now on display at Disney World) to look at a tract of nondescript swampland as a potential site for Disney World. Disney lacked sufficient space to expand Disneyland in California and, with the help of site selection expert Buzz Price and a group of top managers, established several criteria for the company's second theme park, including a place with good weather throughout most of the year, plenty of land at bargain prices, a location near a major city, and access to major highways and infrastructure for the company's second theme park (dubbed "Project X"). When Disney flew over the intersection of Interstate 4 and Route 192 near Orlando, he knew he had found the ideal location for Disney World, which now encompasses 30,000 acres, an area that is about the size of San Francisco![4] ■

Which region of the country has the characteristics necessary for a new business to succeed? Above all, entrepreneurs must place their customers first when considering a location. As the experience of Johnny's Lunch suggests, facts and statistics, not speculation, lead entrepreneurs to the best locations for their businesses. Common requirements may include rapid growth in the population of a certain age-group, rising disposable incomes, the existence of necessary infrastructure, an available workforce, and low operating costs. At the broadest level of the location decision, entrepreneurs prefer to locate in regions of the country that are experiencing substantial growth. Every year, many popular business publications prepare reports on the various regions of the nation—which ones are growing, which are stagnant, and which are declining. Studying overall trends in population and business growth gives entrepreneurs an idea of where the action is—and isn't. Questions to consider include the following: How large is the population? How fast is it growing? What is the makeup of overall population? Which segments are growing fastest? Slowest? What is the trend in the population's income? Are other businesses moving into the region? If so, what kind of businesses? Generally, entrepreneurs want to avoid declining regions; they simply cannot support a broad base of potential customers.

One of the first stops entrepreneurs should make when conducting a regional evaluation is the U.S. Census Bureau (http://www.census.gov/). There entrepreneurs can access for specific locations vital demographic information such as age, income, educational level, employment level, occupation, ancestry, commuting times, housing data (house value, number of rooms, mortgage or rent status, number of vehicles owned, and so on), and many other characteristics. With a little practice, entrepreneurs can prepare customized reports on the potential sites they are considering. These Web-based resources give entrepreneurs instant access to important site-location information that only a few years ago would have taken many hours of intense research to compile. In 2012, the Census Bureau ceased publication of the *U.S. Statistical Abstract* (published annually since 1878), which contained about 1,400 useful data sets about the United States, ranging from basic population characteristics and leisure activity expenditures to poverty rates and energy consumption. However, ProQuest, an information gateway company founded in 1943, now publishes in both print and online formats the *ProQuest Statistical Abstract of the United States* (http://cisupa.proquest.com/ws_display.asp?filter=Statistical%20Abstract), which closely resembles the discontinued Census Bureau publication.

The Census Bureau's American FactFinder site (http://factfinder.census.gov) provides easily accessible demographic fact sheets and maps on nearly every community in the United States, including small towns. The Census Bureau's American Community Survey provides annual updates on the demographic and economic characteristics of areas with populations of at least 65,000, three-year updates on areas with populations between 20,000 and 65,000, and five-year updates on areas with populations of less than 20,000. Both the American FactFinder and the American Community Survey allow entrepreneurs to produce easy-to-read, customizable maps of the information they generate in their searches.

Entrepreneurs also can use nongovernment sources to research potential locations. Zoom-Prospector (www.zoomprospector.com) is a useful Web site that allows entrepreneurs to search for the ideal location using a multitude of factors, including population size, job growth rate, number of patents issued, venture capital invested, education level, household incomes, and proximity to interstate highways, railroads, and airports. Once entrepreneurs locate a city that matches their customer profiles, they can find other cities across the United States that have similar profiles with a single mouse click. Entrepreneurs who are considering a particular region can display "heat maps" that visually display the areas that have the highest concentrations of people who have a particular characteristic, such as a bachelor's degree or the highest household incomes.

ENTREPRENEURIAL PROFILE: Steve Sarowitz: Paylocity Steve Sarowitz, CEO of Paylocity, a provider of human resources and payroll services to small and medium-size businesses, uses ZoomProspector to find the best locations across the United States for the rapidly expanding company's new offices. Sarowitz says ZoomProspector helps his company answer the important question, Would this be a good market for us? "What's great about ZoomProspector is that we can get so much information about each individual market we are considering—market demographics, which industries are strongest, education levels, and more, "says Sarowitz. Founded in 1997, Paylocity, which is based in Arlington Heights, Illinois, and has appeared on *Inc.*'s list of the 5,000 fastest-growing companies seven times, now has 14 locations and, with ZoomProspector's help, is looking to add more.[5] ∎

Zipskinny (www.zipskinny.com) is a Web site that provides quick census data profiles of various ZIP codes across the United States and allows users to compare the demographic profiles of the people who live in different ZIP codes. The Population Reference Bureau (www.prb.org)

provides a detailed breakdown of the most relevant data collected from the most recent census reports. The Population Reference Bureau's DataFinder is a database that includes 244 variables for the United States and 132 variables for 210 other nations. The site includes easy-to-generate maps and charts and helpful articles that discuss the implications of the changing demographic and economic profile of the nation's (and the world's) population, such as the impact of aging baby boomers on business and the composition of the U.S. workforce.

Other helpful resources merit mention as well. *Lifestyle Market Analyst,* a four-part annual publication, matches population demographics with lifestyle interests. Section 1 provides demographics and lifestyle information for 210 "Designated Market Areas" across the United States. Section 2 gives demographic and geographic profiles of 77 lifestyle interests that range from avid readers and dieters to wine aficionados and pet owners. Section 3 describes the dominant lifestyle interests for each of the 210 market areas. Section 4 provides comparisons of other activities that correspond with each lifestyle interest. Entrepreneurs can use *Lifestyle Market Analyst* to determine, for example, how likely members of a particular market segment are to own a dog, collect antiques, play golf, own a vacation home, engage in extreme sports, invest in stocks or bonds, or participate in a host of other activities.

Other sources of demographic data include Nielsen Marketplace, *Editor and Publisher Market Guide*, *The American Marketplace: Demographics and Spending Patterns*, and *Zip Code Atlas and Market Planner*. Nielsen Marketplace provides a comprehensive tool for market analysis, allowing customers to generate customized reports and maps that show basic demographics, lifestyle patterns, and purchasing behavior for almost any market in the United States. The site also includes several unique statistics. Effective buying income (EBI) is a measure of disposable income, and the buying power index (BPI) is a unique measure of spending power that takes population, EBI, and retail sales into account to determine a market's ability to buy goods and services.

The *Editor and Publisher Market Guide* includes detailed economic and demographic information, ranging from population and income statistics to information on climate and transportation networks for all 3,096 counties in the United States and more than 1,600 key cities in both the United States and Canada.

The American Marketplace: Demographics and Spending Patterns provides useful demographic information in eight areas: education, health, income, labor force, living arrangements, population, race and ethnicity, and spending and wealth. Most of the tables in the book are derived from government statistics, but *The American Marketplace* also includes a discussion of the data in each table as well as a forecast of future trends. Many users say the primary advantage of *The American Marketplace* is its ease of use.

The U.S. Census Bureau also offers the Zip Code Tabulation Areas (ZCTA) Web site (http://www.census.gov/geo/ZCTA/zcta.html) that organizes the wealth of census data by Zip code. The database of 33,120 ZCTAs across the United States allows users to create tables and plot maps of census data by Zip code.

Site Selection magazine (www.siteselection.com) is another useful resource that helps entrepreneurs determine the ideal location for their companies. Issues contain articles that summarize the incentive programs that states offer, profiles of each region of the country, and the benefits of locating in different states.

States now provide geographic information systems (GIS) files online that allow entrepreneurs to identify sites that match the criteria they establish for the ideal location. GIS packages allow users to search through virtually any database containing a wealth of information and plot the results on a map of the country, an individual state, a specific city, or even a single city block. The visual display highlights what otherwise would be indiscernible business trends. For instance, using GIS programs, entrepreneurs can plot their existing customer base on a map with various colors representing the different population densities. Then they can zoom in on those areas with the greatest concentration of customers, mapping a detailed view of Zip code borders or even city streets. GIS street files originate in the U.S. Census Department's TIGER (Topographically Integrated Geographic Encoding Referencing) file, which contains map information broken down for every square foot of Metropolitan Statistical Areas (MSAs). TIGER files contain the name and location of every street in the country and detailed block statistics for the 345 largest urban areas. In essence, TIGER is a massive database of geographic features such as roads, railways, and political boundaries across the United States that, when linked with mapping programs and demographic databases, gives entrepreneurs incredible power to pinpoint existing and potential customers on easy-to-read digital maps.

The Small Business Administration's Small Business Development Center (SBDC) program also offers location analysis assistance to entrepreneurs. These centers, numbering more than 900 nationwide, provide training, counseling, research, and other specialized assistance to entrepreneurs and existing business owners on a wide variety of subjects, all at no charge. They are an important resource, especially for those entrepreneurs who may not have access to a computer. (To locate the SBDC nearest you, contact the SBA office in your state or go to the SBA's Small Business Development Center locator page at http://www.sba.gov/local-assistance.)

For entrepreneurs interested in demographic and statistical profiles of international cities, Euromonitor International (http://www.euromonitor.com/) and the Organization for Economic Development and Cooperation (http://www.oecd.org) are excellent resources. Plant Location International publishes a report, *The World's Most Competitive Cities*, that analyzes 100 top cities around the world on their suitability as locations for various types of businesses.

Once an entrepreneur has identified the best region of the country, the next step is to evaluate the individual states in that region.

Choosing the State

Every state has an economic development office working to recruit new businesses. Even though the publications produced by these offices will be biased in favor of locating in that state, they still are an excellent source of information and can help entrepreneurs assess the business climate in each state. Some of the key issues to explore include the laws, regulations, and taxes that govern businesses, costs of operation, workforce availability, and incentives or investment credits the state may offer to businesses that locate there.

ENTREPRENEURIAL PROFILE: Terry Douglas: ProNova Solutions After investing a year looking at potential sites for a new $52 million manufacturing plant, ProNova Solutions, a company that is developing next-generation proton therapy cancer treatment technology, selected a location in Pellissippi Place, a technology research and development park in Maryville, Tennessee. The area, dubbed Innovation Valley because of its proximity to the University of Tennessee and the Oak Ridge National Research Laboratory (ORNL), which is conducting research in the field, is ideally suited for ProNova's needs. Tennessee's pro-business culture and the area's talented workforce and existing infrastructure, including the Pellissippi Parkway, a highway that connects the R&D park with ORNL, sold ProNova's CEO Terry Douglas on the location. Because of ORNL, workers in the area already are familiar with the technology that ProNova uses, including linear accelerators and cyclotrons.[6] ■

Factors that entrepreneurs often consider when choosing a location include proximity to markets, proximity to raw materials, wage rates, quantity and quality of the labor supply, general business climate, tax rates, Internet access, and total operating costs.

PROXIMITY TO MARKETS Locating close to markets they plan to serve is extremely critical for manufacturers, especially when the cost of transporting finished goods is high relative to their value. Locating near customers is necessary to remain competitive. Service firms also often find that proximity to their clients is essential. If a business is involved in repairing equipment used in a specific industry, it should be located where that industry is concentrated. The more specialized a business or the greater the relative cost of transporting the product to the customer, the more likely it is that proximity to the market will be of critical importance in the location decision.

The ability to get finished products to customers quickly is an important location consideration for many companies.

ENTREPRENEURIAL PROFILE: Alan Yu: Lollicup USA Alan Yu, founder and CEO of Lollicup USA, a manufacturer of premium beverage and disposable food service products such as napkins, cups, and utensils, recently relocated to Chino, a city in California's San Bernardino Valley, to be closer to its customers, many of whom are quick-service restaurants. Yu notes that in Southern California, the company's customer base has grown exponentially, and the ability to get its products to a large number of customers quickly was a critical factor in Lollicup's location decision. Access to a qualified workforce and lower taxes than those in the company's former Los Angeles location added to the area's attractiveness.[7] ■

PROXIMITY TO ESSENTIAL SERVICES AND RAW MATERIALS   For some entrepreneurs, locations near suppliers of essential services are vital. Fashion designer Trina Turk, whose company produces 11 distinct collections each year, located her business in Alhambra, California, a suburb of Los Angeles, rather than in the bustling city center for several reasons, including safety (she employs a significant number of young women who sometimes work after normal business hours) and low rental rates. However, the location's main draw is its proximity to Los Angeles's garment district, where many of the company's sewing contractors are based. Although Turk says her company's neighborhood is not glamorous or known as a fashion center, the location does give her company a competitive advantage.[8]

Splash News/Newscom

If a business uses raw materials that are difficult or expensive to transport, it may require a location near the source of those raw materials. Transporting heavy, low-value raw material over long distances is impractical—and unprofitable. For products in which bulk or weight is not a factor, locating manufacturing operations in close proximity to suppliers facilitates quick deliveries and reduces inventory holding costs. Chobani, a maker of Greek yogurt founded by Hamdi Ulukaya in 2005, recently opened its second factory in the United States in Twin Falls, Idaho. The main reason that Ulukaya chose Idaho as the location for the factory, which, at 1 million square feet, is the largest yogurt production facility in the world, is that Idaho is the third largest milk-producing state in the United States. Chobani, the leading maker of Greek yogurt in the United States, requires 4 to 5 million pounds of milk each day to produce 3 million cases of Greek yogurt each week. Other factors that led to the decision to locate the factory in Twin Falls included easier and faster access to markets on the West coast (the company's other U.S. factory is in central New York), a skilled labor force with a strong work ethic, and low operating costs.[9] The value of products and materials, their cost of transportation, and their unique functions interact to determine how close a business should be to its suppliers.

WAGE RATES   Existing and anticipated wage rates provide another measure for comparison among states. Wages can sometimes vary from one state or region to another, significantly affecting a company's cost of doing business. For instance, according to the Bureau of Labor Statistics, the average hourly compensation for workers (including wages and benefits) ranges from a low of $27.14 in the South to a high of $34.79 in the Northeast.[10] Wage rate differentials within geographic regions can be even more drastic. When reviewing wage rates, entrepreneurs must be sure to measure the wage rates for jobs that relate to their particular industries or companies. In addition to surveys by the Bureau of Labor Statistics (www.bls.gov), local newspaper ads can give entrepreneurs an idea of the pay scale in an area. Entrepreneurs also can obtain the latest wage and salary surveys with an e-mail or telephone call to the local chambers of commerce for cities in the region under consideration. Entrepreneurs should study not only prevailing wage rates but also *trends* in rates. How does the rate of increase in wage rates compare to those in other states? Another factor influencing wage rates is the level of union activity in a state. How much union organizing activity has the state seen within the last two years? Which industries have unions targeted in the recent past?

ENTREPRENEURIAL PROFILE: Bombardier Inc.   Bombardier Inc., based in Montreal, Canada, recently built a manufacturing plant in what was once dry cactus fields in Querétaro, Mexico, to produce the Learjet 85, the company's newest corporate jet. Bombardier was attracted by lower wage rates, a pool of trained aeronautics engineers from the local National Aeronautics University of Querétaro, and proximity to customers in both North and South America. The availability of a trained labor force and wage rates that are 25 to 30 percent lower than those in the United States were driving factors in the company's location decision.[11] ■

SIZE AND QUALITY OF LABOR FORCE   For many businesses, especially technology-driven companies, two of the most important characteristics of a potential location are the size and composition of the local workforce. The number of workers available in an area and their levels of education, training, and experience determine a company's ability to fill jobs with qualified workers at reasonable wages. For example, Provo, Utah, home to Brigham Young University (BYU), hosts a large concentration of technology and software companies, second only to California's Silicon Valley but without the high costs. One reason that software companies find Provo attractive is the city's high concentration of college graduates; nearly 39 percent of its residents have a bachelor's degree or higher (compared to 28.5 percent in the United States as a whole).[12] Another feature that attracts technology companies to Provo is access to Google Fiber, the super high-speed Internet connection currently available in just a handful of cities.

ENTREPRENEURIAL PROFILE: Scott and Ryan Smith and Stuart Orgill: Qualtrics Scott and Ryan Smith and Stuart Orgill launched Qualtrics, a market research software company, from their Provo, Utah, basement in 2002. "We had 20 people working in the basement at one time," recalls Orgill, "so we moved to another building and continued to hire." Qualtrics soon outgrew that space and now has 350 employees and more than 5,000 clients worldwide. The company benefits from the steady supply of college graduates from nearby BYU and the University of Utah to meet its needs for well-educated employees, 95 percent of whom are locals. "This market is filled with a lot of very educated people and is home to a very strong work ethic," says Orgill. The area also boasts a high quality of life, offering outdoor activities such as mountain biking, skiing, snowboarding, hiking, and fishing, hobbies that appeal to the young people Qualtrics hires.[13] ∎

Before selecting a location, entrepreneurs should know how many qualified people are available in the area to perform the work required in their businesses. Some states have attempted to attract industry with the promise of cheap labor. Unfortunately, businesses locating in those states find unskilled, low-wage workers who are ill suited for performing the work the companies need and are difficult to train.

Knowing the exact nature of the workforce needed and preparing job descriptions and job specifications in advance help business owners to determine whether there is a good match between their companies' needs and the available labor pool. Reviewing the major industries already operating in an area provides clues about the characteristics of the local workforce as well. Checking educational statistics to determine the number of graduates in relevant fields of study tells entrepreneurs about the available supply of qualified workers.

BUSINESS CLIMATE What is the state's overall attitude toward your kind of business? Has it passed laws that impose restrictions on the way a company can operate? Do "blue laws" prohibit certain business activity on Sundays? Does the state offer small business support programs or financial assistance to entrepreneurs?

ENTREPRENEURIAL PROFILE: Eclipse Aerospace Eclipse Aerospace, maker of "the world's most efficient very light jet," selected Albuquerque, New Mexico, as the location for its new 215,000-square-foot manufacturing facility because of the state's business-friendly environment. The state legislature passed legislation that eliminated the sales tax on aircraft parts, services, and finished aircraft. Because the base price of Eclipse Aerospace's newest jet is $2.9 million, the exemption saves the company hundreds of thousands of dollars annually. The company's factory is conveniently located next to Albuquerque's International Sunport Airport, which boasts one of the longest runways in the United States, and access to a railroad spur and to two major interstate highways. In addition, as one CEO points out, Albuquerque treats entrepreneurs like rock stars.[14] ∎

Some states and cities create policies that are more small business friendly than others. Texas is the birthplace of many business start-ups, especially technology firms, because it offers entrepreneurs ready access to venture capital; quality colleges and universities; a young, well-educated workforce; and a variety of programs designed to encourage entrepreneurship. Texas was an early participant in the Startup America program, which is designed to encourage start-up companies and to help them succeed. Austin, Texas, is home to Indeed.com, the world's leading job search site. Launched in 2004 by Paul Forster and Rony Kahan, the company attracts more than 140 million unique visitors to its Web site each month. Forster and Kahan mainly bootstrapped Indeed.com but landed $5 million in venture capital and grew the company to more than 800 employees before selling it to Tokyo-based human resources services company Recruit Co. Ltd. for a reported $1 billion.[15]

TABLE 14.1 Most and Least Small-Business-Friendly States

States *Most* Friendly to Small Businesses

1. South Dakota	6. Washington
2. Nevada	7. Alabama
3. Texas	8. Indiana
4. Wyoming	9. Ohio
5. Florida	10. Utah

States *Least* Friendly to Small Businesses

41. Connecticut	46. Hawaii
42. Oregon	47. New York
43. Iowa	48. Vermont
44. Maine	49. New Jersey
45. Minnesota	50. California

Source: Raymond J. Keating, *Small Business Policy Index 2013*, Small Business & Entrepreneurship Council, 18th Annual Edition, December 2013, p. 2.

The Small Business & Entrepreneurship Council publishes an annual "small-business-friendly" ranking of the states and the District of Columbia that includes a composite measure of 47 factors, ranging from a variety of taxes and regulations to crime rates and energy costs (see Table 14.1).

TAX RATES Another important factor that entrepreneurs must consider when screening states for potential locations is the tax burden they impose on businesses and individuals. Does the state impose a corporate income tax? How heavy are the state's property, income, and sales taxes? Income taxes may be the most obvious tax that states impose on both business and individuals, but entrepreneurs also must evaluate the impact of payroll taxes, sales taxes, property taxes, and specialized taxes on the cost of their operations. Figure 14.1 shows how each state's overall tax burden measured by 100 variables ranks. Currently, seven states impose no state individual income tax (two others do not tax wage income), and three states have no corporate income tax, but state governments always impose taxes of some sort on businesses and individuals.[16] In some cases, states offer special tax credits or are willing to negotiate fees in lieu of taxes (FILOTs) for companies that create jobs and stimulate the local economy. The Outdoor Group LLC, a maker of high-end archery equipment, received $900,000 in tax credits from New York by building a new manufacturing facility in the Rochester suburb of Henrietta.[17]

ENTREPRENEURIAL PROFILE: Clint Greenleaf: Greenleaf Book Group Clint Greenleaf, founder of Greenleaf Book Group, a book publisher dedicated to independent authors and small presses, moved his company from Ohio to Texas to escape the high tax burden Ohio imposed and to capitalize on the highly educated workforce in Texas. Since making the move, Greenleaf Book Group's annual revenue has grown by a factor of 10.[18] ■

HIGH-SPEED INTERNET ACCESS Speedy, reliable Internet access is an increasingly important factor in the location decision (See Figure 14.2). In fact, 95 percent of small businesses that have computers have broadband Internet access.[19] Fast Internet access is essential for high-tech companies, those that rely on cloud computing, and those that engage in e-commerce; however, even companies that may not sell to customers over the Internet find high-speed Internet to be a valuable business tool. Companies that fall behind in high-speed Internet access find themselves at a severe competitive disadvantage. According to a recent study, 48 percent of small business owners in rural areas and 37 percent of business owners in metropolitan areas say they are not satisfied with their Internet speed.[20] Google Fiber, a high-speed fiber network from Google that runs 100 times faster (1 gigabyte per second) than current broadband, is already in place in Kansas City (Kansas and Missouri), Austin, Texas, and Provo, Utah, and is proving to be an

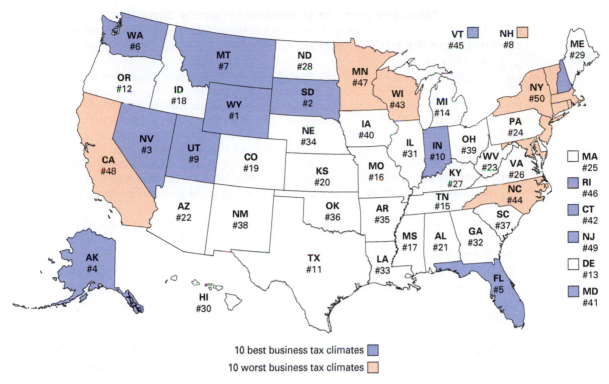

FIGURE 14.1

State Business Tax Climate Index

Source: Scott Drenkard and Joseph Henchman, *2014 State Business Tax Climate Index*, Tax Foundation, October 9, 2013, p. 2.

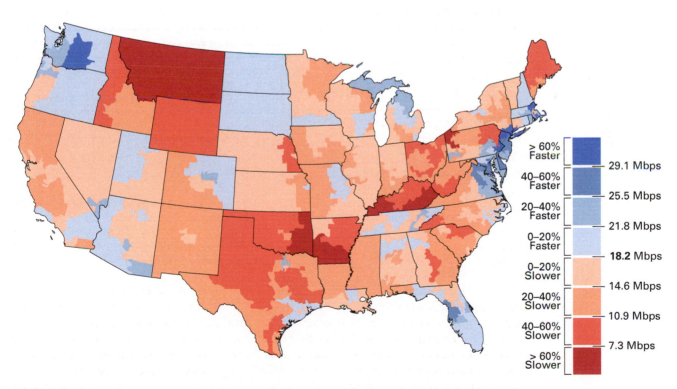

FIGURE 14.2

Internet Download Speeds Across the United States

Source: Reuben Fischer-Baum, "A Map of Who's Got the Best (and Worst) Internet Connections in America," *Gizmodo*, September 15, 2013, http://gizmodo.com/americas-internet-inequality-a-map-of-whos-got-the-b-1057686215.

important factor in many entrepreneurs' decisions to locate in these cities. Google currently is working with other cities, such as Atlanta, Charlotte, Phoenix, Portland, Raleigh-Durham, San Antonio, and San Jose, to bring Google Fiber to their businesses and residents.[21]

ENTREPRENEURIAL PROFILE: Brandon Schatz: SportsPhotos.com Brandon Schatz, founder of SportsPhotos.com, a company that organizes and helps photographers sell photos of a variety of athletic events, decided to move his business from Springfield, Missouri, to the Kansas City Startup Village to take advantage of Google Fiber's speed. SportsPhoto.com uploads hundreds of photos of each event, which requires a fast Internet connection. In Springfield, the slow Internet connection always created a bottleneck for the company. However, with Google Fiber, which costs 83 percent less than his slower connection did, Schatz can download a batch of photos that would have taken 30 to 40 hours in just 30 minutes. SportsPhoto.com's increased efficiency not only has improved its profitability but also has enabled Schatz to grow the company faster.[22] ■

TOTAL OPERATING COSTS When scouting a state in which to locate a company, an entrepreneur must consider the total cost of operating a business. For instance, a state may offer low utility rates, but its labor costs and tax rates may be among the highest in the nation. To select the ideal location, entrepreneurs must consider the impact of a state's total cost of operation on their business ventures. After Feel Golf, a company that makes golf clubs and grips, acquired Pro Line Sports, a Sanford, Florida, business that markets the IGOTCHA golf ball retriever, CEO Lee Miller decided to relocate Feel Golf to Florida from Salinas, California, where the company had operated for 15 years. Miller made the move because he was concerned about the effect that the high cost of doing business in California had on his company.[23]

The state evaluation matrix in Table 14.2 provides a handy tool designed to help entrepreneurs determine which states best suit the most important location criteria for their companies. This same matrix can be adapted to analyze individual cities as well. Claremont McKenna College's Kosmont-Rose Institute Cost of Doing Business Survey reports that cities in Texas tend to offer

TABLE 14.2 State Evaluation Matrix

Location Criterion	Weight	Score (Low = 1, High = 5)	State 1	State 2	State 3
			State-Weighted Score (Weight × Score)		
Quality of labor force					
Wage rates					
Union activity					
Property/building costs					
Utility costs					
Transportation costs					
Tax burden					
Educational/training assistance					
Start-up incentives					
Raw material availability					
Quality of life					
Other:					
Other:					
		Total Score			

Assign to each location criterion a weight that reflects its relative importance to your company. Then score each state on a scale of 1 (low) to 5 (high). Calculate the weighted score (weight × score) for each state. Finally, add up the total weighted score for each state. The state with the highest total score is the best location for your business.

TABLE 14.3 Best and Worst States for Doing Business

Top 10 States for Doing Business

Rank*	State	Taxes and Regulations	Workforce Quality	Living Environment
1	Texas	*****	****	****
2	Florida	****	****	****
3	Tennessee	****	****	****
4	North Carolina	****	****	****
5	South Carolina	****	****	****
6	Indiana	****	****	****
7	Arizona	****	****	****
8	Nevada	****	****	***
9	Louisiana	****	****	****
10	Georgia	****	****	****

Bottom 10 States for Doing Business

Rank*	State	Taxes and Regulations	Workforce Quality	Living Environment
41	Maryland	**	***	***
42	Pennsylvania	**	***	***
43	Hawaii	**	**	****
44	Connecticut	**	***	***
45	Michigan	**	***	***
46	Massachusetts	**	***	***
47	New Jersey	**	***	**
48	Illinois	*	***	***
49	New York	*	***	***
50	California	*	***	***

*Rank is the result of a survey by *Chief Executive* magazine that asked 650 business leaders to rank the states on factors such as taxes, regulatory burden, quality of workforce, and quality of life. Five stars is best; one star is worst.

Source: "2014 Best and Worst States for Business," *Chief Executive*, May 4, 2014, http://chiefexecutive.net/best-worst-states-for-business-2014.

the lowest cost of operation (6 cities among the 20 least expensive), while cities in California are among the most expensive (12 cities among the 20 most expensive).[24] Austin, Abilene, and Fort Worth, Texas; Cheyenne, Wyoming; Eugene, Oregon; and Yakima, Washington, are among the cities that offer the lowest cost of doing business, and New York City, New York; Los Angeles and San Francisco, California; Philadelphia, Pennsylvania; and Newark, New Jersey, are those with the highest costs of doing business.[25]

Table 14.3 shows the states that CEOs rank as the 10 best states and the 10 worst states on factors that include taxes and regulations, quality of workforce, and living environment.

Choosing the City

POPULATION TRENDS Analyzing over time the lists of "best cities for business" compiled annually by many magazines reveals one consistent trend: Successful small companies in a city tend to track a city's population growth. In other words, more potential customers mean that a small business has a better chance of success. The Census Bureau recently named San Antonio, Texas; Orlando, Florida; Raleigh, North Carolina; Houston, Texas; and Austin, Texas, as the fastest-growing cities in the United States.[26] Austin, a thriving university town that is home to many technology-related companies, including Dell, Apple, IBM, and Samsung, is a haven for entrepreneurial start-ups. With its funky culture, progressive music scene, abundant festivals (including the quirky South by Southwest Interactive Festival), and temperate climate, the city has become a magnet for young, creative people. The median age of Austin's population is 31.1, well below the national average of 37.2. A highly educated workforce, large concentrations of angel and venture capital, and an entrepreneurial support system that includes business incubators and accelerators such as Capital Factory add to the city's attractiveness for entrepreneurs.

ENTREPRENEURIAL PROFILE: Alan Knitowski: Phunware Serial entrepreneur Alan Knitowski started Phunware, a fast-growing mobile apps company, in Austin, Texas, in 2009, in the jaws of the Great Recession. Knitowski was drawn to Austin's highly educated workforce, entrepreneurial culture and support system, access to start-up capital, and quality of life. With annual sales approaching $50 million, Phunware's software facilitates more than 1 trillion transactions on mobile devices worldwide each year for many companies, such as NASCAR, E! Entertainment, ESPN, Adobe, TCM, Discovery Channel, Disney, and many others, helping them engage and market to their mobile customers in creative ways. The company has grown to more than 150 employees and has raised $43 million in capital in five rounds of financing. From company headquarters in Austin, Knitowski has a vision to make Phunware the industry leader in branded mobile applications and a plan to set up offices across the United States, expand its operations in Europe and Asia, and perhaps make an initial public offering.[27] ■

By analyzing population and other demographic data, entrepreneurs can examine a city in detail, and the location decision becomes more than just an educated guess or, worse, a shot in the dark. Studying the trends and the demographics of a city, including population size and density, growth trends, family size, age breakdowns, education, income levels, job categories, gender, religion, race, and nationality, gives entrepreneurs the facts they need to make an informed location decision. Useful information is available from the U.S. Census Bureau for cities of all sizes, including metropolitan and micropolitan areas (those with an urban core of between 10,000 and 50,000 people) and small towns. There are 536 micropolitan areas in the United States, and Table 14.4 shows the states that have the greatest number of micropolitan areas listed in the top 100.

In fact, using only basic census data, entrepreneurs can determine what home values are in an area, how many rooms they contain, how many bedrooms they contain, what percentage of the population own their homes, and how much residents' monthly rental or mortgage payments are. Imagine how useful that information would be to someone about to launch a bed-and-bath shop!

A company's location should match the market for its products or services, and assembling a demographic profile tells an entrepreneur how well a particular site measures up to his or her target market's profile. For instance, an entrepreneur planning to open a fine art shop would likely want information on a city's household income, size, age, and education level. To succeed, this art shop should be located in an area where people appreciate its products and have the discretionary income to purchase them.

TABLE 14.4 States with the Most Top Micropolitan Areas

State	Number of Top 100 Micropolitan Areas
Ohio	15
Georgia	9
Michigan	9
North Carolina	8
Tennessee	8
Iowa	7
Kentucky	7
Nebraska	7
Minnesota	6

Source: Ron Starner, "The Ladder Effect," *Site Selection*, March 2014, pp. 116–127.

ENTREPRENEURIAL PROFILE: Texas Roadhouse, Anchorage, Alaska
Texas Roadhouse, a 410-unit casual dining chain, recently opened its first restaurant in Anchorage, Alaska, the state's largest and wealthiest city. With a per capita income of nearly $55,000 and a population of nearly 300,000 people, Anchorage is capturing the attention of several restaurant chains in the Lower 48 states. Texas Roadhouse executives say that although somewhat remote, the market is underserved and represents a huge growth opportunity. The chain's theme, a steak-oriented menu and country music, fits well with Alaska's culture. The Anchorage restaurant incorporates several modifications that reflect the region's unique characteristics. The restaurant is bigger than those located in the Lower 48; it needs more storage space because supply deliveries are less frequent in remote locations. The lights also are brighter to offset the long periods of darkness (an average of nearly 18½ hours per day in January) the region experiences in the winter months. The menu features the chain's signature steaks and ice cold beer but also includes several local items, including salmon and crab legs.[28] ■

Courtesy of Texas Roadhouse

The amount of available data on the population of any city or town is staggering. These statistics allow entrepreneurs to compare a wide variety of cities or towns and to narrow the choices to those few that warrant further investigation. Analyzing all of this data makes it possible to screen out undesirable locations and to narrow the list of suitable locations to a few, but it does not make the final location decision for an entrepreneur. Entrepreneurs must see the potential locations on their "short list" *firsthand*. Only by seeing a potential location can an entrepreneur add the intangible factor of intuition into the decision-making process. Spending time at a potential location tells an entrepreneur not only how many people frequent it but also what they are like, how long they stay, and what they buy. Walking or driving around the area will give an entrepreneur clues about the people who live and work there. What are their houses like? What kinds of cars do they drive? What stage of life are they in? Do they have children? Is the area on the rise, or is it past its prime?

Following are other factors that entrepreneurs should consider when evaluating cities as possible business locations.

COMPETITION For some retailers, locating near competitors makes sense because similar businesses located near one another may serve to increase traffic flow to both. This location strategy works well for products for which customers are most likely to comparison shop. For instance, in many cities, auto dealers locate next to one another in a "motor mile," trying to create a shopping magnet for customers. The convenience of being able to shop for dozens of brands of cars all within a few hundred yards of one another draws customers from a sizable trading area. Locating near competitors is a common strategy for restaurants as well.

ENTREPRENEURIAL PROFILE: George Stathakis: Stax Omega When George Stathakis opened his sixth restaurant, Stax Omega, in Greenville, South Carolina, he chose a site at the intersection of an interstate highway and a busy road where several other popular restaurants were already operating. With years of experience in the restaurant business, Stathakis knows that a cluster of restaurants create business for one another. "I always liked the idea of locating my restaurants near competitors," he says.[29] ■

Of course, this strategy has limits. Overcrowding of businesses of the same type in an area can create an undesirable impact on the profitability of all competing firms.

Studying the size of the market for a product or service and the number of existing competitors helps an entrepreneur determine whether he or she can capture a sufficiently large market share to earn a profit. Again, census reports can be a valuable source of information. *County Business Patterns* gives a breakdown of businesses in manufacturing, wholesale, retail, and service categories and estimates companies' annual payrolls and number of employees broken down by county. *ZIP Code Business Patterns* provides the same data as *County Business Patterns* except it organizes the data by ZIP code. The *Economic Census*, which is produced for years that end in 2 and 7, gives an overview of the businesses in an area—their sales (or other measure of output), employment, payroll, and form of organization. It covers eight industry categories, including retail, wholesale, service, manufacturing, construction, and others, and gives statistics not only at the national level but also by state, Metropolitan Statistical Area, county, places with 2,500 or more inhabitants, and Zip code. The *Economic Census* is a useful tool for helping entrepreneurs determine whether the areas they are considering as a location are already saturated with competitors.

clusters
geographic concentrations of interconnected companies, specialized suppliers, and service providers that are present in a region.

CLUSTERS Some cities have characteristics that attract certain industries, and, as a result, companies tend to cluster there. **Clusters** are geographic concentrations of interconnected companies that share specialized supply chains, resources, labor force, distribution networks, and service providers that are present in a region.[30] Businesses in a cluster build on the same pool of resources and strengthen the entire business ecosystem in the area. According to Harvard professor Michael Porter, clusters allow companies in them to increase their productivity, gain a competitive edge, and increase their likelihood of survival. "Specialization in a region increases the number of patents and business formations and leads to higher wages,"* adds Harvard's Rich Bryden, who has helped develop a map of business clusters in the United States. Northeastern Ohio is home to dozens of companies, most of them small businesses, in the flexible electronic components (those that can be bent, folded, and stretched) field, many of them inspired by the world-renowned work of Kent State University's Liquid Crystal Institute and the pioneering work in polymer science at the University of Akron and Case Western Reserve University.[31] California's Napa Valley boasts more than 300 wineries, many of them small, family-owned operations that are among the best in the United States. The region's climate and soil, both of which are ideal for growing grapes, led entrepreneurs to establish wineries as early as 1861. As in most clusters, over time these vintners shared both knowledge and best practices, leading to the formation of more wineries, increased productivity and innovation, and the resulting competitive advantages.[32]

Once a concentration of companies takes root in a city, other businesses in those industries tend to spring up there as well. Ogden, Utah, hosted some events for the 2002 Olympics in Salt Lake City. With its bountiful mountains, canyons, and rivers and a population devoted to outdoor activities ranging from hiking and biking to mountain climbing and skiing, Ogden has become the hub of a cluster of outdoor sports companies. It offers the ideal location for testing new products, and a nearby airport provides direct international flights for entrepreneurs who are engaged in international business.

ENTREPRENEURIAL PROFILE: Steve Flagg: Quality Bicycle Products Steve Flagg, founder of Quality Bicycle Products, a small wholesale bicycle distributor based in Bloomington, Minnesota, chose Ogden for his company's second location. Flagg, whose company serves 5,000 independent bicycle shops, was drawn to Ogden by its cluster of companies that make outdoor gear, its strong pool of labor, its growing retail base, and its easy access to the West Coast market.[33] ■

COMPATIBILITY WITH THE COMMUNITY One of the intangibles that can be determined only by a visit to an area is the degree of compatibility a business has with the surrounding community. In other words, a small company's image must fit in with the character of a town and the needs and wants of its residents. For example, Beverly Hills's ritzy Rodeo Drive or Palm Beach's Worth Avenue are home to shops that match the characteristics of the area's wealthy residents. Exclusive shops such as Cartier, Jimmy Choo, Versace, Louis Vuitton, and Tiffany & Company abound, catering to the area's rich and famous residents.

LOCAL LAWS AND REGULATIONS Before settling on a city, entrepreneurs must consider the regulatory burden local government will impose. Government regulations affect many aspects of small business's operation, from acquiring business licenses and building permits to erecting business signs and dumping trash. Some cities are regulatory activists, creating so many rules that they discourage business creation; others take a more laissez-faire approach, imposing few restrictions on businesses. Andy Puzder, CEO of CKE Restaurants, owner of the Carl's Jr. and Hardee's quick-service restaurant chains, says getting a building permit in Texas requires 60 days; in Shanghai, China, the permitting process takes 63 days, and in Novosibirsk, Russia, the process takes 125 days. In Los Angeles, however, Puzder says getting a building permit requires

---

*Emily Maltby, Where the Action is, *The Wall Street Journal*, August 23, 2011.

285 days, pointing out the irony of being able to open a restaurant on Karl Marx Prospekt in Russia faster than the company can open one on Karl Archer Boulevard in California.[34]

ENTREPRENEURIAL PROFILE: Damien Graf and Robyn Semien: Bibber and Bell Wine and Spirits Copreneurs Damien Graf and Robyn Semien found the ideal location for their wine and spirits shop, Bibber & Bell Wine and Spirits, in the Williamsburg neighborhood in Brooklyn, New York. Negotiating a lease for the building, which is located in a high-traffic area just one block away from a busy subway station, took time and patience but was nothing compared to the gyrations the couple had to go through to get a retail liquor license from the State Liquor Authority. The paperwork they were required to submit took the Authority took three months to process while Graf and Semien continued to pay rent (about $14,000) and other expenses (about $6,000) so that they would not lose their desired location. The couple persisted and ultimately opened their shop, which they continue to operate successfully.[35] ■

Zoning laws can have a major impact on an entrepreneur's location decision. New York City passed the first comprehensive zoning laws in 1916, and most cities now have **zoning laws** that divide a city or county into cells or districts to control the use of land, buildings, and sites.[36] Their purpose is to contain similar activities in suitable locations. For instance, one section of a city may be zoned residential, whereas the primary retail district may be zoned commercial and another zoned industrial to house manufacturing operations. Before selecting a particular site within a city, entrepreneurs must explore local zoning laws to determine whether there are any ordinances that would place restrictions on business activity or that would prohibit establishing a business altogether. Zoning regulations may make a particular location out of bounds.

In some cases, an entrepreneur may appeal to the local zoning commission to rezone a site or to grant a **variance** (a special exception to a zoning ordinance), but this is risky and could be devastating if the board disallows the variance. Stan Freemon, opened his first Eggs Up Grill, a franchise that serves an extensive breakfast menu as well as sandwiches and salads, on a busy road with a high concentration of retail shops in Greenville, South Carolina, in 2014. Several months later, Freemon opened his second franchise in Greenville's vibrant downtown district, drawn by its youthful population, art galleries, live theaters, and eclectic mix of retail shops. Because zoning laws restricted downtown businesses' operating hours, Freemon had to secure a variance from the city's Board of Zoning Appeals to open his restaurant between midnight and 5 A.M.[37] As the number of home-based businesses has increased in the last several years, more entrepreneurs have found themselves at odds with city zoning regulations.

APPROPRIATE INFRASTRUCTURE AND UTILITIES Business owners must consider the quality of the infrastructure and availability of utilities in a potential location. Is an airport located nearby? Are flights available to the necessary cities, and are the schedules convenient? If a company needs access to a railroad spur, is one available in the city? How convenient is the area's access to major highways? What about travel distances to major customers? How long will it take to deliver shipments to them? Are transportation rates reasonable? In some situations, double or triple handling of merchandise and inventory causes transportation costs to skyrocket. Are sufficient supplies of necessary inputs such as water and natural gas available? Are utility rates reasonable? What impact will utilities costs have on the company's operation?

ENTREPRENEURIAL PROFILE: Providencia USA Providencia USA recently built a $70 million factory that makes nonwoven fabric in Statesville, North Carolina, because the location offered all of the necessary infrastructure that is important to the factory's success. An international airport is just 45 minutes away, and two major interstate highways make transporting finished goods to customers along the East Coast fast and efficient. Railway access was also an important factor because railroad delivery is the least expensive way to deliver the pelletized polypropylene raw material that Providencia uses in its production process. Finally, the availability of low-cost electricity was the "tipping factor" in the company's location decision.[38] ■

INCENTIVES Many states, counties, and cities offer financial and other incentives to encourage businesses that will create jobs to locate within their borders. These incentives range from job training for workers and reduced tax rates to financial grants and loans. To gear up its economic development effort, Minnesota recently included more than $86 million in business incentives in

zoning laws
laws that divide a city or county into small cells or districts to control the use of land, buildings, and sites.

variance
a special exemption to a zoning ordinance.

Ethics and Entrepreneurship

"Wait, You Can't Take Our Location . . . Can You?"

As children, Jo-Ann Morlando and Dominica Clementi, both residents of Charlotte, North Carolina, learned how to bake from their beloved Italian grandmothers, affectionately known as Nonas. As adults, both women chose professional careers but retained their love for baking, often creating delectable sweets for their children's school events or for church gatherings. Before long, their reputation as stellar bakers led to a constant barrage of requests for goodies from family members and friends. Sometimes the women would work a full day at the office and stay up all night baking. In 2004, after one marathon baking session, Morlando turned to Clementi and said, "Let's start a bakery."

They did and named their bakery Nona's Sweets as a tribute to their grandmothers, whose recipes they used to create the variety of sweet treats they offered. Although their original shop was small, it was in a good location that drew plenty of customers. The bakery thrived, and in the midst of the Great Recession, the family decided to expand to a new, carefully chosen location in Charlotte's fast-growing University City neighborhood. The building they rented was in a prominent location in a high-traffic area. In addition, the local university had announced plans to build a football stadium nearby, and the city had announced that it was going to build a station for the LYNX Blue Line, the city's light rail system (which carries 16,000 people on a typical weekday) that it was expanding. Although the bakery was profitable, no banks would lend money for the expansion, so Morlando and Clementi invested nearly $400,000 in transforming their new location, on which they had signed a 10-year lease, into the quaint bakery they had always dreamed of. They worked 14-hour days, experimenting with new products, improving their grandmothers' recipes, and building their clientele. They added a wedding cake service, a cupcake bar, and a section called Papa's Eats that serves breakfast and lunch. Within months, their business was booming; sales and profits were higher than ever.

Then in 2012, Morlando and Clementi received a letter from the city of Charlotte, telling them that the plans for the light rail expansion had changed. In a cost-cutting move, the city was shortening the expansion by 1.2 miles and was going to build a five-story parking garage where their building sat. They had 90 days to move their bakery out of the building. Morlando and Clementi were stunned and contacted their lawyer. They soon learned that, despite investing hundreds of thousands of dollars in their new location, they were powerless to save it because the city could invoke the power of eminent domain, which allows a government entity to expropriate private property for public use as long as the government pays "just compensation." Because the entrepreneurs were renting the building, they were not entitled to any compensation. As word spread throughout the community that the building that housed the bakery was being torn down, sales began to decline.

Morlando and Clementi wanted to stay in the University City area and began searching for a new location, but many sites, particularly those in shopping centers, were off limits because their tenants included grocery stores, which typically have their own bakeries, that had negotiated lease provisions that prevent landlords from leasing space to other bakeries. They finally found another suitable building in University City in The Shoppes at Worthington, a shopping center with no grocery store. The city did reimburse Morlando and Clementi for the cost they incurred to move their business to the new location, but they received no compensation for the additional costs of outfitting their new location and advertising it or the sales they lost while the bakery was closed during the transition.

Although the entrepreneurs say they would not want to go through another forced move, the tenacious pair is finding reasons to be excited about their new location, which allowed them to create a space that is warm, welcoming, and relaxing. Shelving allows them to boldly display their intricately decorated cakes, tempting smells lure passersby, and old photographs of nonas from past generations line the walls and give customers a sense of nostalgia.

1. Should a government entity have the power to "take" a business's location if it better serves the public good? Explain.

2. Use the resources of the Internet to learn more about the concept of eminent domain. What benefits does it produce? What are the risks associated with it?

Sources: Caitlin McCabe, "Nona's Sweets Gets Derailed, Starts Over at a New Site in Charlotte," *Charlotte Observer*, June 23, 2013, http://www.charlotteobserver.com/2013/06/23/4124634/nonas-bakery-gets-derailed-starts.html#.U5DBUnZrTOs; Lindsay Ruebens, "Lynx Parking Deck to Bump Nona's Bakery," *Lake Norman News*, November 4, 2012, http://www.charlotteobserver.com/2012/11/04/3637266/lynx-parking-deck-to-bump-nonas.html#.U5DCW3ZrTOs; Coleen Harry, "Blue Line Extension Forcing Businesses Out," *14 News*, October 4, 2012, http://www.14news.com/story/19740507/blue-line-extension-forcing-businesses-out.

its budget, but companies have to earn the incentives through capital investments or job creation. Emerson Process Management, which manufactures pressure, temperature, flow, level, and wireless measurement instruments, earned more than $2.7 million in incentives by investing $70 million in a factory in Shakopee, Minnesota, that created 500 new jobs. Shutterfly, a California-based company that provides personalized digital photo solutions, qualified for a $1 million loan through the Minnesota Investment Fund by locating a production and distribution center in Shakopee that created 330 jobs.[39] Although incentives are not the primary driver of companies' location decisions, they often are the "tie-breaker" between similar sites.

Companies that accept incentives must be aware of "clawback" provisions that require them to repay the state the value of some or all of the incentives if the company fails to create a minimum number of jobs or make a minimum capital investment. State and local government entities approved nearly $270 million in incentives to convince Dell Inc. to build a computer assembly plant in Winston–Salem, North Carolina, on the condition that the company create at least 900 jobs. Four years later, however, in a move to improve its efficiency, Dell decided to close the factory, which required the company to repay $28 million under the contract's clawback provision.[40]

QUALITY OF LIFE A final consideration when selecting a city is the quality of life it offers. For many entrepreneurs, quality of life is one of the key determinants of their choice of locale. Cities that offer comfortable weather, cultural events, colleges and universities, museums, outdoor activities, concerts, unique restaurants, and an interesting nightlife have become magnets for entrepreneurs looking to start companies. Over the last two decades, cities such as Austin, Boston, Seattle, San Francisco, Washington, Dallas, Minneapolis, and others have become incubators for creativity and entrepreneurship as educated young people drawn by the cities' quality of life have moved in.

Not only can a location in a city offering a high quality of life be attractive to an entrepreneur, but it can also make recruiting employees much easier. According to a study of the importance of location on recruiting employees conducted by the Human Capital Institute, the three most important factors in attracting talent are job opportunities, a clean and safe community, and an affordable cost of living.[41]

ENTREPRENEURIAL PROFILE: **K.C. Walsh: Simms Fishing Products.** A few years ago, K.C. Walsh, CEO of Simms Fishing Products, a company launched by entrepreneur and fly fisher John Simms in 1980 that makes fishing waders and accessories, relocated its headquarters to Bozeman, Montana. The quality of life (and superb fly fishing) in and around Bozeman was the primary factor in the decision. Walsh, a lifelong fly fisher, said his dream was to live, work, and play in Montana. Because most of the company's 120 employees are avid fly fishers and outdoor enthusiasts, Bozeman's access to some of the best trout rivers and streams, mountains, and natural beauty make it an ideal location for Simms. Montana is a business-friendly state, and Simms can field-test its products under real-world conditions quite easily.[42] ■

Choosing the Site

The final step in the location selection process is choosing the actual site for the business. Once again, entrepreneurs must let the facts guide them to the best location. Every business has its own unique set of criteria for an ideal location. A manufacturer's prime consideration may be access to raw materials, suppliers, labor, transportation, and customers. Service firms require access to customers but can generally survive in lower-rent properties. A retailer's prime consideration is sufficient customer traffic. For example, an entrepreneur who is planning to launch a convenience store should know that generating a sufficient volume of sales requires a population of at least 500 to 1,000 people who live within a one-mile radius of the outlet and choose a location accordingly.[43] The one element common to all three types of businesses is the need to locate where customers want to do business.

Some entrepreneurs test the suitability of potential locations by opening "pop-up" stores, shops that are open for only a few days, weeks, or months before shutting down. These temporary stores open in available spaces, sell their merchandise quickly, close, and move on to the next location; they are low-cost, efficient ways for an entrepreneur to test a location as a potential site for a permanent business.

ENTREPRENEURIAL PROFILE: **Stephen Robins: Pelindaba Lavender** Stephen Robins, founder of Pelindaba Lavender, a company that sells more than 250 lavender-based products from its farm store on San Juan Island in northwestern Washington, recently opened a pop-up store in Pacific Place, a downtown retail center in Seattle, to test the area as a site for a permanent store location. In addition to serving as a test site, the pop-up store serves as a showcase for the company's unique products and introduces them to customers the company normally would not reach, including tourists. Because of the pop-up store's success, Robins is looking for a location with 900 to 1,000 square feet to house a new permanent Pelindaba Lavender store.[44] ■

Rental or lease rates are an important factor when choosing a site. Of course, entrepreneurs must be sure that the rent or lease payments for a particular location fit comfortably into their budgets. Although "cheap" rental rates can be indicative of a second-class location (and the resulting poor revenues they generate), entrepreneurs should not agree to exorbitant rental rates that jeopardize their ability to surpass their break-even points.

ENTREPRENEURIAL PROFILE: Claude Esnault: Au Grande Richelieu Boulangerie
Claude Esnault, owner for the last 43 years of the Au Grand Richelieu Boulangerie, recently closed the landmark bakery, which opened in 1811, because the annual rent had nearly doubled from €18,000 ($22,860) to €35,000 ($44,450) per year. The landlord claims the new rent is in line with that of other locations in the fast-growing neighborhood, which is situated near the Opera Garnier and the Louvre museum. Unfortunately, Esnault says the bakery, Paris's oldest, could not support rent that high, prompting the decision to close the historic bakery's doors.[45] ■

Many businesses are downsizing their outlets to lower their start-up and operating costs and to allow for a greater number of location options that are not available to full-size stores. Franchises such as Cinnabon and Burger King are finding success by placing smaller, less expensive outlets in locations that cannot support a full-size store. Burger King recently opened six Whopper Bars in the United States and three international locations in Venezuela and Singapore. At just 700 square feet, a Whopper Bar is one-fifth the size of a traditional Burger King outlet and is ideal for locations in theme parks, airports, museums, casinos, cruise ships, and shopping malls. A Whopper Bar, which sells beer and includes a Whopper topper area in which customers customize the company's signature sandwich with 22 different toppings, costs between $600,000 and $800,000 to build, which is 30 percent less than the smallest traditional Burger King restaurant. Despite its size, the Whopper Bar's sales per square foot exceed those of its full-size franchise outlets.[46]

Finally, an entrepreneur must be careful to select a site that creates the right impression for a business in the customers' eyes. A company's location speaks volumes about a company's "personality."

ENTREPRENEURIAL PROFILE: Charlene Dupray and Pascal Siegler: South'n France
When copreneurs Charlene Dupray and Pascal Siegler saw an old diner in downtown Wilmington, North Carolina, with its salmon pink concrete exterior, 13-foot ceilings, and diner stools, they knew they had found the perfect building to house their chocolate bonbon business, South'n France. In addition to its unique character, the building came equipped with freezers capable of holding 20,000 bonbons, provided sufficient space for Dupray and Siegler to manufacture their chocolate delicacies, and included rooms they could convert into a retail storefront. Even though their business is on the verge of outgrowing the space, Dupray says, "We love it so much that we're considering adding another story or buying nearby residences because this old luncheonette really is a workhorse for us."[47] ■

LO2
Describe the location criteria for retail and service businesses.

Location Criteria for Retail and Service Businesses

Few decisions are as important for retailers and service firms as the choice of a location. Because their success depends on a steady flow of customers, these businesses must locate their businesses with their target customers' convenience and preferences in mind. The following are important considerations:

Trade Area Size

trading area
the region from which a business can expect to draw customers over a reasonable time span.

Every retail and service business should determine the extent of its **trading area**, the region from which a business can expect to draw customers over a reasonable time span. The primary variables that influence the scope of the trading area are the type and size of the business. If a retail store specializes in a particular product line and offers a wide selection and knowledgeable salespeople, it may draw customers from a great distance. In contrast, a convenience store with a general line of merchandise has a small trading area because it is unlikely that customers will drive across town to purchase items that are available within blocks of their homes or businesses. As a rule, the larger the store, the greater its selection, and the better its service, the broader is its trading area. Cabela's, the outdoor outfitter, has nearly 60 stores across the United States and Canada (with more on the way) that average 127,500 square feet (one store is 247,000 square feet) and carry more than 225,000 SKUs, ranging from outdoor apparel and hunting and fishing gear to boats and home furnishings. With their extensive inventories and unique features (museum-quality wildlife displays and huge aquariums),

You Be the Consultant

"Pop" Goes the Store

Pop-up stores are temporary locations that are open for only a few hours, days, or weeks before shutting down. For entrepreneurs who operate highly seasonal businesses (think Halloween costume stores and Christmas décor shops), pop-up stores are a way of life, but other entrepreneurs use them to test new business ideas or potential locations, create brand awareness, clear out excess inventory, and promote their full-time locations. Rick Martin used a pop-up store to test Pacific Place, a popular shopping, dining, and entertainment center in downtown Seattle, Washington, as a potential location for his gourmet olive oil and balsamic vinegar business, 11 Olives. Martin's pop-up store proved to be so successful that he has begun looking for a permanent location in Pacific Place.

The Academy of Art University in San Francisco periodically opens a pop-up shop to showcase the work of its students and alumni. The temporary boutique is filled with a wide array of merchandise, including jewelry, gifts, clothing, and accessories and gives students the opportunity to learn firsthand what is required for fashion to go from an idea to actual products that end up in customers' shopping bags. The pop-up shop has proved to be so popular that university officials are considering opening a permanent location in San Francisco.

Before hip-hop artist Kanye West's Yeezus tour opened in New York City, the entertainer used Storefront, a company that specializes in helping entrepreneurs and businesses find locations for pop-up stores, to find a suitable spot for a pop-up shop to sell his merchandise. Four days later, when the tour moved on to its next venue, the shop closed, but not before selling thousands of T-shirts, tote bags, caps, and hats.

Claire Winkler, owner of the Greenville, South Carolina, location of Ten Thousand Villages, a business that sells handmade gifts and crafts created by artisans in developing countries, operates her company from a full-time location on busy Augusta Street. Although only two miles from Greenville's vibrant downtown district, the Augusta Street location rarely draws downtown residents and tourists. Winkler opened a pop-up Ten Thousand Villages store in a vacant building that once housed offices in the downtown district from October to December to take advantage of the pedestrian traffic generated by the many fall festivals and events the city held downtown, the area's live performances, and the busy holiday shopping season. In addition to generating additional sales, her goal was to expand the awareness of her Augusta Street location. The first weekend, the store was extremely busy. Winkler says many of the pop-up shop's customers were people who lived in Greenville but had never heard of her Augusta Street store and its interesting collection of inventory. She considers the pop-up to be a huge sales—and brand awareness—success.

Even online merchants are opening pop-up stores, and many are finding that the opportunity to spend face-to-face time with customers enables them to gain valuable feedback on their product lines, get ideas for new products, and determine whether they are ready to open brick-and-mortar stores. Jon Crawford, founder of Storenvy Inc., an online platform where small businesses can set up e-commerce stores and sell their products, partnered with Storefront Inc. to set up a physical store in which five of Storenvy's more than 50,000 e-commerce business owners would operate their own real-world shops for one month. Each month, five new businesses move into the retail space, which is located in downtown San Francisco. Crawford says the retail space has become a type of retail incubator that allows e-commerce merchants to test the viability of a physical store.

When Laura Bruland, who makes unique laser-cut jewelry from recycled books (she ran a successful Kickstarter campaign to raise the money to purchase her first laser cutter), opened her pop-up shop, Yes & Yes Designs, in the retail space, she realized that she needed a much bigger and bolder display for her innovative designs. Her one-month experience with the physical store gave her the confidence to start selling her jewelry successfully at festivals and craft fairs. Bruland, who operates the online company from her own studio in Oakland, California, with the help of her partner, Julien Shields, and their wonder dog, Toto, also has benefitted from her in-depth conversations with customers, many of whom have given her ideas for new designs and new products. After one customer asked about a gift for her husband, Bruland created a line of cufflinks. Several early participants in the program have gone on to create physical stores to supplement their online sales.

1. What advantages and disadvantages do pop-up stores such as the ones described here offer entrepreneurs?

2. What types of businesses would be successful opening pop-up stores temporarily on your campus or on a nearby campus? What advice would you offer entrepreneurs who are considering opening the store? When should it open and for how long?

3. Would a pop-up store such as the ones that 11 Olives and Ten Thousand Villages used be successful in your community? Explain. Work with a team of your classmates to identify three products or product lines that would be successful in your community if they were sold from a pop-up store.

Sources: Based on Jeanne Lang Jones, "Retail Pop-Up Stores in Demand," *Puget Sound Business Journal,* November 30, 2012, http://www.bizjournals.com/seattle/print-edition/2012/11/30/retail-pop-up-stores-in-demand.html?page=all; Joshua David Stein, "No Space Too Small, No Lease Too Short," *New York Times,* December 20, 2013, http://www.nytimes.com/2013/12/22/fashion/Pop-Up-Stores-Storefront.html; "Young Designers Debut at Academy of Art University Pop-Up Shop," *7X7SF,* May 28, 2014, http://www.7x7.com/music-nightlife/young-designers-debut-academy-art-university-pop-shop; Tony Bravo, "Academy of Art University Pop-Up Shop," *SF Gate,* May 23, 2014, http://blog.sfgate.com/chronstyle/2014/05/23/academy-of-art-university-fashion-pop-up-shop/#23693101=0; Amy Westervelt, "A Shot at the Real World," *Wall Street Journal,* February 3, 2014, p. R5; Anna Lee, "Here Today, Gone Tomorrow," *Greenville News,* October 19, 2013, pp. 1A, 3A.

Cabela's stores are destination stores, often drawing shoppers from 100 or more miles away.[48] Businesses that offer a narrow selection of products and services tend to have smaller trading areas. For instance, the majority of a massage therapist's clients live within 3 to 5 miles of the location, with a secondary tier of clients who live within 5 to 10 miles. Clients who are willing to travel more than 15 minutes for a session are rare.[49]

ENTREPRENEURIAL PROFILE: Greg Carafello: Cartridge World When Greg Carafello became a master franchiser for Cartridge World, an Australia-based company that sells new and remanufactured printer cartridges, he opened franchises in suburban New Jersey in strip malls located near concentrations of small businesses, which make up 95 percent of his customers. When Carafello began opening stores in downtown Manhattan, where rental rates are *much* higher, he discovered that the best locations are those on the first floor of high-rise buildings that house at least 60 floors of business space. The high concentration of small business customers in close proximity generates a high volume of business for his Cartridge World locations.[50] ∎

Retail Compatibility

retail compatibility
the benefits a company receives by locating near other businesses that sell complementary products and services or that generate high volumes of traffic.

Shoppers tend to be drawn to clusters of related businesses. That's one reason shopping malls and outlet shopping centers are popular destinations for shoppers and are attractive locations for retailers. The concentration of businesses pulls customers from a larger trading area than a single freestanding business does. **Retail compatibility** describes the benefits a company receives by locating near other businesses that sell complementary products and services or that generate high volumes of foot traffic. Clever business owners choose their locations with an eye on the surrounding mix of businesses. For instance, grocery store operators prefer not to locate in shopping centers with movie theaters, offices, and fitness centers, all businesses whose customers occupy parking spaces for extended time periods. Drugstores, nail salons, and ice cream parlors have proved to be much better shopping center neighbors for grocers.

ENTREPRENEURIAL PROFILE: Carol Buie-Jackson and Jay Jackson: Birdhouse on the Greenway Carol Buie-Jackson and her husband, Jay Jackson, spent months screening potential locations for their wild bird product shop, Birdhouse on the Greenway. They chose a 1,600-square-foot space in The Shops at Piper Glen, a shopping center on the fast-growing south side of Charlotte, North Carolina, which offers two prime advantages. The store is located in the middle of one of the city's most affluent residential areas that contains large numbers of their target customers, people who are in their 50s and 60s with above-average incomes and are environmentally conscious. It also sits at the entrance of Four-Mile Creek Greenway, a popular walking trail that winds through natural habitat and has connectors to local neighborhoods. The other businesses in the shopping center complement Birdhouse on the Greenway because they draw the same customers the Jacksons target. Trader Joe's is just two doors down, and other stores include Starbucks and Great Harvest Bread Company. Because of their wise choice of a location for their shop, the Jacksons say Birdhouse on the Green is thriving.[51] ∎

Degree of Competition

The size, location, and activity of competing businesses also influence the size of a company's trading area. If a business will be the first of its kind in a location, its trading area might be quite extensive. However, if the area already has 8 or 10 nearby stores that directly compete with a business, its trading area might be very small because the market is saturated with competitors. Market saturation is a problem for businesses in many industries, ranging from fast-food restaurants to convenience stores. Red Mango, an upscale yogurt chain based in Los Angeles, recently saw four of its franchises in that city close because of poor location choices. The company is continuing with its expansion plans but will focus on other cities that are less saturated with frozen yogurt shops.[52]

The Index of Retail Saturation

index of retail saturation
a measure of the potential sales per square foot of store space for a given product within a specific trading area; it is the ratio of a trading area's sales potential for a product or service to its sales capacity.

One of the best measures of the level of saturation in an area is the index of retail saturation (IRS), which takes into account both the number of customers and the intensity of competition in a trading area. The **index of retail saturation** is a measure of the potential sales per square foot of store space for a given product within a specific trading area. It is the ratio of a trading area's sales potential for a particular product or service to its sales capacity:

$$\text{IRS} = \frac{C \times RE}{RF}$$

where

  C = number of customers in the trading area

  RE = retail expenditures, or the average expenditure per person ($) for the product in the trading area

  RF = retail facilities, or the total square feet of selling space allocated to the product in the trading area

This computation is an important one for every retailer to make. Locating in an area already saturated with competitors results in dismal sales volume and often leads to failure.

To illustrate the index of retail saturation, suppose an entrepreneur who is looking at two sites for a shoe store finds that he needs sales of $175 per square foot to be profitable. Site 1 has a trading area with 25,875 potential customers who spend an average of $42 on shoes annually; the only competitor in the trading area has 6,000 square feet of selling space. Site 2 has 27,750 potential customers spending an average of $43.50 on shoes annually; two competitors occupy 8,400 square feet of space:

Site 1

$$\text{Index of retail saturation} = \frac{25{,}875 \times 42}{6{,}000}$$

$$= \$181.12 \text{ sales potential per square foot}$$

Site 2

$$\text{Index of retail saturation} = \frac{27{,}750 \times 43.50}{8{,}400}$$

$$= \$143.71 \text{ sales potential per square foot}$$

Although site 2 appears to be more favorable on the surface, the index shows that site 1 is preferable; site 2 fails to meet the minimum standard of $175 per square foot.

Reilly's Law of Retail Gravitation

Reilly's Law of Retail Gravitation, a classic work in market analysis published in 1931 by William J. Reilly, uses the analogy of gravity to estimate the attractiveness of a particular business to potential customers. A business's ability to draw customers is directly related to the extent to which customers see it as a "destination" and is inversely related to the distance customers must travel to reach it. Reilly's model also provides a way to estimate the trade boundary between two market areas by calculating the "break point" between them. The break point between two primary market areas is the boundary between the two where customers become indifferent about shopping at one or the other. The key factor in determining this point of indifference is the size of the communities. If two nearby cities have the same population sizes, then the break point lies halfway between them. The following is the equation for Reilly's Law:[53]

$$BP = \frac{d}{1 + \sqrt{\dfrac{P_b}{P_a}}}$$

where

  BP = the distance in miles from location A to the break point

  d = the distance in miles between locations A and B

  P_b = the population surrounding location B

  P_a = the population surrounding location A

For example, if city A and city B are 22 miles apart and city A has a population of 25,500 and city B has a population of 42,900, the break point according to Reilly's law is

$$BP = \frac{22}{1 + \sqrt{\dfrac{42{,}900}{25{,}500}}} = 9.2 \text{ miles}$$

The outer edge of city A's trading area lies about nine miles between city A and city B. Although only a rough estimate, this simple calculation using readily available data can be useful for screening potential locations.

Transportation Network

For many retail and service businesses, easy customer access from a smoothly flowing network of highways and roads is essential. If a location is inconvenient for customers to reach, a business located there will suffer from a diminished trading area and lower sales. Entrepreneurs should verify that the transportation system works smoothly and is free of barriers that prevent customers from reaching their shopping destinations. Is it easy for customers traveling in the opposite direction to cross traffic? Do traffic signs and lights allow traffic to flow smoothly?

E-commerce companies also must consider accessibility to trucking routes, such as interstate highways, and airports so that they can expedite customers' orders. Zappos, the online shoe retailer, moved its fulfillment center to Louisville, Kentucky, so that the company can ship orders almost anywhere in the United States within one day. The Zappos center is located just 12 miles from the UPS Worldport, the world's largest automated package-sorting facility (it can sort 416,000 packages per hour) in the Louisville International Airport. From this airport, flights can reach 75 percent of the population of the United States in just 2.5 hours and 95 percent of the population in 4 hours. The city also has three interstate highways and two railways. Because of Zappos's location, a package that leaves UPS Worldport by 12:45 A.M. can arrive at the home or business of any customer in the United States that same day, giving the company a competitive edge in customer service.[54]

Physical and Psychological Barriers

Trading area shape and size also are influenced by physical and psychological barriers. Physical barriers may be parks, rivers, lakes, bridges, or any other natural or man-made obstruction that hinders customers' access to the area. Locating on one side of a large park may reduce the number of customers who will drive around it to get to a store. Psychological barriers include areas that have a reputation for crime and illegal activities. If high crime areas exist near a site, potential customers will not travel through them to reach a business.

Other factors retailers should consider when evaluating potential sites are discussed next.

Customer Traffic

Perhaps the most important screening criterion for a potential retail (and often for a service) location is the number of potential customers passing by the site during business hours. To be successful, a business must be able to generate sufficient sales to surpass its break-even point, and that requires an ample volume of customer traffic going past its doors. The key success factor for many retail stores is a high-volume location with easy accessibility. Entrepreneurs should use traffic counts (pedestrian and/or auto) and traffic pattern studies (usually available from state highway departments) to confirm that the sites they are considering as potential locations are capable of generating sufficient sales volume.

ENTREPRENEURIAL PROFILE: IHOP IHOP, the restaurant chain best known for its breakfast offerings, recently opened an IHOP Express, a downsized version of its restaurants, in Atlanta's Hartsfield-Jackson International Airport. Located outside the security checkpoint in the Main Terminal Food Court, the 3,000-square-foot restaurant is open 24 hours a day, seven days a week and features both sit-down and "grab-and-go" meals. The IHOP Express benefits from the high volume of traffic created by the 90 million passengers who pass through the world's busiest airport each year and the 60,000 employees who work there. Rental rates are much higher than those in traditional locations, but average sales per square foot for restaurants and retailers at Hartsfield-Jackson are an impressive $2,215, seven times the average at a typical mall (and three times the average at top-performing malls).[55] ∎

Adequate Parking

If customers cannot find convenient and safe parking, they are not likely to shop in the area. Many downtown areas lose customers because of inadequate parking. Although shopping malls average five parking spaces per 1,000 square feet of shopping space, many central business districts get by with 3.5 spaces (or fewer) per 1,000 square feet. In addition, some central business districts require visitors to feed meters to pay for parking, another deterrent to shoppers. Even when free parking is available, some potential customers may not feel safe on the streets, especially after dark. Some large city downtown business districts become virtual ghost towns at the end of the business day. A location where traffic vanishes after 6 P.M. may not be as valuable as mall or shopping center locations that mark the beginning of the prime sales time at 6 P.M.

ENTREPRENEURIAL PROFILE: Chris Wysocki and Robert Fulbright: Yarnhouse Chris Wysocki and Robert Fulbright opened Yarnhouse, a specialty knitting, crocheting, and fiber art shop in 2008 in a building on North Davidson Street located in the heart of Charlotte, North Carolina's arts district (known as "NoDa"). The arts district location provided significant exposure and attracted a large number of the entrepreneurs' target customers, but customers often complained about the scarcity of available parking. They knew their sales were suffering because many customers were not willing to walk several blocks to shop at their store. Wysocki and Fulbright decided to move their store, but they did not go far—just a half-mile down North Davidson Street to a building surrounded by ample parking spaces and just three doors away from one of Charlotte's most popular restaurants, Amelie's French Bakery. Their rent actually is 20 percent lower, customer traffic at Yarnhouse already has increased, and Wysocki says the new location is proving to be "monumental."[56] ■

Reputation

Like people, a site can have a bad reputation. Sites in which businesses have failed repeatedly create negative impressions in customers' minds; many people view the business as just another one that soon will be gone. Sometimes previous failures are indicative of a fundamental problem with the location itself; in other cases, the cause of the previous failure was the result not of a poor location but of a poorly managed business. When entrepreneurs decide to conduct business in a location that has housed previous failures, it is essential that they make many highly visible changes to the site to exorcise the "ghosts" of the failed businesses that came before them and to give customers the perception of a company making a "fresh start."

ENTREPRENEURIAL PROFILE: James and Julie Petrakis: The Cask and Larder When copreneurs James and Julie Petrakis, owners of The Ravenous Pig, a restaurant in Winter Park, Florida, decided to open a second restaurant, The Cask and Larder, they selected a landmark building only a half a mile away from their existing restaurant. Although the building was well known to locals and was in a high-traffic location, the Petrakises had some misgivings about it because it had been home to five failed restaurants over the previous decade. However, the couple was able to negotiate a favorable lease and invested in a major renovation to erase the memory of past failures from customers' minds. Two years later, the Cask and Larder is going strong with a diverse menu that includes meats cured in-house, locally sourced fresh seafood, homemade preserves and jams, and craft beers brewed onsite by an experienced brewmaster.[57] ■

Visibility

A final characteristic of a good location is visibility. Highly visible locations simply make it easy for customers to find a business and make purchases. A site that lacks visibility puts a company at a major disadvantage before it ever opens its doors for business.

Location Options for Retail and Service Businesses

LO3

Outline the location options for retail and service businesses: central business districts, neighborhoods, shopping centers and malls, near competitors, shared spaces, inside large retail stores, nontraditional locations, at home, and on the road.

There are nine basic areas where retail and service business owners can locate: the central business district, neighborhoods, shopping centers and malls, near competitors, shared spaces, inside large retail stores, nontraditional locations, at home, and on the road. According to Reis Inc., the average cost to lease space in a shopping center is about $19 per square foot, and at malls, lease rates average $39 per square foot. In central business locations, the average cost is between $22 and $45 per square foot (rental rates vary significantly, depending on the city).[58] Of course, cost is just one factor a business owner must consider when choosing a location.

Central Business District

The central business district (CBD) is the traditional center of town—the downtown concentration of businesses established early in the development of most towns and cities. Entrepreneurs derive several advantages from a downtown location. Because the business is centrally located, it attracts customers from the entire trading area of the city. In addition, a small business usually benefits from the customer traffic generated by the other stores in the district. Many cities have undertaken revitalization efforts in their CBDs and have transformed these areas into thriving, vigorous hubs of economic activity that are proving to be ideal locations for small businesses. However, locating in some CBDs does have certain disadvantages. Many CBDs are characterized by intense competition, high rental rates, traffic congestion, and inadequate parking facilities.

ENTREPRENEURIAL PROFILE: David and Margaret Smith: Blowin' in the Wind David Smith, a fourth-generation carpenter and artist, and his wife, Margaret, moved to Las Vegas, New Mexico (not to be confused with its casino-laden namesake in Nevada) in 2006 to realize David's dream of opening a business. With a population of 14,000, Las Vegas, which was settled in the 1830s while still a part of Mexico, is unique in that its central business district features an uninterrupted avenue of well-preserved commercial buildings from the late nineteenth and early twentieth centuries that reflect a variety of styles, including Victorian, Mission Revival, Queen Anne, and others. More than 900 of the town's buildings are listed on the National Register of Historic Places, and its main street recently was named one of the top 10 Great American Streets. The unique architecture and intriguing colors of the buildings that line historic Bridge Street reflect Las Vegas's frontier history as an important hub of commercial and transportation activity on the famous Santa Fe Trail. The Smiths considered many different locations in the small town before choosing a 7,500-square-foot building at the foot of historic Bridge Street, which connects the "Old Town" with the "New Town," as the site for their gallery and boutique, Blowin' in the Wind, because of its large windows that allow them to feature their merchandise. The copreneurs have filled the space with an eclectic collection of merchandise ranging from wind sculptures and furniture (all made by David) to jewelry and clothing.[59] ■

Beginning in the 1950s, many cities saw their older downtown business districts begin to decay as residents moved to the suburbs and began shopping at newer, more conveniently located malls. Today, however, many of these CBDs are experiencing rebirth as cities restore them to their former splendor and shoppers return. Many customers find irresistible the charming atmosphere that traditional downtown districts offer with their rich mix of stores, their unique architecture and streetscapes, and their historic character. Cities have begun to reverse the urban decay of their downtown business districts through proactive revitalization programs designed to attract visitors and residents alike to cultural events by locating major theaters and museums in the downtown area. In addition, many cities are providing economic incentives to real estate developers to build apartment and condominium complexes in the heart of the downtown area. Vitality is returning as residents live and shop in the once nearly abandoned downtown areas. The "ghost-town" image is being replaced by both younger and older residents who love the convenience, culture, and excitement of life at the city center.

ENTREPRENEURIAL PROFILE: Nello Gioia: Ristorante Bergamo *Forbes* recently named Greenville, South Carolina, one of America's Best Downtowns, but 30 years ago, the city's central business district was a far different place. Nello Gioia, owner of Ristorante Bergamo, an upscale Italian restaurant, took a chance on a downtown location on Main Street in Greenville in 1985 when the city was just beginning an ambitious revitalization of its central business district. Unlike the busy, vibrant, highly desirable location Greenville's downtown is today, what Gioia saw then was a seedy-looking street spattered with offices, a few longtime resident businesses, and lots of shuttered and vacant stores. "The month before we opened, I got cold feet," recalls Gioia. "But I was up to my neck. I had to do it." Gioia had considered locating in a nearby regional mall and a strip mall but decided that those locations were inconsistent with the image he wanted to create for his restaurant. "The one place that resembled where I came from [Bergamo, Italy] was downtown," says Gioia.[60] ■

Today, Gioia is glad he took the chance on a downtown location; Greenville's central business district, with its eclectic mix of restaurants, small shops, and cultural events, has become a well-known success story, and many other cities across the United States are using it as a model for reclaiming their own downtowns.

Neighborhood Locations

Small businesses that locate near residential neighborhoods rely heavily on the local trading area for business. Businesses that provide convenience as a major attraction for customers find that locating on a street or road just outside major residential areas provides the needed traffic counts essential for success. Gas stations and convenience stores thrive in these high-traffic areas. One study of food stores found that the majority of the typical grocer's customers live within a five-mile radius. The primary advantages of a neighborhood location include relatively low operating rent and close contact with customers.

ENTREPRENEURIAL PROFILE: Jodi Hamilton: Dream Dinners Jodi Hamilton, who owns two Dream Dinners franchises, a chain that allows busy parents to assemble fast meals for their families using fresh, pre-prepped ingredients, selected the locations for her two Chicago-area outlets with her target customers in mind. Both of Hamilton's stores are in neighborhood locations, but each one is unique. Her Roscoe Village store, just north of Chicago, is near hundreds of single-family homes characterized by the typical suburban lifestyle. Hamilton's Ukranian Village store is just four miles away but is in a more densely populated area that is home to a younger population with smaller families and young professionals who are not interested in cooking for themselves. The Roscoe Village store is busiest in the mornings, while the Ukranian Village store begins to buzz in the afternoons and is open on Sundays. Hamilton's choice of locations that are convenient for her target customers has played a significant role in her stores' success.[61] ■

Shopping Centers and Malls

Until the early twentieth century, central business districts were the primary shopping venues in the United States. As cars and transportation networks became more prevalent in the 1920s, shopping centers began popping up outside cities' central business districts. Then in October 1956, the nation's first shopping mall, Southdale, opened in the Minneapolis, Minnesota, suburb of Edina. Designed by Victor Gruen, the fully enclosed mall featured 72 shops anchored by two competing department stores (a radical concept at the time), a garden courtyard with a goldfish pond, an aviary, hanging plants, and artificial trees. With its multilevel layout and parking garage, Southdale was a huge success and forever changed the way Americans would shop.[62] Today, shopping centers and malls are a mainstay of the American landscape. Approximately 113,000 shopping centers and 1,513 traditional enclosed malls operate in the United States.[63] Because many different types of stores operate under one roof, shopping centers give meaning to the term "one-stop shopping." In a typical month, nearly 187 million adults visit malls or shopping centers, generating $2.4 trillion in annual sales, an amount that represents more than half of all retail sales in the United States.[64] There are nine types of shopping centers (see Table 14.5):

- *Strip shopping centers.* Strip shopping centers are made up of attached rows of retail stores or service outlets that provide local shoppers a narrow range of goods and services. Although they tend to be the smallest of all shopping centers with an average size of 13,375 square feet of space, they make up the bulk of the centers in the United States, with a total count of more than 66,600.[65]

- *Neighborhood shopping centers.* The typical neighborhood shopping center is relatively small, containing from 3 to 12 stores and serving a population of up to 40,000 people who live within a 10-minute drive with a focus on convenience. The anchor store in these centers is usually a supermarket or a drugstore. Neighborhood shopping centers serve primarily the daily shopping needs of customers in the surrounding area. More than 32,200 neighborhood shopping centers operate across the United States.[66]

- *Community shopping centers.* A community shopping center contains from 12 to 50 stores and serves a population ranging from 40,000 to 150,000 people. The leading tenant often is a large department or variety store, a super-drugstore, or a supermarket.

TABLE 14.5 Types of Shopping Centers

Type of Shopping Center	Concept	Square Footage (Including Anchors)	Acreage	Typical Anchor		Anchor Ratio (%)[a]	Primary Trade Area (Miles)[b]
				Number	Type		
Enclosed Malls							
Regional center	General and fashion merchandise; mall (typically enclosed)	400,000–800,000	40–100	2 or more	Full-line department store; junior department store; mass merchant; discount department store; fashion apparel	50–70	5–15
Superregional center	Similar to regional center but offers more variety	>800,000	60–120	3 or more	Full-line department store; junior department store; mass merchant; fashion apparel	50–70	5–25
Open-Air Centers							
Strip Shopping Center	Convenience	10,000–25,000	2–12	1	Drugstore	30–50	1
Neighborhood center	Convenience	30,000–150,000	3–15	1 or more	Supermarket	30–50	1–3
Community center	General merchandise; convenience	100,000–350,000	10–40	2 or more	Discount department store; supermarket; drug; home improvement; large specialty or discount apparel	40–60	3–6
Lifestyle center	Upscale national chain specialty stores, dining, and entertainment in an outdoor setting	150,000–500,000 but can be larger or smaller	10–40	0–2	Not usually anchored in the traditional sense but may include bookstore; large specialty retailers; multiplex cinema; small department store	0–50	8–12
Power center	Category-dominant anchors; few small business tenants	250,000–600,000	25–80	3 or more	Category killer; home improvement; discount; department store; warehouse club; off price	75–90	5–10
Theme/festival center	Leisure; tourist oriented; retail and service	80,000–250,000	5–20	Unspecified	Restaurants; entertainment	N/A	25–75
Outlet center	Manufacturers' outlet stores	50,000–400,000	10–50	N/A	Manufacturers' outlet stores	N/A	25–75

[a]The share of a center's total square footage that is occupied by its anchors.
[b]The area from which 60% to 80% of the center's sales originate.

Source: Table adapted from *U.S. Shopping Center Definitions*, April 2009. Copyright © 2009 by the International Council of Shopping Centers. Reprinted with permission.

Community shopping centers sell more clothing and other soft goods than do neighborhood shopping centers. Of the eight types of shopping centers, community shopping centers take on the greatest variety of shapes, designs, and tenants. Nearly 9,500 community shopping centers operate across the United States.[67]

- *Power centers.* A power center combines the drawing strength of a large regional mall with the convenience of a neighborhood shopping center. Anchored by several large specialty retailers, such as warehouse clubs, discount department stores, or large specialty stores, these centers target older, wealthier baby boomers who want selection and convenience. In the United States, there are more than 2,000 power centers, where anchor stores usually account for 80 percent of power center space, compared with 50 percent in the typical community shopping center. Just as in a shopping mall, small businesses can benefit from the traffic generated by anchor stores, but they must choose their locations carefully so that they are not overshadowed by their larger neighbors. William James recently opened the Arms Room gun shop, which includes a shooting range, in a former Circuit City store in a power center in Houston, Texas. James spent $5 million to purchase and renovate the 20,000-square-foot building, a bargain compared to what it would have cost to build.[68]

- *Theme or festival centers.* Festival shopping centers employ a unifying theme that individual stores display in their decor and sometimes in the merchandise they sell. Entertainment is a common theme for these shopping centers, which often target tourists. Many festival shopping centers are located in urban areas and are housed in older, sometimes historic buildings that have been renovated to serve as shopping centers.

- *Outlet centers.* As their name suggests, outlet centers feature manufacturers' and retailers' outlet stores selling name-brand goods at a discount. Unlike most other types of shopping centers, outlet centers typically have no anchor stores; the discounted merchandise they offer draws sufficient traffic. Most outlet centers are open air and are laid out in strips or in clusters, creating small "villages" of shops. Nearly 350 outlet centers operate in the United States.[69]

- *Lifestyle centers.* Typically located near affluent residential neighborhoods where their target customers live, lifestyle centers are designed to look less like shopping centers and malls and more like the busy streets in the central business districts that existed in towns and cities in their heyday. Occupied by many upscale national chain restaurants such as P. F. Chang and specialty stores such as Talbots, Coach, and many others, the 392 lifestyle centers in the United States combine shopping convenience and entertainment ranging from movie theaters and open-air concerts to art galleries and people watching. The typical lifestyle center generates between $400 and $500 in sales per square foot compared to $370 in sales per square foot in traditional malls. The first lifestyle center, The Shops of Saddle Creek, opened in Germantown, Tennessee, in 1987.[70]

- *Regional shopping malls.* The regional shopping mall serves a large trading area, usually from 5 to 15 miles or more in all directions. These enclosed malls contain from 50 to 100 stores and serve a population of 150,000 or more living within a 20- to 40-minute drive. The anchor is typically one or more major department stores with smaller specialty stores occupying the spaces between the anchors. In the United States, 828 regional malls currently are in operation.[71] Apparel and accessories are the most popular items sold in regional shopping malls.

- *Superregional shopping malls.* A superregional mall is similar to a regional mall but is bigger, containing more anchor stores and a greater variety of shops selling deeper lines of merchandise. Its trade area stretches up to 25 or more miles out. Currently, 685 superregional malls operate in the United States.[72] Canada's West Edmonton Mall, the largest mall in North America, with more than 800 stores and 100 restaurants, is one of the most famous superregional malls in the world. In addition to its abundance of retail shops, the mall, which draws an average of nearly 31 million visitors a year, contains an ice skating rink, a water park, an amusement park, an aquarium, a bungee tower, miniature golf courses, and a 21-screen movie complex.

Major department or mass merchandising stores serve as anchors and attract a significant volume of customer traffic to malls and shopping centers, allowing small businesses with their unique, sometimes quirky product offerings, boutique atmospheres, and marketing approaches to thrive in their shadows. In fact, as mall vacancy rates have climbed, mall owners are eager to rent space to small businesses, tenants that in the past many of them had shunned in favor of large brand-name retailers.

ENTREPRENEURIAL PROFILE: John Myers: Party Palace John Myers had a successful but highly seasonal business renting inflatable bounce houses and other equipment for backyard parties. His goal was to secure an indoor location, and in 2010, he rented a space that had once housed an Old Navy store in Aviation Mall in Queensbury, New York. Myers converted the 18,000-square-foot space into the ideal home for the Party Palace, which hosts children's parties and offers a full line of inflatables, miniature golf, playhouses, kids' rides, and a stuffed animal center.[73] ■

When evaluating a mall or shopping center location, an entrepreneur should consider the following questions:

- Is there a good fit with other products and brands sold in the mall or center?

- Who are the other tenants? Which stores are the anchors that will bring people into the mall or center?

- Demographically, is the center a good fit for your products or services? What are its customer demographics?

- How much foot traffic does the mall or center generate? How much traffic passes the specific site you are considering?

- What is the mall's average sales per square foot (a common metric for measuring a mall's attractiveness)? The average for all malls is $370 per square foot, but one-third of malls generate less than $300 per square foot in sales. Only 27 percent of malls generate sales per square foot of $535 or more.[74]

- How much vehicle traffic does the mall or center generate? Check its proximity to major population centers, the volume of tourists it draws, and the volume of drive-by freeway traffic. A mall or center that scores well on all three is more likely to be a winner.

- What is the mall's vacancy rate? What is the turnover rate of its tenants?

- How much is the rent, and how is it calculated? Most mall tenants pay a base amount of rent plus a small percentage of their sales above a specified level.

A mall location is no guarantee of business success, however. Malls have been under pressure lately, especially from online retailers and fast-growing discount stores, and mall vacancy rates have been slow to recover from the Great Recession. Many weaker malls (known as "grayfields") have closed or have been redeveloped. The basic problem is an oversupply of mall space; there is 23.5 square feet of mall retail space for every person in the United States![75] The last new enclosed shopping mall opened in 2011. Another problem is that many malls are showing their age, requiring mall owners to remodel them, adding more restaurants, upscale movie theaters, and supermarkets—experiences that shoppers cannot get online.[76] In addition, the demographic makeup of an area's shoppers often changes over time, creating a new socioeconomic customer base that may not be compatible with a small company's target customer profile. As a result, many malls have undergone extensive renovations to transform themselves into "entertailing" destinations, adding entertainment features to their existing retail space in an attempt to generate more traffic. For instance, in addition to its 520 retail shops and 60 restaurants, Minneapolis's Mall of America, the second-largest mall in the United States (located only a few miles from Southdale, the nation's first mall), includes a seven-acre Nickelodeon Universe amusement park at its center, the Sea Life Minnesota Aquarium, a Star Trek exhibition, a CSI Experience based on the popular television show, and a 14-screen movie complex in its 4.2 million square feet of space.[77]

Near Competitors

One of the most important factors in choosing a retail or service location is the compatibility of nearby stores with the retail or service customer. For example, stores selling cars, antiques, and other shopping goods find it advantageous to locate near competitors to facilitate comparison shopping. Locating near competitors can be a key factor for success in those businesses selling goods that customers shop for and compare on the basis of price, quality, color, and other factors.

Although some business owners avoid locations near direct competitors, others see locating near rivals as an advantage. For instance, restaurateurs know that successful restaurants attract other restaurants, which, in turn, attract more customers. Many cities have at least one "restaurant row," where restaurants cluster together; each restaurant feeds customers to the others.

Locating near competitors has its limits, however. Clustering too many businesses of a single type into a small area ultimately erodes their sales once the market reaches the saturation point. When an area becomes saturated with competitors, the shops cannibalize sales from one another, making it difficult for any of them to be successful.

Shared Spaces

Because outstanding locations can be expensive or hard to find, some small companies are sharing spaces with other small businesses, a trend known as **coworking**. Entrepreneurs can reduce their rent and maintenance costs (and, therefore, their financial risk) by operating in a shared space. Entrepreneurs often find that sharing space with other businesses sparks creativity because their employees have the opportunity to interact with people outside of their industries. Others who share space with businesses that sell complementary products often see their sales increase. Shoe designer Rebecca Anderson, founder of Chaos & Harmony, and fashion designer Teresa Hodges, founder of BLAK, operated their businesses from their respective homes before teaming up to share a single workspace in Mt. Maunganui, New Zealand, that included enough space for them to open a retail store, BLAKCHAOS. By sharing workspace, Anderson and Hodges not only lower their operating expenses but also draw inspiration from each other's designs, enabling them to offer customers a complete, put-together look.[78]

coworking
a situation in which two or more small companies share the same space.

Inside Large Retail Stores

Rather than compete against giant retailers, some small business owners are cooperating with them, locating their businesses inside the larger company's stores. These small companies offer products that the large retailers do not and benefit from the large volume of customer traffic the large stores attract. The world's largest retailer, Wal-Mart, is a host to several small businesses, including franchisees of national chains Subway, McDonald's, Seattle's Best Coffee, and others.[79]

Nontraditional Locations

Rather than select a location and try to draw customers to it, many small businesses are discovering where their customers already are and setting up locations there. These nontraditional locations include airports, museums, office buildings, churches, casinos, college and university campuses, athletic arenas, and others that offer high concentrations of potential customers. Mark Talarico, a successful Domino's Pizza franchisee, recently set up interactive pizza-ordering kiosks (not vending machines) in high-traffic areas near residence halls on the campuses of the University of California Santa Barbara and Santa Barbara City College. Students who order pizzas through the kiosks receive a $1 discount.[80] In many cases, nontraditional locations are smaller and less expensive to build but generate much more in sales per square foot than traditional, full-size stores. Daniel Mancini, who left a successful career in the apparel business to open a restaurant using his Italian grandmother's meatball recipes, operates Meatball Obsession in New York City's Union Square neighborhood from a tiny 212-square-foot location that is barely bigger than a counter. Given his space limitations, Mancini keeps his menu simple, offering just four types of meatballs with a dozen sauces.[81]

Dunkin' Donuts has more than 500 nontraditional locations out of 6,800 outlets in the United States, including theme parks, military bases, universities, travel centers on interstate highways, and others. About 8,000 of Subway's 35,000 restaurants worldwide are in nontraditional locations, including a high school in Detroit in which students operate the outlet and a church in Buffalo, New York; these locations account for 20 percent of the chain's total sales. Subway also has an outlet on the MS *Stolzenfels* riverboat that cruises the Rhine River in Germany.[82]

Home-Based Businesses

For millions of entrepreneurs, home is where the business is, and their numbers are swelling. One recent study from the Small Business Administration reports that 52 percent of all small companies are home based.[83] Although a home-based retail business usually is not a good idea, locating a service business at home is quite common. Many service companies do not have customers come to their places of business, so an expensive office location is unnecessary. For instance, customers typically contact plumbers or exterminators by telephone, and the work is performed in customers' homes.

Entrepreneurs locating their businesses at home reap several benefits. Perhaps the biggest benefit is the low cost of setting up the business. Most often, home-based entrepreneurs set up shop in a spare bedroom or basement, avoiding the cost of renting, leasing, or buying a building. With a few basic pieces of office equipment—a computer or tablet, printer, copier, and smart phone—a lone entrepreneur can perform just like a major corporation.

ENTREPRENEURIAL PROFILE: Jen Joas: UrbanHalo Jen Joas describes herself as an accidental entrepreneur, saying that she never intended to launch a business. Instead, the active stay-at-home mom merely wanted a headband stylish enough to wear out but that would stay in place during a workout without giving her a headache. After searching for the perfect headband with no success, Joas sat down at her sewing machine and made one. Soon other people noticed her stylish headwear and asked her to make headbands for them. Joas realized that she had discovered a business opportunity, started a home-based business named UrbanHalo, and began selling her headbands through local boutiques and salons. Joas, who continues to operate her business from home, relies on her company's Web site and Facebook page and attending marathon expositions to market UrbanHalo; she recently expanded her company's product line to include headbands for men and studio scarves.[84] ∎

Choosing a home location has certain disadvantages, however. Interruptions are more frequent, the refrigerator is all too handy, work is always just a few steps away, and isolation can be a problem. Another difficulty facing some home-based entrepreneurs involves zoning laws. As their businesses grow and become more successful, entrepreneurs' neighbors often begin to complain about the increased traffic, noise, and disruptions from deliveries, employees, and customers who drive through their residential neighborhoods to conduct business. Many communities now face the challenge of passing updated zoning laws that reflect the reality of today's home-based businesses while protecting the interests of residential home owners.

On the Road

Some entrepreneurs are finding that the best location is not a permanent location but a mobile business that takes products and services to its customers. Veterinarians, dentists, restaurants, and others are outfitting mobile units and taking their businesses on the road. Although mobile entrepreneurs avoid the costs of building or renovating permanent locations, they must incur the expense of setting up their mobile businesses. They also face other obstacles, such as finding suitable parking spaces in high-traffic areas, complaints from owners of nearby businesses, and securing the necessary permits to operate. Some communities welcome mobile businesses, while others restrict them or even forbid them to operate.

ENTREPRENEURIAL PROFILE: Neil Parish: The Kibitz Room and Reuben on Rye Neil Parish, owner of the Kibitz Room, a classic Jewish delicatessen in Cherry Hill, New Jersey, took his operation on the road after he purchased a used truck and spent $50,000 to outfit it, which he says is a bargain because setting up a food truck usually cost $100,000 or more. Parish often takes the truck, which he dubbed Reuben on Rye, into neighborhoods from which he does not typically draw customers to his restaurant. A favorite spot is in nearby Camden, near three courthouses, a hospital, and a college campus that are served by very few restaurants. Parish uses social media and his Web site to promote the truck and its daily location. Not only does Parish's food truck increase his company's sales and profits, but it also serves as a rolling advertisement for the Kibitz Room.[85] ∎

LO4

Explain the site selection process for manufacturers.

The Location Decision for Manufacturers

The criteria for the location decision for manufacturers are very different from those of retailers and service businesses; however, the decision can have just as much impact on the company's success. In some cases, a manufacturer has special needs that influence the choice of a location.

For instance, when one manufacturer of photographic plates and digital cameras was searching for a location for a new plant, it had to limit its search to those sites with a large supply of available fresh water, a necessary part of its process. In other cases, the location decision is controlled by zoning ordinances. If a manufacturer's process creates offensive odors or excessive noise, it may be even further restricted in its choices.

The type of transportation network required dictates location of a factory in some cases. Some manufacturers may need to locate on a railroad siding, whereas others may need only reliable trucking service. If raw materials are purchased by the carload for economies of scale, the location must be convenient to a railroad siding. Bulk materials are sometimes shipped by barge and consequently require a facility convenient to a navigable river or lake. The added cost of using multiple shipping methods (e.g., rail to truck or barge to truck) can significantly increase shipping costs and make a location unfeasible for a manufacturer.

As fuel costs escalate, the cost of shipping finished products to customers also influences the location decision for many manufacturers, requiring them to open factories or warehouses in locations that are close to their primary markets to reduce transportation costs. Thermo-Pur Technologies, a small company that has developed a new stainless-steel heat exchanger core that makes automotive radiators lighter, more efficient at transferring heat, and less expensive to manufacture, recently selected the Clemson University International Center for Automotive Research in Greenville, South Carolina, as the location for its headquarters and first North American factory. Company managers considered other locations but selected Greenville because of its growing reputation as a knowledge center for automotive products, excellent transportation network, proximity to potential customers (including BMW, Mercedes Benz, Kia, and others), cost of operation, and overall quality of life.[86]

Foreign Trade Zones

Foreign trade zones can be an attractive location for small manufacturers that engage in global trade and are looking to reduce or eliminate the tariffs, duties, and excise taxes they pay on the materials and the parts they import and the goods they export. A **foreign trade zone** (see Figure 14.3) is a specially designated area in or near a U.S. customs port of entry that allows resident companies to import materials and components from foreign countries; assemble, process, manufacture, or package them; and then ship the finished product back out while either reducing or eliminating completely tariffs and duties. As far as tariffs and duties are concerned, a company located in a foreign trade zone is treated as if it is located outside the United States. For instance, a maker of speakers can import components from around the world and assemble them at its plant located in a foreign trade zone. The company pays no duties on the components it imports or on the speakers it exports to other foreign markets. The only duties the manufacturer pays are on the speakers it sells in the United States; the duty the company pays is either on the finished speakers or the imported component parts, whichever is less. There are 258 foreign trade zones and 498 subzones, which are special foreign trade zones that are established for limited purposes, operating in the United States. More than $730 billion worth of goods are shipped into FTZs in the United States annually.[87]

foreign trade zone
a specially designated area in or near a U.S. customs port of entry that allows resident companies to import materials and components from foreign countries; assemble, process, manufacture, or package them; and then ship the finished product while either reducing or eliminating tariffs and duties.

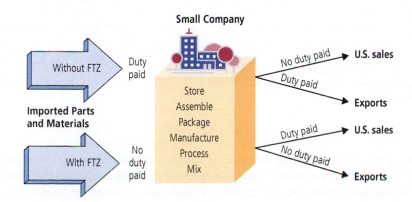

Small Company

Without FTZ
Duty paid

Imported Parts and Materials

With FTZ
No duty paid

Store
Assemble
Package
Manufacture
Process
Mix

No duty paid → U.S. sales
Duty paid → Exports

Duty paid → U.S. sales
No duty paid → Exports

FIGURE 14.3

How a Foreign Trade Zone Works

Business Incubators

business incubator

an organization that combines low-cost, flexible rental space with a multitude of support services for its small business residents.

For many start-up companies, a business incubator may make the ideal initial location. A **business incubator** is an organization that combines low-cost, flexible rental space with a multitude of support services for its small business residents. The primary reason for establishing an incubator is to enhance economic development by growing new businesses that create jobs and diversify the local economy. An incubator's goal is to nurture young companies during the volatile start-up period and to help them survive until they are strong enough to go out on their own. Common sponsors of incubators include colleges or universities (32 percent), economic development organizations (25 percent), government entities (16 percent), and others. Most incubators (54 percent) are "mixed use," hosting a variety of start-up companies, followed by incubators that focus on technology companies (37 percent).[88] Some incubators operate virtually with no physical presence much like a social network, providing entrepreneurs with mentoring and the opportunity to collaborate with other entrepreneurs.

In addition to discounted lease rates, incubators also offer tenants valuable resources, such as telephone systems, computers and software, high-speed Internet service, meeting and conference rooms, and sometimes management consulting services and financing contacts. Not only do these services save young companies money (reducing a small company's start-up costs in some cases by 40 to 50 percent), but they also save them valuable time. Entrepreneurs can focus on getting their products and services to market faster than competitors rather than searching for the resources they need to build their companies. The typical incubator has entry requirements that prospective residents must meet. Incubators also have criteria that establish the conditions a business must maintain to remain in the facility as well as the expectations for "graduation" into the business community (usually within three to five years).

More than 1,250 incubators operate across the United States (and 7,000 incubators worldwide), up from just 12 in 1980; they house an estimated 49,000 start-up companies.[89] Perhaps the greatest advantage of choosing to locate a start-up company in an incubator is a greater chance for success; according to the National Business Incubation Association, graduates from incubators have a success rate of 87 percent, and 84 percent of the companies that graduate stay in the local community.[90]

ENTREPRENEURIAL PROFILE: Jonni Lynch: Pie Bird Sweet and Savory Jonni Lynch, a mother with a full-time job at a law firm in Covington, Kentucky, started a business making pies from her home simply because she loved baking pies. Less than a year after starting Pie Bird Sweet and Savory, Lynch moved into the Northern Kentucky Kitchen Incubator where she shares space with other food-related small businesses, including companies that make marshmallows, granola, and vegan zucchini bread. Not only do the incubator tenants have access to professional kitchen equipment, but they also benefit from lower overhead costs and combine their purchases whenever possible to negotiate better discounts from vendors.[91] ■

LO5

Describe the criteria used to analyze the layout and design considerations of a building, including the Americans with Disabilities Act.

layout

the logical arrangement of the physical facilities in a business that contributes to efficient operations, increased productivity, and higher sales.

Layout and Design Considerations

Once an entrepreneur chooses the best location for his or her business, the next issue to address is designing the proper layout for the space to maximize sales (retail) or productivity (manufacturing or service). **Layout** is the logical arrangement of the physical facilities in a business that contributes to efficient operations, increased productivity, and higher sales. Planning for the most effective and efficient layout in a business environment can produce dramatic improvements in a company's operating effectiveness, efficiency, and overall performance. An attractive, effective layout can help a company's recruiting efforts, reduce absenteeism, and improve employee productivity and satisfaction. The comprehensive *U.S. Workplace Survey* by global design firm Gensler reports that employees believe that the quality and the quantity of their work would increase by an average of 25 percent with better workplace design.[92] The changing nature of work demands that work space design also changes. Although many jobs require the ability to focus on "heads-down" individual tasks, collaboration with coworkers is becoming a more significant component of work. An effective work space must be flexible enough to accommodate and encourage both types of work. Increasingly, work is becoming more complex, team based, technology dependent, and mobile; work spaces must adapt to accommodate these character-istics. The study by Gensler concludes that top-performing companies have work spaces that are more effective than those of average companies, particularly for collaboration. Gensler also reports that employees at top-performing companies spend 23 percent more time collaborating with their coworkers than do employees at average companies.[93]

The design of a company's work space should reflect its character and culture, which is es-pecially important for start-ups that are trying to recruit employees or attract investors. The "cube farms," rows of impersonal cubicles in expansive open spaces, dominated office designs for de-cades but are disappearing in favor of smaller work spaces that are more informal and contain workstations and furniture that employees can rearrange quickly and easily. Research shows that open offices, with their distractions and lack of privacy, actually impede employees' productivity, reduce their creativity, and increase their stress levels.[94] Modern, flexible work spaces encourage collaboration among employees, look less like a traditional office and more like a comfortable living room, and can be rearranged easily to accommodate different tasks, technology, and types of work.

ENTREPRENEURIAL PROFILE: Mark Zuckerberg: Facebook Facebook recently moved into its new headquarters on a 57-acre tract in Menlo Park, California, whose design en-courages creativity, productivity, interaction, and collaboration among its more than 4,000 work-ers. The goal is to create a headquarters that more closely resembles a college campus than a corporate office. Designers took out interior walls, cubicles, and private offices in the existing building to create an open space, covered the walls with whiteboard paint, and sprinkled com-fortable sofas and hundreds of small breakout rooms throughout the space where workers can conduct informal meetings and brainstorming sessions. In a tribute to Facebook's "hacker cul-ture," the design features exposed beams and ductwork and plywood-covered corridors to re-mind employees that their work is never done. Free-style artwork throughout the space signals the value of creativity and self-expression. The renovated building features a glass roof that pro-vides plenty of natural light and a central courtyard with cafés, dry cleaners, a fitness center, a medical clinic, and other services to maximize employee convenience—even a giant, outdoor screen on which employees can watch movies after hours. Facebook recently announced the ad-dition of a 494-unit housing community, Anton Menlo, that is within walking distance of its head-quarters. Like company headquarters, the community's layout encourages people to interact and share ideas.[95] ∎

When creating a layout, managers must consider its impact on the space itself (comfort, flexibility, size, and ergonomics), the people who occupy it (type of work, special requirements, need for interaction, and tasks performed), and the technology they use (communication, Internet access, and equipment).[96] The following factors have a significant impact on a space's layout and design.

"Sure I get the open concept idea. I just don't
think we need a watering hole."

Scot Richie/Cartoon Stock

Size and Adaptability

A building must offer adequate space and be adaptable enough to accommodate a business's daily operations. If it is too small at the outset of operations, efficiency will suffer. A space must have enough room for customers' movement, inventory, displays, storage, work areas, offices, and restrooms. Haphazard layouts undermine employee productivity and create organizational chaos. Businesses that launch in locations that are too small at the outset must make premature and costly moves to larger spaces, interfering with their ability to maintain a loyal customer base. Although entrepreneurs want spaces capable of accommodating their companies' growth, they should avoid spaces that are too big because they waste valuable resources. Many businesses are reducing the space they allocate to office workers because technology allows some people to work from almost anywhere rather than from a traditional office. In the 1970s, the average amount of office space per worker was 600 square feet; today, it is 200 square feet, and experts predict that by 2021, the typical employee will work in just 150 square feet of space.[97] Companies are moving away from private offices and even cubicles to unassigned works spaces, such as communal tables or desks that workers share and can rearrange easily to suit the task at hand. Research shows that employees' cubicles are unused more than 60 percent of the time and that private offices sit empty about 80 percent of the time.[98] Some entrepreneurs have done away with the concept of "the office" entirely.

ENTREPRENEURIAL PROFILE: Jill Bluming: The Creative Type Although Jill Bluming's graphic design company, The Creative Type, is based in New York City, her eight employees have no office space. Instead, her creative team, which is made up of copywriters, designers, illustrators, and others, work together "virtually" from their homes or wherever they are. When Bluming needs a conference room for a client meeting, she uses a Web-based service to rent one by the hour. Bluming says The Creative Type is driven by flexibility rather than a particular structure, pointing out that her company's low overhead costs give it a competitive advantage.[99] ■

Construction and Appearance

Is the construction of the building sound? Having an expert look it over before buying and leasing the property can pay big dividends. Beyond the soundness of construction, does the building have attractive external and internal appearances? The physical appearance of the building provides customers with their first impression of a business. Retailers and service providers, in particular, must recognize the importance of creating the proper image for their stores and how their shops' layouts and physical facilities influence this image. A store's external appearance contributes significantly to establishing its identity among its target customers. Does the building convey the appropriate signals to potential customers about the type of company it houses? Physical facilities send important messages to customers. Should the building project an upscale image or an economical one? Is the atmosphere informal and relaxed or formal and businesslike?

Communicating the right signals through layout and physical facilities is an important step in attracting a steady stream of customers. Retail consultant Paco Underhill advises merchants to "seduce" passersby with their storefronts. "The seduction process should start a minimum of 10 paces away," he says.[100]

A store's window display and in-store displays can be powerful selling tools if used properly. Often, a store's displays are an afterthought, and many business owners neglect to change their displays often enough. The following tips help entrepreneurs create window displays that sell:

- *Keep displays simple.* Simple, uncluttered, and creative arrangements of merchandise draw the most attention and have the greatest impact on potential customers.

- *Keep displays clean and current.* Dusty, dingy displays or designs that are outdated send a negative message to passersby.

- *Change displays frequently.* Customers do not want to see the same merchandise on display every time they enter a store. Experts recommend changing displays at least quarterly, but stores selling trendy items should change their displays twice a month.

- *Get expert help if necessary.* Not every business owner has a knack for designing displays. Their best bet is to hire a professional or to work with the design department at a local college or university.

Entrances

Entrances to a business should *invite* customers into a store. Wide entryways and attractive merchandise displays that are set back from the doorway draw customers into a business. A store's entrance should catch passing customers' attention and draw them inside. "That's where you want somebody to slam on the brakes and realize they're going someplace new," says retail consultant Paco Underhill.[101] Retailers with heavy traffic flows, such as supermarkets or drugstores, often install automatic doors to ensure a smooth traffic flow into and out of their stores. Retailers must remove any barriers that interfere with customers' easy access to the storefront. Broken sidewalks, sagging steps, mud puddles, and sticking or heavy doors create not only obstacles that might discourage potential customers but also legal hazards for a business if they cause customers to be injured. The goal is to eliminate anything that creates what one expert calls "threshold resistance."[102]

The Americans with Disabilities Act

Approximately 12.3 percent of people in the United States are disabled.[103] The **Americans with Disabilities Act (ADA)**, passed in 1990, requires practically all businesses, regardless of their size, to make their facilities available to physically challenged customers and employees. Most states have similar laws, many of them more stringent than the ADA, that apply to small companies as well. The rules of these state laws and the ADA's Title III are designed to ensure that mentally and physically challenged customers have equal access to a firm's goods or services. For instance, the act requires business owners to remove architectural and communication barriers when "readily achievable" (accomplished without much difficulty or expense). The ADA allows flexibility in how a business achieves this equal access, however. For example, a restaurant could either provide menus in Braille or offer to have a staff member read the menu to blind customers. A small dry cleaner might not be able to add a wheelchair ramp to its storefront without incurring significant expense, but the owner could comply with the ADA by offering curbside pickup and delivery services at no extra charge for disabled customers.

> **Americans with Disabilities Act (ADA)**
> a law that requires practically all businesses to make their facilities available to physically challenged customers and employees.

The Department of Justice revised the ADA in 2010, and all newly constructed or renovated buildings that are open to the public and were occupied after March 15, 2012, must comply with the 2010 requirements. For example, in retail stores, checkout aisles must be wide enough—at least 36 inches—to accommodate wheelchairs. Restaurants must have at least 5 percent of their tables accessible to wheelchair-bound patrons. Miniature golf courses must make at least 50 percent of the holes on the course accessible to disabled customers.

Complying with the ADA does not necessarily require businesses to spend large amounts of money. The Department of Justice estimates that more than 20 percent of the cases customers have filed under Title III involved changes the business owners could have made at no cost, and another 60 percent would have cost less than $1,000.[104] In addition, companies with $1 million or less in annual sales or with 30 or fewer full-time employees that invest in making their locations more accessible qualify for a tax credit. The credit is 50 percent of their expenses between $250 and $10,250. Businesses that remove physical, structural, and transportation barriers for disabled employees and customers also qualify for a tax deduction of up to $15,000.

Echo/Getty Images

Signs

One of the lowest-cost and most effective methods of communicating with customers is a business sign. Signs serve as guideposts for a business, telling potential customers what it does, where it is, and what it is selling. Ideally, a sign conveys a positive image of the company's brand. In a highly mobile society, a well-designed, well-placed sign can be a powerful tool for reaching potential customers. The Viva McDonald's restaurant on Las Vegas Boulevard (or "the Strip") includes an oversized sign and four jumbo display screens—all with video playback ability—mounted on the front of the store. Designers recognized that a restaurant located in a city known for gaudy neon light displays required a sign that would stand out to attract customers.[105]

A sign should be large enough for passersby to read from a distance, taking into consideration the location and speed of surrounding traffic arteries. To be most effective, the message should be short, simple, and clear. Including the company's Web site URL on the sign promotes its e-commerce business. A sign should be legible both in daylight and at night; proper illumination is a must. Contrasting colors and simple typefaces are best. The most common problems with business signs are that they are illegible, poorly designed (including unattractive color schemes and type that is hard to read), improperly located, and/or poorly maintained.

Before investing in a sign, an entrepreneur should investigate the local community's sign ordinance. In some cities and towns, local regulations impose restrictions on the size, location, height, and construction materials used in business signs.

Building Interiors

Designing a functional, efficient interior layout demands research, planning, and attention to detail. Retailers in particular have known for a long time that their stores' layouts influence their customers' buying behavior. Retailers such as Cabela's, Barnes & Noble, and Starbucks use layouts that encourage customers to linger and spend time (and money). Others, such as Lowe's, Aldi, and Wal-Mart, reinforce their discount images with layouts that communicate a warehouse environment, often complete with pallets, to shoppers. Luxury retailers, such as Tiffany and Company, Coach, and Nordstrom, create opulent layouts in which their upscale customers feel comfortable.

Building interiors send important signals to shoppers about a business's image, and cleanliness and order are essential. In restaurants, for example, dining areas or bathrooms that are dirty send customers scurrying. Studies consistently show that the most common reason that customers refuse to return to a restaurant has nothing to do with food or service; it is dirty bathrooms![106] ("If the bathrooms are this bad, the kitchen must be worse.") Because entrepreneurs are in their buildings every day and are focused on the "big picture," overlooking details in the physical space can happen easily but can be deadly for sales. Is the carpet in need of cleaning or replacement? Are displays and decorations dusty and disheveled? Would a coat of fresh paint brighten the space? Does clutter detract from a good first impression?

Coordinating an effective layout is not a haphazard process. **Ergonomics**, the science of adapting work and the work environment to complement employees' strengths and to suit customers' needs, is an integral part of a successful design. For example, chairs, desks, and table heights that allow people to work comfortably can help employees perform their job faster and more easily. Design experts claim that improved lighting, better acoustics, and proper climate control benefit the company as well as employees. An ergonomically designed workplace can improve workers' productivity significantly and reduce days lost due to injuries and accidents. A study for the Commission of Architecture and the Built Environment and the British Council for Offices reports that simple features, such as proper lighting, reduce absenteeism by 15 percent and increase productivity between 2.8 and 20 percent.[107]

Unfortunately, many businesses fail to incorporate ergonomic design principles into their layouts, and the result is costly worker's compensation claims, absences from work, and lost productivity. The good news for employers, however, is that preventing injuries, accidents, and lost days does *not* require spending thousands of dollars on ergonomically correct solutions. Most of the solutions actually are quite simple and inexpensive, ranging from installing equipment that eliminates workers' repetitive motions to introducing breaks during which workers engage in exercises designed by occupational therapists to combat injuries.

Drive-Through Windows

For many businesses, a drive-through window adds another dimension to the concept of customer convenience and is a relatively inexpensive way to increase sales. In the quick-service restaurant business, drive-through windows are an essential design component, accounting for 70 percent of sales, an increase from 60 percent in 2002.[108] Although drive-through windows are staples at quick-service restaurants, other businesses, including fast-casual restaurants, drugstores, convenience stores, hardware stores, and even wedding chapels benefit from them. Managers at fast-casual restaurant chain Panera Bread studied and tested drive-through windows for 10 years before introducing them throughout the chain because they did not want to diminish the dining experience for drive-through customers or in-store customers, who might be distracted by the noise of a drive-through window. Panera's strategy includes drive-throughs that are isolated from the dining room, sufficient staff dedicated solely to serving drive-through customers, technology

---

ergonomics

the science of adapting work and the work environment to complement employees' strengths and to suit customers' needs.

to support fast, accurate orders, and special packaging designed to ensure the integrity of custom-ers' food. Panera says sales at outlets with drive-through windows have experienced double-digit sales, and all new outlets include drive-through windows.[109]

Sight, Sound, Scent, and Lighting

Retailers can increase sales by sending important subconscious signals to customers using what design experts call "symbolics." For instance, when shoppers enter a Whole Foods supermarket, the first items they see are displays of fresh flowers. Not only are the flowers' colors and the smells pleasing, but they also send a clear message to customers: "You are embarking on an adventure in freshness in our store—flowers, produce, meats, seafood, *everything*."[110] Layouts that engage all of customers' senses also increase sales. Retail behavioral expert Paco Underhill, founder of Envirosell, a market research company, says most of customers' unplanned purchases come after they touch, taste, smell, or hear something in a store. For example, stores that sell fresh food see sales increase if they offer free samples to customers. One study reports that of-fering shoppers free samples increases not only sales of the item offered but also sales of other products.[111] Research also shows that customers are willing to pay more for products they can see, touch, taste, or try.[112] "If somebody doesn't try 'em, they're not going to buy 'em," quips Underhill.[113] Sight, sound, scent, and lighting are particularly important aspects of retail layout.

SIGHT A business can use colors and visual cues in its interior designs to support its brand and image in subtle yet effective ways. At the Vermont Country Deli in Brattleboro, Vermont, wooden bookshelves and odd tables filled with colorful displays of jams, jellies, and desserts greet customers as they enter the store. The mismatched tables and shelves give the store an authentic, down-home look, and signs such as "Life is short. Eat cookies." entice customers to make purchases. At Whole Foods, prices for fresh fruits and vegetables appear to be hand scrawled on fragments of black slate, a tradition in outdoor markets in Europe—as if a farmer had pulled up that morning, unloaded the produce, and posted the price before heading back to the farm. Some of the produce also is sprinkled with water droplets. When customers at the restaurant Tallulah on the Thames in Newport, Rhode Island, are seated, waiters hand them a rustic clipboard with a handwritten list of the daily "farm-to-table menu."[114] The subtle message these symbolics send to customers is *freshness*.[115]

SOUND In an attempt to engage all of their customers' senses, companies are realizing the impact that sound has on shoppers and are incorporating it into their layouts. Research shows that a business's "soundscape" can have an impact on the length of time customers shop and the amount of money they spend. Background music that appeals to a company's target customers can be an effective marketing tool, subtly communicating important messages about its brand to customers. Playlists differ depending on the company's target customers and the mood the business wants to create. Quaker State & Lube, a chain of 45 casual dining restaurants that feature an automotive theme, hired experts at Ambiance Radio to create playlists for its outlets for different parts of the day (lunch, dinner, and late night). At peak times, Quaker State & Lube plays upbeat, fast-tempo music to encourage faster dining and to speed up the number of table turns.[116] To reinforce its image with its target audience, 18- to 30-year-olds who appreciate its funky, often edgy styles,

retail clothing company Urban Outfitters uses playlists that feature obscure, independent artists whose work is available on online platforms such as SoundCloud and Spotify.[117] Thomas Pink, an upscale London-based retailer known for its branded shirts and ties with stores in major cities in Europe, Asia, the United States, and the Middle East, plays an eclectic list of songs that is designed to be part of customers' interaction with the brand. The company worked with soundscape specialty company Mood Media to create a customized playlist that is far-reaching, ranging from The Beatles and David Bowie to The Jam and the Mystery Jets, but is decidedly British. The company also launched a Web radio channel that streams its in-store playlists.[118] For most retail soundscapes, one rule is clear: Slow is good. People's biorhythms reflect the sounds around them, and soothing classical music encourages shoppers to

David Lyons/Alamy

relax and slow down, meaning that they will shop longer and spend more. Classical music also makes shoppers feel more affluent and increases sales more than any other type of music.[119]

SCENT Research shows that scents can have a powerful effect in retail stores. The Sense of Smell Institute reports that the average human being can recognize 10,000 different odors and can recall scents with 65 percent accuracy after one year, a much higher recall rate than visual stimuli produce.[120] In one experiment, when Eric Spangenberg of Washington State University diffused a subtle scent of vanilla into the women's department of a store and rose maroc into the men's department, he discovered that sales nearly doubled. He also discovered that if he switched the scents, sales in both departments fell well below their normal average.[121] Vanilla connotes warmth and comfort, and citrus scents tend to be energizing and invigorating.

Many companies—from casinos to convenience stores—are beginning to understand the power of using scent as a sales tool. Bakeries use fans to push the smell of fresh-baked breads and sweets into pedestrian traffic lanes, tempting them to sample some of their delectable goodies. Panera Bread, a chain of 1,800 restaurants in 45 states, recently switched bread-baking in its stores from the night shift to the day shift so that customers could smell the enticing aroma of freshly baked bread (and watch the bakers at work). Cinnabon, a chain of franchised restaurants located mainly in shopping malls that specialize in fresh cinnamon buns, locates its ovens in the front of its stores so that the delectable smell of baking cinnamon buns can draw in customers.[122] Select Comfort, the company that markets the Sleep Number mattress in 400 stores across the United States, worked with ScentAir, a company that designs scents for retailers, to infuse its retail outlets with a blend of cashmere wool, amber, cardamom, cinnamon, and bergamot that conveys a sense of "quiet repose."[123]

LIGHTING Good lighting allows employees to work at maximum efficiency. Proper lighting is measured by the amount of light required to do a job properly with the greatest lighting efficiency. Efficiency is essential because lighting consumes 21 percent of the total energy used in the typical commercial building.[124] Traditional incandescent lighting, which Congress banned on January 1, 2014, is least efficient. Only 10 percent of the energy it generates is light; the remaining 90 percent is heat. Compact fluorescent lights (CFLs) generate far less heat, use 75 percent less energy, and last 10 times longer than traditional incandescent lights. Technology advances are increasing the popularity of light-emitting-diode (LED) lighting. Although still more expensive to purchase, LEDs use just 20 percent of the electricity of incandescent lights and 50 percent of CFLs. They also last six times longer than CFLs and 25 times longer than incandescent lights. LEDs generate the least amount of heat, reducing business's cooling costs.[125] Joseph Banker, owner of Creative Dental Care, a boutique dental practice in Westfield, New Jersey, invested $700 to switch his entire lighting system to LEDs. Because LEDs are more efficient and burn much cooler than incandescent and CFL bulbs, Banker's cooling bill decreased, saving him $1,800 in the first year.[126]

Lighting provides a good return on investment given its overall impact on a business. Few people seek out businesses that are dimly lit because they convey an image of untrustworthiness. Layouts that use natural light not only are less expensive to operate but also give businesses an open and cheerful look and actually can boost sales. A series of studies by energy research firm Heschong Mahone Group found that stores using natural light experience sales that are 40 percent higher than those of similar stores using fluorescent lighting.[127] In a retail environment, proper lighting should highlight featured products and encourage customers to stop and look at them.

Sustainability and Environmentally Friendly Design

Businesses are designing their buildings in more environmentally friendly ways not only because it is the right thing to do but also because it saves money. Companies are using recycled materials; installing high-efficiency lighting, fixtures, and appliances; and using Leadership in Energy and Environmental Design (LEED) principles in construction and renovation. LEED principles cover every phase of construction and include concepts ranging from installing self-contained, solar-powered energy sources and water-conserving plumbing fixtures to collecting rainwater for use in landscape irrigation to using renewable and recycled construction materials.

Starbucks, the popular chain of coffee shops, built its latest roasting plant in Sandy Run, South Carolina, to LEED standards and has built several LEED-certified outlets out of old shipping containers that otherwise would have gone to a landfill. Some of these outlets are micro drive-throughs. At just 380 square feet, they are the smallest Starbucks stores in existence, but they allow the company to access high-traffic locations that otherwise would be out of reach and can be operating in just one week. Other outlets are larger, made of several shipping containers connected to or stacked on top of one another. Each "recycled" outlet contains all of amenities of a "regular" Starbucks store and is decorated to reflect the local character of each location. The company plans to build more "green" outlets in the future.[128]

Richard Ellis/Alamy

Layout: Maximizing Revenues, Increasing Efficiency, or Reducing Costs

LO6

Explain the principles of effective layouts for retailers, service businesses, and manufacturers.

The ideal layout for a building depends on the type of business it houses and on the entrepreneur's strategy for gaining a competitive edge. An effective layout can reinforce a brand and contribute to a company's desired image.

ENTREPRENEURIAL PROFILE: John Kunkel: Lime Fresh Mexican Grill John Kunkel, founder of Lime Fresh Mexican Grill, a small chain of casual burrito restaurants that Ruby Tuesday recently purchased, was repulsed by the hard plastic interiors of other quick-service Mexican restaurants. He contends that the design sends a clear signal to customers: "Finish your food quickly and make room for the next customer." Instead, Kunkel wanted to create a comfortable, welcoming environment that supported his company's image. He says he took cues from Starbucks and tried to make a Lime Fresh Mexican Grill a social place where people can come to hang out. A large tub filled with ice and bottled beverages sits on a countertop, reminding customers of a friendly backyard cookout. Large windows that diffuse natural light, golden-toned walls, warm hammered-copper and brick accents, and comfortable chairs invite customers to linger inside, and umbrella-covered sidewalk tables beckon hungry customers to sit and relax. Dining room attendants called "fronters" greet customers and provide café-style service, delivering beverage refills, chips, salsas, and desserts.[129] ■

Retailers design their layouts with the goal of maximizing sales revenue and reinforcing the brand; manufacturers see layout as an opportunity to increase efficiency and productivity and to lower costs.

Layout for Retailers

Retail layout is the arrangement of merchandise and displays in a store. For retailers, layout is all about understanding a company's target customers and crafting every element of a store's design to appeal to those customers. Retail expert Paco Underhill says "a store's interior architecture is fundamental to the customers' experience—the stage upon which a retail company functions."[130] A retail layout should pull customers into the store and make it easy for them to locate merchandise; compare price, quality, and features; and ultimately make a purchase. This is another area in which small stores may have an advantage over their larger rivals. Small stores allow customers to find the products that they want to purchase quickly and easily. (One study reports that the average shopper in a cavernous Wal-Mart Supercenter spends 21 minutes in the store but finds only 7 out of 10 items on his or her shopping list![131])

In addition, a floor plan should take customers past displays of other items they may buy on impulse. Customers make a significant percentage of their buying decisions once they enter a store, meaning that the right layout can boost sales significantly. One of the most comprehensive studies of impulse purchases found that one-third of shoppers made impulse purchases. The median impulse purchase amount was $30 but varied by product category, ranging from $6 for food items to $60 for jewelry and sporting goods. Although the urge to take advantage of discounts was the most common driver of unplanned buying decisions, the location and attractiveness of the display also were important factors.[132]

Retailers have always recognized that some locations within a store are superior to others. Customer traffic patterns give the owner a clue to the best location for the highest gross margin items. Generally, prime selling space should be reserved for products that carry the highest mark-ups. If customers come into the store for specific products and have a tendency to walk directly to those items, placing complementary products in their path boosts sales. Diane Holtz, CEO of Pet Supermarket, a retailer of pet supplies founded in 1962 with 124 locations in the Southeast, redesigned the layout of the company's stores, placing essential items such as pet food and kitty litter at the rear of the store to draw customers past attractive displays of pet toys, treats, and supplies. The new design features a clean, colorful look with space to feature new products each week and to encourage interaction with pets and their owners. One year after the redesign, the company's sales had increased almost 16 percent.[133]

 **Hands On . . . How To**

Create the Ideal Layout

As the world shifts to a knowledge-based economy, more workers are engaging in office work, in which measuring productivity sometimes proves difficult. Research shows that a well-designed office is one of the simplest and most cost-effective ways to increase workers' productivity and satisfaction. For instance, if a company builds and operates an office building, the cost of initial construction accounts for just 2 percent of the building's total cost over 30 years. Operating expenses account for 6 percent. The remaining 92 percent of the total cost of operating the building over 30 years goes to paying the salaries and benefits of the people who occupy the space! The implication of this research is that top-performing companies recognize that their employees account for the largest portion of the total cost of a work environment and make adequate investments to ensure that the work space maximizes their efficiency, satisfaction, and productivity. Unfortunately, many other companies remain stuck in the antiquated cubicle culture that provides the fodder for so many Dilbert cartoon strips and that squelches individual expression, collaboration with colleagues, and creativity.

In the early to mid-twentieth century, companies used office layouts that resembled factory layouts with workers sitting in long rows performing repetitive tasks. The layout reflected management's attitude that workers were simply parts in the company machinery. In the 1960s and 1970s, the landscape office emerged, featuring a design in which managers and their staffs sat together so that they could accomplish related tasks efficiently. In the 1980s, as real estate prices escalated, companies used cubicles as an efficient way to pack lots of workers into a limited amount of space, giving cubicles the reputation of housing employees in the same way that a hive houses bees. Today, office designs reflect the changing nature of work: small teams of employees collaborate on projects, and creativity improves when employees from different parts of the company exchange ideas as a result of impromptu encounters. Modern offices employ furniture, features, and designs that are more flexible, allowing employees to shift them according to the tasks they need to perform.

At Big Spaceship, a creative agency in Brooklyn, New York, the design includes open spaces to which employees are naturally drawn and that encourage collaboration. Walls are covered in whiteboard paint and markers are everywhere so that employees can sketch their ideas while working together. It also includes private and semi-private rooms with couches and beanbag chairs to which people can escape when they need a quiet space in which to work. Cross-disciplinary teams sit along with their backs to aisles so that they can concentrate on a project or simply spin their chairs around to collaborate with colleagues. The goal of Big Spaceship's layout is to encourage collaboration, stimulate creativity, and capture as many ideas as possible.

What principles make for a good office design and allow a company to get the most out of its investment in designing a work space?

Observe How Employees Use the Existing Space

The nature of employees' work changes over time, and so do their work space needs. A design that was suitable a few years ago may be inappropriate today. Entrepreneurs should take the time to observe employees at work. When do workers use office space? Which spaces are at maximum capacity, and which ones are underutilized? Why? Does the existing design support employees' ability to do their jobs or hinder it? Red flags include the following:

- People whose work requires collaboration do not naturally interact with their colleagues during the course of a day.

- Employees waste a lot of time in transit to meeting rooms, printers, copiers, and other office equipment.

- Workers are competing for the use of certain pieces of office equipment.

- An area is either typically overcrowded or empty.

- Employees schedule meetings at nearby coffee shops or restaurants because these places provide better common space for collaboration.

Hands On . . . How To *(continued)*

Involve Employees in the Redesign

One of the worst mistakes designers make is creating a new layout without the input of the people who will be working in the space. Asking employees up front for ideas and suggestions is essential to producing an effective layout. What barriers to their work does the existing design create? How can you eliminate them? One surefire way to alienate employees is to fail to involve them in the redesign of their work space.

Plan the New Design

Redesigning a work space can be a major undertaking. The process goes much more smoothly, and the end result is superior for companies that invest in significant planning than for those companies that do not. Successful designs usually result when entrepreneurs and their employees define two to five priorities, such as increased collaboration, enhanced productivity, reduced absenteeism and turnover, or improved energy efficiency, for design professionals to achieve.

Creating an effective design does not have to be expensive, but it does demand a good plan. An extensive report, *Innovative Workplace Strategies*, from the General Services Administration, lists the following hallmarks of the productive workplace:

- **Spatial equity.** Do workers have adequate space to accomplish their tasks and have access to privacy, natural light, and aesthetics?

- **Healthfulness.** Is the work space a healthy environment with access to air, light, and water? Is it free of harmful contaminants and excess noise?

- **Flexibility.** Can workers adjust their work environment to respond to important functional changes?

- **Comfort.** Can workers adjust light, temperature, acoustic levels, and furnishings to their individual preferences?

- **Technological connectivity.** Can on-site and off-site workers stay connected with one another and gain access to the information they need? Does technology enhance their ability to collaborate on projects?

- **Reliability.** Does the workplace have dependable mechanical and technological systems that receive proper support?

- **Sense of place.** Does the workplace decor and atmosphere reflect the company's mission and brand? Does the space create a culture that is appropriate for accomplishing the tasks at hand?

At OpenTable, the restaurant reservation site based in San Francisco, the design reflects the company's food-centric culture. The lobby doubles as a large break room and includes a wall filled with employees' quotations about their favorite restaurant experiences. A "menu of the day" chalkboard invites employees to share creative ideas. Conference rooms, which carry names such as "Food Truck" and "Buffet," feature flexible designs that employees adjust to suit their needs. Comparing the company's new space to its previous headquarters, one manager says the new space reflects OpenTable's culture and encourages employee interaction, which has enhanced creativity in the company.

Create a Design That Helps People Get Their Work Done

A work space should *never* impede employees' productivity—although many designs do. A proper layout should *enhance* employees' ability to do their jobs. At animated film company Pixar, the work space, which includes large open areas with large couches and high-top tables that encourage impromptu meetings, is designed to encourage collaboration among employees. Even the company's volleyball and basketball courts encourage employee interaction, making Pixar headquarters a haven of creativity. However, recognizing that sometimes employees must work "heads down" without interruption, Pixar also created more private, quiet spaces.

Rely on Continuous Improvement

A redesign project is not finished just because the work is complete. Smart entrepreneurs resist the temptation to sit back and admire the finished product and think about how happy they are to be "done." Instead, they recognize that no redesign, however well planned, is perfect. They are willing to tweak the project and to make necessary adjustments to meet employees' changing needs.

Sources: Based on Stephanie Orma, "Branding at Work," *Entrepreneur*, February 2014, p. 20; Lisa Ward, "Design for Working," *Wall Street Journal*, April 28, 2014, p. R6; Ben Kesling and James R. Hagerty, "Say Goodbye to the Office Cubicle," *Wall Street Journal*, April 3, 2013, pp., B1, B6; "How to Design an Office That Makes Everyone Happy," *Inc.*, November 2013, p. 60; Aaron Herrington, "Pixar Is Inspiration for Modea's New Headquarters," *Modea*, September 19, 2011, http://www.modea.com/blog/pixar-is inspiration-for-modeas-new-headquarters; Jane Hodges, "How to Build a Better Office," *BNET*, 2007, http://www.bnet.com/2403-13056_23-190221.html; Julie Schlosser, "The Great Escape," *Fortune*, March 20, 2006, pp. 107–110; Michael Lev-Ram, "How to Make Your Workspace Better," *Business 2.0*, November 2006, pp. 58–60; Jeffrey Pfeffer, "Thinking Outside the Cube," *Business 2.0*, April 2007, p. 60; and *Innovative Workplace Strategies*, General Services Administration, Office of Governmentwide Policy, Office of Real Property, Washington, DC, 2003, p. 70.

Layout in a retail store evolves from a clear understanding of customers' buying habits. Observing customer behavior helps entrepreneurs identify "hot spots" where merchandise sells briskly and "cold spots" where it may languish indefinitely. Winn-Dixie stores, a supermarket chain, recently remodeled its stores to capitalize on its primary hot spot, the front section of the store to the right of the front door. Because market research shows that produce is the most important factor in choosing a grocery store and winning customer loyalty, Winn-Dixie located its produce section there and expanded it by 30 percent. Bananas, one of the most commonly purchased produce items, are located at the back of the section to draw customers through it. Produce displays also use wood shelves, carts, and display tables as symbolics to send a message of freshness.[134]

Business owners should display merchandise as neatly and attractively as possible. Customers' eyes focus on displays, which tell them the type of merchandise the business sells. It is easier for customers to relate to one display than to a rack or shelf of merchandise. Open displays of merchandise can surround a focal display, creating an attractive selling area. Spacious aisles provide shoppers an open view of merchandise and reduce the likelihood of shoplifting. One study found that shoppers, especially women, are reluctant to enter narrow aisles in a store. Narrow aisles force customers to jostle past one another (experts call this the "butt-brush factor"), making them extremely nervous. The same study also found that placing shopping baskets in several areas around a store can increase sales. Seventy-five percent of shoppers who pick up a basket buy something, compared to just 34 percent of customers who do not pick up a basket.[135]

Retailers can also boost sales by displaying together items that complement each other. For example, displaying ties near dress shirts or handbags next to shoes often leads to multiple sales. Placement of items on store shelves is important, too, and store owners must keep their target customers in mind when stocking shelves. For example, putting hearing aid batteries on bottom shelves where the elderly have trouble getting to them or placing popular children's toys on top shelves where little ones cannot reach them hurts sales. Retailers also must avoid wasting prime selling space on nonselling functions (e.g., storage, office, fitting rooms, and others). For a typical retailer, the ratio of selling to nonselling space is 80/20. Although nonselling activities are necessary for a successful retail operation, they should not occupy a store's most valuable selling space. Shoppers who use fitting rooms to try on garments make purchases 67 percent of the time, compared to a 10 percent purchase rate for shoppers who do not use a fitting room. Clothing retailer Ann Taylor recently revamped its fitting rooms, enhancing their lighting to be more flattering, enlarging them to accommodate shoppers' and their friends, and making them more like a shopper's walk-in closet. The company also added displays of complementary merchandise, such as camisoles, underwear, and shapewear, to its fitting room areas. Many retailers place their nonselling departments in the rear of the building, recognizing the value of each foot of space in a retail store and locating their most profitable items in the best-selling areas.[136]

The checkout process is a particularly important ingredient in customer satisfaction and often ranks as a sore spot with shoppers. Research shows that shoppers tend to be impatient, willing to wait only about four minutes in a checkout line before becoming exasperated. One study reports that 43 percent of customers say long checkout lines make them less likely to shop at a store.[137] Retailers are discovering that simplifying and speeding up the checkout process increases customer convenience, lowers shoppers' stress levels, and makes them more likely to come back. Some retailers, including Apple, use roving clerks equipped with handheld credit card–swiping devices, especially during peak hours, to hasten the checkout process. Studies conclude that having shoppers form a single line that leads to multiple cashiers results in faster checkout times than having shoppers form multiple lines in front of multiple cashiers.[138]

The value of a store's space for generating sales depends on floor location in a multistory building, location with respect to aisles and walkways, and proximity to entrances. Space values decrease as the distance from the main entry-level floor increases. Selling areas on the main level contribute a greater portion to sales than those on other floors in the building because they offer greater exposure to customers than either basement or higher-level locations. Therefore, main-level locations carry a greater share of rent than other levels.

Space values also depend on their position relative to the store entrance. Typically, the farther away an area is from the entrance, the lower is its value. Another consideration is that in North America, most shoppers turn to the right entering a store and move around it counterclockwise. (This apparently is culturally determined; studies of shoppers in Australia and Great Britain find that they turn *left* on entering a store.) Finally, only about one-fourth of a store's customers will go more than halfway into the store. Based on these characteristics, Figure 14.4 illustrates space values for a typical small store.

Retail layout is a never-ending experiment in which entrepreneurs learn what works and what doesn't.

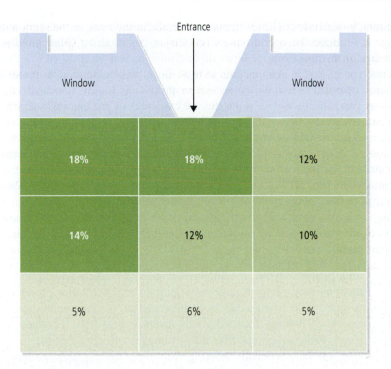

FIGURE 14.4

Space Values for a Small Store

Source: From *Retailing*, 6th edition, by Dale M. Lewison. Copyright © 1997 by Dale M. Lewison. Reprinted with permission.

Layout for Manufacturers

Manufacturing layout decisions take into consideration the arrangement of departments, work stations, machines, and stock-holding points within a production facility. The objective is to arrange these elements to ensure a smoothly flowing, efficient, and highly productive work flow. Manufacturing facilities have come under increased scrutiny as companies attempt to improve quality, reduce inventory, and increase productivity through layouts that are integrated, flexible, and efficient. Facility layout has a dramatic effect on product processing, material handling, storage, production volume, and quality.

FACTORS IN MANUFACTURING LAYOUT The ideal layout for a manufacturing operation depends on several factors, including the following:

- *Type of product.* Product design and quality standards, whether the product is produced for inventory or for order, and the physical properties, such as the size of materials and products, special handling requirements, susceptibility to damage, and perishability.

- *Type of production process.* Technology used, types of materials handled, means of providing a service, and processing requirements in terms of number of operations involved and amount of interaction between departments and work centers.

- *Ergonomic considerations.* Ensure worker safety, avoid injuries and accidents, and increase productivity.

- *Economic considerations.* Volume of production; costs of materials, machines, work stations, and labor; pattern and variability of demand; and minimizing cycle time, the amount of time between receiving a customer's order and delivering the finished product.

- *Space availability within the facility itself.* Ensure that the space will adequately meet current and future manufacturing needs.

TYPES OF MANUFACTURING LAYOUTS Manufacturing layouts are categorized either by the work flow in a plant or by the production system's function. There are three basic types of layouts that manufacturers can use separately or in combination—product, process, and fixed position—and they are differentiated by their applicability to different conditions of manufacturing volume.

product (line) layout
an arrangement of workers and equipment according to the sequence of operations performed on a product.

Product Layouts In a **product (line) layout**, a manufacturer arranges workers and equipment according to the sequence of operations performed on the product. Conceptually, the flow is an unbroken line from raw material input or customer arrival to finished goods or customer departure. This type of layout is applicable to rigid-flow, high-volume, continuous-process or a mass-production operation or when the service or product is highly standardized. Automobile assembly plants, paper mills, and oil refineries are examples of product layouts. Product layouts offer the advantages of low material handling costs; simplified tasks that can be done with low-cost, lower-skilled labor; small amounts of work-in-process inventory; and relatively simplified production control activities. All units are routed along the same fixed path, and scheduling consists primarily of setting a production rate.

Disadvantages of product layouts are their inflexibility, monotony of job tasks, high fixed investment in specialized equipment, and heavy interdependence of all operations. A breakdown in one machine or at one work station can idle the entire line. This layout also requires business owners to duplicate many pieces of equipment in the manufacturing facility, which for a small firm can be cost prohibitive.

process layout
an arrangement of workers and equipment according to the general function they perform, without regard to any particular product or customer.

Process Layouts In a **process layout**, a manufacturer groups workers and equipment according to the general functions they perform, without regard to any particular product or customer. Process layouts are appropriate when production runs are short, when demand shows considerable variation and the costs of holding finished goods inventory are high, or when the service or product is customized. Process layouts offer the advantages of being flexible for doing custom work and promoting job satisfaction by offering employees diverse and challenging tasks. Its disadvantages are the higher costs of materials handling, requirement of more skilled labor, lower productivity, and more complex production control.

ENTREPRENEURIAL PROFILE: C.C. Filson C.C. Filson, a company that began supplying gold miners with outdoor gear in 1897, recently moved into a new 57,400-square-foot factory in which the company manufactures its line of durable luggage and bags. The new factory uses an efficient process layout that is divided into three departments, each of which focuses on making 10 similar types of products. Workstations are arranged so that products flow smoothly from one to the next without having to double-back (as they did in the old, cramped factory). Quality manager Teresa Whittaker says making this change alone saved the company huge amounts of time and money. In the new factory, workers use rolling carts to move bundles of fabric and leather to their workstations, which are equipped with special chairs designed for a sewing operation, rather than hauling them by hand in the old factory. Managers say that since moving into the new factory, employee productivity has increased by more than 50 percent. ■

fixed position layout
an arrangement in which materials do not move down a production line but rather, because of their weight, size, or bulk, are assembled on the spot.

FIXED POSITION LAYOUTS In a **fixed position layout**, materials do not move down a line as in a production layout but rather, because of the weight, size, or bulk of the final product, are assembled in one spot. In other words, workers and equipment go to the material rather than having the material flow down a line to them. Aircraft assembly plants and shipyards typify this kind of layout.

DESIGNING PRODUCTION LAYOUTS Two important criteria for selecting and designing a layout are workers' productivity and material handling costs. An effective layout allows workers to maximize their productivity by providing them the tools and a system for doing their jobs properly. For example, a layout that requires a production worker to step away from the work area in search of the proper tool is inefficient. An effective manufacturing layout avoids what lean manufacturing principles identify as the seven forms of waste:

- *Transportation.* Unnecessary movement of inventory, materials, and information
- *Inventory.* Carrying unnecessary inventory
- *Motion.* Engaging in motion that does not add value to the product or process
- *Waiting.* Periods of inactivity when people, materials, or information are idle

- *Overproduction.* Producing more than customer demand dictates

- *Processing.* Using tools and procedures that are inappropriate for the job

- *Defects.* Producing poor-quality products, which requires scrapping or reworking material

In its newest factory in Miyagi, Japan, Toyota positioned cars on the assembly line side by side rather than tip to tail, reducing the required length of the production line by 35 percent and increasing worker productivity by allowing employees to walk shorter distances between cars.[139]

Manufacturers can lower materials handling costs by using the following principles that are hallmarks of a lean, efficient manufacturing layout:

- Planned materials flow pattern

- Straight-line layout where possible

- Straight, clearly marked aisles

- "Backtracking" of products kept to a minimum

- Related operations located close together

- Minimum amount of in-process inventory on hand

- Easy adjustment to changing conditions

- Minimum materials handling distances

- Minimum of manual handling of materials and products

- Ergonomically designed work centers

- Minimum distances between work stations and processes

- No unnecessary rehandling of material

- Minimum handling between operations

- Minimum storage

- Materials delivered to production employees just in time

- Materials efficiently removed from the work area

- Maximum visibility; maintain clear lines of site to spot problems and improve safety

- Orderly materials handling and storage

- Good housekeeping; minimize clutter

- Maximum flexibility

- Maximum communication

Using the principles of lean manufacturing can improve efficiency, quality, and productivity and lower costs.

ENTREPRENEURIAL PROFILE: Bensonwood Homes Bensonwood Homes, a premier designer and builder of energy-efficient timber frame homes based in Walpole, New Hampshire, applies "5S" principles (sort, shine, simplify, standardize, and sustain) that world-class automaker Toyota uses in its lean manufacturing process. (Bensonwood also added a sixth "S" principle, safety.) As the company's 65 employees began to buy into the process, improvements quickly became apparent. Employees applied lean and 5S principles to processes for both standard and custom products; productivity increased by 40 percent, setup time for several machining process decreased by 90 percent, and the company experienced dramatic reductions in costs associated with the seven forms of waste.[140] ■

Chapter Summary by Learning Objective

1. **Explain the stages in the location decision: choosing the region, the state, the city, and the final site.**

   - The location decision is one of the most important decisions an entrepreneur will make given its long-term effects on the company. An entrepreneur should look at the choice as a series of increasingly narrow decisions: Which region of the country? Which state? Which city? Which site? Choosing the right location requires an entrepreneur to evaluate potential sites with his or her target customers in mind. Demographic statistics are available from a wide variety of sources, but government agencies such as the Census Bureau have a wealth of detailed data that can guide an entrepreneur in his or her location decision.

2. **Describe the location criteria for retail and service businesses.**

   - For retailers, the location decision is especially crucial. Retailers must consider the size of the trade area, the compatibility of surrounding businesses, the degree of competition, the suitability of the surrounding transportation network, physical and psychological barriers, volume of customer traffic, adequacy of parking spots, a site's reputation, and the site's visibility.

3. **Outline the location options for retail and service businesses: central business districts, neighborhoods, shopping centers and malls, near competitors, shared spaces, inside large retail stores, nontraditional locations, at home, and on the road.**

   - Retail and service businesses have nine basic location options: central business districts; neighborhoods; shopping centers and malls; near competitors; shared spaces; inside large retail stores; nontraditional locations, such as museums, sports arenas, and college campuses; at home; and on the road.

4. **Explain the site selection process for manufacturers.**

   - A manufacturer's location decision is strongly influenced by local zoning ordinances. Some areas offer industrial parks designed specifically to attract manufacturers. Two crucial factors for most manufacturers are the reliability (and the cost of transporting) raw materials and the quality and quantity of available labor.

   - A foreign trade zone is a specially designated area in or near a U.S. customs port of entry that allows resident companies to import materials and components from foreign countries; assemble, process, manufacture, or package them; and then ship the finished product while either reducing or eliminating tariffs and duties.

   - Business incubators are locations that offer flexible, low-cost rental space to their tenants as well as business and consulting services. Their goal is to nurture small companies until they are ready to "graduate" into the business community. Many government agencies and universities sponsor incubator locations.

5. **Describe the criteria used to analyze the layout and design considerations of a building, including the Americans with Disabilities Act.**

   - When evaluating the suitability of a particular building, an entrepreneur should consider several factors: size (Is it large enough to accommodate the business with some room for growth?), construction and external appearance (Is the building structurally sound, and does it create the right impression for the business?), entrances (Are they inviting?), legal issues (Does the building comply with the Americans with Disabilities Act? If not, how much will it cost to bring it up to standard?), signs (Are they legible, well located, and easy to see?), interior (Does the interior design contribute to our ability to make sales? Is it ergonomically designed?), and lights and fixtures (Is the lighting adequate for the tasks workers will be performing? What is the estimated cost of lighting?).

6. **Explain the principles of effective layouts for retailers, service businesses, and manufacturers.**

   - Layout for retail stores and service businesses depends on the owner's understanding of his or her customers' buying habits. Some areas of a retail store generate more sales per square foot and therefore are more valuable.

   - The goal of a manufacturer's layout is to create a smooth, efficient work flow. Three basic options exist: product layout, process layout, and fixed position layout. Two key considerations are worker productivity and materials handling costs.

Discussion Questions

14-1. Buzz Price, the location expert who helped Disney and other entrepreneurs find the ideal locations for their businesses, described the location decision in the following way: "Guessing is dysfunctional. Using valid numbers to project performance is rational." How can entrepreneurs find "valid numbers" to help them project the performance of their businesses in different locations?

14-2. What factors should a manager consider when evaluating a region in which to locate a business? Where are such data available?

14-3. Outline the factors important when selecting a state in which to locate a business.

14-4. What factors should a seafood processing plant, a beauty shop, and an exclusive jewelry store consider in choosing a location? List factors for each type of business.

14-5. What intangible factors might enter into the entrepreneur's location decision?

14-6. What are zoning laws? How do they affect the location decision?

14-7. What is the trade area? What determines a small retailer's trade area?

14-8. Why is it important to discover more than just the number of passersby in a traffic count for a potential location?

14-9. What types of information can the entrepreneur collect from census data?

14-10. Why may a "cheap location" not be the "best location"?

14-11. What is a foreign trade zone? A business incubator? What advantages and disadvantages does each one offer a small business locating there?

14-12. Why is it costly for a small firm to choose a location that is too small?

14-13. What function does a small company's sign serve? What are the characteristics of an effective business sign?

14-14. Explain the Americans with Disabilities Act. Which businesses does it affect? What is its purpose?

14-15. What is ergonomics? Why should entrepreneurs apply the principles of ergonomics in the design of their facilities?

14-16. Explain the statement, "Not every portion of a small store's interior space is of equal value in generating sales revenue." What areas are most valuable?

14-17. According to market research firm NPD Group, in 1985, women purchased 70 percent of all men's clothing; today, women buy just 34 percent of men's apparel. What implications does this have for modern store layouts?

14-18. What are some of the features that determine a good manufacturing layout?

Beyond the Classroom . . .

14-19. Select a specific type of business you would like to go into one day and use census data to choose a specific site for the business in the local region. What location factors are critical to the success of this business? Would it be likely to succeed in your hometown?

14-20. Interview a sample of local small business owners. How did they decide on their particular locations? What are the positive and negative features of their existing locations?

14-21. Visit the Web sites for *Entrepreneur* or *Fortune* magazine and find articles about the "best cities for (small) business." (For *Entrepreneur*, it is usually the October issue, and for *Fortune*, it is normally an issue in November). Which cities are in the top 10? What factors did the magazine use to select these cities? Pick a city and explain what makes it an attractive destination for locating a business there.

14-22. Select a manufacturing operation, a wholesale business, or a retail store and evaluate their layouts using the guidelines presented in this chapter.

What changes would you recommend? Why? How does the new layout contribute to a more effective operation? How much would the changes you suggest cost?

14-23. Every year, *Site Selection* magazine selects the states with the top business climates. Use the Internet to locate the latest state rankings. Which states top the list? Which states are at the bottom of the list? What factors affect a state's ranking? Why are these factors important to entrepreneurs' location decisions?

14-24. Visit the Web site for the Census Bureau at www.census.gov. Go to the census data for your town and use it to discuss its suitability as a location for the following types of businesses:

- A new motel with 25 units
- A bookstore
- An exclusive women's clothing shop
- A Mexican restaurant
- A residential plumber

- A day care center
- A high-quality stereo shop
- A family hair care center

14-25. Visit the Census Bureau's Web site and use the American FactFinder section to prepare a demographic profile of your hometown or city or of the town or city in which you attend college. Using the demographic profile as an analytical tool, what kinds of businesses do you think would be successful there? Unsuccessful? Explain.

Endnotes

Scan for Endnotes or go to www.pearsonhighered.com/scarborough

15

Global Aspects of Entrepreneurship

Mike Kemp/Getty Images

Learning Objectives

On completion of this chapter, you will be able to:

1. Explain why "going global" has become an integral part of many small companies' marketing strategies.

2. Describe the principal strategies small businesses have for going global.

3. Discuss the major barriers to international trade and their impact on the global economy.

4. Describe the trade agreements that will have the greatest influence on foreign trade in the twenty-first century.

Until recently, the world of international business was much like astronomy before Copernicus, who revolutionized the study of the planets and the stars with his theory of planetary motion. In the sixteenth century, the Copernican system replaced the Ptolemaic system, which held that the earth was the center of the universe with the sun and all the other planets revolving around it. The Copernican system, however, placed the sun at the center of the solar system with all of the planets revolving around it. Astronomy would never be the same.

In the same sense, business owners across the globe have been guilty of having Ptolemaic tunnel vision when it came to viewing international business opportunities. Like their pre-Copernican counterparts, owners saw an economy that revolved around the nations that served as their home bases. Market opportunities stopped at their homeland's borders, and global trade was only for giant corporations. American small businesses lag behind their counterparts in most countries around the globe when it comes to exporting. Only 3.9 percent of U.S. small businesses engage in exporting. In contrast, an average of 8 percent of small and medium enterprises in the European Union engage in exporting. Estonia, Slovenia. and Finland have about 20 percent of small and medium businesses engaging in exporting.[1] The most common barriers keeping U.S. small businesses from exporting are regulations, rising and unpredictable transportation costs, tariff and other trade barriers, time-consuming foreign customs procedures, language and cultural differences, and lack of knowledge of foreign markets.[2] The majority of small businesses in the United States are content to focus on the domestic market. However, 95 percent of the world population lives outside of the U.S borders!

ENTREPRENEURIAL PROFILE: Ron Ward: Western Forms Western Forms, a family-owned business in Kansas City, Missouri, that manufactures forms for pouring concrete for the construction industry, exports to more than 30 countries. The company's initial foray into global markets was modest, tapping Canada and Mexico, the closest international markets geographically. CEO Ron Ward says that customers in Canada and Mexico now account for more than half of Western Forms's sales.[3] ∎

Today, the global marketplace is as much the territory of small upstart companies as it is that of giant multinational corporations. The world market for goods and services continues to grow, fueled by a global economy that welcomes consumers with new wealth. By 2025, more than 1 billion people globally will join the ranks of middle-class consumers, creating a tremendous opportunity for small businesses.[4] Powerful, affordable technology; the Internet; increased access to information on conducting global business; and the growing interdependence of the world's economies have made it easier for small companies, many of which had never considered going global, to engage in international trade. These micromultinational companies are proving that even the smallest companies can succeed in the global marketplace.

As globalization transforms entire industries, even experienced business owners and managers must rethink the rules of competition on which they have relied for years. To thrive, they must develop new business models and new sources of competitive advantages and be bold enough to seize the opportunities that the global marketplace offers. Opportunities for global trade can come from anywhere. Many small businesses focus on markets that are nearby and/or share a common language, including Canada, the United Kingdom, and Australia. However, entrepreneurs also should pay attention to the top emerging markets, which include China, South Korea, Malaysia, Chili, Thailand, Panama, Peru, Latvia, Poland, and Czech Republic.[5]

Entrepreneurs are discovering that the tools of global business are within their reach, the costs of going global are decreasing, and the benefits of conducting global business can be substantial. Nearly 67 percent of the world's purchasing power lies *outside* the borders of the United States![6] By 2020, global middle-class consumption will increase from $21 trillion to $35 trillion, with more than 80 percent of that growth occurring outside of North America and Europe.[7] Worldwide, countries trade nearly $18 trillion in goods and services annually, a dramatic increase from $58 billion in 1948.[8] There has never been a better time for small companies to become players in the global marketplace.

LO1

Explain why "going global" has become an integral part of many small companies' marketing strategies.

Why Go Global?

Failure to cultivate global markets can be a lethal mistake for modern businesses, whatever their size. A few decades ago, small companies had to concern themselves mainly with competitors who were perhaps six blocks away; today, small companies face fierce competition from companies that may be six *time zones* away! As a result, entrepreneurs find themselves under greater pressure to expand into international markets and to build businesses without borders. Today, the potential for doing business globally for companies of all sizes means that where a business's goods and services originate or where its headquarters is located is insignificant. Operating a successful business increasingly requires entrepreneurs to see their companies as global citizens rather than as companies based in a particular geographic region. For small companies around the world, going global is a matter of survival, not preference. To be successful, small companies must take their place in the world market. Unfortunately, most small companies follow a *reactive* approach to going global (engaging in global sales because foreign customers initiate the contact) rather than pursue a *proactive* global sales strategy that involves researching and analyzing foreign markets that represent the best fit for their products and services.[9]

Going global can put a tremendous strain on a small company, but entrepreneurs who take the plunge into global business can reap many benefits, including the ability to offset sales declines in the domestic market, increase sales and profits, improve the quality of their products to meet the stringent demands of foreign customers, lower the manufacturing cost of their products by spreading fixed costs over a larger number of units, and enhance their competitive positions to become stronger businesses. In fact, companies that sell their goods and services in other countries generate more sales revenue, are more profitable, have higher levels of productivity, and are less likely to fail than those that limit their sales to the domestic market.[10]

Success in a global economy requires constant innovation; staying nimble enough to use speed as a competitive weapon; maintaining a high level of quality and constantly improving it; being sensitive to foreign customers' unique requirements; adopting a more respectful attitude toward foreign habits and customs; hiring motivated, multilingual employees; and retaining a desire to learn constantly about global markets. In short, business owners must strive to become "insiders" rather than just "exporters."

Becoming a global entrepreneur requires a different mindset. To be successful, entrepreneurs must see their companies from a global perspective and must instill a global culture throughout their companies that permeates everything the business does. To these entrepreneurs and their companies, national boundaries are irrelevant; they see the world as a market opportunity. An absence of global thinking is one of the barriers that most often limit entrepreneurs' ability to move beyond the domestic market. Indeed, learning to *think globally* may be the first—and

"I don't call expanding to New Jersey thinking globally."

Roy Delgado/www.Cartoonstock.com

most challenging—obstacle an entrepreneur must overcome on the way to creating a truly global business. Global thinking is the ability to appreciate, understand, and respect the different beliefs, values, behavior, and business practices of companies and people in different cultures and countries. This requires entrepreneurs to "do their homework" to learn about the people, places, business techniques, potential customers, and culture of the countries in which they intend to do business. Several U.S. government agencies, including the Department of Commerce, offer vast amounts of information about all nations, including economic data that can be useful to entrepreneurs searching for market opportunities. Doing business globally presents extraordinary opportunities only to those who are prepared.

LO2

Describe the principal strategies small businesses have for going global.

Strategies for Going Global

Small companies pursuing a global presence have 10 principal strategies from which to choose: creating a presence on the Web, relying on trade intermediaries, establishing joint ventures, engaging in foreign licensing arrangements, franchising, using countertrading and bartering, exporting products or services, establishing international locations, importing and outsourcing, and becoming an expat entrepreneur (see Figure 15.1).

CREATING A WEB SITE In our technology-rich global environment, the fastest, least expensive, and lowest-cost strategic option to establish a global business presence is to create a Web site. As you saw in Chapter 9 on e-commerce, the Internet gives even the smallest business the ability to sell its goods and services all over the globe. By establishing a presence online, a local candy maker or a home-based luxury boat broker gains immediate access to customers around the world. With a well-designed Web site, an entrepreneur can extend his or her reach to customers anywhere in the world—without breaking the budget! A company's Web site is available to potential customers everywhere and provides exposure to its products or services 24 hours a day seven days a week. For many small companies, the Internet has become a tool that is as essential to doing business as the telephone.

Establishing an Internet presence has become an important part of many small companies' strategies for reaching customers outside the United States. Internet World Stats estimates the number of Internet users worldwide to be 2.4 billion. Just 273 million of them live in the United States, leaving more than 2 *billion* potential Internet customers outside this country's borders (see Figure 15.2)![11] A study by the World Retail Congress reports that 23 percent of global retail sales will take place online by 2015.[12]

Just as business owners who conduct international business in person must be sensitive to the cultural nuances and differences in the business practices of other countries, entrepreneurs who conduct business online must take these same factors into account when they design their companies' Web sites. Entrepreneurs must "think local" when they create Web sites that target customers in other countries. Although having a single domain name with separate "language"

FIGURE 15.1

Ten Strategies for Going Global

FIGURE 15.2

Internet Users Worldwide

Source: http://www .internetworldstats.com/stats .htm

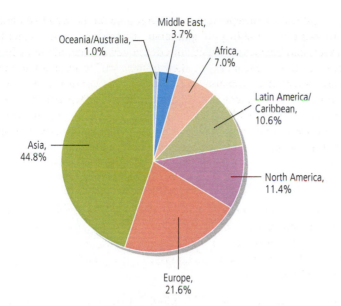

buttons for translations is simpler and less expensive, e-commerce experts say having separate domain names for each targeted country produces better sales results. The design of Web sites that target foreign customers must reflect the local culture, customs, and language. For instance, not all cultures read from left to right, and colors that may be appropriate in one culture may be offensive to customers in another. A U.S. entrepreneur won't have much luck listing "soccer cleats" for sale on a Web site aimed at customers in the United Kingdom, where customers would search for "football boots." Although there are online tools to help translate keywords and Web site content into multiple languages, the subtleties of language and culture require getting help from people with specific expertise in a new market.

Before the advent of the Internet, small businesses usually took incremental steps toward becoming global businesses. They began selling locally and then, after establishing a reputation, expanded regionally and perhaps nationally. Only after establishing themselves domestically did small businesses begin to think about selling their products or services internationally. The Internet makes that business model obsolete because it provides small companies with a low-cost global distribution channel that they can use from the day they are launched.

TRADE INTERMEDIARIES Although many small businesses handle their foreign sales efforts in-house, another alternative for getting into international markets with a minimum of cost and effort is to use a trade intermediary. **Trade intermediaries** are domestic agencies that serve as distributors in foreign countries for domestic companies of all sizes. They rely on their networks of contacts, their extensive knowledge of local customs and markets, and their experience in international trade to market products effectively and efficiently all across the globe. These trade intermediaries serve as the export departments for small businesses, enabling the small companies to focus on what they do best and delegate the responsibility for coordinating foreign sales efforts to the intermediaries. They are especially valuable to small companies that are getting started in the global arena, often producing benefits that far outweigh their costs. Lawrence Harding, president of High Street Partners, a trade intermediary that manages foreign sales for small companies, points to the example of a company that imported telecommunications equipment into the United Kingdom to sell to its customers there. The deal triggered a hefty 17.5 percent duty that Harding says the company could have avoided paying if it had imported the equipment in a different way.[13]

Although a broad array of trade intermediaries is available, the following are ideally suited for small businesses.

Export Management Companies **Export management companies (EMCs)** are an important channel of foreign distribution for small companies just getting started in international trade or for those that lack the resources to assign their own people to foreign markets. Most EMCs are merchant intermediaries, working on a buy-and-sell arrangement with domestic small

trade intermediaries
domestic agencies that serve as distributors in foreign countries for domestic companies of all sizes.

export management companies (EMCs)
merchant intermediaries that provide small businesses with a low-cost, efficient, off-site international marketing department

You Be the Consultant

Going Global from the Outset

Entrepreneurs are discovering that doing business globally is not just for large corporations. Some entrepreneurs take their companies global from the outset, and their micro-multinational companies are reaping the benefits.

Zee Wines USA

Roy Goslin and his wife, Dianne Ferrandi, grew up in South Africa, where both had connections to that country's wine industry. Ferrandi's parents owned vineyards and sold grapes to local vintners, and Goslin worked in materials and process management for one of South Africa's largest wineries. Both Goslin and Ferrandi grew up with wine as an integral part of meals. In 1998, recruited by a large information technology consulting firm, the couple moved to Minneapolis, Minnesota, but they never lost their passion for the fine wines of South Africa. Because few people in the United States knew about the storied winemaking tradition and superb vineyards of South Africa, Goslin and Ferrandi had difficulty finding wines from their homeland in Minnesota. Their solution: start their own wine import business that specializes in wines from South Africa. They announced their decision at a dinner with friends, where one friend suggested that they name their company "Z Wines." (You've got zee food, and we have zee wine," he joked.)

In 2006, Goslin and Ferrandi started Zee Wines USA as a home-based business with the goal of importing wines from South Africa that they knew were the best the country had to offer and wholesaling them to retail stores. Many of the wineries the company buys from have been operating for hundreds of years. With its diverse climate, rich soil, amazing biodiversity, and rich winemaking tradition, South Africa produces some of the world's finest, most distinctive wines. The couple knew they could import wines from South Africa and sell them for just $10 to $15 per bottle in the United States.

In addition to the South African wines they import, Goslin and Ferrandi also sell domestic wines from Washington, Oregon, and California. With $500,000 in annual sales, their total portfolio of wines numbers only about 100. Although the owners could have pursued a more aggressive growth strategy, they chose to focus on wines that fit their business model of providing high value for their customers. The company only accepts 1 to 2 percent of the wines its owners evaluate.

Somnio

When Sean Sullivan was an executive at The North Face and Specialized Bicycle Components, he noticed that international sales accounted for the majority of sales in some product categories. Learning from his corporate experience, Sullivan decided that when he launched his own company, he would operate it as a global business from the start. Sullivan, an avid runner, came up with the idea for his business after visiting his doctor, Andy Pruitt, founder of the Boulder Center for Sports Medicine in Boulder, Colorado, for treatment for chronic foot pain. Pruitt told Sullivan that his running shoes were the cause of his foot problem, and the two worked together to design a better running shoe using biomechanics, custom padding, and inserts to create customized shoes that accommodate runners' foot shape and running style. For instance, they developed insoles that are tailored to fit each customer's arch height. They launched Somnio in 2009 and immediately began developing strategies to sell their running shoes in Europe and Asia.

After a four-month search, Sullivan hired Saskia Stock, who had been in charge of biomechanical research at MBT Shoes, a Swiss footwear maker, to manage Somnio's European division in Zurich, Switzerland. The reason that Sullivan wanted a veteran of the shoe industry to manage the company's European operations was to enable Somnio to enter into direct sales relationships with retailers rather than sell through foreign distributors. Sullivan is concerned that selling through distributors will cost him too much over the long run. When Somnio entered Asian markets, however, Sullivan opted to use foreign distributors there because they had established connections that would take Somnio years to develop and understood the nuances of doing business locally.

Somnio, which is headquartered in La Selva Beach, California, manufactures its running shoes in China and sells them in 20 countries, throughout the Americas, Europe, and Asia. The company generates $10 million in annual sales, more than half of which comes from Europe.

1. As the global market grows, more small businesses are expanding into other markets. What are the implications for small companies that have the potential to conduct business globally?

2. What advice can you offer the founders of Zee Wine USA about selling their products globally?

3. Notice that Sean Sullivan used a direct sales approach to enter the European market but relied on foreign distributors in the Asian market. What are the advantages and the disadvantages of each approach? Why do most small companies that sell internationally use trade intermediaries?

Sources: Based on John Garland, "Roy Goslin and Dianne Ferrandi of Z Wines," *Heavy Table,* March 2, 2011, http://heavytable.com/roy-goslin-and-dianne-ferrandi-of-z-wines; Phil Bolsta, "Small Business Success Stories: Z Wines USA," *Twin Cities Business,* December 2008, http://www.tcbmag.com/superstars/smallbusinesssuccessstories/106542p1.aspx; and Ryan Underwood, "Made to Travel: Why More Start-Ups Are Going Beyond Borders, *Inc.,* March 2011, pp. 96–98.

companies, taking title to the goods and then reselling them in foreign markets; others work on commission. More than 1,000 EMCs operate across the United States, and many of them specialize in particular industries, products, or product lines as well as in the foreign countries they target. For instance, Dorian Drake International, an EMC started in 1947, specializes in selling equipment around the world for U.S.-based companies in four industries—automotive, food service, lawn and garden, and environmental. For more than 40 years, Dorian Drake has managed global sales for American Lawn, the leading U.S. maker of manual reel lawn mowers, a family-owned business founded in Shelbyville, Indiana, in 1895.[14]

EMCs provide small businesses with a low-cost, efficient, independent international marketing and export department, offering services that range from conducting market research and giving advice on patent protection to arranging financing and handling shipping. The greatest benefits that EMCs offer small companies are ready access to global markets and an extensive knowledge base on foreign trade, both of which are vital for entrepreneurs who are inexperienced in conducting global business. In return for their services, EMCs usually earn an extra discount on the goods they buy from their clients or, if they operate on a commission rate, a higher commission than domestic distributors earn on what they sell. EMCs charge commission rates of about 10 percent on consumer goods and 15 percent on industrial products. Although EMCs rarely advertise their services, finding one is not difficult. The Federation of International Trade Associations provides useful information for small companies about global business and trade intermediaries on its Web site, including a listing of EMCs. Industry trade associations and publications and the U.S. Department of Commerce's Export Assistance Centers also can help entrepreneurs to locate EMCs and other trade intermediaries.

Export Trading Companies Another tactic for getting into international markets with a minimum of cost and effort is through export trading companies. **Export trading companies (ETCs)** are businesses that buy and sell products in a number of countries, and they typically offer a wide range of services, such as exporting, importing, shipping, storing, distributing, and others, to their clients. Unlike EMCs, which tend to focus on exporting, ETCs usually perform both import and export trades across many countries' borders. Although EMCs usually create exclusive contracts with companies for a particular product line, ETCs often represent several companies selling the same product line. However, like EMCs, ETCs lower the risk of exporting for small businesses. Some of the largest ETCs in the world are based in the United States and Japan. In fact, many businesses that have navigated successfully Japan's complex system of distribution have done so with the help of ETCs.

In 1982, Congress passed the Export Trading Company Act to allow producers of similar products to form ETC cooperatives without the fear of violating antitrust laws. The goal was to encourage U.S. companies to export more goods by allowing businesses in the same industry to band together to form ETCs.

Manufacturer's Export Agents **Manufacturer's export agents (MEAs)** act as international sales representatives in a limited number of markets for various noncompeting domestic companies. Unlike the close, partnering relationship formed with most EMCs, the relationship between the MEA and a small company is a short-term one, and the MEA typically operates on a commission basis.

Export Merchants **Export merchants** are domestic wholesalers who do business in foreign markets. They buy goods from many domestic manufacturers and then market them in foreign markets. Unlike MEAs, export merchants often carry competing lines, meaning that they have little loyalty to suppliers. Most export merchants specialize in particular industries, such as office equipment, computers, and industrial supplies.

Resident Buying Offices Another approach to exporting is to sell to a **resident buying office**, a government- or privately owned operation of one country established in another country for the purpose of buying goods made there. Many foreign governments and businesses have set up buying offices in the United States. Selling to them is just like selling to domestic customers because the buying office handles all the details of exporting.

Foreign Distributors Some small businesses work through foreign distributors to reach international markets. Domestic small companies export their products to these distributors, who

export trading companies (ETCs) businesses that buy and sell products in a number of countries and offer a wide variety of import and export services to their clients.

manufacturer's export agents (MEAs) businesses that act as international sales representatives in a limited number of markets for noncompeting domestic companies.

export merchants domestic wholesalers who do business in foreign markets.

resident buying office government- or privately owned operations of one country established in another country for the purpose of buying goods made there.

handle all of the marketing, distribution, support, and service functions in the foreign country. The key to success is screening potential distributors to find those that are reliable, financially sound, and customer focused.

ENTREPRENEURIAL PROFILE: Dr. Roy Archambault: DryCorp DryCorp, located in Wilmington, North Carolina, manufactures products that help waterproof other products. DryCorp, which was founded by Dr. Roy Archambault, developed its first line of products to waterproof casts, bandages, ostomies, and prosthetics using a rubber sleeve. The product allows patients to swim, bathe, shower, and to receive hydrotherapy without any damage to the medical product protected by the sleeve. DryCorp then developed a line of crystal clear bags that vacuum-seal electronic devices while still allowing them to be fully functional. Products include cases for tablets, earphones, and backpacks. Because DryCorp's products are highly seasonal, the company relies on foreign distributors in markets such as Australia that have opposite seasons to the United States.[15] ■

THE VALUE OF USING TRADE INTERMEDIARIES Trade intermediaries such as these are becoming increasingly popular among small businesses attempting to branch out into world markets because they make that transition much faster and easier. Most small business owners simply do not have the knowledge, resources, or confidence to go global alone. Intermediaries' global networks of buyers and sellers allow their small business customers to build their international sales much faster and with fewer hassles and mistakes. Entrepreneurs who are inexperienced in global sales and attempt to crack certain foreign markets alone quickly discover just how difficult the challenge can be. However, with their know-how, experience, and contacts, trade intermediaries can get small companies' products into foreign markets quickly and efficiently. The primary disadvantage of using trade intermediaries is that doing so requires entrepreneurs to surrender control over their foreign sales. However, by maintaining close contact with intermediaries and evaluating their performance regularly, entrepreneurs can avoid major problems.

The key to establishing a successful relationship with a trade intermediary is conducting a thorough screening to determine which type of intermediary—and which one in particular—will best serve a small company's needs. Entrepreneurs should look for intermediaries that specialize in the products their companies sell and that have experience and established contacts in the countries they have targeted. An entrepreneur looking for an intermediary should compile a list of potential candidates using some of the sources listed in Table 15.1. After compiling the list, entrepreneurs should evaluate each one using a list of criteria to narrow the field to the most promising ones. Interviewing a principal from each intermediary on the final list should tell entrepreneurs which ones are best able to meet their companies' needs. Finally, before signing any agreement with a trade intermediary, it is wise to conduct thorough background and credit checks. Entrepreneurs with experience in global trade also suggest entering short-term agreements of about a year with new trade intermediaries to allow time to test their ability and willingness to live up to their promises. Many entrepreneurs begin their global business initiatives with trade intermediaries and then venture into international business on their own as their skill and comfort levels increase.

JOINT VENTURES Joint ventures, both domestic and foreign, lower the risk of entering global markets for small businesses. They also give small companies more clout in foreign lands. In a **domestic joint venture**, two or more U.S. small businesses form an alliance for the purpose of exporting their goods and services. For export ventures, participating companies get antitrust immunity, allowing them to cooperate freely. The businesses share the responsibility and the costs of getting export licenses and permits, and they split the venture's profits. Establishing a joint venture with the right partner has become an essential part of maintaining a competitive position in global markets for a growing number of industries.

In a **foreign joint venture**, a domestic small business forms an alliance with a company in the target nation. The host partner brings to the joint venture valuable knowledge of the local market and its method of operation as well as of the customs and the tastes of local customers, making it much easier to conduct business in the foreign country. Sometimes foreign countries place certain limitations on joint ventures, for example, requiring host companies to hold a majority stake in the venture.

domestic joint venture
an alliance of two or more U.S. small companies for the purpose of exporting their goods and services abroad.

foreign joint venture
an alliance between a U.S. small business and a company in the target nation.

TABLE 15.1 Resources for Locating a Trade Intermediary

Trade intermediaries make doing business around the world much easier for small companies, but finding the right one can be a challenge. Fortunately, several government agencies offer a wealth of information to businesses interested in reaching into global markets with the help of trade intermediaries. Entrepreneurs looking for help in breaking into global markets should contact the International Trade Administration, the U.S. Commerce Department, and the Small Business Administration first to take advantage of the following services:

- *Agent/Distributor Service (ADS).* Provides customized searches to locate interested and qualified foreign distributors for a product or service. (Search cost, $250 per country)
- *Commercial Service International Contacts (CSIC) List.* Provides contact and product information for more than 82,000 foreign agents, distributors, and importers interested in doing business with U.S. companies.
- *Country Directories of International Contacts (CDIC) List.* Provides the same kind of information as the CSIC List but is organized by country.
- *Industry Sector Analyses (ISAs).* Offer in-depth reports on industries in foreign countries, including information on distribution practices, end users, and top sales prospects.
- *International Market Insights (IMIs).* Include reports on specific foreign market conditions, upcoming opportunities for U.S. companies, trade contacts, trade show schedules, and other information.
- *Trade Opportunity Program (TOP).* Provides up-to-the-minute, prescreened sales leads around the world for U.S. businesses, including joint venture and licensing partners, direct sales leads, and representation offers.
- *International Company Profiles (ICPs).* Commercial specialists will investigate potential partners, agents, distributors, or customers for U.S. companies and will issue profiles on them.
- *Commercial News USA.* A government-published magazine that promotes U.S. companies' products and services to 400,000 business readers in 176 countries at a fraction of the cost of commercial advertising. Small companies can use *Commercial News USA* to reach new customers around the world for as little as $499.
- *Gold Key Service.* For a small fee, business owners wanting to target a specific country can use the Department of Commerce's Gold Key Service, in which experienced trade professionals arrange meetings with prescreened contacts whose interests match their own.
- *Platinum Key Service.* The U.S. Commercial Service's Platinum Key Service is more comprehensive than its Gold Key Service, offering business owners long-term consulting services on topics such as building a global marketing strategy, deciding which countries to target, and serving the needs of customers in foreign markets.
- *Matchmaker Trade Delegations Program.* This program helps small U.S. companies establish business relationships in major markets abroad by introducing them to the right contacts.
- *Multi-State/Catalog Exhibition Program.* The Department of Commerce presents companies' product and sales literature to hundreds of interested business prospects in foreign countries for as little as $450.
- *Trade Fair Certification Program.* This service promotes U.S. companies' participation in foreign trade shows that represent the best marketing opportunities for them.
- *Globus and National Trade Data Bank (NTDB).* Most of the information listed above is available on the NTDB, the U.S. government's most comprehensive database of world trade data. With the NTDB, small companies have access to information that once only *Fortune* 500 companies could afford for an annual subscription rate of just $200.
- *Economic Bulletin Board (EBB).* Provides online trade leads and valuable market research on foreign countries compiled from a variety of federal agencies.
- *U.S. Export Assistance Centers.* The Department of Commerce has established 19 export centers (USEACs) in major metropolitan cities around the country to serve as one-stop shops for entrepreneurs who need export help.
- *Trade Information Center.* The center helps locate federal export assistance, provides export assistance, and offers a 24-hour automated fax retrieval system that gives entrepreneurs free information on export promotion programs, regional market information, and international trade agreements. Call USA-TRADE.
- *Office of International Trade.* Through the Office of International Trade, the Small Business Administration works with other government and private agencies to provide a variety of export development assistance, how-to publications, online courses, and information on foreign markets.
- *Export-U2.com.* This Web site offers free export webinars to business owners on topics that range from the basics, "Exporting 101," to more advanced topics such as export financing arrangements. The site also provides links to many useful international trade Web sites.
- *U.S. Commercial Service.* The U.S. Commercial Service, a division of the International Trade Administration, provides many of the services listed in this table. Its Web site is an excellent starting point for entrepreneurs who are interested in exporting.
- *Export.gov.* This Web site from the U.S. Commercial Service is an excellent gateway to myriad resources for entrepreneurs who are interested in learning more about exporting, including market research, trade events, and trade leads.
- *Federation of International Trade Associations (FITA).* The FITA Global Trade Portal is an excellent source for international import and export trade leads and events and provides links to about 8,000 Web sites related to international trade.

ENTREPRENEURIAL PROFILE: Sean "Diddy" Combs and Diageo Beverages: DeLeon Tequila Sean "Diddy" Combs, a successful entertainer and entrepreneur, formed a joint venture with the British beverage company, Diageo Beverages, to purchase the Mexican tequila brand DeLeon. DeLeon tequila sells at prices that range from $120 to more than $1,000 a bottle. Both parties contributed cash to the transaction and are equal owners in the joint venture. In addition to the cash he invested, Combs offers strong marketing skills and connections to the entertainment industry. In addition to its cash contribution, Diageo brings its industry leadership in the adult beverage market.[16] ■

The most important ingredient in the recipe for a successful joint venture is choosing the right partner. Taking the following steps will help avoid problems:

- Select a partner that shares the company's values and standards of conduct.

- Define at the outset important issues such as each party's contributions and responsibilities, the distribution of earnings, the expected life of the relationship, and the circumstances under which the parties can terminate the relationship.

- Understand their partner's reasons and objectives for joining the venture.

- Spell out in writing exactly how the venture will work and where decision-making authority lies.

- Select a partner whose skills are different from but compatible with those of the company's.

- Prepare a "prenuptial agreement" that spells out what will happen in case of a "business divorce."

FOREIGN LICENSING Rather than sell their products or services directly to customers overseas, some small companies enter foreign markets by licensing businesses in other nations to use their patents, trademarks, copyrights, technology, processes, or products. In return for licensing these assets, a small company collects royalties from the sales of its foreign licenses. Licensing is a relatively simple way for even the most inexperienced business owner to extend his or her reach into global markets. Licensing is ideal for companies whose value lies in its intellectual property, unique products or services, recognized name, or proprietary technology. Although many businesses consider licensing only their products to foreign companies, the licensing potential for intangibles, such as processes, technology, copyrights, and trademarks, often is greater. Some entrepreneurs earn more money from licensing their know-how for product design, manufacturing, or quality control than they do from actually selling their finished goods in a highly competitive foreign market with which they are not familiar. Foreign licensing enables a small business to enter foreign markets quickly and easily and with virtually no capital investment. Risks to the company include the potential loss of control over its manufacturing and marketing processes and creating a competitor if the licensee gains too much knowledge and control. Securing proper patent, trademark, and copyright protection beforehand can minimize those risks.

INTERNATIONAL FRANCHISING Franchising has become a major export industry for the United States. Over the last several decades, a growing number of franchises have been attracted to international markets to boost sales and profits as the domestic market has become increasingly saturated with outlets and much tougher to wring growth from. Franchisors should consider expanding into global markets when foreign markets present an important growth opportunity for the franchise. Yum! Brands, the franchisor of KFC, Pizza Hut, and Taco Bell restaurants, has a significant global presence with more than 40,000 restaurants in 117 countries. International franchising, particularly in fast-growing markets such as India and China, has been essential to the company's growth; in fact, China alone accounts for 40 percent of Yum! Brands' profits.[17] To be successful in global markets, a franchisor should have the following characteristics:

- Sufficient managerial and financial resources to devote to globalization

- A solid track record of success in the United States

- Adequate trademark protection for the franchise's brand

- Time-tested training, support, and reporting procedures that help franchisees succeed[18]

Franchisors that decide to expand internationally should take these steps:

1. *Identify the country or countries that are best suited to the franchisor's business concept.* Factors to consider include a country's business climate, demographic profile, level of economic development, rate of economic growth, degree of legal protection, language and cultural barriers, and market potential. Franchisors making their first forays into global markets should consider focusing on a single nation or a small group of similar nations.

2. *Generate leads for potential franchisees.* Franchisors looking for prospective franchisees in foreign markets have many tools available to them, including international franchise trade shows, their own Web sites, trade missions, and brokers. Many franchisors have had success with trade missions, such as those sponsored by trade groups like the International Franchise Association or the U.S. Department of Commerce's Gold Key Program. These trade missions are designed to introduce franchisors to qualified franchise candidates in target countries. Others rely on brokers who have extensive business contacts in specific countries.

3. *Select quality candidates.* Just as in any franchise relationship, the real key to success is choosing the right franchisee. Because of the complexity and cost of international franchising, selecting quality franchisees is essential to success. Establishing an intranet allows franchisors to stay in contact with their international franchisees across time zones.

4. *Structure the franchise deal.* Franchisors can structure international franchise arrangements in a variety of ways, but three techniques are most popular: direct franchising, area development, and master franchising.

   - Direct franchising, common in domestic franchise deals, involves selling single-unit franchises to individual operators in foreign countries. Although dealing with individual franchisees makes it easier for the franchisor to maintain control, it also requires more of the franchisor's time and resources.
   - Area development is similar to direct franchising except that the franchisor allows the franchisee to develop multiple units in a particular territory, perhaps a province, a county, or even an entire nation. A successful area development strategy depends on a franchisor selecting and then supporting quality franchisees. In 2001, brothers Manpreet and Gurpreet Gulri entered into an area development agreement with Subway to expand the sandwich chain's presence in India; they now operate more than 200 stores there. "We work closely with local chefs and regional suppliers to ensure a good balance of vegetarian and non-vegetarian items, along with many traditional Subway menu items, all specifically selected to appeal to the Indian palate," says Manpreet.[19]
   - Master franchising is the most popular strategy for companies entering international markets. In a master franchising arrangement, a franchisor grants an experienced master franchisee the right to sell outlets to subfranchisees in a broad geographic area or sometimes in an entire country. Franchisors use this method to expand into international markets quickly and efficiently because their master franchisees understand local laws and customs and the nuances of selling in local markets. Although master franchising simplifies a franchisor's expansion into global markets, it generates less revenue for franchisers than direct franchising and gives them the least amount of control over their international franchisees. Domino's Pizza, with more than 5,000 outlets in 70 countries outside the United States, relies on master franchises, especially in emerging markets such as India, China, Malaysia, and Turkey. Jubilant FoodWorks Limited, Domino's Pizza's master franchisee in India, operates nearly 450 outlets, but Richard Alison, Domino's Pizza's international president, says the country has the potential to have at least 1,000 locations.[20]

Just as they do in the United States, franchisors in international markets sell virtually every kind of product or service imaginable—from fast food to child day care. In some cases, the products and services sold in international markets are identical to those sold in the United States. However, most franchisors have learned that adaptation is the key to making sure their goods and services suit local tastes and customs. Traveling the world, one discovers that American fast-food giants such as Domino's, KFC, and McDonald's make significant modifications in their menu to remain attractive to the demands of local customers.

ENTREPRENEURIAL PROFILE: Tony Chew: KFC Vietnam One of the more active regions for international franchising is Southeast Asia. Indonesia, Thailand, the Philippines, Malaysia, Singapore, Vietnam, Myanmar, Brunei, Cambodia, and Laos are experiencing rapid growth in American franchised restaurants. One of the most popular franchises is KFC, which first came to Vietnam in 1997 through the vision of Singapore entrepreneur and franchisee Tony Chew. When Chew opened the first KFC in Vietnam, there was a limited power supply, poor roads, an untrained workforce, and a weak business climate. KFC Vietnam (KFCV) currently operates 140 restaurants and employs 4,000 workers.[21] ■

countertrade

a transaction in which a company selling goods in a foreign country agrees to promote investment and trade in that country.

COUNTERTRADING AND BARTERING A **countertrade** is a transaction in which a company selling goods in a foreign country agrees to promote investment and trade in that country. The goal of the transaction is to help offset the capital drain from the foreign country's purchases. As entrepreneurs enter more and more developing countries, they will need to develop skills at implementing this strategy. In some cases, small and medium-size businesses find it advantageous to work together with large corporations that have experience in the implementation of this marketing strategy.

Countertrading suffers numerous drawbacks. Countertrade transactions can be complicated, cumbersome, and time consuming. They also increase the chances that a company will get stuck with merchandise that it cannot move. They can lead to unpleasant surprises concerning the quantity and quality of products required in the countertrade. Still, countertrading offers one major advantage: sometimes it's the only way to make a sale!

Entrepreneurs must weigh the advantages against the disadvantages for their company before committing to a countertrade deal. Because of its complexity and the risks involved, countertrading is not the best choice for a novice entrepreneur looking to break into the global marketplace.

bartering

the exchange of goods and services for other goods and services.

Bartering, the exchange of goods and services for other goods and services, is another way of trading with countries lacking convertible currency. In a barter exchange, a company that manufactures electronics components might trade its products for the coffee a business in a foreign country processes, which it then sells to a third company for cash. Barter transactions require finding a business with complementary needs, but they are much simpler than countertrade transactions.

EXPORTING For many years, small businesses in the United States focused solely on the domestic market, never venturing beyond its borders. However, growing numbers of small companies, realizing the growth and profit potential that exporting offers, are making globalization part of their marketing plans. Although small and medium-size companies account for nearly 98 percent of the 302,000 U.S. businesses that export goods and services, they generate just one-third of the nation's export sales. Their impact is significant, however; small companies generate $2.1 billion in day in export sales. Owners of small companies that export say that two of the main benefits their companies reap are increased sales and profits and larger, more diversified customer bases.[22]

Many more small companies have the potential to export but are not doing so. The biggest barrier facing companies that have never exported is not knowing where or how to start, but entrepreneurs have a treasure trove of resources, training, and consulting on which they can draw. The International Trade Administration's *Export Programs Guide* provides entrepreneurs with a comprehensive list of 100 federal programs in 20 agencies designed to help U.S. exporters. The U.S. Commercial Service Web site is an excellent starting point for entrepreneurs who are looking for international business partners to help their companies expand into global markets. Many entrepreneurs also find the U.S. Small Business Administration's Export Business Planner, a comprehensive set of worksheets that guides users through the process of building an export business plan, to be a valuable resource.

Another source of useful information are the U.S. Export Assistance Centers that serve as single contact points for information on the multitude of federal export programs that are designed to help entrepreneurs who want to start exporting. The U.S. government's export Internet portal gives entrepreneurs access to valuable information about exporting in general (finance, shipping, documentation, and others) as well as details on individual nations (market research, trade agreements, statistics, and more). Learning more about exporting and realizing that it is within the realm of possibility for small companies—even *very* small companies—is the first and often most difficult step in breaking the psychological barrier to exporting. The next challenge is to create a sound export strategy:

Step 1. ***Recognize that even the tiniest companies and least experienced entrepreneurs have the potential to export.*** Many entrepreneurs never considering exporting because they think their companies are too small; however, a business's size has nothing to do with the global potential of its products. In fact, 33 percent of the

You Be the Consultant

Selling a Simple Product to a Global Market

Courtesy of John Aron

The Pasta Shoppe, located in Nashville, Tennessee, manufactures and distributes pasta. John Aron and his wife Carey, cofounders of The Pasta Shoppe, first came up with the idea for a pasta business while on their honeymoon in Italy. They were inspired by the many shapes of pasta they discovered as they traveled throughout the many regions of Italy. What differentiates The Pasta Company from its competitors is that it makes pasta in a variety of fun shapes that are tied to people's favorite college sports teams and to various holidays, such as Christmas, St Patrick's Day, Halloween, and Thanksgiving. The Arons found a way to Americanize the variety of pasta shapes that had caught their imaginations while on their honeymoon.

Rather than compete with other mass production pasta businesses, the Arons chose to build the company by focusing on small batch production using high-quality ingredients and a carefully designed manufacturing process. The company buys all of its wheat from the Dakotas and uses specially designed bronze tools to cut the pasta into the various shapes. The Pasta Shoppe dries the pasta overnight in carts, rather than using the speed drying machines favored by large manufacturers. Its products are sold online, through specialty retailers, and as a fundraising product for schools and youth programs. The Pasta Shoppe is able to more favorably price its products by avoiding selling through mass retailers, which typically demand discounts. The company has experienced strong growth in the U.S. market since it was founded in 1994, even during economic downturns.

Then in 1998, The Pasta Shoppe entered its first international market, Japan, which remains its largest market outside the United States. Its success in Japan is due to Japanese interest in Western celebrations and holidays. John Aron recognized that international markets would extend the company's season for its holiday products due to the earlier production needed to move its product to Japanese distributors. The company quickly learned that to be successful, it had to customize its products and packaging to fit the Japanese consumer market.

The Pasta Shoppe's first entry into Japan had to be cut short in 2000 due to the outbreak of Asian flu. Because the two years it sold in Japan were highly successful, the company reentered the Japanese market in 2003 after the Asian flu scare had passed.

Based on its success in Japan, The Pasta Shoppe now exports to Canada, Australia, the United Kingdom, Mexico, Chile, and Guam. The company is currently attempting to develop distribution into the Philippines and South Korea. However, although the Arons have tried, they have made no headway into exporting to China.

When considering a move into a new international market, the Arons use specific criteria to assess its attractiveness. In addition to the quality of the foreign distributor and projected cash flow, timing is everything. The company looks for international sales that do not conflict with sales in the domestic market, which peak from September through December, because the U.S. market remains its most profitable market.

Pricing is key to success in international markets for The Pasta Shoppe. "It's our toughest priced sales channel," says Aron.

1. Identify the risks and the benefits The Pasta Shoppe faces by operating as a global business.

2. Identify some of the barriers that companies such as The Pasta Shoppe encounter as they expand internationally. What steps can entrepreneurs take to overcome these obstacles?

3. What steps do you recommend that entrepreneurs such as John Aron take before they make the decision to take their companies global?

Sources: Based on John Aron, personal communication, May 20, 2014; Brian Reisinger, "Pasta Shoppe elbows in on international markets," *Nashville Business Journal,* November 12, 2010, www.bizjournals.com/nashville/print-edition/2010/11/12/pasta-shoppe-elbows.html?page=all; Carey Aron, "Why Fun Pasta—The Pasta Shoppe," *Readable,* n.d., www.allreadable.com/vid/why-fun-pasta-the-pasta-shoppe%2C-nashville-tn-489722.html.

TABLE 15.2 Assessing Your Company's Export Potential

1. *Does your company have a product or service that has been successfully sold in the domestic market?* A product's or service's success in the domestic market is a good indicator of its potential success in markets abroad. However, because selling domestically and internationally are entirely different ventures, entrepreneurs should read *A Basic Guide to Exporting* (http://www.export.gov/basicguide/) to learn what to expect when selling internationally.

2. *Does your company have or is your company preparing an international marketing plan with defined goals and strategies?* Many companies begin export activities haphazardly, without carefully screening markets or options for market entry. A marketing plan allows your company to find and focus on the best export opportunities. Formulating an export strategy based on good information and proper assessment increases the chances that you will choose the best options, that you will use your company's resources effectively, and, therefore, that your efforts will successful. To find market research on the countries you are interested in selling to, visit the Market Research Library (http://export.gov/mrktresearch/index.asp).

3. *Does your company have sufficient production capacity that can be committed to the export market?* To export successfully, your company must meet the demand that it creates in foreign markets. You may need more space and equipment to manufacture for the specific countries you are selling to (who have their own product standards and regulations). Expanding into the international marketplace will result in a higher number of units to manufacture, and you do not want this increase in production to lower your company's quality of output.

4. *Does your company have the financial resources to actively support the marketing of your products in the targeted overseas markets?* Developing foreign markets requires financial resources. This is a big hurdle for many small companies because it involves activities such as international travel, participation in trade shows, market research, and international business training. However, there are many government programs to help finance companies' export sales, including the Export-Import Bank (Ex-Im Bank) (www.exim.gov), the U.S. Small Business Administration (www.sba.gov/content/export-loan-programs), the U.S. Department of Agriculture (www.fas.usda.gov), and the Overseas Private Investment Corporation (www.opic.gov).

5. *Is your company's management committed to developing export markets and willing and able to dedicate staff, time, and resources to the process?* Management commitment is the number one determining factor for export success. Developing an export market takes time and effort, and managers must be certain they can afford to allocate sufficient time to exporting. Whether managers are willing to invest the time to build an export business plan is a good indicator of their commitment to an export initiative.

6. *Is your company committed to providing the same level of service to foreign customers that it gives to domestic customers?* This is a commitment every business must make before it begins selling in foreign markets. Successful exporters treat their foreign customers with the same commitment and service as their domestic customers. They are responsive to inquiries from international customers, work hard to build positive relationships with them, and establish systems to provide the same top-notch service they provide to their domestic customers.

7. *Does your company have adequate knowledge in modifying product packaging and ingredients to meet foreign import regulations and cultural preferences?* Selecting and preparing your product for export requires not only product knowledge but also knowledge of the unique characteristics of each market your company is targeting. Sound market research and input from foreign representatives tell a company about the potential to sell its products or services in specific target countries. Before the sale can occur, however, a company may have to modify its products and services to satisfy customers' tastes, needs, or preferences and legal requirements in foreign markets. Entrepreneurs can learn about regulations and export controls at http://export.gov/regulation/index.asp.

8. *Does your company have adequate knowledge in shipping its product overseas, such as identifying and selecting international freight forwarders and freight costing?* When shipping a product overseas, entrepreneurs must be aware of packaging, labeling, documentation, and insurance requirements. Violating these requirements often means severe and expensive penalties. This is where international freight forwarders can help. These agents understand the export regulations of the U.S. government, the import rules and regulations of foreign countries, appropriate methods of shipping, and the documents related to foreign trade. Freight forwarders assist exporters in preparing price quotations by advising on freight costs, port charges, consular fees, costs of special documentation, insurance costs, and handling fees. To find a freight forwarder, entrepreneurs can visit the National Customs Brokers and Freight Forwarders Association of America at www.ncbfaa.org.

9. *Does your company have adequate knowledge of export payment mechanisms, such as developing and negotiating letters of credit?* Experienced exporters have extensive knowledge of export payment mechanisms and extend credit cautiously. They evaluate new customers with care and continuously monitor existing customers' accounts. For general information on ways to receive payments, methods of payment, and currency issues and payment problems, see *A Basic Guide to Exporting* (http://export.gov/basicguide/) and other resources described in this chapter. Conducting a credit check of potential buyers is essential because collecting delinquent accounts receivable from foreign customers is more difficult than collecting them from domestic customers. Exporters can use the U.S. Commercial Service's International Company Profiles (ICPs) to gain insight into the creditworthiness of potential customers. ICPs contain financial profiles of foreign companies and information on their size, capitalization, and number of years in business.

Source: Adapted from: "Export Questionnaire," Export.gov, http://export.gov/begin/assessment.asp.

small companies that are exporters have no employees.[23] If a company's products meet the needs of global customers, it has the potential to export. Studies suggest that small companies that export are stronger and grow markedly faster than those that do not. Table 15.2 provides nine questions designed to help entrepreneurs assess the export potential of their companies.

ENTREPRENEURIAL PROFILE: William Haynes: Sabai Technology After William Haynes was laid off during the financial crisis, he started Sabai Technology, a company based in Simpsonville, South Carolina, that develops and sells wireless routers and network equipment, with himself as the sole employee. Initially, Haynes sold only to domestic customers until one of his customers, Strong VPN, opened the door to orders from companies in China. International sales took off after people involved in an Egyptian uprising discovered that Sabai Technology's wireless routers could send and receive information that was blocked by government filters. Haynes began working with the U.S. Commercial Service and U.S. Export Assistance Centers, which led him to advertise his products in *Commercial News USA*, a publication that goes to more than 400,000 readers in 178 countries. Today, international sales account for 80 percent of Sabai Technology's sales, and the company, which exports to 120 countries, has grown to 14 employees. Haynes uses superior customer service and speedy delivery to set his company apart from the competition, most of which are much larger businesses.[24] ■

Step 2. *Analyze your product or service.* Is it special? New? Unique? High quality? Priced favorably because of lower costs or favorable exchange rates? Does it fit well with the culture and traditions of a country or region? Process Barron, owned by Cliff Moss and Ken Nolen, manufactures large fans used to clean air in factories. The company, located in Pelham, Alabama, struggled when first attempting to sell its products internationally. Moss and Nolen realized they lacked the knowledge needed to be successful exporters. After sending members of the management team to export seminars at a local university, the company began to have success negotiating financing and payment terms with international customers. Its international accounts helped the company to grow even in the midst of the Great Recession, which was not the case for many companies operating in the industrial sector.[25]

In many foreign countries, products from the United States are in demand because they have an air of mystery about them! In some cases, entrepreneurs find that they must make slight modifications to their products to accommodate local tastes, customs, and preferences. For instance, when Joseph Zaritski, owner of an Australian juice company, began marketing his company's products in Russia, he met with limited success until he realized that package size was the problem. Willing customers simply could not afford to purchase the two-liter bottles in which the juice was packaged. Zaritski switched to one-liter bottles and saw sales climb by 80 percent within six months![26]

Step 3. *Analyze your commitment.* Are you willing to devote time and energy to develop export markets? Does your company have the necessary resources? Patience is essential. An exporting initiative can take from six to eight months (or longer) to get off the ground, but entering foreign markets isn't as tough as most entrepreneurs think.

Step 4. *Research markets and pick your target.* Fifty-five percent of small businesses that export sell to just four or fewer countries (see Figure 15.3). Before investing in a costly sales trip abroad, however, entrepreneurs should search the Internet or make a trip to the local library or the nearest branch of the Department of Commerce. Exporters can choose from a multitude of guides, manuals, books, newsletters, videos, and other resources to help them research potential markets. Market research must include more than just the size of the potential market; it should include a detailed analysis of the demographic and buying habits of the customers in it as well as the cultural nuances of selling there.

FIGURE 15.3

Number of Countries to Which U.S. Small Businesses Export

Source: Based on data from 2013 Small Business Exporting Survey, National Small Business Association and Small Business Exporters Association, p. 6.

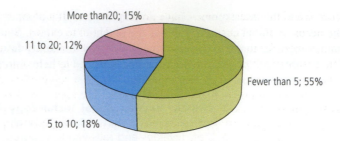

ENTREPRENEURIAL PROFILE: Wood Stone Ovens Wood Stone Ovens, based in Bellingham, Washington, sells its restaurant cooking equipment to customers in more than 75 countries. The company realized an unexpected benefit from its international sales activities: As its sales team traveled to meet with customers around the globe, they came back with many new product ideas. Exports account for 25 percent of Wood Stone Ovens's annual revenues.[27] ■

Armed with research, entrepreneurs can avoid wasting time and money on markets with limited potential for their products and can concentrate on those with the greatest promise. The nations that account for the greatest export volume for U.S. businesses are Canada, Mexico, China, Japan, and Germany.[28] Some of the most helpful tools for researching foreign markets are the Country and Industry Market Reports available at the U.S. government's export Web portal; these reports provide detailed information on the economic, political, regulatory, and investment environment for countries ranging from Afghanistan to Zimbabwe. Research tells entrepreneurs whether they need to modify their existing products and services to suit the tastes and preferences of their foreign target customers. Sometimes, foreign customers' lifestyles, housing needs, body size, and cultures require exporters to make alterations in their product lines. Making just slight modifications to adapt products and services to local tastes can sometimes spell the difference between success and failure in the global market. Entrepreneurs also should consider traveling to trade shows in the countries they are targeting to witness firsthand customers' responses to their products and services.

Step 5. *Develop a distribution strategy.* Should you use a trade intermediary or sell directly to foreign customers? As you learned earlier in this chapter, many small companies just entering international markets prefer to rely on trade intermediaries to break new ground. Using intermediaries often makes sense until an entrepreneur has the chance to gain experience in exporting and to learn the ground rules of selling in foreign lands.

ENTREPRENEURIAL PROFILE: John Burke: Louisiana Caviar Company The Louisiana Caviar Company, founded by John Burke, sells its product to customers in an unlikely foreign market: Russia. Louisiana Caviar Company harvests its caviar from bowfin fish in Louisiana's Atchafalaya Swamp, which is the largest wetland in the United States. The company sells caviar with a Cajun twist, flavoring the delicacy with various Cajun spices. The Russian market opened up due to efforts to ban caviar from the Caspian Sea in Russia. Overfishing and pollution have endangered sturgeon, which are the traditional source of Russian caviar. Louisiana Caviar Company exports 80 percent of its product, with half of its exports going to Russia.[29] ■

Step 6. *Find your customer.* According to a study by the U.S. International Trade Commission, one of the most common problems among small business exporters is finding prospective customers.[30] After all, establishing a network of business contacts takes time and resources. Small businesses can rely on a host of export specialists to help them track down foreign customers. The U.S. Department of

Commerce and the International Trade Administration should be the first stops on any entrepreneur's agenda for going global. These agencies have the market research available for locating the best target markets for a particular company and specific customers in those markets. Industry Sector Analyses, International Market Insights, and Customized Market Analyses are just some of the reports and services global entrepreneurs find most useful. These agencies also have knowledgeable staff specialists experienced in the details of global trade and in the intricacies of foreign cultures. GlobalEDGE (http://globaledge.msu.edu), an international trade information portal, also offers useful information on doing business in more than 200 countries, including directories, tutorials, online courses, and diagnostic tools designed to help companies determine their potential for conducting global business. The International Finance Corporation's Enterprise Surveys give entrepreneurs useful profiles of the business environments in 135 countries, ranging from overviews of basic infrastructure and business regulations to corruption and business obstacles. Through its Gold and Platinum Key services, the U.S. Commercial Service provides entrepreneurs who want to take their companies global with a list of prescreened distributors and potential customers and arranges face-to-face meetings with them.

One of the most efficient and least expensive ways for entrepreneurs to locate potential customers for their companies' products and services is to participate in a trade mission. These missions usually are sponsored by either a federal or a state economic development agency or an industry trade association for the purpose of cultivating international trade by connecting domestic companies with potential trading partners overseas. A trade mission may focus on a particular industry or may cover several industries but target a particular country. Pactrans Air & Sea, Inc., a small business headquartered in Bensenville, Illinois, participated in a trade mission to China organized by the SBDC office at Governors State University. During the trade mission, Pactrans managers had 95 business appointments, generated 450 sales leads, negotiated two joint ventures, and closed contacts worth more than $1 million during the trade mission. Pactrans owner Alex Pon anticipates adding 5 or 6 employees to his existing staff of 45 to accommodate the increased business activity that resulted from the trade mission.[31]

Step 7. *Find financing.* One of the biggest barriers to small business exports is lack of financing. Access to adequate financing is a crucial ingredient in a successful export program because the cost of generating foreign sales often is higher and collection cycles are longer than in domestic markets. The trouble is that bankers and other providers of capital don't always understand the intricacies of international sales and view financing them as excessively risky. In addition, among major industrialized nations, the U.S. government spends the least per capita to promote exports.

Several federal, state, and private programs are operating to fill this export financing void, however. Loan programs from the Small Business Administration's include its Export Working Capital program (90 percent loan guarantees up to $5 million), International Trade Loan program (90 percent loan guarantees up to $5 million) and Export Express program (75 to 90 percent loan guarantees up to $500,000). In addition, the Ex-Im Bank, the Overseas Private Investment Corporation, and a variety of state-sponsored programs offer export-minded entrepreneurs both direct loans and loan guarantees. The Ex-Im Bank, which has been financing the sale of U.S. exports since 1934, provides small exporters with export credit insurance and loans through its working capital line of credit and a variety of preexport loan programs. The Overseas Private Investment Corporation provides loans and loan guarantees up to $250 million to support foreign investments by small and medium-size companies and offers businesses discounted political risk insurance. The Bankers Association for Foreign Trade is an association of banks around the world that matches exporters in need of foreign trade financing with interested banks.

ENTREPRENEURIAL PROFILE: Lisa Howlett: Auburn Leather Company Auburn Leather Company, located in Auburn, Kentucky, manufactures leather laces for footwear and sporting equipment. Auburn Leather expanded its international sales with the help of a small business insurance policy from the Ex-Im Bank, which assigns and insures Auburn Leather's export accounts receivable. This insurance gives lenders the confidence to provide working capital financing for Auburn Leather's export sales. Growth in international sales has created more than 30 new jobs at Auburn Leather and has increased its annual revenues from $7.4 million to more than $11 million. Export sales have grown from 33 percent of total sales to 45 percent. Auburn Leather's President, Lisa Howlett, says the growth from international sales has created 20 new jobs at her company.[32] ■

Step 8. *Ship your goods.* Export novices usually rely on international freight forwarders and customs brokers—experienced specialists in overseas shipping—for help in navigating the bureaucratic morass of packaging and regulatory requirements, tariffs, and paperwork demanded by customs. These specialists, also known as transport architects, are to exporters what travel agents are to travelers and normally charge relatively small fees for a valuable service. They not only move shipments of all sizes to destinations all over the world efficiently, saving entrepreneurs many headaches, but also are well versed in the regulations that govern exported products and services. For example, packaging for Ganong Brothers, Canada's oldest candy maker, must read "5 mg" (with a space between the number and unit of measurement) for products sold in Canada. To sell the same product in the United States, just across the border from its factory, the company's packaging must read "5mg" (with no space between the number and unit of measurement).[33] Exporters can find local freight forwarders and customs brokers at the National Customs Brokers and Freight Forwarders Association of America's Web site.

Shipping terms, always important for determining which party in a transaction pays the cost of shipping and bears the risk of loss or damage to the goods while they are in transit, take on heightened importance in international transactions.

Step 9. *Collect your money.* A survey by the National Small Business Association and the Small Business Exporters Association reports that the top concern of companies that export is collecting payment for the goods and services they sell.[34] Collecting foreign accounts can be more complex than collecting domestic ones; however, by picking their customers carefully and checking their credit references closely, entrepreneurs can minimize bad-debt losses. Businesses that engage in international sales use four primary payment methods (ranked from least risky to most risky): cash in advance, a letter of credit, a bank (or documentary) draft, and an open account. The safest method of selling to foreign customers is to collect cash in advance of the sale because it eliminates the risk of collection problems and provides immediate cash flow. However, requiring cash payments up front severely limits a small company's base of foreign customers.

letter of credit
an agreement between an exporter's bank and the foreign buyer's bank that guarantees payment to the exporter for a specific shipment of goods.

bank draft
a document the seller draws on the buyer, requiring the buyer to pay the face amount either on sight or on a specified date.

A **letter of credit** is an agreement between an exporter's bank and the foreign buyer's bank that guarantees payment to the exporter for a specific shipment of goods. In essence, a letter of credit reduces the financial risk for the exporter by substituting a bank's creditworthiness for that of the purchaser (see Figure 15.4). A **bank draft** is a document the seller draws on the buyer, requiring the buyer to pay the face amount (the purchase price of the goods) either on sight (a sight draft) or on a specified date (a time draft) once the goods have been shipped. With either letters of credit or bank drafts, small exporters must be sure that all of the required documentation is present and accurate; otherwise, they may experience delays in the payments due to them from the buyer or the participating banks. Rather than use letters of credit or drafts, some exporters simply sell to foreign customers on open account. In other words, they ship the goods to a foreign customer without any guarantee of payment. This method is riskiest because collecting a delinquent account from a foreign customer is even more difficult than collecting past-due payments from a domestic customer.

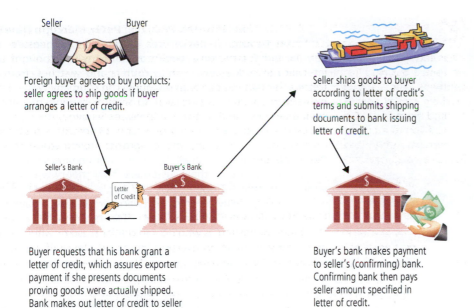

FIGURE 15.4

How a Letter of Credit Works

Source: A Basic Guide to Exporting, 10th edition, Washington DC: U.S. Department of Commerce, International Trade Administration, 2008, p. 5.

One way that small exporters can minimize the risk of bad-debt losses on foreign credit sales is to purchase export credit insurance, which protects a company against the nonpayment of its foreign customers' open accounts. The cost of export credit insurance typically is a small percentage of the amount of the foreign sale a company is insuring. Private insurers and the Ex-Im Bank offer export credit insurance.

ESTABLISHING INTERNATIONAL LOCATIONS Once established in international markets, some small businesses set up permanent locations there. Establishing an office or a factory in a foreign land can require a substantial investment reaching beyond the budgets of many small companies. In addition, setting up an international office can be an incredibly frustrating experience in some countries where business infrastructure is in disrepair or is nonexistent. Hayden Hamilton, founder of GreenPrint Technologies, a company that sells software that reduces printing costs by eliminating unnecessary pages, opened an office in India, where he can get bargain rates on quality software programming. He was frustrated when it took three hours to apply for a telephone line—and one month to get it installed. Because power outages in India are common, GreenPrint also had to purchase expensive backup generators.[35]

In some countries, securing necessary licenses and permits from bureaucrats often takes more than filing the necessary paperwork; in some nations, bureaucrats expect payments to "grease the wheels" of commerce. American entrepreneurs consider payments to reduce the amount of red tape involved in an international transaction to be bribery, and many simply avoid doing business in countries where "grease payments" are standard procedure. In fact, the Foreign Corrupt Practice Act, passed in 1977, considers bribing foreign officials to be a criminal act. One study by the World Bank of grease payments for the purpose of minimizing the red tape imposed by foreign regulations concludes that the payments do not work; in fact, companies that actually used them experienced greater government scrutiny and red tape in their international transactions.[36] Finally, finding the right person to manage an international office is crucial to success; it also is a major challenge, especially for small businesses. Small companies usually have lean management staffs and cannot afford to send key people abroad without running the risk of losing their focus.

Small companies that establish international locations can reap significant benefits. Start-up costs are lower in some foreign countries (but not all!), and lower labor costs can produce significant savings. In addition, by locating in a country, a business gains a firsthand understanding of local customers' preferences, tastes, and habits and the nuances of how culture influences business practices. In essence, the business becomes a local corporate citizen.

Courtesy of Peter Marcum

ENTREPRENEURIAL PROFILE: Peter Marcum: DevDigital DevDigital has offices in Nashville, Tennessee, and Baroda, India. DevDigital began as company that bought used Internet network assets, such as routers and switches, from distressed companies at a steep discount. The company would refurbish the hardware and resell it to small independent network companies. Eventually the company expanded into operating digital networks. As profit margins for network operators became razor thin, the company made another major strategic shift. DevDigital purchased a small Web site programming shop in India being sold by one of their customers. "My theory was that the larger companies—Google, IBM, and Apple—were and had been diversifying globally in their software production," says Peter Marcum, cofounder of DevDigital. "The problem for a smaller U.S.-based operation, is who do you call, or trust, or where do you go to get started, in an overseas location?" DevDigital made the move into Web site development for smaller companies. It took about four years to fully integrate the two locations. Due to its cost advantage and stable employment, the company has been able to grow in the highly competitive market of Web site development. DevDigital does about 80 percent work for hire, and the remainder are projects in which they take equity in exchange for Web site development. "My strongest advice to anyone wanting to set up off shore is find a local way in," says Marcum. "By that I mean you need a core group that will stay long-term as you build a team, just as you would here in the U.S."[37] ■

IMPORTING AND OUTSOURCING In addition to selling their goods in foreign markets, small companies also buy goods from distributors and manufacturers in foreign markets. In the United States alone, companies import more than $2.7 trillion worth of goods and services annually.[38] The intensity of price competition in many industries—from textiles and handbags to industrial machinery and computers—means that more companies now shop the world market looking for the best deals they can find. Because labor costs in countries such as Mexico, Taiwan, and India are far below those in other nations, businesses there offer goods and services at very low prices. Increasingly, these nations are home to well-educated, skilled workers who are paid far less than comparable workers in the United States or Western Europe. For instance, a computer programmer in the United States might earn $100,000 a year, but in India, a computer programmer doing the same work earns $20,000 a year or less. As a result, many companies either import goods or outsource work directly to manufacturers in countries where costs are far lower than they would be domestically.

Alibaba.com, an online trading platform started in Hangzhou, China, in 1999, has enabled millions of small companies to find reliable suppliers and vendors around the globe for the products and services they sell. Alibaba.com boasts nearly 37 million registered users in more than 240 countries.

Courtesy of Scott Kuyper

ENTREPRENEURIAL PROFILE: Nuvar Nuvar Inc., located in Holland, Michigan, develops and designs office furniture and healthcare products. Nuvar's in-house engineering assists its customers with product development and design. Through a global network of manufacturing suppliers, Nuvar sources component parts manufacturing from Europe (France, Germany, and Italy), Asia (China, Taiwan, and Malaysia), and North America (Mexico and Canada). Parts are then shipped to its facilities in Michigan, where they are assembled, packaged, and shipped to the final customer. Although Nuvar does not ship to international customers, its customers ship around the globe. "We still deal with the repercussions of dealing internationally," says Scott Kuyper, International Supply Chain Lead at Nuvar. "Different markets may have different requirements for testing, standards, etc. Because we're involved with product development, we really see this first hand." With the breadth of international relationships, Nuvar has learned the importance of being open minded and flexible when it comes to differences in culture strategy and economies of their various global partners.[39] ■

Entrepreneurs who are considering importing goods and service or outsourcing their manufacturing to foreign countries should follow these steps:

- *Make sure that importing or outsourcing is right for your business.* Even though foreign manufacturers often can provide items at significant cost savings, using them may not always be the best business decision. Some foreign manufacturers require sizable minimum orders, sometimes hundreds of thousands of dollars' worth, before they will produce a product. Entrepreneurs sometimes discover that achieving the lowest price may require a trade-off of other important factors, such as quality and speed of delivery.

- *Establish a target cost for your product.* Before setting off on a global shopping spree, entrepreneurs first should determine exactly what they can afford to spend on manufacturing a product and make a profit on it. Given the low labor costs of many foreign manufacturers, products that are the most labor intensive make good candidates.

ENTREPRENEURIAL PROFILE: Tom Haarlander: ARCiPLEX ARCiPLEX, headquartered in Nashville, Tennessee, is a medical manufacturing company. ARCiPLEX works with entrepreneurs and established companies to invent, design, develop, and produce health and wellness products. Tom Haarlander, President and cofounder, made the strategic decision to move its manufacturing from China to Mexico in early 2014. The company had been using a Chinese manufacturer for a little over a year but found a lack of consistency in the products from China, which resulted in warranty issues after the products were delivered to customers. Haarlander sent team members to live in China to monitor quality control, but the problems persisted. In an effort to improve its product quality and its team's quality of life, Haarlander decided to move manufacturing back to North America. Haarlander was able to find manufacturers in the United States and sourced some work to a company in Mexico. "This has allowed us to cut travel and various other overhead costs," says Haarlander. "Our cost per unit has risen, but our testing, quality control, headaches, and rework of product has dropped dramatically, cutting the overall cost. In the long run, we know we have made the best strategic decision for building a strong foundation for our company and we are proud to be supporting work in North America."[40] ■

- *Do your research before you leave home.* Investing time in basic research about the industry and potential suppliers in foreign lands is essential before setting foot on foreign soil. Useful resources are plentiful, and entrepreneurs should use them, including the Internet, the Federation of International Trade Associations, industry trade associations, government agencies (e.g., the U.S. Commercial Service's Gold Key Matching Service), and consultants.

ENTREPRENEURIAL PROFILE: Jim Greene: Richland, LLC Richland, LLC, located in Pulaski, Tennessee, is an industrial service company that supplies, assembles, fabricates, installs, paints, sandblasts, and tests equipment that contains mechanical or electrical components. Richland has contracts with TSKE Tsukishima Kankyo Engineering Ltd., a Japanese company, and Moritani, a German company. Tsukishima Kankyo and Moritani engage in many joint projects around the globe. Richland recently partnered with the two companies in a wastewater project for a client in Dubai that was developing a recreation area and golf course for a multinational community in Dubai. Richland provided manufacturing and test assembly for the water and wastewater treatment equipment that was shipped to Dubai. Jim Greene, a partner and president of Richland, LLC, admits that the language barrier can be difficult when dealing with partners from two different countries working for a client in another part of the world. "Foreign nationals appreciate it when you attempt to learn their language," says Green, "Even if it is only 'My name is Jim and welcome to Richland, LLC.'"[41] ■

- *Be sensitive to cultural differences.* When making contacts, setting up business appointments, or calling on prospective manufacturers in foreign lands, make sure you understand what constitutes accepted business behavior and what does not. This is where your research pays off; be sure to study the cultural nuances of doing business in the countries you will visit.

- *Do your groundwork.* Once you locate potential manufacturers, contact them to set up appointments and go visit them. Preliminary research is essential to finding reliable sources of supply, but "face time" with representatives from various companies allows entrepreneurs to judge the intangible factors that can make or break a relationship. Entrepreneurs who visit foreign suppliers often find that they receive better service because their suppliers know them personally.

- *Protect your company's intellectual property.* A common problem that many entrepreneurs have encountered with outsourcing is "knockoffs." Some foreign manufacturers see nothing wrong with agreeing to manufacture a product for a company and then selling their own knockoff version of it that they manufacture in a "ghost shift." Securing a nondisclosure agreement and a contract that prohibits such behavior helps, but experts that securing a patent for the item in the source country itself (not just the United States) is a good idea.

- *Select a manufacturer.* Using quality, speed of delivery, level of trust, degree of legal protection, cost, and other factors, select the manufacturer that can do the job for your company.

- *Provide an exact model of the product you want manufactured.* Providing a manufacturer with an actual model of the item to be manufactured will save lots of time, mistakes, and problems.

- *Stay in constant contact with the manufacturer and try to build a long-term relationship.* Communication is a key to building and maintaining a successful relationship with a foreign manufacturer. Weekly teleconferences, e-mails, and periodic visits are essential to making sure that your company gets the performance you expect from a foreign manufacturer.

EXPAT ENTREPRENEURS   Some entrepreneurs take advantage of opportunities in foreign markets by actually moving to a country and starting a new business. People who take up residence and work in a foreign country are known as expatriates, or more commonly, expats. **Expat entrepreneurs** are entrepreneurs who keep their citizenship in their home country but live and run their businesses on foreign soil. American expat entrepreneurs can be found living in countries on every continent. Expats from the same home country often form social groups to offer each other support and keep a little bit of their homeland's culture active in their lives. American expats use social networking sites such as Facebook to help build community and share common challenges faced by expat entrepreneurs. Some countries have been making it easier to become an expat entrepreneur to encourage economic development. For example, Spain recently cut the red tape associated with expats starting businesses to help ease its chronic unemployment and low rate of entrepreneurial activity. Although being an expat entrepreneur creates unique hurdles and problems, those with an adventurous spirit can find amazing experiences starting and growing companies in other countries. The following *You Be the Consultant* feature highlights three expat entrepreneurs who started businesses in Argentina, as told in David English's book *Expat Entrepreneurs in Argentina.*

expat entrepreneurs
entrepreneurs who keep their citizenship in their home country but live and run their businesses on foreign soil.

Barriers to International Trade

LO3
Discuss the major barriers to international trade and their impact on the global economy.

Governments traditionally have used a variety of barriers to block free trade among nations in an attempt to protect businesses within their own borders. The benefit of protecting their own companies, however, comes at the expense of foreign businesses, which face limited access to global markets. Numerous trade barriers—domestic and international—restrict the freedom of businesses in global trading (see Figure 15.5). Even with these barriers, global trade of goods and services has grown to nearly $19 trillion.[42]

Domestic Barriers

Sometimes the biggest barriers potential exporters face are those right here at home. Three major domestic roadblocks are common: attitude, information, and financing. Perhaps the biggest barrier to small businesses exporting is the attitude that "My company is too small to export." That's just for big corporations." The first lesson of exporting is "Take nothing for granted about who

You Be the Consultant

Expat Entrepreneurs Find Opportunity in Argentina

Business owners featured in the book, *Expat Entrepreneurs in Argentina*
Courtesy of David English

Entrepreneurs who start new businesses in a foreign country, expat entrepreneurs, can be found in countries all around the globe. Expat entrepreneurs start new ventures in a foreign land for many different reasons—the specific opportunity, the desire to live in a different country, the wish to leave their home country, or life circumstances. Whatever the reason, entrepreneurs face unique challenges operating businesses in a country other than their homeland. What follows are profiles of three entrepreneurs from a book, Expat Entrepreneurs in Argentina, by David English, who is an expat himself.

Michael Evans

Michael Evans's career as an expat entrepreneur in Argentina began with what he thought was going to be a one-week vacation in Mendoza, which is the heart of wine country. What he found was that Mendoza had none of the amenities of other wine destinations he had visited.

"I came here expecting a consumer-friendly experience like I had in Napa, Italy, and France," says Evans. "But, I couldn't find it anywhere. Argentina felt like a new frontier."

Evans decided to stay in Mendoza for six months to do research with a potential partner he had met, Pablo Giménez Riili, whose family had been in the wine business for several decades. In addition to having skills, knowledge, and local credibility that Evans needed for this business, Giménez Riili's approach to business meshed well with Evans's business philosophies.

The two developed a business plan for a start-up to serve the emerging wine industry and its associated tourism. The concepts of a small hotel, a wine tasting room, and a direct wine sales business emerged from their work together.

"We developed these concepts to solve the problems I had as a consumer," says Evans.

The business, The Vines of Mendoza, was successful beyond any of their plans. The Vines of Mendoza has grown to include operating a wine store in the Park Hyatt Mendoza, managing more than 100 private vineyard estates, overseeing a direct wine sales business that exports Argentinian wine to the United States, and operating their own winery. They also have opened their own five-star resort for wine tourists.

Carolyn Gallagher

Carolyn Gallagher grew up in Sacramento, California. While she was in high school, she became close friends with an exchange student from Argentina. Gallagher went to visit her friend in Argentina after finishing school, fell in love with the country, and envisioned moving there some day to settle down. Gallagher went to college at the University of California at Santa Barbara, where she studied geography and linguistics. After college she went to work as a river guide, winery worker, and English tutor for construction companies to save money for her move to Argentina.

In 1998, Gallagher bought a one-way ticket to Mendoza.

"I said to myself, 'OK, I'm going on an adventure! I don't know what I'll end up doing, but I'll figure it out,'" recalls Gallagher.

For two years she taught English. However, she wanted to do more than teach. She wanted to start a business. Gallagher returned to California to study cooking, wine making, and business, while she worked in the wine industry.

In 2004, Gallagher returned to Argentina ready to find an opportunity.

"I was on the lookout for niches I could fill in wine and education," she says. "I saw that tourism was taking off, and nobody was doing multifaceted tours that combined outdoor adventure with cooking classes and great wine."

Gallagher launched her business, Uncorking Argentina, which has been successful since it opened. In the meantime, Gallagher married her Argentine boyfriend. The two are now happily raising their two children in the country she envisioned living in back when she first visited it right after high school.

David English

David English was a technology consultant for Qwest Communication in New York City on his way to meet with executives of CitiGroup to close a contract for a new project. On that sunny morning, everything changed. It was September 11, 2001. As he left his offices on the way to the meeting, ashes began to fall. People were saying that someone had flown a small plane into one of the towers of the World Trade Center. English did not think much about it. He hopped on the subway to go to his meeting. When he emerged from the subway, the city was in chaos from

(continued)

You Be the Consultant (continued)

the attack on the World Trade Center's Twin Towers. Although it was several more years before English left America to start his new life in Argentina, he sees the events of that day as the turning point in his life that led him down the path to eventually becoming an expat entrepreneur.

After graduating from college, English had traveled to Argentina in 1997 through an exchange program run by the Rotary Club. English spent six weeks in Argentina visiting Rotarians in Argentina and touring their businesses.

"When I returned home, I dreamed about Argentina every night for weeks and immediately made plans to go back and see more of the country with which I had fallen in love," says English.

He got that opportunity in 2003. He discovered a niche helping American businesses by serving as their connection with local Argentines. He launched English & Associates with a single client who was developing a wine business in Argentina. English enrolled in an MBA program in Argentina that he credits with teaching him about doing business within the culture of Argentina and honing his Spanish communication skills.

The scope of his business broadened over time. English & Associates provides due diligence for foreigners buying real estate

in Argentina, prepares and files tax returns for nonresident investors, consults with entrepreneurs looking to start a business in Argentina, and develops study-abroad programs in Mendoza for leading universities from around the world.

"Being an expat in a place like Argentina is about a lot more than running a business," reflects English. "It's also about playing an active role in the community and looking for opportunities to be a positive influence."

1. How are expat entrepreneurs' assumptions about conducting business internationally different than entrepreneurs pursuing more traditional international strategies? Explain.

2. What advice would you give to someone who wants to become an expat entrepreneur? Explain.

3. What lessons did each of these expat entrepreneurs learn that would be useful for others interested in this type of lifestyle? Explain.

Source: Based on David English, *Expat Entrepreneurs in Argentina* (Mendoza, Argentina: Expat Books, 2013). Available on Amazon.com.

FIGURE 15.5

Most Frequently Encountered Impediments to International Trade

Source: U.S. International Trade Commission, *Small and Medium-Sized Enterprises: Characteristics and Performance,* Publication 4189, November 2010, pp. 6–8.

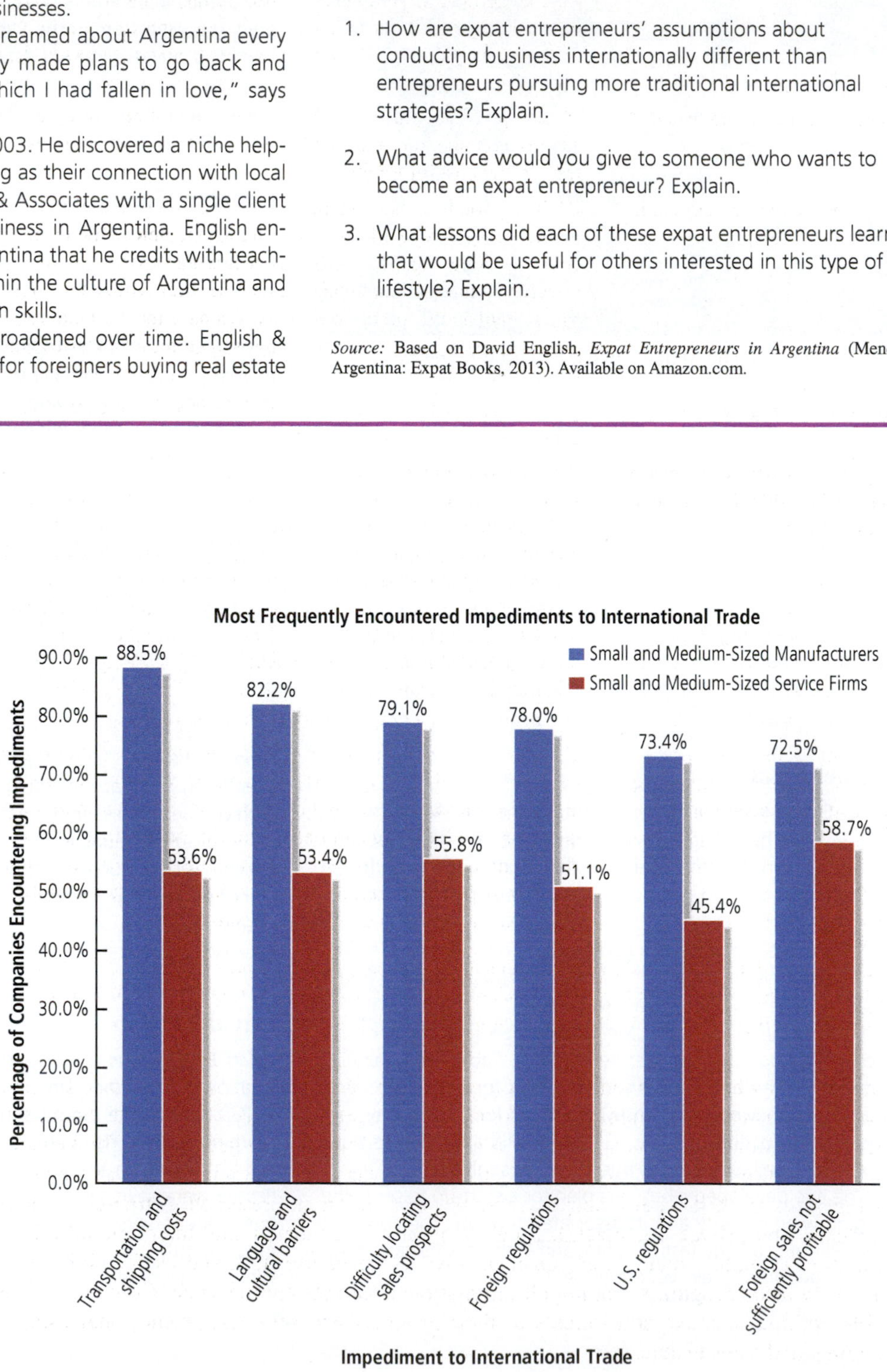

Most Frequently Encountered Impediments to International Trade

Legend:
- Small and Medium-Sized Manufacturers
- Small and Medium-Sized Service Firms

Y-axis: Percentage of Companies Encountering Impediments

Data:
- Transportation and shipping costs: 88.5% / 53.6%
- Language and cultural barriers: 82.2% / 53.4%
- Difficulty locating sales prospects: 79.1% / 55.8%
- Foreign regulations: 78.0% / 51.1%
- U.S. regulations: 73.4% / 45.4%
- Foreign sales not sufficiently profitable: 72.5% / 58.7%

X-axis: Impediment to International Trade

TABLE 15.3 **Global Business Assumptions**

Old Assumption	New Assumption
Exporting is too risky for my small company.	Exporting to "easy" markets such as Canada is no more risky than selling to companies in the United States. Each international market has its own level of risk. Entrepreneurs can identify the most significant risks their companies face and reduce them by using the extensive amount of affordable export assistance that is available now.
Getting paid is cumbersome, and I'll lose my shirt.	Trade finance and global banking have evolved to the point where buying and selling goods and services internationally is routine, safe, and efficient. Reliable collection methods, including credit cards, online payments, and letters of credit, are readily available. Some delivery firms will collect payment from customers at the time of delivery.
Exporting is too complicated.	Most exporting requires minimal paperwork. Often, entrepreneurs can research markets and find buyers from their computers using free or low-cost information.
My domestic market is secure. I don't need to export.	Globalization has made buying and selling goods in multiple markets easy. Few markets remain static, and new markets are constantly opening. Most U.S. businesses are involved in or affected by international markets, whether they realize it or not. More small and medium-size companies have the potential to benefit from going global, but doing so requires an international marketing strategy.
I'm too small to go global.	No company is too small to go global. In fact, 72 percent of U.S. exporters have fewer than 20 employees.
My product or service probably won't sell outside the United States.	If your product or service sells well in the United States, there is a good chance you can find a foreign market in which it will sell. In addition, help is available for entrepreneurs who want to test the appeal of their products and services in more than 100 countries around the globe. In some markets, entrepreneurs must make modifications to their products and services because of cultural, regulatory, or other differences. However, most modifications are small and simple to make. In addition, by learning to sell successfully in other markets, small companies become stronger and better able to compete in all of their markets.
I won't be successful because I don't speak another language and have never been abroad.	Cultural knowledge and business etiquette are important, but you can learn as you go. English is the language of business in many countries, but you can easily hire translators and interpreters when necessary. Researching cultural differences before engaging in foreign transactions helps prevents embarrassing faux pas, but a friendly disposition, a sense of humor, and a willingness to learn can make up for many unintended mistakes.

Source: Based on "Table 1.1: Global Business Assumptions," *A Basic Guide to Exporting*, 10th ed., 2008, U.S. Department of Commerce, International Trade Administration, p. 7; "U.S. Export Loan Programs," U.S. Small Business Administration, http://www.sba.gov/content/export-loan-programs.

can export and what you can and cannot export" (see Table 15.3). The first step to building an export program is recognizing that the opportunity to export exists. Another reason entrepreneurs neglect international markets is a lack of information about how to get started. The keys to success in international markets are choosing the correct target market and designing the appropriate strategy to reach it. That requires access to information and research. Although a variety of government and private organizations make volumes of exporting and international marketing information available, many small business owners never use it. A successful global marketing strategy also recognizes that not all international markets are the same. Companies must be flexible, willing to make adjustments to their products and services, promotional campaigns, packaging, and sales techniques.

Hands On . . . How To

Build a Successful Global Company

Brothers Jeff and Tony Logosz grew up enjoying water sports in the Columbia River Gorge in the state of Washington. They ultimately found a way to turn their passion into a business, launching Slingshot Sports to design and manufacture kiteboards.

Slingshot Sports helped to create a market for kiteboards, which were the focus of a relatively new sport at the time. Slingshot Sports soon began to find success promoting kiteboarding and selling its products to a growing market.

One day, a distributor from the United Kingdom showed up at the Slingshot Sports offices in North Bonneville, Washington, wanting to import its products. Like many small business owners, the Logosz brothers had no idea how exporting worked. However, the request prompted them to learn how to export their products. When they did, they found strong growth in demand for kiteboards around the globe. Distributors from around the world came clamoring for contracts to sell Slingshot Sports Kiteboards.

The company eventually expanded its product line by adding wakeboards. Unlike kiteboards, wakeboards were a well-established product in a market with many competitors. Rather than having global distributors seeking out Slingshot Sports at the national trade show, the company had to develop a sales strategy in which the founders traveled to markets around the globe to pitch their new wakeboards. The strategy was successful, and sales of Slingshot Sports wakeboards soon exceeded all of the Logosz's projections. Following are some of the lessons the Logosz brothers and other entrepreneurs have learned about operating a global small business.

Don't assume that your company has to be big to be an international player. As the Logosz brothers learned, even very small companies have the opportunity to be successful in the global arena. Success in international markets does not require size, but it does require commitment and a sound strategy.

Know what you don't know. Perhaps the most important item in a global entrepreneur's briefcase is *knowledge*. Before embarking on any international business initiative, entrepreneurs should take the time to educate themselves and their employees. This chapter is filled with useful resources, many of which are free, that are designed to help business owners get their global business efforts off to a good start. The starting point for conducting international business successfully is learning about best practices for key issues such as identifying target markets, developing distribution strategies, complying with regulations, adapting products when necessary, collecting payments, and providing customer service.

Build a network of connections. Having a contact in a foreign country who can open doors to potential suppliers and customers greatly reduces the risk involved in international business. Mia Abbruzzese, founder of Morgan & Milo, a children's shoe company, had launched several shoe lines during her days as an executive for three large global shoe companies and knew that success in the shoe business requires an extensive network of connections in all corners of the globe. Using her industry contacts, Abbruzzese found a Taiwanese investor who provided start-up capital for Morgan & Milo and introduced Abbruzzese to the owner of the factory in southern China that makes many of the shoes that Morgan & Milo designs. Two other advisers on whom Abbruzzese relies are industry veterans who have an extensive network of contacts in the shoe industry that have proved to be extremely valuable to her company.

Learn about the cultural aspects of conducting business in the countries in which your company operates. Business dealings are a reflection of a country's culture, and entrepreneurs should educate themselves about the nuances of doing business in the host country to avoid committing embarrassing cultural blunders. In the United States, businesspeople are transaction oriented. They want to set up an appointment, negotiate a deal quickly and efficiently, sign a contract, and leave. In many other countries, landing a deal takes much longer because businesspeople expect to get to know their potential partners first. Particularly in Asia, businesspeople tend to be relationship oriented, doing business only with people they know, like, and respect. Developing relationships can take time, making a network of connections all the more important. When doing business in Asia, entrepreneurs quickly learn that formal contracts, which are the foundation of business deals in the United States, are not as important. They also learn to adjust the speed at which they close deals and take more time to build relationships with reliable suppliers.

Go there. As Slingshot Sports learned when it expanded into wakeboards, building a global business usually requires entrepreneurs to travel to the countries in which they plan to do business. It's an excellent way to build a network of contacts. Participating in international trade missions, attending international trade shows, and using matching services such as the U.S. Department of Commerce's Gold Key and Platinum Key services are ideal methods for connecting with potential customers, distributors, and suppliers.

Recognize that foreign sales often put additional demands on a company's cash flow. Expanding a company's sales efforts into international markets can strain a company's cash flow, and many traditional lenders are hesitant to extend loans to cover foreign credit sales because they perceive the risk to be too great. Help is available for small companies, however. The Small Business Administration and the Ex-Im Bank offer loan and loan guarantee programs to finance small companies' foreign credit sales. CellAntenna Corporation, a maker of cell phone jamming and control technology in Coral Springs, Florida, secured a $250,000 line of credit through the Small Business Administration's Export Working Capital loan guaranty program to finance its export sales. The company recently landed a $100,000 order from a prison in Australia. "Having a $250,000 line of credit makes it

Hands On . . . How To (continued)

easy for us to produce the equipment while receiving orders from around the world," says CEO Howard Melamed.

Make sure you collect payments from foreign sales. Collecting payments on delinquent foreign sales is more involved than collecting payments on delinquent domestic sales. The best way to avoid this problem is to sell to customers who pay their bills on time. That means that conducting credit checks before selling to international customers is just as important as it is before selling to domestic customers. In addition, small companies can reduce the risk of foreign credit sales by purchasing export credit insurance from either private insurers or from the Ex-Im Bank. CellAntenna Corporation routinely sells to foreign customers on open account

but purchases export credit insurance from the Ex-Im Bank to mitigate the risk of nonpayment.

Sources: Based on "Slingshot Sports," Export Washington, n.d., www.exportwashington .com/why-export/success-stories/Pages/Slingshot-Sports.aspx; Diana Ransom, "Five Tips for Getting Started in Exporting," *Entrepreneur,* May 17, 2011, http://www .entrepreneur.com/article/219650; Ian Mount, "Tips for Increasing Sales in International Markets," *New York Times,* April 21, 2010, http://www.nytimes .com/2010/04/22/business/smallbusiness/22sbiz.html; John Jantsch, "Around the Block or around the World," Duct Tape Marketing, September 21, 2010, http://www .ducttapemarketing.com/blog/2010/09/21/around-the-block-or-around-the-world; Anita Campbell, "Preparing Your Business to Go Global," Small Business Trends, November 19, 2010, http://smallbiztrends.com/2010/11/preparing-your-business-to-go-global.html; Allessandra Bianchi, "Small & Global: The World as a Factory," *FSB,* June 2004, pp. 40–42; Sheri Qualters, "Operating on a Shoestring," *Boston Business Journal,* June 10, 2005, http://boston.bizjournals.com/boston/stories/2005/06/13/smallb1.html; and *2011 National Export Strategy: Powering the National Export Initiative,* Trade Promotion Coordinating Committee, Washington, DC, June 2011, p. 23.

An additional obstacle is the inability of small firms to obtain adequate export financing. Financial institutions that serve small companies often are not experienced in financing international sales and are unwilling to accept the perceived higher levels of risk they create for the lender.

International Barriers

Domestic barriers aren't the only ones that export-minded entrepreneurs must overcome. Trading nations also erect obstacles to free trade. Two types of international barriers are common: tariff and nontariff.

TARIFF BARRIERS A **tariff** is a tax, or duty, that a government imposes on goods and services imported into that country. Imposing tariffs raises the price of the imported goods—making them less attractive to consumers—and protects the domestic makers of comparable product and services. Established in the United States in 1790 by Alexander Hamilton, the tariff system generated the majority of federal revenues for about 100 years. Currently, the *Harmonized Tariff Schedule,* which sets tariffs for products imported into the United States, includes 37,000 categories of goods. The average U.S. tariff on imported goods is 1.74 percent (compared to the global average of 2.69 percent).[43] American tariffs vary greatly and depend on the particular type of good. For instance, inexpensive men's acrylic sweaters imported into the United States carry a 32 percent tariff, but the tariff on cashmere sweaters is 4 percent; cheap sneakers are taxed at 48 percent, but golf shoes carry an 8.5 percent tariff.[44] Tariff rates also vary among nations. Singapore, Switzerland, and Hong Kong impose no tariffs at all on imported goods, but Bermuda's is 15.2 percent.[45]

tariff
a tax, or duty, that a government imposes on goods and services imported into that country.

NONTARIFF BARRIERS Many nations have lowered the tariffs they impose on products and services brought into their borders, but they rely on other nontariff structures as protectionist trade barriers.

Quotas Rather than impose a direct tariff on certain imported products, nations often use quotas to protect their industries. A **quota** is a limit on the amount of a product imported into a country. Those who favor quotas argue that they protect domestic industries and the jobs they create. Those who oppose quotas say that they artificially raise prices on the restricted goods, imposing a hidden tax on customers who purchase them. China imposes a quota on foreign films, allowing only 34 foreign films to be released each year. Before 2012, the quota was 20 foreign films per year. China's total box office sales are $3.57 billion annually, the third largest in the world, and its box office sales are predicted to exceed $5 billion by 2015. China has 4,582 cinema complexes and 18,195 movie screens, with more than 5,000 screens added just in 2013. Despite pressure from the World Trade Organization (WTO) to eliminate the film quota, Chinese officials have refused, expressing concern that removing the barrier would unleash a flood of foreign films that might wipe out the local film industry.[46]

quota
a limit on the amount of a product imported into a country.

embargo

a total ban on imports of certain products into a country.

Embargoes   An **embargo** is a total ban on imports of certain products. The motivation for embargoes is not always economic; it also can involve political differences, environmental disputes, war, terrorism, and other issues. For instance, the United States imposes embargoes on products from nations it considers to be adversarial, including Cuba, Iran, Iraq, and North Korea, among others. An embargo on trade with Cuba, started in 1962 when Fidel Castro nationalized all U.S. businesses on the island nation and formed an alliance with the Soviet Union, still exists today. In 1994, the United States lifted a total trade embargo on Vietnam that had stood since 1975, when Saigon fell into communist hands at the end of the Vietnam War. Today, the United States imports $24.6 billion worth of goods from Vietnam and exports goods worth $5.0 billion.[47]

Embargoes also originate from cultural differences. For instance, the United States imposes embargoes on any harp seal products from Norway under the Marine Mammal Protection Act. Norway, where seal products make up a multi-million-dollar industry, has pushed for the elimination of the embargo, arguing that harp seals are not an endangered species.[48]

dumping

selling large quantities of goods at prices that are below cost in foreign countries in an effort to grab market share quickly.

Dumping   In an effort to grab market share quickly, some companies have been guilty of **dumping** products: selling large quantities of them at prices that are below cost in foreign countries. The United States has been a dumping ground for steel, televisions, shoes, and computer chips from other nations in the past. Under the U.S. Antidumping Act, a company must prove that the foreign company's prices are lower here than in the home country and that U.S. companies are directly harmed. Disputes over dumping brought before the WTO have increased significantly over the last five years, and China has been the target of most of the complaints from WTO member nations. The U.S. Department of Commerce, without the involvement of the WTO, recently ruled that government-subsidized makers of solar cells and panels in China were guilty of dumping their products in the United States at prices that average 31 percent below "fair value." SolarWorld Industries America and six other U.S.-based solar cell and panel manufacturers initiated the charge, claiming that artificially low prices on solar products from China are crippling the domestic industry. As part of its ruling, the U.S. Department of Commerce imposed punitive dumping margins (the difference between the fair value of the items and their actual export price) of 31 percent on the Chinese companies.[49]

Political Barriers

Entrepreneurs who go global quickly discover a labyrinth of political tangles. Although many U.S. business owners complain of excessive government regulation in the United States, they are often astounded by the onerous web of governmental and legal regulations and barriers they encounter in foreign countries. One entrepreneur who established a business location in Russia says he had to visit more than two dozen agencies to complete the necessary paperwork and get 90 different documents signed.[50]

Companies doing business in politically risky lands face the very real dangers of government takeovers of private property; coups to overthrow ruling parties; kidnapping, bombings, and other violent acts against businesses and their employees; and other threatening events. Their investments of millions of dollars may evaporate overnight in the wake of a government coup or the passage of a law nationalizing an industry (giving control of an entire industry to the government).

Business Barriers

American companies doing business internationally quickly learn that business practices and regulations in foreign lands can be quite different from those in the United States. Simply duplicating the practices they have adopted (and have used successfully) in the domestic market and using them in foreign markets is not always a good idea. Perhaps the biggest shock comes in the area of human resources management, in which international managers discover that practices common in the United States, such as overtime and employee benefits, are restricted, disfavored, or forbidden in other cultures. Business owners new to international business sometimes are shocked at the wide range of labor costs they encounter and the accompanying wide range of skilled labor available. In some countries, what appear to be "bargain" labor rates turn out to be excessively high after accounting for the quality of the labor force and the benefits their governments mandate: from company-sponsored housing, meals, and clothing to profit sharing and extended vacations. For instance, laws in many European countries mandate a minimum of 20 days of vacation in addition to paid holidays, giving workers there an average of nearly 35 days off per year.[51] Some countries' labor laws make it extremely difficult or even impossible to terminate employees once hired. Hefty taxes, ineffective legal systems, corruption, and shady business associates can make doing business in foreign countries difficult.

Cultural Barriers

Even though travel and communications technology has increased the ease and the frequency with which entrepreneurs engage in global transactions, the potential for cultural blunders has increased. The **culture** of a nation includes the beliefs, values, views, and mores its inhabitants share. Differences in cultures among nations create another barrier to international trade. The diversity of languages, business philosophies, practices, and traditions make international trade more complex than selling to the business down the street. Consider the following examples:

culture
the beliefs, values, views, and mores that a nation's inhabitants share.

- A U.S. entrepreneur, eager to expand into the European Union, arrives at the headquarters of his company's potential business partner in France. Confidently, he strides into the meeting room, enthusiastically pumps his host's hand, slaps him on the back, and says, "Tony, I've heard a great deal about you; please, call me Bill." Eager to explain the benefits of his product, he opens his briefcase and gets right down to business. The French executive politely excuses himself and leaves the room before negotiations ever begin, shocked by the American's rudeness and ill manners. Rudeness and ill manners? Yes—from the French executive's perspective.

- Another American business owner flies to Tokyo to close a deal with a Japanese executive. He is pleased when his host invites him to play a round of golf shortly after he arrives. He plays well and manages to win by a few strokes. The Japanese executive invites him to play again the next day, and again he wins by a few strokes. Invited to play another round the following day, the American asks, "But when are we going to start doing business?" His host, surprised by the question, says, "But we *have* been doing business."

- An American businesswoman in London is invited to a party hosted by an advertising agency. Unsure of her ability to navigate the streets and subways of London alone, she approaches a British colleague who is driving to the party and asks him, "Could I get a ride with you?" After he turns bright red from embarrassment, he regains his composure and politely says, "Lucky for you I know what you meant." Unknowingly, the young woman had requested a sexual encounter with her colleague, not a lift to the party![52]

- One pharmaceutical company was about to market a weight loss pill under the name Tegro, which sounds harmless enough in English. However, phonetically, the word sounds identical to the French phrase *t'es gros*, which translates "You are fat." Another global company attempted to market a technology training system whose name sounded exactly like the Korean phrase for "porn movie."[53]

When American businesspeople enter international markets for the first time, they often are amazed at the differences in foreign cultures' habits and customs. In the first scenario above, for instance, had the entrepreneur done his homework, he would have known that the French are very formal (backslapping is *definitely* taboo!) and do not typically use first names in business relationships (even among longtime colleagues). In the second scenario, a global manager would have known that the Japanese place a tremendous importance on developing personal relationships before committing to any business deals. Thus, he would have seen the golf games for what they really were: an integral part of building a business relationship.

Understanding and heeding these often subtle cultural differences is one of the most important keys to international business success. Conducting a business meeting with a foreign executive in the same manner as one with an American businessperson could doom the deal from the outset. Business customs and behaviors that are acceptable, even expected, in the United States may be taboo in others, and entrepreneurs who fail to learn the differences in the habits and customs of the cultures in which they hope to do business are at a distinct disadvantage.

Courtesy of Tyler Seymour, Aloompa

ENTREPRENEURIAL PROFILE: Aloompa Aloompa is an app development business located in Nashville, Tennessee, that specializes primarily in apps for music festivals. Its first customer was the Bonnaroo Music and Arts Festival in Manchester, Tennessee. The app includes a map of the festival grounds, including the location of food vendors, bathrooms, retail spaces, and stages. It also includes bios of performers, audio samples of performers' music, and reviews that can be pushed out to Facebook, Instagram, and Twitter. After growing to more than two dozen music festivals in the United States, Aloompa expanded to international festivals. The first was the Playa del Carmen in Mexico. The app for this festival is available in both English and Spanish. Aloompa is quickly adding new festivals for customers in Asia, Europe, and South America. "As Aloompa expanded into the international market, it has had to learn how to communicate across culture barriers and familiarize itself with a variety of business practices across the globe," says Caleb Jones in Business Development for Aloompa. "For example, as we expanded we found it necessary to start our deals in the South American market a full month prior due to slower timelines. As we move further into the international market, it has given us an appreciation for the vast array of cultures that make up international commerce, and a great desire to continue business ventures abroad."[54] ∎

Culture, customs, and the norms of behavior differ greatly among nations, and making the correct impression is extremely critical to building a long-term business relationship. Consider the following examples:

- In Europe and China, just as in the United States, punctuality for business meetings is important. In Latin America, Africa, and many Middle Eastern countries, however, business meetings rarely start at the scheduled time, something that does not seem to bother locals.

- In Great Britain, businesspeople consider it extremely important to conduct business "properly"—with formality and reserve. Boisterous behavior such as backslapping or overindulging in alcohol and ostentatious displays of wealth are considered ill mannered. The British do not respond to hard-sell tactics but do appreciate well-mannered executives. Politeness and impeccable manners are useful tools for conducting business successfully.

- In Colombia, foreigners are expected to be on time for meetings, although native Colombians are rarely punctual. Be ready to wait. Once the meeting begins, Colombians stand closer together when talking. However, unlike many other South Americans, they engage in less physical contact during a conversation. Be ready for relaxed conversation before getting down to business. It is considered rude to jump right into business discussions.[55]

- In India, a limp handshake and avoiding eye contact are not signs of weakness or dislike; they convey respect.[56]

- When doing business in Greece, U.S. executives must be thoughtful of their hand gestures; the hand-waving gesture that means "good-bye" in the United States is considered an insult in Greece.[57]

- In Japan and South Korea, exchanging business cards, known in Japan as *meishi*, is an important business function (unlike in Great Britain, where exchanging business cards is less popular). A Western executive who accepts a Japanese companion's card and then slips it into his pocket or scribbles notes on it has committed a major blunder. Tradition there says that a business card must be treated just as its owner would be—with respect. Travelers should present their own cards using both hands with the card positioned so that the recipient can read it. (The flip side should be printed in Japanese, an expected courtesy.)

- Business attire is very important when doing business in Argentina. Business dress is conservative, with men and women generally wearing dark suits. Eye contact should be maintained throughout a business conversation.[58]

- Exercise caution when giving gifts. Although gift giving is standard practice in Japan, businesspeople in other countries, such as Malaysia, may see a gift as a bribe. In many countries, gifts of flowers are considered inappropriate because they connote romantic attention. In South Korea, giving a clock as a gift is considered good luck, but in China, it is considered a bad omen.[59] Avoid giving gifts to business associates that are traditional symbols of their own cultures, such as chocolates to the Swiss or tea to the Chinese.

- In China, entrepreneurs will need an ample dose of the "three Ps": patience, patience, and patience. Nothing in China—especially business—happens fast, and entrepreneurs wanting to do business there must be persistent! In conversation and negotiations, periods of silence are common; they are a sign of politeness and contemplation. The Chinese view personal space much differently than Americans; in normal conversation, they will stand much closer to their partners. At a business meal, sampling every dish, no matter how exotic, is considered polite. In addition, do not expect to conduct business the week before or after the Chinese New Year ("Yuandan"), whose dates vary from year to year, when many businesses are closed.

- Starting business relationships with customers in the Pacific Rim usually requires a third-party contact because Asian executives prefer to do business with people they know. In addition, building personal relationships is important. Many business deals take place over informal activities in this part of the world. American entrepreneurs doing business in the Pacific Rim should avoid hard-sell techniques, which are an immediate turnoff to Asian businesspeople. Harmony, patience, and consensus make good business companions in this region. It is also a good idea to minimize the importance of legal documents in negotiations. Although getting deals and trade agreements down in writing always is advisable, attempting to negotiate detailed contracts (as most American businesses tend to do) would insult most Asians, who base their deals on mutual trust and benefits.

International Trade Agreements

LO4
Describe the trade agreements that will have the greatest influence on foreign trade in the twenty-first century.

With the fundamental assumption that free trade among nations results in enhanced economic prosperity for all parties involved, the last 50 years have witnessed a gradual opening of trade among nations. Hundreds of agreements have been negotiated among nations in this period, with each contributing to free trade across the globe. Although completely free trade across international borders remains elusive, the following trade agreements have reduced some of the barriers to free trade that had stood for many years.

WORLD TRADE ORGANIZATION The World Trade Organization (WTO) was established in January 1995 and replaced the General Agreement of Tariffs and Trade (GATT), the first global tariff agreement, which was created in 1947 and was designed to reduce tariffs among member nations. The WTO, currently with 160 member countries, is the only international organization that establishes rules for trade among nations. Its member countries represent more than 97 percent of all world trade. The rules and agreements of the WTO, called the multilateral trading system, are the result of negotiations among its members. The WTO actively implements the rules established by the Uruguay Round negotiations of GATT from 1986 to 1994 and continues to negotiate additional trade agreements. The ninth round of negotiations, the Doha Development Agenda, began in 2001. As of 2014, there was still no definitive conclusion to this round of negotiations. Through the agreements of the WTO, members commit themselves to nondiscriminatory trade practices and to reducing barriers to free trade. The WTO's agreements spell out the rights and obligations of each member country. Each member country receives guarantees that its exports will be treated fairly and consistently in other member countries' markets. The WTO's General Agreement on Trade in Services addresses specific industries, including banking, insurance, telecommunications, and tourism. In addition, the WTO's intellectual property agreement, which covers patents, copyrights, and trademarks, defines rules for protecting ideas and creativity across borders.

In addition to the development of agreements among members, the WTO is involved in the resolution of trade disputes among members. The WTO system is designed to encourage dispute resolutions through consultation. If this approach fails, the WTO has a stage-by-stage procedure that can culminate in a ruling by a panel of experts.

NORTH AMERICAN FREE TRADE AGREEMENT The North American Free Trade Agreement (NAFTA) created a free trade area among Canada, Mexico, and the United States. A **free trade area** is an association of countries that have agreed to eliminate trade barriers, both tariff and nontariff, among partner nations. Under the provisions of NAFTA, these barriers were eliminated for trade among the three countries, but each remained free to set its own tariffs on imports from nonmember nations.

NAFTA forged one of the world's largest free trade areas, a unified United States–Canada–Mexico market of 465 million people with a total annual output of $20.1 trillion in goods and services.[60] This important trade agreement binds together the three nations on the North American continent into a single trading unit stretching from the Yukon to the Yucatan. NAFTA's provisions called for the reduction of tariffs to zero on most goods traded among these three nations. NAFTA's provisions have enhanced trade among the United States, Canada, and Mexico. Since NAFTA's passage in 1994, total trade between the United States and Mexico has increased 522 percent, and total trade with Canada has increased 200 percent.[61] It also has made that trade more profitable and less cumbersome for companies of all sizes and has opened new opportunities for many businesses. Since NAFTA's passage, trade among the three nations has more than tripled; these countries now conduct nearly $3.1 billion in trilateral trade each day![62]

ENTREPRENEURIAL PROFILE: Tanya Shaw: Unique Solutions In 2002, Tanya Shaw launched Unique Solutions, a company based in Dartmouth, Nova Scotia, that markets the Intellifit Virtual Fitting Room, a high-tech scanner that is capable of capturing 200,000 measurements on a fully clothed person in just 20 seconds. After a visit to a mall or retail store for a brief scan, customers receive a report that gives them key body measurements they can use to purchase made-to-measure garments from a database of companies that Unique Solutions maintains or to make shopping for off-the-rack clothing more a more pleasant and efficient experience. The company's Me-Ality shopping guide matches shoppers' body shapes with specific sizes at retailers ranging from Banana Republic and Coldwater Creek to J. Crew and Talbot's. Shaw decided to leave the company's headquarters in Nova Scotia, but because NAFTA created opportunities in the United States and Mexico, she moved her marketing and sales division to California and partnered with a New Zealand company, TJ's Jeanswear, that has a factory in Parras, Mexico. TJ's Jeanswear produces and delivers custom-made jeans to Unique Solutions customers. Shaw credits the collaborative business environment created by NAFTA as her small business sought the formation of international partnerships.[63] ∎

DOMINICAN REPUBLIC–CENTRAL AMERICA FREE TRADE AGREEMENT The Dominican Republic–Central America Free Trade Agreement (CAFTA-DR) is to Central America what NAFTA is to North America. The agreement, which was implemented in stages between 2006 and 2008, is designed to promote free trade among the United States and six Central American countries: Costa Rica, El Salvador, Guatemala, Honduras, the Dominican Republic, and Nicaragua. In addition to reducing tariffs among these nations, CAFTA-DR protects U.S. companies' investments and intellectual property in the region, simplifies the export process for U.S. companies, and provides easier access to Central American markets.

Conclusion

To remain competitive, small businesses must assume a global posture. Global effectiveness requires entrepreneurs to be able to leverage workers' skills, company resources, and customer know-how across borders and throughout cultures across the world. They also must concentrate on maintaining competitive cost structures and a focus on the core of every business—the *customer!* Although there are no surefire rules for going global, small businesses that want to become successful international competitors should observe these guidelines:

- Take the time to learn about doing business globally before jumping in. Avoiding mistakes is easier and less expensive than cleaning up the results of mistakes later.

free trade area

an association of countries that have agreed to eliminate trade barriers, both tariff and nontariff, among partner nations.

- If you have never conducted international business, consider hiring a trade intermediary or finding a local partner to help you.

- Make yourself at home in all three of the world's key markets: North America, Europe, and Asia. This triad of regions is forging a new world order in trade that will dominate global markets for years to come.

- Appeal to the similarities within the various regions in which you operate but recognize the differences in their specific cultures. Although the European Union is a single trading bloc composed of 28 countries, smart entrepreneurs know that each country has its own cultural uniqueness and do not treat the nearly 507 million people in them as a unified market. "Gone are the days when you could just roll out one product for the global market," says Hamad Malik, Middle East marketing director for the South Korean electronics company LG.[64]

- Develop new products for the world market. Make sure your products and services measure up to world-class quality standards.

- Familiarize yourself with foreign customs and languages. Constantly scan, clip, and build a file on other cultures: their lifestyles, values, customs, and business practices.

- Learn to understand your customers from the perspective of *their* culture, not your own. Bridge cultural gaps by adapting your business practices to suit their preferences and customs.

- "Glocalize." Make global decisions about products, markets, and management but allow local employees to make tactical decisions about packaging, advertising, and service.

- Recruit and retain multicultural workers who can give your company meaningful insight into the intricacies of global markets. Entrepreneurs with a truly global perspective identify, nurture, and use the talents and knowledge multicultural workers possess.

- Train employees to think globally, send them on international trips, and equip them with state-of-the-art communications technology.

- Hire local managers to staff foreign offices and branches.

- Do whatever seems best wherever it seems best, even if people at home lose jobs or responsibilities.

- Consider using partners and joint ventures to break into foreign markets you cannot penetrate on your own.

- Evaluate opportunities to become an expat entrepreneur.

By its very nature, going global can be a frightening experience. Most entrepreneurs who have already made the jump, however, have found that the benefits outweigh the risks and that their companies are much stronger because of it.

Chapter Summary by Learning Objective

1. Explain why "going global" has become an integral part of many small companies' marketing strategies.

- Companies that move into international business can reap many benefits, including offsetting sales declines in the domestic market; increasing sales and profits; extending their products' life cycles; lowering manufacturing costs; improving competitive position; raising quality levels; and becoming more customer oriented.

2. Describe the principal strategies small businesses have for going global.

- Perhaps the simplest and least expensive way for a small business to begin conducting business globally is to establish a Web site. Companies that sell goods on the Web should establish a secure ordering and payment system for online customers.

- Trade intermediaries, such as EMCs, ETCs, MEAs, export merchants, resident buying offices, and foreign distributors, can serve as a small company's "export department."

- In a domestic joint venture, two or more U.S. small companies form an alliance for the purpose of exporting their goods and services abroad. In a foreign joint venture, a domestic small business forms an alliance with a company in the target area.

- Some small businesses enter foreign markets by licensing businesses in other nations to use their patents, trademarks, copyrights, technology, processes, or products.

- Franchising has become a major export industry for the United States. Franchisers that enter foreign markets rely on three strategies: direct franchising, area development, and master franchising.

- Some countries lack a hard currency that is convertible into other currencies, so companies doing business there must rely on countertrading or bartering. A countertrade is a transaction in which a business selling goods in a foreign country agrees to promote investment and trade in that country. Bartering involves trading goods and services for other goods and services.

- Once established in international markets, some small businesses set up permanent locations there. Although they can be very expensive to establish and maintain, international locations give businesses the opportunity to stay in close contact with their international customers.

- Many small companies shop the world for the goods and services they sell. The intensity of price competition has made importing and outsourcing successful strategies for many small businesses.

- Some entrepreneurs choose to exploit opportunities in foreign markets by moving to those countries and becoming expat entrepreneurs.

3. **Discuss the major barriers to international trade and their impact on the global economy.**

- Three domestic barriers to international trade are common: the attitude that "we're too small to export," lack of information on how to get started in global trade, and a lack of available financing.

- International barriers include tariffs, quotas, embargoes, dumping, and political, business, and cultural barriers.

4. **Describe the trade agreements that will have the greatest influence on foreign trade in the twenty-first century.**

- The WTO was established in 1995 to implement the rules established by the Uruguay Round negotiations of GATT from 1986 to 1994, and it continues to negotiate additional trade agreements. The WTO has 160 member nations and represents more than 97 percent of all global trade. The WTO is the governing body that resolves trade disputes among members.

- NAFTA created a free trade area among Canada, Mexico, and the United States. The agreement created an association that knocked down trade barriers, both tariff and nontariff, among the partner nations.

- CAFTA-DR created a free trade area among the United States and six nations in Central America: Costa Rica, El Salvador, Guatemala, Honduras, the Dominican Republic, and Nicaragua. In addition to reducing tariffs among these nations, CAFTA protects U.S. companies' investments and intellectual property in the region, simplifies the export process for U.S. companies, and provides easier access to Central American markets.

Discussion Questions

15-1. Why must entrepreneurs learn to think globally?

15-2. What forces are driving small businesses into international markets?

15-3. What advantages does going global offer a small business owner?

15-4. What risks does going global offer a small business owner?

15-5. Outline the ten strategies that small businesses can use to go global.

15-6. Describe the various types of trade intermediaries that small business owners can use.

15-7. What functions do each type of trade intermediary perform?

15-8. What is a domestic joint venture?

15-9. What is a foreign joint venture?

15-10. What advantages and disadvantages does taking on an international partner through a joint venture offer?

15-11. What mistakes are first-time exporters most likely to make?

15-12. Outline the steps a small company should take to establish a successful export program.

15-13. What are the benefits and challenges of establishing international locations?

15-14. Describe the barriers businesses face when trying to conduct business internationally.

15-15. How can a small business owner overcome the obstacles of conducting business internationally?

15-16. What is a tariff?

15-17. What is a quota?

15-18. What impact do tariffs and quotas have on international trade?

15-19. What impact has agreements such as WTO, NAFTA, and CAFTA had on small companies that want to go global?

15-20. Summarize the key provisions of WTO.

15-21. Summarize the key provisions of NAFTA.

15-22. Summarize the key provisions of CAFTA.

15-23. What advice would you offer an entrepreneur interested in launching a global business effort?

Beyond the Classroom . . .

15-24. Go to lunch with a student from a foreign country and discuss what products and services are most needed there.

15-25. Ask a student from a foreign country how business systems there differ from ours.

15-26. Ask a student from a foreign country about government regulation and how it affects business in his or her country.

15-27. Ask the student from a foreign country about the cultural differences between the United States and his or her country.

15-28. Ask the student from a foreign country about trade barriers that his or her government has erected.

15-29. Review several current business publications and prepare a brief report on which nations are the most promising for U.S. entrepreneurs.

15-30. What steps should a small business owner take to break into the most promising markets for U.S. entrepreneurs?

15-31. Identify those nations that are currently the least promising for U.S. entrepreneurs.

15-32. Describe why the least promising nations are not attractive markets.

15-33. Select a nation that interests you and prepare a report on its business customs and practices.

15-34. Explain the similarities with business customs and practices in United States.

15-35. Explain the differences with business customs and practices in United States.

Endnotes

Scan for Endnotes or go to www.pearsonhighered.com/scarborough

Morsa Images/Getty Images

Learning Objectives

On completion of this chapter, you will be able to:

1. Explain the challenges involved in the entrepreneur's role as leader and what it takes to be a successful leader.

2. Describe the importance of hiring the right employees and how to avoid making hiring mistakes.

3. Explain how to create a company culture that encourages employee retention.

4. Describe the steps in developing a management succession plan for a growing business that allows a smooth transition of leadership to the next generation.

5. Explain the exit strategies available to entrepreneurs.

Leadership: An Essential Part of an Entrepreneur's Job

LO1

Explain the challenges involved in the entrepreneur's role as leader and what it takes to be a successful leader.

To be successful, an entrepreneur must assume a wide range of roles, tasks, and responsibilities, but none is more important than the role of leader. Some entrepreneurs are uncomfortable assuming this role, but they must learn to be effective leaders if their companies are to grow and reach their potential. **Leadership** is the process of influencing and inspiring others to work to achieve a common goal and then giving them the power and the freedom to achieve it. Without leadership ability, entrepreneurs—and their companies—never rise above mediocrity. Entrepreneurs can learn to be effective leaders, but the task requires dedication, discipline, and hard work. In the past, business owners often relied on an autocratic management style, one built on command and control. Today's workforce is more knowledgeable, has more options, and is more skilled and, as a result, expects a different, more sophisticated style of leadership. Mark Leslie, founder of Veritas Software and under whose leadership the company grew from $95,000 in annual sales to more than $1.5 billion in sales in just 11 years, says leadership is no longer about command and control. Companies must attract the best and brightest people and create an environment in which they can use their intelligence and judgment to make decisions.[1]

leadership
the process of influencing and inspiring others to work to achieve a common goal and then giving them the power and the freedom to achieve it.

The rapid pace of change shaping the economy also is placing new demands on leaders. Technology is changing the ways in which people work, the ways in which the various parts of an organization operate and interconnect, and the ways in which competitors strive for market dominance. To remain competitive, companies must operate at a new, faster speed of business, and that requires a new style of leadership. Leaders of small companies must gather information and make decisions with lightning-fast speed, and they must give workers the resources and the freedom to solve problems and exploit opportunities as they arise. Effective leaders delegate authority and responsibility and empower employees to act in the best interest of the business. In this way, leaders demonstrate trust in employees and respect for their ability to make decisions. Many entrepreneurs have discovered that the old style of leadership has lost its effectiveness and that they must develop a new, more fluid, flexible style of leadership that better fits the needs of modern workers and competitive conditions.

Until recently, experts compared a leader's job to that of a symphony orchestra conductor. Like the symphony leader, an entrepreneur made sure that everyone in the company was playing the same score, coordinated individual efforts to produce a harmonious sound, and directed the orchestra members as they played. The conductor (entrepreneur) retained virtually all of the power and made all of the decisions about how the orchestra would play the music without any input from the musicians themselves. Today's successful entrepreneur, however, is more like the leader of a jazz band, which is known for its improvisation, innovation, creativity, and freewheeling style. "The success of a small [jazz band] rests on the ability to be agile and flexible, skills that are equally central to today's business world," says Michael Gold, founder of Jazz Impact, a company that teaches management skills through jazz.[2] Business leaders, like the leaders of jazz bands, should exhibit the following characteristics:

Innovative. Leaders must step out of their own comfort zones to embrace new ideas; they avoid the comfort of complacency.

Passionate. One of entrepreneurs' greatest strengths is their passion for their businesses. Members of their team feed off of that passion and draw inspiration from it.

Willing to take risks. Playing it safe "is not an option in jazz or for any company that wants to be solvent ten years from now," says Gold.[3]

Adaptable. Although leaders must stand on a bedrock of resolute values, like jazz band leaders, they must adapt their leadership styles to fit the situation and the people involved.

Management and leadership are not the same, yet both are essential to a company's success. Leadership without management is unbridled; management without leadership is uninspired. Leadership gets a small business going; management keeps it going. In other words, leaders are the architects of small businesses; managers are the builders. Some entrepreneurs are good managers yet are poor leaders; others are powerful leaders but are weak managers. The best bet for the latter is to hire people with solid management skills to help them to execute the vision they have for their companies. Stephen Covey, author of *Principle-Centered Leadership*, explains the difference between management and leadership in this way:

> Leadership deals with people; management deals with things. You manage things; you lead people. Leadership deals with vision; management deals with logistics toward that vision. Leadership deals with doing the right things; management focuses on doing things right. Leadership deals with examining the paradigms on which you are operating; management operates within those paradigms. Leadership comes first, then management, but both are necessary.[4]

Leadership and management are intertwined; one without the other means that a small business is going nowhere. Leadership is especially important for companies in the growth phase, when entrepreneurs are hiring employees (often for the first time) and must keep the company and everyone in it focused on its mission as growth tests every seam in the organizational structure.

Effective leaders exhibit certain behaviors:

- ***They define and then constantly reinforce the vision they have for the company.*** Effective leaders have a clear vision of where they want their companies to go, and they concentrate on communicating that vision to those around them. Unfortunately, this is one area in which employees say their leaders could do a better job. Clarity of purpose is essential to a successful organization because people want to be a part of something that is bigger than they are; however, the purpose must be more than merely achieving continuous quarterly profits. Nick Saban, one of the most successful college coaches in recent memory, says a clear vision is the first ingredient for any successful organization. The others are a plan to implement the vision, a leader who sets a good example and develops principles and values that support the vision, and convincing people to buy into the vision.[5]

  In the 1930s, Walt Disney asked his team of animators to stay late one evening because he had a vision that would transform his company: Rather than continue making the short cartoons the company had become known for, he wanted to make the first full-length animated movie, a concept that at the time was revolutionary. Over the course of three and a half hours, Disney created an unmistakable vision for the young company by acting out all of the parts of the characters in *Snow White and the Seven Dwarfs*. Not only was the movie a commercial and critical success (becoming the top grossing movie of all time until it was unseated in 1939 by *Gone with the Wind*) and winning a special Academy award (a full-size Oscar accompanied by seven "dwarf" Oscars), it paved the way for dozens of other full-length animated films and transformed the entire company into an entertainment powerhouse.[6]

- ***They create a set of values and beliefs for employees and passionately pursue them.*** Values are the foundation on which a company's vision is built. Leaders should be like beacons in the night, constantly shining light on the principles, values, and beliefs on which they founded their companies. Whenever the opportunity presents itself, entrepreneurs must communicate with clarity the company's bedrock values and principles to employees and other stakeholders. Some entrepreneurs may not think that it is necessary to do so, but successful leaders know they must hammer home the connection between their companies' values and mission and the jobs workers perform every day.

- ***They establish a culture of ethics.*** One of the most important tasks facing leaders is to mold a highly ethical culture for their companies. They also must demonstrate the character and the courage necessary to stick to the ethical standards they create—especially in the face of difficulty.

- ***They develop a strategic plan that gives the company a competitive advantage.*** Ideally, employees participate in building a successful strategic plan, but the leader is the principal strategic architect of the company. The leader also is responsible for implementing the plan with flexibility and the ability to adapt it to changing conditions.

- ***They respect and support their employees.*** To gain the respect of their employees, leaders must first respect those who work for them. Successful leaders treat every employee with respect. They know that a loyal, dedicated workforce is a company's most valuable resource, and they treat their employees that way.

- **They set the example for their employees.** Leaders' words ring hollow if they fail to "practice what they preach." Few signals are transmitted to workers faster than a leader who sells employees on one set of values and principles and then acts according to a different set. This behavior quickly undermines a leader's credibility among employees, who expect leaders to "walk their talk." That is why integrity is perhaps the most important determinant of a leader's effectiveness.

- **They are authentic.** Employees quickly see through leaders who only pretend to be what they are not. Authenticity does not make someone a leader, but a leader cannot be successful without it. Authenticity is a vital part in developing trust among employees. Successful leaders follow the philosophy of Popeye, the spinach-munching, crusty sailor who first appeared in a cartoon strip in 1929 and was famous for saying, "I yam what I yam, and that's all what I yam."[7]

- **They create a climate of trust in the organization.** Leaders who demonstrate integrity win the trust of their employees, an essential ingredient in the success of any organization. Honest, open communication and a consistent pattern of leaders doing what they say they will do serve to build trust in a business. Research suggests that building trust among employees is one of the most important tasks of leaders wherever they may work. A recent survey of the CEOs of the 500 fastest-growing small companies in the United States, top managers said the most important traits of outstanding leaders were trustworthiness, sincerity, and the capacity to inspire.[8]

- **They build credibility with their employees.** To be effective, leaders must have credibility with their employees, a sometimes challenging task for entrepreneurs, especially as their companies grow and they become insulated from the daily activities of their businesses. To combat the problem of losing touch with the problems their employees face as they do their jobs, many managers periodically return to the front line to serve customers. *Undercover Boss*, a popular television show, disguises CEOs and sends them to work in frontline jobs in their companies. In addition to seeing just how difficult many jobs can be, all of the CEOs get a superb refresher course in how important every worker's role is to the success of the company and how the policies they and other top managers create often make workers' jobs harder. Michael Rubin, founder and CEO of GSI Commerce, a company that provides distribution and call center services, learned so much from his frontline experience that he now requires all of the GSI's executives to spend time working in the company's warehouses and call centers. The idea is that top managers will make better decisions about policies and procedures if they see firsthand the impact of those decisions on customers and frontline employees. When 7-Eleven CEO Joe DePinto went undercover, an encounter with a talented night-shift clerk who was considering leaving the company for a brighter future elsewhere led him to implement a "talent identification program" designed to promote promising employees within the company.[9]

- **They focus employees' efforts on challenging goals and keep them driving toward those goals.** When asked by a student intern to define leadership, one entrepreneur said, "Leadership is the ability to convince people to follow a path they have never taken before to a place they have never been—and upon finding it to be successful, to do it over and over again."[10]

- **They provide the resources employees need to achieve their goals.** Effective leaders know that workers cannot do their jobs well unless they have the tools they need. They provide workers not only with the physical resources they need to excel but also with the necessary intangible resources, such as training, coaching, and mentoring.

- **They communicate with their employees.** Leaders recognize that helping workers to see the company's overarching goal is just one part of effective communication; encouraging employee feedback and then *listening* is just as vital. In other words, they know that communication is a two-way street. Open communication takes on even greater importance when a company faces a difficult or uncertain future.

- *They value the diversity of their workers.* Smart business leaders recognize the value of their workers' varied skills, abilities, backgrounds, and interests. When channeled in the right direction, diversity can be a powerful weapon in achieving innovation and maintaining a competitive edge. Good leaders get to know their workers and to understand the diversity of their strengths. Especially important to young workers is a leader's capacity for empathy, the ability to see things from another person's viewpoint.

- *They celebrate their workers' successes.* Effective leaders recognize that workers want to be winners, and they do everything they can to encourage top performance among their people. The rewards they give are not always financial; in many cases, it may be as simple as a handwritten congratulatory note.

- *They are willing to take risks.* Entrepreneurs know better than most that launching a business requires taking risks. They also understand that to remain competitive, they must constantly encourage risk taking in their companies. When employees try something innovative and it fails, they don't resort to punishment because they know that doing so would squelch creativity in the organization.

- *They encourage creativity among their workers.* Rather than punish workers who take risks and fail, effective leaders are willing to accept failure as a natural part of innovation and creativity. They know that innovative behavior is the key to future success and do everything they can to encourage it among workers.

- *They maintain a sense of humor.* One of the most important tools a leader can have is a sense of humor. Without it, work can become dull and unexciting for everyone.

ENTREPRENEURIAL PROFILE: Richard Branson: Virgin Group Sir Richard Branson, founder of Virgin Group, a diversified company whose businesses range from airlines and bridal gowns to cosmetics and consumer electronics, is famous for creating a work environment of fun for himself and his employees. Branson has put on a wedding dress, bungee jumped, and hosted off-site events designed strictly to allow employees to have fun. The culture of fun at Virgin Group has built an ésprit de corps that gives the company a unique advantage that competitors find difficult to match, and crown prince Richard Branson is its architect.[11] ∎

- *They create an environment in which people have the motivation, the training, and the freedom to achieve the goals they have set.* Leaders know that *their* success is determined by the success of their followers. The goal is to make every employee the manager of his or her job. The leader's role is to provide employees with the resources and support they need to be successful.

- *They create a work climate that encourages maximum performance.* Leaders understand that they play a significant role in shaping a company culture that sets high standards of performance. Anne Wojcicki, founder of 23andMe, a genetic testing company, says her primary role is to get everyone in the company to think bigger.[12]

- *They become a catalyst for change.* With market and competitive climates changing so rapidly, entrepreneurs must reinvent their companies constantly. Although leaders must cling to the values and principles that form the bedrock of their companies, they must be willing to change, sometimes radically, the policies, procedures, and processes within their businesses. If a company is headed in the wrong direction, the leader's job is to recognize that and to get the company moving in the right direction.

- *They develop leadership talent.* Effective leaders look beyond themselves to spot tomorrow's leaders and take the time to help them grow into their leadership potential. A vital component of every leader's job is to develop the next generation of leaders.

- *They keep their eyes on the horizon.* Effective leaders are never satisfied with what they and their employees accomplished yesterday. They know that yesterday's successes are not enough to sustain their companies indefinitely. They see the importance of building and maintaining sufficient momentum to carry their companies to the next level. "A leader's job is to rally people toward a better future," says Marcus Buckingham, who has spent nearly two decades studying effective leaders.[13] Just like winning athletes, good leaders visualize a successful future and then work to make it happen.

Table 16.1 presents 12 questions leaders should address if they want their companies to excel.

TABLE 16.1 12 Questions That Every Leader Should Address

Jim Collins, coauthor of business best-sellers *Good to Great* and *Great by Choice*, has spent 25 years researching great companies and has integrated the results of his research into 12 questions that leaders must address if they want their companies to excel. Collins advises leaders to discuss one of the following questions every month and repeat the process annually:

1. ***Do we want to build a great company, and are we committed to doing the things that are required to make our company great?*** Becoming a great company starts by making this fundamental choice, understanding the implications of choosing to build a great company, and then making the commitment to take the necessary steps to achieve greatness.

2. ***Do we have the right people on the bus and in the key seats?*** Leaders must decide whether the people who will carry the company forward are the *right* people. Are they capable? Motivated? Committed? Leaders must answer this question before they decide *where* they want the business to go, and that sometimes means getting the *wrong* people *off* the bus.

3. ***What are the brutal facts?*** Leaders cannot make good decisions unless they have access to facts, both good and bad. Confronting the negative, most troubling issues is essential because ignoring them represents a serious threat not only to a company's success but also to its survival. The key is to confront the facts without losing faith.

4. ***What are we best at, and what do we have an unbounded passion for?*** By answering this question, leaders are defining their companies' fundamental economic engine. Isaiah Berlin wrote, "The fox knows many things, but the hedgehog knows one big thing."* In other words, a fox is easily distracted, but a hedgehog, like an outstanding company, is focused, determined, and relentless. A company's hedgehog combines its passion and its distinctive competence with what it can make money doing (its economic engine). What is the company's hedgehog?

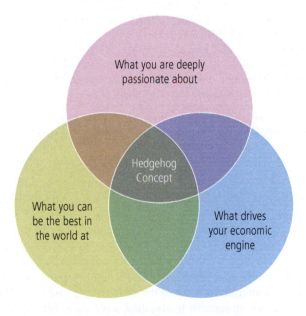

5. ***What is our company's 20-Mile March, and are we hitting it?*** Collins refers to Roald Amundsen's successful attempt in 1911 to be the first person to reach the South Pole by committing to traveling 20 miles a day, no matter what the weather or other obstacles he and his team encountered. Every company has a specific performance goal it must hit year in and year out to be successful. Has the company identified that goal and committed to achieving it? How successful has the company been in achieving the goal? Measuring performance in the 20-Mile March means that leaders must develop a meaningful set of metrics and monitor them constantly.

6. ***Where do empirical data tell us that we should be placing our big bets?*** A company should invest major resources in a new initiative only if leaders already know that it is likely to succeed. That requires conducting low-cost, low-risk tests on a range of possible options ("shooting bullets") to figure out what works before unleashing the full power of the organization's resources on an initiative ("firing a cannonball"). The empirical evidence from the tests guides leaders' decisions about where to aim the cannon.

(continued)

TABLE 16.1 12 Questions That Every Leader Should Address *(continued)*

7. *What are the core values and core purpose on which we want to build this enterprise over the next 100 years?* The challenge is not only to build a company that can endure the long haul but also to build one that is *worthy* of enduring. Leaders must identify the core values and core purpose they would be willing have their companies built around 100 years in the future no matter what changes occur in the external environment.

8. *What is our 15- to 25-year BHAG?* A BHAG is "big, hairy audacious goal." To build a great, enduring company, leaders must have a BHAG that is tangible, energizing, and highly focused and that people can understand immediately with little or no explanation. The BHAG should be linked to the company's core values and purpose. In addition, achieving the BHAG should require a company to make a quantum leap in its capabilities and its aptitude.

9. *What could kill our company, and how can we protect our flanks?* Paranoia is productive when it helps a business survive the inevitable bad surprises that come along and avoid the disasters they are capable of producing. The idea is for leaders *not* to be plagued by constant fear but to be sensitive to changing conditions in the environment and ask, "What if . . .?" Great leaders are always watching the horizon for the threat of storms—and opportunities. They also prepare for the inevitable stormy times by building up cash reserves.

10. *What should we stop doing to increase our discipline and focus?* Effective leaders are disciplined when it comes to pursuing business opportunities. They know that determining what their companies should *not* do is as important as determining what they *should* do. Although an "opportunity of a lifetime" may arise, excellent leaders know that pursuing it is meaningless (and downright dangerous) unless it fits inside the three circles of their "hedgehog."

11. *How can we increase our return on luck?* All companies are affected by both good luck and bad luck. What counts is what a company does with the luck it encounters—good *and* bad. How can the company glean the greatest benefit from good luck and minimize the damage that a run of bad luck causes?

12. *Are we becoming a Level 5 leadership team and cultivating a Level 5 management culture?* Collins calls the highest level of leadership Level 5, which builds enduring greatness in a company through a paradoxical blend of personal humility and professional will. "The central dimension for Level 5 is a leader who is ambitious first and foremost for the cause, for the company, for the work, not for himself or herself; and has an absolutely terrifying iron will to make good on that ambition," says Collins. Are you and your management team providing Level 5 leadership?

*Archilochus, (c680 BC– c. 645 BC) Greek poet and mercenary. Translated by Isaiah Berlin, "The Hedgehog and the Fox: An Essay on Tolstoy's View of History" **© Isaiah Berlin 1953** (London: Weidenfeld and Nicolson Ltd.1953)

Source: Bo Burlingham and Jim Collins, "Hedgehogs, Cannonballs, BHAGs, and Bullets," *Inc.*, June 2012, p. 71; Neil Phillips, "The Entrepreneur's Hedgehog," *The Coach Toolkit*, October 20, 2009, http://www.thecoachtoolkit.com/2009/10/the-entrepreneurs-hedgehog; Troy Schrock, "*Great by Choice* and Strategy Execution," *CEO Advantage*, December 8, 2011, http://www.ceoadvantage.com/blog/tag/jim-collins; Jim Collins, *Vision Framework*, 2002, p. 2; Stephen Blandino, "Productive Paranoia: Lesson #3 from Jim Collins' *Good to Great*," *Stephen Blandino*, January 3, 2012, http://stephenblandino.com/2012/01/productive-paranoia-lesson-3-from-jim-collins-great-by-choice.html; Jim Collins, "Jim Collins and Level 5 Leadership," Management-Issues, January 3, 2006, http://www.management-issues.com/2006/5/24/mentors/jim-collins-and-level-5-leadership.asp; and "Roald Amundsen, Alone on the Ice," WGBH Educational Foundation, 1999, http://www.pbs.org/wgbh/amex/ice/peopleevents/pandeAMEX87.html.

servant leadership
a leadership style in which a leader takes on the role of servant first and leader second.

Leading an organization, whatever its size, is one of the biggest challenges any entrepreneur faces. Yet for an entrepreneur, leadership success is one of the key determinants of a company's success. Research suggests that there is no single "best" style of leadership; the style a leader uses depends, in part, on the situation at hand. Some situations are best suited for a participative leadership style, but in others, an authoritarian style actually may be best. Research by Daniel Goleman and others suggests that today's workers tend to respond more to adaptive, humble leaders who are results oriented and who take the time to cultivate other leaders in the organization.[14] The practice is known as **servant leadership**, a phrase coined by Robert Greenleaf in 1970. Servant leaders are servants *first* and leaders second, putting their employees and their employees' needs ahead of their own. They are concerned more about empowering others in the organization than about enhancing their own power bases. "Servant-leaders ask, 'What do people need? How can I help them to get it? What does my organization need to do? How can I help my organization to do it?'" explains Kent Keith, CEO of the Greenleaf Center for Servant Leadership. "Rather than embarking on a quest for personal power, servant-leaders embark on a quest to identify and meet the needs of others."[15] At ENGEO, a geotechnical and hydrologic engineering consulting firm in San Ramon, California, managers see themselves as servant leaders whose jobs are to "lead from the bottom" by supporting employees as they perform their daily work. That means managers train and empower workers to make decisions that in many other companies only managers are authorized to make.[16]

One business writer explains servant leadership this way:

Real leadership is grounded in a higher level of self-interest that's tied to the interests of those who trust and follow their leader. It [creates] an atmosphere of confidence and light of clarity that flows from and surrounds the leader and that fills the room with the exhilaration of possibility.[17]

To tap into that exhilaration of possibility, an entrepreneurial leader must perform many important tasks, including the following:

- Hire the right employees for the entrepreneurial team and constantly improve their skills.

- Create a culture for motivating and retaining employees.

- Plan for "passing the torch" to the next generation of leadership.

Building an Entrepreneurial Team: Hiring the Right Employees

LO2

Describe the importance of hiring the right employees and how to avoid making hiring mistakes.

As a company grows, the people an entrepreneur hires determine the heights to which the company can climb—or the depths to which it will plunge. Experienced managers understand that the quality of their workforce affects the company's ability to thrive. Acquiring that human capital, however, can be difficult. In a recent survey, North American human resource managers ranked acquiring necessary talent as their top concern.[18] The problem is particularly acute for small companies, which usually cannot afford to match the salaries and benefit packages their larger rivals offer employees. More than one-third of small business owners say their companies are somewhat or significantly understaffed.[19] In addition, 11 percent of business owners report that the job searches they conduct never produced a suitable candidate, and 28 percent say the positions for which they were hiring remained vacant for up to three months.[20]

The decision to hire a new employee is an important one for every business, but its impact is magnified many times in a small company. One new employee represents a significant investment and a significant risk. Adding just one or two employees can significantly increase a company's ability to generate sales. However, in a small company, one bad hiring decision can poison the entire culture, reduce employee productivity, and disrupt any sense of teamwork. Unfortunately, hiring mistakes in business are all too common: 66 percent of companies in the United States report that they made a bad hire within the last year.[21] The culprit in most cases? The company's selection and hiring process.

Hiring mistakes are incredibly expensive, and no company, especially small ones, can afford too many of them. The higher the position is in an organization and the longer the tenure of the person who holds that position, the higher the cost associated with replacing a "bad hire." Employers report that their hiring mistakes result in lower productivity (36 percent), negative impact on employee morale (32 percent), time lost and cost incurred in recruiting and training another worker (31 percent), and diminished customer satisfaction (18 percent).[22] Even the best training program cannot overcome a flawed hiring decision. One study reported in the *Harvard Business Review* concludes that 80 percent of employee turnover is caused by bad hiring decisions.[23] The most common causes of a company's poor hiring decisions include the following:

- Managers who rely on candidates' descriptions of themselves rather than requiring candidates to demonstrate their abilities.

- Managers who fail to follow a consistent, evidence-based selection process. Forty-seven percent of managers admit they make hiring decisions in 30 minutes or less, and 44 percent of managers say they rely on their intuition to make hiring decisions.

- Managers who fail to provide candidates with sufficient information about what the jobs for which they are hiring actually entail, which results in a job-skill mismatch.[24]

- Managers who succumb to pressure to fill a job quickly.

- Managers who fail to check candidates' references.[25]

FIGURE 16.1

Annual Growth Rate in the U.S. Labor Force

Source: Bureau of Labor Statistics, 2012.

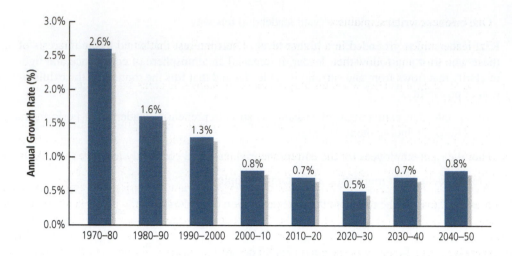

As crucial as finding good employees is to a small company's future, it is no easy task because entrepreneurs face a labor shortage, particularly among knowledge-based workers. The severity of this shortage will become more acute as baby boomers retire in increasing numbers and the growth rate of the U.S. labor force slows (see Figure 16.1). According to the National Commission for Employment Policy, the impact of these demographic changes will be a "skilled worker gap" (in which the demand for skilled workers outstrips the supply) of 14 million in 2020.[26] The result is that small businesses already find themselves pursuing the best talent not just across the United States but across the globe. A recent study by ManpowerGroup reports that 35 percent of companies around the world have difficulty filling jobs because of a lack of available talent. The United States is above the global average with 39 percent of companies having difficulty filling jobs because of a lack of talent.[27]

Unfilled jobs are expensive; the average company loses more than $14,000 for every job that is vacant for at least three months. Employers report that their extended job vacancies result in a negative impact on employee morale (41 percent), work that does not get done (40 percent), delays in delivery times (34 percent), diminished customer service (30 percent), lower quality of work because remaining employees are overworked (30 percent), and diminished employee motivation (29 percent).[28]

ENTREPRENEURIAL PROFILE: Kevin Madden: Group One Safety and Security Kevin Madden, president of Group One Safety and Security, a 16-employee company in Stuart, Florida, that installs security and video surveillance systems in homes and commercial properties, has two job openings for technicians that have gone unfilled for 18 months. Although hourly pay rates for the jobs range from $16 to $30, depending on qualifications and experience, the jobs remain unfilled. Madden frequently declines new projects, costing his Group One sales, because he is not willing to jeopardize his company's reputation for providing excellent customer service due to a lack of technical support staff.[29] ■

High employee turnover rates cost companies as well. The voluntary turnover rate for employees is 16.6 percent, which means that the average employee's tenure at a company is about six years. The average cost that a company incurs when an employee leaves is 20 percent of the employee's annual salary (for employees who earn less than $50,000 annually) and 213 percent of the annual salary for an executive who leaves.[30] A company with 25 employees can expect to lose, on average, about four employees per year. If those employees earn an average of $40,000, the cost to the company is $32,000 per year ($40,000 × 20% = $8,000 per employee. 4 employees × $8,000 = $32,000). To reduce their employee turnover rates, companies can employ the following strategies:

- Provide rewarding and challenging work.

- Pay employees fairly.

- Provide training opportunities and mentoring relationships.

- Offer flexible work schedules.

- Provide simple (and inexpensive) rewards such as thank-you notes for extra effort or "good job" notes for jobs well done.

- Conduct exit interviews when employees leave to determine areas that require improvement.

A recent study by IBM reports that 71 percent of CEOs across the globe say the most important factor in their companies' ability to provide sustained economic value to their customers is the quality of their employees.[31] Smart business owners recognize that the companies that have the most talented, best-trained, and most motivated workforces will be the winners.

As a result of the intense competition for quality workers among businesses, employers often feel pressured to hire someone, even if that person is not a good fit for the job. A study by Development Dimensions International reports that 34 percent of hiring managers admit to making bad hiring decisions because they were under pressure to fill a job.[32] The result is the almost always an expensive hiring mistake for the company. Smart entrepreneurs maintain their hiring standards even when the pressure is on to fill a position.

ENTREPRENEURIAL PROFILE: Dane Atkinson: SumAll Dane Atkinson, cofounder of SumAll, a business analytics company in New York City, believes that hiring "fast" increases the odds of hiring mistakes. At SumAll, every new employee goes through a 45-day probationary period, during which time he or she is assigned to a mentor and receives regular reviews from a dedicated selection committee. At the end of the probationary period, selection committee members vote on whether to hire the candidate permanently. If the candidate passes that vote, the remainder of the employees in the company vote, and one "no" vote sends the candidate packing. About 70 percent of candidates make it through the process and are hired permanently. The process works; in the two years since it has been in place, only one employee has left the company.[33] ∎

How to Hire Winners

Even though the importance of hiring decisions is magnified in small companies, small businesses are most likely to make hiring mistakes because they lack the human resources experts and the disciplined hiring procedures that large companies have. In many small businesses, the hiring process is informal, and the results often are unpredictable. In the early days of a company, entrepreneurs rarely take the time to create job descriptions and specifications; instead, they usually hire people because they know or trust them rather than for their job or interpersonal skills. As the company grows, business owners hire people to fit in around these existing employees, often creating a very unusual, inefficient organization structure built around jobs that are poorly planned and designed.

The following guidelines can help entrepreneurs to become employers of choice and to hire winners as they build their team of employees.

COMMIT TO HIRING THE BEST TALENT Smart entrepreneurs follow the old adage, "A players hire A players; B players hire C players." They are not threatened by hiring people who may be smarter and more talented than they are. In fact, they recognize that doing so is the best way to build a quality team. What skill sets do CEOs say are essential to employees' success? According to the IBM study of global CEOs, the most important skills are the ability to collaborate with others (75 percent), the ability to communicate effectively (67 percent), creativity (61 percent), flexibility (61 percent), and analytical and quantitative skills (50 percent).[34]

ELEVATE RECRUITING TO A STRATEGIC POSITION IN THE COMPANY The recruiting process is the starting point for building quality into a company. Chris McCann, cofounder of NextDigest, a company that publishes newsletters for technology entrepreneurs, says that after finding money the most difficult challenge start-ups face is finding talent.[35] Assembling a quality workforce begins with a sound recruiting effort. By investing time and money in the crucial planning phase of the staffing process, entrepreneurs can generate spectacular savings down the road by hiring the best talent. Recruiting is so important that many entrepreneurs are actively involved in the process themselves. Visionary entrepreneurs *never* stop recruiting because top-quality talent is hard to find and is extremely valuable. Tom Bonney, founder of CMF Associates, a fast-growing financial consulting firm in Philadelphia, knows that finding superior talent is essential to the success of his service business and says he never stop recruiting.[36] Unfortunately, Bonney is in the minority; only 38 percent of hiring managers say they constantly recruit. Their principal barrier: lack of time.[37]

Attracting a pool of qualified job candidates requires not only constant attention but also creativity, especially among smaller companies that often find it difficult to match the more generous offers large companies make. With a sound recruiting strategy and a willingness to look in new places, however, smaller companies *can* hire and retain high-caliber employees. The following techniques will help:

Look inside the company first. One of the best sources for top prospects is inside the company itself. A promotion-from-within policy serves as an incentive for existing workers to upgrade their skills and to produce results. In addition, an entrepreneur already knows the employee's work habits, and the employee already understands the company's culture. Unfortunately, companies fill only one-third of their job vacancies from within.[38]

Look for employees with whom your customers can identify. For an entrepreneur whose company sells women's shoes, hiring young women straight out of college to manage the company's social media presence makes sense; however, hiring young women for sales positions in a company that sells makeup to middle-age women does not. At the Vermont Country Store, a business in Rockingham, Vermont, now in its fifth generation of family ownership, half of the employees are older than 50, which benefits the company because the average customer is in his or her 60s.[39]

ENTREPRENEURIAL PROFILE: Greg Selkoe: Karmaloop Greg Selkoe, founder and CEO of Karmaloop, a Boston-based e-commerce company that operates a growing hipster media empire representing more than 500 brands, looks for employees who resemble the company's target customers, members of verge culture. "What makes us successful is that our employees reflect the street culture that we market to," says Selkoe. "Some are DJs or musicians or artists. They're young; the median age here is 26, and from almost every race, religion, and ethnicity. Basically, they are the market we sell to."[40] ∎

Encourage employee referrals. To cope with the shortage of available talent, many companies are offering their employees (and others) bonuses for referring candidates who come to work and prove to be valuable employees. Employees serve as reliable screens because they do not want to jeopardize their reputations with their employer. Employee referrals have proved to be an excellent source of quality employees. Although employee referrals are the source of only 6.9 percent of applicants, they account for 39.9 percent of those hired. Employees hired through employee referrals also have higher retention rates than those hired by job Web sites and job boards.[41] The Nerdery, a Web design firm in Bloomington, Minnesota, finds about 25 percent of its new hires through referrals from existing employees.[42] To encourage employee referrals, many companies offer incentives for successful hires. Rewards companies offer to employees for successful referrals range from cash and iPads to big-screen televisions and exotic vacations. At CarGurus, a Web site that helps car buyers navigate the often intimidating process of researching and purchasing a car, founder and serial entrepreneur Langley Steinert offers employees cash bonuses for recommending quality job candidates.[43]

Make employment advertisements stand out. Getting employment ads noticed in traditional media is becoming more difficult because they get lost in the swarm of ads from other companies.

ENTREPRENEURIAL PROFILE: Amy Rees Anderson: MediConnect Global When Amy Rees Anderson was CEO of MediConnect Global, a fast-growing medical records retrieval and electronic document management company, she created several offbeat videos that featured brief, home-made clips of employees demonstrating their silly and unusual talents (for example, one employee balanced a toilet plunger on one finger and then suctioned it to his stomach) to make her company's recruiting ad stand out and to communicate the sense of fun in the company's culture. The videos opened with a graphic that said,

NICK Wass/Invision/AP

"Featuring the Elite Talent of MediConnect Global" before showing the employees' "talents" and closing with a graphic that said, "What's your elite talent? Apply now." The low-cost ads were successful, not only producing many new hires that Anderson says the company would have missed otherwise but also improving employee morale.[44] ■

Use multiple channels to recruit talent. Although newspaper ads still top employers' list of job postings, many businesses are successfully attracting candidates through other media, particularly the Internet. The goal is to spread wide a company's recruiting net. Posting job listings on the company's Web page, on its social media accounts, on career-oriented Web sites such as Monster, CareerBuilder, and others not only expands a small company's reach far beyond ads in a local newspaper but also is very inexpensive. A recent survey by Jobvite reports that 98 percent of recruiters use LinkedIn to recruit employees, 42 percent use Facebook, and 33 percent use Twitter. In addition, 73 percent of the companies used these social media tools to make successful hires, and 42 percent say adding social media as a recruiting tool increased the quality of the applicant pool.[45] Employers also are connecting with potential employees (not all of whom are actively seeking new jobs) through their employees' social media sites and network of contacts. A social media recruiting strategy works well for technology companies such as Red Hat Inc. (the company that distributes the Linux operating system), which finds 50 percent of its new hires through social networks.[46] Mobile apps and technology such as smart phones provide another mechanism for reaching job candidates. One recent survey reports that 72 percent of job seekers want to receive career opportunity information on their smart phones (and 45 percent of job seekers have applied for a job using their smart phones).[47]

Recruit on campus. For many employers, college and university campuses remain an excellent source of workers, especially for entry-level positions. In a recent survey, 39 percent of college graduates say a small or medium-size business would be the ideal place to work (compared to 27 percent who believe a large corporation would be the ideal place to work).[48] After screening résumés, a recruiter can interview a dozen or more high-potential students in just one day by conducting on-campus interviews. Entrepreneurs must ensure that the recruiters they send to campuses are professional, polished, and prepared to represent their companies well because 42 percent of students say their impression of a recruiter is the primary determinant of their perception of the company.[49]

Forge relationships with schools and other sources of workers. Internships and co-op programs can be excellent sources of future employees. As colleges and universities offer students more internship and co-op opportunities, small businesses can benefit from hosting one or more students for a semester or for a summer. Internships and co-op programs offer companies low-risk opportunities to "test-drive" potential employees, observe students' work habits, and sell top performers on permanent positions on graduation. A recent study by the National Association of Colleges and Employers reports that employers offer full-time jobs to 56.5 percent of their interns. In addition, 72.9 percent of interns who are hired for full-time positions are still working for the same companies five years later.[50]

ENTREPRENEURIAL PROFILE: Burnstein von Seelen Burnstein von Seelen, a precision castings company located in Abbeville, South Carolina, that specializes in producing cast products from copper-based materials, faced a shortage of skilled machine tool operators, and three-fourths of its machinists were at or near retirement age. Managers worked with the Metal Trades Department at a local technical college, Piedmont Technical College, to create a co-op apprenticeship program in which students could attend classes for a semester and work for a semester. Kenny Price, the first student to participate in the program, started as an apprentice with Burnstein von Seelen and now has a full-time job as a machine tool operator. The co-op apprenticeship program has been so successful that the company is expanding it.[51] ■

Recruit "retired" workers. By 2020, 20.4 percent of workers in the United States will reach retirement age.[52] Many of these baby boomers plan to continue working after reaching retirement age to maintain their lifestyles, however. The Bureau of Labor Statistics estimates that 13.2 million people over the age of 65 will be in the workforce in 2022, an increase from 7.3 million today, and small businesses should be ready to hire them.[53] With a lifetime of work experience, time on their hands, and a strong work ethic, "retired" workers can be the ideal solution to many entrepreneurs' labor problems and can be a valuable asset to small firms.

Consider using offbeat recruiting techniques. To attract the workers they need to support their growing businesses, some entrepreneurs have resorted to creative recruiting techniques. As part of its recruiting efforts, Range Resources Corporation, a natural gas company, sponsors a unique float in the local Fourth of July parade, invites prospective employees to mingle with current employees at cookouts, and sends employee representatives prepared to talk about working at the company to more than 1,000 community events each year.[54] Other ideas include the following:

- Sending young recruiters to mingle with college students on spring break. Deloitte, an accounting and consulting firm, takes dozens of college students to various locations for Spring Break. Rather than party on the beach, however, the students work alongside Deloitte employees in a program called Maximum Impact, focusing on community projects ranging from sprucing up community parks and repairing homes for the elderly to preparing taxes and assisting in soup kitchens. Sara Ferguson, who took part in a Maximum Impact trip to Galveston, Texas, while she was a college student, now works for Deloitte. Ferguson says the experience gave her unique insight into the company's culture and assured her that Deloitte was the type of company for which she wanted to work.[55]
- Using social networks, such as Facebook, LinkedIn, Twitter, and company blogs to reach potential employees, especially young ones.
- Sponsoring a "job-shadowing" program that gives students and other prospects the opportunity to observe firsthand the nature of the work and the work environment.
- Inviting prospective employees to a company tailgating party at a sports event.
- Inviting potential candidates to participate in a company-sponsored event. Corey Reese, cofounder of Ness Computing, a company that makes practical apps for the iPhone, sponsors "hackathon" events on college campuses that attract the technologically savvy computer software engineers he must hire for the fast-growing company.[56]
- Posting "what it's like to work here" videos created by current employees on the company's Facebook page, YouTube, and other video sites.
- Inviting potential candidates to meet and mingle with a company's workforce at informal, fun events. Ness Computing regularly invites potential employees to company-sponsored barbecues and picnics.
- Keeping a file of all of the workers mentioned in the "People on the Move" column in the business section of the local newspaper and then contacting them a year later to see whether they are happy in their jobs.[57]

Offer what workers want. Adequate compensation and benefits are important considerations for job candidates, but other, less tangible factors also weigh heavily in a prospect's decision to accept a job. To recruit effectively, entrepreneurs must consider what a McKinsey and Company study calls the "employee value proposition," the factors that would make the ideal employee want to work for their businesses. Flexible work schedules and telecommuting that allow employees to balance the demands of work and family life attract quality workers to small companies. Human resource managers say the most important factor in a company's ability to attract and retain the best workers, especially young ones, is a flexible work schedule. (The second most important factor is a culture characterized by trust, open communication, and fairness.)[58] Employees agree. In a recent survey, 83 percent of workers say they would be more loyal to their companies if they had flexible work schedules.[59]

Many of the companies listed on *Fortune*'s "100 Best Companies to Work For" offer low-cost but valuable (from their employees' perspectives) benefits, such as take-home meals, personal concierge services that coordinate everything from dry cleaning to auto maintenance for employees, exercise facilities, and discounts on the merchandise they sell.[60]

TABLE 16.2 Affordable Alternative Benefits

Although small companies typically cannot match their larger rivals on the employee benefits packages they offer, with some creativity entrepreneurs can provide less expensive options that increase employee retention, motivation, and morale.

Perhaps You Cannot Offer . . .	But You Might . . .
Tuition reimbursement for college classes	Implement a flex-time schedule that allows employees to attend classes at a nearby college or university
Paid leave	Use job sharing so that two part-time employees share one full-time job
Comprehensive health insurance	Hold a wellness day in which a local health care provider performs basic health screens for employees
An on-site fitness center	Set up a basketball goal in a corner of the parking lot or a ping-pong table in the office or negotiate a reduced fee for employees at the local YMCA
401(k) retirement plan with employer match	Invite a local investment adviser to provide financial counseling and retirement advice to employees
Counseling services	Allow employees to bring their dogs to work; research shows that allowing pets in the workplace reduces stress and increases job satisfaction
Child care subsidies	Negotiate discounts at a local preschool for employees' children or allow employees to telecommute from home several days a week

Source: Based on Paula Andruss, "Affordable Alternatives," *Entrepreneur*, May 2012, p. 57; "Pets at Work Keep Workers Happy," *U.S. News and World Report*, April 2, 2012, http://health.usnews.com/health-news/news/articles/2012/04/02/pets-at-work-keep-workers-happy.

ENTREPRENEURIAL PROFILE: April Kumzelman: Fat Wallet Fat Wallet, an online discount retailer, provides employees with a valuable, low-cost benefit—the flexibility they need to achieve work–life balance. The company's "no-miss" policy tells employees not to miss important family or school events because of work. "It doesn't cost us any money, and people really appreciate it," says human resources director April Kunzelman. "Flexibility pays huge benefits for a small company like ours."[61] ■

Table 16.2 provides examples of affordable alternative benefits that small businesses can offer employees.

Create Practical Job Descriptions and Job Specifications

Business owners must recognize that what they do *before* they interview candidates for a position determines to a great extent how successful they will be at hiring winners. The first step is to perform a **job analysis,** the process by which a firm determines the duties and nature of the jobs to be filled and the skills and experience required of the people who are to fill them. Without a proper job analysis, a hiring decision is, at best, a coin toss. The first step in conducting a job analysis is to develop a **job description,** a written statement of the duties, responsibilities, reporting relationships, working conditions, and methods and techniques as well as materials and equipment used in a job. A results-oriented job description explains what a job entails and the duties the person filling it is expected to perform. A detailed job description includes a job title, job summary, primary responsibilities and duties, nature of supervision, the job's relationship to others in the company, working conditions, the job's location, definitions of job-specific terms, and a description of the company and its culture.

Preparing job descriptions is a task that most small business owners overlook; however, this may be one of the most important parts of the hiring process because it creates a blueprint for the job. Without this blueprint, managers tend to hire the person with experience whom they like the best.

ENTREPRENEURIAL PROFILE: Sherri Comstock: The Cheshire Cat and The Spotted Crocodile Sherri Comstock, owner of The Cheshire Cat and The Spotted Crocodile, two jewelry and gift boutiques in Grayslake, Illinois, admits to failing to write meaningful job descriptions. "One of the biggest mistakes we've made is not defining the job as well as we should," she says. "If the position is not well-defined before you hire the person to fill it, a bad fit is all but inevitable."[62] ■

job analysis
the process by which a firm determines the duties and nature of the jobs to be filled and the skills and experience required of the people who are to fill them.

job description
a written statement of the duties, responsibilities, reporting relationships, working conditions, and methods and techniques as well as materials and equipment used in a job.

You Be the Consultant

Avoid These Hiring Mistakes

One week after hiring a shipping manager for her online personalized gifts business, The Younique Boutique, Brina Bujkovsky knew something was wrong. Other employees saw the new hire slipping in and out of the building with a backpack. One day at lunch, he left to "make a personal call" but did not return for several hours. When he finally showed up, he was extremely intoxicated. Bujkovsky fired him immediately.

Hiring mistakes like the one Bujkovsky made are quite common and can be expensive, especially for small companies. Spotting problem employees before they are hired, however, is not always easy because bad employees often are adept at hiding their problems until well after they are hired. What steps can entrepreneurs take to avoid making critical hiring mistakes?

- *Know what you want.* Before hiring anyone, an entrepreneur should create a job description and a job specification. These important documents spell out the duties and responsibilities of the job and define the skills, traits, and experience of the ideal candidate.

- *Don't be in a hurry.* Rushing through the hiring process almost always guarantees a hiring mistake. Hiring a new employee is a long-term commitment; make sure you devote sufficient time to making the right decision.

- *Involve others in the selection process.* Involving others in the selection process lowers the probability that "warning signs" about a candidate will go unnoticed. After her hiring mistake, Bujkovsky changed the selection process in her company to include her entire team in the interview process.

- *Ask the right questions and listen carefully to candidates' answers.* Smart entrepreneurs always prepare for interviews and have a set of prepared questions that are designed to probe each candidate's experience, personality, background, and work ethic. They also listen carefully (even for what candidates don't say) and watch their body language during the interview.

- *"Test drive" candidates whenever possible.* Internships and apprenticeships allow employers to observe candidates to determine whether they are likely to make good full-time employees. When internships or apprenticeships are not practical, some companies use interviews that put candidates into situations they are likely to encounter on the job to see how they handle them.

- *Check references—always.* Checking candidates' references takes time, but the payoff can be huge. Some companies check "one-off" references, those people with whom a candidate worked but are not listed as references on the application. Asking listed references for other potential references and searching social media sites such as LinkedIn and Facebook can produce these valuable unofficial references.

- *Look for candidates' profiles on social media platforms.* Social media can be useful not only for finding candidates but also for learning more about them. Although it is not a good idea to ask for candidates' social media passwords (it actually is illegal in six states), reviewing their social media profiles can be quite revealing. A recent survey by Jobvite reports that 94 percent of recruiters use or plan to use social media to hire employees. In another study, 43 percent of hiring managers say they have found information on social media that caused them not to hire a candidate. Conversely, 20 percent of hiring managers say they found information on social media that led them to hire a candidate.

1. Why are hiring mistakes so expensive for companies, particularly small businesses?

2. Suppose your best friend is about to hire someone to work in his or her company. List at least three other tips that will enable him or her to avoid making a hiring mistake.

Source: Based on "5 Ways to Spot Bad Employees Before They're Hired," *All Business Experts*, January 1, 2013, http://experts.allbusiness.com/5-ways-to-spot-bad-employees-before-theyre-hired/#.U6w6C0BrTOs; *2013 Social Recruiting Survey Results*, Jobvite, 2013, p. 2; Kristin Piombino, "Social Media Costs Candidates Their Jobs, Report Says," *Ragan*, July 9, 2013, http://www.ragan.com/Main/Articles/Social_media_costs_candidates_their_jobs_report_sa_46973.aspx; Greg Fisher, "Eight Reasons You Made a Bad Hire," *Perspectives*, June 24, 2013, http://blog.betterweekdays.com/blog/employers/324758/eight-reasons-you-made-a-bad-hire.

Useful sources of information for writing job descriptions include the manager's knowledge of the job, the worker(s) currently holding the job, and the *Dictionary of Occupational Titles*, which is available online. This dictionary, published by the U.S. Department of Labor, lists more than 20,000 job titles and descriptions and serves as a useful tool for getting a small business owner started when writing job descriptions. Internet searches also are a valuable tool for finding resources for writing job descriptions. There, entrepreneurs can find templates and descriptions they can easily modify to fit their companies' needs. Table 16.3 provides an example of the description drawn from the *Dictionary of Occupational Titles* for an unusual job, a worm picker.

TABLE 16.3 A Sample Job Description from *the Dictionary of Occupational Titles*

Worm Picker—gathers worms to be used as fish bait; walks about grassy areas, such as gardens, parks, and golf courses and picks up earthworms (commonly called dew worms and nightcrawlers). Sprinkles chlorinated water on lawn to cause worms to come to the surface and locates worms by use of lantern or flashlight. Counts worms, sorts them, and packs them into containers for shipment. (# 413.687-014)

The second objective of a job analysis is to create a **job specification**, a written statement of the qualifications and characteristics needed for a job stated in terms such as education, skills, and experience. A job specification shows the small business manager the kind of person to recruit and establishes the standards an applicant must meet to be hired. In essence, it is a written "success profile" of the ideal employee. Does the person have to be a good listener, empathetic, well organized, decisive, and a "self-starter"? Should he or she have experience in Python programming? One of the best ways to develop this success profile is to study the top performers currently working for the company and to identify the characteristics that make them successful. Before hiring new sales representatives, sales managers at Blackboard, Inc., a Washington, D.C., company that sells software for the educational market, study their top sales producers to identify the characteristics they demonstrate in four areas—skills, experience, knowledge, and personality traits. Table 16.4 provides an example that links the tasks for a sales representative's job (drawn from the job description) to the traits or characteristics an entrepreneur identified as necessary to succeed in that job. These traits become the foundation for writing the job specification.

job specification
a written statement of the qualifications and characteristics needed for a job stated in terms such as education, skills, and experience.

Plan an Effective Interview

Once an entrepreneur knows what to look for in a job candidate, he or she can develop a plan for conducting an informative job interview. Research shows that planned interviews produce much more reliable hiring results than unstructured interviews in which interviewers "freewheel" the questions they ask candidates. Unstructured interviews produce no better results than flipping a coin to decide whether to hire a candidate, but structured interviews produce highly valid hiring results.[63] Too often, business owners go into an interview unprepared, and as a result, they fail to get the information they need to judge the candidate's qualifications, qualities, and suitability for the job. A common symptom of failing to prepare for an interview is that the interviewer rather than the candidate does most of the talking.

Conducting an effective interview requires an entrepreneur to know what he or she wants to get out of the interview in the first place and to develop a series of questions to extract that information. The following guidelines will help entrepreneurs develop interview questions that will give them meaningful insight into an applicant's qualifications, personality, and character:

Involve others in the interview process. Solo interviews are prone to errors. A better process is to involve other employees, particularly employees with whom the prospect would be working, in the interview process either individually or as part of a panel.

TABLE 16.4 Linking Tasks from a Job Description to the Traits Necessary to Perform a Job Successfully

Job Task	Trait or Characteristic
Generate and close new sales	"Outgoing"; persuasive; friendly
Make 15 "cold calls" per week	"Self-starter"; determined; optimistic; independent; confident
Analyze customers' needs and recommend proper equipment	Good listener; patient; empathetic
Counsel customers about options and features needed	Organized; polished speaker; "other oriented"
Prepare and explain financing methods	Honest; "numbers oriented"; comfortable with computers and spreadsheets
Retain existing customers	Customer oriented; relationship builder

ENTREPRENEURIAL PROFILE: Richard Sheridan: Menlo Innovations At Menlo Innovations, a successful custom software company in Ann Arbor, Michigan, collaboration among workers is paramount because employees typically work together on projects in pairs all day. Menlo Innovations's hiring process reflects its emphasis on collaboration in what cofounder Richard Sheridan calls "extreme interviewing." Candidates team up in pairs to tackle 20-minute exercises that are typical of the projects they would work on at Menlo Innovations while employees and managers observe them. To drive home the company's focus on teamwork, each team of candidates shares a single pencil. Candidates complete three exercises so that employees can observe them. After an extreme interviewing session, employees collectively decide which candidates to invite back. Those selected spend a day working for pay with two employees on a project. Those who pass that test come back for a three-week trial employment period. Only after completing the trial successfully do they become Menlo Innovations employees.[64] ■

Develop a series of core questions and ask them of every candidate. To give the screening process more consistency, smart business owners rely on a set of relevant questions they ask in every interview. Of course, they also customize each interview using impromptu questions based on an individual candidate's responses. "The most effective way to hire fantastic, loyal employees who will fit into your company culture and help you meet your goals is to hire them for their inherent abilities (which can't be taught), such as personality, learning style, and core values," says Mike Michalowicz, a successful serial entrepreneur who started his first business at age 24. "You do this by identifying behavior patterns during the interview process. If you ask questions designed to identify the patterns, you can predict how prospective employees will behave."[65]

Ask open-ended questions (including on-the-job "scenarios") rather than questions calling for "yes or no" answers. These types of questions are most effective because they encourage candidates to talk about their work experience in a way that will disclose the presence or the absence of the traits and characteristics the business owner is seeking. Peter Bregman, CEO of Bregman Partners, a company that helps businesses implement change, says one of the most revealing questions that an interviewer can ask candidates is, "What do you do in your spare time?" The answer to this question offers unique insight that helps interviewers differentiate between those who are merely competent and those who are stars. Bregman points to the example of Captain C. B. "Sully" Sullenberger, the pilot who safely landed a disabled jet with 155 passengers on the Hudson River using skills that he learned from his hobby: flying gliders.[66]

situational interview
an interview in which the interviewer gives candidates a typical job-related situation (e.g., a job simulation) to see how they respond to it.

Create hypothetical situations that candidates would be likely to encounter on the job and ask (or better yet watch) how they would handle them. Building the interview around these kinds of questions gives the owner a preview of the candidate's actual work habits and attitudes. Some companies take this idea a step further and put candidates into a simulated work environment to see how they prioritize activities and handle mail, e-mail, and a host of "real-world" problems they are likely to encounter on the job, ranging from complaining customers to problematic employees. Known as **situational interviews**, their goal is to give interviewers keener insight into how candidates would perform in the work environment.

ENTREPRENEURIAL PROFILE: Andy Dunn: Bonobos Andy Dunn, cofounder and CEO of clothing company Bonobos, says that situational interviews are the most important screening tool his company uses. The company asks candidates to perform the jobs for which they are interviewing. For instance, a person who applies for a job as a Customer Service Ninja has the chance to respond to e-mail questions and complaints from actual customers. At the executive level, Bonobos invites candidates to offer advice on a big decision the company faces and has even allowed them to run meetings to develop solutions to specific problems.[67] ■

Kathy Willens/AP Photo

Probe for specific examples in the candidate's past work experience that demonstrate the necessary traits and characteristics. A common mistake interviewers make is failing to get candidates to provide the detail they need to make an informed decision.

Ethics and Entrepreneurship

Honesty in Job Descriptions

Explorer Ernest Shackleton reportedly placed this advertisement in a British newspaper to recruit the crew for his 1914 expedition with the goal of "crossing the South Polar continent from sea to sea," a distance of 1,800 miles in the face of some of the most grueling and dangerous conditions possible. Nearly 5,000 men applied, from which Shackleton selected 28 of the most capable men, carefully matching their skills and abilities to the challenges that the journey would present. On August 1, 1914, Shackleton and his crew left London on their ship, the *Endurance*, to document the largely unexplored Antarctic. On October 27, 1915, after watching the *Endurance* splinter after being stuck in pack ice for 10 months, Shackleton and his crew began a harrowing journey of survival that would not end until August 20, 1916, 22 months after their expedition began. Even though Shackleton's ad stated "safe return doubtful," Shackleton and his entire crew returned safely to London after an amazing adventure.

Like Shackleton, smart entrepreneurs know that writing job descriptions that make jobs sound more interesting, glamorous, and exciting than they really are not only is misleading but also creates problems for their businesses. To avoid high turnover rates, low morale, and abysmal productivity rates among their employees, entrepreneurs must paint realistic pictures of jobs when they create job descriptions. Recruiters at Lindblad Expeditions, a company that takes guests on adventure cruises to exciting destinations around the globe, makes sure that job applicants get an unvarnished picture of what their jobs would entail—warts and all. Prospective employees receive a DVD that shows crew members performing their daily tasks—from serving meals to guests and seeing wildlife on the Galapagos Islands to washing windows and swabbing toilets. "The things you see and the places that you

go are amazing, but you're still doing this incredibly hard work," says one employee. "You're going to put in 10- to 12-hour days," adds another. The video discourages most applicants, but those who do apply tend to be just the kind of young people Lindblad is looking for to take on a six-month assignment of taking care of guests' safety and comfort. "If they get on board and say, 'This is not what I expected,' then shame on us," says Kris Thompson, vice president of human resources.

Tony Hsieh, CEO of Zappos, the online shoe retailer whose 10 core values include "deliver WOW through service" and "create fun and a little weirdness," relies on an unusual policy to make sure his company hires only those employees who are most committed to fulfilling the company's mission. After the first week of the company's four-week training program, during which employees earn a full salary, Zappos presents them with "The Offer": Stay with the company or take a $3,000 payout to leave, no strings attached. Only about 10 percent of new employees take the money and leave. Hsieh says that those who remain are more likely to believe in Zappos's values and to commit themselves to upholding the company's commitment to customer service. Every year, Zappos publishes the *Zappos Culture Book*, in which employees have the opportunity to write anything they want about Zappos's core values and its culture, what the values and culture mean to them, and what they do to uphold them. In the foreword of a recent edition of the *Zappos Culture Book*, Hsieh wrote, "For us to succeed as a service company, we need to create, maintain, and grow a culture where employees want to play a part in providing great service. . . . As we grow as a company and hire new people, we need to make sure that they understand and become a part of our culture."

1. Why is it important for entrepreneurs to create honest job descriptions to potential employees? What are the implications for entrepreneurs who fail to do so?

2. Is it ethical for small companies to present to potential employees only the "fun" aspects of a job and to gloss over its less appealing components?

3. Lindblad Expeditions and Zappos sometimes receive criticism for being too extreme in the honesty of their recruiting approaches. Do you agree? Explain.

Sources: Based on *Shackleton's Expedition*, NOVA, http://www.pbs.org/wgbh/nova/shackleton/1914; Boost Retention with Honest Job Previews," *Manager's e-Bulletin*, July 24, 2008, pp. 1–2; "Would You Give an Employee $1,000 to Quit?" *Marketing Profs*, June 2, 2008, pp. 1–2; Lisa Everitt, "Zappos Tells New Employees: Please Go Away," *BNet*, May 21, 2008, http://industry.bnet.com/retail/100066/zappos-tells-new-employees-please-go-away; Bud Bilanich, "Zappos and Employee Engagement and Commitment," Common Sense Solutions to Tough Business Problems, November 20, 2007, http://bbilanich.typepad.com/blog/2007/11/last-week-i-blo.html; and Matt Rosoff, "Tony Hsieh: Don't Rule Out a Zappos Airline," *Business Insider*, September 28, 2011, http://articles.businessinsider.com/2011-09-28/tech/30211874_1_customer-service-tony-hsieh-virgin-brand.

Experienced interviewers use the phrase "Tell me more" to harvest meaningful information about candidates.

Ask candidates to describe a recent success and a recent failure and how they dealt with them. Smart entrepreneurs look for candidates who describe their successes and their failures with equal enthusiasm because they know that peak performers put as much into their failures as they do their successes and usually learn something valuable from their failures.

Arrange a "noninterview" setting that allows several employees to observe the candidate in an informal setting. Giving candidates a plant tour, setting up a coffee break, or taking them to lunch gives more people a chance to judge a candidate's interpersonal skills and personality outside the formal interview process. These informal settings can be very revealing.

ENTREPRENEURIAL PROFILE: Scott Lerner: Solixr Scott Lerner, founder of Solixr, an all-natural energy drink company, says that he learns a great deal about job candidates in noninterview settings and often invites candidates to several lunches or to accompany him on in-store demonstrations. These informal settings give Lerner better insight into candidates' qualifications and personalities and how well they will fit into his company's culture.[68] ∎

Table 16.5 shows an example of some interview questions one business owner uses to uncover the traits and characteristics he seeks in a top-performing sales representative.

Conduct the Interview

An effective interview contains three phases: breaking the ice, asking questions, and selling the candidate on the company.

BREAKING THE ICE In the opening phase of the interview, the manager's primary job is to diffuse the tension that exists because of the nervousness of both parties. Many skilled interviewers use the job description to explain the nature of the job and the company's culture to the applicant. Then they use "icebreakers," questions about a hobby or special interest, to get the candidate to relax and begin talking.

ASKING QUESTIONS During the second phase of the interview, the employer asks the questions from the question bank to determine the applicant's suitability for the job. The interviewer's primary job at this point is to listen. Effective interviewers spend about 25 percent of the interview talking and about 75 percent listening. They also take notes during the interview to help them ask follow-up questions based on a candidate's comments and to evaluate a candidate after the interview is over. Experienced interviewers also pay close attention to a candidate's nonverbal clues, or body language, during the interview. They know candidates may be able to say exactly what they want with their words but their body language does not lie!

TABLE 16.5 Interview Questions for Candidates for a Sales Representative Position

Trait or Characteristic	Question
Outgoing; persuasive; friendly; self-starter; determined; optimistic; independent; confident	How do you persuade reluctant prospects to buy?
Good listener; patient; empathetic; organized; polished speaker; "other" oriented	What would you say to a fellow salesperson who was getting more than his share of rejections and was having difficulty getting appointments?
Honest; customer oriented; relationship builder	How do you feel when someone questions the truth of what you say? What do you do in such situations?
Other questions:	If you owned a company, why would you hire yourself?
	If you were head of your department, what would you do differently?
	How do you recognize the contributions of others in your department?
	If you weren't in sales, what other job would you be in?

Some of the most valuable interview questions are designed to gain insight into a candidate's creativity and capacity for abstract thinking. Known as **puzzle interviews**, their goal is to determine how candidates think by asking them offbeat questions, such as "You are shrunk to the height of a nickel and thrown into a blender. Your mass is reduced so that your density is the same as usual. The blades start moving in 60 seconds. What do you do?" (a classic interview question at Google).[69] "How many cows are in Canada?" is another favorite Google interview question. Other companies use questions such as "A penguin walks through that door wearing a sombrero. What does he say, and why is he here? (asked at Clark Construction Group)," "If we came to your house for dinner, what would you prepare for us?" (a question asked by interviewers at Trader Joe's), "How would you design Bill Gates's bathroom?" (a favorite at Microsoft), or "What is the angle of the two hands on a clock when the time is 11:50? (asked at Bank of America)."[70] The logic and creativity that candidates use to derive an answer to these questions is much more important than the answer itself.

puzzle interview
an interview that includes offbeat questions to determine how job candidates think and reason and to judge their capacity for creativity.

Entrepreneurs must be careful to avoid asking candidates illegal questions. At one time, interviewers could ask wide-ranging questions covering just about every area of an applicant's background. Today, interviewing is a veritable minefield of legal liabilities waiting to explode in the unsuspecting interviewer's face. Although the Equal Employment Opportunity Commission, the government agency responsible for enforcing employment laws, does not outlaw specific questions, it does recognize that some questions can result in employment discrimination. If a candidate files charges of employment discrimination against a company, the burden of proof shifts to the employer to prove that all pre-employment questions are job related and nondiscriminatory. In addition, many states have passed laws that forbid the use of certain questions or screening tools in interviews. To avoid trouble, business owners should keep in mind why they are asking a particular question. The goal is to identify individuals who are qualified to do the job well. By steering clear of questions about subjects that are peripheral to the job itself, employers are less likely to ask questions that will land them in court. Wise business owners ask their attorneys to review their bank of questions before using them in an interview. Table 16.6 provides a quiz for you to test your knowledge of the legality of certain interview questions.

SELLING THE CANDIDATE ON THE COMPANY In the final phase of the interview, the employer tries to sell desirable candidates on the company. This phase begins by allowing the candidate to ask questions about the company, the job, or other issues. Experienced interviewers note the nature of these questions and the insights they give into the candidate's personality. This part of the interview offers the employer a prime opportunity to explain to the candidate why the company is an attractive place to work. Remember that the best candidates will have other offers, and it's up to you to make sure they leave the interview wanting to work for your company. Pointing out the benefits of working for a small company, such as a flexible work schedule, regular feedback, the opportunity to contribute directly to a meaningful mission, and the chance for growth and advancement, can influence a candidate's decision. Finally, before closing the interview, the employer should thank the candidate and tell him or her what happens next (e.g., "We'll be contacting you about our decision within two weeks.").

Contact References and Conduct a Background Check

Entrepreneurs should take the time to conduct background checks and contact candidates' references. Background checks are inexpensive to perform but can save companies many thousands of dollars by identifying "red flags" in candidates' backgrounds, helping them avoid making expensive hiring mistakes. By performing a basic background check, employers can steer clear of candidates with criminal or other high-risk backgrounds. Although some states ban the practice, conducting credit checks on job candidates (which legally require the candidates' written permission) also can be quite revealing, giving employers insight into candidates' dependability and trustworthiness. A recent study by the Society of Human Resource Managers reports that 69 percent of employers conduct criminal background checks on all of their job candidates and 47 percent of employers conduct credit checks. Fourteen percent of businesses do not conduct background checks on any job candidates, and small businesses are less likely to conduct background checks than large businesses.[71] One expert says failing to conduct background checks on potential employees is the equivalent of walking up to a stranger and handing him or her the keys

TABLE 16.6 Is It Legal?

Some interview questions can lead an employer into legal problems. Test your knowledge concerning which questions are legal to ask in an interview using the following quiz.

Legal	Illegal	Interview Question
☐	☐	1. Are you currently using illegal drugs?
☐	☐	2. When was the last time you used illegal drugs?
☐	☐	3. Have you ever been arrested?
☐	☐	4. Have you ever been convicted of a crime?
☐	☐	5. Do you have any children or do you plan to have children?
☐	☐	6. Are you willing to travel as part of this job?
☐	☐	7. When and where were you born?
☐	☐	8. Is there any limit on your ability to work overtime or travel?
☐	☐	9. How tall are you? How much do you weigh?
☐	☐	10. Do you drink alcohol?
☐	☐	11. How much alcohol do you drink each week?
☐	☐	12. Would your religious beliefs interfere with your ability to do the job?
☐	☐	13. What contraceptive practices do you use?
☐	☐	14. Are you HIV positive?
☐	☐	15. Have you ever filed a lawsuit or workers' compensation claim against a former employer?
☐	☐	16. Do you have physical/mental disabilities that would interfere with doing your job?
☐	☐	17. Are you a U.S. citizen?
☐	☐	18. What is your Facebook password?

Answers: 1. Legal. Employers can screen candidates on their current use of illegal drugs. **2.** Illegal. Employers cannot ask about a candidate's past drug addiction because drug addiction is covered by the Americans with Disabilities Act; casual drug use, however, is not covered. **3.** Illegal. Employers cannot ask about an applicant's arrest record, but they can ask whether he or she has ever been convicted of a crime. **4.** Legal. Although employers cannot ask about a candidate's arrest record, they can ask whether he or she has been convicted of a crime. **5.** Illegal. Employers cannot ask questions that could lead to discrimination against a particular group (e.g., women, physically challenged, and so on). **6.** Legal. **7.** Illegal. The Civil Rights Act of 1964 bans discrimination on the basis of race, color, sex, religion, or national origin. **8.** Legal. **9.** Illegal. Unless a person's physical characteristics are necessary for job performance (e.g., lifting 100-pound sacks of mulch), employers cannot ask candidates such questions. **10.** Legal. **11.** Illegal. Notice the fine line between question 10 and question 11; this is what makes interviewing so challenging. **12.** Illegal. This question violates the Civil Rights Act of 1964. **13.** Illegal. What relevance would this have to an employee's job performance? **14.** Illegal. Under the Americans with Disabilities Act, which prohibits discrimination against people with disabilities, people who are HIV positive or have AIDS are considered "disabled." **15.** Illegal. Workers who file workers' compensation suits are protected from retribution by a variety of federal and state laws. **16.** Illegal. This question also violates the Americans with Disabilities Act. **17.** Illegal. This question violates the Civil Rights Act of 1964. **18.** Currently legal—but creepy—and creates the possibility that employers would have access to information about which they cannot legally ask, such as religion, marital status, and others, which creates a potential legal liability. Six states have banned employers from asking job candidates for their social media passwords.

to your house.[72] To avoid legal problems, employers must be able to show a connection between the type of background check conducted and the applicant's job duties and must conduct the background check for *all* applicants for the job. Employers also should have applicants sign a separate disclosure document authorizing the employer to conduct a background check.

Checking potential employees' social networking pages such as Facebook, Twitter, and LinkedIn also can provide a revealing look at their character. A study by CareerBuilder reports that 39 percent of employers investigate job candidates' social networking sites and that 43 percent have discovered something there that caused them to reject a candidate (see Figure 16.2).[73]

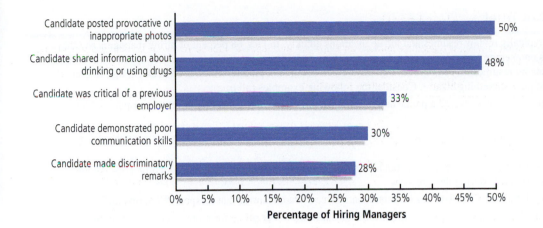

FIGURE 16.2

Why Hiring Managers Rejected Job Candidates' after Checking Their Social Media Profiles

Source: Based on "More Employers Finding Reasons Not to Hire Candidates on Social Media, Finds CareerBuilder Survey," *CareerBuilder*, June 27, 2013.

Although many business owners see checking references as a formality and pay little attention to it, others realize the need to protect themselves (and their customers) from hiring unscrupulous workers. Is it really necessary? Yes! According to a survey of hiring professionals, 53 percent of candidates either exaggerate or falsify information on their résumés.[74] Yahoo Inc. once fired its CEO just five months after hiring him when the company's board of directors discovered that his résumé contained false information about his academic credentials.[75] Checking references thoroughly can help employers uncover false or exaggerated information. Rather than contacting only the references listed, experienced employers call applicants' previous employers and talk to their immediate supervisors to get a clear picture of the applicant's job performance, character, and work habits. At Bonobos, an online menswear company, managers conduct "off-list" reference checks, contacting people who have worked with a candidate but are not listed as references on the candidate's résumé. Andy Dunn, cofounder and CEO, says that in most cases, these off-list references enhance a candidate's application, but on occasion they have alerted the company to problem areas in a candidate's background. Using LinkedIn to find common connections to former employers, colleagues, or employees is an efficient way to expand a candidate's reference pool.[76]

Many employers implement a probationary trial period for new hires that may range from two weeks to several months. Doing so increases the probability that the company has found the right person for the job. After two weeks on the job at Whole Foods Market, team members of new hires vote on whether to keep the new employees or to let them go.[77]

Experienced small business owners understand that the hiring process provides them with one of the most valuable raw materials their companies count on for success—capable, hardworking people. They know that hiring an employee is not a single event but rather the beginning of a long-term relationship. Table 16.7 features some strange but true incidents that employers have encountered during the selection process.

Creating an Organizational Culture That Encourages Employee Motivation and Retention

Culture

A company's **culture** is the distinctive, unwritten, informal code of conduct that governs its behavior, attitudes, relationships, and style. It is the essence of "the way we do things around here." In many small companies, culture plays as important a part in gaining a competitive edge as strategy does. Culture has a powerful impact on the way people work together in a business, how they do their jobs, and how they treat their customers. Company culture manifests itself in many ways—from how workers dress and act to the language they use. For instance, at some companies, the unspoken dress code requires workers to wear suits and ties, but at others employees routinely come to work in jeans and T-shirts. At CustomInk, a company founded by three former college classmates, Marc Katz, Mike Driscoll, and Dave Christensen, that makes custom T-shirts, the dress code includes jeans, flip-flops, and (no surprise) T-shirts. However, the company

LO3

Explain how to create a company culture that encourages employee retention.

culture

the distinctive, unwritten, informal code of conduct that governs an organization's behavior, attitudes, relationships, and style.

TABLE 16.7 Strange but True!

Human resource managers typically review résumés and job applications quickly. In fact, 68 percent of hiring managers say they spend less than two minutes on average reviewing a résumé or application, and 17 percent of hiring managers spend no more than 30 seconds on average reviewing resumes. If you read enough résumés, conduct enough interviews, and check enough references, sooner or later you will encounter something bizarre. Consider the following examples (all true):

- During the interview, one candidate answered a phone call to set up an interview with a competitor of the company with which he was interviewing.
- One candidate for a management position listed "gator hunting" as a skill on his résumé. Another candidate included "versatile toes" as a strength on her résumé.
- One applicant's résumé was written in Klingon, a fictional language spoken by humanoid warriors from *Star Trek*. Another candidate acted out a *Star Trek* role during the interview.
- When interviewing for a job that required working in Antarctica, one candidate claimed that he spoke "Antarctican."
- After having lunch with a job candidate, a business owner took the applicant to her office for more discussion. The discussion ended, however, when the applicant dozed off and began snoring.
- One candidate decorated her résumé with pink rabbits. Another applicant revealed that her résumé was set up to be sung to the tune of "The Brady Bunch."
- One candidate walked into the interviewer's office, picked up the candy dish on her desk, and emptied its entire contents into her pocket.
- When asked what person, living or dead, he would most like to meet, one candidate replied, "The living one."
- One applicant checked his Facebook page during the interview, and another kept her iPod headphones in her ears during the interview.
- One candidate popped his false teeth out of his mouth when discussing dental benefits with the interviewer.
- One candidate wore a Boy Scout uniform to his interview but never explained to the interviewers why.
- A candidate explained that promptness was one of her strengths—even though she showed up 10 minutes late for the interview.
- On his résumé, a candidate for an accounting position described himself as "detail-oriented" and spelled the company's name incorrectly.
- During an interview, one candidate asked the interviewer, "What company is this again?" Another asked the interviewer if he could have a sip of the interviewer's coffee.
- During the interview, one candidate told the interviewer that he wanted a job that did not require him to "work a lot."
- One candidate asked if he could bring his rabbit to work with him, adding that the rabbit was focused and reliable but that he himself had been fired before.
- One man who forgot to wear socks to his interview remedied the problem by coloring his ankles with a black felt-tip marker.
- One candidate asked the interviewer for a hug at the end of the interview.

Recommendations from previous employers can sometimes be quite entertaining too. The following are statements from managers about workers:

- "Works well when under constant supervision and cornered like a rat in a trap."
- "This young lady has delusions of adequacy."
- "A photographic memory but with the lens cover glued on."
- "If you were to give him a penny for his thoughts, you'd get change."
- "If you stand close enough to him, you can hear the ocean."
- "He's so dense that light bends around him."

Sources: Based on "Employers Share Most Memorable Interview Blunders," CareerBuilder, January 16, 2014, http://www.careerbuilder.com/share/aboutus/pressreleasesdetail.aspx?sd=1/16/2014&id=pr798&ed=12/31/2014; "CareerBuilder Releases Study of Common and Not-So-Common Resume Mistakes That Can Cost You the Job," CareerBuilder, September 11, 2013, http://www.careerbuilder.com/share/aboutus/pressreleasesdetail.aspx?id=pr780&sd=9/11/2013&ed=09/11/2013; "Hiring Managers Rank Best and Worst Words to Use in a Résumé in New CareerBuilder Survey," *CareerBuilder*, March 13, 2014, http://www.careerbuilder.com/share/aboutus/pressreleasesdetail.aspx?sd=3%2f13%2f2014&siteid=cbpr&sc_cmp1=cb_pr809_&id=pr809&ed=12%2f31%2f2014; "10 Strangest Job Interview Fails," *CBS News*, January 7, 2013, http://www.cbsnews.com/pictures/10-strangest-job-interview-fails/2/; "CareerBuilder Releases Study of Most Outrageous Resume Mistakes and Creative Techniques That Work," CareerBuilder, July 11, 2012, http://www.careerbuilder.com/share/aboutus/pressreleasesdetail.aspx?sd=7/11/2012&id=pr707&ed=12/31/2012; "Hiring Managers Share Most Unusual Résumé Mistakes in Annual CareerBuilder Survey," *CareerBuilder*, August 24, 2011, http://www.careerbuilder.com/share/aboutus/pressreleasesdetail.aspx?id=pr653&sd=8/24/2011&ed=8/24/2099; "Survey Reveals Wackiest Job Interview Mistakes," *SmartPros*, March 13, 2008, http://accounting.smartpros.com/x61115.xml; "Hiring Horrors," *Your Company*, April 1999, p. 14; Mike B. Hall, "From Job Applicants," Joke-of-the-Day, December 8, 2000, http://www.jokeoftheday.com; Karen Axelton, "L-L-L-Losers!," *Business Start-Ups*, April 2000, p. 13; "Great Places to Work: Interview Horror Stories," *Washingtonian*, November 1, 2005, http://www.washingtonian.com/articles/businesscareers/2159.html; and "Hiring Managers Share the Most Memorable Interview Mistakes in Annual CareerBuilder Survey," *CareerBuilder*, February 22, 2012, http://www.careerbuilder.com/share/aboutus/pressreleasesdetail.aspx?id=pr680&sd=2/22/2012&ed=12/31/2012.

slogan, "Don't let the flip-flops fool ya,'" characterizes the company's strong work ethic and expectation of high performance.[78] Although it is an intangible characteristic, a company's culture has a powerful influence on everyone the company touches, especially its employees, and on the company's ultimate success.

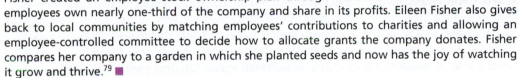

ENTREPRENEURIAL PROFILE: Eileen Fisher: Eileen Fisher At Eileen Fisher, a clothing company named for its dynamic founder, the culture conveys a strong sense of family, unity, and social responsibility. Founder Eileen Fisher relies on a participative style of management, and employees, who work in six offices and 63 stores across the United States, enjoy flexible work schedules and a unique set of benefits, including a generous $3,000 clothing allowance on top of their employee discounts and paid sabbaticals. They also receive an annual $1,000 wellness allowance and free in-office or in-store massages every month. In 2006, Fisher created an employee stock ownership plan through which her employees own nearly one-third of the company and share in its profits. Eileen Fisher also gives back to local communities by matching employees' contributions to charities and allowing an employee-controlled committee to decide how to allocate grants the company donates. Fisher compares her company to a garden in which she planted seeds and now has the joy of watching it grow and thrive.[79] ■

An important ingredient in a company's culture is the performance objectives an entrepreneur sets and against which employees are measured. If entrepreneurs want integrity, respect, honesty, customer service, and other important values to be the foundation on which a positive culture can flourish, they must establish measures of success that reflect those core values. *Effective executives know that building a positive organizational culture has a direct, positive impact on the financial performance of an organization.* The intangible factors that make up an organization's culture have an influence, either positive or negative, on the tangible outcomes of profitability, cash flow, return on equity, employee productivity, innovation, and cost control. An entrepreneur's job is to create a culture that has a positive influence on the company's tangible outcomes.

Sustaining a company's culture begins with the hiring process. Beyond the normal requirements of competitive pay and working conditions, the hiring process must focus on finding employees who share the *values* of the organization. In winning workplaces, entrepreneurs build a culture of trust, treat their workers fairly, respect their personal lives, provide opportunities for growth and advancement, and provide them with jobs that are interesting, meaningful, and fun. The result is a team of people who give their best ideas and efforts to the business.[80]

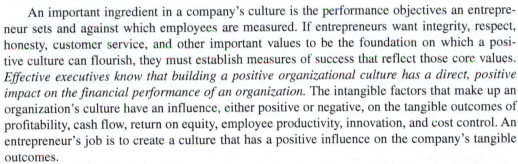

ENTREPRENEURIAL PROFILE: Aaron Levie and Dylan Smith: Box.net At Box.net, a cloud software development company in Los Altos, California, cofounders Aaron Levie and Dylan Smith expect their employees to invest long hours to meet their weekly project deadlines. In their hiring process, they look for software engineers who are highly competitive and hard driving—the "I-can't-rest-until-I've-noodled-out-an-answer" types. To attract those types of workers, Levie and Smith say they spend a significant portion of their time building the right culture. They reward their hardworking employees with perks such as swing sets and ping-pong tables to relieve stress, free dinners, and facilities so that workers can sleep and shower if they stay late to work on a project. Box.net also encourages collaboration and innovation with its semiannual Hackathon, an event in which teams of employees take new product ideas from early stage to implementation in a single night. Levie and Smith have successfully created a culture of "we're all in this together" in which the company's approval rating among employees is an impressive 97 percent.[81] ■

Creating a culture that supports a company's strategy is no easy task, but entrepreneurs who have been most successful at it believe that having a set of overarching beliefs serves as a powerful guide for everyday action. Culture arises from an entrepreneur's consistent and relentless pursuit of a set of core values that everyone in the company can believe in. "Values outlive business models," says management guru Gary Hamel.[82]

Nurturing the right culture in a company can enhance a company's competitive position by improving its ability to attract and retain quality workers and by creating an environment in which workers can grow and develop. As a new generation of employees enters the workforce, companies are discovering that more relaxed, open cultures have an edge in attracting the best workers. These companies embrace nontraditional, fun cultures that incorporate concepts such as casual dress, team-based assignments, telecommuting, flexible work schedules, free meals, company outings, and many other unique options. Barbara Corcoran, a regular on the television show *Shark Tank*, built her company, The Corcoran Group, into the largest residential real estate brokerage firm in New York by creating a fun, engaging culture, which is a reflection of her leadership style. "The more fun I created in the company, the more creative and innovative it became," she says. "Fun is the most underutilized tool in the leadership tool belt," according to Corcoran, who started her business with a $1,000 loan and ultimately sold it for $66 million.[83]

Modern organizational culture relies on several principles that are fundamental to creating a productive, fun workplace that enables employees and the company to excel.

RESPECT FOR WORK AND LIFE BALANCE Successful companies recognize that their employees have lives away from work. Generation X and Millennial workers, in particular, want to work for companies that erase the traditional barriers between home life and work life by making it easier for them to deal with the pressures they face away from their jobs. These businesses offer flexible work schedules, part-time jobs, job sharing, telecommuting, sabbaticals, and on-site day care and dry cleaning.

ENTREPRENEURIAL PROFILE: Pamela Noble: Noble-Davis Consulting Noble-Davis Consulting, a retirement plan administration and consulting service founded by Pamela Noble, not only attracts top-quality talent but also reaps the benefits of high productivity and employee retention by emphasizing work–life balance. The company provides its employees with flexible work schedules, self-determined vacations, and the opportunity to work from home when appropriate, benefits that allow employees to more easily balance their work–life demands. Meeting team goals calls for special celebrations, including bowling and movie nights or Whirlyball outings. Employees also can earn year-end performance bonuses, some of which have exceeded $20,000.[84] ∎

A SENSE OF PURPOSE As you learned in Chapter 5, one of the most important jobs an entrepreneur faces is defining the company's vision and then communicating it effectively to everyone the company touches. Effective companies use a strong sense of purpose to make employees feel connected to the company's mission. Anne Wojcicki, founder of 23andMe, a company based in Mountain View, California, that provides genetic testing services, emphasizes the importance of linking every employee's job to the company's mission ("to be the world's trusted source of personal genetic information"). Everyone in the company, including Wojcicki, sets individual and team goals for the next six months that are distributed throughout the company. Each week, everyone in the company writes a weekly summary of his or her progress toward those goals. Every employee receives the summaries, and Wokcicki spends an hour reading them and following up with questions.[85]

A SENSE OF FUN For some companies, the line between work and play is blurred. The founders of these businesses see no reason for work and fun to be mutually exclusive. In fact, they believe that a workplace that creates a sense of fun makes it easier to recruit quality workers and encourages them to be more productive and more customer oriented. "Healthy and sustainable organizations focus on the fundamentals: quality, service, fiscal responsibility, leadership—but they didn't forget to add fun to that formula," says Leslie Yerkes, a consultant and author.[86] Once a month, former collegiate athlete Missy Park, founder of Title Nine, a maker of women's fitness and athletic apparel, and her employees in the company's Berkeley, California, offices participate in impromptu exercises, such as bouncy ball races. Once a year, employees compete in the Title Nine Olympics, which includes kickball, dodge ball, tugs-of-war, office chair foosball, and other unusual sports. The winning team gets a paid day off.[87]

ENGAGEMENT Employees who are fully engaged in their work take pride in making valuable contributions to the organization's success and derive personal satisfaction from doing so.

Although engaged employees are a key ingredient in superior business performance, just 30 percent of employees in North America are fully engaged in their work, and 18 percent actually are disengaged.[88] Research shows that disengaged employees have higher turnover, accident, and absenteeism rates than the average employee, are more likely to steal from their employers, and are more likely to drive customers away. Disengaged workers also are less productive than engaged employees, costing U.S. companies between $450 billion and $550 billion a year.[89] Employees become disengaged when they are disconnected from the company's culture, when they lack opportunities for growth and advancement, when they don't believe the company values, and when they believe they are not compensated fairly for their contributions. What can managers do to improve employee engagement?

- Recognize and reward employees for top performance.

- Constantly communicate the purpose and vision of the organization and why it matters.

- Challenge employees to learn and advance in their careers and give them the resources and the incentives to do so.

- Create a culture that encourages and rewards engagement.

Engaged employees are the drivers of innovative ideas and new customers and revenues that every company, especially small ones, require to thrive. Research shows that companies with higher percentages of engaged employees generate higher earnings per share than those with lower percentages of engaged employees.[90] Figure 16.3 shows the factors that drive employee engagement.

DIVERSITY Companies with appealing cultures not only accept cultural diversity in their workforces but embrace it, actively seeking out workers with different backgrounds. Today, businesses must recognize that a workforce that has a rich mix of cultural diversity gives the company more talent, skills, and abilities from which to draw. A study of the demographics of the United States reveals a steady march toward an increasingly diverse population. In fact, demographic trends suggest that by 2043, minority groups, including Hispanics, African Americans, Asians, and other nonwhite groups, will make up the majority (53 percent) of the U.S. population.[91] For companies to remain relevant in this environment, their workforces must reflect this diversity (see Figure 16.4). Who is better equipped to deal with a diverse, multicultural customer base than a diverse, multicultural workforce?

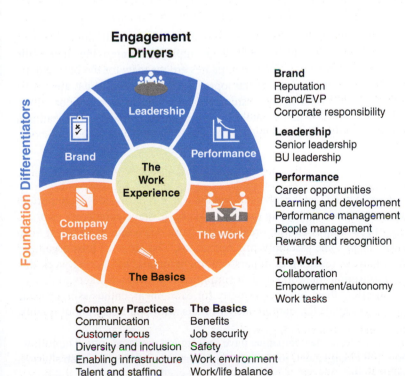

Engagement Drivers

Foundation Differentiators

Brand
Reputation
Brand/EVP
Corporate responsibility

Leadership
Senior leadership
BU leadership

Performance
Career opportunities
Learning and development
Performance management
People management
Rewards and recognition

The Work
Collaboration
Empowerment/autonomy
Work tasks

Company Practices
Communication
Customer focus
Diversity and inclusion
Enabling infrastructure
Talent and staffing

The Basics
Benefits
Job security
Safety
Work environment
Work/life balance

FIGURE 16.3

Drivers of Employee Engagement

Aon Hewitt, a leading human resources consulting firm, has developed the following model of employee engagement on the basis of responses from more than 7 million employees in more than 6,000 companies around the world. The model shows six drivers of engagement (the basics, company practices, the work, performance, leadership, and brand) in employees' work experience and their outcomes: *Say* – Engaged employees speak positively about the organization.
Stay – Engaged employees have an intense sense of belonging to the organization.
Strive – Engaged employees are motivated and work to achieve success in their jobs.
The model also identifies four categories of positive business outcomes (talent, operational, customer, and financial) that result from highly engaged employees.

Source: From *Trends in Global Employee Engagement,* 2011, p. 7. Copyright © 2011 by Aon-Hewitt Associates. Reprinted with permission from Aon-Hewitt.

FIGURE 16.4

Composition of U.S. Workforce

Source: Based on Crosby Burns, Kimberly Barton, and Sophia Kerby, "The State of Diversity in Today's Workforce," Center for American Progress, July 12, 2012, p. 4; Steve H. Murdock, "Population Change in the United States: Implications for Education, the Labor Force, and Economic Development," Hobby Center for the Study of Texas at Rice University, November 10, 2011, p. 59.

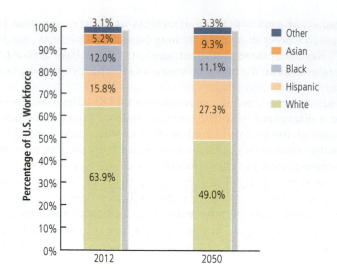

INTEGRITY Employees want to work for companies that stand for honesty and integrity. They do not want to check their own personal values systems at the door when they report to work. Indeed, many workers take pride in the fact that they work for companies that are ethical and socially responsible. People want to work for a company that makes a difference in the world rather than merely making a product or providing a service. Putney, a Portland, Maine, company that makes generic drugs for pets, gives both money and time back to the local community and gives its 57 employees paid time off to volunteer at local nonprofit organizations, including its partner agency, the Animal Refuge League of Greater Portland.[92]

PARTICIPATIVE MANAGEMENT Today's workers do not respond well to the autocratic management styles of yesteryear. Company owners and managers must learn to trust and empower employees at all levels of the organization to make decisions and to take the actions they need to do their jobs well. As a company grows, managers must empower employees at all levels to act without direct supervision. A study by consulting firm McKinsey and Company reports a strong correlation among the quality of a decision, clarity concerning the person responsible for implementing the decision, and that person's involvement in the decision-making process.[93]

LEARNING ENVIRONMENT Progressive companies encourage and support lifelong learning among their employees. They are willing to invest in their employees, improving their skills and helping them to reach their full potential. These companies are magnets for the best and the brightest young workers who know that to stay at the top of their fields, they must always be learning. Every year, Noble-Davis Consulting, the retirement plan administration and consulting firm, creates a budget for each employee to participate in outside training, classes, and educational courses. To enhance employees' skills, the company also sponsors monthly in-house workshops, seminars, and Webinars.[94]

Job Design

Over the years, managers have learned that the job itself and the way it is designed is an important factor in a company's ability to attract and retain quality workers. In some companies, work is organized on the principle of **job simplification**, breaking the work down into its simplest form and standardizing each task, as in some assembly-line operations. The scope of jobs organized in such a way is extremely narrow, resulting in impersonal, monotonous, and boring work that creates little challenge or motivation for workers. Job simplification invites workers to "check their brains at the door" and offers them little opportunity for excitement, enthusiasm, or pride in their work. The result can be apathetic, unmotivated workers who don't care about quality, customers, or costs.

To break this destructive cycle, some companies have redesigned workers' jobs. The following strategies are common: job enlargement, job rotation, job enrichment, flextime, job sharing, and flexplace.

job simplification
the type of job design that breaks work down into its simplest form and standardizes each task.

Job enlargement (horizontal job loading) adds more tasks to a job to broaden its scope. For instance, rather than an employee simply mounting four screws in computers coming down an assembly line, a worker might assemble, install, and test the entire motherboard (perhaps as part of a team). The idea is to make the job more varied and to allow employees to perform a more complete unit of work.

Job rotation involves cross training employees so that they can move from one job in the company to others, giving them a greater number and variety of tasks to perform. As employees learn other jobs within an organization, both their skills and their understanding of the company's purpose and processes rise. Cross-trained workers are more valuable because they give a company the flexibility to shift workers from low-demand jobs to those where they are most needed. As an incentive for workers to learn to perform other jobs within an operation, some companies offer skill-based pay, a system under which the more skills workers acquire, the more they earn.

Job enrichment (vertical job loading) involves building motivators into a job by increasing the planning, decision-making, organizing, and controlling functions—traditionally managerial tasks—that workers perform. The idea is to make every employee a manager (at least one of his or her own job).

To enrich employees' jobs, a business owner must build five core characteristics into them:

- *Skill variety* is the degree to which a job requires a variety of different skills, talents, and activities from the worker. Does the job require the worker to perform a variety of tasks that demand a variety of skills and abilities, or does it force him or her to perform the same task repeatedly?

- *Task identity* is the degree to which a job allows the worker to complete a whole or identifiable piece of work. Does the employee build an entire piece of furniture (perhaps as part of a team), or does he or she merely attach four screws?

- *Task significance* is the degree to which a job substantially influences the lives or work of others—other employees or final customers. Does the employee get to deal with customers, either internal or external? One effective way to establish task significance is to put employees in touch with customers so they can see how customers use the product or service they make.

- *Autonomy* is the degree to which a job gives a worker the freedom, independence, and discretion in planning and performing tasks. Does the employee make decisions affecting his or her work, or must he or she rely on someone else (e.g., the owner, a manager, or a supervisor) to "call the shots"? At Intuit, employees have the autonomy to spend 10 percent of their time working on projects they believe will benefit the company.[95]

- *Feedback* is the degree to which a job gives the worker direct, timely information about the quality of his or her performance. Does the job give the employee feedback about the quality of his or her work, or does the product (and all information about it) simply disappear after it leaves the worker's station?

A study conducted by researchers at the University of New Hampshire and the Bureau of Labor Statistics concludes that employees of companies that use job enrichment principles are more satisfied than those who work in jobs designed using principles of simplification.[96]

Flextime is an arrangement under which employees work a normal number of hours but have flexibility about when they start and stop work. Most flextime arrangements require employees to build their work schedules around a set of "core hours," such as 10 a.m. to 2 p.m., but give them the freedom to set their schedules outside of those core hours. For instance, one worker might choose to come in at 7 a.m. and leave at 3 p.m. to attend her son's soccer game, and another may work from 11 a.m. to 7 p.m. Flextime not only raises worker morale but also makes it easier for companies to attract high-quality young workers who want rewarding careers without sacrificing their lifestyles. In addition, companies using flextime schedules often experience lower levels of tardiness, turnover, and absenteeism.

ENTREPRENEURIAL PROFILE: Pamela Blackwell: Blackwell Consulting Services
Pamela Blackwell, president of Blackwell Consulting Services, an information technology consulting firm in Chicago that her father Bob started in 1992, says flextime plays an important

job enlargement (horizontal job loading)
the type of job design that adds more tasks to a job to broaden its scope.

job rotation
the type of job design that involves cross training employees so that they can move from one job in the company to others, giving them a greater number and variety of tasks to perform.

job enrichment (vertical job loading)
the type of job design that involves building motivators into a job by increasing the planning, decision-making, organizing, and controlling functions that workers perform.

flextime
an arrangement under which employees work a normal number of hours but have flexibility about when they start and stop work.

part in attracting skilled, high-tech workers whom the company relies on for its success. "We're more focused on the job and delivering on client expectations than on how, when, and where our employees work," she says.[97] ■

Flextime is becoming an increasingly popular job design strategy, especially among small companies. A recent study by the Families and Work Institute found that 77 percent of U.S. businesses give at least some of their employees flexible schedules, up from 68 percent in 1998. However, 32 percent of small companies (fewer than 100 employees) offer most or all of their employees flexible schedules, compared to just 16 percent of large companies (more than 1,000 employees).[98] The number of companies using flextime will continue to grow as companies find recruiting capable, qualified full-time workers more difficult and as technology makes working from a dedicated office space less important. Research shows that when considering job offers, candidates, particularly members of Generation Y, weigh heavily the flexibility of the work schedule that companies offer.[99]

Job sharing is a work arrangement in which two or more people share a single full-time job. For instance, two college students might share the same 40-hour-a-week job, one working mornings and the other working afternoons. Salary and benefits are prorated between the workers sharing a job. Because job sharing is a simple solution to the growing challenge of life–work balance, it is becoming more popular. Companies already using it are finding it easier to recruit and retain qualified workers.

Flexplace is a work arrangement in which employees work at a place other than the traditional office, such as a satellite branch closer to their homes or, in many cases, at home. Flexplace is an easy job design strategy for companies to use because of **telecommuting**. Using modern communication technology such as WiFi, smart phones, texting, intranets, e-mail online workspaces, and project management software, employees have more flexibility in choosing where they work. Today, connecting electronically to the workplace (and to all of the people and the information there) from practically anywhere on the planet is quite simple for many workers. Research by market research firm Ipsos shows that 60 percent of employees around the world would telecommute if their employers allowed it.[100] The Telework Research Network estimates that 45 percent of workers in the United States have the potential to telecommute at least some of the time.[101] However, only 4 percent of employees in North America telecommute full-time (26 percent telecommute at least once per week), well below the global average of 7 percent (36.5 percent telecommute at least once per week).[102] Telecommuting employees get the flexibility they seek, and they also benefit from reduced commuting times and expenses, not to mention a less expensive wardrobe (bathrobes and bunny slippers compared to business suits and wingtips). Companies reap many benefits as well, including improved employee morale, less absenteeism, lower turnover, higher productivity, and more satisfied, more loyal employees. Studies show that telecommuting can reduce employee turnover by 20 percent and increase productivity between 15 and 20 percent.[103] Even though many small companies are ideally suited for telecommuting, large companies use this job design strategy more than small companies.[104]

ENTREPRENEURIAL PROFILE: Anne Wojcicki: 23andMe Anne Wojcicki, founder of 23andMe, the genetic testing service, offers her company's 70 employees both flextime and flexplace options. Wojcicki herself often works from home, not coming into the office until late morning or early afternoon. She says she actually encourages people to work wherever they can be most productive, whether it is at a café, at home, or in the office.[105] ■

Motivating Employees to Higher Levels of Performance: Rewards and Compensation

Another important aspect of creating a culture that attracts and retains quality workers is establishing a robust system of rewards and compensation. The rewards that an employee gets from the job itself are intrinsic rewards, but managers have at their disposal a wide variety of extrinsic rewards (those outside the job itself) to attract, retain, and motivate workers. The keys to using rewards to motivate are linking them to performance and tailoring them to the needs and characteristics of the workers. Entrepreneurs must base rewards and compensation on what is really important to their employees. For instance, to a technician making $30,000, a chance to earn a

---

job sharing
a work arrangement in which two or more people share a single full-time job.

flexplace
a work arrangement in which employees work at a place other than the traditional office, such as a satellite branch closer to their homes or at home.

telecommuting
an arrangement in which employees working remotely use modern communications equipment to connect electronically to their workplaces.

$3,000 performance bonus would most likely be a powerful motivator. To an executive earning $175,000 a year, it may not be.

One of the most popular rewards is money. Not surprisingly, a recent survey by the Society for Human Resource Management reports that 96 percent of employees rated compensation as either important or very important to their job satisfaction.[106] Cash is an effective motivator—up to a point. Simple performance bonuses are a common reward at many companies. The closer the bonus payment is to the action that prompted it, the more effective it will be.

Some companies have moved to **pay-for-performance compensation systems**, in which employees' pay depends on how well they perform their jobs. In other words, extra productivity equals extra pay. By linking employees' compensation directly to the company's financial performance, a business owner increases the likelihood that workers will achieve performance targets that are in their best interest and in the company's best interest. Pay-for-performance systems work only when employees see a clear connection between their job performance and their pay, however. That's where small businesses have an advantage over large businesses. Because they work for small companies, employees can see more clearly the impact that their performances have on the company's profitability and ultimate success than their counterparts at large corporations.

Some companies offer their employees financial rewards in the form of **profit-sharing plans** in which employees receive a portion of the company's profits. At Badger Mining, a family-owned sand extractor located in Berlin, Wisconsin, employees participate in a generous quarterly profit-sharing plan. The company also offers performance-based bonuses in addition to the profit-sharing program. The result is an employee turnover rate that is virtually nil, with 95 percent of employees saying they intend to retire from Badger Mining.[107] A few companies have gone even further, coupling profit sharing plans with **open-book management**, a system in which entrepreneurs share openly their companies' financial results with employees. The goal is teach employees how their job performances have a direct impact on profits and to give them an incentive for improving the company's bottom line. "Open book [management] gives everyone the chance to see what we need to do to succeed," says Jack Stack, CEO of SRC Holdings, a holding company of 26 employee-owned businesses and a longtime advocate of open-book management.[108]

Money isn't the only motivator business owners have at their disposal, of course. In fact, money tends to be only a short-term motivator. In addition to the financial compensation they provide, most companies offer their employees a wide array of benefits, ranging from stock options and health insurance to retirement plans and tuition reimbursement. **Stock options**, a plan under which the employees can purchase shares of a company's stock at a fixed price, have become a popular benefit for employees. Employees at Putney, Inc., a business in Portland, Maine, that makes generic drugs for pets, receive stock options in the fast-growing company.[109] Stock options take on real value once the market price of a company's stock exceeds the exercise price, the price at which employees can purchase stock. (Note that if the fair market price of a stock never exceeds the exercise price, the stock option is useless.) When trying to attract and retain quality employees, many small companies rely on stock options to gain an edge over larger companies offering bigger salaries. Stock options produce a huge payoff for employees when companies succeed. Workers at highly successful companies such as Microsoft, Google, and Dell have retired as multimillionaires thanks to stock options.

Benefits packages also are an important part in attracting and retaining quality workers and achieving high productivity. A recent survey by MetLife shows that employees who are satisfied with their benefits demonstrate more loyalty to their employers and are less likely to leave than those who are not. The most important benefit? Health insurance.[110] Integrated Project

pay-for-performance compensation systems compensation systems in which employees' pay depends on how well they perform their jobs.

profit-sharing plan a reward system in which employees receive a portion of the company's profits.

open-book management a system in which entrepreneurs share openly their companies' financial results with employees.

stock options a plan under which employees can purchase shares of a company's stock at a fixed price.

Management, a project management consulting firm based in Burr Ridge, Illinois, not only covers 100 percent of healthcare premiums for its employees and their families but also offers a comprehensive wellness program designed to keep workers healthy.[111]

In an economy in which they must compete aggressively for employees, entrepreneurs must recognize that compensation and benefits no longer follow a "one-size-fits-all" pattern. The diversity of today's workforce requires employers to be highly flexible and innovative with the compensation and benefits they provide. To attract and retain quality workers, creative entrepreneurs offer employees benefits designed to appeal to their employees' particular needs. This diversity has led to the popularity of **cafeteria benefit plans**, in which employers provide certain base benefits and then allocate a specific dollar amount for employees to select the benefits that suit their needs best. To provide the best package of benefits most efficiently, employers should survey their employees periodically to discover which benefits are most important to them and then build their benefits package to include them. Online shoe retailer Zappos, which is consistently listed as one of *Fortune*'s "Top 100 Companies to Work For," conducts benefits surveys of its employees throughout the year and adjusts its benefits package accordingly.[112]

Beyond flexible benefits plans, many small companies are setting themselves apart from others by offering unique benefits, including the following:

- At every five-year anniversary with the company, employees at Ruby Receptionists, an agency based in Portland, Oregon, that provides virtual receptionist services for small businesses, receive a five-week paid sabbatical during which they are encouraged to explore some aspect of the company's core values ("foster happiness, create community, innovate, and practice WOW-ism") and apply them to a goal that they might not otherwise have time to accomplish. The company also supplements employees' sabbaticals with $1,000 to help them reach their goals, whether it involves traveling to a far-away land, taking a class, or assisting a nonprofit organization.[113]

- ENGEO, an engineering consulting company in San Ramon, California, provides a "dream manager," who works with employees to help them realize their personal and professional goals, from buying a home to advancing in their careers. Employees also own a portion of the company through an employee stock ownership plan and participate in company-sponsored ice cream socials and chili cook-offs.[114]

- Employees at ClifBar, a company founded by copreneurs Gary Erickson and Kit Crawford that makes energy bars, can scale a 22-foot-high climbing wall in the company gym. Employees also get 2.5 hours of paid time each week to work out in the gym, which is staffed by five personal trainers. To celebrate the company's twentieth anniversary, Erickson and Crawford gave all 340 employees commuter bicycles.[115]

Many small business owners whose companies may not be able to afford benefits such as these find other ways to reward their employees, including vacation days on their birthdays, an occasional catered lunch (especially after completing a big project successfully), and free tickets to a local game, movie, or performance.

Besides the wages, salaries, and attractive benefits they use as motivators, creative entrepreneurs have discovered that intangible incentives can be more important sources of employee motivation. After its initial impact, money loses its effectiveness; it does not have a lasting motivational effect (which for small businesses, with their limited resources, is a plus). For many workers, the most meaningful motivational factors are the simplest ones—recognition, praise, feedback, job security, promotions, and others—things that any small business, no matter how limited its budget, can do. Dylan Johnson, a bartender at the Truck Yard, a unique bar in Dallas, Texas, that includes an indoor bar and an outdoor beer garden with a tree house bar and an Airstream bar, says simple recognition from a manager, such as a "thank you" for staying an extra hour or doing something beyond the normal requirements of the job inspires workers to excel.[116] One recent study concludes that recognition leads to increased employee satisfaction. The study also shows that employees who have been recognized at work within the previous six months are more likely to be highly engaged in their work.[117]

Praise is another simple yet powerful motivational tool. People enjoy getting praise, especially from a manager or business owner; it's just human nature. As Mark Twain said, "I can live

cafeteria benefit plan
a plan under which employers provide certain basic benefits and then allocate a specific dollar amount for employees to select the benefits that best suit their needs.

for two months on a good compliment."* Praise is an easy and inexpensive reward for employees who produce extraordinary work. A short note to an employee for a job well done costs practically nothing, yet it can be a potent source of motivation. Barbara Corcoran, founder of The Corcoran Group, awarded her company's top performers each week with colored ribbons and annual "Salesperson of the Year" trophies as if they had just won an Olympic event. Corcoran realized that recognition often is a better motivator than money after visiting her top salesperson's home and seeing a large cabinet in the middle of her living room in which she proudly displayed the five "Salesperson of the Year" trophies she had won.[118] How often have you had an employer recognize you and say "thank you" for a job you performed well?

Because they lack the financial resources of bigger companies, small business owners must be more creative when it comes to giving rewards that motivate workers. In many cases, however, using rewards other than money gives small businesses an advantage because they usually have more impact on employee performance over time. Rewards do not have to be expensive to be effective. At ENGEO, the engineering consulting firm, employees who provide extraordinary service to clients receive the coveted "ENGEO Rocks" traveling rock award, an actual rock (the company provides geotechnical and hydrologic consulting services) that the outstanding employee proudly displays at his or her work station.[119] Managers are not the only ones who can provide rewards. At Etsy, the online marketplace for handmade artisanal products based in Brooklyn, New York, workers recognize one another's accomplishments by sending an e-mail to the Ministry of Unusual Business, a secretive group that rewards high-performing individuals (and sometimes the entire company) with prizes and gifts.[120]

Entrepreneurs tend to rely more on nonmonetary rewards, such as praise, recognition, game tickets, dinners, letters of commendation, and others, to create a work environment in which employees take pride in their work, enjoy it, are challenged by it, and get excited about it. In other words, the employees act like owners of the business.

Management Succession: Passing the Torch of Leadership

More than 80 percent of all companies in the world are family owned, and their contributions to the global economy are significant. Family-owned businesses account for 70 to 90 percent of global GDP. In the United States alone, family businesses make up 90 percent of all businesses, create 64 percent of the nation's gross domestic product, employ 62 percent of the private sector workforce, and account for 65 percent of all wages paid. Not all family-owned businesses are small, however; 33 percent of *Fortune* 500 companies are family businesses. Family-owned companies such as Wal-Mart, Ford, Mars, Cargill, and Winn-Dixie employ thousands of people and generate billions of dollars in annual revenue.[121] Family firms also create 78 percent of the U.S. economy's net new jobs and are responsible for many famous products, including Heinz ketchup, Levi's jeans, and classic toys, such as the Slinky and the Wiffle Ball.[122]

Unfortunately, the stumbling block for most family businesses is management succession. Just when they are ready to make the transition from one generation of leaders to the next, family businesses are most vulnerable. Only about 30 percent of first-generation businesses survive into the second generation; of those that do survive, only 12 percent make it to the third generation, and just 3 percent make it to the fourth generation and beyond.[123]

ENTREPRENEURIAL PROFILE: Mark Valade: Carhartt Carhartt, a maker of more than 800 products ranging from rugged canvas clothing and fire-resistant apparel to hoodies and boots, is a family business that has beaten the odds and survived into the fourth generation of family ownership. CEO Mark Valade is the great-grandson of Hamilton Carhartt, who started the company in 1889 when he came up with the idea of making durable overalls for railroad workers. Every generation of Carhartt leaders since has overcome demanding challenges such as surviving the depths of the Great Depression and battling the influx of cheap, imported competing goods from the Far East in the 1980s. Valade says one key to Carhartt's longevity and continued success is its consistent commitment to its core values and a focus on making the best apparel for active workers. Valade's daughter, Gretchen, representing the fifth generation of family ownership, recently graduated from college and now works for Carhartt.[124] ∎

LO4

Describe the steps in developing a management succession plan for a growing business that allows a smooth transition of leadership to the next generation.

---

*Source: Mark Twain, *Letter to Gertrude Natkin*, 2 March 1906.

Hands On . . . How To

Make Your Small Business a Great Place to Work

Smart entrepreneurs know that although they may be the driving force behind their businesses, their highly committed and engaged employees are the *real* keys to their companies' success. As a result, these entrepreneurs carefully select their employees, develop their talents through training and education, and create a culture that reflects the central role their employees play in the success of their businesses. Following are 10 lessons for creating a great workplace drawn from small companies that have been recognized as some of the best places to work.

Lesson 1. Take a long-term view of your business.
Owners of small, privately held companies have a distinct advantage over managers in large, publicly held firms in that they can make decisions that are in the best interest of their companies and their employees for the long haul rather than managing to meet quarterly financial expectations. These companies are willing to sacrifice short-term results for long-term stability and success. The entrepreneurs behind them also know that their companies' success hinges on their employees, and their company cultures reflect their emphasis on their workers. At CustomInk, the customized T-shirt company, the founders show their confidence in their employees by following a promotion from within policy; 65 percent of the company's current managers started in entry-level positions with the company. Great companies also create a culture of trust among their workers. Nugget Market, a small chain of grocery stores in Sacramento, California, has never had a layoff since the father-son team of William and Mack Stille opened the first store in 1926. Nugget Market's employee turnover rate (a huge expense without an invoice) is just 14 percent per year, compared to the industry average of 38.7 percent.

Lesson 2. Recognize your company's responsibility to society.
These leading small companies strive for more than profitability; they aim to make a difference in the world, both locally and globally, and they get their employees involved in their efforts. Etsy, the Web site that provides an online marketplace for artisans to sell their creations, recently became certified as a B corporation, a company that meets rigorous standards of social and environmental responsibility and transparency in its operations. Employees receive 40 hours of paid time off each year to volunteer for the nonprofit organization of their choice. A group of employees recently traveled to Alaska to teach artisans there how to sell their work on Etsy as part of a program designed to help people in remote locations with limited resources become successful entrepreneurs.

Lesson 3. Honest, open, two-way communication helps your company in good times and bad times.
Managers at these small companies recognize that good communication is a key to building trust with employees and to encouraging employees to participate in making decisions that make the workplace better. At Ideal Printers,

a second-generation family-owned commercial printing company in St. Paul, Minnesota, sisters Lana Siewert-Olson and Joan Siewert-Cardona, use open-book management, sharing with employees all of the company's financial statements and teaching them how to read them. They say opening the company's books allows employees to see how their jobs directly affect the company's profits and their compensation because Ideal Printers also offers a profit-sharing plan. During a recent recession, when business slowed, the company reduced everyone's pay by 10 percent (and has since restored the reduction) but did not resort to layoffs, unlike many of its competitors.

Lesson 4. Teamwork counts.
Managers at leading small companies understand that a genuine team spirit leads to innovation, unparalleled productivity, and a fun atmosphere of camaraderie. They rely on team-based awards and recognition to encourage a team spirit and help employees understand how their jobs fit into the "big picture." At Nugget Market stores, every day begins with a motivational rally, during which team leaders and employees share important information and get energized for the day.

Lesson 5. Investing in your employees is one of the best investments you can make.
Great companies understand that enhancing their employees' skills benefits both the employee and the business. Managers at SmartPak, an online and catalog retailer of nutritional supplements, medicine, tack, and other equestrian supplies in Plymouth, Massachusetts, know that understanding the needs of horses and their riders is essential to the company's success. Although most of the company's employees own, ride, and show horses, not all do. SmartPak created SmartPak University, through which it offers a variety of courses to educate its employees about horses, their owners, and their unique

Lana Siewert-Olson and Joan Siewert-Cardona, second-generation owners of Ideal Printers.
ZUMA Press, Inc. / Alamy

Hands On . . . How To (continued)

needs. The company's New Hire Start Groups are designed to get new employees off to a good start, and its Barn Buddy program pairs non-riding employees with employees who are experienced equestrians to learn about horses—and to better understand the customers with whom they interact.

Lesson 6. Give your employees a real sense of ownership. Every employer's dream is to have employees who act like owners of the company. The best way to achieve that is to make them owners of the company! Stan Sheetz, the second-generation owner of Sheetz, a chain of 437 convenience stores in six states, believes that allowing Sheetz employees to own part of the company increases their level of engagement. Sheetz created an employee stock ownership plan (ESOP), and employees who work at least 1,000 hours in a calendar year receive shares in the company through the ESOP based on their earnings and years of service. Even in the leading small companies that do not offer ESOPs, employees receive some kind of performance-based compensation, such as profit sharing or stock options. The result is an ownership mentality and a workforce that is dedicated to making the company successful.

Lesson 7. Encourage your employees to stay healthy. With health care costs rising rapidly, smart business owners know that anything they can do to help their employees stay healthy not only lowers costs but also helps their employees lead better personal and work lives. Many of the leading small companies pay 100 percent of the cost of their employees' health insurance. Others provide incentives for employees to improve their health by quitting smoking, reaching and maintaining an ideal weight, or exercising regularly. Some companies provide on-site exercise facilities or pay for employees memberships at local gyms. Etsy, the online marketplace for artisans, pays 80 percent of employees' and their families' health insurance premiums and encourages employees to live healthy lives by providing yoga classes ("EtsYoga") and fitness classes ("Fitsy" and "Sweatsy"), locally sourced gourmet lunches every Tuesday and Thursday, and a kitchen stocked with healthy snacks and drinks. Employees also enjoy bringing their dogs to work.

Lesson 8. Recognize your employees' stellar performances publicly and privately—and often. The best small businesses make recognizing employees' accomplishments a top priority and use a unique system of rewards to reinforce a positive company culture. At The Clymb, an online marketplace for outdoor gear and adventure travel in Portland, Oregon, employees can recognize one another's accomplishments by giving coworkers recognition cards called "Fist Bumps" that are posted in the kitchen for all to see. Company founders Kelly Dachtler and Cec Annett recently took their entire staff to Hawaii's North Shore on a "workcation" as a reward for achieving an aggressive business goal. Employees worked shorter days and had the opportunity to

take surfing lessons, snorkel, sight-see, and hang out on the beach. At Torch Technologies, recognition is not as elaborate but no less effective. CEO Bill Roark recognizes employees' outstanding performances with a handwritten thank-you letter sent to their homes. "I get notes back from kids and wives that bring tears to my eyes," he says.

Lesson 9. Let your employees have fun. Just because you are at work does not mean you cannot have fun. OtterBox, a fast-growing company in Fort Collins, Colorado, that makes protective cases for smart phones, e-readers, and tablets, is known for its fun-based culture. The company's headquarters features a spiral slide in addition to stairs, scooters that employees can use to get around, a self-service latte machine and soda fountain, game rooms with pinball and foosball machines, and aquariums. Employees participate in impromptu events such as Flash Fitness Sessions and Star Wars Starship flying contests. There is a business purpose behind all of the fun. CEO Brian Thomas says the goal is to create a culture that fosters innovation and inspires passion. OtterBox also encourages employees to give back to their community by giving them 24 hours of paid time off each year to volunteer at a nonprofit organization and provides weekly updates on nonprofits in need of help.

Lesson 10. Give your employees the flexibility they need for work–life balance. Small companies that offer flextime, job sharing, telecommuting, and other flexible work arrangements have an edge when it comes to hiring the best workers. At outdoor retailer REI, employees enjoy flexible work schedules. Many of the company's employees are outdoor enthusiasts and are committed to REI's core values that include a passion for the outdoors. That's why managers have no problem with workers going out for bicycle rides, quick kayak trips, or taking their dogs out for a game of fetch on "Doggy Row" during "work hours" as long as the work gets done. Generous benefits such as health insurance (including coverage for part-time employees who work at least 20 hours per week), employee discounts on REI products, wellness programs, and sabbatical leaves make working at REI more than just a job.

Sources: Based on "Recreational Equipment, Inc," Great Rated, December 30, 2013, http://us.greatrated.com/recreational-equipment-inc; Paul Wozniak, "Fort Collins OtterBox Named Best Place to Work," Tri-102.5, October 26, 2012, http://tri1025 .com/fort-collins-otterbox-named-best-place-to-work/; "OtterBox," Great Rated, April 18, 2013, http://us.greatrated.com/otterbox; "The Clymb" Great Rated, September 12, 2013, http://us.greatrated.com/the-clymb; "Etsy – Great Perks, Great Rated, September 12, 2013, http://us.greatrated.com/etsy/great-perks; "Custom-Ink," Great Rated, August 6, 2013, http://us.greatrated.com/customink; "Sheetz," Great Rated, December 20, 2013, http://us.greatrated.com/sheetz; "SmartPak," Great Rated, February 6, 2014, http://us.greatrated.com/smartpak; "Nugget Market," Great Rated, January 14, 2014, http://us.greatrated.com/nugget-market; Todd Nelson, "Culture Helps Printing Firm Survive," Star Tribune, December 25, 2011, http://www .startribune.com/business/136171088.html#jlfMzZ7YOFeW2h5U.97; Gabrielle M. Blue, Dave Smith, and Drew Gannon, "2011 Top Small Company Workplaces," *Inc.,* June 2011, http://www.inc.com/top-workplaces/index.html; Kelly K. Spors, "Top Small Workplaces 2008," *Wall Street Journal,* February 22, 2009, http://online.wsj .com/article/SB122347733961315417.html; and *2008 Guide to Bold New Ideas for Making Work Work* (New York: Families and Work Institute, 2008), pp. 3–6, 42.

The average life expectancy of a family business is 24 years, although some last *much* longer.[125] For instance, the oldest family business in the world is Houshi Ryokan, an inn and spa that was built near a hot spring in Komatsu, Japan, in 718 by Gengoro Sasakiri. Today, the forty-sixth generation of Sasakiri's descendants operate the inn, which can accommodate 450 guests in its 100 rooms.[126]

The primary causes of lack of continuity among family businesses are inadequate estate planning, failure to create a management succession plan, and lack of funds to pay estate taxes.[127] In addition, sibling rivalries, fights over control of the business, and personality conflicts often lead to nasty battles that can tear families apart and destroy once thriving businesses. The best way to avoid deadly turf battles and conflicts is to develop a succession plan for the company. Numerous studies have found a positive relationship between the existence of a management succession plan and the longevity of family businesses.

Most of the family businesses in existence today were started after World War II, and their founders are ready to pass the torch of leadership on to the next generation. Experts estimate that between 2012 and 2050, $27 trillion in wealth will be transferred from one generation to the next, much of it through family businesses.[128] For these companies to have a smooth transition from one generation to the next, they must develop management succession plans. Unfortunately, only slightly more than half of all business owners have created succession plans, and, somewhat surprisingly, younger business owners are more likely to have a plan than older owners (see Figure 16.5). Often, the reason for failing to develop a succession plan is that entrepreneurs are unwilling to make tough and potentially disruptive family-oriented decisions that require selecting their successors. Family feuds often erupt over who is (and is not) selected as the successor in the family business. Without a succession plan, however, family businesses face an increased risk of faltering or failing in the next generation. Family businesses with the greatest probability of surviving are the ones whose owners prepare a succession plan well before it is time to pass the torch of leadership to the next generation. Succession planning also allows business owners to minimize the impact of estate taxes on their businesses and on their successors' wealth as well.

Succession planning reduces the tension and stress of a transition by gradually "changing the guard." A well-developed succession plan is like the smooth, graceful exchange of a baton between runners in a relay race. The new runner still has maximum energy; the concluding runner has already spent his or her energy by running at maximum speed. The athletes never come to a stop to exchange the baton; instead, the handoff takes place on the move. The race is a skillful blend of the talents of all team members; the exchange of leadership is so smooth and powerful that the business never falters but accelerates, fueled by a new source of energy at each leg of the race.

HOW TO DEVELOP A MANAGEMENT SUCCESSION PLAN Creating a succession plan involves the following steps:

Step 1.   *Select the successor.* There comes a time for even the most dedicated company founder to step down from the helm of the business and hand the reins over to the next generation. The entire population of the Baby Boomer generation (born

FIGURE 16.5

Percentage of Business Owners Who Have Succession Plans in Place, by Age

Source: Small Business Owner Report, Spring 2014, Bank of America, p. 8.

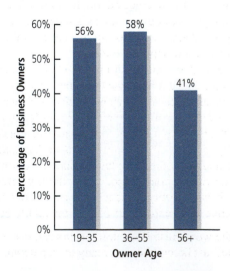

between 1946 and 1964), some 76.4 million people, will be 65 or older by 2030, and 60 percent of small business owners are Baby Boomers. As those Baby Boomers retire (a Baby Boomer business owner retires every 57 seconds), they are creating a tidal wave of business transitions and sales as they look either to hand them over to the next generation or sell them.[129] Unfortunately, many of these soon-to-retire family business owners who intend to turn over their businesses to the next generation of family members have not yet identified their successors. They resist thinking about stepping away from the businesses they have built, but in the end, every business owner exits the company he or she created.

At age 63, Richard Branson, the brash founder of the Virgin Group, a collection of about 400 companies in industries that range from air travel and wine to balloon flights and space travel, has yet to name his successor. However, Branson's daughter Holly, who left a career as a doctor, now works for the Virgin Group as a special projects manager and is learning about the vast collection of companies in the Virgin portfolio and honing her financial management skills.[130]

Terry Bradford/Solo/ZUMAPRESS/Newscom

Entrepreneurs should never assume that their children want to take control of the family business, however. It is critical to remember at this juncture in the life of a business that children do not necessarily inherit their parents' entrepreneurial skills and interests. By leveling with the children about the business and their options regarding a family succession, the owner will know which heirs, if any, are willing to assume leadership of the business.

When naming a successor, merit is a better standard to use than birth order or gender. More than one-third of family business founders say the next leader will be a woman, quite a change from just a generation ago.[131] The key to selecting the right successor is to establish standards of performance, knowledge, education, and ability and then identify the person who most closely meets those standards.

When considering a successor, an entrepreneur should consider taking the following actions:

- Let family members, especially children, know that joining the business is not mandatory nor guaranteed. Family members' goals, ambitions, and talents should be foremost in their career decisions, and the business does not owe jobs to people just because they are family members. Andrew Cornell, CEO of Cornell Iron Works, a family business that started in 1828 as a blacksmith shop and now makes overhead doors for industrial, commercial, and residential customers, says part of the company's success is its objective approach to hiring family members. He points out that successful family businesses cannot be homes for wayward family members.
- Do not assume that a successor must always come from within the family. Simply being born into a family does *not* guarantee that a person will make a good business leader. A recent survey by PriceWaterhouseCoopers reports that 34 percent of leaders of family businesses in North America with succession plans say the next top manager will come from outside the family.[132]
- Give family members the opportunity to work outside the business first to learn firsthand how others conduct business. Working for others allows them to develop knowledge, confidence, and credibility before stepping back into the family business. Seventy percent of the successors who have been identified have full-time work experience outside the family business.[133]

One of the worst mistakes entrepreneurs can make is to postpone naming a successor until just before they are ready to step down. The problem is especially acute when more than one family member works for the company and is interested in assuming leadership of it. Sometimes founders avoid naming successors because they don't want to hurt the family members who are not chosen to succeed them. However, both the business and the family will be better off if, after observing the family members as they work in the business, the founder picks a successor on the basis of that person's skills and abilities.

ENTREPRENEURIAL PROFILE: Irwin and James Monroe Smucker: J. M. Smucker Company J. M. Smucker Company, the well-known maker of jams and jellies, has had five CEOs since James Monroe Smucker started the company in Orrville, Ohio, in 1897, and every one of them has been a member of the Smucker family. Well before Paul, the grandson of founder J. M., stepped down from the company's helm in 1961, he named both of his sons, Timothy and Richard Smucker as co-CEOs. Timothy and Richard currently are grooming their sons, Mark Smucker and Paul Smucker Wagstaff, to become the fifth-generation coleaders of the company. Mark and Paul, both in their early forties, have held a variety of positions in the company and currently are in charge of two major divisions. "We would like for them to share the CEO job," says Richard, "but it's not a *fait accompli*."[134] ∎

Step 2. *Create a survival kit for the successor.* Once he or she identifies a successor, an entrepreneur should prepare a survival kit and then brief the future leader on its contents, which should include all of the company's critical documents (wills, trusts, insurance policies, financial statements, bank accounts, key contracts, corporate bylaws, and so forth). The founder should be sure that the successor reads and understands all of the relevant documents in the kit.

Step 3. *Groom the successor.* Typically, founders transfer their knowledge to their successors gradually over time. The discussions that set the stage for the transition of leadership are time consuming and require openness by both parties. In fact, grooming a successor is the founder's greatest teaching and development responsibility, and it takes time and deliberate effort. To create ability and confidence in a successor, a founder must be:

- patient, realizing that the transfer of power is gradual and evolutionary and that the successor should earn responsibility and authority one step at a time until the final transfer of power takes place;
- willing to accept that the successor will make mistakes;
- skillful at using the successor's mistakes as a teaching tool;
- an effective communicator and an especially tolerant listener;
- capable of establishing reasonable expectations for the successor's performance; and
- able to articulate the keys to the successor's successful performance.

Grooming a successor can begin at an early age simply by involving children in the family business and observing which ones have the greatest ability and interest in the company.

ENTREPRENEURIAL PROFILE: Rudolph, Tommy, and Thomas Young: Young Office Young Office, an office supply and furnishings business in Greenville, South Carolina, is in its third generation of family ownership. Thomas Young, who became CEO in 2008, began working in the business as a child, joined the company full-time as a sales representative after graduating from college, and gradually worked his way up the ladder. His father, Tommy, started working at Young Office as a warehouse employee and truck driver, learning the business from his father, Rudolph, who founded the company in 1953. Thomas's father, Tommy, invested years preparing Thomas to take over the family business, which each successor has reinvented to accommodate changes in the marketplace. When asked about his success, Thomas is quick to credit his father for teaching him the nuances of the business and then stepping away to allow him to lead the company according to his vision, which is built on the bedrock of the company's values he learned growing up.[135] ∎

Step 4. *Promote an environment of trust and respect.* Another priceless gift a founder can leave a successor is an environment of trust and respect. Trust and respect on the part of the founder and others fuel the successor's desire to learn and excel and build the successor's confidence in making decisions. Developing a competent successor typically requires at least 5 to 10 years. Dan Cathy, now Chairman and CEO of Chick-fil-A, the highly successful chicken sandwich chain founded in 1967 by his father, Truett, started working in the family business at age 9. He joined the company full-time after graduating from college, starting as a director of operations, where he opened 50 new stores. Over the next several years, Dan moved up the ranks as vice president of operations and senior vice president. In 2001, he became president and CEO. In 2013, as part of a long-planned succession, Dan assumed the mantle of chairman of the board from his then 92-year-old father.[136]

Empowering the successor by gradually delegating responsibilities creates an environment in which all parties can objectively view the growth and development of the successor. Customers, creditors, suppliers, and staff members develop confidence in the successor. The final transfer of power is not a dramatic, wrenching change but a smooth, coordinated passage. Founders must be careful at this stage to avoid the "meddling retiree syndrome" in which they continue to report for work after they have officially stepped down and take control of matters that are no longer their responsibility. Doing so undermines a successor's authority and credibility among workers quickly.

Step 5. *Cope with the financial realities of estate and gift taxes.* The final step in developing a workable management succession plan is structuring the transition to minimize the impact of estate, gift, and inheritance taxes on family members and the business. Entrepreneurs who fail to consider the impact of these taxes may force their heirs to sell a successful business just to pay the estate's tax bill. Recent tax legislation may reduce the impact of taxation on the continuity of family businesses. Currently, without proper estate planning, an entrepreneur's family members incur a painful tax bite that can be as high as 40 percent (or more if the state also imposes an estate tax) when they inherit the business (see Table 16.8).

TABLE 16.8 Changes in the Estate and Gift Taxes

As the following table illustrates, Congress is constantly tinkering with the often punishing structures of estate and gift taxes. The federal estate tax is actually interwoven with the gift tax; the impact of the two taxes began differing in 2004. Congress repealed the estate tax originally in 2010 but reinstated it in 2011. The following table shows how the exemptions and the maximum tax rates for the estate and gift taxes have changed over time.

Year	Estate Tax Exemption	Gift Tax Exemption	Maximum Tax Rate
2001	$675,000	$675,000	55%
2002	$1 million	$1 million	50%
2003	$1 million	$1 million	49%
2004	$1.5 million	$1 million	48%
2005	$1.5 million	$1 million	47%
2006	$2 million	$1 million	46%
2007	$2 million	$1 million	45%
2008	$2 million	$1 million	45%
2009	$3.5 million	$1 million	45%
2010	Tax repealed	$1 million	35% (gifts only)
2011	$5 million	$1 million	55%
2012	$5.12 million	$5.12 million	35%
2013	$5.25 million	$5.25 million	40%
2014	$5.34 million	$5.34 million	40%

However the federal laws governing estate taxes may change over the next few years, entrepreneurs whose businesses have been successful cannot afford to neglect estate planning. Even though the federal estate tax burden has eased somewhat, some states have increased their estate taxes.

Source: Based on data from the Internal Revenue Service, United States Government.

Entrepreneurs should be actively engaged in estate planning no later than age 45; those who start businesses early in their lives or whose businesses grow rapidly may need to begin as early as age 30. A variety of options exist that may prove to be helpful in reducing the estate tax liability. Each operates in a different fashion, but their objective remains the same: to remove a portion of business owners' assets from their estates so that when they die, those assets will not be subject to estate taxes. Many of these estate planning tools need time to work their magic, so the key is to put them in place early on in the life of the business.

BUY-SELL AGREEMENT One of the most popular estate planning techniques is the buy-sell agreement. A **buy-sell agreement** is a contract that co-owners often rely on to ensure the continuity of a business. In a typical arrangement, the co-owners create a contract stating that each agrees to buy the others out in case of the death or disability of one. That way, the heirs of the deceased or disabled owner can "cash out" of the business while leaving control of it in the hands of the remaining owners. The buy-sell agreement specifies a formula for determining the value of the business at the time the agreement is to be executed. One problem with buy-sell agreements is that the remaining co-owners may not have the cash available to buy out the disabled or deceased owner. To resolve this issue, many businesses purchase life and disability insurance for each of the owners in amounts large enough to cover the purchase price of their respective shares of the business.

ENTREPRENEURIAL PROFILE: Larry Jaffe and Bob Gross: Jaffe and Gross Larry Jaffe and Bob Gross, co-owners of Jaffe and Gross, a successful jewelry store in Dayton, Ohio, failed to create a buy-sell agreement backed by insurance for their business. When Gross died suddenly of a heart attack, Jaffe did not have enough cash to purchase Gross's share of ownership in the business. Gross's heirs, who inherited his shares of the business, had no interest in operating the jewelry store, and without a buy-sell agreement or a succession plan in place, the 27-year-old company folded. Jaffe has since launched his own jewelry store, Jaffe's Jewelers, but admits that things would have been much easier had he and Gross taken the time to create a succession plan.[137] ■

LIFETIME GIFTING The owner of a successful business may transfer money to his or her children (or other recipients) from the estate throughout his or her life. Current federal tax regulations allow individuals to make gifts of $14,000 per year, per parent, per recipient that are exempt from federal gift taxes. The recipient is not required to pay tax on the $14,000 gift he or she receives, and the donor must pay a gift tax only on the amount of a gift that exceeds $14,000. For instance, husband-and-wife business owners could give $1,680,000 worth of stock to their three children and their spouses over a period of 10 years without incurring any estate or gift taxes at all. To be an effective estate planning strategy, lifetime gifting requires time to work, meaning that business owners must create a plan for using it early on.

SETTING UP A TRUST A **trust** is a contract between a grantor (the company founder) and a trustee (generally a bank officer or an attorney) in which the grantor gives to the trustee legal title to assets (e.g., stock in the company) that the trustee agrees to hold for the beneficiaries (the founder's children). The beneficiaries can receive income from the trust, the property in the trust, or both at some specified time. Trusts can take a wide variety of forms, but two broad categories of trusts are available: revocable trusts and irrevocable trusts. A **revocable trust** is one that a grantor can change or revoke during his or her lifetime. Under present tax laws, however, the only trust that provides a tax benefit is an **irrevocable trust**, in which the grantor cannot require the trustee to return the assets held in trust. The value of the grantor's estate is lowered because the assets in an irrevocable trust are excluded from the value of the estate. However, an irrevocable trust places severe restrictions on the grantor's control of the property placed in the trust. Although recent changes in tax laws have eliminated certain types of trusts as estate planning tools, business owners use several types of irrevocable trusts to lower their estate tax liabilities:

- *Irrevocable life insurance trust (ILIT).* This type of trust allows business owners to keep the proceeds of a life insurance policy out of their estates and away from estate taxes, freeing up that money to pay the taxes on the remainder of their estates. To get the tax benefit,

buy-sell agreement
a contract among co-owners of a business stating that each agrees to buy out the others in case of the death or disability of one.

trust
a contract between a grantor (the company founder) and a trustee in which the grantor gives the trustee assets (e.g., company stock) that the trustee holds for the trust's beneficiaries (e.g., the grantor's heirs).

revocable trust
a trust that a grantor can change or revoke during his or her lifetime.

irrevocable trust
a trust in which a grantor cannot require the trustee to return the assets held in trust.

business owners must be sure that the business or the trust (rather than the owners themselves) owns the insurance policy. The primary disadvantage of an ILIT is that if the owner dies within three years of establishing it, the insurance proceeds become part of the estate and *are* subject to estate taxes. Because the trust is irrevocable, it cannot be amended or rescinded once it is established. Like most trusts, ILITs must meet stringent requirements to be valid, and entrepreneurs should use experienced attorneys to create them.

- *Irrevocable asset trust.* An irrevocable asset trust is similar to a life insurance trust except that it is designed to pass the assets (such as stock in a family business) in the parents' estate on to their children. The children do not have control of the assets while the parents are living, but they do receive the income from those assets. On the parents' death, the assets in the trust go to the children without being subjected to the estate tax.

- *Grantor retained annuity trust (GRAT).* A GRAT is a special type of irrevocable trust and has become one of the most popular tools for entrepreneurs to transfer ownership of a business while maintaining control over it and minimizing estate taxes. Under a GRAT, an owner can put property (such as company stock) in an irrevocable trust for a minimum of two years. While the trust is in effect, the grantor (owner) retains the benefits associated with the assets in the trust (e.g., the voting rights associated with the stock) and receives interest income (calculated at a fixed interest rate that is determined by the Internal Revenue Service [IRS]) from the assets in the trust. At the end of the trust, the property passes to the beneficiaries (heirs). The beneficiaries are required to pay a gift tax on the value of the assets placed in the GRAT. However, the IRS taxes GRAT gifts only according to their discounted present value because the heirs did not receive use of the property while it was in trust. The primary disadvantage of using a GRAT in estate planning is that if the grantor dies during the life of the GRAT, its assets pass back into the grantor's estate. These assets then become subject to the full estate tax. A GRAT is an excellent tool for transferring the appreciation of an asset such as a growing company to heirs with few tax implications.

ENTREPRENEURIAL PROFILE: Mark Zuckerberg: Facebook Mark Zuckerberg, founder of Facebook, and seven other major shareholders in the company recently created GRATs that will save an estimated $240 million in estate taxes in the future. By setting up a GRAT with 3.4 million pre-IPO shares of Facebook stock valued at just $1.85 per share, Zuckerberg alone will avoid nearly $68 million in estate taxes (at current estate tax rates).[138] ∎

Establishing a trust requires meeting many specific legal requirements and is not something business owners should do on their own. It is much better to work with experienced attorneys, accountants, and financial advisers to create them. Although the cost of establishing a trust can be high, the tax savings they generate are well worth the expense.

ESTATE FREEZE An **estate freeze** minimizes estate taxes by having family members create two classes of stock for the business: (1) preferred voting stock for the parents and (2) nonvoting common stock for the children. The value of the preferred stock is frozen, whereas the common stock reflects the anticipated increased market value of the business. Any appreciation in the value of the business after the transfer is not subject to estate taxes. However, the parent must pay gift taxes on the value of the common stock given to the children. The value of the common stock is the total value of the business less the value of the voting preferred stock retained by the parent. The parents also must accept taxable dividends at the market rate on the preferred stock they own.

estate freeze
a strategy that minimizes estate taxes by creating two classes of stock for a business: preferred voting stock for the parents and nonvoting common stock for the children.

FAMILY LIMITED PARTNERSHIP Creating a **family limited partnership (FLP)** allows business-owning parents to transfer their company to their children and lower their estate taxes while still retaining control over it for themselves. To create an FLP, the parents (or parent) set up a partnership among themselves and their children. The parents retain the general partnership interest, which can be as low as 1 percent, and the children become the limited partners. As general partners, the parents control both the limited partnership and the family business. In other words, nothing in the way the company operates has to change. Over time, the parents transfer company stock into the limited partnership, ultimately passing ownership of the company to their children.

family limited partnership (FLP)
a strategy that allows business-owning parents to transfer their company to their children (lowering their estate taxes) while still retaining control over it for themselves.

One of the principal tax benefits of an FLP is that it allows discounts on the value of the shares of company stock the parents transfer into the limited partnership. Because a family business is closely held, shares of ownership in it, especially minority shares, are not as marketable as those of a publicly held company. As a result, company shares transferred into the limited partnership are discounted at 20 to 50 percent of their full market value, producing a large tax savings for everyone involved. The average discount is 40 percent, but that amount varies, depending on the industry and the individual company involved.

Because of their ability to reduce estate and gift taxes, FLPs have become one of the most popular estate planning tools in recent years. The following tips will help entrepreneurs establish an FLP that will withstand legal challenges:

- Establish a legitimate business reason other than avoiding estate taxes—such as transferring a business over time to the next generation of family members—for creating the FLP and document it in writing.

- Make sure that all members of the FLP make contributions and take distributions according to a predetermined schedule. Owners should not allow FLP funds to pay for personal expenses nor should they time partnership distributions with owners' personal needs for cash.[139]

- Do not allow members to put all of their personal assets (such as a house, automobiles, or personal property) into the FLP. Commingling personal and business assets in an FLP raises a red flag to the IRS.

- Expect an audit of the FLP. The IRS tends to scrutinize FLPs, so be prepared for a thorough audit.[140]

Developing a succession plan and preparing a successor require a wide variety of skills, some of which the business founder will not have. That's why it is important to bring experts into the process when necessary. Entrepreneurs often call on their attorneys, accountants, insurance agents, and financial planners to help them build a succession plan that works best for their particular situations. Because the issues involved can be highly complex and charged with emotion, bringing in trusted advisers to help improves the quality of the process and provides an objective perspective.

LO5

Explain the exit strategies available to entrepreneurs.

Exit Strategies

Most family business founders want their companies to stay within their families, but in some cases, maintaining family control is not practical. Sometimes, no one in the next generation of family members has an interest in managing the company or has the necessary skills and experience to handle the job. Under these circumstances, the founder must look outside the family for leadership if the company is to survive. Whatever the case, entrepreneurs must confront their mortality and plan for the future of their companies. Having a solid management succession plan in place well before retirement is near is absolutely critical to success. Entrepreneurs should examine their options once they decide it is time to step down from the businesses they have founded. Entrepreneurs who are planning to retire often use two strategies: sell to outsiders or sell to (nonfamily) insiders. We turn now to these two exit strategies.

Selling to Outsiders

As you learned in Chapter 6, selling a business to an outsider is no simple task. Done properly, it takes time, patience, and preparation to locate a suitable buyer, strike a deal, and make the transition. Advance preparation, maintaining accurate financial records, and timing are the keys to a successful sale. Too often, however, business owners, like some famous athletes, stay with the game too long until they and their businesses are well past their prime. A "fire-sale" approach rarely yields the maximum value for a business.

A straight sale may be best for those entrepreneurs who want to step down and turn the reins of the company over to someone else. However, selling a business outright is not an attractive exit strategy for those who want to stay on with the company or for those who want to surrender control of the company gradually rather than all at once.

ENTREPRENEURIAL PROFILE: Michael and Joseph Orseno: CVM Companies After investing more than 25 years leading CVM Companies, a maker of industrial fans in Carol Stream, Illinois, brothers Michael and Joseph Orseno, both members of the Baby Boom generation, grew tired of their 70-hour workweeks and decided to sell their business. Although the brothers had children, none were interested in taking the reins of CVM Companies. Within weeks of putting the company up for sale, the Orsenos provided information about their business to 70 potential buyers before receiving four offers, one of which they accepted. ■

Selling to Insiders

When entrepreneurs have no family members to whom they can transfer ownership or who want to assume the responsibilities of running a company, selling the business to employees is often the preferred option. In most situations, the options available to owners are a leveraged buyout and an employee stock ownership plan.

LEVERAGED BUYOUTS In a **leveraged buyout (LBO)**, managers and/or employees borrow money from a financial institution and pay the owner the total agreed-on price at closing; then they use the cash generated from the company's operations to pay off the debt. The drawback of this technique is that it creates a highly leveraged business. Because of the high levels of debt they take on, the new management has very little room for error. Too many management mistakes or a slowing economy has led many highly leveraged businesses into bankruptcy.

If properly structured, LBOs can be attractive to both buyers and sellers. Because they get their money up front, sellers do not incur the risk of loss if the buyers cannot keep the business operating successfully. The managers and employees who buy the company have a strong incentive to make sure the business succeeds because they own a piece of the action and some of their capital is at risk in the business. The result can be a highly motivated workforce that works hard and makes sure that the company operates efficiently.

EMPLOYEE STOCK OWNERSHIP PLANS Unlike LBOs, **employee stock ownership plans (ESOPs)** allow employees and/or managers (i.e., the future owners) to purchase the business gradually, freeing up enough cash to finance the venture's future growth. With an ESOP, employees contribute a portion of their salaries and wages over time toward purchasing shares of the company's stock from the founder until they own the company outright. In leveraged ESOPs, the ESOP borrows the money to buy the owner's stock either all at once or over time. Then, using employees' contributions, the ESOP repays the loan over time (with pre-tax dollars), using the shares of the company's stock as collateral for the loan. An advantage of a leveraged ESOP is that the principal and the interest the ESOP borrows to buy the business are tax deductible, which can save thousands or even millions of dollars in taxes. Transferring ownership to employees through an ESOP is a long-term exit strategy that benefits everyone involved. The owner sells the business to the people he or she can trust the most, his or her managers and employees, and the managers and employees buy a business they already know how to run successfully. In addition, because they own the company, the managers and employees have a huge incentive to see that it operates effectively and efficiently. One study of employee stock ownership plans in privately held companies found that the ESOPs increased sales, employment, and sales per employee by 2.4 percent a year.[141] Approximately 10,900 ESOPs operate in U.S. companies, and they involve 10.3 million employee owners. In half of the companies, the ESOP controls a majority of the ownership.[142]

ENTREPRENEURIAL PROFILE: Tom Hirons: Hirons & Company Tom Hirons, who in 1978 founded the advertising and public relations firm that bears his name, created an ESOP through which he will transfer ownership to his 29 employees over several years. At 61, Hirons did not want to sell the company, based in Indianapolis, Indiana, to outsiders. The ESOP allows him to gradually make the transition out of his business and put it into the hands of the people who contributed so much over time to make it successful.[143] ■

---

leveraged buyout (LBO)

a situation in which managers and/or employees borrow money from a financial institution to purchase a business and then use the money from the company's operations to pay off the debt.

employee stock ownership plan (ESOP)

an arrangement in which employees and/or managers contribute a portion of their salaries and wages over time toward purchasing shares of a company's stock from the founder until they own the company outright.

Chapter Summary by Learning Objective

1. Explain the challenges involved in the entrepreneur's role as leader and what it takes to be a successful leader.

- Leadership is the process of influencing and inspiring others to work to achieve a common goal and then giving them the power and the freedom to achieve it.

- Management and leadership are not the same, yet both are essential to a small company's success. Leadership without management is unbridled; management without leadership is uninspired. Leadership gets a small business going; management keeps it going.

2. Describe the importance of hiring the right employees and how to avoid making hiring mistakes.

- The decision to hire a new employee is an important one for every business, but its impact is magnified many times in a small company. Every new hire a business owner makes determines the heights to which the company can climb—or the depths to which it will plunge.

- To avoid making hiring mistakes, entrepreneurs should develop meaningful job descriptions and job specifications, plan and conduct an effective interview, and check references before hiring any employee.

3. Explain how to create a company culture that encourages employee retention.

- Company culture is the distinctive, unwritten code of conduct that governs the behavior, attitudes, relationships, and style of an organization. Culture arises from an entrepreneur's consistent and relentless

pursuit of a set of core values that everyone in the company can believe in. Small companies' flexible structures can be a major competitive weapon.

- Job design techniques for enhancing employee motivation include job enlargement, job rotation, job enrichment, flextime, job sharing, and flexplace (which includes telecommuting).

- Money is an important motivator for many workers but not the only one. The key to using rewards such as recognition and praise to motivate involves tailoring them to the needs and characteristics of the workers.

4. Describe the steps in developing a management succession plan for a growing business that allows a smooth transition of leadership to the next generation.

- As their companies grow, entrepreneurs must begin to plan for passing the leadership baton to the next generation well in advance. A succession plan is a crucial element in successfully transferring a company to the next generation. Preparing a succession plan involves five steps: (1) select the successor, (2) create a survival kit for the successor, (3) groom the successor, (4) promote an environment of trust and respect, and (5) cope with the financial realities of estate taxes.

5. Explain the exit strategies available to entrepreneurs.

- Family business owners wanting to step down from their companies can sell to outsiders or to insiders. Common tools for selling to insiders (employees or managers) include LBOs and ESOPs.

Discussion Questions

16-1. What is leadership? What is the difference between leadership and management?

16-2. What behaviors do effective leaders exhibit?

16-3. Why is it so important for small companies to hire the right employees? What can small business owners do to avoid making hiring mistakes?

16-4. What is a job description? A job specification? What functions do they serve in the hiring process?

16-5. Outline the procedure for conducting an effective interview.

16-6. What is company culture? What role does culture play in a small company's success? What threats does rapid growth pose for a company's culture?

16-7. Explain the differences among job simplification, job enlargement, job rotation, and job enrichment.

What impact do these different job designs have on workers?

16-8. Is money the "best" motivator?

16-9. How do pay-for-performance compensation systems work? What other rewards are available to small business managers to use as motivators? How effective are they?

16-10. Why is it so important for a small business owner to develop a management succession plan? Why is it so difficult for most business owners to develop such a plan? What are the steps that are involved in creating a succession plan?

16-11. Briefly describe the options a small business owner wanting to pass the family business on to the next generation can take to minimize the impact of estate taxes.

Beyond the Classroom . . .

6-12. Visit a local business that has experienced rapid growth in the past three years and ask the owner about the specific problems he or she had to face because of the organization's growth. How did the owner handle these problems? Looking back, what would he or she do differently?

6-13. Contact a local small business with at least 20 employees. Does the company have job descriptions and job specifications? What process does the owner use to hire a new employee? What questions does the owner typically ask candidates in an interview?

6-14. Ask the owner of a small manufacturing operation to give you a tour of his or her operation. During your tour, observe the way jobs are organized. To what extent does the company use the job design concepts of job simplification, job enlargement, job rotation, job enrichment, flextime, and job sharing? Based on your observations, what recommendations would you make to the owner about the company's job design?

6-15. Find *Fortune*'s "100 Best Companies to Work For" or *Inc.*'s "Top Small Company Workplaces" issue. Read the profiles of the companies included on the list and develop a list of at least five ideas you would like to incorporate into the company you plan to launch.

6-16. Contact five small business owners about their plans for passing their businesses on to the next generation. Do they intend to pass the business along to a family member? Do they have a management succession plan? When do they plan to name a successor? Have they developed a plan for minimizing the effects of estate taxes? How many more years do they plan to work before retiring?

6-17. Entrepreneurs say they have learned much about leadership from the movies! "Films beg to be interpreted and discussed," says one leadership consultant, "and from those discussions business-people come up with principles for their own jobs." A recent survey of small company CEOs by *Inc.* magazine[*] resulted in the following list of the best movies for leadership lessons: *Apollo 13* (1995), *The Bridge on the River Kwai* (1957), *Dead Poets Society* (1989), *Elizabeth* (1998), *Glengarry Glen Ross* (1992), *It's a Wonderful Life* (1946), *Norma Rae* (1979), *One Flew over the Cuckoo's Nest* (1975), *Twelve Angry Men* (1957), and *Twelve O'Clock High* (1949). Rent one of these films and watch it with a group of your classmates. After viewing the movie, discuss the leadership lessons you learned from it and report the results to the other members of your class.

---

[*] Leigh Buchanan and Mike Hofman, "Everything I Know about Leadership, I Learned from the Movies," *Inc.*, March 2000, pp. 58–70.

Endnotes

Scan for Endnotes or go to www.pearsonhighered.com/scarborough

Appendix

The Daily Perc Business Plan*

This sample business plan has been made available to users of *Business Plan Pro*®, business planning software published by Palo Alto Software, Inc. Names, locations, and numbers may have been changed, and substantial portions of the original plan text have been omitted because of space limitations and to preserve confidentiality and proprietary information.

You are welcome to use this plan as a starting point to create your own, but you do not have permission to resell, reproduce, publish, distribute, or even copy this plan as it exists here.

Requests for reprints, academic use, and other dissemination of this sample plan should be e-mailed to the marketing department of Palo Alto Software at marketing@paloalto.com. For product information, visit our Website: www.paloalto.com or call: 1-800-229-7526.

*"The Daily Perc," from Business Plan Pro. Copyright © 1995–2012 by Palo Alto Software, Inc. Reprinted with permission.

1.0 Executive Summary

The Daily Perc (TDP) is a specialty beverage retailer. TDP uses a system that is new to the beverage and food service industry to provide hot and cold beverages conveniently and efficiently. TDP provides its customers the ability to drive up and order (from a trained Barista) their choice of a custom-blended espresso drink, freshly brewed coffee, or other beverage. TDP offers a high-quality alternative to fast-food, convenience store, or institutional coffee.

The Daily Perc offers its patrons the finest hot and cold beverages, specializing in specialty coffees, blended teas, and other custom drinks. In addition, TDP will offer soft drinks, fresh-baked pastries, and other confections. Seasonally, TDP will add beverages such as hot apple cider, hot chocolate, frozen coffees, and more.

The Daily Perc will focus on two markets:

The daily commuter. Someone who is traveling to or from work, shopping, delivering goods or services, or just out for a drive.

The captive consumer. Someone who is in a restricted environment that does not allow convenient departure and return for refreshments or where refreshments stands are an integral part of the environment.

The Daily Perc will penetrate the commuter and captive consumer markets by deploying drive-through facilities and Mobile Cafés in highly visible, accessible locations. The drive-through facilities are designed to handle two-sided traffic and dispense customer-designed, specially ordered cups of premium coffee in less time than is required for a visit to a locally owned café or one of the national chains.

In addition to providing a quality product and an extensive menu of delicious items, we will donate up to 7.5 percent of revenue to local charities to increase customer awareness of and loyalty to our business and to generate good publicity coverage and media support.

The Daily Perc's customer service process is labor intensive, and TDP recognizes that a higher level of talent is essential to success. The financial investment in its employees will be one of the greatest differentiators between TDP and its competition. For the purpose of this plan, the capital expenditures of facilities and equipment are financed. We will maintain minimum levels of inventory on hand to keep our products fresh and to take advantage of price decreases when they should occur.

The Daily Perc anticipates an initial combination of investments and short- and long-term financing of $365,670 to cover start-up costs. This will require TDP to grow more slowly than might be otherwise possible, but our growth will be solid, financially sound, and tied to customer demand.

The Daily Perc's goal is to become the drive-through version of Starbucks between the mountains, eventually obtaining several million dollars through a private offering that will allow the company to open 20 to 30 facilities per year in metropolitan communities in the North, Midwest, and South with populations of more than 150,000. The danger in this strategy is that competitors could establish a foothold in a community before the arrival of TDP, causing a potential drain on revenues and a dramatic increase in advertising expenditures to maintain market share. Knowing these risks—and planning for them—gives TDP the edge needed to make the exit strategy viable.

By year 3, we estimate a net worth of $1,075,969, a cash balance of $773,623, and earnings of $860,428, based on 13 drive-throughs and four Mobile Cafés. At that point, a market value of between $3.5 million and $8.6 million for the company is reasonable. At present, coffee chains are trading in multiples of 4 to 10 times earnings. Using the midpoint of that range (7) provides an estimated value of $6 million by the end of year 3.

The figure on page 654 summarizes the forecasts for TDP's sales, gross profit, and net income for the first three years of operation.

1.1 Objectives

The Daily Perc has established three objectives it plans to achieve in the next three years:

1. Thirteen drive-through locations and four fully booked Mobile Cafés by the end of the third year

2. Gross profit margin of 45 percent or more

3. Net after-tax profit above 15 percent of sales

1.2 Mission

The Daily Perc's mission is threefold, with each being as integral to our success as the next.

- *Product mission.* Provide customers the finest quality beverages in the most efficient way

- *Community mission.* Support the local communities in which we operate

- *Economic mission.* Operate and grow at a profitable rate by making sound business decisions

1.3 Keys to Success

There are four keys to success in this business, three of which are virtually the same as in any food service business. It is the fourth key—the Community Mission—that gives TDP the extra measure of respect in the public eye.

1. The best locations, characterized by highly visible, high traffic counts, and convenient access

2. The best products, featuring the freshest coffee beans, cleanest equipment, premium serving containers, and most consistent flavor

3. The friendliest servers who are well trained, cheerful, skilled, professional, and articulate

4. The finest reputation that generates word-of-mouth advertising and promotes our community mission and charitable giving

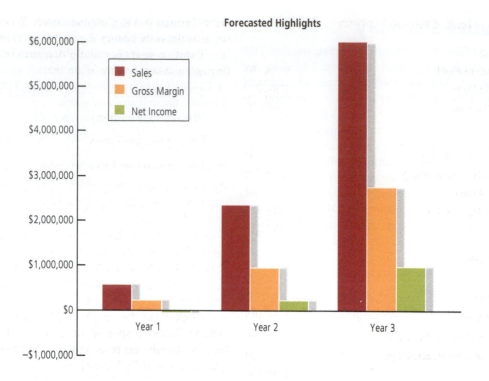

Forecasted Highlights

2.0 Company Summary

The Daily Perc is a specialty beverage retailer. TDP uses a system that is new to the beverage and food service industry to provide hot and cold beverages conveniently and efficiently. TDP provides its customers the ability to drive up and order from a trained Barista their choice of a custom-blended espresso drink, freshly brewed coffee, or other beverage. TDP offers a high-quality alternative to fast-food, convenience store, and institutional coffee.

2.1 Company Ownership

The Daily Perc is a limited liability company. All membership shares are currently owned by Bart and Teresa Fisher, who intend to use a portion of the shares to raise capital.

The plan calls for the sale of 100 membership units in the company to family members, friends, and private (angel) investors. Each membership unit in the company is priced at $4,250, with a minimum of five units per membership certificate, or a minimum investment of $21,250 per investor.

When TDP completes its financing, Bart and Terri Fisher will maintain ownership of 51 percent of the company.

2.2 Start-Up Summary

The Daily Perc's start-up expenses and funding are shown in the following tables and charts. The majority of these funds will be used to build the first facility, pay deposits, and provide capital for six months of operating expenses, initial inventory, and other one-time expenses. The Daily Perc also will need operating capital for the first few months of operation.

Table: Start-Up Expenses and Assets

Start-Up Requirements	
Start-Up Expenses:	
Legal	$3,500
Office Equipment	$4,950
Drive-Through Labor (6 months)	$65,000
Drive-Through Finance Payment (6 months)	$12,300
Drive-Through expenses (6 months)	$8,520
Land Lease (6 months)	$7,200
Vehicle Finance (6 months)	$3,700
Administration Labor (6 months)	$54,000
Web Site Development and Hosting	$5,600
Identity/Logos/Stationery	$4,000
Other	$5,000
Total Start-Up Expenses	$173,770
Start-Up Assets:	
Cash Required	$25,500
Start-Up Inventory	$35,000
Other Current Assets	$0
Long-Term Assets	$131,400
Total Assets	$191,900
Total Requirements	$365,670

Table: Start-Up Funding

Start-Up Funding	
Start-Up Expenses to Fund	$173,770
Start-Up Assets to Fund	$191,900
Total Funding Required	$365,670
Assets	
Noncash Assets from Start-Up	$166,400
Cash Requirements from Start-Up	$25,500
Additional Cash Raised	$0
Cash Balance on Starting Date	$25,500
Total Assets	$191,900
Liabilities and Capital	
Liabilities	
Current Borrowing	$9,000
Long-Term Liabilities	$131,400
Accounts Payable (Outstanding Bills)	$0
Other Current Liabilities (Interest Free)	$0
Total Liabilities	$140,400
Capital	
Planned Investment	
Partner 1	$10,000
Partner 2	$10,000
Partner 3	$10,000
Partner 4	$10,000
Partner 5	$11,500
Partner 6	$10,000
Partner 7	$11,500
Partner 8	$10,000
Partner 9	$11,500
Partner 10	$10,000
Partner 11	$11,500
Partner 12	$11,500
Other	$97,770
Additional Investment Requirement	$0
Total Planned Investment	$225,270
Loss at Start-Up (Start-Up Expenses)	($173,770)
Total Capital	$51,500
Total Capital and Liabilities	$191,900
Total Funding	$365,670

2.3 Company Locations and Facilities

The Daily Perc will open its first drive-through facility on Manchester Road in the Colonial Square Shopping Center. We will locate 12 more drive-through facilities through-out the metropolitan area over the next three years. The drive-through in the Colonial Square Shopping Center will serve as the commissary for the first mobile unit.

The demographic and physical requirements for a drive-through location are the following:

- Traffic of 40,000+ cars per day on store side
- Visible from roadway
- Easy entry, preferably with a traffic light
- Established retail shops in area

The founders identified TDP's first location with the help of MapInfo's Spectrum Location Intelligence Module, a mapping and geographic analysis software package that enables users to visualize the relationships between demographic and traffic count data and geography to produce maps that show the best locations for businesses. We will use this software to choose the company's future locations in the metropolitan area. As TDP expands into other cities, managers will supplement the insight that MapInfo provides with the tools in ZoomProspector, another useful location analysis tool, to identify the cities that are most likely to be home to other successful TDP locations.

3.0 Products

The Daily Perc provides its patrons the finest hot and cold beverages, specializing in specialty coffees and custom-blended teas. In addition, TDP will offer select domestic soft drinks, Italian sodas, fresh-baked pastries, and other confections. Seasonally, TDP will add beverages such as hot apple cider, hot chocolate, frozen coffees, and more.

3.1 Product Description

The Daily Perc provides its customers, whether at a drive-through facility or at one of the Mobile Cafés, the ability to custom-order a beverage that will be blended to their exact specifications. Each of TDP's Baristas will be trained in the fine art of brewing, blending, and serving the highest-quality hot and cold beverages with exceptional attention to detail.

Besides its selection of coffees, TDP will offer teas, domestic and Italian sodas, frozen coffee beverages, seasonal specialty drinks, pastries, and other baked goods. Through the Web site and certain locations, TDP will market premium items bearing the TDP logo, such as coffee mugs, T-shirts, sweatshirts, caps, and more.

3.2 Competitive Comparison

The Daily Perc considers itself to be a player in the retail coffeehouse industry. However, we understand that competition for its products range from soft drinks to milk shakes to adult beverages.

The Daily Perc's primary competition will come from three sources:

1. National coffeehouses, such as Starbucks and Panera

2. Locally owned and operated cafés

3. Fast-food chains and convenience stores

Two things make TDP stand out from all its competitors: The Daily Perc will provide products in the most convenient and efficient way, either at one of the two-sided drive-through shops or at one of the Mobile Cafés. This separates TDP from the competition in that its customers won't have to find parking places, wait in a long lines, jockey for seats, and clean up the mess left by previous patrons. The Daily Perc's customers can drive or walk up, order their beverages, receive and pay for them and quickly be on their way.

The second differentiator is TDP's focus on providing a significant benefit to the community through a 7.5 percent contribution to customer-identified charities, schools, or other institutions.

3.3 Sourcing

The Daily Perc purchases its coffees from PJ's Coffee. It also has wholesale purchasing agreements for other products with Major Brands, Coca-Cola, Big Train, Al's Famous Filled Bagels, L&N Products, and Royal Distribution.

The drive-through facilities are manufactured by City Stations, and the Mobile Cafés are manufactured by Tow Tech Industries.

Fulfillment equipment suppliers include PJ's Coffee, City Stations, Talbert Ford, and Retail Image Programs. The Daily Perc's computer equipment and Internet connectivity are provided by NSI Communications.

3.4 Technology

The Daily Perc's delivery system uses state-of-the-art, two-sided drive-through facilities to provide convenience and efficiency for its clientele. An architectural exterior diagram of the drive-through building can be found in the appendix (not included in this sample plan).

The Daily Perc also has designed state-of-the-art Mobile Cafés that will be deployed on high school and college campuses, on corporate campuses, and at special events.

3.5 Future Products

The Daily Perc will offer products that reflect the changing seasons and customers' changing demand for beverages. During the warm summer months, TDP will offset lower hot beverage sales with frozen coffee drinks as well as soft drinks and other cold beverages. The Daily Perc will also have special beverages during holiday seasons, such as eggnog during the Christmas season and hot apple cider in the fall.

The Daily Perc's primary desire will be to listen to its customers to ascertain which products they want and to provide them.

4.0 Market Analysis Summary

The Daily Perc will focus on two markets:

1. *The daily commuter.* Someone traveling to or from work, out shopping, delivering goods or services, or just out for a drive

2. *The captive consumer.* Someone who is in a restricted environment that does not allow convenient departure and return while searching for refreshments or where refreshment stands are an integral part of the environment

4.1 Market Segmentation

The Daily Perc will focus on two different market segments: commuters and captive consumers. To access both of these markets, TDP has two different delivery systems. For the commuters, TDP offers the drive-through coffeehouse. For the captive consumer, TDP offers the Mobile Café.

Commuters are defined as anyone in a motorized vehicle traveling "from point A to point B." The Daily Perc's principal focus will be on attracting commuters heading to or from work and those on their lunch breaks.

Captive consumers include those who are tethered to a campus environment or to a restricted-entry environment where people's schedules afford limited time to make purchases. Examples include high school and college campuses, where students have limited time between classes, and corporate campuses, where the same time constraints are involved.

The following table and pie chart reflect the number of venues available for the Mobile Cafés and the growth we expect in those markets over the next five years. For an estimate of the number of Captive Consumers, we multiplied the total number of venues by 1,000. For example, in year 1, we estimate that there are 2,582 venues at which we might position a Mobile Café. That would equate to a captive consumer potential of 2,582,000 people.

Similarly, there are more than 2,500,000 commuters in the metropolitan area as well as visitors, vacationers, and others. Some of these commuters make not just one beverage purchase a day but, in many cases, two and even three beverage purchases.

The chart also reflects college and high school campuses, special events, hospital campuses, and various charitable organizations. A segment that the chart does not show (because it would skew the chart greatly) is the number of corporate campuses in the metropolitan area. There are more than 1,700 corporate facilities that employ more than 500 people, giving us an additional 1,700,000 potential customers, or a total of 2,582 locations at which we could place a Mobile Café.

Table: Market Analysis

Market Analysis		Year 1	Year 2	Year 3	Year 4	Year 5	
Potential Customers	Growth						CAGR
Public High School Campuses	1%	80	81	82	83	84	1.23%
Private High Schools	0%	88	88	88	88	88	0.00%
College Campuses	0%	77	77	77	77	77	0.00%
Golf Courses	0%	99	99	99	99	99	0.00%
Special Events	3%	43	44	45	46	47	2.25%
Nonprofits with $500K+ Budgets	2%	362	369	376	384	392	2.01%
Hospital Campuses	0%	100	100	100	100	100	0.00%
Total	1.10%	849	858	867	877	887	1.10%

CHART: MARKET ANALYSIS (PIE)

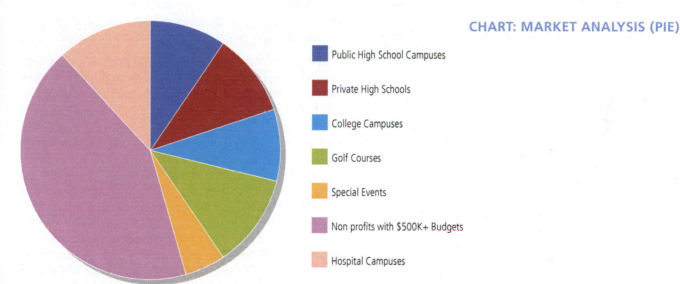

- Public High School Campuses
- Private High Schools
- College Campuses
- Golf Courses
- Special Events
- Non profits with $500K+ Budgets
- Hospital Campuses

Source: Based on data from the National Coffee Association.

4.2 Target Market Segment Strategy

The Daily Perc's target market is the mobile customer who has more money than time and excellent taste in the choice of a beverage but no desire to linger in a café. By locating the drive-throughs in high-traffic/high-visibility areas, these customers will patronize TDP and become our regular guests.

Our Mobile Cafés will allow TDP to take the café to the customer! By using the community support program that TDP is instituting, we will make arrangements to visit high schools, college campuses, or corporate campuses once or twice a month. (We also will offer to visit these facilities for special games, tournaments, recruiting events, or corporate open houses.) We will return a portion of the revenue from each beverage or baked goods sold to the high school or college, allowing the institution to reap a financial reward while providing a pleasant and fulfilling benefit to their students or employees.

4.2.1 MARKET TRENDS Nearly 20 years ago, a trend toward more unique coffees began to develop in the United States. There had always been specialty coffee stores, such as Gloria Jeans and others, but people began to buy espresso machines for their homes and offices. Coffee tastings in stores became popular, and later espresso bars began to appear. Then along came Starbucks, the quintessential bastion of upwardly mobile professionals who wanted to take control over how their beverages were made.

Since Starbucks arrived on the scene, people have become more pressed for time. The same customers who helped push Starbucks's sales to nearly $10 billion are now rushing to get their kids to soccer practice and basketball games, running to the grocery store, and trying to get to work on time and back home in time for dinner—or to get to the next soccer game. Yet they still have the desire for that refreshing, specially blended coffee each morning.

Recently, we have seen the introduction of beverage dispensers at convenience stores that spit out overly sweet, poorly blended cappuccinos in flavors such as French vanilla or mocha, and consumers are paying as much as $3.00 for these substandard beverages.

The market is primed for the introduction of a company that offers a superior quality, specially blended product in a convenient, drive-through environment at a price that is competitive with national coffeehouses.

The Daily Perc is a member of the National Coffee Association and the National Specialty Coffee Association. These two trade associations provide useful information on the relevant trends in the industry, information for making comparisons to other companies on financial performance, and educational workshops and seminars.

4.2.2 MARKET GROWTH

The 183 million Americans who drink coffee consume 146 *billion* cups of coffee per year. In addition, more than 173 million people in the United States drink tea. According to industry statistics, the consumption of coffee and flavored coffee products is growing rapidly, and 34 percent of coffee drinkers go to "premium" coffee outlets to purchase their beverages.

The segment of the market we are targeting is the commuter, and the number of people who commute to work is increasing by about 6 percent per year. In the metropolitan area, as with many metropolitan areas in the country, there is a migration away from the cities as people choose to live in quiet suburban areas and drive to work in the city.

The United States is home to 128.3 million commuters. Using census data, we estimate that more than 2.5 million commuters drive to and from work each day in our defined market. In addition, research shows that 54 percent of Americans drink coffee every day and that the typical coffee drinker consumes three nine-ounce cups of coffee per day. Nearly 65 percent of coffee consumption takes place in the morning, 30 percent occurs between meals, and 5 percent occurs between meals. Therefore, TDP has a significant daily target for its beverages, particularly during the morning drive time.

4.2.3 MARKET NEEDS

The United States is a very mobile society. With the introduction of the automobile, we became a nation that thrived on the freedom of going where we wanted when we wanted. The population of the United States is 315 million people, and there are more licensed vehicles in the country than there are people. The population's mobility has created a unique need in our society for products available "on the go."

Our market is made up of consumers who have busy schedules, a desire for quality, and adequate disposable income. As much as they would like the opportunity to sit in an upscale coffeehouse and sip a uniquely blended coffee beverage and read the morning paper, they don't have the time. However, they still have the desire for a uniquely blended beverage as they hurry through their busy lives.

4.3 Industry Analysis

Consumers in the United States drink *450 million cups* of coffee per *day* and spend *$40 billion* a *year* on coffee-based drinks. The coffee industry in the United States has grown rapidly in the United States over the last five years. Sales of specialty coffees are growing at a rate of 20 percent per year. Even general coffee sales have increased, with international brands such as Folgers, Maxwell House, and Safari coffee reporting higher sales and greater profits. The United States is the leading coffee-consuming nation in the world, and the coffee industry is reaping the rewards.

4.3.1 DISTRIBUTION PATTERNS

The café experience comes from the Italian origins of espresso. The customer enters a beautifully decorated facility surrounded by wondrous aromas and finds himself or herself involved in a sensory experience that, more often than not, masks an average product at a premium price. However, the proliferation of cafés in the United States proves the viability of the market. It is a duplication of the same delivery process as currently exists in Europe.

4.3.2 COMPETITION AND BUYING PATTERNS

There are four general competitors in TDP's drive-through market. They are the national specialty beverage chains, such as Starbucks and Panera; local coffeehouses—or cafés with an established clientele and a quality product; fast-food restaurants; and convenience stores. There is a dramatic distinction among the patrons of each of these outlets.

Patrons of Starbucks or of one of the local cafés are looking for the "experience" of the coffeehouse. They want the ability to "design" a custom coffee, smell fresh pastries, listen to soothing Italian music, and read a newspaper or visit with a friend. It is a relaxing, slow-paced environment.

Patrons of fast-food restaurants or convenience stores expect just the opposite. They have no time for idle chatter and are willing to overpay for whatever beverage the machine spits out—as long as it's quick. They pay for their gas and are back on the road to work. Although they have ability to differentiate between a good cup of coffee and a bad one, time is more valuable to them than quality.

Competitors of the Mobile Cafés on campuses include fast-food restaurants (assuming that they are close enough so that customers can get there and back in the minimal allotted time), vending machines, and company or school cafeterias. The customers in this environment are looking for a quick, convenient, fairly priced, quality beverage that allows them to purchase the product and return to work, class, or other activity.

Competitors of the Mobile Cafés at events such as festivals and fairs include all the other vendors who are licensed to sell refreshments. Attendees of these events expect to pay a premium price for a quality product.

4.3.3 MAIN COMPETITORS

The Daily Perc has no direct competitors in the drive-through segment of the market in the metropolitan area. The Daily Perc will be the first double-sided, drive-through coffeehouse in the city. However, we face significant competition from indirect competitors in the form of traditional coffeehouses, convenience stores, fast-food outlets, and other retailers.

National Chains: In 2013, Starbucks, the national leader, operated more than 11,400 retail outlets in the United States (and nearly 8,400 foreign outlets) that generated operating revenue of $14.9 billion, which represents an increase of 12 percent over 2012. The average annual revenue for a Starbucks outlet is $754,000, or $89,558 in revenue per employee.

Panera Bread had revenues of $2.11 billion, an increase of 12.2 percent over 2012. Annual sales at the average Panera Bread outlet are $2.5 million. Coffee beverages are not the primary focus of Panera Bread's menu.

Despite its name, Dunkin' Donuts's primary emphasis is on selling coffee. The company has more than 11,000 outlets worldwide, 7,000 of which are in the United States. Constructing a Dunkin' Donuts retail store costs about $500,000, and average sales at a Dunkin' Donuts outlet in the United States are $845,000. The company's stronghold on market share is greatest in the Northeast, where it originated.

The Daily Perc believes it has a significant competitive advantage over these chains because of the following benefits:

- Drive-through service
- Superior customer service
- Community benefit
- Mobile Cafés
- Greater selection
- Higher product quality

Local Cafés: The toughest competitor for TDP is the established locally owned café. The Daily Perc knows the quality and pride that the local café has in the products their customers purchase. Local cafés typically benefit from their loyal, highly educated customers. The quality of beverages served at an established café surpasses those of the regional or national chains.

The competitive edge TDP has over local cafés is based on the following:

- Drive-through service
- Supply discounts
- Mobile Café
- Consistent menu
- Community benefit
- Quality product

Drive-Through Coffeehouses: There are no drive-through specialty beverage retailers with a significant market presence in the central United States. The only company

with similar depth to that of TDP is Quikava, a wholly owned subsidiary of Chock Full 'o Nuts. However, Quikava has limited its corporate footprint to the East Coast and the Great Lakes region.

In the drive-through specialty beverage market, TDP has a competitive edge over these competitors, including Quikava, because of the following:

- Mobile Cafés
- Consistent menu
- Community benefit
- Quality product
- Supply discounts
- Valued image
- Greater product selection

Fast-Food and Convenience Stores: Most national fast food chains and national convenience store chains already serve coffee, soda, and some breakfast foods. The national fast-food chains understand the benefits and value that drive-through service provides customers; 70 percent of the typical fast-food outlet's sales come from drive-through customers. In addition, nearly 80 percent of the growth in the fast-food industry in the last five years has come through outlets' drive-through windows. Customers who buy coffee at fast-food and convenience stores shop primarily on the basis of price rather than quality and, therefore, are not TDP's primary target customers. The Daily Perc's advantage is that the quality of the products it sells is much higher than those sold at fast-food and convenience stores. Soft-drink sales for the typical quick-serve store account for a large portion of beverage sales. The Daily Perc believes that the quality of its products and the convenience of speedy drive-through service give it a competitive edge over fast-food and convenience stores.

Other Competition: The Daily Perc understands that once it has entered the market and established a presence, others will try to follow. However, TDP believes that although imitators will appear, they cannot duplicate its corporate mission, organizational design, or customer value proposition. The Daily Perc will constantly evaluate its products, locations, service, and mission to ensure that it remains a leader in the specialty beverage industry in its market segment.

4.3.4 INDUSTRY PARTICIPANTS There is only one national drive-through coffee franchise operation in the United States that poses a threat: a subsidiary of Chock Full 'o Nuts called Quikava. Quikava operates primarily on the East Coast and in the upper Great Lakes region. The East and West coasts and even some Mountain and Midwest states have smaller local drive-through chains such as Caffino, Java Espress, Crane Coffee, Java Drive, Sunrise Coffee, and Caffe Diva. However, other players in the premium coffee service industry include Starbucks, Gloria Jean's, Caribou Coffee, Panera Bread, and locally owned and operated coffee shops or "cafés."

5.0 Strategy and Implementation Summary

The Daily Perc will penetrate the commuter and captive consumer markets by deploying drive-through facilities and Mobile Cafés in highly visible, high-volume, accessible locations. The drive-throughs are designed to handle two-sided traffic and dispense customer-designed, specially ordered cups of specialty beverages in less time than required for a visit to the locally owned café or one of the national chains.

The Daily Perc has identified its market as busy, mobile people whose time is already at a premium but who desire a refreshing, high-quality beverage or baked item while commuting to or from work or school.

In addition to providing a quality product and an extensive menu of delicious side items, TDP pledges to donate up to 7.5 percent of revenue from each cup sold in individual drive-throughs to the charities that its customers choose.

5.1 Strategy Pyramid

The Daily Perc's strategy is to offer customers quality products, convenient accessibility, and a community benefit. To execute this strategy, TDP is placing the drive-throughs and Mobile Cafés in well-researched, easily accessible locations throughout the metropolitan area. The Daily Perc is pricing its product competitively and training the production staff to be among the best Baristas in the country. Prices for TDP's products are at or slightly below the national average. Through coupons and display ads at its locations, TDP will involve customers in community support efforts by donating a portion of each sale to a charity of their choosing.

In so doing, TDP has accomplished the following:

1. Provided a customer with a quality product at a competitive price

2. Provided customers with a more convenient method for obtaining their desired products

3. Demonstrated how TDP appreciates their loyalty and patronage by donating money to a meaningful cause

5.2 Value Proposition

The drive-through facilities provide a substantial value proposition because our customers do not have to find parking places, exit their vehicles, stand in long lines to order, pay premium prices for average products, find places to sit, clean up the previous patron's mess, and then enjoy their coffee—assuming that they have sufficient time to linger over the cup.

The Daily Perc's concept is that the customer drives up, places an order that is filled quickly and accurately, receives a high-quality product at a competitive price, and drives away, having invested little time in the process.

The Daily Perc is also providing a significant community value on behalf of customers who patronize TDP. For every purchase a customer makes from us, TDP will donate up to 7.5 percent of each sale to a local charity selected by our customers.

5.3 Competitive Edge

The Daily Perc's competitive edge is simple. TDP provides a high-quality product at a competitive price in a drive-through environment that saves customers valuable time.

5.4 Marketing Strategy

The Daily Perc will be placing its drive-through facilities in highly visible, easily accessible locations. They will be located on high-traffic commuter routes and near shopping centers and concentrations of complementary retail shops to catch customers who are traveling to or from work, going out for lunch, or venturing on a shopping expedition. The drive-throughs' design is very unique and eye-catching, which will be a branding feature of its own.

As the following chart indicates, TDP's target audience skews older.

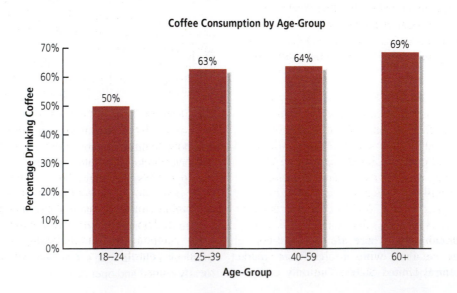

Coffee Consumption by Age-Group

Therefore, TDP will implement a low-cost advertising campaign that includes traditional advertising media, such as drive-time radio and a few strategically located outdoor ads. However, because a significant portion of our target customers is younger than 40, we also will use social media tools extensively.

The Daily Perc will rely on building relationships with schools, charities, and companies to provide significant free publicity through its community support program. When TDP makes charitable contributions to these institutions, they will get the word out to their students/faculty/employees/partners about TDP. Word-of-mouth advertising has long been one of the greatest advertising techniques a company can use. In addition, we will encourage the media to cover the charitable aspects of TDP, giving the company the opportunity for more exposure every time TDP writes a check to a nonprofit organization.

The Daily Perc will use social media marketing tools such as Twitter and Facebook as well, particularly to promote the locations of its Mobile Cafés. We will send tweets to our followers to alert them to the location of our Mobile Cafés. We also will post the Mobile Cafés' locations on Facebook.

5.4.1 PROMOTION STRATEGY
The long-range goal is to gain enough visibility to expand the TDP brand into other regions and generate inquiries from potential inventors. To do that, TDP must employ the following:

- A public relations service at $1,000 per month for the next year to generate awareness of TDP among newspapers, magazines, bloggers, and reviews. We anticipate that the school fund-raising program will generate a publicity on its own and eventually will minimize—or even eliminate—the need for a publicist.

- Advertising expenditures of $1,000 per month focused on drive-time radio and strategically selected billboards. The Daily Perc will experiment with different stations, keeping careful track of results. We will select billboards that are near our existing locations to serve as reminders of our locations for passing motorists. As with the school fund-raising program, TDP expects its storefronts and signage to be a substantial portion of our advertising.

- A social media presence on Facebook, Twitter, and YouTube. We can use these tools to reach our target customers at very little expense. We will promote daily specials on selected items on Facebook and Twitter and will post videos of our Best Barista Contest on YouTube. We also plan to involve our customers through a contest that offers free coffee for one year to the customer who posts the best YouTube video promoting TDP. We also will sponsor a "Fan of the Day" contest by randomly drawing one person who likes TDP on Facebook to receive a free cup of coffee and announcing the winner on Facebook and on Twitter.

5.4.2 DISTRIBUTION STRATEGY
The Daily Perc will locate its drive-through facilities in high-traffic areas of the city where it knows working commuters will be passing. Our first outlet will be located at the corner of Main Street and Broughton Road, which has a traffic count of 42,200 cars per day.

The Daily Perc will also make arrangements for the Mobile Cafés to be at as many schools, businesses, and events as possible every year to promote TDP to new customers.

5.4.3 MARKETING PROGRAMS
Distinctive Logo: Our logo, "Papo," is a very happy and conspicuous sun. The sun touches every human being every day, and TDP wants to touch its customers every day. Papo is already an award-winning logo, having won the "New Artist Category" of the 2013 Not Just Another Art Director's Club (NJAADC).

Distinctive Buildings: The Daily Perc is using diner-style buildings for its drive-through facilities and has worked closely with the manufacturer to make the building distinctive so that it is easy to recognize and functional.

The Mobile Café: The Mobile Café will be a key marketing tool for TDP. The similarities between the Mobile Cafés and the drive-through facilities will be unmistakable. The exposure that these units provide is difficult to measure directly but is extremely important to the company's growth. The Daily Perc will negotiate visits for its mobile units at schools, hospitals, companies, and special events. A portion of all sales made while at these locations will go to a nonprofit entity of the organization's choice. The organization will promote its presence to its constituency and encourage them to frequent TDP's drive-through establishments to support their charitable cause. This will give those patrons an opportunity to taste the products and become regular customers of the drive-through facilities. The Mobile Cafés will also appear at community events, such as fairs, festivals, and other charitable events.

Advertising and Promotion: In the first year, TDP plans to spend moderately on advertising and promotion, with the program beginning in June, prior to the opening of the first drive-through. This would not be considered a serious advertising budget for any business, but TDP believes that the exposure will come from publicity and promotion, so we will spend most of the funds on a good publicist who will get the word out about the charitable contribution program and how it works in conjunction with the Web site. The Daily Perc also believes that word-of-mouth advertising and free beverage coupons will be better ways to drive people to the first and second locations.

In the second year, TDP will increase the budget because it will need to promote several locations, with particular emphasis on announcing these openings and all the other locations. The Daily Perc will continue to use publicity as a key component of the marketing program because TDP could be contributing more than $70,000 to local schools and charities.

In the third year, TDP will double its advertising and promotion budget, with the majority of the advertising budget being spent on drive-time radio to reach our commuting target audience. As in the previous years, TDP will get substantial publicity from the donation of nearly $200,000 to local schools and charities.

5.4.4 PRICING STRATEGY

The national average price for a cup of brewed coffee is $1.38, and the average price of an espresso-based drink is $2.45. The Daily Perc's pricing will be slightly below those of the national chain coffeehouses but very similar to those of local cafés to reflect the value-added feature of immediate, drive-through service and convenience. Costs to make a 6-ounce cup of coffee are as follows:

Coffee	$0.25
Cup, lid, and sleeve	0.22
Milk	0.21
Total	$0.68

Additional ingredients add anywhere from $0.02 (sugar) to $1.08 (mocha syrup) to the cost of a single 6-ounce cup of coffee for a total cost that ranges from $0.70 for a basic cup of premium coffee to $1.76 for a café mocha.

5.5 Sales Strategy

We will rely on several in-store sales strategies, including posting specials on high-profit items at the drive-up window. The Daily Perc also will use a customer loyalty program that awards a free cup of coffee to customers who have accumulated the required number of points by purchasing 12 cups of coffee. Customers also can earn points by telling others about their purchases at TDP on Facebook, Twitter, and other social media sites. The Daily Perc will also develop window cross-selling techniques, such as the Baristas asking whether customers would like a fresh-baked item with their coffee.

5.5.1 SALES FORECAST

In the first year, TDP anticipates having two drive-through locations in operation. The first location will open on July 15. The second drive-through will open six months later. The Daily Perc is building in a few weeks of "ramp-up" time for each facility while commuters become familiar with its presence. The drive-throughs will generate 288,000 checks in the first year of operation.

In the second year, TDP will add two more drive-throughs, and in the third year, TDP will add an additional nine drive-through facilities. The addition of these facilities will increase the revenue from drive-throughs with a total of more than 1,000,000 checks in the second year and 2,675,000 checks in the third.

In addition to the drive-throughs, TDP will deploy one mobile unit in the fourth quarter of the first fiscal year and expects this mobile unit to generate 10,000 checks at an average check of $2.45 (including baked goods).

In the second quarter of the second fiscal year, TDP will deploy its second and third mobile units and expects all three mobile units to generate a total of 150,000 checks in the second year. In the third fiscal year, with the addition of a fourth mobile unit, TDP expects to generate 264,000 mobile unit checks.

The Daily Perc also will generate revenue from the sale of "The Daily Perc" T-shirts, sweatshirts, insulated coffee mugs, prepackaged coffee beans, and other items. The Daily Perc is not expecting this to be a significant profit center, but it is an integral part of the marketing plan and an important part of developing our brand and building product awareness. The Daily Perc expects revenues from this portion, which will begin in the second fiscal year, to reach as much as $3,000 per month in the third fiscal year.

We forecast total first year unit sales will reach 298,402 cups. The second year will see unit sales increase to 1,177,400 cups. The third year, with the addition of a significant number of outlets, we will see unit sales increase to 2,992,000 cups.

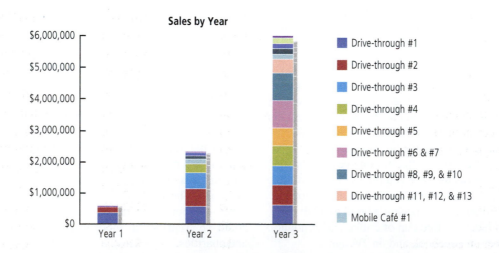

Sales by Year

Legend:
- Drive-through #1
- Drive-through #2
- Drive-through #3
- Drive-through #4
- Drive-through #5
- Drive-through #6 & #7
- Drive-through #8, #9, & #10
- Drive-through #11, #12, & #13
- Mobile Café #1

Table: Sales Forecast

Sales Forecast			
	Year 1	Year 2	Year 3
Unit Sales			
Drive-Through 1	202,913	300,000	325,000
Drive-Through 2	85,489	300,000	325,000
Drive-Through 3	0	275,000	325,000
Drive-Through 4	0	150,000	325,000
Drive-Through 5	0	0	300,000
Drive-Throughs 6 and 7	0	0	450,000
Drive-Throughs 8, 9, and 10	0	0	450,000
Drive-Throughs 11, 12, and 13	0	0	225,000
Mobile Café 1	10,000	60,000	66,000
Mobile Café 2	0	45,000	66,000
Mobile Café 3	0	45,000	66,000
Mobile Café 4	0	0	66,000
Web Site Sales/Premium Items	0	2,400	3,000
Total Unit Sales	298,402	1,177,400	2,992,000
Unit Prices	Year 1	Year 2	Year 3
Drive-Through 1	$1.85	$1.90	$1.95
Drive-Through 2	$1.85	$1.90	$1.95
Drive-Through 3	$0.00	$1.90	$1.95
Drive-Through 4	$0.00	$1.90	$1.95
Drive-Through 5	$0.00	$1.90	$1.95
Drive-Throughs 6 and 7	$0.00	$1.90	$1.95
Drive-Throughs 8, 9, and 10	$0.00	$1.90	$1.95
Drive-Throughs 11, 12, and 13	$0.00	$1.90	$1.95
Mobile Café 1	$2.45	$2.50	$2.55
Mobile Café 2	$0.00	$2.50	$2.55
Mobile Café 3	$0.00	$2.50	$2.55
Mobile Café 4	$0.00	$2.50	$2.55
Web Site Sales/Premium Items	$0.00	$11.00	$12.00
Sales			
Drive-Through 1	$375,389	$570,000	$633,750
Drive-Through 2	$158,154	$570,000	$633,750
Drive-Through 3	$0	$522,500	$633,750
Drive-Through 4	$0	$285,000	$633,750
Drive-Through 5	$0	$0	$585,000
Drive-Throughs 6 and 7	$0	$0	$877,500
Drive-Throughs 8, 9, and 10	$0	$0	$877,500
Drive-Throughs 11, 12, and 13	$0	$0	$438,750
Mobile Café 1	$24,500	$150,000	$168,300
Mobile Café 2	$0	$112,500	$168,300
Mobile Café 3	$0	$112,500	$168,300
Mobile Café 4	$0	$0	$168,300
Web Site Sales/Premium Items	$0	$26,400	$36,000
Total Sales	$558,043	$2,348,900	$6,022,950

(continued)

Table: Sales Forecast (*continued*)

Sales Forecast

	Year 1	Year 2	Year 3
Direct Unit Costs	Year 1	Year 2	Year 3
Drive-Through 1	$0.64	$0.61	$0.59
Drive-Through 2	$0.64	$0.61	$0.59
Drive-Through 3	$0.00	$0.61	$0.59
Drive-Through 4	$0.00	$0.61	$0.59
Drive-Through 5	$0.00	$0.61	$0.59
Drive-Throughs 6 and 7	$0.00	$0.61	$0.59
Drive-Throughs 8, 9, and 10	$0.00	$0.61	$0.59
Drive-Throughs 11, 12, and 13	$0.00	$0.61	$0.59
Mobile Café 1	$0.64	$0.61	$0.59
Mobile Café 2	$0.00	$0.61	$0.59
Mobile Café 3	$0.00	$0.61	$0.59
Mobile Café 4	$0.00	$0.61	$0.59
Web Site Sales/Premium Items	$0.00	$6.50	$6.50
Direct Cost of Sales			
Drive-Through 1	$129,864	$183,000	$191,750
Drive-Through 2	$54,713	$183,000	$191,750
Drive-Through 3	$0	$167,750	$191,750
Drive-Through 4	$0	$91,500	$191,750
Drive-Through 5	$0	$0	$177,000
Drive-Throughs 6 and 7	$0	$0	$265,500
Drive-Throughs 8, 9, and 10	$0	$0	$265,500
Drive-Throughs 11, 12, and 13	$0	$0	$132,750
Mobile Café #1	$6,400	$36,600	$38,940
Mobile Café #2	$0	$27,450	$38,940
Mobile Café #3	$0	$27,450	$38,940
Mobile Café #4	$0	$0	$38,940
Web Site Sales/Premium Items	$0	$15,600	$19,500
Subtotal Direct Cost of Sales	$190,977	$732,350	$1,783,010

5.5.2 SALES PROGRAMS

Corporate Tasting Events. The Daily Perc plans to host at least one tasting event for customers each quarter. In addition, TDP will adjust its menu to reflect the changing seasons in the flavors it served.

Drink Coupons. At fund-raising events for schools and corporate events, we will give away drink coupons as door prizes or awards. These giveaways are inexpensive and encourage new customers to come in to claim a free beverage and bring a friend or buy a baked item or a package of our premium coffee. The drive-through units will also distribute coupons for special menu items or new product introductions.

Chamber of Commerce and Professional Membership. Because of the need to promote its drive-through locations and its Mobile Café services, TDP will be an active member in the regional and local chambers of commerce, food service associations, and two national coffee associations. The exposure and education that these organizations provide is outstanding, but equally important are the contacts and opportunities made available for deploying a Mobile Café—or even two—at a special event.

5.6 Milestones

The Milestone table reflects critical dates for occupying headquarters, launching the first drive-through and subsequent drive-throughs as well as deploying the mobile units. The Daily Perc also defines our break-even month, our Web site launch and subsequent visitor interaction function, and other key markers that will help us measure our success.

Table: Milestones

Milestones

Milestone	Start Date	End Date	Budget	Manager	Department
Launch Web Site	6/1/2015	8/15/2015	$5,600	COO	Marketing
Open First Drive-Through	7/15/2015	8/31/2015	$105,400	COO	Administration
First Break-Even Month	12/1/2015	12/31/2015	$0	COO	Finance
Open Second Drive-Through	12/15/2015	2/1/2015	$105,400	COO	Administration
Receive First Mobile Unit	3/1/2016	3/30/2016	$86,450	COO	Administration
Launch Web Site Voting	5/1/2016	6/1/2016	$12,500	COO	Marketing
Open Third Drive-Through	4/15/2016	6/1/2016	$105,400	COO	Administration
Receive Second and Third Mobile Units	7/15/2016	9/1/2016	$172,900	COO	Administration
Open Fourth Drive-Through	12/15/2016	2/1/2017	$105,400	COO	Administration
Install Point-of-Sale System	12/1/2016	2/1/2017	$21,000	CIO	MIS
Occupy Headquarters	4/1/2017	5/15/2017	$45,000	COO	Administration
Open Fifth Drive-Through	4/15/2017	6/1/2017	$105,400	COO	Administration
Receive Fourth Mobile Unit	4/15/2017	6/1/2017	$86,450	Equipment	Administration
Open Drive-Throughs 6 and 7	7/15/2017	9/15/2017	$210,800	COO/Director	Management
Open Drive-Through 8, 9, and 10	10/15/2017	12/15/2017	$316,200	COO/Director	Management
Open Drive-Throughs 11, 12, and 13	1/15/2018	3/1/2018	$316,200	COO	Administration
Expand to Kansas City	1/15/2018	6/1/2018	$176,943	COO	Management
Open First Franchise	10/31/2017	9/1/2018	$45,000	CFO	Finance
Initiate Exit Strategy	10/1/2018	1/1/2019	$100,000	CFO	Management
Totals			$2,122,043		

6.0 Management Summary

The Daily Perc will maintain a relatively flat organization. Overhead for management will be kept to a minimum, and all senior managers will be "hands-on" workers. We have no intention of creating a top-heavy organization that drains profits and complicates decision making.

At the end of year 3, TDP will have four executive positions: chief operating officer, chief financial officer, chief information officer, and director of marketing. There will be other midmanagement positions, such as district managers for every four drive-throughs and a facilities manager to oversee the maintenance and stocking of the Mobile Cafés and the equipment in the drive-through facilities.

6.1 Management Team

The Daily Perc has selected Mr. Barton Fisher to perform the duties of chief operating officer. Bart has an entrepreneurial spirit and has already started a company (NetCom Services, Inc.) that was profitable within three months of start-up and paid off all of its initial debt within six months. Bart's experience, leadership, and focus and three years of research in specialty drinks and drive-through service make him the ideal chief operating officer for TDP.

Ms. Mary Jamison will fill the position of bookkeeper and office manager. Mary has been the business administrator of Jones International, Inc., for the last four years. Jones is a $4 million company that retails vitamins and other nutritional products. During her four years with Jones International, Mary has written numerous corporate policies and directed the financial reporting.

Mr. Tony Guy will perform the duties of corporate events coordinator on a part-time basis. Tony has more than five years of experience in business-to-business sales. Last year he sold more than $250,000 in sales of promotional material to corporate and educational clients.

Mr. Chuck McNulty will fill the position of warehouse/trailer manager. Chuck has been working for Nabisco, Inc., as a service representative for more than 10 years; before that, he was involved in inventory control for a Nabisco factory. His experience in account services, merchandising, and inventory control is a welcome addition to the TDP team. Chuck will use his knowledge to establish inventory and warehouse policies. The warehouse manager is responsible for the inventory of all products sold by TDP. In addition, knowledge of regulations and health requirements are important. Chuck will be responsible for ensuring that TDP maintains proper levels of inventory. He will work closely with the mobile and drive-through Baristas to make sure that all of the products they sell are fresh, appetizing, and available in the appropriate quantities at the right time.

6.2 Management Team Gaps

The Daily Perc will require several additional management team members over the next three years. We will hire one district manager for every four drive-throughs. These district managers will oversee the quality of the products sold, the training of the Baristas, inventory management, and customer satisfaction. Eventually, the goal is to promote from within, particularly from our Mobile Café and drive-through teams, for these positions.

By the beginning of the third year, TDP will have hired three key senior managers: a chief financial officer, a chief information officer, and a director of marketing. We will discuss the roles of each of these managers in subsequent sections of this plan.

6.3 Organizational Structure

The organization will be relatively flat; most of TDP's employees are involved in production, and our goal is to maintain a small core of qualified managers who empower employees to make decisions that are in our customers' best interest.

There are three functioning groups within the company: production, sales and marketing, and general and administrative. For purposes of this plan—and to show the details of adding senior-level management—TDP has broken management down as a separate segment, but it is an integral part of the general and administrative function.

Production involves the Baristas, or customer service specialists, who will be staffing the drive-throughs and Mobile Cafés and blending the beverages for the customers. The sales and marketing staff will coordinate the promotion and scheduling of the Mobile Cafés as well as the promotion of the drive-throughs and the Community Contribution program. General and administrative personnel will manage the facilities, equipment, inventory, payroll, and other basic, operational processes for the company.

6.4 Personnel Plan

The Daily Perc forecasts its first year to be rather lean because we will have only two locations and one mobile unit,

none of which will be in operation for the entire year. The total head count for the first year, including management, administrative support, and customer service (production) employees, is 15. The payroll expenditures are shown in the following table.

In the second year, with the addition of two drive-throughs and two mobile units, TDP will add customer service personnel, its first district manager, and some additional support staff at headquarters, including an inventory clerk, equipment technician, and administrative support staff. The head count will increase by nearly 100 percent in the second year to 29, causing a significant increase in payroll expense.

In the third year, we will see the most dramatic growth in head count—180 percent over year 2—because of the addition of nine drive-throughs and another mobile unit. Total payroll for the third year will reflect this increase as well as the significant increase in the senior management team with the addition of a chief financial officer, a chief information officer, and a director of marketing. The Daily Perc also will add two more district managers and a corporate events sales executive. Total personnel will reach 81.

The chief financial officer will be brought in to manage the growing company's finances. The chief information officer will be responsible for the expansion of our existing point-of-sale computerized cash register system that will make tracking and managing receipts, inventory control, and charitable contributions more robust. Ideally, this person will have both point-of-sale and inventory control experience that will allow him or her to provide real-time sales and inventory control information for accurate decision making at every level in the company. In addition, the chief information officer should begin building the foundation for an Internet-based information system that will support franchisees in the future.

The director of marketing will be charged with managing the relationships with advertising agencies, public relations firms, the media; keeping the TDP Web site current; and coordinating the company's social media marketing efforts.

Personnel Plan			
	Year 1	Year 2	Year 3
Production Personnel			
Drive-Through Team	$135,474	$439,250	$1,098,650
Mobile Café Team	$9,400	$172,800	$225,600
Equipment Care Specialist (Headquarters)	$0	$22,000	$77,000
Other	$0	$12,000	$24,000
Subtotal	$144,874	$646,050	$1,425,250
Sales and Marketing Personnel			
District Manager (Four Drive-Throughs)	$0	$22,000	$77,000
Corporate Events Sales Executive	$0	$0	$36,000
Director of Marketing	$0	$0	$72,000
Other	$0	$0	$0
Subtotal	$0	$22,000	$185,000

Personnel Plan

	Year 1	Year 2	Year 3
General and Administrative Personnel			
Bookkeeper/Office Administrator	$24,500	$46,000	$54,000
Warehouse/Site Manager	$7,000	$42,000	$48,000
Inventory Clerk	$0	$12,000	$42,000
Other	$0	$6,000	$12,000
Subtotal	$31,500	$106,000	$156,000
Other Personnel			
Chief Operating Officer	$66,000	$72,000	$78,000
Chief Financial Officer	$0	$0	$96,000
Chief Information Officer	$0	$0	$84,000
Other	$0	$0	$0
Subtotal	$66,000	$72,000	$258,000
Total People	15	29	81
Total Payroll	$242,374	$846,050	$2,024,250

7.0 Financial Plan

Although we forecast a loss of about $29,000 for TDP in its first year of operation, the company's long-term financial picture is quite promising. Because TDP is a cash business, its cash requirements are significantly less than other companies that must carry extensive amounts of accounts receivable. However, because our process is labor intensive, TDP recognizes that we must hire employees with more talent. The financial investment in our employees will be one of the greatest differentiators between TDP and its competitors. In this plan, we assume that we are financing the cost of our facilities and equipment. These items are capital expenditures and will be available for financing. We will maintain a minimum of inventory to ensure the freshness of our coffee products and baked goods and to take advantage of price decreases when and if they occur.

The Daily Perc forecasts that the initial combination of investments and long-term financing will be sufficient without the need for any additional equity or debt investment other than the purchase of additional equipment and facilities as it grows. This strategy will require TDP to grow more slowly than might be otherwise possible, but the company's expansion will be solid, financially sound growth based on its success in meeting customers' needs.

7.1 Important Assumptions

The following table shows the underlying assumptions used to build the financial forecasts for TDP:

- A slow-growth economy but no major recession.

- No unforeseen changes in public health perceptions of its products.

- Access to equity capital and financing sufficient to maintain its financial plan as shown in the tables.

Table: General Assumptions

General Assumptions	Year 1	Year 2	Year 3
Short-Term Interest Rate	8.00%	8.00%	8.00%
Long-Term Interest Rate	9.00%	9.00%	9.00%
Tax Rate (LLC)	0.00%	0.00%	0.00%

7.2 Key Financial Indicators

The following chart shows changes in key financial indicators: sales, gross margin, operating expenses, and inventory turnover. The expected growth in sales exceeds 250 percent each year. The Daily Perc forecasts its gross profit margin in year 1 to be 40 percent; by year 3, we expect it to reach 45 percent.

Projections for inventory turnover show that TDP will maintain a relatively stable amount of inventory in its warehouse so that it has no less than one week of inventory on hand but no more than two weeks of inventory so that products stay fresh. The only time we will consider holding larger stores of inventory is if there is some catastrophic event that would cause shortages in the supplies of its coffees or teas.

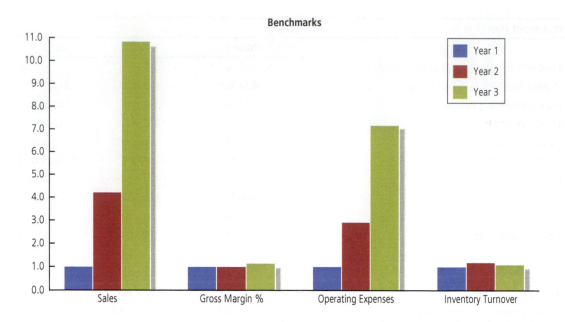

Benchmarks

7.3 Break-Even Analysis

Assuming average revenue per unit of $1.87 and fixed operating costs of $19,457 per month, TDP estimates its break-even point to be $29,580 per month. This is the equivalent of selling 15,817 cups of coffee per month, or 527 cups per day.

Break-Even Analysis	
Monthly Units Break-Even	15,817
Monthly Revenue Break-Even	$29,580
Assumptions:	
Average Per-Unit Revenue	$1.87
Average Per-Unit Variable Cost	$0.64
Estimated Monthly Fixed Cost	$19,457

7.4 Projected Profit and Loss

The Daily Perc is expecting dramatic growth in the next three years, reaching strong sales and a healthy gross profit margin by the end of its first year of operation. Expenses during the first year will, however, produce a net loss of about $29,000.

Aside from production costs of 60 percent, which include actual purchases of products and commissions for sales efforts, the single largest expenditures in the first year are in the general and administrative (G&A) area, which total 23 percent of sales. G&A includes expenses for rents, equipment leases, utilities, and payroll for all employees.

Sales increase by nearly 400 percent in the second year because of the addition of two more drive-throughs and two more Mobile Cafés. Although operating expenses double in the second year, TDP forecasts a net profit of $217,000, which represents a net profit margin (net income ÷ sales) of 9.24 percent. In that same year, TDP will make substantial charitable contributions in the communities in which it operates.

The third year is when TDP has the opportunity to break into markets outside the metropolitan area. The Daily Perc will open nine additional drive-through facilities in the third year, which will increase sales faster than production costs, which improve the company's gross profit margin. Several expenses increase substantially in year 3, including advertising, charitable donations, and payroll (because TDP will add several key management team members). Once again, the company's two largest expenses are production costs and G&A expenses. However, the G&A expenses decrease from 23 percent of sales in year 1 to 18.5 percent of sales in year 2 and 15.0 percent of sales in year 3. By year 3, operating efficiencies push the company's net profit margin to 16 percent.

Pro Forma Profit and Loss			
	Year 1	Year 2	Year 3
Sales	$558,043	$2,348,900	$6,022,950
Direct Cost of Sales	$190,977	$732,350	$1,783,010
Production Payroll	$144,874	$646,050	$1,425,250
Sales Commissions	$1,416	$35,234	$90,344
Total Cost of Sales	$337,267	$1,413,634	$3,298,604

Pro Forma Profit and Loss

	Year 1	Year 2	Year 3
Gross Margin	$220,776	$935,267	$2,724,346
Gross Margin %	39.56%	39.82%	45.23%
Operating Expenses			
Sales and Marketing Expenses			
Sales and Marketing Payroll	$0	$22,000	$185,000
Advertising/Promotion	$18,000	$36,000	$72,000
Web site	$1,000	$15,000	$22,000
Travel	$4,000	$7,500	$15,000
Donations	$3,332	$70,467	$180,689
Total Sales and Marketing Expenses	$26,332	$150,967	$474,689
Sales and Marketing %	4.72%	6.43%	7.88%
General and Administrative Expenses			
General and Administrative Payroll	$31,500	$106,000	$156,000
Sales and Marketing and Other Expenses	$0	$0	$0
Depreciation	$21,785	$92,910	$196,095
Leased Offices and Equipment	$0	$6,000	$18,000
Utilities	$9,640	$19,800	$41,100
Insurance	$12,570	$32,620	$63,910
Rent	$16,800	$50,400	$126,000
Payroll Taxes	$36,356	$126,908	$303,638
Other General and Administrative Expenses	$0	$0	$0
Total General and Administrative Expenses	$128,651	$434,638	$904,743
General and Administrative %	23.05%	18.50%	15.02%
Other Expenses:			
Other Payroll	$66,000	$72,000	$258,000
Consultants	$0	$0	$0
Legal/Accounting/Consultants	$12,500	$24,000	$36,000
Total Other Expenses	$78,500	$96,000	$294,000
Other %	14.07%	4.09%	4.88%
Total Operating Expenses	$233,483	$681,605	$1,673,431
Profit before Interest and Taxes	($12,707)	$253,662	$1,050,915
EBITDA	$9,078	$346,572	$1,247,010
Interest Expense	$16,165	$36,639	$77,102
Taxes Incurred	$0	$0	$0
Net Income	($28,872)	$217,023	$973,812
Net Income/Sales	-5.17%	9.24%	16.17%

7.5 Projected Cash Flow

As in any business, managers must manage cash extremely carefully; however, TDP has the benefit of operating a cash business. Forecasts show that the business generates positive cash flow, even in year 1. The greatest challenge that TDP faces in managing cash flow results from the seasonal dips in coffee sales during warm weather, but TDP will attempt to offset those declines by adding seasonal menu items, such as iced cappuccinos, iced mochas, and others.

With sufficient initial financing, TDP anticipates no cash flow shortfalls for the first year or beyond. In year 1, the months of March and May produce the greatest cash drains because TDP will incur the cost of adding second drive-through and a second mobile unit. In addition, TDP experiences heavier-than-normal cash disbursements in December and January because accounts payable come due then.

Pro Forma Cash Flow			
	Year 1	Year 2	Year 3
Cash Received			
Cash from Operations			
Cash Sales	$558,043	$2,348,900	$6,022,950
Subtotal Cash from Operations	$558,043	$2,348,900	$6,022,950
Additional Cash Received			
Sales Tax, VAT, HST/GST Received	$0	$0	$0
New Current Borrowing	$0	$0	$0
New Other Liabilities (interest Free)	$0	$0	$0
New Long-Term Liabilities	$181,463	$253,970	$729,992
Sales of Other Current Assets	$0	$0	$0
Sales of Long-Term Assets	$0	$0	$0
New Investment Received	$0	$0	$0
Subtotal Cash Received	$739,506	$2,602,870	$6,752,942
Expenditures			
Expenditures from Operations			
Cash Spending	$242,374	$846,050	$2,024,250
Bill Payments	$273,191	$1,236,069	$2,880,058
Subtotal Spent on Operations	$515,565	$2,082,119	$4,904,308

Pro Forma Cash Flow

	Year 1	Year 2	Year 3
Additional Cash Spent			
Sales Tax, VAT, HST/GST Paid Out	$0	$0	$0
Principal Repayment of Current Borrowing	$1,500	$2,000	$5,000
Other Liabilities Principal Repayment	$0	$0	$0
Long-Term Liabilities Principal Repayment	$26,469	$27,000	$50,000
Purchase Other Current Assets	$0	$0	$0
Purchase Long-Term Assets	$191,850	$429,700	$1,356,993
Dividends	$0	$0	$0
Subtotal Cash Spent	$735,384	$2,540,819	$6,316,301
Net Cash Flow	$4,122	$62,051	$436,641
Cash Balance	$29,622	$91,673	$528,315

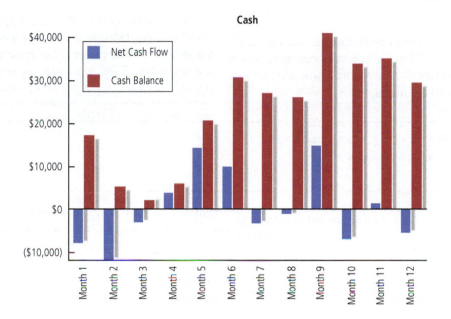

Cash

7.6 Projected Balance Sheet

The Daily Perc's projected balance sheet shows a significant increase in net worth in year 2, at which point the company will generate an impressive 90.5 percent return on investment (ROI). As the financial projections indicate, TDP expects to build a company with strong profit potential and a solid balance sheet that will be asset heavy and flush with cash at the end of the third year. The Daily Perc has no plan to pay dividends before the end of the third year; instead, the company will use the cash it generates to fuel its growth.

Pro Forma Balance Sheet

	Year 1	Year 2	Year 3
Assets			
Current Assets			
Cash	$29,622	$91,673	$528,315
Inventory	$35,159	$134,826	$328,253
Other Current Assets	$0	$0	$0
Total Current Assets	$64,781	$226,499	$856,568

(continued)

Pro Forma Balance Sheet

	Year 1	Year 2	Year 3
Long-Term Assets	$323,250	$752,950	$2,109,943
Accumulated Depreciation	$21,785	$114,695	$310,790
Total Long-Term Assets	$301,465	$638,255	$1,799,153
Total Assets	$366,246	$864,754	$2,655,721
Liabilities and Capital			
Current Liabilities			
Accounts Payable	$49,724	$106,240	$248,402
Current Borrowing	$7,500	$5,500	$500
Other Current Liabilities	$0	$0	$0
Subtotal Current Liabilities	$57,224	$111,740	$248,902
Long-Term Liabilities	$286,394	$513,364	$1,193,356
Total Liabilities	$343,618	$625,104	$1,442,258
Paid-In Capital	$225,270	$225,270	$225,270
Retained Earnings	($173,770)	($202,642)	$14,381
Earnings	($28,872)	$217,023	$973,812
Total Capital	$22,628	$239,651	$1,213,463
Total Liabilities and Capital	$366,246	$864,754	$2,655,721
Net Worth	$22,628	$239,651	$1,213,463

7.7 Exit Strategy

There are three scenarios for the investors and managers to recover their investment, two of which produce significant returns on each dollar invested.

Scenario 1: The Daily Perc becomes extremely successful and begins selling franchises. When one considers the wealth that successful franchisers such as McDonald's, Wendy's, Five Guys Burgers and Fries, and others have created, the potential to franchise a well-run system is considerable. However, developing a franchise can be extremely costly, takes years to build, and can be diminished by a few franchisees who fail to deliver the consistency or value on which the founding company has built its reputation.

Scenario 2: The Daily Perc becomes the drive-through version of Starbucks, obtaining several million dollars through a private offering that allows the company to open 20 to 30 outlets per year in the region of the country between the mountain ranges in both metropolitan and micropolitan communities. This is the preferred exit strategy of the management team. The danger with this exit strategy is that once TDP becomes successful, competitors will attempt to enter high-potential markets with copycat concepts before TDP can expand into those markets, resulting in lower revenues and a dramatic increase in advertising expenditures to maintain market share. Understanding these risks—and planning for them—gives TDP the edge required to make this scenario work.

Scenario 3: By the third year, the growth and community support for TDP is creating a buzz in cities beyond the metropolitan area. Competitors such as Starbucks or Quikava will realize the value proposition that TDP offers its customers and identify the company an attractive target for buyout.

Taking a conservative approach to valuation, we estimate that TDP would be valued at $7.5 million. Assuming that all 250 units of ownership in TDP are distributed to investors, a cash purchase of TDP would net each unit $30,000. With each unit selling at $4,250, that price constitutes an ROI of 705 percent over the three years. However, any buyout will most likely involve a cash/stock combination, which is preferable because tax consequences of the transaction for the sellers would be more favorable than in an all-cash deal.

Pro Forma Cash Flow

	Month 1	Month 2	Month 3	Month 4	Month 5	Month 6	Month 7	Month 8	Month 9	Month 10	Month 11	Month 12
Cash Received												
Cash from Operations												
Cash Sales	$0	$0	$0	$32,375	$42,637	$44,769	$42,530	$42,637	$77,144	$85,167	$95,392	$95,392
Subtotal Cash from Operations	$0	$0	$0	$32,375	$42,637	$44,769	$42,530	$42,637	$77,144	$85,167	$95,392	$95,392
Additional Cash Received												
Sales Tax, VAT, HST/GST Received (0.00%)	$0	$0	$0	$0	$0	$0	$0	$0	$0	$0	$0	$0
New Current Borrowing	$0	$0	$0	$0	$0	$0	$0	$0	$0	$0	$0	$0
New Other Liabilities (Interest Free)	$0	$0	$0	$0	$0	$0	$0	$0	$0	$0	$0	$0
New Long-Term Liabilities	$0	$0	$5,300	$0	$0	$0	$0	$0	$98,184	$0	$77,979	$0
Sales of Other Current Assets	$0	$0	$0	$0	$0	$0	$0	$0	$0	$0	$0	$0
Sales of Long-Term Assets	$0	$0	$0	$0	$0	$0	$0	$0	$0	$0	$0	$0
New Investment Received	$0	$0	$0	$0	$0	$0	$0	$0	$0	$0	$0	$0
Subtotal Cash Received	$0	$0	$5,300	$32,375	$42,637	$44,769	$42,530	$42,637	$175,328	$85,167	$173,371	$95,392
Expenditures												
Expenditures from Operations												
Cash Spending	$5,500	$5,500	$5,500	$16,000	$18,100	$17,050	$18,800	$19,500	$28,624	$30,700	$38,200	$38,900
Bill Payments	$112	$3,349	$2,987	$7,228	$10,030	$17,719	$27,251	$24,342	$26,320	$54,407	$46,831	$52,615
Subtotal Spent on Operations	$5,612	$8,849	$8,487	$23,228	$28,130	$34,769	$46,051	$43,842	$54,944	$85,107	$85,031	$91,515
Additional Cash Spent												
Sales Tax, VAT, HST/GST Paid Out	$0	$0	$0	$0	$0	$0	$0	$0	$0	$0	$0	$0
Principal Repayment of Current Borrowing	$0	$0	$0	$0	$0	$0	$0	$0	$0	$0	$500	$1,000
Other Liabilities Principal Repayment	$0	$0	$0	$0	$0	$0	$0	$0	$0	$0	$0	$0
Long-Term Liabilities Principal Repayment	$2,500	$3,116	$0	$5,166	$0	$0	$0	$0	$0	$7,216	$0	$8,471
Purchase Other Current Assets	$0	$0	$0	$0	$0	$0	$0	$0	$0	$0	$0	$0
Purchase Long-Term Assets	$0	$0	$0	$0	$0	$0	$0	$0	$105,400	$0	$86,450	$0
Dividends	$0	$0	$0	$0	$0	$0	$0	$0	$0	$0	$0	$0
Subtotal Cash Spent	$8,112	$11,965	$8,487	$28,394	$28,130	$34,769	$46,051	$43,842	$160,344	$92,323	$171,981	$100,986
Net Cash Flow	($8,112)	($11,965)	($3,187)	$3,981	$14,507	$10,000	($3,521)	($1,205)	$14,984	($7,156)	$1,390	($5,594)
Cash Balance	$17,388	$5,422	$2,236	$6,217	$20,724	$30,724	$27,203	$25,998	$40,982	$33,826	$35,216	$29,622

Case 1

Panda Sunglasses

How Should a Start-Up Business with a Social Mission Market Its Sunglasses with Bamboo Frames?

Vincent Ko showed his entrepreneurial potential in high school in Rockville, Maryland, when, as a young hockey player, he invented a drying rack for hockey pads that he sold to his teammates, then on eBay, and finally on a Web site for the company he created. A few years later, while attending George Washington University in Washington, D.C., Ko and two friends, Luke Lagera and Mike Mills, were inspired by the growing social entrepreneurship movement and the success of companies such as TOMS shoes, a company founded by Blake Mycoskie that donates a pair of shoes to someone in need for every pair it sells. One day while walking through the Georgetown shopping district, the friends noticed a display of sunglasses and decided to create a business that would market cool sunglasses and provide eye examinations to someone in need for every pair sold. In keeping with the idea of a socially responsible company, Ko suggested that they make their sunglasses frames from eco-friendly bamboo, a lightweight, sturdy wood that grows extremely fast. Having grown up in China, Ko was familiar with the properties of the renewable wood and knew that it was the perfect material from which to make sunglasses frames.

They created a company, Panda Sunglasses, and set out to find companies that could make the product they envisioned. Ko knew bamboo was the most commonly used wood in China, so the team began looking for a company in China to manufacture the frames to their specifications. Not only did they find a Chinese wood shop that would make their sunglasses frames, but they also located a Chinese eye wear manufacturer to produce the polarized lenses. Pairing the two companies gave them their unique, stylish sunglasses, which float. They created a Web site and began selling them at $120 a pair. Through a connection that Lagera had, the young entrepreneurs found an ideal partner in the Tribal Outreach Medical Association (TOMA), a nonprofit organization that provides eye examinations and other health services for tribal communities. They quickly reached a deal: For every pair of Panda Sunglasses sold, the company would pay for one eye exam through TOMA.

The entrepreneurs' next challenge was to market their unique sunglasses and their potential to help people in need. They knew that without sales, their effort at "conscious capitalism" would be for naught. None of the three cofounders had any experience in the retail industry, but they learned quickly on the job. The young men had just graduated and took "regular" jobs to pay their bills, but they remained

dedicated to making Panda Sunglasses a success. After testing sales of their sunglasses online, the trio began applying for spots in various trade shows geared toward accessories. One of the shows they applied to was the prestigious ENK International trade show, which attracts more than 250,000 buyers and press members from across the globe. Companies that are accepted to the juried show find sales leads that generate total sales of more than $1 billion. Mills sent Ko an e-mail in which he joked that they would be willing to set up in a broom closet at ENK if their application were accepted. Ko forwarded that e-mail to executives at ENK, who responded with, "We'll find you a booth instead." At the ENK show, Ko says he and his cofounders, fresh out of college, created a booth that featured a giant bamboo backdrop that attracted a great deal of attention. At one point, they struck up a conversation with three women, who they learned were buyers from the retail chain Nordstrom. The trade show opened many doors for the young company, and less than two years after starting, Panda Sunglasses was generating annual sales of $350,000.

Questions

1. How can social entrepreneurs such as the founders of Panda Sunglasses use their companies' social missions to attract customers and promote their businesses?
2. How should the founders of Panda Sunglasses define a unique selling proposition for their company that resonates with customers?
3. Write a brief memo to the founders of Panda Sunglasses outlining a bootstrap marketing plan for the company.
4. Use the business model canvas to illustrate Panda Sunglasses's business model. Can you identify other revenue streams that could support the company? How can the company strengthen its relationships with customers?
5. How should the founders of Panda Sunglasses use social media to market their company and its products? What can they do to increase the traffic to and generate more sales from their company's Web site?

Sources: Based on Nancy Dahlberg, "Start-up Spotlight: Panda," *Miami Herald,* June 29, 2014, http://www.miamiherald.com/2014/06/29/v-print/4207736/startup-spotlight-panda.html; Olga Khazan, "Panda Glasses Are TOMS Shoes for Your Face," *Washington Post,* May 24, 2012, http://www.washingtonpost.com/blogs/on-small-business/post/panda-glasses-are-toms-shoes-for-your-face/2012/05/23/gJQAsOPhlU_blog.html; Alicia Ciccone, "Vincent Ko, Panda Sunglasses: Sustainable Bamboo Eyewear That Gives Back," *Huffington Post,* May 25, 2012, http://www.huffingtonpost.com/2012/05/25/vincent-ko-panda-sunglasses_n_1544043.html; "Panda Sunglasses Are More Than Meets the Eye," *Asian Fortune,* April 25, 2014, http://www.asianfortunenews.com/2014/04/panda-sunglasses-are-more-than-meets-the-eye/; Zach Gordon, "Alums' Business Aims to Help the Needy," *The Hoya,* May 17, 2012, http://www.thehoya.com/alums-business-aims-to-help-the-needy/.

674

Oxitec

Should a Company Be Able to Release Genetically-Altered Mosquitoes into the Environment?

Oxitec, a British biotech company founded by Dr. Luke Alphey, develops innovative approaches for insect-borne diseases and agricultural pests plaguing developing countries.

Oxitec developed a new approach to tackling the mosquito-borne disease dengue fever. There are 50 million to 100 million cases of dengue fever every year, with a death rate of about 2.5 percent. There is no treatment or vaccine for dengue fever; patients are treated for their symptoms and the disease must run its course. Many pests are becoming resistant to insecticides, and concerns are growing over the long-term environmental and health impact of consistent use of insecticides. Using advanced genetics, Oxitec breeds and releases "sterile" male mosquitos of the disease-carrying species. The company claims that this new approach is a highly targeted form of biological control that is safe to other species, causes no lasting impact on the environment, and is cost-effective. In 2010, Oxitec released 3 million genetically altered mosquitos into the Cayman Islands, resulting in a reported 80 percent reduction in the incidence of dengue fever.

In 2009 the Florida Keys suffered an outbreak of dengue fever. Although no one died from the outbreak, 93 people became ill in Key West. To avoid future outbreaks, the Florida Keys Mosquito Control District decided to contract with Oxitec to release its genetically altered mosquitos in the Florida Keys. Key West would be only the fourth location worldwide to use this approach to control the local mosquito population.

Some critics raised concerns about releasing genetically altered mosquitos into the environment. Others questioned the ecological impact of removing insects from an ecosystem. These critics argued that no one knows the impact on animals that feed on these mosquitos and cannot know what other organisms may move in to fill the ecological void once the mosquitos are gone. The Florida Keys Environmental Coalition wrote to Florida Governor Rick Scott, asking him to stop Oxitec, pointing out that ". . . biting female mosquitoes could inject an engineered protein into humans along with other proteins from the mosquitos' salivary gland. Oxitec has yet to conduct or publish any study showing that this protein is not expressed in the salivary gland and therefore cannot be passed on to humans."

A local real estate agent collected more than 117,000 signatures on a petition she posted on Change.org against the release of the genetically-altered mosquitos in the Florida Keys.

Advocates of the plan pointed to the research conducted by Oxitec that has been published in peer-reviewed scientific journals, which highlights the problems associated with traditional spraying with insecticides. The use of the altered mosquitos cannot move ahead until the FDA gives its formal approval.

Local residents also are concerned about the ecological impact of Oxitec's approach to insect control. They argue that officials should take a wait-and-see approach by observing the ecological impact of the treatment used in the Cayman Islands.

Questions

1. Is it ethical for a company to expose people to products that have not been definitively proven to be safe? Explain.

2. Is it ethical for community leaders to put citizens at risk for a deadly disease, such as dengue fever, when there is a proven approach to reducing the impact of the disease? Explain.

3. How should companies test the safety of products before they are introduced? Explain.

4. Create a detailed diagram of all of the stakeholders of Oxitec. How is each of the stakeholders affected by Oxitec's actions? Explain. What conclusions can you draw from this analysis?

5. Describe the business model of Oxitec using the Business Model Canvas. What recommendations might you make for the company's business model going forward?

Sources: http://www.oxitec.com/; The World Health Organization, "Dengue and Severe Dengue: Fact Sheet," November 2012, http://www.who.int/mediacentre/factsheets/fs117/en/; Maria Cheng, "GM Mutant Mosquitoes Fight Dengue Fever in Cayman Islands," *Huffington Post*, November 11, 2010, http://www.huffingtonpost.com/2010/11/11/gm-mosquitoes-fight-dengu_n_782068.html; Chris Sweeney, "Genetically Modified Bugs Glow Red and Self-Destruct, but Can They Keep Away Disease?" *Broward Palm Beach NewTimes News*, Thursday, May 31 2012, http://www.browardpalmbeach.com/2012-05-31/news/genetically-modified-bugs-glow-red-and-self-destruct-but-can-they-keep-away-disease/; "Oxitec Wants to Release Genetically Modified Mosquitoes into Florida Keys," *Huffington Post*, July 16, 2012, http://www.huffingtonpost.com/2012/07/16/oxitec-mutant-mosquitoes_n_1676344.html.

Source Outdoor

Should a Small Company's Business Model Include a Channel of Distribution That Competes with Its Retail Customers?

Entrepreneurs never know when a business idea will come to them. Gerald Shvartsman came up with the idea for his wicker and outdoor furniture business, Source Outdoor, in 2009 when he went shopping at several Miami, Florida, stores for outdoor furniture for the balcony of his apartment. Shocked by the high prices of couches, wicker chairs, and chaise lounges, Shvartsman decided to open a business that imported low-cost, high-end outdoor furniture. He found a low-cost supplier in China and placed an order. When the four containers arrived, Shvartsman unloaded them himself and then switched roles, becoming his company's one-man sales force and calling on every furniture store within a 60-mile radius. Within a few months, every store that he had visited had some of Source Outdoor's furniture in their showrooms or were selling from his company's catalog.

To expand his company's reach, Shvartsman began selling through local interior designers and decorators and to hotel and condominium owners at discounts of 50 percent of the normal retail price. After working with one online furniture retailer, he began filling orders (by drop shipping) for other online retailers. Like the brick-and-mortar retail stores he supplied, Shvartsman offered online furniture retailers discounts of 60 percent off retail prices. In addition, six or seven times each year, Shvartsman would haul a truckload of his overstocked merchandise and sell it directly to the public at a large Florida home show. Most of the sales to the public were at full retail price, generating impressive profit margins of more than 300 percent. By 2011, Source Outdoor's sales had reached $4.4 million; in 2013, they doubled to $9 million.

As Source Outdoor's sales volume increased, Shvartsman began to notice that his manufacturer in China was shipping aluminum chairs and tables that had flaws, such as discolored metal coatings, mismatched fabrics on cushions, and weak metal supports. Because he had built his company on the premise of selling high-end, quality furniture at moderate prices, he knew that the quality problems could threaten Source Outdoor's reputation and success. Shvartsman decided that the best way to address the quality problems with his supplier was to manufacture those items himself. He cleared out a section of the company's warehouse, purchased $60,000 worth of equipment, including metal lathes for forming curved table legs and other parts, welding torches, grinders, and an oven for warming vinyl. Soon Source Outdoor was making much of the same furniture in his converted Miami warehouse that he had been importing from China but the quality of the products was much higher. In addition, Shvartsman could now fill orders much faster (shipments from China took months to arrive) and could offer custom-designed finishes and cushions, a feature that was appealing to many of his interior designers, decorators, and retail furniture store customers. Although Shvartsman wants to expand the percentage of his company's products made in-house, he realizes that he will have to continue to import items that are labor-intensive, such as handcrafted woven wicker furniture, from China and other countries with low labor costs.

One day, Shvartsman received a call from one of his best retail customers who complained about Source Outdoor selling directly to customers at the Florida home show. The store owner said Source Outdoor was taking potential sales from his store and all of the other nearby stores to which Shvartsman sold. He realized that similar calls from other retail customers were likely to come and began weighing his options. The home show sales were important to his company and generated impressive profit margins. So far, he had encountered none of the retail stores he supplied at the home show. Shvartsman was able to move slow-selling merchandise at attractive margins, but was doing so worth alienating his primary customer base, the retail furniture stores that carried his company's products?

Questions

1. Is Shvartsman's entrepreneurial story typical of the way that other entrepreneurs come up with the ideas for their businesses? Explain.
2. Use the business model canvas to illustrate Shvartsman's business model. Do you notice any areas that require strengthening?
3. What advantages and disadvantages did Shvartsman encounter by "reshoring" some of his company's manufacturing?

4. Should Source Outdoor consider exporting its products? If so, what steps should Shvartsman take to develop an export strategy?

5. Refer to the "Channels," "Customer Segments," and "Revenue Streams" segments of the business model canvas that you created in question 2. Do you see any potential conflicts?

6. Write a one-page memo to Gerald Shvartsman explaining how you recommend that he resolve the issue that the retail store owner raised over Source Outdoor's direct sales to customers at the Florida home show.

Sources: Based on Douglas Hanks, "Furniture Importer Likes Flexibility of 'Made in Miami,'" *Miami Herald*, April 28, 2013, http://www.miamiherald.com/2013/04/28/3368540/furniture-importer-likes-flexibility.html; John Grossman, "A Wholesaler Finds Himself in Competition with Retail Clients," *New York Times*, April 24, 2013, http://www.nytimes.com/2013/04/25/business/smallbusiness/reconciling-retail-success-in-wholesale-business.html?pagewanted=all; John Grossman, "A Wholesaler Decides to Abandon His Most Profitable Sales Channel," *New York Times*, May 1, 2013, http://boss.blogs.nytimes.com/2013/05/01/a-wholesaler-decides-to-abandon-his-most-profitable-sales-channel/?_php=true&_type=blogs&_r=0; Ashley D. Torres, "Source Outdoor Has Expansion Plans for South Florida," *South Florida Business Journal*, April 19, 2013, http://www.bizjournals.com/southflorida/news/2013/04/19/source-outdoor-looks-to-expand.html.

Father and Son Pizzeria

Should the Owner of a Pizzeria Remodel and Expand, Move to a New Location, or Focus on Selling the Restaurant's Popular Red Sauce Through Retail Outlets?

When Carlos Vega was in high school, he worked part-time at a small pizza shop, Father and Son Pizzeria, in Guttenberg, New Jersey, where he learned the value of hard work. As a young man, Vega demonstrated entrepreneurial tendencies, operating a disc jockey business on weekends, launching an Internet dating service (that he sold), and flipping houses. After graduating from Montclair State University with a degree in business administration, Vega went to work in his family's printing business for several years before taking jobs with KPMG and Thomson Financial, where he managed the company's printing operations.

Many years later, Vega stopped by Father and Son Pizzeria to buy a pizza and began talking with his former boss, who still operated the business but wanted to retire. The founder's son had no interest in taking over the business, and the founder confided to Vega that he did not want to sell the business to just anyone. Before he knew it, Vega bought the tiny pizzeria, which was housed in just 900 square feet of space and had room for only eight tables. Vega immediately expanded the menu to include a broad range of Italian dishes and a line of desserts, began accepting Internet orders, added credit card sales, and introduced "take-and-bake" pizzas that customers could pick up and bake at home. He also tweaked the recipe for the pizzeria's red sauce, known by the locals as "gravy," that he had learned to make as a teenager working there.

One problem facing Vega was that Father and Son Pizzeria had no liquor license. Acquiring one would cost $250,000, and Vega doubted that, with just eight tables, selling alcohol would generate enough revenue to offset the cost of the license. Nearby competitors not only had liquor licenses but also operated from larger buildings and had their own parking lots, which allowed them to generate more sales. However, the biggest problem the small pizzeria faced was more difficult to solve: no parking lot and a location in a densely populated six-block central business district where parking spaces were scarce. It was as if the little business were caught in a small three-square-mile trap. Vega was making the best of the location, however, and the small restaurant was generating a profit, albeit a meager one.

Vega spotted another business opportunity as growing numbers of customers asked to purchase the classic red sauce that he used on his pizzas. He began making 40 quarts a week that sold out quickly. Then he began making 120 or more quarts a week to satisfy customer demand. Profit margins on the quarts of sauce, which he sold at $8.99 per jar, were higher than those on the items on the pizzeria's menu.

Vega faced an important decision in the life of his business. He could expand his pizzeria by adding a second story at the current location, move to a larger building down the block that had room for more tables, or turn his focus to selling jars of his red pizza sauce, which he was marketing on the side as Jersey Italian Gravy. If he chose to focus on selling his sauce, he knew that he would have to learn a new set of skills concerning food manufacturing, packaging, and shipping. He also knew that the pizza sauce market is crowded, highly price-sensitive, and dominated by several large brands. His local market tests showed that customers would buy his Italian gravy, but would that translate into profitable sales across a larger geographic area where the tiny business had no name recognition? In addition, would he be able to get the product onto the shelves of enough stores to make a difference?

Questions

1. Analyze the advantages and the disadvantages of each of the three options that Carlos Vega has identified.
2. Based on your analysis in question 1, write a short memo to Vega explaining which of the three options he should pursue and why.
3. Suppose that Vega chooses to relocate his business. Should he expand his analysis of potential sites beyond the central business district of Guttenberg? What criteria should he establish for screening potential sites?
4. Suppose that Vega chooses to focus on selling his red sauce. Work with a team of your classmates to brainstorm ideas for a unique selling proposition (USP) that Vega could use to market the sauce effectively.
5. If Vega focuses on marketing his red sauce, what steps should he take to protect the Jersey Italian Gravy brand name he has been using?

Sources: Based on John Grossman, "A Business Owner Seeks an Alternative to Seven-Day Weeks," *New York Times*, January 1, 2014, http://www.nytimes.com/2014/01/02/business/smallbusiness/a-business-owner-seeks-an-alternative-to-working-seven-day-weeks.html; John Grossman, "For a Former Pizzeria Owner, It's All Gravy," *New York Times*, January 7, 2014, http://boss.blogs.nytimes.com/2014/01/07/for-a-former-pizzeria-owner-its-all-gravy/.

Jimmy Beans Wool

Can an Online Yarn Retailer Get Its Groove Back?

In 2002, Laura Zander, a former software engineer, decided to turn her recently acquired knitting hobby into a business. She and her husband, Doug, who also has a background in technology, invested $30,000 of their own money to open a 500-square-foot knitting store, Jimmy Beans Wool, in Truckee, California, a small town of 14,000 people near the Lake Tahoe resort area. To expand the reach of their business, the Zanders built a Web site and used social media and instructional videos to drive traffic to the company's Web site. As evidenced by Jimmy Beans Wool's tag line, "Your local yarn store—online," Laura's strategy was to offer the same personalized customer service that she offered in the store online. She wrote newsletters to keep customers up to date on trends, fashions, and techniques and created 1,100 free instructional videos made in a simple, friendly, homespun style that resonated with her target customers. The videos are posted on YouTube and on the company's Web site. Internet sales soon made up 98 percent of the company's total sales. As the company grew, Laura added a customer service line that customers could call to have their questions answered by a friendly, well-trained employee.

By 2005, Jimmy Beans Wool had grown so much that Doug quit his technology job and began working for the business full-time. By 2007, annual sales had reached $1 million and in 2013, sales had grown to $7 million. Consultants told the Zanders that Jimmy Beans Wool could become a $100 million business, and that became the co-preneurs' goal. They decided to add fabric to their product line, investing $150,000 in inventory, with the anticipation that fabric sales would double the company's revenue within three to five years. The Zanders also decided to create a flagship retail store in Reno, Nevada. The 20,000-square-foot store housed the company's offices, warehouse, and retail space. Laura began to move out of her day-to-day role in the business, leaving those tasks to the company's rapidly growing staff, to become the "face" of Jimmy Beans Wool and its spokesperson. The Zanders also embarked on several rather costly marketing initiatives, including partnerships with the United States Ski and Snowboard Association and the National Institutes of Health. They also doubled the size of the company's marketing staff to eight and hired a chief technology officer to allow Doug to focus more on expanding the company.

The Zanders were confident that the changes they had implemented would increase sales. However, the company's sales growth evaporated, and then sales began to decline, all while expenses increased. Laura soon realized that they were spending too much money to spread the Jimmy Beans Wool message. The company was headed for a cash crisis; the Zanders stopped drawing salaries and had to meet payroll for their employees out of their savings. They had to get Jimmy Beans Wool back on track.

The Zanders put their growth plans on hold and began to look closely at what had made their business successful and what it had become. Jimmy Beans Wool had lost its small, family business feel and was operating like a big, impersonal corporation. Employee morale was flagging. The Web site had been neglected, and its bounce rate had increased. Jimmy Beans Wool's search engine optimization strategy was outdated and ineffective, and its social media presence had faded without Laura's attention to drive it. Overall, the Zanders realized that in the midst of their growth plans, their company had lost touch with the people who were most important—its customers who loved to knit. To revitalize their business, the Zanders faced several important questions: Should Jimmy Beans Wool become a $100 million company? Should they drop their line of fabric and stick to selling wool and knitting supplies? Should the company build its brand online, perhaps by focusing on international sales, or should it open other retail stores around the country, perhaps by franchising? The Zanders hired a consultant and found themselves and some of their employees sitting before a whiteboard ready to generate potential ideas for solving the company's problems.

Questions

1. Is the Zanders's dilemma—expansion goals causing the company to lose the character that made it successful in the first place—a common one that entrepreneurs face? Why?
2. Assume the role of the Zanders's consultant. What advice would you offer them concerning the fundamental questions they have about their business?

3. What steps should the Zanders take to redesign their Web site and to get their company back on the first page of search results for the three largest search engines?

4. What should the Zanders do to address their company's cash flow problems? What steps can they take to avoid cash flow problems in the future?

5. Write a brief report for the Zanders outlining your recommendations for getting their business back on track.

Sources: Based on Adriana Gardella, "Seeking Even Faster Growth, an E-Commerce Company Stumbles," *New York Times*, April 2, 2014, http://www.nytimes.com/2014/04/03/business/smallbusiness/seeking-even-faster-growth-an-e-commerce-company-stumbles.html; Adriana Gardella, "Jimmy Beans Wool Decides to Get Back to Knitting," *New York Times*, April 9, 2014, http://boss.blogs.nytimes.com/2014/04/09/jimmy-beans-wool-decides-to-stick-to-its-knitting/; Angela Haines, "Goat Farms, Wool, and Making a Living at What You Love," *Forbes*, March 6, 2012, http://www.forbes.com/sites/85broads/2012/03/06/goat-farms-wool-and-making-a-living-at-what-you-love/; Laura Zander, "Jimmy Beans Wool—Made a Fortune Spinning Yarn," *The Story Exchange*, 2014, http://thestoryexchange.org/laura-zander-jimmybeanswool/.

Case 6

James Confectioners—Part 1

Squeezed by Rising Costs, a Confectioner Struggles to Cope

Telford James and his wife, Ivey, are the second-generation owners of James Confectioners, a family-owned manufacturer of premium chocolates that was started by Telford's father, Frank, in 1964 in Eau Claire, Wisconsin. In its 50 years, James Confectioners has grown from its roots in a converted hardware store into a large, modern factory with sophisticated production and quality control equipment. In the early days, all of Frank's customers were local shops and stores, but the company now supplies customers across the United States and a few in Canada. Telford and Ivey have built on the company's reputation as an honest, reliable supplier of chocolates. The prices they charge for their chocolates are above the industry average but are not anywhere near the highest prices in the industry even though the company is known for producing quality products.

Annual sales for the company have grown to $3.9 million, and its purchases of the base chocolate used as the raw materials for their products have increased from 25,000 pounds 20 years ago to 150,000 pounds. The Jameses are concerned about the impact of the rapidly rising cost of the base chocolate, however. Bad weather in South America and Africa, where most of the world's cocoa is grown, and a workers' strike disrupted the global supply of chocolate, sending prices upward. There appears to be no relief from high chocolate prices in the near future. The International Cocoa Organization, an industry trade association, forecasts world production of cocoa, from which chocolate is made, to decline by 7.2 percent this year.[1] Escalating milk and sugar prices are squeezing the company's profit margins as well. Much to James and Ivey's dismay, James Confectioners's long-term contracts with its chocolate suppliers have run out, and the company is purchasing its raw materials under short-term, variable-price contracts. They are concerned about the impact these increases in cost will have on the company's financial statements and on its long-term health.

Ivey, who has the primary responsibility for managing James Confectioners's finances, has compiled the balance sheet and the income statement for the fiscal year that just ended. The two financial statements appear below:

[1]"Cocoa Forecasts," International Cocoa Organization, May 27, 2009, http://www.icco.org/about/press2.aspx?Id=0ji12056.

Balance Sheet, James Confectioners December 31, 20xx

	Assets
Current Assets	
Cash	$ 161,254
Accounts Receivable	$ 507,951
Inventory	$ 568,421
Supplies	$ 84,658
Prepaid Expenses	$ 32,251
Total Current Assets	$ 1,354,536
Fixed Assets	
Land	$ 104,815
Buildings, net	$ 203,583
Autos, net	$ 64,502
Equipment, net	$ 247,928
Furniture and Fixtures, net	$ 40,314
Total Fixed Assets	$ 661,142
Total Assets	$ 2,015,678
	Liabilities
Current Liabilities	
Accounts Payable	$ 241,881
Notes Payable	$ 221,725

(continued)

	Liabilities
Line of Credit Payable	$ 141,097
Accrued Wages/Salaries Payable	$ 40,314
Accrued Interest Payable	$ 20,157
Accrued Taxes Payable	$ 10,078
Total Current Liabilities	$ 675,252

Long-Term Liabilities

Mortgage	$ 346,697
Loan	$ 217,693
Total Long-Term Liabilities	$ 564,390

Owner's Equity

James, Capital	$ 776,036
Total Liabilities and Owner's Equity	$ 2,015,678

Income Statement, James Confectioners

Net Sales Revenue		$3,897,564
Cost of Goods Sold		
Beginning Inventory, 1/1/xx	$ 627,853	
+ Purchases	$ 2,565,908	
Goods Available for Sale	$ 3,193,761	
− Ending Inventory, 12/31/xx	$ 568,421	
Cost of Goods Sold		$ 2,625,340
Gross Profit		$ 1,272,224
Operating Expenses		
Utilities	$ 163,698	
Advertising	$ 155,903	
Insurance	$ 74,065	
Depreciation	$ 74,043	
Salaries and Benefits	$ 381,961	
E-commerce	$ 38,976	
Repairs and Maintenance	$ 58,463	
Travel	$ 23,385	
Supplies	$ 15,590	
Total Operating Expenses		$ 986,084
Other Expenses		
Interest Expense	$ 119,658	
Miscellaneous Expense	$ 1,248	
Total Other Expenses		$ 120,906
Total Expenses		$ 1,106,990
Net Income		$ 165,234

To see how the company's financial position changes over time, Ivey calculates 12 ratios. She also compares James Confectioners's ratios to those of the typical firm in the industry. The table below shows the value of each of the 12 ratios from last year and the industry median:

Ratio Comparison

Ratio	James Confectioners Current Year	James Confectioners Last Year	Confectionery Industry Median*
Liquidity Ratios			
Current ratio		1.86	1.7
Quick ratio		1.07	0.8
Leverage Ratios			
Debt ratio		0.64	0.7
Debt-to-Net-Worth ratio		1.71	1.0
Times-Interest-Earned ratio		2.49	2.3
Operating Ratios			
Average Inventory Turnover Ratio		4.75	4.9
Average Collection Period Ratio		34.6	23.0 days
Average Payable Period Ratio		31.1	33.5 days
Net-Sales-to-Total-Assets Ratio		2.17	2.1
Profitability Ratios			
Net-Profit-on-Sales Ratio		7.40%	7.1%
Net-Profit-to-Assets Ratio		9.20%	5.6%
Net-Profit-to-Equity Ratio		29.21%	16.5%

*from Risk Management Associates Annual Statement Studies.

"How does the financial analysis look for this year, Hon?" Telford asks.

"I'm about to crunch the numbers now," says Ivey. "I'm sure that rising chocolate prices have cut into our profit margins. The question is 'How much?'"

"I think we're going to have to consider raising prices, but I'm not sure how our customers will respond if we do," says Telford. "What other options do we have?"

Questions

1. Calculate the 12 ratios for James Confectioners for this year.
2. How do the ratios that you calculated for this year compare to those that Ivey calculated for the company last year? What factors are most likely to account for those changes?
3. How do the ratios you calculated for this year compare to those of the typical company in the industry? Do you spot any areas that could cause the company problems in the future? Explain.
4. Develop a set of specific recommendations for improving the financial performance of James Confectioners using the analysis you conducted in questions 1 to 3.
5. What pricing recommendations can you make to Telford and Ivey James?

James Confectioners—Part 2

Forecasting Cash Flow for a Small Confectioner

Telford James and his wife, Ivey, the second-generation owners of James Confectioners, a family-owned manufacturer of premium chocolates that was started by Telford's father, Frank, in 1964 in Eau Claire, Wisconsin, have become increasingly concerned that turmoil in the banking and financial industries could have a negative impact on their business. They have read the headlines about bank closures, heightened government scrutiny of the banking industry, and tight credit conditions, especially for small businesses. The company has a $150,000 line of credit with Maple Leaf Bank, but the Jameses want to increase it to $250,000 as a precautionary move. Last week, they contacted Claudia Fernandes, their personal banker at Maple Leaf, about increasing the line of credit. In addition to reviewing James Confectioners's most recent balance sheet and income statement, Fernandes said she would need a cash flow forecast for the upcoming year.

Although Telford and Ivey have prepared budgets for James Confectioners and have analyzed their financial statements using ratio analysis, they have not created a cash flow forecast before. They expect sales to increase 6.2 percent next year to $4,139,213. Credit sales account for 96 percent of total sales, and the company's collection pattern for credit sales is 8 percent in the same month in which the sale is generated, 54 percent in the first month after the sale is generated, and 34 percent in the second month after the sale is generated. The Jameses have gathered estimates from their budget for the upcoming year.

Actual sales for the last two months, November and December, were $459,913 and $553,454, respectively. The company's cash balance as of January 1 is $22,565. The interest rate on James Confectioners's current line of credit is 8.25 percent, and the Jameses have established a minimum cash balance of $10,000.

Questions

1. Develop a monthly cash budget for James Confectioners for the upcoming year.
2. What recommendations can you offer Telford and Ivey James to improve their company's cash flow?
3. If you were Claudia Fernandes, the Jameses' banker, would you be willing to increase the company's line of credit? Explain.

	Jan	Feb	Mar	Apr	May	Jun	Jul	Aug	Sep	Oct	Nov	Dec
Sales	$264,910	$447,035	$289,745	$293,884	$190,404	$318,719	$281,466	$231,796	$335,276	$409,782	$488,427	$587,768
Other cash receipts	105	55	60	75	85	55	65	60	65	85	95	110
Purchases	365,280	174,400	294,300	190,750	193,745	125,350	209,825	185,300	152,600	220,725	269,774	321,549
Utilities	13,600	14,100	13,700	13,200	13,200	13,600	14,800	15,900	14,900	14,100	13,800	14,000
Advertising	18,000	11,000	10,000	7,000	9,000	10,000	12,000	12,000	15,000	20,000	22,000	24,000
Insurance	0	0	19,650	0	0	19,650	0	0	19,650	0	0	19,650
Salaries and benefits	33,583	33,583	33,583	33,583	33,583	33,583	33,583	33,583	33,583	33,583	33,583	33,583
E-commerce	2,700	4,500	2,900	3,000	1,900	2,400	3,200	3,300	3,400	3,900	5,000	6,000
Repairs and maintenance	5,000	5,000	5,000	5,000	5,000	5,000	5,000	5,000	5,000	5,000	5,000	5,000
Travel	4,100	2,700	2,700	2,000	3,000	2,600	2,200	3,100	3,800	4,500	5,500	6,500
Supplies	1,088	1,836	1,190	1,207	782	1,309	1,156	952	1,377	1,683	2,006	2,414
Interest	10,000	10,000	10,000	10,000	10,000	10,000	10,000	10,000	10,000	10,000	10,000	10,000
Other cash disbursements	125	125	125	125	125	125	125	125	125	125	125	125

Case 8

SocialToaster

Where Should the Founder of a Social Media Marketing Company Turn for Financing to Fuel His Fast-Growing Business?

As a Web developer, Brian Razzaque recognized the power and efficiency of social media marketing and wanted to make social media marketing easier for companies but wasn't sure exactly how to achieve his goal. Then an employee asked to be notified every time Razzaque made a post to the company blog so that he could then share the post with his social network. Razzaque realized that every company has "super fans," customers with a strong affinity for a company and its brand, who will readily share content about the company if it is easy and convenient to do so. That realization was the beginning of Razzaque's company, Baltimore-based SocialToaster, a platform that sends simple e-mails notifying super fans of new content, such as blog posts, articles, events, promotions, and awards, that fans can, in turn, share with members of their own social networks with just one click. SocialToaster magnifies a company's social media efforts many times over, drives traffic to its Web site, enhances customer engagement, and improves brand recognition and loyalty at minimal cost. In essence, SocialToaster allows a company's super fans to increase exponentially the visibility of the content that the company creates through the fans' social networks. Razzaque says promoting a business through a company's super fans using SocialToaster is as easy as making toast.

Razzaque began promoting SocialToaster's power and began landing clients around Baltimore. As success stories began to spread, SocialToaster landed bigger clients, including the Baltimore Ravens, the Baltimore Symphony Orchestra, the Detroit Lions, Lifetime Network, A&E, VH1, Sony Pictures, Universal Music, Johns Hopkins University, and many others. Clients report that their fans share 60 to 74 percent of the content they promote, providing exposure that is almost impossible for companies to achieve through their own social media accounts alone. In its first year of operations, SocialToaster generated $300,000 in sales, an amount that more than doubled to $800,000 in its second year.

Razzaque is at an important crossroads in the life of his company. He needs financing to fuel its rapid growth, but he wants to ensure that he selects the right sources of financing. He estimates that he will need $500,000 as bridge financing to fuel the company's short-term growth. That financing will give him time to raise the $2 million he will need to increase the size of SocialToaster's sales force, hire account managers, increase the company's marketing efforts across the globe to land more clients, and hire more technical staff to constantly upgrade and improve the product and enhance its features.

Razzaque has called on several wealthy individuals in New York City, Boston, and Silicon Valley. None were willing to invest in SocialToaster, but they did offer Razzaque helpful feedback that enabled him to improve his pitch. He also discovered the differences in how potential investors in Silicon Valley and on the East Coast view start-up companies. Razzaque says investors in Silicon Valley were not impressed by SocialToaster's existing (but modest) revenue stream. Instead, they were looking at the company's growth rate as an indicator of market potential. Does the company have the potential to become a billion-dollar business? East Coast investors, however, were more interested in the company's fundamentals, its revenue stream as proof that the product is viable, its "burn rate" (how quickly the company's monthly expenditures were burning through its capital), the soundness of its business model, and its staying power.

Questions

1. What tips can you offer Brian Razzaque for creating a business plan that will attract the capital SocialToaster needs to fuel its growth?
2. What advice can you offer Razzaque about presenting his plan to potential lenders and investors?
3. Write a brief memo to Razzaque describing the advantages and disadvantages of using debt capital and equity capital.
4. Which sources of debt capital offer the greatest potential for SocialToaster's financing needs? In what order would you prioritize the sources you have listed (from greatest potential to least potential).
5. Which sources of equity capital offer the greatest potential for SocialToaster's financing needs? In what order would you prioritize the sources you have listed (from greatest potential to least potential)?
6. What advice can you offer Razzaque about avoiding potential dangers and pitfalls in accepting outside financing for a business?

Sources: Based on Kara Ohngren, "SocialToaster Lands Some Bread," *Entrepreneur*, January 2013, p. 65; "SocialToaster Closes Series A Funding in the Amount of $1.975M," *City Biz List: Baltimore*, June 28, 2012, http://baltimore.citybizlist.com/article/socialtoaster-closes-series-funding-amount-1975m; Sarah Gantz, "SocialToaster Nears Another $1M in Funding, Targets Up to $8M More," *Baltimore Business Journal*, August 29, 2013, http://www.bizjournals.com/boston/how-to/funding/2013/06/social-toaster-raises-1m-targets-up.html?page=all; Scott Dance, "'How I Got Started' with Brian Razzaque, *Baltimore Business Journal*, April 15, 2011, http://www.bizjournals.com/baltimore/print-edition/2011/04/15/how-i-got-started-with-brian-razzaque.html?page=all.

The Evolution of CoolPeopleCare's Business Model

How Should the Founder of a Social Enterprise Increase the Visibility of His Company?

The original idea for CoolPeopleCare came to Sam Davidson after he had taken a trip to Washington, D.C., for a Save Darfur Rally in April 2006. While at the rally he saw a man holding a cardboard sign declaring "Cool People Care" and was struck by the power of the phrase. It had a really persuasive ring to it. Returning home to Nashville, Tennessee, Davidson couldn't stop thinking about the phrase, "Cool People Care." Initially he thought it would be appealing to build a Web site as a platform to sell "Cool People Care" T-shirts and ask people what they care about.

Davidson approached Stephen Moseley, whom he had met while working at a nonprofit in Nashville, for help to build a Web site to promote his CoolPeopleCare idea. A 15-minute conversation turned into a 3-hour planning session in which Davidson and Moseley mapped out what the first version of the Web site would look like.

Davidson had observed by working in nonprofits that people tended to give two main excuses for not volunteering or actively supporting a worthy cause: (1) "I don't have enough time," and (2) "I have no idea how to get started." He believed that the CoolPeopleCare Web site could potentially eliminate the excuses. Through the Web site, Davidson wanted to enlighten and connect his audience. He envisioned that CoolPeopleCare would pair people who want to make a difference with organizations and opportunities that need their help. He recognized a need in the nonprofit sector for young, passionate people to connect with these organizations with the aim of making a positive difference in the world. He believed the Web site would be a good way to connect young people with causes they could help and support.

In May 2007, Davidson decided it was time to leave his full-time job and dedicate himself to building and growing CoolPeopleCare. He set up the business as a social for-profit venture. Davidson chose this form of business entity to ensure that his company did not compete for funds with the organizations it sought to help. He wanted the company to be self-sustaining from its own revenue streams. He also wanted to prove that a for-profit business could be successful with a social mission.

The Web site initially had two main features. The first was *5 Minutes of Caring,* which highlights a single action a person could take in less than five minutes to make the world a better place. The second feature is customized content for more than 40 cities, which includes a community calendar, volunteer and job opportunities, and a nonprofit directory specific to each city.

After Davidson committed to working on CoolPeopleCare full-time, it became apparent that he would have to change his business model to make the business viable. Over time, he had added several new revenue streams to the business. Davidson began to offer speaking engagements and soon added training sessions for nonprofits to help them create revenue streams that would alleviate the need for traditional fund-raising. Moseley also rolled his nonprofit consulting practice into CoolPeopleCare. Next, Moseley and Davidson wrote a book, *New Day Revolution: How to Save the World in 24 Hours,* and began to sell it through the Web site. They have sold thousands of copies of their book.

They realized they could also offer more value to the nonprofit community. They added "Partner Pages," where nonprofits could highlight their organizations, consolidated event and volunteer listings, contact information, links to their own Web sites, donation buttons, national e-mail announcements, and job listings. Nonprofits pay $1 a day to list on this page. Dozens of nonprofits soon took advantage of this new feature. Davidson and Moseley also added "Cool Pages" to allow corporate sponsors to highlight their support of social causes.

The most significant change to the business model was the addition of merchandise to the Web site, although at the time they did not realize its eventual impact. In addition to the book, the CoolPeopleCare store sells merchandise with the CoolPeopleCare logo, including T-shirts, coffee mugs, and reusable shopping bags. The site also sells fair trade coffee.

In May 2010, Nashville was hit by a devastating flood. The Thursday after the flood, CoolPeopleCare began selling "We Are Nashville" T-shirts to help raise money for flood relief. Davidson and Moseley had hoped to sell 1,000 shirts; they reached that goal the first day. Eventually, CoolPeopleCare made more than $100,000 in profits from T-shirt sales, which Davidson and Moseley donated to the Nashville Community Foundation for flood relief. The site also sold "We Are Nashville" prints and bumper stickers that raised more money for this cause. In addition to the good that the new product line delivered for the people of Nashville, it helped put CoolPeopleCare on the map on a national and even global scale as orders came in from around the world for "We Are Nashville" products. This visibility helped take CoolPeopleCare to another level and reach a much broader audience.

From this experience with the flood relief effort, Davidson recognized the need to pay more attention to promoting CoolPeopleCare to build awareness for the brand. By doing so, the company could help more nonprofits and reach more volunteers. He also saw the need for new products that reinforced the company's social mission. However, with a bootstrapped business, he also had to find creative ways to market CoolPeopleCare without the benefits of a large advertising budget.

Questions

1. Identify several bootstrapping marketing techniques that would help CoolPeopleCare build brand awareness and help the company grow. Explain how each approach to bootstrap marketing would work for this business.

2. Develop a detailed bootstrap marketing plan for CoolPeopleCare that offers specific ideas on how to promote the business. Why do you think the elements of your plan will be successful?

3. Generate ideas for new products that would be consistent with CoolPeopleCare's business model and mission. Explain each idea in detail.

4. Why did the business model of CoolPeopleCare change over time? Explain why each of the changes in the business model was successful.

5. Develop a business model canvas for the current operations of CoolPeopleCare.

6. What specific recommendations would you make to change the business model of CoolPeopleCare going forward? What is your rationale for each of these recommendations?

Sources: Based on Cornwall, J., Gonzalez, J., and Brown, S. "CoolPeopleCare: A Social Venture," United States Association for Small Business and Entrepreneurship, Proceedings, 2009; "CoolPeopleCare, Inc. Business Plan," 2008; "Cool People Care Does Way More Than Sell T-shirts", November 19, 2010, http://www.wkrn.com/Global/story.asp?S=13539331; Ray Chung, "Young People Spotlight," *Ray Chung's Online Journal*, February 13, 2008, http://raychung22.com/blog/2008/02/11/young-people-spotlight-sam-davidson/.

InQuicker

How Can a Fast-Growing Small Company Maintain Its Unique, Employee-Friendly Culture?

InQuicker provides an online waiting room service for emergency rooms and urgent care centers. Its software enables patients to check-in and wait at home based on projected treatment times. InQuicker also offers online appointment scheduling services for medical clinics.

Michael Brody-Waite, cofounder and CEO, wants to make InQuicker a cool and fun place to work. The first thing visitors see when they walk into the InQuicker office is a ping-pong table. The workspace is open, with no cubicles, to facilitate collaboration and teamwork.

InQuicker has a "culture club" that is responsible for leading activities to facilitate building a strong culture. Team members of InQuicker have weekly lunch meetings at a local restaurant. Once a month an employee hosts the rest of the staff for a cookout at his or her home. Employees dress up and eat sweets for each person's birthday and for various holidays, and every year, the team spends a week together away from the office on a retreat.

The company offers employees flextime and flexspace, which employees to separate family time and work time. When employees are with family and friends, they are expected *not* to answer e-mails and phone calls from work.

In its early stages of InQuicker's growth, Brody-Waite often rejected the opportunity to grow the business more quickly and to take on outside investments to preserve the culture of the business.

However, the company did soon experience significant growth. Revenues grew from about $2 million in 2011 to more than $5 million in 2013. Part of its growth came from market expansion into new applications for its software beyond just emergency rooms into other segments of the healthcare industry. InQuicker offers software that facilitates referrals to specialists. When physicians refer patients to specialists, InQuicker enables patients to make appointments from iPads while sitting in their doctors' offices.

Employment grew from 21 employees to 35 during this two-year period. The growth in the number of employees has created challenges for a company so focused on its employee-friendly culture. InQuicker has continued to focus just as much on the cultural fit of job candidates as it does on their skills and experience.

Brody-Waite has always been cautious about raising money from venture capitalists or other outside investors, preferring to grow through bootstrapping. He knows investors want to see significant returns on their investments that most often require an exit plan. Brody-Waite's primary focus always has been on building a strong culture. His concern with equity investors is that they might pressure him to focus on growth, even if it jeopardizes his commitment to intentionally developing InQuicker's culture. However, the pace and demands of its rapid growth may mean that InQuicker may have to look seriously at seeking equity investment.

Questions

1. Many entrepreneurs believe that corporate culture can be a strong competitive advantage. Do you agree? Explain.
2. Why do company cultures, like the culture at InQuicker, appeal to employees, particularly members of Generation X and Generation Y? Explain.
3. What steps can Brody-Waite take to maintain InQuicker's unique culture as the company grows?

Source: Based on E. J. Boyer, "What I Learned about InQuicker in 10 Minutes," *Nashville Business Journal*, February 15, 2013, http://www.bizjournals.com/nashville/blog/2013/02/what-i-learned-about-inquicker-in-10.html; Annie Johnson, "Case Study: For InQuicker, Success Means Taking It Slow," *Nashville Business Journal*, July 13, 2012, http://www.bizjournals.com/nashville/print-edition/2012/07/13/for-inquicker-nashville.html?page=all; Zina Moukheiber, "Health Tech Startup InQuicker Shuns Venture Money and Hype," *Forbes,* August 20, 2012, http://www.forbes.com/sites/zinamoukheiber/2012/08/20/health-tech-start-up-inquicker-shuns-venture-money-and-hype/.

Name Index

Subject Index